THE
HERITAGE OF
ARMENIAN
LITERATURE

This Publication Was Made Possible By a Generous Grant
From the Dolores Zohrab Liebmann Fund.

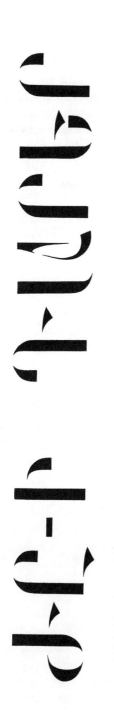

THE
HERITAGE OF
ARMENIAN
LITERATURE

VOLUME III

FROM THE
EIGHTEENTH
CENTURY TO
MODERN TIMES

Agop J. Hacikyan, Coordinating Editor

Gabriel Basmajian

Edward S. Franchuk

Nourhan Ouzounian

Wayne State University Press   Detroit

© 2005
by Agop J. Hacikyan,
Edward S. Franchuk, and Nourhan Ouzounian.
Published by Wayne State University Press, Detroit, Michigan 48201.
Manufactured in the United States of America.
09 08 07 06 05   5 4 3 2 1

Library of Congress Cataloging-in-Publication Data

The heritage of Armenian literature: From the oral tradition to the golden age / Agop J. Hacikyan, coordinating editor; Gabriel Basmajian, Edward S. Franchuk, Nourhan Ouzounian.

    p. cm.

    Includes bibliographic references.

    ISBN 0-8143-2815-6 (alk. paper)

    1. Armenian literature—Literary collections. 2. Armenia—History—Sources. I. Hacikyan, A. J. (Agop Jack), 1931– . II. Basmajian, Gabriel. III. Franchuk, Edward S. IV. Ouzounian, Nourhan.

    PK8532.H47 2000

    891'.99208—dc21   99-033544

ISBN 0-8143-3221-8 (Volume III)

♾ The paper used in this publication meets the minimum requirements of the American National Standard for Information Sciences—Permanence of Paper for Printed Library Materials, ANSI Z39.48-1984.

For credits see Permissions Acknowledgments, page 1071.

*in memory of the Armenian
writers whose lives were cut
short on 24 April 1915*

*to Alice Nigoghosian
in recognition of her dedication
and service to Armenian letters*

CONTENTS

Preface xix

Acknowledgments xxiii

Transcription of the Armenian Alphabet xxv

AN OVERVIEW FROM THE EIGHTEENTH TO THE BEGINNING OF THE TWENTIETH CENTURY 1

ABRAHAM KRETATSI (D. 1737) 109

from The Chronicle: A Brief History of Nader Shah's Early Reign 110

STEPANOS ROSHKA (1670–1739) 120

from Chronicle, or Ecclesiastical Annals 121

PAGHTASAR DPIR (1683–1768) 128

Money 129

Song 130

ABRAHAM YEREVANTSI (EIGHTEENTH CENTURY) 131

from History of the Wars 132

HOVHANNES KAMENATSI (EIGHTEENTH CENTURY) 141

from History of the War of Khotin 142

MOVSES BAGHRAMIAN (EIGHTEENTH CENTURY) 147

An Appeal to the Reader 148

SIMEON YEREVANTSI (1710–80) 151

Confession of the True and Orthodox Faith of the Armenian Holy Church and Myself 152

PETROS GHAPANTSI (D. 1784) 156

To My Honorable Nation, Under the Metaphor
   of the Rose 157

SHAHAMIR SHAHAMIRIAN (1723–97) 160

from Snare of Glory 161

JOSEPH EMIN (1726–1809) 168

from Life and Adventures of Joseph Emin 168

MIKAYEL CHAMCHIAN (1738–1823) 174

from History of Armenia 175

HOVHANNES KARNETSI (c. 1750–1820) 180

Song One 181

Hymn to Love (Ten) 181

Hymn to Love (Fifteen) 183

HOVHANNES VANANDETSI (1772–1841) 184

from The Light of Armenia 185

GRIGOR PESHTIMALCHIAN (1778–1837) 189

from The Path of Enlightenment 190

HARUTIUN ALAMDARIAN (1795–1834) 195

Spring 196

Dream 197

HOVHANNES TEROYENTS (1801–88) 199

from Critic 200

MESROP TAGHIADIAN (1803–59) 203

Parable 3 204

Parable 11 205

Parable 15 205

Parable 18 206

Lazy Pupil 206

from The Diary: Bangala 1830—Second Navigation to
   Dacca—The Project of the Mesrovbian College 207

KHACHATUR ABOVIAN (1809–48) 211

from The Introduction to Wounds of Armenia 214

The Fortress of Yerevan 216

STEPANOS NAZARIAN (1812–79) 219
On Childhood 220

KHACHATUR MISAKIAN (1815–91) 223
National Progress 224

NAHAPET RUSINIAN (1819–76) 226
Cilicia 227

GHEVOND ALISHAN (1820–1901) 229
The Lily of Shavarshan 231
The Nightingale of Avarayr 234

MKRTICH KHRIMIAN (HAYRIK) (1820–1907) 236
Crowned by Grandpa in the Field 238
from Invitation to the Promised Land 242

NIKOGHAYOS ZORAYAN (1821–59) 246
Association 247

TZERENTS (HOVSEP SHISHMANIAN) (1822–88) 250
from Toros Levoni 252

KARAPET IUTIUCHIAN (1823–1904) 261
The Task of National Advancement 262

STEPAN VOSKANIAN (1825–1901) 264
Our Shortcomings 266

GABRIEL SUNDUKIAN (1825–1912) 268
The Ruined Family 270

HOVHANNES HISARIAN (1827–1916) 280
from Antichrist, or the End of the World 281

MKRTICH PESHIKTASHLIAN (1828–68) 286
A Plaint 288
We Are Brothers 289
Spring 290

MIKAYEL NALBANDIAN (1829–66) 291
Freedom 294
Days of Childhood 295

SARGIS VANANDETSI (c. 1830–71) 297
Nerses the Great, Patron of Armenia 298

MATTEOS MAMURIAN (1830–1901) 305
from English Letters, or the Destiny of an Armenian 307

RAFAYEL PATKANIAN (1830–92) 316
The Woe of Araxes 318
from The Vacant Yard 320

GEVORG DODOKHIAN (1830–1908) 327
Swallow 328

HARUTIUN SVACHIAN (1831–74) 330
August Guiné 331

NARPEY (KHOREN GALFAYAN) (1832–92) 336
Armenia 338
The Exile to the Swallow 339

GRIGOR OTIAN (1834–87) 341
London and Paris 342

RAFFI (HAKOB MELIK HAKOBIAN) (1837–88) 345
from The Fool 348

PERCH PROSHIAN (1837–1907) 354
A Matter of Bread: Sako, the Publican 356

MKRTICH ACHEMIAN (1838–1917) 362
The Misguided 363

GRIGOR CHILINKIRIAN (1839–1923) 366
from Journey to Constantinople: Woman in the
    Nineteenth Century 367

GAREGIN SRVANDZTIANTS (1840–92) 372
Lament over the Heroes Fallen in the Battle
    of Avarayr 374

SMBAT SHAHAZIZ (1840–1907) 377
Dream 379

TOVMAS TERZIAN (1840–1909) 380
The Chraghan Palace 381

GHAZAROS AGHAYAN (1840–1911) 383
Tork Angegh and Haykanush the Fair 385

SRBUHI DUSSAP (C. 1841–1901) 399
from Mayta 401

HAKOB PARONIAN (1843–91) 404
Honorable Beggars 407

GRIGOR ARTZRUNI (1845–92) 420
A Couple of Words on the Education of Girls 422

RETEOS PERPERIAN (1848–1907) 428
The Blind Youth's Grief 429

ATRPET (SARGIS MUPAHIACHIAN) (1850–1937) 431
Tzhvzhik 432

PETROS DURIAN (1851–72) 440
Complaint 442
The Lake 444
My Death 445

YEGHIA TEMIRCHIPASHIAN (1851–1908) 447
The Song of the Vulture 449

ARPIAR ARPIARIAN (1852–1908) 452
I Have Seen So Many . . . 454

MINAS CHERAZ (1852–1929) 459
Loxandra Pandelis 460

HOVHANNES SETIAN (1853–1930) 467
Lament 468

MURATSAN (GRIGOR TER-HOVHANNESIAN) (1854–
1908) 470
from Gevorg Marzpetuni 472

SHIRVANZADÉ (ALEKSANDR MOVSISIAN) (1858–1935) 480
from For the Sake of Honor 483

MELKON (HRAND) KIURCHIAN (1859–1915) 489
from The Emigrant's Life 490

TLKATINTSI (HOVHANNES HARUTIUNIAN) (C. 1860–1915) 495

The Village and the Winter 497

YEGHISHÉ DURIAN (1860–1930) 500

The Travelers of Emmaus 502

LEO (ARAKEL BABAKHANIAN) (1860–1932) 506

from Melik's Daughter 508

GRIGOR ZOHRAP (1861–1915) 517

Armenisa 520

HRAND ASATUR (1862–1928) 531

Grigor Zohrap 532

To Zapel Khanchian-Tonelian from Hrand Asatur 538

SIBIL (ZAPEL ASATUR) (1863–1934) 541

from The Bride 542

A Letter from Sibil (Zapel Asatur) to Hrand Asatur 547

LEVON MANUELIAN (1864–1919) 550

from Shattered Life 551

HOVHANNES HOVHANNISIAN (1864–1929) 559

Araxes Came Devouringly 560

A Gentle Sleep 561

ALEKSANDR TZATURIAN (1865–1917) 562

Don't Cry, Bulbul 564

The Armenian Poet's Prayer 564

GEGHAM TER-KARAPETIAN (MSHO GEGHAM) (1865–1918) 565

from A Moonlit Journey to Mush 567

VRTANES PAPAZIAN (1866–1920) 570

The Source 572

HAKOB HAKOBIAN (1866–1937) 577

My Land 578

TIGRAN KAMSARAKAN (1866–1941) 580

from The Teacher's Daughter 581

AVETIS AHARONIAN (1866–1948) 592
Judgment 594

NAR-DOS (MIKAYEL HOVHANNISIAN) (1867–1933) 602
Hoopoe 604

LEVON BASHALIAN (1868–1943) 611
Angel 612

HOVHANNES TUMANIAN (1869–1923) 619
My Friend Neso 623
Akhtamar 626
My Song 628

YERVAND OTIAN (1869–1926) 630
from Comrade Panjuni: In Lieu of a Preface 632

LEVON SHANT (1869–1951) 642
from Ancient Gods 645

YERUKHAN (YERVAND SRMAKESHKHANLIAN) (1870–
    1915) 658
Crayfish 660

KHNKO APER (1870–1935) 664
The Golden Spindle 665

VAHAN MALEZIAN (1871–1966) 669
from In the Fields 670
The Blouse 671

ANAÏS (YEVPIMÉ AVETISIAN) (1872–1950) 673
from My Recollections 674

ARSHAK CHOPANIAN (1872–1954) 680
from Gregory of Narek 683
The Bond 685
To the Moon 686
Ode to My Native Tongue 687

ARTASHES HARUTIUNIAN (1873–1915) 690
from Art and Literature 691

RUBEN VORBERIAN (1873–1931) 693
from All the Way to Argaeus 694

RUBEN ZARDARIAN (1874–1915) 701
The Seven Singers 702

ONNIK CHIFTÉ-SARAF (1874–1932) 709
Crucifixion 711

YEVTERPÉ (ZARUHI KALEMKIARIAN) (1874–1971) 719
Agony of a Horse 720

INDRA (TIRAN CHRAKIAN) (1875–1921) 722
from The Inner World 723

MARI SVACHIAN (NINETEENTH–TWENTIETH
CENTURIES) 728
Khamsin 729

AVETIK ISAHAKIAN (1875–1957) 734
Saadi's Last Spring 736
Abu Ala al-Mahari 740

SUREN PARTEVIAN (1876–1921) 744
The Vow 745

SHUSHANIK KURGHINIAN (1876–1927) 748
The Workers 749

ARANDZAR (MISAK KUYUMCHIAN) (1877–1913) 752
The Story within the Story 753

MIKAYEL MANUELIAN (1877–1944) 760
Luck 761

DERENIK TEMIRCHIAN (1877–1956) 765
King Aram 767

SIAMANTO (ATOM YARCHANIAN) (1878–1915) 774
Prayer to Anahit on the Feast of Navasard 776
The Glory of Invention 778
The Dance 780

VAHAN TEKEYAN (1878–1945) 783
It Is Raining, My Child 785

To the Armenian Nation 786

Ode to Verlaine 786

Dark Hours 787

Prayer on the Threshold of Tomorrow 788

Dear Brother in the Bond: A Letter of Tekeyan to
  Varuzhan 789

ZAPEL YESAYAN (1878–1943) 792

from Shirt of Fire 794

ARAZI (MOVSES HARUTIUNIAN) (1878–1964) 799

In the Cages 800

ARAM ANTONIAN (1879–1951) 804

In Those Black Days 805

MIKAYEL KIURCHIAN (1879–1965) 812

The New Outfit 814

GEGHAM BARSEGHIAN (1883–1915) 826

Journal 827

HAKOB OSHAKAN (1883–1948) 830

Topich 833

DANIEL VARUZHAN (1884–1915) 843

The Red Soil 846

The Oriental Bath 848

The Lamp 850

TIGRAN CHEOKIURIAN (1884–1915) 852

The Monastery: The Diary of an Archimandrite 853

RUBEN SEVAK (1885–1915) 858

The Crane 860

Letters from a Student 862

VAHAN TERIAN (1885–1920) 866

I Love Your Dark and Wicked Eyes 869

Coming to Terms (or Reconciliation) 869

In the Style of Sayat-Nova 870

Carousel 870

This Time Like a Sister 871

Farewell Song 872

The Gallows 872

KOSTAN ZARIAN (1885–1969) 874

Istanbul 878

The Man 882

MISAK METZARENTS (1886–1908) 885

A Winter's Serene Night 886

Nameless 887

The Hut 888

Prayer for the New Year 889

AHARON TATURIAN (1886–1965) 891

Ancient Longing 892

My Shoes 893

HAKOB MNDZURI (1886–1978) 894

The First Born 896

HAKOB ANTONIAN (1887–1967) 900

Moments 900

The Waves 901

STEPAN ZORIAN (1889–1967) 903

Grandfather and Granddaughter 905

HAKOB SIRUNI (1890–1973) 910

The Caravan 912

HRACH ZARDARIAN (1892–1986) 918

Grandmother and Grandson 919

MATTEOS ZARIFIAN (1894–1924) 927

The Crazy Boy 928

VAHAN TOTOVENTS (1894–1938) 935

The Divine Comedy 937

AZAT VSHTUNI (1894–1958) 941

The Camel 942

BENIAMIN NURIKIAN (1894–1988) 946

The Sun for You 947

HAMASTEGH (HAMBARDZUM GELENIAN) (1895–1966) 951

The Blue Bead 953

YEGHISHÉ CHARENTS (1897–1937) 958

from Land of Nayiri 963
I Love the Sun-Baked Taste of Armenian Words 970
Ocean Song 971
Ode for the Dead 972
Hairdresser's Charms 974

TOROS AZATIAN (1898–1955) 975

Solitude 976

SHAVARSH NARDUNI (1898–1968) 978

The Tower of Babylon 979

NSHAN PESHIKTASHLIAN (1898–1972) 984

The Smile 985

AKSEL BAKUNTS (ALEKSANDR TEVOSIAN) (1899–1937) 988

The Alpine Violet 990

ARAM HAYKAZ (1900–1986) 1000

Happiness 1001

ZAREH VORBUNI (1902–80) 1007

from The Persecuted (The Candidate) 1008

GURGEN MAHARI (1903–69) 1013

from Barbed Wire in Flower 1015
On Guard, People 1020

SHAHAN SHAHNUR (1903–74) 1022

from Retreat without Song 1026

NIKOGHOS SARAFIAN (1905–73) 1031

On the Road to Insomnia 1032
At Farewell 1033

Bibliography 1035
Index 1047

PREFACE

This volume of *The Heritage of Armenian Literature* is the final install-
ment of a three-volume series aimed at providing an organized basis for
the systematic study of Armenian letters. Its purpose is to provide a collection of great Armenian writings, representing the power of Armenian
literature during the modern period, from the beginning of the eighteenth century. It is predominantly an anthology of imaginative literature: unlike the first two volumes of *The Heritage of Armenian Literature*,
it contains very few samples of historiography, theology, or philosophy.
In the eighteenth and especially in the nineteenth century, imaginative literature began to make an impact on and define the character of
the epoch in which it was written. In fact it has been mainly through
this type of literature that Armenian writers have led the reader deeper
into the meaning of past ages. At the same time they have gradually
communicated their aspirations and intuitions as well as their conscious
theorems and ideals.

Although literary merit was the final criterion for selection, every
effort was made to assure that the range of readings is both wide and diversified, in order to represent the major authors of the period in the fullness of their stature and with as much variety as possible. In addition to
the literary titans of the age, the volume includes writers of lesser stature
whose works nevertheless endure. The most discerning of literary critics,
however, remains, as it has always been, the passage of time. In order to
ensure a certain degree of objectivity to this volume, the authors included
were all, with a few major exceptions, born before the end of 1900. The
exceptions were such towering literary figures and were born so soon
after the turn of the century that to exclude them would have been merely
arbitrary. On the other hand, the selections from the literature of the
eighteenth century exclude the writings of Sayat-Nova, who, as a major
figure of "folk poetry," was included in the previous volume of the anthology, together with introductions that incorporate material from Hasmig
Injejikian's thesis, "Sayat Nova and Armenian Musical Tradition."

Effective understanding of any author depends upon studying an autonomous and substantial piece of his or her work: a whole drama, a whole story, or a whole canto or book of a long poem; as for lyric poems, one needs to have access to as many representative pieces as possible. Unfortunately, an anthology is always limited in the number of pages it can devote to a specific author, and inevitably concessions must be made. Consequently, it has often been necessary to represent a long work by extracts. In such cases every effort was made to choose texts that are interesting and worth reading in themselves while at the same time characteristic, both contextually and stylistically, of the works from which they are drawn. In some cases, then, complete short stories or long narrative poems are given; in others entire acts, chapters, or full cantos are offered for the reader's appreciation and enjoyment.

As in previous volumes the aim of the editors has been to produce an ideal companion to Armenian studies, and with this in mind they have included a comprehensive introduction to the political, social, cultural, and literary developments of the times. This overview, the biographical notes on individual authors, and the endnotes have two purposes: to provide enough background to facilitate reading and make it more enjoyable; and to make it more informative by emphasizing the relation between the literary works and the general directions of Armenian cultural and intellectual history. In the textual annotations, as in the introductory overview and the biographical sketches, the editors strove for as much objectivity as possible. They have been rather liberal in their furnishing of endnotes, believing that their function as editors requires that they elucidate obscurities that would handicap a reader who lacked immediate access to the appropriate reference books. Words in Armenian and other foreign languages are usually glossed in the body of the text so that the translations may be assimilated without interrupting the flow of the reading.

Naturally, it is possible to organize the study of Armenian literature in a number of different but equally acceptable ways. As in their two previous volumes, the editors arranged the selections chronologically, believing this organization to be the most logical, practical, and useful. In the overview at the beginning of the book, however, they have grouped authors together under topical headings such as "Romanticism," "Realism," "Literature in Translation," "The Historical Narrative," "Armeno-Turkish Literature," and so on.

The contents of this volume, as well as of volumes I and II, comprise Armenian literature in English translation. Every effort was made to select the best translations; sometimes the editors revised older translations in order to give them a more idiomatic form and thus make them more accessible to the non-Armenian or non-specialist reader. In many instances no English translation was available (either because it does not exist or because it was impossible to procure), and it was therefore necessary to translate the works directly from Armenian. Many of these selections are here offered to the English-speaking reading public for the first time. The first endnote for each selection indicates whether the piece in question is being reprinted, was revised, or is newly translated. The sources for all of the texts included are provided both in endnotes and in the bibliography.

Furthermore, when presenting literature in a language other than that in which it was written, an anthologist has to be selective: the translations chosen should respect the style and attitudes of the original, but they should also be idiomatic and readable texts in the target language, in this case English. The editors have attempted to respect these two principles while providing samples of several different periods and styles of translations.

In scholarly translations, certain words and expressions are enclosed in square brackets ([ ]) to indicate that they were supplied by the translator. Throughout *The Heritage of Armenian Literature*, these square brackets have been suppressed; the editors' aim is to ensure the smooth reading of the text.

Furthermore, the editors applied the transcription system used in their first and second volumes. However, for authors' names that are not Armenian in origin, the editors supplemented the transliteration obtained by the application of this system with a transcription based on the pronunciation of the names in their languages of origin; this second transcription appears in parentheses at the beginning of each biographical sketch and, when deemed necessary, within the texts.

Finally, the editors repeat the hopes that they expressed in the first two volumes of *The Heritage of Armenian Literature:* that as readers journey through the period represented in this volume they will find the adventure stimulating and rewarding; that they will see stretched out before them the rich panorama of Armenian literature in historical perspective; and that the varied experience communicated by Armenian literature of the recent past will supplement and illuminate their experience of the literature of other nations.

ACKNOWLEDGMENTS

The editors wish to acknowledge the support, encouragement, and invaluable suggestions they received from many sources, too numerous to list here. To all those who in any way contributed to the production of this anthology, our heartfelt thanks. There are, however, a few individuals whom we feel compelled to name individually for their very special help.

It is a pleasure to express our gratitude for the continual assistance and advice of the Very Reverend Dr. Krikor Maksoudian, director of the Krikor and Clara Zohrab Information Center. Likewise, our special thanks go to Aram Arkun, the assistant director of the same center, for providing us with much needed references and texts, and for guiding us to other sources of information. We owe much also to the expert and friendly guidance of Professor Kevork Bardakjian of the University of Michigan, as well as for the precious information contained in his *Reference Guide to Modern Armenian Literature, 1500–1920*. In the selection of texts we were occasionally guided by the discriminating taste exhibited in Minas Teoleolian's *Dar me grakanutiyun* (A century of literature, 2 vols.). A personal word of gratitude also goes to Edmond Y. Azadian, who helped us on numerous occasions with invaluable suggestions.

We also gratefully acknowledge our indebtedness to the scholars, poets, and writers who generously granted us permission to make use of their translations and scholarship in this volume. Particular thanks are owed to Aris Sevag and Hagop Giuludjian for their highly valued contributions.

Gabriel Basmajian, one of the editors of the first two volumes of *The Heritage of Armenian Literature,* died in 2001. Although he had no direct part in the editing and writing of the present volume, as a small token of our esteem we have included him as an editor of this volume as well.

Finally, we express our very special thanks for the support of the Dolores Zohrab Liebmann Fund, whose generous grant made this publication possible.

TRANSCRIPTION OF THE ARMENIAN ALPHABET

The transcription system used in *The Heritage of Armenian Literature* is the Armenian Review transliteration key, which is based on the phonetic values of Eastern and Classical Armenian and omits the use of diacritics.

All texts included in this anthology have been normalized accordingly, and diacritical signs have been omitted.

Ա	ա	a	Յ	յ	y & h
Բ	բ	b	Ն	ն	n
Գ	գ	g	Շ	շ	sh
Դ	դ	d	Ո	ո	o & vo
Ե	ե	e & ye	Չ	չ	ch
Զ	զ	z	Պ	պ	p
Է	է	e & é	Ջ	ջ	j
Ը	ը	e	Ռ	ռ	r
Թ	թ	t	Ս	ս	s
Ժ	ժ	zh	Վ	վ	v
Ի	ի	l	Տ	տ	t
Լ	լ	l	Ր	ր	r
Խ	խ	kh	Ց	ց	ts
Ծ	ծ	tz	Ւ	ւ	v
Կ	կ	k	Փ	փ	p
Հ	հ	h	Ք	ք	k
Ձ	ձ	dz	Օ	օ	o
Ղ	ղ	gh	Ֆ	ֆ	f
Ճ	ճ	ch	Ու	ու	u & v
Մ	մ	m	Իւ	իւ	iu & iv

1. The transliteration of diphthongs is simplified.
2. Armenian names ending in (yan) are normalized to (ian).
3. The transliteration of proper names may vary from the system, according to widely accepted usage.

ARMENIA

AND THE NEIGHBORING COUNTRIES

An Overview from the Eighteenth to the Beginning of the Twentieth Century

As the eighteenth century opened, Armenia was partitioned between the Persian and Ottoman empires. During the previous two hundred years Armenia was the battleground between these two rivals, who fought on a land that belonged to neither of them and utterly devastated it. The political, social, demographic, and cultural changes that occurred during the eighteenth century were shaped or dictated by the events of previous centuries. In order to place them in historical perspective, it might be helpful to go back a bit and briefly examine some of the major circumstances that played portentous roles in the destiny of the Armenian people.

Armenia: Battleground between Rival Neighbors

From the fifteenth to the seventeenth century there was no central power in Armenia proper, except in a few locations where a descendent of an ancient feudal lord retained his rule over a hereditary estate or a fortress. The entire country seemed open to hordes of marauding Mongol and Turkoman tribes from Central Asia, who poured in and lived off the land, looting and terrorizing the inhabitants. At the beginning of the fifteenth century these tribes were grouped into two rival confederacies, the Black Sheep (*Kara-Koyunlu*) and the White Sheep (*Ak-Koyunlu*), which established themselves as rulers over Armenia (eastern Anatolia) and northwestern Persia, respectively. As Muslim domination of the region from central Asia to the Balkans increased, and as the Ottomans and the Persians emerged as powers in this territory, a power struggle was inevitable.

Their deadly rivalry began in the early sixteenth century, when Shah Ismail I (1502–24) of Persia, the founder of the Safavid dynasty (1502–1736), led his troops, known as the *Kizil-bash* (redheads, because of the red caps they wore), against the White Sheep and ended their rule over Persia. Then he raided Eastern Armenia and occupied almost the entire country, causing considerable devastation. The Persians also captured much of Georgia, consolidating their position in the Caucasus.

These developments were naturally most unwelcome to the other great power of the region, the Ottoman Empire, which had its own plans to expand to the east and to the south. The conflicting ambitions of these two forces set the stage for a series of continuous wars that were fought on Armenian soil and lasted for two centuries.[1]

In 1512 the Ottoman sultan, Selim I (1512–20), launched a great offensive against Persia. This was motivated by religious animosity as well as by the pursuit of territorial conquest: the Ottoman Turks belonged to the Sunni faction of Islam, whereas the Persians adhered to the Shi'ite faction, and each considered the other a heretical sect.[2]

Selim commanded a formidable army of Janissaries,[3] whose conquests brought the central and southern provinces of Armenia under Ottoman rule. For the first time, the Ottomans crossed the Euphrates River and set foot on Armenian soil. Shah Ismail was forced to retreat

---

1. In the course of less than two centuries (from 1512 to 1746), there were eleven major wars between the Ottomans and the Persians: 1512–16, 1533–34, 1547–52, 1553–55, 1578–90, 1602–12, 1616–18, 1623–39, 1723–27, 1730–36, and 1743–46. All of them were fought on Armenian territory, depopulating and laying waste to large areas.

2. As a preliminary measure to his campaign, Sultan Selim put to death some 40,000 of his subjects who were suspected of belonging to the heretical sect. Another irritant was the fact that the Ottomans saw the emergence of Safavid power as a threat to their own claim to the caliphate and the leadership of the Muslim world.

3. The Janissaries (*yenicheri*, new troops, in Turkish) were a branch of the Turkish infantry that came into existence in the fourteenth century. Originally composed of slaves and prisoners of war, their ranks were later stocked with Christian youths abducted from their families at a very young age, Islamized, and trained to be ferocious warriors. They formed the empire's main fighting force, but later, as they acquired more power, they raised insurrections and palace revolts, and eventually became its scourge. They were abolished by Sultan Mahmud II in 1826.

from Erzinjan (Erzincan) and Erzurum to the Araks River, but as he left he devastated the entire country. The crucial battle took place in 1514 on the plain of Chaldiran (Çaldiran), northwest of Tabriz, where the shah was defeated. Tabriz was taken and the Persian kings' gorgeous throne was carted to Constantinople, where it can still be seen.

Retaliation was not long in coming. In 1516 Shah Ismail invaded Georgia and the Caspian coast of Shirvan (Şirvan), and a short while later Shah Tahmasp (1524–76) raided Armenia as far as Kars, Erzurum, and Terjan (Tercan). This was countered by a campaign by Sultan Suleiman ("the Magnificent": 1520–66) in 1533, which resulted in the recapture of Erzurum and adjacent regions, and the seizure of the fortress of Van.

The next Ottoman campaign began in 1547–48, when more Armenian territories were seized. This, in turn, provoked another vicious counterraid by Shah Tahmasp. In Armenia proper, the immediate consequence of these attacks and counterattacks was the great famine of 1552–53.

The historian Dickran Kouymjian characterizes the Turkish attack of 1553 to 1555 as "one of the most consciously violent recorded in the annals of the Ottoman Empire."[4] He quotes the Turkish historian Ibrahim Pechevi, whose history of these campaigns vividly describes the seizure and burning of Yerevan, the capture of Nakhijevan, and the total destruction of all the provinces between Tabriz and Maragheh and details the willful devastation carried out by the Turks. Here is a section of Pechevi's entry for the year AH 962 (AD 1553–54):

> The region had become very prosperous, having many rich villages with cultivated lands. The victorious Ottoman army destroyed and ruined those prosperous villages and leveled them to the ground. From there the army . . . arrived on the seventeenth day at the city of Yerevan, which was the soul of Persia. . . . Everything was burned to the ground. On the twenty-third day it moved on to the Arpa Chaï, and in that area too everything was pillaged and destroyed. . . . On the twenty-fifth day it entered the land called Karabagh, which, with its mountains and rich orchards, is a very famous region of the Persian lands. . . . The local population had scattered and disappeared without a trace . . . yet, the army seized enormous riches and spoils. . . . On the twenty-seventh day it reached the plain of Nakhijevan. From

---

4. Dickran Kouymjian, "Armenia from the Fall of the Cilician Kingdom (1375) to the Forced Emigration under Shah Abbas (1604)" in Richard G. Hovannisian, ed., *The Armenian People from Ancient to Modern Times* (New York, 1977), 2:16.

dread of the victorious army, the towns and villages, the houses and habitations were so deserted and desolate that the area had become a haven for owls and crows, striking terror amongst those who viewed such a sight. . . . The army, thirsty for booty, again looted and destroyed, not leaving one stone upon another. Besides this, for a distance of four to five days' march from the main route, all villages and hamlets, fields and construction were destroyed and ruined to such a degree that not a trace of building or any life remained. . . . But in addition to this, uncountable quantities of valuable property and stores were looted and destroyed. And the number of handsome young boys and lovely, gentle young girls who were enslaved was of such a large portion that it is impossible for this writer to describe. In no other campaign did such a quantity of wealth come to the Ottoman army. There was not a soldier's tent in which the number [of slaves] . . . was less than three, and the number of tents with five or more than ten was beyond counting.[5]

On May 29, 1555, a peace treaty was signed at Amasya, whereby the Ottomans dominated most of Armenia and western Georgia, and the Persians kept Shirvan and Tabriz. Taking advantage of the quarrels of succession that erupted in Persia following the death of Shah Tahmasp in 1576, the Ottomans launched a new campaign into Armenia (1578–90) and took most of Transcaucasia. During this campaign tens of thousands of the native Armenian population were sent into exile or taken prisoner, and most of the survivors migrated.

When Shah Abbas the Great (1587–1629) acceded to the throne, he tried to recapture lost territory. He forced the Ottomans out of Transcaucasia and regained a number of cities; he had similar successes in the province of Nakhijevan, including Julfa. The local Armenians, who had been laid destitute by heavy Ottoman taxes, and the Shi'ite Moslems, who had been persecuted for their beliefs, welcomed the Persians as liberators. For the Armenians, however, a greater tragedy awaited. In 1603 Shah Abbas laid siege to the fortress of Yerevan. In the summer of 1604, at the news of an Ottoman counteroffensive, Abbas ordered the entire Armenian population of Bayazit (Beyazit), Van, and Nakhijevan to be displaced, as part of a scorched earth policy. The number of Armenians removed from this area between 1604 and 1605 is estimated at

---

5. Ibrahim Pechevi, *Ta'rikh* (History), quoted in A. Safrastian, ed., *Turkakan aghbiurnere Hayastani, hayeri yev Andrkovkasi mius zhoghovrdneri masin* (Turkish sources on Armenia, Armenians, and other peoples of Transcaucasia) (Yerevan, 1964), 1:33 ff. See Hovannisian, *Armenian People*, 2:16–17.

close to 300,000. Thousands perished crossing the Araxes River. Most of the displaced Armenians were gradually settled in various parts of Persia. However, one group, comprised mostly of merchant families from Julfa, was settled near Isfahan, the Safavid capital, and a new town was built for them, which they called New Julfa.

Persian-Ottoman hostilities were renewed in the 1620s, but the Ottomans did not have a chance against Shah Abbas's newly refurbished army. In 1639 the Treaty of Zuhab (Zuhabad and also known as Qasr-i Shirin) put an end for a time to the perennial policy of mutual despoilment and initiated a period of peace, albeit shaky, which lasted about eighty years. In accordance with this treaty, Armenia was partitioned between the Ottoman and the Persian empires along a border that ran from the Javakhk mountains in the north to the junction of the Araxes and Akhurian (Arpaçay) rivers, passed through the twin summits of Ararat, and descended south to the mountains of Vaspurakan. The Ottomans acquired Akhaltskha (Akhaltsikhe), Kars, Bayazit, and Van, and the Persians kept the provinces of Yerevan, Nakhijevan, and Karabagh.

Early in the 1720s the Safavids were in decline. This encouraged Peter the Great of Russia to invade the coastal regions of the Caspian Sea, and the Afghans to move to occupy Isfahan. This was also an opportune moment for the Ottoman sultan, Ahmed III (1673–1736), to break the peace accord of 1639 and invade Eastern Armenia, which he did in 1723. Within two years the Ottomans were in control of the entire region except Karabagh and Siunik, where the Armenian *meliks*, under the military leadership of such men as David Beg, Avan Yüzbashi (Captain Avan), and Mkhitar Sparapet, mounted vigorous opposition and forced the Turks out of these domains.

In 1734–35 Nadir, the de facto ruler of Iran (he was shah 1736–47, establishing the Afshar dynasty), invaded Eastern Armenia and Georgia, dealing a crushing blow to the Ottoman forces and regaining all the territory lost in 1723. The two imperial rivals, who for more than a century had shifted borders back and forth, leaving death and devastation in their wake, eventually settled on the borders established by the treaty of 1639.

As reward for their heroic defense, Nadir Shah recognized the semiautonomous status of the Armenian *meliks* of Karabagh[6] and granted exemption from taxes and other privileges to the Holy See of Etchmiadzin.

---

6. The five Armenian melikdoms of Karabagh—Gulistan, Jraberd, Khachen, Varanda, and Dizak—originated in the principality of Khachen, an ancient feudal institution that existed from the tenth to the sixteenth century. Eastern (or Persian) Armenia was organized administratively into four khanates (provinces): Yerevan,

The assassination of Nadir Shah in 1747 triggered a struggle for succession and provided an opportunity for Turkic tribes, such as the Qajars in Yerevan, Ganja, and Nakhijevan, and the Javanshirs in Karabagh, to assert themselves. However, they were subdued in 1762 by Karim Khan Zand of Persia.

The Russo-Turkish wars of 1768–74 and 1787–91, which occurred during the reign of Catherine the Great (1762–96) and ended with the defeat of the Ottomans, kept both sides busy in the Balkans and Crimea and their hands off Eastern Armenia.

Emancipation Movements

The search for ways and means to emancipate Armenia from the Ottoman and Persian yokes preoccupied a number of religious and secular leaders as early as the sixteenth century, and the Armenian Church played an important role in this struggle. It is interesting to note that despite the fact that the Roman Catholic Church was energetically engaged in spreading Catholicism among Armenians at the time, a number of Armenian leaders believed that the European powers could be persuaded to help in the liberation of Armenia only through the mediation of the papacy, even if that would entail compromise on certain religious matters. Between 1547 and 1585 two missions, each headed by a catholicos, Stepanos V Salmastatsi (1545–67) and Mikayel I Sebastatsi (1567–76) respectively, and delegates of the Armenian princes and *meliks* visited Venice, Rome, and the major European courts to plead the Armenian cause. Some of these powers saw an independent or autonomous Armenia as consistent with or helpful to their own political aims, but a major obstacle to its realization came from the Vatican, which made unification of the Armenian Church with the Roman Catholic Church the sole condition of assistance.

The next serious attempt at an emancipation project was launched in 1678 by Catholicos Hakob Jughayetsi (Hakob of Julfa, 1655–80), who invited the leading *meliks* of Siunik and Artsakh (Karabagh) and the

---

Nakhijevan, Karabagh (including Zangezur), and Ganja. In 1603 Shah Abbas I recognized their special status. They played an important role in military expeditions. In the second half of the eighteenth century, *melik* Shahnazar of Varanda allied himself with Panah Khan Javanshir, the chieftain of a Turkic tribe, against the other *meliks*, and this led to the downfall of autonomous Karabagh. The heroes of Karabagh inspired the historical novels *The Melikdoms of Khamsa* (1882) and *David Beg* (1882) by Raffi; an opera, *David Beg* (1950), by Armen Tigranian; and another historical novel, *Mkhitar Sparapet* (1961), by Sero Khanzadian. See George A. Bournoutian, *A History of Qarabagh: An Annotated Translation of Mirza Jamal Javanshir Qarabagh's Tarikh-e Qarabagh* (Costa Mesa, Calif., 1994).

prominent religious and secular leaders of Armenia to a secret meeting in Etchmiadzin. There he proposed leading a delegation to Europe in search of a protector for Armenia. The group proceeded to Constantinople, where further consultations were to take place, but upon the sudden death of the catholicos the delegation was dispersed.

Some twenty years later, however, the son of the *melik* of Zangezur, Israel Ori (1659–1711), a member of the defunct delegation, dedicated himself wholeheartedly to the pursuit of the emancipation project that was cut short by Hakob Jughayetsi's death. From Constantinople Ori proceeded to Venice, then to France, where he served in the army of Louis XIV, rising to the rank of major, and fought against the English in the 1688–95 Franco-English war. He later settled in Prussia as a merchant. His contacts with individuals in power led him to Prince Johann Wilhelm of the palatinate in Düsseldorf, to whom he presented his plans for the eventual independence of Armenia. The prince responded favorably and was instrumental in involving others in this project: the Holy Roman Emperor, Leopold I (1640–1705); the grand duke of Tuscany; and the pope, who, however, did not show much interest. Then, in 1701, Ori went on to Russia, where his deliberations with Russian officials led him to conclude that Christian Russia, as a country with major political and economic interests in the Middle East, would be best disposed to help Armenia. He managed to obtain an audience with Peter the Great (1689–1725), who dispatched a delegation to Armenia to examine a proposed expedition against the Ottomans and the Persians. But the Russo-Swedish War (1700–21) delayed the project. Ori entered the service of the tsar, was given a military title, and in 1708 was sent to Isfahan, Persia, as a special envoy. Although he worked hard to realize his plans, he eventually failed, as a result of French conspiracy. Ori left Persia and was on his way to St. Petersburg for further consultations when he died in Astrakhan in 1711.[7]

In the 1720s an uprising in Siunik, Eastern Armenia, led by two Armenian professional military leaders, David Bek and Mkhitar Sparapet, dislodged the Persians, chased away the invading Ottoman Turks, and acquired a short-lived autonomy for Karabagh.

Even though Israel Ori's efforts failed, they inspired another man of vision, Hovsep (Joseph) Emin. Born in 1726 in Hamadan, Iran, he emigrated with his parents to Calcutta, where his merchant father

---

7. Israel Ori's life and political activities are the subject of an eponymous novel (1959) by Arazi (Movses Harutiunian, 1874–1964). For documentary evidence of Ori's correspondence with Peter the Great see George A. Bournoutian, *Armenians and Russia, 1626–1796* (Costa Mesa, Calif., 2001).

established a business. By this time there was a flourishing Armenian community in India, mainly in Madras and Calcutta, where the merchant class gained eminence through their high level of prosperity and culture. At an early age Joseph Emin, deeply committed to the emancipation of his own people and having decided to pursue a military career, went to England (1751) and attended the Royal Military Academy at Woolwich. He established a number of contacts with government leaders, including the war minister, William Pitt, but soon realized that extending help to Armenia was not compatible with Britain's political interests. In 1760 Emin toured Armenia to propagate his ideas of liberation and, realizing that it could not be achieved without Russia's help, went to St. Petersburg, where he explained to Chancellor Vorontsov and other dignitaries his plan of liberating Armenia and creating an Armenian-Georgian federative republic under Russian protection. In spite of some apparent sympathy, Russia dismissed the plan. Encouraged by the supportive attitude of the Georgian king, Heracle II, Emin tried to organize armed resistance units in various regions from Karabagh to Mush, but the plan failed because of the strong opposition of Catholicos Simeon I Yerevantsi (1763–80), who did not wish to cause provocation, and the Georgian nobility, who feared they would lose their feudal rights.

In 1773 Emin, back in India, joined the Madras Group, an association of politically inclined intellectuals dedicated to the cause of Armenian emancipation.[8] Their ultimate aim was the creation of an Armenia freed from the feudal order and ruled by a constitutional government. To expound these ideas and inspire the youth with patriotism, they published three pamphlets—considered the first in Armenian political literature—one after the other: *Nor tetrak vor kochi hordorak* (A new booklet, called Exhortations), *Vorogayt parats* (Snare of glory), and *Tetrak vor kochi Nshavak* (A booklet called Target). In 1780 a draft constitution for "an Armenian state under Russian protection" was presented to the Russian government, followed, in 1783, by a similar document by Archbishop Hovsep Arghutian; despite some favorable reaction, neither of these bore fruit. In 1788 Joseph Emin published a book in English titled *The Life and Adventures of Joseph Emin, an Armenian*, with the aim

---

8. The Madras Group was created in the 1770s by Movses Baghramian, Shahamir and Hakob Shahamirian, and other intellectuals, with the financial support of wealthy merchants. Its aim was to sensitize the public to the plight of Armenians in both Persia and the Ottoman Empire, and to propagate the ideas of the European Enlightenment. An Armenian press, established in 1772 by Shahamir Shahamirian, helped immensely in spreading their message by the printed word.

of acquainting Europeans with Armenian realities and aspirations. He died in Calcutta in 1809.

Eastern Armenia under Russian Rule

At the close of the eighteenth century, the Eastern Armenian khanates of Yerevan, Nakhijevan, Karabagh, and Ganja were under Iranian rule.[9] In 1801, however, a major change occurred in the political scene that was destined to have momentous consequences. In its drive to move beyond the Caucasus mountains, a cherished aim pursued since the days of Peter the Great, Russia annexed Georgia and subsequently invaded the khanate of Ganja, triggering the Russo-Iranian war of 1804–13. This conflict, fought intermittently on various fronts, brought into play the sharp rivalries and hidden agendas of France, Great Britain, Russia, Turkey, and Iran. While Russia was fighting on two fronts—the Caucasus in the east and the Danube basin in Europe—France and Great Britain, their conflicting interests notwithstanding, were independently supplying military aid to both Iran and Turkey, in an effort to restrain Russian expansion. Having signed a peace treaty with the Ottomans and repelled Napoleon in the disastrous retreat of 1812, the Russians concentrated on the Caucasian front and defeated the Iranian armies. Through the Treaty of Gulistan (a fortified town in Karabagh), signed in 1813, Russia acquired the mostly Armenian-populated khanates of Ganja and Karabagh. Despite the many attempts of the Russian army, the khanates of Nakhijevan and Yerevan, including Etchmiadzin, remained under Iranian rule. As the result of an administrative reorganization, Russia incorporated Ganja into Georgia and Karabagh into the (Muslim) Caspian Province.

None of the parties involved was happy with the Treaty of Gulistan. Russia had not acquired enough, Iran had lost too much, and Eastern Armenia had not achieved complete union with Russia, as planned by Armenian leaders headed by Bishop Nerses of Ashtarak (later elected catholicos, 1843–57). In fact, the ultimate plan was to achieve autonomy for Armenia under Russian suzerainty, a plan which had its supporters even at the Russian court. Taking advantage of the death of Tsar Alexander I (1777–1825) and the Decembrist uprising of 1825 in Russia, the Iranians invaded Karabagh, igniting the second Russo-Iranian war (1826–28). The Russian army, to which a number of Armenian armed

---

9. See George A. Bournoutian, *The Khanate of Erevan under Qajar Rule, 1795–1628* (Costa Mesa, Calif., 1992).

units and thousands of volunteers had been joined, placed under the command of Ivan Paskevich by the new tsar, Nicholas I (1796–1855), crossed the Araxes River and beleaguered Tabriz, the capital of Iranian Azerbaijan. The shah sued for peace, and the Treaty of Turkmanchaï was signed in 1828, according to the terms of which the khanates of Yerevan and Nakhijevan were annexed to Russia. Thus almost all of Eastern Armenia became part of Russia, with the Araxes River marking the boundary between Armenia and Iran. These delineations remain to the present day.

As presaged by the Treaty of Turkmanchaï, the union of Eastern Armenia with Russia triggered a massive displacement of Armenians. According to one source,[10] between 1828 and 1830 some 130,000 Armenians from Persian and Turkish Armenia immigrated to Eastern Armenia to seek relief from Persian and Turkish oppression, a move that also helped replenish the depleted Armenian population in the regions of Yerevan and Nakhijevan, which were integrated into an administrative unit called the Armenian Province (*Armianskaia Oblast*). These migrations began a trend that resumed after the Crimean War (1853–56) and the Russo-Turkish War (1877–78), and eventually created a solid Armenian majority in part of the Armenian homeland—a development that was later to have great political significance.[11]

The victories against Iran in 1813 and 1828 and the unification of Eastern Armenia with Russia raised strong hopes for the realization of an autonomous Armenia under Russian protection, but both Nicholas I and Paskevich (who later became governor-general of the Caucasus) were staunch centralists and proponents of the Russification of all non-Russian elements. Although Nerses of Ashtarak was decorated for his efforts in the war, he was exiled to Bessarabia as "the prelate of the Armenian Church." In 1849, as the result of administrative changes, the regions of Yerevan and Nakhijevan were incorporated into Yerevan Province, and the remaining regions of Eastern Armenia were included in the provinces of Tiflis and Ganja (Elizavetpol/Kirovabad). This arrangement remained basically unchanged until 1917.

The unification of Eastern Armenia with Russia brought about a policy change in the Russian government's attitude toward Armenians

---

10. M. G. Nersissian, ed. *Hay zhoghovrdi patmutiun* (The history of the Armenian people) (Yerevan, 1972), 340.

11. See George A. Bournoutian, *A History of the Armenian People* (Costa Mesa, Calif., 1994), 2:66–70.

and particularly the Armenian Church. Realizing very well the important role of the Armenian Church and its authority over the Armenian people—not only in religious matters but in political, social, and cultural matters as well—and recognizing that the catholicos who resides in Etchmiadzin is acknowledged as their supreme head by all Armenians—including those living in the Ottoman Empire and Persia—the Russian government decided to take advantage of these circumstances in shaping its policies in the Near and Middle East.

In 1836 Tsar Nicholas I enacted a set of regulations, known as the *Polozhenie,* to oversee the activities of the Armenian Church. It declared freedom of belief for the Armenian Church and granted it an autonomy that was denied the Georgian Church, which became subordinate to the Russian Orthodox Church. The *Polozhenie* also had a further, much wider impact, encompassing as it did the educational and cultural activities of all Armenians within the boundaries of Russia. As a recognized, distinct religious community, Armenians now had the right to preserve their language and national heritage and were allowed to open and maintain Armenian schools under the supervision of the clergy. The Church was exempted from taxes, and its property was secure. The catholicos, as supreme head of the Church, was to be elected by the entire Armenian nation, including those living outside of Russia, by means of representatives to a general assembly composed of clergy and laymen. The assembly was to present two candidates to the tsar, one of whom he would certify: obviously, the one who would be more loyal to him. A restriction on the catholicos' power was the Synod of Etchmiadzin, which was under the supervision of a procurator appointed by the tsar. Thus, on the one hand the *Polozhenie* granted religious, educational, and cultural autonomy to Armenians living in Russia. Yet on the other hand, by placing this autonomy under the supervision of the Church, it ensured that that autonomy would serve as a political tool for the tsar's own purposes.[12]

Armenians in the Ottoman Empire and in India resented the *Polozhenie,* considering its provisions contrary to the traditional practices of the Church. The *Polozhenie* remained in force, however, until 1903, when Tsar Nicholas II (1868–1918), in an effort to speed up the Russification of national minorities, abrogated it. He ordered the confiscation of Armenian Church property and the transfer of Armenian schools to

---

12. Cf. A. H. Shaghgamian, ed. *Hay Zhoghovrdi patmutiun* (History of the Armenian people) (Yerevan, 1974), 5:214.

Russian jurisdiction, measures that provoked strong reactions. Catholicos Mkrtich Khrimian (known as Khrimian Hayrik, 1892–1906) refused to sign the decree and mobilized the Church and the people against it. After two years of protests and violent demonstrations, the tsar rescinded the decree in 1905.

Western Armenia under Ottoman Rule

By the beginning of the nineteenth century the Ottoman Empire was in sharp decline. After centuries of misrule, its public administration had become rife with corruption. Top government positions were customarily acquired by bribery: each position had a price, and the aspiring candidate had to pay it in full into the sultan's treasury. Since this practice prevailed from the highest to the lowest level, each official had to extort bribe money from his subordinates; as a result, the common people at the very bottom of the scale were the ones who were most preyed upon. These extortions were, of course, imposed on top of numerous other taxes and duties extracted from the people under different guises.

The armed forces, known as the Janissaries, had become a group of thugs who toppled or killed sultans and viziers at will. The central power had been weakened to such an extent that the pashas and the Kurdish chieftains exercised absolute rule in the interior provinces, oppressing and enslaving the people and refusing to pay imperial levies. The Ottoman Empire had become the worst kind of feudal state, and the segment of the population most cruelly oppressed comprised the non-Muslim subjects, who were denied security of life and property and equal standing before the courts. This situation was exploited by the foreign powers—mainly France, Great Britain, and Russia—each pursuing its own interests behind the facade of what was called "humanitarian intervention,"[13] and the religious factor played an important role. As it had since the days of Catherine the Great (1729–1796), Russia took it as a duty to protect the Orthodox Russians, Serbs, Bulgarians, and Rumanians, whereas France claimed to be protecting the Roman Catholics. The decaying empire also faced two major threats: financial bankruptcy and political unrest among its subjugated nations. The Ottoman Empire was no longer able to conquer countries and bring back spoils of war to replenish the treasury. On the contrary, the conquered countries were now struggling to cast off the Ottoman yoke, and the sultans were trying hard to suppress them with bloodbaths.

---

13. Cf. Vahakn N. Dadrian, *The History of the Armenian Genocide* (Oxford, 1995), 7 ff.

The rapid deterioration of the empire and increased foreign pressure eventually persuaded Sultan Selim III (1789–1807) to introduce European-style reforms. He established a new corps (called *Nizam-i Jedid,* the New Order), opened a military academy, and reorganized the fleet. But there was an immediate and vehement counterreaction from the radicals and the Muslim clergy, and Selim was assassinated by the Janissaries. His successor, Mahmud II (1808–39), proclaimed reforms and ordered that the people and their *rayahs* (the subjugated non-Muslims) be treated with justice. In the 1820s Mahmud also succeeded in eliminating by force some of the rebellious feudal lords of the interior provinces, and in 1826, almost in one night, he massacred the Janissaries assembled in the capital and began to form a modern army, with European help.

By this time, however, the dismemberment of the Ottoman Empire had already begun. It started with the Serb revolt (1815–17), which invited Russian intervention and assured autonomy for Serbia, Moldavia, and Wallachia under Russian protection. Next came the Greek uprising, which eventually, with British intervention, led to total independence (1830). The greatest loss was the separation of Egypt under Mohammed-Ali, governor general of Egypt, and the ensuing Turko-Egyptian wars (1831–33 and 1839–40). This was followed, in 1861, by the autonomy of Lebanon, negotiated by France, and many more losses. All these events clearly demonstrated to the sultans that urgent and serious reforms were necessary if the Ottoman Empire were to survive.

In 1839 the young Sultan Abdul-Mejid I (1839–61), upon the advice of officials who favored reforms, issued the *Hatt-i Sherif-i Gülhane* (Edict of the Rose Chamber), which gave unprecedented guarantees of liberty and security of life and property to all subjects of the empire. It promised military and fiscal reforms, a centralized administration, an assembly of leading citizens (*ayan mejlisi*), the establishment of provincial councils, and mixed tribunals. The *Hatt-i Sherif* thus initiated reform and ushered in the *Tanzimat* (reorganization or reform) period. The edict was strongly opposed by Muslim religious leaders, on the grounds that it broke with Islamic tradition; furthermore, it was not enacted by legislation but implemented by a decree of the sultan, who could rescind it at will.[14] In 1856, at the Paris Peace Conference convened after the Crimean War,[15] Turkey was forced by the European powers to pass a

---

14. Cf. Bournoutian, *History of the Armenian People,* 2:17.

15. The Crimean War (1854–56) was fought mainly in the Crimean Peninsula; the combatants were Russia on one side and Great Britain, France, and Turkey on

new "Reform Act" (called the "*Hatt-i Humayun*," imperial edict), which was almost a replica of the *Hatt-i Sherif*, with the addition of articles addressing the problems in the Balkans and, more particularly, eliminating discrimination against non-Muslims in the empire. In fact these reforms were only words on paper, aimed at appeasing the great powers. As admitted by Abdurrahman Sheref, an official Ottoman historian and president of the State Council, "The reforms of the *Tanzimat*, i.e. the idea of the organization of the legal state, is to be framed on paper. Let them deliver speeches, compose advertisements, and temporize with people inside and outside the country. But they themselves [the authors of the *Tanzimat*] will proceed as they please. This is the meaning many people will give to the idea of a legal state."[16] Militant Islamic nationalism was opposed to introducing European-style legal reforms: the principles on which they were based were not compatible with the customs and traditions of Muslim society, where the idea of equality between Muslim and non-Muslim was a foreign concept.[17]

In fact, by 1876 the *Tanzimat* was no more than a smoke screen, and after it was abolished by Sultan Abdul-Hamid II (1876–1909), the Ottoman Empire carried on its despotic and oppressive rule. Oppression reached a climax in 1894–96, with the massacre of some 200,000 Armenians in the interior provinces.

Social, Economic, and Political Conditions

A country that had been turned into a battleground by two powers viciously fighting each other for two centuries could hardly be expected to develop viable socioeconomic conditions. Devastation caused by marauding armies as they moved back and forth, atrocities committed by the new rulers every time a province changed hands, forced population displacements, and the heavy emigration of native Armenians, to the extent that it changed the ethnographic nature of the land,[18] all contributed to the ravage of Armenia.

---

the other. The war arose from a series of misunderstandings and diplomatic errors concerning conflicts among the interests of the great powers in the Near East, including a dispute over the protection of the holy places in Palestine. Cf. "The Crimean War," *Encyclopaedia Britannica* (1963), 6:759.

16. Dadrian, *History of the Armenian Genocide*, 34.
17. For more on this subject see ibid., 21–23, 32–34.
18. At the turn of the sixteenth to the seventeenth century, a large number of nomadic Turkic tribes were brought in to repopulate western Anatolia. See Ahmed Refik, *Anadoluda Türk aşiretler* (Turkic tribes in Anatolia) (Istanbul, 1932), vi–x.

Both Eastern and Western Armenia, ruled by the Persians and the Ottomans respectively, were administratively divided into khanates, each headed by a *khan,* in Persia, and into *eyalets* (provinces), each headed by a pasha, under the Ottoman Empire. These officials were appointed by and were accountable only to the shah or the sultan, and the favors they enjoyed were proportionate to the tribute they paid to the shah's or the sultan's treasury. These feudal lords, some of whom, particularly on the Persian side, enjoyed hereditary succession, exercised absolute power over their domains, with rights to impose and collect taxes, conduct military actions, and rule on judicial and civic matters. Each khanate or *eyalet* had numerous levels of administration, on each of which the official in charge could appoint his subordinates. Most of these appointments were acquired by bribery, and the bribe money was ultimately extorted from the people.

From the sixteenth to the eighteenth century the great majority of the population in Western Armenia were peasants, considered by their Muslim rulers as *rayahs,* tax-paying, non-Muslim subjects of the Empire. Numerous levies were imposed on them, such as *harach,* for being a non-Muslim; *ashar* (tithe), a tax on produce; *jizie,* a head tax on each member of a family; *bahra,* a tax for working on the land; *salarlik,* a tax on civil servants; a tax on marriage; and many others, according to the whims of the pashas. In addition, many tolls, duties, and "gifts" (called *peshkesh*) were extorted from the people by violent means whenever a grandee happened to visit the place. In almost every province[19] large expanses of land were granted, with hereditary rights, to various Turkish and Kurdish *begs* (tribal chiefs). The recipients had autonomy over the land, and the peasantry living on it was considered their personal property. These feudal lords appropriated most of the produce of the land, fed and sheltered their armed units at the expense of the peasants, and exacted from the meager sustenance of the peasants various taxes in arbitrary amounts, to be paid in produce, cattle, or forced labor. A peasant did not have the right to leave the land and move elsewhere; if he did, for a period of ten years the lord had the right to force him back and penalize him for losses suffered. Armenian monasteries or abbeys were allowed to own land for cultivation, on the condition that they paid *bahra,* the agrarian tax, directly into the state treasury.

A calamity that struck the peasantry periodically was the practice of gathering male children from Christian households and taking them

---

19. The only exceptions were the mountainous regions of Sasun, in the province of Bitlis, and Zeytun, in Cilicia.

away to be trained in warfare to replenish the ranks of the Janissaries. An anonymous chronicler of the sixteenth century describes such a scene: "The child's parents, brothers, and relatives were weeping with the greatest sadness, and everyone present broke into a heart-rending lamentation that no human tongue can describe. They wore black garments and sack cloth, sat on ashes, and wished that death had spared them from such a tragic scene."[20]

The status of the Armenian peasantry in the Ottoman Empire remained unchanged as late as the nineteenth century. In a few large seaports such as Constantinople, Smyrna (Izmir), and Trebizond (Trabzon), and in cities on the main overland trade routes such as Karin (Erzurum) and Yerznka (Erzincan), Armenians, along with Greeks and Jews, fared much better, since they held important positions in domestic and international trade. In these cities most of the Armenians were engaged in trades and crafts, where they excelled as jewelers, goldsmiths, silversmiths, and metal workers. They formed their own trade guilds to coordinate their activities and protect their interests and the quality of their work. These trade guilds gradually acquired power and began to exert considerable influence on social issues, even at times finding themselves in conflict with the Patriarchate.

Armenians in Constantinople

Constantinople, the capital of the Ottoman Empire, has occupied a very prominent place in the history of Western Armenia. It eventually contained the greatest concentration of Armenians and became the center of the cultural, religious, intellectual, and political life of Western Armenia.

The Armenian presence in Constantinople goes back to the beginning of the fifth century. When the Roman Empire was split in two in 395, its role and interests in the east were assumed by Byzantium, which also inherited all of Rome's pretensions and claims with regard to Armenia. This resulted in an active exchange of envoys, military men, clerics, students, merchants, and hostages. There is reason to believe that a significant number of Armenians established themselves in Constantinople between the ninth and the eleventh centuries, when there were a number of ruling emperors from a Macedonian dynasty that had Armenian origin, and when Armenian generals fought the empire's battles with contingents of Armenian soldiers. By the tenth century,

---

20. Levon S. Khachikian, ed., *Hay zhoghovrdi patmutiun* (History of the Armenian people) (Yerevan, 1972), 4:292.

when the number of Armenians had increased considerably, a strong wave of fanaticism, inspired by the Greek clergy, swept the country and drove out the Armenians and other non-Orthodox minorities. However, when Michael VIII Palaeologus came to power in the second half of the thirteenth century (1261–82), he introduced religious tolerance and even tried to find terms of reconciliation with the pope, in an effort to unite Christendom against the ominous threat of invasion by Mongol hordes from the east. Around the middle of the fourteenth century, in the quarter of Galata that was under Genoese rule, there was an Armenian church, St. Sarkis, where Armenian manuscripts were copied.[21] The next oldest church in that quarter is that of St. Gregory the Illuminator, built in 1436 on property purchased from the Genoese by a certain Koms, an Armenian merchant from Kaffa (Theodosia), Crimea. This church, renovated and rebuilt many times, was expanded with adjoining buildings, and a college that opened in 1886 has served up to the present day.

The organization of the Armenian communities within the Ottoman Empire into a distinct nation (*millet*) materialized only after the occupation of Constantinople in May, 1453, by Sultan Mohammed II (1451–81).[22] Realizing that the Armenians would be useful in the reconstruction of the capital because of their skills in the arts and in trade, the sultan moved large numbers of them from various regions and settled them within the walls of the city, mostly near the gates. In 1461 he established an Armenian Patriarchate and appointed the Primate of Brusa (Bursa), Bishop Hovakim, as the patriarch (1461–78), with full jurisdiction over religious and civic matters. This arrangement also had a political aim: to create a rival or counterbalance to the Greek Patriarchate. The date 1461 can be considered the beginning of the Armenian community in Constantinople as an organized, distinct, and legal entity.[23] According to statistics supplied by Yeremia Chelepi Keomiurchian (Kömürdjian,

---

21. Cf. Hakob J. Siruni, *Polis yev ir dere* (Constantinople and its role) (Beirut, 1965), 1:88, 91.

22. The fall of Constantinople marked the end of the Byzantine Empire, which had lasted for more than a thousand years. For three days Ottoman soldiers had license to pillage and kill as they pleased. Two eyewitnesses to the occupation, Armenian priests who lived in Constantinople, left vivid descriptions of the tragic events. Abraham Argiuratsi's *Voghb i vera arman Kostandnupolso* (Lament on the fall of Constantinople) and Arakel Baghishetsi's *Voghb mayrakaghakin Stampolu* (Elegy on the capital city of Stambol), both in verse, are included in part III of volume 2 of the present anthology.

23. There is compelling evidence that from as early as the eleventh century up to the fall of Constantinople there were Armenian bishops in the capital. Their presence indicates the existence of a sizable Armenian community and religious center. See Siruni, *Polis yev ir dere*, 90 ff.

1637–95) in his *History of Stambol,* by 1478, about twenty-five years after the occupation, Constantinople contained 817 Armenian households and 267 households of immigrants from Kaffa, most of whom were Armenians.[24]

As the Ottomans conquered more territories, the authority of the Armenian patriarch was extended over the Armenian communities of the newly acquired provinces, both in Anatolia and in Rumeli (European Turkey). Whenever a new patriarch was appointed a new edict was issued by the sultan, specifying his rights and duties in detail. The oldest such edict extant was issued in 1764 by Sultan Mustafa III (1717–74); it gives Patriarch Grigor Pasmachian (Basmadjian) full jurisdiction over all religious and civic matters pertaining to Armenians, including the appointment of primates, the levying of taxes and duties, the right to rule on judiciary cases, and the management of Church property. It also contains an article that was quite significant for the time, stating that no Christian should be forced to convert to Islam without the consent of the individual. In return, the patriarchs themselves had to pay considerable sums of money in tribute to the sultan, the vizier, and other high-ranking officials. It is fair to say, however, that in Constantinople, under the watchful eyes of the sultans and foreign embassies, the Armenian Church enjoyed a large degree of autonomy.

SOCIAL CONDITIONS

The Armenian population in the Ottoman capital was never a homogeneous mix. One should bear in mind that while Constantinople, Smyrna, and a few other cities were flourishing centers, the peasant population of the interior provinces languished in oppression and poverty under ruthless feudal lords and pashas. There was always a constant flow of migrants from the provinces, some forced to relocate, others lured by economic opportunities, and still others attempting to escape oppression. Each group had its own customs, traditions, dialect, and manners, and a many-colored social fabric was soon created, which resisted attempts to integrate. By the eighteenth century a wide range of social classes had emerged: the merchants who wielded considerable economic power; the *amiras,* wealthy bankers who managed the finances of the viziers, pashas, and the charities of the community; an elite class of intellectuals educated in European centers and imbued with democratic ideas; the ecclesiastic establishment; tradesmen who formed trade guilds for almost every profession; as well as shopkeepers, artisans, and common laborers. A society with so much diversity but no overarching

---

24. See Khachikian, *Hay zhoghovrdi patmutium,* 4:301.

regulatory instrument was rife with clashes, dissensions, and conflicts of interest. In the Ottoman Empire Armenians were considered an ethnic religious community (*millet*), and all authority—religious, civic, and judicial—was concentrated in the patriarch, whose jurisdictional limits were defined by a sultan's edict. In the 1830s a major conflict erupted between the *amiras* and the trade guilds, when the latter demanded to have a voice in the administration of a school and prevailed.

The Amiras

One group of notable Armenians, called *amiras* (from Arabic *amir*, chief or commander), played an important role in the developing relationships between the sultans and the patriarchs. Toward the end of the seventeenth century, a class of wealthy magnates emerged in Constantinople, most of them from the Armenian province of Aken; they acted as bankers, loaning money to viziers, pashas, and tax farmers. It had become an unwritten rule in the empire that top government appointments and lucrative positions were acquired by bribery, and it was the *amiras* who provided aspiring candidates with security. The wealthiest *amiras* also lent money to the sultan, thus becoming influential at the court. Many of them—such as the Palian (Balian), Tiuzian (Düzian), and Tatian (Dadian) families—held highly responsible positions; their members became the chief imperial architect, the director of imperial mint, and the director of the gunpowder mill, respectively.

The *amiras* maintained their Armenian identity and the Christian religion and contributed generously to the needs of the Armenian community in Constantinople. They built churches, schools, and hospitals, and sponsored charities. However, by virtue of their humanitarian works and the influence they exerted at the Court, they felt entitled to interfere with the affairs of the Patriarchate, even to the extent of having the sultans depose or appoint patriarchs according to their own choice. Around the 1840s a sharp conflict arose between the *amiras* and the trade guilds (generally known as the *esnaf*) when the guilds became critical of the patriarchate for its compliance with the wishes of the *amiras*. The rule of the *amiras*—there had been some 160 of them since their emergence—came to an end around the middle of the nineteenth century, when the Armenian community in Constantinople was in the throes of cultural and social evolution.[25]

---

25. For a detailed and authoritative study of the *amiras*, see Pascal Carmont, *Les amiras, seigneurs de l'Arménie ottomane* (The amiras, the lords of Ottoman Armenia) (Paris, 1999).

RELIGIOUS DISSENT

A factor contributing to the social conflict was the series of long and acrimonious disputes between the Patriarchate and the members of the Armenian community who belonged to the Catholic Church. Catholic inroads into Armenia had a long history, beginning with the Crusaders in the time of the Cilician Kingdom and continuing through the Middle Ages with the Unitors,[26] who set up missions in various locations in Armenia proper. Their penetration into the Ottoman Empire began in the seventeenth century, when the Jesuit priest Clemens Galanus was sent by *De Propaganda Fide* to the Caucasus in order to learn the Armenian language; in 1640 he was assigned to Constantinople for the specific purpose of converting Armenians to the Catholic faith. The ensuing divisions were fueled by attitudes that failed to distinguish between religion and nationality. In 1831 the situation eventually resulted in the formation of a new and separate *millet* of Catholic Armenians, a solution backed by the foreign powers and, therefore, readily conceded by the sultan.

A similar situation, though with less violent repercussions, was repeated some fifteen years later, this time with the Protestants. In the 1820s American Evangelical missionaries began to establish contacts with Armenians. In the 1830s and 1840s new missionaries arrived in Constantinople and other centers. With the help of newly converted local preachers, and sustained by schools and publications, they waged an active campaign. Even though some converts initially wished to remain in the fold of the Armenian Mother Church, intransigent attitudes prevented them from doing so. In 1848 the Protestants broke their ties with the Armenian Patriarchate and formed a Protestant *millet,* also approved by the sultan.

THE ARMENIAN NATIONAL CONSTITUTION

The period from the first decade of the nineteenth century to about 1870 is very significant in the history of the Ottoman Empire. For the first time a number of political and social reforms were introduced, albeit under the pressure of the European powers. These reforms were aimed at eliminating discrimination between Muslim and non-Muslim subjects before the courts, guaranteeing security of life and property, suppressing the excesses of the feudal lords, and ushering in a constitutional

---

26. The name, from the Latin word for unifiers, was given to a brotherhood formed in various Christian Churches with the aim of uniting them to the Catholic Church.

monarchy. They were implemented in stages under successive sultans—Selim III, Abdul Mejid I, and Abdul Aziz—and were collectively called the *Tanzimat* (reform in Arabic).[27] These reforms introduced a breath of freedom and raised the hopes and aspirations of the people for a harmonious future. The *Tanzimat* was ineffective, however, and turned out to be nothing more than window dressing to appease the European powers. It was entirely abrogated in 1876 by Sultan Abdul-Hamid II.

While the *Tanzimat* was in force, however, it invigorated the social and cultural life of the Armenian communities in Constantinople and Smyrna. In 1841 a committee comprising twenty-four merchants and intellectuals was established to assist the *amiras* in administering the finances of the community. By 1847 two more bodies, a religious council and a civic council, were formed to supervise affairs in their respective domains. After the Crimean War, the treaty signed in Paris in 1856 forced Turkey to grant its non-Muslim subject nations autonomy over their internal affairs. By this time a large number of Armenians who had studied in European universities and had been imbued with the liberal ideas of the 1789 and 1848 revolutions had returned to Constantinople and initiated a cultural and ideological revival. Around 1850 a group of prominent intellectuals—such as Nikoghayos Zorayan (1821–59), Grigor Otian (1834–87), Nahapet Rusinian (1819–76), Stepan Voskanian (1825–1901), Serobé Vichenian (1815–94), and others—was already working on a code of laws that would concentrate legislative power in a national assembly, to be elected on a representative basis, which would set up religious and secular councils that would define the jurisdiction of the Patriarchate. It took a long time to iron out the thorny issues. Finally in 1863 an abridged version of the constitution, based mainly on French and Belgian civil law, was ratified by Sultan Abdul-Aziz (1836–76) and became part of Ottoman law. The document contained ninety-nine articles and was known among Armenians as the National Constitution (*Azgayin sahmanadrutiun*, in Turkish: *Nizamnamei milleti ermenyan*). The assembly consisted of 140 members, mostly from Constantinople, forty clerics, and forty representatives from other major centers, along with educational and economic councils. Despite a number of shortcomings, this constitution, based on liberal and democratic principles, was a notable achievement.

In 1872 Patriarch Mkrtich Khrimian (1869–73) tried to increase the number of the provincial representatives, but his proposal was rejected. The National Constitution was abolished by Sultan Abdul-Hamid in

---

27. The *Tanzimat* is discussed in detail in the historical section of this introduction.

1896, the year of the massacres in the Armenian provinces. It was reinstated in 1908 when the Young Turks came to power, and it ceased to exist in 1915, the year of the genocide, when the National Assembly was dispersed and most of its members deported or killed. The National Constitution, with certain abridgments and readjustments, is still used in a number of communities in the Armenian diaspora. After 1915, and even after the establishment of the Republic of Turkey, the Armenian Patriarchate lost all its properties and privileges. At the present time its role is confined solely to the religious supervision of the Armenian community concentrated in Constantinople.

♦

In Eastern Armenia, which was under Persian rule, the socioeconomic conditions in the four Armenian khanates were more tolerable. The majority of Armenians lived as peasants, whereas most of the Kurds and Turkic tribes led a traditional nomadic existence. Taxes and duties were as numerous as in Western Armenia, but under Persian rule the Armenians enjoyed greater security. Early in the seventeenth century the population of Eastern Armenia decreased, mainly as a result of the massive emigration of Armenians whom Shah Abbas forced to settle in Persia. They enjoyed the shah's protection, and he settled the most skilled artisans and tradesmen in the new city of New Julfa, near the capital city of Isfahan. The population soon grew to about 50,000. Here there emerged a class of Armenian merchants known as *khodjas* (notables), who were granted trading privileges, particularly monopoly of the silk trade between Asia and Europe. Through these activities and the opening of trade routes, the economy prospered, and there was a fallout effect on Eastern Armenia as well. The *khodjas* also played a prominent role in cultural and political spheres.

Early in the eighteenth century, as Safavid rule declined and eventually fell, Eastern Armenia regressed. In violation of the 1639 treaty, Ottoman raids began again, triggering massive waves of Armenian migration to Russia, the Crimea, and eastern Europe. The peace and prosperity that Eastern Armenians enjoyed under Persian rule had lasted only eighty-five years, from the signing of the agreement of 1639 to its violation by Ottoman Sultan Ahmed III in 1723. Major improvements in socioeconomic conditions began to appear only after 1828, when Eastern Armenia was united with Russia.

The Armenian Question

The Armenian Question is foreshadowed by the Eastern Question, a term used to describe the international problems caused by the chaotic conditions that prevailed in the Ottoman Empire in the nineteenth century. Following the French Revolution and the Napoleonic wars, the treaties of Paris and the Congress of Vienna (1814–15) tried to establish an international system and redraw the map of Europe. The Ottoman Empire constituted a field of potential conflict between the great powers and thus, as Vahakn Dadrian puts it, "the Eastern Question began to crystallize itself around crisscrossing trends of imperialism, nationalism, repressive despotism, and Great Power interventionism."[28]

The key to understanding the Eastern Question and its corollary, the Armenian Question, is that the governmental structure of Europe was entirely different from that of the Ottoman Empire, which was based on Islamic law and practice. This was also why various attempts at reform of the *Tanzimat* did not work. To quote Dadrian again:

> In the final analysis, these twin questions arose . . . because of the clash of two disparate and incompatible legal-political systems. [In the West] religious dogmas were subordinated to the legal principle, thus concentrating secularism as the arch foundation on which to build the system of a family of nations. But the Ottoman Empire, for most of its reign, was, and remained, a theocracy, which, by definition and fact, cannot be secularized; laws that are predicated upon permanently fixed and intractable religious precepts cannot be modified, much less reformed.[29]

The Eastern Question occupied the political agenda of all the major powers throughout the nineteenth century. The conflicting interests of the powers on the one hand and the decadence and corruption of the Ottoman state on the other played against each other, resulting in armed confrontations in various sensitive locations such as the Balkans, the Mediterranean, the Caucasus, and the Middle East. Another aggravating factor was the brutality to which the Turks resorted to quell the uprisings of some non-Muslim subject nations aspiring to autonomy or independence.[30]

The Armenians were one of the groups that suffered most under Ottoman misrule and oppression. Throughout the centuries of Ottoman domination, Armenians and other non-Muslim peoples were considered *rayahs* (serfs), and as such subjected to humiliation and exploitation.

---

28. Dadrian, *History of the Armenian Genocide,* 21. For more details, see 21–37.
29. Ibid., 22.
30. Some examples are the 1822 massacres in Chios, prior to Greek independence; the 1845 massacre of 10,000 Christian Syrians in Hakkiari, an eastern province of Turkey; the 1860 massacre of about 40,000 Maronite Catholics in Lebanon and Syria; and the 1876 massacre of close to 20,000 Bulgarians in Plovdiv.

Particularly in the interior provinces, notorious pashas and Kurdish chieftains, with their armed bands, were given a free hand to raid Armenian towns and villages to rob, rape, kidnap, and kill. In many provinces, such as Trebizond (Trabzon), Karin (Erzurum), Baghesh (Bitlis), Vaspurakan (Van), and Hamshen, there were forced conversions to Islam, under threat of torture or death. Even though in the early years of the *Tanzimat* efforts were made to eliminate some of the most rebellious and despotic feudal lords, those who replaced them were just as bad. The Armenian Patriarchate of Constantinople was flooded with reports of atrocities and mass murders, which were transmitted to the Sublime Port and then totally ignored.

One strong reaction to the silence of the government was the rebellion of the Armenian autonomous enclave of Zeytun,[31] in the mountainous region of Cilicia, in 1862. A large Turkish army unit attacked the region but was defeated, suffered heavy losses, and was forced to retreat. The news of the victory spread fast and inspired similar outbreaks in other places, such as Van (1862), Erzurum (1863), and Mush (1864). The victory of Zeytun also energized Armenian intellectuals in Constantinople, who were going through the turbulence of the great cultural and political revival.[32] It stimulated patriotism and inspired many writers, notably Mkrtich Peshiktashlian (Beshiktashlian, 1828–68), to produce exquisite poetry.

Although the main cause of these insurrections—not only in Armenia but also, on a much larger scale, in the Balkans—was Ottoman misrule and oppression, there was another: the surge of nationalism in Europe that had been triggered by the revolutionary movements of 1848. In the 1860s and 1870s the Ottoman Empire was plagued with revolt and internal turmoil: Serbian uprisings; insurrections in Bulgaria, followed by Turkish atrocities; the agrarian revolt of Christian peasantry in Bosnia-Herzegovina, where the landowners were mostly Bosnian Serbs who had converted to Islam; the detachment of Wallachia and Moldavia to form the new state of Romania; the granting of autonomy to the island of Crete; the financial collapse of the empire; and, eventually, the

---

31. Zeytun (presently Süleymanye, in the province of Marash, Turkey, and known as Ulnia in Byzantine days) was a mountainous region populated by Armenians. In 1626, in an attempt to win the inhabitants over to his side against the Jalalis, Sultan Murad IV granted autonomy to the region in exchange for a tribute to be used to keep the lamps of the Hagia Sophia Mosque in Constantinople supplied with oil.

32. The Armenian Revival (or Renaissance, as some call it) will be discussed separately.

dethronement of Sultan Abdul-Aziz in 1876 as a result of his despotism and extravagant spending. All these events contributed to the reduction of the Ottoman Empire to what was described at the time as "the sick man of Europe."[33]

In 1876, the year Abdul-Hamid II acceded to the throne, Great Britain convened a conference of the major powers in Constantinople with the purpose of settling the Balkan conflicts. Although the new constitution contained a few articles confirming the sultan's authority, it nevertheless guaranteed civil rights, religious freedom, security of life and property, and equality before the courts. The proclamation of this constitution was a stratagem of the sultan to defeat the conference, which was indeed shortly disbanded. Two weeks later the sultan banished Mithat Pasha and suspended the constitution.

In exasperation, Russia declared war on Turkey on April 24, 1877. The war was fought both in Eastern Europe and in Western Armenia, and the Turks were defeated on both fronts. Parts of Western Armenia were liberated, and the Russian army in Europe came within reach of Constantinople. By this time atrocities committed against the Armenians in the provinces had become so frequent and violent that Armenian leaders in Constantinople, headed by Patriarch Nerses Varzhapetian, asked Russia to include certain propositions for the security of western Armenians in the peace talks. On March 3, 1878, the Treaty of San Stefano (a suburb of Constantinople, presently Yeşilköy) was signed, granting total independence to Serbia, Romania, and Montenegro, and complete autonomy to a larger Bulgaria. As for Western Armenia, the Russians annexed Kars, Ardahan, Alashkert, and Bayazit (Beyazit). A major gain for Armenians was article 16 of the treaty, "which provided for Russian troops to remain in the Armenian provinces until the Turkish Government carried out the reforms requested by the Armenian inhabitants, and to protect them against Kurdish and Circassian raids."[34]

Sadly, however, these provisions of the treaty remained on paper. Great Britain and Austria, unhappy at Russian gains, denounced the treaty and threatened war. Russia, already troubled with revolutionary agitations, agreed to a conference in Berlin brokered by the German chancellor, Otto von Bismarck (1815–98). An Armenian delegation, led by Mkrtich Khrimian (a former Patriarch of Constantinople and later catholicos), visited various European capitals to solicit support for

---

33. This phrase was apparently coined by Tsar Nicholas I, who applied it to the Ottoman Empire in 1833.

34. Bournoutian, *History of the Armenian People,* 2:91.

local autonomy for Western Armenia. However, the great powers had made separate agreements in secret meetings prior to the conference, and when the delegates arrived at the Berlin Congress (June 1878), the fate of the Balkans and of the Armenians was already decided. Russian gains were curtailed, and the boundaries of some Balkan countries were redrawn. But what was most disastrous for Armenia was the introduction of Article 61, which forced Russia to return Alashkert and Bayazit to Turkey and renounce the right to keep troops in the Armenian provinces. The implementation of reforms in these provinces was made a collective European responsibility—without direct supervision.[35]

This loose promise of "supervision under collective responsibility" never materialized. The major aim of the great powers convened at Berlin was to oppose Russian expansion and secure for themselves generous morsels of the crumbling Ottoman Empire. In fact, Great Britain acquired the administration of Cyprus, giving it an important base in the Mediterranean, and France was granted the right to occupy Tunis. The great powers had no interest in resolving the Armenian question: it would serve them well to keep the sick man alive and vulnerable. But Sultan Hamid had other plans. As A. George Bournoutian says, "He viewed all Armenians as a threat. He . . . used his position as Caliph to unite all Muslims in the empire against Christian revolutionaries in the Balkans and Anatolia."[36] Realizing that the European powers would not intervene, Sultan Hamid recruited Kurdish criminals and prison convicts into irregular cavalry units, known as the *Hamidiye*, to carry out pogroms against the Armenians.

The Berlin Congress was a great disappointment to Armenians. In despair, a number of Armenian intellectuals who were active in the Armenian cultural revival of the 1860s and were also influenced by the socialist and revolutionary trends in Russia began to organize defense groups and revolutionary parties. The first was the Armenakan, formed in Van in 1885, followed by the Social Democratic Hnchakian Party (1887, Geneva), and the Armenian Revolutionary Federation (Dashnaktsutiun, 1890, Tiflis). None of these organizations advocated independence for Armenia; their aims were self-defense against oppression, drawing the attention of the European powers to their failed promises, pressing the sultan for reforms, and, eventually, local autonomy.

Despite disagreements regarding the best course of action, the Armenian revolutionaries organized a number of demonstrations in the

---

35. Cf. ibid., 91–92.
36. Bournoutian, *History of the Armenian People,* 93.

capital, to which the government responded with bloody reprisals. Betrayed and frustrated, the Armenians organized a number of self-defense campaigns that erupted into armed conflicts in the interior provinces, such as those in Sasun, a mountainous enclave in the province of Marash (1894); Zeytun in Cilicia (1985); and Van (1896). Assured of the non-intervention of the European powers, in 1895–96 Abdul-Hamid unleashed a series of massacres in the Armenian provinces, in which no fewer than 200,000 Armenians were killed and hundreds of churches were destroyed. Also in 1896 the sultan organized a massacre in the capital city of Constantinople, where some 6,000 Armenian civilians were killed in broad daylight, under the watchful eyes of foreign embassies. All the major powers sent formal protest notes, but they refused to intervene.

Between 1895 and 1902 a number of Turkish leaders who had been exiled to Europe formed a group formally called the Committee of Union and Progress but generally known as the Young Turks. Their aim was to depose the sultan and establish a constitutional government with equal rights for all nationalities and religions. But when they acceded to power through a bloodless coup in 1908, they reneged on their promises and adopted a violent stance against minorities, particularly the Armenians, on whose behalf the European powers had begun to intercede. The most violent manifestation of this attitude was the organized massacre in Adana (1909), during which an aroused mob killed some 30,000 Armenians. The hidden policy of the Ittihadist (Young Turks) leaders, as revealed in a secret discussion at the 1910 annual Ittihadist Congress in Saloniki, was to "Ottomanize" or "Turkify" the entire country by eliminating minorities, thus forestalling foreign intervention. In fact, some historians see the Adana massacres as a rehearsal for the great genocide that followed.[37]

The Armenian Genocide (1915–22)

Turkey's defeat in the Balkan War of 1912 and the resulting loss of more territory triggered a coup led by the ultranationalists on January 23, 1913. This gave dictatorial powers to a triumvirate consisting of Enver Pasha (minister of war), Talaat Pasha (minister of the interior), and Jemal (Djemal) Pasha (minister of the marine). Their first act was to abrogate the constitution. Since the beginning of its decline, the Ottoman Empire had lost a great deal of territory, as one subjugated

---

37. Cf. Dadrian, *History of the Armenian Genocide*, 179 ff.

nation after another declared its independence. Yet all these countries were peripheral to the empire. By contrast, Armenia represented its heartland, and the elimination of this sole Christian enclave, with its aspirations for independence, would remove forever the threat of further fragmentation and would also open up the way to the Caucasus and central Asia for the eventual creation of a Pan-Turkic or Pan-Turanian Empire. The First World War (1914–18) provided Turkey with a unique opportunity to carry out the long intended genocide of the Armenian people.

The starting signal was given in Constantinople on the night of April 24, 1915, when over 200 Armenian intellectuals and community leaders, including members of parliament, were arrested, deported to the interior, and brutally killed. The number of victims soon reached 600. Armenian soldiers serving in the army were forced to dig trenches in isolated places and then shot to death while standing in them. Explicit orders were cabled to the governors and military commanders of the provinces to deport the Armenians. First all the able-bodied men were rounded up, led under heavy guard to remote mountains, valleys, or caves, and shot dead. Others were crowded into churches which were set on fire. Then all the women, children, and the aged were moved from their homes and, "guarded" by special brigades of Turkish gendarmes, were forced into a death march toward the Syrian desert.

This pattern was repeated in every city, town, village, and hamlet, from one end of the country to the other. The deportees were treated with untold cruelty, and thousands upon thousands of Armenians perished. Most of those who survived the march died in the desert camps of Deir el Zor. In a few places the Armenians offered armed resistance, but they eventually suffered a martyr's death. In only two places was resistance successful. The first was Van, where the Armenians, about 30,000 strong, barricaded themselves and managed to resist the Turkish army until the arrival of Russian troops in mid-May 1915. The second was Cilicia, on the shores of the eastern Mediterranean. Six Armenian villages on the slopes of Musa Dagh decided to fight and held back a large Turkish army unit for forty days, until, in mid-September, 4,000 of them were rescued by the French navy.[38] By the end of 1916 the entire Armenian population of Turkey had been eradicated, with the exception of those in Constantinople and Smyrna; they were spared because of

---

38. The heroic resistance of these Armenians was immortalized by the Austrian writer Franz Werfel in his novel *The Forty Days of Musa Dagh* (New York, 1933).

the presence in those cities of foreign embassies, consulates, and trading companies.[39]

The Armenian genocide, the first of the twentieth century, was the greatest tragedy that has ever struck the Armenian people. What were the losses? A million and a half people were killed by the sword, fire, famine, disease, and death marches. A three-thousand-year-old ancestral homeland was lost, along with the cultural and traditional heritage, both material and spiritual, that was rooted and had flourished in that homeland. An untold amount of personal and communal wealth was destroyed, stolen, or confiscated by the government. All the history, legends, and myths that had evolved in that land and had forged the specific character of the nation were erased from its collective memory. More than two thousand churches and convents, with all their sacred treasures and illuminated manuscripts, were looted or destroyed. Some forty dialects of the language were wiped out. Above all, a moral and psychological trauma was inflicted on the entire nation, from which second and third generations of Armenians are still suffering.

The Armenian Diaspora

The Armenian diaspora is a direct result of centuries of subjugation by foreign powers, successive waves of invasion by marauding tribes, and continuous battles fought by rival empires on Armenian soil. Beginning with the Seljuks's arrival in Asia Minor around the middle of the eleventh century and continuing to the eighteenth century, cycles of invasions and battles—such as the invasion of the Mongols; the savage raids of Tamerlane; the internal fights of the Black Sheep, White Sheep, and other Turkic tribes; the century-long wars between the Ottoman and Persian empires; and the insurrection of the Jalalis against the Ottomans—left behind a scorched land, extreme devastation, and a decimated population. Brief periods of independence, achieved with great heroism after long intervals of subjugation, periodically allowed the Armenians to rebuild the country and regain prosperity, but these achievements were destroyed by the next wave of conquerors. Mass murders, deportations, forced conversions to Islam, tens of thousands enslaved— particularly by the Arabs and the Mamluks—and the fact that under Muslim rule all subjugated peoples were designated *rayahs* or *dhimmi*, akin to slaves or servants, and deprived of civic rights: all these played

---

39. Most of the Greek and Armenian population of Smyrna perished or was driven out to sea when Kemalist forces set fire to the Christian quarters in 1922.

important roles in forcing large masses of the Armenian population to abandon their ancestral homeland and emigrate to foreign countries in search of peace, security, and prosperity.

Since very early times Armenian communities have been established in many countries. A distinction should be made, however, between those who emigrated voluntarily, for purposes of trade, education, and economic opportunities, and the masses who were forced to abandon their homeland because of deportations, oppression, and massacres. The Armenian migrations have followed the life cycle of all diasporas: genesis, development, and extinction. The duration of each stage of this cycle depends on the ideology, social conditions, cultural influences, and economic structure of the host country, and also on the inherent and collective determination of the migrants to adhere to and preserve their national identity. What follows is a brief description of some of the major Armenian diasporas around the world. Some of them have been extinguished by assimilation, but others persist and are evolving.

ARMENIANS IN THE MIDDLE EAST

The Armenian presence in Mesopotamia dates back to the time of King Tigran II (96/95–55 BC), when part of Syria was under Armenian rule and cities like Antioch, Edessa (Urfa), and Amida (Diyarbekir) attracted students and merchants. In fact, Mesrop Mashtots went to Edessa and Amida early in the fifth century, in search of a model for the Armenian alphabet. In the ninth century the Byzantines settled a large number of Armenians in northern Syria as a buffer against the Arabs. The fall of the Bagratunis and the marauding raids of the Seljuks were additional reasons for Armenians to emigrate. During the Cilician Kingdom, there were close relations between the crusader states, but after they collapsed when they were overrun by the Mamluks, waves of Armenian migrants headed to northwestern Syria and settled in the larger cities, particularly Aleppo, which was on a main trade route. After the Ottoman conquest of Syria (1517), the treaty with France (1535) further opening the region to trade, encouraging many Armenians to settle there. From 1616 to 1652 the Armenian population of Aleppo increased from 6,000 to more than 20,000, mainly because of migrants from Jugha, Sivas, Erzurum, and Marash, who were mostly either traders in raw silk or artisans working with jewelry and leather. Other centers, like Alexandretta, Homs, Latakia, Kessab, and Musa Dagh were engaged primarily in agriculture and crafts. The decline of New Julfa in Iran, the Napoleonic wars, the campaigns of Mohammed Ali Pasha and Ibrahim Pasha in Syria, and the opening of the Suez Canal all adversely affected the economy of Aleppo. By the end of the nineteenth century, however, the city had bounced back, thanks to the commercial and banking activities of the Armenian merchants of Constantinople, and new settlers were attracted to the city. The number of churches, schools, and community centers, and the cultural activity of the city all demonstrate that Aleppo became one of the most vibrant centers in the Armenian diaspora.

The beginnings of the Armenian community in Lebanon go back to the turn of the twelfth to the thirteenth century, when Armenian merchants settled in the port cities of Tripoli and Sidon, and their numbers gradually increased after the fall of the Cilician Kingdom. In the seventeenth century Druse and Maronite lords who were struggling to shake off Ottoman rule provided refuge to a large number of Armenians who were fleeing from Turkey, in order to create a stronger basis for autonomy. In 1736 the Maronite Church united with Rome and opened its territories to more Christian refugees, particularly Armenian Catholics, who were then being harassed by the Armenian Orthodox Church. In 1742 the Vatican established an Armenian Catholic Patriarchate in Lebanon, and in 1749 an abbey was opened in Zmmar, which became a center of learning. Religious strife, which had erupted between the Druses and the Maronites in 1860, was quelled by the Ottoman massacre of some 40,000 Christians, prompting the French to send forces to Lebanon in 1861. Under strong pressure from the French and other European powers, the Ottomans accepted Lebanese autonomy under a Christian governor-general, two of whom were Armenians: Karapet Artin Pasha Da'ud, 1861–68, and Hovhannes Kuyumchian (Kuyumdjian) Pasha, 1912–15, both members of the Armenian Catholic community.

Thanks to the hospitality and benevolence of the Arab people, Armenian communities in Lebanon and other Arab countries increased in great numbers as the survivors of the 1896 massacres and the 1915 genocide found shelter and protection there. The survivors reorganized themselves with amazing energy and self-reliance, and within a couple of decades most of them achieved economic stability. Churches and schools were built, benevolent and youth organizations and artistic societies sprang up, newspapers began to be published, and a vigorous social and cultural life started to flourish. In the 1930s the Catholicosate of Sis, with its affiliated seminary, was reestablished in Antilias, a suburb of Beirut, making Lebanon, and particularly Beirut, with its close to 200,000 Armenians, an important center in the Armenian diaspora.

ARMENIANS IN JERUSALEM

The Armenian presence in Jerusalem can be traced back as far as the time of King Tigran the Great, when there were already commercial ties between Armenia and Palestine. At the beginning of the fourth century, when Armenia declared Christianity as her state religion, large numbers of Armenians went to Jerusalem as pilgrims and residents. In these early times all Christians, regardless of ethnic group, were under the spiritual authority of the Patriarch of Jerusalem, and the holy places were used by all. Even after the wide breach caused by the controversy regarding the nature of Christ at the Council of Chalcedon (451), Jerusalem maintained religious harmony among all Christian communities. There is evidence that by the mid-fifth century the Armenians had founded a scriptorium in Jerusalem. This and an extant Armenian lectionary, a translation of the Greek liturgy, attest to the presence of a fully organized Armenian religious community. In the sixth century, however, Emperor Justinian (527–65) began to persecute the monophysites, most of whom abandoned their monasteries and moved to neighboring countries. Those who remained established a separate episcopal hierarchy, independent of the Greek patriarch. As a consequence, the See of Jerusalem was split into the Greek Patriarchate, with jurisdiction over diophysite Christians, regardless of nationality or language, and the independent Armenian hierarchy, with authority over the monophysite communities: the Armenians, the Jacobite Syrians, the Copts, and the Abyssinians. By the seventh century there was already a considerable Armenian community, with a number of monasteries, in Jerusalem and its environs.

After the Arab invasion, Greek domination was subdued, and the first Armenian Patriarchate was established in 638, under Archbishop Abraham.[40] This triggered an influx of Armenians, mostly traders and artisans, into the city. Control of the Christian holy places was a cause of bitter conflict between the Greek (i.e., Byzantine) and Armenian communities. Although the Armenians in Jerusalem numbered fewer than the Greeks, the Arabs, who considered the Byzantines a common enemy, granted the Armenians custodianship of a number of important Christian shrines. Rivalries between the religious communities (later the Catholic Church became involved as well) for control of the holy sites has continued unabated for centuries.

---

40. There are two chronologically consecutive lists of the Armenian patriarchs of Jerusalem; the first, which covers the period from 638 to 1281, is a "traditional" list, and still requires meticulous research. The second, which goes from 1281 to the present, is indisputable.

During the Latin Kingdom of Jerusalem (established by the crusaders in 1099 and destroyed by the Mamluks in 1291), many Armenians from Cilicia who had fought alongside the crusaders settled in Jerusalem and other Palestinian cities; this raised the Armenian population to one thousand families and five hundred monks. Marriage ties between the royal houses of the two kingdoms facilitated these exchanges. The major accomplishment of this prosperous period was the construction of the large Armenian Cathedral of St. James, which contains the relics of the apostles James the Great and James the Lesser.

When Saladin (1174–93) occupied Jerusalem in 1187, Armenian Patriarch Abraham (1180–91) and his leading clerics hastened to pledge loyalty to the sultan and pay the prescribed toll tax. In return Saladin granted the Armenian patriarch a charter guaranteeing the community's security and freedom of worship throughout his entire domain and greater privileges on the holy sites. This situation lasted until the beginning of Mamluk rule. The Mamluks's increasing intolerance of Christians and the tax collectors' constant extortions impoverished the Armenian population, reducing it to small enclaves scattered throughout Syria and Palestine.

Ottoman rule, which lasted about four centuries, did not much change the status of Jerusalem. The charters issued in 1517 to the Armenian and Greek patriarchates by Sultan Selim I (1467–1520) confirmed the status quo: the monasteries of St. James were recognized as the exclusive jurisdiction of the Armenians, but the principal shrines, such as the Church of the Holy Sepulcher, the Church of St. Mary at Gethsemane, and the Grotto of the Nativity in Bethlehem were considered Armenian possessions in the charter given to the Armenians and as Greek possessions in the charter given to the Greeks. Thus it was assumed that jurisdiction over these sanctuaries were to be shared by the two communities, a situation that created major controversies between the two camps. With the revival in 1847 of the Latin Patriarchate of Jerusalem, the conflict about jurisdiction over the sanctuaries was intensified, to the extent that it became one of the causes of the Crimean War. Although the issue was on the agenda of the Council of Paris in 1856, no agreement was reached between the contesting communities.

The nineteenth century witnessed a phenomenal growth of cultural activities in Jerusalem's Armenian community. In 1833 the first printing press was established at the Patriarchate; its output consisted mainly of liturgical and ecclesiastical works, and a number of ancient manuscripts, which appeared in print for the first time. In 1857 a seminary was opened within the St. James monastery complex, and it became a leading institution for the training of Armenian clergy. The seminary has continued to operate up to the present, except for a short interval (1917–20) when it was closed because of the First World War and the Armenian genocide. Boys' and girls' schools were founded in 1840 and 1862 respectively; these were later united under the name of Holy Translators' School, which also still exists. The monthly review *Sion*, the organ of the See of Jerusalem, was established in 1866 and is still being published. Today the Armenian community in Jerusalem has been reduced to a bare minimum, but the Patriarchate and its institutions play a prominent role in the Armenian diaspora.

ARMENIANS IN EGYPT

The first Armenian to set foot on Egyptian soil was probably King Artavazd II (d. 31 BC), who, after waging war against Rome, fell victim to a plot of the Roman general Marcus Antonius (Mark Anthony, c. 83–30 BC), was carried to Alexandria as a prisoner, and was beheaded on the order of Cleopatra in 31 BC. In the fifth and sixth centuries, when Alexandria was a Christian center, it attracted Armenian clergy and students, who were welcomed by the Egyptian Copts. Very little is known about Armenians in Egypt during the Arab conquest (640–969), except for the existence, early in the seventh century, of a unit of five hundred Armenian soldiers under the command of an Armenian officer, and of two highly placed government officials of Armenian origin, Vardan al-Rumi and Hasan al-Armani. In the ninth century mention is made of an Islamized Armenian governor, Ali ibn Yahya Abul-Hasan al-Armani.

Under Fatimid rule (969–1171), Christians were tolerated, and a large number of Armenian merchants and tradesmen from Cilicia settled in Cairo and Alexandria; a period of prosperity ensued. According to Matteos Urhayetsi, an Armenian chronicler of the eleventh to twelfth century, there were then some 30,000 Armenians in Egypt. This was a time when the Arabs were cooperating with Byzantium against the Turkish threat in Syria and Anatolia. Some Armenians reached the higher ranks of government and the military, and a few of them became viziers, such as Badr al-Jamali (1074–94), his son Avdal (1094–1121), and Bahram al-Armani (Vahram Pahlavuni [1135–37]), a relative of the great churchman Nerses Shnorhali (c. 1101–73) of Cilicia, the last of whom also held the post of commander of the army. However, the Ayyubids (1169–1250), who followed the Fatimids, considered the Armenians allies of the crusaders, and their harsh treatment forced many Armenians to return to Cilicia.

The condition of the Armenians in Egypt worsened drastically under Mamluk rule (1250–1517). The Mamluks (from the Arabic word *mulk,* possession) were originally recruited from white slaves, Islamized, and trained as bodyguards in the service of the Ayyubid sultans. In 1250 they assassinated the last Ayyubid sultan, al-Muaddam, and established their own sultanate. They destroyed the remaining crusader states and began a relentless and lengthy campaign against the Armenian Kingdom of Cilicia, which they eventually toppled in 1375, carrying tens of thousands of Armenians to Egypt as servants and slaves. The children of these slaves were converted to Islam and enlisted in the army. Some of them later occupied important positions at court.

Following the Ottoman conquest of Egypt by Selim I in 1517, the conditions of the Armenian community deteriorated further. However, toward the end of the seventeenth century when the region was stabilized, the economic situation improved for a short while, and Armenian merchants from Aleppo and Constantinople ventured to start businesses in Egypt. Armenian fortunes began to improve around the middle of the nineteenth century, during the viceroyalty of Mohammed Ali Pasha and his son, Ibrahim Pasha, when many enterprising Armenian merchants and craftsmen, encouraged by the economic, educational, and military reforms, poured into Cairo and Alexandria and set the stage for economic and social progress.

A number of Armenians reached high positions in the Egyptian government. Among the most notable were Poghos Yusufian, who was Mohammed Ali Pasha's personal adviser and director of foreign affairs and commerce—whose responsibilities were later taken over by Artin Chrakian—and Poghos Nupar, a French-educated diplomat who, during the reign of Ismail Pasha (1863–79), the *khedive* of Egypt, became minister of foreign affairs then prime minister, and was elevated to the rank of pasha. These individuals rendered innumerable services to the Armenian community.

By the end of the nineteenth century the Armenian community in Egypt numbered over 50,000. With a number of schools, churches, and community centers, a printing press, and a wide range of cultural and artistic activities, Egypt was one of the best organized and most progressive centers in the Armenian diaspora.

ARMENIANS IN INDIA

There is a record stating that the main chandelier of the cathedral of Ani (built by King Smbat II in 980–89) was imported from India through Armenian merchants.[41] This indicates that trade relations

---

41. See Khachikian, *Hay zhoghovrdi patmutian,* 4:337.

between the two countries existed as far back as the tenth century and perhaps even earlier. It was only in the sixteenth century, however, that the tolerant and progressive policies of Mogul emperor Akbar (1556–1605) encouraged Armenian merchants to settle and invest in India. Akbar trusted the Armenians, gave them certain privileges in the free circulation of merchandise, and also appointed a number of them to high positions in the government. Armenians also acted as interpreters for European envoys who arrived in India on commercial or diplomatic missions. Most Armenians settled in Agra, the center of the Mogul dynasty, where the first Armenian church was built in 1562. One of Akbar's queens, Maryam Begun, was Armenian. Akbar appointed Abdul Hai, an Armenian, as his chief justice, and engaged an Armenian woman doctor, Juliana, to look after his family. He adopted an Armenian boy, naming him Mirza Zul-Qarnain, who attained the position of *amir* (commander) and later became governor of Punjab and was known for his numerous charitable works.

The Armenian influx to India increased in the seventeenth century, when many merchant families from New Julfa in Iran migrated to India. Those who came by the maritime route settled in Surat and Bombay and in time spread out, forming communities in cities like Delhi, Lucknow, Saidabad, Dhaka, Calcutta, and Madras. The Armenians mainly traded in jewels, spices, and silk. The jute trade was almost entirely in the hands of the Armenians of Bengal, and they formed an important link on the South Asia-Iran-Europe trade route. Churches were constructed in almost every community, all linked to the Holy See of Etchmiadzin.

By the seventeenth century a number of trading posts had been established by Europeans such as the Portuguese and the Dutch, providing ample opportunities to Armenian merchants. However, a deadly rivalry broke out when the British entered the scene. By 1619, after defeating the Portuguese navy a few years earlier, the English had established trading posts and factories in Surat, Agra, and later in Bombay (1661), and Surat became the headquarters of the English East India Company. In 1688 an agreement was signed in Bombay between the English East India Company and Khoja Panos Kalantar, representing the Armenian merchants, whereby trade was diverted from traditional routes to the British-dominated route of the Persian Gulf and the Cape of Good Hope. The company trusted the Armenian merchants and permitted them to trade throughout their territories in South Asia. In 1715 Armenians helped the British establish their enterprises in Bengal and make Calcutta a new commercial center. It is a little known fact that in 1715 the British delegation from Calcutta to the court of Emperor

Farrukh Siyar in Delhi included an Armenian merchant named Khoja Israel Sarhad.

Madras is another important city where an Armenian community flourished. Soon after the Portuguese established a trading center there in 1504, an Armenian community started taking shape. The city was occupied by the British in 1602 and became home to a large number of Armenians. There is a story among the Malabar Christians of India that an Armenian named Tomas Cana (presumably from *kahana,* priest) who had landed on the Malabar Coast in south India was responsible for the revival of Christianity in the region. The Christians of Madras also credit Armenians with locating the tomb of the Apostle Thomas, who brought the Christian faith to India in AD 52. In the 1720s an Armenian trader, Khoja Petrus Woskan, built broad stone steps leading to the hilltop tomb of Saint Thomas and also a bridge across the river Aydar, to provide easy access to pilgrims.

The Armenians of Madras and Calcutta were prosperous and intellectually inclined. Their contacts with the British opened up opportunities for higher education and exposure to liberal thinking. In 1771 Shahamir Shahamirian (1723–97) established a printing press in Madras and published three political documents, one of which, *Vorogait parats* (Snare of glory), is a constitution in 521 articles for an independent Armenian republic based on democratic principles and promoting, among other things, an elected parliament, a judicial system, and mandatory education for girls. Prominent Armenians in India include Shahamir Shahamirian, Movses Baghramian, Mkrtich Murat, and Edward Raphael, the last two of whom made the initial donation for the establishment of the Murat-Raphaelian School in Venice. Madras was the birthplace of Armenian journalism: the first Armenian periodical, *Azdarar* (Monitor), was published there by Father Harutiun Shmavonian in 1794. Armenian intellectuals in Madras and Calcutta initiated a national revival in the second half of the eighteenth century, when Joseph Emin committed himself to a mission of emancipation for Armenians suffering under the Persian and Ottoman yokes.

Late in the eighteenth century, as England was expanding its influence into Burma, the Punjab, and Afghanistan, Calcutta became a more important center than Madras, and the Armenian community in that city was revived. An Armenian printing press began to operate there in 1797, publishing both original and translated works. A second school was opened in 1798; an Armenian weekly, *Mirror of Calcutta,* began in 1818; and by 1821 an Armenian college was in operation. Despite all these developments, the anglicization of Armenian-Indian culture had already begun to take a toll. Furthermore, the British campaign to remove all the independent principalities and occupy Hindu states triggered a rebellion by the native troops (sepoys) in 1856. The real cause of the rebellion, known as the Sepoy Mutiny, was westernization, as Hindus and Muslims alike revolted against encroachments on their traditional religious and social values and practices. The mutiny spread throughout India, and many British soldiers and their families were killed. The Armenian merchants, who were regarded as associates of the British, suffered a great deal of property loss during the looting of European businesses.

A prominent Armenian from Delhi known as Colonel Jacob Petrus (1775–1870), the son of a merchant from Yerevan, commanded the First Brigade of Scindhiah and fought on the side of his adopted country against the British colonialists. He and his army of 12,000 soldiers and forty Armenian officers held the central Indian city of Gwalior, south of Agra. His tomb is in the Armenian cemetery in Gwalior.

In 1858 the British government abolished the East India Company, took complete control of India, and made it a crown colony.[42] British businessmen and administrators flooded the country, and Indians were trained to work under British supervisors. Consequently, Armenians lost their economic advantages. By the end of the century the Armenian community in Calcutta numbered about one thousand and was barely able to maintain its college, church, and other institutions. Armenians in other parts of India fared much worse, and began to emigrate to join associates in Burma, Indonesia, and even China, where some, particularly in Burma, succeeded in establishing new businesses. But by the end of the nineteenth century, as the colonial governments of South and East Asia sent more of their own officials to manage these regions, the Armenians had been marginalized, and their numbers dwindled.[43]

ARMENIANS IN EASTERN EUROPE: THE CRIMEA

The fall of the Bagratuni Kingdom, successive invasions of Tatar, Mongol, and Turkoman tribes, and the interminable Iran-Ottoman wars of the sixteenth and seventeenth centuries forced Armenians to emigrate from their native lands for several centuries. One favored place was the

---

42. British colonial rule, known as the Raj, continued until 1947, when India gained independence.

43. For more details about the Armenians in India see Bournoutian, *History of the Armenian People*, 2:43–50 and David Zenian, "The Armenians in India: A Historical Journey," *AGBU Magazine* 2, no. 2 (July 2001): 3–12.

Crimea (historically known as Tauric Chersonese: peninsula), where Armenian settlements consisting of soldiers in the service of Byzantium and their families already existed as early as the eighth century. In fact, an Armenian commander named Vardan toppled Byzantine Emperor Justinian II in 711 and occupied the throne as Philippicus Bardanes for two years.

In the eleventh century, as a result of the intolerance of the Greek Orthodox Church in Constantinople and the Seljuk invasion of Armenia proper, and with the fall of Ani, a large number of Armenians migrated to the Crimea and settled mainly in Kaffa (Theodosia) and other cities, such as—using their modern names—Simferopol, Armiansk, and Belogorsk. These Armenians were engaged mostly in commercial enterprises. By the middle of the thirteenth century the Genoese had a trade monopoly on the Black Sea by virtue of a number of agreements with the Byzantines and the Tatars of the Crimea, which provided Armenian merchants with lucrative trade opportunities. Among the Armenian migrants were many artisans and farmers. The region possessed ten Armenian banks and some forty churches, along with parish schools. The Armenian communities were given their own prelacy, and the Holy Cross Monastery in Surkhat became a bishopric. In 1333, with the support of the pope, a Dominican abbey was established. The Armenians enjoyed a certain autonomy, and their civic affairs were run according to their own rules and traditions. There was also an Armenian militia for security.

After the Ottoman occupation of the Crimea in 1475, Genoese control came to an end, and a Tatar khanate, subordinate to Ottoman rule, emerged in 1478. Many Armenians lost their lives in defense of Kaffa, and many were exiled to Constantinople. Their churches were transformed into mosques, and many migrated to various centers in Poland, Galicia, and Transylvania, where they previously had commercial links. Thus the number of Armenians in the Crimea, which had once been about 300,000, dwindled drastically. The 1768–74 Russo-Turkish war was fatal to the Armenians. According to the Treaty of Küchuk Kaynardja, the Tatar khanate acquired independence and fell under Russian influence. To cripple the economy and develop the southern flatlands, Catherine the Great encouraged Armenian and Greek merchants to migrate to Russia before she annexed the Crimea in 1783. Some 12,600 Armenians settled on the right bank of the Don river, in an area called Rostov-on-Don, which the Armenians renamed Nor Nakhijevan (New Nakhijevan). They were granted exemption from taxes for ten years, freedom to practice their religion and establish their own schools, and, in 1811, local autonomy. Nor Nakhijevan played an important role in the development of Armenian intellectual life in Transcaucasia.

The Crimea was an important center of Armenian manuscript illumination, as evidenced by some 240 manuscripts that are extant. The seventeenth-century artist Nikoghos Melanavor is particularly renowned for having continued the tradition of the famous Cilician illuminator Toros Roslin.

Besides Greek and Italian, the language of business in the Crimea was mainly Kipchak Turkish, the language of the Tatars. Armeno-Kipchak, written in Armenian script, was the language of the Armenian merchants.

Ukraine and Poland[44]

Because large territories have switched back and forth between Poland and Ukraine during the course of their eventful histories, the Armenian communities of these two countries cannot be studied in isolation from each other. In fact, the ancestors of most of the Armenians who settled in Poland were from Kievan Russia. Following the Seljuk invasion of Armenia in the eleventh century and the fall of Ani, large numbers of Armenians emigrated to Kiev and some to Kamenets-Podol'skiy. After the sacking of the city of Kiev by the Mongols in 1240, many Armenians were resettled in the regions of Galicia, Podolia, and Volhynia, and in the city of Lvov. In 1340, the king of Poland, Casimir the Great, occupied Galicia and Volyniya; recognizing the Armenians' contributions to commerce, he granted them local autonomy to observe their own laws and traditions. Armenians were settled in more than a dozen cities in Poland, but the heaviest concentrations were in Kamenets-Podol'skiy and Lvov. By 1250 there was already a functioning Armenian church in Kamenets-Podol'skiy. Soon after that, King Vladislav III granted trading permits to Armenian merchants, and the community was allowed to manage its own judicial affairs. By 1575 there were some 300 Armenian households in Kamenets-Podol'skiy, a number which had risen to 1200 households, about half the population of the city, by 1635, at which date King Vladislav IV allowed the Armenians to organize their own magistracy. This liberal course was cut off in 1672, when the city was invaded by the Ottoman Turks, who carried out a brutal massacre and exiled

44. The information in this section is derived mainly from the following sources: Khachikian, *Hay zhoghovrdi patmutiun*, 4:359–79, and Bournoutian, *History of the Armenian People*, 2:74–76.

most of the remaining population to Macedonia. Later John Sobieski[45] managed to bring the exiles back and resettle them, but the Armenian community did not revive.

Another Armenian community that flourished in Poland was Lvov (now in Ukraine), where Armenians, mostly artisans and farmers, settled as early as the thirteenth century. By the middle of the fourteenth century they had built two churches, St. James and Holy Cross, a monastery, bridges, and bathhouses. A cathedral, still standing, was built in 1365. In later centuries more Armenians arrived in eastern Poland from Cilicia, the Crimea, and Armenia proper. Armenians were recognized as skilled artisans, jewelers, painters, and weavers, and their merchants played an important role in promoting trade with many European and Asian countries.

It has been estimated that by the end of the seventeenth century there were about 300,000 Armenians in Poland. The Armenian communities in each city or district were allowed their own courts and permitted to conduct their civic affairs according to their own laws and traditions. In 1519 King Sigismund I (1467–1548) extended this privilege to all Armenians in the kingdom and allowed them to use Armenian judicial law, based on Mkhitar Gosh's (c. 1120–1213) *Datastanagirk* (Book of judgments)[46] from the late thirteenth century, with some changes. Armenians also enjoyed certain trading privileges. The community prospered, churches and schools were built, manuscripts were copied, a printing press was established in 1616, and cultural life flourished. Some of the better known historians, theologians, and poets were Stepanos Lehatsi (d. 1689), Simeon Lehatsi (1548–c. 1637), Stepanos Roshka (1670–1739), and Minas Tokhatetsi (1510–1622). The Armenian prelacy in Poland was linked to the Holy See of Etchmiadzin.

Early in the seventeenth century, the Catholic Church launched a campaign to convert Armenians to Catholicism. It is a long and sensitive story, with players and contributing factors as many and diverse as the papacy, the Polish court and civic authorities, the Jesuit order, wealthy Armenian laymen who had already embraced the Catholic faith but still

---

45. King John III Sobieski of Poland (1624–96) ascended to the throne in 1676. He signed a treaty with the Roman Emperor Leopold I that was the prelude to the most glorious episode of his life: the relief of Vienna and the liberation of Hungary from the Ottoman yoke on March 21, 1683. A battalion of 5,000 Armenian soldiers joined Sobieski's army to participate in lifting the siege of Vienna.

46. Medieval Armenian writers are included in volume 2 of the present anthology.

controlled Armenian Church property, and certain weaknesses on the part of Etchmiadzin. In 1629 Archbishop Nicholas Torosowicz, scion of a wealthy family who had illegally become primate of the Polish Armenian Church, accepted the supremacy of Rome, at the same time superficially maintaining his links with Etchmiadzin. Soon after this, a seminary was established in Lvov to prepare young Armenian Catholic priests, who gradually replaced the older priests of the Armenian Apostolic Church. Through massive conversions, Armenians were gradually assimilated into Polish society. After the death of Nicholas Torosowicz the new prelate of the Armenian Church, Archbishop Vardan Hunanian, imposed on the community by the papal legate to Poland, finally broke with Etchmiadzin and declared the Armenian Church of Poland and western Ukraine united with the Church of Rome.

Drastic changes in the political situation also played a decisive role in the demise of the Armenian community. The Turkish occupation of Podolia in 1672 led to an economic decline, causing many Armenians to emigrate. In 1772, when part of Poland, including Lvov (renamed Lemberg), fell to the Austro-Hungarian Empire, Armenian courts and civic autonomy were abolished. Further dispersal of Armenians occurred when Catherine the Great occupied eastern Poland in 1784. All these events—religious, political, and economic combined—spelled the end of the once prosperous Armenian community in Poland. Some of the migrants found their way to Transylvania (presently part of Romania), where the city of Gherla, also called Armenopolis, became an important Armenian center. Many other migrants settled in Bulgaria and Hungary.

⚓

What has been presented here is a brief survey of some major diaspora centers that emerged in various countries throughout the tragic history of the Armenian people, up to the nineteenth century. Some of these centers have vanished, others have survived, and new ones have sprouted. There is hardly a country in the world where Armenians have not set foot at one time or another and have not flourished, either as individuals or as a community, aided by their instinct for survival and their resiliency. Another major wave of migration involved the survivors of the 1915 genocide, which, however, is beyond the scope of this volume.

The Cultural Revival

The great Armenian cultural revival known as the *Zartonk* (awakening) blossomed in Constantinople in the second half of the nineteenth century. It derived its vigor from various centers of the diaspora, where its seeds were sown in the eighteenth century. As a result of their contacts with foreign cultures, Armenian communities in Italy, the Netherlands, Poland, Ukraine, and India played an important role in opening the Armenian mind to western ideas and political thinking. Armenian merchants, mainly those of New Julfa, with their network of trade routes and their wealth, were instrumental in promoting culture and education by financing printing presses and schools in cities with major Armenian communities. Enlightened by contacts with different cultures and ideologies, new generations were now attempting to reaffirm their national identity and preserve their history and culture. Aware of the dangers of assimilation, intellectuals encouraged people to become acquainted with their past and familiarize themselves with European revolutionary concepts, in the hope of one day regaining an autonomous homeland. They anticipated a double liberation of Armenia: from ignorance and from political oppression. The vigorous initiatives of Israel Ori, Joseph Emin, the Madras Group, and some religious leaders, discussed earlier, focused on this noble purpose.

Other important factors helped to promote the Awakening in various centers of the Armenian diaspora including the founding of the Mkhitarist Order in Venice in 1717 and the enactment by the Ottoman Empire of what was called *Azgayin sahmanadrutiun* (The National Constitution) in Constantinople.

THE ORIGINS OF ARMENIAN PRINTING

Although the Armenians understood and appreciated the importance of the printed word and ardently pursued the idea to establish publication centers in Armenia, the devastating conditions prevailing in the war-torn homeland did not allow them to materialize their dreams.

The man who pioneered Armenian printing was Hakob Meghapart (Hakop the Sinful, as he called himself; sixteenth century). In 1512, some sixty years after Gutenberg's epoch-making invention of movable type, Hakob Meghapart established an Armenian press in Venice. He chose that city for two main reasons: first, compared to other centers, the Catholic Church censorship there of material printed in foreign languages was more relaxed; second, there was already an Armenian community in the city, which was a transit point for Armenian merchants. The first five books printed by Hakob Meghapart, and still extant, are *Urbatagirk* (Friday book), consisting mainly of prayers and remedies for the sick together with long quotations from the *Narek* (the poems of Narekatsi); *Pataragatetr* (The Missal); *Akhtark* (An astrological treatise); *Parzatumar* (The calendar); and *Tagharan* (Song book), which contains poems and hymns by Shnorhali (c. 1101–73), Frik (1230–1310), Hovhannes Tlkurantsi (fourteenth to fifteenth century), Mkrtich Naghash (c. 1394–c. 1475), and others. The choices seem to have been dictated by popular taste. Unfortunately, Hakob's press lasted for only three years.

The second Armenian printer was Abgar Dpir Tokhatetsi (d. c. 1572), who led a delegation (which included his son Sultanshah) sent by Coadjutor Catholicos Mikael I Sebastatsi (1567–76) to Rome in 1564 to secure permission from Pope Pius IV (1555–65) to set up a printing press for the publication of religious books. After obtaining permission, Abgar went to Venice and tried to recommence Hakob Meghapart's work, which had been abruptly discontinued some fifty years earlier. In 1565, with the financial support of a few wealthy merchants from New Julfa, he printed a broadsheet calendar entitled *Kharnapntiur tomari* (Confusion of the calendar) and a *Saghmosaran* (Psalter). After these two publications, Abgar transferred his press to Constantinople, where, he thought, he would have more success in the midst of a large Armenian community. His enterprise lasted until 1569, by which time he had printed half a dozen religious books. He was the first to establish an Armenian press in the Ottoman capital.

In the meantime, Abgar's son, Sultanshah (now known as Marc-Antonio), who had settled in Rome after his father's departure and enjoyed the patronage of the pope, had acquired a mastery of Latin and the art of printing. In 1583 he joined Hovhannes Terzntsi, a priest from Amida, in southern Armenia, who had come to Italy with his son Khachatur to establish himself in the printing business. With the encouragement of the Vatican, Abgar and Hovhannes set themselves the task of translating and printing the famous *Gregorian Calendar* devised by the pope of the day, Gregory XIII (1572–85), which was to replace the old Julian Calendar. The book was printed on the press of Dominicus Basa in black and red type cut in 1579 by Sultanshah and Robert Granjon, a French type designer. This new type, unlike the style used by Hakob Meghapart, which was designed to imitate manuscript, was closer to the print type (*bolorgir*) used today. In 1586 Hovhannes and his son moved to Venice, where they published a new psalter. It is not known when and under what circumstances this press ceased to exist.

Early in the seventeenth century, as the Catholic Church launched a campaign to bring Eastern Christians into its fold, a large number of books were required. To meet this demand, several Italian printing houses began to publish Armenian books. The most prominent among them was operated by *De Propaganda Fide* in Rome; it was established in 1623 by Pope Urban VIII and continued until the 1890s. Other printers were Juan Batista Bovis, Michelangelo Barboni, Stephan Orlando, and Antonio Bortoli. Before the Mkhitarist Fathers established their own press in Venice in 1789, most of their printing was done at Antonio Bortoli's.

Although the books published during the seventy years between Meghapart and Terzntsi were few, they contributed much valuable experience and fostered self-confidence among those who would pursue the work with greater success. In 1616–18 Fr. Hovhannes Karmatanents established a new press for the Armenian communities of southeastern Europe in Lvov. The books published there included a prayer book in the Kipchak language but written in the Armenian alphabet, as this, the language of the Crimean Tatars, was also used by Armenian traders.

In 1636, far from Lvov, in New Julfa, a certain Khachatur Kesaratsi (1590–1646) and his associates set up a printing press. With no outside help, and relying only on their own skills and ingenuity, they mounted the press, cut their own type, manufactured their own paper, and, in 1638, published their first book, a *Saghmosaran* (Psalter). This was the first printing press in Iran. One very important book that Armenian ecclesiastics were keen to see printed was the Bible. There were a limited number of manuscript copies in circulation, and such a voluminous tome was not easy to reproduce by hand. In 1630 Catholicos Movses III Tatevatsi (1629–32) and, coincidentally, the clergy of New Julfa, wrote to the pope for permission to have the Armenian Bible printed in Rome, at the expense of the Armenian merchants of New Julfa. The request was rejected by the Vatican, which set a condition that changes be made to harmonize the text with the Vulgate. Upon this refusal, the people of New Julfa sent a promising monk named Hovhannes Jughayetsi to Livorno, Italy, to learn the art of printing. Upon his return, he did all the preliminary work and, in 1650, set himself diligently to the task of printing the Bible. As the work progressed, unforeseen difficulties arose, and the task was abandoned because of its enormity and complexity.

In 1656 Catholicos Hakob IV Jughayetsi (1655–80) sent Matteos Tzeretsi to Rome in a second attempt to arrange for the printing of the Bible. He stayed there for thirteen months but failed to achieve his purpose; once again the Vatican refused permission. Some twenty years earlier a certain Hovhannes Ankiuratsi, a translator for the ambassador of the Republic of Venice in Smyrna and a printing enthusiast, had suggested that the "heretical Protestant Dutch" would be more amenable to printing the Armenian Bible. Matteos went straight to Amsterdam and, overcoming formidable difficulties (in his words "working to death day and night for four years and eight months"), he set up a printing press. He had new fonts prepared by the Dutch font designer Christopher Von Dyck and acquired precious engravings of biblical illustrations prepared by Christoffel Van Sichem. In 1660 Matteos was ready to begin. As a trial, he began to print the poem "*Hisus vordi*" (Jesus the Son) by Nerses Shnorhali, but he died in 1661, without seeing the completion of his most cherished project.

Fortunately, the press was saved by the intervention of Avetis Ghlijents, an Armenian merchant in Amsterdam, who paid the accumulated debts and invited his brother, Voskan Yerevantsi, a man of learning who was the abbot of St. Sarkis Monastery in Ushi, Armenia, to assume responsibility for running the press. He arrived in 1664, and, after producing a few books as a trial, on March 11, 1666, with the help of two colleagues, Karapet Andrianatsi (born c. 1630) and Voskan Yerevantsi (1614–74), he began printing the Bible. It took more than two years to complete the job, but at long last the Armenian Bible saw the light on October 13, 1668. This was achieved with the financial support of three merchants from New Julfa. The volume consisted of 1470 double-column quarto pages, almost square, with 159 illustrations, and was the crown of Armenian printing, to be classed among the most famous early printed Bibles in the world. Voskan Yerevantsi based his text on the manuscript of King Hetum II (d. 1307) of Cilicia, dated 1295. The Old Testament was originally translated from the Greek Septuagint in the fifth century; in order to harmonize it with St. Jerome's Latin translation from the Hebrew, known as the Vulgate, Voskan Yerevantsi made changes in the division into chapters and verses, added certain passages from the Latin translation, and included some books of the Old Testament that were previously excluded from the Armenian canon, such as the Fourth Book of Esdras,[47] and the Book of Sirach (also known as the Book of Ecclesiasticus), which he translated from the Latin into an unrefined Armenian. These changes can probably be explained by his cautious desire to evade the censorship of the Inquisition. It must have paid off, because the Armenian Bible spread far and wide; it was reprinted in Constantinople in 1705 and in Venice in 1733 by Mkhitar Sebastatsi (1676–1749), the founder of the Mkhitarist Order. A version of the Armenian Bible based on the original fifth-century translation was published in Venice in 1805 by Hovhannes Vardapet Zohrapian (1756–1829). After printing about a dozen new titles, Voskan Yerevantsi became plagued with financial problems; he moved his press to Livorno in 1669, then in 1673 to Marseilles, where he died the following year.

---

47. According to Armenian numbering.

In 1685 one of Voskan's pupils, Matteos Vanandetsi, revived Armenian printing in Amsterdam, ordered new type from the renowned Hungarian type founder, Nicholas Kish, and increased his staff by recruiting a few family members. By 1695 he had produced a number of books. Two of his productions were epoch-making: one was the first Armenian map of the world, *Hamataratz ashkharhatsuyts* (1695), representing the two hemispheres, a work of excellent craftsmanship; the second was Movses Khorenatsi's *History of the Armenians* (1695), which appeared in print for the first time. After Matteos's death the press continued under the direction of Tovmas Vanandetsi, a learned professional, who visited London in 1707, was introduced to Queen Anne, and received an honorary Doctor of Divinity degree from the University of Oxford. On this occasion he presented the Bodleian Library a set of books printed by his press. He died in 1711. The press continued six more years, then collapsed financially. Many years passed before Armenian printing was revived in Europe. The Mkhitarist Fathers established their own printing presses in Trieste and Venice (San Lazzaro) in 1776 and 1789, respectively, by acquiring Tovmas Vanandetsi's equipment from the Dutch creditors.[48]

In order to survive, Armenian printing had to be established in or close to centers of Armenian concentration. Books printed in Amsterdam reached Armenia by a circuitous route: by boat to Smyrna and from there to various cities. Since conditions were still unfavorable in Armenia proper, printing activities began to concentrate in Constantinople.

More than a century elapsed after Abgar Dpir's initial press there ceased to function in 1569. In 1677 a new one was established by the scholar Yeremia Keomiurchian (Kömürdjian, 1637–95), but it lasted only two years. In the last decade of the seventeenth century, Grigor Marzvanetsi of Baghesh (Bitlis), a scribe and manuscript illuminator, spent four years mastering the arts of printing and engraving, prepared new Armenian fonts and plates, and, in 1698, published his first book, *Tagharan* (Hymnal or song book), a work of high quality. Marzvanetsi established a high standard of professionalism and began the practice of making printing a family business that passed from one generation to the next. In fact, his press lasted forty years. This tradition continued in Constantinople until the nineteenth century.

Another famous name in the history of Armenian printing is Astvatzatur Dpir, who opened his publishing house in 1700. Continued by

48. See Vrej Nersessian, *Early Armenian Printing (1512–1800),* a brochure published on the occasion of the Exhibition of Oriental Manuscripts and Printed Books at the British Museum library, July–December 1980.

his successors until the 1770s, the press published some eighty titles by classical authors, most of them printed for the first time. Other outstanding printer-publishers include the Arabian family (three generations, 1766–1851). The founder of the dynasty, Boghos Arabian (1742–1835), also designed Turkish type, and was appointed superintendent of the imperial press by Sultan Mahmut II in 1816. Another publisher, Janik Aramian (1820–79), founded presses in Constantinople, Paris, and Marseilles; he is known for the Aramian simplified type face, which is still in extensive use. Hovhannes Muhentisian (Mühendisian, 1810–91) was another pioneer; his press was in operation from 1839 to the First World War.

Presses were also established in Smyrna, a seaport city on the Aegean Sea, where the Armenian presence goes back to the 1620s. With its large Armenian community, Smyrna became the second capital, after Constantinople, of the Revival Movement. The first press there was founded in 1759 by Mahtesi Marcos; it was followed by the Mesropian, Teteyan (Dedeyan), and Mamurian print shops, which produced a prolific amount of literature.

The first Armenian press on the Indian subcontinent was established in Madras in 1772 by Shahamir Shahamirian. Marking a departure from tradition, this press produced material of a political nature, promoting ideas of emancipation and freedom for Armenia. Such books as *Nor tetrak vor kochi hordorak* (New booklet of exhortations), and *Vorogayt Parats* (Snare of glory), both written by Shahamirian himself, were blueprints for independence. *Snare of Glory* bears the date 1773 on the title page and was published under the name of Hakob Shahamirian, who was Shahamir Shahamirian's son; he died at a young age (1745–74). (The publication date has been disputed by some, who date it 1788–89.) This work comprises an elaborate and meticulously prepared constitution, in 521 articles, for a future independent Armenian state. It is based on democratic principles and advocates an elected parliament, an independent judicial system, and mandatory education for boys and girls. It is notable that this document preceded the United States Constitution by fourteen years. Shahamirian's press lasted until 1783, and had a primarily educational and historical output.

The second Armenian press on the subcontinent was established in 1789 by Fr. Harutiun Shmavonian (1750–1824), the priest of St. Mary's church in Madras. Born in Shiraz, Iran, Shmavonian was ordained in New Julfa and served as pastor in his native city. In 1777, after the death of his two sons, he spent his time in solitude, studying oriental languages, philosophy, and theology, and becoming adept in various crafts. In 1784 he returned to his pastoral duties in Madras. In 1789 he established a printing press almost from scratch, preparing the matrices and the typeface himself. The books he printed comprise a long list of religious, historical, and philosophical works. The crowning achievement of his career, however, was the publication of the first Armenian monthly journal, *Azdarar* (The monitor), whose initial issue appeared on October 16, 1794. Eighteen issues appeared between 1794 and 1796, and were primarily devoted to strengthening ties between Armenian communities, and promoting social and cultural awareness. The press functioned until 1818, by which time the Madras community was beginning to decline, ceding its place to Calcutta.

Because of its sizable Armenian community, Calcutta became the second Armenian cultural center in India. The first press there was founded in 1796, and the first book it published was the *History* of Catholicos Abraham Kretatsi (d. 1737). In the first half of the nineteenth century more than ten Armenian printing presses operated in Calcutta. The one that lasted longest (1816–53) was the press of *Mardasirakan chemaran* (Philanthropic college). The first Armenian newspaper, *Hayeli Kalkatian* (Mirror of Calcutta) was published in 1820.

Armenian presses were also established in St. Petersburg (1781); Nor Nakhijevan (1789); Astrakhan (1795), through the efforts of Hovsep Arghutian, primate of the Armenian Church; and Moscow (1829), at the Lazarian Academy.

Political, social, and economic conditions in the Armenian homeland did not encourage the development of the art of printing. It was only in the second half of the eighteenth century, during the pontificate of Catholicos Simeon Yerevantsi (1763–80), that a printing press was established in the Mother See of Etchmiadzin. A learned and widely traveled man, Simeon Yerevantsi had been to Constantinople, Smyrna, and Madras, and was well acquainted with the cultural life and the printing facilities of these centers. His decision to establish a press in Etchmiadzin was an audacious project, which he materialized within the space of a few years. With the financial support of Grigor Mikayelian-Chakikian, a merchant from Madras, and the assistance of local craftsmen, the work began in earnest. Equipment was assembled, a typefoundry was built, a press was installed, plates were prepared, other printing accessories were acquired, and a printing house was built to accommodate the operation. A few years later a paper mill was added. The press began functioning in 1771 and, after trials and adjustments, the first successfully printed book, *Zbosaran hogevor* (Spiritual recreation), basically a prayer book by Simeon Yerevantsi, came out in 1772, in an ornate leather-bound edition. The colophon of the book describes at length the circumstances of its printing and also the war of 1768–71 between the khanate of Yerevan and King Herakl of Georgia, which caused great suffering to the Armenian population and delayed the opening of the press.

During the next twenty years the printing house of Etchmiadzin, named after St. Gregory the Illuminator, produced several volumes of major works, including a 564-page *Tonatsuyts* (Calendar of feasts), *Saghmosaran* (Psalter), *Khorhrdatetr* (Missal), *Sharaknots* (Hymnal), and Stepanos Lehatsi's (d. 1689) translation into Armenian of Josephus's *History of the Jewish War.* Initially the output of the press was not prolific, but significantly, after two centuries of wanderings from country to country, the Armenian press was at last established on native soil. In 1792, troubled times caused the activities of the press to be suspended. Printing was resumed in 1818, through the efforts of Catholicos Yeprem I Dzorageghtsi (1809–30). The press of the Holy See of Etchmiadzin continues to the present day.

THE MKHITARIST (MEKHITARIST) ORDER

A prominent forerunner of the Armenian intellectual revival was the Mkhitarist Order, established in Venice in 1717 by Mkhitar Sebastatsi. Born in 1676 in Sebastia (Sivas), he received his religious education in Etchmiadzin, then moved to Karin (Erzurum) and was ordained a celibate priest of the Armenian Apostolic Church in 1696.

From his youth, Mkhitar Sebastatsi had cherished the idea of establishing a monastic order that would serve the spiritual and intellectual needs of his people and bring about a cultural revival. In order to realize his project, he wandered from place to place in search of favorable conditions and a suitable location. He did not find encouragement from the Armenian clergy, and the adverse political and economic conditions prevailing in Armenia forced him to look elsewhere. He got in touch with Latin missionaries in Aleppo and accepted the Catholic faith. In 1700 he went to Constantinople, gathered around him a dozen students, and founded, in secret, a religious order that was later to be called by his name.[49]

In 1703 he and his pupils moved to Morea (the ancient name of the Peloponnesus, southern Greece) and established his order in the city

---

49. The traditional date of the founding of the Mkhitarist Order is 1701. However, new evidence suggests that the actual date was 1700. See *Bazmavep*, 1–4 (2000), 55–71.

of Meton, which was under Venetian rule at the time. Two years later, when they had acquired a monastery and adopted the Benedictine Rule, he petitioned Pope Clement XI for recognition of the order. Mkhitar Sebastatsi always maintained that there was no conflict between practicing Catholicism and being faithful to the Armenian nation and its values. However, the Vatican interpreted this view as dual loyalty and tampering with the rites of the Church, and the pope's recognition of the order was delayed until 1712. In 1715 the Ottoman Turks invaded Morea, and the Mkhitarists fled to Venice. In 1717 the Venetian Senate recognized the order and granted it the island of San Lazzaro as its permanent home. The following year Mkhitar traveled to Rome to defend the order against continuing rumors, and he successfully convinced the Vatican of its orthodoxy. Construction of the monastery complex on the island soon started, laying the foundations of a movement that was destined to have a tremendous impact on Armenian culture and to last uninterrupted to the present day.

As the order's first abbot, Mkhitar Sebastatsi efficiently conducted the administrative, educational, and religious activities of the congregation, finding little time for writing. He did, however, produce two books of grammar (1727, 1730), a commentary on the Gospel of St. Matthew, and a few religious books. He was also the motivating force behind the publication of the Armenian Bible in 1735. His monumental work is *Bargirk haykazian lezvi* (Dictionary of the Armenian language), published posthumously. Sebastatsi died on April 27, 1749. His tomb on San Lazzaro has become a shrine for thousands of visitors.

In 1772 a disagreement about certain amendments to the constitution of the Mkhitarist Order led some twelve of its members to separate. Under the leadership of Fr. Astvatzatur Papikian, the group moved to Trieste, which was under Austrian rule at the time, where they established a branch of the Mkhitarist Order in 1773. In 1811 they settled in Vienna, were recognized as an independent congregation by an imperial decree of Emperor Franz Joseph, and soon acquired their own building.

The two branches of the Mkhitarist Order, equally concerned with preserving Armenian culture and reviving Armenian studies and research in history and language, pursued their own programs. These were not competitive but rather complemented each other in various fields. Each established its own printing press and scholarly review: *Bazmavep* (Polyhistor: many stories) in Venice (1846), and *Handes Amsorya* (Monthly review) in Vienna (1887), both of which are still in existence.

Understandably, the earliest publications of the Mkhitarist Fathers were religious in nature. This aspect of their activities was never neglected, but after a couple of decades of stabilization, as the congregation grew and their ranks filled with highly educated members, their intellectual output began to encompass a wide range of studies and research. The Venetian order became particularly noted in the fields of history, the arts, and literature, whereas the Vienna branch emphasized philology and language. These orientations were perhaps influenced by the Italian penchant for the arts and the German for rational thinking, respectively. Their activities can be classified into the following major categories:

Armenian Classics

With the purpose of reviving the Armenian literary language (*grabar*) and making the ancient classics accessible to the public, the Mkhitarists began to publish a series of "Golden Age" and medieval authors,[50] such as Koriun, Pavstos Buzand, Yeghishé, Yeznik, Movses Khorenatsi, Grigor Narekatsi, Nerses Shnorhali, Nerses Lambronatsi, and many others. The aim was to familiarize the Armenian people with their history and develop in them an appreciation of their national values.

Western Classics

In a period when familiarity with ancient Greek and Latin classics was considered an essential element in the education of a cultured person, the Mkhitarists thought it important to produce Armenian translations of such famous works as Homer's *Iliad* and *Odyssey*, Virgil's *Aeneid* and *Georgics*, Plato's *Phaedo*, Sophocles' *Oedipus*, and classic European works, such as Milton's *Paradise Lost*, Fénelon's *Télémaque*, Bossuet's *Oraisons funèbres*, some of Racine's and Voltaire's tragedies, and many more. Almost all of these were translated into classical Armenian by fathers of the order, including Manuel Jakhjakhian (1770–1835), Harutiun Avgerian (1774–1884), Yeghia Tovmajan (1777–1848), Arsen Bagratuni (1790–1866), and Yedvard Hiurmiuz (1799–1876). However, most of this huge corpus of translated material regrettably remained inaccessible to the public. By the 1840s classical Armenian was in decline except among the learned elite, and the trend toward a modern literary language was gaining momentum. Hence the Mkhitarists of both Venice and Vienna gradually switched to modern Armenian, in the evolution of which they played an important role.

Poetry

Although poetry was not a major genre explored by the Mkhitarist Fathers, a few were captivated by it. One who stands out as a poet

---

50. See volumes 1 and 2 of the present anthology.

and erudite man of letters is Arsen Bagratuni (1790–1866), a staunch classicist. His first book, *Taghk* (Poems), appeared in 1852; in five parts, it is saturated with religious and moral sentiment. His best work is *Hayk diutsazn* (The epic hero Hayk), a long poem epitomizing the sacredness of the fatherland, in which Hayk is represented as a historic figure who fights for freedom. Its beautiful and elegant style is an example of classical Armenian at its best, used to create richly ornate poetic imagery. Among others who wrote poetry, Manuel Jakhjakhian (1770–1835) and Yedvard Hiurmiuz (1799–1876) stand out as representatives of classicism. A three-volume anthology of poetry, *Taghk mkhitarian vardapetats* (Poems by Mkhitarist Fathers), was published between 1852 and 1854.

The person who broke ranks with the classicists was Ghevond Alishan (1820–1901). He wrote poetic works in verse and prose early in his career before dedicating himself to historical and philological research. These works reflect pronounced romanticism combined with ardent patriotism. The poems *"Voghbam zkez hayots ashkharh"* (I weep for you, Armenia), *"Hraztan," "Plpuln Avarayri"* (The nightingale of Avarayr), *"Shushann Shavarshana"* (Shushan of Shavarshan), and *"Hushikk hayrenyats hayots"* (Memories of the Armenian homeland), the latter written in prose, are among his best.

History and Philology

An important figure in the revival of Armenian historiography is Mikayel Chamchian (1738–1823), whose three-volume, 2760-page *Patmutiun Hayots* (History of the Armenians), published between 1781 and 1786, was an attempt to write a comprehensive history of Armenia from the time of the biblical Creation to his own days. Some have likened this *History,* in concept and in scope, to that of Movses Khorenatsi, which was written in the fifth century and on which Chamchian bases the earlier part of his narrative. For the rest he makes use of numerous Armenian and non-Armenian sources, some of which, particularly those by Greek and Latin authors, he treats with a critical approach. He accepts as reliable only those events cited by at least two independent sources, and he indicates those sources in the margins. The text is divided into historical periods according to the Armenian royal dynasties and the periods of domination by invading powers. Judging by the criteria of his own time, this book is a great achievement in Armenian historiography.

What Chamchian did for history, Ghukas Inchichian (Indjidjian, 1758–1833) did for geography with his books *Storagrutiun hin hayastaniayts* (Description of ancient Armenia), and *Hnakhosutiun ashkharhagrakan Hayastani* (Archeology of geographic Armenia), in three volumes, which gives a historical description of the geography of the Armenian provinces. Another famous name is that of Ghevond Alishan, mentioned above, an erudite scholar who commanded a number of languages; he first made his name as an ardent patriotic poet, deriving his inspiration from Armenian history, and later concentrated on studies of Armenian history, philology, and antiquities. His *Shirak, Sisvan, Ayrarat,* and *Sisakan,* all published between 1881 and 1883, deal with the history and geography of these Armenian provinces with amazing accuracy, despite the fact that Alishan never visited them himself. Most of his philological works have been collected in a series comprising twenty-two small volumes called *Soperk haykakank* (Armenian stories). Also to be noted are his *Hin havatk kam hetanosakan kronk hayots* (The ancient beliefs or pagan religion of Armenians, 1895) and *Haybusak* (Armenian flora, 1895), which describes some 3400 species of plants that grow in Armenia.

These and related books by Mkhitarist authors helped revive a deep attachment within the people for their homeland and forge a sentiment of national identity. Great credit should also be given to the Mkhitarists of Vienna for the Armenian philological and historical studies contained in their series *Azgayin matenadaran* (The national library), which comprises close to two hundred volumes.

Language

For more than a century (1700–1820) after the establishment of the Mkhitarist Order, its intellectual output was almost exclusively in classical Armenian (*grabar*). This was still the age of classicism, and modern literary Armenian was in its very early stages of development. Mkhitar Sebastatsi's monumental work is the dictionary of the Armenian language (*Bargirk haykazian lezvi*), in classical Armenian, which was published posthumously (1749–69). It comprises all the words contained in Armenian manuscripts, together with their etymology and their equivalents in Greek and Latin.

The original dictionary was subsequently edited and meticulously revised by Frs. Gabriel Avedikian (1750–1827), Khachatur Surmelian (1751–1827), and Mkrtich Avgerian (1762–1854), and published in two large volumes in 1836–37, under the title *Nor bargirk haykazian lezvi* (New dictionary of the Armenian language). Along with the dictionaries came grammar books, such as Arsen Bagratuni's *Tarerk hayeren kerakanutyan* (Elements of Armenian grammar, 1846) and *I petes zargatselots* (For the use of the educated, 1852). Although these works were intended to improve the use of classical Armenian, they were also instrumental in establishing a solid basis for the formation of modern Armenian in the 1860s. In this respect the *Knnakan kerakanutiun ashkharabar lezvi* (A critical grammar of modern Armenian, 1866), a monumental work by Arsen Aydenian (1825–1902), abbot of the Mkhitarist Congregation in Vienna, became an authentic source and guidebook for the development of modern Armenian. The numerous publications of the Mkhitarist Fathers contributed a great deal to the refinement of western literary Armenian.

Education

From the earliest days of the order, education has been one of the Mkhitarists' main concerns. In 1732, fifteen years after it was established in Venice, the order opened an academy that later became a well-known educational center, where even some European men of letters came to familiarize themselves with Armenian and other eastern languages. The academy's most famous visitor was Lord Byron (1788–1824), who studied Armenian with the Mkhitarist Fathers while he was in Venice. In 1833 the Muratian School opened in Padua, in northern Italy, and in 1836 the Raphaelian School opened in Venice; in 1873 these were united as the Murat-Raphaelian School. In 1846 another school, also known as the Muratian School, opened in Paris. Neither congregation spared any effort to establish a network of schools, from elementary to college level, in cities in the diaspora that had large Armenian populations and also in the Armenian provinces where conditions allowed. This necessitated another task: the preparation of textbooks in literature, history, religion, and even the sciences. By the beginning of the First World War the Mkhitarists of Vienna were operating twenty-six schools worldwide. The graduates of the Mkhitarist schools include numerous poets, essayists, novelists, journalists, and activists, who helped usher in the great intellectual and social reawakening of the mid-nineteenth century. Today only six Mkhitarist schools continue to function: those of Venice, Paris, Istanbul, Aleppo, Buenos Aires, and Los Angeles.

For the past three hundred years the Mkhitarist Order, with its twin branches in Venice and Vienna, has dedicated itself to an admirable vocation and contributed immensely to the cultural, intellectual, and spiritual development of the nation. What has been attempted here is only a cursory survey of a momentous movement that commands admiration and pride. It should be noted that the Venetian and Viennese branches of the order, which separated in 1772, reunited in July 2000, under the abbotship of Venice.

THE INTELLECTUAL REVIVAL

By the beginning of the nineteenth century a sizable class of Armenian merchants and entrepreneurs had emerged in Constantinople and Smyrna. They sent their sons to be educated in European centers, mainly France and Italy, where they were influenced by the revolutionary ideas sweeping across Europe. The French Revolution had already shaken the foundations of the monarchic state, and Italy was struggling to rid itself of Austrian hegemony and establish national unity. When these Armenian youths returned home imbued with new ideas and ideals, they brought with them the Promethean fire, as it were. With the awakening of national consciousness, this new generation began to shake up ancient and stagnant patriarchal attitudes, and it initiated a movement that soon blossomed into an intellectual revival.

Journalism

The first manifestation of this revival occurred in journalism, regarded as the most effective means of reaching the general public. The first Armenian newspaper in Constantinople was *Ditak Biuzandian* (The Byzantine observer), a biweekly, published in 1812 by the Mkhitarist Fathers; it lasted for three years. In 1832 *Newspaper* appeared; this was a translation into colloquial Armenian of the daily news bulletins issued by the government; it disappeared after one year. In the meantime two periodicals began in Smyrna: *Shtemaran pitani giteliats* (Warehouse of useful knowledge, 1839–54), which was mainly religious in nature, and *Arshaluys Araratian* (Dawn on Ararat, 1840–87), a periodical of political, literary, and commercial content founded by Ghukas Baltazarian. A high point of Armenian journalism in Smyrna was the *Arevelian mamul* (Eastern press), founded in 1871, and edited by Matteos Mamurian (1830–1901), historian, educator, translator, and social activist. His paper became a strong proponent of democratic ideology and lasted for thirty years, until the editor's death. As new print shops opened and the demand for literature increased, more and more journals appeared. Prior to 1922, the year of the massacre of the Greek and Armenian populations of Smyrna and the burning of the city by the Kemalist Turks, a total of thirty-six journals were being published.

The first Armenian publication in Constantinople that can justifiably be called a newspaper was the *Surhandak Costandnupolso* (Constantinople courier), established in 1846 as the organ of the Patriarchate, under the editorship of Hovhannes Teroyents and Mkrtich Aghaton. Its name was soon changed to *Hayastan* (Armenia), and it continued for six years, with content that maintained a high intellectual level. In 1852 it was acquired by Karapet Iutiuchian (Ütüdjian, 1823–1904), one of the luminaries of the revival period, who assumed the editorship of the paper and renamed it *Masis*. Many intellectuals became editors or contributors: Arpiar Arpiarian (1852–1908), Grigor Zohrap (1861–1915), Hrand Asatur (1862–1928), Levon Bashalian (Pashalian, 1868–1943), Arshak Chopanian (Arshag Tchobanian, 1872–1954), among others. Until its demise in 1908, *Masis* continued to be a forum for liberal ideas, social issues, and literary criticism, and a highly influential molder of public opinion.

The year 1855 saw the initial publication of a weekly religious and literary magazine, *Avetaber* (Messenger), financed by the Evangelical missionaries, which continued until 1915. Also in 1855 Mkrtich Khrimian, later patriarch and catholicos) began to publish a monthly magazine in Constantinople under the title *Artzvi Vaspurakan* (The eagle of Vaspurakan); its aim was to acquaint the intelligentsia of the capital with the dismal conditions in the Armenian provinces and promote the education of youth in national values. After Khrimian was appointed abbot of St. Karabet monastery in Taron and had established a seminary there, he moved the paper to Van, renamed it *Artzvik Tarono* (The eaglet of Taron), and entrusted the editorship to his former pupil Garegin Srvandztiants (1840–92). The paper focused on advocating the rights of the peasants. It continued until 1865.

In 1856 Harutiun Svachian (Svadjian, 1831–74), a French-educated writer and political activist, founded a biweekly magazine in Constantinople called *Meghu* (The bee), which, besides its literary, social, and economic content, also had a feature that was a first in the Armenian press: a section devoted to satire. A few years before the paper folded in 1874 the editorship was assumed by Hakob Paronian (Baronian, 1843–91), renowned satirist of the time, who would later publish his own satirical paper, *Khikar* (1884–88).

During this period two major publications were established by the Mkhitarist Fathers. In 1843 the Venice Congregation began to publish *Bazmavep* (Polyhistor), a learned historical and literary monthly, and *Yevropa* (Europe), launched in 1847 and which lasted until 1863. In 1887 *Yevropa* was replaced by *Handes amsoria* (Monthly review), a philological and linguistic journal. *Bazmavep* and *Handes amsoria* are still being published.

In the last decade of the nineteenth century, as literary orientations were being crystallized and modern Armenian was gradually stabilizing, two major papers saw the light. The first was a daily, *Hayrenik* (Fatherland), founded in 1891 by the prominent writer Arpiar Arpiarian, the dean of realism. *Hayrenik* attracted a large number of progressive writers, whose ideas did not please the ruling sultan, Abdul Hamid; the paper was closed in 1896. That same year a new paper appeared, *Biuzandion* (Byzantium), founded and edited by Biuzand Kechian, who drew to the paper intellectuals who were principally inclined to conservatism. *Biuzandion* played an important role in keeping alive the debate between different schools of thought. It closed in 1918, immediately after the genocide.

The preceding list of newspapers and periodicals is not exhaustive. At least a dozen more journals of various types were published between 1880 and the end of the century, mostly on individual initiatives. Each in its own way contributed to the engagement of the public in the Revival Movement. Moreover, throughout the nineteenth century and even before that, an immense amount of literature was produced in Armeno-Turkish, that is in the Turkish language written in Armenian characters.

Armeno-Turkish Literature[51]

From the seventeenth to the end of the nineteenth century an important Armeno-Turkish literature and periodical press, written in Armenian characters, developed. This phenomenon can best be understood within the framework of Western Armenian political conditions.

During centuries of Ottoman domination, the authorities imposed restrictions on Armenians, forcing them to use Turkish instead of their mother tongue. At the same time, the persecutions inflicted upon the Armenian populations of certain provinces by Ottoman and local authorities led the people to gradually stop speaking Armenian.[52]

In certain regions of Anatolia, especially in the provinces of Caesarea (Kayseri), Adana, and Angora (Ankara), a large portion of the Armenian population became Turkish-speaking. Although they retained their religion and national traditions, they lost their mother tongue. To save the population of these regions from alienation, the Armenian religious leaders felt obliged to translate religious literature from Armenian into Turkish. The resultant flood of religious literature written in Turkish

---

51. Armenian literature written in the Turkish language but using the Armenian alphabet.
52. See Gabriel Basmajian's articles: "*Hayatar Turkeren mamul*" (The Armeno-Turkish press), *Abaka* (Future), (March 31, 1997), 7, and "*Agapi arevmtahayots arajin vepe yev ir antzanot heghinake* (*Agapi*, the first novel of Western Armenians and its little known author)," *Abaka* (July 7, 1997), 6 and 9.

but using Armenian characters, a phenomenon at times exaggerated by the leaders of the Armenian Catholic Church, accelerated the loss of the mother tongue among the population. In fact, a huge number of Turkish-speaking Armenian Catholics identified themselves with the Catholic *millet* (nationality), defining themselves by their religion rather than their nationality.

With the appearance of Armeno-Turkish religious literature, a number of writers began to produce original works written in Turkish in Armenian characters. One of the best-known works in this category is *Agapi* (1851), a novel by Hovsep Vardanian.[53] During the Ottoman period Armenian minstrels wrote their lyrics in Turkish with Armenian characters, and in time these became part of Armenian folk culture.

Armeno-Turkish literature was also enriched with translations of European (mainly French) writers. From the twelfth to the nineteenth century, historical and political circumstances led some Armenian settlements to use the Armenian alphabet to express themselves in Kipchak,[54] Latin, Greek, Assyrian, Iranian, Arabic, Polish, Hungarian, Russian, and Azerbaijani. The most renowned bard of Transcaucasia during the eighteenth century was Sayat-Nova, who wrote in three languages (Armenian, Azerbaijani, and Georgian). His Azerbaijani poems were composed in the Armenian alphabet.

The Armeno-Turkish Press

In the mid-nineteenth century around ten periodicals and newspapers appeared with the mission of informing the Turkish-speaking Armenian population, especially that of Constantinople. This Armeno-Turkish press reported on religious, moral, national, and social issues of the time. Although they did not last long, some were published until the beginning of the twentieth century. *Madjmuayi Havadis* (News magazine, 1852–63) was published in Constantinople by the author of *Agapi*, Hovsep Vardanian. *Zohal* (Saturn, 1855–57) was edited by Teroyents Hovhannes Patveli Chamurchian (Chamurdjian). In 1857 the

---

53. Hovsep Vardanian (1815–79) and Hovhannes Hisarian (1827–1916) are considered the first Western Armenian novelists. *Agapi* is a simple story of the love between Agapi and Hakob: an impossible and discouraging love because of their confessional differences.

54. The (now extinct) language of the Kipchaks belonged to the family of Turkic languages. It was spoken in the Black Sea region, in the Crimea, and in the Balkan peninsula. The Kipchaks had no alphabet of their own, so Armenians who were fluent in Kipchak used Armenian characters when they wrote in that language.

paper changed its name to *Yerevak* (also Saturn, but in Armenian). It published mainly educational, philological, and religious articles. At first *Yerevak* was a bimonthly journal, then it became a weekly (1857–62 and 1864–66). *Manzumei Efkâr* (Course of opinion, 1866–1917) was edited by Karapet Panosian and published in Constantinople, first as a daily then as a weekly. It was the first Turkish-Armenian daily and maintained a rather liberal view, criticizing the dire economic, political, and social conditions of the interior provinces. In 1880, however, as a result of Sultan Hamid's imposition of censorship, the liberal stance of the paper shifted. Despite its Turkish name, beginning in 1896 it became an Armenian paper, and five years later Misak Gochunian assumed its editorship.[55]

Terdjümane Efkâr (Translator of opinions, 1877–84) was published by T. Chivelekian (Djivelekian) and S. Sakayan in Constantinople; *Djerideyi Sharkiye* (Eastern journal, 1885–1913) was published as its continuation. T. Djivelekian was the first editor, but in 1907 H. Varzhapetian took over. Although the paper catered to Turkish-speaking Armenians, in 1890 it began to publish some Armenian articles. The paper maintained its liberalism until the end.

The Armenians of Adana and other regions of Cilicia had gradually become Turkish-speaking. *Adana* (1910–15) was published specifically for them. After the Armistice several other Armenian journals and dailies were published there (1919–21), but they all came to an abrupt halt in 1922, when Armenian life in Adana ceased to exist.

In addition to the aforementioned publications, some journals composed in Armenian carried Turkish supplements written in Armenian characters. Worth mentioning are *Mamul* (The press), a periodical published in Constantinople by G. Ayvazian, and *Tatron* (Theater), a weekly published by the well-known humorist Hakob Paronian (Baronian). In 1875 Paronian wrote of these Armeno-Turkish supplements: "It is with the utmost sadness that an Armenian has to resort to a foreign language in order to communicate with another Armenian. Yes, it is regrettable, but it is the way things are."

This tradition continued well into the twentieth century, but after the Armenian genocide of 1915, as the remainder of the Armenian population scattered all over the Middle East—some to Constantinople, others to Europe and the United States—Armeno-Turkish literature disappeared completely.

---

55. Misak Gochunian (1863–1913) founded *Zhamanak* (Time) in 1908. Despite some interruptions, the paper continues as an Istanbul daily.

THE DEVELOPMENT OF MODERN ARMENIAN
Middle Armenian (Mijin hayeren)

Classical Armenian, known as *grabar,* was the literary language that ruled supreme from the fifth to about the middle of the nineteenth century. During this period the Armenian language went through various stages, such as the Golden Age, the post-Golden Age, the Hellenistic stage, and later the medieval stage, when a large number of colloquialisms and dialectal elements penetrated the spoken and written languages.

The period between the twelfth and the sixteenth centuries can be distinguished as the age of middle Armenian, and can be divided into two stages: a) from the twelfth to the fourteenth century, when it was refined, normalized, and became the state language of the Cilician Kingdom; and b) from the fifteenth to the sixteenth century, when, deprived of state usage and protection and spreading into Greater Armenia, it deteriorated into a mixture of various dialects. Two new letters, corresponding to the sounds [o] and [f], were added to the alphabet, and some phonetic and declensional changes occurred. A number of the grammatical forms of *grabar* were retained, though others suffered dialectal mutations, and many popular locutions and foreign words were introduced. Although an abundance of literature was produced in middle Armenian, classical Armenian retained its position as the language of religion and scholarship. Many Cilician authors, such as Nerses Shnorhali, Mkhitar Gosh, and Nerses Lambronatsi, wrote their major works in classical Armenian. By contrast, Smbat Sparapet's *History* and the poems of Hovhannes Pluz were written in the popular language. As middle Armenian spread abroad after the collapse of the Cilician Kingdom, it gradually mixed with local jargon and a large number of Arabic and Turkish words slipped in. The period between the sixteenth and eighteenth centuries was a low point for culture in Armenia proper, because of the devastating wars between the Ottomans and the Persians. Despite this, however, a significant amount of literature was produced, in prose and in verse, mainly on secular themes, all written in middle Armenian.[56]

Modern Armenian (Ashkharhabar)

In the late eighteenth and early nineteenth centuries the Mkhitarist Fathers and other intellectuals made a vigorous effort to revive classical Armenian. As mentioned earlier, the Mkhitarists produced two

---

56. See vol. 2 of the present anthology for excerpts from medieval authors translated from middle Armenian.

monumental works, the *History of the Armenians* and the *Dictionary of the Armenian Language*, both in classical Armenian, and a number of grammar books. The books they authored and the translations of ancient and European classics on which they worked fastidiously were all in classical Armenian. However, this noble effort failed to bring forth the expected result. All this work, unintelligible to the general public, was destined to remain in the cloister. The dominance of classical Armenian was long since over, and a popular vernacular mixed with foreign intrusions was already imposing itself. Now it was time to take this crude vernacular, rid it of the dross of dialect and jargon, refine and enrich it with vocabulary drawn from the classical roots of the language, and adorn it with a simplified, consistent, and elegant grammar. This is what the young intellectuals of the revivalist generation, both in Constantinople and Smyrna, did.

The transition was not smooth. Among the staunchest supporters of reviving classical Armenian were such educators and scholars as Matatia Karakashian (1818–1903), Hakob Gurgen (1850–1915), and Reteos Perperian (Berberian, 1851–1907). The modernists were represented by a host of prominent intellectuals, including Nahapet Rusinian (1819–76), Mkrtich Khrimian, Ghevond Alishan, Nikoghayos Zorayan (1821–59), Tzerents (1822–88), Mkrtich Peshiktashlian (Beshiktashlian), Grigor Otian, Grigor Chilinkirian (Chilingirian, 1839–1923), Tovmas Terzian (1840–1909), Petros Durian (1851–72), and Minas Cheraz (1852–1929).

Although the traditionalists were few in number, the clash between them and the modernists was strong and the debates were sharp. The development of modern literary Armenian was a painful process. Its proponents were not always unanimous on how to proceed. The idea, advanced by some ultra radicals, of completely abandoning classical Armenian as a dead language and allowing the modern version to follow its natural course was unacceptable. Neither could modern Armenian be based on the vernacular of Constantinople, since that was already a mixture of dialects, debased with numerous Turkish words. The wisest thing to do would be to go back to the roots of the language, that is to *grabar* and the ancient dialects, to draw from them a genuinely Armenian vocabulary, and, by applying the rules of a simplified and consistent grammar, derive or coin new words, maintaining the specific characteristics of the Armenian language. This was a difficult task, but it was accomplished, and the first comprehensive grammar of modern Armenian was written by Mkhitarist Father Arsen Aydnian (Aytnian) in 1866. And so was created a purified and well-structured literary language that still commands respect.

Contributing Factors

Several factors contributed to the speedy development and spread of modern Armenian. Perhaps the most important was the printing press. As mentioned earlier, its profusion after the 1840s served as a powerful instrument for the growth of modern Armenian and also provided a school and a testing ground for it, as it was gradually shaped, normalized, and popularized.

Schools. Another significant factor was the Armenian school. The first Armenian school in Constantinople was established in 1715 through the efforts of Patriarch Hovhannes Kolot. Although its main purpose was to prepare priests, its curriculum contained courses in philosophy, literature, and the sciences. It flourished under Paghtasar Dpir (1683–1768), who assumed its directorship in 1741. Other early academies were the Tarkmanchats and Hripsimiants schools (for boys and girls, respectively, now combined as the Tarkmanchats school), whose beginnings may go back to 1785; the Levonian school (1820, now known as the Levon-Vartuhian school); the *Usumnaran* (Institute of learning), which opened in 1828 adjacent to the patriarchate, with Grigor Peshtimalchian (Peshtimaldjian), an erudite educator, as its headmaster; the Pezchian (Bezdjian) school, named after Harutiun Amira Bezdjian, who built it in 1830; the Nunian girls' school (1831, now known as the Sahakian-Nunian school and coeducational); the Nersesian school (1836); and the *Jemaran* (academy) in Scutari (Üsküdar, 1838). These schools were scattered through the various suburbs of the capital. According to a report issued by the Educational Council in 1865, there were then forty-six Armenian schools in Constantinople, with over 5,500 students.[57] Nevertheless, the need for higher education was acute. Starting from 1865, a number of schools were opened at the lycée and college levels, such as the Nupar-Shahnazarian school (1866), the Akabian (1869) and Mezpurian (Mezburian, 1879) schools (both for girls), and the Perperian (1876) and Kedronakan (1886) schools. The medium of instruction was modern Armenian, although the teaching of *grabar* continued. The Mkhitarist Fathers of Venice and of Vienna opened three schools, one at the lycée level, in 1825.

Educational revival in the cities spread to the provinces. The Sanasarian academy was established in Karin (Erzurum) in 1881 with the financial support of Mkrtich Sanasarian (1818–89), an industrialist from Tiflis and a graduate of the Lazarian college in Moscow. The curriculum, spread over nine grades, was oriented toward the humanities and

---

57. See Siruni, *Polis yev ir dere,* 3:310.

sciences. There were also two-year courses for training teachers and vocational courses that met local requirements. The school was equipped with laboratories and an ample library. It lasted until the 1915 genocide, when most of its teachers were massacred and the building was ruined. Two schools were opened in Van in 1870: the Haykazian (for boys) and the Sandukhtian (for girls), followed by the Yeramian (1880) and the Kedronakan (1881). These also came to an end in 1915. Kharberd (Harput) was famed for its National Central School, built in 1887, which produced a host of writers, including Tlkatintsi (1860–1915) and Ruben Zardarian (1874–1915), who, with the entire school, perished in the 1915 carnage.

The significant contribution made to the educational revival by Protestant missionary organizations should also be noted. The main institutions that played a role in raising several generations of well-educated and Western-oriented youth were Robert College (1840) and the Home School (for girls) in Constantinople; Euphrates College (1878–1915) in Kharberd, a prestigious institution solely for Armenian students, with a wide-ranging and enriched curriculum; a Girls' College in Marash (1884–1915); Anatolia College in Marzvan (Merzifon, 1886–1915); and the Theological Seminary at Ayntap (1855–1915).

Literature in Translation. Another potent factor in the development, enrichment, and popularization of modern Armenian was the vast amount of literature, mainly by French authors, that appeared in translation. When the public began to experience the joy of reading a comprehensible language, there were not enough books in print. Armenian authors could not keep up with the demand. The short-term solution was to produce popular translations: not the kind over which the Mkhitarist Fathers struggled for so many decades such as Homer's *Iliad* and *Odyssey*, Fénelon's *Télémaque*, and Milton's *Paradise Lost*.

A vast number of translations were produced between 1840 and 1890. An important milestone, which had a significant influence on the development of modern Armenian, was the translation of the Bible from *grabar* (classical Armenian) into *ashkharhabar* (modern Armenian) by Andreas Papazian, assisted by Ghukas Baldazarian, in Smyrna (Izmir).

It is impossible to ignore the colossal work done by major Armenian literary figures during this period; they made a number of the masterpieces of European literature accessible to Armenian readers in modern Armenian. It is interesting to note that Armenian translators often adapted works by their European contemporaries rather than writers of former times. What the public wanted was contemporary books, and

French novels often met this desire. Both in Constantinople and in Smyrna frantic efforts were made to translate the works of such authors as Victor Hugo, Eugène Sue, Ludovic Halévi,[58] Alexandre Dumas the elder, Jules Verne, Octave Feuillet,[59] Alfred de Musset, Lamartine, and others, whose works captivated the public.

Hovhannes Teroyents (1801–88), an ardent defender of the Armenian Apostolic Church, translated 150 books and pamphlets between 1840 and 1846. His translation of Pascal's *Pensées* (Thoughts) is among his major contributions.

Grigor Chilinkirian, Mesrop Nuparian (1842–1929), and Matteos Mamurian were Smyrna translators who made important contributions. Interestingly, some French writings were translated into Armeno-Turkish. Karapet Iutiuchian (Ütüdjian) and other well-known literary figures, such as Nikoghayos Zorayan, Stepan Voskanian, Nahapet Rusinian, Mkrtich Peshiktashlian (Beshiktashlian), Tovmas Terzian, and Grigor Otian, also made important translations.

The reputations of the translators often equaled those of authors who produced original works. This may in part be because Armenian writers of the Revival Movement did not have the opportunity to collect their works into books, whereas the works that were being translated were the most renowned pieces of the time. Armenian writers simply could not compete. A few examples are sufficient to indicate the rich repertoire of European literature being translated at the time.

Among the works translated by Matteos Mamurian are Goethe's *Die Leiden des Jungen Werthers* (The sorrows of young Werther, 1774); Eugène Sue's *Les mystères de Paris* (The mysteries of Paris, 1842); the elder Alexandre Dumas's *Les trois mousquetaires* (The three musketeers, 1844), *Vingt ans après* (Twenty years later, 1845), and *Le vicomte de Bragelonne* (The viscount of Bragelonne, 1848–50); Sir Walter Scott's *Ivanhoe* (1819); and Jules Verne's *Le tour du monde en quatre-vingts jours* (Around the world in eighty days, 1873).

---

58. A French librettist and novelist (1834–1908) who collaborated with Henri Meilhac on the librettos for most of Offenbach's operas and Bizet's *Carmen*. His novels include *L'Abbé Constantin* (Abbé Constantin, 1882) and *La Famille Cardinal* (The cardinal family, 1883). He was elected to the Académie Française in 1884.

59. A popular French novelist (1821–90) whose works include the novels *Roman d'un jeune homme pauvre* (Story of a poor young man, 1858), *Monsieur de Camors* (1867) and *Julia de Trécoeur* (1872), and the plays *Le pour et le contre* (For and against, 1853), *La belle au bois dormant* (The beauty of the sleeping woods, 1867), and *La partie de dames* (The ladies' party, 1884). He was elected to the Académie Française in 1862.

Grigor Chilinkirian translated twenty-seven books, including Victor Hugo's *Les Misérables* (1862), Eugène Sue's *Mathilde* (1841), Abbé Prévost's *Manon Lescaut* (1731), Lamartine's *Raphaël* (1849), and Alfred de Musset's *La confession d'un enfant du siècle* (The confession of a child of the century, 1836).

Mesrop Nuparian translated numerous works: among them are Victor Hugo's *Notre Dame de Paris* (1831), Racine's *Esther* (1689), Boileau's *Le lutrin* (The lectern, 1674, 1683), the first part of Goethe's *Faust* (1808), and La Fontaine's *Fables* (1668–94).

In Smyrna, Harutiun Teteyan (Dedeyan) published Molière's *L'Avare* (The miser, 1669) and *Le médecin malgré lui* (The involuntary physician, 1666); Victor Hugo's *Lucrèce Borgia* (1833), and the elder Alexandre Dumas's *Le Comte de Monte Cristo* (The Count of Monte Cristo, 1844–45).

Grigor Mserian (1846–1893) translated Octave Feuillet's *Roman d'un jeune homme pauvre* (Story of a poor young man, 1858).

Among the volumes translated by Nahapet Rusinian, *Ruy Blas* (1838) by Victor Hugo is important.

Karapet Iutiuchian (Ütüdjian) translated more than fifty European works; important among them are Eugène Sue's *Le juif errant* (The wandering Jew, 1844–45) and Silvio Pellico's *Le mie prigioni* (My prisons, 1844).[60]

Some of these translators had no significant literary output apart from their translations. In this respect they resemble Edward Fitzgerald (1809–83), the English man of letters whose chief work was the English poetic version (from Persian) of the *The Rubáiyát of Omar Khayyám* (1859), and Sir Richard Burton (1821–90), whose almost thirty volumes of translations included *The Thousand and One Nights* (1885–88).

As modern Armenian gradually emerged and increased its vocabulary, there was a great need for dictionaries, particularly French-Armenian ones. In 1884 Norayr (Noraïr) Biuzandatsi published such a dictionary, in which many classical Armenian words and expressions could still be found. Other dictionaries soon followed. That of Yeghia Temirchipashian (Demirdjibashian) in 1886, with subsequent printings, and those of Mesrop Nuparian (1892), and Gwiton Lusignan (1900–1903, in two volumes) were French-Armenian dictionaries; the compilers, under the compulsion to find an Armenian equivalent for every French word, had to coin new words and introduce neologisms. A large

---

60. Garo Sasuni, *Patmutiun arevmtahay ardi grakanutyan* (History of modern Western Armenian literature [Beirut, 1951]), 116–17.

number of these fitted harmoniously into modern Armenian; others did not survive. Simon Gabamachian's (Kapamadjian) *Nor baregirk Hayeren lezvi* (New lexicon of the Armenian language), first published in Constantinople in 1892, was a worthy effort to promote modern Armenian. The first comprehensive and authoritative dictionary of modern Armenian, both Eastern and Western, was compiled by Stepan Malkhasiants and published in four volumes in Yerevan in 1942.

The translators earned a place in the history of the development of Armenian culture and language. The influence of their work on Armenian literature was immense. Literature in translation remained popular for almost fifty years, and the translators realized the importance of their mission: to use *ashkharhabar* with purity, to show the endless artistic and literary possibilities of this modern version of Armenian, and to promote its use and acceptance. The translators revised and adapted the existing Armenian vocabulary, inventing words and expressions as needed. This was a monumental linguistic task, which introduced European masterpieces to Armenian readers. It should also be noted that the Mkhitarist Fathers contributed to the translation movement by translating not only into *grabar* but also into modern Armenian.

As the school of realism gained ground in modern Armenian literature around 1885, enthusiasm for literature in translation waned, and the fervent era of translation—the outcome of forty years of revival fever—came to an end.

THE REVIVAL IN EASTERN ARMENIA

The cultural revival in Eastern Armenia kept pace with economic and social conditions that were much more tolerant there, particularly after the Russo-Persian wars of 1813 and 1828, when some provinces of Eastern Armenia and the khanates of Yerevan and Nakhijevan were annexed to Russia. The Eastern Armenian population was mainly rural. Intellectuals and the merchant class were concentrated in urban centers of the Caucasus such as Tiflis, Baku, Batum, and Astrakhan, as well as in St. Petersburg and Moscow. A generation of Armenian youths who grew up in these centers received their education in foreign universities that filled them with liberal and progressive ideas. Some of these young men, fired by a vision and moved by the plight of their native land, returned home and ignited the spark of cultural revival.

The first step was to establish schools. As early as 1805 and 1810 Armenian schools were begun in Tiflis and Astrakhan by the renowned educator Serovbé Patkanian (1769–1836). It soon became apparent that a college (*chemaran*) was needed for higher education and that it was best to establish it in Tiflis, the cultural center of the Caucasus at the time. This was the cherished project of Nerses Ashtaraketsi (1770–1857), Primate of Tiflis (elected catholicos in 1843), but fifteen years passed before it was realized. In the meantime, an important institution of higher education came into existence in Moscow: the Lazarian academy, founded in 1815 by the Lazarian family, a dynasty of wealthy and enlightened businessmen who were originally from New Julfa. The academy offered the full program of a Russian gymnasium, under the able leadership of Harutiun Alamdarian (1795–1834), a writer, educator, and activist. The academy's curriculum gradually shifted in the direction of Eastern and Armenian studies, and it soon became a research center with a highly qualified staff, attracting scholars and students from all over Russia. Among those who taught or studied there were Mkrtich Emin (1815–90), Stepan Nazariants (1812–79), Mikayel Nalpantian (Nalbandian, 1829–66), Kerovbé (1833–89) and Rafayel Patkanian (1830–92), Smbat Shahaziz (1840–1907), and many others, who played prominent roles in the intellectual revival that ensued. The Lazarian academy had its own printing press and an extensive library. It was closed in 1918 by the Communist government.

Nerses Ashtaraketsi's dream of a college in Tiflis was not realized until 1824, when the Nersisian school (named after him) was established. Its first principal was Harutiun Alamdarian. Over the years, as more grades were added and the curriculum was enriched and diversified, the number of students rose to about seven hundred. Although it offered courses in religion, it was a secular school, and quite a few of the faculty were liberal-minded intellectuals. Among the graduates were such notables as Khachatur Abovian (1809–48), Stepan Nazariants, Perch Proshian (1837–1907), Ghazaros Aghayan (1840–1911), Hovhannes Tumanian (1869–1923), Derenik Temirchian (Demirdjian, (1877–1956), Anastas Mikoyan (1895–1978), Gabriel Sundukian (1825–1912), Tzerents, Leo, Manuk Abeghian (1865–1944), Stepan Malkhasiants (1857–1947), and Hakob Manandian (1873–1952), all of whom contributed immensely to the cultural reawakening. The school continued operating until 1925.

The education of boys and girls was a major preoccupation of both religious and secular leaders; this resulted in the opening of many parish and local schools in Yerevan, Shushi, Alexandropol, and other centers. One school, however, the Gevorgian Chemaran, deserves special mention. Founded in 1874 by Catholicos Gevorg IV of Etchmiadzin, the college was originally intended as a seminary for preparing priests and teachers. Over time its curriculum expanded to include the physical and social sciences, literature, and languages. The trend toward the secularization of the educational program opened the way to liberal-democratic ideas, and around the turn of the century these gave rise to a number of student protests against the college's conservative teachers. The school administration wisely introduced changes to avert disorder. From time to time the number of students exceeded three hundred. Many of its graduates later became important writers, historians, scientists, and activists. The school was closed in 1917 as a result of the drastic political changes that occurred in the country.

The press also played a major role in fueling the Cultural Revival, particularly in the second half of the nineteenth century. Two newspapers began publication in Moscow: *Chrakagh* (The gleaner, 1853–62), a conservative literary and religious journal written mostly in classical Armenian, and *Hiusisapayl* (Aurora Borealis, 1858–62, 1864), edited by Stepan Nazariants and written in modern Armenian. The latter had a progressive, anticlerical orientation and counted among its contributors Mikayel Nalbandian, the revolutionary, and other democratic-minded intellectuals. In 1868 the monthly review *Ararat* (1868–1919) began publication in Etchmiadzin as the official organ of the catholicate; this was a prestigious periodical, almost entirely dedicated to Armenian studies. Journalistic activities were concentrated in Tiflis, where two periodicals appeared in quick succession: *Meghu Hayastani* (The bee of Armenia, 1858–86); and *Mshak* (The tiller, 1872–1921), a daily newspaper founded by Grigor Artzruni (1845–92), a graduate of Heidelberg University, who edited the paper until his death. *Mshak* played a prominent role in advocating social democracy and initiating reforms in labor organizations. *Nor dar* (New age, 1883–1916), another daily, which, although conservative in its outlook, defended laborers against exploitation by the lords of industry; it also strongly protested the savage treatment of Armenians in the Ottoman Empire and the hypocritical conduct of European diplomacy, especially during the 1894–96 massacres. Another monthly review, *Murch* (The hammer, 1889–1907), was basically a literary magazine inclined to realism, aimed at developing a popular literature. Famed writers such as Perch Proshian, Vrtanes Papazian (1866–1920), Ghazaros Aghayan, Hovhannes Tumanian, and Derenik Demirdjian were among its contributors.

The development of modern Armenian into a literary language proceeded relatively smoothly in Eastern Armenia, mainly because Eastern Armenian was directly based on the Ararat dialect, which had already become popular in the 1860s. But Western and Eastern Armenian writers were not entirely isolated from each other; on the contrary, writers in both camps published articles in both Constantinople and Tiflis.

It must be noted that many of the pioneers of the Cultural Revival in Eastern Armenia received their education in European centers of learning. Just as Armenian youths in the West were attracted to Italy and France, Armenian youths in the East were drawn to the German University in Dorpat (presently Taru, in Estonia). Each center influenced its students in its own specific way and according to its own philosophy, and this provided greater enrichment and a wider perspective to the Armenian intellectual elite.

The Literary Scene

In Armenia the first four decades of the eighteenth century were the context for the development of the nation's version of the Age of Enlightenment.[61] The dominant tendency in Armenian literature during this period was a variant of European neoclassicism: a form of artistic expression that reflected an awareness of Armenian idealism, which began in the early seventeen hundreds and lasted for almost two centuries.[62]

This movement, while reflecting some distinctly national realities, was a powerful echo of the European Renaissance and Enlightenment. In Europe the Renaissance occurred roughly between the middle of the fourteenth century and the end of the sixteenth, the neoclassical Enlightenment during the seventeenth and early eighteenth centuries. In Armenia though, the eighteenth century ushered in a gradual national reawakening, one of the consequences of which was a drive to educate and enlighten the nation in order to secure its survival. Just as Europe had looked to the classical past for most of its renaissance principles, Armenian idealism focused upon the forgotten Armenian past. Quickened

---

61. The purpose of this section, as well as the sections on romanticism, realism, Armeno-Turkish literature, historical fiction, and so on, is to discuss broad literary movements, not individual authors. Although major authors are mentioned here for purposes of illustration, individual authors are discussed elsewhere in the anthology.

62. The editors acknowledge their indebtedness to Vahé Oshagan's "Modern Armenian Literature and Intellectual History from 1700 to 1915," in Hovannisian, *The Armenian People from Ancient to Modern Times*, 2:139–74; to "*Grakanutiun yev arvest*" (Literature and art), in Tz. P. Aghayan et al., *Hay Zhoghovrdi patmutiun* (History of the Armenian people) (Yerevan, 1974), 598–634; to Mesrop Chanashian's *Hay grakanutyan nor shrjani hamarot patmutiun* (Concise history of Armenian literature: modern phase, 1701–1920) (Venice, 1973); to Minas Teoleolian's *Dar me grakanutiun: 1850–1920* (A century of literature: 1850–1920) (Boston, 1977), vol. 1; and to Sasuni, *Patmutiun arevmtahay ardi grakanutyan* (History of west Armenian modern literature).

by a renewal of spiritual and temporal life, the movement brought to light ancient, dust-laden manuscripts and scrolls. It reinvented *grabar* (classical Armenian) as the language of cultivated literary expression, and in so doing it engraved the outlines of the future fatherland—the Armenian utopia—on the national consciousness.

In Europe, the neoclassical movement took as its point of departure the conviction that mankind had fallen from virtue and should return to the standards of classical antiquity, developing respect for the ancient past and its discipline. It posited that the ancients had attained an excellence later writers had not even come close to equaling. In literature and the other arts, European neoclassicists focused on such traditionally classic values as sense of form, balance, discipline, the dominance of reason, unity of design and aim, clarity, proportion, restraint, "noble simplicity," quiet grandeur, and a view that art should be focused on man. For a neoclassicist such as Voltaire or Racine in France or Addison, Steele, or Pope in England, literature was the product of careful study, not only of the world around the observer but also of the past, and local bias could be redressed by looking back to Greece and especially Rome.

Although similar principles also inspired eighteenth-century Armenian writers, it is not easy to classify Armenian artistic expressions as belonging to one specific literary movement rather than another; they present an overlapping mixture of the neoclassical, romantic, realistic, and other new movements. It is also important to note that "the absence of national political life for over 400 years had developed strong centrifugal and individualistic tendencies among Armenians and had given rise to an incipient xenophilia that had been the major cause of a permanent desire to emulate Western cultural models, resulting in a certain 'alienation' of the ethnic literature."[63]

Despite their understanding of European literary principles, Armenian writers of the period could not take up the European revolutionary spirit, at least in the beginning. They were thwarted by a religious mentality that looked to the venerated past and to the security of divine providence for the realization of national ideals. Yet in time the neoclassical movement found a place within the Armenian reality. It discovered a wealth of subjects within the works of the ancient Armenian writers Khorenatsi, Pavstos Buzand, Yeznik Koghbatsi,[64] and others. From them nineteenth-century writers gleaned subjects and episodes of epic

---

63. Oshagan, "Modern Armenian Literature," 2:142.
64. All are outstanding figures of the Golden Age. See vol. 1 of the present anthology.

dimensions based on historical Armenian entities. Besides stimulating novel creative efforts, these writers also provided a visible philosophical foundation, which encouraged and fostered a national awakening.

As mentioned earlier, the founding of the Mkhitarist Order in Venice, dedicated to piety, literary scholarship, and service to the nation; the cultural awakening of Armenian communities in India; and the gradual revival of Eastern Armenia in the mid-eighteenth century all contributed immensely to the shaping of an intelligentsia that would advance the political, cultural, and literary development of the nation.

The first visible figure of the pre-revival period was theologian and philosopher Khachatur Erzrumtsi (1666–1740). The tenets of the movement also interested several literary figures and scholars among the Mkhitarist Fathers. For example, Yedvard Hiurmiuz, considered the essential theoretician of Armenian "neoclassicism," systematically examined the various literary views, genres, styles, and languages in his *Ardzern banasteghtzutiun hamarotyal* (Short manual of poetry, 1839). Another eminent figure of this period was Arsen Bagratuni, whose poems, particularly his masterpiece, *Hayk diutsazn* (Hayk the hero), reflect the pure classical tradition of Homer, Virgil, and Tasso.[65]

Armenian poetry of the time was collected into *Musayk Araratian* (The muses of Ararat), published by the alumni of the Lazarian academy in Moscow in 1829, and the three-volume *Taghk Mkhitarian vardapetats* (Poems by Mkhitarist fathers, 1852, 1853, 1854). Although the poetry produced by the adherents of this movement suffered from a certain internal malaise and monotony of form, it nevertheless promoted the use of regular meter and spurred the future development of Armenian verse with nationalistic motifs. According to Manuk Abeghian, Armenian neoclassical poetry is a sort of infantile babbling, but it heralds a time when the babbling will turn into a full-fledged language. It makes clear that the muses love and express much more than metrical moral preaching and the Gospels; they are also inspired by our past. They have already grasped the idea of a homeland, and they are proud of it because that homeland is paradise.[66]

These literary efforts were more fruitful in the fields of Armenian drama and fiction, which focused on various political phases of historical Armenia. The plays expressed ideas of liberation and concentrated more on national themes than on human passions and emotions. The first Armenian play of this era, *Argatzk Tigrana* (The adventures of

---

65. See Oshagan, "Modern Armenian Literature," 153.

66. Manuk Abeghian, *Hay hin grakanutyan patmutiun* (History of ancient Armenian literature) (Yerevan, 1945), 2:509.

Tigran), was staged by the Mkhitarist school theater in 1776. During the following decades dramatists such as Manvel Jakhjakhian (1770–1835), Yeghia Tovmachan (1777–1848), and others produced interesting historical tragedies.

Hovhannes Vanandetsi (1772–1841), in epic poems such as *Voski dar Hayastani* (The golden age of Armenia), *Tesaran handisitsn Hayka, Arama, yev Arayi* (Scenes of splendor depicting Hayk, Aram, and Ara), and *Arpiakan Hayastan* (Sunlit Armenia), depicted events of ancient Armenian history and introduced the political motif into Armenian literature.

An important figure in Armenian drama was the playwright Petros Minasian (1779–1867). In historical tragedies such as *Khosrov metz* (Khosrov the great), *Smbat arajin* (Smbat the first), *Arshak yerkrord* (Arshak the second), and *Yervand,* he analyzed and interpreted historical Armenian themes from moral and nationalistic viewpoints. He also wrote a few comedies.

However, the national, patriotic, and political views of Armenian pre-revival literature, its aesthetic principles vis-à-vis historical instruction, and its exclusive use of *grabar* limited the scope and duration of the movement.

ROMANTICISM

In Armenia as elsewhere, neoclassicism was followed by romanticism. This necessitated removing reliance on divine providence from "Armenian Idealism" and establishing a new school of artistic expression. Since Armenian neoclassicism had not yet come to a definable end, these two movements ran parallel to each other for some time. In this respect, both movements in Armenia differed from their European counterparts.

Around the turn of the century, the German critic Friedrich Schlegel (1772–1829) was the first to use the term romanticism to designate a school of literature opposed to neoclassicism. From Germany the movement spread to England and France. One of the fundamentals of romanticism was belief in the natural goodness of man: that in a "state of nature" mankind would behave well, but it had been corrupted by civilization. From this belief sprang not only admiration for the primitive and the child, but also romantic faith in the emotions. If man is inherently sinful, reason should govern the passions, but if he is naturally good, the emotions can be trusted. Romanticism is too diverse and too full of contradictions to be characterized in simplistic or accurate terms, but in a very general way a romantic may be described as one who seeks not the clarity and certainty of classical antiquity, but the mystery and longing of the medieval era. The main characteristics of romanticism are belief in the innate goodness of man, individualism, reverence for nature, primitivism, philosophic idealism, a paradoxical tendency toward both free thought and religious mysticism, revolt against political authority and social convention, exaltation of physical passion, the cultivation of emotion and sensation for their own sakes, and a persistent attraction to the supernatural, the morbid, the melancholy, and the cruel.[67]

As mentioned previously, the first signs of Armenian romanticism appeared in Venice, in five volumes of verse by Fr. Ghevond Alishan. Two poems in this collection, "*Bnuni*" (On nature) and "*Hayruni*" (On the fatherland), both written in classical Armenian, display an ardent love of nature and the nation. A great deal of Alishan's romanticism derived from French writers and the influence of the 1848 republican revolution in Paris. Alishan was directed to nature not by aesthetics but philosophically: he found in nature the mystery of moral education and beauty.

In Constantinople, *Masis,* the most influential daily, under the editorship of Karapet Iutiuchian (Ütüdjian) and *Meghu* (The bee), a bimonthly published by Harutiun Svachian (Svadjian) gathered together a generation of young writers and intellectuals who had recently returned from studying at European universities. Around the same time, the poet Mkrtich Peshiktashlian (Beshiktashlian), a graduate of the Mkhitarist college in Padua, where he had been exposed to European romanticism, distinguished himself as a leader of the Armenian romantics. He played an important role in founding Western Armenian theater in Constantinople, and during the Zeytun rebellion (1862) he aroused the public with his patriotic poems, popularizing the romantic mood.

Another noted poet of the era was Petros Durian (1851–72), who began by writing a few historical plays but earned his fame with poetry in very refined modern Armenian on the themes of love, solitude, nature, and death, in the romantic tradition of Lamartine. His untimely death, as well as his talent, patriotism, poverty, and desperate love of life made him a symbol of the Armenian romantic poet.

Other leaders of the movement were the poet Tovmas Terzian, who continued to write in *grabar,* and the novelist Hovsep Shishmanian (Tzerents), who tried to impart the concept of freedom through the ideological characters he created. Srbuhi Dussap (c. 1841–1901),[68] the

---

67. See *Benét's Reader's Encyclopedia,* 3rd ed. (New York, 1987), 840.
68. Srbuhi Dussap, Zabel Yesayan, and Sibil were the most influential women writers in Constantinople at the time. They explored issues confronting the Armenians of Constantinople.

first feminist in Armenian literature, wrote three novels that advocated the emancipation of Armenian women.

At first the Western Armenian poets sang about nature, love, and life's adversities. They also wrote nationalistic poems, in some of which the classical spirit still dominated, despite their romantic contexts. Their delicate verse at times becomes tempestuous oceans, volcanic eruptions, blasphemies, and bitter tirades—rare moments in Western Armenian romantic poetry. They wrote poetry in a popular literary language, tasteful and clear, and, especially Durian, introduced into Armenian poetry the use of artistic imagery to reinforce thought.

Romanticism also began to spread to Eastern Armenian literature in the early 1840s. The pioneer there was Khachatur Abovian, a graduate of Dorpat University, who wrote lyric poetry in classical Armenian but switched to the popular language for his prose. The language, style, and characters of his masterpiece, *Verk Hayastani* (Wounds of Armenia, written 1841, published 1858), marked a turning point in Armenian literature. By means of this novel and his patriotic poems, Abovian placed the tragedy of the Armenian experience in the center of the Enlightenment effort.

A crucial literary event of the time was the publication of Stepan Nazariants's journal *Hiusisapayl* (Aurora borealis) in Moscow in 1858. Nazariants and Mikayel Nalbandian represented two approaches to the democratization of Armenian society: Nazariants favored a moderate approach to social change, whereas Nalbandian was committed to radical and revolutionary change. Both, however, pursued the goal of *ashkhar-habar*. Another romantic of the same period was the poet Smbat Shahaziz, whose literary career was tied to Nazariants's journal.

Eastern Armenian literature can be described as romantic, patriotic, and populist. In the second half of the nineteenth century these elements continued to appear, as new novelists gradually honed them into a dominant literary style of "descriptive, didactic, and socially oriented prose that has characterized the novels, the short stories, the plays, and even to some extent the poetry of Eastern Armenians."[69]

Meanwhile, a literary event similar to the publication of Nazariants's journal took place in Tiflis: Grigor Artzruni founded the periodical *Mshak* (The tiller)—an organ of westernization, European Enlightenment, and liberalism, as well as a literary vehicle—to promote promising writers of the time.

---

69. Oshagan, "Modern Armenian Literature," 163.

Raffi (Hakob Melik Hakobian, 1837–88), the most talented and prolific novelist of the nineteenth century, wrote several historical and ethnographic novels that voiced the deplorable situation of Armenians in the Ottoman Empire, in order to inspire his compatriots with their historical past. His novels contributed immensely to the Armenian revolutionary movement.

Perch Proshian was another romantic. He concentrated on the ills of society rather than on the ideas of Enlightenment and political awakening that preoccupied Raffi. In the field of drama, Gabriel Sundukian was the major figure whose contribution heralded the coming of the realist movement.

During this period, Abgar Hovhannisian's (1849–1904) *Ardzagang* (The echo) also began its crusade of modernization, soon followed by Mkrtich Barkhudarian's (1862–1927) *Handes grakanakan yev patmakan* (Literary and historical review) and several other periodicals that contributed to the movement.

During the last decade of the nineteenth century, when the realist movement was in full swing in the West, Eastern Armenian literature entered a new phase with the writings of Hovhannes Hovhannisian (1864–1929). His passionate love of nature, concern for the suffering of mankind, and tender lyricism prepared the ground for Vahan Terian (1885–1920), Avetik Isahakian (1875–1957), and Hovhannes Tumanian, who became the voice of the "national conscience" and the symbol of "national unity."

Eastern Armenian poetry echoed the temper of the age: the voice of the people, their cries, their complaints, their protests. It also championed the ideas of liberty and enlightenment. Many poets tried to awaken a dormant population, to console an abandoned and afflicted nation with their songs. They laid the foundation of Eastern Armenian poetry, which in time developed stylistically and in terms of expression, becoming more profound in the works of Tumanian, Terian, and Isahakian.

The Realist Movement

Around the 1880s, inspired by European models and spurred on by political, social, and intellectual developments within its own sphere, Armenian literature began to follow new directions, especially in the areas of theme and subject matter. A new literary movement was being born—realism. It is difficult, however, to assign a specific date when romanticism ended and realism began, especially with Armenian writers, in whose writings the two tendencies are mixed. In effect, there was not enough time for Armenian romanticism to mature, reach fruition, and be succeeded; as a result the various stages overlapped each other. That is why it is not possible to classify certain authors with the same ease and conviction as it is with the writers of the neoclassical era. Romantic and realistic works were produced simultaneously, with the latter school only gradually taking over the former.

Armenian literature before 1880 had attained several significant achievements. There was an important bulk of translated literature. The endless flood of European literature in translation in *ashkharhabar* attracted a vast number of readers. Writers such as Karapet Iutiuchian (Ütüdjian), Tovmas Terzian, Grigor Otian, Mesrop Nuparian, and Stepan Voskanian had translated more than a hundred European master-pieces.[70]

In the political arena, as a result of the revival of the Armenian Question, the Treaty of San Stefano,[71] and Article 61 of the Congress of Berlin,[72] Armenians lived in hope that their long-sought rights would be achieved. The enthusiasm created was tempered by pessimism. On one side stood Patriarch Nerses Varzhapetian,[73] who was optimistic about the expectations that emerged from San Stefano; on the other stood Khrimian Hayrik, whose realistic and disillusioned attitude gave new momentum to Armenian political life by guiding the thinking of the younger generation. The expectations of a national life prepared Arme-nian intellectuals for a more realistic recognition of the peculiarities of the Armenian identity.

European writers had already left romanticism behind and were producing a new kind of literature. They recorded life as it was and refrained from imposing a predetermined pattern upon its materials. They were free of romantic subjectivity and emphasized truthfulness of detail. Balzac, Daudet, Zola, de Maupassant, and others exercised a profound influence on the new world of Armenian letters that blossomed in Constantinople between 1880 and 1890. Another healthy sign of the creative works that were to come was the fact that by that time modern Armenian had developed into a full-fledged language of literary expression.

---

70. See the section on literature in translation.

71. The treaty that ended the Russo-Turkish war in 1878, on terms beneficial to Russia.

72. The Treaty of San Stefano so alarmed the western powers that they invoked the Congress of Berlin (June 13–July 13, 1878) to revise it. Article 61 dealt with reforms in Turkey's Armenian provinces.

73. Armenian patriarch (1837–1884). He became Patriarch of Constantinople in 1874.

It was in such an atmosphere that Armenian journalists, poets, novelists, and short story writers turned toward the school of realism, and strove to develop and popularize the new movement. They denounced the mediocrity of the romantics and worked diligently to promote the new literature with its innovative forms, style, and principles. A sizable group of writers resisted, however, and united to criticize the new school: Reteos Perperian (Berberian), Yeghia Temirchipashian (Demirdjibashian, 1851–1908), Hovhannes Setian (1853–1930), Khoren Narpey (Narbey, 1832–92), Tovmas Terzian, and Mkrtich Achemian (Adjemian, 1838–1917). These authors continued to write according to their usual practice and principles, and showed little inclination for realism. On the other hand, some of their contemporaries—Hakob Paronian (Baronian) and Matteos Mamurian, for example—because of their use of realistic local images and color, qualify as realistic writers. They were not, however the flag bearers of the movement. That distinction belongs to the new generation.

Around 1884, several well-known Western Armenian writers—Arpiar Arpiarian, Grigor Zohrap, Biuzand Kechian, Levon Bashalian (Pashalian), Tigran Kamsarakan (1866–1941), Hrand (Melkon), Mikayel Kiurchian (Gürdjian, 1879–1965), Hrand Asatur, and Sibil (Zapel Asatur, 1863–1934)—became contributors to the *Arevelk* (The east) daily and *Masis* weekly newspapers. In 1891, H. Shahnazarian founded the *Hayrenik* (The homeland, 1891–96) daily. Writers such as Tlkatintsi, Ruben Zardarian, and Arshak Chopanian (Arshag Tchobanian) gained prominence. They spared no effort to shape modern Armenian and bring it to its final stage. Influenced by the political atmosphere and the events of the time, they did their utmost to realistically reflect Armenian life. By the 1890s, under the influence of newly created political parties, the Armenian press and written opinion had assumed a firmly rooted popular stance.

Like their European counterparts, the Armenian realists looked at life objectively and opposed works burdened with exaggerated emotionalism. They sought to understand life as it really was, and consequently presented their interpretations of it by documenting real characters, events, or scenes. Their writings depicted the tragic, painful lives of the Armenian peasant, laborer, artisan, and the expatriate or deportee, all of whom found a place in contemporary literature and in the consciousness of readers.

As devoted missionaries of the realist school, writers assumed the responsibility of expressing the national anguish. By means of the periodical press they echoed Armenian aspirations and thus created a new psychology. They became literary activists combating the privileged classes; they expressed what they thought, and often paid dearly for their boldness. Because of them national organizations and the privileged classes began to feel the weight of harsh judgment, which they could have ignored a couple of decades earlier. Hakob Oshakan (1883–1948) emphasized this phenomenon and pointed to Arpiar Arpiarian's *"Orhnyal gerdastane"* (The blessed dynasty) as an example: "It is not a satire but a bomb!" Realism, however, was not accepted blindly, for these writers shaped their material into a form that also revealed their personal visions of reality.

In these conditions and within these circles the realist movement in Armenian literature had its start. Arpiar Arpiarian's chronicles can be considered the precursors of this movement. Grigor Zohrap's novel *Anhetatatz serund me* (A vanished generation) appeared in 1884 and 1885. It was followed by Tigran Kamsarakan's *Varzhapetin aghjike* (The teacher's daughter), the subject of which was taken from real life. Its author, at the age of nineteen, became an overnight sensation.

The new active youth were not only enthusiastic about questions of education but were also interested and very much involved in trends that had begun in the Caucasus, led by Grigor Artzruni and Raffi. Raffi's novels were blueprints of the liberation movement, and Artzruni's views kept alive the hope that Russia would intervene to help realize reforms in the Armenian provinces.

It should be noted that realism developed almost simultaneously in Eastern and Western Armenian literature. The relationship between Eastern and Western Armenians at that time is significant. Arpiarian, under the pen name Haykak, dispatched writings to *Mshak* (The tiller) describing Western Armenian life and its concerns. In return, the life, situation, and experiences of Armenians in the Caucasus found a place in the Armenian press of Constantinople. These crucial and worthwhile exchanges shaped Armenian opinion as a whole.

These complex times produced several famous figures of the realist movement. In Western Armenia the novel and the short story developed in the hands of Arpiar Arpiarian, Hakob Baronian, Yervand Otian, Grigor Zohrap, Levon Pashalian, Tigran Kamsarakan, Yerukhan (Yervand Srmakeshkhanlian, 1870–1915), Zavel Yesayan (1878–1943), and others. At the same time Shirvanzadé (1858–1935), Avetis Aharonian (1866–1948), Muratsan (1854–1908), Vrtanes Papazian, Nar-dos (1867–1933), Levon Shant (1869–1951), and others made important contributions to the development of the Eastern Armenian novel. All these writers were free of romantic subjectivity and allowed their stories to tell themselves, letting truth emerge from the events they described rather than inventing stories to illustrate reality. For example, in his famous novel *Kaos* (Chaos, 1896), Shirvanzadé depicted the ills of rural society and the corrupt state of the bourgeoisie due to the emergence of the industrial proletariat. It is important to note that in both Eastern and Western Armenia realism first became a trend in the novel and the short story.

The theater also matured during the realist years in Eastern Armenia. Gabriel Sundukian ridiculed the iniquities of the middle class as well as the superstitions of the lower class and its exploitation by the bureaucracy. His influence on future playwrights was immense. Another crucial figure of Eastern Armenian theater was Aleksandr Shirvanzadé, who began as a novelist but after 1900 turned to theater, where he treated social themes similar to those of his twenty-six novels and novellas. Levon Shant, born in Constantinople and educated in Armenia, where he was exposed to Eastern Armenian, was also a major figure. His dramas are mostly history plays and products of the symbolist school. His genuine interest in and preoccupation with Armenian history and disunity is reflected in his dramatic work. In Western Armenian Hakob Paronian (Baronian) was a major satirist and playwright. He was an uncontested master of hilarious plays based on urban life, with picturesque characters marked with a distinct ethnic stamp.

In poetry, the realist and symbolist movements first began to supplant romanticism in Constantinople. The principal figure to adapt foreign influences to his personal experiences and thence to Armenian literature was Yeghia Temirchipashian. He was capable of and indeed tried all literary genres, but poetry best suited his romantic tendencies, realistic approach, and symbolist sensibility. Poets such as Sibil, Arshak Chopanian, Indra (Tiran Chrakian, 1875–1921), Siamanto (1878–1915), Vahan Tekeyan (1878–1943), Daniel Varuzhan (1884–1915), Misak Metzarents (1886–1908), and Matteos Zarifian (1894–1924) brought a new direction to Armenian poetry. Some of these poets, such as Sibil and Chopanian, exemplified both romantic and realist currents. In fact, despite their realist tendencies, many other poets, such as Tekeyan, made use of symbolist conventions; still others leaned toward the new school of aestheticism. For example, Vahé Oshagan considers Varuzhan's poetry, "a synthesis of controlled classical beauty and of romantic emotion and imagination," and of Metzarents, the great aesthete, he says: "He had a totally individual and lyrical temperament, intoxicated with sounds, smells, and pure sensations, a creature of nature destined to die very young, the equivalent of John Keats in Armenian poetry."[74]

---

74. Oshagan, "Modern Armenian Literature," 173.

Eastern Armenian realist poetry had its beginning in the 1880s, when it was featured in the literary journal *Murch* (The hammer). The editor, Avetik Araskhanian (1857–1912), was educated in Germany, and attracted young poets and novelists to contribute to his journal. The poets of the preceding era had sung of freedom in their works, but in a manner that was perceived as pedantic. The new poets concentrated more on personal experiences, rarely giving expression to nationalistic ideas. In time the expression and style of their poetry developed, and it deepened in thought, especially with Hovhannes Tumanian, Vahan Terian, and Avetik Isahakian. Other romantics were Hovhannes Hovannesian, Aleksandr Tzaturian (1865–1917), Levon Manuelian (1864–1919), Lerents (Avetis Nazarbekian, 1866–1939), Ghazaros Aghayan, Aram Charek (Charik, 1874–1947), Hakob Hakobian (1866–1937), and Shushanik Kurghinian (1876–1927). Like their Western Armenian counterparts, some, such as Terian and Isahakian, became aestheticists,.

After the Constitution of 1908, the former intellectual and artistic animation of Constantinople began to revive. Armenian intellectuals who had been living abroad returned to the capital. Their homecoming resulted in additional journals, newspapers, books, and other artistic activities that heralded the beginning of a new movement. The struggle for "liberation" became a way of life. The genocide was still seven years in the future.[75]

AESTHETICISM

Around the end of the nineteenth century a fresh trend appeared in Armenian literature: writers became part of a new movement called aestheticism. This flourished until the 1915 genocide and was extended by about a decade by some of the few writers who survived the massacres. Some of the prominent practitioners were Archbishop Yeghishé Durian (1860–1930), Indra, Levon Shant, Sibil, Misak Metzarents, Daniel Varuzhan, Matteos Zarifian, and Vahan Tekeyan, who, with several others, transformed prose and especially poetry into exquisite arts.

In Western Armenia the realists had finally succeeded in leaving aside *grabar*, turning Armenian into a language of current literary expression. The aesthetes embellished and beautified the language used by their realist colleagues. They also purified the language by ridding it of Turkish linguistic conventions. For the poets and prose writers grouped under the label of the Aesthetic Movement, language became a goal, an objective in itself. They promoted reverence for beauty, inspired, to

---

75. See Teolelian, *Dar me grakanutian*, 1:454.

some degree, by their European counterparts, who took the phrase *ars gratia artis* (art for art's sake) as their credo. It is important to emphasize that these artists, especially in England and France, were also concerned with matters of form; they rejected theories which held that the value of literature is somehow related to morality or utility.

SYMBOLISM

Other Armenian poets also adhered religiously to the school of symbolism, under the influence of the Symbolist Movement, which first arose in France in the second half of the nineteenth century. Proponents of this school presupposed the existence of an invisible world beyond that of concrete phenomena. For poets and writers such as Tekeyan and others, the function of imaginative writers was to express an unseen reality in words and sounds. Their descriptions were intended as expressions of their own spiritual states. They sought to make poetry more subtle, more suggestive, and at the same time more precise. They realized the necessity of creating clear and precise images—ones that were absolutely precise in what they referred to physically and at the same time endlessly suggestive in the meanings they set up because of their relationship to other images. The combination of precision and symbolic suggestion in the poetry of some late nineteenth-century French poets attracted and influenced them.

They, in turn, influenced future poets and writers. Acceptance of these movements was facilitated by the simultaneous trend toward realism, which opened the door to literary novelty and different artistic principles.

THE LITERATURE OF THE PROVINCES

Provincial literature played a crucial and compelling role in the development of realistic literature and modern Armenian prose. While the realist movement was giving Armenians a feeling of integrity and legitimacy about their understanding and expression of life, the influence of European subject matter and style was threatening the character of Armenian literature centered in Constantinople. The search for integrity and legitimacy needed to be centered in the actual life of the nation if it were to bear the stamp of authenticity in the face of the immensely popular French literature of the 1890s that threatened to overwhelm it.

Masis, a Constantinople daily, and *Tzaghik* (The flower) and *Anahit,* periodicals published in Paris, turned the question of provincial literature into a literary wrangle. Arguments promoting and deploring it inundated Armenian intellectual circles. Artashes Harutiuninan (1873–1915) considered the literature of the provinces *indigenous* and *Armenian*. On the other hand, Arshak Chopanian (Arshag Tchobanian) defended the literature produced in the cities under foreign influence; according to him, municipal centers had produced works full of Armenian spirit, despite the fact that their authors had never lived in the provinces. As he saw it, only those who lived in the cities, amidst the great mass of the nation, could endow literature with aesthetic expression, writing works that were at once magnificent and noble. However, he admitted that this literature should be informed by the provincial spirit, gaining authenticity by drawing inspiration from and reflecting the national character, life, and models.

Writers such as Garegin Srvandstiants had already mined the provincial spirit in their popular writings. A bit later Tlkatintsi became notable for his dispatches from the provinces. His *Émile* was especially popular and was considered a work of great artistry, and his example inspired many others. Ruben Zardarian perfected Tlkatintsi's genre, depicting scenes from the pastoral life of Kharberd (presently Harput); the province of Mush was represented by the writer Gegham Ter-Karapetian (1865–1918).[76]

Later on, in 1914, a group of young writers who had written for *Mehyan* (The temple),[77] convinced of the importance of provincial literature, promoted the movement through a more modern approach. Hakob Oshakan, Gegham Barseghian (1883–1915), and Kostan Zarian (1885–1969) wrote both fiction and poetry in support of the movement.[78]

The literature of the provinces depicts the struggle of the peasant against the forces of nature, and the exploitation caused by imbalances in the world order and by social injustice. These writings depict rustic characters in all their disappointments as well as in their happy moments. Provincial writers knew only too well the hardships and the poverty experienced by the Armenian peasant: they had a close affinity with the people, their traditions, and their everyday life. The writings of these authors vary from affectionate lightheartedness to tender sadness and

---

76. Much of the information in this section is drawn from Chanashian, *Hay Grakanutyan nor shrchani hamarot patmutiun 1701–1920*, 317–18.

77. A literary and art journal published in Constantinople.

78. Garegin Srvandztiants (1840–92), Gegham Ter-Karapetian (1865–1918), Melkon Kiurchian (Gürdjian, 1859–1915), Tlkatintsi (c. 1860–1915), Ruben Zardarian (1874–1915), Hamastegh (1895–1966), Hakob Oshakan (1883–1948), Kostan Zarian (1885–1969) are among the well-known writers included in the present anthology who enriched the genre.

even to fervent patriotism. The works reflect the simple dignity and touchingly humane sentiments of village life.

The soil with which these writers were so intimately acquainted was never far from their thoughts. Their works, although sometimes uneven, are distillations of the new realistic style and expression. At their best they paint a warm, dignified picture of the loves, the everyday life, and the bucolic activities of the village people. It must be admitted, however, that at times their authors succumb to the occupational hazard of those who practice the genre, a tendency to sentimentality.

They are at their best when they use the local dialect, and in this they paved the way for the realist writers. Many of the latter also followed their use of the past and the rustic environment as backgrounds. Provincial literature will continue to appeal to and captivate readers, and it will remain of interest to the student of literature.

Nineteenth-Century Armenian Historical Fiction[79]

The Armenian historical novel developed in a relatively peculiar way compared to its European counterpart. This is because it is hard to identify an established Armenian prose fiction tradition before the emergence of the historical novel. Consequently, rather than evolving from other forms of narrative, the genre of narrative fiction in Armenian emerged from historical, political, and epic subjects.[80] There are few Armenian historical novelists, but those who cultivated the genre had a great influence on the nation's political future.

The State of Affairs in Armenia

In the early nineteenth century, Eastern Armenia was mainly under Persian rule. People suffered greatly under local governors and tribal chiefs, and the instability of Persian state structures. The Armenian provinces of the Ottoman Empire were in even worse condition. However, the situation in Eastern Armenia improved after its annexation to Russia in 1828. Despite this, cultural life remained almost exclusively in the hands of the Church. In the 1840s young Armenians who were returning from northern universities—particularly that of Dorpat (Estonia)—attempted to start a cultural awakening. Their first aim was to modernize and expand education, in order to inform their fellow countrymen.

---

79. This section is an abridged version of a study written by Hagop Gulludjian especially for the present volume.

80. The only antecedent was historical drama, which often had a religious theme. Such plays were presented within the context of a lively theatrical movement throughout much of the nineteenth century.

Among them were Mesrop Taghiadian (1803–59) and Khachatur Abovian, both of whom attempted to develop the historical novel in their quest to shape national public opinion, with the help of periodical presses in Moscow and Tiflis.

One of the first steps in this improvement was the development and use of *ashkharabar* in order to make literature accessible to the masses. In the East, the new language was put into circulation through serial novels—especially those of Raffi—which played a prominent role in encouraging the public to read. They exercised a highly refined, rich, and picturesque influence on the final formation of literary Eastern Armenian.

In Western Armenia *ashkharhabar* achieved victory particularly in Constantinople. After the adoption of the National Constitution in 1863, the education system expanded enormously and began supplying great numbers of talented young intellectuals to an increasingly passionate and liberal urban press, and groups of new writers established the foundations of the Western Armenian cultural awakening. The situation was less promising in remote provinces, which not only suffered under the rule of a hostile government but lacked effective means to attempt improvement.

Antecedents and Development of the Historical Novel

The historical novel was essentially a nineteenth-century development, established on the rising wave of nationalistic sentiment. It is widely believed that its emergence is linked to pivotal historic events. The French Revolution and the Napoleonic wars made people ask questions about their identity and how they perceived themselves as groups. National armies proliferated and developed under a single centralized command. This appealed to rising national consciousness by galvanizing public will around a common leader and project. This affected both conquerors and defenders.

A definitive conclusion about the cause and effect relationship between historical events and the historical novel is unreachable. The thesis that literary expression arose as a result of historical conditions may not be the whole truth. Especially in the case of the historical novel, literary works themselves have often exercised a profound influence on the development of certain historical events. Armenian authors, for instance, had as their obvious goals a national political awakening and the creation of a resistance movement.

Writers tried to use historical facts from their national heritages as background for their novels, although there was still no agreement on the precise characteristics of the genre. The main point of discord was about which of the two main components of such writing ought to have more weight: fidelity to history or the freedom to develop fiction to its fullest extent.

The historical novel as we know it first appeared with the Waverley series, inaugurated in 1814 by Sir Walter Scott. The new type of literary expression he developed quickly caught the attention of readers and writers all over Europe. Armenian authors began practicing this genre quite late. We know that many of them read Scott's works, especially *Ivanhoe*, as well as Flaubert, Hugo, Dumas, and others. Many of these works were published in Armenian in Smyrna and Constantinople, in a translating frenzy led by Matteos Mamurian.

The Armenian Historical Novel

Except for the early translation of pseudo-Callisthenes's *The Novel of Alexander* and its derivatives, the Armenian historical novel had no antecedents before the nineteenth century comparable to European chivalric or gothic novels. Nevertheless the historical novel was an exceptional phenomenon in Armenian literature. Despite relatively few examples, the form exerted a profound influence on Armenian literary, linguistic, social, and political life.

Of prime importance was the historical novel's role in the political revival, the surge of national self-consciousness, and the emergence of guerrilla liberation movements. Except for the writings of Raffi, it is hard to find a case where such a small number of books exercised a strong influence on the political thinking of contemporary and subsequent generations, constituting a direct inspiration for the formation of resistance movements. The creation of Armenian political and revolutionary parties began immediately after the publication of Raffi's works. Perhaps this, along with the relative political freedom of Eastern Armenians, is one of the reasons that the roots of these movements can be traced to the Caucasus region. So influential were Raffi's works that the typist of his novel *Khente* (The fool, 1880), once he had completed the task, abandoned his job and rushed off to volunteer as a guerrilla fighter in defense of Turkish Armenian rights.

The Armenian historical novel consists mainly of didactic works. Authors openly admitted the intention of their novels and even proclaimed that the form was not important, so long as they succeeded in delivering their social and political message. Muratsan's testimony in this respect is characteristic: "I was moved by the idea of being useful to my contemporary brothers, and not by the desire to join the ranks of immortal writers."[81]

Among the main ideas pursued by Armenian novelists are the importance of education and information; the suffering of Armenians in Turkey; and the role of women in society. The Armenian historical novel is, in fact, a *national* historical novel. Almost no novelists wrote about non-Armenian issues except Vrtanes Papazian and Yervand Otian, who referred mainly to contemporary history.

Beyond the requirements of historical content and fictional treatment, among literary critics there are no rules about how distant in time the subject should be. Many believe that the author should not have lived through the time covered in the novels, while others consider that "the really trustworthy historical novels are those which were a-writing while the history was a-making," as in the case of *Uncle Tom's Cabin*.[82] But the Armenian historical novelists were not aiming at stimulating the historical curiosity of their readers: they wanted to work over the readers' historical consciousness. These novelists wished to awaken their fellow countrymen, to instruct rather than delight, to make them enthusiastic about the nation's future, and push them to action, rather than just update their historical knowledge. Therefore the Armenian category includes works that are historically contemporary but constitute literary and political milestones, such as Raffi's *Jalaleddin* and *Khente* (The fool), and even the futuristic and almost utopian *Kaytzer* (Sparks).

There are no realistic historical novels in nineteenth-century Armenian literature. Nonetheless, some realistic strokes are occasionally visible against their wide romantic background. In general, however, the historical novel was increasingly disfigured by descriptive and objectivist excesses. Later on, with the expansion of the realistic movement in Europe, the genre went through a decline, until new approaches appeared. The hiatus lasted much longer in Armenia. Between the early 1900s and 1940, almost no historical novels were produced. This may be the result of two factors: Western Armenian literature was devastated by the First World War and the Armenian genocide, and it was extremely

---

81. Muratsan, "*Inknakensagrutiun: ughghvatz Minas Perperianin*" (Autobiography, addressed to Minas Perperian), in *Yerkeri zhoghovatzu* (Collection of works) (Yerevan, 1962–65), 7:138.

82. Brander Matthews, *The Historical Novel and Other Essays* (New York, 1901), 18.

difficult to overcome the resultant state of paralysis, with perhaps no recovery at all in some fields of literature. Moreover, writers in Eastern Armenia, then part of the Soviet Union, had no means to fight against brutal government measures that prevented them from embarking on projects that involved national issues. Only during the Second World War did Armenian writers probably get the regime's green light (perhaps even orders) to tackle historical novels, with the aim of motivating the people to participate in the war effort. It was a prompting long awaited by local writers. Thus, in 1944 Temirchian's (Demirdjian) *Vardanank* and Zorian's *Pap Tagavor* (King Pap) appeared, and, in 1947, Arazi's (Movses Harutiunian, 1878–1964) *Israel Ori*.

Typology of Armenian Works

Because of its special features, the Armenian historical novel might be considered to include three broad categories of works:

(1) historical novels proper: works based on documented historical facts and characters, using fiction to express their authors' points of view about historical periods to readers of (preferably) a later period;

(2) novels whose primary aims are to define and clarify questions regarding national identity, mission, and purpose in history, and to suggest strategies for the accomplishment of those objectives. These works openly state their objectives within the text and sometimes use long asides to editorialize in a sort of conversation with the reader. And

(3) national-revolutionary narratives. These works were produced mostly during the first two decades of the twentieth century, especially from the 1908 Turkish revolution until the First World War, a short but amazingly fertile period for Armenian literature. Novels from this period depict the vicissitudes of revolutionary life and the struggle against the regime of Sultan Abdul Hamid II (ruled 1876–1909). They are the weakest of all, at times a confusing mix of fiction, fantasy, and documentary.

Armenian Historical Novelists

Most of the important historical novels of the nineteenth century were published between 1877 and 1897. There were, however, a few predecessors, particularly Tzerents's *Toros Levoni*.

Mesrop Taghiadian (1803–58),[83] who may be considered the first writer of Armenian historical fiction, wrote in *grabar*. Yet he also founded the Calcutta *Azgaser* (The patriot), one of the first newspapers to include texts in *ashkharhabar*. The paper published *Vep Vardgesi* (The story of Vardges, 1846), a historical novel inspired by Movses Khorenatsi's account of Prince Vardges Manuk, who married King Yervand's sister after putting down a conspiracy against the ruler. The novel highlights early ideals of national unity and state cohesion, while criticizing the Church.

Nineteenth-century critics argued that this work is an adaptation of the Russian variation on Johann Heinrich Zschokke's gothic novel *Aballino* (1793), with the action transferred to the Armenian Armavir.[84] Taghiadian was fairly familiar with German and English literature, however, so the possibility cannot be discounted that he read *Aballino* in the original German or in its English translation by Matthew Gregory ("Monk") Lewis, *The Bravo of Venice* (1805). Zschokke, in turn, is believed to have modeled his novel on Schiller's (1759–1805) play *Die Räuber* (The robbers, 1781). Adapting other literary works was a common practice of nineteenth-century literature, and Taghiadian should be regarded as a pioneer in this aspect in Armenian literature.

His novel *Vep Varsenka* (The story of Varsenik) was published in Calcutta in 1847. Rather than classifying it as a historical novel, it may be better to consider it a predecessor of the Armenian historical novel, much as medieval romances prefigured the genre in Europe. The story is about the Aghvan King Vachagan, his daughter, and three of his subjects, who are caught up in a series of supernatural adventures, the aim of which is to impart moral examples.

Khachatur Abovian (1809–48) is regarded as one of the founders of Eastern Armenian *ashkharhabar*, with his milestone work *Verk Hayastani kam Voghb hayrenasiri* (Wounds of Armenia, or lamentation of the patriot). This was published in 1858, although it was written in 1841 and read before its publication by Armenian students in Dorpat.

---

83. Biographical information about Taghiadian and the other novelists mentioned here is given elsewhere in this anthology, immediately preceding the selection(s) from each author's works.

84. Vrtanes Papazian, *Patmutiun hayots grakanutian skzbits minchev mer orere* (History of Armenian literature from the beginning to our times) (Tiflis, 1910), 333; Ghazaros Aghayan, *Horizon* (1910), 169, qtd. in H. B. Muradian, "Khachatur Abovian," in *Hay nor grakanutyan patmutiun* (History of modern Armenian literature) (Yerevan, 1962), 1:344.

Abovian was very young when he left the religious seminary in Etchmiadzin for the University of Dorpat. He pursued a wide-ranging program of studies, mainly in German. For six years he read voraciously and learned every subject he could, without concentrating on any specific program. On returning to Armenia he began to prepare textbooks and courses. But his greatest achievement came with *Verk Hayastani*.

The novel focuses on the struggle of Aghasi, a young Armenian guerrilla from Kanaker, who, together with his friends, resists the criminal oppression of a local Persian ruler until the occupation of the Yerevan district by the Russians in 1827. It is a singular creation and does not fit into any specific literary genre. Although the work is based on historical events, Abovian's style and rhythm go beyond the representation of history and reach heroic proportions, lending an epic tone to his book. Despite being a first expression, almost a tryout, of the weak and barely organized structure of a regional dialect, *Verk Hayastani* demonstrates new heights of language and style, enhanced especially by its highly emotional tone. Its rhythm is so intense and atypical that at times it approaches poetry. Hakob Oshakan, one of the most rigorous critics of Armenian literature, characterized the work as an "epic in prose: tragic, poetic, and primitive at the same time," with a "popular, communicative (non-rhetorical), and pathetic style similar to that of the Iliad; . . . dynamic, pictorial, firm, and rhythmical."[85]

Abovian was an early precursor of Raffi in writing about the unheard-of idea of rising in arms against the enemy. As throughout his life, his goal here was to enlighten and educate, at the same time gravitating toward Russia rather than Persia and Turkey, as a precondition of freedom. His opinions permeate the book: sometimes diverting, sometimes editorializing, then picking up the thread with an apology to the reader, in a manner reminiscent of the early European romantics.

Anonymous. *Voch vok chi karogh nakhasahmanutyan karge pokhel* (No one can alter the order established by Providence, 1850) is probably the first published historical novel in *ashkharhabar*.[86] It was printed as

---

85. Hakob Oshakan, *Hayots grakanutiun* (Armenian literature) (Jerusalem, 1957), 601.

86. The first literary critic to mention this forgotten work could not discover its author. The copy he had was missing the final pages, which were replaced by a handwritten copy that lacked a signature: see Papazian, *Patmutiun hayots grakanutyan,* 365. Sergei Sarinian also fails to identify the author: *"Ayl ardzakagirner"* in *Hay nor grakanutian patmutiun,* 2:426. However, as Papazian asserts, the novel's language is consistent with that of the Tiflis *Ararat,* a blend of Eastern and Western Armenian with a strong mix of *grabar,* and reflects the background of its editor, Gabriel

a serial in the *Ararat* weekly of Tiflis (vols. 12–15), run by Gabriel and Rafayel Patkanian (1830–92). The novel treats the story of the twelfth-century Cilician princes, Levon I and his son Toros, and relates how the latter returned from Constantinople to reclaim his father's usurped principality. Tzerents used the same subject in 1877, but to convey a different message. The *Ararat* novel imparted the medieval concept that whatever is determined will happen: *che sarà sarà.*

Hovsep Vardanian (Hovsep Vardan Pasha, 1815–79) was one of the authors who wrote in the Armenian alphabet but in the Turkish language. His *History of Napoleon Bonaparte* (6 vols.: 1855–56) is not a historical novel in the strict sense. Nevertheless it is an unusual work for its time: a well documented history narrated in an artistic and literary manner.

Ghevond Alishan (Kerovbé Alishanian, 1820–1901) attempted to make his own incursions into the historical narrative with short novels such as *Vahan Goghtnatsi,* but his main contribution was his personal influence over Tzerents from the time when they were both students in Venice. He also inspired a great number of Western Armenian writers with his *Hushikk hayrenyats hayots* (Memories of the Armenian home-land),[87] which laid the foundation of the romantic movement in Armenian literature.

Hambardzum Karian published the first two volumes of *Gaghtnik siraharats kam Ararata aytselun* (Lovers' secret, or visitor to Ararat) in Constantinople in 1871–72. The work was planned to comprise five volumes, but it was unfinished. Nevertheless, it is an interesting novel, in which the pre-Christian Armenian King Artavazd meets characters from modern Van. The author relies on a popular myth that Artavazd is imprisoned in the slopes of Ararat. The demigod, like Prometheus, represents the drive for freedom.

Matteos Mamurian (1830–1901) published *Sev lerin marde* (The man from Black Mountain) in 1872. The novel is set during the 1828 Russo-Turkish war. Like other Armenian writers, Mamurian generally applauds the Russian occupation of Eastern Armenia, but in the second part of the book his hero is persecuted by the Russian regime, and the novelbecomes anti-Russia. In the preface, the author asserts that he received the manuscript of the novel from a certain Hayr Taparik, a

---

Patkanian. There is, then, reason to infer that the author may have been the editor himself, who was a priest.

87. *Hushikk hayrenyats hayots* (Memories of the Armenian homeland), 2 vols. (Venice, 1869–70).

mysterious, wandering cleric from the Rshtunik region, who in turn got it from an old, half-Kurdish, half-Armenian man. This was either an attempt on Mamurian's part to avoid Turkish government persecution or a late imitation of the authors of early European historical novels, whose practice was to hide behind the credibility of a third person, hoping to deter readers' mistrust. It appears that Mamurian was trying to write an adventure novel similar to those of Dumas the elder.

Armenak Haykuni (Hambardzum Chizmechian, Djizmedjian, 1835–66) was the author of *Eliza, kam Verjin arevelyan paterazmi zhamanak teghi unetsatz depk me* (Eliza, or an incident that occurred during the recent eastern war), published in 1861. A romance set against the historical background of the Crimean War, this is the second novel written in Western Armenia. Haykuni had previously written several historical tragedies that were printed in the theater magazine *Musayk masyasts* (Muses of Masis), including *Ara Keghetsik* (Ara the fair), *Olimbiada* (Olympiada), and *Yernjak* (Common).

Tzerents (Hovsep Shishmanian, 1822–88) is the first writer wholly identified with historical novels. His writing fits in with the romantic movement, and the lyrical quality of his nationalistic thinking is inspired by the ideas of the Mkhitarists, whose school in Venice he attended. That explains why his treatment of the topic of liberation is slightly different from that of other rebellious historical novelists.

At the age of fifty-five Tzerents wrote his first historical novel, *Toros Levoni,* published in Constantinople (1877). The novel was possibly inspired by his stay in Cilicia and his long-term strategy to convert that region into a springboard for economic and political reform. Although it was written in the space of only three months, it is his most fully realized work. The Turkish government attempted to suppress the novel, but it was reprinted eight times before 1939, not counting Soviet Armenian editions. Its story is based on Matteos Urhayetsi's history of twelfth-century Cilician Armenian princes and their struggle to reinstate autonomous rule. The romance element is not well realized, and some characters lack definition, including the Greek teacher Dionisio, himself a physician, through whom Tzerents editorializes profusely. The novel has been criticized for lack of drama, a dearth of intimate personal feelings, and for being tendentious. However, its narrative elements are successful and have assured what is the first Armenian historical novel a wide dispersion.

The year 1878 was a milestone for Tzerents. After failing to obtain anything concrete from the Congress of Berlin, Catholicos Khrimian delivered his well-known homily about "paper and iron spoons."[88] That is why Tzerents does not adopt political authority as the focal point of national defense in his next novel, *Yerkunk innerord daru* (Ninth-century labor pains, 1879). Armenians had been without political or military power for centuries, so Tzerents concentrated on the idea of a popular uprising, inspired by the ninth-century works of Tovma Artzruni and Hovhannes Draskhanakerttsi. This novel is mainly based on Artzruni's description of the uprising of the people of Sasun against Arab invaders. Hovnan Khutetsi comes forward as a popular leader and tries to wage a war of liberation independently from the Bagratuni princes and the catholicos, inducing them to become part of the movement.

Tzerents's last novel, *Teodoros Rshtuni* (1881), is full of continuous judgments, sometimes at the expense of narrative and character development. The story, adapted from Ghevond (eighth century), is about the Rshtuni princes' battles for the survival of Armenia in the seventh century. The attempt to mix a thesis novel with military adventure weakens the book.

Tzerents represents the conservative wing of the Armenian intellectuals of his time. Throughout his novels, he advocates centralization and a strong and unified state. He believed that unity was the remedy for all of Armenia's problems.

Raffi (Hakob Melik Hakobian, 1837–88) was the greatest of the Armenian historical novelists, with unprecedented and unmatched influence upon readers. He was a master at gaining the attention of readers and inspiring them, despite having written most of his works on the run. It is important to remember this point. He wrote his novels on a day-to-day basis, as newspaper serials, sometimes adapting them to the commercial necessities of the papers where they first appeared,[89] mainly *Mshak* (The tiller) and *Ardzagang* (Echo) of Tiflis.

Despite lacking a formal university education, he was widely read in both classical and contemporary European literature, from Shakespeare to Scott, Hugo, Tolstoy, Dostoevsky, and Turgenev. The last author

---

88. He called attention to the fact that the nations that had risen up against the empire carried "iron spoons" to the Congress, while the only thing Armenians had to show were petitions and letters: that is, a "paper spoon." The implication was obvious: if Armenians expected to get anything, they had to arm themselves like everyone else.

89. Raffi's novels usually began to appear in December, to motivate readers to buy a subscription for the following year.

seems to have especially influenced Raffi's work, particularly his anticipation of a "bright" future, and the significant role he assigns to women
in its social order. Many critics also attribute to Turguenev's influence
a hypothetical "Hamletism" in his novel *Samuel.* On the other hand,
Raffi claimed to have composed *Khachagoghi hishatakarane* (Racketeer's
memoir), written 1869–70 and published 1882–83, while still caught up
in the excitement caused by his reading of Eugène Sue's *The Wandering
Jew* (1845).

Only two of his novels, *Davit Bek* and *Samuel,* and one novella,
Paruyr Haykazn (Paruyr the Armenian), can be strictly defined as historical, but in a broader sense, some Raffi's fiction novels with contemporary themes may also be considered as such, given that many of them
had the same aim: to stimulate awareness of the struggle for national
liberation. Moreover, they represent stages on the novelist's journey to
purely historical novels.

Raffi wrote *Jalaleddin* in 1878. During teaching assignment in Agulis, he gathered eyewitness accounts of the brutal incursion of Sheik
Jalaleddin into the Aghbak region and the subsequent destruction and
slaughter of numerous Armenian villages. *Jalaleddin* is full of the ideas
advanced by Grigor Artzruni, the editor of *Mshak*) and Stepan Nazariants: its principal aim is to encourage Armenians to raise their heads and
defend themselves.

Khente (The fool, 1880) is based on an episode from the 1877
Russo-Turkish war. Once again, most of the characters are historical
figures. The main character is an Armenian volunteer who helps the
Russian Army avoid defeat during a siege. He pretends to be a fool and
succeeds in getting a request for reinforcements to the commander in
Yerevan. The text describes the horrors of war and the miserable state of
refugees in Etchmiadzin. The hero, Vardan, has a characteristic dream:
he imagines a future utopian society that is educated, enlightened, has
full employment, and knows neither persecutions nor oppressors.

Raffi's most expansive work is *Kaytzer* (Sparks). While his previous
writings advocated relying on Russian assistance, this and subsequent
novels recommend looking for a way of salvation to the people themselves, once they had become sufficiently educated and organized to
pursue the ideal of a free and happy society. The book does not lack
interest, despite the absence of a well-defined plot, thanks to the author's
superior narrative skills. The hunter Avo, a descendent of the medieval
Rshtuni princes, guides the progress of a group of distinctive characters:
Hamo has literary inclinations and looks for the key to the people's
salvation in the arts and letters; Garo is hot-blooded and impatient, and

believes that everything can be solved by arms; Aslan is wiser and intends to instruct the people; while Farhad dedicates his time more to listening, doubting, and querying, assimilating and acting like the average person: dumbfounded at first, but gradually internalizing an entirely new way of thinking. Maro, the hunter's daughter, who takes some part in the action, impresses the reader by her open attitude and her ideological preparation; she is a girl worthy of the dawning age. Raffi was especially fond of this book; he even tried to raise a public subscription to get it published. He believed, and facts later justified this belief, that *Kaytzer* was a milestone in national thinking about liberation and how to achieve it.

After *Voski Akaghagh* (The golden rooster, 1879), devoted to dirty commercial practices in Tiflis, Raffi began to publish *Davit Bek* as a serial (1880–1882) in *Mshak*. He continued to promote the idea of armed patriotism outlined in his previous novels, reaching back to the 1720s uprisings in Zangezur and Karabagh and transforming them into a saga of extraordinary political and military planning and execution. At the time, the historical facts were almost unknown, except for a 1879 booklet, but Raffi personally questioned local elders, collecting information for the work.[90]

Although written in a relatively simple style, *Davit Bek* is a singular phenomenon in the tradition of Armenian prose narrative because of its almost forty characters. Some of them, such as Melik Davit, Melik Frangiul, and the Persian Aslamaz Kuli Khan, are fully rounded, with individual qualities. Davit Bek himself remains distant and is not a well developed character. Raffi may have intended this, for this lack of definition creates a remoteness that safeguards the novel from the risk of anachronism implicit in rendering historical characters; at the same time, it instills a certain sense of respect for authority and power.

In 1881 Raffi published *Khamsayi melikutiunnere* (The five melikdoms of Khamsa), a nonfiction investigation of the Armenian principalities that managed to survive continuously until the arrival of the Russians in Karabagh. He considered this the centerpiece of his quest to restore national pride to a devastated Armenia, because he believed that it demonstrated the continuity of Armenian statehood.

90. See Nicolas Adonts, "*Davit Bek vepi patmakan hime yev gaghaparakan arzheke*" (The historical basis and ideological value of the novel *Davit Bek*), in *Raffi, kyanke, grakanutiune, hishoghutiunner* (Raffi, his life, his literature, memories) (Paris, 1937), 122–148. The book was prepared by the committee in charge of commemorating Raffi's fiftieth anniversary; the editor is unnamed.

Paruyr Haykazn (Paruyr the Armenian, 1883) is a short novel that, like its predecessors, represents a response to the contemporary political situation. Raffi, a citizen of Persia, had already been investigated by the Russian government in Tiflis, and on one occasion he was put under house arrest for his opinions. Thus he could not openly express his views about school closings and other restrictions intended to Russify Armenia. Instead, he reached back to the fifth century, implicitly pointing out the parallel between the two epochs: during both periods Armenia was divided by two great powers (the Russian and Ottoman empires now, the Persian and Byzantine empires then), under threat of cultural suffocation, and, at the same time, experiencing a remarkable renaissance. The focal point of *Paruyr Haykazn* is the friction between the contradictory stances of Movses Khorenatsi and Paruyr the Armenian.[91] The former chooses to work for the national culture, while the latter argues from the standpoint of someone who has devoted himself to the service of humanity as a whole, without consideration of national boundaries.

Raffi devoted more time to his next novel, *Samuel* (1884), and this may be why it is his most successful work. It is based on the histories of Pavtos Buzand and Movses Khorenatsi. Choosing a secondary historical figure as his main character, Raffi selects a powerful theme, the killing of fourth-century Prince Vahan Mamikonian and his wife by their son Samuel. The story becomes a debate about complex issues, within the context of a tragedy reminiscent of Shakespeare.

Despite the opinion of some critics that Samuel is narcissistic, he has a substantial and distinct personality, particularly with regard to his ideological hesitations about his father's execution, which he hardly questions. His psychological state revolves more around his need to discover and learn his role—the need to convince himself that his judgment is legitimate: there is no other way to prevent his father's crimes against the state or to persuade him to reconsider his plans.

It may be suggested that Samuel's motive is the Middle Eastern preoccupation with restoring family honor by ending the disgrace caused by one of its members. It is only a small step from there to the implication, suggested by some critics,[92] that Samuel is troubled not so much by treason itself as by the fact that the traitor is his father—but this interpretation is not explicit in Raffi's text.

---

91. Paruyr is the Armenian name of the orator Proerecius (275–367), who lived in Athens.

92. See Sarinian's broad psychological portrait of Raffi's characters in his *Raffi* (Yerevan, 1957), 295–314.

Raffi's earliest novel, *Salbi*, was not published until 1911, although he began to write it in early 1855, even before the publication of Abovian's *Verk Hayastani* (1858).[93]

Raffi was aware of the importance of his works: "I was the first who had the confidence to transform our as-yet unrefined, unpracticed literary dialect [i.e., modern Eastern Armenian] into the language of novels."[94] Another of his achievements was the rhythm of his narration: "Raffi's books come to an end almost violently, and only through the author's intervention, so powerful is the breath that rises and strains the pages from inside."[95] On the other hand, his language is vigorous, striking, and jarring, because a "pioneer cannot be mild and polite."[96] Although long asides to describe details of natural beauty, customs, and traditions are characteristic of romantic writers, Raffi manages to incorporate them with barely an interruption to his narrative rhythm, at times applying the rule of "one step back, two steps forward" to increase the intensity of the next episode.

During the last three decades of the nineteenth century, Raffi was criticized by adherents of the realistic movement for the psychological shallowness of his characters and their less than faithful links to history. Nevertheless, even though his works have such definite romantic features as idealized characters, authorial subjectivism, and ideological polarization, his writings exhibit some similarities to the practices of the realists.

All of Raffi's works are rooted in the understandings and compulsions of his times. He did not like the new trend very much and believed that it would soon disintegrate.[97] Raffi had this to say about the relationship between history and fiction in his novels: "The poet

---

93. The first volume of *Salbi* was published in 1911, by Raffi's wife Anna. In her foreword she says that she adapted most of the work's antique language to the language Raffi used in his later novels. However, Khachik Samuelian mentions that the novel was first written in *grabar*, and later changed by the author: see Khachik Samuelian, *Raffi: hamarot aknark* (Raffi: a brief consideration) (Yerevan, 1957), 3–20.

94. Raffi, *"Vipagrutiune rusahayeri mej"* (Fiction among the Russian-Armenians), in *Vepikner yev patkerner* (Novellas and images), (Tiflis, 1891), xiv.

95. Hakob Oshakan, *"Mardots kovn i ver"* (In people's company), in his *Raffi, kyanke, grakanutiune, hishogutiunner* (Raffi, the life, the literature, memories) (Paris, 1937), 75.

96. Zaven Avetisian, *Hay nor patmavepi poetikan* (The poetics of the modern Armenian historical novel) (Yerevan, 1986), 139.

97. Shirvanzadé, *"Raffi—Hakob Melik Hakobian,"* in *Raffi, Khente, grakanutiune, hishoghutiunner* (Raffi, *The Fool*, his literature, memories) (Paris, 1937), 41.

is free; he should not be the slave of history. . . . Otherwise, he becomes a scribe. . . . On many occasions he even has the right to ignore demonstrated historical truth, because what he needs are ideal truths."[98] Nevertheless, he rejected the "manifest proclaiming of ideas," and was not obsessed with creating "pure art." This balanced approach was a novelty in the Armenian literary context of his time. He maintained that the novelist "has the right to gather evidence and, based on probability, to create from it a whole new picture, which, although not technically conforming to what actually happened, has the nature and authenticity of those events." That is, an author has the right to prefer verisimilitude to verity. Raffi drew an example from fifth-century historians: "Even Yeghishé's Vardan differs from [his contemporary] Ghazar Parpetsi's Vardan."[99]

Perch Proshian (Hovhannes Ter-Arakelian, 1837–1907) was a prolific novelist, dedicated mostly to regional and social issues. Three of his novels can be included in the broad category of historical fiction. *Krvatzaghik* (Battle-flower, 1876) follows Abovian's formula. The story is about the fight against Persian domination in Etchmiadzin and Yerevan at the end of the eighteenth century. The novel's hero, Vard, is reminiscent of the Aghasi character in Abovian's *Verk Hayastani. Shahen* (1880) can be classed in the same group, while *Skizbn yerkants* (The onset of labor, 1892) recalls Raffi's *Kaytzer.* In some ways all three novels are dated, because the ideas they tried to plant were already deeply rooted in the public.

Tevkants (Sedrak Sargsents, 1851–1937) was among the writers from the Armenian districts of Turkey rather than its capital. He tried writing a novel similar to Abovian's *Verk Hayastini. Shahenn i Sipir kam Gaghtakan haye* (Shahen in Siberia, or the Armenian expatriate, 1877),[100] written in Western Armenian, recounts the journey of Shahen from his native Van to Eastern Armenia in order to escape prison. It tells of his successful career in the Russian army and his deportation to Siberia for his nationalistic views. Beyond the action, the novel develops several

---

98. Quoted in Avetisian, *Poetics of the Modern Armenian Historical Novel,* 97–101.

99. Pavtos (Raffi's pseudonym), *"P. Haykunu kritikan yev 'Kaytzere"* (P. Haykuni's criticism and *Kaytzer*), in *Raffi: Collected Works* (Yerevan, 1964), 67–147. For an in-depth analysis of Raffi's views see also Yeghishé Petrosian, *Raffi, kyanke yev steghtzagortzutiune* (Raffi: his life and work) (Yerevan, 1959), 462–500.

100. Sarinian, *"Ayl ardzakagirner"* (1979), 3:641–50. *Shahenn i Sipir* was banned by the government after its publication in Constantinople; unsold copies were confiscated and burned.

themes, such as the error of moving away from the homeland, the necessity of self-reliance, the danger of letting Russia continue to increase its assimilation policy, and the call for a national liberation struggle against the Turkish state. In his preface, Tevkants sums up the position of most Armenian historical novelists when he asserts that Armenian national novels should have a different orientation from European novels, a "revolutionizing" mission.

Muratsan (Grigor Ter-Hovhannesian, 1854–1908) was the last major historical novelist of the nineteenth century. He was the most conservative of Armenian novelists, and he tried to delve into his characters' personalities. But the nearly obsessive dogmatism about religious and national unity conveyed by the majority of his works made them quickly outdated; the exception is his novel *Gevorg Marzpetuni*.

After approaching historical subjects in the play *Ruzan kam hayrenaser oriord* (Ruzan, or the patriotic damsel, 1896), which deals with the thirteenth-century Karabagh invasions, Muratsan wrote the novel *Andreas Yerets* (Andreas the priest, 1897), about a religious conflict in seventeenth-century Agulis. Andreas, an exemplary and commendable friar from the Armenian national Church, Andreas, collides with Erasmus, a Catholic priest proselytizing in the region. The extravagant plot ends with Andreas's martyrdom on orders of the sovereign, the shah of Persia. Erasmus has apparently instigated the execution. He arrives at the last minute with an order from the shah in his hand, promising to reprieve Andreas if he disowns his Church and converts to Catholicism. Andreas rejects the offer, stating that to accept would be the same as converting to Islam for the shah.

Muratsan's principal work, *Gevorg Marzpetuni* (1896), was possibly prompted by the Turkish massacres of Armenians in 1895–96. It deals with the tenth-century Armenian King Ashot Yerkat (Ashot the Iron). The novel's theme is the clash between personal interests and passions and the social and public responsibilities of a statesman, with heavy emphasis on the ideal of national unity. The story is based on the medieval historical works of Ghevond, Tovma Artzruni, and Hovhannes Draskhanakerttsi. Ashot has to cope with a military revolt by several of Armenia's local rulers and simultaneously take care of many serious problems occasioned by an Arabic invasion.

In *Gevorg Marzpetuni*, Muratsan depicts Armenia's problems as not so much the result of political, economic, and sectarian interests as of the king's indecent behavior. Ashot has had an illicit affair with the wife of one of the regional rulers; as a result his father-in-law has joined forces with the cheated husband to avenge the honor of the queen, his daughter.

The king, who does not hesitate to blind his father-in-law and brother-in-law, nevertheless has serious reservations concerning how his actions have affected the public well-being. All of his emotions and values are subordinated to the public interest: the monarch has the responsibility of caring for the future of his nation. The author's position gets tougher as he highlights the conflict between private necessities, passions, and vices, and public responsibility and morality. As he faces external menace, the king feels the gravity of his acts, which have exposed the nation to the enemy by causing disunity and discord.[101] Marzpetuni, a powerful prince and the commander of the royal forces, represents positive values, such as moral fiber, impartiality, and political farsightedness. Even though the novel was written at the peak of the realist movement, the author adheres to romanticism. His characters have intense personalities, unambiguous positions, and polarized opinions.

Muratsan also became involved in the debate over the historical novel. During a discussion against the objectivist scheme endorsed by Leo, he highlighted the disparity between the concepts of verity and verisimilitude: "While in historical works it is history that creates people, in works of artistic creation it is man who creates history,"[102] adding that "the artist can reconstruct historical facts. . . . In his works, he [should give] the first place not to historical truth but to ideal truth," and he agrees with Raffi that "one can say much more to the public through novels than by means of distant leaders."[103]

Leo (Arakel Babakhanian (1860–1932), best known as a historian, also produced a series of historical novellas and tales, including: *Hayi vrezh* (Revenge of the Armenian, 1887), which he later expanded into the novel *Meliki aghchike* (Melik's daughter); *Vahan Mamikonian* (1888); *Spannvatz hayre* (The assassinated father, 1891); *Verjin verker* (The last wounds, 1891); *Tatakhman gishere* (The night of breaking Lent, 1892); *Lerntsinere* (Mountaineers, 1896). He also wrote the historical play *Vardanank* (1916).

His principal historical novel is *Melik's Daughter,* published as a serial in *Mshak* (1897–98). It tells the story of the struggles for liberation conducted by the *meliks* of Karabagh during the first half of the eighteenth century. Critics have generally accepted the explanation of the tale's

101. See Sarinian, "Muratsan," in *Hay nor grakanutyan patmutiun,* 4:172–75.

102. Avetisian, *Hay nor patmavepi poetican,* 35.

103. Muratsan, *"Namak khmbagrutian Ruzani knnadatutyan aritov"* (Letter to the editor regarding Ruzan's criticism), in *Yerkeri zhoghovatzu* (Collected works) (Yerevan, 1961–65), 7:108, and *"Inknakensagrutiun"* (Autobiography), 138.

source that Leo gives in his preface: "*Meliki aghchike* (Melik's daughter) is not based on written history, but on a tradition of the village of Avetaranots in Karabagh. I don't know if it is still to be found there, but twenty years ago I acquired a thick notebook in Shushi, which had only recently been written in Avetaranots, in a very disorganized, crude, and awkward fashion, but which related the tale in great detail. I used that text like a dry skeleton, as the underlying structure.[104] The nineteenth-century reader was all too familiar with mysterious manuscripts, texts of unknown origin, and other inexact clues planted by authors of historical novels at the beginning or the end of their tales. These inventions were intended to support the "contract" between the author and the reader. This contract involved a "pact of verisimilitude" as opposed to the "pact of verity" expected of historical works. This was important for a genre that met with a good deal of resistance in terms of credibility, a result of its particular and unusual blend of history and fiction. Footnotes are resources of the same type, used by most authors, including Raffi, to reinforce the idea that the narrative can be anchored in history by means of a reference.

Leo vigorously criticized the romantic novelists, but he adopted some of their typical ways. Later in his life he abandoned fiction almost entirely and established himself as one of the first Armenian historians of modern times.

Bagrat Ayvazian (1862–1934) is one of the forgotten writers of Armenian historical novels. He spent all his life in Tiflis, Georgia, and began to write in *Meghu Hayastani* (The bee of Armenia) in 1882. He published three historical novels. *Ashot Yerkat* (1893–94) has the same subject as Muratsan's later *Gevorg Marzpetuni* (1896). Ayvazian's other two novels are *Hiusisi artzive* (The northern eagle, 1801–1829, 1901), about the Russian annexation of Eastern Armenia in 1828, and *Anii kortzanume* (The destruction of Ani, 1891, 1905), reprinted as *Anin tzakhvetsav* (Ani is sold). The latter deals with the fall of Armenia's capital city in the eleventh century. Ayvazian also wrote a short novel, *Sev haghtanak* (Black victory, 1903) and a play, *Sasune ayrvum e* (Sasun is burning, 1913). Paying little attention to philosophical perspective, character building, or other artistic concerns, Ayvazian focused on action and adventure. His books were widely popular at the turn of the century, enjoying several reprints.

Khanzadé (Levon Khansanamian, 1873–1938) was another Eastern Armenian historical novelist, albeit not so successful as others. His

104. Leo, *Meliki aghchike* (Melik's daughter) (Boston, 1933), 1.

Zakaria Dzagetsu orere (The days of Zakaria Dzagetsi, 1904) was published in St. Petersburg. The novel deals with events that took place during the ninth century. Khanzadé also published short novels on contemporary national issues.

Sargis Kamalian (1860–1934) was an intellectual based in Tiflis and educated in Dorpat and Berlin. He focused mainly on popular tales and fables. In 1900 he published an adaptation of Tzerentz's *Yerkunk innerord daru* as *Sasuntsi Hovnan* (Hovnan of Sasun).

Nerses Andrikian was the author of *Hangatz Yekeghetsin* (The muffled church), a historical novel published in Venice in 1906.

Smbat Biurat (Smbat Ter-Ghazarents, 1862–1915) was one of a series of writers who recounted the decaying days of the sultans' regime after the 1908 revolution brought some freedom to publish previously forbidden texts. His works acclaimed the heroic deeds and adventures of a once secret network of revolutionaries, acts of revenge, and government persecution. He and a number of other writers, such as Armen Shitanian and Sev-Vost, may be included in the late romantic movement.

Biurat's *Sasunen yetke* (After Sasun) was published in Constantinople in 1911. It comprises two volumes: *Diakaputnere* (Body snatchers) and *Depi Yltez* (Toward Yiltiz). These books portray many of the historical figures who took part in anti-regime struggles before 1908. They are often confusing, overwhelming the reader with details of journalistic information and neglecting the fictional element. As a whole, they bear testimony to the ultimate defiance in the history and character of Zeytun, of which Biurat was a native.

Others of his works in the same vein include *Yltezen Sasun* (From Yildiz to Sasun, 1910); *Ariuni chambun vra* (On the bloody road, 1911); *Azatutyan hamar: Zeytuni vrezhe* (For liberty: the revenge of Zeytun, 1911); *Bante bant* (From prison to prison, 5 vols., 1910); *Yltezi pompan* (The Yildiz bombing, 1912); *Innesunvets: ariuni mejen* (The bloodbath of ninety-six, 1911); the short novel *Ariuni dzore* (Blood canyon, 1919); and the historical tragedy *Verjin berde: kottatsogh verker hayutyan srtin mej* (The last fortress: wounds stabbing at the Armenian heart, 1914).

Biurat's poetry appeared in *Banasteghtzakan yerker* (Poetic works), vol. 1, 1908, and *Burgeren* (From the pyramids). He also wrote a historical play, *Avarayri artzive kam Vardanank* (The eagle of Avarayr, or Vardanank, 1909); *Haykakan endhanur patmutiun* (General Armenian history, 1912); and the biographical works *Vegharavor herose* (Hooded hero, 1909) and *Zeytuntsi vardapet* (The priest from Zeytun). Many other of his writings remain scattered, under the pseudonyms of Hayk-

Levon, Tab, Mtrak, and Lernordi, in a series of periodicals he edited in Constantinople and Egypt (*Piunik, Nor or, Gaghapar*). Biurat also translated Émile Zola's *Fécundité* (Fecundity, 1899) in 1910.[105]

Ultimately the Turkish partners of the anti-regime revolution changed their course. Biurat was murdered in the initial days of the Armenian genocide, and his dreams of a burgeoning Armenian population were brutally crushed.

Armen Shitanian (Abraham Shitanian, 1870–1928), also known as Fakir in Hnchakian Party circles, was another author from the provinces. Although he moved to Constantinople and spent most of his life in Bulgaria, he was a native of Shitan, a village near Van. Incarcerated in 1896 by the Turks, he had the rare "privilege" of being sued by Sultan Hamid in a Bulgarian court for his serialized satirical work *Sultan Hamit* (1903).[106] Shitanian wrote a series of works in the manner of Biurat, but with even less literary value and more public appeal because of his more sensational and melodramatic effects and his undue emphasis on his characters' heroism and adventures. Most of his works are about revolutionary fighters during the last decades of the nineteenth century.

Although he does not appear regularly in literature courses, Shitanian is one of the most frequently published and best selling Western Armenian novelists. Some of his works were reprinted and sold out even a hundred years after their first editions.

His novels, mostly labeled "historical," "national," or "national-revolutionary," were usually published in Varna, first in the periodical *Iravunk* (Rights), with reprints in Constantinople, Sophia, and Beirut. These include *Kakhaghanen yetk* (After the gallows, 1898); *Gnuni* (1898); *Gharip akhpere* (The expatriate, 1898); *Andunde* (The precipice, 1898); *Avazakapete* (The bandit chief, 1898); *Tiaparte* (The convict, 1898); *Tiapart kam vanakan* (Convict or monk, 1910); *Vashkharun* (The usurer, 1910); *Aksorakane* (The exile, 1910); *Matniche* (The informer, 1910); *Taparakan haye* (The wandering Armenian, 1914); *Taparakan hayu vordin* (The wandering Armenian's son, 1925); *Paterazme* (The war, 1926); and the novels *Fatma* (1925), *Anitzyale* (The cursed, 1926),

---

105. Zola (1840–1902) was one of the founding members of the National Alliance for the Growth of the French Population. Biurat had a political purpose in selecting his translations.

106. Ultimately he prevailed, because the court ruled that the sultan should be personally present. When he failed to appear, the sultan was ordered to pay a fine of 11 *levas*.

Nedelka (1926), and *Tamara* (1930). Shitanian also wrote two historical plays: *Vani haydukner* (The fighters of Van, 1897), and *Arabo yev Andranik* (Arabo and Andranik, 1905).

Sev-Vost was the author of a rare novel about the 1915 genocide, published immediately after the First World War. *Leran vogin. Hay yeritasardi me arkatznere metz paterazmi entatskin* (The spirit of the mountain: the journey of a young Armenian during the Great War) was printed in Constantinople in 1920. It covers the vicissitudes experienced by the hero during the liberation of Erzurum, the "Great Retreat" of the Russian army, the battles in Armenia, and the proclamation of independence.

Vrtanes Papazian (1866–1920) was a prolific author who also wrote historical fiction. He too began writing about the human rights of Turkey's Armenian population. Later, by the last decade of the nineteenth century, he embraced the realist cause and criticized with contempt, even to the point of denying any artistic value in, the literary production of Raffi and other writers had any hint of romantic facade. Papazian's historical fiction includes the short novels *Asi* (1897), *Alemgir* (1900, published 1904), and *Azerfeza* (1905), about popular uprisings in Persia in the nineteenth century. His realist zeal laid stress on the descriptive elements.

Tigran Kamsarakan (1866–1941) was one of the 80s generation of Constantinople writers who specialized in realist novellas. His only work of historical fiction is the short novel *Levon Metzagortze* (1919), published as a serial in the newspaper *Arev* (The sun) of Cairo.

Yervand Otian (1869–1926). His voluminous literary production includes two historical narratives: *Abdul Hamid yev Sherlock Holmes* (Abdul Hamid and Sherlock Holmes, 1911) and *Saliha hanem kam Banake brnavorin dem* (Saliha Hanem, or the army versus the tyrant, 1912). Otian described these works as "contemporary historical novels." Both are about the 1904–8 struggles against Sultan Hamid's oppression, with some historical background and characters, but mostly invented situations. They are modeled after the detective and adventure novel made popular by Dumas the elder's *The Three Musketeers*, but with no interval between the time of the story and the author's own age. Some literary historians consider that a work can rightly be considered a historical novel if there is a significant historical situation or turning point dividing the action of the story from the time it was composed—in this case, the 1908 revolution. In their treatment of the sultan as the principal villain and their highlighting of certain aspects of the former regime, these two fictional works go beyond detective adventures, becoming more like political novels.

Both novels gained instant acclaim, and they were translated into French, Turkish, and Greek. Far from being cheap spy-and-police novels, they benefited from Otian's celebrated skills of artistic observation and sharp reasoning. His literary record includes a number of fine works and translations of Tolstoy, Zola, Dostoevsky, and Gorky.

Derenik Temirchian (Demirdjian, 1877–1956) published his first historical novel, *Vardanank* (1943, completed in 1946), when he was sixty-seven. It centers on the fifth-century religious war between Armenia and Persia. Although he wrote the play *Vasak* on the same subject in 1912, his ideas became more mature, and in *Vardanank* he developed them into, in his words, a way of explaining "the puzzle of the existence of the Armenian people."[107] Temirchian tried to reconstruct the passions and psychological journeys of his characters as well as the historical events from a realistic perspective, which gives his work an ideological stance.

The history of Vardan's war against Persia is a meticulously prepared and constructed novel that the author revised continuously until 1954. The personalities of the characters, particularly that of Vasak the traitor, mature through a colorful psychological evolution, complete with ups and downs, against a background rich in epical qualities and philosophical considerations. As for the political conflict—whether to side with Persia or the Byzantine state—despite the ideological conditioning around him Temirchian arrives at the wisdom displayed by Raffi in his final years. In his work notes for *Vardanank,* he says: "Only we can love us more than any others can. Our personality is us. We are us, and others are not us. This has a huge, huge significance. . . . Think about it."[108]

Temirchian planned a trilogy on the events of the fifth century, but he died leaving the second novel, *Mesrop Mashtots* (1956) unfinished. The third title, *Vahanants paterazme* (The war of Vahanants) was only in the planning stage.

Arazi (Movses Harutiunian, 1878–1964) wrote a historical novel *Israel Ori* (3 vols., 1959–63). Earlier, he produced *Ayrvogh horizon* (Burning horizon, 1940), a "historical-revolutionary" novel on the subject of pre-Soviet-era insurgency movements.

---

107. Qtd. in Avetisian, *Hay nor patmavepi poetikan*, 311.
108. Ibid., 239.

Stepan Zorian (Arakelian, 1889–1967), completed a trilogy of historical novels: *Pap tagavor* (King Pap, 1944), *Hayots berde* (The fortress of Armenians, 1959), and *Varazdat* (1967). The first of these was especially well received. It continued the story of *Samuel* from the point where Raffi had left it. Though it is somewhat influenced by Raffi, it is quite dissimilar. Zorian's approach is realistic, with an attempt to make his characters' speech typical of their own epoch. This occasionally imparts a forced naturalness to his narrative. In accordance with Soviet Communist ideology, he tries to make ordinary people the main actors of history, with special emphasis on the importance of centralized statehood. His narrative is remarkable for its battle scenes, perhaps inspired by modern translations he made of Tolstoy. He also translated Turgenev and Mark Twain.

The First Decades of the Twentieth Century

For Armenian writers the beginning of the twentieth century was not easy; they experienced harsh government censorship in both the West and the East. Despite the precarious conditions and cataclysmic events—displacements, massacres, the Great War, and the politics of the Young Turks—Armenian writers and scholars continued to be productive during the first few decades of the twentieth century. Scholars such as Hrachya Acharian (1876–1953), Manuk Abeghian (1865–1944), and Nikoghayos Adonts (1871–1942), contributed impressively to Armenian philology. Literary activities revived when several Armenian writers returned to Constantinople after the proclamation of the 1908 Constitution.

Literary criticism and history made an impact. Criticism developed from reviews in the popular press to more intricate analyses and monographs. Arshak Chopanian (Arshag Tchobanian) and, most famous of all Armenian literary critics, Hakob Oshakan defined the canon of Western Armenian literature, while Vahan Nalbandian (1876–1902), Nikol Aghbelian (1873–1947), and others did the same for Eastern Armenian literature.[109]

Some of the greatest names of Armenian poetry surfaced during the period—their works added new dimensions both of form and of content: Siamanto, Daniel Varuzhan, Misak Metzarents, and Vahan Tekeyan in the West, and Hovhannes Tumanian, Avetik Isahakian, Vahan Terian,

---

109. See Kevork Bardakjian, *A Reference Guide to Modern Armenian Literature, 1500–1920* (Detroit, 2000), 152.

and Yeghishé Charents (1897–1937) in the East. Symbolism, aestheticism, naturalism, and futurism influenced many of them. The plays of Levon Shant and Shirvanzadé revived Armenian drama and created a discerning theater audience. Short-lived periodicals such as *Mehyan* (The temple) and *Navasard,* both published in Constantinople on the eve of World War I, contributed immensely to the revival of the literary scene, but the genocide brought this dynamic literary atmosphere to an abrupt end. The genocide was intended to destroy Armenian life and intellect, and the perpetrators succeeded, at least temporarily, in their objective.

With the Armistice, however, new life gradually started to stir. Genocide survivors tried to revive the old cultural movement. Some of the writers and poets, including Levon Shant, Yervand Otian, Vahan Tekeyan, Arshak Chopanian, (Arshag Tchobanian) Hakob Oshakan, Levon Bashalian (Pashalian), Tigran Kamsarakan, Kostan Zarian, Hamastegh (1895–1966), and Matteos Zarifian, were spared the horror of the genocide because some were already in Europe and others had managed to escape the tragedy and moved abroad.

A new generation was born amidst the ashes and the ruins of the human cataclysm—a generation who founded the postwar Armenian communities in Paris, the Middle East, and the United States. Unfortunately, after only two decades of peace the world was immersed in a second World War. By that time Armenia was a Soviet Republic.

Armenian literature produced during the early decades of the twentieth century bears the stamp of alienation. It was written in Paris, Boston, New York, Beirut, Aleppo, Alexandria, and other outposts of the diaspora, and it was deprived both of the conditions essential to the expression of national character and the inspiration derived from a homeland. Undoubtedly, those who settled in the Middle East found it easier to preserve the Armenian character, color, and spirit than those who found themselves in France and the USA, but even that area of the world was far from fully representative of their homeland.

The literature reborn in the diaspora was written by a group of authors whose major preoccupations were longing for the homeland or their native provinces and memories inspired by the great tragedy. These preoccupations were expressed especially by prose writers. Vahé Hayk (1896–1983), Beniamin Nurikian (1894–1988), Aram Haykaz (1900–1986), and Hamastegh in particular used their stories as a way to maintain ties with their past, the homeland and national traditions. Another concern was to create a literary reaction to what had happened by thwarting defeatism and ascending to new literary heights. Even while prose writers described expatriate Armenians, the tragic events of the recent past, the dangers of alienation, and falls on the slippery road to recovery, they tried to lift the Armenian spirit. Shahan Shahnur (1903–74), Hrach Zardarian (1892–1986), and Zareh Vorbuni (1902–80) were the militants of this movement.

This was true also of poetry. Almost all poets wrote of the tragic past, painting horrific images of the desert, and directly or indirectly mixing in their own emotional experiences, with a view to inspiring the new generation with the spiritual enthusiasm to endure.

The literary life that emerged between the two world wars resumed after the second, both in the diaspora and in the Armenian Soviet Republic, but under different circumstances, different conditions and directions. The new generation felt the pressure of modern spiritual and intellectual demands, and, influenced by contemporary European currents, tried to respond to those demands in new ways. This was the beginning of the new era of sensitivity and artistic feeling. It took some time, however, for these changes to fill the gaps that were created in the Armenian intellectual and psychological environment.

However, the intellectual and ideological revolution gradually invigorated a new generation of Armenian writers, for whom the art of the previous period seemed less than irrelevant. Many of these writers were born between the two wars. A literary movement is valid only insofar as it allows artists to express the spirit of the times truly and sincerely. If that expression is just, time, which separates the bad from the good like chaff from wheat, will judge it worthwhile. It will have become literature.[110]

---

110. For more details see Bardakjian, *Reference Guide,* 150–200; Chanashian, *Hay grakanutyan nor shrjani hamarot patmutiun,* 377–83; Teoleolian, *Dar me grakanutiun,* 1:454–85.

Abraham Kretatsi

(Abraham of Crete)

(d. 1737)

Abraham Kretatsi was born in Candia, on the island of Crete. He was or-dained as a celibate priest, and in 1709 was appointed Prelate of Rodosto (Tekirdagh), in eastern Thrace. He retained this position until 1734, when he undertook a pilgrimage to Etchmiadzin with the intention of also visiting the monastery of Glak in Taron. At the insistence of Catholicos Abraham II Khoshabetsi (1730–34), he postponed his de-parture, which turned out to be providential. A few months later the catholicos was struck by an epidemic, and Kretatsi, who had earned esteem and respect for his integrity and vast knowledge, was elected catholicos, in which position he was known as Abraham III.

His years as catholicos (1734–37) happened to be a troubled period in Eastern Armenia, because of the devastating wars between Persia and the Ottoman Empire.[1] The Persians, fighting under Tahmaz Ghuli Khan (who later became Nadir Shah), recaptured the territories previ-ously lost to the Ottomans, including the province of Yerevan. Abra-ham Kretatsi developed warm relations with the shah and gained his confidence. In return the shah honored him with the title of Father

---

1. From 1512 to 1746 eleven major wars were fought between the Ottoman Empire and Persia for the domination of Armenia and the Transcaucasus. As all of these battles were fought on Armenian soil, the country was utterly devastated.

and often sought his counsel. The catholicos's wise and tactful dealings with the shah earned him prestige, which he used to good advantage: he succeeded in asserting Etchmiadzin's right to ownership of Church treasures and property, and obtained certain privileges for the Holy See, including authorization for an Armenian banker, Melik Hakobjan, to establish a mint in Yerevan. Abraham Kretatsi met Nadir Shah for the last time in 1736 in the field of Mughan, prior to the shah's coronation, to which he had been invited as one of the dignitaries. As thousands of people gathered in preparation for the coronation, he noticed close to seven thousand Armenian and Georgian youths, boys and girls, whom provincial lords had brought to present to the shah as slaves. He immediately intervened and arranged for the return of these youths to their homes. He gave his blessing to the shah and returned to Etchmiadzin, delegating a priest to attend the coronation.

Abraham Kretatsi's principal work is *Patmagrutiune* (Historiography), an eyewitness account in minute detail of the events of the Turko-Persian war of 1734–36, including the military operations and other activities of Nadir Shah. It also includes descriptions of the Persian court as well as the shah's coronation and its the accompanying festivities.[2] The *Historiography* was published in Calcutta in 1796 and in Etchmiadzin in 1870. A French translation by Marie Brosset was published in *Collection d'historiens arméniens* in 1876. A Russian translation was published with the Armenian original in Yerevan in 1973.

FROM THE CHRONICLE[3]

A Brief History of Nader Shah's Early Reign
Composed by Our Patriarch Abraham of Tekirdagh

---

2. In Muslim countries a sovereign is confirmed by girding him with a sword rather than by crowning him. As Abraham Kretatsi did not attend this ceremony in person, it is likely that the detailed description in his book is based on the report of his delegate. It is worth noting that Nadir Shah was a Sunni Muslim, whereas the overwhelming majority of Persians were Shiite. He struggled to unite the two sects, but without success. He made a compromise by inviting a Christian patriarch to his coronation.

3. Abraham Kretatsi, *Patmutiun: Katoghikos Abraham Kretatsi* (The chronicle of Catholicos Abraham of Crete) in George A. Bournoutian, annotated translation from the critical text with introduction and commentary, *The Chronicle of Abraham of Crete* (Costa Mesa, Calif., 1999), 11–23. All footnotes are by Bournoutian.

Chapter I

According to the Holy Scriptures, that which God has pre-destined is inviolable. God does whatever He wishes. "Who has directed the Spirit of the Lord, or as His counselor has instructed Him?"[4]

The Holy Scriptures also declare that "The Lord makes poor and makes rich,"[5] and so forth. We humans are humble and nat-urally weak. Our knowledge is ridiculously inadequate and, as is stated in the Scriptures, "We can hardly guess at what is on earth."[6]

Thus, some men who are born virtuous turn wicked, while others who are born vile become righteous. The worthy ones, how-ever, are those who are born good and remain good. The all-loving God, the source of all goodness, supplied us with good will in our nature, even though some use the gift of the Lord inappropriately.

Thus, if people follow goodness, God, according to the testi-mony of the apostle, "will make all things work together for good."[7]

The yearning I had from childhood to visit the Holy See, the monasteries, and other holy places in the land of Armenia, was instilled in my unworthy self by God. At first, in the year 1168 (1719),[8] I was sent to Holy Jerusalem. I spent two years there.[9] This occurred during the time of the feast of the Restoration of the Universal Church of the Holy Resurrection and the Holy Places. It was in my tenth year as the prelate (bishop) of the diocese of the city of Trakia (Thrace). The Patriarch of Holy Jerusalem was the gentle-spirited Grigor;[10] the Patriarch of Constantinople was the tireless theologian, Hovhannes,[11] both of whom were students of *Vardapet*[12] Vardan of Baghesh from the monastery of Amrdolu.

---

4. Isa. 40:13.

5. I Sam. 2:7.

6. Sol. 9:16.

7. Rom. 8:28.

8. The Armenian Church calendar is reckoned from the autumnal equinox of the year 552. It is, therefore, 551 years behind that of the West.

9. According to a colophon written by Abraham, he stayed in Jerusalem from 1719–21.

10. Grigor of Shirvan (Shghtayakir) (1715–49).

11. Hovhannes (Kolot) of Baghesh (1715–41).

12. A celibate cleric in the Armenian Church who has completed his studies at the seminary. A doctor of the Church.

On 27 April 1183 (1734), 21 left Trakia and journeyed to Holy Etchmiadzn via the sacred monastery of Glak[13] in Taron, the site of the church of St. Karapet, erected by our Illuminator, St. Gregory. On the hundredth day, on Saturday August third, at the third hour of the day after sunrise, we reached the holy and all-sustaining refuge of Etchmiadzin.

Chapter II

ON THE DEPARTURE OF MY FELLOW TRAVELERS FROM ETCHMIADZIN TO ST. KARAPET

Following our arrival at the Holy See, after we had kissed the threshold of the holy cathedral and had worshiped at the spot where Jesus Christ had descended, as well as at other holy places, we were taken to the supreme and holy leader, Catholicos Abraham.[14] He was sitting in the garden in the center of a large veranda and on seeing us he rejoiced and was rejuvenated. It was as if the great affection, which had been developed in my heart over the last twenty years, had suddenly burst into flame. At the conclusion of our talk, which included questions regarding the condition of our brother, the Patriarch of Constantinople,[15] the great city of Constantinople, its churches, princes, and priests, he the Patriarch sent me to my cell.

I was directed to the chamber of the late and saintly Catholicos Agheksandr (Alexander),[16] which was located inside the residence of the Catholicos. The bell for the Divine Liturgy was rung and we went to hear Mass. After that we sat for our meal. From then on, the Catholicos met with me on a daily basis and we talked in his room. Twenty days passed in this manner.

I then sought permission to return to the St. Karapet Monastery. The Catholicos, however, did not permit it, stating, "God Himself, seeing the weak state of my health, has sent you to me. Therefore, at least for this year, I shall not let you go. Wait! Stay in the bosom of Our Mother, the luminous and Holy Etchmiadzin. Be

---

13. Glakavank, also known as St. Karapet, is located in Western Armenia in the Mush Province,
14. Catholicos Abraham II of Khoshab (1730–34).
15. Hovhannes of Baghesh.
16. Catholicos Agheksandr of Julfa (1706–14).

my advisor and sympathize with my woes. I have known for some time that you feel close to me. My soul knows this. I have heard for many years, and during my residence at the Holy See, that you are my friend and are loyal to me and to those who hold my views." No matter how much I begged, there was no chance of changing his mind. He did not give me permission or alter his directive. But he did state "If God wishes, and with His help, I would like to visit Taron next year. Stay here with me and we shall journey together to St. Karapet and after you have made your pilgrimage there I shall send you to your diocese."

I begged him to at least permit those who had accompanied me, *Vardapet* Harutiun, Father Hovhannes, the senior priest of Tekirdagh, Father Hovnan, Father Poghos, Father Gaspar of Boghazhisar and others from Istanbul and T'ekirdagh, some twenty altogether, to go on their pilgrimage to St. Karapet, and from there back to their own homes. We entrusted them to God and to *Vardapet* Hovhannes, the prelate of Kaghzovan.[17] He acted as their leader and guide and on Saturday, 23 August, he took them via Kaghzovan to their destination. I promised them that I would follow at the end of the grape harvest. The blessed one the Catholicos laughed and said, "Fine, let it be so."

Chapter III

On Visiting the Monasteries Near Etchmiadzin and on the Reconsecration of the Altar of St. Karapet in Hovhannavank[18]

The first Monday after the departure of my fellow travelers to the St. Karapet Monastery, 27 (25) August, the Catholicos ordered his servants to prepare for a journey to visit some monasteries. He said, "I have not traveled anywhere for a long time and my heart is very heavy." He took me and more than ten *vardapets* and we all left in good spirits.

At first we went to Hovhannavank, since the prior of the monastery, *Vardapet* Hakob, had come to Etchmiadzin and had

---

17. Kagizman in Turkish. A town located on the banks of the Araxes in the province of Kars.

18. The monastery of Hovhannavank is located in the Ashtarak region in the village of the same name in present-day Armenia.

invited His Holiness to consecrate anew the renovated altar and communion table on the northern side of the St. Karapet church built by our Illuminator, Gregory. The church possessed holy relics including some bones of St. John the Baptist. With great celebration we reconsecrated the altar.

Two or three days after savoring this spiritual and corporal happiness we went to the church of St. Sargis in Ushi.[19] While we were there, Hakobjan, the melik[20] of Yerevan, who had been summoned by the Catholicos, arrived.

A horseman arrived from Tiflis (Tbilisi) the same day. He brought the news, as well as an official letter to inform us, that Isak Pasha,[21] had, without any reason, ordered the strangling of Ashichal Bek, the melik of our people the Armenians in Tiflis. He had kept his corpse hanging on the city gate until he received 50,000 *kurush*[22] which he had permitted the body to be buried.

The next day, at my request, we went to Parpi[23] and from there to Karbi,[24] where we spent the night at the residences of Paron[25] Khachatur and Paron Ohazar. The next day we traveled to Mughni[26] to visit the Church of St. Gregory. Melik Hakobjan, who accompanied us, was not feeling well and we stayed the night there. In the morning, after services, we went down to Oshakan.[27] The melik went to Yerevan via Yeghvard,[28] but we stayed the night there. We left at dawn and arrived at Holy Etchmiadzin.

Chapter IV

On How I Once Again Visited a Monastery

Because of the love that the Catholicos had for me, the ill-fated one, he took me with him and as a diversion we went to visit

---

19. A village southeast of Mt. Aragats on the banks of a tributary of the Araxes.

20. An Armenian petty prince, feudal lord, or secular leader.
21. Isak Pasha was a Jaqeli Muslim from Samtskhe, who set himself up as prince in Tiflis.
22. Small Turkish coin.
23. A village in the Ashtarak region.
24. A large village in the Ashtarak region, which was a trade center.
25. From the Latin *baron*, the term synonymous with the Persian *aga*. In modern times it signifies mister (*monsieur*).
26. A village in the Ashtarak region.
27. A large village in the Ashtarak region.
28. The center of the Nairi region, it contains numerous medieval sites.

large and small monasteries. We could not remain long in these holy cloisters, however, for the Catholicos was highly preoccupied with the affairs of and news from the Holy See. There were more than thirty people in our party and just as many beasts of burden. Since His Holiness was an astute and thoughtful person regarding his subordinates, he did not wish to burden anyone else with the problems at Etchmiadzin.

He, therefore, hastened to return to the Holy See, particularly since those were troubled times and His Holiness had been informed of the appearance of Tahmaz Khan and the advance of the Persian army. He, the Catholicos, rushed back to Etchmiadzin to care for its needs. We have become accustomed it seems from time immemorial to leave all of our problems to our leaders. We do not think or worry about anything but our own safety and comfort. The fact is that as long as one is alive one delegates all one's concerns to one's superior. It seems to me that one does this for one's own benefit and for one's own prosperity. But, after the death of such a person, he is not remembered; instead of tears and lamentations, he is criticized and ridiculed. This is part of the character of our people; and the reasons are ignorance and ingratitude and nothing else.

I was once more commanded by His Holiness to proceed alone to the monastery of the Illuminator Hovhannavank and to remain there for a week before returning to Etchmiadzin. When I had his leave to go, the prior of the monastery, *Vardapet* Hovhan, arrived on behalf of His Holiness. He took me to his monastery and after a week's stay I returned to the Holy See.

Chapter V

On My Pilgrimage to Distant Monasteries in the Araratian Province

A few days later I was again ordered by the Patriarch to visit several distant monasteries in the Araratian province. His Holiness wished to visit these places himself, for he had not seen them since he had become the Supreme Patriarch, and did not wish me to go alone. Despite the fact that this Blessed Soul, wished, for a number of reasons, to go to these monasteries, troubled times and other concerns prevented him from leaving the Holy See. He, therefore, asked me to go.

Although ill, I departed the Holy See. I hoped that during my journey I would be cured from my painful fever. At first I went to Yerevan, this was on 16 October 1734, and I spent one night there. The next day I went to holy Virap[29] and from there to Akori[30] and to the spring of St. Hakob[31] on Masis Ararat. Having concluded my pilgrimage there, I celebrated Mass, and after our prayers were completed we returned to the Akori settlement.

After a short respite we returned to Virap. I descended into the pit, a necessary obligation for all devotees, and led a service down there. After ascending, I spent the night. In the morning, taking one of the monks as my guide, I went to Havuts Tar,[32] that is, the All Savior Monastery, where I spent two days. From there I traveled to the monastery of Aghchots,[33] and after that to Holy Geghard,[34] where I stayed two nights. From there I journeyed to Garni where I spent one night. From there I went to Nork, where I also spent one night. From Nork[35] I went to Yerevan where I also passed one night.

I then traveled to Getargel.[36] The messengers of the Catholicos caught up with me there. He had two or three times sent men to seek me and to ask me to rush back to him. The first reason was that he missed me. The second was the arrival of the *nvirak* (legate) of Tokhat,[37] *Vardapet* Agheksandr and *Vardapet* Sargis, a student of the Patriarch of Constantinople, later known as the overseer of Caesarea.[38] The third was due to his illness. It seems the air that year was still and full of disease. The entire congregation of

---

29. Khor Virap of "Deep Pit," where according to tradition, King Trdat III imprisoned Gregory the Illuminator.

30. An old settlement on one of the slopes of Mt. Ararat in the Surmalu district in present-day Turkey.

31. The monastery of St. Hakob was on a slope of Mt. Ararat, not far from Akori.

32. The monastery is near Garni (present-day Abovian district in Armenia).

33. A monastery near Garni which was damaged in the 1679 earthquake.

34. A monastery located twenty-five miles from Yerevan. It was also called Ayrivank (Grotto Monastery).

35. Nork was a suburb of Yerevan located on the side of a hill also called Nork.

36. A monastery, currently in ruins, near the village of Dizak. Tradition has it that a small part of the Holy Lance was stored there.

37. Present-day Tokat in Turkey.

38. The capital of Cappadocia, present-day Kayseri in Turkey.

the Holy See was taken ill. The disease had spread and many in the village of Vagharshapat had died. Among them was *Vardapet* Sargis from Tekirdagh, *Vardapet* Zakaria from Baghesh, and a number of pilgrims. Avetis, a member of the Holy Council, other pilgrims, as well as many villagers became sick. Some patients were ill for a long time and were barely well by Easter 1735.[39]

After receiving the messengers and after reading the letter, I rushed back to Yerevan and on 4 November arrived at Etchmiadzin. Although I wished to visit Bchni,[40] Karenis,[41] and other monasteries, I cut my journey short, for the Catholicos had summoned me. I thus rushed to the Holy See to see His Holiness.

Chapter VI

ON MY ARRIVAL AT ETCHMIADZIN, THE ILLNESS OF THE CATHOLICOS, HIS DEATH AND BURIAL

I arrived at Etchmiadzin on Monday, 4 November, and found the Catholicos sick in bed. He had become ill two days before. During my visit I asked him the cause of the sickness and which part of his body was in pain. His Holiness responded, "My entire body aches. I do not know the cause of my fever."

Sad and confused, I tried to reassure and comfort him. Thus passed part of the night, until he told me three or four times, "Go and rest, you are weak and tired from your journey, you have just arrived." Thinking that he would be distressed and unhappy if I did not leave him, I got up and went to my room.

Day and night, until Sunday, we were all in a state of anxiety and confusion. On Sunday we all quietly sat around his deathbed with grief-stricken faces and glanced worriedly at each other. We stayed there that night until the hour of four or five after sunset. The lay brothers told me, "Go to your room. Let him rest for a while. Your grief distresses him." I got up and went to my cell. My spiritual son, *Vardapet* Hovhannes and Father Hakob stayed with

---

39. An unspecified epidemic killed the Supreme Patriarch, a number of clergymen, as well as some residents of Vagharshapat and Yerevan.

40. Bjni was the main center of the Pahlavuni clan and was a center of learning during the Middle Ages.

41. The previous name of the village of Gumush, located on the bank of the Hrazdan (Zangi) River, present-day Hrazdan region of Armenia.

His Holiness. They came to my cell after that night and said, "Go to His Holiness, he has a strange look and we are all worried."

I got up immediately, went to his side, and saw that he was near death. I begged him to bless us all and to grant us absolution. I sought his instructions regarding the Holy See, the members of the congregation, and his intimate companions. His Holiness speaking in a weak voice, or by moving his head made it clear that he understood my supplication.

Placing his right hand in my hands, he quietly and peacefully gave up his unblemished soul to the benevolent angel. It was like someone giving an apple from his bosom to another or to a beloved one. This occurred at nine or ten on the night of Monday, 11 November 1734.

At dawn we informed the melik of Yerevan, Paron Hakobjan, who sought the instructions of the governor of Yerevan, the *defter-dar*.[42] Ali Pasha the governor was sick and bedridden. As they came to ask his permission to bury His Holiness, the governor passed away during the hour of the morning prayer. His Holiness had died in the night and the pasha died that morning in Yerevan. The *kekhia* (*kadkoda*)[43] of Vagharshapat had, therefore, to order the burial of the Catholicos.

Hajji Husein Pasha, of Terent, was named governor the next day. He had been the *mafaz*[44] or guardian of Yerevan.

Melik Hakobjan arrived accompanied by one of the *chukha-tars*[45] of the pasha. On Tuesday, I, the unworthy, led the service and anointed the Catholicos with *meron* (Holy chrism). We buried him in the Church of St. Gayané.[46] I could not attend for I was stricken with fever and returned almost unconscious to bed.

The next day Wednesday, 14 November, I, together with the entire congregation of the Holy See went to the Church of St.

---

42. This title in this context refers to a commissary general of a province. The pasha was known as Defterdar Ali Pasha.

43. The *katkoda* was a respected and well-to-do elder of a community. He acted as the head of a village, quarter, district.

44. Actually the Arabic *muhafiz*, which translates as defender, guardian, commander, governor, or warden.

45. This Turkish term translates as "lackey."

46. The Church of St. Gayané was built in 630 AD by the order of Catholicos Ezr of Parazhnakert (630–641) on the site where, according to tradition, St. Gayané was martyred.

Gayané and conducted a memorial service, after which we returned to the monastery.

After that they took five or six *vardapets* and me by force to Yerevan. When we passed by the church where His Holiness was buried (St. Gayané),[47] we saw many citizens of Yerevan, Armenian men and women refugees who had fled from there. Seeing them we were filled with horror and felt helpless at their defenseless position. We wished to return to the monastery for we feared that the arrival of Persian troops would strand us in the Yerevan fortress. We begged the melik and the accompanying lackey, who was our former *mubashir,*[48] to let us leave. We thus reached Parakar[49] and rested for a while by a stream. I managed to gather five gold coins and gave them to him (lackey). After much begging we finally got rid of him and returned to the monastery.

---

47. The text has the church of the deceased (*hangutsyal*).

48. Arabic term meaning manager, supervisor, inspector, and in this case, superintendent.

49. A village in the suburbs of the Etchmiadzin region, presently on the Yerevan Etchmiadzin highway.

Stepanos Roshka

(1670–1739)

Stepanos Roshka was born in Kamenits, Poland, and received his early education there. In 1690 he went to Rome, and the following year he was accepted at the college De Propaganda Fide, an institution established by Pope Urban VIII to train priests for foreign missions. He graduated with a doctorate in philosophy and theology, and was ordained a Catholic priest. After a short visit to Constantinople, he returned to Poland and was assigned to various pastoral positions in the Armenian communities of Lemberg, Kamenits, and Stanislavov. He was very effective at establishing churches and promoting cultural activities. He had close ties with Khachatur Erzrumtsi (1666–1740), an erudite scholar and prolific author who was his fellow student in Rome.

Stepanos Roshka produced works on a variety of subjects, such as his *Kerakanutiun* (Grammar, 1718), *Tramabanutiun* (Logic), *Baroyakan astvatzabanutiun* (Moral theology, 1725), *Kensagrutiun hayots yepiskoposats i lehs* (Biographies of Armenian bishops in Poland), and *Zhamanakagrutiun kam tarekank yekeghetsakank* (Chronicle, or ecclesiastical annals, 1739). He also compiled a dictionary in two parts, Armenian-Latin and Latin-Armenian, which he called *Gandz lezvin hayots kam bararan Stepanian* (A treasury of the Armenian language, or Stepanos's dictionary).[1]

---

1. For a critical analysis of this dictionary see Mesrop Chanashian, *Bazmavep* (Polyhistor) 113 (1955): 129–38, 185–91, 249–55.

Most of the works of Stepanos Roshka, including the dictionary, remain unpublished. The only published work (1964) is the *Chronicle,*

> a record of the Roman Catholic Church, with a brief, complementary, and concurrent history from a Catholic point of view, including the chronology of the Armenian "heretics," namely the Church of Armenia. It begins with the birth of Christ and concludes with the year 1739. The format records the year, the reigning pope, emperor (Roman, Holy Roman, etc.), head of the Armenian Church, and Armenian king, followed by pertinent ecclesiastical-religious and political information. There is much on the Armenians of Poland. . . . His entries expand as he deals with events closer to his own time.[2]

FROM CHRONICLE, OR ECCLESIASTICAL ANNALS[3]

Sanatruk, King of Armenia, did nothing worth remembering other than renovating Nisibin, which had been greatly damaged by an earthquake. He razed the town and rebuilt its fortifications with splendid ramparts, and inside them he placed a statue of himself holding money in one hand, to indicate that he had spent his entire treasury to rebuild the city. After a reign of thirty years, he died on a deer hunt when he was shot with an arrow in the abdomen, perhaps in revenge for the tortures his daughter, St. Sandukht, had undergone. A great many legendary tales have been told about his upbringing and also that he was named Sanatruk after Sanot, his nurse (Khorenatsi, 189).

After a short period of instability, Yervand acceded to the throne of Armenia in the eighth year of the reign of Darius, king of Persia. Yervand's mother, who was a descendant of the Arsacids, was a vigorous and coarse-featured woman who refused to marry anybody, and she bore two illegitimate sons: Yervand and Yervaz. Yervand was a courageous, robust youth, and Sanatruk, who greatly appreciated his many praiseworthy deeds, made him an

---

2. Kevork B. Bardakjian, *A Reference Guide to Modern Armenian Literature, 1500–1920* (Detroit, 2000), 90.

3. Stepanos Roshka, *Zhamanakagrutiun kam tarekank yekeghetsakank* (Chronicle, or ecclesiastical annals)(Vienna, 1964), 11–16. Translated by Arminé Kuechguerian and edited by the editors of the present anthology.

overseer. He became the first satrap of the entire Armenian army, and his humility and the boundless generosity he exhibited gained him the sympathy of all, until finally he became king. After Sanatruk's death, however, Yervand killed Sanatruk's sons on suspicion of treason, perhaps in revenge for the assassination of Abgar's sons; but one of Sanatruk's sons, Artashes, escaped the slaughter through the efforts of his nurse, who took him to the province of Her, where they found refuge in a community of shepherds, and they sent news of their whereabouts to Smbat, the child's tutor (Khor. 191).

The second year of Yervand's reign

When Smbat, the son of Biurat Bagratuni, heard about the death of Sanatruk and the massacre of his sons, he took his two daughters to the fortress of Bayberd and, leaving them in safety there, he went in search of Artashes, taking with him only his wife and a few of his men. When King Yervand learned of this, he sent spies after them, but they were unable to find any trace of him. Meanwhile Smbat, who had found the child and wandered with him through the mountain country and the fields, continued to hide in the shepherd community. At last, at an opportune moment, he took Artashes to Darius, king of Persia. The Persian generals were very well acquainted with Smbat as a brave and valiant soldier, so he was received as a highly respected guest at the king's court, and all due attention and honors were paid to Artashes, as befitting the son of a king (Khor. 191–92; also see 76).

The fifth year of Yervand's reign

The apostle Bartholomew, who had preached the doctrine of Christ in India, came to Armenia and converted many to the faith of Christ, for which reason he was skinned alive. . . . [O]n August 25 his body was decapitated by order of the king and taken first to Libar, then to Penevent, and later to Rome. This took place in the town of Arevbenos (Khor. 185; Briet. 71n.).

The tenth year of Yervand's reign

Now when Yervand, King of Armenia, heard that Smbat had taken Sanatruk's son to Darius, king of Persia, and that he was being received with honor there, he was sorely grieved, imagining the malice against himself that might be stirred up in the Persian court. Accordingly he sent presents to Darius, asking to send him the child, who, he claimed, was the son not of Sanatruk but of a shepherd. He sent a similar message to Smbat. When he did not receive an answer that pleased him, Yervand grew furious and ordered that the guards in Bayberd be slain. He took Smbat's daughters captive and confined them in the fortress of Ani.

In order to forestall further danger, Yervand ceded Mesopotamia to Vespasian and Titus, thus entering into an alliance with the Romans. That is when the Armenians lost their sovereignty over Mesopotamia, and the tribute that Yervand had to pay increased greatly (Khor. 193–94).

The eleventh year of Yervand

The Roman officers completely equipped the town of Edesa, establishing treasuries and places to keep the tribute paid by Armenia, Assyria, and Mesopotamia. There they built an archive and opened schools, one for the Assyrians and another for the Greeks; they also transferred there the archives of the tributes and of the temples, which had been kept in Sinop of Pontus (Khor. 194).

The twelfth year of Yervand[4]

By that time, Yervand had transferred his court to the hill of Armavir, which was a safer place, and fortified its citadel with high ramparts. He erected copper doors inside the walls and hidden traps under the stairs, which operated differently depending on whether one went and came by day or by night, so that he might be safe from unwanted intruders and impostors. Later, he transferred all the temples of Armavir to a new city that he had founded by the River Akhurian, some forty stades (*asparez*) from Armavir, and had named Bagaran, which means "place of altars"; he appointed his brother, Yervaz, high priest over them (Khor. 195, 196).

The fifteenth year of Yervand

King Yervand of Armenia planted a huge fir tree by the River Akhurian, surrounded it with walls, and filled the enclosure with

---

4. The manuscript has two sections titled "The twelfth year of Yervand" between the eleventh year and the thirteenth year; this is the second of those sections.

wild goats, various kinds of stags, hinds, wild asses, and wild boars, and he delighted to spend his time hunting them. He also constructed a beautiful city with elegant structures and splendid buildings, and he named it Yervandakert, after himself. He and a great many other people resided in the center of the valley, and he adorned the surroundings with gardens of fragrant flowers and vineyards that were praiseworthy indeed, for royal revels (Khor. 197).

The eighteenth year of Yervand

When Artashes the son of Sanatruk, who was being educated in Persia, reached the age of twenty, the Persian noblemen entreated their king to place him on the throne of Armenia because he was a kinsman of Smbat Bagratuni, who had performed great deeds of heroism and bravery. Darius consented, and put Smbat in command of some troops from Assyria and Atropatene charging them with the task of restoring Artashes to his father's throne (Khor. 199).

The nineteenth year of Yervand

When Yervand, who was then in the region of Uti, received the news that the king of Persia had placed so many troops under Smbat's command for the purpose of restoring Artashes to his kingdom, he left many of his governor-satraps there and hurried to his own city in order to assemble troops from Armenia, Georgia, Caesarea, and Mesopotamia. He pleaded with, presented gifts to, and bestowed honors upon the *nakharars* and enticed the soldiers with gifts. Since it was springtime, the army gathered quite rapidly. Argam Muratsian also arrived before long with an army of infantry. When Smbat and Artashes rapidly advanced to the frontiers of Uti, the soldiers and dignitaries whom Yervand had left there as guards came out to meet them. When, in turn, the other Armenian *nakharars* heard this, they also considered deserting Yervand, for they saw that the Roman army had not come to their help. Yervand, meanwhile, continued to distribute presents, but the more he gave the more he was despised, because it was understood that he was squandering his money only out of fear (Khor. 200).

The twentieth year of Yervand

Once in Armenia, Smbat Bagratuni and Artashes hurried to reach Yervand's army. Smbat had high regard only for Prince Argam Muratsian, who was a brave soldier and had many lancers under his command. Artashes appealed to him, promising, through his ambassador, that if he left Yervand he would receive whatever was taken from Yervand and even more. Argam followed this counsel, and Smbat, whom the other *nakharars* had already joined, defeated Yervand's army in a fierce battle. Yervand barely escaped death, and fled to his own city. The brave Smbat followed him, reached the gate of the city during the night, and kept it under guard until Artashes arrived with all his troops. A fight ensued, ending with the surrender of the townsfolk. When they had entered the city, one of the soldiers cut Yervand's head off with his sword, scattering his brains, and so Yervand died, after a reign of twenty years. Bearing in mind that Yervand was an Arsacid, Artashes ordered that he be buried in a tomb and that a monument be erected over his resting place.

The first year of Artashes of Armenia

Artashes, son of Sanatruk, was crowned king, acceding to his father's throne at the age of twenty-two, in the twenty-ninth year of Darius's reign. He sent the Persian and Median troops back to their homelands, having lavishly rewarded them with gifts. To Argam Muratsian he granted, as he had promised, the rank of lieutenant, as well as a crown adorned with hyacinths, earrings for both ears, a red boot for one foot, and the right to eat with a golden spoon and fork and drink from a goblet of the same metal. To Smbat, his tutor, he granted, in addition to the two earrings and the red boot, the privilege of crowning the king, a knighthood, and command of the western army, entrusting him with all Armenian troops, and many other things, of which you may read (Khor. B. 44, 47).

Artashes ordered Smbat to go to Bagaran and kill Yervand's brother, Yervaz, the high priest. Smbat carried out the order by casting Yervaz into a whirlpool in the river, and he appointed a man named Mokapasht, who was friendly to Artashes, in his place. Then, Smbat seized the treasures and the five hundred servants of

Yervaz, as well as the treasures of the temples, and brought them all to Artashes. Artashes gave the servants to Smbat and ordered that the treasures, with some additions from his own treasury, be taken to Darius as a sign of gratitude. In this way he honored him as a father and as a supporter. It was Smbat who carried all these offerings to King Darius in Persia (Khor. 208 and 88, and, for the departure, 90).

The third year of Artashes

While Smbat was in Persia, the tax-collectors of the Roman emperor arrived in Armenia with a great army. Artashes appeased them with his pleas and made peace by paying double the amount of the tribute. Later, he went to the place where the Yeraskh and Mamor rivers merge, and built a city there, which he called Artashat, after himself. He raised a temple, transferred all the idols from Bagaran there, and furnished the city with Jewish slaves. He adorned Artashat with all the luxury, elegance, and splendor of Yervand's city and made it his place of residence and the capital of Armenia (Khor. 209, 210; the Latins call the town Artakasta).

The fourth year of Artashes

By that time the Alans, together with the people who lived in their mountains and a few Georgians, were making incursions into Armenia. Artashes rode against them with his troops, and a war ensued, with the rival armies encamped on opposite banks of the river. When the Armenians captured the son of the Alan king and brought him to Artashes, the father asked that his son be released, promising to give Artashes whatever he wanted and to establish an everlasting alliance and peace, with oaths that the Alans would never again sack Armenia. When Artashes did not agree to return the king's son, his sister, Satenik, came and stood on a promontory on the opposite bank of the river, from which she addressed the Armenian king in the following words: "Oh valiant Artashes, come, trust me: hear my words and return the youth. For it is not just, for the sake of a mere grudge, to destroy families of royal blood and establish perpetual enmity between two nations." Artashes was moved by the girl's clever speech, made peace with the Alans, and married Satenik. She was first among the wives of

Artashes, and gave birth to Artavazd and many others. At their wedding gold coins were handed out in front of the temple and pearls were scattered around, something the birds sang about (and even now, that is, in 1738, the Armenians of Bughtan still sing those songs at wedding feasts) (Khor. 211, etc.).

Paghtasar Dpir

(1683–1768)

Paghtasar Dpir was born in Constantinople. As a poet, musician, educator, and social activist, he became a leading figure of the pre-revival era. He was educated in local schools and continued his studies with Bishop Astvatzatur Jughayetsi, legate of the catholicos of Etchmiadzin. In 1741 he was appointed headmaster of the secular school of the Armenian Patriarchate, founded by Patriarch Hakob Nalian. A number of noted writers and leaders were among his students, including the future Catholicos Simeon Yerevantsi and the poet Petros Ghapantsi.

Paghtasar Dpir, along with Naghash Hovnatan (1661–1722), occupies a prominent place among the late medieval poet-musicians by virtue of his efforts to simplify the literary language without resorting to the vernacular. He introduced the themes of freedom and liberalism into poetry, dwelling not merely on the theme of love, as the ancient bards (*ashughs*) used to do, but also treating social, national, religious, and moral issues. For the melodies of his love songs he chose traditional oriental and Armenian tunes. His *Tagharan pokrik* (A small book of odes, 1723) has gone through seven editions, with successive revisions and additions. One of his famous odes, *I nnjmaned arkayakan zartir* (Arise from your royal slumber) is a love song, but it can also be interpreted allegorically as a message to his people to awaken from their torpor and resist foreign domination.

His educational and historical output is imposing. Some of his most important works in these areas are: *Parzabanutiun kerakanutian karcharot yev diurimats* (A simplified grammar, concise and easy to understand, 1736) in two volumes, a grammar of classical Armenian written in that language; *Girk kerakanutian* (A grammar book, 1760), a grammar of classical Armenian written in modern Armenian; *Hamarot meknabanutiun tramabanutiun* (Concise commentary on logic, 1822); *Zhamanakagrutiun* (Chronology, 1951); and *Hamarotutiun patmutyan Movses Khorenatzvo* (Summary of Movses Khorenatsi's history). In the 1760s he published a series of textbooks for teaching the Armenian language; they have been used by many generations of students.

Paghtasar Dpir also contributed to Armenian printing in Constantinople. Under his supervision the works of a number of classical writers —such as Zenob Glak, Arakel Siunetsi, Grigor Narekatsi, Simeon Jughayetsi, Grigor Tatevatsi, and David Anhaght—were published there.

Money[1]

Where did you come from, Oppressor?
Nothing else like you has come along.
Without the touch of your hand
no one becomes happy or strong.

Kings and caesars lust
for the strength you wield.
Without you they remain powerless
as cattle in the field.

You deal in evil but men crave
to stay your middlemen,
unwittingly do good,
while you steal their souls from them.

Willingly, lovingly, men bind
themselves with your chains.

---

1. Diana Der Hovanessian and Marzbed Margossian, eds. and trans., *Anthology of Armenian Poetry* (New York, 1978), 104–5. Final poetic versions of this and all poems in the book are by Diana Der Hovanessian (*Anthology of Armenian Poetry*), vii.

No matter how much rope you toss
they agree to be enmeshed with more.

Should someone undo your cords,
you lead him into war,
to wound himself or other men
with your gift, the sword.

SONG[2]

From your royal sleep, wake,
Wake, my gracious one, wake,
The sun has come and reaches out,
Wake, my gracious one, wake.

Lovely picture, oval vision,
Perfect as the full moon—
No one can be found who equals you,
Wake, my gracious one, wake.

The very sight of you possesses me,
Bewitches me, makes me your slave;
And lest you burn beneath the sun,
Wake, my gracious one, wake.

Heartbroken, how long must I cry,
O rose, O unfading red rose?
Only see how pitiful I am,
Wake, my gracious one, wake.

Hot and evil winds swept down,
To burn your tender leaves,
But the dark night has passed now—
Wake, my gracious one, wake.

My noble love is peerless,
Her ring the most precious jewel;
In this year 1708,
Wake, my gracious one, wake.

---

2. Aram Tolegian, ed. and trans., *Armenian Poetry Old and New* (Detroit, 1979), 93.

Abraham Yerevantsi

(Abraham of Yerevan)

(Eighteenth century)

Very little is known about the life of the historian Abraham Yerevantsi. His only known work is *Patmutiun paterazmatsn vor yeghev hosmantsvots i vera kaghakatsn hayastanyayts yev parsits* (History of the wars fought by the Ottomans over Armenian and Persian cities), which relates the events between 1721 and 1736, from the Afghan invasion of Persia to the coronation of Nadir Shah at Mughan, including all the details of the Turko-Persian war. Of particular importance is the second chapter, an eyewitness account of the heroic resistance mounted by the inhabitants of Yerevan against the Ottoman invaders in 1724. It also contains interesting information about the city of Yerevan itself. His accurate description of military preparations and operations indicates that Abraham Yerevantsi had a clear understanding of the art of warfare, and his brilliant style suggests that he was a well educated man.

The original manuscript of *History of the Wars* is preserved in the library of the Mkhitarist Congregation in Venice. It was published in Yerevan in 1938, followed by a Russian translation in 1939.

FROM HISTORY OF THE WARS[1]

I

INITIATED BY THE OTTOMANS TO SEIZE ARMENIAN AND PERSIAN TOWNS FOLLOWING THE CAMPAIGN OF SULTAN MAHMUD AFGHAN[2] AGAINST THE PERSIAN KING, SHAH SOLTAN HOSEIN[3]

Chapter One is about how Shah Tahmasp,[4] the son of the Persian King Hosein, undertook to regain his father's throne which was usurped by the Afghans, and how the town of Tiflis, after being devastated by the Lesghian Tatars,[5] fell to the Ottomans.

II

THE SIEGE OF THE TOWN OF KARBI AND DEVELOPMENTS IN ETCHMIADZIN

Having seized Tiflis on 26 December of the year 1172 of the Armenian calendar (1723), the Ottomans secured their position there. Saru Mustafa Pasha was then told that the Afghan leader, having captured the city of Isfahan, had moved on to Hamadan and was planning to attack Transcaucasia. Saru Mustafa Pasha sent a message to Sultan Ahmet warning him that, "The Afghan is preparing to march on Yerevan and if he succeeds in taking it he would then easily attack Tiflis and take it away from us." Learning this, the Sultan appointed Abdullah Pasha, who was a member of the Köprülü family, as commander-in-chief and dispatched him with a 75,000-man army to Yerevan.

Abdullah Pasha took the field and reached Erzurum, where he stayed for a month, since it was winter. On 7 February he began to prepare his advance on Yerevan. On 6 March 1173 (1724)

---

1. Abraham Yerevantsi, *Patmutiun paterazmatsn* (History of the Wars), in George A. Bournoutian, annotated trans. from the original eighteenth-century texts with introductory notes, *History of the Wars, 1721–1738* (Abraham Yerevantsi's *Patmutiun paterazmatsn*) (Costa Mesa, Calif., 1999), 11–27. All footnotes are by Bournoutian.

2. Mahmud (d. 1725) was the elder son of Mir-Vais, chief of the Ghalzai Afghans. After murdering his uncle he took over the tribe and invaded Persia in 1719 and again in 1721.

3. Safavid Shah (1696–1722).

4. Safavid Shah (1722–32) known as Tahmasp II, hereinafter Tahmasp.

5. Muslim tribesmen in southern Daghestan (also "Lesghian").

his army reached the river that the local people call Arpa Çay.[6] He dispatched two of his military commanders, one of whom was called Yalguz Hasan, a citizen of Erzurum, and the other, Güç[7] Ali, to cross the Arpa Çay. Each had approximately 1,800 men. When they reached a place called Yeghvard,[8] the commander of Yerevan, who was called Mehr Ali Khan,[9] was informed of their presence and marched against them with 12,000 men. The antagonists clashed against each other and both sides left many wounded on the field. The Ottomans overcame and slaughtered more than 11,000 Persian troops. Only 800 men were left. The Persians took flight and together with their commander sought refuge in Yerevan, where they fortified themselves and did not venture out again.

Güç Ali and Yalguz Hasan advanced and laid siege to the town of Karbi,[10] which was located near Yerevan, with plans to plunder it and enslave its Armenian population. The citizens of Karbi, seeing the enemy, were seized with terror and began to worry about their sons and daughters. The men of Karbi, therefore, fortified their settlement, the walls, and their gates and planned to resist the Ottomans. Those among them who were believers prayed to God to spare them and not to subject their sons and daughters to death or captivity. The elders of Karbi, among them the Paron Aqa Baba and Paron Stepan, conferred amongst themselves and decided to send a man to the Khan of Yerevan with the following message: "The Ottoman army has arrived and has laid siege to Karbi. If you are willing to send troops we are ready to defend our town with our lives. We shall attack the enemy and shall drive them out." The Khan of Yerevan, however, did not respond to their request and did not send any troops. The citizens of Karbi did not think of sending someone to the Ottomans to offer their submission. Instead, they hurriedly began to fortify their homes and to close the entrance and passageways into their settlement, giving the impression that they were prepared to give battle.

---

6. That is, the Akhuryan River, which was one of the borders (agreed upon in 1639) between Persia and Ottoman Empire.

7. A variation of the Turkish term *güç*, meaning "strength."

8. A village in the Ashtarak region, the site of two major battles fought between the Persians and the Ottomans.

9. The Khan of Yerevan from 1719 to 1724.

10. A settlement in Ashtarak region.

They remained in this guarded condition and resisted the Turks for forty days until Abdullah Pasha, who was the commander-in-chief of the entire Ottoman force, arrived with his large army. The citizens of Karbi still hoped that the governor of Yerevan would send troops to defend them, not realizing that he was totally helpless and needed every soldier to defend his citadel. It was God's will that Abdullah Pasha did not immediately attack Karbi to destroy it. Instead, he sent envoys with a proposal of peace, stating, "You were our subjects in the past, why have you now risen against us? Why do you fight for a State that does not belong to you and put your settlement in risk of death and captivity? Return to your former citizenship and I shall not only order my troops not to harm you, but will leave a detachment of troops to protect you." Paron Mkrtum and Paron Poghos were filled with doubt, fear and hope. They began to confer among themselves. Paron Manuk, son of Hovhannes, asked, "What if after such promises the Pasha goes against his word and enslaves us, our wives, and our children?" Paron Aqa Baba, Paron Sargis, Paron Avak, Paron Mkrtum, and Paron Poghos said, "We should surrender Karbi to the Ottomans, for we lack the forces to resist such a large army and no help has arrived." They thus agreed to give the following answer: "Give us ten days' time to convince all our subjects to submit." The Pasha conceded to their honest request, for he had no intention of destroying the village and depopulating the land.

In the meantime, the elders of the village secretly sent a man to the governor of Yerevan, Mehr Ali, with the following message: "Besieged by the Ottoman forces, we had to give our word to the Turkish commander that we would surrender Karbi in ten days, for we cannot withstand such a large army. Tell us what to do?" Mehr Ali did not accept this and ordered that they fight bravely and not surrender. He promised to send them gunpowder and small cannons. To further inspire them he added, "Your Catholicos, Astvatzatur,[11] has gone to see Shah Tahmasp to seek advice on this dangerous conflict which is upon us. Have patience, therefore, until we hear some news of assistance from them."

It was true that the Armenian Catholicos, Astvatzatur, was summoned by Shah Tahmasp and had gone to see him, but the

---

11. Astvatzatur of Hamadan (1715–25).

mentioning of this supposedly reassuring fact by the godless governor of Yerevan was totally useless and senseless. This wretched man was leading them to slaughter. He was a man of a different race and an unbeliever. He did not care if our Christian people were subjected to death and captivity. For if he was of the same faith and blood and was a true guardian of his subjects, why would he lead them like sheep to slaughter? For how could one equate a village that lacked fortifications and soldiers to the large army which surrounded it, even though the village had many men who could fight as soldiers?

The elders of the settlement, after conferring among themselves, rightly disregarded the words of the governor of Yerevan and rather than being enslaved decided to submit to the Ottomans. After the ten days had elapsed, the Ottomans sent word stating, "Prepare to submit and surrender your arms." The Armenians prepared gifts of gold, silver, and precious stones for Abdullah Pasha. On the appointed day they sent Paron Aqa Baba, Paron Sargis, Paron Avak, and Paron Poghos, whom they had elected as envoys. They were admitted to the presence of the Pasha who asked, "How many citizens are in your village?" Aqa Baba responded, "There are some 6,000 souls." The Pasha then said, "If you are truly to become our subjects, remove all weapons from the home of every person and give them to us." They agreed to fulfill that command. The Pasha sent a detachment of troops with Aqa Baba. They entered the village and took the swords and guns of every defender. The Pasha then ordered that Paron Aqa Baba, Paron Poghos, and three or four other notables be given *kalats*[12] and be escorted back to Karbi. The Pasha ordered six companies of troops to safeguard the village, while he himself marched on Yerevan.

III

THE SIEGE OF YEREVAN AND THE RESISTENCE OF ITS POPULACE: HOW THE ARMENIANS BRAVELY FOUGHT OUTSIDE THE CITADEL AND ROUTED THE OTTOMANS

Abdullah Pasha moved from the plain of Yeghvard and three days later reached Yerevan. His army camped at a site called Sambek Dalma, which was half an hour's distance from Yerevan, and

---

12. A robe of honor made of expensive material.

was named after a water canal (Dalman) located in the vicinity. All those who lived in the villages and farms around Yerevan fled and took refuge in the city.

After seven days of positioning his troops around Yerevan, the Pasha decided to march to Etchmiadzin. A decree, however, arrived from the Ottoman Sultan in which he ordered the Pasha not to attack Etchmiadzin. Instead, he ordered the Pasha to place some of his troops to guard it and not to allow anyone to damage it. No one was to loot it or to harm anyone residing in Etchmiadzin. The Catholicos of the Armenians. Astvatzatur, was not in Etchmiatzin at that time for he had gone to see Shah Tahmasp in Tabriz.

This occurred as a result of God's grace. For when the Ottoman army invaded Armenia, a pious Armenian notable called Seghbos, a most distinguished Armenian in Constantinople, who was an influential man and who held the rank of purveyor in the Sultan's court, interceded on behalf of Etchmiadzin. The Sultan cared for the Armenian people, and in the interest of the State, gave the order to the Pasha to protect Holy Etchmiadzin and to forbid his soldiers to invade that holy place. The Pasha, following the Sultan's decree, forbade his troops to attack Etchmiadzin and appointed a detachment of soldiers to guard it.

When Abdullah Pasha marched forward with the intention of taking the fortress of Yerevan, he sent delegates beforehand to discuss conditions for the peaceful surrender of the fortress. The governor of Yerevan, who was called Mehr Ali, replied, "We shall submit your offer to our Shah and if he approves we shall surrender the fortress to you. If not, we cannot give it up on our own." When the Pasha realized that the city would not surrender he prepared for war.

The Pasha brought his army forth and prepared the siege of Yerevan. The next day he approached the fortress. He placed twelve cannons in the direction of the All Savior monastery, twenty-nine cannons near St. Madr,[13] and seven cannons on top of the three hills across the river, thus surrounding and bombarding Yerevan from four locations.

Mehr Ali then ordered the Muslims (Turks) to join the Armenians and give battle. They fought against the Ottomans for

---

13. Persian for "mother"; refers to the Monastery of St. Anne (the Mother of Virgin Mary).

sixty days, killed many of the assailants, and did not allow them to enter the city. When Abdullah Pasha saw that his army was being slaughtered, he sent envoys to Bayazit and the Kurds to ask assistance. Thirty-five thousand armed men arrived, but even with their help he could not conquer Yerevan.

When the Pasha witnessed the firm resolve of the citizens of Yerevan and his own casualties, he decided not to continue the battle. He sent a message to the Sultan stating, "Yerevan has too many defenders and I cannot take it." The latter arrived with 10,000 armed men and camped near the city.

Three days later the two Pashas joined forces and after conferring, decided not to delay, but to move forward. At sunrise on a Thursday they prepared the army for an assault on Yerevan. A large river called Zengi[14] lies before the city, and when the Ottoman hordes began to cross it, the width of the river was covered with such a multitude that the water was not visible and it appeared as if the river had dried out. Although the Ottomans had crossed the river, they could not proceed much further, for the defenders of Yerevan attacked them. These were the Armenians, who fought them for half a day, for the Persians and the governor of the city had fled into the citadel and had left the Armenians to do battle in town. Two thousand Christians fell to the sword on that day. The Armenian commanders were the following: Hovhannes Hundibekian, Poghos Kijibekian, Hovhannes Karjik, and Davit Mirzejanian.

There was a certain *vardapet*[15] in Yerevan, called Grigor. He went to the St. Sargis Church,[16] which was located in the neighborhood called Dzoragegh. He summoned and gathered a crowd of Armenians. At the first hour of the night the citizens sought the advice of the *vardapet* and asked, "What are we to do? Tomorrow the Ottomans will kill all of us and will take our wives and children into captivity." In Yerevan, in the district called Kond, there lived some one hundred households of Christian *Boshas*.[17] They were wealthy, brave, and had armed men. Their leaders at that time were Paron Ghazaros Baburian, Paron Klduz, Paron Davit, Paron Beyram,

---

14. Present-day Hrazdan River.

15. Armenian celibate priests, who have graduated from a seminary, equal to archimandrites in the Orthodox Church.

16. Also known as Hovhannavank.

17. The Armenian gypsies were called *bosha*. Some one hundred households lived in Yerevan as late as the nineteenth century.

and Paron Petros. They and their men came to *Vardapet* Grigor. The Armenians, along with the *vardapet*, were in tears and begged the armed men to save them, their wives and their children from those who had besieged the town and were preparing to loot it. Ghazaros said the following to Grigor: "*Vardapet!* I have two hundred brave young men. They are armed and capable of fighting with swords and guns. I shall gather them and shall fight with all my ability." Hovhannes Hundibekian of Dzoragegh began to gather men as well. Other Armenian notables followed his lead and promised to resist with their followers. These were Paron Pirigul, Paron Arzumbek, Paron Tadevos, Paron Mghum, Paron Mkrtich, Paron Malkhas, Paron Alexan, Paron Agham, Paron Galust, Paron Aghazadé, Paron Nuri, Paron Zohrab, Paron Nikoghayos, Paron Avetis Srapionian, and Paron Yeram.

The Armenians gathered that night, conferred, and prepared their defenses against the Ottomans. At daybreak God's mercy spared them, for it was Friday and the Ottomans did not attack. The Armenians gathered brave young men from the various villages around Yerevan: from Parakar, Gök-Gumbed, Kanaker, Arinj, Avan, Gavan, Tzak, and Noragegh. Nine thousand armed troops, that is, all the able-bodied men from the above villages, gathered outside Yerevan to do battle. Young Armenians from the district called Old Yerevan came around under the command of their chiefs, Nikoghos, Andon son of Maryam, Butik son of Khatun, and the priest Ter-Movses. On Saturday morning, Bosha Ghazaros, Bosha Klduz and Bosha Davit Bedik came to Dzoragegh with 234 men. *Vardapet* Grigor ordered them to hold the road leading to the Forty Mills. The men from Dzoragegh, three thousand strong, armed with swords or guns were to defend Tzak. The men from Kond were to defend the road to the Tappakhana district. Nine hundred fifty-five men from the Juhair neighborhood, with swords and guns, under the command of Ter-Movses, guarded the Darbinots road. Four thousand men from Old Yerevan were under the command of three men: Pahlavan Nikoghos, who was a horseshoe maker, Andon son of Maryam, and Butik son of Khatun. There were a total of 9,423 men with guns and swords, who were capable of fighting. The rest, some 28,000, were not trained. They stayed to guard their homes.

All of them left their wives, children, and those men who were unfit to fight and gathered with their commanders in a suburb of

Yerevan that was called Dzoragegh. They were ready to battle for their own sake and that of their wives and their children. They placed detachments in different parts of the city with instructions to block the entrance to Yerevan. They waited in readiness to give battle should the enemy manage to enter the city and, if not, to hold their positions.

The Ottomans surrounded the city on four sides. Dense gardens, orchards, and numerous ancient willow trees, which had been planted a long time ago for the defenses of the town, surrounded the city. Behind the tree line flowed the big Zangi River. Because of this the Ottomans were afraid to move on Yerevan, for they could not operate their guns because of the trees. They therefore set up their positions across the river and opened fire on the city. They sought a way to advance and occasionally they managed to move forward, but only in the direction of Dzoragegh, which had no gardens or trees and from where they attacked the town.

The governor of Yerevan and all the notables were in the citadel and fought using their cannons. However, when the Ottomans came near the city, the cannons of the citadel were useless, for cannons fired from a height cannot hit the enemy if he is too near, but are effective only if he is located a certain distance away. The governor of Yerevan, Mehr Ali Khan, had taken twelve Armenian families with him into the citadel. The most important individuals were Melik Sahak, who was the son of Melik Aqamal, and his brother Aqa-Veli, Paron Karapet, Mikayel Barkhudarian, Babajan Motsakian, and other notables. The lesser nobles remained outside and prepared to fight. Harutiun, the son of Yesaman, was sent as envoy to the Pasha. When Harutiun, the Armenian, crossed the Zangi, the Ottoman janissaries killed him.

The Armenians then prepared for renewed attacks. Meanwhile, 3,000 Egyptian troops came to the aid of the Ottomans. They pitched camp near the villages defended by the Armenians. Being more courageous than the Turks, the Egyptians, ignoring discipline and without the permission of the commander-in-chief, Abdullah Pasha, attacked the wild beasts with the intention of breaking into Yerevan from Dzoragegh. Many Turks followed their lead and moved *en masse* without formation. They thought that they alone would be able to achieve victory, gain glory, and at the same time be among the first to take booty and to accomplish their evil deeds. When the attack on the Dzoragegh district commenced, the defenders could not hold and retreated to the Forty Mills district. News of this reached the Armenian gypsies, who were guarding other districts. They were afraid to move, but *Vardapet* Grigor shed tears and begged them to aid the defenders. Finally, 234 Armenian gypsy warriors rushed to defend the road leading to the Forty Mills. They attacked with swords and guns and with God's help managed to defeat the enemy and kill 6,000. The rest fled across the Zangi, for the Christians held the high ground and the enemy the low ground. The Christians, however, also lost some 1,300 men that day. Witnessing the disorganized behavior of the Egyptians, Abdullah Pasha was extremely incensed and ordered that no one attack without his express order.

Hovhannes Kamenatsi

(John of Kamen)

(Eighteenth century)

The eighteenth-century Armenian historian Hovhannes Kamenatsi lived and worked in Kamenets-Podol'skiy.[1] His major work, written in *grabar* (classical Armenian) at the suggestion of his father, is *Patmutiun paterazmin Khotinu, i zhamanaks sultan Osmanin tachkats, yev i katoghiko-sutyan Hayots Melkisedi srpo Etcmiadzni* (History of the war of Khotin in the time of the Turkish sultan Osman, during the patriarchate of Melkised, the Armenian catholicos of holy Etchmiadzin). This work is an excellent source for information on the victory of Polish-Ukrainian soldiers over Turkish invaders near the city of Khotin[2] in 1621, and on the eventual peace treaty. The book also contains source material, in Polish and other languages, concerning the battle. It consists of an introduction and eighteen chapters and colophons. The last chapter describes the assassination of Sultan Osman II[3] in Constantinople in 1622. Some parts of the work are based on personal experience and on what the author has himself heard from others.

---

1. In present-day Ukraine.
2. In present-day Ukraine.
3. Ottoman sultan 1604–22.

The manuscript (the third copy)[4] was discovered in the St. Mesrop Mashtots Matenadaran library in Yerevan in 1953. It was published for the first time in Russian in 1958, and with the original manuscript in 1964.

It is unfortunate that there is little biographical information about Hovhannes Kamenatsi.

FROM HISTORY OF THE WAR OF KHOTIN, IN THE TIME OF THE TURKISH SULTAN OSMAN, DURING THE PATRIARCHATE OF MELCHIZEDEK, THE ARMENIAN CATHOLICOS OF HOLY ETCHMIADZIN[5]

Chapter I

AN ACCOUNT OF THE DESPOTISM OF THE ISMAELITES AND OF SULTAN OSMAN'S INTENTION TO ATTACK POLAND, FORGETTING HIS VOW TO KEEP THE PEACE

After Sarah had expelled her maidservant Hagar,[6] when the barbarous Saracens became stronger, they settled down and increased greatly in number, appropriating everything to the right and to the left of them, according to the truthfully related account of Holy Scripture, subjugating the principal part of the universe and many territories of the world's population and making them their tributaries.

They rapidly subjugated the land of Ararat, both Greater and Lesser Armenia, ancient Babylonia and Egypt, Damascus and Palestine, Georgia and Albania,[7] and many others (of which to speak now would lengthen my report), especially the entire territory of the Greeks and the country of the invincible Byzantine

---

4. Manuscript 2644.

5. Hovhannes Kamenatsi, *Patmutiun paterazmin Khotinu* (The history of the war of Khotin) (Yerevan, 1964), 34–38. Translated by Arminé Keuchguerian and edited by the editors of the present anthology.

6. See Gen. 16. Hagar was the mother of Ishmael, through whom, in Muslim tradition, the Arabs trace their ancestry back to Abraham.

7. Aghvank in Armenian; also known as Caucasian Albanians.

emperors. And thus all the Christians were removed from power, many being deceived by the perverted faith of the diabolic and iniquitous Mohammed; some were seduced with fraudulent promises, others with threats or menace, and thus the prediction of the prophet who lamented over Israel was fulfilled: "The heathen are come into thine inheritance; thy holy temple they have defiled," etc.[8] But why do I spend so much time stating what many authors have already predicted? I believe that this was the practice of all of our past historians, who handed everything down to us with three-dimensional precision and willingly passed the story of the present age to future generations. This is what I humbly propose to do here.

Of course, this work is not intended to serve the interests of the heathens, but instead to inspire people with hope and faith in their vigor and with strength in their defeat, because the wicked people of Ismael have not yet curtailed their pillage of the country and, having conquered the universe, they continue to boast haughtily and growl greedily like savage beasts.

One of them, the nineteenth who ruled over Constantinople, the capital, was a malicious, arrogant individual, a minor, and defective in stature. Like his predecessors, he was called Sultan Osman, son of Ahmet, grandson of Mahmet. With his accession to power, the lamentations of the sage who mourned over the city were fulfilled: "Woe to thee, 0 land, when thy king is a child."[9]

And so he brought much suffering and calamity upon the entire world, and these misfortunes were rampant not because the evil genius had inherited them from his predecessors, but rather because he followed their policies and deeds insofar as they opposed peace and the welfare of mankind: as it is written, "A good tree bringeth not forth corrupt fruit; neither doth a corrupt tree bring forth good fruit," and also, "Every tree is known by his own fruit."[10]

In the third year of his reign this monarch grew corrupt and absorbed in evil thoughts, constantly resenting the pious population of Sarmatia (that is, the Dalmatians), who confess the Roman faith. They inhabit the western territory that borders the countries of the Germans, the Bughtans, the Machars, and the Russians, who are

---

8. Ps. 79:1 (in the Vulgate numbering Ps. 78:1: Deus, venerunt gentes).
9. Eccles. 10:16.
10. Luke 6:43, 44.

called Muscovites. When this malevolent idea of the wicked king took root in his heart, he grew shameless and insolent, and undertook impossible, unattainable projects out of a desire to destroy the sovereignty of Poland and subjugate its population, thus rupturing the treaty of friendship and peace that had been settled between the two nations long ago.

And so, he was overcome by the plot he had planned himself; as a philosopher has observed: "He who is consumed with the desire to increase his inheritance will be struck down by a poisonous snake." By the time we reach the end of our narrative we will, as promised, have related, in its place, the bitter death of that evil monarch on his return from the battle.

As for now, we put aside the subject of our sovereign, having described him in a few, brief words, in order not to hamper the report with an exuberance of description.

THE ABOVE REMARKS ARE REPEATED IN FIFTEEN STANZAS OF RHYMED VERSE, COMPOSED BY HOVHANNES.

> The uncreated God, Who is incorruptible,
> Incomprehensible and inaccessible,
> Has sated with miraculous deeds
> The human race in modern times.
>
> As Habakkuk has told us in his song,
> The world was filled with hatred on all sides;
> Alas! why did He not unite
> All the creatures He had given life?[11]
>
> Instead, He invigorated the ignoble
> And failed to bolster up the docile,
> He let His people languish
> . . . . [12]
> He encouraged the arrogant
> And enriched their followers,
> Depriving the prosperous of their wealth
> . . . . [13]

---

11. See Habakkuk 1:2–4.
12. This line is missing from the manuscript.
13. This line is missing from the manuscript.

And many others who resemble them,
On whom so much was bestowed from heaven,
Making them remarkably magnificent,
Which, it seems to us, was quite immoral.

But in this way He had shown to all
That He meant to put them to the test,
Forewarned them of the inevitable,
That those who saw should learn thus to be wise.

And now you have the proof,
The word of the prophet, who also warned
How the lowly would be raised up
Much higher than Lebanon, so firm and stout.

Then all would pass in silence,
No traces of what happened would be seen;
The lowliest of all would be at rest,
And peacemakers would be regarded best.

An example somewhat like to this
Can be found in the words of our Savior:
. . . . [14]
But many who are first will then be last."[15]

Just so are Hagar's children,
Descendants of the handmaid,
Who now rise up, storming highest heaven,
Although, in fact, resembling deepest hell.

But our spiritual father Nerses
Bequeathed to us the hopeful thought
That the valiant Dalmatians
Would take revenge on the Mohammedans.

One of the latest among these,
Osman by name, like his predecessors
Who sat on the throne of Rome,
Wanted to reign over many lands.

---

14. The final word of this line is illegible in the manuscript, making the line incomprehensible.
15. Matt. 19:30.

The splendor of our country
Tormented his evil spirit,
Stimulating him like a wolf
To plunder the glory of others.

He greatly desired our homeland
And wished to wipe out the Sarmatians,
Until, like a tumultuous river
In his bosom, the troubled waters raged.

And now from within my heart I beseech
The Holy Spirit, the hope of the faithful,
To enlighten this my path,
Until I have achieved what I have promised.

Movses Baghramian

(Eighteenth century)

It is not known when Movses Baghramian was born or died, and there is very little information about his early life except that he studied in Jugha under a certain *vardapet* called Gevork. In the years 1762–67 he collaborated with Hovsep Emin (1726–1809) in the liberation movement, which was mainly based on armed resistance. Finding this project unfeasible, however, he moved to Madras, India, where in 1770, in association with Shahamir Shahamirian (1723–97), he formed a political circle, known as the Madras Group. Convinced that an ideological platform was necessary for the launching of a liberation movement, in 1772 he published *Nor tetrak vor kachi hordorak* (New booklet called exhortations),[1] in which he expounds his ideas about how to establish a constitutional democracy in which supreme authority resides with parliament. Such an idea was not even thought of before his time. He emphasizes the importance of inculcating youth with patriotism and promoting their education in democratic principles. He also has some advice for parents, encouraging them to give their children the best education possible. In his review of the history of Armenia, he analyzes

---

1. An abbreviated version was published in Russian translation in St. Petersburg in 1786.

the causes of the failures and successes and derives precious lessons for the future. He condemns feudalism and despotism, considering them contrary to nature. Nor does he have much sympathy for clericalism, accusing the religious establishment of leading the people into fatalistic submission. Because of his "heretical" ideas he and the Madras Group were considered undesirable by the catholicos of the day, Simeon Yerevantsi (1710–80). Baghramian believed in the unity of the Armenian people, and he felt that liberation could only be achieved by united effort. He asks the perennial question: "If the people does not fight for its freedom, who will?"

As a progressive thinker, an ardent activist, and a visionary, Movses Baghramian was far ahead of his time.

AN APPEAL TO THE READER[2]

Now, prostrating ourselves humbly, we beseech the learned and ingenuous holy fathers, who are adorned with God-instructed intelligence, as well as you, dear brothers, who are fortified with eloquent, perceptive knowledge, that whoever comes upon this book not blame us for its faults and reproach us. The fact is, we do not deny that there are a lot of mistakes in the present work, because not only is the composition unbecoming, but the expression is also, because of the improper use of the letters, syllables, and words. Besides, there is lack of agreement in the conjugation of the verbs, and the writing is not correct, with many words spelled incorrectly, and some of the adjectives do not agree with the nouns that precede or follow them, and sometimes a single noun has two or three adjectives modifying it, while governed by only one preposition, while others have none. The same thing occurs with agreement when unsuitable, bombastic adjectives are used needlessly.

There are many other such discrepancies, such as with prefixes and declensions, either resulting from our lack of skill or introduced intentionally, for some reason. The imperfection of our knowledge is already evident to readers and grammarians, but if, in several

---

2. Movses Baghramian, "*Argahadank ar entertsoghsn*" (An appeal to the reader), in *Hay Girke 1512–1800 tvakannerin* (Armenian letters, 1512–1800), ed. R. A. Ishkhanian (Yerevan, 1988), 490–91. Translated by Arminé Keushguerian and edited by the editors of the present anthology.

cases, we have repeated many words, mainly verbs and nouns, this has been done with the intention of making them intelligible, easily understood. The reason we have proceeded in this way is that many of our compatriots have a very poor knowledge of classical Armenian and others know nothing at all about it. That is why you may come across several words that have been provided with their foreign equivalents in order to help the reader comprehend the meaning, if not by means of the original, at least through the foreign words.

Some errors in spelling may be found; this does not mean, however, that we did not know the correct spelling; the reason is that we did not have lead type for all the characters of the alphabet and were sometimes obliged to substitute others. Many other deficiencies can also be found, concerning the paper, for instance, which is not uniform in quality: some of it is smooth and thin, while some is rather rough and thick. It must not be thought that this was the result of our desire to save money by not buying the most suitable and best kind. The truth is, we could not find high-quality paper in the country, and the paper we used was sought for a rather long time and found with great difficulty. Other imperfections that you may encounter were caused by the lack of skilled craftsmen. For the same reason, some parts of the text look rather ugly, and in various places here and there, the pages may be stained with ink spilled during the printing process; in addition, we did not possess the tools or other necessities required to bring the work to a successful realization.

Now the cause of these faults is the following: first of all, we knew absolutely nothing about the task we took on, and must also confess that we had neither experience nor the necessary instruction in our university studies. Nevertheless, constantly hoping to do something useful for our people, we confided in God's help, which enabled us to complete our task. In undertaking this heavy responsibility, we placed importance not so much on the book's appearance as on its being published as quickly as possible. In fact, it was completed within the space of seven months. As if being pressured by higher authorities, we were in such a rush to finish it that we did not even have time to make corrections, and the text was published just as it was, being printed without any corrections or amendments.

We know quite well that many of our compatriots could write much better or help our tortured, miserable people in some other way. We are not envious or jealous of them; on the contrary, we are happy and delighted when we hear of anyone's contribution, for it is something that our shrunken and afflicted heart desires so much.

Oh, ingenuous and zealous young people, dear, charming youngsters of our nation, we humbly implore you, over and over again, that whenever you come upon this work you not disregard our humble prayer that you recall the labor we have performed with so much hope and longing. God knows what great expense it put us to, not to mention the difficult, onerous labor and fatigue we endured, working day and night. Therefore accept this work of ours with unflagging love and consideration, and may God, Who is the guardian and overseer of the distressed, satisfy all your desires. We demand nothing from you in return and offer it freely, for the privilege of serving you; and to the Giver of that privilege we raise our prayers and hymns of praise, together with the angels and the other celestial beings, now and always, for ever and ever. Amen.

Simeon Yerevantsi

(Simeon of Yerevan)

(1710–80)

An outstanding figure of the Armenian Church, Simeon Yerevantsi was born in Yerevan, received his education in Etchmiadzin, and went to Constantinople to pursue his studies under Baghdasar Dpir. He served as legate to Constantinople and Madras, and was elected catholicos in 1763. His first task was to consolidate the authority of the See of Etchmiadzin and reorganize its administration to make it a strong religious and cultural center. To this end, he was the first to establish a printing press in Etchmiadzin (1771), followed by a paper mill (1776); these were enormous achievements in a country that at the time was under hostile foreign rule and far from industrial centers. He struggled consistently to preserve the Armenian Church from the encroachments of Catholic missionaries in Eastern Armenia. For political reasons he disapproved of the emancipation movements promoted by the Madras Group, believing that Armenia could only be liberated with the assistance of a powerful Christian state.

One of his significant works was what he called *Jambr* (from the French *chambre*), a word he used in the sense of register, record, or archives. In twenty-five chapters he compiled a historical retrospective of the Armenian Church, including the history of the Catholicosate and its rival sees; the list of dioceses, their jurisdictions, and financial status;

lists of edicts and permits granted by Persian and Turkish authorities; and the histories of twenty-one monasteries situated in the Khanate of Yerevan. A valuable source book for historical research, it was printed in Vagharshapat in 1873.

His other works include *Hishatakaran* (Records), a compilation of the correspondence conducted by the Mother See in the years 1763–79; *Girk vor kochi partavchar* (A book called acquittal, 1779), which deals with doctrinal issues; *Tonatsuyts* (Calendar of feasts, 1774), in which he introduced a few changes to ensure uniformity of observation and prepared a calendar for a cycle of 523 years; and *Girk aghotits vor kochi zbosaran hogevor* (A book called spiritual recreation, 1771), a compilation of prayers for various occasions that radiate piety and patriotism. One of his poems begins with the words "Arise, O God of our fathers" (*Ari, Astvatz hartsn merots*) and entreats the Lord to help his nation. It is a favorite of Armenians and is sung in the liturgy of the Armenian Church.

CONFESSION OF THE TRUE AND ORTHODOX FAITH OF THE ARMENIAN HOLY CHURCH AND MYSELF[1]

Oh, most Blessed Holy Trinity and one God, who are the beginning and the end, the first and the last, the only one bringing forth and terminating everything, for which reason this small, supplicatory speech resembling a copper coin.[2] I start from You and finish with You, confessing therein the very declaration of my faith that I have in You.

Here then, I confess and believe with true faith. I trust in God with indisputable hope and adore with pure love the Holy and inseparable Trinity which is the one God, without beginning and end, infinite and eternal, unlimited and everlasting; the only creator of all beings—celestials and terrestrials—out of nothing, the only lord and king of all the lords and kings; the only provider and ruler of the

---

1. Simeon Yerevantsi, "*Davanutiun chshmarit yev ughghapar havato srpo yeke-ghetsvo Hayastanyats yev im sharadroghis isk*" (Confession of the true and orthodox faith of the Armenian Holy Church and myself), in Shahé Achemian, *Tetrak aghotits* (Prayer book), *Etchmiadzin* 56, no. 1 (January 2000), 97–101. Translated by Arminé Keuchguerian and edited by the editors of the present anthology.
2. *Luma* in Armenian.

entire world; the only judge of the living beings and the deceased, the only crowner of innocents and the condemner of sinners, who must be repeatedly knelt and worshiped unto ages of ages.

I believe in You as the same and one God divided into three persons, represented by the Father, the Son and the Holy Spirit; not three gods but only one, one divinity, one nature, one will, one domination and one power; not any of them being great or prior and the other inferior or posterior, but as much as the Father, so is the Son and the same is the Holy Spirit, all three being consubstantial, that is, united in nature and in glory.

I believe in You, Father, as the very God uncreated, unbegotten and eternal, without beginning and in unlimited time, being the originator of your Son and the source of the Holy Spirit.

I believe in You, only-begotten Son and truly God born from the Father ahead of eternity, uncreated and without beginning. And, in time, by the will of the Father and the contentment of the Holy Spirit, You descended to earth with your own self and through the purest blood of the Holy Virgin became incarnate and marvelously united with your divinity.

You, who were the perfect and the very God, then became the perfect and the very man with your soul, mind and body— one person, one countenance, one will and one nature uniting in You the two natures—the divine and the human. Therefore, You were called one Christ, that is, God and man. After nine months of abstinence in the womb of the Holy Virgin You were born in flesh, through immaculate conception and incorruptible birth. Thirty years later You came to be baptized by John, in the river Jordan, witnessed by God the Father and the descent of the Holy Spirit, professing yourself to be truly God and Son of God.

You, the same Jesus Christ our God, then became incarnate humbly walking around on earth and preaching to the people. You toiled, felt hungry and were thirsty like a man, and then, with your own will suffered for our salvation; being an eternally living and impassible God, You took flesh, underwent tortures, were crucified, died and were buried in the grave, then descended into hell to redeem the souls. After three days You were resurrected in flesh and appeared to your disciples. Forty days later, with that same body of yours, You ascended to heaven and sat at the right of your Father, from whom You were never separated.

This was because You, Jesus Christ our God, though dwelt in the womb of the Holy Virgin, were born in a manger, humbly walked around on earth, endured tortures, were crucified and put in the grave as a corpse, all like a human being, You were, with your divinity, inseparable from God the Father and the Holy Spirit, sitting in heaven on the cherubic throne and receiving the adoration of all the creatures, as You are being now worshiped for your divine and human natures, unto ages of ages.

Hence, as there was no beginning for your divinity, there is also no end for your humanity, because You have been Jesus Christ yesterday, today and will be the same forever. I also believe that You will come in flesh at the end of time, in the glory of your Father, to judge the living and the dead, and that will be the resurrection of every creature. You will judge each individual according to his/her deeds; the righteous will then be rewarded with eternal life, while the sinners will be condemned to everlasting tortures.

I also believe in You, Holy Spirit, the very God gushed out without beginning and timelessly from the Father; having, in time, descended into Jordan and the upper room, You revealed the divinity of Jesus Christ who is consubstantial with You; consoled the disciples and enriched them with wondrous graces. You spoke in the Law, in the Prophets and in the Gospels, filling and adorning the church of your faithful with various graces and pious favors.

Now, this is my faith that I believe in, confess and worship the Holy Trinity and one God—the Father, the Son and the Holy Spirit—and the one of the three persons—the Son of God, incarnated in time to redeem the human beings.

We believe also in only one catholic and apostolic Church founded by Christ, the rock. It is here that You, Lamb of God, offer yourself to the Father in sacrifice for reconciliation and to remove the sins of the world. Here, we are being baptized in the name of the holiest Trinity and reborn affiliated with eternal life. Here, all the seven sanctifying and salutary sacraments You taught are being performed through the influence of the Holy Spirit; three of them—the Baptism, the Confirmation and the Extreme Unction—are for the mysterious rebirth, according to the tradition of the Holy Apostolic Armenian Church. The remaining four sacraments—the Repentance, the Religious Order, the Matrimony and the Holy Communion—come each in its time. With them we are justified and set free from the first inciting, mortal and remissible sins, we grow stronger and have courage against the enemy, we become freed from his traps, enlightened and improved, and are united spiritually with You, Christ, the always living God.

In this Holy Church we celebrate the feasts of all your celestial and terrestrial saints and beloved ones. We believe to attain in this Church the remission of sins, confessing them through repentance and the intercession of all the saints whom we commemorate as long as we live.

We believe that through this Church we will enter the supernal Sion, which is the abode of the righteous. I also believe and profess Mary, the Holy Virgin who became the conceiver and immaculate bearer of Jesus Christ our Lord—staying that same spotless Virgin after giving birth to Him—to be the ingenuous mediator and intercessor with her Son for us, the believers in You.

Now, at the end of these words of declaration of my faith I beseech You, Holy Trinity and one God, asking for your bountiful mercy to keep me, who is your unworthy servant, firm and unbending in this faith; and give me the courage and prudence to achieve virtuous deeds pleasing You, for the vitality of this faith; grant me, also, the favor of coming to You with this faith after my terrestrial existence and be accorded the eternal life; and let me glorify, with all the saints, the Father, the Son and the Holy Spirit unto ages of ages. Amen.

I, being an Armenian by birth and of Christian creed, confess the religion of St. Gregory the Illuminator of whom I have obtained this true doctrine and confession of faith, which I possess while living and will also have when deceased; St. Gregory the Illuminator, that special witness of God, Christ's fourteenth apostle who sprouted forth as a luminary from Thaddeus and Bartholomew, our first enlighteners, the two of the twelve Superior Apostles of Christ our Lord, to whom be glory for ever. Amen.

Petros Ghapantsi

Peter of Ghapan

(d. 1784)

Petros Ghapantsi was a priest, poet, and composer, about whose early life very little is known. Born in Ghapan (Siunik) in Eastern Armenia, he became a friar of the Etchmiadzin brotherhood and served as legate to various places, such as Constantinople, Adrianopolis (Edirne), Armash, and the Crimea, settling eventually in Constantinople. In 1780 he was appointed prelate of Nicomedia (presently Izmit, in Turkey).

He was a disciple of Baghdasar Dpir (1683–1768). Although he used new forms and expressions in his poetry, the influence of his master is perceptible; both lived in the same environment and were conditioned by the same sociocultural realities. His only known work is *Grkuyk vor kachi yergaran* (A booklet called the song book), published in Constantinople in 1772. It contains 110 poems, thirty-six of which gained great popularity and some of which are still sung. Ghapantsi's verses explore all the nuances of sorrow, yearning, and dreaming, artistically expressed in masterful rhyme, rhythm, and meter.

Petros Ghapantsi perfected the use of such allegorical motifs as the rose and the nightingale, where the author considers himself a nightingale expressing his love for the rose, which represents his lost fatherland. In some poems he discloses the hidden allegories with subtitles such as

"To My Beloved People" or "On the Deep Grief of our Country." In the poem "To My Sweet Partridge," under the guise of praising the bird, he asks it to dispel his grief for his homeland.

Ghapantsi wrote his poems in "soft" classical Armenian—a transition between classical and modern Armenian—and in a very clear style.

To My Honorable Nation, Under the Metaphor of the Rose[1]

Oh, my little rose, I mourn for you every year.
The winds greet your beauty with hostility:
They want to uproot your branches, scatter your petals.
    Atone for it,
    Preserve yourself,
    And win my self.

Intemperate heat and drought reside with you forever:
Your beauty marks them as excessive faults;
Age-old familiarity does not adapt them to our nature.
    Atone for them,
    Preserve yourself,
    And win my self.

Your dainty, delicate petals
The fiery wind and drought try to sacrifice;
That's why I'm always in tears, forever mourning.
    Now, be informed
    Through me, a diviner,
    And think of a strategy.

In Carmel, Lebanon, and Sanir too,
An army makes camp and abides;
Take care of yourself till the winter snows pass away.

---

1. Petros Ghapantsi, "*Ar azgn im patvelí khorhrdabar nshanakutyamb vardi*" (To my honorable nation, under the metaphor of the rose), in *Hayreniki yev bnutyan yerger* (Songs of homeland and nature), ed. Shushanik Nazarian (Yerevan, 1969), 24–26. Translated by Arminé Keushguerian and edited by the editors of the present anthology.

Recognize yourself,
Resemble the light:
Do not act too quickly.

I constantly endeavor to keep your spirit high,
In case my desires should find a way;
That is the object of my prayers and constant pleas.
    With extreme anxiety,
    Forever exiled,
    In a foreign country.

When I perceive your splendid beauty,
I rejoice to the bottom of my soul;
My life, as long as it shall last,
    I'll give it all to you,
    That you may dwell there,
    As in a lodge.

Oh, inexhaustible treasure of my soul, and most kind,
Wake up quickly and listen to the good news!
Look how the chill vanishes from your face.
    Like the disabled,
    Suffering always,
    For ever and ever.

In grief and mourning I sit in a far-off place;
Fixing my eyes on you, I tread in your daring steps:
My love for you has made me a slave of letters.
    Becoming a captive,
    I brought this to you,
    Faultless and complete.

The strong winds smite my body instead of yours;
The smoke of hostility has not yet dispersed for the brave one,
Who is mistreated, scorched, and suffers unjustly,
    Ailing with pain,
    As if at sea,
    Growing vexed.

For me, your captive, many snares they set,
My miserable self through intrigues they seek to entrap,
And, imitating flocks of birds, they stretch their wings.

With pebbles they stone,
With fire they brand,
And with salt they parch.

My heart will rejoice if I see you fine,
And all these mischiefs I'll forget ere long:
Coming back from the past, I'll be renewed again.
I'll play the swell,
Will gain in strength,
And rise to power.

Shahamir Shahamirian

(1723–97)

A staunch proponent of the emancipation of Armenia, Shahamirian was originally from New Julfa, Iran. He immigrated to India and settled in Madras where, by about the age of forty, he built a fortune as a merchant. A learned man, he acquired his education by hiring private teachers, both Armenian and English.

Of great historical importance was the founding in the early 1770s of a group of concerned liberal intellectuals called the Madras Group. Inspired by the ideas of Hovsep (Joseph) Emin (1726–1809), they dedicated their energies to the cause of the emancipation of Armenia and began to frame its ideological foundations. Their aim was first to sensitize the Armenian communities to democratic principles and procedures, then to form a political and military alliance with a sympathetic and mutually beneficial power. The most prominent members of the Madras Group were Movses Baghramian (eighteenth century), Shahamir Shahamirian, his son Hakob Shahamirian, and Joseph Emin; the group also had close connections with Hovsep Arghutian (1741–1801), prelate of Russia, and Hovhannes Lazarian (1735–1801), a government functionary. In 1771–72 Shahamir Shahamirian founded the first Armenian printing press in Madras, which greatly facilitated the propagation of the Madras Group's ideas. A tract published in 1773, called *Nor tetrak vor kochi hordorak* (New tract called exhortations) and attributed to Movses Baghramian, presented an analysis of the causes of the historic subjugation Armenians have suffered, the rationale of the emancipation movement, and an appeal to revive patriotism; these were all aimed at fostering self-confidence among the people and rallying them to shake off the Persian and Ottoman yokes.

Another book of the Madras Group, published in 1783 and authored by Shahamir himself is *Tetrak vor kochi nshavak* (A tract called target), which basically consists of bylaws for the administration of the Armenian community in Madras, advocating the separation of religious and civic authority, regulating the placement of new immigrants, and dealing with other matters related to commerce and society.

The most important book produced by the Madras Group was *Vorogayt parats* (Snare of glory), written by Shahamir Shahamirian and published under the name of his son, Hakob Shahamirian. The date on the title page is 1773, though some scholars place it in 1788–89. It is the world's first known blueprint for a constitutional democracy, and is remarkable for having appeared in the East. In the lengthy introduction the author denounces feudal and despotic rule as practiced in the Persian and Ottoman empires and advocates the principles of democracy. The main part of the book consists of a 521-article constitution for a democratic government, intended to be the basis of the future independent Armenia. The proposed constitution encompasses a wide range of provisions. It covers the formation of a representative parliament; political, military, and social issues; other aspects of the new state, including education, the economy, and national security; and such topics as justice and taxation. All the provisions are based on respecting the rights and freedoms of the individual. This valuable document of democratic thought was far too advanced for its time, particularly for the Eastern mentality. It was republished in Tiflis in 1919.

FROM SNARE OF GLORY[1]

I, the writer, who am one of the subordinate Armenians and your humble servant, first of all confess before God and mankind

---

1. Hakob Shahamirian, *Vorogayt Parats* (Snare of glory), in Raphael Hambardzumian, *Sources, Relevance and Peculiarities of Vorogayt Parats* (Yerevan, 1999), 9–20. Translated by Aris Sevag in *Armenian Reporter International*, March 16, 23, 30, and April 6, 2002, through the sponsorship of Madras Group PA.

that I do not have personal desire for either power or wealth and fame; rather, I am merely connected with total love to my own nation and our land. But the unsettled times took me to a foreign land, where I lived under the rule of free, foreign Christian nations. By comparing one country to another, one man to another, one plant to another, by paying attention to, or reading about (becoming acquainted) with the individual worthiness of numerous countries and various nations of the world, I found that the best, the sweetest and most excellent of all the countries under the sun is the land of Ararat. It can he said that the Lord designated the land of Ararat, with lofty Masis, as king of the entire world and all mountains. Just as the Garden of Eden became the first abode for our forefather Adam, so too did Ararat, along with Masis, become the second principal abode for our second father Noah. Therefore, it is not without reason that the Creator of all tall mountains and the Lord deigned to have our forefather Noah, the only just and beloved man, descend on Mt. Ararat and give his blessing to the province of Nakhijevan (First Descent) and the land of Ararat.

It was not without reason that the first valor and courage against willful autocracy was shown by our ancestor; well-curled, strong-armed and mighty powerful Hayk, who brought down the haughty Bel from the heights of arrogance and detestable pride and knocked him to the ground in the place called Gerezman (Grave), at the site called Armenian Valley, at the foot of Mt. Sim, within the confines of our region of Turuberan.

It was not without reason that King Abgaros, son of Arsham, believed in Christ, the incarnation of the Word, Jesus of Nazareth, son of the living God, without having heard the sermons of the *vardapets* and the predictions of the prophets, without having been an eyewitness to miracles, and without having the slightest knowledge.

It was not without reason that the singularly exceptional and ineffable miracle occurred in the land of Ararat. For Anak, the father of St. Grigorios Pahlavuni, so loved that which was worldly that, taken with the promise of a frivolous gift from Persian king Artashir, he betrayed his relative, going so far as killing the Armenian king Khosrov, just for the sake of winning praise from the Persian king. However, his virtuous son, contrary to his father's wishes, and considering all worldly glory detestable, put himself in the sweet-smelling garden of humility and underwent so many agonizing tortures, the likes of which only he endured on this earth and under the sun.

After fifteen years of torment, he was still alive, despite having been administered many body blows, and he finally was deemed worthy of the Lord's mercy, for he baptized the Armenian king Trdat, neophyte of Christ, along with the noble princes and countless commoners, in the Euphrates River, which flows from (the plain of) Ararat toward the ocean (Persian Gulf).

It should not seem such a small surprise that a time period of approximately four hundred years has passed until now, during which a kingdom has not existed in the land of Armenia and among the Armenian nation. That has been replaced by subjugation at the hands of the ungodly, who are enslaving our sons and daughters, plundering our entire luxury, property and possessions, covetously subjecting us to a heavy tax burden and reducing us to utmost wretchedness. However, our praiseworthy nation, enduring everything threatening its physical existence, has completely kept its faith in the Lord God. It professes all the sacraments of the holy Church, which were handed down by Christ our Savior, just as our holy Armenian Church sends out shoots among us in (the land) of Ayrarat until the present. Thus, we entertain hope that the Lord will protect us with the same complete love and faith until eternity.

According to all manner of national customs and according to the Holy Bible, we are of the conviction that everything is confirmed through two or three witnesses. Behold I am placing before the honorable readers the aforementioned five strongest and most reliable testimonies, which can confirm in your mind the grace, love and mercifulness of the omnipotent Creator toward the land of Ararat, and that none of these testimonies appeared anywhere else on this earth under the sun at any time. Through these testimonies everybody can become convinced that the land of Ararat and its inhabitants, along with their heirs who worship the most holy Trinity and one Deity, have particularly their protector, savior and dispeller, in accordance with the Lord's saying, that the torments of those who build their own house won't be in vain.

Also I wish to reflect on and relate to you the excellence and generosity of the Armenian nation, in particular. First of all, the nation of Japheth is loved by all because of its natural human disposition, since he was a desirable boy; i.e., he was the younger among our forefathers Seth and Ham. Even if he had been older, Japheth, along with his heirs Torgom, Hayk, Tigran, Armen and others, was worthy of honor. Let me say with praise that this honey-tongued nation, from the very beginning until the present, has such a steadfast custom of hospitality, which forces me to believe that such a grace in the world has been especially handed down from our Lord Creator only to the Armenians so that mankind would know their hospitality in particular, in accordance with the Lord's saying that the one who comes to him will not be turned aside.

This honorable youth Japheth, son of Noah, our ancestor, together with his descendants, reigned over his home, over his personal inheritance of Ararat and the Armenian people, for more than two thousand years until the time of the kingdom of Vahes, son of Vahan. But, as is unique to human nature, pursuing his wishes and pleasure—feeling free in his thoughts, let your will prevail; as is currently pleasing, think in your own minds about his being deprived of his kingdom; however, that thing happened like this, since this Vaheos [*sic*], resisting Alexander the Great, was killed by him. It was at that time that the Japhethian kingdom ceased belonging to the tribe of Hayk and Aram, after existing for two thousand years. Arshak's brother, Vagharshak Pahlavuni, then came to us, promising to lead us with paternal compassion. The same custom and kindness, about which I spoke above, obliged the Armenians, according to their characteristic hospitality, to lovingly accept Vagharshak who, with his successors, reigned over the Armenian homeland for five hundred years, more or less, until the time of the kingdom of Artashes III. The Armenian Arshakuni kingdom ceased to exist, and then there appeared among us Ashot, the son of Smbat Bagratuni. The Armenians received Ashot Bagratuni with the same hospitality and love, and he, together with his successors, ruled over the Armenians for three hundred fifty years, more or less, until the time of the kingdom of Gagik II. Thereafter the Armenian kingdom ceased to belong to the Bagratuni dynasty and no longer existed in the land of Ararat. But, presently, they are not all that unknown to us, like the tribe and lineage of Japheth or Vagharshak. For, until now, there is a royal scion from the Bagratuni dynasty on the Georgian throne, and may the Lord support him.

Thereafter, the brave Armenian prince Ruben, from the same Bagratuni dynasty, grew in strength, took control of our territory, and occupied the Armenian throne, together with his descendants, in the land of Cilicia for two hundred twenty years, more or less, until the time of Levon VI, after which, namely in 1381, the Armenian kingdom ceased to exist until the present.

Let it also be known to you that starting with the lineage of our ancestor Japheth, the first Armenian king of the house of Ararat Hayk, son of Torgom, son of Thiras, son of Gomer, son of Japheth, son of Noah, having been the first to descend from the ark on the face of the land of Ararat, down to the last king Levon VI, along with the *marzpans* (governors), make a total of one hundred twenty-four persons from the dynasties of Hayk, Vagharshak, Bagrat and Rubinians; as well as the various clans of *marzpans*. During that period of time, there also emerged in our land numerous loyal, victorious and famous individuals, such as the Gnunis, the Artzrunis, Mamikonians, Orbelians and many many others, about whom the sincere historian Movses Khorenatsi has specifically written. All of them, in turn, proceeded diligently with their princely affairs on the Armenian throne to the extent that their intelligence and ability were able to promise them, such that we can now admit that many of them have (a record of) service and legacy with regard to the Armenian throne, owing to their good works. On the other hand, many of them, because of their lack of intelligence, became weak and were destroyed and became the cause of numerous acts of harm that were committed against the Armenian throne.

So, therefore, let us get up and enter the abode of love and peace, not propelled by the desire of our body and the partiality of princely personalities, but by the will of the one whose sincere human nature confesses justice, and according to the custom of the entire world and all prudent persons, who wish to establish peace among opponents. Thus, we too are obligated to forgive our ancestors—kings and princes—for their good and bad works, and let no one praise the service and legacy of those ancestors with regard to the land and people of Armenia; and let no one despise the harmful and wicked laziness of our princes of old, since all of them did not refrain from doing that which they were capable of doing, based on their individual capability. Whatever happened has passed, and that was the lot that fell to us under the sun. Therefore, right and justice demand that we always exalt the honorable name

of Hayk by honoring him and demanding same; he was the originator and he made us famous with his name, since it was through
him that the world recognized the Armenian nation and we were
called Hayk; furthermore, it was through his lineage that we were
called Armenians by foreign nations.

Also worthy of honor among us are Vagharshak Arshakuni,
Ashot Bagratuni and the Rubinians, along with their entire lin-
eages, since they held the Armenian nation together, while maintaining the honor of our ancestor Hayk and reigning over the
land of Ararat for approximately three thousand years, more or
less. And because none of the descendants of the aforementioned
princes came forth in defense of the Armenian nation and the land
of Ararat which, becoming deserted under the authority of foreigners, exists and persists down to the present, therefore it will be good
for the Armenian nation, with its present farsightedness, to turn
its attention to the wrongs committed in the past and learn about
the huge harm which came to the land of Armenia and Armenian
nation owing to autocratic monarchy and autocratic authority and
as a result of arbitrary actions. If, on the other hand, we sometimes
encountered situations where kind men ruled, our benefit did not
extend beyond existing and being their servants. Also, from time
to time, according to variable human nature, we were subjected to
extreme torment at their hands; or, on the contrary, if it was a situation whereby wicked and stupid men reigned, they humiliated us
to the point where we lost our honor and the bliss of freedom, and
became reduced to an abject state. Through just the commission
of that wrong alone, not only did they severely debase us but they
made us slaves to foreigners, an insult to other humans, and an
object of scorn for those who saw us. And just as there is no one
from our nation ruling over us as king, let it not be desirable and
acceptable for us that, hereafter, a king or prince commander again
emerge from the Armenian nation, no one at all with autocratic
power, because no man has been born who doesn't commit sin,
except Christ the Savior.

Thus, it will be very good for our country and us, if the Armenian nation together, as a whole, reign in their country freely, with
their natural nature, eliminating ill will, jealousy and avarice, so
that one will not be superior and the other inferior but, rather, all
together, from the moment of their birth, will equally receive regal

respect and will forever remain king in their own land throughout the days of their lives. I know full well that whoever reads this will shudder at the thought of how an entire nation can be king of one country. I ask those who think like this, how can only one man reign over an entire nation and free people, when he has nothing more within himself than the strength of an ordinary man? If we wish to live and remain free, as the Creator, God, created us from the beginning, then no one should be allowed to reign over us according to his will and whim, if he can not compensate us in a lawful manner according to the value of our accomplishment, so that every one may achieve honor or punishment, without weariness, depending on the worthiness of his work. That kind of kingdom was granted to us by our Lord, the Creator, from the beginning of creation, from the time of our forefather Adam, when with his omnipotent power he made everything that he created on the earth and under the sun subject to man's natural nature; he, in turn, reigned over our nature according to the Law which says that man may eat of the fruit of all trees, except the fruit of evil. Only this law became king over us; that is why our nature fell from that supreme authority of freedom into the service of death, for no other reason than the unlawful act committed by us. By doing so, we violated the law of the Lord and, being scattered, we fell on the face of the earth under the yoke of service, we agreed to accept death and descend into the earth, from which we arose to give recompense for the transgression committed by our hand, in the life hereafter forever and ever.

Joseph Emin

(1726–1809)

FROM LIFE AND ADVENTURES OF JOSEPH EMIN[1]

XI

LORD HUNTINGDON AND FREDERICK OF PRUSSIA'S COMPLEXION—LORD HUNTINGDON INVITES EMIN TO DINNER—AND MEETS HIS MATCH—H. R. H. WANTS TO HELP EMIN—THE DUKE OBJECTS—VOYAGE WITH A MUTINOUS CREW.

He [Emin] stayed in London about eight months, very busy all the time to find ways and means for going to Petersburg. The late Earl of Bath, after dinner at Mr. Montagu's, saw Emin much dejected. Mr. Montagu said to his lordship, "Our friend Emin cannot get a letter of recommendation from any gentleman to Russia." His lordship immediately answered, that he would give him one to Mr. Keith, envoy to that court. Mr. Jonas Hanway,[2] author of the *History of Nadir Shah,* procured him a pass from Prince Gallitzin, the Russian minister, to whom Emin had before the honor of being

---

1. For Joseph Emin's biography see the overview in the present anthology. Joseph Emin, *Life and Adventures of Emin Joseph Emin—1726–1809,* ed. Amy Apcar (Calcutta, 1918), 162–68. This piece was written in English by Emin himself and edited by his great-great-granddaughter.

2. A philanthropist who became partner of an English merchant at Petersburg in 1743, in 1743–44 he made a mercantile journey to Persia, where he suffered many misfortunes, publishing an account of his travels in 1753. His later years were occupied with many philanthropic schemes, especially on behalf of poor children.

introduced by the late Lady Yarmouth. Dr. Seeker, then Archbishop of Canterbury, wrote a letter to Doctor Dumaresque, chaplain to the factory; Miss Talbot to the Princess of Georgia; and Dr. Mounsey of Chelsea hospital, to Dr. Mounsey, his relation, chief physician to the late Empress Elizabeth. When he had secured all these letters, he waited upon his patron the duke, who was much surprized and equally glad of the success he had met with.

Two years before his proceeding on this journey, it happened one day, that the foreign ministers, after waiting on His Majesty, came to Lady Yarmouth's apartment, to pay their respects to her ladyship, and among them was Lord Huntingdon. In conversation the King of Prussia became the subject. His lordship said, "It is singular that we cannot have an exact likeness of His Majesty painted, nor can I discover the reason of it." Emin said, "My lord, the reason is very plain, a child may know it very easily by looking at his face about half an hour." His lordship smiled, and the rest of the gentlemen were somehow startled; they had taken but very little notice of him before; they asked him if he could tell the reason. He said, "Yes," and added, "that the king was not made like the rest of mankind, that he changed complexion with every thought that passed in his mind; that sometimes he looked pale, and at another time fresh-colored, white, black, yellow, in short he answered all sorts of colors like a chameleon; wherefore it would be impossible for a painter to draw a true picture of him." On this solution, every one of the company cried out, "that is the very reason, well said! this is Asiatic penetration": then they took proper notice of him; and this pleased Lady Yarmouth as much, who took that opportunity to introduce him to all of them in form; and among the rest, to Prince Gallitzin.[3] His lordship putting a second question, "What is the cause of his assuming those different colors?" Emin answered, "When he looks fresh, he thinks he is sure of conquest; when pale as ashes, he is afraid of being crushed by the united powers of Europe; when yellow, he fears Voltaire will publish a scandalous book again to smite his mind, and so forth." On the second explanation, his lordship with both hands moved his chair, and sat close to him, and invited him to dinner that day, if he was

---

3. Russian ambassador to England during the reign of the Empress Elizabeth of Russia.

not otherwise engaged. The foreign ministers spoke in French to Lady Yarmouth, with a satisfied pleasing countenance; and said, "Although we thought before he was not worthy of the notice taken of him by the nobility of England, now we are very well convinced that he deserves to have honors conferred upon him, and that His Royal Highness the duke, and the Earl of Northumberland, had really great merit in patronizing him. The levee broke up; the gentlemen went away; and though Emin understood what they said, yet Lady Yarmouth took pains, with great good-nature and satisfaction, to express it to him.

According to his promise, he went to Lord Huntingdon's;[4] at dinner there were two brothers, Doctor and Captain Hamilton, the second of whom was equerry to his present Majesty, at that time Prince of Wales, and Lord Huntingdon was then his master of the horse.

When they had dined, the conversation turned upon various subjects, and his lordship in a bantering good-natured way, said to Emin, "Your best method will be to compose a new sort of religion like Mohamed, and reform your countrymen to your way of thinking; otherwise the religion they have now will never suffer them to follow your example, so as to become a free nation. I dare to say, you know of the reformation among the English; who if they had continued papists, might have been retained slaves to this day." This proposition, though delivered in jest, agitated him not a little, by mentioning the polluted name of that Arabian impostor; and he said, "If your lordship will not be displeased with my boldness, I will tell my opinion on that head?" His lordship said, "Not in the least." Then Emin began with his rough comparison, proceeding thus:

"My lord, it appears to me that you are very learned, and your elegant conversation is most improving to the minds of every hearer; but you seem exactly like a sirloin of beef turning upon a spit, and roasting before a very large fire in a chophouse; where the customers coming in one after another, the master of the house, with a sharp carving knife in his hand, like a Turkish executioner, cries out, 'What will you please to have gentlemen?' 'Roasted beef,

---

4. Francis, tenth Earl of Huntingdon, b. 1728–29. Carried sword of state at coronation of George III, 1761; died without issue 1789, succeeded by his sister Elizabeth, who married the Earl of Moira.

master,' they say. He cuts the outside and inside of it, where it is best done, serving his customers; who being satisfied, and the reckoning paid, the beef still going round on the spit by the help of the jack, till at last it is eaten up, and reduced to the very bone, without the least benefit to itself. Now, one may look upon you just in the same light; and nothing surprises one so much as to find her ladyship, your mother, so very religious,[5] and your lordship so irreligious. Several free speakers like you have brought down the true Christian character of the most noble English nation to the lowest degree of heathenism and even propagated a notion all over the eastern quarter of the world, that (which God forbid) the English are not Christians." This grave repartee made his lordship hang down his head, and both the brothers cried out laughing, "He serves you right, my lord, upon our honor; we will acquaint His Royal Highness with every word Mr. Emin has said to you." Some days after Captain Hamilton sent for him, and acquainted him that he had been very industrious in giving an account to his Royal Highness, of every syllable that passed at dinner, between him and Lord Huntingdon; that His Royal Highness was greatly pleased, and said to his lordship, "I am very glad you have at last met with your match." He graciously inquired, if it was the Emin who had been in the late campaign in our service and whether he was rewarded for his trouble or not? "We said," added the captain, "that we believed not; and now, my friend, it is high time for you to inform your patron, that the prince is much interested in your behalf; so that his lordship, who attends every levee day, may agree with his Royal Highness to do something for you."

Emin mentioned this to the duke, who went to the prince; his Royal Highness favorably inquired about the matter, and expressed himself very ready to assist Emin. The duke said, "He is already provided for," meaning by his Grace; and added, "He shall have any sum of money he chooses." The duke told Emin what his Royal Highness had said; adding, "It is not proper you should have more money than is necessary; you came hither without any; without language or friends; and, by your own activity,

---

5. Selina, Lady Huntingdon (1707–91), daughter of Washington Earl Ferrers. Celebrated after her husband's death for her Methodistical religious convictions. Founded many chapels and became the leader of a sect of Methodists known as "Huntingdonians," and the "Countess of Huntingdon's Connection."

made yourself known to the greatest princes in Europe: you have letters of recommendation to the court of Russia, who will certainly write to Prince Heraclius, and he immediately will employ you in his service; by which means you will be as rich as any prince in Asia." Emin said, "My lord, your advice is excellent, but I shall never be able to compass my design without money, or being independent; at least that country is very well known to be poor; if not, Prince Heraclius' father would not have gone to Russia, to solicit like a beggar for assistance." The duke said, "No, my dear Emin, you are mistaken; he is gone for some greater affair unknown to us." Emin said, "My lord, when I was in Armenia at Etchmiadzin, the Archbishop of Tiflis told me, that King Tahmuras of Georgia, through mere necessity being at variance with his son, was sent to Moscow to be maintained by the Russians. Has not your lordship read of *Sir John Chardin's Travels*, which say that the Georgians are the handsomest, the worst, and the poorest of kind?"

"No, no, Mr. Emin, you will do very well with Prince Heraclius." "Yes, my lord, if I were independent, I should do better with all the world; but since your lordship has that great opinion of your humble servant, that he can live upon air, he says no more about it; he is ready to obey your command in gratitude; even if you order him, he is ready to shoot himself at the feet of your lordship, that the world may have the pleasure to say, Emin behaved obediently and gratefully to his breath, to his princely patron."

This consultation being over, the duke gave him a hundred guineas, and promised him two hundred more, to remit after him a hundred each year, and to continue for three years and no longer. What could Emin do, but make much of a little? Mrs. Montague, Lady Sophia Egerton, and Miss Talbot made up about sixty pounds; Lady Anson, his valuable friend, was dead; he was therefore worth 160—deducting 30—for fitting himself out; paid five guineas to the captain of the ship; took leave of his friends, and set out on the 15th of October 1761. He arrived with moderate wind in eight days at Elsinore, a sea-port town in Denmark, where he stayed two days; on the third day setting sail, on the fourth a storm arose with such fury, that nothing could equal it; in a few days more made the Island of Bornholm.

Here, the sailors embracing the opportunity (which was very near proving fatal to the ship, and all who were in it), half a dozen of them got drunk, set the whole place in an uproar, and did not care a pin for the captain. Emin had much ado to quiet them. At last every one of them got on board and no sooner was the anchor weighed, than a contrary wind began to blow three times stronger than before; half of the crew mutinied, and laid a scheme to kill Emin (the only passenger) and the captain, because they advised them not to drink more than was necessary, and then to carry the ship to France, at that time engaged in war with England. Emin finding no other remedy to quiet them, he, with the captain, resolved to shoot the ringleader, a very stout young man, a deserter from a man-of-war; the rest seeing what was going on, submitted to join Emin's and the captain's party, and with much ado the young lion was secured in irons. The captain drew up an affidavit of their unruly behavior, and the poor fellows every one of them signed a paper, confessing themselves guilty of a conspiracy. Exactly in fifty days, they with great difficulty came to an anchor at Riga.[6]

---

6. After two days Emin hired a cart going toward St. Petersburg, where he arrived in twelve days, and met Count Worronzoff, the Russian chancellor.

Mikayel Chamchian

(1738–1823)

The noted historian, linguist, grammarian, and theologian Mikayel Chamchian was born in Constantinople. He joined the Mkhitarists of Venice in 1757 and was ordained priest in 1762. He was sent to the Middle East as a missionary and, after serving the Armenian Catholic community in Basra, Iraq, for six years as their pastor, he returned to Venice to recover from ill health. He served as supervisor of the Mkhitarist schools in Venice and Transylvania, and in 1795 moved to Constantinople and organized a Mkhitarist school there, where he taught Armenian language and grammar. He was also unofficially involved in unity talks between the Armenian Apostolic and Armenian Catholic communities, which did not bear fruit. He remained in Constantinople until his death, at the age of eighty-five.

Mikayel Chamchian was a prolific writer, producing more than ten works, some multivolumed, among which two stand out above the others. The first, *Kerakanutiun haykazian lezvi* (Grammar of the classical Armenian language), published in Venice in 1779 and in fifteen subsequent editions by 1859, has long been regarded as the best textbook for teaching classical Armenian. Relying on the authentic language of the authors of the fifth to seventh centuries, he reinstated genuine grammatical forms and eliminated Latinisms that had crept in over the course of time. He also appended a section called *"Hamarotutiun kerakanutyan"* (An abridged grammar), which lists all the grammatical rules.

His second important work, the monumental *Patmutiun hayots* (History of the Armenians) in three volumes, was published in Venice from 1781 to 1786; this was an attempt to write a comprehensive history of Armenia from Creation to his own time. Chamchian bases the earlier part of his narrative on Movses Khorenatsi's *History* (fifth century). For the rest he utilizes a variety of Armenian and non-Armenian sources, some of which, particularly the foreign authors, he treats critically. He accepts as factual only events cited by at least two independent sources, which he cites in the margins. Chamchian's *History* is divided into periods according to the Armenian royal dynasties and times of foreign domination by invading powers. Written with patriotic love and pride, it represents a great achievement.

Chamchian's other works are religious and educational in nature.

FROM HISTORY OF ARMENIA[1]

Chapter XXV

THE EXPLOITS OF DAVID PRINCE OF THE SIUNIK

About this period (AD 1722, Armenian era 1171) the powers who domineered over that part of Armenia called Artsakh, and the country of the Siunik, oppressed the original inhabitants in a most intolerable manner. Of all the Armenians who resided in these countries none felt so keenly the degradation and oppression of his nation as David,[2] prince of the Siunik, a man of undaunted bravery and strong mental powers. Determined on making an effort to shake off the yoke which was then so galling, he secretly gathered troops, and attacking the oppressors, succeeded in expelling them from Artsakh and Siunik. He then built a fort in the village of Halidzor in the country of the Siunik, and garrisoning it with a

---

1. Mikayel Chamchian (Michel Chamich), *History of Armenia—From* BC *2247 to the Year of the Christ, 1780, or 1229 of the Armenian Era* (Calcutta, 1827), 466–74. Translated by Johannes Avdall. Spelling is normalized by the editors of the present anthology. The translator appended a continuation of the history from the year 1780 to the date of publication.

2. The famed military leader known as David Beg (?–1728), who defended Siunik against Persian and Ottoman invaders and ensured its autonomy.

competent number for its defense, confided it to one of his followers named Mkhithar, a man of courage and great military talent. From the time of his appearing in arms until he had driven the enemies out of his country, a period of four years elapsed, during which many severely contested battles were fought between them.

In this year (AD 1726, Armenian era 1175) the enemies who had been expelled from Artsakh and Siunik, returned thither in greater numbers than had been ever before seen, in consequence of which David was deserted by almost all his followers, being left in the fort of Halidzor with only seventeen men, one of whom was Mkhithar. Not at all daunted by this circumstance, he prepared to contend with the enemy with as much resolution as he had shown in the outset of his career. Previously, however, to any battle taking place between the two parties, David was joined by a number of Armenians, who, like himself, detested living under the yoke of foreigners. His number in all amounted to 454 fighting men, among whom was Melik Pharsadan, a valiant chief, and Ter-Avetik, who although a clergyman, had been obliged by the disturbed nature of the times to take up arms, in which it is said he excelled. The castle, besides these, held many of the wives and relations of the men, together with three bishops, thirteen priests, and about forty nuns. The number of the invaders amounted to 70,000 men, many of whom were Armenians, who conceiving that resistance was fruitless had abandoned the cause of their country. These advanced and encamped near the river Halidzor, intending to besiege the fortress in which David and his brave associates had placed themselves. On the number of their enemies becoming known to the people within the fort, one hundred of them basely deserted to the enemy. This, however, did not much affect the remainder, who determined to hold out while a man remained to defend the walls. The enemy crossed, surrounded the fort on all sides, and commenced battering it with artillery. David, however, defended it so well, that in the first six days the enemy lost 1,800 men, while there only fell eight of his party. The enemy perceiving that it was not possible to make a breach in the walls, determined to attempt to scale them. For this purpose they prepared ladders of immense width, capable of holding several hundreds of men in a row, and assaulted the fort in three different places at once. They were bravely met by the besieged under the heroic David, and hundreds of them were precipitated from the walls, as they reached the top of the ladders. They were, however, so numerous, that as the foremost fell their places were immediately taken up by those who followed, and although thousands of therm perished, yet their numbers appeared undiminished. David perceiving this, and fearful of the result, if they should continue to come on with the same resolution, directed Avetik and Mkhithar to take two hundred men and issue out of the fort and attack the besiegers in the rear. This order was immediately executed, and the enemy on finding themselves placed between two fires, quitted the assault and took to flight. David then with the remainder of his brave little garrison sallied out, and joining Avetik and Mkhithar went in pursuit of the fugitives. A horrible slaughter ensued, the enemy losing 13,000 men in their retreat, who were all killed by the pursuers. The whole of their camp equipage, together with forty-eight standards, fell into the hands of the victors.

Twenty-two thousand of the defeated army took refuge in Meghri. News of this being brought to Holi, David dispatched thither a small party, consisting of but sixty-six men under the command of Avetik and Mkhithar, directing the leaders to act as circumstances should suggest. On their approach to the city of Meghri, they disguised themselves, and entered it as if they were simple citizens. On looking around them, Avetik and Mkhithar discovered that the greatest disorder reigned amongst the remnant of the wing which had taken refuge here, and that it required only a little audacity to clear the city of the whole of them. Determined to signalize themselves by a bold act, they assembled their men, and seeing them well provided with arms, directed them to rendezvous at a certain spot on the dawn of the next morning. The time being arrived, the two brave leaders at the head of their little band made a furious attack on the enemy, who being taken by surprise, and uncertain of the number of their assailants, by the dim light which prevailed at that early hour, made little resistance, most of them fleeing without striking a blow. All the fugitives after escaping without the walls of Meghri directed their course toward the river Arax. Mkhithar's party kept up the pursuit with the utmost ardor, killing the invaders of their land with the most unsparing revenge. There was a remarkably narrow defile leading to the river Arax, called Uzum Pent, by which the wretched fugitives were obliged to pass. Hither the Armenians had gathered on the news of the expulsion and flight of the enemy from Meghri; and as the latter entered the pass, they were cut down with all the eagerness of a foe smarting under the recollection of recent oppression and bondage. Many of those who effected their way through the defile were drowned in the river: indeed this part of the enemy's army was almost annihilated. The spoil which the victors acquired after this affair was immense. Horses, camels, mules in great numbers, with a variety of all the weapons and ornaments as well of man as of beast, used in war, fell into their hands, and all was taken to David at Halidzor. When the news of this brilliant affair was made known in the adjacent countries, a general rendezvous of the troops of the enemies of David and the Armenians was appointed to take place on a certain day, in the province of Goghtn. Immense bodies of cavalry and infantry were hereupon marshaled, and the whole brought against the fortress of Halidzor. In the meantime the Armenians residing in Siunik and Artsakh, struck with admiration at the skill and courage displayed in its defense by David in his late contest with the enemies of his country, flocked to Halidzor to assist in its defense. Unfortunately dissensions broke out amongst the adherents of this valiant and truly disinterested chief, so that on the arrival of the enemy's army before the fort, the garrison was a scene of universal discord, and it was chimerical to attempt any enterprise with followers mutually jealous of each other's pretensions. David attempted to allay the ferment amongst his men, but all was fruitless.

In this dilemma he determined to try a stratagem to annoy the enemy, so as to make them defer the erection of their batteries. Having selected sixty mares, he caused them to be secretly conducted by night to the camp of the enemy and there let loose. In consequence, the stallions on which part of the cavalry were mounted broke from their picquets as soon as the mares began to neigh, and running here and there in the dark made the besieging army believe that the garrison had made a sortie. All the camp was in a state of confusion, which being perceived by David, he with a select band made a furious attack upon it. The enemy in disorder, by reason of the darkness of the night knew not the extent of the force brought against them, and making little resistance took to flight. A vast number was killed and all their battering train and camp equipage fell into the hands of David and his party. Thus was a second army discomfited by the resolution and genius of one man; and if he had but half of the resources possessed by his enemies, he would have restored Armenia to her right place among the political states of Asia.

The next year (AD 1727, Armenian era 1176) the enemies again took the field against David, assembling on the plains of Marad in greater numbers than before. David's followers having also increased, he boldly came out of his fortress, and took up a position near that on which his enemies were encamped. When the latter observed the Armenians, they divided their army into three parts, intending to surround them; David seeing this movement, formed his small army also into three divisions, commanding all, on the advance of the enemy to turn about and make a feint of flight, in order to make them believe that they were afraid to encounter them, by which means the adverse army would be lulled into a state of carelessness. "Then," said David, "we can return and attack them!"

This was done, and the invaders imagining that the Armenians wished to avoid a battle, returned to their camp and gave themselves up to amusement. At the close of the day David returned with his army, and attacking the enemy while they were feasting, obtained an easy victory. After a faint resistance they abandoned their camp and fled, pursued with great slaughter by the victorious Armenians. This was the last exploit which distinguished the life of the valiant David, who was thenceforward permitted to remain at ease in his fort of Halidzor. He died six years after this event at the age of fifty-four (AD 1728, Armenian era 1177).

Hovhannes Karnetsi

(John of Karin)

(c. 1750–1820)

Poet, educator, and a notary by profession, Hovhannes Karnetsi was born in the city of Karin (Erzrum). He started writing in the early 1770s, and his last work bears the date 1779. He spent most of his life teaching and earned the epithet "the just teacher."

His known literary heritage consists of five epic poems based on historical events: *Haghags umemn Merser kochetsyal Sahak mankan* (On the youth Sahak, called Merser, 1788), *Haghags Varvar anun ariasirt aghjkan* (On a courageous girl called Varvar, 1810), etc. He also composed 130 poems, mostly to be sung, on the theme of love, with titles such as "*Tap siro ko zis tochoryats*" (The ardor of your love has burned me), "*Tagh siro*" (Ode to love), "*I ser sireluyd*" (For the sake of your love), and "*Hayim sers vor chems aryal*" (I watch my love as she walks in the sun). He is credited with a score of beautiful quatrains in the style of ballads and a number of religious songs.

Because in the late eighteenth century a large segment of the Armenian population was Turkish-speaking, Hovhannes Karnetsi produced a number of original works and translations in Turkish, but written in the Armenian alphabet. Among these translations are some of the *sharakans* (spiritual hymns) of Catholicos Komitas and the poem *Aravot luso* (The morning of light) by Nerses Shnorhali. Hovhannes Karnetsi's odes were collected and published by Shushanik Nazarian in Yerevan in 1962.

"Hovhannes Karnetsi's songs may not reflect artistic perfection from the point of view either of form or of content, but their language and simplicity give them the characteristics of popular songs and give the poet's pen a unique quality."[1]

Song One[2]

I'll offer you *sherbet:*[3] drink it in goblets most precious!
My treasure, you have knocked me out with your love!
You deserve goblets studded with stones, my precious,
Because your wine-drenched ardor has made me drunk with
    love.
The smoke of my sighs has seeped into the valleys,
The bearer of love has leapt over rivers and passes,
And so the flames of love jumped over valleys
And your scorching love converted me to ashes.

My darling love, my radiance is you:
I've never met another so bright as you!
With rays of light you shine upon my heart,
And with your love you've driven me insane.

Your love has filled me with yearning fire;
My heart looks out with nothing but desire,
While my poor self your road so long walks down.
But the torment of your love can't break me down.

Hymn to Love (Ten)[4]

My ardent love for you has burned me out, my lovely treasure,
My longing after you has worn me out, my jewel without
    measure,

---

1. Shushanik Nazarian, ed., *Hovhannes Karnetsi, Tagharan* (Hovhannes Karnetsi: hymns) (Yerevan, 1962), 43.
2. Ibid., 67. Translated by the editors of the present anthology.
3. Sweet, fruity drink (Arabic).
4. Nazarian, *Hovhannes Karnetsi,* 80–81. Translated by Arminé Keuchguerian and edited by the editors of the present anthology.

To behold your noble manners and bright looks is such a
pleasure.
That is why I feel conquered by your love, my dear,
And, rising from my lips, this song of praise you hear.

I could never see enough of your noble face, my dame,
The longer my passions were stirred up, the more I burned in
love's flame,
As deep within my heart I cherish your charming name.
That is why I feel conquered by your love, my dear,
And, rising from my lips, this song of praise you hear.

You have my yearning, my desire, my admiration;
Like the bright and shining sun, you bring illumination,
Like a priceless string of pearls, a sparkling constellation.
That is why I feel conquered by your love, my dear,
And, rising from my lips, this song of praise you hear.

You have become a source of joy for me, my lovely rose;
Like that of the love-sick nightingale, my singing swells and
grows;
The sweet fragrance of your fair and rosy nature fills my nose.
That is why I feel conquered by your love, my dear,
And, rising from my lips, this song of praise you hear.

Your voice, so like the nightingale's, falls sweetly on the air;
To hear the music of your precious words is my only care;
Words drop from your lips like honey and fill me with joy, my
fair.
That is why I feel conquered by your love, my dear,
And, rising from my lips, this song of praise you hear.

I am attached to you by love, like the nightingale to the rose;
Your love revives my heart, and as the river of time flows,
Day by day increasing, into a mountain my old love grows.
That is why I feel conquered by your love, my dear,
And, rising from my lips, this song of praise you hear.

HYMN TO LOVE (FIFTEEN)[5]

My most precious and desirable sweetheart,
The love I cherish for you has made me miserable:
Your rejection of me fills me with deepest grief.
That is why I sing this song of lamentation.

Pondering my passion for you fills me with constant torment,
The agitation that love causes me sets my poor self on fire,
More and more I long to see your dear and noble face.
That is why I sing this song of lamentation.

I resemble the unfortunate nightingale
Consumed with love for the pretty flower,
But my suffering is even deeper than the grief of that bird.
That is why I sing this song of lamentation.

I am given up to solitude in my sad, unhappy dwelling,
With no companion, like a mournful turtle-dove,
Or like an owl that watches over ruins.
That is why I sing this song of lamentation.

This life we lead in the glare of the sun,
Is more painful to me than to anyone else,
For I am deprived of my sweetheart's noble face.
That is why I sing this song of lamentation.

I am thirsty, my entire being longs for your love
Like the unicorn that approaches the water spring,
For my heart is tumultuous, burning with your love.
That is why I sing this song of lamentation.

---

5. Ibid., 90–91.

Hovhannes Vanandetsi

(John of Vanand)

(1772–1841)

Hovhannes Vanandetsi was born in Van and orphaned at the age of four. He was placed in the care of the brothers of the Ktuts monastery, where he grew up and received his early education. He was a gifted and eager student, became a deacon, and, at the age of about twenty, moved to Constantinople to further his education. There he studied at the Dpratun school (operating under the Patriarchate of Constantinople), where he studied grammar, rhetoric, and logic. His teachers saw great abilities in him and persuaded the school supervisor, Mkrtich *Amira* Mirichanian, to sponsor his studies. Happy with his progress and demeanor, the *amira* welcomed him into his own home. Vanandetsi had already begun to make a name for himself with his poems and speeches. He graduated in 1798, and the following year he was appointed teacher at the newly opened Mesropian school in Smyrna, where he taught for eighteen years. In 1817 he was ordained a married priest. He remained in Smyrna for the rest of his life and died there in 1841, after a long illness.

His first work was *Char nerboghakan i surb khachn Kristosi* (Eulogy on the Holy Cross of Christ), written in 1816 and published in Moscow in 1853 by one of his students, Mser Mserian, a journalist and author, in gratitude to his teacher. Half lyric and half narrative, it is a work that extols the role Christianity has played in the life of the Armenian people, including the history of the Holy Cross of Varag and some commentary.

Hovhannes Vanandetsi established his fame in poetry. His style is that of the old school, and the lack of artistry in his works is partially compensated for by his rich imagination and mastery of words. Unfortunately, he did not learn any European languages and was thus deprived of contact with the Western classics. In his day, for example, Homer and Virgil had not yet been translated into Armenian. However, he was well versed in Turkish, Arabic, and Persian, and indeed translated poetry from Persian. Some of his poems are read as prose set to verse.

His best known works are epic poems, all of which derive their themes from Armenian history and are aimed at reviving patriotism and national pride among the people by recalling past glories: *Tesaran handisitsn Hayka, Arama yev Arami* (Scenes of splendor depicting Hayk, Ara, and Aram), written in 1829 and published in Smyrna in 1856; *Arpiakan Hayastani* (To sunlit Armenia Constantinople, 1836), a lengthy epic poem based on Agathangelos's account of Armenia's conversion to Christianity (which takes some liberties with certain details, in order to enhance the story); and *Voski dar Hayastani* (Armenia's golden age), a 5000-line poem published posthumously in Smyrna in 1841. All these works are typical examples of Armenian classicism.

The merit of his poetry lies not so much in its form as in its content: Vanandetsi introduced new ideas and new sensitivities, sowing them like seeds in the consciousness of the people, where they would eventually blossom.[1]

FROM THE LIGHT OF ARMENIA[2]

Preface

Having come of age, St. Gregory asks his nurse about his origin and family. The nurse narrates his life, beginning with his birth. She tells him of the battle of the Armenian King Khosrov against Artashir the Sasanit, of Anak's falsehood and his killing

---

1. For an extensive analysis of Hovhannes Vanandetsi's work see Manuk Abeghian, *Yerger* (Works) (Yerevan, 1970), 4:592–610.
2. Hovhannes Vanandetsi, "Nakhadrutiun" (Preface), in *Arpiakan Hayastani* (To sunlit Armenia) (Constantinople, 1836), 1–5. Translated by Arminé Keuchgue-rian and edited by the editors of the present anthology.

of Khosrov, the extermination of Anak's family, the rescue of St. Gregory from the carnage, and his being brought to Caesarea, where he was raised in the Christian faith. Then she tells about Artashir's invasion of Armenia, the massacre of Khosrov's family, the rescue of Tiridates, and his bravery and great deeds in Rome; this is followed by Gregory's becoming King Tiridates' loyal servant and the duel of Tiridates with the tyrant of the Goths, whom he captures and takes to Emperor Diocletian.

Canto One[3]

The refreshing heavenly breeze which gently blew
Inspired my soul to give forth a new song,
Making a nosegay of our Illuminator's splendid deeds
To cheer our people with the tale of what he has done.

This perpetual desire to earn my nation's ardent love
Gave a new motive to my waves of agony:
To turn scenes of the past into a spectacle of praise,
To change their rhapsody into a quiet meditation.

And first we visit the border of Kotayk. Ensnared within its pit
Is Armenia's radiant fount, destined to be its light.
Thenceforth to that brilliant offspring and clever scion
All have desired to sing his praise in worthy song.
Therefore I sing a fitting, gracious heavenly tune,
Starting with the occasion when our light was born.
But first, troubled by my state of tense anxiety,
I ask the Supreme Being for an enlightened, tranquil mind.

What Eternal Light You first created from that somber pit!
It shines on all, that Light of yours, with radiance sublime!
On bended knee, from the depths of my soul, I beg:
Enable me to praise in verse the splendid light of Armenia.

May Divine Wisdom, sublime creative power,
I earnestly entreat You, guide this work of mine.
My heart rejoices, aflame with unfeigned ardor
That quickens, like a seraph, the flow of words in my distressed
  mind.

---

3. Ibid.

Why did the spoilers defile our land with evil deeds,
And plunder the very truth, with torment of adversity?
The land that constantly endured the curse of obscurity
By the wondrous grace of heaven began to shine like snow with
    goodness.

While expanding melodies once more reached the people,
And agitated passions of the Court were locked in discord,
Our luminary was zealously seeking the people's salvation,
And our native land threw off its load of obligation.

Tall and well-built, a comely youth in prime of life,
A handsome man, broad-shouldered, with firm hips and noble
    face,
The blood of epic heroes flowing amply in his veins,
Appeared to the people as someone wonderful, most glorious.

While living in Cappadocia, an ignorant suckling,
Along with milk he had sucked the sacred laws of grace divine.
His lively face gave all who looked on him the hope
He would be honest, eloquent, robust, with strength of mind.

Caesarea became his home, where he was fed with dual knowl-
    edge;
He held home life in high esteem, giving respect where due,
Because he still knew nothing of his origin or lineage,
And what had happened in the past was hidden from his
    knowing.

His nuptial bed, shared with a wife according to decent custom,
Produced descendants of that same blood, as a service to our
    land.
The sons grew and flourished like high branches, resembling
    their father,
Who fed them with ever more substantial food for mind and
    soul.

His nurse appeared to him in sleep and told him all
About the branches rising from his grandsires' roots,
In what castle of Caesarea, in refuge, he was raised,
With what pure faith, as at his mother's bosom.

How fortunate! the new idea was sent by God to our holy
  father:
God's Will inflamed his righteous heart with sacred love,
And so the clever nurse let loose a flood of words,
Making him comprehend the great events the past had swal-
  lowed up.

She then told why he had been kept in darkness,
And revealed the truth that was concealed till then.
"You are the seed of noble heroes, boy," she said,
"Believing in our Father, in lineage pure, unsullied.

"Your father, Anak Bahlav, the famed Surenian minister,
Supported his brother-in-law, his noble relative
Artashir. He, savage with greed, audaciously betrayed his kin
And dethroned the Armenian king, of Persia's Arsacid line.

"The Armenian king, Khosrov, of the same Arsacid blood,
Not knowing of the plot, continued to govern prudently,
Delighting in his kinfolks' loyalty to Artavan,
Hoping firmly in his heart for lasting unity."

Grigor Peshtimalchian (Peshtimaldjian)

(1778–1837)

Grigor Peshtimalchian, an educator mainly known for his erudition in the Armenian language, theology, and philosophy, was a prominent figure of the pre-revival period. He was born in Constantinople, and devoted his entire life to writing and teaching. He became principal of the Pezchian (Bezdjian) Armenian school, where he also taught language, rhetoric, philosophy, and religion. In 1828, soon after the establishment of the religious school attached to the Patriarchate of Kum Kapu, he was appointed head teacher and chief administrator there. As an educator, he worked on textbooks and curriculum organization and wrote regulations for discipline in the schools and the fair treatment of students.

Early in his life he started to compile a dictionary of classical Armenian, intended to comprise two volumes, but the project was discontinued.

He lived at a time when the intelligentsia were actively engaged in sharp disputes about classical versus modern Armenian. It is interesting to note that in his publications Grigor Peshtimalchian alternates between the two. In 1829 he published *Kerakanutiun haykazian lezvi* (A grammar of the Armenian language), in essence a grammar of classical Armenian. His *Tramabanutiun kam arvest banakan* (Logic, or the art of reason), a philosophical treatise, is also in classical Armenian. Yet his other works, such as *Krtutiun kaghakavarutyan* (Education in civility) and *Lusashavigh* (The path of enlightenment), are written in a very clear modern Armenian. Indeed, Peshtimalchian's works reflect the crucially important transition in Armenian letters during the early nineteenth century.

He also taught, and wrote on, philosophical topics, tending to adhere to the European philosophers of the Age of Reason. Although he was a layman, his knowledge in matters of religion and theology far exceeded that of most clerics. Living at a time when several schismatic movements arose, he came forward as a staunch defender of the Armenian Apostolic Church, her doctrines, and her traditions, attempting to preserve the national and religious unity of the people.

FROM THE PATH OF ENLIGHTENMENT[1]

According to the order of God's providence, no one is able to comprehend the substance of the faith all by himself nor adhere to it, except through the mediation of preaching and instruction. But if pastors are neglectful of preaching and teachers are careless in teaching, then how should the ignorant comprehend the essence of the faith and the salvation of humanity be accomplished? As the Scriptures say, "And how shall they believe in him of whom they have not heard? and how shall they hear without a preacher?"[2] Because, as St. Gregory the Illuminator says, "The ears are doors of faith, assuring the entrance of pure morals."[3]

If an adult who possesses the knowledge needed to teach the doctrine of the faith does not exert himself vigorously, he may be considered guilty of a crime, because for the salvation of mankind it is not enough to recite the Creed, pronouncing the words only with the lips, but rather it is necessary to comprehend and perceive the most important attributes of the faith, enclosed within the Creed.

Thus, pastors and tutors who possess the expertise to teach but show indolence cannot escape reproach and blame, for in accordance with their ministerial obligations they should preach and

---

1. Grigor Peshtimalchian, *Lusashavigh . . .* (The path of enlightenment) (Constantinople, 1848), 1–4. Translated by Arminé Keuchguerian and edited by the editors of the present anthology.
2. Rom. 10:14 [KJV].
3. *Hachakhabatum* (Dogmatical sermons).

teach. As the Scriptures say, "Woe is unto me, if I preach not the gospel!"[4]

The command that was given by God to love one's neighbor as oneself[5] is not fulfilled only by providing necessities and giving money or by showing compassion for sorrows with words of consolation, because these things, being corporeal, are all temporal and destined to vanish. Of those who are qualified for the purpose it is also required that they teach their "neighbors" the doctrine of the faith—which serves as nourishment for the spiritual life, pure morals, and the integrity of rational abilities. In short, they must be taught to become perfect, loving God with all their hearts, with all the faculties of their minds, and with all the strength of their souls.

Since God desires "all men to be saved, and to come unto the knowledge of the truth,"[6] we feel incessantly compelled, being stirred within our hearts by the perpetual motion of his favors through the preaching of pastors and the instruction of intelligent tutors, to comprehend the mystery of the faith, which is confirmed by the delight of inheriting eternal felicity.

First of all, we must learn the Creed, which is the basis and the source of all divine and human virtues. Then come the other teachings, one by one, because "without faith it is impossible to please Him."[7]

As the doctrines of the faith are extremely deep and inscrutable, beyond our comprehension, it is a mere delusion to think that we are able to penetrate those depths through human reasoning or that we can discern the obscure notions through keen observation: "For who hath known the mind of the Lord? or who hath been his counselor?"[8] Therefore, we must content ourselves with the inspiring words of the Scriptures that encourage us to have faith; as the Holy Bible says, "You may take our case as an example, and learn the true meaning of 'nothing beyond what stands written.' "[9] And so, as Nerses the Gracious says, "The way to comprehend the unintelligible is none other than to believe in everything the Holy

---

4. 1 Cor. 9:16 [KJV].
5. Mark 12:33.
6. 1 Tim. 2:4 [KJV].
7. Heb. 11:6 [KJV].
8. Rom. 11:34 [KJV].
9. 1 Cor. 4:6 [REB].

Bible says, and not to scrutinize the inscrutable with painstaking investigation."

Moreover, it is very impudent to prefer the scrutiny of the intellect to the revelation of God in the Scriptures: "Your faith should not stand in the wisdom of men, but in the power of God."[10] And so St. Gregory the Illuminator says: "Let us put an end to vain and useless scrutiny and listen to the precepts of the sacred testaments, both the old and the new, . . . because I am your God, says the Lord, . . . and there is no one else to proclaim the laws."[11]

In this concise survey we present an explanatory commentary on the essential attributes of the faith, necessary for any adult Christian; as the Scriptures say: "Believe in God, believe also in me."[12] Explanations, referring to the Christian religion, are also given, for the use of teachers.

In fact, we had no intention of taking such a hard, trying, and difficult task upon our feeble self and were reluctant to cast, with all our shortsightedness, an eagle eye on the shining rays of the sun. It is indeed an impudence that deserves to be reprimanded ten thousand times and more, for only perfect minds and those closely attuned to divine realities should speak of sacred things.

We are taught, however, to obey our superiors, to respect them and comply with their commands, because they are more concerned with the salvation of our souls, for which they have to render an account to God.

Therefore, in accordance with an irrevocable order of our holy father, His Blessedness Poghos (Paul), the renowned patriarch, we felt obliged to take on this task, for no other reason than to dispel the resentment of those who, without knowing me, thought I had stumbled in the faith and considered me a stray.

Accordingly, the good faith that I possess through baptism and the sound doctrine that I learned from the sainted illuminator of the Armenian Church I am now proclaiming to everyone, addressing those who live both far away and close at hand, but chiefly because Petros (Peter) the Apostle instructs us to do so: "Be ready always to give an answer to every man that asketh you a reason of the hope that is in you."[13]

---

10. 1 Cor. 2:5 [KJV].
11. *Discourses.*
12. John 14:1 [KJV].
13. 1 Pet. 3:15 [KJV].

Perhaps I will be criticized for using the language of the Scriptures here and, in some places, for writing in a philosophical style that needs clarification, making it difficult for most readers to understand. Prior to this survey, in our *I kristoneakan hamarotutyan* (Abridged outlook on Christianity), which was written at the monastery of Ortagiugh (Ortaköy),[14] I wrote in a rural dialect, as if feeding children on milk. Now, I am writing in the literary language, as if giving solid food to proper adults, for there is much about the faith that is obscure and difficult to understand, requiring explanations that make use of literary language sprinkled with philosophy. The following are a few examples of such terms, encountered in this survey and in the writings of many others: *existence, correlation, manifested property, active* or *passive meaning, reason to, reason for, impressed* or *portrayed image,* and so on.

Perhaps some might say that the faith should be elucidated in a simple way that can easily be understood by everybody, and that in consequence it is not proper to use words the meaning of which it is difficult to grasp. In fact, the ideas of the faith that every Christian should know are clear and plain, at least in their essentials and their most important details, as the Creed illustrates.

When I say clear, I am not referring to the substance or the inner meaning, because the essence of the faith is the substance of divinity in three persons and the substantial union of divinity and human nature in one Christ, who is uncompounded and indivisible; and the sanctifying sacraments of Baptism, Holy Communion, Penitence, and so on, are all also unintelligible and incomprehensible. They are clear only in relation to the construction of the words used to explain them and their external meanings.

The notions that are necessary for the Christian but not for any single individual include the thorough knowledge of the attributes of the faith and the sacraments of the Church, the reasoning behind the doctrines, the causes of conformity and impropriety, the various attempts to establish the truth and refute aberrations, and the solution of many other knotty problems; none of these can be expressed in the vernacular, which is not capable of conveying the meaning with clarity. Therefore, even skillful weaving of such words or terms, instead of clarifying the obscurity of the meaning and making the difficult easy to understand, renders the work

---

14. A suburb of Istanbul, inhabited at the time mainly by Armenians.

totally unintelligible, not to mention that vulgar and mean words cast disrepute on the dignity of the royal ring, scepter, and throne. Henceforth flawless literary terms are needed to illustrate the conformity of divine and spiritual ideas with purity and elegance.

That it is important for the Church not only to possess knowledge of the essential attributes of the faith, but also to possess great erudition concerning the divine and human actions that serve to establish sound doctrine and refute the contradictions of opponents, is evident from the following words of the apostle: "He must keep firm hold of the true doctrine, so that he may be well able to appeal to his hearers with sound teaching and to refute those who raise objections."[15]

We had all these things in mind, intending not to mix the attributes of the faith with fictitious narratives, but only to repeat the sayings of the holy fathers and the *vartapets* (doctors of divinity), supporting those sayings by the Scriptures.

But some opponents might say: "There are many such writings; what is the use of this one?" In fact, there are not few such writings, but some of them are very concise, dealing only with issues, but omitting the principal, the essential; others are extremely long, to the extent that they become tedious with the repetition of ideas.

Our present survey, being midway between the verbose and the succinct, sets forth all that is considered important and also, to a moderate and reasonable degree, the fundamental essence of some teachings, in such a way that we will not be criticized but rather commended for our diligence. If, however, anyone finds it useless, let him not consider the work entirely worthless: perhaps it will be of some value to others; for if a certain kind of food does not please a particular individual, that does not mean that it is totally inedible.

Finally, I humbly ask my noble readers to remember me kindly for having given an account of the truth of the orthodox teaching of our Holy Armenian Church.

---

15. Titus 1:9 [REB].

Harutiun Alamdarian

(1795–1834)

Harutiun Alamdarian was born in Astrakhan, received his education at the local Aghababian Armenian school, and, in 1813, moved to Moscow, where he associated himself with the founding of the Lazarian school, which began to function in 1815. He was ordained a married priest in 1814. He stayed at the Lazarian till 1824, by which time the school had grown to the level of a Russian gymnasium. He studied under the renowned scholar Serovbé Patkanian (1814–95) and also attended a series of lectures at the University of Moscow. He began teaching before he had completed his studies.

In 1824 Nerses Ashtaraketsi, the primate of Tiflis (later catholicos, 1843–58), asked Alamdarian to assume the principalship of the newly founded Nersisian school, which opened its doors in January 1825. He remained in that position till 1830 and raised the school to a high standard. The first five years of the school are known as the "Alamdarian era."

In 1827, during the Russo-Iranian war, he helped organize Armenian volunteer units for the Russian army. Although his orientation was Russian, he actively defended the rights of Armenian religious and cultural institutions against the assimilation policies of the tsars. In 1830, at the instigation of Ivan Paskevich, the governor of the Caucasus, he was banished to the monastery of Haghpat as a collaborator of Ashtaraketsi, who was similarly exiled to Bessarabia. After staying in Haghpat for a while, he became superior (1832–34) of the Surb Khach (Holy Cross) monastery in Nor Nakhijevan (Rostov-on-Don), where he was killed under mysterious conditions.

His literary output is mainly poetry and is considered a transition from classicism to sentimentalism-romanticism. The greatest blow in his life was his wife's untimely death in 1828, after which he took a vow of celibacy. Her death was a source of inspiration for his highly sensitive poems. He used the traditional theme of the rose and nightingale, with the sad twist that no spring would ever bring the rose to life again. In poems expressing religious sentiments he tends to mysticism, while at the same time protesting against destiny.

His other works consist of a Russian-Armenian dictionary (1821); a Russian-Armenian grammar (unpublished); a booklet of "Proposed Regulations for the Armenian School in Tbilisi" (1825) that includes administrative, curricular, and ethical rules; and a number of primers and other teaching material.

SPRING[1]

At the end of April I opened the window
And saw the snowy field adorned with flowers.
My cheeks burned with hot tears flowing down,
As they recalled my unchangeable captivity.

Bitter was my sinking heart, like an acrid aftertaste,
Benumbed my senses, almost lost my breath.
"Alas!" I repeated endlessly, in pity of myself,
Cursing again and again the unfortunate day of my birth.

Faded and worn, I was overcome with sleep,
The anguish of my poor existence cast into the deep.
The glorious queen of immortals came to me in a vision:
It seemed she drew me up out of a deep rut.

---

1. Harutiun Alamdarian, *"Garun"* (Spring), in *Entir ejer Hay grakanutyan* (Select pages of Armenian literature) (Yerevan, n.d.), 324–25. Translated by Arminé Keuchguerian and edited by the editors of the present anthology. The Armenian text is an acrostic, with the first letter of each stanza, read consecutively, spelling out "by Alamdarian."

Unfearing, I drew near to kiss her feet,
My rescuer, whose mystical powers had saved me.
Flights of sweet-singing birds warbled in harmony,
Magnifying the glory of the life-giving Mother of God.

Happy the rose that glows so red
To give me heart and to praise my patron saint!
How wretched I am for wailing peevishly:
Why did I think myself alone and incurably lost?

My tormentors' barbs turned back upon themselves,
And their plotting ensnared them in their own nets.
All you who suffer and are heavy laden, bless the Lord forever:
Console yourselves that hope flows from the Holy Cross.

DREAM[2]

Since break of day, as I lay in bed,
    I've been tortured with my sweetheart's love.
I had spent a sleepless night,
    For thoughts of her tormented me.

With dry mouth and dry spirit
    I lay down, feeble in body.
In my light sleep, sweet dreams
    Brought tears of joy to my eyes.

Ever in turmoil, ever in love,
    I resemble a boat upon a stormy sea.
The cure for these sufferings is my precious love,
    But of her presence I see not a sign.

Water from the garden, splashing into my room,
    Disturbed the slumber of my misty eyes.
I listened closely, and I heard
    The treading footsteps of my beloved.

---

2. Alamdarian, "*Anurchk*" (Dream), ibid., 325. Trans. ibid. The Armenian text is an acrostic with the first letter of every second line spelling out "by Alamdarian."

"Is this a dream?" Gently I jostled
    My tormented soul fully awake.
"Alas, my prince!" she woefully exclaimed,
    "Why do you dwindle so, my dearest one?"

The voice of my beloved in my ear
    Stirred sparks of life within my heart.
Soon both my body and my soul
    Were overcome with great exultation.

Hovhannes Teroyents

(1801–88)

One of the last representatives of the traditionalist, conservative school of Armenian intellectuals of the 1840s, Hovhannes Teroyents Chamurchian (Chamurdjian), also known as Ter-Karapetian, was born in Brusa (Bursa), where he attended the local school and pursued his education (1817–19) at the Armash Monastery. He accumulated an enormous amount of knowledge in theology, Church history, and philosophy, mostly through self-education, and he also became fluent in a number of languages.

In 1830, having decided to make teaching his life's work, he moved to Constantinople and joined the *Jemaran* (educational institution) in Scutari (Üsküdar), where he served first as teacher (1838–49) then as principal (1841–46). In 1846 he and Mkrtich Aghaton (1818–90) founded and edited *Hayastan* (Armenia), a weekly with literary, religious, and political content. This was the first periodical to be published under the auspices of the Patriarchate of Constantinople. After its cessation in 1852, he launched a new journal, *Zohal* (Saturn), written in Turkish but printed in Armenian characters, which lasted for one year; it resurfaced later (1857–66), written in Armenian, under the Armenian name *Yerevak*. Its editorial stance was strongly conservative, supporting the clerical establishment and the *amiras*.

Teroyents lived through a time when the entire Armenian community was in social, religious, and intellectual turmoil. Liberal trends, the creation of the National Constitution, the emergence of literary schools, and especially the establishment of Catholic and Protestant communities composed of Armenians made him very uneasy. His main concern was not so much to initiate debate as to defend the old, well established order, fearing that otherwise the nation would lose its identity and stability. He staunchly defended the integrity and orthodoxy of the Armenian Apostolic Church.

He was a prolific writer: his writings, whether original or translations, in classical or modern Armenian, printed or still in manuscript, amounted to about 150 works. Some of his best known are a translation of Blaise Pascal's *Pensées* (*Khorhrdatzutiunk Paskala*, Pascal's *Thoughts*, 1844); a translation of Jean-Jacques Rousseau's *Du contrat social* (*Hasarakakan dashink*, *The Social Contract*); a series of works on grammar, philosophy, religion, and morality; *Iravakhoh* (The arbitrator, 1866–72), a study in three volumes of the differences between the Catholic and Armenian Apostolic churches; and *Endhanur yekeghetsakan patmutiun* (General church history), thirty unpublished volumes, the manuscript for which is in the library of the Armenian Patriarchate of Jerusalem. The best study of his life and work is Harutiun Mrmrian's *Tasnevinnerord dar yev Hovhannes Prusatzi Teroyetz* (The nineteenth century and Hovhannes Teroyents of Brusa, 1908).

FROM CRITIC[1]

The Worship of Images

This is a term to be found neither in the writings nor in the mouths of religious writers. The Protestants have created it in

---

1. "*Patkerapashtutiun*" (The worship of images) is from Hovhannes Teroyents's *Banadat—Pan Tiarn Tiarn Matteosi Srbazan Katoghikosi Amenayn Hayots: "Bari mard bari kristonya" grkin dem boghokakanneren nuyn anun grkin gnnutiun* (Critique: examination of the Protestant rebuttal of the treatise of His Holiness Matthew, Catholicos of all Armenians, identically titled *A Good Man Good Christian*) (Constantinople, 1860).

This book is a reply to Protestant criticisms of Catholicos Matteos's book *Bari mard yev bari kristonya* (Good man and good Christian) that accused the Armenian Church of endorsing "the worship of images." See Minas Teoleolian, *Dar me grakanutiun 1850–1920* (A century of literature, 1850–1920) (Boston, 1977), 1:107–8. Translated by the editors of the present anthology.

order to persuade their followers that the Church of the faithful worships images just as idolaters worship idols. It has often been explained that the faithful do not worship images; they merely use them to remind themselves of the virtue behind the images, and hence they show only respect for the persons represented in them. They know that it is not a sin to show respect for those whom God has glorified.

But say what one will, the Protestants know their scriptures. When your rival slanders you, says Voltaire, you lose even if the slander is not believed, because it leaves a trace in the listener's mind and that is a gain for your enemy. I do not mean to say that the Protestants learned to do this from Voltaire; it is a very old tactic, dating back to the Tondrakians and Paulicians, who accused the Orthodox of worshiping the subjects of images. Since this lie is so ancient, how can we eradicate it or stop the liars from telling it? They are like the men of the tribe of Ephraim, who learned to pronounce the word Sibboleth: their tongue is unable to pronounce it Shibboleth, even under threat of death.[2]

They repeat over and over, in order to make the basis of their objection clear, that God forbids the worship of idols in the Ten Commandments, and that therefore the making of images contravenes God's law. They have been told a thousand times that the purpose of that commandment is to prevent confusing the true God with lies, and that our images do not mean that we worship a false god instead of the true God. It is not a question of disobeying Our Lord and Savior's commandment; rather, it is a way of reaching those who behold the images, especially the illiterate, reminding them of the deeds of the saints whom God has found acceptable, so that they too might believe and become His followers. But the Protestants continue to sing the same tune.

Tell them that when images remind one of God and His miracles they have never been forbidden, either at the time of the Old Testament or at the time of the New. Tell them that He ordered Moses to cure those who had been bitten by serpents by making a brazen serpent and putting it on a pole where all might look on it.[3] And that Our Lord declared that this was a symbol of His

2. Judg. 12:5–6.
3. Num. 21:8–9. "If a serpent had bitten any man, when he beheld the serpent of brass, he lived."

crucifixion.[4] And that when the Israelites began to worship it and offer it sacrifices, then it deserved to be destroyed, and Hezekiah the king broke it into pieces and had the pieces thrown away.[5] Say that the prophet Moses had two cherubim made of gold and placed on the two ends of the mercy seat (the Ark of the Covenant).[6] And when Solomon had the temple built he also placed two cherubim, not on the Ark of the Covenant as Moses did, but within the sanctuary called the Holy of Holies.[7] Say that the New Testament also contains accounts of the very ancient practice of using images. Remind them of the portrait that Our Lord sent to King Abgar,[8] as Khorenatsi relates, based on the archives of Edessa.[9] Remind them also of numerous other examples in the records of the Church.

What kind of reaction do you get? The same. God forbade the raising up of idols in the Ten Commandments, they say. This is also a logical error: changing the meaning of a word within the same sentence. God forbade the raising up of idols; so to say that the making of images is a sin means accepting that an image and an idol are the same thing. But in general all Protestants since Carlstadt[10] and Zwingli[11] understand the terms in that way. However, it is they whose understanding is at fault, and they cannot make something wrong that is right. All this shows that those who speak that way are tenacious in their error. It is frivolous to hope that one might be able to convince these people by reasoning with them. We can, however, warn the children of the church not to be taken in by their warped ideas.

---

4. John 3:14: "And as Moses lifted up the serpent in the wilderness, even so must the Son of man be lifted up."

5. 2 Kings 18:4.

6. Exod. 25:18–20.

7. 1 Kings 6:23–28.

8. According to an ancient tradition, Abgar V (4 BC–AD 50), one of the kings of Edessa, wrote a letter to Christ, asking Him to visit and cure him of an illness; although Christ declined to come, He wrote back promising that He would send a disciple to cure the king and preach the Gospel to the people. A variation of this story is recorded by Eusebius (*History of the Church*, 1:13). A later version adds that along with His reply Christ also sent His portrait, miraculously imprinted on canvas. See F. L. Cross and E. A. Livingstone, eds., *The Oxford Dictionary of the Christian Church*, 2nd ed. (Oxford, 1982), 5.

9. Movses Khorenatsi (c. 410–end of the fifth century), *Hayots patmutiun* (History of the Armenians), (Yerevan, 1940), 2:32.

10. Real name Andreas Rudolf Bodenstein (c. 1480–1541), German reformer known especially for his iconoclastic zeal.

11. Huldreich Zwingli (1484–1531), Swiss reformer.

Mesrop Taghiadian

(1803–59)

The writer, traveler, and teacher Mesrop Taghiadian[1] was born in Yerevan, studied in Etchmiadzin under Poghos Gharadaghtsi (c. 1790–c. 1850–60), and traveled through the villages of the area to collect popular songs and legends. He became a deacon but did not take holy orders. He had an inquisitive mind and an adventurous nature, which led him to Calcutta (1826–30), where he studied at the Bishop's College and graduated with a master's degree in arts. While studying, he worked at the college print shop and published a number of translations from English (his favorite authors were Shakespeare, Chesterfield, John Milton, John Locke, Alexander Pope, and Robert Burns) and, from Latin, Hugo Grotius's *De Veritatae Religionis Christianae* (On the truth of the Christian faith). From 1831 on he was an itinerant educator, teaching in Calcutta, New Julfa, Etchmiadzin, Tabriz, and Constantinople. His frequent travels and many contacts helped him acquire a wider worldview. Returning to Calcutta, he became employed at Bishop's College, in charge of the Armenian section of the print shop. In 1845 he founded a periodical, *Azgaser* (Patriot), later renamed *Azgaser Araratyan* (Ararat patriot), which emphasized the importance of education and promoted

---

1. For some of the details in this biography the editors are indebted to Kevork B. Bardakjian, *A Reference Guide to Modern Armenian Literature, 1500–1920* (Detroit, 2000), 133–35.

the idea of rallying around the ancestral homeland to work for its development and stability. The paper also provided information and commentary on current political and social issues. It lasted till 1852. In 1846 he established a school in Calcutta, named after St. Sandukht, for boys and girls, where instruction was based not on the old scholastic system but on modern European methods that Taghiadian extolled in his booklet "Discourse on the Education of Girls" (1847). He rejected the idealistic approach that assumed moral characteristics to be innate; he maintained they were acquired gradually, by means of education.

Mesrop Taghiadian was a prolific writer. Other than primers, language and grammar textbooks, a small dialectal dictionary, and other teaching material, he produced some major works: *Ditsabanutiun* (Mythology), *Patmutiun hin Hndkastani hanhishatak daruts anti i hardzakumn mahmetakanats* (History of Ancient India from immemorial ages to the invasion of Mohammedans) (1841), *Patmutiun Parsits* (History of the Persians) (1846), *Zvarchakhos arakk parsits* (Humorous Persian fables) (1846), and *Vkayabanutiun srbuyn Sandkhto* (The martyrdom of St. Sandukht) (1847). He also left extensive records and "diaries" about his travels in Armenia, Iran, and India. He also tried his hand at fiction; the two novels he wrote, *Vep Vardgisi* (The story of Vartges, 1846) and *Vep Varsenkan* (The story of Varsenik, 1847), are among the earliest examples of modern Armenian fiction. The first one, an adaptation from Heinrich Zschokke's *The Great Bandit*, "illustrates national unity and personal integrity," whereas the second, based on a Middle Eastern tale, extols "persistence, industry and self-reliance."[2] As for poetry, all his poems written after 1830 were collected in *Tutak taghiadiants* (The Taghiadian parrot) and published in 1847. His poetry, written in Classical Armenian bears the influence of romanticism and is imbued with sincere humanism.

In 1858 Mersrop Taghiadian decided to return to his native land and spend the rest of his life there. On his journey to Yerevan he became ill and died in Shiraz, Iran.

PARABLE 3[3]

A scholar, who was to leave for a foreign country, entrusts his 1,000 piastres to a pharmacist. On his return, when he wants the

---

2. Bardakjian, *Reference Guide*, 134–35.
3. Mesrop Taghiadian, in *Gegharvestakan yerker* (Artistic works) (Yerevan, 1965), 395–403. Translated by Arminé Keuchguerian and edited by the editors of the present anthology.

money back, the pharmacist denies having received anything and everybody mocks the scholar. Not capable of solving the problem, the scholar writes down an account of the incident and delivers it to the king. The latter orders him to go and sit speechless nearby the place of the pharmacist, for three days. "On the fourth day," he says, "I will pass by that place and greet you. You also must give me a salute, but without standing up." The scholar does as he was told. On the fourth day the king, while pompously passing thence, stops to greet the scholar and says: "Oh, my brother, why don't you come to see me and relate some particulars about you?"

After the king leaves, the pharmacist, who was shuddering with fear, finds out ways to return the deposit and free himself from the king's wrath.

PARABLE 11

A robbery takes place in a house and the owner complains to the judge. The judge summons all the accused and, giving each a stem of the same measure, says: "Now, you may go; the one who is the thief will have his stem extended at a finger depth." The next day he calls them back and notices that one of the accused, fearing that his stem would grow during the night, had cut off a finger depth at the extremity, thus betraying himself.

So, the judge not only makes the culprit return the stolen goods, but also punishes him.

PARABLE 15

Certain merchants offer the king some horses for sale. Finding them very nice, the king buys them and after paying the required sum, he also gives an additional 200,000 piastres for more horses to be brought later. The merchants depart and the king, who had given himself to feasting and drunkenness, orders his minister to set down the names of the idiots of his realm in a list. "I have already prepared such a list," says the minister, "and have placed the name of Your Majesty at the top." "But why?" asks the king. "Because," replies the minister, "you paid 200,000 piastres without requesting guarantee, and also without asking whence those merchants came or where they went."

"And if they bring the horses, what then?" asks the king.

"Then," answers the minister, "I will wipe Your Majesty's name off the list and put the names of the merchants instead."

PARABLE 18

People ask the hunchback whether he would prefer to have his hump straightened or to see everybody hunchbacked like himself.

"I would like everybody to be hunchbacked," he says, "so that I might look at them in the way they are now looking at me."

LAZY PUPIL[4]

O, Athena, gruff-looking,
>   Why treat me so severely?
>   Me, having no wish and will
>   To acquire wisdom and understanding.

The hell with your Alphabet,
>   Which takes my soul almost away.
>   O, how I would like to be
>   The dumb ox drawing the plough,

Instead of seeing, to my grief,
>   That inflexible countenance of yours,
>   And corrupt my blooming youth
>   With your frantic discoveries.

Your teachings and your principles—
>   Why should we need them today?
>   When gold and silver may alone
>   Make humans Worthy Gentlemen.

O, when those good times shall come
>   When we'll not have A and Z?
>   So that we might enjoy well
>   The dance and play, with no shame.

---

4. Ibid., 59

Arsham, a fool greater than me,
   Is not an honored prince glorified?
   Then why should I study
   That knowledge of yours, useless, futile?

FROM THE DIARY[5]

' **Bangala 1830—Second Navigation to Dacca—The Project
of the Mesrovbian College—August 20, 1830[6]**

Being prepared for a travel to my homeland with the intention
of establishing there a college named after St. Mesrop, I wrote
and circulated a letter addressed to our community of Calcutta,[7]
asking for financial aid to buy materials needed for a printing press.
Only a sum of 228 *ska* (Indian monetary unit) was collected, which
would not cover half the expenses; so, I had to pay over 400 rubies
(rupees), from my pocket, completely spending the money destined
for the journey.

LEAVING FOR Dacca—August 25—My sleeplessness resulted in
my becoming ill. Following the doctor's advice that I needed some
change of air, on August 30 I left for Dacca,[8] without telling anybody and with the hope of getting financial aid from our compatriots

---

5. Mesrob Taghiadian, *Divan* (Archives) (New Julfa, 1979), 3–7. Translated
by Arminé Keuchguerian and edited by the editors of the present anthology.

6. This is the first time Mesrop Taghiadian's diary of the years 1830–38 is being
published. There was reference to its existence, but it was not known to specialists
of Armenian literature. The diary belongs to the archives of the Catholicate of
Cilicia. They have been copied by Mesrop Seth and kept in the archive of the priest
Hovhannes Mkrian and were taken, together with his other books, to Antelias,
in 1932. This publication is based on four copybooks, with an attempt to keep
the orthography and the punctuation unchanged. At times, we have referred to Fr.
Hovhannes Mkrian's copies, mainly to verify the proper names, though not always
with much success, especially for the Indian toponyms.

7. Calcutta: the "capital" of Armenians in India. Their commercial, national,
cultural, and religious center was the Armenian Church, built with the financial support of Agha Nazareth, in 1724, and named after St. John the Baptist (Hovhannu
Karapet). This church was called "Church of Nazareth," in order to distinguish it
from the Church of Chichra, bearing the same name.

8. Dacca: Armenians were first established here as merchants, at the beginning of the eighteenth century. The Armenian Church of Holy Resurrection (Surp
Harutiun), built in 1781, is on the street Armenitola.

there. On Monday, at 9 P.M., I left the Bishop's College[9] and arrived in Balu Ghat.

AUGUST 31—TUESDAY. From Balu Ghat I went to Sirampur, but could not meet there Mr. Begdan Sarkisiants. Soon after, I left for Chichra,[10] arriving late during the night. The next day I had breakfast with Martiros Ter-Stepanosian, whom I tried to persuade to remove with his family to Armenia. Having convinced him I then passed my day with Rev. Fr. Hovhan Arakelian. I also visited M. Shirkhorian and that same evening left Chichra.

SEPTEMBER 2—We sailed having a fair wind.

SEPTEMBER 3—I arrived in Chogtan. After casting anchor, I hired a boat, paying a silver coin, and dispatched Shikdar, my servant, to Novsara, to deliver to the royal mailing personnel the enclosed fragments of my *Mythology,* as well as a printed letter addressed to Sayks of the Bishop's College. There resided a certain Englishman, by the name Davis, who cultivated coffee. There are some 3,000 Indian families in Chogtan.

The climate is unhealthy. In a moment I witnessed the death of six individuals whose bodies were then burned, according to the Indian custom. Yesterday, the weather being fine we reached Hardam, on the river bank of Churnia. The sight of an old but lofty building pushed me to cast anchor there. Here I met Raja Ajidchndra, the son of Bjiachndra and the grandson of Sumnchndra, descendants of the Brahmans. We went together to visit the temple of their deities; there was the statue of the goddess Kalki, on her right was Ganesa, on her left was Rama, and Linga was under her feet. A great number of Brahmans were gathered there, quite ignorant of the principles of their religion. I talked to them long enough about their faith, speaking both in Indian and Persian languages. Raja Achidchndra was pleased with my Persian speech very much. He asked from me a letter of recommendation. He sent sweets, as a present. Today I bought a sheep, and slaughtering it shared with my sailors.

---

9. Bishop's College: established in 1820, through the efforts of Middleton, the primate of the Anglican Church. It served as a seminary for Anglican clergymen and teachers. Mesrop Taghiadian studied and worked there.

10. Chichra (Chinsura): a town on the bank of the river Hougli, where the Armenians were established prior to 1645, and had built the first Armenian Church in 1695.

SEPTEMBER 4—At noon I arrived in Rahnagat, paid one ruby and 8 *ska,* as row-charge. I knew through the tax-registration book that Mr. A. Nazar and Mr. R. Shirkhor had left the previous day, and therefore urged the sailors to pursue them. There being nothing particular, I offered medicine to two Indian patients, bought a goat and continued to sail.

SEPTEMBER 5—I arrived in Hanskali, a large borough lying to the north and south of the river Churnia. It has 1,700 residents, in all. The leading business of the place is the manufactory of indigo,[11] belonging to an Englishman by the name Marlis, who was then absent, because of some judicial problems. I bought fish for my sailors.

SEPTEMBER 6—While leaving Hanskali I narrowly escaped death as the river was flowing most violently and it had overflowed covering some four miles of the nearby fields and one of my sailors was almost drowned. Thence, from Churnia we sailed into the river Kunkunia. Today, at two o'clock, I reached Shipni-Bas—a former borough, and now a village where fairs were organized every Monday and Friday. There were three sumptuous temples here, narrow and long in shape, built in the Bengalese year 1644. In one of the temples stood the statue of the god Ram, four-winged, holding a bow and two barnacles. It represented a kneeling man, having his wife by him. This place was the property of Maharaja Kishinchndra Bhadri Ndiula. Jndra Brahman of this place seemed to be a good-natured person, with whom I had a rather long conversation about the mystical sign of Ling. Today I left Kunkunia and sailed to the river Isamut. I passed the night in Gospur, which is a village of herdsmen, with a small mosque, for the Muslims. Here I met the servants of Mr. Sahakian Malkhasiants, the owner of the indigo factory. The wind is blowing in the opposite direction.

SEPTEMBER 7—From Gospur we sailed East and after a troublesome and difficult navigation we came to Kethia. Here I met Messrs. Avetik Nazarian and Raphael Zakarian Shirkhoriants whom I was glad to take on board my ship. Their companionship was a real solace for me. By the evening, I reached Gishanspur, and passed the night there.

---

11. Indigo: Indian hemp; its cultivation began in Bengal, in the years 1780. The Armenians possessed large factories which gradually passed to the English.

SEPTEMBER 8—Wednesday. We left Gishanspur, where a fair is being organized on Wednesdays. The water of the river which here whirled round and round, was obstructing the navigation; that is why the State Company of East India had opened a broad passage leading to the river Poyrap, opposite Ramendra—the Indigo factory of Harris the Englishman. Today, at noon we arrived at Damurda, a big village in the south of the river, where there was a market selling olive oil, rice and all kinds of pulse.[12] We did not find here anything worthy to purchase and left, arriving, after many whirling passages, in Summu Teganch. I did not see there anything that deserved to be mentioned, except a Greek whom I met, by the name Maniram; he was the head of a large family, counting 40 members; he had four sons, all of them with sons and grandsons. To them I presented my *Book of Travels* in full.[13]

SEPTEMBER 9—Thursday. Today we began our navigation with greater success. Mr. Avetik Nazarian showed me, among various narratives, particulars regarding religions.

At 1:00 we arrived at Dunayi-Ganj. Here lived together with his family, Elen the Englishman who had an indigo factory. Within a mile distance, between the rivers Gadiakala and Ismat (which would take about three days to go from Dacca, but we could not risk it as the winds blew in the opposite direction) there was the indigo factory of McDonald, the Englishman of the village of Ratnpur. Traveling by land for one and a half miles, taking approximately four turns of the river, we came to Calcutta.

---

12. The edible seeds of leguminous plants cultivated for food (peas, beans, lentils).

13. It becomes obvious that this diary of Mesrop Taghiadian is an abridged version of a more extended one.

Khachatur Abovian

(1809–48)

Khachatur Abovian was born in the village of Kanaker, now a suburb of Yerevan. When he was ten his father took him to the clerical school in Etchmiadzin to study for the priesthood, but after five years he escaped the suffocating atmosphere there and went to the Nersisian College in Tiflis, where he took up Armenian studies and languages under the guidance of Harutiun Alamdarian (1795–1834). Abovian graduated in 1826 and was ready to go to Venice to further his education, but the outbreak of the Russo-Persian war destroyed his dream. After teaching for a while at Sanahin, he was employed as the secretary and translator of the catholicos.

In 1829 fortune smiled on him. Friedrich Parrot, a naturalist and a professor at the University of Dorpat (now Taru, in Estonia), traveled to Armenia to climb Mount Ararat for geological studies, and he required a guide and translator for the expedition. Khachatur Abovian was assigned these tasks. Highly impressed with him and aware of his thirst for knowledge, Parrot arranged for him to be accepted as a student at Dorpat.

Abovian's years in Dorpat (1830–35) were fruitful: he studied the social and natural sciences, mastered Russian, German, French, and Latin, studied European literature and philosophy, and established numerous contacts with European intellectuals. In 1836 he returned home, keen to launch a mission of enlightenment among his own people. He was well equipped for the task, but his dreams met an implacable wall of conservatism and superstition, mostly on the part of the clergy, and all his efforts were thwarted. He married a German woman in 1839, entered the civil service, and was appointed supervisor of a school in Tiflis. Upon his dismissal in 1843 he moved to a similar position in Yerevan, but there too he was treated either with apathy or antagonism. In 1845 he applied for a job at the Catholicate of Etchmiadzin but was turned down. On April 2, 1848, he left his house early in the morning as if going for a walk. He never returned. The puzzle of his mysterious disappearance remains unsolved.

Despite the neglect and disregard he experienced during his lifetime, Khachatur Abovian was a pioneer of the Revival Movement in Eastern Armenia. Deeply aware of the plight of his nation under the brutal rule of the Persian khans, and cognizant also of the backwardness of his native land, he regarded intellectual enlightenment and political emancipation as inseparable aims. The annexation of Eastern Armenia to Russia in 1828 raised his hopes for a better future because it provided security of life and property. Yet in the 1830s and 1840s political developments adversely affected the Armenians[1] and greatly disillusioned Abovian. These developments further stimulated his patriotism.

Given the difficult conditions under which he lived, his literary production is impressive; it consists of poetry, essays, and articles on historical, social, educational, and folkloric subjects. His poetry, mostly in classical Armenian, represents the transition from classicism to romanticism. His earliest poems on love and yearning are reminiscent of the medieval *gusans,* but gradually his poetry embraces the people and evolves to the stage where his lyricism is saturated with sociopolitical thought. He expresses pain over the fate of his people and homeland, and over the disparity between his dream and brute reality.

Some of his significant works are *Nakhashavigh krtutian* (Introduction to education: in two parts, written 1837–40, published 1862); *Parap vakhti khaghalik* (Leisure entertainment, written 1838–41, published 1864), a collection of fables in verse castigating moral degradation; *Hazarpeshen* (The wine jug, 1840), a poem that criticizes the

---

1. Among these can be cited the Russification policies; the imposition of the *Polozhenie* in 1836, concentrating all activities in the Armenian Church and placing it under a synod ruled by the tsar; and, in 1840, the abolition of the administrative unit called *Armianskaya Oblast* (the Armenian Province).

state bureaucracy; and *Turki aghjike* (The Turkish girl), in which he talks about a rational society where religion fosters love, friendship, and brotherhood.

His masterpiece is *Verk Hayastani* (Wounds of Armenia, written 1841, first published 1858), the first Armenian novel. It relates the abduction of a young woman by a group of thugs sent by the Persian governor of Yerevan, which eventually triggered an uprising led by the hero, Aghasi. Though symbolic, the incident was sufficiently potent to arouse sentiments of patriotism, national pride, and dignity. The book reads like a poem, in which the author, like a son, is having an honest, forthright talk with the people, in their own Kanaker dialect. Its message is direct and strong: an appeal from the bottom of the heart.

Here are Abovian's own words describing how the idea for the novel came to him while he was living in Tiflis:[2]

"In my capacity as teacher I found that no matter what Armenian book I gave my pupils they understood nothing of it. At the same time Russian books dealt with human qualities and attachments such as love, friendship, devotion to one's soil, while Armenian books spoke only of God and the saints. Yet Armenia had many heroes with whose life and career it was worthwhile to acquaint the reader. . . . The unfortunate position in which Armenian literature found itself caused me great anguish. I would seek solitude, roaming in the hills and valleys, all the time thinking, planning. . . . I had made up my mind to write a book in which I could glorify my nation. It was to be a book about a national hero.

"But who was I to write for? My people would not understand what I wrote. What was to be done? Everybody I spoke to was of the opinion that our people had no longing for education, no desire to read. Yet I had seen them devour such books as *Robinson Crusoe* and *Copper City*.

"Almost every nation has two languages, an old and a new. I knew how our people enjoyed the songs of our wandering minstrels at their weddings, at the fairs and other gatherings. After much reflection I decided to throw overboard grammar and rhetoric and become a minstrel.

"Once at Shrovetide, when I dismissed my pupils I plunged into recollections of all I had seen and heard in my childhood. Aghasi, the Armenian hero, came to my mind and I decided to make him the principal character in my book. I had hardly jotted down a page of writing

---

2. The following lines are taken from Robert Hewsen's article, "Khachatur Abovian: Father of Modern Armenian Literature," *Ararat* 23, no. 4 (Autumn 1982): 5–6. Original source also quoted by Robert Hewsen: *Friedrich Parrot, Journey to Ararat* (London, 1846), 110–11.

when Dr. Agafon Smbatian, a friend of mine, walked in. I wanted to hide my page of writing but it was too late. He asked me to read it to him. I trembled with excitement as I read, fearing that after I finished I would get a headshake, a frown and that like others, if not to my face, then up his sleeve, he would laugh at me. However, nothing of the kind happened. 'If you will go on writing like this, the result will be splendid,' was his judgment."

Khachatur Abovian was far ahead of his time, which may be why almost none of his works was published during his lifetime. Not until the establishment of the Armenian SSR was he accorded the recognition and stature he merited.

FROM WOUNDS OF ARMENIA[3]

The Introduction

My beloved nation, my blessed forefathers, for twenty or thirty years, my heart has been afire, burning day and night, my eyes have been struck with grief and sorrow, my tongue has been constantly moaning. My brothers, if only I could voice my mind, my dreams and my hopes, I could then die peacefully. Every passing day would bring my grave closer to me; hour by hour, death's fiery sword would hover over my head; minute by minute, your heart's pain and suffering would burn and erode away my being. But still I would hear your sweet voice, picture your fair countenance, feel your kind thoughts and desires, and take pleasure in your holy love and friendship. In my mind's eye, I would see our holy land's, our Fatherland's, miracle and splendor: that chosen nation's unsurpassed character of brave acts; the succession of its magnificent kings and princes, with all their lives and works.

Alas, all that splendor and mightiness is lost now. Masis always stood steadfast before me, as a reminder of what nation's son I was born to be. I would remember that heavenly place which, in my imagination as well as in reality, has always asserted our nation's honorable name for me. In my sleep, Hayk, Vardan, Trdat

---

3. Khachatur Abovian, from *Verk Hayastani* (Wounds of Armenia), *Ararat* 23, no. 4 (Autumn 1982): 8–10. Translated by Sonia Harlan and Hourig Jacob in *Ararat* 23, no. 4 (Autumn 1982): 8–10.

(Tiridates) and Lusavorich (Illuminator) would be telling me that I was their son. Europe and Asia would be constantly reminding me that I was Hayk's son, Noah's grandson, Etchmiadzin's offspring and a dweller of Eden. As I would think of those places where my people walked (and still do), even the stones of the fields and the desert, the church and home, would compel me to pull out my heart from my bosom in grief. Each time I would see an Armenian, I would want to give him my breath, my inspiration. Alas, my tongue would be tied, my mouth sealed, my heart saddened. I would be unable to express my heart's yearning by means of the written word because our literary language is *Grabar* (Classical Armenian) and our new tongue is dishonorable and disqualified.

Just then, God sent me a few children as students. My heart was distressed because I was at a loss as to what text to choose for them. I realized that they enjoyed whatever they read in Russian, German, or French. My anger intensified (I felt like pulling all my hair out) when I saw that they liked foreign tongues better than ours. However, the reason was simple. As they read famous works by authors, their innocent hearts were enchanted by words and deeds they read about. And why not? Every reader enjoys emotional tales. Who does not take pleasure in reading about love and hate, friendship, patriotism, death, family and children? Alas, there are no such pleasures to be found in our language. How would one, therefore, go about inspiring these students with the love of their mother tongue?

Finally, one day during *Barekendan* (Shrovetide), after I had dismissed my students, I wracked my brains trying to go back to my own childhood experiences for an answer. There I found our hero, Aghasi, and with him, thousands of brave Armenian lads. All raised their heads and told me to go to them. Now, Aghasi had passed on in poverty, may he rest in peace, and the boys were grown men, most of them still alive, thank God. I told myself not to be ungrateful and decided to choose them for my models. My heart was in my mouth. I observed how only a few people still spoke and read Armenian. Yet, what preserved a nation was its tongue and faith. If we were to lose those, God help us. It was as though our mother tongue was running ahead of me, like Croesus, with me in pursuit. My mouth that had been sealed for thirty years, now, Aghasi had opened.

My soul was on fire. It was ten in the morning. I could not think of food. Nothing could stand in my way; not even a fly. If one came before me, I would kill it! Armenia stood before me, urging me to soar. My past (home, family and childhood) had become so animated that the present had lost its reality. All my lost thoughts had been revived. I was just then comprehending how *Grabar* and other similar tongues had sealed and chained off my mind until now. Whatever I said or wrote up to this moment had been borrowed or translated. That is why even a single page that I wrote bored me, tired my hand. I stayed up until five in the morning without food or tea. My pen and my writing were my nourishment. I did not pay attention to the begging, complaints or disapproval of my family until thirty pages were filled; nature prevailed and my eyes fell shut.

My dear beloved nation, now my tongue is unleashed. Henceforth let those who are compatible with each other, write to please each other and call me ignorant. They understand one another. I am your lost and bewildered child: I will write to please you. Whosoever has a sword, let him strike me, let him pierce my heart, for as long as I can speak I will roar: "Who are you drawing your sword on, do you not know that great Armenian Nation?" I only ask that you, my precious nation, love your son's utterances; that you accept them as a loving father would his child's words and would not trade them for the whole world. When I grow up, I will use a more sophisticated language. Aghasi is your young son; you have many other great and famous sons. Encourage me, I beg of you. Watch and see how I am going to bring them all back, present them to you, and then, you will be amazed. You will wonder how anyone could despair in this world, having such sons. Let me kiss your holy hand so that you may forgive me. Then we will go and meet Aghasi. . . .

The Fortress of Yerevan

On the stony river bank, Yerevan's thousand-year-old fortress stands erect, as if calmly scanning the surroundings. The walls, eighteen feet deep, are reinforced with towers and surrounded by a moat. The fortress looks like a thousand-headed monster, with sharp teeth on its dried-up sky-scraping head, resting one foot on Kond, the other on Damurbulagh, its two jaws gaping wide on the north and on the south, its large skirt wrapping the land. Its thousand and one eyes look angrily from its insolent unabashed face. With its twin claws it hugs to its chest, like a hairless, speechless cannibal, the stony and frightening Zanga gorge.

This monster hides its yellowish tinge from faraway places; its sordid eyes cast down, it lures the unsuspecting spectator, draws him close to its bosom and then, suddenly, without a sound or a warning, it swallows and destroys him.

Did the cunning and tricky Persians build it or did the savage Ottomans lay its foundation? There is no inscription nor date. History has enveloped it in her darkness; no one has heard or knows of its origin. For a thousand years the cannon balls have struck its rough back, its soft bosom, its unprotected head. Nothing has affected its brave, fearless, strong facade. It has resisted all blows like an insolent beast.

Having its lost limbs recovered, its broken bones mended, its head held high, the fortress stood up, straightened its shoulders, took another breath and struck back. This adobe fortress stood up, and pointed its finger threateningly, mocking at the importance of all those who had the audacity and the narrow-mindedness to poke at it. Its revolting countenance remained undaunted; yet its broken limbs fell to block the Zanga's mouth. The enraged Zanga, in turn, spent sleepless days and nights rambling, ferociously, beating upon the fortress' bare chest and unjust heart, eroding it as if it were a sword without its blade. Realizing that efforts for revenge and destruction were futile, first she roared, shrieked and complained, then withdrew quietly, entering Zangibasar's bosom without a whisper. Discouraged, disheartened and saddened, she altered her course to flow through the orchards, blessing the land with goodness and plenty. The needy and thirsty people of Yerevan greeted her with love and coaxed her to stay on the plain so that they might wash their bitter sweat of their brows with her sweet waters and be refreshed.

My beloved people, I would gladly die for you. My beloved land, my beloved nation, who gave birth to you? Whose milk nourished you, who embraced you and bestowed blessings upon you? You are the manifestation of a miraculous soul and spirit in this world. By what insensitivity can one be blinded so as to miss your worthiness? By what indifference can one become mute and not praise you and exalt your name? Only a heart of stone would not sacrifice oneself for your love.

Love the Russians! Love and support one another because you are the sons of a nation which amazed the world and continues to do so. Protect and defend the honor of your brethren. Remember your forefathers, worship your land and your people.

Now it is time for me to go back to my tale. I am weary. For if your love for each other has decreased and dried up, then my task will be left unaccomplished, my heart's desire will go to my grave with me. Let us go to Yerevan's fortress. The hour is late and it grows dark. My heart is crushed and I feel faint. The desolation and sufferings of my birthplace pierce my heart and my eye like a dagger. Unlike the bird who delights in his nest, I feel displaced in my fatherland. I am consumed by fire as I look upon the injuries that befall my people. The land and the water surrounding the fortress of Yerevan is tarnished by their blood. How am I to endure this affliction as guilt and sorrow gnaw at my very being? Death will be easier to bear.

Stepanos Nazarian

(1812–79)

Stepanos Nazarian was a great revivalist of Eastern Armenian culture, an orientalist, an educator, and a publicist. He was born in Tiflis and educated at the Nersisian school (1824–29), the gymnasium in Torpat (now Tartu, Estonia) (1833–34), and in the faculties of medicine (1835–36) and philosophy (1836–40) of the university there. He held the chair in Armenian studies at the University of Kazan (1842–49), where he acquired his master's (1846) and doctoral (1849) degrees. He returned to Moscow and taught Persian language and literature and oriental studies at the Lazarian Institute (1850–79), where he also served as director (1869–71).

His greatest contribution to the Eastern Armenian Revival Movement was to found and assume the editorship of *Hiusisapayl* (Northern lights) in Moscow. As its masthead proclaimed, this was a review dedicated to "national enlightenment and education." With the close collaboration of Mikayel Nalbandian and the contribution of many intellectuals such as Raffi, Rafayel Patkanian, Smbat Shahaziz, and others, and despite its short life (1858–64), the review became a powerful instrument for the dissemination of the ideas and principles of liberal democracy. Headed by Nazarian, the *Hiusisapayl* team advocated renouncing the patriarchal mode of life, embracing the best European social and political concepts, and bringing about a cultural and educational evolution that would ensure the survival of a stateless nation. It was no surprise that *Hiusisapayl* soon found itself under attack by the religious establishment and the traditionalists, who enrolled two conservative papers, *Chrakagh* (Gleaner) of Moscow and *Meghu Hayastani* (The bee of Armenia) of Tiflis in their cause. Fortunately, youth was on its side.

Nazarian's learning encompassed many fields: philosophy, education, religion, and social and political studies. He had ideas that were ahead of his time, and not only within the Armenian context. With regard to education, he suggested that school programs should be tailored to fit individual students' abilities and capacities rather than being rigid forms in which all students are molded alike. With respect to religion, although he was a firm adherent of the Armenian Church, he believed that Christianity should be reduced to its purest form, eliminating some of the traditional and ritualistic frills, and that the intellectual level of the clergy should be raised. He also tried to reconcile religion and science, faith and rationalism. He thought that the emancipation of Armenia would be achieved not through armed revolution but through diplomacy, a prerequisite of which was consolidating the nation through enlightenment and higher education.

In addition to the editorials, reviews, and essays that appeared in *Hiusisapayl,* he wrote *A Brief Survey of Thirteenth-Century Armenian Literature* (1844, in Russian), *A Survey of Armenian Literature of the Modern Period* (1846, in Russian), *Haghags pordzakan hogebanutyan char* (Lecture on experimental psychology, 1851), *Arajin hogeghen kerakur hayazgi yerakhaneri hamar* (First spiritual food for Armenian children, 1853), *Vardapetaran kroni* (Source book of religion, 1853), and *Handes nor hayakhosutyan* (Review of Modern Armenian) in two parts (1857). He was an ardent defender of modern Eastern Armenian and contributed immensely to its development.

On Childhood[1]

In his obituary of his mother, Manushak, Stepanos Nazarian also wrote about his childhood: how much he learned and developed

1. Stepanos Nazarian, in Smbat Shahazizian, *Hraparakakhos dzayn* (Voice of the publicist) (Moscow, 1881), 4–6. Translated by the editors of the present anthology.

at home and from his teachers. The following excerpt deals with these matters.

Our father, the priest Yesayi Kahana,[2] was a well-intentioned, kind-hearted, spiritual man. He was a caring father, filled with love for his children. . . . Himself a product of the eastern educational system, the only way he knew of educating children was through painful and effective means: with a stick and a slap.

I loved to play. I used to take advantage of his noontime siesta by setting my studies aside and climbing onto a rooftop. I really enjoyed flying kites. When he woke up and saw that I was not studying, he would look for me, and when he found me he would tie me up and beat me in a fabulous, glorious rage.

My tender-hearted mother got involved on those occasions and defended us from our father's punitive blows.

Like other priests, my father had no formal education to speak of, because of the educational system in those days. But he had his own unique kind of "higher" education, acquired through personal diligence. Night and day he would spread out his papers on a pastry board, since desks did not exist in those days, and copy out texts, both handwritten and typed, in his simple but elegant handwriting. He wrote an ornate old Armenian, which was all that was known in his day, and the ideas he expressed were typical of Armenian religious education, both before and during his time.

The materials that supplied my primary education were quite miserable and poor compared to the present variety of reading materials: they were in Armenian only, and in a variety of Armenian that was incomprehensible to our childish minds.

My earliest religious education was from a book of stories from the New Testament, full of pictures, that was published in St. Petersburg during the days of Primate Hovhannes Arghutian. The selection was not bad. But I think that learning the sacred stories by heart, as my father required, especially when they are only half understood, did more harm than good.

When I was fourteen my father sent my elder brother and me to the great grammarian Poghos Vardapet from Karabagh, whose

---

2. Armenian married priest.

teaching was based on Chamchian's grammar book, a copy of which father bought us at the cost of ten silver manets.[3]

My father gave us as much education and foundation as those poor, simple times permitted. But to me the greatest lessons we learned were from the example he set for us: his particular love for knowledge, his fondness for studying, his lively conversations and advice. My father was not a rich man, and he never strove for riches and a comfortable life. Our everyday life was modest. At least we children were happy and led a contented life. Our parents' love satisfied our needs. The thousand imaginary needs of the children of today were unknown to us. But no innocent joy, no delightful playtime activity was denied us, especially during the high holidays.

My father liked to take his children on field trips, to mountains and valleys. These trips, seasoned with cheerful conversations, were like consummate wedding feasts. How happy the days of childhood, when life's pains and worries had not yet filled our hearts and minds. . . .

---

3. Ten rubles.

Khachatur Misakian

(1815–91)

Khachatur Misakian was born in Constantinople,[1] where he received his early schooling in a religious atmosphere. An avid reader, he acquired his education through self-instruction and the private tutoring of two renowned teachers, Grigor Shekerchian (Shekerdjian) and Grigor Peshtimalchian. In 1838 he obtained a position at the Scutari (Üsküdar) College (*chemaran*), where he taught Armenian language and literature. A number of his students became leaders of the Revival Movement.

In 1845, after his father's death and the remarriage of his mother, he became a solitary, dedicating himself to literary and philological studies. In 1848 he was hired by a wealthy merchant and sent to Paris as guardian and private tutor to the merchant's children, who were studying there. He remained in Paris until 1871. Despite the fact that the period from the 1848 revolution to the Franco-German war of 1870 was a turbulent and eventful time, Misakian remained isolated from his surroundings and abandoned himself to his mystical inclinations. He cherished the idea of publishing a periodical and prepared close to two thousand pages of manuscript, but the project never materialized. Upon his return to Constantinople he resumed his teaching position, and for a while he was an elected member of the Armenian National Assembly.

---

1. Hrand Asatur and Hakob Oshakan accept 1805 as his birthdate.

In addition to the articles and essays he published in *Masis,* some of his works are *Yepimendes i Vospor* (Epimendes in the Bosphorus), *Kurats dastiarakutiun* (The education of the blind), *Tknutiunk hayrinasiri* (Wakefulness of a patriot), and a novel called *Sophia* (unpublished). It should be pointed out that what he published does not do justice to his erudition. He was praised by his contemporaries as a learned and competent teacher. He is known for his firm stand for the importance of education and as a contributor to the development of modern Armenian.

NATIONAL PROGRESS[2]

There has never been an earnest attempt to give our nation an educational system, but there has been so much talk and research expended on it that one day it will be done precipitously, as a starving lion pounces upon its prey, devours it, and has done with it.

Here is a people whose entire patrimonial inheritance and wealth consists of a name and a language. It has no land, no sovereignty, and hence no civil laws of its own; most grievous of all, there is no unity within the population. Throughout its entire extent, from east to west and from north to south, walls are thrown up, impassable and unyielding to other nations, breaking the entire area into pieces and almost completely preventing communication. The country is in urgent need of attention and care on a national level, and for this it requires a national education system. It is not right to reserve knowledge to the legislators and leave the common people in ignorance, for the legislators and the people are one; in other words, the legislators and the people together are the nation. It appears that the people have also felt this need; that is why boatmen and porters, the old and the young, men and women have all taken up reading and writing.

We cannot deny the devotion and goodwill of our educators; but that does not prevent us from reiterating that the essential element of an educational system has not yet been devised for our country; hitherto we have not expended sufficient care and

---

2. Khachatur Misakian, *"Azgayin harajdimutiun"* (National progress), 1861, in Minas Teoleolian, *Dar me grakanutiun* (A century of literature), vol. 1 (Boston, 1977), 111–12. Translated by the editors of the present anthology.

effort to persuade people, especially callow youth, to acquire solid knowledge and skills before they become frustrated. Well! Who does not know that the fire dies when the fuel runs out? Likewise, any human thing whatsoever—be it desire, ardor, or passion—will, alas! be hard to sustain without adequate nourishment. On the one hand, regular studies and classes, which spread the love of education in its true sense, have not been put in place; on the other hand, nothing is done to adapt the upcoming youth to their sacred obligations. Certainly, either we have to establish public lectures or impromptu talks, or we have to send out preachers who have a store of knowledge and science in their heads, to wander around rhapsodizing, like the Greek peripatetic philosophers. It is the job of the press to make the essence of knowledge accessible to the people in every possible way through its editorials.

Nahapet Rusinian

(1819–76)

Nahapet Rusinian was a physician, writer, activist, and one of the pillars of the Revival Movement. He was born in Efkere, Caesarea, moved to Constantinople with his parents in 1828, completed his secondary education there, and, in 1840, won a scholarship to study medicine in Paris. Since he was interested in the arts and letters as well, he followed courses in literature and philosophy at the Sorbonne, and was actively involved in the social and intellectual aspects of the revolution then raging in Paris. These experiences exerted a strong influence on his future activities.

When he returned to Constantinople in 1851, he again found himself in the midst of social and intellectual upheaval; he plunged right into it, and became a leading exponent of constitutional reform. The issue was to put an end to the arbitrary rule of the *amiras* and bishops and establish a representative national assembly based on democratic principles. He joined a group headed by Grigor Otian (1834–87), another pioneer and statesman, and they set themselves the difficult task of preparing a draft constitution. These efforts eventually bore fruit when, in 1863, the final version of the constitution, comprising ninety-nine articles, was ratified by Sultan Abd-ul Aziz.[1] After the establishment

---

1. For details of the Armenian National Constitution see the overview of the present volume.

of the National Assembly, Rusinian served alternately as speaker and secretary.

He was also very active in the field of education. Beginning in 1853 he was a member of the newly organized Educational Council and relentlessly pursued the aim of opening new schools, raising standards, and publishing textbooks. Another of his great concerns was the development of modern Armenian. To this end, in 1858 he published *Ughghakhosutiun* (*Orthologia:* correct speech), followed by two volumes of *Taretsuyts* (Yearbook), which contained a series of arbitrary rules and suggestions for simplifying and modernizing the grammar and vocabulary of modern Armenian. Plausible as his aim was, in many cases he went to extremes, producing an artificial language. Although his suggestions were rejected by the Educational Council, he is nevertheless responsible for a great many neologisms that are still used both in popular and literary language. He also helped to found an Armenian Benevolent Society and a musical association called *Knar* (Lyre) in Constantinople.

The Ottoman government entrusted him with weighty missions. During the unrest in Lebanon in 1857, when Fuat Pasha was dispatched there to calm the place down, he chose Nahapet Rusinian to lead the commission that was to arrange for the return to their original faith of Christians who had been forced into Islam. After completing the mission, he was instrumental in the election of Karapet Da'ud Pasha as governor of Lebanon, the first Armenian to fill that position.

Rusinian produced a number of translations from French literature: Victor Hugo's *Ruy Blas* and a collection of poems by various authors. He is also the creator of the famous poem and song "*Kilikia*" (Cilicia), which, although an adaptation of a French poem dedicated to Normandy, is both nationalistic and emotionally gripping.

Nahapet Rusinian also taught philosophy at the Medical School in Constantinople, and he wrote a *Textbook of Philosophy*, in French, for his courses, bringing together the various philosophical doctrines that prevailed at the time. He decided to translate it into Armenian and completed the translation just a few days before his death.

CILICIA[2]

**When the gates of hope are opened
And winter takes leave of our homeland,**

---

2. Nahapet Rusinian, "Cilicia," in *Goharner Hay Grakanutyan*, Biuzand T. Engapapian (Boston, 1916), 157–58. Translated by the editors of the present volume.

When our beauteous land of Armenia
Beams its euphoric, delightful days;
When the swallow returns to its nest;
When the trees are clothed in leaves,
I yearn to see my Cilicia,
World that deluged me in eternal sun.

I saw the meadows of Syria,
The mountains of Lebanon and its cedars;
I saw the land of Italy,
Venice and its gondolas;
No other island is like our Cyprus,
But truly compared can be nowhere
With my exquisite land Cilicia,
World that deluged me in eternal sun.

There is an age in our lifetime
When every desire dissipates in air,
An age when the yearning soul
Aspires to reach the memory's trail.
When my lyre quivers and chills,
Sending love its final smile.
Let me go rest in my Cilicia,
World that deluged me in eternal sun.

Ghevond Alishan

(1820–1901)

Ghevond Alishan, poet, philologist, historian, educator, and translator, was born in Constantinople and, at age twelve, was sent to the Mkhitarist school in Venice. He completed his studies in 1841 and joined the order. He held administrative positions at the Monastery of St. Lazarus, taught and supervised at the Rafaelian and Muratian schools in Venice and Paris respectively, and edited the review *Bazmavep* (*Polyhistor*) for a brief period (1849–51). In 1852 he embarked on an educational mission, visiting a number of European cities. While in London he took time for research and made a list of Armenian manuscripts in the libraries of Oxford and Cambridge universities.

Alishan's early literary output was almost exclusively poetry. He was the first Mkhitarist writer to make the transition from classicism to romanticism. The poems he published in *Bazmavep* from 1847 to 1860, under the pen name Nahapet, are inspired by a deep yearning for his native land, which he tries to transmit to the reader with emotion and love. His poems, collected under various titles—*Mankuni, Maghtuni, Khohuni, Bnuni, Hayruni, Teruni,* and *Tkhruni*—have been compiled in five volumes under the general title of *Nvagk.* His other literary work is *Hushikk hayrenyats hayots* (Memories of the Armenian homeland, 1869), written in prose, which derives patriotism and devotion to the mother country from historical events. His love for Armenia and his desire to see it free is particularly expressed in a few poems in which one can neither miss the martial tone nor remain unaffected. Though he was a promoter of modern Armenian, he chose to write most of his poetry in the classical language (*grabar*), because of its elegance and artistic expressiveness.

Alishan was proficient in several languages and produced a number of translations, such as a section of John Milton's *Paradise Lost;* the fourth canto of George Byron's *Childe Harold's Pilgrimage;* a ballad by Schiller, "Das Lied von der Glocke" (The song of the bell); and a collection of poems by Longfellow and others under the general title *Knar amerikyan* (The American lyre).

It appears that in the 1870s Alishan bade farewell to poetry and thenceforth dedicated all his time to historical and philological research. One of his major projects was to prepare a volume on each of the fifteen provinces of ancient Armenia, complete with historical, geographic, ethnographic, and cultural information. Only four volumes were published, however: on the provinces of Shirak, Sisvan, Ayrarat, and Sisakan. The minute and accurate description of topography and historical sites contained within these works is amazing, considering that the author never set foot in the places he described. Among his other accomplishments are: *Soperk haykakank* (Armenian stories), a set of twenty-two small volumes, each dealing with a well researched historical topic or figure; *Teghagir hayots metzats* (Topography of Greater Armenia); *Hay busak* (Flora of Armenia), an encyclopedic compilation of more than 3,400 species of plants and flowers, some with illustrations; *Hin havatk kam hetanosakan kronk hayots* (The ancient beliefs or heathen religion of the Armenians); *Arshaluys kristoneutyan hayots* (The dawn of Christianity in Armenia); critical publications of two medieval Armenian historical works, Kirakos Gandzaketsi's *Hamarot patmutiun* (Abridged history) and Khosrov Andzevatsi's *Meknutiun aghotits pataragin* (Interpretation of the prayers of the Mass); and also a translation from Armenian into modern French of *Antioki asizner* (Assies d'Antioch).[1]

Ghevond Alishan received international recognition for his erudition. He was made a laureate of the Legion of Honor of the French

---

1. According to Alishan, the code book called *Assises d'Antioch* (Assises of Antioch) was compiled between 1201 and 1233, during the reign of Bohemond IV of the principality of Antioch. It was written in Old French. Early in the second half of the thirteenth century, it was translated into Armenian by Smbat Sparapet (constable) of Cilicia. By the time of Alishan, the Old French was incomprehensible, hence the need to retranslate it from Armenian to modern French.

Academy (1886), an honorary member and doctor of the Academy of Philosophy of Jena, Germany (1897), and a member of Italian and Russian academic associations.

Alishan's literary, historical, and philological output is immense and varied: the above summary is far from exhaustive. He was an intellectual giant of the nineteenth-century Enlightenment Movement.

THE LILY OF SHAVARSHAN[2]

Armenian maidens, come and view
    In Shavarshan[3] a lily new!

The radiant type of maidenhood,
    Crown of Armenia's pride!
From the fair brow beneath her veil
    The wind-stirred curls float wide.
With little steps, like turtle dove,
    She walks the dew-bright plain;
Her lips drop honey, and her eyes
    Effulgent glances rain.

The beauty of Armenia,
    A sun-like mirror clear,
Our Northern star is bright Sandukht,
    The king's fair daughter dear.
She has come forth, the graceful bride
    On whom the East and West
Desire to look, while fires of love
    Consume the gazer's breast.

---

2. Ghevond Alishan, "The Lily of Shavarshan," in *Armenian Poems* (Boston, 1917), 103–6, edited and translated by Alice Stone Blackwell, with a preface and introduction. There is also a facsimile reproduction of the 1917 edition by Caravan Books (Delmar, N.Y., 1978). This is an extract from a long poem in the classical Armenian, describing the conversion to Christianity by the Apostle Thaddeus, in the first century AD of Sandukht, the daughter of the Armenian King Sanatruk. Both the princess and the apostle were put to death by the king. According to Armenian tradition, Sandukht was the earliest Christian female martyr.

3. Province of Shavarshan. The ancient name of the province of Artaz in Armenia.

Less fair the bright and morning star,
    'Mid cloudlets small and fine;
Less fair the fruit whose rosy tints
    'Mid apple leaves outshine;
Araxes' hyacinthine flower
    That chains of dew doth wear,
All are less beautiful than she,
    With gracious mien and air.

At sight of her, the snowy peaks
    Melt and are flushed with rose;
Trees, flowers bud forth; the nightingales
    All sing where'er she goes.
The bell-flowers open myriad eyes
    When she comes through the bowers;
Beneath her breath, the vales and hills
    Alike are clad in flowers.

Before her have been bent to earth
    Foreheads with diadems;
The valley has become a hill
    Of scattered gold and gems.
Where passes by with humble grace
    Armenia's virgin sweet,
Fine sands of pearls come longingly
    To spread beneath her feet.

Full many a monarch's valiant son
    Has left his palace home
In Persia or Albania,
    In India or in Rome.
Admiringly they gaze on her,
    Exclaiming, "Happy he
Who wins the fair Armenian maid
    His bride beloved to be!"

But palace worthy of Sandukht
    The earth can nowhere show,
And for the arches of her brows
    This world is all too low.
The Sky says, "Let her on my throne

Reign queen o'er every land."
The Ocean says, "My purple waves
    Shall bow to her command."

There is one greater than the earth,
    More wide than sea-waves run,
Higher and vaster than the heavens,
    And brighter than the sun.
There is a formidable King
    Whose power no bound has known;
The royal maid Sandukht shall be
    For him, and him alone.
Her halls of light are all prepared,
    And for a footstool meet
The azure sky adorned with stars
    Awaits her dove-like feet.

. . . .

The sharp sword glitters in the air,
    And swift the red blood flows;
Sandukht, who was a lily fair,
    Falls to the earth, a rose.
The sword flashed once, and aspects three
    Were in Sandukht descried;
Her heart dropped blood, and roses red
    Sprang up on every side;
Her eyes were violet chalices,
    Sweet e'en while they expire;
Her face, like lilies half unclosed,
    But on her lips what fire!

The heaven and earth shine white and red;
    Come forth and gather, maids,
The rose and lily joined in one,
    This peerless flower that fades.
Lay in the tomb that youthful corpse,
    With Thaddeus, good and brave.
Sweet maiden of Armenia,
    Her sweet soil be thy grave.
Armenian maids, a lily new
    Is brought to Shavarshan for you!

THE NIGHTINGALE OF AVARAYR[4]

Whence dost thou come, O moon, so calmly and softly,
    Spreading o'er mountain, valley, and plain thy light,
And over me tile Patriarch, wandering sadly,
    With wandering thoughts, in Avarayr tonight?

Here where our matchless, brave Armenian fathers
    Fell as giants, as angels to rise anew,
Com'st thou to spread o'er the bones of the saints a cover
    Of golden thread, from thy cloud of snowy hue?

Or dost thou think, though thy brow be bright already,
    Adornment of heroes' blood becomes it well?
Or dost thou still, in silence and secret, wonder
    To think how the great and terrible Vardan fell,

Giving his enemies' lives to the shades of darkness,
    And giving his spirit into the hands of God?
And thou, O River Teghmut, thou flowest lamenting
    Amid thy reeds, sad river bestained with blood.

And thou, O wind from Mankuran's upland blowing,
    Or Ararat's sacred summit, gray-haired and hoar,
Thou, too, like me, uncertain and trembling movest,
    On faint wings passing the mountains and valleys o'er.

From forest to forest, from leaf to leaf, lamenting,
    Thou comest upon the plains, in pale moonshine,
To carry unto Armenian hearts the echo
    Of the last sighs of this worn heart of mine.

Nightingale, voice of the night, little soul of the roses,
    Friend of all mournful hearts that with sorrow are sighing!
Sing, little nightingale, sing me a song from that hillock,
    Sing with my soul of Armenia's heroes undying!

Thy voice in the cloister of Thaddeus reached me and thrilled
me
    My heart, that was close to the cross, in a reverie grave,

---

4. Ibid., 107–9.

Suddenly bounded and throbbed; from the cross I hastened to
  seek thee—
    Came forth and found thee here, on the field of Vardan the
      brave.

Nightingale, this is the tale that of thee our fathers have told
  us:
    That Avarayr's nightingale, singing so sweetly at daylight's
      dim close,
Is not a bird, but a soul,—it is Yeghishé's[5] sweet-voiced spirit,
    That sees the image of Vardan for aye in the red-blooming
      rose.

In winter he walks alone, and mourns in the midst of the desert;
    In spring comes to Avarayr, to the bush with roses aflame,
To sing and to call aloud, with Yeghishé's voice, upon Vardan,
    To see whether Vardan perchance will answer when called
      by his name.

If like the voice of a nightingale faint and weary,
    Sons of Togarmah, my voice shall reach your ears,—
Sons of the great, whose valiant and virtuous fathers
    Filled plains, books, and the heavens, in former years,—

If one small drop of blood from Armenia's fountain,
    The fount of Pahlav, flow into your bosoms' sea,—
If you would that your country's glories for you be written,
    Come forth to Artaz with your Patriarch, come with me!

5. An Armenian historian of the fifth century, a contemporary of Vardan. In
his history of the Persian invasion he compares Vardan, drenched in his blood, to
the red rose.

Mkrtich Khrimian (Hayrik)

(1820–1907)

Mkrtich Khrimian was born in Van and became one of the most famous and beloved national-religious figures of his time. His compassionate dedication to his people and relentless efforts for their well-being earned him the title "*Hayrik*" (the diminutive of *father*). He lost his father at an early age, and his uncle provided for his education at the Varag monastery, near Van, where he studied classical Armenian, history, and ecclesiastical literature. He soon married and had a daughter. His thirst for knowledge and higher education led him to Constantinople. Before he arrived there, however, he traveled through Persia, Eastern Armenia, Shirak, and Etchmiadzin, in order to acquaint himself thoroughly with the living conditions of Armenians. In 1847 he was in Constantinople, where he was shocked at the indifference and disdain with which the Armenian elite and bourgeois classes in the capital viewed their kinsmen in the provinces.

He taught in a suburban school for two years, at the same time writing articles and preaching sermons to arouse patriotism among the people. In 1850 he published his first work, *Hravirak Araratian* (Convoker to Ararat), a verse essay in classical Armenian in which he assumes the role of guide and leads a group of youths through the history and geography of the ancestral homeland, extolling its ancient glories and exquisite beauty in an attempt to instill a love and passion for the mother country in the young generation. In 1851, after a trip to the Holy Land, he published a similar verse essay, *Hravirak yerkrin avetiatz* (Convoker to the Promised Land), in which he leads youths on a tour of the holy sites, teaching them the essence of Christianity as they go. After a short trip to Cilicia on an educational mission, Khrimian returned to Van in 1853 to discover that both his wife and his mother had died. In 1854 he took vows of celibacy and returned to Constantinople.

His next project was the publication, in 1855, of a periodical called *Artzvi Vaspurakan* (The eagle of Vaspurakan), the goal of which was to sensitize the elite community of the capital to the plight of the provinces. In 1857, after being appointed abbot there, he moved the paper and the entire printing press to the Varag monastery near Van, and the paper continued until 1864. In 1862 he became Primate of Taron (Mush). His vision and organizational skills enabled him to revitalize the place, transforming it into a flourishing center equipped with a school, a printing press, and a new newspaper, *Artzvik Tarono* (The eaglet of Taron). One of Khrimian's achievements at this time was his intervention with the governor of Karin (Erzrum), which resulted in the removal of excessive taxes on the people.

In 1868 he was ordained bishop by Catholicos Gevorg IV in Etchmiadzin, and a year later he was elected Patriarch of Constantinople (1869–73). He helped to clear the debt of the patriarchate and fought hard to increase the number of provincial representatives in the Armenian National Assembly. He also prepared a detailed report documenting instances of oppression, persecution, and miscarriage of justice in the Armenian provinces; as the recognized leader of Armenians in the Ottoman Empire, he presented this document to the Port.

His integrity and outspokenness annoyed not only the Ottoman authorities but some of the Armenian "lords" as well. In 1873 he resigned from the patriarchal throne and dedicated his time to literary pursuits. He completed two small works, *Vanguyzh* (Bad tidings from Van) and *Hayguyzh* (Bad tidings from Armenia), both written to give consolation to and inspire faith and courage in the survivors of the fire in Van and the massacres in Bagrevand and Alashkert.

In 1878 Khrimian headed an Armenian delegation to the Congress of Berlin, whose mission was to present a memorandum to the European powers concerning the implemention of essential reforms in the Armenian provinces. The mission failed, prompting Khrimian to deliver a speech, famed for its allegories, on his return to Constantinople; it is considered the first signal of revolution.

Soon after his return from Berlin he was appointed Primate of Van and Abbot of St. Karapet monastery (1879–85). He opened new schools and established an agricultural school, a first for Armenia; the printed word began to spread, and an intellectual revival was set afoot. These activities, however, were not looked upon with favor by the authorities. In 1885 he was suspended by government order and sent to Constantinople, later (1890) to be exiled to Jerusalem under pretense of being on a pilgrimage. While thus isolated he wrote *Papik yev tornik* (Grandfather and grandson), his best known work.

In 1892, upon the death of Catholicos Makar I, Khrimian was unanimously elected Catholicos of Etchmiadzin. Fearing excessive manifestations of jubilation by the Armenians, the Ottoman authorities did not allow Khrimian to travel through Turkey to his new post; instead, he journeyed through Europe and Russia, and was welcomed in Etchmiadzin with great honors. His new position brought him into conflict with the tsarist authorities when, in 1903, in a frenzy to Russify all ethnic minorities, they ordered that all Armenian schools be closed and that the property of the Armenian Church be confiscated. Khrimian defied the tsar's order so resolutely that it was soon rescinded. Among his other accomplishments were the renovations of numerous ancient monasteries and churches and the uninterrupted publication of the review *Ararat*. It was also he who established the Diocese of the Armenian Church of America, in 1902.

In addition to the literary works mentioned above, he also published the following: *Khachi char* (Discourse on the Cross, 1876); *Zhamanak yev khorhurd yur* (Time and its mystery, 1876); *Drakhti entanik* (The family of paradise, 1876); *Sirak yev Samuel* (Sirak and Samuel, 1878), a treatise on child education; *Tagavorats zhoghov* (The meeting of kings, 1900); and *Verjaluysi dzayner* (Sounds of twilight, 1901), a collection of his poetry.

Khrimian was one of the few truly great figures in the history of the Armenian Church.

CROWNED BY GRANDPA IN THE FIELD[1]

My dear grandson, I'm going to crown[2] you again, for the second time; you mustn't think that being crowned in the church by

---

1. Mkrtich Khrimian (Hayrik), "*Papké psak i dasht,*" in *Amboghjakan yerker Khrimian Hayriki* (Complete works of Khrimian Hayrik) (New York, 1929), 740–43. Translated by the editors of the present anthology.

2. As part of the wedding ceremony of the Armenian Church, the presiding priest places crowns on the heads of the bride and groom.

a priest is enough. Oh, I know—according to religious and divine law it's more than enough! But if your grandpa does not set his own crown on top of the wedding crown, you'll die of starvation. There you have it: the chapel is open for business! Ask the local farmers to provide you with a plow and get yourself to the field near you. That piece of land has to be plowed and fertilized now, to prepare it for a crop of vegetables in the spring.

Yoke the ox, my grandson, and you'll see how I crown you! First go and kiss the buffaloes and oxen on the forehead; then bend right over next to the plow handle and kiss the land of your fathers. My hand will be on that handle; kiss your grandpa's hand and the plow handle. That man, your grandpa, has plowed for forty years; today he entrusts you with the sublime responsibility of plowing, which the Almighty gave to Adam, our great ancestor, so that he would cultivate and preserve the homeland.

Let me, with my own hand, plait a beautiful crown for you out of wheat stalks. Bend over toward me, grandson, and let me place it on your head: it's your grandpa's crown and reminder—never take it off your head until the day you die. And when you too get old like your grandpa, place the crown on the head of your eldest grandson, and so let it be passed down from grandson to grandson. Let me tell you about the meaning of the crown, so you'll understand it completely and remember this day.

My gentle grandson, the meaning of my curious crown is this: it unites you to the earth, to the plow, to the cultivation of the fields. The priest has united you to Shushan, and from now until you die you will never be able to leave her. In the same way, your grandpa's crown unites you to the land, which you will never be able to abandon: it's the land of our fathers. Adam said and everyone says that it's the land that gives women life. But isn't it the land that also gives life to everyone? Bread gives life to everyone in this world. Shushan will bring forth your children, and the land will bring forth your bread; the cow and the sheep grazing in the field will bring forth milk in abundance, and you'll make butter and cheese with the milk. Isn't the land the source of all these good things?

So now, my grandson, tell the farmers to take the plow and the oxen, and we'll go home; I have to tell your mother and Shushan about the mystery of the crowning in the field.

Listen to what I'm saying, gentle housewife and Shushan. Today I took the new bridegroom to the field. I had the ox yoked, put the plow handle in the hands of my grandson, placed my hand on his head, gave him my patriarchal blessing, and crowned him again with the fruits of the earth, uniting him to the plow and the land— and you know, nothing can undo a grandpa's crowning. Now my grandson has two wives, and you have to understand this: one wife is Shushan, to whom he was united through the crown of holy matrimony, and the other wife is the land he has inherited from his fathers, to which I united him with the blessing of Father Abraham. Shushan will give my grandson children; the land will give the whole family bread. I pray that God will watch over Shushan, so that she might live for many long years. But Shushan is mortal; if she dies, my grandson will find another Shushan. But if the land dies, grandpa's home dies, and the whole family dies with it. And how does the land, which has existed since Adam and is everlasting, die? I'll tell you when the land dies: on that unfortunate day when the grandson lets go of the plow handle and stops cultivating the land; or when he gets rich and stuck-up and is ashamed to live in a village. He leaves the village and the land and becomes a city-dweller. Or hard times fall upon him, he piles debt on debt, and his creditor seizes the land, leaving the grandson landless.

On that day the land will die to the grandson, but to the one who confiscates it, it will remain alive. On that day, yes, the lamp in grandpa's home will be extinguished, and the grandson who owns the property will become a hired man. Alas! the grandson's bride, pretty Shushan, will go to work as a baker in the village; in the evening she'll put a few loaves of bread in her apron and bring them home to her children. Mother of my grandson, gentle housewife, die immediately after grandpa does, so you'll never see that day!

Do I hear you asking, my grandson: "Papik,[3] what kind of evil prophecy is that to give your grandson? Please open your mouth again and say a few good things!" No, my grandson, God forbid that my prediction ever comes true in your case. I pray that you never see that black day. I have painted this sad, gloomy picture of life to ensure that the flour always flows. To make you see, and remember your grandpa's far-fetched prophesy, and work with all your might never to let go of your land. You need not only the land, which provides your bread and enables you to live in this world,

---

3. Grandfather (Armenian).

but may the Lord also grant you abundant sunshine. When you die you'll also need a couple of permanent plots of land for your grave; people also fight over burial grounds. Pity the man who dies and has no plot to be buried in! A man also deserves a piece of land in the cemetery. What I'm trying to say, my grandson, is that from the day he is born a man needs land, and when he dies he still needs a piece of land to lie under.

That's how it is, my grandson: land is a matter of life and death. So I say again: to ensure an abundant supply of flour, your grandpa united you to the land and crowned you to make sure you clasp it firmly; never let anyone take it from you and make you landless, or you'll become a slave. That's when your grandpa's mysterious prophecy will come back to you. And then you'll come to your senses and remember that you once owned it but didn't heed your grandpa's patriarchal advice, and, like the prodigal son, became a hired shepherd, leaving your own flock behind in order to graze the flocks of others and once a week going from door to door to collect your earnings.

And yet, my grandson, when your luck turns and you become a humble servant, a grazer of others' sheep, don't bemoan your condition; after all it's the condition of a hired village shepherd: he takes home bread for the table, he has a cow he can milk, at least a few sheep and a goat, and his family lives quite comfortably.

But when there's no chance that the unfortunate landowner will work as a shepherd, he remembers his former condition and says: "I used to be a landowner; how can I now become a hired shepherd in the same village? I'd better leave the village and go to the city as an unknown pauper, mingle with the rest of the poor on the street, and become a beggar. But if I manage to get a certificate saying that I'm a *devletden düşgün*[4] from the primate, it could be a great opportunity for me: I could go from one world to the other, to churches, to rich folks, and collect enough money to return home, pay my debt, and take care of my family."

And so, my grandson, this is the hard and bitter predicament when the landowner allows himself to become a beggar, convinced that by the dishonorable means of panhandling he'll be able to raise

---

4. Somebody who has seen better days; literally a person thrown out of government service (Turkish).

enough money to rebuild his livelihood: do you believe that the destroyed home of the farmer can be rebuilt by begging? In my whole life, from youth to old age, I've never seen any such thing. For the solid grounding of a farmer is farming. When the person who owns land abandons it, he is already destroyed and can never get back on his feet. He will live in poverty until the day he dies.

Well, dear grandson, I've said enough, let's put an end to the crowning in the field and the farming lessons. I also have to tell the village elders and the other villagers, so that everyone will know what a strange thing Papik has done: he has taken his grandson, the newlywed bridegroom, to the field, and has crowned him beside the plow. No one has ever heard of that kind of crowning: with no priest, with no cross or Bible or witnesses, and performed in the middle of a field!

Let the peasants think what they want! Grandson, it's enough for me that you understand the meaning of this crowning. I'll die, but you'll go on living, and understand. Then the peasants will understand too, and will bless Papik's soul!

FROM INVITATION TO THE PROMISED LAND[5]

The Cathedral of St. James (Jerusalem)

Kind children, after touring with me thus far around the various places related to the (earthly) life of the Lord, the Incarnate Son of God, you have come to the end. Now I invite you and your fellow bearers of the Cross to the shrine of the martyrs, the lofty and magnificent See of St. James, a site given to the Armenians (by the Emperor Constantine), as a gracious gift to Sts. Gregory and Trdat. Fittingly situated atop Mt. Zion, (it is the place) where the head of the venerable Apostle James is laid to rest, the one who with his brother promised to drink of the same cup (as did Jesus) (Matt. 20:22).

First, entering the chapel, we kiss the place of his head, a place of which the Armenian people are proud, a place where people

---

5. Khrimian Hayrik, *"Hravirak Yerkrin Avetyats,"* (Invitation to the promised land), in *Amboghjakan yerker Khrimian Hayriki*, 625–29. Translated by Abraham Terian.

come to fulfill their vows. There they plead (in his name), for God honors his servant. Here I shall tell of the goodly blossom stemming from Zebedee, I mean the venerable James who surpassed his ancestors (in piety). This Apostle did not forsake the One who was sought—not even for a night; he never wished to do such a thing, it never entered his heart. For three full years, day and night, he was inseparable (from the Lord), wandering with the One sought after, filling his heart with the love (of the Lord). (Unlike his namesake, Jacob), the one stricken in the hip, who did not let the Lord go so as not to limp after Him, since he could no longer run to grab Him (Gen. 32:23–32), typifying his weak progeny who were limping willfully, (wavering) between two lanes, in their quest for truth. He distinguished himself from them; appearing with much grace, he waxed strong and pursued the holy faith boldly and without limping; he followed Christ and the way of life that leads to heaven. Whereas the former physically fathered twelve sons for this world, the latter became an Apostle and went, as was his lot, to Spain. There he preached the Word to those religiously wayward, the godless, and begot children born of the Spirit, a whole nation for heaven. The one who promised Jesus to drink willingly of the cup of death, hastened to return to Jerusalem, where the Lord himself drank (the bitter cup) at the hands of his obstinate people. Thus he resembled his Lord, who came to suffer willingly. He was arrested by Herod and imprisoned like John (the Baptist), and drank of the same bloody cup by laying down his head for Christ's sake. Longing for its embrace, the wakeful host of heaven came to attend to it; they lifted it up on a bright, white sheet and brought it to Jerusalem, where the mourners were assembled, weeping: the Mother of God, (his brother) John, and the (other) Apostle James, before whom they laid the sacred head soaked in blood. How much more was the grief of his associates, who wept and wept and then buried here the unattainable treasure.

. . . .

Let us now approach the relics of St. James the Just (the brother of the Lord; Clement of Alexandria, writing in the second century, was first to call him "the Just"), gathered beneath the main altar, under the immovable slab of stone: these pieces of tireless bones, quarried from the rebellious nation; small, but great in their measureless grace; righteous, for he proceeded irreproachably in his path of life. (We call him) the brother of the Lord for he was a close relative of Christ, nurtured in unwavering love, descended from that same family. Because of this, he was honored by being among the apostolic circle, the first to be privileged to sit on the throne of the Son of David in Jerusalem. In love resembling Jesus, he resided here, the house of James, where he preached, endeavoring to lead Israel to the Light. But through his hortatory words he was writing and speaking to those far away, to the newly called twelve Hebrew tribes in the dispersion (James 1:1); counseling that trusting in faith alone is futile, unless one necessarily brings forth the fruits of good works. "You are a new tree planted by Christ, you who now are blossoming in faith. Bring forth fruit lest you be terminated by the sharp axe laid low (cf. James 3:12–18; Matthew 3:10). Light your hearts with the immaterial flame of the zeal of Elijah and become like him (cf. James 5:17), not by running away from the enemy nation but by staying firm like a rock among those who scandalize (you), those builders who are confounded, those who disallowed the cornerstone (cf. 1 Pet. 2:6–8)." Again, in love, he pleaded (with people) to choose that building, to join in faith and be added to the immovable Rock. "Say not 'when you stumble on that (Rock) you shall be broken to pieces and shall be lost, shall be scattered here and there by the wind of (His) wrath'" (cf. 1 Pet. 2:8; James 1:6).

When the people in the palace had enough of his rebukes, they contrived to kill the blessed (Apostle): to come up with a snare for the righteous one, thus severing themselves from his blessing. Deceitfully they brought him to the pinnacle of the Temple and threw off the one who was already uplifted to heaven by the Spirit. Because he survived miraculously, they quickly smashed his head. They saw to it that the righteous one was taken away from the world, for (they thought) he was disturbing them very much (according to the first-century Jewish historian Josephus, this happened in AD 62, during the interval between the death of the Roman governor Festus and his replacement by Albinus; cf. Hegesippus, writing ca. 180 and as quoted by Eusebius, *Church History*, 11.23.4–18).

. . . .

My children, you who have responded to my inviting song to come to Jerusalem in the spirit, where the love of God, which is beyond description, was revealed to all: may the image of God's love be reprinted in your souls; the image of the Manger of Bethlehem; the image of the Cross of Calvary; that of the great Church of the Holy Sepulcher; the image of the sacred Tomb. Blessed are you who cherish these images in your souls. These memories shall remain forever, like sculpture in the rock.

O children of the new Zion, ponder these things in your hearts. Hasten to Jerusalem with the love of Christ ablaze in your souls. My children whom I begot through the Spirit and invited through my song: I leave for you this volume as a memorial. I shall soon die and go to be with the Bridegroom. Please remember Jerusalem as often as you read this. I did remember, and so I came to see Jerusalem three times. I toured, I kissed the places touched by Jesus' feet. I vowed, like David, never to forget Jerusalem (Ps. 137:5).

I now direct my words to you, O my love, Jesus. I shall gracefully conclude my book with your seal (of approval). I confess that it is your grace that inspires poetically, even a useless elder like myself. Being prompted by you, O Lord, I walked in through this gate at the start (of my spiritual journey); and as I exit, to you I give my thanks. O for your love! Could it be fire, which you hurled at people on earth, which has since engulfed the whole earth, beginning from Jerusalem? You also set me ablaze while my spirit was already burning within me; but now you are blazing my body and soul from Jerusalem. When I was young in age, a spark of your love shielded me and lit for me the lamp of your Word, which lighted unto me the path of life. Now I have reached an old age, past seventy. I beg you, O my light Jesus, keep my lamp burning. O (my Lord); surely I would have stumbled in the dark were it not for your light that keeps my lamp burning. Draw not your Spirit from me while I am not yet dead. For I have loved your Incarnation with all my heart, and I remembered Jerusalem, the holy Mount Zion, and the word of the Cross.

Nikoghayos Zorayan

(1821–59)

Nikoghayos Zorayan, economist and educator and a leading figure in the Revival Movement, received his early education in Constantinople, but, unhappy with the archaic methods of teaching, he quit school at the age of thirteen and then studied under private tutors. In 1838 he was employed as a translator in a government department; in 1843 he went to Europe to experience Western civilization. After visiting Manchester and Venice, he moved to Paris, where he stayed from 1844 to 1848. At that time Paris was a gathering place for young Armenian intellectuals, mostly from Constantinople, who were imbued with liberal ideas and who would later help to bring about the Armenian intellectual renaissance. Zorayan felt very much at home in the group.

On his return to Constantinople, he began to publish articles in the periodicals *Bazmavep* (*Polyhistor*), *Hayastan* (Armenia), and *Masis* on economic, political, and pedagogical issues, while at the same time developing and analyzing certain philosophical views. In his essay "*Teghekutiunk tntesagitutyan vra*" (Information about political economics), influenced by Adam Smith and David Ricardo—according to whom economy is the wealth producer of a nation and is contingent on rules regulating labor and values—he advanced the thesis that since social and economic development is based on productivity, Western Armenia should be industrialized to European standards.

In the field of education, his essay *Nkaragir azgayin dastiarakutyan* (The Nature of national education) starts with the premise that all human beings are born equal, and it goes on to reject the idealistic dogma that goodness and other virtues are innate. In the debate over "nature versus nurture" he was on the side of "nurture," hence his strong emphasis on education. He encouraged the preparation of language and history textbooks in modern Armenian, even though his views on history got him into trouble with the clergy. However, his textbooks *Varzhutiun entertsanutyan* (Exercise in reading) and *Entertsasirutiun* (Love of reading), prepared according to modern pedagogical principles, were appreciated by teachers. He was an active promoter of the use of modern Armenian.

Nikoghayos Zorayan was one of the pioneers of the Revival Movement. Most of his writings remain scattered in the periodicals of the time. He died of cerebral paralysis in Constantinople, at the age of thirty-eight.

ASSOCIATION[1]

It must not be looked upon as an exaggeration when I say that even a slip of straw would not grow without association. If the combination of merchandise, craft work and labor is needed in order to construct a three-story vessel, a similar combination is required for the making of a small needle; let us see, therefore, how it works.

When we have some work to accomplish but do not know how to carry it out, we seek the advice of someone who has the necessary knowledge. In other words, we associate, combine ourselves with his intelligence. When we try to lift something heavy and realize that our strength does not suffice to do it, we ask someone to help us; that is, we associate ourselves with his power. When we do not possess the needed merchandise to start an enterprise, we borrow it or rent it from someone else; that is, we associate ourselves with his merchandise. Thus, when the intelligence, power and merchandise of different persons are united to accomplish something, we consider the latter as to have been completed through

---

1. Nikoghayos Zorayan, *"Enkerutiun"* (Association), in *Dar me grakanutiun,* ed. Minas Teolelolian, vol. 1 (1850–1920) (Boston, 1977), 117–18. Translated by Arminé Keushguerian and edited by the editors of the present anthology.

association. Therefore, association is the unification of the means of two or more individuals, with the intention of attaining a certain purpose.

Intelligence, power and merchandise—these three substantial elements being almost impossible to be possessed by a single individual, companionship is necessary for all kinds of business and, moreover, for industrial and commercial enterprises. These elements being more important for the industrial and commercial enterprises, association is the only basis and best way to start and develop such huge undertakings.

Merchandise, intelligence and labor are each, by themselves, of enormous power, but when combined they become even more powerful and capable of carrying out very great enterprises. When left alone, they often lose strength, their ability is annihilated and they become useless; because if the human mind does not have these three elements in unison, it will mostly not be capable of carrying out ideas of great importance.

When I speak of associations, I do not allude to those which consist of only two or three persons existing in our country since a rather long time, and for all kinds of trade. I likewise do not allude to the artificial, unnatural assemblies where a few individuals behave as contractors, while the others are merely submitted to obedience. When I say *association,* I have in view a companionship not only of four or five persons, but much more, who are all equally sharing the profit. Because, in the associations of the first category, the combined means are, in their turn, so limited that they not only cannot undertake a great business but often would not afford the necessary means for the successful development of a small business. At this point, the association for industrial enterprises is rather harmful than beneficial.

The bond uniting the members of the second category of associations, especially of the artificial assemblies, is the necessities of life. Public benefit, which is the basic characteristic for legal associations destined to attain successfully the goal, does not exist here; the profit is very little both from the labor and for the laborer.

The best associations, most suitable to undertake huge industrial enterprises, are those of the third category. Through them it is possible, first of all, to bring together the three most important elements—the intelligence, power and labor, utilizing them in combination, and for the same purpose. Besides, a cordial advice of a fellow member, his encouragement and praise revives the hope of boosting the profit of the association, because everybody is convinced that he will be a partaker of the profit.

Tzerents (Hovsep Shishmanian)

(1822–88)

Hovsep Shishmanian, better known as Tzerents, was born in Constantinople, attended the Mkhitarist school in Venice (1837), taught for a while in Constantinople, visited Tiflis in 1843, spent some time traveling through Armenia, and eventually, in 1848, went to Paris to study medicine. This was the year when the revolution in France and the emancipation movements in Italy were in full swing, and young Shishmanian fell under their ideological sway. Along with Nahapet Rusinian and others, he founded the Ararat Society in Paris (1849). After graduating from the University of Pisa in 1853, he returned to Constantinople and involved himself in cultural, educational, and literary activities. At that time the Armenian community of Constantinople was going through a serious crisis resulting from religious factionalism, which ended in the separation of Catholics and Protestants from the Armenian Church. Shishmanian worked hard to establish unity and harmony among the groups and for the implementation of the Armenian National Constitution, and to these ends he published numerous articles. He also collaborated with the poet Mkrtich Peshiktashlian (Beshiktashlian) in founding the National (*Hamazgiatz*) Union for culture and education. He was a fervent promoter of national unity.

Late in the 1870s he made a trip to Cilicia to investigate the possibility of establishing an agricultural school there. Knowing that he was under suspicion by the government, he went on to Cyprus, where he occupied a medical post (1876–78). He then returned to Constantinople for a short while and finally moved to Tiflis, where he spent the rest of his life. His daughter's death in 1884 was a hard blow to him and affected his health very adversely. He died of a heart attack in 1888.

Hovsep Shishmanian's literary legacy consists mainly of three historical novels. The first, *Toros Levoni* (1877), is based on the restoration and expansion of the mid-twelfth-century Cilician kingdom under Toros II of the Rubenid dynasty; this work advocates cooperation among feudal lords to strengthen the central power. The background of the second, *Yerkunk innerord daru* (The ninth century in labor, 1879), is ninth-century Armenia under Arab rule, focusing on the revolt of 851. The popular hero, Hovnan (a fictional figure), has contempt for the ruling class and nobility because of their conceited and arrogant demeanor, and he arouses the people to rebellion. Although he is martyred, freedom is eventually assured. The third novel, *Teodoros Rshtuni* (1881), is based on the events of the seventh century, mainly from 620 to 660, when Armenia was caught between Byzantine pressure for religious and political subordination and the Arab incursions. Prince Teodoros Rshtuni, a historical figure who was both commander-in-chief of the army and *marzpan* (governor or viceroy) of Armenia, tried hard to maintain a political equilibrium between the two adversaries, a task that was complicated by the shifting loyalties of the feudal lords. Although these novels may not always depict historical events faithfully, they were nevertheless a powerful inspiration of patriotism and the spirit of cooperation and unity among the people.

"Tzerents is the father of the Armenian historical novel. Despite his failure to reach the artistic excellence of Raffi, in Eastern Armenian literature, his literary labors gave birth to the genre and put it on a respectable basis."[1]

See the section on the historical novel in the overview part of this volume.

---

1. James Etmekjian, "The Historical Novel," *Ararat* 19, no. 4 (Autumn 1978): 39. See the section on historical fiction in the overview of the present anthology.

| *FROM* TOROS LEVONI[2]

Haven or Trap?

Editor's note—Toros has just been freed from prison. His jailor was bribed by an unknown man to hand the prisoner over to him. In the selection that follows, we find Toros and his servant in the house of his mysterious protector.

Thus, the two Greeks, followed by Toros and his servant (Babken), passed through the palace gate that led to the square, then through triumphal arches again, and finally entered the city proper. There, long, high walls with huge gates indicated palaces or residences of high dignitaries, sometimes followed by small wooden houses. From time to time, they encountered gatherings of people, as is usual in large cities, and entered deserted streets again. At last, they arrived in front of a door set in a high, square wall. It opened promptly when they knocked, revealing the customary garden with its giant trees and many rosebushes. At the end of the garden was a two-storied house whose windows looked out on the garden on three sides. The servants' quarters, a one-story structure, stood at the right of the garden entrance, next to the wall.

The man who opened the door was, to judge by his clothes, an average domestic in a cleanly kept house. When the four persons entered, an old woman, sticking her head out of the kitchen door, peered at them with natural curiosity. As soon as they were inside, the leader turned to the short man and said:

"Friend, now you know the house. Do you want anything else?"

"No, but. . . ."

"Then our private agreement has been carried out," he said and assumed an attitude that indicated to the other that there was no time for long conversations. The other understood it and departed, leaving his companions in the solitude of the four walls of the house that, except for its smallness, resembled a harem or a convent. When the door closed, the stranger, simply but full of respect, turned to Toros and, pointing to the door of the house,

---

2. Tzerents (Hovsep Shishmanian), Toros Levoni, *Ararat,* ibid., 40–43. Translated and footnotes by James Etmekjian.

asked, "Do you wish to see your quarters, my prince, and order your servant to get you whatever you wish?"

Toros, who had not been treated with such respect for years by anyone but Babken, stepped forward indifferently without showing any surprise whatsoever. He found himself in a small vestibule with a room on either side. One was the dining room and the other the living room, both appropriately furnished. At the other end of the vestibule was a staircase leading upstairs, where there were two more rooms, a bedroom and a study, in which besides the sofas and other necessary furniture, one could see polished arms hanging on the wall. In the bedroom, there were all the clothes that a young nobleman needed. The simple but tasteful bed covers proved that an alert woman with a delicate touch had been there. At one end of the bedroom, there was a door which led into a small bathroom. After they had seen all this, the leader turned again to the prince and said, "If you need anything else, my prince, please command." The prince, turning his penetrating eyes for the first time toward the man, replied, "Let us go into this room for a moment." Entering the other room for the second time, he went directly to a gigantic curved sword, removed it from the wall, drew it partly from its scabbard, examined it, and, recognizing his father's sword, replaced it on the wall.

"Friend," he said, enunciating each word clearly, "tell the person who prepared this house for me that, if she is an angel, half of my heart belongs to her."

"When you let me know your commands through this servant, I shall always be at your service," said the man and left with a respectful gesture.

"Did you notice the position of this house?" asked Toros, turning to Babken. "Go out before darkness sets in, walk around the house, observe without seeming to observe, and see without looking. Find out what there is behind this house, and whether there is a house or garden behind this wall. Hurry, so that you may be back in time for dinner."

After Babken had left, Toros began to examine the wooden walls carefully. The slightest crack was subject to minute scrutiny by his eagle eyes. Finally, he stopped before a section of one of the walls in the bedroom, and a scornful smile appeared on his lips. "This is what I was looking for," he said. "Treacherous wood, you are a Byzantine door, but what are you hiding? Truly, this bed, these muslin curtains, and even the folds of these clothes indicate the presence of an angel's hand. It was said a thousand years ago that there are angels of darkness that assume the guise of angels of light, but what an impossible dream to find angels of light in this cursed city, in this Babylon. Then there is my father's sword hanging in the other room. What does it all mean? Who is behind it? A woman? That sword has been taken from the room where victory trophies are kept. What kind of woman can she be?

"What an eventful day it has been. I have left prison; I have seen the betrayer of my brother scorn me; and I have been in the presence of the emperor and heard his arrogant words. He wishes to make me renounce being an Armenian. This man has stolen his people's soul and distributed it among his priests. Would that he knew what the welfare of his throne, as well as his people, demanded. Would that I could take his place. If that royal head had learned what I learned from my father in prison concerning my people's past and had had the knowledge I acquired from the dusty worm-eaten books in their monasteries of the Greeks, he would not have spoken those concerning words to me. Instead of humiliating me with his scorn and persecuting my people, he would form an army of Eastern Christians, uniting us around him, in order to resist attacks from the east and the west. Unfortunately, he is destined to fall at the feet of one or the other, and this capital will become a ravished and plundered Ani.[3]

"Who called me, a forgotten prisoner, to the attention of that childish emperor, who grants me sunlight and freedom? Oh, brilliant sun of Black Mountain, when will I stand on your rocky peaks and see my people, as well as foreigners, not as a boy who is scrutinized from head to foot, but as a giant to whom people must look up when they wish to speak to him? That Andronicus[4] must be convinced that the cub is a lion. Traitors, my brother, my Ruben, was truly a lion's cub with the blood of a lion, the strength of a lion, and the heart of a lion. You blinded him when he was at my age. There were three of us when we entered prison. They wasted

---

3. Ani was the capital of the Bakratuni kingdom. It was captured by the Seljuk Turks in 1064. It was a city of many churches which at one time numbered 1,001, according to tradition.

4. The cousin of the Byzantine emperor Manuel Comnenus (1145–80).

away and died,[5] and I alone have come out having learned from
their example and their mistakes. O, Lord, enable me to remain
unrecognized until I plant the banner with the Rubenian cross on
the peaks of the Taurus. My first steps have already revealed to
me a friendly hand that extends toward me in the darkness as I
stand alone and helpless in this hostile country. However, were
there not a thousand friendly hands ready to help my brother? He
was handsome, personable, vigorous, fearless, and created for love
and friendship only. Who could say that there was a single person
who hated him? The women were in love with him. The youth
sought his aid. O, Byzantine love! O, Byzantine friendship! How
many cursed passions are harbored within the walls of this city!
The shiny golden cupolas of that palace are so many tombs of ugly
corruption.

"My father's sword moved me. I wonder whether it is Andronicus, himself, who has caused that sword to be hung on the wall in
order to dispatch me in the same manner he dispatched Ruben and
to escape from the vengeance of his brother should that brother be
like Ruben. But where are my brothers Steban and Mleh? Perhaps
if they had given signs of life, there would not have been anyone to
save me from prison. . . . What is the situation in Cilicia? I wonder
who will bring me news. . . . I must go there personally, but until
that day I must be like the Roman who feigned insanity in order
to save his country. I'll pretend to be a fool, and if he thinks that
I am a fool, probably everyone in the palace will also think so.
But can a fool love a woman? The person who put that (secret)
door there and hung that sword on the wall undoubtedly wishes to
unmask me. . . . Let us see who will succeed in this game, who will
be the victor. I shall be. I must be, for I shall rule over land and
sea. That is the prophecy. . . . Yes, the prophecy of a dream. But
what is a dream? Who knows where it comes from, and what its
meaning is? . . . I am convinced that dreams have meaning, and my
magnificent old man had something truly godlike on his dignified
and lighted face, with his luxuriant beard and brilliant eyes, whose
gaze had transformed me from a boy to a man. 'Well,' said my
father, Levon, 'the bread is your paternal land, the fish represents
the sea. You will rule over land and sea, and I shall not see it.'

---

5. Ruben was assassinated.

Indeed, he died a few days later, and I was left alone, a stranger and a prisoner surrounded by all his enemies, all the enemies of the Armenians. . . .

"It was the love of that Armenian people that moved my ancestors who, full of hatred and vengeance for the Greeks, placed the banner of freedom on the peaks of the Taurus. I have the same sentiments. I feel, as the heir of my ancestors, and as a product of my Greek readings, that they do not know their Lycurguses, their Leonidases, and their Aristideses. They argue for hours and weeks and persecute their co-religionist brothers for the interpretation of a drop of water, a little bread *dough*,⁶ and an incomprehensible *word*. They are madmen. If God permits me to realize my dreams, I know what I shall do. However, my aspirations are high, but my position difficult. We'll see. . . ."

He was in the midst of these meditations when Babken entered. Silently, Toros took him into the next room and asked him what he had seen, and as he had suspected, Babken had seen nothing but high walls. Without losing any time, they went downstairs for dinner, for it was already past dinner time, and they had not eaten since morning. Although very hungry, Toros was even more curious to know what kind of food was prepared in this singular house, where one noticed a secret hand behind everything. When they were in the dining room, he asked Babken to sit at the table with him, and upon the latter's hesitation, "Father Babken," he said, "if circumstances so dictate, I shall let you know when you are not to share the table with me. Otherwise, we'll not change our prison habits. I also want you to know that it is a greater pleasure for me to eat bread and cheese with my father's faithful servant and my childhood guardian than to enjoy royal viands with strangers."

The food was choice and tasty without being extravagant. The wine was excellent and the fruit delicious. Toros left the table without saying a word. When the servant asked what his wishes were for the next day's menu, he simply answered, "Ask the person who ordered you to prepare today's meal."

After he had directed Babken to place a bed in the living room and to spend the night there in wakeful sleep, he went upstairs, "Although," he added with a smile, "such an order was unnecessary

---

6. These have to do with the wine and bread used in communion.

for a man who has taken part in every one of my uncle's or father's wars since the age of twelve and knows that it is necessary to be cautious when one is surrounded by the enemy." Then, without giving it further thought, he went to bed as if he were in his paternal fortress of Vahk, where he had spent his childhood. Although he lay awake for several hours, he was still at an age when he was unable to resist indefinitely the emotional fatigue resulting from the events of the day, and he fell asleep. When he awoke, he jumped out of bed, as had been his custom since childhood, and naturally his eyes turned toward the secret door that seemed like a wall. He opened the window and saw Babken strolling calmly in the garden. Upon a motion of the young man's hand, he came up, and his first glance, like that of Toros, was directed toward the door.

"Father Babken," said the prince, "why are you looking at that door? What did you see?"

"I didn't see it now," answered Babken. "I saw the trap yesterday, but things didn't turn out the way I had imagined."

"What do you mean?"

"I thought that an enemy would come out of that door armed with a sword. It is true that an enemy came out but not the kind I had thought."

"Babken, I don't understand a thing you're saying."

"You told me to spend the night in wakeful sleep, which is what I had intended to do. However, what was the point of lying on a bed downstairs in that room in wakeful sleep? I had to be in a position from which I could see the activity in the house and watch over the only hope of the Armenian people. Thus, when silence settled over the city, 'Let's change beds,' I said to myself, went quietly to the garden, and unable to find a more appropriate bed than the tree, I climbed it. Everything was dark and quiet until midnight. Suddenly, I saw your wall open and a faint glimmer of light was outlined in the darkness. I gripped my sword. 'Saint Gregory,' I said, 'give me patience. . . .'"

"Were you going to shout?"

"God forbid. I was going to jump into the house. We are good jumpers on Black Mountain, but the distance was too great, and the window too narrow. The intruder could escape, especially since the light was faint and the intruder timid. Therefore, it was necessary to wait. A minute seemed like a year. The long line of light began to move just slightly, and then I saw a head. 'Thank you, Saint Gregory,' I said, and put the sword back in the scabbard. The head belonged to a woman. But what did she want? She listened. She wanted to know whether you were asleep. When she was reassured, the door opened all the way, and she entered the room, holding a light which she was shielding with her hand. She first examined the room, then approached you slowly, and when I saw her, I began to tremble."

"Why, what did you notice on her face?"

"It was as beautiful as the sun. I am frightened when Satan is beautiful, especially now. She observed you. She prayed over you. I prayed, too, that Saint Gregory rescue you from the hands of that beautiful devil. She stayed for a few minutes, and as if shaken by someone, she took her light and disappeared as quietly as she had entered. The vision vanished."

"This was the sum total of your vision and fear Father Babken?" laughed Toros.

"If that woman had not been so beautiful, I would not have been afraid."

"I see. You are afraid that I'll fall in love with her and forget our mountains, aren't you?"

"Yes, I am. If that woman leaves this city and comes with you, if she gives up her cursed religion and accepts Saint Gregory's religion, we'll make her queen of the mountains. But Greek women are cursed. You, on the other hand, our prince, are good, prudent, and learned. You read much and know as much as a *vardapet* but you have not seen women. I am afraid that, just as you forgot our Armenian books as you spent your time reading the Greek books in the monastery prison, you will forget our Armenian women. I used to say to your late father, 'Sire, our prince, Toros, is intelligent, but he is reading that cursed nation's books, and I am afraid that he will forget Saint Gregory's religion.' He used to reply, 'Babken, do not be afraid for Toros. He is more intelligent than I. He is like his uncle. He will be braver and better than we. Some day, he will make you forget us. Don't worry. You'll see.' I didn't worry, but when I saw you leave your Narek[7] and read those dusty, worm-

---

7. Gregory of Narek (951–1010), a saint in the Armenian Church and the author of *Lamentations,* translated into several languages.

eaten Greek books secretly, I used to say, 'Lord, protect our prince.'
When I saw that woman, with her blond hair hanging down her
back in golden braids, as she tried to charm you, I became afraid.
May God protect you, and may Saint Gregory enlighten you."

"Don't worry, Father Babken. God will protect me. I feel more
secure. Just as the Greek books protected me from the danger of the
Greek religion, so will Greek women protect us against the danger
from their men. You did well last night to borrow your bed from
the birds. You can now sleep in peace at night, for the enemy is not
as strong as you thought. Who knows, she may even be an ally."

"The Lord save us from a Greek ally," said the old man crossing himself. "Ask the Franks how helpful their assistance was. The
Greeks readily promised friendship and abundant provisions on
the one hand, and on the other, they secretly burned the grass and
the crops, dumped the wheat and barley into the sea, and made
deserts out of the towns and villages. My father used to tell that
during your grandfather's reign (God rest both their souls), when
the Franks reached Cilicia, they had no horses, for they had all died
on the way. The men had wasted away, as if they were suffering
from an illness, and we thought that they would all die. Those
brave barons and freres would never have succeeded in capturing
Jerusalem if they had not been fed by the Armenians. Your father,
who was a very intelligent man, went to see their king and took
care of all his needs, for God's sake as well as his own. They ate and
drank freely, and before a week had gone by, they had become as
strong as bulls, and they went and conquered everything, including
the Holy Sepulcher. What a pity! These Franks are brave and
strong, but their heads are empty. They have no brains. The Greeks
are the opposite. They are not strong, but they know much, they
see much. Look at the eyes of their priests. They look like torches
from hell. You'd think that Satan, himself, were there. Since last
night, I am more afraid of Greek women than men."

"All this is in vain, Babken," said Toros seriously. "Just now
we don't have a friend in the world. We must prepare to leave
this cursed city. We have no money to pay for our passage. As
you say, if we do not act intelligently by taking advantage of the
opportunity that presents itself, we'll be as empty-headed as your
Franks. Take a stroll today, and observe the city. Perhaps you'll
meet an Armenian. Don't listen to every Armenian. You may find a

great many Armenian-speaking people who have renounced their religion. There are very few true Armenians. Be especially wary of priests. The good among them are saints, the bad are worse than Satan. If people mention me, tell them that I am a fool, that my mind is hazy, that I have changed since my father's illness. Talk about me. Express sadness and pity for me. If you meet someone who is true and sincere, inform me after you have seen him several times, telling me his name, address, and past history. Then, when I am ready, you'll bring him to me. Now go."

"Fine," said Babken, and got up to go.

Since Levon's father's death, he had not had such a long conversation with his young master. Thus, he was happy in his heart, although his face had forgotten how to smile. Toros called him as he was leaving.

"Father Babken, do you have any money?"

"I have none whatsoever, but God is merciful."

"What do you mean?"

"When we had no feet, God gave us feet. Now we have no money. God is great. He will provide for us. Don't worry."

Karapet Iutiuchian (Ütüdjian)

(1823–1904)

The journalist Karapet Iutiuchian was born in Balat, an Armenian suburb of Constantinople. He attended the local school, then studied at the *Jemaran* in Scutari (Üsküdar, 1839–40), but his education was interrupted when the institution closed as a result of internal dissensions. With diligent effort he educated himself and became a teacher. In 1848 he went to Paris to study commerce, returning home in 1851 after a short visit to London.

His return coincided with the resignation of Hovhannes Teroyents (1801–88), his former teacher, from the editorship of *Hayastan* (Armenia), the organ of the Patriarchate. He was offered the position and accepted with some conditions, such as a certain degree of editorial autonomy, a broadening of the issues addressed by the publication, and changing its name to *Masis* (Mount Ararat). The first issue under the new name and format appeared early in 1852, and the paper continued, as a daily or a weekly, without interruption, for thirty-two years under his editorship. With its wide range of contents—political, social, and literary—and with its balanced position, it became a prestigious and respected paper. From 1884 to 1908 it was published jointly with Arpiarian's *Arevelk* (The Orient), and eventually merged with it.

Iutiuchian was a political moderate. He opposed despotism and harshly condemned the atrocities committed by the Ottoman government against the Armenians. He supported the National Constitution and was a member of its preliminary committee, but he was against revolutionary emancipation activities.

His greatest contribution was in the development and refining of modern Western Armenian. He tried to expunge all colloquial and non-Armenian expressions from everyday language and replace them with equivalent terms, either by coining new words or by borrowing from classical Armenian. In order to encourage reading among the general public, he set himself to the task of translating a number of popular works, mostly by contemporary European authors. Some of the works he translated were *Vingt mille lieues sous les mers* (*20,000 Leagues under the Sea*) and *De la Terre à la Lune* (*From the earth to the moon*), both by Jules Verne; *Le Juif errant* (*The Wandering Jew*) by Eugène Sue; *Sans famille* (No family) by Hector Malot; *La marquise* (The marquise) by Edmond About; and *Le Serment des hommes rouges* (The oath of the red men) by Ponson du Terrail.

However, it was the longevity and prestige of *Masis*, and Iutiuchian's invaluable contribution to the development of modern Armenian that earned him fame.

THE TASK OF NATIONAL ADVANCEMENT[1]

Two things educate peoples: the schools and the press; one is the vital midwife of instruction, the other the arena of public enlightenment.

An examination of the current state of our national education system reveals three categories of schools. Although none of them is really distinguished in the area of traditional studies, it is not appropriate to think of them together, because the differences are enormous. The first category comprises the small village and town schools of Armenia; these do not even deserve to be called schools, for there the pupils learn only grammar and the psalms. The second category consists of a few schools in Armenian cities where, despite the fact that instruction is given in both Armenian and Turkish, one notices little improvement, and that is so ineffectual that only a few master the art of spelling. The third category includes schools

---

1. Karapet S. Iutiuchian, "*Azgayin harajdimutyan gortze*" (The task of national advancement), *Masis*, May 17, 1865. Translated by the editors of the present volume.

in different districts of the capital and elsewhere where languages and the elements of science are taught in addition to Armenian.

. . . The nation needs leadership, however; that is why the education council must draw up a plan, specifying the purpose of such institutions, what their expenses are, and how they can be financed. In addition, the education council must supervise schools, examine the qualifications of teachers, and adopt textbooks. In other words, they must take charge of everything (too numerous to list individually here) on which educational improvement—and consequently the future advancement of the nation—depends.

. . . It might be thought that we do not consider the education of girls important, because it has not yet been mentioned. But how can we neglect the foundation of all civilization? Girls must learn to write and read in order to obtain the moral education that is so necessary for a mother. We do not know exactly how many girls' schools there are, but it is safe to say that in general there is still no instruction for girls in the provinces. And in Constantinople and Smyrna, at most twenty per cent of the girls know how to write, while still lacking what we usually refer to as the enrichment that would justify calling a young girl educated. So it is obvious that we have not advanced much in this field either, to the point that it is no exaggeration to say that the education of girls has yet to be put into place, and it will require continuous national effort in this area as well, if the desired result is to be attained. It must be pointed out that before we can educate our girls we need women educators, and we still do not have them. We therefore have to find a way of meeting this need, and then we have to open dedicated schools everywhere.

Presently all three categories of schools are unsatisfactory; therefore, those who wish to see the nation advance should first and foremost turn their attention to the establishment of a regular education system; without this not only is advancement impossible, but so are all attempts to civilize the nation. No matter how much we sacrifice in order to expand education, it will never be enough. This means that there is a huge task before us, a task for which we not only lack what is needed, but for which we have to invent everything anew. The same thing has to be done in other areas vital to the nation. Some things can be postponed, however; education cannot. For a nation that desires to become civilized, this is a matter of life and death.

Stepan Voskanian

(1825–1901)

Editor, translator, teacher, and a democrat far ahead of his time, Stepan Voskanian was born in Smyrna (Izmir). He was educated at the local Mesropian school and taught there for a number of years. In 1846 he went to Paris, entered Sainte-Barbe College, and also followed courses in history and philosophy at the Sorbonne, under such professors as Jules Simon, Auguste Comte, and Jules Michelet. He graduated with a bachelor's degree. His liberal contacts led him to join the revolutionary movement, and during the insurrection of February 1848 he fought at the barricades alongside the students. His natural propensity to defend the cause of the downtrodden, his education, and his experiences in France combined to give him liberal ideas, a strong belief in democracy, and a firm character: qualities that shaped him into the outspoken journalist and polemicist he became.

In 1852 he left France and returned first to Constantinople then to Smyrna, where, in 1853 and 1854 respectively, he published two pamphlets, *Nerkin hamozum* (Inner conviction) and *Hromeakan pargev* (A gift from Rome), that were aimed mainly at the Mkhitarists, condemning their critical attitude toward the Armenian Apostolic Church.

In 1855, once again in Paris, he began to publish a biweekly journal, *Arevelk* (Sunrise), in which he exposed ignorance and corruption in high places, at the same time offering ways and means for reform. He was a staunch advocate of education, the establishment of democratic order, and confining the authority of the clergy to religious matters. As expected, the reaction from the traditionalists was swift and nasty, and the journal folded after fourteen issues. But Voskanian did not give up. In 1859 he started a new journal, this time called *Arevmutk* (Sunset), to carry on his crusade against decadence and the obscurantism of the clergy. While in Paris he got to know the great democrat Mikayel Nalbandian (1829–66), some of whose articles he published in his journal. But *Arevmutk* met the same fate as its predecessor: it ceased publication after twenty issues.

The story did not end there, however. In 1860 Voskanian was in Turin, working as editor of the French newspaper *L'Italie*. He became acquainted with Count Camillo Benso di Cavour, the statesman and architect of Italian unification, and was engaged by him to tutor his son in French. After Cavour's death in 1861, Voskanian returned to Paris, and in 1865 he resumed publication of *Arevmutk* as a last effort to propagate his democratic ideas. This time the series lasted only nine months.

Voskanian was a man of strong and noble character, fully conscious of the dire conditions under which Armenians lived under Ottoman rule, particularly in the provinces. He realized that before it could be politically emancipated, the nation must free itself of ignorance, inept leaders, and a decadent clergy that by and large surrendered to fatalism and were slavishly subservient to the ruling authority. He made it his vocation to promulgate and fight for these ideas. His opponents—most of them holders of prestigious positions acquired by unholy means, who attended to their own interests rather than those of the nation—were afraid of his ideas and fought him with all the meanness they could muster. During all these years, Voskanian earned his living by teaching French to private students.

Discouraged and despondent, Voskanian returned to Smyrna in 1866, where he was offered the principal's position and teaching assignments at the Mesropian and Hripsimiants schools. Despite the bitterness he had experienced, he was still animated by the spark of journalism. In 1867 he began to publish a paper in French, *La Réforme* (Reform), which he continued to publish, uninterrupted, for thirty-four years, until the end of his life. One day in 1898, when he was in a depressed mood, he confided to Ruben Vorberian (1874–1931), a fellow writer: "For the past thirty-five years I have not written a single word in Armenian, except for a few obituaries. Everyone was ungrateful to me; in disgust, I vowed to hate what I had loved in the past. My compatriots left me hungry, and I began to write in French, to earn my living from strangers."[1]

Despite the fact that Voskanian's ideas were not appreciated during his lifetime and he was even persecuted for them, they exerted a profound influence on the young generation of intellectuals. His maxim was "A moral or physical wound has to be exposed before it can be cured."[2] He clearly distinguished between nationhood and religion: he believed in and respected the Armenian Church, but was against the hegemony of clerics. In order to achieve emancipation, the nation, particularly Western Armenians, would have to be well prepared in all respects and would need outside support to rely upon. Education was of primary importance, both for men and women. The development of the arts and sciences and political and economic thought were essential parts of education. These were his main tenets, which he iterated relentlessly.

He wrote in modern Armenian and contributed to its refinement. Apart from his numerous articles, he also wrote poetry, short stories, and some satire. He also translated substantial amounts of such European (mainly French) authors as Eugène Sue, La Fontaine, Alexandre Dumas *fils*, Chateaubriand, John Locke, and others. He died in Smyrna in 1901.

OUR SHORTCOMINGS[3]

The Armenian critic finds himself in a curious situation these days, and he doesn't really know for sure in which direction to proceed and how to do his job. If he expresses his opinion somewhat arbitrarily, and if he exposes a shortcoming or erroneous opinion and refutes it, he is quickly regarded as an enemy; he is accused and condemned mercilessly. For an Armenian, making a correct judgment is tantamount to being inimical to him or setting a trap for him, with nefarious intent and nefarious will.

It's the same thing in literature. The Armenian still cannot imagine that there's no relationship between an author's honor and his thoughts. An author can be a respectable person, and his

1. Minas Teoleolian, *Dar me grakanutiun* (A century of literature) (Boston, 1977), 1:129.
2. *Arevmutk* (West) 3 (1859): 17. Quoted in *Haykakan Sovyetakan hanragitaran* (The Soviet Armenian encyclopedia) (Yerevan, 1985), 8:626.
3. Stepan Voskan, in *Dar me grakanutiun*, 1:129. Translated by Aris Sevag.

thoughts disrespectful or irrational, just as a lovely tree can give tasteless fruit and a plain bush, a very tasty harvest. The Armenian doesn't understand or doesn't wish to understand this basic truth. Praise or be silent; this is his will.

For sensitive persons, the barbs of the tongue, which manifest themselves here in the form of a whisper, there in the form of disgust, and elsewhere with a biting reference, are considered most unbearable and, barely a short while later, we learn of the wound inflicted. Until their echo reaches us, the falsehood becomes rooted in people's hearts, and thereafter, if you can, try to eradicate it. Pulling weeds from the vicinity of wild flowers is easier, and doesn't subject our hands to as many thorns. Some will say this is due to a lack of education. Yes, but when that deficiency takes on the appearance of an old disease overstepping the boundary of incivility and poisons domestic life, it falls to virtuous people to stem it, respecting the codes of honor like religious commandments. One must not permit, with an indifferent heart, biting tongues to shred a good name publicly, because being careless in matters of honor, or saying "that doesn't concern me" and looking the other way, is the result too of a selfish attitude. One should always imagine that this disease has no mercy, it spreads everywhere and spares nothing; it endeavors to attack everyone, in order, and sticks on rich and poor alike like dog fleas. Honor is the legacy of society; the one wishing to go against it finds himself in the hypothetical situation in which a criminal breaks the law; it is everyone's obligation to have this law respected because everyone's peace is dependent on it.

A people cannot establish a norm and trample upon overall morality. If it dares to do so, it is subject to further contempt for adding perfidy to its other shortcomings. It is preferable for that people to attempt to arrest them and one day become freed from it. A wound, whether moral or material, must be revealed in order to be healed. Praiseworthy for us is that individual who reveals a shortcoming, describes it, and searches for a remedy. That person can never be castigated when he passes judgment on the aberration of the mind and the filth of the heart, and condemns the moral pollution according to the laws of true civilization.

Gabriel Sundukian

(1825–1912)

Gabriel Sundukian was a towering figure of the Armenian stage, the first to embrace realism and to expose and ridicule the vice and corruption of the wealthy classes. Born in Tiflis, he received his early education (1832–40) in private schools, where he learned classical and modern Armenian, Russian, French, and Italian. He attended the Russian gymnasium in Tiflis (1840–46), and in 1846 enrolled at the University of St. Petersburg, in the Department of Philology and Eastern Studies, also learning Arabic, Turkish, and Persian. He graduated in 1850, after submitting a thesis on Persian prosody. His favorite authors were Pushkin, Lermontov, Shakespeare, Schiller, and Molière. He maintained a correspondence with Victor Hugo and the younger Alexandre Dumas, and greatly esteemed Nikolai Gogol, of whom he wrote: "my best memories are linked with his name and I owe much to him for my devotion to the theater." A close literary friend was the Russian playwright Aleksandr Ostrovski (1823–66), who later prepared Sundukian's famous play *Pepo* for the Moscow stage: the project was not realized because of Ostrovski's untimely death.

After graduating from university, Sundukian returned to Tiflis, taught for a while at the Nersisian College, and then entered the civil service as a translator. After some time he was sent to the North Caucasian port of Derbent on an assignment, and when he returned to Tiflis in 1858 he obtained a position in the Caucasian Railroad Administration. He married, had five children, and dedicated his literary life to the theater.

Sundukian is unique in that he created his own type of theater, refusing to follow traditional models that used religious and historical themes and heroes to extol the virtues of patriotism and morality. The intellectual revival of the mid-nineteenth century ran parallel to a social evolution; as a result, most literary and artistic creations, far from being art merely for the sake of art, were intended as didactic tools to help bring about desired social and behavioral changes. It was important for the people first to recognize themselves, to know who they were, where they had come from, where they were going, and where they should be going. With these goals in mind, Sundukian drew his themes and characters from his immediate surroundings, criticizing in the most humorous way the life and manners of the Armenian community of Tiflis, whose customs and dialect he depicted accurately.

Sundukian's first play, *Gishervan sabre kher é* (A sneeze at night is good luck, 1866) is a farce constructed around a marriage-and-dowry situation, a traditional and contentious issue that was further developed in his next play, *Khatabala* (Quandary), where matchmaking, courtship, money, and family interests all join to create a hilarious entanglement. (An expanded and revised version of this play was staged in 1879.) This was followed, also in 1866, by *Oskan Petrovichn en kyankume* (Oskan Petrovich in the afterlife), which, together with *Yev ayln kam nor Diogines* (Etcetera, or the new Diogenes, 1869), examines the topic of marriage from different social perspectives. These plays represent the first phase of Sundukian's drama, in which farce or vaudeville dominates, despite a pointed social message in each act.

After 1870 Sundukian began to write serious comedies, in which laughter was often accompanied by tears. He still dealt with social conditions, but as abstractions. *Eli mek zoh* (Yet another victim, 1884, 1888, 1902) focuses on the clash between fathers and sons in what is, in fact, the first Armenian drama to examine the conflict of ways of living and concepts between different generations and layers in society. Sundukian's best known play, *Pepo* (1871), is a confrontation between Zimzimov, a wealthy usurer, and Pepo, a simple fisherman who has entrusted his sister's dowry to Zimzimov as collateral for a promissory note that has temporarily been lost. Zimzimov's lying and cheating contrasts with Pepo's honesty, and the stage is set for a dramatic confrontation between two social classes: the rich and the poor. In fact, Sundukian was inspired to create *Pepo* by the opposition to the tsarist regime organized by the trade guilds in 1865.

Sundukian's other dramas are *Kandvvats ojakh* (Ruined family, 1883), *Amusinner* (Spouses, 1893), *Baghnesi bokhcha* (Bath bag, 1907), and his last work, *Ser yev azatutiun* (Love and liberty, 1910). He also translated Molière's *Georges Dandin* and published a number of satirical articles in the *Mshak* (The tiller) review under the pseudonym Hammal.

One of the main theaters in Yerevan is named after him.

THE RUINED FAMILY[1]

ACT I

The Ruined Family deals with the disaster that befalls the family of Osep, a merchant, when his frivolous and socially ambitious wife, Salome, agrees to pay a dowry that is more than the family can afford in order that their daughter, Nato, might marry above her station. One of Sundukian's main themes in this play as elsewhere (indeed, it is a characteristic theme of most Armenian provincial literature of this period) is the conflict between old and new, between rural tradition and citified modernity, between native values and foreign-inspired superficiality. The following scenes from Act One are fine examples of how Sundukian handles this theme, so representative of the author, the literary movement of which he was a part, and the time in which he wrote. As scene 5 opens, Osep and his wife (Salome) have been having a rather heated argument about how much dowry he can afford to offer the object of his daughter's matrimonial desires. Khakho is Osep's aunt.

(*Well-furnished room with open door is center and anteroom behind. To the left in foreground a window looking out upon a garden. To the right a sofa, in front of which is a table. To the left a* takhta[2] *with a* kecha[3]

---

1. Gabriel Sundukian, *The Ruined Family,* in Robert Arnot and F. B. Collins, eds., *Armenian Literature,* trans. F. B. Collins, with a special intro. by Robert Arnot, (New York, 1901), 81–109. Armenian text in Gabriel Sundukian, *Yergeru zhogho-vatzu* (Collected works) (Yerevan, 1974), 117–27. The names of the characters have been adjusted to be consistent with the Armenian-English transcription system used in the present anthology.

2. Broad, low sofa.

3. Carpet.

and several mutakas[4]. *A side door. The first and third acts take place in Ossep's house.*)

SCENE V

KHAKHO. (*Enters, left.*) What's all this noise about?

OSEP. O aunt, you are here?

KHAKHO. Yes, it is I, as I love and live. How are you, my son?

OSEP. Pretty well, thank God. And how are you, aunt?

KHAKHO. My dear son, I am very feeble. But what is going on here? They must have heard your voices in the street.

SALOME. Do you not know that married people often have little quarrels?

KHAKHO. That I know a hundred times better than you. And only a blockhead takes a dispute between man and wife seriously. That is true; but that you two have already had time to get used to each other is also true.

OSEP. Sit down dear aunt. Tell me, rather, whether a wagon can be moved when one ox pulls to the right and the other to the left.

KHAKHO. It will not stir from its place any more than I will now. (*Sits down with legs planted firmly.*) What can move me away from here?

OSEP. Now, is it not true? One must help the other, for one alone cannot accomplish much, be he ever so strong and ready to work.

SALOME. Oh, yes! And you are the one ready to work and I am the lazy one, I suppose.

OSEP. For heaven's sake, do not fly into a passion like that!

KHAKHO. (*To Salome.*) Tell me, can we count ourselves among those persons who can give their daughter 10,000 rubles for a dowry? Are we able to do that?

SALOME. Eight thousand is surely not 10,000.

OSEP. Both are too much for me.

SALOME. Oh, it is all the same to me; it is not for myself; it is for your daughter.

(*Sits down, ready to cry, upon the sofa.*)

OSEP. It is a beautiful thing, the way you look out for your daughter; but everything has its time and place. We have, remember, two other daughters to provide for.

---

4. A long veil, covering the head and upper part of the body.

KHAKHO. Dear Osep, why are you so obstinate?

OSEP. I am not obstinate; but you two are. Yes, you are obstinate, and will pay no attention at all to what I say.

KHAKHO. Since when have you become such a niggard? You should have economized when you gave the *sazandars*[5] something like ten rubles for a fee.

OSEP. Those times have passed and won't come back again, dear aunt. At that time I was able to do it; but not now. Trade is dull and my business is going badly.

KHAKHO. Possibly with your enemies, dear son; but there is nothing the matter with your business.

OSEP. (*Aside.*) There you have it! They insist that I let them inspect my books.

(*Aloud.*) Do you know what, aunt? What I say I first consider, for I do not like to speak to no purpose. If that young man pleases you and my daughter, and you will have him at all hazards, I have nothing against it. So therefore go to him; and if you can settle the affair with 6,000 rubles, do it. I will gladly make the best of it; but mind, this is my last word, and if you hang me up by the feet, I will not add a single shilling.

KHAKHO. What has come over you, Osep. If you are willing to give 6,000 rubles, you will surely not let the whole thing go to pieces for the sake of 500 or 1,000 more?

OSEP. Do you know what, aunt? Even if a voice from heaven were to demand it of me, that is my last word. Even if you flayed me alive, I would not give another shilling.

KHAKHO. Do not excite yourself, dear son. Let us first see. Perhaps it can be settled with 6,000 rubles.

OSEP. Yes, to that even I say yes.

SALOME. If a man can give 6,000, he can surely give 1,000 or 2,000 more. Why do you fret yourself unnecessarily?

OSEP. (*Aroused.*) God deliver me from the hands of these women! They say that one woman can get the best of two men; and here I am alone and fallen into the hands of two of you. Where, then, have you discovered this confounded fellow of a son-in-law? That comes of his visits. What has he to do with us? We are entirely different kinds of people. (*To Salome.*) He is neither your

---

5. Musicians.

brother nor your cousin; why, then, does he come running into our house? I believe he has been here as many as three times. I decline once and for all his visits. May his foot never cross my threshold!

KHAKHO. Do not get excited, my son. Do not be vexed.

OSEP. Now, aunt, you come so seldom to our house, and just today you happen in: how does that come?

KHAKHO. If you are so vexed about my visit, go down in the cellar and cool yourself off a little.

OSEP. I am a man; do you understand me? If I tell you that I can give no more, you should believe me.

KHAKHO. We believe it, truly, we believe it; but we must say to you, nevertheless, that the dowry that a man gives his daughter means a great deal. It does not mean buying a house, when it is laudable to be economical. No; where the dowry is concerned, a man must think neither of his pocket nor of his money-box. You were acquainted with Jegor? Did he not sell his last house and afterward lived like a beggar to give his daughter a proper dowry? When he died, was there not money for his burial? That you know yourself very well. Are you any poorer than he, that you grumble like a bear about 2,000 rubles?

OSEP. O great Heavens! they will bring me to despair yet. Isn't this a punishment of Providence, to bring up a daughter, spend a lot of money on her education, and when you have done everything, then hang a bag of gold around her neck, so that she may find someone who is kind enough to take her home with him? A pretty custom!

SALOME. Against the manners and customs of the world you can do nothing, however.

OSEP. The devil take your manners and customs! If you hold so fast to old ways, then stick to all of them. Is it an old custom to wear, instead of Georgian shoes, little boots—and with men's heels, too? And that a girl should be ashamed to go with her own people and should walk around on the arm of a strange young man: is that also one of the good old customs? Where can we find anything of the good old manners and customs of our fathers, in the living or eating or housekeeping, or in the clothing, or in balls and society? What! was it so in old times? Do *you* still talk about old manners and customs? If once we begin to live after the new fashion, let us follow it in all things. Why do we still need to have bedclothes for twenty-four beds for guests? Why do we use the old cupboard and cake-oven and sofa-cover? Why does one not visit a mother with a young baby and stay whole months with them? Why does one invite one hundred persons to a wedding and give funeral feasts and let eighty women mourners come and howl like so many dervishes? And what is that yonder? (*Points to the furniture.*) That one is old-fashioned and the others new-fashioned. If we can have one kind, why do we use the other? (*Silent awhile.*)

SALOME. Well, well! don't be angry! So you will give 6,000 rubles— you have promised it. What is lacking I will procure.

OSEP. You will procure it? Where, then, will you get it? Not some of your own dowry, I hope.

SALOME. I had no dowry. Why do you tease me with that? No, every- thing I have I will sell or pawn. The pearls, my gold ornaments, I will take off of my katiba. The gold buttons can be melted. My brooch and my necklace, with twelve strings of pearls, I will also sell; and, if it is necessary, even the gold pins from my velvet cap must go. Let it all go. I will sacrifice everything for my Nato. I would give my head to keep the young man from slipping through my hands. (*Exit hastily at left.*)

SCENE VI

OSEP. Have you ever seen anything like it, aunt? I ask you, aunt, does that seem right?

KHAKHO. My son, who takes a thing like that to heart?

OSEP. She is obstinate as a mule. Say, does she not deserve to be soundly beaten, now?

KHAKHO. It only needed this—that you should say such a thing! As many years as you have lived together you have never harmed a hair of her head; then all of a sudden you begin to talk like this. Is that generous?

OSEP. O aunt! I have had enough of it all. Were another man in my place, he would have had a separation long ago. (*Sits down.*) If she sees on anyone a new dress that pleases her, I must buy one like it for her; if a thing pleases her anywhere in a house, she wants one in her house; and if I don't get it for her she loses her senses. It is, for all the world, as though she belonged to the monkey tribe. Can a man endure it any longer?

KHAKHO. The women are all so, my son. Why do you fret yourself so much on that account?

OSEP. Yes, yes; you have the habit of making out that all women are alike—all! all! If other people break their heads against a stone, shall I do the same? No; I do what pleases myself, and not what pleases others.

KHAKHO. Osep, what nonsense are you talking? As I was coming here, even, I saw a laborer's wife so dressed up that a princess could hardly be compared with her. She had on a lilac silk dress and a splendid shawl on her head, fine, well fitting gloves, and in her hand she held a satin parasol. I stood staring, open-mouthed, as she passed. Moreover, she trailed behind her a train three yards long. I tell you my heart was sad when I saw how she swept the street with that beautiful dress and dragged along all sorts of rubbish with it. I really do not see why they still have street-sweepers. It was a long time before I could turn my eyes from her, and thought to myself, Lord, one can't tell the high from the low nowadays! And what can one say to the others if a laborer's wife puts on so much style?

OSEP. I said that very thing. I have just spoken of it. A new public official has just arrived. She sees that others want to marry their daughters to him, and she runs, head first, against the wall to get ahead of them.

KHAKHO. You are really peculiar. You have, you say, not enough money to provide a dowry for your daughter, and yet you brought her up and educated her in the fashion. For what has she learned to play the piano, then? Consider everything carefully.

OSEP. Devil take this education! Of what good is this education if it ruins me? Is that sort of an education for the like of us? Ought we not to live as our fathers lived and stay in our own sphere, so that we could eat our bread with a good appetite? What kind of a life is that of the present day? Where is the appetizing bread of earlier times? Everything that one eats is smeared with gall! For what do I need a salon and a parlor, a cook and a footman? If a man stretches himself too much in his coat the seams must burst!

KHAKHO. If you don't want to have all those things can't you manage the house another way? Who is to blame for it?

OSEP. Have I managed it so? I wish he may break his neck who brought it all to pass! I haven't done it; it came of itself, and how it happened I don't know. Oftentimes when I look back over my early days I see that things were very different twenty years ago. It seems to me I have to live like an ambassador! (*Stands up.*) We are all the same, yes, we all go the same pace. Wherever you go you find the same conditions, and no one questions whether his means permit it. If a man who has 10,000 rubles lives so, I say nothing; but if one with an income of 1,000 rubles imitates him, then my good nature stops. What are the poorer people to learn from us if we give them such an example? Weren't the old times much better? In a single *darbas*[6] we all lived together; three or four brothers and their families. We saved in light and heat, and the blessing of God was with us. Now in that respect it is wholly different. If one brother spends fifty rubles, the other spends double the sum, so as not to be behind him. And what kind of brothers are there now, as a rule? And what kind of sisters and fathers and mothers? If you were to chain them together you could not hold them together a week at a time. If it is not a punishment from God, I don't know what is.

KHAKHO. My dear Osep, why do you revive those old memories? It gives me the heartache to recall those old times. I remember very well how it was. In the room stood a long broad sofa that was covered with a carpet. When evening came there would be a firepan lighted in the middle of the room and we children would sit around it. That was our chandelier. Then a blue tablecloth was spread on the sofa and something to eat, and everything that tasted good in those days was placed on it. Then we sat around it, happy as could be: grandfather, father, uncle, aunt, brothers, and sisters. The wine pitcher poured out sparkling wine into the glasses, and it wandered from one end of the table to the other. Many times there were twenty of us. Now if for any reason five persons come together in a room one is likely to be suffocated. (*Points to the ceiling.*) With us there was an opening for smoke in the ceiling that was worth twenty windows. When

6. Hall.

it became bright in the morning the daylight pressed in on us, and when it grew dark the twilight came in there, and the stars glimmered through. Then we spread our bed-things out, and we went to sleep together with play and frolic. We had a kettle and a roasting-spit in the house, and also a pot-ladle and strainer, and the men brought in the stock of provisions in bags. Of the things they brought, one thing was as appetizing as the other. Now, it seems the cooks and servants eat all the best bits. God preserve me from them! Our homes are ruined by the new ways!

OSEP. Do you know what, aunt? I wager it will not be long before the whole city is bankrupt. On one side extravagance and the new mode of life will be to blame, and on the other our stupidity. Can we go on living so? It is God's punishment, and nothing more. You will scarcely believe it when I tell you that I pay out ten rubles every month for pastry for the children alone.

KHAKHO. No! Reduce your expenses a little, my son. Retrench!

OSEP. That is easily said. Retrench, is it? Well, come over here and do it. I would like to see once how you would begin. Listen, now! Lately I bought a pair of children's shoes at the bazaar for three *abaces*.[7] The lad threw them to the ceiling. "I want boots at two and a half rubles," said the six-year-old rascal. He was ready to burst out crying. What could I do but buy new ones? If others would do the same I could let the youngster run in cheap boots. How can one retrench here? Twenty years, already, I have struggled and see no way out. Today or tomorrow my head will burst, or I may beat it to pieces against a stone wall. Isn't it an effort at retrenchment when I say that I cannot afford it? But with whom am I to speak here? Does anyone understand me? Yes, reduce your expenses!

(*Goes toward the anteroom to the right and meets Nato with four sheets of music in her hand.*)

SCENE VII

OSEP. Yes, yes, reduce your expenses!

KHAKHO. Little girl, how quickly you have come back!

NATO. I did not go far, aunt.

KHAKHO. What have you in your hand, sweetheart?

---

7. Twenty kopecks.

278 The Heritage of Armenian Literature

NATO. I have bought some new music.

OSEP. (*Stepping up to them.*) Yes, yes, retrench! (*Taking a sheet of music out of her hand.*) What did you pay for this?

NATO. Four *abaces*.

OSEP. And for this? (*Taking another.*)

NATO. (*Looking at it.*) Six *abaces*.

OSEP. (*Taking a third.*) And for this?

NATO. (*Fretfully.*) One ruble and a half.

OSEP. (*Taking the last.*) And certainly as much for this?

NATO. No, papa; I paid two rubles and a half for that.

OSEP. (*Angrily.*) And one is to economize! Am I to blame for this? What have you bought four pieces for? Was not one or two enough?

NATO. (*Frightened.*) I need them.

OSEP. (*Still more angrily.*) Tell me one thing—is this to be endured? If she could play properly at least, but she only drums two or three pieces and says she can play. I cannot play myself, but I have heard persons who played well. They could use these things, but not we. I wish the devil had the man who introduced this! (*Throws the music on the floor.*) I'll cut off my hand if she can play properly.

KHAKHO. There, there, stop, now!

OSEP. Whatever she tries to do is only half done: music, languages— she has only half learned. Tell me, what can she do? Is she able to sew anything? Or to cut out a dress for herself? Yes, that one seems like a European girl! Ha! ha! Five times I have been in Leipzig, and the daughter of the merest pauper there can do more than she can. What have I not seen in the way of needlework! I gaped with admiration. And she cannot even speak Armenian properly, and that *is her mother* tongue! Can she write a page without mistakes? Can she pronounce ten French words fluently? Yes, tell me, what can she do? What does she understand? She will make a fine housekeeper for you! The man who takes her for his wife is to be pitied. She will be able to share with him the troubles of life! Some day or other she will be a mother and must bring up children. Ha, ha! they will have a fine bringing-up! She is here to make a show; but for nothing beside! She is an adept at spending money. Yes, give her money, money, so that she can rig herself out and go to balls and parties!

(*Nato cries.*) Can I stand this any longer? Can I go oil with these doings? Retrench, you say. What is this? (*Taking a corner of Nato's tunic in his hand.*) How is this for a twelve-story building? Does it warm the back? How am I to reduce expenses here? And if I do it, will others do it also? I'd like to see the man who could do it!

(*Nato still crying.*)

KHAKHO. Do all these things you have said in my presence amount to anything? You yourself said that you troubled yourself little about what others did. What do you want, then? Why should you poison the heart of this innocent girl?

(*All are silent awhile.*)

OSEP. (*Lays his hand on his forehead and recovers self.*) O just heaven, what am I doing? I am beside myself. (*Goes up to Nato.*) Not to you, not to you, my Nato, should I say all this! (*Embraces her.*) No, you do not deserve it; you are innocent. We are to blame for all. I am to blame, I! because I imitated the others and brought you up as others brought up their daughters. Don't cry! I did not wish to hurt you. I was in bad humor, for everything has vexed me today, and unfortunately you came in at the wrong moment. (*Picks up the music and gives it to her.*) Here, take the music, my child. (*Embraces her again.*) Go and buy some more. Do what you wish everywhere, and be behind no one. Until today you have wanted nothing, and, with God's help, you shall want nothing in the future. (*Kisses her and turns to go.*)

KHAKHO. Now, Osep, think it over; come to some decision in the matter.

OSEP. I should like to, indeed; but what I cannot do I cannot do. (*Goes off at the right.*)

Hovhannes Hisarian

(1827–1916)

Hovhannes Hisarian, writer and editor, was born and educated in Constantinople. He became a teacher and served in a number of educational institutions, including government schools. In 1851 he began to publish a monthly review in refined modern Armenian, *Banaser* (Philologist), edited entirely by him, that pursued the aim of "spreading intellectual light, promoting education, and thus contributing to the progress of the nation." After one year, however, it ceased to operate and he tried to launch another periodical, this time in French, called *Journal asiatique de Constantinople* (Asiatic journal of Constantinople). It, too, was short-lived.

He is considered the first romantic novelist in modern Armenian literature because of his novel, *Khosrov yev Makruhi* (Khosrov and Makruhi, 1851). It is the saga of a fictional family, in which serious complexities arise from the clash of personal interests, love and betrayal, and family feuds; eventually three lives are lost in a shipwreck. It is a worthy attempt at a romantic novel. What is lacking in literary style is compensated for by a rich imagination, flowing language, and a captivating narrative.

His second novel, *Nern kam kataratz ashkharhi* (Antichrist, or the end of the world, 1867) is religio-moralistic and sentimental in nature but shares with its predecessor the distinction of being known as one of the first romantic novels in Western Armenian literature.

His poems, written in classical Armenian, are collected in a volume called *Divan.*

Hisarian's numerous articles, essays, and lectures on social and political themes, with a few on archaeological topics, are written in clear and simple modern Armenian and reflect compelling, well reasoned thinking.

FROM ANTICHRIST, OR THE END OF THE WORLD[1]

Chapter I

The Rumelian ramparts.[2]

The Anatolian and Rumelian fortifications, or fortresses, stand on the shores of the narrow strait of the Bosporus and dominate them with their spacious towers, solidly built thick, wedge-shaped bastions, the foundations of which almost reach the water, and their outlines fall on the glassy surface like an image in a mirror. These two strongholds, the junction between two worlds, are alike in appearance, a unified work of architecture, similar in shape, as if constructed on the same foundation but then separated with a flood of water. This illusion is even stronger when one sails along the winding Bosporus and observes the fortresses frequently change position as if by the wave of a magic wand, and through a delightfully compelling optical illusion sometimes join together and sometimes hide one behind the other. But our purpose is to make a few historical comments, not to indulge in topographical descriptions. I wonder which is better? By not going into details are we not writing trivial words? Our intention is to be as brief as possible.

Late in the fourteenth century, a century prior to the conquest of Constantinople, Sultan Bayazit the Thunderbolt, who

---

1. Hovhannes Hisarian, *Nern kam kataratz ashkharhi* (Antichrist, or the end of the world) (Constantinople, 1867), 7–16. Translated by Ardashes Shelemian and edited by the editors of the present anthology. Footnotes are by the editors.
2. The Rumelian fortifications at Rumeli Hisar, along the shores of the Bosporus in Istanbul.

was famous for his victories, built the Anatolian Fortress on the Anatolian shore of the strait as a barricade and spearhead for his newly expanded territory, which extended from Iconium (Konya) to Adrianopolis (Edirne); then, like a menacing eagle, he would be able to destroy every obstacle in his path and challenge the principal city of the Greeks.[3] The Byzantine emperors watched these formidable and ominous threats with apprehension. From then on, the inconstant luck of battle did not well serve the arrogant intentions of the conqueror, whose life came to an end in the cage of Tamerlane, the Tatar.

Fifty years later Fatih Sultan Mehmet the Conqueror built a similar fortress on the opposite shore. The fortress on the Anatolian side of the strait became known as "Güzelce Hisar," and the one on the Rumelian side as "Boğaz Kesen." The two fortresses stood as landmarks of the Ottoman Empire's incursion into Europe, like the Pillars of Hercules.[4] Yildirim Bayazit the Thunderbolt and Fatih the Conqueror chose the narrowest part of the strait for the location of the opposing fortresses, the place where Darius' three hundred rafts were destroyed and his formidable army drowned in the deep waters.[5] It seems that the erection of the fortresses was intended to defend each side, Asia and Europe, against incursions and feuds initiated by the other: events that would leave an abundance of traces in the pages of modern history.

According to tradition, pleading the healthy climate of Rumeli Hisar, Mehmet the Conqueror persuaded the Greek[6] emperor to grant him a piece of land the size of an ox hide, which he then sliced into thin strips, making a line as long as the periphery of the fortress. It is also said that the sultan made several houses inside

---

3. I.e., Byzantium.

4. Like these two fortresses, the Pillars of Hercules are situated one on either side of a narrow body of water separating two continents: Europe and Asia in the former case, Europe and Africa in the latter.

5. In 492 BC, during the Persian Wars (499–479 BC), Darius the Great (550–486 BC) of Persia sent 600 ships through the Hellespont (now known as the Dardanelles), half of them were destroyed before they reached Greece. In 480 BC Xerxes (Darius's son) tried to transport land troops across the Hellespont by building two bridges made of ships lashed together with cables. The bridges were destroyed but eventually rebuilt, and the troops crossed successfully. Hisarian is conflating these events and transferring them to the Bosporus, at the opposite end of the Sea of Marmara.

6. I.e., Byzantine.

Rumeli Hisar available to Armenian migrants, and that there are still families that bear their names. Based on what we know of how the present inhabitants make their living, we can be certain that many of those Armenians were farmers and fishermen. It is also true that Hisar is quite noteworthy for its moderate weather. As to its panoramic position, its summer houses overlooking the sea, and its shaded cemeteries on the seaside, overlooking the turbulent waters, nothing need be said. Referring to these cemeteries, a talented writer, Théophile Gautier,[7] has said, "One would like to be buried there!"

Human life and everything else is predetermined: there is pleasure and sadness, there is satisfaction for some and privation for others. Similarly, these bastions were built against the enemy and destined for bloodshed, and later served as a prison and place of execution for convicts: no one who was sent in would ever come out alive. The galleys of the Bostandji Bashi (sultan's body guard), filled with convicts, would approach the seashore of Rumeli Hisar, where the wretched ones would be disembarked with their hands tied behind their backs and their feet hobbled and led to the underground prisons in the fortress, from which, during the night, they were taken out to be strangled and thrown, all tied together, into the sea. Many times, especially during the Greek disturbances and Janissary massacres, the waters off these shores became sluggish with the terrible bloodshed, and the great number of strangled corpses jammed between the rocks on the shore impeded navigation.

Here and there the shores along the narrow passes have caused accidents, both known and unknown, the memories of which are carved on each piece of rock and pile of sand. It is horrible to envision the water stained by the flow of blood from the fall of Constantinople to its attempted revival. That was the Greek revolution. Who is capable of describing the bravery of those heroes, who amazed the world with their immortal valor? These brave young men from the archipelago and Iberian regions, together with troops of Klepht lancers in their wide fustanellas[8] and crimson fezzes tilted to one side, with tassels hanging over their

7. French poet and writer (1811–72).
8. Stiff full petticoats of white cotton or linen worn by men in modern Greece.

shoulders and with their frightful weapons to battle against the yataghan,[9] surprised the opponents and proved their heroic valor. They excelled their forefathers, to whose amazing patriotism they were worthy heirs. They were slaughtered when sword clashed against sword, they were pursued and scattered along the shores, holding on to rocks to keep their chins above water, protected by the cypress trees, which cast their shadows upon the waters and broke the reflection of the moon at night, and their woeful songs filled the air, just as once happened with the Israelites by the waters of Babylon.[10] Although ordinary in style, these songs were not unrelated in skill and in spirit to those on which Homer and Pindar were brought up, and have been played on horn and reed until our times. Suddenly a deep, loud noise interrupted the tranquility of the night. A window or light-shaft on one of the summer houses opened, and closed again instantly after a bag was thrown hurriedly into the sea. The rough sea waves, striking fiercely upon the threshold of the shore, broke open the bundle by brute force. Then the tumultuous waters gradually subsided and it was all over. . . . Who was the doorkeeper or night watchman, and what was in the bag he threw into the sea? Could it be a useless piece of furniture or inanimate household object, or was it perhaps something alive? Was it an unruly prisoner, an unfortunate youngster, or a lover cleaving to another? No one could describe it but one could look back and remember the hatred of tyranny and restraints that existed within the domain of this capital city that was governed by absolute authority.

And even recently, in AD 18——,[11] the underground gates opened one night and four people came out, two with hands tied and feet chained, as is usual with convicts sentenced to death; they were taken away by the other two, who were executioners under the command of the Bostandji Bashi. When they reached the seaside, a noose was placed around the neck of one of the convicts; he was swung back and forth as if in a cradle, to gain momentum, and then he was hurled into the sea. A terrible splash was heard in the darkness of the night, and the swelling waters surged up to the

---

9. The sword of Muslim countries, having a handle without a guard and often a double-curved blade.

10. See Ps. 137 (136 in the Vulgate numbering): *Super flumina.*

11. The lacuna is by Hisarian.

feet of the executioners, who had taken a break to wipe away their sweat. After ascertaining that the sea had swallowed the prey they had thrown it, they prepared to do the same thing with the other convict.

All of a sudden a three-oared boat quickly drew in to shore and a huge figure got out, came ashore, halted the actors of the somber scene, and stood there like a tombstone. It was the sultan's body guard, wearing his huge helmet. No one knew the reason for his unexpected appearances, and his subordinates were used both to his habitual unexpected appearances and to carrying out his orders faithfully and without hesitation. He signaled his intentions to the two guards, then took the surviving convict with him to the waiting boat and swiftly departed from the shores of Hisar.

All this happened in the dark of night, and no one witnessed the shadowy scene. Thereafter nothing interrupted the tranquility of those places except the winds blowing through the cypresses, making them nod their heads as if continually encouraging the age-old inconsolable laments of the forever grieving mourners.

Mkrtich Peshiktashlian (Beshiktashlian)

(1828–68)

Poet, playwright, and activist, Mkrtich Peshiktashlian was born in Constantinople, received his early education in the local Mkhitarist school, then completed the Muratian school in Padua, Italy (1839–45), where his most influential teacher was the erudite classicist Arsen Bagratuni (1790–1866). After spending some time in Venice doing research on ancient Armenian literary texts, he returned to Constantinople and began teaching Armenian language, literature, and French in local schools. At this time the Armenian community was in turmoil because of confessional disputes and schisms, and Peshiktashlian became closely involved in community affairs, supporting the unity of the nation and preaching brotherhood, to which end he also helped establish, in 1846, a pan-national (*hamazgyats*) association that transcended denominational boundaries, to promote culture and education. He was also one of the founding members of the Armenian Benevolent Society (*Baregortzakan enkerutiun Hayots*), established in 1860, whose membership, recruited from all religious groups, grew to 700 in one year. The aim of the society was to reach out to destitute people in the provinces, particularly those in Zeytun, Cilicia.

In 1856 Peshiktashlian staged his first play, *Kornak,* which he called a tragedy, in the Lusavorchian school where he was teaching. It was a true success, mostly because it was written in modern Western Armenian. This in itself was a break from tradition, as hitherto all theatrical performances were in classical Armenian. The play depicted the deadly conflict between patriots and traitors that flared up after the death of King Trdat (Tiridates) the Great in the fourth century. His other plays, *Arshak* (based on the life of Arshak II), *Vahé,* and *Vahan* (both rulers from the Mamikonian dynasty) were all written in modern Armenian; they revolve around historic events, which the author revives and relates to contemporary issues of unity, patriotism, and liberation. Even though the plays seem to have been written according to classical norms, the ideological content, suffused with humanistic ideas, is rather romantic. Peshiktashlian tries to arouse in the spectator a sense of national identity and self-consciousness. This is evident also in the plays he chose to translate, such as Voltaire's *La mort de César* (The death of Caesar) and Alfieri's *Saul.* His plays filled a very important educational and social need in his time, but in today's context they do not possess much literary value.

The crown of Peshiktashlian's work is his poetry. It is interesting to note that while he was a staunch supporter of modern Armenian and wrote his tragedies in that idiom, he used classical Armenian for most of his poetry, obviously captivated by its charm and beauty. His poetic legacy is not extensive (some sixty poems in all), but they fascinate the reader by their varied content, delicate sentiment, and poetic expressiveness. His patriotic poems were inspired mainly by the 1862 uprising of Armenian peasants in Zeytun, which shook the entire nation. He holds the heroes up as examples and crowns them with glory as martyrs in a great cause. His other poems deal with nature, love, and sadness, the emanations of a very sensitive soul. Some of his poems are still favorites, including a few, such as *"Garun"* (Spring) and *"Yeghbayr yemk mek"* (We are brothers), that have been set to music by Tigran Chukhachian (Chukhadjian, 1837–98) and have become popular songs.

In his earlier years, in order to supplement his income, Peshiktashlian tutored private students from aristocratic families. One of these students was Srbuhi Vahanian (1840–1901), the future feminist writer Srbuhi Dussap, who greatly admired and respected her teacher, with whom she developed a close sentimental, if platonic, tie. From early youth his health was fragile, and in 1867 his illness was definitely diagnosed: consumption. Srbuhi Vahanian was always at his bedside, reading, comforting, and trying to take his mind off the inevitable. He died in 1866, at the age of forty. The entire community mourned his death, and the most touching obituary was that of Srbuhi Vahanian.

Peshiktashlian's works—plays, poems, lectures, and articles—were collected and published in one volume in 1870, as a result of the efforts of Tzerents. The second edition was published by Arshak Tchobanian in Paris in 1904.

A Plaint[1]

Were I a springtime breeze,
 A breeze in the time when the song-birds pair,
I'd tenderly smooth and caress your hair,
 And hide from your eyes in the budding trees.

Were I a June-time rose,
 I'd glow in the ardor of summer's behest,
And die in my passion upon your breast,
 In the passion that only a lover knows.

Were I a lilting bird,
 I'd fly with my song and my joy and my pain,
And beat at your lattice like summer-rain,
 Till I knew that your inmost heart was stirred.

Were I a winged dream,
 I'd steal in the night to your slumbering side,
And the joys of hope in your bosom I'd hide,
 And pass on my way like a murmuring stream.

Tell me the truth, the truth,
 Have I merited woe at your tapering hands,
Have you wilfully burst love's twining strands,
 And cast to the winds affection and ruth?

'Twas a fleeting vision of joy,
 While you loved me you plumed your silvery wings,
And in fear of the pain that a man's love brings
 You fled to a bliss that has no alloy.

---

1. Mkrtich Peshiktashlian, "A Plaint," in Robert Arnot and F. B. Collins, eds., *Armenian Literature,* trans. F. B. Collins, with a special intro. by Robert Arnot (New York, 1901), 47.

WE ARE BROTHERS[2]

From glorious Nature's myriad tongues
    Though songs be breathed by lips of love
And though the maiden's fingers far
    Across the thrilling harp-strings rove,
Of all earth's sounds, there is no other
So lovely as the name of brother.

Clasp hands, for we are brothers dear,
    Of old by tempest rent apart;
The dark designs of cruel Fate
    Shall fail, when heart is joined to heart.
What sound, beneath the stars aflame,
So lovely as a brother's name?

And when our ancient Mother-Land
    Beholds her children side by side,
The dews of joyful tears shall heal
    Her heart's sad wounds, so deep and wide.
What sound, beneath the stars aflame,
So lovely as a brother's name?

We wept together in the past;
    Let us unite in harmony
And blend again our tears, our joys;
    So shall our efforts fruitful be.
What sound, beneath the stars aflame,
So lovely as a brother's name?

Together let us work and strive,
    Together sow, with toil and pain,
The seed that shall, with harvest blest,
    Make bright Armenia's fields again.

---

2. Beshiktashlian, "We Are Brothers," in *Armenian Poems* (Boston, 1917, 1978), 64–65. Translation by Alice Stone Blackwell. This poem has been quoted over the years by Armenians in referring to their political divisions. But it was originally written at the time of a sectarian rift between Catholic and Apostolic Armenians, and was published in 1870. See *Anthology of Armenian Poetry*, ed. and trans. Diana Der Hovanessian and Marzbed Margossian (New York, 1978), 116.

What sound, beneath the stars aflame,
So lovely as a brother's name?

SPRING[3]

How cool and sweet, O breeze of morn,
    Thou stirrest in the air,
Caressing soft the dewy flowers,
    The young girl's clustering hair!
But not my country's breeze thou art.
Blow past! Thou canst not touch my heart.

How sweetly and how soulfully
    Thou singest from the grove,
O bird, while men admire thy voice
    In tender hours of love!
But not my country's bird thou art.
Sing elsewhere! Deaf to thee my heart.

With what a gentle murmur,
    O brook, thy current flows,
Reflecting in its mirror clear
    The maiden and the rose!
But not my native stream thou art.
Flow past! Thou canst not charm my heart.

Though over ruins linger
    Armenia's bird and breeze,
And though Armenia's turbid stream
    Creeps 'mid the cypress-trees,
They voice thy sighs, and from my heart,
My country, they shall not depart!

---

3. Ibid., 62.

Mikayel Nalbandian

(1829–66)

Mikayel Nalbandian, writer, activist, and revolutionary democrat, was born in Nor Nakhijevan (Rostov-on-Don, Russia). He received his early education in Father Gabriel Patkanian's private school (1837–45) and complemented it with self-instruction. In 1848 he was appointed secretary to Archbishop Matteos Vehapetian, primate of Bessarabia. He abandoned his plans to become a priest and, in 1853, after passing examinations at the University of St. Petersburg, he moved to Moscow and obtained a teaching position at the Lazarian College, at the same time (1854–58) auditing medical courses at Moscow University. In 1858 he collaborated with Stepanos Nazarian (1812–79), a graduate of Dorpat University, in the founding and editing of the monthly journal *Hiusisapayl* (Northern lights, 1858–64), which became an influential publication. This collaboration, however, did not last long because of an ideological disagreement with Nazarian.

In 1859 he visited a number of cities—Warsaw, Berlin, Paris, London, and Constantinople—to gain a close acquaintance with social and political conditions abroad, and he made contacts among the leading activists of the day. He returned to St. Petersburg to defend his dissertation at the Faculty of Eastern Studies (1860), and shortly thereafter he traveled to Calcutta, to arrange for the transfer of a considerable sum that had been bequeathed to the Armenian community of Nor Nakhijevan. He collaborated with the leaders of the Armenian revival movement, including Stepan Voskanian (1825–1901), editor of the bi-weekly review *Arevmutk* (Occident), in Paris, and Harutiun Svachian (Svadjian, 1831–74), editor of *Meghu* (Bee), in Constantinople. His long travels (1860–62) through Europe and in Eastern and Western Armenia allowed him to establish contacts with a number of illustrious people, such as Grigor Otian (1834–87), Mkrtich Peshiktashlian (Beshiktash-lian, 1828–68), and Matteos Mamurian (1830–1901) in Constantino-ple; Ghazaros Aghayan (1840–1911) in Tiflis; the Garibaldi partisans in Italy; Aleksandr Herzen;[1] Nicolai Ogariov; the so-called "London Propagandists"; Mikhail Bakunin;[2] and Ivan Turgenev. He also partic-ipated in the underground organization *Zemlia i volya* (Land and will) with Nicolai Tchernishevski. He was a passionate revolutionary and was certainly taking many risks. In a letter dated 1 October 1861 and ad-dressed to Harutiun Svachian (1831–74), he wrote: "Etna and Vesuvius are still smoking; is there no fire left in the old volcano of Ararat?" The inevitable happened: in 1862, as he was returning to Nor Nakhijevan, he was arrested by the tsarist government as a "collaborator of Russian revolutionaries," imprisoned in St. Petersburg (1862–65), and then ban-ished to Kamyshin, in Saratov, where he died of tuberculosis in 1866. His remains were interred in the Armenian monastery of Surb Khach (Holy Cross) in Nor Nakhijevan. His profile has been deftly drawn by Kevork B. Bardakjian:

> In both his literary and journalistic pieces, Nalbandian emerges as an unrelenting champion of freedom and equality; a fearless opponent of despotism, imperialism, and serfdom; an interpreter of human life from materialistic positions; a tireless propagandist of enlightenment, science, and the scientific approach; a believer in agriculture as the key to prosperity and independence; uncompromisingly anti-clerical; and a zealous supporter of Modern Armenian.[3]

It must be noted, however, that his anticlericalism did not mean that he was anti-Christian; in fact, he considered Christianity a means of abolishing despotism and a source of love and freedom.

His literary output is diverse in genre and subject matter. He wrote poems on patriotism, novels that expose social ills, essays and articles

---

1. Aleksandr Ivanovich Herzen (1812–70), Russian philosopher and writer.
2. Russian revolutionary and anarchist leader (1814–76).
3. Kevork B. Bardakjian, *A Reference Guide to Modern Armenian Literature, 1500–1920* (Detroit, 2000), 138.

on national and political issues, economics, philosophy, and education, and a series of pieces of literary criticism. He even wrote a few satiric pieces. His most popular poems are *"Azatutiun"* (Freedom), *"Mankutyan orer"* (Childhood days), and *"Yeraz"* (Dream), which are saturated with nostalgic yearnings for freedom and the homeland. Another poem, *"Mer hayrenik"* (Our fatherland), with some changes to the text, has become the national anthem of the modern Republic of Armenia.

He wrote two novels, *Minin khosk, miusin harse* (A bride promised to one but given to another, 1857), which ridicules old superstitious attitudes, and an unfinished work, *Merelahartsuk* (The necromancer), which attacks ignorance and popular beliefs.

While in Paris he wrote *Yerkragortzutiune vorpes ughigh chanaparh* (Agriculture as the right path, 1862), in which he argues that the agrarian reform introduced in 1861 by the tsarist government was detrimental to the peasants and expresses his own views on social and economic justice and how they can be achieved. He promotes the establishment of an agricultural industry in Armenia proper as the only means of economic independence.

During his prison years (1862–65), he wrote *Azgayin tshvarutiun* (National misery) and *Hegel yev ir zhamanake* (Hegel and his time, 1863), which points out a number of contradictions in Hegel's philosophy. He also found time to translated a number of works by Pushkin, Lermontov,[4] Pierre Béranger,[5] Heinrich Heine, and Eugène Sue.[6]

Nalbandian's ideas on literature, the arts, aesthetics, and education are expressed in several essays and lectures known as *Critica* (Criticism). In one of these pieces, which discusses Perch Proshian's novel, *Sos yev Varditer* (Sos and Varditer), he advocates the creation of a national literature, which he defines as one that deals with the past and present realities of the nation and the struggles for realization of its aspirations. He finds in Khachatur Abovian's *Wounds of Armenia* the perfect exemplar of such a literature. For him the essential purpose of literary criticism is to promote realism in literature. He highlights the importance of theater as an educational medium when he says: "the theater stage is no less than a teacher's podium." He promotes the creation of a national theater; the raising of scholastic standards, mainly in the teaching of modern Armenian; equal rights for men and women; and many other improvements consistent with his democratic concepts.

---

4. Mikhail Yurevich Lermontov (1814–41), Russian poet.
5. Pierre-Jean de Béranger (1780–1857), French poet.
6. French novelist (1804–57).

He fought tirelessly for reform and renewal. In his short but tumultuous life he was not swayed by diverse influences, but remained faithful to his only source of inspiration: his fatherland and his people.

Nalbandian's *Complete Works,* in four volumes, were first published in Armenia in the period 1940–49.

FREEDOM[7]

From the day that God, serene and unconstrained,
Was pleased to course His breath
Into my earthly elements
And grant me my life,

I, an infant, too young to speak,
Lifted my arms,
And with my weak new hands
Grasped Freedom.

Restless at night,
Swaddled in my cradle,
I cried endlessly,
Disturbing my mother's sleep;

I constantly begged her
To release my arms,
And from that day on I vowed
To love Freedom.

As the restraints on my stammering tongue
Began to loosen, to unbind,
As my parents smiled
And grew joyful at my voice,

The very first word I cried out
Was not father, nor mother nor anything else:
Freedom leaped out
Of my innocent mouth.

---

7. Mikayel Nalbandian, in "Freedom," Aram Tolegian, ed. and trans., *Armenian Poetry Old and New* (Detroit, 1979), 107–8.

Above me Destiny
Repeated "*Freedom?*
Would you like to be a soldier,
From this day on, for Freedom?

"O your path will he rock-strewn,
Many mishaps lie in the way;
For the one who loves freedom
This world is a narrow road."

"Freedom!" I called out,
"Let lightning, fire, flares, and iron
Burst over my head,
Let the enemy plot—

"Until death, until the gallows,
Until dropped from the scaffold of death,
I will shout out over and over,
Endlessly, Freedom!"

DAYS OF CHILDHOOD[8]

Days of my childhood, like a dream
    Ye fleeted, to return no more.
Ah, happy days and free from care,
    Ye brought but joy in passing o'er!

Then Science came, and on the world
    He gazed with grave, observant looks;
All things were analyzed and weighed,
    And all my time was given to books.

When to full consciousness I woke,
    My country's woes weighed down my heart.
Apollo gave me then his lyre,
    To bid my gloomy cares depart.

Alas! that lyre beneath my touch

---

8. Nalbandian, "Days of Childhood," *Armenian Poems* (Boston, 1917), 41–42.
Translated by Alice Stone Blackwell.

Sent forth a grave and tearful voice,
Sad as my soul; no single chord
Would breathe a note that said "Rejoice!"

Ah, then at last I felt, I knew,
There never could be joy for me,
While speechless, sad, in alien hands,
My country languished to be free.

Apollo, take thy lyre again,
And let its voice, amid the groves,
Sound for some man who may in peace
Devote his life to her he loves!

To the arena I will go,
But not with lyre and flowery phrase;
I will protest and cry aloud,
And strive with darkness all my days.

What boots today a mournful lyre?
Today we need the sword of strife.
Upon the foeman sword and fire,—
Be that the watchword of my life!

Sargis Vanandetsi

(c. 1830–71)

A playwright, actor, and editor also known as Sargis Mirzayan, he was born in Smyrna. He was an active member of various organizations in Smyrna, such as the *Hashtenits* Association—he edited the association's review, *Miutiun* (Unity), and their journal, *Iravunk* (Rights, 1868)—and the *Aghkatasirats* (benevolent) Society, which he served as secretary. He founded the Vaspurakan *Tatron* (theater) and was also one of its leading actors. The first play staged at this theater was *Metzn Nerses kam Hayastani barerare* (Nerses the Great, patron of Armenia), a tragedy written by him in 1857, published in 1858, and staged in Moscow in 1859 (under the name *Aristakes:* i.e., Arshak), in Smyrna in 1861, and in Baku in 1871. His two other plays, both tragedies, are *Mihrdat,* staged in such cities as Smyrna, Tiflis, Constantinople, and Yerevan between 1859 and 1870, and *Virgenia,* staged in Smyrna in 1862.

As an actor, he played leading roles at the Vaspurakan Theater (1861–62), including those of King Arshak in Mkrtich Beshiktashlian's (i.e., Peshiktashlian) *Arshak II,* Nerses and Mihrdat in his own plays, and the title character in Alfieri's *Saul.*

NERSES THE GREAT, PATRON OF ARMENIA[1]

DRAMATIS PERSONAE

ST. NERSES[2]
TEOTOS—[3]Greek emperor
PAP—King of Armenia
ZARMANDUKHT—Pap's wife
ARSHAK—Pap's son
SMBAT BAGRATUNI andMUSHEGH MAMIKONIAN—Armenian
generals
TERENTIANOS—Greek general
NERUZHAN—Armenian traitor
GAVAN—Nerses the Great's faithful servant
VAGHARSH—Pap's servant
KOSTAND—Terentianos's servant
SOLDIERS and GUARDS

ACT 1
Constantinople. In the palace of Emperor Teotos.

SCENE I
(*NERSES and GAVAN.*)
NERSES is asleep on a chair. GAVAN enters with a letter in his hand.
GAVAN: My lord, there's a letter from Armenia.

Strange, he never sleeps at this hour; I must wake him. . . .
But no: I might disturb his rest. O sleep! people call you their
repose, but I disagree, because your appearance is horrible, like
that of death; you affect people's hearts. . . .

---

1. Sargis Nirza Vanandetsi, *Metzn Nerses kam Hayastani barerare* (Nerses the
Great, patron of Armenia) (Jerusalem, 1887), 6–23. Translated by the editors of
the present anthology.
2. St. Nerses (sometimes spelled Narses in English) the Great lived from c.
326 to 373. He was a descendant of St. Gregory the Illuminator (c. 240–c. 326)
and the father of St. Isaac the Great (c. 347–438). Tradition has it that c. 329 he
was deposed for denouncing the crimes of King Arshak III, was restored to his post
by Arshak's son, King Pap—only to feel compelled to denounce Pap as well—and
was eventually poisoned by Pap.
3. Presumably Byzantine Emperor Theodosius I (the Great), but the dates are
wrong: Theodosius reigned 379–95.

What do the furrows on this venerable face reveal? Why is this face so creased with sorrow? The cause could not be imaginary—for what harm can imagination do at night?—so of necessity they have natural causes.

Who then is the man who calls sleep repose? let him draw near and see. Here you see the repose that sleep confers—a repose that makes my saintly patriarch wander through a sea of sadness and perplexity. A rest—come and see!—that makes tears roll down onto my lord's chin.

I can stand it no longer; I cannot be so merciless as to leave my lord in the claws of imagination and let him grow more and more disturbed. . . . I'll wake him, but . . . it will be to put an end to his oppressive dreams. . . . No, I won't wake him: he's moving; he's waking up.

(*ST. NERSES wakes up.*)

ST. NERSES: Where have you been?

GAVAN: I've been watching your movements for an hour, my lord, but I didn't dare to wake you.

ST. NERSES: I've been having bad dreams about my country, Gavan. I put no store in dreams, but such dreams have often come true. How I would like to hear from Armenia!

GAVAN: My lord, there's a letter from Armenia; here.

ST. NERSES: Bravo! I feel like leaping for joy! You know how much I've longed for news from my homeland ever since I returned there. (*He tries to open the letter.*) When did it get here?

GAVAN: I got it only an hour ago.

ST. NERSES: Good! Who gave it to you?

GAVAN: The Emperor himself.

ST. NERSES: Did he say anything?

GAVAN: No, but he seemed sad when he handed it to me. He told me to give it to my lord, Your Holiness. But he had a sad look on his face.

ST. NERSES: Gavan, did you do anything to upset him?

GAVAN: No, my lord, never! Besides, you know how much he likes me.

ST. NERSES: I suspect there's another cause.

GAVAN: What could that be?

ST. NERSES: Was there another letter from Armenia?

GAVAN: Yes, I noticed an opened letter in his hand.

ST. NERSES: That means my suspicion is right. He must have been upset by that letter; that letter, I'm afraid, will also sadden me. . . . My God, what does this letter say? (*He opens it without further delay.*) Oh! I dare not even read it. . . . What tragic news. . . . Alas! Oh, I can read no more! I have to control myself, and not cry out at the heart-rending misfortunes of my homeland. True, during my exile I had many unhappy experiences; I was beset with a great many stormy situations and reached the point of death; I roamed about hungry, thirsty, helpless, and weary in an alien land filled with savage monsters. But none of these upset me as much as the present state of Armenia. Oh, my wretched homeland! Is this what I was looking forward to hearing? The children of our glorious homeland seek to ruin and destroy you. My heart breaks when I see virtue overcome by jealousy.

GAVAN: (*On his way out.*) What new tragedy has befallen Armenia?

SCENE 2

[*TERENTIANOS and KOSTAND*]

TERENTIANOS: Where are you going?

KOSTAND: To enforce the Emperor's command, my lord.

TERENTIANOS: What command?

KOSTAND: That no one should enter his room.

TERENTIANOS: Why?

KOSTAND: I don't know why, my lord. I know only what my orders are, and I'm obliged to make sure those orders are carried out.

TERENTIANOS: Is anyone with him?

KOSTAND: He's alone, my lord—and wants to remain alone for a while.

TERENTIANOS: He must have a reason for wanting to be alone, of course. But don't you know what it is?—or have you been ordered to pretend that you don't?

KOSTAND: Never, my lord! All I know is that he seemed sad today.

TERENTIANOS: Why do you think he's sad?

KOSTAND: I wouldn't know. And now, if you'll please excuse me, I must be on my way to enforce the Emperor's command, my lord.

TERENTIANOS (*Alone.*): I wonder. The state is completely at peace; there's no hostility between the ministers and princes; tranquility reigns in the palace. So why is he sad? There must be someone in the palace who knows why the Emperor is sad. Let me get busy, then, and find out! (*He exits.*)

SCENE 3

[*GAVAN, then ZARMANDUKHT, and then PAP and ST. NERSES.*]

GAVAN: Pernicious letter . . . you'd have to have a heart of stone to read it without moaning. Arshak, king of our homeland! How is it that your licentious life did not end before this? Maybe then Armenia would not have to suffer so many misfortunes today. What a great thing it would have been if Armenia had been spared a tyrant like you!

You may be dead, but the injustices you have wrought will live on. Bow down before the heavenly King; bow down in fear, and give Him an account of all your crimes: the poverty you caused, and the assassinations.

I should go to find His Grace, and see how he is. He had reason to be in so much pain. What patriot could hear of such tragedies and remain unmoved? Poor Armenia! unlucky state! miserable nation! occasionally superb and sumptuous kingdom! I grieve with you in your misery; I grieve that with all your magnificent buildings, you have become a heap of ruins. Alas! alas. . . .

ZARMANDUKHT: (*Standing at the door.*) Who is that I hear groaning? . . . (*She enters.*) Gavan, Gavan, is that you crying? . . . You, weeping? But what's the reason for this sobbing? Where's the saintly patriarch? Oh, my heart races! Speak to me, Gavan: why?

GAVAN: It's nothing, my lady.

ZARMANDUKHT: Don't try to hide it from me. I heard you mutter the word *Armenia*. That's what you were crying about; please, tell me! Why? What evil are you bewailing? what tragedy has occurred? why are you crying? Speak up, Gavan! What loss has befallen our worthy fatherland?

GAVAN: It has lost its glory, its splendor—and peace.

ZARMANDUKHT: Oh God! How?

GAVAN: Forgive me, my lady: forgive me if I say nothing, lest I cause you grief.

ZARMANDUKHT: No, no, go ahead; although the news you bring may be sad, even though it wither my heart, I want to know how things are in my homeland.

GAVAN: The sun of peace and love no longer shines on Armenia. Armenia is on her death bed, my lady. . . .

ZARMANDUKHT: Armenia is on her death bed. . . . What has happened to her rulers: where are her ministers? where is Arshak, that Armenia is dying?

GAVAN: The state has no head; every minister thinks only of himself; and Arshak has surrendered to the Persians and committed suicide in the fortress of Anhush.

ZARMANDUKHT: He has killed himself? Arshak? At the fortress of Anhush? What are you talking about, Gavan?

GAVAN: You begged me to tell you, my lady. Now let me say what I know.

ZARMANDUKHT: Oh, merciful heavens! (*She closes her eyes.*)

GAVAN: The Persians, under Meruzhan, who hates Armenia, invaded Armenia. . . . Where there was life death now reigns. Where once laughter and happiness resounded, cries and tumult now reverberate. The sword is at its head and blood beneath its feet, and scorching fire turns my pleasant homeland into a desert. . . . Oh, woe is me. . . .

ZARMANDUKHT: Shh, Gavan, quiet, please. . . . But where did you hear this? Who brought you this dreadful news?

GAVAN: There were two letters from Armenia.

ZARMANDUKHT: Addressed to whom?

GAVAN: To the Emperor and His Grace.

ZARMANDUKHT: That means that His Grace has heard the news.

GAVAN: Yes, my lady: he had barely finished reading the letter when sorrow and grief compelled him to withdraw to his room.

ZARMANDUKHT: O misery! you fall more terribly on the exile, for whom you are like the tolling of a death knell in the depths of his heart. . . . Come, Gavan! take me to His Grace, so that I might console him; we must not let his bitter grief endanger his health in his old age. Let's trust to the mercy of Heaven, the sole protector of the wretched. Come!

GAVAN: But I think His Grace is coming here. I hear his footsteps.

ZARMANDUKHT: Yes, it's him. And Pap is with him, but both are mournful and sad.

(*PAP and ST. NERSES enter.*)

PAP: This unfortunate news turned my blood to ice, Your Grace.

ST. NERSES: And made our land run red with blood.

PAP: Arshak, my father . . .

ZARMANDUKHT: . . . has killed himself.

GAVAN: And peace has died with him.

ST. NERSES: There you see the fruits of selfishness and hatred, which can demolish a world and leave its population in ruins . . . and both of these things have happened to Armenia. That Armenia should fall victim to them, and its glory, splendor, and peace be blackened and unhinged? Oh, no! No, sweet Armenia! No, holy place! you must not fall prey to such a pitiful situation. Meruzhan may be uprooting your monasteries and churches, your miserable inhabitants may be being persecuted and massacred, but God, the beloved Creator, has not deserted you. The flame that consumes you now may be extinguished with Meruzhan's own blood. . . . And you, my children, do not despair! Let us place our trust and hope in Heaven, even though our aspirations and expectations are now buried beneath Armenia's desolate ruins.

PAP: Let us go, Your Grace: the time has come for you to open the storehouse of your incomparable wisdom and find a remedy for these tragedies. I want to return to Armenia: every minute I remain here drains away my life. What if my weapons have not yet tasted blood; what if the steel of war has not yet dazzled my eyes: I am ready to sacrifice both heart and arms to benefit our motherland. . . . I'll revenge your miserable, vile death, Arshak, my father!

ZARMANDUKHT: Calm down, Pap! Dear husband, don't upset yourself.

ST. NERSES: Yes, you *shall* return to Armenia! You must avenge your sovereign father's death, and, even more, the loss of your homeland. For your father, Arshak, did not die defending our homeland; it was his unruly behavior, his sinful conduct that destroyed Armenia's peace, together with his own and many other lives.

GAVAN: Arshak was responsible for the blood of Kamsarakans and Gnels and the other innocent victims.

PAP: But Arshak, my father. . . .

ST. NERSES: Wait, Pap: at such terrible times and before such an important task, we mustn't be ruled by passion, but by caution.

I'll go to see the Emperor and try to move him to pity; I'll ask him to help us by crowning you king of Armenia in place of your father.

ZARMANDUKHT: King of Armenia! oh, how wonderful!

ST. NERSES: Yes, King of Armenia—but not a king like Arshak, mind you, Pap; it would be much better to be poor and humble than to act like King Arshak. But let us go: my heart is heavy, and my country is in such a state that to waste time would be unforgivable.

GAVAN: Good conduct and a good name are the royal qualities my country has greatest need of.

CURTAIN

Matteos Mamurian

(1830–1901)

The writer, editor, translator, and educator Matteos Mamurian was born in Smyrna (presently Izmir, Turkey), which harbored the second largest Armenian community in the Ottoman Empire, after Constantinople. He received his early education in the local Mesropian school, where he was recognized as a bright student and was selected to be sent to Paris to continue his education at the Muratian Mkhitarist school. At his graduation he received his diploma from the famed French poet, Lamartine,[1] who was an invited guest. He returned to Smyrna in 1850 and opened a school in collaboration with Marcos Aghabekian. In 1853 he went to Constantinople as principal of the Nersesian school in the suburb of Khasgiugh (Hasköy). In 1856–57 he served as a translator during the Crimean war and then went to England, where he attended courses at Cambridge University as a scholarship student. After an extensive tour of Europe, including a visit to St. Petersburg, he returned to Constantinople in 1860 and was appointed head of the secretariat of the Patriarchate. During this time he organized a fundraising campaign in support of the fighters in the Zeitun uprising of 1862 and published

---

1. Alphonse Marie Louis de Lamartine (1790–1869), French poet, statesman, and historian.

articles condemning the atrocities committed in Cilicia by Aziz Pasha. In 1868 he returned to Smyrna, occupying two positions: principal of the Mesropian school and supervisor of the Hripsimiants girls' school. He also taught English, French, and world history. In 1871 he established a printing press and launched a monthly journal, *Arevelyan mamul* (Oriental press), which rapidly became a very influential periodical. He managed it as publisher and editor for thirty years, until his death in 1901.[2]

Mamurian's literary career started early. His first works are translations of Voltaire's *Zadig, Jeannot et Colin,* and *Micromégas,* which were serialized in *Masis* (Mount Ararat). While in England (1857–58) he wrote *Angliakan namakani* (English letters), a series of philosophical letters highlighting patriotism and enlightenment. This was followed by *Haykakan namakani* (Armenian letters, 1872), which is a compilation of his columns in various papers such as *Masis, Meghu* (Bee), *Kilikia* (Cilicia), *Tzaghik* (Flower), and others. These pieces reflect his observations, views, and criticisms of the events and the attitudes of the previous decade and expressively sketch the main personalities of the time, camouflaging them with pseudonyms. Hrant Asatur considered this work Mamurian's masterpiece.

His novel, *Sev lerin marde* (The man from the black mountain), was serialized in *Arevelyan mamul* (1871–81), but remained unfinished. It is set against the background of the Russo-Persian war of 1826–28, during which Eastern Armenia was emancipated from the Persian yoke, only to be later subjugated to tsarist rule. His political and social views find ample expression in the novel. As an educator, he published *A Concise History of the World, A Concise History of Armenia,* and *Key to Armenian Composition* for use as textbooks. He also tried his hand at theater with a play called *Sefilents tune* (The house of Sefils), which was staged in 1882 but was not successful.

A few members of the intellectual elite of Smyrna (Izmir) made it their mission to translate some of the most popular novels by foreign authors, mostly French, in order to encourage reading among the common people. Translations also enriched the vocabulary of modern Armenian as new words were coined and the grammar was standardized. Grigor Chilinkirian (Chilingirian), the translator of Victor Hugo), and Mesrop

---

2. The journal was published as a bimonthly from 1894 to 1902. After Mamurian's death it was continued (1903–9) by his successors as a weekly, and after a ten-year interruption it was revived as a daily, continuing as such until 1922, the year of the Smyrna massacre.

Nuparian (compiler of French-Armenian dictionaries), the trailblazers of this movement, were joined by Matteos Mamurian, himself a staunch supporter of modern Armenian. The list of his translations is impressive: Alexandre Dumas's *Les trois mousquetaires* (The three musketeers), *Vingt ans après* (Twenty years later), and *Le vicomte de Bragelonne* (The viscount of Bragelonne); Eugène Sue's *Les mystères de Paris* (The mysteries of Paris); Beaumarchais' *Le barbier de Séville* (The barber of Seville); Jules Verne's *Le tour du monde en quatre-vingt jours* (Around the world in eighty days) and *L'Île mystérieuse* (The mysterious island); Sir Walter Scott's *Ivanhoe;* and Goethe's *Faust.* The translation movement, joined by many other writers, contributed tremendously to the popularization of literature.

Matteos Mamurian's fame, however, derives from the area of journalism. *Arevelyan mamul,* the review he established in 1871 and continued to publish for thirty years, was an achievement indeed. It became a prestigious paper, an opinion maker, not only in Smyrna but throughout the Armenian diaspora. His personal characteristics of fortitude, analytical thinking, and acute but tactful observation are reflected on every page of the paper. It was one of the most forward-looking, balanced periodicals of the Revival Movement.

FROM ENGLISH LETTERS, OR THE DESTINY OF AN ARMENIAN[3]

Smyrna, 17 April 1881
Dear Tzerents
Many years ago, when I was in London, I had begun to write this series of letters, whose plan I showed to you upon my return to Constantinople, as my longtime mentor who, for the first time, had inspired me with the taste of free thought, and as my bosom buddy, who has always been sympathetic to my situation. At that time, you exhorted me to finish and publish this series of letters, barely one part of which (some 16 of them), called English Letters,

---

3. Matteos Mamurian, *Ankliakan namakani kam Hayu me chakatagire* (English letters or the destiny of an Armenian) (Smyrna, 1881), 8–18. Translated by Aris Sevag. English letters "highlight patriotism and the cause of enlightenment in Armenia and the dire consequences of emigration." See Kevork B. Bardakjian, *A Reference Guide to Modern Armenian Literature, 1500–1920* (Detroit, 2000), 121.

was published in the *Miutiun* periodical of Smyrna, and then in the *Hayots Ashkharh Krnkan,* whereas the majority of them (some 90 letters) remained in manuscript form in my desk.

As you see, dear friend, this is an old work which perhaps appears bland next to new works and writers, but it has a value, at least for me, because it is one product of your encouragement and one memory of my days as an émigré.

It is this encouragement and memory, which prompt me today to not only assemble all the letters and publish them in book form but also to dedicate them to you.

I hope you accept this gift as a token of my affinity and respect.

Your friend, M. Mamurian

Letter 1, Constantinople
Nelson to Wood

Last week I was near you, friend, there in London; this morning the steamship brought me here, covering a distance of three thousand miles in nine days. Many persons can fill many tiresome pages in order to give a description of the journey, but I shall avoid that; suffice it to say that I found the motion of the steamship to be rough. I wonder, when will the day come when people will fly like birds? Of course, Great Britain shall give wings to the world. This discovery of mine pertains to that country's ingenuity.

Well, I realized my wish. I'm Armenian by language and I have the opportunity to write in Armenian to you, an Armenophile. If you didn't know I was an Englishman, I think you would take me for a native Armenian, by reading my letter. However, I'm not totally sure of this because, indeed, the man is not apparent behind the pen. The more skilled he is and the more clearly he writes, if the writer is of a foreign nationality, he can come up with such an innovative meaning, style or phrase that will immediately betray his real identity. This applies especially to the Englishman, who is the most extraordinary of the world's rational creatures, who is a unique phenomenon among nations owing to his makeup and nature, and who, no matter what curtain he goes under, is revealed a mile's distance away just by his shadow. His face, manner of walking, style of hat, the tone of his voice and even his breath make him evident to everyone. While our behavior, our work resembles a foreigner's, if you throw an Englishman among a million Europeans,

I will point him out to you from afar. Take him to one end of the world and he takes with him his natural and native customs and ideas. If someone has found a new, inaccessible and unknown land, like Trek, you can be sure he's an Englishman; another set foot on the North Pole, like (Sir John) Franklin, he's an Englishman; the idea of splitting the (Atlantic) Ocean and connecting the Old and New Worlds by cable came from England; it was at the instigation of the English that companies came into being to enclose the entire universe in a glass palace and present it; to establish an imposing floating city[4] on a precipice. It is behind this that the Englishman can say, "When I, the lion, wear a cow's skin for a special purpose, I'm saddened that my mane and my roar reveal my true identity." Friend, isn't it a glory for man to be recognized always and everywhere in terms of his humanity and nationality? Don't you prefer to roam and appear in your English nakedness rather than appropriate the skin of a foreigner, especially if the skin is hot and seeks to stick to your body? Indeed, it's a pleasant state to willingly turn from a human to an animal. There are individuals and peoples who consider it a good policy to grow stupid for a time; when that time doesn't come to an end, the policy becomes routine and, of course, they can't see their tails.

Therefore, don't worry; don't let your national pride be insulted for seeing me as an Armenian writer for a moment. Don't fear; I have neither a tail nor the desire to get one. I'm not considered a wild boar like Trdat, for speaking the same language as he. The stock of an Englishman is very hard and strong, and it remains pure and immaculate even in other sour dough. It is easier to cause a lofty Himalayan mountain to tumble than to efface my innate English vanity, which is mixed with my patriotism. It is not the first time that I am moving about among nations, as you know, and my purpose this time is an educational investigation, which I shall explain below.

The Greeks called non-Greeks barbarians and steered clear of them, but they weren't more patriotic than us. We don't hate foreign nations; rather, we examine them, as a botanist does plants, so that if we find a natural property, use, or wish that is unknown to us, we can benefit from it. Our fatherland won't suffer a great

---

4. Huge Leviathan or Great Oriental ship.

loss if those like me leave it and go elsewhere in the world. It has in its bosom worthy and fine individuals who are turning the wheel of its government. There's no shortage of champions there to defend its rights and freedom. And, let's say, when I'm far away and keep the memories and principles of old England in my heart, will I not always have worked for my free fatherland, no matter what undertaking and job I'm involved in? Before being a world traveler, the Englishman is a man, an Englishman, and whatever effort, whatever sweat he makes, whatever manly activities he engages in, that which stems from their beneficial source accrues to British greatness and increases British well being. So many individuals, owing to the strength of their courage and talent, invincible courage, were the cause of the spread of our motherland's influence and world conquest! The retreat of the ten thousand, the Thermopylae affair, seem to be trifling and ordinary matters, next to their exploits. Instead of giving us the command of a Spartan woman, i.e., "Defeat your enemy, and may your shield be either your victorious throne or your coffin," our mothers say, "Your fatherland is your wet-nurse and protector, and just deeds will find an echo in our heart and in our history, go forth." And behold, Cook, an invincible captain, makes a trip around the world; Hudson discovers North America and new, unknown paths; Lord Clive, who strikes terror upon all of India with just a few regiments; Livingstone, who explores the depths of Africa. But, friend, you would say that it would not be boasting to ask, what is the reason why other nations are amazed at this liberalism, intrepidity and activity of ours? I can guess your response; they are not educated like us, you will say. Because one becomes great and courageous, or base, evil and stupid, based on fine or faulty education; I know this because, aside from the same old stimulus, there is lacking in our soul a stimulus that propels us to commit continuous magnificent deeds. I think, to a certain extent, it is our country's location, our system of government and, especially, our curious and self-confident soul that prompt us to go elsewhere and, by overcoming difficulties, to open new doors, harbors for British commerce, to spread the spirit of freedom among nations and to investigate the nature and cause of everything. And all these reasons are crowned by the profit motive, and it is this motive that stupid people contemptuously throw up into our faces. Which man, no matter how noble his calling, how virtuous his work, doesn't look for profit or glory in this world? Without a doubt, when Newton was discovering the law of the planets, when Galileo was becoming the victim of truth, and Abelard a martyr to love, a noble purpose, the love of wisdom and immortality had greater appeal than actual profit; however, once again, don't their effects win our gratitude and respect, and don't the mind and heart of man profit from them? And what are seasoned and illuminated minds, if not the source and storehouse of future regular operations, and therefore their success and meritoriousness?

Now don't think that I, being close to the tower of Leander[5] and Aya Sophia (Saint Sophia), will do something great, and don't think that I have the ambition to be included in the class of our prominent compatriots (the praising of which was superfluous and pleasing only to my national pride, which is lurking under the fashionable veil of the Armenian language) in this journey of mine.

Mine is a simple undertaking born of curiosity, because we confess to each other that sometimes the sickness of strange visions overcomes us. I hope you won't laugh at me if I briefly explain to you the purpose of my first letter.

Indeed, I did not invade these parts to find either fortune or the philosopher's stone, either the golden fleece[6] or Ero.[7] I'm afraid, however, that what I'm seeking may turn out to be something more difficult to find than them, although it has a beginning and place in history. I came here in search of the grandsons of Haik, my friend, and although I imagined that the Armenians had shared a similar fate to the Assyrians, Chaldeans and Romans, who disappeared in time beneath the ruins, however, in England, when the traces of living Armenians caught my eye in a few books, I made inquiries and found out that, especially in Constantinople, they move about in large crowds and are a living and breathing people. I was surprised because, while I was examining the relics and bones of the Armenians in histories and in Armenia, who

---

5. Kiz Kulesi in Istanbul.

6. In classical mythology, this was a fleece of pure gold kept at Colchis, to the north of Armenia, by King Aeetes. Jason and the Argonauts stole it with the help of Aeetes's daughter, Medea.

7. Ero (Hero). In classical mythology, Hero was the lover of Leander, who was drowned while swimming the Hellespont.

effected their resurrection? If this resurrection is certain, hereafter I shall believe in other resurrections. Therefore, I, who became the first Armenology student of Cambridge University, along with you; I, who have more or less devoured the literature and history of said nation, and am now making some marks on paper to practice their language, I must experimentally verify what I know and have learned. Is there a nation, which wishes to see work and proof as much as us, to be convinced, especially about ancient historical realities, which must be believed only with the utmost degree of caution? Ignorant people are gullible concerning many a legend, which are copied from one another and don't even have the value of novelty, as pure history. Are not hearing the living language from the mouths of Armenians, observing their customs and values, and culling information from them about historical and present-day Armenia both, perhaps sufficient means of shedding light on certain obscure bits of knowledge received by us? For that called history is an image which makes the color of man and individuals dark or very bright, and the same is more or less understandable to the eye of the mind, according to the partiality or sincerity of the artist.

However, when we bring to mind the authors of the actual events, right away we determine the true version by comparing them with the image. Now, because I have interest in knowing the Armenians and have been seen with them only in history, why shouldn't I personally look for their original image, since they are living breathing beings till now, they say? One of the principal stimuli of this interest of mine, in turn, became my finding partial similarity of the Armenian's nature with ours, not at the time when we were half naked, living in huts and engaged in hunting and roaming the forests, but by comparing our new condition with their old one. For when we were wearing wild animal skins and worshiping the oak tree, they were bedecked in silks and jewels, they were living in palaces, they had temples and theaters, and they were worshiping a better creature—the sun. Although the Armenians were not a seafaring people like us, they extended their overland trade as far as India, and we learn from history that their nature, domestic and political life were not very different from ours. The Armenians are a tough, energetic, industrious, clever and serious people; they are devoid only of our patience, love of unanimity, and ingenuity, and therefore they have very easily fallen under the yoke of foreign bloodthirsty rulers. What was the difference between an Armenian and our John Bull? As a patriarch, being the lord of families and the manor, winning the love and confidence of his own people, he acted as lawmaker, judge and protector, as the situation demanded, and if his selfishness took hold quickly, he would confine himself to his home, which was the castle, without thinking about the public interest. When we see the land of Armenia divided into separate principalities and the king's authority naturally limited by their influence, doesn't that bring to mind one version of our landed system, the rule of our Normans? What Vagharshak Partev did was practically identical to William the Conqueror's action. The former divided up the beautiful provinces of Armenia among certain princes who were his comrades in arms, and whom he had brought with him to said land; the latter did the same to England with his Norman soldiers. It is a fact that, since the spirit of freedom has not reached the fringes of the populace, they (the Armenians) have not been able, with the progression of time, to establish national courts and assemblies like us; to defend their rights, interests and independence, by putting an end to internal civil unrest and warring against foreign invaders.

Rather, the vast majority, which gradually had fallen prey to a class of privileged and despotic individuals; i.e., prince, *nakharar,* and clergyman, in recent times especially, they endeavored to snatch the people from each other's hands, as if they were not the sons of the same fatherland, descendants of the same Haik. It is true that more wonderful peoples than the Armenian nation have died off. Where are your Romans, the Carthaginians? Rome fell to an elderly priest; Hannibal's shadow wanders in the deserts, while the Armenians, who are older than them, still exist. Like people, governments likewise succeed each other. However, that country which is born, expands, shines, and, leaving behind its history to the human race, is buried without a trace under the dust of time, has run its course, we say, thinking in human terms, and is worthy of our attention. Now, when a nation approaches its death, and having fallen into the clutches of beasts due to its carelessness, you look at its last hour from all sides and see that, no matter how many heads they cut off, a new one takes its place, like a seven-headed beast; it rises and stands up out of blood and tears, and, from one century to the next, it reaches the present, void of the legacy of the fatherland, true, and carrying only its flotsam and jetsam and relics, then it is obligatory to not only marvel at that nation but also to consider the function and mission of said nation among nations unfulfilled in the secret verdicts of Providence. It is worth seeing the generation of such a nation, I think, and, like the apostle Thomas, I came to touch its wounds so I could believe. Put aside the importance that it already has in the eyes of antiquarians, on account of Ararat, the Garden of Eden and Noah's Ark being in its bosom. For a nation's pride and existence do not consist of such antiquities as these; they should be honored without examination. I think they are the little bells of the Armenians' imagination, which perhaps only strike the ear without convincing the mind. In order to know a nation, it doesn't happen by measuring the length of a ship or a mountain; its soul is to be sought in its values, institutions, deeds and genius.

But I just arrived here and sat down, dusty and dirty, to write to you and I don't wish to get up from my seat, and especially to become separated from this charming scene of the Bosphorous that I have, which is shining before me like a mirror. I am in Tarabia, friend, or better yet, the fifth heaven of the prophet, this cradle of pleasure, where all my feelings and imagination are being lulled, and my eyes try in vain to embrace this serpentine strait, verdant hills, seaside gardens, which seemingly are waving in the air, releasing colorful glimmers. But, no matter how bright your sky is, oh Byzantium, how marvelous your natural location is, I wouldn't exchange your sun for the fog of Albion, behind which the burning torch of civilization illuminates mind and soul, whereas yours leads to dreams and slackness.

I talked enough, this is our custom; when we're near each other, we remain speechless because our conduct speaks, whereas we become garrulous once there is distance between us. Give me news about England; the opening of the Parliament is near, so what issues shall be discussed this year?

Also, go see my sweetheart Lili (Shushan) and console her, because I know that my departure affected her greatly, but what's the use; even if I were there, I wouldn't have been able to overcome her parents' perversity and conceit, and we would have always remained apart. Gold is a lord's law; our hearts burn only with sincere love.

Please don't leave me without a written response. I am eager to receive from you a meditation, a piece of news about the Armenians. Therefore, be supportive of my purpose. I'm sure that you would have come with me if I had expressed my intention to you beforehand.

Accept my heartfelt greetings.

Rafayel Patkanian

(1830–92)

Rafayel Patkanian came from a distinguished family of letters. Born in Nor Nakhijevan (Rostov-on-Don, Russia), he was the grandson of Serovbé Patkanian, poet and educator, and the son of Gabriel Patkanian, priest, writer, and social activist. Rafayel received his early education in the private school founded by his father, then attended the Lazarian College in Moscow (1843–49). Before completing his studies there, however, he moved to Tiflis with his father, who had been appointed principal of the Nersisian College. He continued his education intermittently at the University of Dorpat (now Tartu, Estonia, 1851–52) then at the University of Moscow (1852–54), and completed his higher studies at the University of St. Petersburg (1855–60), in the field of Eastern Studies.

In his first poems he sang of youth, fun, and pleasure, but very soon he left these behind. He began to reflect seriously on the plight of his people and dedicated all his abilities to the task of the intellectual enlightenment and emancipation of his countrymen by igniting in them the spark of patriotism. His earlier poems appeared in the *Ararat* weekly (1850–51), the first modern Armenian periodical in the Caucasus, which was founded and edited by his father. While he was in Moscow he and two fellow students, Gevorg Kananian and Minas (or Mnatsakan) Timurian, formed a small literary group to publish their own works. They called the group Gamar-Katipa, an acronym formed of the first letters of their first names and the first syllables of their surnames. The first pamphlet published under this acronym appeared in 1855 with the motto "Write as you speak; speak as you write," which represented the group's literary credo: to give the written word the immediacy and dynamic expressiveness of spoken language. By 1857 five pamphlets in succession had been published under this collective name, most of them written by Patkanian. Starting in 1860, he began to contribute to a number of periodicals, and in 1863 he founded a review called *Hiusis* (The north), which lasted only one year. In 1864 he published his first collection of poems, which received an enthusiastic reception. In 1866 he moved back to Nor Nakhijevan, his birthplace, where he concentrated on his writing and involved himself in educational projects as a teacher at the local parish school. In 1879 he helped establish a vocational school for the children of poor families, which he directed until his death at the age of sixty-two.

Rafayel Patkanian lived at a time when Armenian literature was expected to serve a number of purposes other than art: communication, education, exhortation, and patriotism. In serving these ends Patkanian was allied with a number of his contemporaries—Khachatur Abovian 1809–48), Perch Proshian (1837–1907), and Ghzaros Aghayan (1840–1911), to mention a few—who assumed the role of writer-teacher in order to fulfill a self-imposed mission of enlightening the people. Patkanian's patriotic poems include "*Araksi artasuke*" (The tears of the Araxes or The woe of Araxes), a dialogue between the poet and Armenia's sacred river, and "*Kaj Vardan Mamikoniani mahe*" (The death of Vardan Mamikonian the brave), an epic poem based on the Battle of Avarayr between the Armenians and the Persians in 451; these are aimed at dissipating the age-long lethargy of the people and invigorating them with a new vision of the future. His second collection of poems, *Azat yerger* (Free songs, 1878), written in reaction to the Turkish atrocities on subjugated peoples in the 1870s, were intended to rouse the national consciousness and reestablish pride and self-respect.

Both in poetry and prose he depicted the tragic fate of his country-men with a view to leading them away from darkness and blood to light and victory. Every major event was reflected in his works: his elation at the uprising in Zeytun (1862) as well as his disappointment and anger at the indifference and treachery manifested by the European powers at the Congress of Berlin (1878), as expressed in his poem *Boghok ar Yevropa* (Protest to Europe). Sometimes he reproaches his countrymen for their sluggishness, as in *Dzayn barbaro hanapati* (A voice crying in the wilderness); at other times he delivers a rousing revolutionary message, as in *Vanetsots aghotke* (The prayer of Vanetsis). His poems, mostly written in the vernacular, may be a bit crude poetically, but they all contain a social, national, or political message. Some of them have been set to music and are popular even to this day.

As well as the poetry mentioned above, Rafayel Patkanian wrote novels, short stories, memoirs, textbooks, and poems and songs for children. Most of his short novels—such as *Paraser* (Fond of glory), *Yes nshanatz ei* (I was engaged), and *Tikin yev nazhisht* (The lady and the maid)—reflect social mores that sometimes clash with moral principles. Some of his stories are written in the Nor Nakhijevan dialect. His collected works, in eight volumes, were published in Yerevan from 1963 to 1974.

THE WOE OF ARAXES[1]

Meditating by Araxes,
Pacing slowly to and fro,
Sought I traces of the grandeur
Hidden by her turgid flow.
"Turgid are thy waters, Mother,
As they beat upon the shore.
Do they offer lamentations
For Armenia evermore?

"Gay should be thy mood, O Mother,
As the sturgeons leap in glee:
Ocean's merging still is distant,
Shouldest thou be sad, like me?

"Are thy spume-drifts tears, O Mother,
Tears for those that are no more?

---

1. Rafayel (Raphael) Patkanian, "The Woe of Araxes," in Robert Arnot and F. B. Collins, eds., *Armenian Literature,* trans. F. B. Collins, with a special intro. by Robert Arnot (New York, 1901), 49–51.

Dost thou haste to pass by, weeping,
This thine own beloved shore?"

Then uprose on high Araxes,
Flung in air her spumy wave,
And from out her depths maternal
Sonorous her answer gave:

"Why disturb me now, presumptuous,
All my slumbering woe to wake?
Why invade the eternal silence
For a foolish question's sake?

"Know'st thou not that I am widowed;
Sons and daughters, consort, dead?
Wouldst thou have me go rejoicing,
As a bride to nuptial bed?

"Wouldst thou have me decked in splendor,
To rejoice a stranger's sight,
While the aliens that haunt me
Bring me loathing, not delight?

"Traitress never I; Armenia
Claims me ever as her own;
Since her mighty doom hath fallen
Never stranger have I known.

"Yet the glories of my nuptials
Heavy lie upon my soul;
Once again I see the splendor
And I hear the music roll.

"Hear again the cries of children
Ringing joyfully on my banks,
And the noise of marts and toilers,
And the tread of serried ranks.

"But where, now, are all my people?
Far in exile, homeless, lorn,
While in widow's weeds and hopeless,
Weeping, sit I here and mourn.

"Hear now! while my sons are absent
Age-long fast I still shall keep;
Till my children gain deliverance,
How I watch and pray and weep."

Silent, then, the mighty Mother
Let her swelling tides go free
And in mournful meditation
Slowly wandered to the sea.

FROM THE VACANT YARD[2]

Rafayel Patkanian's story concerns the destruction of a grocer, Sargis, and his family by the unscrupulous practices of a con man known as Hemorrhoid Jack. The excerpt below is narrated by an old nurse who used to live with the family. One evening the family is visited by the trickster, who presses the grocer to receive merchandise from him, promising that it will make the family's fortune. As the nurse continues her story, Hemorrhoid Jack is speaking:

" 'You may seek a thousand times and you will not find again such good goods and such a favorable opportunity. I speak from experience. You must not let this chance slip by or you will throw gold out of the window with your own hands. I am talking about great gains, great profits; do you think it is a joke?'

" 'We shall see,' said poor Sargis. 'We have many days before us. Yes, we will surely do something.'

" 'What you do now is not worth much,' cried Hemorrhoid Jack. 'I see that if I leave the thing to your decision, in five years you will not have reached one. Isn't that true? In the morning I will send you one load of goods and the rest later.'

"With these words he seized his cap, quickly made his adieus, and went away.

---

2. Rafayel Patkanian, ibid., 37–44. Translated by F. B. Collins. This translation is now a century old. It has not been modernized, however, as its language and style are typical of the period when the story itself was written.

"It was nearly one o'clock; Mayram and Takush[3] were sitting there asleep and I also was very sleepy, but I fought against my sleepiness to watch that devil of a Hemorrhoid Jack. Mankind can be a priest to mankind, also a Satan!

"When he was in the street, Sargis said to me, 'What a wonderful conversation we have had this evening. Of all this man has said, I understand nothing. His purposes are not exactly bad, but I don't know how it happens my heart presages something of evil.'

"I was just going to answer him when suddenly I sneezed; but only once.

" 'See now,' I said to Sargis; 'I was right in saying he was going to trick you. Now it has proved itself.'

" 'If one sneezes only once by day that is a bad sign, but at night it means something good,' he interrupted me.

" 'Oh,' I said, 'do not, I pray, give me lessons; don't teach me what a sneeze is the sign of. Whether it is in the daytime or at night it is a bad sign, and if one just made up his mind to do anything, he should let it drop.'

"Sargis would not give in that I was right, but began to chatter about a sneeze at night being a good thing. I said no and he said yes, and so it went on until I finally gave it up."

" 'Oh,' I said, 'have your own way, but when misfortune comes to you do not blame me for it.'

" 'I have really begun nothing,' he observed. 'That was only a talk. We have only discussed something. I have really no desire to try my hand with the tea and tobacco.'

"That he said to me, but heaven only knows! perhaps in his thoughts he was already counting the thousands he hoped to earn. Money has such power that my blessed grandmother always said that the devil had invented it. He had racked his brains to find a way to lead mankind into wickedness and did not succeed until he invented money. Then he was master of our souls. How many men money has deprived of reason! Sargis was not of so firm a mind that he would be able to stand out against such rosy hopes.

"The next day, early in the morning, the shop-boy came running into the house in a great hurry, and said that nine cart-loads

3. Mayram and Takush are Sargis's wife and daughter, respectively. He also has a son, Toros.

of goods were standing at the gate. The man who was in charge of them was asking for Sargis.

" 'What kind of an invasion is this!' cried Sargis. 'I must go and see who it is. Perhaps the loads are not for me at all. God knows for whom they are!'

"He went out, and we after him. Although I had not seen the loads of goods, I knew the whole story in a moment.

"Before we had reached the gate a man met us and said:

" 'My master sends you greeting and begs you to take these nine wagon-loads of goods and sign for them.'

" 'Who is your master?' we asked, all together.

" 'Hemorrhoid Jack. Don't you know him? He was at your house last evening.'

"I was ready to burst with anger.

" 'You fellow,' I said, 'who told your master to send these goods here? Have we ordered anything? Turn at once and get out of the room.'

" 'Is that so!' said the man. 'After a thing is settled you can't take back your word. Where shall I put the goods now?'

" 'Where you brought them from, take them back there!' "

" 'The coach-house is closed.'

" 'That does not concern us; that is your master's affair.'

" 'If he were here I would tell him, but he is not here.'

" 'Where is he then?' I asked.

" 'He has gone to Taganrog.'

" 'When did he start?

" 'About two hours ago. He will not be back for two months, for he has very important business in the courts.'

"It could not be doubted now that this villain of a John had already begun his tricks; but that innocent Sargis did not see through his devilish purposes. Had I been in his place I would have run immediately to the City Hall and told every detail of the business, and the thing would have come out all right. But Sargis was not the man for that.

" 'Well, if that is the case drive into the yard and unload. The goods cannot stand in the street. When Jack comes back from Taganrog I will arrange things with him in some way.'

"The wagons came into the yard with a clatter and the driver unloaded the goods and piled them up in the coach house. I stood as if turned to stone and silently watched this move in their game. 'What will come of it?' I thought to myself.

"Ah, but I would rather have died than see what did come of it!

"When the goods were unloaded the clerk demanded a receipt, which Sargis gave him without hesitation, whereupon the clerk went away satisfied. "Later we heard that Jack had not gone to Taganrog at all, and had only ordered the clerk to say so.

"That same day when we were sitting at dinner, Sargis turned to me and said: 'See, Hripsimé, your sneeze has cheated you. Did you not say that Jack was going to play a trick on me? You see something very different has happened. This forenoon four or five persons came into my shop who wished to buy tea and tobacco. I told them the matter was not yet settled; that we had not agreed on the price; as soon as the agreement was made I would begin business. Do you see? I have not advertised that I was going to handle the goods, yet everybody knows it and one customer after another comes into my store. How will it be when the goods are put on sale? They will fight for them. It will give me a great deal to do; I must only go to John and settle on the terms. Yes, little mother, such a wholesale trade is not to be despised; the wholesaler can often make more money in a moment than the retailer makes in two years. Yes, my love, in business that is really so!'

" 'God grant that it may be so!' I said, and nothing more was said about Jack.

"Several months passed by and November came. One evening we were sitting together chatting comfortably when the door opened softly and an old woman entered. I knew immediately that she was a matchmaker. In three days Takush was betrothed to a plain, middle-rate man. The wedding was to take place the next winter on her father's name-day. As a dowry her parents promised 3,000 rubles—1,500 in cash, and the rest in jewels.

"Takush was at that time fifteen years old. Although I had lived in her parents' house I had never looked right attentively at her face, scarcely knew, in fact, whether she was beautiful or ugly; but when on her betrothal day she put on a silk dress and adorned herself as is customary at such a festive time; when she had put on her head a satin fez with gold tassels, and a flower set with brilliants, I fairly gaped with admiration. I am almost eighty years old, but in all my life I have never seen a more beautiful girl.

"I am no dwarf, but she was a few inches taller than I. She was slender as a sweet-pine tree. Her hands were delicate and soft, her fingers were like wax. Hair and eyebrows were black, and her face like snow. Her cheeks were tinged rose-red, and her glance! That I cannot forget even to this day. It was brighter than a genuine Holland diamond. Her eyelashes were so long that they cast shadows on her cheeks. No, such a charming creature I have never seen in dreams, let alone reality. She was—God forgive my sins—the pure image of the Mother of God in our church; yes, she was even more beautiful. When I looked at her I could not turn my eyes away again. I gazed at her and could not look enough. On the betrothal day I sat in the corner of the room with my eyes nailed on Takush.

" 'How sorry I am,' thought I, 'that you with that angel face are to be the wife of a commonplace man, to be the mother of a family and go into a dirty, smoky kitchen. Shall your tender hands become hard as leather with washing, ironing, kneading, and who knows what housework beside? Shall your angel cheeks fade from the heat of the oven and your eyes lose their diamond-shine from sewing?' Yes, so thought I, and my heart bled within me for this girl who ought to wear a queen's crown and live in a palace. Surely, if this rose maiden had lived in olden times she would certainly have married a king or a king's son. And the poor thing stood there like a lamb, for she did not understand what life was. She thought marriage would be nothing more than a change in her dwelling-place. Oh, but I was sorry that evening that she was going to marry only an ordinary, but still eligible, young man, and yet it would have been a great good fortune for her if this had come to pass. Had we thought at that time that great misfortunes were in store for the poor child! And that cursed Hemorrhoid Jack was the cause of them all!

"That betrothal day was the last happy day of the poor wretches. I never afterward saw smiles on their faces, for from that day their circumstances grew worse and worse and their business became very bad. They lost house and ground, moved about for several months from one rented house to another, until finally they disappeared from the city.

"The day after the betrothal Hemorrhoid Jack sent word to Sargis by his clerk that Sargis must pay 2,700 rubles for the tobacco and tea and 184 rubles for the manufactured goods. I have forgotten to tell you that among the latter were old-fashioned dress-goods, taxed cloth, linen, satin, and some silk. The clerk also said that if Sargis did not pay the 184 rubles the ring and watch[4] would be retained.

"Poor Sargis was completely dazed.

" 'Have I bought the goods?' he asked.

" 'Certainly you have bought them,' answered the unscrupulous clerk. 'Otherwise you would not have sold a chest of tea and a bale of tobacco. Beside, the coat your boy is wearing was made from our cloth.'

"This was true. On the third day after receiving the goods, Sargis had sold a bale of tobacco and a chest of tea, and had cut off several yards of cloth. It was very singular that in the course of three months Sargis had not once caught sight of Hemorrhoid Jack to call him to account for the delivery of the goods. He had been several times to his house, where they said, 'He is at the store.' At the store they said Jack was at home. It was very evident that he wished to defraud Sargis. After much talk back and forth the matter came into the courts, and since Sargis had sold part of the goods and had given a receipt for them, he had to pay the sum demanded.

"For several months past business had been going very badly with the poor fellow and he could not raise the required sum, so he had to give up his property. First they drove the poor man out of his house and emptied his store and his storehouse. Then they sold the tobacco and tile tea, for which no one would give more than fifty rubles, for both were half rotten. The store and all that was in it were then auctioned off for a few hundred rubles, and finally the house was offered for sale. No one would buy it, for among our people the praiseworthy custom rules that they never buy a house put up at auction till they convince themselves that the owner sells it of his own free-will. The household furniture was also sold, and Sargis became almost a beggar, and was obliged, half naked, to leave his house, with his wife and children.

"I proposed that they should occupy my house, but he would not have it. 'From to-day the black earth is my dwelling-place,' he

---

4. Sargis had previously given Hemorrhoid Jack a prized ring with a watch, ostensibly so the latter could have copies made and then return them.

326 The Heritage of Armenian Literature

said, and rented a small house at the edge of the town near where the fields begin.

"When the neighbors found out the treachery of Hemorrhoid Jack, they were terribly angry, and one of them threw a note into his yard in which was written: that if he took possession of poor Sargis's house they would tear or burn it down. That was just what John wished, and he immediately sent carpenters to tear down the house and stable and then he sold the wood.

"At this time I became very sick and lay two months in bed. When I got up again I thought to myself, 'I must go and visit the poor wretches!' I went to their little house, but found the door locked and the windows boarded up. I asked a boy, 'My child, do you know where the people of this house are?' 'Two weeks ago they got into a wagon and drove away,' answered the lad. 'Where are they gone?' I asked. 'That I don't know,' he said.

"I would not have believed it, but an old woman came up to me on the street, of her own accord, and said:

"'They all got into a wagon and have moved away into a Russian village.'

"What the village was called she could not tell me, and so every trace of them was lost.

"Many years later a gentleman came from Stavropol to our city, who gave me some news of the poor wretches. They had settled in a Cossack village—he told me the name, but I have forgotten—where at first they suffered great want; and just as things were going a little better with them, Mayram and Sargis died of the cholera and Takush and Toros were left alone. Soon after, a Russian officer saw Takush and was greatly pleased with her. After a few months she married him. Toros carried on his father's business for a time, then gave it up and joined the army. So much I found out from the gentleman from Stavropol.

"Some time later I met again one who knew Takush. He told me that she was now a widow. Her husband had been a drunkard, spent his whole nights in inns, often struck his poor wife, and treated her very badly. Finally they brought him home dead. Toros's neck had been broken at a horse-race and he was dead. He said also that Takush had almost forgotten the Armenian language and had changed her faith. That is the history of the Vacant Yard."

Gevorg Dodokhian

(1830–1908)

The educator and poet Gevorg Dodokhian was born in Simferopol, Crimea, received his early education in the local parish school and at the gymnasium, then enrolled at the Lazarian Institute in Moscow, from which he graduated in 1848. He manifested a talent for painting and developed it by attending the Academy of Fine Arts in St. Petersburg (1848–51). Next he attended the University of Dorpat (presently Taru in Estonia), where he studied economics and law. He adopted the teaching profession and taught almost all his life, serving in various schools in St. Petersburg, the northern Caucasus, and Crimea, where he also helped promote the cultural life of the Armenian community.

He began to write while still a student, making translations of Heinrich Heine and Ivan Krylov. He is best known for his poems, one of which in particular, "*Tzitzernak*" (Swallow), written in 1854 and set to music, has become one of the most popular songs among Armenians around the world and is sung even today. In Armenian folklore the swallow is the symbol of the migrant or exile who, away from his native land and in deep yearning, awaits its arrival every spring, a messenger from home.

A considerable amount of Dodokhian's verse and prose remains unpublished.

SWALLOW[1]

Swallow, swallow,
Fine bird of spring,
Tell me, where
Are you flying, so fast?

Ah swallow, fly
To Ashtarak,[2] where I was born,
Weave your nest there
Beneath your native roof.

There, far away, I have
An aging father who mourns,
Who waits out the days
For his only son.

When you see him
Bring him all my love;
Tell him he must sit and weep
Over his luckless son.

Tell him that I'm
Bereft and miserable,
Always crying, always wretched,
My life worn down, half gone.

For me, the day
Passes in darkness,
And no sleep comforts
My eyes at night.

Tell him I am fading
Before I ever came to bloom,

---

1. Gevorg Dodokhian, "Swallow," in Aram Tolegian, ed. and trans., *Armenian Poetry Old and New* (Detroit, 1979), 125.
2. City near Yerevan, Armenia.

A splendid small flower
Wrenched from its native ground.

Well, pretty swallow,
Be gone, fly away fast
To the land of Armenia,
To Ashtarak, where I was born.

Harutiun Svachian (Svadjian)

(1831–74)

During the course of his fairly brief life, Harutiun Svachian managed to achieve a lot as a writer, activist, teacher, and humorist. Born in Constantinople, he lost both parents at an early age. After completing his initial education in his native city under the sponsorship of Khachatur Partizpanian and with the help of the Otian family, he was sent to study at Collège Ste. Barbe in Paris. Upon his return to Constantinople in 1852 he became part of Nahapet Rusinian's enlightenment group and helped in the movement against the clerics and amiras.[1]

After becoming a teacher at the Beshiktash school in Constantinople, he devoted himself to promoting liberal ideas and studying Rusinian's textbook of modern Armenian, *Ughghakhosutiun* (Correct speech). He was convinced that modern rather than classical Armenian should be used in literary expression. In the meantime, he started a psychological, literary, economic, and satirical bimonthly journal called *Meghu* (Bee),[2] which he used to promote his favorite causes: the struggles against Armenian regression, pro-clerical movements, the Armenian bourgeoisie, and the sultanate. Here he published his aphorisms, *Aptakk* (Slaps),

---

1. A title bestowed on notable Armenians by the sultan.
2. Published 1856–65 and 1870–74.

and *Aské anké* (About here and there), a series of political chronicles criticizing the European political position on the Armenian issue. He also devoted considerable space to the writings of Mikayel Nalbandian and to Grigor Otian's satirical pieces, among many others.

Svachian was also a member of the committee that prepared the National Constitution (1859). He remained extremely active in several national political organizations that promoted his principles, above all the ideal of liberating Western Armenia. He was a champion of the rights of the working and peasant classes and the artisans as against those of the bourgeoisie.

Apart from his founding of *Meghu* and his efforts to introduce and promote Armenian writers, Svachian made other important contributions to Armenian literature and literary criticism. "*Hayastan Mayr*" (Mother Armenia), a narrative poem, and a poem entitled "*Arik Haykazunk*" (Brave Armenians) are among his most notable works. The latter piece was set to music and became the foundation of the National Constitution. *Katina,* a novella; *Arandzar Amatuni,* a historical tragedy; *Matnutiun* (Betrayal), a political pamphlet; and several satirical pieces are also important parts of his literary repertoire. Svachian was, in fact, among the founders of Armenian political humor. He was also one of the earliest practitioners of popular theater.

In 1981 Soviet Armenia observed the 150th anniversary of Harutiun Svachian's birth.

August Guiné[3]

One night last summer I was on the ferry to Büyük Deré. Near me sat two young men, facing each other. One of them had a handsome face and was dressed decently but modestly; he seemed an agreeable, dignified gentleman. The other was a modern, fashionable young man: people call the type a *Lionis*. The fez he wore was so black that it looked as if it had just come out of a coal mine. And he was wearing it so askew that his left eye and half his face were hidden. His hair was so greasy and disheveled that one might think he had put a piece of black cloth under his fez. And his pale

---

3. Harutiun Svachian, "August-Guiné," *Meghu* 1, no. 1 (15 September 1856), 19–24. The story makes extensive use of wordplay. Translated by the editors of present anthology.

thin cheeks were so sunken that, as they say, it looked as if he had two jaws. Instead of eyelashes, blood-red rings seemed to encircle his eyes. Despite his big nose, the ends of his collar protruded so far from under his chin that it seemed smaller than average. There was a tie around the collar, colored in every existing hue, as if it were a color chart. He wore a green jacket and white trousers, and over them a *setré*,[4] which measured one-third his height. The sleeves were so large that they were not much different from the sleeves of ancient *djüppé*s.[5] His gloves were so small that I think he tore them the very first time he put them on. His trousers were so very narrow that they clung to his body; on the other hand his shoes were so long that his knees, calves, and the tips of the shoes were the points of an equilateral triangle. He was sitting in a chair, resting his hands on a cane as thick as a broomstick.

The young man remained in the same position for some time, inspecting his surroundings. Baron[6] Hovhannes turned and said to him:

"Was your outfit made by August?"

"Who's August? What's he called in Armenian?"

"I really don't know, but I think those who prefer to speak Armenian might call him *Okosdos*."

"I don't know anybody by that name."

"For heavens sake! Haven't you ever heard of the famous August! There's no one like him in the world."

"Oh yes, now I get you. But did he really make clothes?"

"Who?"

"Augustus, the first Roman emperor, who has been dead for more than 1800 years."

"Heavens, no! I didn't say Emperor Augustus: I just asked if your outfit was made by August or *Okosdos*."

"Got it! No, no: it was made last May. I don't have my suits made at any specific time. I have something made whenever I need it. August, September, January—they're all the same to me."

"For God's sake, I didn't mean the month of August. There's a master tailor in Beyoghlu. He's French. He has two names; one is

---

4. An old fashioned type of frock coat (Turkish).
5. Robes worn by imams and judges (Turkish).
6. Mister (Armenian).

August or *Okosdos* and the other. . . . Oh, I can't remember it now. No, no I remember: Guiné. . . . Yes, Guiné."[7]

"Oh: so the tailor's a woman!"

"Who said so?"

"You did. But August isn't a woman's name."

"No, brother, no. It's a he, not a woman. His name is Guiné. They call him Augustus Guiné."

"Oh, yeah, now I see. No, I don't know him. Where's his shop?"

"On the main street in Beyoghlu. How can I explain, let me see. If you walk from Taksim Square in the direction of the four roads, Galatasaray is to your left, right?"

"Yes."

"No, no: this is even better. If you walk up from Tophané through Yeni Charshi to Beyoghlu, it's on your right, not your left . . . or, even better, let me explain it this way. . . ."

"I know, I know: Isn't that straight boulevard?"

"Hah! yes."

"The big store next to Baron Hulis?"[8]

"Yes, yes, that's it."

"And on the other side is Baron September?"

"No, who said so?"

"My calendar. That's what it says. On one side of August is *Hulis* and on the other is September."

"My God! I don't mean the August in your calendar."

"Don't wear yourself out for nothing. I don't want to know the man and I don't care where his shop is. To me, my own tailor is worth forty Augusts, especially since he is much less expensive than your man."

"Who is your tailor? Honestly, he has done such a terrific job: you'd swear August had outfitted you. I don't know, though, if he could make a *setré* as short as mine."

"He's so skillful he can even make it as long as a *djüppé*, or as short as a monkey suit, although he's Armenian."

"Did you say he's Armenian?"

---

7. *Guiné* is Armenian for "she is a woman." But here it is used as a proper noun.
8. July (Armenian).

"Yes."

"You don't say, brother! Do the Armenians possess such a master tailor? I don't believe it: I don't believe he can make a *setré* as short as this one. For heaven's sake, where's his shop? Can you explain it easily?"

"It's very easy to get there. . . ."

"What's his name?"

"We call him Khachatur Brother."

"No. If I go there and call him Khachatur Brother, don't you think he might get angry and do a bad job?"

"No, don't worry. He's not like that. He's an Armenian."

"I really will have to go to him. August is costing me a lot."

They stopped talking for a minute or two.

"I passed your store the other day," said Mr. Hovhannes. "But you weren't there."

"That's right," said the other. "Now I'm working for another boss, in Uzun Charshe. My old boss paid me fifty *ghrush*[9] a week. At this new place I make seventy a week. I wouldn't have left my old boss, but I couldn't stand his meddling. Talk, talk, talk . . . he meddled in everything I did. He never liked anything I did. 'Why is your *setré* so short? Why do you wear your fez so crooked?' He had to comment on everything. Otherwise he was a very nice man. I am sure he would have given me seventy *ghrush* if I had asked."

"Do you make any money on the side?"

"It happens sometimes, when people order things and I deliver them to their homes: they give my five or six *ghrush*. But it doesn't happen very often. And sometimes I sell things for more than the price set by the boss and pocket the difference."

"That's about three or four hundred *ghrush* a month."

"Yes," he said, laughing. "What can you do? Everything's expensive. Everything costs twice as much these days, not like before. You can only afford the bare necessities. If you want a suit in the latest fashion, it's 1,500 or 2,000 *ghroush*. Young people like us have to keep up with fashion a little. We're at the age when . . . you know what I mean. . . ."

---

9. The Armenian pronunciation of *kurush,* a unit of Turkish currency. There are 100 kurush or piastres in a lira or pound.

"Do you have to pay for your lodgings?" interrupted Baron Hovhannes.

"Of course! what do you think? I make little enough as it is, and on top of everything I also have to pay for my lodgings. At least thirty *ghrush* a month."

"That's not so bad."

"No, not really. My mother takes care of a lot of the expenses. She sews all day. She's quite old, but she never stops working."

"Don't you feel sorry for your mother? Why do you let her work so much? Why don't you pay a little more?"

"How can I pay more on what I make?" he said, a bit offended, and looked over his shoulder to see if the boat had arrived at Büyük Deré. "We're here." He got up and walked through the crowd, pushing himself past the other passengers. With their swearing ringing in his ears, he left.

Baron Hovhannes watched him carefully and laughed, making a face as if he felt sorry for him.

Narpey (Narbey) (Khoren Galfayan)

(1832–92)

Narpey, né Khoren Galfayan (Kalfayan), was born in Constantinople, received his education at the Mkhitarist school in San Lazzaro, Venice, and became a member of the Mkhitarist Congregation. After he was ordained a priest, he was sent to Paris to assume the position of director of the Muradian school. There he got to know the famed French poet Lamartine,[1] whose *Harmonies poétiques et religieuses* (Poetic and religious harmonies) he translated into Armenian under the title *Dashnakk*, in 1859. He also published a few translations of Victor Hugo and Vittorio Alfieri.[2]

In 1857 Narpey left the Mkhitarist order after a dispute with the leadership and became a celibate priest of the Armenian Apostolic Church. In this he followed in the steps of three other clerics who had left the order: Bishop Gabriel Aïvazovski (the brother of the renowned seascape painter, Hovhannes [Ivan] Aïvazovski), who was the founder and first editor (1843–48) of the review *Bazmavep* (*Polyhistor*); his own brother, Ambrosius Galfayan (known as Prince Guiton Lusignan, the

---

1. Alphonse Marie Louis de Lamartine (1790–1869), French poet, statesman, and historian.

2. Count Vittorio Alfieri (1749–1803), Italian poet and dramatist.

name he adopted, claiming descent from the French Lusignan dynasty related to the kings of Cilicia), who authored a two-volume French-Armenian dictionary; and Sargis Teodorian. While still in Paris, he continued his teaching and contributed to the journal *Masyats aghavni* (Dove of Masis), founded in 1855 by Gabriel Aïvazovski.

In 1861 he went to Theodosia (Crimea), where he taught at the newly opened Khalibian school and continued his collaboration with *Masyats aghavni*, which had moved to Theodosia in 1860. A few years later he visited Etchmiadzin and Jerusalem, where he was elevated to the rank of bishop in 1867. He served a brief term as Primate of Rumania, but eventually returned to Constantinople and decided to remain there for the rest of his life.

He experienced his greatest triumphs and the saddest tragedy of his life in the Turkish capital. An eloquent orator and popular poet, he was much sought after in lecture halls and the salons of the Armenian aristocracy. For a time he was secretary of the Religious Council and later a member of the Armenian delegation to the Congress of Berlin (1878), in the capacity of translator. Even though he was honored by the sultan with a medal, he was suspected of espionage on behalf of Russia and placed under police surveillance. In 1888 his house was searched and all his papers confiscated. His trip to Tiflis in 1889 to attend the funeral of the great philanthropist Mkrtich Sanasarian, the founder of the Sanasarian college in Karin (Erzurum), and his reception of a medal from Tsar Alexander made things worse. Under the circumstances, the Armenian Patriarch, Archbishop Ashekian, saw fit to defrock him. In 1892 he was summoned to the police station for further questioning, and there, it is said, he died from drinking poisoned coffee.

His literary output consists mainly of three volumes of poetry: *Vardenik* (Rose garden, 1863), *Knar pandukhtin* (The expatriate's lyre, 1868), and *Stverk haykakank* (Shadows of the homeland, 1874). The first book contains melancholy poems inspired by his sister, Varduhi, to whom he expresses fraternal love and dedication, finding solace in this love from the disappointments of life. In the second book patriotism, religion, and nature join to console the expatriate with visions of the homeland. The third volume reveals the author's deep nostalgia for the land of his ancestors and its glories, heroes, and saints. The language is modern Armenian, sometimes weighed down with classical expressions. Despite his capacity for feeling, his excessive patriotism and lack of imagination prevented him from achieving great poetic heights.

He also tried his hand at theater. His play, *Arshak II* (1862), written for the students of the Armenian school in Theodosia, lacks dramatic and literary merit, whereas *Alafranca* (1862), a satire about provincials who ape French manners, is more polished.

ARMENIA[3]

If a scepter of diamond, a glittering crown,
Were mine, at thy feet I would lay them both down,
    Queen of queens, O Armenia!

If a mantle of purple were given to me,
A mantle for kings, I would wrap it round thee,
    Poor Armenia, my mother!

If the fire of my youth and its sinews of steel
Could return, I would offer its rapture and zeal
    All to thee, my Armenia!

Had a lifetime of ages been granted to me,
I had given it gladly and freely to thee,
    O my life, my Armenia!

Were I offered the love of a maid lily-fair,
I would choose thee alone for my joy and my care,
    My one love, my Armenia!

Were I given a crown of rich pearls, I should prize,
Far more than their beauty, one tear from thine eyes,
    O my weeping Armenia!

If freedom unbounded were proffered to me,
I would choose still to share thy sublime slavery,
    O my mother, Armenia!

Were I offered proud Europe, to take or refuse,
Thee alone, with thy griefs on thy head, would I choose
    For my country, Armenia!

---

3. Khoren Galfayan Narpey de Lusignan, "Armenia," in *Armenian Poems* (Boston, 1917), 43–44. Translated by Alice Stone Blackwell.

Might I choose from the world where my dwelling should be,
I would say, Still thy ruins are Eden to me,
    My beloved Armenia

Were I given a seraph's celestial lyre,
I would sing with my soul, to its chords of pure fire,
    Thy dear name, my Armenia!

THE EXILE TO THE SWALLOW[4]

Swallow, swallow, was it thine,
    This nest, all cold and drear,
That empty in this niche I found
    When first I entered here?
At sight of it mine eyes o'erflowed
    With bitter teardrops, horn
Of the sad thought that my nest too
    Lies empty and forlorn.

O swallow, hasten to thy nest,
    And have no fear of me!
In me a comrade thou shalt find;
    A wanderer I, like thee.
I know the longing of thy heart,
    The yearning for thy home;
I know the bitter pains of those
    As exiles forced to roam.

Happy art thou, O bird, to find
    Thy little nest at last!
The time of thy brief pilgrimage
    Is over now and past.
Forget thy woes, chirp merrily!
    Let grief be left to me,
Who know not of my wanderings
    When there an end shall he.

---

4. "The Exile to the Swallow," in ibid., 222–23.

Swallow, thou hadst the hope of spring,
    To reach thy home nest here;
My winter ends not; spring I lost,
    Losing my country dear.
Oh, dark to me this foreign light!
    The air is dull and dead,
Flitter the water that I drink,
    And like a stone my bread!

Swallow, when thou shalt seek again
    This nest, to thee so dear,
Wilt thou still hear my trembling voice
    Bidding thee welcome here?
If thou shalt find my humble cot
    Empty and silent stand,
Bear to my grave a drop of dew
    Brought from my fatherland!

Grigor Otian

(1834–87)

One of the most prominent figures of the Revival period, Grigor Otian was born in Scutari (Üsküdar), a suburb of Constantinople, to a venerable aristocratic family. He received his education at home, under private tutoring by some of the most competent teachers of the day, acquiring a well-rounded education. When he went to Paris for further studies, he witnessed the 1848 revolution unfolding before his eyes. He followed it with keen interest, and it had a profound influence on the shaping of his democratic ideas. He returned to his native city in 1854.

By the 1850s the Armenian community of Constantinople had become embroiled in social upheavals, religious fragmentation, constitutional disputes, and the throes of cultural evolution. Otian jumped into this turmoil, maintaining, however, his serenity and his clear and analytical thinking, and keeping himself above all factionalism. He wanted to serve the nation. He took to the lecture halls, where he captivated large audiences with his speeches on vital issues. He was a keen observer of European democratic movements and strove to promote and implement them in Armenia. He was also a judicious chairman of councils, an acute political thinker and organizer.

Otian played an important role in the formulation of the Armenian National Constitution, a legal instrument that for the first time established a democratic system of rule for an ethnic community that was part of a despotic empire. The project started in 1860, and Otian, along with Servichen, Nikoghayos Palian (Balian), Nahapet Rusinian, and others, made a valuable contribution to the preparation of the final draft of the Constitution, which was presented to the Sublime Porte and eventually ratified, in 1863. Once the Constitution was in place, he served for a number of years as chairman of the Armenian National Assembly. In 1864, as a government official, he accompanied Midhat Pasha to Bulgaria on a diplomatic mission. In 1866 he was appointed to the Council of State and became advisor to Midhat Pasha, who by that time had been elevated to the rank of grand vizier. They shared liberal ideas, and Otian assisted him in the preparation of the Ottoman constitution of 1876, which, however, was abolished soon after the accession of the new sultan, Abdul Hamid II. The new sultan also banished Midhat Pasha to exile in Arabia. Sensing the approaching clouds of terror, and on the advice of friends, Otian managed to slip away to Paris, where he lived for the rest of his life.

Otian's writings consist mainly of articles, essays, lectures, committee records, and reviews, which are scattered in numerous journals and periodicals of the day. He was a staunch supporter of modern Armenian, and contributed to its development. As a man of firm principles and convictions, he dedicated his life to the task of bringing to his people the light of European civilization in the social, political, and intellectual realms.

LONDON AND PARIS[1]

Dear Editor,

What I am going to relate is not a Paris or London experience, but a personal one, although it is true that I crossed the Channel to London. To cross the Channel means to cross a hazard, and to travel to London is to travel to a different world. The ocean, especially for me, is so unpleasant—I like neither its somber, gray waves nor its ferocity. I no longer understand Victor Hugo, who says, "When I behold grandeur, I forget my bitterness of heart, That is why I am here: I have come to be a neighbor of the sea." But

---

1. Grigor Otian (signed Vahram), "*London yev Paris*" (London and Paris), in *Hatntirk ardi tohmayin grakanutyené* (Selections from modern national literature) (Constantinople, 1908), 164–68. Translated by the editors of the present anthology.

I do not expect to find sweetness in the harsh waves of any other poet. Not with Virgil either: I like only his "murmuring water," and Milton's "delicate water of the rain." And I am not Byron, to command the ocean's waves: "Roll on, thou deep and dark blue ocean—roll!"[2] Rather let her carry me away. The ocean orders the depths to pour out all their crimes and breakers through this narrow waterway, and drives them against the two shores.

In fact, man can be rescued from the waves of the ocean, and here I am: I have been to London and returned. London, as vast as an empire, and as populous. Paris has two million inhabitants; London four million. And how different these two cities are! Paris is the world's metropolis, London its capital. Paris is lovable, London venerable. The characteristic of Paris is decorum, whereas London's is greater decorum. Paris is mirthful and alive, London sound and pensive. Paris is facetious, London courteous. Paris fickle and impudent, London always solemn and prudent. Today Paris is bold, tomorrow shrewd; London is steady in all it undertakes. . . . Paris is always on the move, London moves but seldom.

Parisians live in the streets; Londoners live at home. In Paris going to church is considered shameful, in London not to go church is shameful. Family and religion: two major factors that promote the greatness of a nation. This island is just a tiny dot on the globe, but that dot at times rules the world, as Fox[3] once said to Napoleon the Great. If I had Thiers's history [4] in hand, I would have copied word for word the interesting conversation between the conquering French emperor and Pitt,[5] the prominent Englishman, in which the arrogance of the son of Albion[6] suddenly awakens. Arrogance: how quick one is to utter such words, going along with the trend of general opinion. The English understand and know themselves, but they are not arrogant. What seems arrogance in them is nothing but shyness, as though they were somehow uncultivated and ashamed of the fact. A friend of mine used to say that they are

---

2. *Childe Harold's Pilgrimage* (1818), canto IV, stanza 179.

3. Charles James Fox (1749–1806), English orator and statesman.

4. *Histoire de la révolution française,* in ten volumes (1823–27), by Louis Adolphe Thiers (1797–1877), first president (1870–73) of the Third Republic.

5. William Pitt "the Younger" (1759–1806), English statesman and prime minister (1783–1801; 1806–06). He and Charles James Fox were bitter rivals.

6. England (poetic).

civilized savages; perhaps this is also one of the secrets of their greatness. Except for this particular quality in their character, it is said that nobody knows how to show respect and to be polite and pleasing better than an English lord. No matter how impregnated with the ideals of democracy an individual might be, it is impossible not to admire an English nobleman. And how can a person not feel a certain greatness or fail to bear the stamp of greatness when he is the scion of six or eight hundred years of ancestors, all of them landed gentry, and their city—London? It is probably in this sense that our forefathers used the word *vostaik;*[7] and called a nobleman *horordi,*[8] as I have read, I think, in Khorenatsi.[9]

In England, everyone is a capital-inhabiting monarch—every individual in this truly free country—whether he be a noble landlord or a simple landowner, is a prince in his own home. There you have it: this is how they exercise the great principle of individual freedom—stable, general, and absolute—that the English possess. I do not know if it is written down anywhere, but it is engraved on every Englishman's heart; it is recorded in traditions and morality, just as the laws of justice are inscribed on the conscience of a judge instead of in legal tomes. A happy nation—they have never needed laws to make them a lawful nation!

---

7. Inhabitant of a capital city.

8. Nobleman, gentleman, literally the son of the father.

9. I.e., in the work of Movses Khorenatsi (Moses of Khoren), a fifth-century Armenian historian.

Raffi (Hakob Melik Hakobian)

(1837–88)

The writer who had the greatest revolutionary impact on Armenian literature was born in the village of Payajuk in Salmast, Persia, descended from a family of *meliks*. His father had a prosperous business and a large family of thirteen children, of whom Raffi was the eldest. He received his early education at a private school run by a teacher called Father Teodik, whose character he later depicted in his novel *Kaytzer* (Sparks). In 1847 he accompanied his father to Tiflis and remained there to complete his education, first at a private Armenian school, then at the Russian gymnasium, where he became well acquainted with ancient and European classics. After four years of study he was forced to return home in 1856 because of financial difficulties his father was experiencing. In 1857–58 he had the opportunity to travel extensively in the Armenian provinces of Turkey and Persia. He visited Taron, Van, Aghtamar, and Varag, where he met Khrimian Hayrik (1820–1907). He also studied local history and traditions and observed at firsthand the everyday life of the peasants, the oppression they were subjected to, and the corruption of their leaders. The wealth of information and the profound impressions he received would later provide material for his novels. By the early 1860s he had already produced a good number of works on poetry and prose, most of them published in periodicals.

Raffi married in 1863 and in 1868 moved to Tiflis. By this time his father's business had collapsed, and as the eldest son he had no choice but to take charge of the situation. But a man like him, dedicated to literature and passionate about patriotic ideas and romanticism, could not save the business, despite his efforts. Eventually it was liquidated, creating a hapless situation for the entire family. All he could do was write for long hours, in order to provide for a large family. He once told the novelist Shirvanzadé (1858–1935), "the day I put aside my pen, my family will die of starvation."[1]

Raffi's first association with Grigor Artzruni (1845–92) was a turning point in his life. When Artzruni founded the weekly review *Mshak* (Tiller) in 1872, Raffi became its most active and appreciated collaborator; this is when he started to use the pen name Raffi. The exchange of ideas and criticism with Artzruni was most beneficial; in his words, "The critical spirit and the beauty of art were combined to make the product more realistic." His novels were first serialized in *Mshak* and became very popular indeed.

Raffi lived a modest life, often beset by financial difficulties. His only income consisted of what he received from the review and the sale of his books; hence he wrote incessantly. He had to care for his wife and two children, as well as for his mother and sisters. For a while he took up teaching in Tiflis (1875–77) and in Agulis (1877–79), but he had to abandon it because of the vehement opposition of fanatical conservatives to his novel *Harem* (1874), in which he criticized the despotism and backwardness of eastern society. He returned to Tiflis and resumed writing full-time. In 1884 he had a falling out with Grigor Artzruni (1845–92) and began to write for another literary-political weekly, *Ardzagang* (Echo). He died in Tiflis. His funeral procession was attended by thousands of people, despite a pouring rain.

Like many writers, Raffi began his literary career with poetry. His most famous poem is "*Dzayn tur ov tzovak, inchu es lrum*" (Cry out, O lake: why are you silent?), which he was inspired to write during a visit to the shores of Lake Van. It has been set to music and is still a popular song.

Raffi is most renowned for his prose, in which he excelled, captivating his readers. He was the precursor or ideologist of the revolution. His works, whether short stories or novels, targeted the rulers for their corruption and cruelty, the clergy for having led the people into slavish servility, the peasants for their prevailing ignorance and poverty, those

---

1. Shirvanzadé, "Raffi-Hakob Malik Hakobian," in *Raffi, kyanke, grakanutiune, hishoghutiunner* (Raffi, his life, his literature, memories) (Paris, 1937), 43.

who exploited them for their own ends, and the existing social and political order, which fed off the misery of the people. Raffi never spoke of armed revolution, knowing full well that the nation was not ready for it. He did not sermonize either. The heroes he created—men of vision who fight in self-defense and for freedom from ignorance and servitude—and the events he depicted are harmoniously and artistically interwoven in each work, making it an exciting literary experience.

He was a prolific writer. Following are some of his major works. In *Voski akaghaghe* (The golden rooster, 1881),[2] the main character, a grotesque bourgeois, personifies the vices of society. In *Khachagoghi hishatakarane* (Memoirs of a robber, 1883) the author defends the thesis that men are born neither good nor bad; society and education shape their characters. *Jalaleddin* (1884) is the true story of the atrocities committed by a Kurdish sheik in the region of Aghbak during the Russo-Turkish war of 1877–78. The hero, Sahrat, fights only in self-defense and is even pitted against his own father as he tries to galvanize the people into a unified force. The novel *Khente* (The fool, 1881) has as its main theme the emancipation of Armenia enacted against the background of the 1877–78 war, when the city of Bayazid (Beyazit) was besieged by the Turks. The hero, Vardan, disguised as a fool, breaks through enemy lines and reaches the Russian commander, who liberates the city. The story is infused with acts of heroism, love, denial, and treachery, making it a captivating novel, one of the author's best.

Davit Beg and *Khamsayi melikutiunnere* (The melikdoms of Khamsa), both published in 1882, are more historical studies than novels. The first is the story of the military campaign (1722–25) mounted in Siunik by Davit Beg against the invading Persian and Ottoman forces, which resulted in the provincial autonomy that continued well into the beginning of the nineteenth century. The second is a historical study of the five Armenian melikdoms of Khamsa (presently Artsakh or Karabagh). Raffi's most popular work is *Kaytzer* (Sparks), in two volumes (1883, 1887), in which a group of students travels through Eastern Armenia and explores ways to alleviate the plight of the people. It is considered a guidebook of the emancipation movement. *Paruyr Haykazn*[3]

---

2. The parenthetical dates represent the year the work was published in book form. Some works were serialized in periodicals much earlier.

3. *Paruyr Haykazn* is the Armenian name of the rhetorician and philosopher Proaeresius (AD 276–368), who was born in Caesarea, Cappadocia, to an Armenian family. He was educated in Athens and became the head of a school of rhetoric. His works have not survived. Information about him comes from his biographer, the Greek rhetorician and historian Eunapius (c. 345–c. 414).

(1884) is a short philosophical work, wherein his thinking echoes that of Movses Khorenatsi when he points out the incompatibility of patriotism and Paruyr Haykazn's cosmopolitanism. He also concludes that the main cause of the nation's tragedies is lack of unity, which may foster treacherous behavior. His last novel, *Samuel* (1884), is a historical novel depicting fourth-century Armenia, which was under great pressure from Persia to renounce her newly adopted religion. Samuel, the hero, a member of the Mamikonian dynasty, fights bitterly against enemies and traitors, even his own kin, to preserve the political and religious integrity of the nation. The complete works of Raffi, in 10 volumes, were first published in Yerevan in 1962–64, with subsequent editions. His works continue to be a source of inspiration. For additional information see the section on the historical novel in the overview essay at the beginning of the present anthology.

FROM THE FOOL

Chapter 43[4]

Now a confusion of dreams crowded in upon his inflamed imagination: hellish visions that filled him with horror, yet also comforted and enchanted him. The cycle of time had seemed to jump forward by many centuries, and he saw Armenia, once nothing but a wasteland full of ruins, now totally transformed and renewed. What kind of miraculous change was this? Could it be that paradise was restored after being lost? Could it be that the golden age which existed before God's earth was polluted with evil and injustice now reigned again? No. This paradise that Vardan saw was not the paradise Jehovah had established between the banks of Armenia's four rivers, where the first human pair lived in perfect innocence and unknowing. This wasn't that paradise in which there was no need to produce anything by labor, where people could simply live off the fruit of the land—feasting at God's rich table, spread out before them by nature.

This was a paradise of a different kind, a paradise created by people out of their own labor and right-livelihood; where instead of

---

4. Raffi (Hakob Melik Hakobian), *The Fool* (Reading, England, and Princeton, N.J., 2000), 206–17. Translated by Donald Abcarian. This excerpt is a condensation based on the final chapter of *The Fool*. It was edited by Abcarian especially for inclusion in the present volume and contains minor changes in wording.

unconsciousness, there was intelligence and consciousness; instead of a simple patriarchal form of life an advanced culture.

Now it seemed that the meaning of those fateful words spoken by the Creator to the first-created had been fulfilled, "You shall earn your bread by the sweat of your brow." Now man didn't simply labor, but had lightened his work so much that sweat was no longer necessary. Now he worked for his own benefit; what he produced was no longer torn out of his hands by a violent oppressor.

And behold, Vardan saw a village. Could it be the village of O— in Alashkert? The surroundings looked familiar: the same mountains and hills, the same river, the same verdant valley—all looked the same.

The passage of centuries had taken nothing away but only transformed things. And how changed the village was! Those miserable cottages, excavated out of the earth and more fit as dens for animals than for human habitation, were no longer to be seen. These houses were made of stone, white as snow, and surrounded by beautiful gardens; broad, straight streets were sheltered by trees ever green, and bordered by crystal-clear brooks.

It was in the morning.

The village children were coming out of their houses, healthy, gay, well dressed; boys and girls together, hurrying off to school with their books slung over their shoulders. Vardan looked at them and was amazed. How well taken care of they looked, and how happy they seemed. They must have had no fear of school or teachers. Could these be the same half-naked and sickly children that Vardan had known?

He stood alone in the street, looking around with wonder, unsure what direction to take. A beautiful sound struck his ear, the sound of the church bell. It appeared the morning service had not concluded yet. This was the first time since leaving the monastery and the monastic order that the sound of invitation to God's house had seemed so sweet to him. His hardened heart was filled with spiritual devotion, and he made his way toward the church, a place he hadn't set foot in for more than ten years.

He was amazed at what he saw. What a plain and humble church it was: no throne for dignitaries, no altar, no adorned sanctuary, no gilded images, no silver crosses or precious vestments. All the magnificence of the Armenian church was absent here; nor were there any choristers, or choirmasters, or deacons to be seen.

There were only two pictures, one of Jesus Christ, and the other of Saint Gregory the Illuminator, both mounted in simple, black frames.

Men and women sat together, holding missals in their hands. The priest was delivering a sermon with the Holy Scriptures opened before him in the pulpit. His attire was no different from that of the congregation. His sermon was so simple and clear that Vardan understood everything he said. God's word flowed from his lips like the pure, living water of a spring. He took for the subject of his sermon those words from the Holy Scriptures, "You shall earn your bread by the sweat of your brow." Vardan was struck by the priest's explanation of this verse. Up until this day, Vardan had been given to understand that these words were a curse placed on the destiny of the first-created, a curse extending to all future generations. He now understood that this was an admonition intended to root out idleness and keep man in a state of indefatigable, industrious, self-motivated activity.

The sermon ended. From the midst of the congregation, an ordinary villager was reciting an extemporaneous prayer, asking God's help for the health, intelligence, and strength necessary to work the land He had created to bring forth its countless blessings. "What a prayer! What do they seek for themselves?" thought Vardan. "They don't ask for anything spiritual. Could it be they expect nothing beyond the grave, that they are asking only for that which meets their physical needs and what is required by real existence?"

The prayer concluded. The entire congregation, men, women, young, and old, started to sing a song with words taken from the Psalms, "Many said, who will show us the goodness of God? The light of your countenance fell upon us, and you granted joy to our hearts. You made us abound with the wealth of wheat and wine, and oil."

"Again, the same material intentions . . ." Vardan thought. "Again, nothing spiritual, . . . The farmer sings of the abundance of the earth, given to him by God to be worked with his own hands. How remarkable that these people have reconciled the abstraction of religion with the demands of real life conditions. . . ."

How beautiful that song was, joined in harmony by the organ's lovely sound. What a sweet anthem flowing from the lips of hundreds of people. It seemed to Vardan that the voice of these people became one with the melody of the seraphim and lofted upward to the Eternal Throne. This was the first time in his life he had heard such holy music.

The service came to an end, and the people started to leave. Now the school teacher stood in the pulpit where the priest had delivered his sermon; and the children of the village filled the pews where the congregation had just been singing and praying. Boys and girls mingled together, listening to their teacher's lecture.

Without waiting for the class to end, Vardan walked out of the church, or rather the school, and went out into the surrounding grounds. Instead of the graves usually found around Armenian churches he found the churchyard filled with the beauty of rare trees and flowers. He stood for a long while looking at the lovely walkways. Noticing that he was a visitor, a villager invited him to his house for breakfast.

The villager's home was one of those tidy houses that contains everything necessary within modest confines, and it was totally ensconced in the shelter of trees. There were several rooms, each suited to the various requirements of life; each plain, clean, appropriately furnished. . . . .

Vartan looked out the window from where Vardan sat surrounded by the happy family of his host; the windows revealed the verdant beauty of the valley, stretching to the foot of the distant mountains. The mountains were covered with thick forests; an awesome sight was presented by the gigantic trees rising up to become one with the clear blue sky. The morning sun poured down its golden rays, and, bathed in its light, many rivers twisted and shimmered like silver snakes, winding their way through the open expanse of the valley. Vardan couldn't take his eyes off this wondrous vista. Cultivated by the hands of a hardworking people, untamed nature had taken on the appearance of a painting by a great artist. . . .

"Do you see those breathtaking mountains?" asked his host. "Well, a century and a half ago, they were totally bare, without so much as a shrub on them. In those days, the trees were destroyed by the barbarians with the same cruelty that the people had been destroyed. Everything was gone; the people used dried dung for fuel, for there wasn't any wood left, and they were forced to dig into the earth to live. But when peace returned, then hosts of people returned to the destroyed towns, and the mountains became covered with forests, all planted by our industrious, dedicated villagers. See that beautiful green valley? It had been turned into a totally dry wasteland, without any water. There was only a little river left, and it would dry up completely in the heat of summer. But from the moment the forests were planted, there was water in abundance. This is now one of the most fertile and fruitful places in the region. Yes, a great deal has changed. . . . Before, there weren't even any roads, but now you can see level roads gleaming like mirrors and connecting all the towns of our province with each other. The vehicles speeding along on those roads are powered by steam, not animals. What we produce here is taken to market hundreds of miles away; and, in turn, we get whatever we need from the outside. . . ."

Vardan's host picked up the newspaper once more and, taking a look at one of the articles, seemed quite disturbed by it.

"What kind of news is it?" Vardan asked, quite curious.

"Nothing unusual. . . . A general convocation of the assembly is going to take place in town tomorrow to discuss some controversial issues. . . ."

Vardan and his host were by now outside the village. Wherever Vardan looked, there were dense crops, beautiful farms, well cultivated fields, and abundant pastures.

They passed by a sawmill where most of the labor was carried out with steam-powered machinery. The mill produced lumber in many different sizes and styles, and supplied all the nearby villages and towns.

"Who owns the mill?" asked Vardan.

"The village owns it. Any enterprise you see here isn't the property of just one individual," replied his host. "All the facilities belong to the entire village community; each villager has a share in it. They are constructed of wood from the nearby forests. These, too, are owned by the entire village. . . ."

But one thing impressed Vardan beyond all else: all the workers in the village conveyed a striking boldness, self-confidence, and hardiness of spirit wherever they were encountered and under whatever circumstances. Judging from their manner, it would seem they had grown up in freedom; that they had never suffered a slap at the hands of a Turk, nor ever had any fear of a Kurdish spear. . . .

Vardan thanked his host and went on alone. He didn't know which way he should go. He saw something that looked like a tramway with people sitting on either side of it. He took a seat among them on finding out that the tram would soon come along and take him to the next station. He suddenly heard a familiar voice ring out from the crowd around him, "Vardan!"

Vardan turned around and saw Mr. Salman. The two old friends embraced.

"And so, my friend, we find each other again after exactly two hundred years. . . ." Mr. Salman said, still holding on to Vardan's hand. "That's been a very long time. You look the same; you haven't changed a bit. . . . But in those two hundred years, there have been great changes in our country. Didn't I used to tell you, Vardan, that Armenia in its infancy was the cradle of humanity, a paradise in the age of innocence, but that the day would come, in humanity's maturity, when it would become a paradise of advancement? Now that has all been fulfilled. Now the existence of the Armenians on their own ancestral land is entirely secure, joyous, and peaceful; if you only knew how hard we had to work to get there. . . . So much work. . . . In these last two hundred years, we passed through so many trials. . . . We won our well-being at the cost of much blood and sweat."

"Where are you going now?" Vardan asked his friend.

"I'm on my way to town to take part in the session of assembly that has been called. I represent my district there. I'm going to deliver a speech. Come along, I'm sure you'll find the debate very interesting."

The final whistle for departure sounded, and they climbed into the tram. It was nighttime. They reached the railway station just before daybreak. The beautiful, lively town was now in slumber. Only a few workers could be seen in the streets, hurrying off to their factories.

"Take us to 'Noah's Dove,'" said Mr. Salman to a coachman.

The coach sped along straight and smooth, through streets lined with splendid, colorful buildings which looked like palaces to Vardan. . . .

"We're late, gentlemen. The assembly is about to begin," said Mr. Salman.

"He's the leader of our freedom-loving party," Tomas Effendi whispered in Vardan's ear, pointing at Mr. Salman. "He has an outstanding speech to make today. Ah, how well he talks. . . ."

"Let me go with you, gentlemen. I want to listen, too, . . ." said Vardan eagerly. . . .

Perch Proshian

(1837–1907)

Also known as Hovhannes Ter-Arakelian, Perch Proshian was born in the village of Ashtarak, to a tailor's family. He received his elementary education at the local school. As he relates in his memoirs, what impressed him most as a student were the visits to the school of the district inspector, Khachatur Abovian (1809–48), whose forbade corporal punishment and introduced modern methods of teaching based on respect for the individuality of each pupil. He was later influenced by Abovian again when he wrote his novels. In 1852 he was sent to the Nersisian school in Tiflis, sponsored by Catholicos Nerses Ashtaraketsi, with the aim of becoming a clergyman. After graduating in 1856, he refused holy orders, desiring instead to continue his education at the Lazarian College in Moscow. Lack of financial means forced him to give up this dream, and, after studying for a year at the Russian gymnasium in Tiflis, he took up the teaching career that occupied the rest of his life. His teaching took him to many places, including Ashtarak, Tiflis (where he also helped to establish a girls' school (1861) and a professional theater troupe), Shushi (where also he opened a girls' school), Agulis, and Astrakhan. In 1879 he was invited to Etchmiadzin, to assume the post of supervisor of the parochial schools of Yerevan and Kars. Throughout his teaching career, which lasted more than forty-five years, he strove to change traditional methods and introduce new concepts of education, making the student rather than the teacher the center of the educational process. In these endeavors he was constantly opposed by narrow-minded clerics.

His many travels as a teacher to villages, cities, and districts gave him the opportunity to study the customs, traditions, and dialects of a wide range of people, to share their everyday life, and to acquaint himself thoroughly with their situations. All this provided background material for his novels.

During some periods of his life he supplemented his income by working as a photographer. However, he still found time for writing. He wrote his first novel, *Sos yev Varditer* (Sos and Varditer), at the age of twenty-three. It is a story of two passionate lovers who eventually succeed in obtaining their parents' consent to marry; at the last minute a miserly relative spoils their plans, and the lovers die tragically. The novel is written in the Ashtarak dialect. Although it is a first novel, it has considerable ethnographic value, as it is a keenly observed reflection of the traditions and customs of village life.

His second novel, *Krvatzaghik* (A bone of contention, 1878), a historic novel influenced by Khachatur Abovian's *Wounds of Armenia*, is set against the background of the oppressive Persian rule in the closing decades of the eighteenth century. It contains tacit criticism of local Armenian leaders and clergymen, and a call to mobilize the youth for education and self-defense.

Proshian's next book, *Hatsi khndir* (A matter of bread, 1880), an articulate and captivating realistic novel, is considered his best. It mirrors life in Ashtarak as it was in the 1840s, '50s, and '60s. The author contrasts two ways of life: the old patriarchal style of village life and the new trend to capitalism, where wealth is concentrated in a few hands. The resultant social imbalance is represented by the conflict between two characters, Khechan and Sako.

His other novels—such as *Shahen* (1883), *Tsetser* (The moths: i.e., the parasites of society, 1889), *Bghdé*, (1890), *Hunon* (1891)—and a number of short stories deal with social and human conditions in villages, tinted with revolutionary ideas. He is also known for his *Hushikner* (Memoirs, 1894), which provide valuable information about the events and persons of his time; two plays; a series of articles on education and theater; and a number of translations, including from Charles Dickens and Dostoyevsky. He spent the last years of his life in Tiflis, where he is buried.

As the famed poet Hovhannes Tumanian (1869–1923) aptly said, "Proshian raised the aesthetics of romanticism to a higher level; his work is an entire album, depicting village life and village characters." His collected works, in seven volumes, were published in Yerevan (1962–64), followed by a second edition (1974–75) in three volumes.

A MATTER OF BREAD: SAKO, THE PUBLICAN[1]

Near the source of the Sev Jur[2] River, I think it is still possible to see what is left of a couple of ruins; they attract the attention of the traveler interested in archaeology, causing him to stop awhile and ponder.

The ruin on the north side is the unforgettable government building to which the people of Sartarapat[3] and Karb[4] resorted to seek justice and to claim their rights.

I should mention that what is today a ruin was an impressive structure a few years back. This was the residence of the governor of the district, the *movrov* as he was called locally; here also were all his assistants, secretaries, and the entire police force, as well as the courthouse.

Across from this large structure, not very far from it but closer to the reedy banks of the Sev Jur River, where the other ruin is, was the tavern of the governor's wine merchant.

This tavern was no less important than the government building. Naturally there had to be a place to receive travelers, to feed and shelter them. Such inns are common on all main roads. We are familiar with only one of the publicans who operated the place; we will have the good fortune of meeting him quite frequently. He is Sako the Publican, and I consider it an honor to introduce him to you.

Some say he was a Kurd; others insist he was from Ashtarak. The latter base their opinion on the fact that he had a couple of vineyards in Ashtarak. But where he came from is of no importance to us. We knew him since he was ten or twelve years old,

---

1. Perch Proshian, "Mikitan Sakon" (Sako the publican), from *Hatsi khndir* (A matter of bread), in *Hay Grakanutiun* (Armenian literature) (Yerevan, 1984), 46–54. Translated by the editors of the present anthology. The Armenian text is in the Ashtarak dialect.

2. Literally black water (Armenian).

3. Sartarapat district is part of the great plain of Ararat, traversed by the Araxes River.

4. A village in Western Armenia, in the Province of Van.

when he used to knock at the doors of the garrison taverns looking for work. They say that no publican was ever able to employ Sako for more than two or three months. Our layabout urchin could pull the wool over anyone's eyes and steal not only from the customers' pockets but even from the publican: the man's purse disappeared from his breast pocket or from under his pillow while he was sound asleep. What fool would put up with that for long?

No one knows how it happened, but one day Sako became the powerful publican of Lake Ayghr. In no time he had won the sympathy of all the inhabitants of government house and its visitors, and his respectability especially increased when everybody heard that he had become the apple of the governor's eye. In consequence Sako became the advisor of the village's valued guests, the support of the landlords, the intimate friend of the district official in charge of water distribution, the crony of the police officers, and even the darling of the assistants. Sako's name was well known throughout the region. All the peasants considered it a duty to give Sako part of their choicest produce whenever they visited the governor. If the peasants did not have anything in stock, they bought something, not wanting to cross Sako's threshold empty-handed.

Not only was Sako respected in this cheerful village and by the brigands who lived in caves and valleys, terrorizing the entire land, but he was a personality they revered. How could one not love Sako? Who else could have his gentle disposition and his wily tongue? Just pay a visit to his tavern, and you too will be convinced!

"Hello there, my dear Sako!"

"Oh, hello, hello; come: welcome a thousand times. Let me be your footstool; treat my place as your own."

Good reader, never think that Sako speaks like this to notables only. Even the worthless may treat Sako's place as their own.

"Quick, boy, quick:" Sako orders his servant, "Take care of Karo Agha's horse, give it lots of hay, loosen its saddle, and bring in what it's carrying.

"Come in, Agha Karo. You've traveled a long way: you must be tired. Come, wet your throat a little, then go to your room to rest for a while. What would you like: wine or *oghi?*"[5]

"Sako Jan (my dear Sako), don't go to any trouble."

5. Ouzo (Greek), Arrack (Arabic).

"My God, what a disgrace! None of that. There's no place for such talk between friends. The entire establishment is at your service! Even were you to drink it dry, no one would dare to say anything, if he's a man."

"Sako Jan, I've brought you a few trinkets. I hope you won't be offended: you deserve much more."

"Why put yourself to the trouble, Karo Jan? I beg you to make this the last; otherwise, you know, we'll fall out," Sako says, taking the bag from his hand and giving it to the servant to empty. And of course this is neither the first nor the last gift that Karo brings to Sako.

Two days later, Karo finishes his business and is ready to leave.

"Sako Jan, I must leave."

"May God speed you on your way, Karo Jan."

"Sako Jan, how much do I owe you?"

"Just remain in good health."

"No, tell me: how much did I spend?"

"Shame, shame! no such questions between us. What are a couple of *manets*?⁶ Not worth mentioning. You came home, enjoyed it, and now you are leaving."

Our Karo's face turns as white as the wall. He thinks it should hardly amount to two *spasis*,⁷ and the word *manet* resounds in his ears.

"No, Sako Jan. I don't like such things—An account should be paid *dinar* for *dinar, bakshish* is *tuman* for *tuman*.⁸ You don't get things for nothing. You pay for them. You too work hard to earn a few pennies. We're brothers, so tell me exactly how much I owe you."

After a few more arguments, Sako pronounces the verdict: "Three and a half *manets*."

Karo gulps, thrusts his hand into his pocket, and loosens the drawstring of his cotton purse. Before coming to Sev Jur, he had borrowed ten *manets* for an unimportant job; now he has only two *manets* left, which he gives to Sako, and promises to send the rest with the first traveler as soon as he gets home.

---

6. Rubles.

7. Persian monetary unit much smaller than a ruble.

8. The dinar and the tuman are monetary units used in the Middle East. The expression means accounts should be tallied accurately, whereas tips depend on a person's generosity.

"Don't trouble yourself. Really, don't bother about it: it doesn't matter—or send it when you have it. I know it's a sure thing," Sako assures him and bids him godspeed. He knows full well that not only the muleteer but even the landlord would not dare to cheat him, not even of a *kopek;* after all, he has already received four or five times what was due him. Furthermore, and in a round-about way, the greater part of the ten *manets* has already made its way into his pocket. Whatever the man has spent has also passed through his fingers.

I do not know whether Sako's predecessors had the same rep-utation and wisdom. Probably not. I think this was Sako's unique genius, and that is what made him so popular. Not everybody can manage such things. Who but Sako, before whom the gover-nor's door would open wide, was capable of conducting business so soundly? Just watch him on one of his visits to the governor.

Night falls and clients peter out; everyone retires to his room. Sako turns over the tavern to his helper and sets out for the gov-ernor's mansion. He does not take the usual direct route; he walks along the wall, poking around here and there, until he ends up in the governor's antechamber. He does not need to signal his intention to visit ahead of time. The guard does not have the right to stop him. Once Sako enters, he leaves the antechamber and inspects the door to make sure that no stranger will interrupt the visit. It is enough that the governor is at home. If the door is locked from inside, Sako knocks on it in a special way. At once the door opens before him. Sako is authorized to go straight into the governor's bedroom and wake him up, which indicates that they have immediate business to discuss.

"Who's there?" the governor shouts to the guard. And again he gives strict orders not to be disturbed by anyone.

Sako enters. He stands in the doorway, brings his hand to his chest, and bows his head. He does not raise his head until the governor asks, "Well, what do you want?"

"Your health!"

"Come on, out with it."

Suppose, my dear reader, that you and I, wearing out magi-cian's hats, have the power to become invisible and listen, standing quietly in a corner. Hush!

Sako does not answer right away.

"Ha!" the governor raises his voice. "Why do you purse your

lips like that? You don't have to pay to speak. Speak! Tell me what's going on."

"Ah, ah, ah . . . nothing. Nothing important, really. I came to see how you are."

"I know you don't give a damn about my health: tell me what's on your mind. Are there lawyers involved?'

"Right on, my Agha!"

"How many? What do they want? Are they fat or skinny?"

"There are three brothers. The problem seems simple, but there's a lot more to it than that. They want to split up, but they can't agree. The eldest brother wants the greatest part of the inheritance. The younger ones refuse. They are here now, to ask you to divide it."

"Why didn't the village elder settle the problem?"

"Didn't I tell you that I was going to order on your behalf that the village elders not dare to handle such matters?"

"As far as I remember, I haven't given you any such right."

"Well, Agha, you take too much on yourself. Is it necessary for you to concern yourself with such trivialities? We're also people: we don't graze in the fields. We understand, and we try to spare you headaches. I've acted on your behalf."

"Didn't you put the order in writing?"

"Am I crazy or what? I told one of them when he was here, and the others I informed through the police."

"Careful, Sako: don't get us into trouble."

"Let the trouble trouble me. If it ever harms you, is there anybody in these parts who knows anything or can do anything about it? They're nothing but a bunch of sheep. Hereabouts your word carries more weight than the king's. You're our lord, our judge, the one who decides whether we live or die. You have the paper and the pen in your hand; you can do whatever you fancy; as they say, whatever you have written is written. Who stays your hand? You can destroy a person by sentencing him to the stocks or exiling him."

"Well, my lad, you're too confident of yourself. If they ever hear of this in Yerevan, can you imagine what they will do? They'll have our lives!"

"Well, Agha, I know that they can't touch a single hair on your head. If they find anyone more benevolent, let them replace you. What do they want, these gluttons? They always want more. On the road to Yerevan, where the police have lined up like a caravan of ants, these people carry off their booty: leather bottles filled wine and *oghi* of Ashtarak, wheat as bright as the Yeghivard sun and butter like the pure amber of Abaran, bolls of pure cotton from Haytagh, choice rice from Molla Dursun, pressed olive oil like the honey of Alibegli, onion heads as red as the apples of Gharkh, and our own onions fill every nook and cranny of the houses of the *shinoviks*[9] in Yerevan. What the hell more do they want? Sweet tea, which the people haven't even tasted, flows from our street (Sako rubs his thumb and index finger together to make him understand that he is referring to bribe money), and this too, which you take from them at the beginning of the week you share with others at the end of the week. If I were my own god and I were in their place, I would simply shut my eyes."

"That's true. You're here for business, Sako; come! let's have a look."

"What more is there to say? I've settled their dispute. The eldest brother is putting his inheritance in your hands; if you encourage the younger ones and force them to acknowledge the respectability of the oldest one, the younger ones will also put their shares of the inheritance in your hands, and may even give you extra for shutting the mouth of their elder brother."

"I don't need their land and fields. You mentioned money."

"Money is all right, but there will be no land; you don't have a plow to yoke your oxen to in order to till the land. It is said that if you don't have a donkey to offer as sacrifice, you can offer its value in money. And so we can turn this dispute into cash."

"He who pays most can have most say in the outcome."

"Of course."

"What should we do now?"

"Very simple. When they come to see you, reproach all three of them for bothering you with every trivial matter. Then order them to be jailed. They stay there for two days, then I intervene and you announce your decision: you oblige the eldest not to deprive the two younger ones; you advise the younger brothers to uphold the honor of the eldest. Then you call me and ask me to reconcile them as I see fit. Naturally, not before the bribe has been paid."

---

9. Russian civil servants.

Mkrtich Achemian (Adjemian)

(1838–1917)

Mkrtich Achemian was born in Ortagiugh (Ortaköy), a suburb of Constantinople, and received his early education in the local Armenian school. He then attended the Murat-Raphaelian school in Venice (1852–58), where he developed his literary talent under Ghevond Alishan. He returned to Constantinople and began working for the State Telegraph Administration, where he stayed for most of his remaining life.

His poems were published in various newspapers and periodicals and eventually collected into three books: *Zhbitk yev artasuk* (Smiles and tears, 1871), *Luys yev stverk* (Light and Shadow, 1887), and *Garnan hover* (Winds of spring, 1892). In 1908 he published these three books as one volume, adding other poems that had been scattered in the periodical press. He also published a collection of translated poems by foreign authors, *Zanazan targmanutiunk* (Diverse translations).

His poems are written in refined modern Armenian; they are delicate and rich in rhymes that impart a certain musicality. He was a poet of the romantic school but retained traces of classicism. He was a renowned poet in his own time, but he seemed unable or unwilling to refresh his poetry with the blowing winds of realism and remained attached to his own genre and style, which, after the 1880s, gradually began to lose favor.

THE MISGUIDED[1]

She was a comely woman, and her eyes were jet:
now and then they sparkled with devoted love, and yet
at other times they spurted lightning flame.
On her milky brow of virgin innocence
roses blossomed from delightful smiles,
as though from noble race they came.
Her walk was stately and her stature splendid,
she had the grace of an eternal bride
and a voice so harmonious and bewitching
it yoked an entire army of paramours
to her opulent carriage and carried them away.
Silk, diamonds, flowers, gems, and gold
she collected like sand from the sea,
which later she strewed by handfuls in the air.
Sitting at table, those debauchees
clinked thousands of wine glasses
and roared love songs, while
Bacchus and Astghik[2] together danced.
There, the sight of her alluring smile
inflamed the blood of drunken guests;
her voluptuous kisses, had for a price,
her lascivious dances, her deceptive touch
laid waste, took spoils and prey,
devouring fortunes, but never satisfied.
She wrenches hearts to shreds but feels no blame:
to crush a soul for her a guiltless game,
and her great joy to tear and pull apart
with rosy fingers young and older heart,
as if to take revenge for ancient wrongs,
to suck their blood with tender lips,
drop by drop . . . and I, a witness
to her triumph, asked in wonder

---

1. Mkrtich Achemian, "*Moloryale*" (The misguided), in *Trtrun hanger* (Thrilling rhymes) (Constantinople, 1908), 17–19. Translated by the editors of the present anthology.
2. Armenian goddess of love, beauty, and fertility.

why cankers gnawed the lily, why from under
the tender bosom of this comely maid
hard-hearted, somber passions burst
and why her beauty was for her a curse?

In the holy chapel, draped in black,
she piously lit candles and drew back
into a corner. She there did kneel
and tried to pray with humble zeal,
her brow against the stone, her heart
swollen with long and painful memories.
She was once a girl with no experience;
when she, surrounded with the scent of innocence
stooped to pick a flower near the pit,
there was no friendly hand to check her fall,
but everything conspired to hasten it.

When with the joy of her first love she shone,
those round her mocked—and the magic was gone;
they seized her throbbing heart while still afire,
and dried up every trace of pure desire.
And, crushed by grief, bowed down by shame,
discouraged, she brought dishonor to her name.
Her silky bed is now a coffin
where, unperturbed, her dead soul rests.
She is a walking corpse wrapped in a golden shroud,
and is called the Wayward Mistress.
Her brow resting against the stone,
suffering weakly from unnumbered woes,
she did not have the strength to drink
that sad and bitter cup, to empty it.
Her hand too weak to cover her head
with her veil, woven of curses,
her brow resting against the stone,
begging pardon, she sobbed pitifully.
When she rose to her feet and shook
her pretty head, she scattered the glittering drops
that slowly flowed down her pale face.
At last she kissed the cross and
moved away with wavering pace.

Go, unhappy woman, to the sea, go
to drown in its deep waves your woe;
or go, disguised and wounded in your soul,
and bury it forever in some dark nunnery. . . .
But alas! A mortal child, it was her lot
to find no way to excise the dark blot
from off her brow, and she became a prey
of her mournful destiny to her last day.
A fiery falling star in the darkness of the night
from time to time streaks heaven with radiant light.
The scorching draft denudes the rose of petals,
leaving of beauty but inconsequential waste.
(29 July 1892.)

Grigor Chilinkirian (Chilingirian)

(1839–1923)

Grigor Chilinkirian was a prolific translator, who rendered great service in the 1860s and '70s by introducing the French novelists to the Armenian reading public. Born in Smyrna, he attended the local Mesropian school and worked at various jobs to help his father, who was a blacksmith. Keen for education and with a passion for literature, he taught himself Turkish, Greek, French, and Italian. His first translations, made in his early youth, were from Greek to Armenian and from French to Turkish. In 1861 he and Armenak Haykuni, another enthusiast of literature, founded a biweekly periodical, *Tzaghik* (Flower, 1861–67), which had a liberal orientation and provided a forum (especially later, when Matteos Mamurian [1830–1901] became coeditor) for progressive ideas, as represented mainly by European authors. For a while he was engaged as a teacher at the Mesropian School, but because of his public criticism of certain practices, this association terminated in 1865.

Grigor Chilinkirian is the foremost of the writers who dedicated much time and effort to translating popular works of European, mostly French, authors. The movement, which flourished between 1850 and 1880, aimed at giving the people access to reading material in their own language (i.e., modern Armenian) that would interest them and develop their taste for literature. Translations would also help refine and embellish modern Armenian and increase its vocabulary. Many others contributed to this movement, such as Matteos Mamurian, Mesrop Nuparian (1842–1929), and Karapet Iutiuchian (Ütüdjian, 1823–1904). The list of Grigor Chilinkirian's translations into Armenian is impressive: *Les misérables* (Victor Hugo), *Raphaël* (Lamartine), *Manon Lescaut* (Abbé Prévost), *La confession d'un enfant du siècle* (Alfred de Musset), *Mathilde* (Eugène Sue), *Mademoiselle de la Quintinie* (George Sand), *Monsieur de Camors* (Octave Feuillet), and works of other writers. His many articles, scattered in various periodicals, deal with social and political issues. He defended the principles of social democracy, analyzed various aspects of the National Constitution, openly discussed serious issues related to education, schools, theater, and the status of women, and cautioned the "leaders" of the community on the dangers that lurked behind Sultan Hamid's policies.

Although he spent most of his time in Smyrna, he kept up a lively correspondence with colleagues in Constantinople and visited them frequently. His letters and impressions are compiled in a volume entitled *Ughevorutiun i Kostandnupolis* (Travels to Constantinople, 1883), which is still of interest. He was an eyewitness to the great tragedy of Smyrna, brought about by the Turkish National Army in 1922.

FROM JOURNEY TO CONSTANTINOPLE: WOMAN IN THE NINETEENTH CENTURY[1]

Among us Armenians, the education of the female sex began only a short while ago, yet the Armenian Woman—and I am referring principally to a class of Armenian Women from Constantinople, Smyrna and Tiflis—owing to a smidgen of enlightenment, sees a pagan divinity about her person and demands the right to love of her own free will instead of being obliged to be loved, or to devote herself legally, as she sees fit, instead of pursuing material well-being. In addition, she notices the indifference resulting from the peculiar will or ignorance of men as regards mitigating and gradually eliminating the repressive customs that have become stacked up against her down through the centuries, so she proposes to

---

1. Grigor Chilinkirian, *"Kinn tasnevinnerord darun mej"* (The woman in the nineteenth century), in *Chashak ardi Hay matenagrutyan* (Taste in modern Armenian literature) (Constantinople, 1888), 355–59. Translated by Aris Sevag.

mitigate and eliminate them herself. She wishes to *think, feel* and *act* freely, namely *live,* in order to succeed, to become an active power by ceasing to be a passive force, to be distinguished from the animal and to rise to the level of an assuredly rational being.

From the right to live arises the triple necessity of constituting a mind, a heart and a social personality.

As a mind, she looks at the current educational laws and institutions and is dissatisfied.

As a heart, she focuses her attention on the prejudices and superstitions which stand in the way of the development of all her natural and noble feelings, and she lets out a cry of indignation.

As a social personality, she tosses an inquisitive glance at the legal restrictions and limitations violating her material and moral interests and crowding the arena of her activity, and says, "I too am a citizen."

Sociologists assert that every human society obeys the law of evolution and that, by necessity, the improvement being produced by the influence of heredity and custom, namely progress, is irresistible in all human groups. However, the woman wishes to function for herself, as if finding a proof against the belated effects of that law, in her centuries-old state of slavery and ignorance, and regretting and feeling sorry for having left the matter of improving her development, i.e., her intellectual, emotional and moral qualities, up till now solely to that law, that social providence.

I wonder, why hadn't she wanted to until now? Because, in order to want, the will is obligated to move at the direction of the mind, and because this movement always corresponds to the class of ideas.

When you see archaic institutions, laws and all kinds of ugliness in a society having been continued undisturbed for centuries, be assured that there is a relative harmony in the ideas generally accepted by them and the members of that society. When this harmony is disrupted owing to a change in ideas, when disagreement prevails in the will that moves according to social realities and the physical and mental laws of man, the transformation begins secretly and silently at first, then in an obvious and irresistible manner, by legal or illegal means in legislative assemblies or *elsewhere,* and does not really end until the harmony is reestablished, until those social realities and life's affairs, in turn, do not consent to change and sufficiently fall in line with the change undergone by ideas and feelings. If the fighting continues, if the realities do not cease resisting mental renewal, the very essence of society becomes at risk, and thus Herbert Spencer is perfectly correct when he says in his famous work, *Introduction to Social Science,* that "there must be sufficient harmony in required institutions and generally accepted ideas in order for a society to be able to survive."

Now it is quite natural to conclude that these institutions, the injustices of civil and political affairs having taken root, always persist if the feeling producing the ability to notice and examine them and become indignant over them, the feeling of moving the human will and having it act, and the ideas inspiring willingness, are not widespread and generalized.

I repeat that, by progress, I understand the gradual improve- ment of these institutions, the gradual disappearance of these in- justices and all the obstacles to human welfare, and this disappear- ance is impossible if man doesn't have the awareness of these, an awareness which is likewise impossible without mental awakening. It follows from this, that the starting point of all human progress is the cultivation of the mind and heart equally, the flourishing of the abilities to think and feel.

The nineteenth-century woman seeks her salvation in this cul- tivation and flourishing. And, in order to be saved, she demands that she too participate in the work of drafting the law and plan of her education and upbringing, so that this law and plan may conform to the natural conditions of her sex and the new demands of her social personality, so that a radical transformation of mind and heart, a way of thinking and feeling, may begin for her too, whereby it will prosper more and more, without totally ceasing to accommodate the conditions of her present progressive state and environment, and so that all intellectual, esthetic and moral aptitudes of man and woman may improve. As we already said, sociologists attribute this improvement to the law of evolution; I, in turn, in my weak judgment, dare to profess it to be principally the result of mental development. I say so, because the idea of im- provements has first been conceived in the mind and then realized in societies, starting with the appearance of the human race on this earth and continuing until now, and because the civilization representing the totality of these improvements is neither totally the *result of procreation,* nor a divine gift having suddenly arrived; rather, it is the fruit of centuries of efforts, ideas conceived and revealed in the mind, struggles and sacrifices. And, finally, it is because, without will and force, neither can the mind be cultivated nor can it understand the lessons and examples offered by scenes from the animal and physical worlds.

The woman, who wishes to advance through education and be equal to man in a different way and with a different status, has seen only one arena in front of her up until now, and that is the family, where, however, she always encounters the infringements of men, yet she sees the realms of not only family but also professions and other situations open to men. Thus, she bitterly complains about the injustices leaving her out of these two realms, as well as the infringements seen in her personal realm.

However, I don't wish to infer from these reflections of mine that all progressive ideas and feelings received concerning the families of the women of enlightened nations, and professions, can be fully accepted as of now among their women and ours alike, become generalized, firmly established and realized, especially among the Armenian women, because the state of the Armenian nation, as well as the environment in which it exists, has an entirely different dimension. "There is a manner of thinking and feeling suited to every single society, and every single manifestation of its evolution, and *any manner of thinking and feeling, if it does not conform to the degree of evolution and the conditions of the evolution,* cannot become permanently established," says Spencer.

However, there are certain indispensable ideas and feelings about family and work; the wish for their realization is not inopportune and premature for the women as of now, if we consider the degree of evolution which they have arrived at and the environmental conditions in which they find themselves, and so the European woman protests against the *old repressions* in opposition to the accomplishments of the past and present.

She protests against the laws and customs of prehistoric, Roman, Hellenistic, barbaric and feudal periods.

She protests against the Athenian law, which, for a while, considered the woman a possession, an object, and designated her to the heir, along with bequeathed items.

She protests against the Roman law, on whose strength a father would marry off his daughter to whomever he wished, and break up that marriage whenever he wished, to give her to another, without obtaining her agreement and approval.

She protests against the feudal law, according to which a girl could not get married without the approval of her father, master and king, and which gave the ruler of the land the scandalous right of tithe on her beauty.

She protests against Moses, who denied the woman's soul, saying, "A woman is not obliged to stick to her oath if she takes an oath."

She protests against a Synod, which asked of itself in the Middle Ages if woman really has a soul.

She protests against the eighteenth century and the authors, philosophers and legislators glorifying it; "against Diderot,[2] for whom the woman is a prostitute; against Montesquieu,[3] for whom the woman is merely a pleasant creature to be caressed; against Rousseau,[4] who considers woman suitable for acts of pleasure; against Voltaire, for whom a woman is zero," and after this rightful protest, she knowingly issues a calm and symbolical verdict: "No, I too have a soul."

Some of the Armenian women of Constantinople seemingly perceive the natural fairness of this major verdict; like the progressive women of Europe, they too wish to protest against the prejudices and injustices having piled up against their person, mind and soul ever since ancient times, in a narrow confine, in a practical manner and with a view toward the conditions of their present state and environment; and to partially at least effect a verdict surely and calmly, which the spirit of enlightenment has won for the female sex after struggles lasting for centuries, they have proposed to get directly involved with the task of women's education and instruction, succeeding in forming two societies, one of which is the *Patriotic Armenian Women,* the other *School Ladies.*

---

2. Denis Diderot (1713–84), French philosopher and encyclopedist.

3. Charles Louis de Secondat Montesquieu (1689–1755), French jurist and philosophical writer on history and government.

4. Jean Jacques Rousseau (1712–78), French philosopher, writer, and social theorist.

Garegin Srvandztiants

(1840–92)

Garegin Srvandztiants, priest, poet, traveler, and ethnographer, was born in Van. Dissatisfied with his early schooling, he ran away to the monastery of Varag and was admitted to the seminary, where, under the tutelage and inspiring influence of Mkrtich Khrimian (1820–1907), he received an excellent education and developed his talents, particularly a strong penchant for literature. At twenty he was already helping Khrimian edit the review *Artzvi Vaspurakan* (The eagle of Vaspurakan). In 1862 he was entrusted with the position of principal-teacher of the school attached to the St. Karapet monastery in Mush, and he assumed the editorship of the institution's journal, *Artzvik Tarono* (The eaglet of Taron), at the same time contributing to *Masis* in Constantinople, *Meghu* (Bee) and *Krunk* (Crane) in Tiflis, and *Arevelyan mamul* (Eastern press) in Smyrna (Izmir).

In 1860–61, in company with Khrimian, he toured the provinces of Eastern Armenia and meticulously described in his notes and letters the grim living conditions of the people. He also collected dialectal expressions, customs, and oral traditions, which he later published periodically. In 1864 Srvandztiants was ordained a celibate priest in Karin (Erzurum). In 1866 he worked as a priest in Constantinople, actively participating in community affairs. From 1867 to 1869 he served as supervisor of Armenian schools in Karin, and in 1869 he was appointed rector of St. Karapet monastery in Mush and also put in charge of implementing the Armenian Constitution in the province of Vaspurakan. In 1879, soon after the Russo-Ottoman war, he was commissioned by Patriarch Nerses Varzhapetian to tour all the Armenian provinces and districts to collect ethnographic, statistical, and historical information about population, churches, schools, convents, customs, dialects, and songs, and to make excerpts of manuscripts and colophons: an extensive project indeed, which produced a tremendous amount of material. He also traced and recorded a number of folk tales and epic stories that had been transmitted from generation to generation; by so doing he saved them from perdition: an extremely valuable service for ethnic studies.

In 1886 Srvandztiants was consecrated bishop in Etchmiadzin and was appointed Primate of Trebizond (Trabzon); he later became Primate of Mush and Abbot of St. Karapet monastery. His nationalistic activities brought him under the suspicion of the sultan's government, and he was sent to Constantinople, where he could be monitored more closely. There he was assigned to Holy Trinity Church in Péra,[1] taught at the Kedronakan Lycée, and was elected chairman of the Religious Council. For his ethnographic and archaeological studies he was made an honorary member of the Imperial Academy of St. Petersburg. He died in Constantinople, after a lengthy illness.

His literary career began with two plays, *Metzn Sahak Partev yev ankumn Artashri Arshakunvo* (Sahak Partev the Great and the fall of Artashir Arshakuni) and *Shushan Shavarshana* (Shushan of Shavarshan), the subject of which is related to the battle of Vardanants. He is best known for his major contribution to ethnographic studies and for the ancient oral literature that he saved from perdition: if this work had been postponed for forty years or so, all traces of the age-old epic tales, customs, and traditions unique to the Armenian people would have been lost forever in the genocide of 1915.

One of his well known works, *Grots-brots* (1874, roughly translated as Bookworm), is a compilation of ancient Armenian traditions and tales from various provinces. One section of the book contains a variant of the epic tale known as *Mheri dure* (The gate of Mher) or *Sasuntsi Davit* (David of Sasun), which Srvandztiants brought to light for the first time. He heard it from a peasant named Krpo, from the village of Arnist in Mush. As he says, "it took him three days to tell the story, in his own dialect, and I took down everything he said, word for word."[2]

---

1. At the time a residential and commercial area in Constantinople.
2. For the full text of this epic tale, with an introduction, see volume 2 of the present anthology.

Another book, *Hnots-norots* (Of old and new, 1874), written in classical Armenian, contains material about two ancient luminaries, Movses Khorenatsi (historian, fifth century) and Davit Anhaght (philosopher, fifth–sixth century), and other valuable philological material. *Manana* (Manna, 1876) contains ethnic songs, songs for social occasions, poems, folk tales, proverbs, riddles, and a dialect dictionary. One section is dedicated to the city of Van; it contains a description of the city as well as samples of and commentary on popular legends written in the Van dialect. A later publication is *Hamov, hotov* (With taste and aroma, 1884), which comprises his impressions and observations as he traveled widely through Armenia. It also contains the epic love story of Siamanto and Khajé Zaré, a Kurdish boy and an Armenian girl. This love story was later turned into a beautiful poem by Hovhannes Shiraz that was published in Yerevan in 1955. Srvandztiants's last work is *Toros Aghbar* (Brother Toros, a popular name for a sea bird) in two volumes (1879, 1884), entirely devoted to his extensive travels in Armenia. It is not a travelogue but a collection of poetic reflections.

Until the 1860s, even though the intellectual revival was progressing in Constantinople, there was still a strong barrier between the provinces and the capital, mostly caused by lack of communication and, to a certain degree, by the snobbishness of the city elite. They simply did not know what was going on in the Armenian provinces. Mkrtich Khrimian and Garegin Srvandztiants broke this barrier and tried to build a bridge between provinces and capital. The interest they aroused eventually resulted in the founding in Constantinople of numerous benevolent societies, especially in the 1880s, to look after the educational and social needs of the provinces.

LAMENT OVER THE HEROES FALLEN IN THE BATTLE OF AVARAYR[3]

If Goghtan's[4] bards no longer crown
Armenia's heroes with their lays,

---

3. Garegin Srvandztian, "Lament over the Heroes Fallen in the Battle of Avarayr," in *Armenian Legends and Poems*, compiled and trans. Zabelle C. Boyajian (London, 1916), 25–26. Reference is to the Battle of Avarayr (451), waged in defense of Christianity against Mazdaist Persia.

4. The famous troubadours of the district of Goghtn (the modern Julfa and Agulis).

Let deathless souls from Heaven come down,
Our valiant ones to praise!

Ye shining angel hosts, descend:
    On Ararat's white summit pause;
Let God Himself the heavens rend,
    To come and judge our cause.

Fly, clouds, from Shavarshan[5] away,
    Pour not on it your gentle rain:
'Tis drenched with streams of blood today
    Shed by our brave ones slain.

Henceforth the rose and asphodel
    No more shall on our plains appear;
But in the land where Vardan[6] fell
    Shall Faith her blossoms rear.

Fit monument to Vardan's name,
    Mount Ararat soars to the sky.
And Cross-crowned convents tell his fame,
    And churches vast and high.

Armenian Legends and Poems,
    Thy record too shall ever stand,
O Yeghishé,[7] for where they fell,
    Thou forthwith camest, pen in hand,
    Their faith and death to tell.

Bright sun, pierce with thy rays the gloom,
    Where Khaghtik's[8] crags thy light repel,
There lies our brave Hmayak's[9] tomb,
    There, where he martyred fell.

---

5. The ancient name of the province of Artaz.

6. Vardan Mamikonian, general, and the hero of the Battle of Avarayr. See volume 1 of the present anthology.

7. A fifth-century Armenian historian. He is the author of *History of Vardan and the Armenian War*.

8. The land of the Kaght people on the Black Sea—the district of Lazistan in present-day Turkey.

9. One of the Mamikonian brothers.

And, moon, thy sleepless vigil keep
    O'er our Armenian martyrs' bones;
With the soft dews of Maytime steep
    Their nameless funeral stones.

Armenia's Stork, our summer guest,
    And all ye hawks and eagles, come,
Watch o'er this land—'tis our bequest—
    We leave to you our home.

About the ashes hover still,
    Your nests among the ruins make;
And, swallows, come and go until
    Spring for Armenia break!

Smbat Shahaziz

(1840–1907)

The educator, poet, and publicist Smbat Shahaziz was born in Ashtarak, Eastern Armenia, the youngest of six brothers. After being taught until he was ten by his father, a priest, he was sent to the Lazarian College in Moscow, and upon his graduation in 1862 he was asked to teach modern and classical Armenian at the primary school level. In the meantime he prepared himself for a university degree, and in 1867 he was granted a degree in oriental languages by the University of St. Petersburg. This qualified him to teach Armenian language and literature at the college level. He obtained a position at his alma mater, the Lazarian College, and retained it for thirty-five years, until his retirement in 1897.

He started writing in his student days and was greatly influenced by Rafayel Patkanian (1830–1920) and Khachatur Abovian (1809–48). He contributed to the journal *Hiusisapayl* (Northern lights, 1858–64), which was founded and was edited by Stepanos Nazarian (1812–79), and gathered around it a group of intellectuals who promoted national enlightenment and education. Shahaziz's articles and essays aroused public interest, and he remained a contributor until the journal's demise.

In 1860 he published his first collection of poems, *Azatutyan zhamer* (Hours of freedom), which consists of thirty-three poems, most in modern Armenian but with a few in classical Armenian. The poems have such themes as love, nature, and the praise of national heroes. His second book appeared in 1865, under the title *Levoni vishte* (Levon's grief), an extended poem imbued with ardent patriotism. Levon is a serious minded, idealistic Armenian youth studying in the far north. He is deeply concerned about and grieved by the dire conditions of his homeland, whereas his frivolous companions carry on a prodigal life, even denying their Armenian identities. Struck with loneliness and grief for his country, he decides to return home and contribute to the struggle against ignorance, servility, moral and religious decline, and corrupt leadership in all domains. This poem, which obviously reflects the reformist ideology emerging in Russia at the time, was very well received. Certain critics assume that Shahaziz was influenced by Byron's *Childe Harold's Pilgrimage* (published 1812–18), for they discern a parallel between Childe Harold's disillusionment and grief and Levon's. Yet as the writer Leo puts it, "Levon's grief and that of Harold both emanate from the same source: a pure and noble heart; however, Levon's grief has a distinctly national character; it is the grief of an Armenian."[1]

Articles, essays, and speeches about the important national and social issues of the times occupy a considerable part of Shahaziz's literary output. He encouraged the use of modern Armenian, criticized archaic methods of education and the conservatism of religious leaders, and denounced despotism and the hypocritical attitude of the European powers with regard to the Armenian question. In 1893 he founded the Abovian-Nazarian Fund for the benefit of needy writers. After his retirement in 1898, he created a committee in Moscow to organize the care and education of children orphaned by the massacres perpetrated by Sultan Hamid in Eastern Armenia. He exposed the anti-Armenian stance of the czarist regime in *Hishogutiunner Vardanants toni artiv* (Recollections from the Feast of Vardanank, 1901) and the duplicity of Turkish diplomacy in *Mi kani khosk im entertsoghnerin* (A few words to my readers, 1903).

These works of Shahaziz served contemporary purposes; today, however, they have lost their relevance, except as historical documents. His best work is the epic poem *Levoni vishte* (Levon's grief), in which is enshrined a delicate verse entitled "*Yeraz*" (Dream), dedicated to his mother, whose tender care and love he enjoyed as the youngest of six brothers. The poem begins with the words "*Yes lsetsi mi anush dzayn . . .*" (I heard a sweet voice . . .); it has been set to music and is still sung in many homes.

---

1. Quoted in Mushegh Ishkhan, *Ardi Hay grakanutiun* (Modern Armenian literature), volume 2 (Beirut, n.d.), 273.

DREAM[2]

Soft and low a voice breathed o'er me,
    Near me did my mother seem;
Flashed a ray of joy before me,
    But, alas, it was a dream!

There the murmuring streamlet flowing
    Scattered radiant pearls around,
Pure and clear, like crystal glowing—
    But it was a dream, unsound.

And my mother's mournful singing
    Took me back to childhood's day,
To my mind her kisses bringing—
    'Twas a dream and passed away!

To her heart she pressed me yearning,
    Wiped her eyes which wet did seem;
And her tears fell on me burning—
    Why should it have been a dream?

---

2. *Smbat Shaaziz,* "Dream," in *Armenian Legends and Poems,* comp. and trans. Zabelle C. Boyajian (London, 1916), 46.

Tovmas Terzian

(1840–1909)

Tovmas Terzian, poet and playwright, was born in Constantinople to a Greek-speaking Armenian father and an Italian mother. After attending the local Mkhitarist elementary school, he was sent to the Murat-Raphaelian school in Venice, from which he graduated in 1858. Both on his own and at school he mastered a number of foreign languages: Italian, Greek, French, Turkish, classical Greek, Latin, and English. On returning home he dedicated himself to teaching. He taught successively at the Nersesian and Nupar-Shahnazarian schools—both in Khasgiugh (Hasköy), a suburb of Constantinople—and later at the Kedronakan lycée. Among his students were Reteos Perberian (Berperian, 1848–1907), Minas Cheraz (1852–1929), Yeghia Temirchipasian (Demirdjibashian, 1851–1908), Grigor Zohrap (1861–1915), Yerukhan (1870–1915), and others who became prominent educators and writers.

Terzian is chiefly known for his plays and poetry. In theater he followed the pattern set by Mkrtich Peshiktashlian (Beshiktashlian, 1828–68), but he excelled him in both style and artistic expression, principally because he wrote under the influence of classical Greek literature. His first play, *Sandukht* (a proper name), written in 1862 and staged several times, is a tragedy based on a historical topic. This was followed by *Hovsep geghetsik* (Joseph the fair, 1872), based on the Biblical story, dealing with the conflict between good and evil; a tragedy entitled *Hripsimé* (1868); and others. These works do not have much appeal today, but at the time they served two great purposes: refining modern literary Armenian and arousing patriotic sentiments.

His most important achievement was the libretto of the first Armenian opera, *Arshak II* (1871), composed by Tigran Chukhachian (Chukhadjian, 1837–98), which was based on the life of the notorious fourth-century Armenian king. Terzian wrote the libretto in 1868, in both Armenian and Italian, and the opera was printed in 1871. Unfortunately, neither the author of the libretto nor the composer ever saw the opera mounted on stage: it premiered at the Spentiarian theater of opera and ballet in Yerevan in 1941.

Terzian's poems are expressions of personal moods, such as sadness, yearning, and affection. Each poem is a literary gem in its perfection of language and esthetic beauty, however lacking in passion, deep emotions, and turbulence. His collected poems, in two volumes, with an introduction and notes by Arshak Chopanian (Arshag Tchobanian), were published posthumously in Venice, in 1929.

THE CHRAGHAN PALACE[1]

Have you ever seen that wondrous building,
    Whose white shadows in the blue wave sleep?
Carrara sent vast mounds of marble,
    And Propontic,[2] beauty of the deep.

From the tombs of centuries awaking,
    Souls of every clime and every land
Have poured forth their rarest gifts arid treasures
    Where those shining balls in glory stand.

Ships that pass before that stately palace,
    Gliding by with open sails agleam,
In its shadow pause and gaze, astonished,
    Thinking it some Oriental dream.

---

1. Tovmas Terzian, "The Chraghan Palace," in *Armenian Poems Rendered into English Verse*, ed. and trans. Elizabeth Stone Blackwell (Boston, 1917, and a facsimile reproduction of the 1917 edition, New York, 1978), 128–29.
2. The ancient name of the Sea of Marmara.

New its form, more wondrous than the Gothic,
    Than the Doric or Ionic fair;
At command of an Armenian genius[3]
    Did the master builder rear it there.

By the windows, rich with twisted scrollwork,
    Rising upward, marble columns shine,
And the sunbeams lose their way there, wandering
    Where a myriad ornaments entwine.

An immortal smile, its bright reflection
    In the water of the blue sea lies,
And it shames Granada's famed Alhambra,
    O'er whose beauty wondering bend the skies.

Oft at midnight, in the pale, faint starlight,
    When its airy outline, clear and fair,
On the far horizon is depicted,
    With its trees and groves around it there,

You can fancy that those stones grow living,
    And, amid the darkness of the night,
Change to lovely songs, to which the spirit,
    Dreaming, listens with a vague delight.

Have you ever seen that wondrous building
    Whose white shadows in the blue wave sleep?
There Marmora sent vast mounds of marble,
    And Propontic, beauty of the deep.

It is not a mass of earthly matter,
    Not a work from clay or marble wrought;
From the mind of an Armenian genius
    Stands embodied there a noble thought.

---

3. Reference is to Karapet Amira Balian, the architect (1800–66).

Ghazaros Aghayan

(1840–1911)

Ghazaros Aghayan received his early education in the Armenian village of Bolnis-Khachen, Georgia, where he was born. At the age of thirteen he was sent to the Nersisian school in Tiflis but left after one year because of his family's financial situation. Unable to stand his father's despotic treatment, he left home to fend for himself. From 1861 on he traveled between Tiflis, Moscow, and St. Petersburg, working as a compositor—an occupation that brought him into contact with a number of writers. In Moscow he worked for Stepanos Nazariants, the editor of the journal *Hiusisapayl* (Northern lights), and in St. Petersburg he joined the Armenian Students' Literary Club. In 1867 he was invited to Etchmiadzin as manager of the *Ararat* monthly. In 1870 he returned to Tiflis, a self-educated and experienced man, and dedicated himself entirely to teaching. He taught in Akhaltskha, Alexandropol, Yerevan, and Shushi (1872–80); was appointed supervisor of the Armenian parochial schools of Georgia; and collaborated on *Aghbiur* (Source), an illustrated monthly for children.

In 1895 Aghayan was arrested by the Russian government on suspicion of belonging to the Hnchakian political party. He was banished to Nor Nakhijevan and Crimea in 1898; two years later he was allowed to return to Tiflis, albeit with ruined health. The fortieth anniversary of the start of his literary career was celebrated in 1902, with massive popular participation, and in the 1905 revolt he sided with the revolutionaries against the tsar. He died in Tiflis in 1911.

His first work, *Arutiun yev Manuel* (Arutiun and Manuel: proper names, 1867, revised and expanded 1888–93), an autobiographical novel that vividly depicts village conditions in the 1840s, is, in essence, an assault on poverty and superstition. This was followed by a shorter novel, *Yerku kuyr* (Two sisters, 1872), the love stories of two sisters, in which the author highlights the issue of women's rights. Various episodes in the novel touch on the question of human justice, particularly as related to the 1861 agrarian reform, which failed to distribute land judiciously among the peasants. In *Keoroghli* (the name of a legendary popular hero), his social philosophy informs the activities of his hero, who, in the author's words, "raises the peasants against the *khans* and *begs*, takes away the lands and moneys they have seized and renders them back to the people, and distributes the tax money to the poor."

Aghayan had a special talent for retelling ancient folk tales in such a way as to emphasize their inherent social and moral messages. The most famous of these retellings is the poem "*Tork Angegh*" (the name of a mythological giant) whose prowess in warding off enemies, tenderness for his kinsfolk, and manner of treating everyone else comprise an exemplary lesson in social harmony. His other stories and folk tales include such works as *Anahit, Aregnazan, Hazaran blbul,* and *Aslan bala* (all proper names). Aghayan's two volumes of poetry, *Hovvakan sring* (Shepherd's pipe, 1882) and *Banasteghtzutiunner* (Poems, 1890), convey profound reflections in very simple language. A typical example is his delicate and touching poem, "*Hishoghutiun*" (Remembrance) about the swallow that returns home every spring to build a new nest: "he sang as he built, and with each twig he fastened he remembered his old nest."[1]

Aghayan contributed greatly to the development of modern Armenian. He prepared a series of textbooks introducing new pedagogical methods at four levels, which have gone through thirty editions in about as many years. His essays "The proper way to teach literacy," "Thoughts on education," "On punishment," "Differences between classical and modern versions," "On Armenian phonetics," and others on orthography and related subjects, along with criticism of contemporary writers,

---

1. For the Armenian pilgrim or migrant, the swallow, like the crane, is a symbol of nostalgic yearning for his homeland and a harbinger whose arrival is eagerly awaited. The swallow that has to build a new nest at every return because the old one has fallen to ruin is a fitting allegory for the fate of the migrant.

aroused great interest. He also wrote a number of children's stories and translated a few works by Krylov,[2] Schiller, Tolstoy, and Pushkin. Another important work was *Im kyanki glkhavor depkere* (The major events of my life, 1893), reminiscences that shed light on details that might otherwise escape the historian.

The main characteristics of Aghayan's writing are popularity, simplicity, and intellectual content.

Tork Angegh

Tork Angegh is a legendary Armenian hero or minor deity, the great-grandson of Hayk. According to Movses Khorenatsi, he was a giant of extraordinary force, who could hurl boulders across the seas, flatten the surfaces of rocks, and draw pictures on them with his fingernails. He was apparently called Angegh (*un-gegh:* not beautiful) because of his physical appearance.

It is generally assumed that Tork Angegh is a combination of two deities who have left traces of themselves in his name: Tarku, the ancient Anatolian deity of fertility, and Angegh, a pagan god venerated mainly in the province of Angegh, in southwestern Armenia. Movses Khorenatsi also states that he was a prince of that province, hence the references in Armenian history to *Angegha tun* (the House of Angegh). According to this view, the name Tork Angegh means Tork of Angegh rather than Tork the Ugly.

It is also interesting to note that in the ancient Armenian translation of the Bible, the name of the Babylonian god Nargal is rendered Angegh (IV Kings 17: 30).[3]

TORK ANGEGH AND HAYKANUSH THE FAIR[4]

Prologue

As spring unfolds, it troubles streams and lakes;
The mountains and the valleys spring to life

---

2. Ivan Andreyevich Krylov (1769–1844), Russian fabulist, whose fables appeared from 1809 onward and have become classics of Russian literature.

3. I.e., 2 Kings 17:30 in the Protestant system of naming the books of the Bible.

4. This English version, by A. J. Hacikyan and Edward S. Franchuk, is based on the recital of the epic *Tork Angegh* by Ghazaros Aghayan in 1888. See Ghazaros Aghayan, *Yerker* (Works) (Yerevan, 1979), 55–86.

As flowers blossom forth in bounteous store;
The swallow finds her nest of seasons past,
She patches and repairs it, lays new eggs;
The frigid snake feels warmth and leaves its pit;
The nightingale awaits the rose's bloom;
The soil in Gugarene[5] rejuvenates;
The snow on Lok[6] and Lalvar[7] starts to melt;
The rivulet in Boghnik, at daybreak
Cascades, quite hidden in its suds and foam.
The Aramian[8] Upert, forest castle,
Is furbished and adorned like a new bride:
Its turrets flow with tears of restless joy,
As though expecting a beloved guest.

    The mistress of the castle, Haykanush,
Is slumbering deeply in her dainty bed,
And dreams of a colossus of a man.
She sees a giant with a massive girder
Borne high upon his broad and mighty shoulder,
Whose feet, as he approaches where she is,
Sink deep into the earth he walks upon.
He shouts, as if in danger: "Haykanush,
you are my love; so kill me with this girder,
Or harken to my plea and grant my prayer!"

    The mistress wakes, and rises from her bed,
Just as the sun arises from the sea:
Her golden locks surround her like a cloud,
Envelop her fine figure to her feet.
A few of her handmaidens then draw near
To help their mistress don her shimmering gown,
Which glimmers with the radiance of her crown.
Her recent dream still preys upon her mind:
She still recalls the giant whom she saw.

---

5. The province of Gugark, which the Greek historians refer to as Gugarene. Chavakh, Kolb, Tsob, Dzor, and Tashir are all in the province of Gugark, which is also one of the four princely states.

6. Mountain range connecting the Kalinino region of Armenia to Bolinisi in Georgia.

7. Mountain in Armenia, eastern part of Georgian Mountains.

8. I.e., belonging to Armenia or Armenians.

"I know," she said, "we'll soon receive a guest,
But I'm convinced we should not let him in;
Tonight, I dreamt about a monstrous giant
Who'll soon be here, and fall down at my feet
To ask if I'll consent to be his wife."

   "If truth be known, the giant that you saw,"
One of her maids said, grinning as she spoke,
"Is just the hero of a lively song
The minstrel sang as you retired last night.
His name is Tork Angegh, of Baskam's kin.[9]
According to your minstrel from the Parkhar Mountains,[10]
He is a most brave shepherd, and his name is Tork;
He is both huge and mighty, more giant than a man,
He has a gentle heart, despite his ugly face
(It doesn't matter if a man is rough-hewn as a chasm,
If his heart is soft and fleecy as a lamb).
He is most dearly loved by man and beast:
Lions and tigers both keep watch upon his flock.
He is a member of your race, and even kin:
For you and he are both the grandchildren
Of one grandfather and his mighty sons.
The minstrel's eulogy perturbed your thoughts last night,
And so you dreamt about your kinsman all night long."

   "Be ready then, no matter what should happen,
And help me gird my fabled weapon[11] on.
Shut tight the gates of this our forest stronghold,
And wash your hair, put on your finest robes.
I realize my dream must come to pass,
So let's permit our guest to enter, if he will:
If he can penetrate through bolted doors
We will have proof our guest is Tork Angegh!"

   The giant in her dream was Tork indeed;
To have a look at him is what we need!

---

9. The founder of the House of Anghegh. See the introduction to the poem, above.

10. I.e., the northern Pontine mountains, on the Georgian border.

11. *Tur Havluni*, a legendary sword which supposedly belonged to Trdat the Great.

Canto One

I

      In times long past, in ancient Hayastan,
There lived a man whom all called Tork Angegh.
He was gigantic and an awesome sight:
No ordinary man, of that you can be sure;
He had blue eyes, clear as the heavenly vault,
Which shimmered with the radiance of the sun,
And over them his pitch-black eyebrows rose,
Heaped on his brow like sombre thunder clouds.
His nose was hooked, a veritable hump,
His teeth like hatchets and his nails like knives,
His chest was thicketed, just like a mountainside,
His waist resembled most a rocky vale,
And his hind quarters seemed a solid beam—
In other words, he was no giant really, but a dev;[12]
Creatures like him were unknown in those parts—
He was ferocious and so very strong
That fifty bulls together were no match.
While still a lad, he penetrated rocks,
Or took hard stones within his massive fists
And crunched them up as if they were just bones,
Or with his nails scraped smooth their surfaces,
And formed them into tablets to receive
The pictures that he drew then with his nails.
      Tork was a shepherd, tending mountain flocks,
A fearless shepherd, not the common sort;
Each time a lion or a tiger came across him
It humbly knelt before him like a hound,
Thinking he was more of a beast than they;
They carried out their mighty master's orders,
And threw themselves in homage at his feet,
And oftentimes they begged with plaintive roars
That he would toss them a few scraps of meat.
He gave them food enough to sate them while
They kept a watchful eye upon his flock;
Then off he went into the woods himself

---

12. Ogre, demon, fiend.

To search out victuals to sustain his strength.
He cut down trees that reached up to the sky
And piled them all together to construct
A palisade that reached into the stars.
The palisade went all around the woods—
Like ancient city ramparts it was built—
Confining all the forest animals:
Deer, roebuck, hart, and every other beast.
He went back to his flock, fatigued and sweating,
With twenty score and ten of wild beasts on his back.
The lions and the tigers ran to him
And threw themselves before the valiant's feet;
They greeted Herculean Tork,[13] and begged him
That they might share in his delicious feast.
He was no glutton, like the ravenous Shara:[14]
His favorite foods were yoghurt, milk, and honey;[15]
And Tork was meek and modest, not a bully:
But Lord help those who thought him dim and woolly!

2

The city-people once enraged our hero:
They called him Foul and ugly, and such names.
Unable to contain his wrath, he pulled up a huge tree
And with it he laid flat the entire city:
Not one inhabitant was spared his ire.
And by "laid flat," I don't mean simply "damaged":

---

13. Hercules is a possible literary model for Tork, as is the biblical hero Samson: both were noted for their superhuman strength, and a famous incident in the career of each involved the subjugation of a lion (see Judges 14:5–6). Tork is more imposing than either of these models, however, since in his case no struggle was needed to subdue the lion, which took one look at him and conceded defeat.

14. A legendary glutton; the son of an Armenian king.

15. These foods are rather significant. The first of them is a kind of geographical marker: the yoghurt-eating countries were mainly those that border on what might be styled the world's yoghurt basin, the Black Sea—Armenia, Turkey, Bulgaria, Rumania, Ukraine, and Georgia—and a few of their immediate neighbors; milk and honey are biblical symbols of abundance (cf. Song of Songs 4:11—"Your lips drop sweetness like the honeycomb, my bride, honey and milk are under your tongue. . . ."—and frequent references to the Promised Land of the captive Israelites as "a land flowing with milk and honey"); here they suggest that Tork's lands were richly endowed with the abundance of nature. Honey is also another link between Tork Angegh and the biblical hero Samson (cf. Judges 14:8 ff.).

The houses, sties, and barns were all destroyed.
The people of the city fled like flies,
For who would be so bold as to fight Tork?
When they beheld his anger growing blacker
They were agreed that they could not withstand him;
Instead they gave him gifts to calm him down,
And danced in honor of their mighty foe:
The boys and girls all joined their hands together,
And swayed to music played to honor Tork.
And it is said that after this his face
Began to look less fearsome, less repellent.

Tork was not vengeful, nor was he unskilled:
He was a goodly mason and an architect;
He levelled hills of stone and brought it to
The town he had destroyed, and built it up again;
As always, he employed his awesome might
To accomplish good and positive results.

In former times our villages and towns
Were thought fair game by bandits and by thieves,
But once let Herculean Tork be on the scene
The robbers disappeared into the crowd.
He threatened them with neither sword nor arrow:
One sight of him sufficed to make them flee!

When the enemy had the upper hand, however,
Tork used his strength and went on the attack:
He lifted heavy stones above his head
And dropped them on the heads of the oppressors,
As persistently as teeming rain or hail.

Around the Sea of Pontus,[16] foreign foes
From countless ships were pillaging the people:
They robbed their houses, then took them as slaves.
They also looted hamlets, suburbs, towns,
And in broad day, abducted pretty maidens.
Some of the local people came to Tork for help
(They were mainly poor and came from humble stock).

---

16. I.e., the Black Sea, on the shores of which the ancient country of Pontus (in northeast Asia Minor, now Turkey) flourished, from the fourth to the first centuries BC.

When Tork Angegh came to the pillaged site,
The ships had lifted anchor and were under sail,
Leaving behind the Sea of Pontus' shore.
Infuriated, Tork let out a howl
And roared just like a lion, hurt or wounded;
He picked up rocks and ice the size of hills,
And threw them at the fast-escaping keels,
The sea was stirred to turmoil, waves swirled round,
The ships were bounced about like spinning tops;
He cast another rock, another turmoil rose,
And boats capsized like tiny shells upon the sea;
Another hill, much larger than the first,
Fell on the foe all unexpectedly.
And rocks kept raining down, in volleys or alone,
Hitting the ships and causing them to sink;
The towering waves which rose from every splash
Caught the remaining ships and dashed them down,
Down to the very bottom of the sea.
Indeed, of all of them one man alone survived;
When he arrived again on his home shores,
A wound was gaping wide upon his head,
And he related tales so marvellous
That all who heard him stood amazed and dumb.
And that is how, at last, the mighty Tork
Brought to an end the pirates' dirty work!

3

Tork's reputation spread both far and wide,
And soon was aired in court, before the king.
The mighty sovereign summoned Tork to court,
That he might present him gifts and see his face.
And so Tork went to court, and carried on his shoulders
A giant tree, the branches hung with game:
Buck, deer, wild lamb, roe, boar, and roe deer too.
In preparation for this strange arrival
The royal town's inhabitants had been warned;
When he arrived in town, the shops and stores poured forth
Horn and trumpet players, and throngs of welcomers:
"He's come, he has arrived, look, look, he's here!"

They heralded the news to one another,
Both young and old, each woman, maiden, child
Had come to see the far-renowned newcomer.
    When Tork the titan strode into the city,
The people thought he was a moving tower,
And, it is true, there are few taller towers:
He seemed a mighty pile of rough-hewn stones.
His stride was leisurely, the tree served as a cane,
And each step spanned four metres and a half.
    He soon walked through the main door of the palace,
Surprising everyone, the king included.
He humbly placed his cane upon the floor,
Approached the king, and fell upon his knees.
The king then spoke: "May you live long, good Tork!
You seem more like an army than a man!"
Tork bowed his head to kiss his sovereign's ring,
And to receive the blessing of his king.

4

    The king had heard that people of the giant race
Were not obedient or very clever,
But as he got to know our Tork a little better,
He found a worthy courtier in the giant.
He kept Tork with him in the palace for three months,
And had him sit beside him when at table.
    "Which do you think," the King asked him one day
(Wishing to test the giant's intelligence),
"Is better: strength of mind or body?"
    "Their worth is equal," valiant Tork replied,
"Those weak in body might be strong in mind,
So it would be a great mistake to think
That a weak man is therefore not a danger;
But what it is to be intelligent—nobody knows,
But only fools ignore the clever man.
A sentry's mind works one way, to be sure,
And a successful thief must think a different way.
But whether he's an idiot or a sage,
Each man has something in him of the brute;
There is one type of wit above all others, though,

And that's the wit of heroes and gallants:
It is inventive and creative too;
It fills its owner with benevolence,
And draws him near the throne of the Creator;
It is the kind of mind which contemplates
The elements of earth, air, fire, water,
And finds a way to form from these four basics
The tools for ploughing and for spreading joy,
For sowing and for tilling and for harvest;
This wit shapes stones and brings forth life,
And that, for me, is true intelligence;
Without it man is nothing but a beast armed with a sword."
The king was most impressed; he listened, full of wonder,
As Tork revealed his cleverness in words and voice of thunder.

5

The king looked out one day and witnessed Tork,
Who carried in his hands a hill-sized rock
So easily it might have been a child.
Tork grasped the rock and split it with his fingers,
And then he used his nails, as sharp as chisels,
To polish it and shape it, hew and sculpt it,
And lo! he made a statue of the king!
It was both beautiful and true to life:
It fit its model like a well made suit of clothes,
And everything was in its proper place.
It was the very sovereign to perfection:
One saw him there in royal robes and cloak,
Bedecked with jewels and other ornaments,
And he was seated on his royal throne,
His sword drawn, and a crown upon his head,
Holding a fine wrought mace, the symbol of his power,
And, best of all, the king's majestic beard
With gold and silver pearls was intertwined.
The king beheld, and marvelled in his mind.

6

"Tork's an enigma!" said the king one day,
"This elephant is huge and canny too!

Who would have thought that God endowed this giant
With height and mind, and also with such talent?
I wonder, though, if love thrives in his heart?
For who, in all the world, could love a man like him?
Among all women living could one find
One who would wish to have him for a husband?
It would, indeed, give rise to a great wonder,
Should such a thing be deemed conceivable,
For she would bear him children just like him!"
        And that is what the king was thinking of
When he summoned Tork to have a talk with him:
"Tork," said the king, "I really don't believe
There's any place for love within your heart."
        At this our giant glowed just like an infant
Which, hungry, hears a sweet maternal voice
Say: "Here's my breast, now suck until you're full";
The coals of love which glowed within his heart
Brought color to his face, red as a rose.
        "My most courageous King," replied our Tork,
"If someone said that they had found a beast,
A flower, snake, or rock that had no breath,
I would most certainly not be surprised,
But I could never make myself believe
That these things could exist if they lacked love:
The heavens and all below them, earth and sea,
The universe itself, without love, would not be!"
        "You speak as though you loved somebody, Tork:
You must have found the woman of your heart."
        "Where could I find a fitting mate for me?
I've yet to meet a woman with a heart that's free!
In distant lands, I hear, live women of my size;
Before much more time passes, I'd like to set my eyes
Upon a woman whom I've often seen in dreams,
Where she awaits me in a deep and lonesome valley:
Like me, she is unlucky and too much alone,
But she is not, as I am, marred and ugly.
For she is beautiful, most fair to look upon,
Like the newborn crimson sun at break of day."
        "What would you like to hear from this most comely
            maiden;

Do you expect that she'd become your wife?"
"Yes, in my dream she promised me she would,
She promised me on one condition:
She said, 'If you can find and vanquish me,
You may be sure I'll wed you right away.'
But I've no inkling where to look for her,
So I can neither fight, defeat, nor wed her."
"Do not despair! I'll summon my *bdeshkhs*[17]
And order them to locate your fair maiden."
Tork was ecstatic, but embarrassed too,
And sat there blushing red as any child.
He humbly kissed the knee of his liege lord,
And took his leave as soon as e'er he could.
The king himself was in a merry mood
That the secrets of the giant's heart had been unglued.

7

As he had said, the king called for the princes,
Who were then staying at the palace, as it happened.
"I wish to know," he said, "about the many peoples
Who live within the borders of our kingdom:
Can there be found among them any giants
For instance, any Torks: both strong and trenchant?"
(The king was not familiar with the land
Because he had been born on foreign soil.)
The first to give his answer was Aran,
Who was the esteemed and mighty prince of Bagh:[18]
"Long live the king!" he said, then made this statement:
"There do indeed survive within our borders,
Gargantuan men, who live quite close to us.
They make their homes in rocky crevices,
Dark hidden valleys, and sequestered places,
Where they have gone in order to stay free
And to avoid the paying of all taxes.
The clerks and elders of our villages
Get nothing from them but a few load roars!

---

17. In ancient Armenia, the heads of four major states (Akhdznik, Gugark, Nor Shizakan, and Korduk), who were higher than all princes and much more independent.

18. I.e., the present region of Siunik, in the Republic of Armenia.

They build their homes beneath the valley floors,
But making use of neither wood nor stone.
Upon the level ground all one can see
Is rising smoke from forty different sources:
A sight hard to explain: what could it be?
No one would ever guess it was a village.
    "You search and find a door and venture in:
Forty or sixty giant men are there,
All throwing tree-sized logs into the fire
And sitting, with long faces, round the hearth.
An ancient giantess, who seems their mother,
Positions a stone caldron o'er the flames,
In which wild boars are being boiled alive;
So she prepares her stew, and stirs it with a pole
Instead of with a ladle as our women do.
The house has countless caverns, in which live
The brides of all the sons, and other maidens:
And all of them are big, nay! all enormous,
Both men and women, little girls and boys.
They are not coarse, like Tork, or so unpolished,
But very beautiful, and well-bred too."
    "What Prince Aran is saying is all true,"
The prince of Gugark[19] took up the tale:
"For giants also fled to our own valleys
In order to escape the tax collectors.
If but the voice of the village clerk is heard,
They melt away, as snow does in the spring—
They seem to shrink in size and disappear—
Our elders cannot catch a single one!
Their own communities have neither clerks nor elders:
That's how they stay so prosperous and huge!"
    "However do they manage without money?"
Inquired the monarch of the Prince of Lor;[20]
"For money is essential to survival:
They surely need to buy both food and clothes."
    "They're skilled in making ploughs, and farm the land;

19. In the northern part of historic Armenia.
20. I.e., the region of Stepanavan, in Armenia.

They have pigs and sheep, and herds to milk and yoke,
And cotton, flax for linen, and silk worms,
They manufacture many dyes, and get crimson from the in-
    sects.
Their women spin, make thread and dyes, and knit,
And wear the clothes they make themselves: the effect is
    exquisite.
They make the clothes for every family member,
And don't forget clothes for their relatives.
They're skilled in weaving: carpets, shawls, and garments;
No item is too large (or small) for them.
They have cows and goats, which give them cream and butter,
They have fruit and seeds and cereal, beets, and flour;
They drink from ice-cold springs, as clear as crystal rivers,
That flow within their chasms and ravines.
They're skilled in surgery and remedies,
And know the recipes for medicines.
If ever there is anything they lack or need,
They soon obtain that thing through bartering.
They don't partake of either wine or *oghi*:[21]
They're free of all addictions, and live long.
Indeed, it seems no member of their race
Has ever suffered ailment or disease:
They're all so healthy that they look like children.
United and attached by lasting love,
They sacrifice themselves for one another;
They are hospitable and generous,
Fond of tradition too, and virtuous."
    "How can these giants be of help to us,
If they refuse to pay the tax collector?"
    "They shun their taxes but are all brave fighters,
And they are always ready to defend their country's honor.
They have an arsenal of arrows, slings, and cross bows,
And go to war as to a wedding feast.
Their favoured strategy is showering their opponents
With arrows from their cross bows and with stones;

---

21. An alcoholic beverage, the Armenian equivalent of the Greek ouzo, the Arab arak, and the Turkish *raki*.

And if perchance it happens that no weapons lie to hand,
They use their superhuman strength in unarmed combat.
Just one of them is strong enough to go against a hundred.
In consequence, a thousand foes can be put down by ten:
Like hungry wolves they fall on them, and they don't have a
    chance!"
    "If what you say is true, leave them alone,
Exempt these giants from the tax collection.
But," said the king, "this freedom has a price:
For Tork, our titan, they must find a bride."
    "That's very hard," replied the prince:
"Perhaps, they will agree to your condition,
But they would never give one of their daughters
In marriage with no test of skill by which
The bridegroom proved himself a worthy husband:
They have a contest and the winner takes the bride;
Moreover, this is not the end—far from it:
For next the bridegroom must take on the bride,
And if it proves he cannot vanquish her,
The woman will consider him no longer."
    "What you have told me, Tork saw in his dream," The king
    said with a grin, when he had finished:
"It's clear Tork, our leviathan, must venture forth,
Go there and test what his great strength is worth!"

Srbuhi Dussap

(c. 1841–1901)

The first Armenian feminist writer, and an activist of the Armenian Cultural Revival, Srbuhi Dussap (née Vahanian), was born in Constantinople to an aristocratic family. She received her education in a French school in Mijagiugh (Ortaköy, a suburb of Constantinople); was tutored by her brother, a chemist, in the natural sciences and history; and also took courses in music. She had a great aptitude for literature. In order to gain mastery of both classical and modern Armenian, in 1861 she began taking private lessons from Mkrtich Peshiktashlian (Beshiktashlian, 1828–68), a well-known and highly respected poet for whom she had great admiration. A mutual affection developed between the two, which, however, was cut short by Peshiktashlian's untimely death in 1868. She was his guardian angel during his long illness, and the eulogy she delivered at his funeral, a highly sentimental poem in classical Armenian, was the best of all the orations. This poem adorns the first page of Peshiktashlian's *Matenagrutiunk* (Works), published posthumously in 1870.

In 1871 she married a French musician and took his surname, Dussap. He was a liberal-minded intellectual and encouraged his wife to pursue her literary interests. Influenced by her teacher, Mkrtich Peshiktashlian, she started with poetry, and one of her poems, *Garun* (Spring), dedicated to Arsen Bagratuni, was printed in *Bazmavep* (*Polyhistor*) in 1864. As she avidly read such French authors as Jean-Jacques Rousseau, Madame de Staël, and Georges Sand, and as she integrated herself into Armenian intellectual circles, her concern began to focus on the status of the Armenian woman: the way she was treated and exploited by an unjust, biased, and even brutal system of male domination. Between 1880 and 1882 she began to publish articles in prestigious Constantinople and Smyrna (Izmir) periodicals, with such titles as "The Education of Women," "A Few Remarks on the Idleness of Women," "The Principle of Working Women," and "Armenian Societies." These articles protested the servility of women and demanded equality with men in the fields of education and labor, and freedom of choice in marriage.

In 1883 she published her first book, *Mayta*, named after its heroine: a romantic novel, the story of which unfolds in a series of letters exchanged between two women—Mayta, a helpless widow who is unable to have a life of her own and consequently suffers in an intolerant society, and her friend Sira, an advocate of freedom for women. The lack of action is amply compensated for by fertile ideas that promote the cause of freedom and equality for women. Soon after it was published, it aroused quite a controversy. This was fostered by Grigor Zohrap (1861–1915), who condemned it as a dangerous book, fearing that granting women equal rights with men would undermine the stability of the traditional family. The dispute between Zohrap and Reteos Perberian (Berperian, 1848–1907), who defended Dussap, continued for approximately two decades. In the meantime, women readers greeted the book with great enthusiasm.

Dussap's second novel, *Siranush*, also named for its heroine, was published in 1884 and was more successful than the first. It represents a much stronger plea for the rights of women and vigorously attacks the despotism of men. Woman is presented here as a victim, sometimes even victimized twice: by her father's greed and by her husband's unfaithfulness.

Her third and last novel, *Araxia kam varzhuhin* (Araxia, or the school teacher, 1887), focuses on situations imposed on women by class distinctions, prejudice, jealousy, malevolence, and nasty rivalries between families. In all cases it is the defenseless woman who suffers. These three books are deficient in action but rich in thought; they are, in fact, thesis novels, the first examples of their kind in Armenian literature.

Srbuhi Dussap was the first woman writer to fight relentlessly for the rights of women in Armenian society. By her time the feminist movement had already made some headway in Europe and, no doubt because of her French education and the influence of liberal authors, she was ahead of her time in the Armenian context and in the Ottoman Empire. Her main audience was the Armenian men and women of Constantinople, who lived in proximity to Europe, while the great masses of the population lived in the provinces, where many of the women were practically illiterate and were still strongly attached to ancient social traditions and customs. Some contemporary critics asserted that the characters in her novels did not represent the typical Armenian woman, but that would have been an impossible task indeed, given the abysmal gaps, both social and educational, between social classes.

She was a staunch supporter of modern Armenian, which she defended in a book published in 1880. Her language is refined and her style elegant. In 1889 she went to Paris for intellectual refreshment and established ties with men of letters and composers such as Charles Gounod and Ambroise Thomas. She returned home in 1891 and suffered the greatest tragedy of her life: the death of her beloved daughter, Dorine, at the age of eighteen. Engulfed in deep sadness, she became a recluse, and wrote no more. She died in 1901.[1]

FROM MAYTA[2]

Mayta to the Count

My greatest wish would have been to live for you, to give what I received from you, and to bring a little happiness to your sad life. But is the dark night capable of giving light? Is a lifeless heart able to grant life, and can what is dead live again? I would be willing to sacrifice a few lives to bring you a little consolation, but, alas, I do not possess a heart to dedicate to you. The pitiless hand of fate dealt a heavy blow to my poor heart, and it has remained lifeless ever since. You overwhelmed me with kindness, and I can do nothing for you. I sincerely wish to help you, but I cannot. To live with you under the same sky, to know you as a brother, and to console you would have been the greatest of my aspirations. But my sky cannot

1. See Victoria Rowe, *A History of Armenian Women's Writing, 1880–1922* (Amersham, Buckinghamshire, 2003).

2. Srbuhi Dussap, extracts from "Mayta," in *Ararat* 19, no. 2 (Spring 1978), 39. Translated by James Etmekjian.

be yours, for I shall live in darkness, whereas you need light. You are beginning your life. I am ending mine.

I shall say farewell to everything. I shall die, and I shall carry the memory of my beloved with me. I can never forget you, Count. When my convent doors close behind me, and when I recall my past memories, your noble image will be one of those that bring me pleasure. My mind will linger on your memory, like a green branch, in arid surroundings, and my heart will sing a song of gratitude and friendship from afar. I can assure you that, when the supreme moment arrives, your name will be uttered with the names of my other loved ones. Farewell, my Count. Why did fate deny me the opportunity of knowing you first? We would have become two happy beings instead of two unfortunate ones. Having been rejected by fate, I hope I shall not be denied a heaven while I am buried alive.

The Count to Mayta

Mayta, do you wish to take leave of your friends and this world by burying yourself in a convent? Do you wish to sacrifice yourself? Very well, but have also the courage to sacrifice the brother who loves you. With you, the universe is mine. Without you, there is nothingness. You are the ears with which I hear. You are the mouth with which I speak. I have a heart that palpitates only for you. Mayta, return the light to my eyes and the words to my mouth. Keep only my heart, for it is yours. However, if you insist upon making your sacrifice, inform me at once so that I may make mine at the same time. Do not fear that my plaints will disturb the peace of your convent. Just the thought of your happiness will make even suffering dear to me. But I cannot remain indifferent as you prepare to wrap your warm heart in a cold shroud. . . . You will always be dear to me in death as in life.

Tigran to Mayta

My dear Mayta, I met you to adore you, to think that you were mine, to lose you, to pine for you, to curse you aloud, and to worship you in silence. I was the victim of a tragic betrayal. I thought that the angel of purity was impure, virtue was vice, beauty was ugliness, and loyalty was treason. . . .

You were accused of being unfaithful. I wrote you to ask for information, but every letter remained unanswered. I went on a trip, and when I returned to Paris with the hope of finally hearing from you, my sorrow was great when my hopes failed to be realized. I wrote you a second time and met the same silence, whereupon I concluded that I was forgotten. Who in my position would not have been the victim of such deception. For six months, I was a lost man. I had become the plaything of roaring waves on a sea of hopelessness. I looked for a seaport. I prayed for a merciful hand to save me, and now, having been extended that hand, I find chains instead of salvation, death instead of life. I am unhappy, Mayta. Have mercy upon me.

When I met you in the church and saw you faint, I was so disturbed, and such a change came over me that my wife looked at me with fear and suspicion. I forgot that I had an unfortunate witness beside me. I forgot that in my mind you were unfaithful to me. I rushed toward you. I wept as I knelt beside you. I worshiped you while I cursed you. I cared for you with compassion. When you were about to recover consciousness, I left you in spite of my heart. I loved you madly even when I thought you to be guilty. . . .

Mayta to Tigran

You ask me for mercy, but did you have mercy upon me when, having crossed the seas to look for you and to ask the reason for your silence, I was lying nearly lifeless because I had heard that your impatience had prepared another love to replace mine? Did you have mercy upon me when strangers were caring for me as I lay between life and death? Did you have mercy upon me when, worshiping the unfaithful person that you are, I had decided to bury myself and to weep over you, whom I considered dead? . . .

In spite of it all, my mouth . . . always prayed for you. Keep happiness for yourself, and leave me the tears.

You have a duty on this earth, which is to make your wife happy. Love her, for she is innocent. She has a right to your love. I do not want my memory ever to disturb her peace. When finally my grieving heart finds its rest in death, I would like her to mingle her tears with yours.

Hakob Paronian (Baronian)

(1843–91)

The first satirist in modern Armenian literature, Hakob Paronian was born in Adrianople (presently Edirne) in 1843. After graduating from the local Armenian school he attended a Greek school for a year (1857) where, as he states, "he succeeded in learning only the difficulties of the Greek language." Nonetheless, in time he learned not only Greek but French and Italian as well. Faced with the struggle between physical survival and intellectual fulfillment, he was forced to abandon formal education and find a job to help his parents. He worked in a pharmacist's shop, then as a bookkeeper in a tobacco company. Moving to Constantinople in 1863, he worked at a telegraph office, taught at the Mezpurian school at Scutari (Üsküdar, 1871–72), was a clerk at the Armenian Patriarchate (1873), and went back to teaching for a short while. He tried his luck in Smyrna (Izmir) for a year (1877–78), then returned to Constantinople in 1879. There he married and remained for the rest of his life.

What he lacked in formal schooling he made up for in self-education. A voracious reader, he took great delight in the literary and theatrical works of Corneille, Racine, Molière, La Bruyère,[1] and other French and

---

1. Jean de la Bruyère (1645–96), French satirist.

Italian classical writers, who exerted a profound influence on him. He chose a literary vocation, particularly the genre of satire, which eventually attracted the ire and rage of certain "prestigious" people, and he ended his life in abject poverty.

Paronian's literary career began with two plays, *Yerku terov tzara me* (A servant of two masters, 1865), which seems to be inspired by a similar work by Goldoni,[2] and *Atamnabuzhn arevelyan* (The oriental dentist, 1868), which treats the subject of an arranged marriage with a bright prospect of wealth. A third play, *Shoghokorte* (The flatterer), begun in 1872, was left unfinished.

Although a career in the theater was a possibility, his gift for satire developed in journalism. His first columns appeared in *Pogh aravotyan* (Morning bugle), *Yeprat* (Euphrates), and Harutiun Svachian's (Svadjian's, 1831–74) famed satirical weekly *Meghu* (Bee), the editorship of which he assumed in 1872. His critical remarks about the way the affairs of the nation were run and about the decay in social mores were published under the general titles of *Khaytvatzk* (Stings) and *Aské anké* (From here and there). After Svachian's death, Paronian continued *Meghu* under a new name, *Tatron* (Theater, 1874–77), in which his own columns appeared under the general title *Ksmitner* (Pinches). In 1874 he began to serialize his *Azgayin jojer* (The big wigs of the nation), one of his major works (printed in book form in 1880), in which he drew satirical portraits of thirty-two contemporary writers, poets, editors, artists, high ranking clergy, political figures, and other celebrities of society against the realities of the day, highlighting their eccentricities with sharp humor. In parallel with *Tatron*, he also published an illustrated magazine for children, *Tatron barekam mankants* (Theater, the children's friend, 1876–78). After the closing of *Tatron*, mainly for financial reasons, he contributed to various journals, such as *Luys* (Light) and *Masis* in Constantinople and *Pordz* (Essay), *Ardzagank* (Echo), and *Paros Hayastani* (The lighthouse of Armenia) in Eastern Armenia, where he avoided Sultan Hamid's censorship.

In the 1870s he sided with Khrimian Hayrik (1820–1907) in support of the revision of the National Constitution and criticized the corruption of the Ottoman officials in the Armenian provinces. As the Balkans erupted into the rebellion that led to the Russo-Ottoman war of 1877–78 (which in turn made the Armenian question an international issue), he attacked Ottoman internal policy and exposed the hypocrisy of

---

2. Carlo Goldoni (1707–93), Italy's notable comic playwright.

the European powers with bitter sarcasm. In 1883, in order to evade censorship, he began to publish a weekly brochure called *Tzitzagh* (Sneer), in which the heroes, all national and international figures, were represented allegorically by animals derived from Armenian folklore, such as the fox, the frog, the ant, and the monkey. The series lasted only for about one year, and his enemies declared victory.

But nothing discouraged him. He established a satirical review, *Khikar*[3] (1884–88) in Adrianople, then moved it to Constantinople. Under Sultan Hamid's regime he refrained from politics and concentrated on social and community problems. His satire spared no one; writers, journalists, teachers, patriarchs, *amiras*, the rich, members of the National Council, all received their share. His keen observation exposed incompetence, hypocrisy, and degenerate behavior in high society. Despite his many enemies, he was very popular. Many read his paper, but very few paid for their subscriptions.

Among Paronian's major works are *Ptuyt me Polso tagherun mej* (A stroll through the quarters of Constantinople, 1880), in which every Armenian quarter (over thirty of them) is visited and its inhabitants of various social classes, its unique characteristics, sights, and sounds are humorously sketched. *Im* (or *hos-hosi*) *dzeratetre* (My notebook, 1880) contains dated entries on political and social events, with sarcastic commentary. The two works *Paghtasar aghbar* (Brother Balthazar), a play, and *Kaghakavarutyan vnasnere* (The dangers of politeness), another play, both appeared first in *Khikar* (1887–88), and tackle social issues. The first deals with the problem of morality in the family of a cheating wife and a deceived husband, and the second exposes the absurdity of fake politeness. His best work, *Metzapativ muratskanner* (Honorable beggars, 1887), is the story of a naive member of the provincial landed gentry who comes to Constantinople to find a suitable bride but is harassed by a number of presumptuous artists, poets, journalists, priests, and other opportunists who exploit him. The author pokes fun at these individuals, but the real target is the society that produces them. This work has been adapted to the stage and is still a very popular comedy.

After the suppression of *Khikar* in 1888, Paronian was compelled to work as a bookkeeper to earn his living, and he also taught for a short

---

3. The name of an Assyrian sage, Ahikar or Achiacharus, assumed to be an officer of King Sennacherib (705–681 BC). His only known work is *The Wisdom of Ahikar*, a collection of proverbs. The oldest version of the text is found in some fifth-century Aramaic papyrus fragments. It was translated into Armenian in the fifth century AD.

while at the Kedronakan lycée. But long years of hard work and deprivation had taken their toll. After a long illness he died of tuberculosis at the age of forty-eight.

Paronian was an honest man and possessed great moral courage. He hated hypocrisy and was compassionate toward the downtrodden. He directed his satire at religious and lay leaders equally, attacking patriarchs and members of the National Assembly for their incompetence, school trustees for their ignorance and favoritism, the wealthy for their depravity, and the sultan's government for its corruption. In addition to the works mentioned above, many of his writings are scattered in the numerous periodicals he contributed to. He had to write fast; consequently he did not have time to polish his language. As a satirist, he is unique in modern Armenian literature; no one preceded him and no one has yet followed him.

His complete works in eleven volumes were first published in Yerevan between 1931 and 1948, and further editions have followed.

Honorable Beggars[4]

For a number of years it has become customary for many to go to France or Germany to receive their education, after which they come to my capital city looking for girls to marry. Of course, the reader already knows that Abisoghom Agha had not come to Constantinople for any other reason. The reader has also not forgotten that Abisoghom Agha was so preoccupied by this issue of marriage that he didn't see the donkeys coming towards him and was hit by one of them. You may ask whether the young donkey which rammed into him may have had marriage-related business on his mind also, which would have accounted for his failure to see a man as large as Abisoghom Agha before his eyes. Those who have little or wide acquaintance with history know that donkeys, one of whose ancestors is purported to have seen an angel once, don't place any importance on us mortals and wish that we would leave the road open to them. Abisoghom Agha, were he well versed in history or were he less concerned with the matter of marriage, surely would have allowed those creatures to pass,

---

4. Hakob Paronian, "Honorable Beggars," *Ararat* 20, no. 2 (Spring 1979), 43–48. Translated by Aris Sevag.

who, because of their ears, enjoy the dubious honor of being King Midas' representatives.

After parting company with the donkeys, Abisoghom Agha inquired of this one and that one how to get to Flower St., this being his first visit to Constantinople. One of his friends living in Trebizond had advised him that he should repair to the street mentioned, to the house mentioned, in order to enjoy good food and comfortable lodging. That friend had written a letter a week earlier to Manuk Agha, informing him that Abisoghom Agha would be staying at his house. Following the directions given him, Abisoghom Agha went up one street and down another; sometimes by mistake he would go up blind alleys, get angry, turn back and, at the same time, wonder whether or not the porters had made off with his bedding and trunks, although he had heard from many people about their faithfulness.

After wandering around the streets of Péra for about an hour, Abisoghom Agha finally succeeded in finding Flower St., which is not to be confused with the street bearing the same name which was reduced to ashes as a result of the Péra fire around 187— I don't remember the exact year. This street was called Flower because on the windowsills of all the houses on the street there were always flower boxes.

"Which house is Number 2?" he inquired of Manuk Agha's wife, without realizing who she was. She, in turn, was waiting in front of the house for the arrival of her husband.

"This is it. Welcome, Abisoghom Agha!" answered the wife.

"Did they bring my bedding and trunks?"

"They brought them, Abisoghom Agha. Come upstairs, Abisoghom Agha. If you wish to rest a bit, sit down in that small room," said the wife, showing him to a room on the ground floor.

"I'm very tired. I'll sit here for a while."

"Do as you wish, Abisoghom Agha. The house is yours. Make yourself at home."

"Thank you."

Abisoghom Agha went into the little room, led by the wife, who was holding a lamp which was just about to burn out of oil.

"How are you, Abisoghom Agha? How's everybody at home? All right?"

"They're fine."

"That's good. How are your children, Abisoghom Agha? Are they going to school?"

"I don't have any children."

"What's your wife doing? Is she all right, Abisoghom Agha?"

"I don't have a wife."

"You're not married, Appisoghom Agha?"

"No."

"Very well, we'll find a nice girl here for you so you settle down here in Constantinople, Abisoghom Agha."

"That's what I'm planning to do," answered Abisoghom Agha, "but before the girl, I'd like to eat something since I haven't had a bite since morning."

"Sure, Abisoghom Agha, sure. I'll bring you some food now."

The wife departed and, opening the door, stood on the threshold waiting for Manuk Agha who, as the readers will recall, had gone looking for the midwife.

Abisoghom Agha, left alone in the room, picked up *Zen, the Spiritual,* which was lying on a cushion, and began to page through it. But, since our hero has stayed hungry for a long while, he can't read a book, just as he is not presently in any condition to write a book; so he replaced the book on the cushion because his stomach informed him that he needed *Zen, the Corporal,* then proceeded to walk around the room.

"I trust, Abisoghom Agha, that you'll make yourself at home," said the wife, entering the room.

"I've got no reason to feel uncomfortable. It's just that I'm hungry and would like to eat something."

"Your dinner is almost ready. I'll bring it to you shortly," said the wife and went out again, waiting in front of the door for her husband.

What kind of a *woman* is this?" said Abisoghom Agha when left to himself. "She keeps me hungry and, on top of that, bids me to be comfortable; can a starving person be at ease? . . ."

"Just think of me as your sister or daughter," said the sixty-year-old woman, again entering the room. "If you want something, don't be shy, tell me and I'll bring to you."

"Thank you."

"I don't want guests who come to my house to feel ill at ease."

"I understand; right this minute I don't want anything else but dinner."

"Dinner is almost ready, don't worry. . . ."

The wife would have still continued to ramble on except that she was interrupted by a knock on the door; in any case, she rushed out so she could open the door, greet her husband, take the vittles he brought and cook supper.

"*Vogjhuyn* (blessings), madam," said someone, as soon as the door was opened.

It is not necessary to say that the person who had come was a priest, because only they use the word *vogjhuyn*.

"Bless, Father," answered the wife.

"How are you? Is everything all right, Madam?"

"Thank God, yes, Father."

"Manuk Agha just approached me and told me you have a guest today, so I came to see him."

"I'm glad you did. Come inside, Father," said the wife, showing him into the small room which Abisoghom Agha was occupying during the course of his starvation.

The priest entered the room.

Abisoghom Agha rose.

"*Voghjuyne*, Abisoghom Agha."

"Bless, Father."

"Being a humble sinner and servant of God, having learned of your pious visit, I came in haste to inquire into your honorable self's devout condition. How are you, Abisoghom Agha?"

"I'm fine."

"Always be that way. May the Lord God grant the heavenly kingdom to your dead ones and longevity to the living."

"Thank you. How are you, Father?"

"Don't ask about our well-being . . . it goes with the times . . . may the Lord God protect you from all temptation and evil; when the people are well, their priests are smiling."

"That's the way it is, Father," answered Abisoghom Agha, never taking his eyes off the door of the room from which he was expecting the food.

"My blessed son, times are very bad, the people have to endure much trouble; for this reason, piety is also waning daily."

"Right."

"But what are we going to do? What else besides being patient are we in a position to do? The Bible says, He that endureth to the end shall be saved."

"That's so."

"If we're not patient, then we have to get angry and the prophet says, 'Get angry but do not sin.'"

"That's true," answered Abisoghom Agha, who wasn't listening at all to the priest's words and, furthermore, was feeling annoyed at the priest's presence because, as our readers know, he didn't need anything but food.

"Man cannot live on bread alone, but on every word that God utters."

The priest took a box of snuff from his inside coat pocket and, using two fingers, filled his nostrils; then, offering the box to Abisoghom Agha, said "Take some, blessed man."

Abisoghom Agha took the box gratefully and breathed in a little snuff.

"You only sniffed a little, Abisoghom Agha. Please, sniff some more—snuff is not harmful."

Abisoghom Agha sniffed once more so that the conversation wouldn't drag on and the guest would leave.

"Why don't you fill your nostrils, Abisoghom Agha?" repeated the priest. "Take a good whiff."

"Thank you, Father, but I'm not used to it."

"I beg of you, don't turn me down. Take a little."

"I notice you're not taking any more either," said Abisoghom Agha as an aside and took a little more.

"The prophet David says that man's days are like those of grass."

"In reference to the snuff?"

"No, he says it in reference to us . . . and we should strive to do good to others during this transitory life, take care of the poor, wretched, homeless souls and sometimes pray for the souls of our dead ones."

"That's so."

"We should be ready to go as soon as we are called."

"True."

"Humble sinner that I am, I'm going to take the liberty of asking a favor of your piety and I hope that you won't refuse because I'm well aware of your piety devotion."

"Please, ask it and it shall be yours."

"May the Good Lord always keep his depthless treasury open to the requests of pious ones like you."

"Thank you."

"May He give a thousand in place of one, in place of a thousand, a million for the building of a holy church for the glory of our nation. My request is that, next Sunday, I want to offer mass for the souls of your beloved deceased ones. Forgive my boldness but it is my duty to remind you that the deceased shouldn't be forgotten.

"You have the right, Father."

"Now, if you wish, tell me so that, accordingly, I can make the arrangements. Don't think that the expense is a big thing. Two gold pieces will do it. For the same I'll serve special notice in church that there'll be a holy and immortal service for the sake of the memory of Abisoghom Agha's deceased ones."

"I'll be thankful."

"It's nothing, it's our obligation."

"Here, take the two gold pieces," said Abisoghom Agha, taking them from his purse and giving them to the priest.

"It could have waited. . . . Why were you in such a hurry?" answered the priest, opening his palm.

"It's okay. Take them."

"Since you insist, I'll take the money so as not to break your heart. God bless you, may He always keep your home cheerful, always fill your purse; whatever is our heart, may God bring it to pass; may your work be successful and may God deliver you from all trials and tribulations."

The priest went out, saying goodbye as soon as he had finished his well-wishing.

"Free at last," said Abisoghom Agha to himself, "from this man. What misfortunes have befallen me today since my arrival in Constantinople. I had hardly gotten off the steamer when along came a newspaper editor who annoyed me for two hours; I got away from him and by the time I found the house, I had a thousand harrowing experiences. I came here to relax a little and eat something and the lady of the house keeps me waiting and, on top of that, she always comes inside and asks me not to bother about a thing but just think about my comfort. As if this weren't enough, this man comes, forces me to inhale some snuff and, while reciting the words of David the Prophet, takes my two gold pieces and leaves. I had to endure all of this on an empty stomach; now why don't they bring me my dinner? Are they going to keep me hungry all night? . . . What a damn shame. . . ."

While Abisoghom Agha is directing these questions to the four walls, the oil lamp, which was giving off a very weak light, went out, leaving our guest in the dark.

"But I shouldn't put up with this," continues our great personage, "either I should go elsewhere or I should call this woman over and say a few things to her. In my hometown I had two servants always at my beck and call; they'd set the table early and carry out my work; why should a man accustomed to servants put up with this humiliation now?"

"What's this? Has the oil burned out?" asked the wife, opening the door to the room.

"Yes, it's all used up," answered Abisoghom Agha, suppressing his growing distress.

"Don't you worry, Abisoghom Agha. It's up to us to look after such things."

"Yes, but I'm hungry and can't wait any longer."

"What did I tell you? Don't trouble yourself; leave everything to me, I'll take care of it."

The wife quickly ran to the neighbor's house and, bringing some fuel, lighted the lamp in Abisoghom Agha's room.

A half hour had not passed since the return of light when there appeared before Abisoghom Agha a young man, who looked neither like a businessman, nor did he resemble a money changer, artisan, or laborer (we might conclude that he looked like something which bears no resemblance to anything). He appeared to be, at the most, thirty-two years old. Blue-eyed and blonde, he also had a beard the length of two fingers which, in my capital city, is either a sign of grief or of indigency. His clothes were so old that the antiquarians would have given a large sum for them. However, if repulsive from point of view of clothes, this person had a certain appeal in his visage.

"I'm your humble servant, honorable sir," shouted this young man, entering the room and approaching Abisoghom Agha.

"What's up? What do you want?" inquired Abisoghom Agha apprehensively.

"Most eminent sir, hearing of your arrival, I rushed over to place my profound respects, for sure, under your feet."

"Under my feet? Very well, go ahead and put them there," said Abisoghom Agha, who thought that he had brought slippers to him.

"Thank you, right honorable sir," said the youth, who took off his hat, got up on the table and stood there.

Apisoghom Agha, completely bewildered by this scene, impatiently waited to see what this man was going to do on the table.

The young man took a piece of paper from his breast pocket and, fixing his eyes on Abisoghom Agha, shouted with all his might:

"Ladies and gentlemen. . . ."

Apisoghom Agha, frightened by this horrid sound, jumped straight up from where he was sitting and, unable to restrain himself, shouted in turn:

"Who is this man? Is he some crazy person who's run from the insane asylum or an idiot who should be sent there?"

"The Armenian nation," continued the young man, lowering his voice a bit, "today is putting on an impressive performance which is dedicated to the bravest Armenian hero. . . ."

"What's on your mind, brother . . . ?"

"There was a time, when darkness fought against it, ignorance against knowledge, the past against the future, the imperative against the indicative, the sword against the pen, hatred against love, fire against water, meat against vegetables, but now those times have passed; they are gone; we are the future; they are darkness; we, light; they are ignorant; we, learned; they the sword; we, the pen; they are hatred; we, love; they are fire; we, water; they are meat; we, vegetables; they are cucumbers; we, apples; they are thorns; we, roses; those centuries have gone before us, during which time humanity rocked in the cradle of ignorance, first to one side, then to the other. . . ."

"What's gotten into you, brother? I haven't done anything to you. What do you want from me? Go and pour out your heart on the one who angered you. . . ."

"Yes, mankind was being tortured, was being outed at the hands of tyrants and didn't know to whom to turn and protest."

"Oh merciful God . . . oh compassionate God!" said Abisoghom Agha to himself, "as if our situation is bearable. . . . I can knock him down from the table now, but I'm afraid that he'll pull out a pistol from his breast pocket and shoot me because he's speaking with decided vehemence."

"And when wisdom arrived on the scene," continued the speaker, "and drove out ignorance, as the light did darkness, love hatred, the pen the sword, the future the past, then, oh at that time . . . yes, at that time, yes, I'm saying, only then was it understood that the words 'humanity,' 'nation' and 'fatherland' were not just made up to fill the dictionaries, but rather were words to be engraved on the mind, the heart and the soul of every man, in iron letters and in an indelible manner. . . ."

"Brother, I beg of you, come down and express the pain in your heart thus. . . ."

Standing there, the speaker was shaking so violently that Abisoghom Agha became worried that the lamp might fall to the floor.

Unable to tolerate this scene any longer, he shouted right up into the face of the self-invited speaker:

"Get down from there."

"I beseech you, don't scold me."

"Get down, and if you don't. . . ."

"Don't break a heart which throbs for our nation."

"Whatever you have to say, come over by me, sit down like a man, and say it. What's to be gained by getting up there?"

"I beg of you, let me finish! Ouch! You don't know how excited I get when I give a speech."

"Get down!"

The orator got down from the "stage" and sat on a chair.

"Now speak to me, what's on your mind?" said Abisoghom Agha indignantly.

"I beg of you, don't get angry."

"What do you want? Tell me, quickly, now!"

"Don't treat me with such wrath. I'll kiss your feet, my heart is heavy, now I'm starting to cry."

And the speaker began to cry.

"What's there to cry about, brother?"

"Your servant desires to serve the nation in the field of literature, but this nation treats its writers with ingratitude."

"Why am I to blame for that?"

"You're not at fault and maybe you're right. . . . I have poems written about the fatherland, lovely verses, honorable lines in which imagination, enthusiasm, inspiration, fire and flame all take wings and fly."

"Very well. Is that something to cry about?"

"Our nation doesn't understand their worth and dignity. It regards them as kid stuff and lets the authors go hungry."

"What am I to do?"

"Please, treat me with kindness."

"What have I done to you?"

"I was going to beseech you to. . . ."

"What? Say it right now. . . ."

"Don't yell at me, for God's sake, Now I'm going to cry. . . ."

Again the writer began to cry.

"God grant me patience," said Abisoghom Agha aside.

"My request was that the speech I just read be published. . . ."

"Go and have it printed. Is there anyone holding you back?"

"I was going to ask you, honorable sir, to give me some money so I could have the speech I just read printed."

"Why. . . . What reason is there for me to give money for your speech? Who's ever heard of one publishing a book for his own profit and Abisoghom Agha paying the cost? . . ."

"I beg of you, my heart is already broken, Don't inflict a new wound there."

"Why should I cause a new wound? Go on about your business, brother. You've become a pain in the back."

"Do you know how heavy this kind of talk weighs upon the heart of a writer?"

"I don't know and I don't want to know."

"The heart of a poet is very delicate. It is injured by the slightest remark. I've written a poem on this subject. I'll read it. Listen."

"Don't have time to listen to a poem."

"I beseech you, don't treat my poem so harshly. I've worked two months on that poem which you don't want to hear and when I hear it insulted like that, my dignity is hurt. I beg of you, don't speak badly about my poem. Please, allow me to read it once."

"I didn't come hear to listen to poems."

"Very well. I've written a tragedy. Let's go through that."

"I don't want to. I'm hungry now. I'm going to eat."

"Very well. I'll give a discourse upon food."

"I don't have time to listen."

"I beseech you, don't say that any more. Nothing is more damaging to an author who desires to read one of its labors of love to another. Please, most honorable sir, treat authors with kindness."

"Do you wish me to sit you on my head?"

"I'll kiss your feet, but don't make fun of me. Why should you sit me on your head?"

"Well, what am I to do? Am I to give you my purse so that I'll have treated authors with kindness?"

"No, only the cost of printing my speech."

"Row many gold pieces do you need to publish your work?"

"It can be done at a cost of four gold pieces. It's nothing. You'll be my patron and I'll put your name with a poem on the title page of the book."

"You're going to put it on the title page?"

"Yes."

"What for?"

"So that every person will know that the book was printed by means of your monetary contribution."

"Very well," answered Abisoghom Agha and took out four gold pieces and handed them to him. The author, offering a thousand respects, went out.

Abisoghom Agha called after him:

"Can't you also have the names of my servants put on the frontispiece and inform the nation that Abisoghom Agha has cows, sheep, donkeys and farms in his hometown?"

"Those remarks of yours fit the category called pastoral poetry."

"I don't understand."

"Poems written about those things; if you desire, I'll write such a poem."

"What am I going to do with the poem?"

"You can have it printed in a newspaper."

"Would they print it?"

"Why shouldn't they print it? If you happen to give half a gold piece, they'll print it forty times."

"Very well. Write it then."

"You can depend on it."

"But make sure it's good."

"Very well."

"In such a way that the reader will like it."

"Sure."

"You'll bring it tomorrow morning?"

"Tomorrow morning? . . . What are you saying? . . . I can hardly finish it in a month's time."

"One month from now?"

"At the earliest. . . . Reading a poem is easy, but writing one is difficult. At the very least, the writing of a beautiful poem takes two months."

"You don't say. . . ."

"Yes, but I'll try to finish it in a month's time."

"What a hard task it is!"

"What did you think? I've got to wait two months for my *musa*[5] to come and inspire me so I can write; a poem isn't written without the *musa*."

"What if the *musa* doesn't come? . . ."

"He'll come for sure."

"Isn't it possible for you to write a letter entreating him to come quickly so you won't have to wait two months?"

"He comes of his own accord. There's no need to write a letter, honorable sir."

"Where does he live? . . . Is it far from here?"

"Yes, it's quite far from here, but he'll come nevertheless."

"By land or by sea?"

"No, honorable sir, no."

---

5. Inspiration, muses (Armenian).

"Well, who is this man who, by rights, should be six feet under. . . . Where's he coming from?. Tell me, we'll figure out a way and have him brought here. If I give one or two gold pieces, will he come this week?"

"Yes, as soon as you give the two gold pieces, everything will be much easier all around, and my *musa* will come running this week," answered the *musa*-less poet as soon as he heard the words gold piece.

"It's as good as done. Goodbye, sir. I'm thankful to you, I'm a servant to your Honor and I pray that you'll accept. . . ."

"No," said Abisoghom Agha angrily, "You've carried on enough. Whatever you said, I accepted. What else do you want me to accept? . . ."

"My deepest guaranteed respect, sir, with which I remain your most humble servant."

"Very well."

The poet departed, promising that two gold pieces would bring the *musa,* whom some people have brought at a lower cost. The daily fee of the *musa* is no more these days than that of a carpenter. Abisoghom Agha, as the readers have observed, forgot about his hunger whenever one spoke to him about putting his name in the newspaper, or serving notice in church; likewise he opened his purse and rewarded all those who promised to propagate his name among the people. Glory is also a kind of hunger which men satiate by expending money. The prestige of being written up in newspapers (which some consider a vice and others a virtue, and which is found today among all classes of our people) had also affected Abisoghom Agha, who, after the departure of the poet, instead of thinking about his real hunger, began to get himself all worked up over the poem.

"I wonder," he asked himself, "whether the poem will be written as I want, whether this man's *musa* will come soon, and, if he doesn't, if another should be brought in his place? . . ."

As he was directing these questions to himself, the lady of the house entered the room and said:

"Dinner is ready. Welcome, Abisoghom Agha."

According to Turkish time it was midnight.

Grigor Artzruni

(1845–92)

The journalist, publicist, and critic Grigor Artzruni was born in Moscow. He received his education at the Tiflis gymnasium and attended the universities of Moscow and St. Petersburg, studying natural sciences. Although the languages spoken at home were mainly Russian and French, he began to improve his Armenian and took a keen interest in Armenian history and the social, political, and intellectual aspects of Armenian life. In 1867 he was admitted into Heidelberg University and graduated in 1869 with a doctorate in political economy and philosophy. Then he spent a year with the Mkhitarists, first in Vienna then in Venice, mastering the Armenian language; late in 1870 he returned to Tiflis. He obtained a teaching position at the Gayanian girls' school and also worked as a columnist at *Meghu Hayastani* (Bee of Armenia) and *Haykakan ashkharh* (The Armenian world).

His most significant step, one that represents a turning point in Armenian journalism, was the founding of the periodical *Mshak* (Tiller) in Tiflis in January 1872. As both editor and publisher, Grigor Artzruni guided the paper in the direction of liberalism and gathered around it some of the best writers of the day, such as Perch Proshian (1837–1907), Ghazaros Aghayan (1840–1911), Gabriel Sundukian (1825–1912),

Shirvanzadé (1858–1935), Vrtanes Papazian (1866–1937), and others. Although it started as a weekly, it soon became a daily and remained so for twenty years under Artzruni's editorship, until his death in 1892. It continued under different editors till 1921 and eventually closed because of changes in the ideological climate.

Artzruni's burning desire was to bring about essential changes—social, economic, political, and cultural—by shaking off archaic customs, ignorance, indifference, despotism, and exploitation by civic and religious rulers. He promoted the reorganization of the economic and social structure in such a way as to provide the productive elements, such as peasants and workers, with protection, incentives, and credit opportunities. He advanced ideas about the distribution of capital to raise the economic level of the peasants.

He was a strong promoter of education and intellectual enlightenment, and was against the conservatism and misconceived piety that prevented progress. He advocated equal education for boys and girls up to the university level, the emancipation of women, who had a major part to play both in the family and in society, and the training of young people for practical work. He believed that literature and arts should teach the reader how to renew and uplift his life, rid him of ignorance and prejudice, reveal his moral and intellectual deficiencies, and help to remedy them. Artzruni emphasized the teaching of the physical sciences for the training of the rational mind. He was in favor of the separation of church and state, and had some less than complimentary things to say about the clergy, whom he advised "to teach the people to live the life of the real doctrine of Christianity, rather than to repeat the lines and motions of the ritual."

In his philosophy, cosmopolitanism and nationalism are not in conflict. He pointed out that a true cosmopolitan does not despise nationalism because he knows full well that it is impossible to serve humanity without serving one's own nation. Consistent with this conviction, he believed that one must always learn one's mother tongue, because that too is a means to contribute to world culture.

On the Armenian question, Artzruni wrote spirited articles, particularly at the time of the Slavic revolts, asking "Isn't it the Armenians' turn now?" But after the Russo-Turkish war of 1877–78, realizing the tragic conditions in Ottoman Armenia and swayed by the hope of implementation of promised reforms in the Armenian provinces under the supervision of the European powers, he reoriented his ideas, believing that implementation would solve the Armenian question. Unfortunately, it did not turn out that way.

Grigor Artzruni also wrote memoirs, a novel entitled *Evelina* (1891), some short stories, and, more important, literary criticism. What made him famous, however, was *Mshak*, considered one of the most prestigious papers of the time. Most of Grigor Artzruni's writings, massive in volume and valuable in content, remain in the pages of this periodical. He exerted a tremendous influence on the social and intellectual life of Eastern Armenians.

A COUPLE OF WORDS ON THE EDUCATION OF GIRLS[1]

Are you familiar with how our girls should be educated? It is extremely easy to remember. Those who have the means should consider it a duty to teach their daughters French and how to play the piano, give them the opportunity to develop good taste to enable them to choose dresses, and above all train them to keep their mouths shut.

There you have it: the trend of contemporary education; according to many, the highest state of education that a girl is capable of attaining! I maintain, however, that such an education is no education at all. What do we expect from our girls? We demand that they contribute to the welfare of the community.

A girl who is educated in our present system will never be able to meet our expectations, because the education she has received does not sufficiently prepare her to contribute to the needs of the community.

We have two sorts of education for girls: general education, which is given outside the home, and the education she receives at home. In other words, a community school or boarding school education, which, like that available anywhere else, is not complete. Throughout their schooling, girls study with the greatest diligence and learn French, the majority of them lose their health, and their heads are filled with trifles and prejudices. Their minds are enlightened very little. They learn everything that is in the books, word for

---

1. Grigor Artzruni, *"Yerku khosk aghjikneru dastiarakutyan vera"* (A couple of words about the education of girls), in *Grigor Artzrunu ashkhatutiunnere* (The works of Grigor Artzruni) (Tiflis, 1904), 1:15–26. Translated by the editors of the present anthology.

word—often without grasping the meaning of what they memorize. Teachers do not consider it their mission to inculcate their pupils with the exact truth and its significance. A girl who wants to be able to assess this or that reality is immediately categorized as a free-thinker and -speaker, or even as crazy. They are expected to remember all the facts without formulating a reasonable point of view about them.

What is the use of such an education? "A person who knows many things," says Bokel, "cannot be called educated if he is not able to profit from what he knows."[2] After receiving such an education, girls do not have the slightest notion about the vocation of women or their obligations as mothers. They do not have the slightest knowledge of the matters and subjects they have studied for so many years.

Such a one-sided education not only fails to develop personal judgment in girls, it often stifles their intelligence. Consequently, this type of education is harmful rather than beneficial. Even women from the lower social classes are better off than those who are educated under such conditions. Women from the lower classes do not lose their natural intelligence, whereas most of the time others who are considered educated have a jaded attitude to any intellectual or even physical challenge. Their views on life have been destroyed; they have only a certain affinity or interest in endless diversions, in having a good time, and a superficial admiration for material things and physical appearances.

There are, however, people who believe that women are not capable of being solidly educated. This is not true. Women (like men) possess the ability to profit from education. And not only that, women's minds have an aptitude for thinking fast. Bokel confirms this when he says: "Women think faster than men. It is true that this particular characteristic of a woman's mind is hidden as a result of bad education, which prevents women from acquiring all kinds of useful knowledge. Contemporary education offers them only insignificant information, to the extent that their beautiful, delicate minds lose their natural capabilities."[3]

---

2. *Women's Influence on the Success of Knowledge.* (No other information is given.)
3. Ibid.

Women of the lower social strata often show the ability to think faster than those of the higher classes. A physician named Girri mentions in his letters that whenever men visited him for treatment with their wives, it was always the wives who answered his questions in a simple and comprehensive way, whereas the husbands had difficulty expressing themselves simply and explaining the nature of their pains and what they were suffering from. I would like to add the observations of a few travelers, which confirm our view. In a foreign country, when you do not speak the native language you are obliged to express yourself through gesture and mimicry. When you do so you will notice that women understand you much better and faster than men. Likewise in a foreign country, whenever you have to ask for directions you receive the simplest explanations from women. Men in such cases cause a great deal of confusion."[4]

Dr. Gertski confirms the opinion that women think faster than men, and he attributes this to their inferior education. In his book we read of a certain countess who says: "Thinking is hard work for women and happens occasionally, but it is not a continuous condition. The reason for this handicap is the lack of a solid formal education."[5]

Now for "home education." The education we give girls at home is even worse than what they receive outside. Nothing has killed so many minds and people as our stupid educational system. Why is that?

We do not lay aside old habits, just as we always hesitate to accept modern tendencies. We borrow only the external facade of European educational principles and we keep the Asian system as the foundation of our education. On the one hand, we teach girls to speak French and play the piano, we make them read useless literature (substantial knowledge is seldom offered) and dress them like Europeans, and on the other hand, the head of the family is still the Asian autocrat, whose orders must be executed without opposition. Children enjoy no freedom of thought or action. And what is the outcome of such conditions? Lack of physical and intellectual advancement, of course. Boys are freed from the yoke

---

4. Ibid.

5. D. Teptseri, *Zonschina* (Women). This is Artzruni's entire entry.

of this regime soon enough, but girls are unable to escape it their whole lives. In the capital, our home education has another evil face: children forget their mother tongue and are deprived of it throughout their formative years. Their love and enthusiasm for their nation is diminished; they may even hate their compatriots. Like their fathers, they are overbearing and conceited. They have neither nation, religion, language, nor healthy minds. On top of all this, another major aspect is lacking in their upbringing: they are deprived of friendship and are alienated from worldly life. Mankind needs friendship: it is damaging for children not to have it. If children experience no other life but that of their own families, their minds are subjected to one-dimensional training. Karl Bokel says, "Isolating people from the world damages them. If the children of prominent citizens are not very developed, the reason lies mainly in their education, which works against the natural needs of humans, removing them from the social milieu at a very early age."[6]

This is the state of our educational system. It is necessary that we change it. No woman educated under such conditions, I repeat, can offer anything beneficial to the community.

What is a woman's role in the community? A man speaks in public, writes, studies, and serves in different fields, etc., all in the public arena. But women have the task of raising their children. "The task of a man," says Adolf Kalachek, "is to influence the masses, but a woman's duty is to educate individuals and cultivate their spiritual aspect."[7] It is possible that these two tasks contradict each other, but in fact they are inseparable. Man educates the masses, woman the individual. But the masses are made up of individuals, so her purpose is ultimately the same: to raise useful members of society, to be of service to the community.

Because a woman fulfills her duty of educating individuals in terms of both spiritual and intellectual needs, she is able to give the necessary moral direction not only to her own children, but also to everyone entrusted to her tutelage. It is clear that the more solid the education a woman receives, the more influence she can exercise on society. Among uneducated nations such influence is almost impossible, as it often is among us Armenians. Our women

---

6. *Fiziologicheskie pisma* (Physiological letters).
7. *Podozhenie zhensh'chine Amerike* (The condition of women in America).

have generally not received good educations, so the majority of them are subject to their husbands' rough, crude treatment. The Armenian man gives endless orders to his family, and his wife and children must obey him without objection. As a result of such circumstances, Armenians have developed certain undesirable qualities, among which the worst are (slavish) respect for authority (arrogance, dictatorship, etc.) and dishonesty. These defects are seen in all their endeavors. Add to these defects their lack of intellectual enlightenment and it becomes clear why we generally do not succeed in our undertakings, even when we undertake the easiest and most agreeable things.

We have said that women educate children and have an influence on the moral development of boys. It is important to note, however, that a woman is able to exercise this influence effectively only when she herself has a solid educational background. In order for her to be able to give a certain direction to the education of children and enlighten their minds, she must first be educated herself. In order to be able to take care of their health, she must have a certain knowledge of the human body. Furthermore, she must know what is bad and what is good for the human body.

For example, if a mother makes her daughter stay at home all the time and forbids her to walk around, or even to run or to ride, because she considers these acts shameful, that mother is unwittingly damaging her daughter, harming her nature as a woman. I have heard that in Tiflis, an Armenian city, women have often been harmed during childbirth. If this is true, it alone proves what I am saying. If, on the one hand, the reason for this is our doctors, on the other hand its major cause is our inadequate education, which does not develop the female body, to which all of Europe pays a great deal of attention.

Teacher has the following explanation: "Instead of educating our girls to become exemplary mothers in time, we mainly offer them a shallow education to keep them busy, and among the needy families we teach them various professions that provide neither intellectual nor physical benefits."[8] The person who wrote this does not mean that professions are useless. What he means is that they are of secondary importance in education.

---

8. *Duchitel* (Teacher), 1862: 13 and 14.

Therefore, if we wish girls to become useful members of society, we must change how they are educated. Instead of filling their heads with silly and useless subjects, we should acquaint them with the exact sciences. Instead of denying them all knowledge of the natural sciences, we should stop considering such things shameful and teach them about nature, the human body, and life. It is not necessary to fill their minds with a lot of fables; on the contrary, we must try to imprint on them a realistic view of life. In short, we must not kill their spirits and bodies with an Asian education; we must put aside prejudices; we must give them a true education and bring them closer to male society—it may offer these girls a better intellectual outlook and thus lay the foundations for a different viewpoint.

But my dear readers, do not imagine that the author of these lines had the intention of giving advice. No! He only wished to express his mind. He is not in the habit of giving advice. He has not yet forgotten what our dear poet wrote:

> Do not criticize the Armenian in your book;
> The Armenian, albeit gentle, abhors advice.
> Do not laugh at his crazy deeds:
> He thinks he is true to his heritage.

Reteos Perperian (Berberian)

(1848–1907)

Reteos Perperian was born in Khasgiugh (Hasköy), an Armenian suburb of Constantinople, and graduated from the local Nersesian school in 1866. With his innate abilities, inclinations, and ideals he was born to be an educator, and from his youngest years he cherished the ambition of founding a school. He realized this dream in 1876, when he founded the Perperian school in Scutari (Üsküdar); over the years it became an educational institution renowned for high standards.

He shaped the curriculum and methodology of the school according to his own educational and pedagogical concepts, which aimed at imparting moral and spiritual values, intellectual excellence, and the traits of character required to conduct a virtuous life. His motto was to pursue what was *good, true, and beautiful* (see Philippians 4:8), and he tried to inculcate this principle in his students. The most convincing source of inspiration for them was the example he set in his own life, which was the embodiment of his teaching. It was indeed an idealistic approach, but it had amazing success in raising a generation of youth that included some of the best writers of the epoch.

The school program was diversified by the addition of foreign languages and social studies, and the graduates reached a level of competency high enough to enable them to enter foreign universities. Perperian remained head of the school until his death in 1907. It continued under new principals: Petros Karapetian (1907–9), followed by Perperian's two sons, Onnik (1909–11) and Shahan (1911–22, with an interruption—1914–18—caused by the First World War and the genocide). In 1924 the school was moved to Cairo, where it continued to function until 1934. It closed for financial reasons.

Reteos Perperian's first book of poetry, *Arajin terevk* (The first leaves, 1877), was written under the influence of French romanticism, particularly of Lamartine, a few of whose poems he had translated. *Mardik yev irk* (Men and objects, 1885) is a compilation of articles that appeared in 1883–84 in the periodical *Yerkragunt* (The globe): metaphysical reflections on his own worldview, nature, the elements, and human beings. *Dastiaraki me khoskere* (Words of an educator, 1901) consists of his speeches and lectures, which emphasize the idealistic approach in education as opposed to the materialistic. In *Khohk yev hushk* (Thoughts and memories, 1903) the poet reveals his deepest emotions: the book was written after the death of his beloved wife. His grief and meditations transcend the personal and become universal. His last work was *Dprots yev dprutiun* (School and schooling, 1907), which contains additional articles on educational matters.

In all his works, whether verse or prose, Perperian wrote with elegance of style and language, often enriched with classical forms that give a unique charm to his writing. He was a poet and a publicist, but first and foremost a great educator. Abp. Maghakia Ormanian (1841–1918) dubbed him "The father of the learned" and "The Head Teacher."

THE BLIND YOUTH'S GRIEF[1]

They say that it is pleasing to see the morn, when it dawns in that reddish brightness with which the East shines in burning brilliancy; the sun's first rays, that gild the summits of the mountains and the domes of the temples; and the dew that glitters like pearls on the grass of the meadows; but that I do not see these things is not what grieves me most.

They say that nature is beautiful in the springtime, and that it is charming to see the rose unfold, to behold the trees adorned

---

1. Reteod Perperian, "The Blind Youth's Grief," *Armenia* 3, no. 8 (July 1907), 3–5. Translated by J. J. Barsamian.

with green leaves; the verdant fields covered with flowers like gems adorning an emerald garment; and the many-hued butterflies flying in the air, or resting on the bosoms of their brothers—the flowers; but that I do not see these things is not what grieves me most.

They say that the sea is wonderful; that in the Strait of Bosporus she reflects in her crystalline waves the palaces and gardens on her shores; that in the broad Marmara, she is limitless in extent, stretching afar to embrace the sky; that in the daylight she sparkles resplendently like molten gold under the rays of the sun, and at night the beams of the stars and the moon slumber in her gentle bosom; that in her calmness she is like a smooth mirror, but when disturbed by the tempest she roars violently, and her mountainous billows foam like ferocious long-maned steeds, and groaning dash themselves upon the rocks; but that I do not see these things is not what grieves me most.

They say that to behold the sky is delightful, that it exalts man, and rouses his mind to sublime thoughts; that when the day is pleasant the sun moves with luminous radiance like a pompous monarch in his kingdom; that when the sky is dark, lightning and thunder come forth; that when the sun sets, the stars appear like heavenly flowers, or hang as if each were a celestial lamp, or as if they were Abigails of the moon, waiting to pay due homage to the Queen of the Night, that rising from the East comes with majestic bearing to make her nightly visit to the ethereal field above us; that she has a thin gauze of clouds spread over her head, and casts a gentle glimmer from her eyes; but that I do not see these things is not what grieves me most.

That which grieves my heart most, and makes me feel the depth of my misfortune is not my inability to behold the morn, the spring, the sea of heavens, but it is, alas! when I cannot see my mother's face.

Atrpet (Sargis Mupahiachian)

(1850–1937)

Sargis Mupahiachian, known by the pen name Atrpet, was born in Kars, received his early education in Alexandropol (now Giumri), moved to Constantinople to continue his education at the Mkhitarist school, then studied at the Ottoman Imperial Lyceum, from which he graduated with a degree in law. Beginning in 1880 he taught in the Armenian schools of a number of cities and towns, from Karin (Erzurum) to Kars, Alexandropol, Akhalkalak, Tiflis, and so on. He spent some time in Tavriz on legal business, and also did research on Iranian history and society for a future book. During the 1890s he was involved in political activities. He was a member of the *Pashtpan Hayreniatz* (Defender of the homeland) organization in Karin, a member of the Central Committee of the Hnchakian Party in Tiflis, and editor (1907–8) of the journal *Apaga* (Future). He was also a regular contributor on historical and philological topics to a number of periodicals such as *Baznavep* (*Polyhistor*), *Mshak* (Tiller), *Handes amsorya* (Monthly review), *Hayastani kochnak* (The call of Armenia), and *Azgagrakan handes* (Ethnographic review). In 1895 he was arrested and exiled to Rostov for his political activities, but soon released. He toured Europe in 1905–6, and during the First World War was a correspondent on the eastern front for the journal *Murch* (Hammer) and some Russian papers.

During the Soviet regime he lived in Giumri, Armenia, and dedicated himself entirely to literature until his death in 1938.

His literary output is varied: novels, short stories, plays, essays on social and political issues, historical and philological studies, and numerous articles in various periodicals. Three of his principal novels are *Khev Karapet* (Crazy Karapet, 1889), *Almast* (1891, in two volumes), and *Javahir* (1904); these last two titles are proper names. His best known short stories include "*Orinakan zharank*" (The legal inheritance, 1903), "*Dimakner*" (Masks, 1904), and "*Charahat*" (The unfortunate, 1905). His most famous short story is "*Tzhvzhik*" (the name of a dish prepared with lamb's lung, 1938), which was made into a movie. *Shushan* (1890) and *Sarraf* (1893) are plays, the first of which was adapted as an opera by Kara-Murza. Among Atrpet's historical works are *Khalifat* (Caliphs, 1906) and *Imarat* (Buildings, 1906), which are historical views of the Sunni and Shiite Muslims, respectively; *Hoghatirutiune Kovkasum* (The ownership of land in the Caucasus, 1906); *Mahmet Ali Shah* (1909), a political, economic, and legal study, in Russian, of contemporary Persia; *Hay tagavorneri dramnere* (Coins issued by Armenian kings, 1913); and a number of other works such as "The Shiite Clergy," "The Papacy," "The Young Turks Movement," and "The Persian Taxation System." He is at his best in his novels and short stories, which reflect village life in all its aspects, in delightful prose rich in ethnographic detail. His written language is Eastern Armenian, despite the fact that he was born and educated in Western Armenia. His collected works, in ten volumes, were published in Tabriz, Giumri, and Tiflis, 1904–11, and in Yerevan in 1964.

TZHVZHIK[1]

Many years ago there lived in Erzurum a certain poor old man named Brother Nerses and a rich man named Nikoghos Agha. The latter, having lived in Constantinople for a number of years, talked fluent Greek, and for this reason and in order to distinguish him from other Nikoghoses in the city, people called him Nikoghos the Greek. Brother Nerses had in his turn once been a very rich man. He was the scion of a distinguished family greatly honored by governors and ministers. But he suffered great misfortunes and

1. Atrpet, "*Tzhvzhik*" (A dish prepared with sheep's lung), in Sarkis Ashjian, ed. and trans., *Great Armenian Short Stories* (Beirut, 1959), 106–13. Translated by Sarkis Ashjian and revised by the editors of the present anthology.

completely failed in life. First his caravans were plundered on the way to Damascus and Constantinople, then his ships were pillaged by pirates in the Black and Mediterranean Seas. Then the Kurds drove his cattle in his own country; furthermore his personal enemies burned his barns and stocks down to ashes. Of his shops and hotels no trace remained. And Brother Nerses was so bewildered, so disappointed and so discouraged that life at last meant absolutely nothing to him, and he led a drab life, loathing all his neighbors. Although his house was dilapidated and in ruins, the signs of past glory could be seen on its exterior. Even his old and shabby clothes showed that they were once first-rate. He had grown old and wrinkled and a bit hunchbacked but he still preserved his magnanimity. He was definitely poor and destitute, needing the help of neighbors and friends, yet he never stooped to beg or live on the pity of other people.

Once, meeting him in the market, at the butcher's, Nikoghos Agha bought a sheep's lung, liver, and heart, which cost him a quarter of a piastre and said to him:

"Take this lung home, Brother Nerses, it's for you!"

"Thank you," he answered and, taking the lung from his hand, he walked homeward with Nikoghos Agha.

The latter had bought a whole sheep, and his servant was following him with the sheep across his shoulders. Although in the distinguished company of Nikoghos Agha, Brother Nerses modestly tried to remain one step to the rear as a sign of honoring him.

When they had left the market and extricated themselves of the circle of ignorant Turks so that they no longer needed to be on their guard against irregular soldiers and Moslem fanatics, Nikoghos Agha said to Brother Nerses, with the air of an experienced man who gives advice to a green young man:

"You know, you must tell my sister, I mean your wife, to scrape off the grease of the lung first with a knife, then let her melt the grease slowly in the frying pan. Let her fry the lung the first day, the liver the following day and the third day let her fry the heart. Advise her to cut the lungs in tiny pieces, otherwise the food won't be palatable. You surely realize, Brother Nerses, that we are close friends and that's why I am giving you my friendly advice. You see with your own eyes how difficult it is to buy anything from those nasty people in the market even if you have got the money. Half your life is destroyed before you finish with them. And then you surely realize how difficult it is to earn one fourth of a piastre. You must live frugally, you see, you mustn't eat much, you ought to put some money aside. Tell my sister (he meant of course Brother Nerses' wife) to put the pan on a slow fire otherwise the grease will turn dark and useless. In that way she will have both economized wood and made sure that the food will be well cooked. When she brings it on table, let her drain off the melted fat for use on the next occasion. And if your wife is economical enough, she may make such use of the melted fat as to be able to cook enough pancakes for the whole family on the fourth day. The lung is exceedingly tasty but you have to season it moderately with salt and pepper and cook it on a slow fire. I think it would be better for your wife to cook half of the white lung the first day and the other half the second day, half of the black lung the third day and the other half the fourth day. How tasty it will be! You must eat it with fresh bread with indescribable joy and appetite! Brother Nerses, tell me, doesn't your mouth water when you think of it?"

Brother Nerses followed his benefactor silently. When Nikoghos Agha asked him questions and looked askance at him, he bent his head as a sign of sheepish agreement. Nikoghos Agha expected him to be grateful and thank him with humbleness; he expected him to express his gratitude in clear and distinct words, yet Brother Nerses couldn't so much as utter a syllable, he was so ashamed. Nikoghos went on with his diligent advice and, thinking he was doing him a good turn, he questioned him and tried to elicit from him words of gratitude, but Brother Nerses was deep in thought and he didn't seem even to hear his words.

"Poor Nerses," he said to himself in self-pity, "there was a time when hundreds of poor and famished people and strangers were filled at your rich tables; they found shelter and protection under your hospitable roof and left your home after being fed and clothed. Hundreds of loafers were given decent jobs at your shops and hostels and thus they fed their families; you helped every acquaintance, neighbor and stranger alike, and you never expected anybody to express gratitude for one moment, and now a certain upstart of a Nikoghos, the son of the cobbler Todor, buys a nasty lung for you to feed your family and reads an obnoxious and trite sermon over your poor head and to crown it all, he expects gratitude!"

To the very door of his house God knows how Nikoghos preached him to be a good economizer, to be content with little, to acknowledge the benevolence of other people and not to be grateful to anybody at all. And he kept repeating: "Do you think you'll lose anything if you send me your son to cut my grass? Surely he won't spoil his hands or die of fatigue? Of course, it is a clear fact that I have more than one servant in my home and so many lick-spittle domestics around me I don't need a new one, yet it is something noble to keep one's self-respect and not be beholden to anybody else. For example, send your daughter one day, let her scrub my floors, what's wrong with it? Do you think her back will break if she scrubs my floors? You surely know that I have about forty maids at my service; the floors of my rooms are so clean you can collect the oil you have spilled on them and you will see it none the worse. My floors are so clean, yet when I propose this to you, my intention is otherwise. I want you to grasp the meaning of the word honor. You'll be great and respected in proportion as you keep your honor. For example, do you think your wife will die of fatigue if she comes to our home some time and washes our linen or bakes our bread? And isn't it sure that my wife will do her best to reward her by some way or another?"

Nikoghos was a smart man by nature, and the fact that he had spent part of his life in Constantinople had rendered him more wily and glib. He talked so much that Brother Nerses stopped listening and said to himself: "I wish I had never met you today; a curse on you and your nasty lung; it would be better for my family to starve than receive your dirty lung!" But Nikoghos was no prophet; he did not guess what was passing through the man's mind and change the subject of his conversation. He looked and strove for one thing alone: he wanted everybody in Erzurum to talk about him and to recognize him as the richest, the noblest, the most generous and most benevolent man in all the city. Nikoghos the Greek wanted to be proclaimed and hailed as Lord and Master of Erzurum, and he wished everybody to genuflect before him in gratitude.

When they arrived at the house of Brother Nerses, he stopped him and said: "You see, the position of your house is wonderful but it is a pity those who built it were stupid and ignorant men; they haven't built it so as to withstand the destruction of centuries."

He intended with these words to wound Nerses' heart and to prove his superiority and farsightedness. When Brother Nerses hurried to go in, finding no other means to stop him, Nikoghos said:

"I wish you good appetite for the sheep's lung!"

"Thank you," said Brother Nerses and entered in with hasty steps. He had a large family. His wife had already prepared the soup. She cooked the lung as well and they left the table hardly filled. The scions of a family once notorious for its riches, they had to appease their hunger with a drop of soup and a nasty sheep's lung. But they were used to enduring every hardship, and no one heard them grumble at their lot.

Toward evening Brother Nerses went to church in slow steps to pray to his Maker, to ask for His help and pity.

On his way he met Nikoghos Agha, who said: "Good evening, Brother Nerses, how is your health? I notice you walk like a vigorous young man. You seem to have received a young man's strength; how was the sheep's lung? Was it tasty? Did my sister, I mean your wife, scrape it well?"

"Very well indeed, my lord, I thank you very much; we all thank you for it very much," answered Brother Nerses in haste, so that Nikoghos Agha would give up talking about the lung and discuss something else. He was terribly afraid that those in the churchyard might hear and that he would be insulted and wounded in his pride.

"It seems you have eaten it with a good appetite; you definitely seem fresher, even the color of your face has changed to a crimson red. Were the salt and pepper added in good proportion?" asked Nikoghos, without considering that his voice might be heard by the bystanders. Brother Nerses, shrinking into himself, wished the ground to open and swallow him alive and bury him forever. "Everything, everything was right," he stammered, wishing to put an end to the conversation. But Nikoghos desired at all costs to let all the church people know that he had given him, as alms, a lung which had cost him one fourth of a piastre.

"My late mother," went on Nikoghos Agha, "was experienced in cooking sheep's lung; so wonderfully did she cook it, I would be satisfied by its odor alone, the moment I entered home. She cooked it so miraculously; ever since her death I always yearn for sheep's lung. But alas! The old are dead and they have taken their skill to the grave along with them. God knows how many times I have wished for a dish of lung; my appetite is always ready for it, yet the women of our own times are unable to cook it palatably. But I hope my sister, I mean your wife, is not like the new fangled women of today. I feel sure she has given you a wonderful chance to taste a glorious meal of sheep's lung today. I think I am not mistaken in my conjecture, am I?" said Nikoghos Agha standing in the churchyard, gazing at him.

"Surely, surely, it was wonderful," answered Brother Nerses and hurried to get into the church. But once in the church, instead of praying he began to reproach God that, as if it was not enough he was in this pitiful and miserable situation, suffering the agonies of utmost poverty and privation, to crown it all, he had fallen into the ruthless clutches of a certain ambitious upstart called Nikoghos the Greek!

On the next morning Brother Nerses went to the market, desiring to sip a cup of coffee. He entered the coffeehouse. There were many kind-hearted people there who knew of his old days of glory and, without being noticed by him, they would wink at the waiter to serve him a cup of coffee on their own account. So without anybody knowing it, this or that man would pay for him from their own purse and he would get out of the coffeehouse honorably as though he had paid for the coffee himself.

He had hardly begun to sip his coffee when Nikoghos Agha entered and, saluting him silently, sat facing him. Brother Nerses felt his coffee turn to poison. He felt he would be sure to talk about benevolence in public. And in fact he was not mistaken.

Holding his coffee cup in his hand in a masterful way and enjoying the smoke of his long pipe, he began:

"Now, how are you, Brother Nerses, did you relish the sheep's lung according to your heart's desire yesterday? One certainly is greatly pleased when one's food is prepared according to one's taste, eh?"

"Surely, surely, there is no doubt about it," he stammered slowly, hoping Nikoghos Agha would be ashamed of himself and would stop repeating the story of that nasty lung. His heart already was madly beating with suppressed anger.

"What are you talking there?" asked one of the habitual loafers in the coffeehouse who had heard the word mentioned.

"Oh! practically nothing," answered Nikoghos Agha, slowly hammering out his words. "You see, yesterday I went to butcher's. There I saw a shapely lung and I bought it to take home. But to tell you the truth I was sorry my people at home couldn't manage to cook it well; so I was turning this over in my mind when I happened to meet our Brother Nerses just at that moment. So I presented the lung to him right away. I said to myself whether it goes to my own home or to that of Brother Nerses makes no difference at all. Glory be to God, we are intimate neighbors and we have never considered ourselves as strangers. Who cares for thine and mine? It all amounts to the same thing. I have always considered Brother Nerses in that light. The fact is I was greatly pleased to think my sister, I mean his wife, would make something nice out of it. You see, what I care for is to see things done in the right way. If I had sent it to my own home they would sure have turned it into something nasty. Who could have eaten it? I like food well cooked and I was sure my sister, I mean his wife, would cook it so nicely Brother Nerses would lick and bite his fingers along with the morsels of the lung, it would taste so nice. And now Brother Nerses tell the rest yourself, I've already finished the part of the story which concerns myself!"

"Well, what do you want me to add? We thank you very much. We cooked it and ate it and that's the long and short of it!" answered Brother Nerses, turning as red as a lobster.

"Well done! I was not talking about that side of the question; I only wanted to be informed whether it was properly cooked or not?" remarked Nikoghos Agha, simulating earnest interest.

"Very well cooked and very appetizing indeed!" answered Brother Nerses, burning in his heart for shame and sweating all over.

"I understand it perfectly well. The greatest pleasure in the world is that of eating what you like, cooked nicely," said Nikoghos Agha.

Being unable to withhold his anger any more, Brother Nerses left the coffeehouse.

On the other hand it was a great pleasure for Nikoghos Agha to hear the story of his famous lung told everywhere! Whenever and wherever he met Brother Nerses, his question would turn upon the subject of the sheep's lung. And he would corner him with irrelevant questions such as this:

"Brother Nerses, do you remember the lung? It was tasty, wasn't it?"

And all the city came to know about it. Nikoghos Agha talked everywhere. A week, a month, three months, six months and at last a whole year passed, and yet Nikoghos Agha would remind him of the lung wherever he met him, whether he was in the street or in the churchyard, in the coffeehouse or in the bath, at meetings or at wedding feasts. So much so that the lung bought for him by Nikoghos Agha became an intolerable curse.

And one day, getting desperately out of temper and patience, Brother Nerses waited before the butcher's door with determination. He had hidden something under his coat. It happened that Nikoghos Agha came along with his servant to buy meat and, noticing Brother Nerses, he said as usual, "How are you, Brother Nerses, I hope you are quite well. Do you remember that greasy lung?"

"Take your nasty lung back and hold your tongue from now on!" roared Brother Nerses, and, taking out the voluminous sheep's lung hidden under his coat, he struck Nikoghos in the face with such unheard of fury that the man was absolutely dumbfounded by the blow. He was struck mute and utterly, absolutely unable to move, and he was a laughingstock to all the passersby, with his face, his turban and his neck covered with blood. . . .

Petros Durian

(1851–72)

A poet, playwright, and aspiring actor, Petros Durian broke new ground in Armenian poetry. In many ways, the modern lyric tradition originates in his work . . . , which is innovative and splendidly spontaneous. His imagery and metaphors are fresh and eloquent, his intimacy charming, and his diction limpid. Beneath his predominantly elegiac and seemingly subdued style, there lurks a tempestuous soul, eagerly but vainly trying to cling to a life sadly cut short by consumption. In his slim collection of verse shine some of the best lines ever uttered in Armenian.[1]

Petros Durian was born in 1851 in Scutari (Üsküdar), a suburb of Constantinople on the Asiatic shore of the Bosporus. His father, a blacksmith, was scarcely able to provide for his large family; however, he acceded to the wishes of his son and sent him to the Armenian academy (*Chemaran*) in Scutari, where his favorite teacher, Hakob Paronian (Baronian, 1843–91), the renowned satirist, discerned his talents and gave him special attention. His penchant for literature was manifested early. At the age of thirteen he wrote his first poem and at fifteen his first play, *Vard yev Shushan* (Rose and Lily: proper names, 1867), a pastoral melodrama which, though lacking artistic merit, depicts an emotional love-hate conflict. He made rapid progress in school, and on graduating he received a volume of Lamartine's works as an award for his excellent performance.

After he completed school, his first concern was to find employment so he could help his family. He worked variously at a pharmacy,

---

1. Kevork B. Bardakjian, *A Reference Guide to Modern Armenian Literature, 1500–1920* (Detroit, 2000), 119–20.

a merchant's office, and for a newspaper editor; he also tutored students, but in this capacity he was treated as an errand boy and exploited. Then, despite his father's opposition, he decided to seek his fortune in the theater, for which he had an innate ability and a great fascination. Armenian theater was flourishing in Constantinople at the time, and he hopefully joined the theatrical troupe founded by actor-director Hakob Vardovian (1840–98). His two plays, *Vard yev Shushan* (Rose and Lily) and *Sev hogher* (Black soil), were staged in 1867 and 1868 respectively, with very little financial benefit to the author. At Vardovian's suggestion he wrote a historical tragedy, *Artashes Ashkharhakal* (Artashes the conqueror, 1869), and its favorable reception encouraged him to write others in quick succession: *Ankumn Arshakunyats harstutyan* (The fall of the Arshakuni dynasty, 1870), *Aspatakutiunk Parskats i Hays kam kortzanumn Ani mayrakaghakin Bagratunyats* (Persian invasions of Armenia or the destruction of Ani, capital of Bagratunis, 1908), *Kortzanumn Hrovma ishkhanutyan* (The overthrow of Roman rule, 1870), *Shushanik* (a proper name), *Tigran II,* and his last play, *Tatron kam tshvarner* (Theater or the wretched, 1871), which deals with social injustice in contemporary life, and whose hero may be seen as a representation of the author himself.

Durian's plays do not accurately reflect his talent: they were written hastily, mainly to satisfy the demands and tastes of the time. The dialogue consists mostly of patriotic orations, laments, or evocations, rather than lively depictions of people and events. The language is poetic and captivating, the style romantic and, particularly in love scenes, spontaneous and highly communicative. These dramas were received with enthusiasm, but unfortunately they failed to benefit the author materially, because some of the directors and publishers denied him his full rights. After his death, the manuscript of another play, *Taragir i Siberia* (Exiled to Siberia), was discovered among his papers; this is an allegorical depiction of the political exile of Mikayel Nalbandian (1829–66) to Saratov.

Petros Durian is famed for his poetry. He is a special phenomenon in Armenian literature. A young man who lived barely twenty-one years and wrote no more than forty poems, he captivated young readers with the sincerity of his heart and the power of his poetry, the kind of poetry that streamed from a troubled soul caught between a boundless love for life, nature, and his "beloved" on the one hand, and his gruesome destiny of premature death on the other. The "beloved," although always referred to in the feminine, is a mysterious and immaterial entity, a poetic abstraction perhaps, which makes his poetry more sublime. His poems reflect the exhausting struggle between an ardent desire to live and fulfill his dreams and the merciless fate that awaits him. He feels that as a youth he is entitled to love, to dream, and to enjoy the exuberance of nature, but even nature betrays him. As he puts it in one of his last poems ("*Trtunj*": grievance): "In vain did the stars spell out *love* in the skies; in vain did the nightingales teach me to love; in vain did the gentle breezes bring me messages of love. In vain did the shrubs fall silent and the leaves cease breathing so as not to disturb my dream of 'her.' Alas! They were all mocking me. . . ." He revolts against God, only to repent with a subdued spirit. All his poems express keen sensitivity, sincerity, and strong emotions, in subdued but eloquent language. Nine of his poems are inspired by patriotic feelings. In one of them he grieves at not being able to serve his fatherland, knowing that death is imminent.

Durian also left behind fifteen letters, written to various individuals between 1869 and 1871 during his illness. They form an exquisite bouquet of prose poetry that complements his poems in verse. He is noted for the purity and elegance of the modern Armenian he used in all his works; in this respect, he was far ahead of many renowned, more experienced writers among his contemporaries.

He died of consumption on 21 January 1872. Four thousand young people followed his funeral procession, accompanied by a choir and band—an event without precedent and in violation of Church rules.[2] Durian's humble life, his broken love, his eternal aspirations, and his undying poetry spurred this outpouring of grief and adoration.

COMPLAINT[3]

Goodbye, Sun, I say to you and the God
who made us both, farewell. I go
to become another constellation in the sky.

What are the stars if not luckless souls that fly up to burn
and curse the forehead of the heavens?

---

2. When Petros Durian died, the youth who organized his funeral asked the patriarch for special permission to have the church choir and an accompanying band lead the funeral procession. The patriarch, Mkrtich Khrimian Hayrik, said, "I do not grant you permission, but if you go ahead and do it, I shall forgive you."
3. Petros Durian, "Complaint," in *Anthology of Armenian Poetry*, ed. and trans. Diana Der Hovanessian and Marzbed Margossian (New York, 1978), 126–27.

God, the root and source of lightning
strikes us to increase the sharp
weaponry of his sky.

I blaspheme. And deserve
to be struck now, oh God.
Shatter the presumption of this climber
of unclimbable heights.

God, I salute you and your world
of waves, dews, words, and
you, my God, who darkens my forehead
even as it blooms, and takes the flame
from my eyes and the tenseness from my lips.

You have promised me at the gate of death
a door to a new life,
a life of vast light and fragrance.

If this is to be my last breath
here in this silent haze,
give me instead the right
to stay here as a fork of lightning
wrapped around your name.
Let me roar forever here.

Let me become a curse.
Let me stick to your side.
Let me thunder at you: Wrathful God!
But I tremble only. And become nothing
but a bitter sigh in the black cypress trees,
a dry leaf or needle falling.

Why don't you give me one spark
so I can live?
I want to live.
What good is such a short dream
consummated by the grave?
Is my fate written only in the ink made of dregs
from that grave?

I want to live, to love.
Dying man wants only two things.

First life. Then, failing that,
a mourner.
God made the moon for those
without mourners. For those
like me he made the stars. But for nothing
they spell "love."
The nightingale echoes "love."
And for nothing the wind inspires "in love"
and the mirror shows me young.

In vain, bushes kept silent
as I walked by.
And in vain the leaves did not breathe,
so as not to disturb my dreams.
Their silence is mockery.
The whole world is nothing
but a mockery of God.

THE LAKE[4]

What shock has stopped you, lake,
and calmed the run
of your waves? Was it pain?
Pain on some beautiful face?

Or do your waves mimic
the placid sky floating on
a foam of clouds?
Let me learn such silence.

Let my wounds,
numberless as your ripples
and my thoughts, substances
as your spray, copy you.

Even when you are filled
with all of heaven's stars
you do not burn
like the lake of fire in my heart.

---

4. Durian, "The Lake," ibid., 124–25.

You keep those stars untarnished;
you keep your flowers unpickable;
unfading, and the clouds rainless
even as you keep me trembling
but peaceful.

"He is trembling and pale."
"All he has is his song."
"He is dying." These rejections
have been my lot.
No one asked, "Why
does he smoulder?" or said
"If he is loved he will not die."

No one said, "Let us listen.
Perhaps his sadness is made
of fire and not from books."
But no. The fire is
only ashes. Ashes.

Swell up and grow stormy,
lake. It is despair now
that you must reflect.

My Death[5]

When the pallid angel of death
Comes to me with his impenetrable smile,
And my pain begins to dissolve, my soul,
Know that I'm still alive.

When shining down from the head of my bed,
A dim small candle lights my dying face,
And gives off only a bitter cold ray,
Know that I'm still alive.

When, all wrapped, I am placed in a dark coffin,
And I lie in my layered shroud, a cold stone,

---

5. Durian, "My Death," in *Armenian Poetry Old and New*, ed. and trans. Aram Tolegian (Detroit, 1979), 141.

My brow now tearless and sanctified,
Know that I'm still alive.

When the peal of the iron bell
Causes a smile on the face of death,
And my coffin makes its silent way,
Know that I'm still alive.

When those men who chant the death songs,
Who wear black and have harsh lines in their faces,
Give prayers and spread incense all around,
Know that I'm still alive.

When they have trimmed my earthly grave,
And, sobbing and grieving,
Turned homeward my family and friends,
Know that I'm still alive.

But if my grave remains unmarked
In a corner of the earth,
And remembrance of me fades away,
Ah, know then that I am dead.

Yeghia Temirchipashian (Demirdjibashian)

(1851–1908)

Yeghia Temirchipashian was born in Khasgiugh (Hasköy), a suburb of Constantinople and one of the intellectual centers of the time. He completed his education at the local Nersesian and Nupar-Shahnazarian schools, and graduated with distinction. From early youth he was a solitary person and an avid reader. He read incessantly—in an unorganized way—many works, from the classics to the moderns, including such authors as Homer, Virgil, Shakespeare, Milton, Byron, Shelley, Spenser, Leopardi, Goethe, Schopenhauer, Georg Buchner, Musset, Lamartine, Madame de Staël, Georges Sand, Balzac, Zola, Auguste Comte, Littré, and Montesquieu, all of whom influenced him in one way or another, sometimes in contradictory ways. He was principally captivated by books that represent the sadder aspects of life, its vanity, and the reality of death, which seemed to suit his melancholy disposition.

Temirchipashian worked for a while as a functionary in a government department, but he quit his job with the intention of going to Paris to acquaint himself with Western civilization. The project failed because of family situations that shook his already delicate psyche and his physical health. Deeply concerned about his condition, his family managed to find the means to send him to Marseille for recuperation in 1874, suggesting that he also study economics. Instead of following their advice, he spent his time reading voraciously and even attempting to publish a paper in French (*Le Moniteur littéraire et financier de Marseille:* The literary and financial monitor of Marseille).

He returned to Constantinople in 1876 and immediately became involved in a dispute that was raging at the time: the new rules for spelling modern Armenian suggested by his old friend and classmate Minas Cheraz (1852–1929), whom he supported. When the Education Council rejected Cheraz's suggestions, however, Temirchipashian conceded. Even though in principal he was a proponent of modern Armenian, all his writings reflect the charm of classical Armenian. "I adore the classical and I defend the modern" he wrote in one of his articles.

In 1879 he began to publish the *Pilisopayakan bararan* (Philosophical dictionary), with the aim of introducing a critical spirit and freedom of thought into literature; sometimes he flirted with atheistic ideas, arousing widespread disapproval. From 1880 on he published a series of critical articles and book reviews on a number of contemporary authors in the periodical *Masis:* some were laudatory, others disapproving, but all were very rigid in their evaluations.

In 1883 Temirchipashian launched a monthly journal called *Grakan yev imastasirakan sharzhum* (Literary and philosophical movement), every issue of which he filled with his own writings. In 1884 he started another periodical, *Yerkragunt* (The globe), on which Grigor Zohrap (1861–1915) and Reteos Perperian (Berberian, 1848–1907) collaborated. Both papers ceased publication in 1888.

Temirchipashian worked diligently as a teacher, writer, editor, and an assemblyman. By 1889 his health had begun to deteriorate, and he sank into despondency. Now all he desired was to die and attain nirvana, a concept to which he referred many times in his writings. A pessimistic mood engulfed him; he wrote about the futility of the world and the "majestic beauty" of death. The loss of his mother in 1890, following the death of his younger brother, aggravated his condition. In 1893 he attempted suicide by throwing himself into the sea, but he was saved by a boatman. Driven by a persecution complex, he frequently changed his place of residence. In 1895, in search of yet another dwelling place, he chanced to ring the bell of a house in Péra. The landlady, a Hungarian named Mrs. Nisen, was impressed by his noble manners, took pity on him, gave him a room in her house, and eventually became his guardian angel, as he himself recognized with the utmost gratitude. In 1897, with the financial assistance of an aunt, he traveled to Geneva, Vienna, and Budapest, but instead of writing about the places he visited he wrote nostalgic pieces about the Bosphorus he longed to return to. He came back to the hospitality of Mrs. Nisen, who lavished compassionate care on him. On 19 July 1908, during Mrs. Nisen's absence, he hanged himself with a scarf that she had given him as a present.

Yeghia Temirchipashian was a talented but eccentric figure. His melancholy and sadness are reflected in his writings; so is his mental and psychic turmoil. He had moments of lucid and fertile inspiration and deep emotion, but they were transitory and leave an impression of incompleteness. Undeniably he had the sensitivity of an artist and was a worshiper of beauty, but he lacked the ability to cultivate and incorporate these feelings into a finished product.

Some of his romantic poetry comprises beautiful verses, but others are dominated by a somber mood that stifles the poetic aspiration. His philosophical writings, composed under the influence of the numerous authors he read, do not constitue a coherent philosophical system. His literary criticism, scattered in periodicals, was mostly written under the immediate influence of the day and the occasion. Though he was respected as a literary critic for ten tears (1875–85) and wrote hundreds of articles, he failed to address the literary trends and concerns of the epoch. He excelled in impressionistic prose, where in harmoniously articulated language he depicted the beauties of nature. It must be added that one of his most important achievements was the preparation of a French-Armenian dictionary (1896), which has gone through many editions and is still in use. Collections of his works were published posthumously in Constantinople (1910), Paris (1955), and Yerevan (1986). The impressive tombstone that marks the last resting place of Yeghia Temirchipashian in the Armenian cemetery of Shishli in Constantinople was erected by his guardian angel, Mrs. Nisen.

THE SONG OF THE VULTURE[1]

A great black bird like to a great black cloud
Hovers forever o'er my spirit bowed.
He is my guardian angel, but alack!
Darker than night he is—than hell more black.

A fearful-looking bird, with wings wide spread,
Ill-omened as the Devil, and as dread;

---

1. Yeghia Temirchipashian, "The Song of the Vulture," in *Armenian Legends and Poems,* ed. and trans. Zabelle C. Boyajian (London, 1916), 98–100.

He hovers round my wasted body, till
I wonder if I yet have life or will.

Upon his wings no spot of white appears,
His plumage black sheds horror down, and fears.
Black are his talons—sharp, like daggers fell;
And like a hound I hear him howl and yell.

His wide-spread pinions hide the light from me;
Heaven dark, and earth a dungeon black I see.
All is in shadow—air and earth and skies—
He even hides the lightning from my eyes.

I cannot see the paleness of my face,
I cannot see the maiden's smiling grace;
Black is the lake, the stars and lilies dark;
What was that cry? The bird's dread calling!—Hark!

I seem to totter on the brink of hell
And think the evil fowl my corpse can smell.
I seem to hear the goblins fight with him—
"Away with thee!—ours is this booty grim!"

But he is cruel, strong, and merciless—
This great black bird;—he heeds not my distress.
Ten years I've lived beneath his deadly wings—
Ten years unceasingly my death-bell rings.

Ten years ago one night it came to pass
On Moda's[2] rock I sat and dreamed; alas,
My foe came to me—Carnal was his name:
He shouted, "Vain are Life and Love and Fame!"

Youthful I was, and armed with Love and Hope
I struggled. "Oh, my soul, arise and cope
With this thy foe, and vanquish him," I cried.
But 'twas in vain, as I full soon espied.

My sun and joy since then are on the wane.
My foe cries out, "I, only I, shall reign

---

2. A seaside resort on the Asiatic shore of Istanbul.

O'er all the universe, none rules but me!"—
Then rose a Siren's voice alluringly.

Nirvana and the flesh held me that hour:
God was asleep—my soul was in their power.
Then on the moon I saw a spot appear;—
It grew, and grew . . . my heart turned sick with fear.

I was as dead. The carrion-eating bird
Had left that heavenly corpse—the moon—allured
To earth by me. It sought my bosom where
The image of Christ crucified lay bare.

Beneath those evil wings I hopelessly
Roam over the earth—my guardian angel he;
No more the cross I wear, nor in my breast
Dwells holy faith; 'tis death: death without rest.

Like to the moon, whether I wax or wane
Still am I lifeless, cursed with this bane.
I give the vulture of my flesh to tear,
And shiver when the name of "love" I hear.

While yet I live he is devouring me.
I cannot bear this pain—Oh, set me free.
I am not dead—Love still dwells with me here.
I am alive—and some call me the "Ner."[3]

---

3. Ner—the Antichrist, concerning whom the Armenians have many traditions.

Arpiar Arpiarian

(1852–1908)

The pioneer of realism in Armenian letters was born aboard ship as his parents, originally from Akn (an Armenian town on the shore of the Euphrates), were traveling from Samsun to Constantinople. They settled in the suburb of Ortakiugh (Ortaköy), where Arpiar attended the local Armenian school. In 1867 he was sent to the Murat-Raphaelian school in Venice, where he studied Armenian language and history under Ghevond Alishan (1820–1901) and also became familiarized with French and Italian literature. On his return home, circumstances forced him to work as an accountant, and later he was offered a secretarial position at the Armenian Patriarchate. His calling was, however, journalism and literature.

By 1878 he was already a regular contributor to dailies and periodicals, mainly the famed *Masis,* of which he became an editor (1884–93) in association with Grigor Zohrap (1861–1915). He also wrote articles for the literary weekly *Mshak* (Tiller), published in Tiflis under the editorship of Grigor Artzruni (1845–1892), about various aspects of Armenian life in Constantinople; these are flavored with witty satire. His articles became so popular among Caucasian Armenians that when he visited Tiflis in 1884 on the occasion of the election of a new catholicos in Etchmiadzin, he was received as a renowned writer. He formed personal acquaintances with the Eastern Armenian authors Artzruni, Raffi (1837–88), Proshian (1837–1907), Aghayan (1840–1911), and others. On returning home, laden with a wealth of impressions and information, he wrote a series of articles entitled *Ughevorutiun i Kavkasia* (Travels in the Caucasus), which appeared in the newly launched daily, *Arevelk* (Orient), in Constantinople. The aim of this series was to promote closer relations between Eastern and Western Armenians.

In cooperation with other intellectuals, he founded *Arevelk* (Orient) in 1884. This was a literary and political newspaper with democratic tendencies, and soon it attracted a number of young writers who formed the core of the school of realism. The paper became a prestigious opinion maker and was published uninterrupted until 1915.

Politically, Arpiarian was a member of the Hnchak Social Democratic party, and along with a group of youths he founded the Ararat Society to spread education in the provinces. In 1890 he was arrested as a revolutionary, but he was released two months later in a general amnesty. The following year he became editor of the daily *Hayrenik* (Fatherland, 1891–96), which was suppressed by the sultan for its democratic ideas. In the turbulent year of 1896, to avoid the fate of other Armenian intellectuals and activists, he left Constantinople for London, where he attempted to publish two monthly reviews, *Mart* (Battle, 1897–1901) and *Nor Kyank* (New life, 1898–1902), both sponsored by the Hnchak party. At this time the party split, and Arpiarian reorganized one of the factions into a viable entity.

He next traveled to Paris, then to Venice (1902–5), where he wrote his most successful work, the novella *Karmir dzamuts* (The crimson offering). In 1905 he went to Cairo, his last haven. He contributed to the local paper, *Lusaber* (Lucifer: light-bearer), and also edited (1906–7) the literary monthly review *Shirak*. His strong stands on national issues embroiled him in controversies and ultimately resulted in his assassination in the streets of Cairo by political enemies.

Arpiarian is considered the founder of realism in modern Armenian literature, the leader of a literary movement without an established school. While many writers were still under the spell of romanticism, he introduced a new trend that revolutionized Armenian literature. He was not an impersonal realist; for him literature was a means to an end: the improvement of the human condition through the exposure of vice and suffering. He was a thinker, and he expressed his thoughts courageously and honestly, traits that earned him the confidence of the people and the animosity of those in power. He became a mentor to a generation of Armenian realist writers, such as Tigran Kamsarakan (1866–1941),

Levon Bashalian (Pashalian, 1868–1943), and Yerukhan (1870–1915), some of whom excelled their master.

Most of his literary output is in the genre of short stories that deal with the working classes and social issues. Some of his better known stories are "*Hogu zavake*" (The adopted child), "*Voski aprjan*" (The gold bracelet), "*Yerazi me gine*" (The price of a dream), "*Khndamolik aghjike*" (The gleeful girl), "*Katak me*" (A joke), and "*Apushe*" (The idiot). His masterpiece is the novella *Karmir dzamuts* (The crimson offering, 1909), in which he depicts the sharp conflict between two philosophies: servile subjection to a despotic authority, as personified by a presumptuous notable of the community, and the belief in self-defense advocated by a humble provincial priest. Arpiarian also wrote numerous journalistic chronicles under the general title *Orvan kyanke* (Daily life), which are pieces of social and political criticism. Most of his writings remained scattered in newspapers and periodicals until after his death. Among his posthumous works, one is a valuable study: *Patmutiun XIX daru Turkio hayots grakanutyan* (A history of nineteenth-century Armenian literature in Turkey, 1943).

As one literary critic has put it: "Although Arpiarian does not lack literary merit, his contribution to literature lies more in his innovations and the impetus and direction he gave to Armenian Realism, than in his own literary achievement, because with him literature was a means to an end rather than an end in itself."[1]

I HAVE SEEN SO MANY . . . [2]

The teacher of Hasköy[3] is the talk of the day. Some people feel sorry for him; others think the man is an outrage, wandering around with a sign hanging from his neck that proclaims his former profession. According to some people he is a lazy vagrant—if not deceitful—for others, a miserable, bitter creature, no longer capable of cold reason. And I am at a loss which opinion to adopt. I only know that whenever misery presents itself, the voice of merciful

---

1. James Etmekjian, ed., *An Anthology of Western Armenian Literature* (New York, 1980), 60.

2. Arpiar Arpiarian, "*Kaniner tesa*" (I have seen so many), in *Patmvatzkner u vipakner* (Short stories and novellas) (Paris, 1931), 64–70. Translated by Ardashesh Shelemian and edited by the editors of the present anthology.

3. A neighborhood in Istanbul.

compassion silences the intellect. Compassion is tolerant even of injustice. Could human society ever exist without mutual toleration? I am reluctant to accept the characterization of that wretched man as ungracious. My memories have made me skeptical: I have seen so many hungry people! Perhaps other hungry teachers were stronger in spirit, but do we have the right to expect such strength of everyone? Weakness of spirit in the teacher is indicative of injustice in society, as a result of which old people and those unable to work go hungry.

♦

Even now, after so many years, I feel sorry whenever I remember those teachers, begging or on the brink of beggary.

After school—twenty-seven years ago—we often used to drop into Barseghian's shop beside the Greek church in Ortaköy[4] to buy a pen or some paper. There was always an old man with a long beard and a thin face, dressed in dirty, worn-out clothes, standing in front of the shop. Obviously he was destitute; but as I recall that face now I detect a hint of arrogance in it. He was always holding a book, faded green in color, but I think the prints were very clear. He tried to sell a copy to everyone who entered the shop . . . to get money for food. I leafed through the book and read a few pages: they were letters, written in classical Armenian. One day the shop owner told me that the man had written the book himself, and "had now ended up like this. . . ." I started to look on the poor man with singular reverence, because he had written a book, and even more because he had done so in classical Armenian!

I do not remember the name of the author of that book in classical Armenian, but he had been a teacher of classical Armenian, and I think his last name was Aliksanian. I have no idea what became of him. I still think of him . . . he may have dropped dead of hunger and, what is worse, have died unknown!

This does not prevent us from declaring that our religion rests on the foundation of classical Armenian, and those who have labored to promote classical Armenian are benefactors of us all.

♦

At Tarkmanchats School in Ortaköy we had a teacher whose work was not difficult but important. He taught reading. Teaching young

---

4. A neighborhood in Istanbul.

children is more repetitive than teaching older ones. Every day I had to stand before him and read the Narek.[5] He would sit calmly in his chair, unsmiling but listening, and, with no trace of ill-will, correct my mistakes and make me continue reading. He was a fatherly man, pleasant and calm, probably kind-hearted as well. He never got angry or disciplined me.

When I returned from many years in Venice, I spotted my old teacher in front of a stonecutter's establishment, chipping stone. He who had once shaped the minds of children was now chipping stone! I felt embarrassed and passed quietly by, pretending not to have seen him.

Then again, years later, I very often used to walk to Galata[6] from Ortaköy. On my way through Findikli[7] one morning, I saw the stonecutting teacher walking ahead of me with his head bent down.

"Nishan Agha, do you remember me?"

"How could I not? I used to teach you Narek."

We had a brief chat about this and that and parted. Some time later, I saw him again in Havyar Han, the office building, standing in front of our office door and peering inside. I ran up to him, led him to a waiting room, and gave him coffee. He explained indirectly why he had come. After that he passed by quite frequently, which I did not regret in the least. His bewildered, fluid face expressed such sadness that I was quite concerned.

Late one evening I saw him again in Findikli, walking ahead of me with a big bag of bread on his shoulder. He would come to see me wherever I happened to be. Then one day he did not show up, and I looked for him in vain. I had no idea where my teacher's corpse had been disposed of.

There was another one, too. Once again, I do not know how his corpse was disposed of or whether he is still alive.

He too was a teacher, rather pedantic, and also from Ortaköy. He was the school director. All day, from morning until late after-

---

5. I.e., *Lamentations of Narek* by Grigor Narekatsi (c. 945–1003), poems in the form of mystic soliloquies addressed to God. For more details, and a selection of these poems, see vol. 2 of the present anthology.

6. A business district in Istanbul.

7. A neighborhood in Istanbul.

noon, he acted as prosecutor and judge, with executive power and authority. He would accuse, pass judgment, sentence, and execute. All the students of that time may still feel, as I do, the shudder in our bones when Mr. Poghos opened his mouth and pronounced his verdict every lunch time: "Kneel for two hours; stand for two hours; only one slice of plain bread for lunch." Each of us would be regularly subjected to that punishment once or twice a week. The offenses were only minor, such as making too much noise coming down the stairs. I do not know why we nevertheless did not hate Mr. Poghos. A few years ago I saw him: skinny, withered, feeble, and dejected. I still carried tender, nostalgic feelings for him: the sight of him awoke so many memories. I shook his hand affectionately and bade him sit. He was looking for a job. I had to do something! I placed an ad in the newspaper, but it brought no response whatsoever. Nor did he come back again. I have not the least idea what might have become of the poor man; but the look of his jobless, hopeless, cast-off teacher's face haunts my memory to this day.

⚓

If that old man—who was known locally for his up-to-date genealogical studies—was not already begging, he was possibly on the brink of beggary.

The protestant preacher was already quite old when he started teaching us. I can never forget the impression this resourceful teacher made upon us. He would speak for one, two, or even three hours, and we, the students, would listen to him without ever getting bored. And whatever he had to say became indelibly sealed in our minds and hearts. He was loved by all of us, and I do not know what educational philosophy led to his dismissal. He went to Rodosto (Tekirda) fell ill there, and returned to Ortaköy to die. This impressive, resourceful teacher was buried during a heavy snowstorm one winter day, with only two or three people in attendance. By now all traces of his grave have probably disappeared. He died at the right time. We knew how hard it would have been for him to have to sell the books he loved so much: so painful, like begging. I cannot imagine what he would have done if his death had been delayed: death spared him much distress and from the shame of imminent vagrancy.

⚓

Following my graduation from Venice, I was preparing to return to Bolis (Istanbul). During a conversation with Fr. Ignatios Kurerghian, the Mkhitarist abbot at the time, he asked me what I intended to do in Bolis, and said: "I'm afraid you may take up teaching. You could never be a better teacher than Peshiktashlian (Beshiktashlian, 1828–68). . . . He died of hunger.

That warning of Fr. Ignatios came back to me. It had been a wake-up call for me to resist the temptation of becoming an educator.

Peshiktashlian died in Ortaköy, in Setrak's home at the bottom of a knoll off Mutevelli Street, in the shade of a pomegranate tree. Every time I walk along that silent, narrow street, I look at the small cottage where the great educator, the great talent, died. Had his death come a bit later, as a result of fatigue and old age, he would have been deprived of his daily bread.

Would Avetis Perperian and Mkrditch Peshiktashlian not, I wonder, have paper signs hanging on their doors, like the sign around the neck of the teacher who wanders the streets of Hasköy?

Minas Cheraz

(1852–1929)

Minas Cheraz, writer, teacher, and a public and political figure, was born in Khasgiugh (Hasköy), an Armenian suburb of Constantinople, to parents descended from a family of *amiras* from the village of Cheraz, near Akn (presently Agin, or Kemaliyé). He received his education at the local Nersesian and Nupar-Shahnazarian schools, where he gained mastery of French and English in addition to Armenian and Turkish. For many years he taught the history of literature and languages in several schools. As secretary and interpreter, he was part of the delegation headed by Mkrtich Khrimian (1820–1907) which the Armenian Patriarchate sent to the Congress of Berlin in 1878 to pursue the Armenian question. In 1880 he was sent to London as the personal envoy of Patriarch Nerses Varzhapetian, to meet with William Gladstone, the British prime minister, to solicit his intervention for the implementation of the reforms in the Armenian provinces promised in the Treaty of Berlin. Cheraz traveled to Italy and France on a similar mission in 1883. He served (1886–89) as the first principal of the newly established Kedronakan lycée in Constantinople, but, feeling that he was under attack by the government, he fled to London, where he began to publish a political journal in French and English, *L'Arménie-Armenia*, to sensitize Europeans to the Armenian question. In 1890 he established an Armenian chair at King's College, London. In 1898 he moved to Paris, where he continued the publication of *L'Arménie* until 1906.

Upon the change of government and the declaration of a new constitution in the Ottoman Empire in 1908, Minas Cheraz returned to Constantinople, where he was elected president of the National Council. In this role he accompanied the newly elected catholicos, Matteos II Izmirlian (1908–10), to St. Petersburg on a diplomatic mission. In 1912 he went to Paris as a member of the Armenian delegation headed by Poghos Nupar Pasha. In 1914 he settled in Paris, then in 1918 he moved to Marseille, where he spent the rest of his life.

Minas Cheraz was destined for literature, but he was dragged into political life and public service, which did not allow him enough time or opportunity to devote to letters to realize his full potential. His productive years were the period before 1878 and the decade beginning in 1918. His *Grakan pordzer* (Literary essays, 1874) is a collection of verse, speeches, and criticism that had appeared in various periodicals, including a seven-page document called *"Entroghakan kerakanutiun"* (Selective grammar), in which he suggests a uniform declension for all words and other radical grammatical changes for modern Armenian. His main works are *Azgayin dastiarakutiun* (National education, 1876); *Inch shahetsank Berlini vehazhoghoven* (What did we gain from the Congress of Berlin?, 1878); *Hayastan yev Italia* (Armenia and Italy, 1879); *Grich yev sur* (Pen and sword, 1881), a book on the language debate; and *Krtakan dasakhosutiunner* (Lectures on education, 1882). But the works that have real literary value are the short stories he wrote in French during his stay in France, collected in two volumes: *Nouvelles Orientales* (Eastern short stories) and *L'Orient inédit* (The unpublished east), the first of which he translated into Armenian himself, under the title *Arevelyan vipakner* (Eastern short stories, 1927). The third and last book he published in France was *Poètes arméniens* (Armenian poets), which includes translations of noted Armenian poets.

LOXANDRA PANDELIS[1]

Based on a True Story

I know the Turks well; I have spent thirty-seven years of my life in their country and, although a stranger to them, was brought into frequent contact with their families through my people.

---

1. Minas Cheraz, "Loxandra Pandelis," *Armenia* 3, no. 4 (February 1907), 18–24. Translated by S———y, revised by the editors of the present anthology.

I was born in Hasköy, on the Golden Horn, and lived on a street that separates the Armenian and Turkish quarters of Süt-lüdjé. There were a lot of Turkish houses in our district, and Turkish women used to drop by and chat freely with my mother and female relatives. As soon as they entered the room my uncles and eldest brother would withdraw into an adjoining one, in accordance with the exigencies of Moslem etiquette. Because I was so young, these women visitors never objected to my presence. But they never doubted for a moment that I was able to listen, observe, and remember. . . .

Eminé Hanim was the most regular of these visitors. She was commonly called Dönmé Eminé (Eminé the Renegade), because she was a Greek from Chio who had converted to Islam. In our parish alone I could point out some twenty Christian women who had been converted by force and sold as slaves after the massacres that drenched that island in blood. They had not altogether forgotten their Greek, and their peculiar accent in Turkish betrayed their Hellenic origin.

I saw Eminé Hanim for the last time in 1866. She was approaching her sixtieth year. Her snowy white hair contrasted sharply with her ocher-colored complexion, and her features were regular and animated. She was tall and thin, the embodiment of a proud and glorious historic people. She paid us frequent visits because, in her own words, she preferred the company of Christians to that of the followers of Mohammed. She told me once that she loved me like a mother because she knew that I hated the Turks as much as she did.

"Who told you I hate them?" I asked.

"My conscience. I'm convinced that no enlightened Christian can feel sympathy for that barbarous and bloodthirsty race. I have often seen you clobbering young Turkish scamps; no need to blush. . . ."

"They call me names because I'm a Christian; they throw stones at me on the way to school. Every once in a while I lose my patience and retaliate."

"Quite right, my boy! It gives me such great pleasure to watch you pick up stones and run after them, I can hardly resist the temptation to kiss you on the forehead, with your cowardly attackers looking on. But the Turks mustn't know how I really feel about them. I have to wear a mask, for strong reasons that I may tell you one day."

What could those strong reasons be? The mystery raised my curiosity to an obsession. I found out soon enough, and to this day a cold shudder runs through me whenever I happen to think of it.

One day I was all alone at home. Someone knocked at the door. I opened it. It was Eminé the Renegade. I told her there was no one home.

"I know, my child," she said, "and that's why I've come. I've been watching all of your people's movements for some time through the slits in my shutters. Christ be praised! I have found you at home by yourself. Now I can tell you my secret before I breathe my last breath. Something tells me that one day you're destined to fight the damned Turks and stand up for the rights of oppressed Christians. I know you're still very young, but I can trust you, and I'm going to tell you the story of my life."

She then took off her *feradjé*[2] and the *yashmak*[3] that covered her head and face, and sat on the divan. I had never seen her so agitated and pale. She asked for a glass of water and, after shutting the door and the windows, motioned for me to sit beside her.

"My son," she said, "my real name is Loxandra and I'm the daughter of Pandelis the chemist. I was born on the island of Chio. In April 1822 I was fifteen years old when Zeybeks and Yörüks[4] and 15,000 Turkish soldiers, incited by Softas and Mollas, carried out horrible massacres on the island. They cut children to pieces, disemboweled women, impaled men. The coast was strewn with gallow posts. . . . 35,000 people were carried into captivity, especially young girls. I was one of them.

"It was breakfast time when the Turkish soldiers broke into our house. We all hid wherever we could. I took refuge in the attic. The first thing I did was to drop a small vial of white powder into my pocket. My father, who had carefully hidden it in the attic, had told my mother in my presence that he had obtained the powder from an old Greek pharmacist who had a monopoly on the formula, which had been preserved in his family since the day one of his

---

2. Dustcoat formerly worn by Turkish women when they went out.
3. Veil worn by Muslim women.
4. Turkish irregular soldiers, mostly recruited from the interior of Smyrna. They are said to be descendants of the ancient Carians.

ancestors concocted it at the request of the Count of Byzantium. He also told us that the powder was a slow-acting poison. It needed to be administered carefully, and it caused loss of appetite, general exhaustion, and death at the end of ten days.

"There was a crack in the floor that I could peek through to see what was happening in the dining room below. The soldiers made themselves comfortable around our table. They raided our provisions and ate freely. They had no difficulty discovering where my terrified father, mother, brother, and sister were. After satisfying their appetites and quenching their thirst, they seized my parents and brother and tied them to the pillars. With them looking on, they raped my little sister, who was twelve years old. She died of the effects of this inhuman treatment. Their next step was to untie my brother, who was fourteen years old. They dealt with him in the same manner, and finished by throwing his corpse into the street. Then they grabbed my mother, raped her, and strangled her to death. It was now my father's turn. He had to suffer unspeakable indignities, and was killed on the spot.

"The fiends took a short rest and then fell to drinking again, after which they inspected the parts of the house they had not yet visited. I heard them reach the attic. I hid under a pile of clothes. They found me, and dragged me out by the feet. I fainted. . . .

"When at last I recovered my senses, I found myself in the custody of an old Turk, who informed me that he was a slave dealer and was getting ready to leave for Constantinople.

"Surfeited with blood and lust, the soldiers had left me untouched. They had sold me to the old slave dealer and divided the payment among themselves.

"Several weeks later I was put up for sale at the slave market in Istanbul. The merchant asked a high price for me, because, as he cried out, I was a Greek beauty. An old pasha bought me, and I was kept in his harem in Scutari.[5]

"When I witnessed the martyrdom of the other members of my family, I swore I would avenge their death. Greek blood runs in my veins. A Greek woman could never allow such affronts to go unavenged. She can be patient, like a camel, abiding her time, then strike . . . even after forty years.

---

5. (Üsküdar), a suburb of Istanbul, on the Asiatic shore.

Every year, on the anniversary of the massacres of Chio, the demon of revenge reawoke within me. My nights were restless. I became obsessed with sacrificing my husband to the *manes*[6] of the Pandelis. But I put off the execution of my sinister project. Besides, the pasha made an ideal husband: he was too old to take advantage of my charms. He showed his affection for me by just softly caressing my head. . . . On the twelfth anniversary of the massacres, I told him of the ghastly scenes that were haunting my memory.

"He replied that the Turks had been well advised to kill the infidels of Chio and should not hesitate to repeat what they had done if the uncircumcised dogs dared raise their heads again. I was livid with indignation. The following day I had recourse to my Byzantine powder. I dropped a small dose of it into his morning *salep*.[7] . . . He gradually lost appetite, withered. . . . At the end of ten days he died, as if carried away by galloping consumption. I had avenged the blood of my sister.

"The Muslim women I knew in Scutari undertook to find me a husband. They acted as go-betweens. I singled out a Turkish official, past middle-age, a resident of the Beshiktash quarter of Constantinople. I broke my relations with Scutari and shut myself up in the harem of that harmless gentleman, who had exhausted all his vigor, sensual and otherwise. He used to buy drugs called aphrodisiacs from Arab shops at exorbitant prices, to restore his departed potency.

The memory of those who were slaughtered never gave me rest. On the eleventh anniversary of our marriage I could not restrain my feelings; I condemned the atrocities. My husband answered that the Turks had committed a great blunder by not exterminating all the infidels at the time of the conquest of Constantinople, but that they had learned from experience and would not shrink from putting this wise policy into practice at the first suitable opportunity. I was in a rage. I mixed some of the blessed powder into his tea. He expired ten days later. I had avenged my brother's death.

"The Turkish women of Beshiktash attributed his death to the infirmities of old age and took a lively part in procuring me

---

6. Spirits or shades of the dead which demand to be propitiated (Latin).
7. A hot drink made from the salep root (*Orchis mascula*).

another husband. As a rule, they mistrusted renegades and wanted to see me married to a Muslim, in order that I might remain solidly attached to my new religion. I placed no obstacles in their way. I still had half my task to fulfill. I married a fruiterer from Yemish-Iskelessi who lived in Ak Seray. I was told this ruffian did not care for women. He expected his wife to be an all-round servant and cook. His earnings were small and every now and then I had to give him one of the jewels my first husband had given me. He would sell it and spend the proceeds in the company of bath-keepers. He never troubled me otherwise.

"Ten years after this marriage, on the anniversary of the Chio horrors, I saw my mother in a dream. She reprimanded me for having forgotten her martyrdom. My husband was very fond of an Albanian drink called *boza*. I poured my powder into it, and he died ten days later. I had avenged my slaughtered mother.

My neighbors in Ak Seray went looking for a fourth husband, for according to Muslim law an unmarried woman does not exist in the eyes of Allah. As I was now advanced in years, my chances of finding a husband were decidedly on the wane. I was becoming a less and less marketable object in the eyes of wife-seekers. I had launched into matrimony by espousing a high ranking pasha, and now I was to share my life with a scavenger. You know that wretch with whom I have lived in Hasköy for the last nine years. He doesn't have a penny, and I have to support him. This is why he obeys me like a puppet. Like my previous husbands, he has never touched me. But this is the month of April, the bloody month in which my family was exterminated. My father has appeared to me in a dream and rebuked me for having forgotten him for so long. I administered a dose of my powder, and in nine days my fourth husband shall be no more, and once my father's death is avenged I'll consider my mission accomplished. There is nothing left to live for. I'll take a similar amount of the same poison and bring my life to a close in the same number of days.

"This is the story of my life. Publish it in the European newspapers after I die. I want everyone to know that Loxandra Pandelis avenged her sister, brother, mother, and father, who were all so brutally raped and murdered on Chio. I want the mighty of the earth to understand that they can't crush the weak with impunity. I'll die a Greek, a Christian, and a virgin, and I'm not afraid to appear before God's judgment seat, having executed His commandment to Moses: 'Eye for eye, tooth for tooth.' "[8]

I sat listening to this story with downcast eyes. I was speechless with emotion. I dared not raise my head to meet Loxandra's eyes. Beads of icy sweat stood upon my brow and neck. Never had I seen crime staring me so closely in the face. It seemed to me as if the avengers were going to sprinkle her homicidal powder on my lips.

Dead silence followed the terrible story, interrupted after some considerable time by a knock at the door. It was Eminé's husband. He had come to fetch her, complaining that he was unwell and begging his wife to return home to nurse him. She quickly put on her veil and mantle, and left without a word.

I felt as if overwhelmed by a terrible nightmare and headed for the garden for a breath of air. It was an exceptionally beautiful day, in the very flush of spring. The sky appeared more serene, the Golden Horn sweetly calm, the sun more radiant, the hills more picturesque. The garden lay spread out with luxurious greenery, blossoming roses, garlands of assorted rare colors and shades. Butterflies with rainbow-like wings amorously pursued one another. Birds of every hue and song warbled around me, insects rustled on the lawn. It seemed the most graceful scene I had ever beheld. It was a all-encompassing hymn before the altar of Beauty. When nature is so benign, how can man be so wicked? Must mankind be a workshop wherein, all through the ages, the chains of hatred and crime are forged, when the voices of nature unite in an appeal to human harmony, happiness, and love?

Nine days later I heard of the death of Eminé's fourth husband, and twenty days after that, that his wife had also died. She was buried in the Turkish cemetery in Hasköy. The *imam* gave a funeral oration, in which he eulogized the piety of the deceased.

"Born an infidel," he said, "Eminé was attached to the glorious religion of Mohammed with all the ardor of her soul. She made four true believers happy, one after the other. May Allah shine on her tomb, and may such a virtuous spouse find numerous imitators among the daughters of Islam!"

---

8. Exod. 21:24; Lev. 24:20. But see Matt. 5:38–39.

Hovhannes Setian

(1853–1930)

The poet Hovhannes Setian was born in Constantinople, acquired his education in the local schools, and dedicated his life to teaching. He managed to escape the 1896 massacres and settled in Cairo, where he stayed until the end of his life.

He belonged to the younger generation of romantics, who, in the 1880s, were attracted to the realists but remained always on the margin of that movement. Setian was on the borderline between the two schools, but he was more inclined to romanticism. In poetry he was a follower of Tovmas Terzian (1840–1909), both in style and language. His short stories, mostly impressions of his immediate surroundings, reflect a deep sensitivity.

Setian's poems are collected in the following volumes: *Grakan zbosank* (Literary leisure, 1882), *Huzman zhamer* (Hours of emotion, 1888), *Blurn i ver* (Up the hill, 1896), and *Taragrin knare* (The lyre of the émigré, 1912). His collected prose was published in Cairo in 1912, in a volume entitled *Arshaluysen verjaluys* (From dawn to dusk). His works contributed to the development of modern Armenian.

LAMENT[1]

We have begun another year; I still do not believe
That you have left us, never to return. Oh, hapless Mariam!
Now tepid tears pour down from out my eyes:
For half a year these tears have filled my head.
You begged me, "Mourn me when I die, Hovhannes,"
And prepared yourself to die with the valor beyond words
That strengthens souls that behold the eternal light.
. . . .
Poor orphan girl, we were but little children,
My brothers and I, when first we went to see you
Where you were. It was a wintry night; they said
You had lost both your parents.
I still recall you, smiling and so gentle:
An angel who knows not yet how to grieve.
Child-like grace adorned your face and gentle gestures:
Although a fragile little child, you shone, poor orphan girl.
And when the tender plant became a lofty shrub,
When the years rolled by and you became a fair young woman,
You were loved by everyone; hearts kindled at your sight,
And the neighbors used to say, "Oh, how gentle is this
   Mariam!"
And friends used to repeat, "How beautiful is Mariam!"
And all agreed you were noble and unblemished,
Chaste and blameless, with not a trace of evil.
You were innocent as a lamb, your gaze was so attractive,
Sensitive, joyous—a solace to those who suffered.
Without doubt on the day when you were born
The universe rejoiced, the sun shone brightly,
And birds slept happily beside your cradle;
All nature had become a lovely, gracious love bouquet;
In that same hour, that multitudes might share in the event,
The desert ceased to mourn, was heard to shout for joy,
Causing souls to dream and quiver with happiness.

---

1. Hovhannes Setian, "*Voghb*" (Lament), in *Hay Grakanutiun*, ed. Hakob Oshakan (Jerusalem, n.d.), 408–10. Translated by the editors of the present anthology.

Alas! Now they have delivered you to the cold earth,
The cold black earth: Ah, Mariam, with your hands as white
    as lilies,
Your head adorned with tresses! You were a rose among roses,
Which we went to pick in the garden of Alemans.[2]
Woe to us! No more now, when spring has come again,
When bud and fragrance, love and life return
With dazzling light, we now no longer shall
Catch sight of you, so fair, along the orchard paths
And in the shady walkways.
No more will evening wind or zephyr kiss
Your delicate brow, which revealed your skill and talents
When we used to talk of life and of the future.
No more will your glittering glances comfort us
When constant yearning for you fills our hearts with aches.
You joyful flower, now withered and faded,
You bird of love, now flown from us, alas!
Wings have borne you away in youth, and
Covered your head in anguish.
And we, when morning spreads its saffron robe,
Or the light evening fog clings to the flank of the hill,
And voices everywhere cease speaking and grow still,
And people are confined to sleep, to spend the night in rest,
We turn our tearful eyes to the top of the dale,
The resting place of the departed,
Where silence is absolute;
We turn our eyes there and we ask,
"Oh, Mariam, where are you?"

---

2. Reference to Germans (German Gardens).

Muratsan (Grigor Ter-Hovhannesian)

(1854–1908)

Grigor Ter-Hovhannesian, who wrote under the pen name Muratsan, was born in Shushi, Karabagh. He graduated from the parish secondary school in 1873 and spent the following year perfecting his French. For two years he taught Armenian language and history at a private school, and in 1877 he toured Artsakh and Siunik for the purpose of conducting historical research. Using the material he collected, he wrote "The Brief Genealogy of the Hasan-Jalalian Dynasty,"[1] which was published in *Pordz* (Essay) magazine in 1880. In 1878 he moved to Tiflis, where he studied accounting and was later employed as bookkeeper. He stayed there for the rest of his life.

His literary talent was first recognized with the publication of *Ruzan kam hayrenaser oriord* (Ruzan, or the patriotic maiden, 1881), a historical drama derived from a thirteenth-century incident that focuses on national pride and dignity.

---

1. The Hasan-Jalalian dynasty, an Armenian princely house, originated in the thirteenth century and established itself in Artsakh, particularly in Khachen. It played a vital role in defending Artsakh against Mongol, Persian, and Turkish invaders, ensuring the autonomy of the region, and preserving the Catholicosate of Gandzasar. The members of this dynasty also founded the three Melikdoms of Artsakh: Jraberd, Khachen, and Gulistan. The dynasty lasted until the nineteenth century.

In the 1880s there was a sharp controversy between conservative and liberal intellectuals concerning what the cultural and social orientation of the Armenian nation should be. Conservatives defended the old order, on the premise that national cohesion could best be assured by uniting the nation around the Armenian Apostolic Church and traditional values; liberals, on the other hand, advocated new social, economic, and political programs that would, they predicted, lead to progress. Some prestigious newspapers took sides in this conflict: *Meghu* (Bee) and *Nor dar* (New age) supported the traditionalists, while Grigor Artzruni's *Mshak* (Tiller) launched a vigorous campaign for liberalism and democracy. Muratsan, firmly convinced that national solidarity could be achieved only by adhering to the moral standards and spiritual values of the past, sided with the conservatives. He believed that social reforms, revolutionary ideologies, and even the acceptance of other Christian traditions such as Catholicism or Protestantism were threats to such national institutions as the Church, the family, and tradition, which had preserved the cohesiveness of the nation for centuries.

This attitude found expression in three of Muratsan's short novels: *Hay boghokakan entanike* (An Armenian Protestant family, 1882), *Im katolik harsntsun* (My Catholic fiancée, 1885), and *Andreas yerets* (Andreas the priest, 1941). The first two depict situations in which family discords are caused by religious incompatibility and end tragically. The third depicts conditions under Persian rule in seventeenth-century Armenia and the martyrdom of Andreas Aguletsi, as recounted by a contemporary historian, Arakel Davrizhetsi (d. 1670).

Only in the late 1880s did Muratsan begin to produce literary works of a caliber that reflected his talent. He believed that the only hope for the survival of the nation lay in preserving its roots: that is, the village, the countryside, and people living on their ancestral land, where national identity was the strongest. He was saddened to see the withering of these roots, and had called upon young people to dedicate themselves to enlightening the rural areas. Three of his works deal with this task, together with the difficulties associated with it. In *Khorhrdavor miandznuhin* (The mysterious sister, 1889), the young heroine, Anna, sacrifices her love and moves from the city to the village in order to advance her education. In *Noyi agrave* (Noah's raven, 1899), a peasant youth educated in Tiflis and St. Petersburg by the enormous sacrifices of his father refuses to help his native village. His father, in great despair, likens him to "the raven released by Noah from the ark, which roams over corpses." The third, *Arakyale* (The missionary, 1902), is about a dedicated youth who works arduously for the betterment of the peasants but eventually flees the village, discouraged by the pressure and the numerous difficulties he encounters. Among Muratsan's other works are *Hasarakats vordegire* (Common adoption, 1884), *Lusavorutian kendrone* (The center of enlightenment, 1892), and *Gtutyan kuyrer* (Sisters of charity, 1902), which all revolve around the theme of the individual versus the community; they all conclude that individual happiness resides not in self-gratification but in working for the good of society. In Muratsan's own words: "In each of my works I kept the Armenian people before my eyes, its past, its history, and its sad present. Whether I did it well or badly, all I wished to do was to communicate my thoughts and feelings to my people."[2]

His masterpiece is the historical novel *Gevorg Marzpetuni* (1896), which is based on the events that shook the Bagratuni kingdom between 920 and 940, as recorded by the contemporary historian Hovhannes Draskhanakerttsi (c. 840–c. 930). In the novel, King Ashot II Yerkat, faced on the one hand with marauding raids by the Arabs and on the other by internal rivalries, has to rely on Prince Gevorg Marzpetuni, who, motivated by national interest, defeats the invading forces and helps the king to reestablish his authority. Although written in a romantic mood, it is a fascinating story. Muratsan entered the literary scene when romanticism was on the ascendancy, and though he witnessed the fading away of this literary movement, he did not abandon his earlier artistic convictions. His works, then, comprise a sort of document of a transitional but crucial period.

See also the section on the historical novel in the overview essay of this anthology.

FROM GEVORG MARZPETUNI[3]

Chapter 1

THE FORT OF GARNI[4]

Built by Haykaz, the ancestor of the Armenians, and later rebuilt and made more formidable by Tiridates the Great[5], the Fort

---

2. Quoted in Minas Teoleolian, *Dar me grakanutiun* (A century of literature), vol. 1 (Boston, 1977), 294.

3. Muratsan (Grigor Ter-Hovanesian), *"Gevorg Marzpetuni,"* *Armenian Review* 5, no. 1 (Spring 1952), 143–48. Translator anonymous. Footnotes and revisions by the editors of the present anthology.

4. Present-day Erzurum in Turkey.

5. Trdat III (287–330), adopted Christianity as the state religion in 301.

of Garni[6], known both in times of war for its service to the state as an impregnable fortress, and in times of peace for sheltering the royal treasures, as well as serving as an asylum for the princely families fleeing from the danger, or as a safe winter quarters for Armenian soldiers—despite the ravages of vile Vasak in the days of Vardan still stood erect and prosperous in those days in which our story begins. . . .

It was the autumn of 923 AD Geghardasar already was stripped of the meager vegetation which in the spring scarcely dared to cover its rocky slopes. It was wholly transformed now into a rugged cluster of bare ridges and rocky embankments in sharp contrast with the beauty of the edifices inside Garni.

The day was waning. There was no sight of a solitary living being on the winding trails through the gorges. The toilers in the fields of Dvin had long since returned to their homes or ceased to appear in the gulches of Ayrivan where the holy fathers provided food and shelter for belated wayfarers, forbidding them to travel in the dark through the defiles of Garin lest they fell prey to the bandits.

For this reason an awesome silence reigned over the surrounding ravines and canyons, interrupted intermittently by the howling autumn winds or the distant rumblings of Azat catapulting from the mountains.

There was not a stir even in crowded Garni. The autumnal dampness and the mountain cold had driven the inhabitants of the fort to the shelter of their homes. Only a few guards, with iron helmets, their heavy swords hanging from their belts, holding in their hand brass-plated shields and long lances, could be seen making their rounds, some in front of the gates of the fort or in front of the barracks, and some circling around the castle where at the time lived Queen Sahakanush, the wife of Ashot Yerkat (Ashot the Iron).

Although the King had just been reconciled with his cousin Ashot the Usurper and together with him, having reconquered the capital city of Dvin, had cleared it of its foreign elements, nevertheless, due to the deterioration of the times, it was impossible to keep the royal family in Dvin since the Arab invaders were likely to attack that city at any time. Dvin in those days was an apple of contention between the conflicting forces. And since the King

---

6. Village in present-day Armenia.

was constantly busy suppressing the rebellions which popped up in various parts of his domain, it was very risky to keep the royal family in the capital when the enemies arrived. It was for this reason that Queen Sahakanush was at the Fort of Garin at this time, together with many ladies of the nobility.

Although the season was cold and it was late in the day, nevertheless the Queen had not yet left the canopy of Tiridates. For the past few days she had spent long hours here, almost alone, at times pacing the floor of the spacious colonnaded salon, and more often sitting on the veranda which overlooked the precipice. From this vantage point, silent and pensive, she watched now the roaring billows of the Azat in the valley which flowed on endlessly, as it kept lashing the willows on either side, and now on the trail which zigzagged the slopes of Mount Kegha, where each mounted wayfarer attracted her attention. She fixed her gaze on each passer to ascertain who he was, and his nationality, as soon as possible, until the latter reached the river and, deflecting his path toward the artery of Garin, disappeared from view.

For two weeks the Queen had been anxiously waiting for someone but that someone had not appeared as yet. This made her very unhappy and intensified the anguish which had been gnawing at her heart for a long time.

There were times when she secluded herself in order to see no one, to speak to no one, and to surrender herself to her stormy meditations. At such times she even got angry if one dared to disturb her lonely meditations or the suffering of her inner agitation. But now? She was tired now, weary of her perpetual sorrow. Now she was looking for anyone to whom she could open her heart and explain her grief. It seemed to her that confiding in someone would allay her pain. But, alas, there was no one in the whole castle, neither in the circle of the women or the young girls in whom she could trust her secret. What was worse, even if such a person could he found, she again would not trust her because she had no faith in the sincerity of any woman, especially if that woman was of a princely family, and consequently her equal by virtue of birth. She believed that such women would sympathize with her only outwardly, while inwardly they would gloat over her misery, because everyone of them had their own reason for such a behavior. She had laid her hope only in one man who, she thought, not only would sympathize with her with complete sincerity, but would be able to alleviate her pain as well. It was this man whom the Queen was awaiting anxiously, who, in spite of his promise and the word which the courier had brought, still failed to appear.

Just then a woman approached the Queen. She was an old woman of medium stature, a benign face with innocent eyes. There was a smile on her lips as she approached the Queen hesitantly, lest she provoke her anger.

This woman was well acquainted with the anguish which was torturing the Queen. She had seen everything from the very beginning, had scrutinized and verified it. She had been sincerely grieved and had wept for her Grand Lady even when the Lady herself, unaware of her misfortune, had surrendered herself to her royal pleasures now at the land of the Siunis, now in the mountains of Gugark. That woman was Seda, the Queen's affectionate foster mother and governess, the most kind and noble-hearted woman among all the women in the castle. All this was known to her, yes, long since, and yet she had never mentioned a word of it to the Queen to this day for the simple reason that, if a person cannot forestall a misfortune (which still is unknown to him), it is better that he never learned about it and thereby embitter his life. But now, when the Queen already was advised about everything, Seda was free to speak with her, commiserate with her and comfort her. And why not? Had she not been the Queen's foster mother and had she not brought her up in her own arms?

Thus meditated Seda, but immediately afterwards she reflected that Sahakanush, the daughter of the Prince of Quardman, no longer was a baby, that she was a Queen today whose feet she could only kiss now, but to sit with her as an equal in rank and share her grief, that of course was something which she could not dare even think. From the day when Seda learned that the Queen was already aware of her misfortune, the poor woman had no rest It is true that she could help her Queen in nothing except the personal care which she could offer, was duty-bound to offer, and which she already was offering. That was, to follow her Grand Lady like a shadow everywhere and try to dispel her worries as much as possible, whereby, she thought she could preserve her health.

"Is that you, Seda?" said the Queen, turning to her somewhat ill at ease.

"Yes, Your Majesty, I came to tell you. . . ."

"Have you been here very long?" the Queen interrupted with a suspicious air, fearing, as it were, that her governess might have overheard some word or sigh which might have betrayed her grief.

"I came in just when the sun swung behind the mountain."

"But I have given strict orders that no one shall disturb my solitude."

"Yes, my lady, I could never dare to ignore your command; but the day is late and the wind is high; you might catch cold. I came to remind you that it is time to return to the castle."

"To remind me? What is the meaning of this, Seda?" asked the Queen, half surprised and half angry.

The good governess was confounded. She had no right to say all this to the Queen, what she thought was the truth. She felt her error, was depressed, and her kindly eyes became hidden in their already cramped hollows; a light crimson lit her pale cheeks like the pale dawn of winter which shines on the snow-clad mountain cliffs. But she soon managed to conceal the external reflection of her inner emotions with her maternal tenderness. It seemed the Queen's serious and unwavering gaze which demanded an explanation was slowly softened by the old woman's kind smile. And indeed, was it not true that she loved her Queen, that she did not follow her in order to learn her secrets, but to take care of her precious health over which she trembled like a tender mother? How could she consider this manifestation of sincere love as an offense? Of course not; therefore, she answered in a firm voice:

"I came to remind you that it is cold, that the Queen might be cold."

"I could have inferred as much myself," the Queen observed.

"No, my Queen, when you plunge into your sad meditations, you no longer feel what is going on around you."

"Seda, Mother Seda, you are raving idle talk," interrupted the Queen, quite surprised.

"That's right, my beloved Queen," repeated Seda in a firmer voice. "The other day in the pelting rain when everyone had hurried to his home, when there was not even a single guard in front of the castle, you were pacing the floor here, as if it was spring time and you were in the paradise lands of our Gardman."[7]

---

7. One of the districts of ancient Armenia located to the northeast of Lake Sevan and along the Kura River.

The Queen made an uneasy gesture; it seemed to her the governess was reproaching her for her useless secrecy, that she was doing it in order to win the favor of one of her antagonist princesses. It could mean that her misfortune already was known to all and that her jealous adversaries had started to scorn her, insulting her queenly pride through her own subordinates.

These thoughts instantly perturbed the Queen's heart, but she hid her emotion and asked in a gentle voice:

"Seda, who told you that the Queen is deep in sad meditations and in such times she does not know what is going on about her?"

"No one, my beloved Lady, I have seen it with my own eyes. Seda must be blind not to see the perpetual grief which is stamped on her Lady's face or the sorrowful wrinkles on her forehead. For a long time I have known what it is that has been gnawing at your noble and kind heart, but I did not dare to tell you, because I knew that, by talking about your troubles I would only further grieve your tender heart, without being able to add anything to my Queen's comfort."

The Queen was moved. Her former suspicion suddenly gave way to a surge of confidence in her good governess. She noted in her voice such a warmth of sincerity and tenderness that it seemed to her the one who was speaking to her was her own mother, and not the woman who had suckled her in her infancy.

Nevertheless she made no reply but rose from her throne, silent and pensive, and straightening herself to her full proud and imperious height, she looked at her governess with affectionate, kindly eyes. At that moment she wanted to hear from her everything, hear with a greater certainty, everything which she had known for a certainty long since. And yet, her queenly pride would not permit her to stoop to such weakness; up to that moment she had talked to no one about her troubles, therefore she was reluctant to start it now; still she heartily craved that her governess would start the conversation without waiting for her command.

Seda did not comprehend the meaning of the Queen's silent and thoughtful gaze; it seemed to her the Queen was offended at her boldness; therefore, to avoid the Queen's gaze, she hastened to pick up the sable cape which had slipped to the floor when the Queen rose, and threw it over her shoulders. "You are too old to attend on me, Mother Seda. Where are my maids?" asked the Queen gently.

"Oh, let me only wait on you, my gentle, my peerless Queen. Is Seda so old that she no longer can be helpful in anything?"

"Mother Seda, such a thought was farthest from my mind."

"That my presence is no longer wanted by my Queen?"

"Seda, you are interrupting me."

"Or perhaps I said something imprudent which offended my Queen."

"No, no, my Seda; your presence is always pleasing to me; the proof lies in the fact that I let no one accompany me in my solitude, but you are always with me, whenever you want; you impose your presence on me whether the Queen wishes it or not."

"And that's the way I will continue, My Lady. You may get angry at me if it pleases you, but to let you sink in deep sad meditation for long hours, that's something I cannot allow, it is harmful to your precious health."

"Precious? Yes, perhaps for you; my good Seda, only to you . . ." the Queen murmured to herself. Then, turning to her governess, she added, "You are right, Mother Seda, I am not angry at you. . . . I really have been too long in the open air. Where are my maids?"

"You have given strict orders that they make no appearance until they receive your summons."

"Call them in, then. Let them bring my palanquin."

The Queen strode to a corner of the canopy and, standing beside the colonnade, she began to watch the golden moon which was slowly rising from behind the distant mountains. Although the cold was piercing and the wind still was howling, the sky was clear and cloudless, the stars had begun to shine, and the disc of the moon, which seemed to be hanging like a magic lantern on top of the mountain, had begun to bathe the jagged mountains and the hills in a pool of limpid phosphorescence. The foaming torrents of the River Azat, precipitating from the mountain heights, were shimmering like a silvery line.

The Queen was enthralled anew with the beauty of the evening moon and again sank into her meditations. A little more of this, and she again would have been tempted to return to the veranda and, sinking into her chair, would surrender herself to the flights of her torturous imagination. But the voices of the maids and the light of the torches borne by the servants of the castle awakened her.

She turned back and looked. Lady Gohar, the Princess Marz-petuni, accompanied by the maids and the governess, was making her appearance. The Princess approached reverently, bowed low before the Queen, and respectfully and gently reprimanded her for her inordinate love of solitude.

"I have been watching the road of Mount Kegha, so that I would be the first to inform you of the arrival of Prince Gevorg," replied the Queen with a gracious smile.

"I shall be very thankful if he only will bring us good news," added Princess Gohar, as she held out her hand to help the Queen come down the steps of the canopy.

"And if he doesn't bring good news?" the Queen asked.

"Then I would wish that you wouldn't open the gates of the fort before him," said the Princess jokingly.

The Queen smiled and said nothing more. . . .

Shirvanzadé (Aleksandr Movsisian)

(1858–1935)

Shirvanzadé, whose birth name was Alexander Movsisian, was born in Shamakhi, the capital of the province of Shirvan in Azerbaijan, from whence he derived his pen name (*Shirvanzadé* means "progeny of Shirvan"). His childhood was not happy. He studied first in a local Armenian parochial school, then in the regular Russian school, but he was obliged to abandon his education in order to help his parents, who were beset by financial difficulties. At the age of about seventeen he went to Baku, a city on the Caspian Sea where the oil industry was booming. He worked for the provincial government as a clerk, then in an oil company as a secretary-bookkeeper. Between 1881 and 1883 he was also the librarian of the Armenian Benevolent Society (*Mardasirakan*) of Baku. During his eight years in Baku, he had ample opportunity to witness capitalism at work, together with its social impact on and exploitation of workers. He made up for his missed schooling by educating himself, establishing contacts with intellectuals and immersing himself in Armenian, Russian, and western literature. Among his favorite authors were Tolstoy, Turgenev, Dostoyevski, Stendahl, Balzac, Flaubert, Zola, Shakespeare, and Dickens. In 1883 he moved to Tiflis and dedicated himself entirely to literature. He contributed articles to various periodicals, such as the conservative *Meghu Hayastani* (Bee of Armenia), the progressive *Mshak*

(Tiller), and the liberal-reformist *Murch* (Hammer); he also assumed the editorship of the cultural magazine *Ardzagank* (Echo) from 1886 to 1891. His first literary work, *"Hrdeh navtagortzaranum"* (Fire in the oil works, 1883) appeared in *Mshak,* followed in 1884 by the story *"Khna-matar"* (The caretaker), both depicting life under capitalism as it relates to the workers and their wealthy bosses. His first major novel, *Namus* (Honor, 1885, adapted for the stage in 1911), is the story of two lovers who become victims of family prejudice, greed, and betrayal. In the story *"Arambin"* (The married woman, 1888), the heroine is abandoned by her husband but cannot remarry because her remarriage would be considered a "stain" on her father's honor, and so she wastes away.

Shirvanzadé produced most of his best work in the 1890s and during the prerevolution period before 1905, which was a time of political and social revival. His novels *Zur huyser* (Vain hopes, 1890), *Arsen Dimaksian* (a proper name, 1893), *Tsavagare* (The epileptic, 1894, turned into a play by the author in 1912 and renamed *Har vogi* (Evil spirit), and *Krak* (Fire, 1896) are realistic reflections of the intellectual, social, and moral contexts of contemporary society. They examine such problems as the decadent morality and family intrigues that result in ruined marriages; the contradictions between ideological trends among intellectuals, which lead to inconsistent action; and the tragic consequences of adhering to a social and economic order that has no relation to the lives of ordinary people.

During the Eastern Armenian massacres of 1895–96, when he was a member of the Hnchakian Social Democratic Party, he wrote articles defending the Armenian cause. He also went to Russia to organize a relief fund for survivors, where he was arrested along with Ghazaros Aghayan and others on suspicion that they were engaged in revolutionary activities and incarcerated in the Metekhi prison, Tiflis. While in prison he wrote *Banti hishatakaran* (Prison memoirs) and planned his next novel, *Kaos* (Chaos), an outstanding, realistic portrayal of the great capitalist city of Baku. He describes it as "a city that is brilliant on the outside but corrupt and extremely harmful on the inside, where the love of gold has completely eradicated all boundaries between light and darkness, morality and immorality, turning it into a monstrous chaos."[1] The book was published in 1898 and became famous both as a work of critical realism and for its ideological and literary qualities. It was adapted for the stage after the author's death.

---

1. Shirvanzadé, *Yerkeri zhoghovatzu* (Collected works) (Yerevan, 1961), 8:243.

In the same year (1898) Shirvanzadé was exiled to Odessa for two years. He used the time to write the novellas *Melania* (1899), *Oriord Liza* (Miss Liza, 1900?), *Artiste* (The artist, 1901), and *Vardan Ahrumian* (1902). The first three portray the conflicts between heart and mind, between love of the arts and money, and the fourth is a satirical depiction of a young man's education by his father in the "ethics" of capitalism.

Once back in Tiflis Shirvanzadé began to produce significant works for the theater. His interest in theater started early, when he began to write critical reviews of the performances of such masters of the stage as Petros Adamian, Siranush, and Hovhannes Abelian. His own plays continued the tradition, established by Gabriel Sundukian, of presenting on the stage all the contradictions and conflicts of society. Shirvanzadé extended the range, including political conflicts and moral-psychological relations as well, and subjecting his characters to deeper analysis. It is also important to note that he wrote in a pure, literary language, rejecting dialect. Although he had written a drama, *Ishkhanuhin* (The princess, published posthumously in 1948), in the early 1900s, now he began to produce plays in quick succession. In *Yevginé* (name of the heroine, 1903) and *Uner iravunk* (Did she have the right?, 1903), and *Patvi hamar* (For the sake of honor, 1905) he treats his female characters with much tolerance and psychological understanding. He was the first to tackle the question of feminism in capitalistic society. In his day women were still abused and enslaved, and had to be submissive, silent, and virtuous to fit the feminine ideal. In his plays women are sometimes allowed to go "off course" and yield to their feelings and intuitions. This drew some criticism from conservative circles, but the attacks only served to increase the popularity of the plays.

In 1905 Shirvanzadé was in Paris, where he remained until 1911, attending literature courses at the Sorbonne and establishing contacts with intellectuals. The defeat of the revolutionaries in the 1905 Russian revolt and the Armeno-Tatar war in the same year once again focused his attention on social conflicts and their nasty consequences. The three serious dramas he wrote during this period—*Kortzanvatze* (The ruined, 1909), *Averakneri vra* (On the ruins, 1911), and *Armenuhi* (proper name, 1916)—and the political comedy *Sharlatane* (The charlatan, 1912) reflect these realities. Profoundly distressed by the First World War and the horror of the 1915 genocide, he wrote numerous articles analyzing the causes of the war and exposing both the savagery of the Turkish perpetrators and the duplicity of the great powers. His book *Arhavirki orerin* (In the days of terror, 1917) is a depiction of these events. His other stories during this period are *"Vorn é mayre"* (Who is the mother?, 1915), *"Herosi veradardze"* (The return of the hero, 1916), and *Alina* (1917).

In 1919 he again went abroad, this time for medical treatment. He visited Constantinople, Smyrna (Izmir), New York (1923–24), and Paris, returned in 1926, and finally settled in Soviet Armenia. In 1930 he published *Morgani khnamin* (Morgan's in-law), the first full-length political comedy in Soviet Armenia, which focuses on wealthy expatriates in Paris who try to speculate on the properties they have left behind. His last years were spent preparing his collected works, in eight volumes, for publication (1930–34), and completing his two-volume autobiography, *Kyanki povits* (Out of the crucible of life, 1930–32).

Shirvanzadé was an important contributor to the development of modern Armenian theater. Some of his dramas—such as *Namus* (Honor, 1925), *Char voki* (Evil spirit, 1927), *Patvi hamar* (For the sake of honor, 1956), and *Kaos* (Chaos, 1972)—were made into films. His works have been translated into a number of languages, and his genius was often recognized. In 1934, one year before his death, he was invited to the First Congress of Soviet Writers in Moscow, where he was awarded the title "People's Writer." He was and remains the greatest writer of realist drama in Eastern Armenian literature.

FROM FOR THE SAKE OF HONOR[2]

Overtones of melodrama in For the Sake of Honor *heighten the action without detracting significantly from its seriousness. The disposition of certain incriminating documents—an often used dramatic device—is central to the conflict. These documents belong to a young man, Artashes Otarian. They presumably prove that his dead father was cheated out of his share of a business by his partner, Andreas Elizbarian. At the play's opening, Otarian is in the midst of pressing a claim to half of Andreas' wealth, but his position is difficult since he is affianced to Andreas' daughter Margarit. At her father's urging, Margarit makes inquiries about the documents. She then borrows them for study, but contrary to her father's expectation she judges her lover's cause to be just. When her extravagant sister Rozalia and her aggressive brother Bagrat ask her to steal the papers in the "family interest," she refuses. Her father, however, with the help of her uncle Saghatel, steals them from her room in the dead of night. Her harried mother and dissolute brother Suren*

---

2. Aleksandr Shirvanzadé (Alexandre Movsesian), *Patvi hamar* (For the sake of honor), excerpt, in *Ararat* 15, no. 1 (Winter 1974), 19–22. Translated by Nishan Parlakian.

tend to side with her and Otarian, but they are powerless to help. In a final confrontation, Margarit vainly pleads with her father to return the papers. For the sake of honor, then, she resolves the dilemma—as the following scene (in a first English translation) indicates.[3]

[*The sitting room of the Elizbarian home.*]

ANDREAS: You are supposed to be ill. Why are you up?

(*Wrapped in her own thoughts, Margarit does not respond to her father.*)

MARGARIT: Father, he's waiting to see me. He's tried three times. I can't see him. I can't face him. Father, it's up to you whether I can ever face him again.

ANDREAS: What are you talking about? What do you want from me?

MARGARIT: (*With a trembling voice, but firmly.*) Decency.

ANDREAS: I am what I am. No more, no less. Who do you think you are, speaking to me like this?

MARGARIT: Don't torture me, father. I can't endure your dissembling.

ANDREAS: If I'm dissembling, you forced me to it.

MARGARIT: I was trying to save your good name.

ANDREAS: (*Sarcastically.*) Save? You were plunging me into total disgrace! You wanted to sacrifice me to your lover.

MARGARIT: (*Wounded.*) Father, don't say that. Don't say it.

ANDREAS: Why shouldn't I say it? Ever since he started with you, you don't think about your parents. A kiss from him is dearer to you than my good name.

MARGARIT: You're wrong, I swear it. Yes, I love him. But the honor of our family means more to me than happiness.

ANDREAS: Silence! Have you no shame? How dare you talk to me about your love? You wanted my money, that's what you wanted, so that you and that adventurer could live together in luxury. My dowry for you was too small.

MARGARIT: Don't say that. You can't believe it. You know I never thought of your wealth.

ANDREAS: (*Mockingly.*) Of course! You're not of this world. You're not born of a mother. Enough! You have no feeling for me. You hate me. You are my enemy.

---

3. Ibid., 19.

MARGARIT: Very well, if that's what you believe. But one day you'll understand that no one cares for you as much as I.

ANDREAS: Why are you plaguing me? Tell me in a word what you want?

MARGARIT: Give the papers back. Give them back.

ANDREAS: (*Laughing bitterly.*) Give them back! Andreas Elizbarian, do you hear that? Give the sword to your enemy; bow your head so he can cut it off. No, my child. God bless us; I'm not insane, yet.

MARGARIT: Father, don't make fun of me. I can't endure it.

ANDREAS: (*Changing his tone.*) What papers do you want? What papers? I haven't seen any papers. I haven't had any papers. And I don't have any papers, now. Tend to your own business.

MARGARIT: (*Wringing her hands.*) My God.

ANDREAS: You've dreamt the whole thing.

MARGARIT: If only it had been a dream! No. I heard the keys in the night and I awoke. I saw your huge figure in the dim light. I could hardly believe my eyes. I was petrified just to see you.

ANDREAS: You must have been dreaming. Yesterday, all day, I wasn't even at home. Your uncle is my witness.

MARGARIT: Father. If I don't count, think of yourself, at least. Those papers will bring down a curse on you.

ANDREAS: That's enough. Don't try my patience. Your attitude is maddening.

MARGARIT: You can't frighten me. Not after what you did last night.

ANDREAS: Get out! You're shameless. Get out before I do something rash.

MARGARIT: Father. Don't think I'm not going to implicate you when I have to tell about the theft of those papers.

ANDREAS: Before you opened your mouth, I'd tear out your vile tongue and throw it to the dogs. So keep your mouth shut, and the devil take it.

MARGARIT: (*Hopelessly.*) I don't know what to do. Don't be so heartless. Father, please give me those papers. I've got to return them today. I've given my word. He's waiting in the other room. I've avoided him like a thief. Give them up if you have the least respect for me.

ANDREAS: Damn you, you devil. I told you I have nothing to give you.

MARGARIT: Father, you don't know me. I can't say all I feel, but I've thought through this whole business. I'd die for your honor. But what about mine? Must I defile it just for your riches? Spare me this shame. That's your duty as my father. Give me my honor. Without it I can't live a moment.

ANDREAS: (*In a great rage.*) Get away from me! My blood's gone to my head!

MARGARIT: I won't go until I get those papers. Deny me everything. Disown me. I'd rather make my own way than be known as a thief. I couldn't bear that. He's good. He thinks I'm a good person. He respects me. I don't want him to think me a thief. Never, father. You're kind and decent and won't let that happen. I'm pleading with you. (*She kneels.*) Pity me. Listen. I'm speaking about my life. Don't do this, father. Don't do this. Stealing is a great sin.

ANDREAS: (*Struggling with himself.*) Get up. Have you no shame? Someone may come in.

MARGARIT: No. I'll stand only if you return me my honor. Listen to your conscience. Don't turn away. I swear I won't judge you. Not with a word. Not with a glance. I'll be silent and I'll respect you as before. I know that you're confused and that you regret what you've done. Father, give me the papers.

ANDREAS: (*With a decisive movement, pulling away.*) I've had enough.

(*He crosses to the desk, opens the strong box and takes out the bundle of documents.*)

MARGARIT:(*Mistakenly, as she stands.*) I knew you couldn't do this. Thank you, father. You've cleared my name.

ANDREAS: Get your hands off. I'm going to end all this once and for all. You're insane.

He tears up the papers and throws them into the stove. This is where they belong.

MARGARIT: What are you doing?

(*She leaps forward, screaming, to save the papers. He prevents.*)

ANDREAS: Get away or I'll throw you in there, too. At last, I'm free of you. Burn! Turn to ashes. You have burnt my heart enough.

(*Father and daughter struggle.*)

MARGARIT: Let go. Let go. You're burning me.

(*She tries to scratch her father's hands.*) I don't have the strength to fight. But I'll shout. I'll call everyone, so they can see your thievery. Let go.

(*Freeing herself from her father's grip, she approaches the stove.*) Ah. It's too late. They're burned. Everything is lost.

(*She calls out loud.*) Come here. Rozalia, Bagrat! Everyone, come here. See what's happened here. A father has burned his daughter's honor. Ah, all is lost.

(*Weakened, she falls into a chair. Silence.*) But let it be.

(*She goes to the doors at left and meets Otarian entering. She is shocked and frozen in her aspect. Bagrat enters by the same doors a little after Otarian. Andreas, arms akimbo, stands at the left.*)

OTARIAN: At last, I've found you. You're not sick. You've been hiding from me. Your father has dishonored me and ordered me out of his house. In his eyes I'm a thief—I'm trying to get his wealth illegally. Show him my papers. Show him I'm in the right. I've been dishonored. Show him my proof.

(*Margarit stands by the wall, silent, pale, trembling, and motionless.*)

Your brother plays a different tune today. We've switched roles. Yesterday, your father wanted to bribe me; today your brother. At least, explain what's happened.

(*Silence.*)

You're silent. You stand there as though you're guilty of something. I swear by my oppressed father's grave that either you or I is insane. Speak. Is this a conspiracy? Didn't I make you a judge in this matter? What have you done with my papers? Bring them here.

MARGARIT: (*Faltering a long moment.*) I don't know.

OTARIAN: Why are you silent? Margarit, go and bring me those papers.

MARGARIT: (*With the coldness of death.*) I burned them. In there.

(*She points to the stove. Full of anguish, she looks long at her father. She turns from her father and with slow steps she leaves by the doors at left. Otarian and Bagrat go to the stove. Bagrat closes the doors of the stove. Sakhatel enters left.*)

OTARIAN: (*Looking surprised from one to the other.*) She burned them? Then this whole thing became a trap for her. Margarit couldn't be an ally of a thief. No, that couldn't be. I'd never suspect her. I know she's a saint. She lied and blamed herself. The culprit here is someone else. (*To Andreas.*) Clear her name before she's destroyed by all this.

ANDREAS: Saghatel, let's go to the club.

(*He strides toward the vestibule. From offstage a gunshot is heard. Everyone is startled.*)

SAGHATEL: What was that?

(*He runs toward the doors, left. Bagrat follows. Otarian and Andreas stand immobile.*)

(*Suren runs in from doors left, pale, faltering. Silence.*)

SUREN: Margarit killed herself.

ANDREAS: (*Bellowing and striking his head.*) I've killed her.

OTARIAN: You burned them. Monster!

(*He tries to leap at Andreas, but Suren comes between them.*)

SUREN: He's punished enough.

(*He looks contemptuously at his father.*)

OTARIAN: Margarit, Margarit.

(*Otarian runs to the left and, leaning weakly on the door, goes out.*)

(*The curtain comes down slowly.*)

END

Melkon (Hrand) Kiurchian (Gürdjian)

(1859–1915)

Born in the village of Havav in the Armenian province of Balu, Melkon Kiurchian attended the local elementary school and in 1870, at the age of eleven, went to Constantinople in pursuit of further education. After completing his studies at the *Chemaran* (academy, also spelled *Jemaran*) and the *Surb Khach* (Holy Cross) school in Scutari, he became a teacher, and from 1878 to 1896 he taught Armenian language and history at various schools, including the Kedronakan lyceum.

In 1893 he was imprisoned for a month for alleged revolutionary activities. Three years later political conditions made it advisable for him to leave for Varna, Bulgaria. While there, with the cooperation of locals, he founded the Artzrunian school for the children of Armenian émigrés. During his absence from Constantinople his house was searched by the police and many of his manuscripts were destroyed. In 1898 he returned, and no sooner had he stepped onto the quay than he was arrested. After six months in prison he was exiled to Kastamonu in northern Turkey, where he remained for ten years. During this time he secretly gave private lessons and labored on his literary works. In 1906, on the basis of an informant's report, his papers were again seized and destroyed. Upon the declaration of the new Constitution of the Ottoman Empire in 1908, he was free to return to Constantinople. There he resumed teaching and participating in civic activities. In 1910 he traveled to Etchmiadzin as an elected delegate to the Armenian National Assembly, on the occasion of the enthronement of the new catholicos. In April of 1915 he was arrested along with hundreds of Constantinople's Armenian intellectuals, who were all deported to unknown destinations and killed by the Turkish gendarmes.

In the 1870s and '80s Constantinople was a haven for thousands of migrants, almost all men, from the Armenian provinces who, because of extreme economic hardships, were forced to leave their families behind and come to the capital to seek their fortune. Unfortunately, they were generally shunned by the established community; many of them worked menial jobs as street porters or water carriers and languished in the dark and damp corners of inns. The writings of Melkon Kiurchian, himself from the provinces and well acquainted with the plight of these people, vividly depict their wretched existence and the dramatic consequences suffered by their families back home. This kind of realism was new for the literati of Constantinople. Arpiar Arpiarian, a realist writer and editor of *Masis,* discovered Kiurchian and encouraged his writing.

Kiurchian's main works are *Pantukhti namakner* (Letters of a pilgrim), *Shinakani namakner* (Letters of a peasant), and *Patmvatzkner* (Short stories). In addition, he published widely in various dailies and periodicals. He greatly enriched migrant literature, not just by describing situations but also by penetrating into the heart and soul of the migrants and feeling their anguish in his own heart. Clarity of language is the most important feature of his style. He wrote in smooth modern Armenian, though traces of classical Armenian, which he mastered and taught, are still present. The first volume of his complete works (*Amboghjakan yerker*) was published in France by the Friends of Martyred Writers in 1931. It contains *Pandukhti namakner* and a few short stories.

FROM THE EMIGRANT'S LIFE[1]

With fraternal love you ask, my dear Arpiar, that I write "From the Lives of Emigrants," to appear in *Masis.* What shall I write? Yesterday, Shakarian gave me an apple from Artamet. With

---

1. Hrand (Melkon) Kiurchian, "*Pandukhti kyanken*" (From the emigrant's life), in *Amboghjakan yerker* (Complete works) (Paris, 1931), 2125. First published in *Masis* 3919 (1888). Translated by the editors of the present anthology.

what awe I stretched forth my hand to take it; and with what care I kept it in my pocket, so that it would not be damaged!

Let me describe it. First it must be regarded as rather extraordinary, when you consider that it has traveled for thirty days across places dear to your heart and the fathomless depths of the Black Sea, and yet still retains its fragrance. But what of its color and skin? It has a faint blush on its cheek, with numerous streaks that gradually merge into a yellowish background. The skin is firm, and yet it has a wrinkled and shrunken appearance. You feel sorry for it.

Your request suggests to me similarities between this apple and the mysterious image of the migrant. The sallowness, withering, and exhaustion of old age seem present in the midst of vigorous youth. What fragrance does such an exile have? And what shall I write?

Would you be pleased if I spread the tattered clothes of the exile at the foot of this paper mountain, if I exposed the wounds to his bloodied and scarred heart, and if one day I passed by, bearing his coffin to the Balikli[2] Cemetery?

Would it satisfy you if I described the suffering existence to which our expatriate countryman is condemned, afflicted more by unjust creditors than by the cold of winter and the heat of summer? The same countryman who is already tormented with longing for his family and by the age-old disease called exile, which, like the legendary falcon, fastens on his liver and gnaws at it constantly. Would you be pleased if I bore you on paper wings and dropped you into the house of the exile, so you could see the heartless moneylender busily writing credit notes, while a woman suffers silently and youngsters grow up without a father until, many long years later, one day, one dark day, a piece of paper drops from the roof at night: an omen of bad news and a miserable ending to so much anxiety and unfulfilled hope? Would you be happy if now and then I used excerpts from the letters of the migrant, allowing him to tell you in his own words about his room, his home, his heart, his wounds? Enabling you to meet, to actually see, the industrious giant from the provinces, with his sunburnt neck and sweat-covered face, shouldering his burden, which is often his

---

2. A suburb of Istanbul.

empty purse—from which he should pay his debts and feed his wife, children, and parents—but often he does not have even so much as a penny? This is what I shall write about, and so you have my plan: but out of necessity and because of the nature of the subject, I shall write about these things in no particular order. Does misery have any order or obey any laws?

But for whom should I write? Will the charming madam ever condescend to cast a glance at the tattered clothes of the exile? Will the wealthy financier deign to acknowledge that the *gharip*,[3] whom he still shuns with disgust, is, in fact, his brother before God? That one Armenian migrant, who commutes between the Bosporus and the city from the healthy years of his youth until he is dried up, dying days, and is able to keep the chimney of his homeland in the mountains smoking, wherever he is, is worth a thousand Armenian emigrants! Let me illustrate this with an example, so you will not think it a figment of my emotional state.

We were old friends, exactly the same age, almost the same height. We both migrated. He took up a trade and I went to school; I lived well and he lived poorly. Today, though, what are we worth to our nation, if we are both weighed on an honest scale, him and me? As I was finishing school, he returned home. His father had died, leaving behind a widow and five little children and, perhaps, also a few debts. Thanks to his hatchet and his sweat, his chimney back in the homeland never stopped smoking. His five little brothers have now grown up and today they are all fine young men: tall and strong, they fill their parental home with joy, with brides, and with children; they are skilled workers, and build houses for others. But I—what have I done for our nation? What can my books, old and new, achieve? Every once in a while I send the press a few pages, written in happy or in troubled moods. Whenever I see my very dear childhood friend, I realize my worthlessness, which he does not even suspect. Is it not phenomenal that this young man is today able to say, "By the strength of my hatchet and my arm, five fine young men and their wives and children, I have raised up to my nation a modest house?" Yes, my dear friend, you are invaluable, beyond price; you are blessed—your arm is blessed.

---

3. *Garip:* poor, needy, destitute person; person away from home (Arabic).

Would you believe that this provincial native, who clings to his home with a troubled soul, is worth a thousand? The tattered clothes of the exile, his calloused hands, the sweat on his face, are worth much more than our decked-out appearances, silky fabrics, and delicate hands when weighed on the scale.

What am I saying? The exiles tell a story that one day a coffin was borne out of an Armenian home—I do not know in which neighborhood of Istanbul. A woman, probably the mother of the deceased, leaned out the window and screamed pitifully, "O my child, weren't there enough bachelors in the *khans?*"[4] Do you see, my dear friend: the migrant from the provinces is not only an Armenian, but he has not even become a man? It is as if he was born of stone and sprouted in the mountains, as if he has never sucked at a mother's breast, as if a mother has never sung him a lullaby, has never sat by his pillow at night to look after him. He has no parents, no children, no home, no place to live.

Was the migrant not forgotten last week? Who raised a glass to the poor porter, who has not only washed the stones of the Church of the Illuminator with his tears and warmed them with his breath, but has even provided oil for the sanctuary lamps with his pennies?

But still, these things must be written about; let us write for the new generation, and from time to time let us sadden their tender young hearts. The new generation is ours. In them one can see a great change. I know from personal experience during my school years that it was agonizing for somebody from the provinces to be a student in any Armenian school in Istanbul. If you had brought with you a pair of strong arms, good! If you were capable of knocking two people down with a singly blow, even better! But if not, you constantly had to endure the insults of all your fellow students. To say nothing of the scornful glance of the hateful tutor. You were subjected to his sharp darts for no reason; you were condemned to hard labor, and your courageous efforts were rewarded with sharp and bitter remarks, which rang always in your ears. Today, however, every Armenian student shows affection and sympathy for his migrant brother; he looks with concern at the needy from

---

4. I.e., could death not have found a bachelor to take, rather than a married man with a family? *Han* or *khan:* in this context, a large commercial building.

Van, Mush, or Sebastia.[5] He often takes care of their needs by giving them paper, pen, and ink. And when I am discouraged by the sight of the granite chins and billowing, brightly colored garments of our glittering society, I shake my head and feel like those Armenian children. With delight I contemplate that tender group, Christ's loved ones, who, like tiny sparks strewn over our heavens, constitute a radiant constellation. Are we not right to say that this is how it is?

So, needless to say, I accept your proposal and will send *Masis* my sketches "From the Lives of Emigrants."

---

5. Present-day Sivas in Turkey.

Tlkatintsi (Hovhannes Harutiunian)

(c. 1860–1915)

Hovhannes Harutiunian, known by his pen name Tlkatintsi, was born in the village of Tlkatin (in ancient times called Til-Kati, now Huylu) near the city of Kharberd (Harput), on the banks of the Aratzani (Murat) River, a tributary of the western Euphrates. His father died while he was still very young, and he was raised by his mother under poor conditions. They moved to Kharberd, where the young boy received his education at the local Smbatian school and dedicated his life to teaching. He taught in Kghi and Balu for a number of years before returning to Kharberd in 1887, where he established a school, known as *Azgayin kedronakan varzharan* (The Central National School), which soon became an important center of education in arts and letters. Here, under his tutoring, was raised a generation of youth, in whom he inculcated love of their native land and in many of whom, such as Ruben Zardarian (1874–1915), Beniamin Nurikian (1894–1988), and Hamastegh (1895–1966), he developed literary skills. He remained at the helm of the school until the end of his life.

Tlkatintsi is one of the most eminent representatives of that genre of literature that comes straight from the land, inspired by its soil and its soul. The cultural revival of the 1860s originated in Constantinople and Smyrna (Izmir) and was led by intellectuals, who for the most part were educated in Europe. The Armenian provinces, where the majority of Armenians lived, were cut off from these centers, and the early revivalists showed very little interest in them. Moreover, the "village folk" were neglected and even despised by the elite and bourgeois classes of the cosmopolitan centers. Although Mkrtich Khrimian (1820–1907) and his pupil Garegin Srvandztiants (1840–92) had already tried to sensitize community leaders and the public to provincial Armenians, Tlkatintsi was the first to cultivate a literary genre entirely centered on the ancestral land, the village, and the peasant. He always lived in the provinces, did not travel far, and did not have the opportunity to learn foreign languages. Although he was in touch with the literary activities of Constantinople and Tiflis and read European authors in translation, he was not influenced by any literary figure or school. These circumstances resulted in writing that was authentic, flowing right from the heart of the countryside.

His literary output consists of short novels (*noravep*), poems, and reports. His best known novels are *Mut ankiunneré* (From dark corners), *Gavat me miayn* (Just one glass), and *Yes kataretsi im partke* (I have done my part). His stories present candidly describe village life, both its pleasant and unpleasant aspects, with characters of different natures and dispositions, all genuine, whether good or bad. His works are examples of realism at its best. In response to those who denigrated provincial literature, he once wrote, in a letter addressed to a colleague: "You must realize that even in these dark corners there are living human beings, loving husbands and wives and loveless couples, fights between the hungry and the well-fed. . . . And all the savory conversations around the fireplace of a village hut, the genial and colorful tales endlessly recounted until the head of the house calls it an evening."[1] All these things provided material for his analysis of human behavior. For him "village literature" was not narrowly confined to the village: through his characters he reaches out to all of humankind, based on the belief that the study of human nature, both good and evil, begins with its primary source: the peasant.

The bulk of Tlkatintsi's work consists of articles he wrote for various newspapers. They consist of descriptions, profiles, short stories, memoirs, traditions, and so on that capture various phases of village life. Similar in nature are his *Geghi namakner* (Village letters), although they have a much wider scope.

---

1. This letter, addressed to Artashes Harutiunian (1873–1915), also known as Malkaratsi Karo, was printed in the Constantinople literary review *Biurakn* (1882–1908) in 1899.

His best plays include *Endi demen* (From the other world), in which a dead man returns to his village to request intercession for his sins, in the process revealing the evil deeds he committed while alive; "*Ktake*" (The will), a one-act play about the clash of heirs over the wealth of a dying man; *Zalem tghan* (The cruel boy), a drama of betrayal and greed; *Depi artasahman* (Going abroad), about the disintegration of a family through emigration to America; and *Vor mekun yeteven* (Whom to follow), a comedy set in a school environment. His poems, fewer than ten in number, are lyric, delicate verses that recall the medieval troubadours. One of these poems, dedicated to his mother, is particularly touching.

His pupil R. Zardarian has this to say about Tlkatintsi's language and style: "Tlkatintsi is the only [provincial writer] to reach the most refined level of art, imparting to the provincial dialect amazing suppleness and beauty. No other Western Armenian writer has been able to preserve native authenticity of language and style without descending to coarseness."[2]

Tlkatintsi had a short life. At the outbreak of the Armenian massacres in 1915 he went into hiding in a friend's house, but he was caught and imprisoned. He was killed outside Kharberd along with a number of other intellectuals, after learning of the deportation of his wife, his only son, and his six daughters, who were never seen again.

His complete works were published in Boston in 1927, in one volume, by the Union of Tlkatintsi's Students, with a preface by Arshak Chopanian (Archag Tchobanian, 1872–1954).

See the section on provincial literature in the overview essay of this anthology.

THE VILLAGE AND THE WINTER[3]

Always the same winter, the same severe cold, with never a delay. It always shows up the same month, driven by the same winds, with the same clouds in the same cold white sky and always in the very same spots: usually hanging over the same sunless valleys and hollows.

---

2. Quoted by Mushegh Ishkhan in *Modern Armenian Literature*, vol. 2 (Beirut, 1982), 138.

3. Tlkatintsi (Hovhannes Harutiunian), "*Geghn u dzmere*" (The village and the winter), in *Giughin Kyanke* (Village life) (Yerevan, 1966), 214–17. Translated by the editors of the present anthology.

It is easy to imagine, then, how the winter and the cold cast a dreadful pall over the run-down houses, where very few are able to pull an extra blanket over themselves and still fewer can wear jackets over their shirts. A few, never more than a few at a time, can warm themselves by the smoky heat of wood cinders smoldering in the fireplace. Many live under the same roof as their hens and chickens; others have had to make room for their cows and calves. The part of the house known as the "heated" or "winter" room is too ugly and untidy even to be called a hellhole.

The soot from the fireplace clings to the ceiling and the walls, leaving a sticky black layer of tar every morning. And what is more, the inhabitants of the house breathe in a great deal of this filthy dust when they try to sweep it up. The stench is so foul it would make even a street mutt sick; it emanates from the mold growing on the bottoms of the water jugs standing in a corner, mixed with the sweaty smell of the old women and children who sit around the fireplace to keep warm.

Who knows when their next chance to sit by the fire will come? Only men dare to approach the fire whenever they want. Only the house cat and the master enjoy the privilege of sitting anywhere in the house, without exception. Women—especially those unfortunate enough to be married—and youngsters have the right neither to speak nor to make their wishes known. Even if the women work until their noses fall from their faces from cold, they are prevented from stretching out their hands or feet to the heat by the fat bodies of the men already congregated around the fireplace. Those who cannot endure this state of affairs might sometimes slip away through the roof and visit the neighbors, in order to warm themselves and thus reinvigorate their bodies at their fire, provided things there are not the same.

Having observed this, we must complete the description of the heated room by adding that the openings in the roof to let the smoke escape also provide an easy passage through which all the hardships of winter can enter. To get an idea of how much snow has fallen without even going outside, people often check the amount of snow that has made its way into the house, melted, and been absorbed by the floor, coating it with another layer of humidity. Rain and snow make their presence felt by means of drops and flakes that fall through the roof openings, mixing with soot as they pour in: spurts of jet-black ink that can sometimes reach the face of an infant who is trying to fall asleep in a cradle and blind an eye.

As if this were not enough, the floor of the heated room remains damp even in July, and in winter it is so damp that even the cat's tender paw leaves a print. Members of the house walk barefoot on the floor. At other times, socks are never considered unnecessary. But if going without them is in a sense fashionable for many, it is another matter when it comes to children: their delicate feet get as red as carrots, and these little ones actually paddle around with their duck-like feet in that dampness all day long.

At night, a family of five to ten—the husband and wife, with the children beside them—bunk down on the bare, humid floor, after performing their evening chores by the light of a foul-smelling oil lamp. Sparks fall on the taut, dirty bed covers, which are patched with bits of rag, but are unable to set them on fire. The family spends the long winter nights in make-shift beds like this. Whenever the dogs in the courtyard bark or howl, the sleepers inside reply with deep, strangled coughs that echo against the outside door; anyone hearing them would form the impression that some diabolic pastime was going on inside, as though someone were throwing huge chunks of rock into a deep well.

Although this is supposed to be when they feel most comfortable, sound asleep in their beds until morning, these choking coughs, sickly wheezes, and snores make them feel as if they have spent the night in their graves.

Beds heavy with dampness from the floor and white frost from the ceiling are folded up in the morning and put aside until once again that evening they rediscover their habitual spots and occupants.

No doubt, reader, you would like me to make an end of this list of details, and wonder if these people do not get sick.

Have you ever compared the peasant in winter to the peasant in summer? In the summer, when his face is tanned by the miraculous rays of the sun, you would swear that he is capable of fathering another seven generations, but if you should see him again in winter it is doubtful that you would recognize him!

1908

Yeghishé Durian

(1860–1930)

The prominent clergyman, poet, educator, and scholar Yeghishé Durian was born in Scutary (Üsküdar), the youngest of six children of a blacksmith. His baptismal name was Mihran. His eldest brother was the famed poet Petros Durian. He received his education at the *Chemaran* school in Scutary (1872–76), where he taught after graduation. A gifted youth and an avid reader, with a precocious intellect and inquisitive mind inclined to religion and philosophy, he decided to take holy orders. In 1879 he was ordained a celibate priest, and in 1880 he was assigned to the parish of Partisak (Bahçecik), an Armenian town not far from Constantinople, both as preacher and as principal of the local Armenian school. He remained in this post for ten years and was instrumental in building up the community and raising the standard of the school. In 1889 he was sent on a pastoral tour to Bulgaria, Austria, France, and England.

In 1890 he was transferred to the newly established seminary of Armash, of which Archbishop Maghakia Ormanian (1841–1918) was the chief administrator. Ormanian's organizational skills and Durian's scholarship helped raise the seminary to its highest level. Durian's tutelage prepared a generation of enlightened clergymen, who played prominent and useful roles during the adversities of the coming years.

In 1904 he was elected Primate of Smyrna (Izmir), where he concentrated on raising the standard of the schools and reviving the educational and spiritual life of the community. In 1908, upon the resignation of Ormanian from the Patriarchal See as a result of the treacheries of the political parties, Durian served as locum tenens until the return of Patriarch Izmirlian from exile. In 1909, when Izmirlian moved to Etchmiadzin to become Catholicos of All Armenians, Yeghishé Durian was elected Patriarch of Constantinople. However, as an intellectual and a man of forthright character and rectitude, he could not abide the ruses, quarrels, and rivalries raised by unscrupulous pseudo-politicians, and he resigned this position within a year. From 1910 on he was active as a preacher, he also taught in various schools, reviving in his students the enthusiasm of the seminary days. He was elected a member of the Armenian National Assembly, where he twice served as chairman of the Religious Council. Although he was spared the tragic fate of other Armenian intellectuals in 1915, he suffered tremendously as he witnessed the carnage of the genocide.

In 1921 the National Assembly unanimously elected him Patriarch of the See of Jerusalem. The See was at its lowest point at the time, and his appointment to this post was a blessing. In a short while he managed to bring about material, moral, and intellectual reforms in the most peaceful and efficient way. The official review of the See, *Sion* (Zion), resumed publication after decades of interruption; scholarly pursuits and research were encouraged. Nine years of relentless effort transformed the See into a prestigious religious center. In 1930 Patriarch Yeghishé Durian died at the age of seventy.

Yeghishé Durian exemplified the devoted clergyman, the ideal teacher, the delicate poet, and the erudite scholar. A diligent student of the Bible and the Church Fathers, he saw Christian doctrine as a way of life, and he exemplified all the principles he was called upon to preach.

The Poet

Durian's poetry is fascinating. In 1909 he published a slim volume entitled *Hovvakan sring* (Pan pipes, 1904–7) that comprised thirty-four of his best poems, all based on biblical themes and episodes, which penetrated their essential message and expressed it in delicately woven language that enhanced its spirituality. With meticulously chosen words, rhythms, and rhymes, each poem is a highly polished work of art. This quality makes him one of the first aesthetes in Armenian literature. A second volume of poems, *Srbazan knar* (Sacred lyre), was published posthumously in 1936.

The Teacher

Durian's intellect ranged over many domains, including theology to philosophy, history, and literature, from all of which he incorporated material into his teaching in order to broaden the horizon of his students. In addition to knowledge, he transmitted moral, spiritual, and national values, helping students build their characters. Indeed, many of his students went on to occupy leading positions in the Church and the community.

The Scholar

Durian owed his erudition to incessant reading and research and to the gift of an analytical mind. Despite his responsibilities as a high ranking clergyman, he produced a number of important works, such as *Drvagner Manuk Hisusi kyanken* (Episodes from the infancy of Jesus, 1926); *Entatsk i krots barbar* (A course in classical Armenian, 1927–29) in three volumes; *Aybubenk hayeren banasirutyan* (The ABC of Armenian philology, 1928); *Azgayin patmutyun minjev XI dar* (History of the nation up to the eleventh century, 1934); *Patmutyun hay matenagrutyan, minjev XIV dar* (History of Armenian literature up to the fourteenth century, 1885); *Hayots hin krone* (The ancient religion of the Armenians, 1933); *Hamarot patmutiun pilisopayutyan* (A concise history of philosophy, 1934); *Dasakan matenagrutyun* (Classical literature, 1935), *Kronneru patmutyun* (The history of religions, 1935); *Haykakan ditsabanutiun* (Armenian mythology, 1935); and *Usumnasirutiunk yev knnadatutiunk* (Studies and reviews, 1935). Some of these works, originally written as textbooks or as supplementary reading material, were published posthumously.

THE TRAVELERS OF EMMAUS[1]

Two men go to Emmaus, sad and weary;
An irresistible grief leads them as guide;

---

1. Yeghishé Durian, "The Travelers of Emmaus," *Sion* (Zion) 45, nos. 9–10 (September–October 1971), 330–32. Translated by M. Manoukian.

What great hopes, Jesus did in His grave bury,
And still He's seen alive by no human sight!

Over the pathway, the sun's fainting orb
Is sinking into the lap of the cloudy skies;
Now and then, they stop in heavy thoughts absorbed,
In a heartrending way, to't lifting their eyes.

—O, Kleopa, His sun too has descended
Into the depths of the marvelous Mystery,
Quenching noiselessly like a shooting star; ended
Th'animated sparks of that Oven fiery!

A little later, darkness was to dominate,
And was to relate with its language thick,
How the profound sunset of the great Faith,
The unseen obscurity of the souls, had to bring.

The two go to Emmaus, sad and weary;
They are led by a remorse of delusion;
Who saw Him coming out from the buried,—
Angel or woman,—O, satan's mad vision!

When the last rays of eve in *dark* were to be submerged,
And slowly crawled on the *black* and Terror,
A stranger approaching, opened a page
From the Cross's Red—Golden sermon to wayfarers.

—Why are your hearts tormented by turbulence great,
In sorrow you fluctuate, as waves ripple,
The hopeless soul is but rejection of faith,
An eye that's stranger to the light of miracle.

What, beforehand, by heaven had been decreed,
The Nazarene executed by His sacrifice,
And on the Cross by His unjustified demise,
Became judge and heir of Father's right indeed.

What is the death of a just man, it's a short night
Where a deep agony dissolves into sunlight.
A night calm and brief than this one of sorrow,
Which fills your soul with impending horror.

Jesus is again living in His glory,
Believe it, testify to God's work great
Th'innocence of Heaven, the earth's love holy,
Angel and woman, each one separate.

Alas the eye that in his light rejoiced,
And yet believes in the Night of Nothingness;
Alas the conscience that heard the Heavenly Voice,
And yet worships the mute solitude immense.

Will you still walk thus weary, in sadness,
Not lifting up your forehead and your heart bold;
Wouldn't you like to be though weak and tardy witness
Of His magnificent greatness untold?

The accent of the stranger's voice affectionate,
Shook the inner world of the travelers;
And when, all of a sudden, He was to bid
Farewell to them, they embraced His feet and said

In anxiety; "Do not depart you hence,
Whoe'er you be, tonight remain with us,
Ah your words dissipated the clouds dense,
That were pushing us into a deep abyss."

They entered a house with a hope secure,
The Stranger took the bread, blessed merrily,
Gave it to them . . . the open eyes saw no more
Th'invisible, evasive Lord of Glory.

—O, Kleopa, then surely it was He
Who met us on the pathway of Despair;
No, it was not an illusory dream;
His breath and life vibrate round us here.

From that vibration taking high-soaring wings,
The two returned in the *dark* of night;
To them, whose eyes still wet, were greeting
The Resurrected God's unquenchable light.

To how many are you still unknown, Jesus,
Who in suspicion of dejection heartrending,

And in hopeless denouncement rebellious,
Clasp the darkness that roams with fluttering wings.

On their nocturnal pathway misled,
Where hides the brightness of your sun unshaded,
Approach as a stranger and do not abate,
The Glory and Mystery of your suffering to relate.

Spread your sublime Fingers' scent of blessing,
O'er the gift of bread on the dining table,
And under the roof where your messages ring,
By your invisible presence be our neighbor.

Sooner or later will come indeed the Day,
The ill-timed day of our fleeting life's end,
But do not let the soul follow the pathway
Of suspicion, along its sunless, gloomy length.

If we go to Emmaus, sad and weary,
Appear and talk to us as a friend on the road;
Resound, reflect deep in our being sincerely,
O, voice and image of the unknown God.

Leo (Arakel Babakhanian)

(1860–1932)

The prominent historian, writer, and literary critic Arakel Babakhanian, who wrote under the name of Leo, was born in Shushi, Karabagh, to a tailor's family. He graduated from the local school in 1878, but his dream of a university education was destroyed when his father died the following year. To assist his family he worked as secretary to the local notary public, and as a telegraph dispatcher. In 1895, after spending two years in Baku, he moved to Tiflis and worked as secretary and journalist for the celebrated periodical *Mshak* (Tiller) until 1906. Though he did not attend university, he worked assiduously to educate himself. He taught for a year (1906–7) at the Gevorgian academy in Etchmiadzin, then returned to Tiflis, where he dedicated himself to historical and literary research and writing. In 1924 he was invited by the State University of Yerevan to teach history and other areas of Armenian studies. He continued to teach, do research, and write until the end of his life.

His early writings, consisting of numerous essays, studies, and criticism, were published in various periodicals. Between 1880 and 1900 his literary output consisted mainly of short stories and novels, such as *Snapashtutyan kurm* (A priest of superstitions, 1884); *Pandukht* (The pilgrim, 1888); *Koratznere* (Those who perished, 1889); *Arnagin* (The price of blood, 1890); a historical novel, *Meliki aghjike* (Melik's daughter,

1898: *melik*—also spelled *malik*—is the Arabic word for the chief or headman of a village or other community); *Aytzaratze* (The goat herd, 1904); *Mi bure mokhir* (A handful of ashes, 1904); and *Karmir gtake* (The red cap, 1904); just to mention a few. Strong realism characterizes all his stories.

From 1900 to 1930 he occupied himself mainly with the writing of history, in which field he earned his reputation. A significant historical work is *Haykakan tpagrutiun* (Armenian printing, 2 vols., 1902), which is, in fact, a history of the cultural, intellectual, and political life of the Armenian people between the sixteenth and eighteenth centuries. This was followed by a host of other studies, such as *Hovsep Katoghikos Arghutian* (Catholicos Hovsep Arghutian, 1902); *Stepanos Nazariants* (2 vols., 1902); *Grigor Artzruni* (3 vols., 1902–5); *Surb Mesrop* (St. Mesrop, 1904); *Hayots hartse* (The Armenian question, 1906); *Hayots hartsi vaveragrer* (Documents related to the Armenian question, 1915); *Vani tagavorutiune* (The Kingdom of Van, 1915); and the historical drama *Vardanank*[1] (1917). To this list should be added his two-volume history of Armenian religious schools in Yerevan from 1837 to 1912 and in Karabagh from 1838 to 1913.

Leo never belonged to a political party; he was a liberal in all his views.

His most outstanding work is the famed *Hayots patmutiun* (History of the Armenians, 1917), a three-volume opus that covers the history of the Armenian people from ancient times to the end of the eighteenth century, with the exception of the period stretching from the sixth to the eleventh century, which he could not complete because of illness.[2] Leo renounced the religio-conservative tradition of writing history and adopted a new approach, placing and evaluating historical events in much wider social, political, and geographic contexts. In his words, "It has been a long time since history was merely the echo of battle drums and kings. It is no longer just pleasant reading; nowadays history is a science. . . . History has a greater and more responsible task to perform: that of depicting the life of the people through the centuries. . . . Kings, princes, and bishops are not the history of the people; they are only an expression of it."[3]

---

1. The reference is to the war waged against the Persians in 451 by the military leader Vardan Mamikonian.

2. Vol. 1 was published in Tiflis in 1917 and vols. 2 and 3 were published posthumously in Yerevan, 1946–47. The hiatus occurs in vol. 2.

3. Leo, *Amboghjakan yerker* (Collected works) (Yerevan, 1966), 1:viii.

During Soviet rule he came under some criticism for not having placed enough emphasis on class struggle in his interpretation of history. However, his works are still considered authoritative.

Leo also wrote a considerable amount of literary criticism on a number of contemporary writers, and many essays on literary trends and attitudes in Armenian, Russian, and western literature. An important work of this kind is *Rusahayots grakanutiune skzbits minchev mer orere* (The literature of Armenian Russians, from its beginning to our times, 1904). Leo regarded literature not as a means of artistic expression, but of moral and intellectual education.

FROM MELIK'S DAUGHTER[4]

PART ONE

It was past noon. The immense shade of the huge walnut tree, which all alone had spread its aged branches over the top of the big hill, extended eastward. That was the sign to resume the games of Vardavar, which had been suspended because of the extreme midday July heat.

A large vegetable garden lay spread out behind the hill, on the high right bank of the babbling brook. In the middle of it, amid low-lying bushes, there appeared a rustic structure, with a sod roof, resting on four rough-hewn crooked wooden columns. A large group of girls and young brides came running out of that covered structure. They all were wearing their most beautiful Sunday dresses. Laughter, gay conversation went with them. That day, the springtime of life had carte blanche: they were all young girls; there was only one old woman and she didn't go near the group.

The swing was ready; a girl stood up in it and began to show off her skill. She rose quickly and folded her knees quickly; after bringing the swing down, she applied all her body's agility to thrust herself forward, ever forward. The rope gradually made an increasingly larger circle and, in a minute's time, the girl was swinging back and forth at a considerable height.

---

4. Leo, *Meliki Aghjike* (Melik's daughter), (Boston, 1933), 13–21. Translated by Aris G. Sevag.

But today the community of girls and young brides had not formed a totally separate group in vain. There were virginal mysteries.

See, a young bride picks up a stick. She's striking the bare feet of the girl on the swing while the remaining girls are demanding that she recite the name of the man she loves.

The one subjected to interrogation does not quickly accede to that demand; she still resists, taking a good beating and only then, when she's tired out and her skin reddened, does she give answers. That's the only way she can get down from the swing and rest. She is engaged and gives the name of her fiancé. That's still not very difficult. Her girlfriends begin to go deeper into her heart and wish to find out without fail what's what—does she love and approve of her fiancé or not? The endless blows make her reveal all the deep dark secrets of her heart.

Also questioned are those who are still not engaged. They are not obligated to give names; they only have to describe the face, figure, clothing and, if possible, even the occupation of the man they desire. The listeners begin to guess who that unknown young man is; one by one, they mention the names of the prospective fiancés in the village, while the girl on the swing, to whom it is positively evident about who has won her heart, torments the questioners, deliberately denying the names given.

There was so much happiness concentrated under the walnut tree that even the old woman was looking on from a distance, laughing, and wishing she were one of those happy young girls.

Now it was the tall girl's turn. It appeared that she was the queen of this festival; no other girl had such beautiful and elegant clothes as she. Two rows of gold coins shined on her chest, whereas silver coins adorned the chests of the others.

"Now we'll start," came voices from left and right.

They all came closer to the swing and gathered more densely. Each one of them wished to grab the beating stick. Like frenzied houris, the entire group wished to torture, beat this girlfriend of theirs.

"There's no sparing her," one said.

"Give me the stick," cried a burly girl. "I'll show how to make human feet murmur." The girl was silent; her marvelous smile expressed acquiescence. And she boldly got up on the rope. The red silk kerchief slid backwards and fell off her head, laying bare her lovely forehead and her thick amber hair. The swing went back and forth twice; the girl was making vigorous efforts; a lovely color came across her face; and her full cheeks became redder, seemingly in an attempt to eclipse the color of the kerchief.

"Who is he?"

Everybody fell silent. With one corner of her little mouth, the girl bit one fold of her kerchief; snow-white teeth appeared between her delicate lips; her smile turned into a lovely mild laugh which caused little dimples to form on her cheeks; she slightly lowered her long and pointed eyelashes on a pair of dark eyes, which were the marvels of that regular round face. She was silent.

"Who is he?" the same question was repeated.

A third blow is struck, then a fourth. But she's not speaking; she's biting tightly on the fold of her kerchief, lifting her shoulders to forget the pain of the blows.

She was agile, flexible. The rope was making impetuous flights, doubling its momentum from the contraction of her knees. The two rows of coins were clinking softly, striking her high and broad chest. A fine wind grabbed a few bunches of her hair and began to play with them softly.

Her stubbornness knew no bounds. The silk she had been biting on in one corner of her mouth had seemingly tied up her tongue. No protest was heard from her, and the blows were not causing her body to jerk. That girl had begun to amaze even her girlfriends. There were now two girls striking her; facing the one armed with the stick was another girl, who was using a twisted belt as a club.

"Baghdasar . . . ," said the girl out loud in a thin voice, suddenly, totally unexpectedly; in an instant, that voice became transformed into a ringing laughter. The redness became more intense, extending to the tips of her ears such that you'd think that blood was going to spurt from them.

"She's lying!" they called out from below.

"Savad!" was heard through the same laughter.

Such a name as this didn't exist. Again questions, again a series of names from above. Everybody was laughing, and the unrestrained joy was giving each one of them the zeal to be stricter in their demand. The girl who was coquettishly swinging and laughing, that beautiful lucky creature, was deriving so much satisfaction from her exquisite stubbornness. . . .

It reached the point where there wasn't anybody left who hadn't struck her and questioned her. And so she gave in and stated that she was now going to say who he was. Silence prevailed but something unusual was heard.

"I don't have anyone," she said.

Laughter, commotion, and cries of discontent ensued.

"She's lying, she's lying! . . . He came to our village yesterday. . . ."

That's what her girlfriends were saying. There was no longer any need to conceal the truth. Twice she flew back and forth in silence; then, gazing upwards, toward the dense walnut branches, she said in a low voice, without any laughter this time:

"Jalal. . . ."

Shouts of joy and triumph greeted that name. The girl arrested the motion of the rope and got down. Now she was metamorphosed. It was a serious individual who quietly went off and withdrew to one side, leaving the rest of the other girls.

But there was no place which could completely shelter her from the sharp penetrating glances that were directed toward her from all sides. The public confession wasn't all that easy; the girl was having difficulty breathing; she felt that her heart wasn't relaxed, that something was burning inside her. She began to put her kerchief and hair in order. No one knew what her situation was but everybody envied her.

The reason was understandable. The lucky beauty was Melik's daughter. . . .

The sun had gotten very close to the mountain, setting behind it. After a few more interrogations, summer's eve would come but the "flowers of Avedaranots" still hadn't completed all the rites of Vardavar. The most interesting of those rites still hadn't taken place; the ever so young at heart were waiting to find out what fate had to say. Each one had revealed her precious secret but . . . it wasn't for nothing that people said, "Never mind what's in your heart; see what fate has to say."

Melik's daughter left the vicinity of the walnut tree and went toward the bottom of the hill. She was followed by the old woman who, until now, had kept her distance. She was the girl's wet nurse. Seeing that the girl began to go hither and thither and was gathering beautiful flowers, the old woman stopped and asked:

"Whom are those for?"

The girl didn't answer until she had a large colorful bunch in hand. Then, approaching the wet nurse, she said:

"They're for our pitcher, which is in the fountain. I will cover it, decorate it, and kiss it so it will predict something good for me. What will it be, Mehri? What will it say for me? I'm afraid, my heart is restless."

"Don't be afraid, Mehri won't let anything bad happen to you," said the old woman with maternal affection and grabbed the girl's hand. "Don't be afraid, my Gayané has a lucky star in the sky over Varanda, the likes of which nobody has yet seen. What will fate say to you, considering you are the good fortune of us all? . . ."

Again and again the old woman reassured her former nursling. Her voice, which had enchanted Melik's children ever since the first years of their childhood, had a marvelous effect on her now as well. Gayané smiled and, full of certitude and faith, looked at the place where the mysterious pitcher was. At this point, the other girls also came over to where Gayané was picking flowers. The old woman became animated, lifted her head and only then noticed that the sun was about to set. She quickly remembered her obligation and, taking Gayané aside, said:

"It's getting dark, and we mustn't stay here."

The girl was stupefied, practically in a state of shock. She didn't think that, at that moment, there existed somebody on earth who would leave in the middle of that day's games.

"But what about the lottery?" she exclaimed in despair. Then she grabbed the wet nurse's hand and, pointing to the west, said:

"There's still sunlight, don't you see? The sun's got a distance of three to four rope lengths yet to travel; then, after setting, a short day begins, a little day of shadows and freshness. The menfolk won't come home until the lamps are lit, and by that time our lottery will have finished."

Mehri was terrified by these last words.

"Until the lighting of the lamps?" she asked in a harsh voice. "That won't do. They're all girls here."

"But our village is very close, a couple of hops, steps and jumps and we'll be there."

"No, no, time is evil. . . . You don't know, you're still a kid. . . . Nowadays it's not safe even in broad daylight. Let's go, the lottery can be drawn at home just as well. . . ."

"There's no bridal fountain at home. . . ."

"We can take the water with us. Hey, what's this I see? . . ." She stopped speaking as she saw something that terrified her.

The mountainous elevation had formed many crooked slopes on the other side of the vegetable garden; the majority of the down-hill area was covered by a forest, whose lower sections had already become engulfed in evening shadows. Below the forest was an open space now covered with yellowed grass; forming little valleys, rough spots and holes, it descended to the brook. Below the forest a rider appeared on horseback. He proceeded a few steps forward but suddenly turned the horse's head around and went in another direction. Evidently he was surveying those parts.

Everything pointed to the fact that he was a dangerous man. Then, as if just noticing the girls scattered about the slope of the hill, he began his slow descent. . . . "For the love of St. Gregory, . . ." murmured the old lady Mehri. . . . "What's a rider on horseback doing here at a time like this? . . ."

Gayané forgot everything; she felt what a little bird feels when a hawk appears in a distant valley. In recent years, she had grown up with those fears; she was always kept out of sight, behind walls; and certain things were whispered in her ears. And she wasn't the only one in that situation; the whole village was in a state of fright and terror. And now, when the danger surfaced, she pressed up against the right arm of her wet nurse, seemingly demanding protection from that weak old woman. The horseback rider had prevented them from moving. Instead of fleeing to save their skins, they stood and watched to see what was going to happen. . . .

At that point, the horseback rider suddenly turned the horse's head around, changed direction and went toward the back of the vegetable garden. The horse was moving fast now. Thank God . . . oh, what joy! . . . Within a minute, another rider on horseback appeared, who quickly went in front of the other. They stopped, apparently engaging in conversation.

Mehri knew that this moment was critical. She had summoned all the saints of Varanda; now she raised her voice, started calling all the girls and brides-to-be, and told them they had to drop everything and flee. The girls had also seen the horsemen and, like birds being chased, quickly began to assemble and move toward the spot where Malik's daughter was standing. But how could they flee . . . when there was no escape route?

Suddenly Gayané laughed and, like someone having escaped from the mouth of a snake, shouted in a loud voice:

"There's nothing to worry about, go and prepare for the lottery. . . ."

Mari would have turned to stone from terror, if Gayané hadn't immediately whispered in her ear:

"I recognized. . . ."

"Who?"

"The one who just came . . ."

No matter how much Mehri concentrated her vision, she wasn't able to make out who the person was.

"Is he from our village?" she asked.

"No!"

And again Gayané prodded the girls to descend quickly and prepare the lottery pitcher.

"I recognized him too," cried out one of the girls and ran downhill.

The terror passed in an instant; it was a storm that suddenly hung over the earth and disappeared just as quickly; again the jumping around and conversation began. The old wet nurse was left stupefied; she didn't know what was happening; dread had become motionless on her wrinkled sunburnt face, and her lips were still uttering, "It's getting dark, what are they saying?" Gayané didn't leave her side and, laughing, asked:

"Don't you recognize him yet?"

"There's no light left in my eyes. Don't you want to tell me?" she replied. "My heart is being torn apart and I don't know what will happen if. . . ."

The poor woman wasn't able to continue and cried. She was pleading to steer clear of danger, to flee, to escape. Gayané hugged her, brought her face up to the kind wet nurse's face as close as possible and, enraptured, uttered:

"It's him, Mehri, it's him! . . ."

"Who?"

"Don't you understand? I said his name back there."

And she pointed toward the walnut tree. But Mehri didn't understand anything, as she was terribly confused.

"You still don't understand? Think carefully, why were our girls beating me?"

Gayané's voice trembled as she spoke these last words; she couldn't look at her wet nurse and turned her face in the other direction.

"Jalal!" Mehri exclaimed after a momentary silence and hugged Gayané tightly.

"Yes! . . . He knows that we're here. . . . His seal is in the lottery pitcher . . . he sent it."

The old woman finally relaxed, wiped her eyes, straightened her kerchief and then began to madly caress her nursling, while uttering countless good wishes for her happiness.

"Jalal!" she repeated in a sweet voice, with a pious feeling, as if he were St. Gregory, whom she had been summoning just a few minutes earlier.

"Yes, he . . . now the dark night is no longer frightening; now, no darkness, no valley and no mountain will bring us any harm, no."

"Yes, Mehri is happy for you . . . but what about Anna-khatun?"

"Doesn't she perhaps believe that this young man alone can protect all of us, all this?"

"Oh, apparently you don't know the Khachen native. Let's go, what have we got to worry about? Lottery takes place only once a year. . . ."

She descended and Mehri no longer dared to make the lovely girl sad with her ill-boding words and presentiments, knowing that her nursling wished to drink from the cup of happiness until the very last drop.

But suddenly Gayané turned back and said in a mysterious low voice:

"Listen, Mehri. If his seal that was tossed into the pitcher doesn't make a good prediction, don't let the Khachen native go away from here sad. Let her know that I know the location of her star in the sky; I see it every night and know what Melik's son is doing and thinking. Tell her only; keep this in your heart, just as I keep. . . ."

Without waiting for an answer, she laughed and ran downhill.

Mehri looked at her, kept looking and, sighing deeply, said:

"Light of my eyes, you're extremely fortunate; that's not good, that much good fortune isn't acceptable in this world of ours."

Grigor Zohrap

(1861–1915)

Lawyer, journalist, polemicist, author, and the most imposing figure of Armenian realism, Grigor Zohrap was born in Constantinople and received his early education in local Armenian schools. He continued his studies at the Galataseray lycée, where he studied engineering, a profession he never practiced. Instead, he entered the newly opened School of Law, and by 1883 he had become a lawyer, specializing in criminal law. In 1895–96 he successfully defended a number of Armenian political prisoners and secured their release. In 1905 he was forbidden to practice law, as a result of having launched a court action against a regional governor who had tortured a peasant. He went to Paris, where he engaged in literary pursuits. In 1908, when the Young Turks came to power and a new constitution was proclaimed, promising freedom and brotherhood, Zohrap returned to Constantinople, was elected to the new Ottoman parliament, and was given a teaching position at the Faculty of Law. He was also elected to the Armenian National Assembly. He was soon recognized as a highly competent lawyer and an eloquent parliamentary orator, fighting relentlessly to introduce legislation that would improve public education; eliminate unjust taxes, feudal privileges, and discrimination among the citizens; and grant equal social and legal rights to all nationalities. Every speech he delivered in parliament or the Armenian Assembly was considered an "event." During the 1909 massacres in Adana, he courageously criticized the government and demanded the punishment of the criminals. He published two textbooks on criminal law in Turkish, and wrote a book in French, under the pseudonym Marcel Léart, entitled *La quéstion arménienne à la lumière des documents* (Documentary clarifications of the Armenian question), published in Paris in 1913.

Early in the 1880s Zohrap began to attract attention with his newspaper articles and critical essays. One target was the way in which the Armenian question was being handled by the patriarch of the day, Nerses Varzhapetian (1837–84), and by Minas Cheraz (1852–1929). In 1883 he and writer-educator Reteos Perperian (Berberian, 1848–1907) began a bitter polemical debate in *Yerkragunt* (The globe) over Srbuhi Dussap's novel *Mayta,* in which the author promoted the rights and freedoms of women. Zohrap's opposition was based on his conviction that such feminist ideas would eventually destroy the traditional role of the woman as keeper of the family and preserver of moral virtue.

Zohrap's strictly literary career began with a novel, *Anhetatsatz serund me* (A vanished generation), which was first serialized in the periodical *Masis* in 1885 and published as a book in 1887. Written in a realistic vein but retaining some traces of romanticism, it portrays a family situation in which love, money, and traditional concepts are in conflict. To this early period also belongs his *Chinakan namakani* (Chinese letters, 1884), an unfinished work in which "he satirizes the Armenian life of Constantinople in a manner reminiscent of Montesquieu's *Lettres persanes* (Persian letters)."[1]

Influenced by French realists like Guy de Maupassant, Alphonse Daudet, and Émile Zola, and encouraged by Arpiar Arpiarian (1852–1908), the pioneer of Armenian realism, Zohrap earnestly embraced the new literary movement and eventually merited the title "prince of short stories" that some of his contemporaries bestowed upon him. His most productive years were 1892–98, when, with Hrant Asatur (1862–1928) and later also with Zapel (Zabel) Asatur (1863–1934), he coedited *Masis,* at the same time contributing to other periodicals such as *Hayrenik* (Fatherland), *Arevelk* (The Orient), and *Azatamart* (The fight for freedom). He produced works in many genres: fiction, editorials, literary portraits, and poems in prose and verse. His short stories, about fifty in number, were collected in three volumes: *Khghchmtanki dzayner* (Voices

---

1. James Etmekjian, ed., *An Anthology of Western Armenian Literature* (New York, 1980), 71.

of conscience, 1909), *Lur tsaver* (Suffering in silence, 1911), and *Kyanke inchpes vor é* (Life as it is, 1911). He summarized his realism as follows: "Literature must be derived from the life of the people and must be used to serve the people."[2] Ara Baliozian, a translator of Zohrap, draws some parallels between Zohrap and other writers: "As a short story writer he was more like Guy de Maupassant, especially in his subtle depiction of feminine psychology, and Anton Chekhov, in his sympathetic treatment of the lower classes."[3] Although most of his short stories are reflections of local life, they have a universal appeal. His sharp eye penetrates the depths of the human soul and discovers the root causes of human behavior. For him women are destined to rise and elevate, to kindness and benevolence, and they are nourished with love; it is society that perverts their moral and psychological image. His stories treat even a fallen woman with respect and dignity. As James Etmekjian says:

> His prose is clear and his imagery powerful. He paints vivid pictures with rapid strokes. He is as skillful at putting sea waves in motion as he is at creating upheavals in the minds and emotions of human beings. His narrative, punctuated by beautiful descriptions and crisp dialogues, leads the reader quickly to the climax of the story. His irony heightens the pathos; his sense of humor brings relief; his symbolism adds depth; while his poetic prose lends beauty to his style. . . . Zohrap remains the incomparable storyteller of his and subsequent generations.[4]

Zohrap also wrote a series of portraits of contemporary writers such as Arpiar Arpiarian, Reteos Perberian, and Yeghia Temirchipashian (Demirjibashian, 1851–1908). These were scattered in various periodicals until they were collected and published as *Tzanot demker* (Familiar figures) in Paris in 1932. Another collection is *Ejer ughevori oragren* (Pages from a travel journal, 1922), which contains impressions and philosophical musings occasioned by his travels in Europe.

On 24 April 1915, when, by the order of the government, more than 200 intellectuals were routed and sent to the interior to be massacred, Zohrap, as a member of parliament, lodged a strong protest and demanded the repeal of the order. On 19 May he had an audience with Talaat Pasha, the minister of the interior, to plead the case. The next day, on the order of Talaat himself, Zohrap was arrested, shipped to the

2. *Masis*, 3956 (1892).
3. Ara Baliozian, *Zohrab* (Kitchener, Ontario, 1985), 7–8.
4. Etmekjian, ibid., 72.

interior, and killed in a brutal fashion somewhere between Diyarbekir and Urfa.

Armenisa[5]

Halki[6] is a Greek island. I met her there. She used to come to Anastas's casino[7] in the evening, to meet her husband arriving on the ferry; at least that short, heavy man in his fifties with whom she returned to the hotel was presumed to be her husband.

Most of the time she was alone; occasionally she brought a little boy with her, about six years old, who must have been her son, whom she talked to and treated as though he were an adult.

She didn't bother with anyone else, and the young men hung about inviting her attention in vain. She never acknowledged their presence in any way.

The casino was built on a terrace that reached out into the sea. She had her own corner there where she sat every evening, alone. That was her place, and considered so by the other guests who seemed disposed to respect the wishes of this foreigner.

I saw her there from time to time, and asked my Greek friends about her.

"Her name is Armenisa, Armenuhi," they told me, and that's all they seemed to know about her.

Questions directed to casino personnel proved no more productive. Others even began coming to me, as a compatriot of hers, for information about her.

The husband, who came to the island twice a week, was more reclusive than the woman. He hadn't exchanged greetings with anyone for the month and a half they had been at the island's Bellevue Hotel. The young men ascribed this isolation to his jealous nature; in their view of the circumstances, the woman emerged as a victim of his constraint.

---

5. Grigor Zohrap, "Armenisa," in *Voice of Conscience: The Stories of Grigor Zohrap*, ed. and trans. Jack Antreassian, intro. Michael Kermian (New York, 1983), 44–57. Footnotes by the editors of the present anthology.

6. Ancient Khalki: present-day Heybeli Ada, one of the islands in the Marmara near Istanbul.

7. In Turkey the word is used for a café, a place serving refreshments, usually outdoors.

And in truth her face was sometimes shaded with a sadness that seemed to confirm that belief.

She didn't appear timid. Her graceful movements and firm walk admirably suited her elegant appearance. With authority in her voice, and not the slightest hesitation in her manner, like one accustomed to being obeyed, she easily commanded the attention of the servants.

From the first I felt more optimistic than the others about the possibility of meeting her.

"You should," my Greek friends insisted, for once envious of my nationality, "you know her language; you'll be able to talk to her."

It was the first time in my experience that there seemed to be some benefit in being Armenian. Immediately, encouraged by this advantage, and urged on by my friends, I began devising ways to meet her.

I went to the casino more often, and found a place at a table near her, and tried to make my presence felt by speaking just loud enough to be heard by her. I always spoke in the very best Armenian, choosing my words with great care; then I turned to French and Turkish; I was not, after all, someone to be dismissed lightly.

I became more fastidious in my dress. I surprised my tailor, who was well aware of my thrift, with an order for five new suits. I purchased a supply of ties, all in the latest style; and white shirt collars, narrow and high, reaching up to my chin and threatening to choke off my breath; handsome, delicately monogrammed handkerchiefs; all worthy of the notice of a woman of good taste.

She was herself always immaculately attired, wearing something different every day, each more striking than the other, all obviously made in the finest shops.

Nothing helped. I was a thoroughly inept suitor. She took no notice of anything I did, not the loud conversation she could not help but hear, not my anxious movements, not the insistent gazes I turned on her. Nothing penetrated her indifference, as she sat there imperturbable as a beautiful marble statue. She never even looked at me.

My lack of success and the snickering it evoked from my Greek friends soured my feelings. Her proud manner seemed like rudeness now, and her reclusive ways a mask for her shortcomings.

I started gossiping about her everywhere. I could say nothing specific; but it was enough to whisper suspicions which her unsociable attitude readily supported. "She is certainly not from any of the respected families of Bolis,"[8] I volunteered at any opportunity. "And that old companion of hers could hardly be her husband." And my friends, themselves disappointed, did not hesitate to circulate similar comments wherever they went.

Fortunately, no echo of the gossip reached her. The interest and curiosity of the islanders did not abate. The style-conscious Greek women tried to imitate her dress, without ever succeeding. And when she passed by, holding her small son by the hand, with the serenity and grace of a goddess, murmurs of admiration moved on everybody's lips, murmurs that fueled my passion.

Her beauty seemed to set her apart. People either adored or detested her; no one remained indifferent. Everything about her, how she moved, talked, looked, had a distinctive character.

She was without curiosity, without the capacity to be surprised. What did she like? How could one please her? It was an impossible puzzle, with this beautiful woman as a prize for anyone who solved it.

Her heart remained buried in her proud breast, an inaccessible treasure.

Armenisa delighted in taking walks, perhaps conscious of the impression made by her delicate grace, her hair swept and gathered under a wide-brimmed straw hat, revealing the smooth whiteness of her neck, the folds of her dress grasped in one hand and her open red parasol in the other, its reflections of the sun highlighting the red tints of her face.

Sunday mornings she always went to Grand Island,[9] where I ran into her one day.

I was going along an immaculate tree-lined road that led from the pier to the Giacomo Hotel. On either side, set among well-groomed flowering gardens, were beautiful homes, actually villas and mansions, whose munificent furnishings were visible through open doors, as were servants got up in black suits and white ties,

---

8. Istanbul in Armenian.
9. Present-day Büyük Ada: the largest of the islands in the Marmara near Istanbul.

and maids as beautifully attired as the woman I pursued, waiting near the doors in white aprons.

Among all these palatial homes was a modest stone structure, conspicuous for its simplicity, the lone plain countenance in an otherwise joyous company.

Everyone was going toward that building, with me following after them. It turned out to be a Catholic Armenian church.

I wondered if this church could really be Armenian. I heard Turkish spoken, and some French. I saw only Europeans around me, gloves in their hands, heads uncovered, standing stiffly like the dressed mannequins in the Shtayni shops. No one seemed to be praying. At the altar a priest was mumbling something in a low, unintelligible dialect. The women leafed casually through their ivory-backed bibles, occasionally nodding toward the altar, unable to bend their bodies which were gathered and bound by corset wires. As for the men, from time to time they bent their left knee barely enough to touch the pew in front of them, a concession to kneeling, unwilling otherwise to disturb the natural folds of their suits, all their attitudes becomingly attentive, as though they were in a theater to see a play.

I saw Armenisa there, looking even more beautiful in this sanctuary setting, her face reflecting warmth and sincerity, a magical, child-like innocence. I averted my admiring gaze, afraid that it might be noticed. But what was I to do? Lost and confused in this constricting atmosphere, taunted by the perfumes emanating from the women, I had to make every effort to keep from doing anything foolish.

I felt uneasy among people who seemed to scorn me as a foreigner. I hesitated to take a seat, and didn't dare to leave the church. I searched through my boyhood years to determine just where in the liturgy we happened to be, without success. It was hopeless. Large drops of sweat began forming on my forehead and slipping down. Then I saw two or three people moving toward the door. I was saved. I couldn't miss this opportunity. I summoned all my courage and moved along with them, only to find myself near Armenisa. She was leaving too. I was at her side as we passed through the door. Before leaving she took some water from a marble basin and crossed herself. I had no idea what it meant, but I followed Armenisa's example. I could not tell whether it was from her or from the water that the promise of happiness suffused my soul. Armenisa looked at me, and a smile, actually a rising sun illuminating a dark horizon, spread across her beautiful red mouth.

This was the beginning of our friendship. A drop of water from that marble basin dissolved the wall of ice that had separated us.

On the return trip to Halki we happened to find ourselves together again. Armenisa spoke to me then, about the weather, about the attractions of the island. I was so deliberate in my answers that I must have seemed a mindless dolt; but I was afraid of endangering the friendship so fortuitously gained.

She was beginning to act as though we were old friends, making fun of the young people of Halki, with candid amiable jokes, some of her sarcasm perhaps meant for me. Then, looking straight at me, she asked:

"You're Catholic, aren't you?"

I had sufficient composure to conceal my surprise.

"Yes," I told her in a tone intended to make the question seem superfluous.

I was surprised myself at not having wavered even a little in telling this lie.

"I could tell from the way you talk. Armenians," and there was contempt in her voice when she uttered the word "can never speak Turkish the way you do."

We had been speaking Turkish.

Armenisa appeared to be a zealous though altogether charming Armenophobe.

I loved Armenisa and became a happy convert.

The question, "You're Catholic, aren't you?" had something irrevocable about it that only a lover's heart could grasp. Without any compunctions, I had kept my religion secret by uttering a simple "yes," in the same way I might have lied about my financial means in front of a wealthy man.

How easy it can be to say "yes," a small word of one syllable and three letters embracing fully half the universe, since "yes" and "no" represent the whole of being. With one word then I had crossed the rubicon, and rejoiced that I had. As I soon became aware, she was not simply a Catholic but also an unrelenting enemy of Armenians. The disgrace of having been born to a people as unfortunate as ours had ignited in her a wild and irreconcilable hatred for them. Catholicism had provided more than the usual satisfaction for her soul: with it she felt she had changed not only her religion, but more significantly her nationality. She would be free of the Armenian stain forever. Any questions regarding her nationality Armenisa answered in the same way:

"I am Catholic."

I never heard her speak an Armenian word. Her convictions, like her beauty, ruled and dominated. Surrendering to her arguments would have been truly pleasurable to me, had I not already been accepted as a Catholic by her.

Now that I was hopelessly in love, my pretense threatened to be more effective than true conversion, so sympathetic did I become to all her rages. She had fantastic notions about the world, which I was careful not to contradict. She regarded papal sovereignty above all else in the world.

Despite being intimidated by this narrow-minded, pietistic woman, I still couldn't shake my resentment of her unjust condemnation of my people and religion. But one caress was enough to make me forget it.

Guilt and self-justification kept swinging back and forth between my love and conscience; I could not completely evade the shadow of that terrible lie, and the probability of its unexpected exposure one day.

Armenisa's love, like her hatred, was warm and passionate. She was not like most women who seem humbled and diminished by defeat. Her disappointments, especially her earlier ones, had given her a maturity far greater than her age might account for.

I don't know why she was attracted to me, but I do know that I became her happiest lover.

The sky was clearer and a deeper blue; the sea calmer, and the sound of the waves softer and more mysterious. My affinity grew for flowers, trees, the mountains, solitude; the stars became intimate friends; I was gentler and more serene; for the first time I was able to sense the majesty of the universe, in reverence; I wrote poems.

Life is a miraculous vision when viewed through an opening we call youth.

I would not thereafter experience such happiness, nor such torments of conscience.

Armenisa's fondness for me grew.

She preferred my confusion and timidity to the daring and enterprise of more worldly men. Perhaps it was her need to feel maternal solicitude for the one she loved, a solicitude that implied a good measure of domination. A shy youth who tentatively presses a woman's hand may be preferred to one who is experienced and audacious.

An impossible thing happened to us. We were both happy. Impossible because in love the happiness of one is often made up of the misery of the other.

I was her constant companion. Everyone was surprised and envious, wondering how I was able to gain this good fortune. They would never know.

We spent time walking together around the island, picking wild strawberries along the way. And at twilight, away from inquisitive and malicious eyes, we sat together under a tree in a small grove, alone above the blue waters of the Marmara. And when it got dark, a young boatman rowed us across the calm surface of the sea to the isolated shores of Prinkipo.[10]

Armenisa had a lovely voice, which could fill a man's heart with joy, his eyes with tears. Her songs were always of love and misfortune.

Sometimes she seemed to have doubts about us.

"We are not for each other," she used to say, shaking her head uncertainly.

She never asked where I was from, or who my parents were. It was enough that I was Catholic. On my part, I knew very little about her, and most of that conjecture.

I used to address her formally in the beginning, and later, as we grew closer, simply "Marie." One day I told her that I first knew her as Armenisa, and that all the islanders referred to her by that name.

I cannot describe her fury.

"I am Catholic," she concluded the matter drily. Her elderly friend still came on certain evenings. They had been together for years. Gradually I became convinced that he was her lover, and that he paid for all her extravagances. He was unendurable, always docile and obedient, like one of those mules, laden with treasure, one comes across everywhere.

---

10. Ancient name of present-day Büyük Ada.

He ate a great deal and talked very little, gave a great deal and received very little, all without complaining. His supreme pleasure was to make Armenisa happy. He had no family of his own and no relatives, and everything he had he was prepared to give to her. He had wanted to marry her, but she was unwilling to surrender her freedom.

Our life was one of love and harmony. Armenisa remained without the slightest suspicion about me, though that did not ease the pain of my deception. Armenians continued to be the principal objects of her scorn. Our language which she didn't understand, our church which she had never entered, suffered her contempt. I tried as much as possible to dispute her wicked judgments, always careful not to arouse her hostility.

In truth I had become the most abject of creatures. And there were times when my conscience was repelled by the extent of my servility. But I was certain that losing Armenisa would be worse than losing life itself.

How long would this deception last, before it was exposed by some innocent word or deed? Every moment, the fear of losing it made my happiness a mixed torment of bitterness and delight.

It was the Sunday of the Holy Cross, a beautiful September morning. We were sitting in the seaside casino. All the women were beautifully dressed. The men, all of them Greek, had on their best suits. A musical group was performing at one end of the large salon. More and more visitors poured out of the ferry at the Halki pier. We watched as they surged boisterously onto the island. I felt very happy, and laughed merrily at all Armenisa's wicked observations. Out of the crowd of figures, a tall man, with a long grey beard, a black coat, and a broad-brimmed hat, suddenly singled me out from the distance, waved and hurried toward me. His gentle smile and kindly face were a thousand times more frightening to me than Banquo's[11] ghost. It was our parish priest, a virtuous, pious, garrulous man who had baptized me, and loved me like his own son. A tempest was about to burst upon us, and I was frantically seeking some escape, to disappear magically perhaps, to become invisible suddenly.

---

11. A character in Shakespeare's *Macbeth:* the ghost of Banquo disrupts a banquet by appearing only to Macbeth, who had ordered his murder.

"Bless you, my son." The priest was already upon us, oblivious to the distress I was in. "I have found you at last. Where have you been staying? You haven't been to confession for a year. I'll be hearing the confessions of your family today, and they will all receive holy communion next Sunday. Who is the lady? I don't know her."

The lady? I didn't have the courage to look into her face. I couldn't open my mouth. I waved toward the Livatia district trying to communicate where our home was.

"Is your father at home?"

I nodded my silent affirmation.

I don't know what he was able to deduce from my dumbfounded condition. I was thankful that he didn't prolong my torment.

"Don't be late," he said, more command than counsel, and went off.

Armenisa hadn't spoken a word the entire time the priest was with us. Not realizing that I was the one he was coming to see, she was getting ready to turn all her scorn on the clerical figure that was drawing near. His greeting and familiar address had stunned her. She couldn't believe what she heard; and she guessed everything.

When the priest departed, she stared at me, her eyes cold, sharp daggers reaching into my heart. Sweat began collecting on my forehead.

"You deceived me all this time by pretending you were Catholic." Anger made her voice unsteady.

The color of my face was sufficient confession of my lie.

"Why won't you answer? You deceived me." She didn't seem to care that there were curious people around us.

I had no answer to give.

"Say something," she repeated, the color fading from her face. People began eyeing us furtively.

"This is not the place to discuss it. Everybody's watching. I'll explain everything later." I tried to reassure her and find a way out of my embarrassment.

"Where?"

"At the hotel."

"Let's go.

Armenisa got up. I followed like a prisoner, trying frantically to think of some explanation I could offer. I could think of nothing.

The time had come to say farewell to my happiness. I knew Armenisa to be stubborn and vindictive and expected no compassion from her. Our parting would be final; my loss irreparable.

We reached the hotel, even while I was hoping that something would prevent our getting there. We went up to the room together, that lovely room, so full of promises, which I entered now as accused, and from which I would emerge a moment later, condemned.

The room was full of memories. I had no thought of continuing the charade. With a single word I had gained this happiness, and with a single word I would surrender it. But I couldn't manage it dispassionately. All the torment of my soul poured out, the immensity of my love and my offense. Armenisa listened intently, allowing me to say whatever I wished. I defended myself with hopeless desperation, finally holding the intensity of her religious beliefs responsible for my deception. I must have known that blaming her piety would make any reconciliation impossible.

"I will love you no matter how much you despise me. My love is truer than yours," I told her. "That will redeem my sin. Yours was only a fanatic idea, not real love."

My boldness startled her. She had never thought of me as brave. For a moment at least my agitation may have touched her. But the thought of having been deceived was too much for her injured piety.

"Very well. Let's not drag this out any longer. You are a heretic who posed as one of the true faith. That's all past. But everything is finished between us. Go and confess your sins to your priest. The poor man is waiting for you."

"If that's the way you want it."

I left, picking my way out of the ruins, afraid the walls might collapse around me. I didn't turn back. On the way I met our cook, who had been looking for me everywhere. The priest was still waiting for me at home, it seemed.

To forgive my sins?

"Let him wait!" I shouted at the servant and, like an idiot who had no idea where he was going, stomped off.

Armenisa was sick for a week. The shock of the truth about me was too much for her. She was in tears, I learned from her servants, when I had left. I dropped by every morning to find out secretly about her health.

Slowly she improved; fever had dissolved her bitterness; reflection had subdued her anger.

The shock had damaged the structure of prejudice that had occupied her mind since childhood. She had come to know and love me; and she began to think that my religion did not make me a different person from the one she knew. She conceded that she had no reason to think of Armenians as a coarse people. She even justified my deceit as having been prompted by my love for her; she understood and counted it a virtue. We were reconciled and, recognizing the extent of the sacrifice I had made, she offered an even greater one. I had pretended being a Catholic; she actually joined the Armenian church. Since we worshiped the same God, she reasoned, there were no real differences of faith, only prejudices, which love overcame, as for a time it had overcome my conscience and convictions.

But our love and intimacy did not last for very long. It was almost as though this self-sacrifice gradually effaced all affection, was in fact an exchange for love, with nothing left over. We never again were able to regain our earlier days. We were friends now, but not lovers.

With the loss of her prejudices, she seemed to lose the most prepossessing of her charms. What was unique about her seemed to fade.

Perhaps we must leave predispositions, faith, even mistaken convictions, undisturbed. Everybody's existence is a unity which cannot survive the removal of any important part.

Becoming sensible and direct, Armenisa ceased to be interesting and charming. Perhaps as time passed it was I who saw her in that light.

She no longer objected to being called Armenisa. Only that remained to cherish from our love. We were at last separated by circumstances, and years passed. One day I heard that Armenisa had married her elderly friend.

Hrand Asatur

(1862–1928)

Hrand Asatur, writer, journalist, and literary critic, was born in Constantinople, received his early education at the Mezburian school, attended Robert College, and studied privately with Minas Cheraz and Biuzand Kechian. In 1879 he published his first literary work, *Patanekan nershnchumner* (Youthful inspirations), and a booklet, *Sahmanadrutiun yev hay zhoghovurde* (The constitution and the Armenian people). In 1881 he went to Paris to study law, and soon after graduation, in 1884, he returned to his native city and published his impressions in the journal *Arevelk* (Orient), under the title "*Kyanke i Fransa*" (Life in France).

From this point on his interests shifted to historical and philological research, which he embraced with passion. His studies examine various cultural domains, from monastic institutions to literature, theater, the press, and all the significant phenomena in the social and intellectual life of the nation. He was a strong proponent of modern Armenian, contributing immensely to its development and refinement; his language reflects the best literary version of the time.

One of his most significant works is *Kostandnupolso hayere yev irents patriarknere* (The Armenians of Constantinople and their patriarchs), which relates the successive migrations of Armenians, beginning with the Byzantine period and concentrating particularly on the period after the twelfth century, and also examining how Armenians fared under the patriarchs of Constantinople, from the establishment of the patriarchate in 1461 to the national and literary revival of 1858. Another interesting historical study, *Hay vankere* (Armenian monasteries), deals with all monastic centers from the time of Gregory the Illuminator to the Cilician period.

In 1892 Asatur became coeditor, with Grigor Zohrap (1861–1915), of the *Masis* weekly, a prestigious journal to which he contributed frequently. From 1898 to 1908 he taught modern Armenian and literature at the Kedronakan lycée in Constantinople. His greatest contribution to education, however, was a series of textbooks for Armenian language and grammar, which he wrote in close collaboration with his wife, Zapel (Zabel) Asatur (1863–1934), herself a writer of great merit. The series, known as *Tangaran* (Treasure house), comprises three levels (elementary, middle, higher), has gone through numerous printings, and has been used by several generations of students. The Asaturs also published a supplement, *Ashkharhabari gortznakan kerakanutiun* (A practical grammar of modern Armenian), which also enjoyed great popularity.

Hrand Asatur is best known for his *Dimastverner* (Portraits), published in 1921: a compilation of seventeen essays, each portraying a contemporary writer, enriched with personal memories and keen observations. He penetrates into the inner self of each subject and sketches a delicate portrait of the individual: not necessarily of the writer, but of the real man.

Two important works of his later years, *Ashkharhabari patmutiun* (The history of modern Armenian) and *Imastasirakan bararan* (Philosophical dictionary), remain unpublished.

GRIGOR ZOHRAP[1]

One night in 1891 I was at Zohrap's home in Kadiköy.[2] Tigran Kamsarakan was also there. We decided that the three of us would form an editorial group and publish *Masis* (The mountain, i.e., Mount Ararat), a literary journal. Zohrap would be the editor-in-chief and I would be the publisher; Kamsarakan did not want

---

1. Hrand Asatur, "Grigor Zohrap," in *Dimastverner* (Portraits) (Constantinople, 1921), 219–50. Slightly abridged, and translated by the editors of the present anthology.
2. A suburb on the Asiatic shore of Istanbul.

an active administrative responsibility. *Masis* would be published and printed at the printing house of *Arevelk* (The Orient), but the administrative board of that paper would have absolutely no power to interfere with the literary or political directions of the journal. That same evening, we prepared an announcement for the newspapers, and Zohrap wrote the statement that would appear on the front page of *Masis*. This statement of editorial principles declared: "Our main purpose is the advancement of literature. The literary content of *Masis* will be derived from the life of the people and will be at the service of the people." Zohrap even promised to write an editorial for the first issue and give us a short story for it.

Masis was supposed to come out on Saturday morning, January 4, but on Thursday evening the editor-in-chief had still not written a line. Early Friday morning, however, Zohrap brought a short story to my office and, sitting at my desk, started to write an editorial. That night we both went to the printing house, and we made the printers work until morning. With the smell of lead and dust in the air, we worked without a break throughout the cold January night, not resting for even a minute. On Saturday morning we had *Masis* distributed to the newstands; all 1,500 issues were sold before dark. On the second day of Armenian Christmas, we had to get the printing house to reopen so 500 more copies could be printed. . . . .

In the second issue of *Masis* Zohrap started the series "Well-Known Figures" with Biuzand Kechian, the editor of *Arevelk*. In certain respects he did not agree with Kechian's ideas, but he recognized and appreciated his intellectual integrity. He wrote: "From his lines sound reasoning distills, condenses, overflows, and threatens to drown the reader." But this "mass of logic," he continued, "is at the same time a rare embodiment of contradiction. Never has the conservative spirit been embodied in such a forceful individual. . . ."

In the third issue of *Masis,* the editor published an article under the title "Immoral Literature." In it he directly contradicted Kechian, without mentioning his name. "Literature," he wrote, "may be considered moral or immoral on the basis of its purpose alone. The description of a voluptuous or lustful scene is not enough to brand an author as immodest and immoral." Otherwise, we would have to begin by dumping all of Greek literature into the fire, along with its mythology. Lucretius, Catullus, and Petronius, who represent the Roman literature of love and passion, are classical authors. Horace and Ovid exceeded all the freedom of modern writers. In French literature also François Rabelais, for all his comical voluptuousness, has not been considered an immoral writer. Fléchier's *Mémoires,* Fénelon's *Télémaque,* and Montesquieu's *Lettres persanes* would not have escaped denunciation; Voltaire, Diderot, Rousseau with his *La nouvelle Héloïse* and *Confessions,* Théophile Gautier with *Madmoiselle de Maupin,* and Dumas with *La dame aux camélias* would be immoral, then, all of them. Among the poets Ronsard, d'Aubigné, and especially Alfred de Musset, the author of "Namouna," and others would not have been spared censure, Zohrap wrote. He also mentioned the Song of Songs in the Bible, Karapet Iutiuchian's (1823–1904) translation of *Gaghtnik havadaknnutyan* (Secrets of the inquisition), and Petros Durian's (1851–72) *Tatrone* (The theater), all of which would have been, according to a narrow perception, immoral. The editor of *Masis* defended his case most skillfully, but in fact Kechian was right when he considered the publication of such writings in our newspapers and periodicals both unsuited to the times and damaging to our development. . . .

Masis gradually became quite interesting. Sibil (Zapel, Asatur, 1863–1934) wrote both prose and poetry for it. Besides his "Well-Known Figures" and editorials, Zohrap contributed short stories and chronicles. Garnik Fnteklian (Findiklian) wrote a few articles analyzing "The Rise of Modern Armenian in the Fourteenth Century"; and on the publication of Mihran Hovhannesian's *Irakan kyanki nvagner* (Melodies of real life) he wrote a critical article on the important role of popular language in literature. In the summer of 1892, Mihran Kamsarakan (1866–1948) left for Europe; so we had to do without his collaboration. At the end of the year, however, after his return, he took part in the publication of the final issues. . . .

At the end of 1892, Zohrap insisted that, beginning the following year, *Masis* become a weekly, and I personally objected. He persisted; we then agreed to draw up an agreement with the administration of *Arevelk,* and he became both publisher and editor-in-chief of *Masis* as of 1893, a situation that lasted only seven months.

Six years later, in 1898, when *Arevelk* was suppressed and *Masis* replaced it as a daily, Zareh Yusufian proposed that Zohrap and I become associates. Zohrap seemed convinced, provided that Sibil, he, and I comprise the editorial board. . . .

In 1898 Zohrap wrote an excellent editorial in *Masis*. In "Edelweiss" he referred to the off-white Alpine flower and described its unfading youth: "Time has not erased the traces of its youth; it remains invariable, like the half-mourning of a widow, which she never takes off because it suits her." He went on to say that edelweiss can also be found among women and the nation. He knew women who were romantic young girls and who now, just as before, try to remain girls, still flirting as they did in former days. They are female edelweiss. Certain Armenians were singled out for public life beginning in their school years, and a quarter century later Zohrap could see the same people around him, always bustling about—they are the nation's edelweiss! "No! I don't like this mountain flower, I don't like that it stays forever young, when everything that resembles it comes and goes so very fast."

Another article, "The Broom," created a big stir. Zohrap criticized Armenian teachers. He said that students who graduated from Armenian schools enter the marketplace with an incomplete education. He advised the Board of Education to look into it more carefully and to get rid of certain incompetent and worthless teachers in the national public schools. This article was widely praised and gave rise to a new expression: "Zohrap's broom." . . .

In his writing as in his private life Zohrap was an enthusiastic aesthete. Whenever he came across a nice little trinket, a stylish building, or a picture by an artist, he could not walk by with indifference. Harmonious music made the hidden strings of his soul resonate, and the sparkle of excitement always gleamed in his eyes. An Armenian talent, regardless of what field it lay in—a Peshiktashlian (Beshiktaslian, (1828–68), a Chukhachian, (Chukhadjian)[3] a Komitas *vardapet*,[4] an Ayvazovsky, a Shirvanzaté,[5] an

---

3. Tigran Chukhachian, composer and educator, the father of Armenian opera (1837–98).

4. Soghomon Soghomonian, composer, musician, and clergyman (1869–1935).

5. Aleksandr Movsesian, writer (1858–1935).

Abelian,[6] or a Siranuysh[7] could always become the object of his devotion, and he knew how to appreciate a great talent wherever he met one, even in the vicinity of his enemies. Everything in his home displayed his good taste. The furnishings of his reception room were ample and finely made, and he loved changing them around according to the latest fashion. Beautiful paintings decorated the walls, especially those by Edgar Shahin, which dominated the rest.

. . . .

His unlimited passion for beauty was especially evident in his writings, where it was revealed in the unique images contained in his short stories, his "Well-Known Figures" series, and his *Ughevori noter* (Travelers' notes) in *Azatamart* (Fight for freedom). Together with a few other talented writers, Zohrap brought the modern spirit into Western Armenian literature: with startling comparisons, with psychological analyses, with real-life snapshots. Zohrap never slavishly imitated foreign writers; he was his own master. Life was his major source of inspiration; his surroundings became the fertile ground from which he gleaned his truly vital, vibrating, palpitating works, which will always be read with a great deal of pleasure. In his short stories, the majority of the characters he introduces are drawn from real life. Often he threw a veil over them so they would not be recognized, but sometimes that veil was very thin indeed and his observations transparent. . . .

I was unable to attend his wedding in 1888, to which he had invited me. Soon after that, however, I went to congratulate him. His wife, Clara, was both beautiful and young; she seemed to be a nice, sincere, sensitive girl—amenable and pleasant, prepared to cater to his caprices and happy to have found her "master"— a master who was superior to her in education, intelligence, and vigor. This was, in fact, an ideal marriage for Zohrap, and he had a deep love for his wife, mixed with a kind of fatherly affection.

Before his first child had been christened, the second and third children were also born. He decided to christen the three of them on the same day. I had the privilege of being the godfather of his

---

6. Hovhannes Abelian (1865–1936) or his brother Aleksandr (1858–1940), actors.

7. Siranush Gantarchian, actress (1862–1932).

daughter, Dolores. Levon Bey Papazian and my brother, Hakob Asatur, were the godfathers of his two boys, Vahan and Aram. One summer day in 1893 we went to the Armenian church on Kinali,[8] because Zohrap had taken his family to Heybeli[9] for the summer. Nothing like it had ever been recorded in the annals of Kinali: a father having three children christened at the same time! The church was already filled with a crowd of curious onlookers. The priest of the island, an old, white-haired man who later died at the age of almost a hundred, looked pleased at having been chosen to preside over this christening, this unusual and fabulous spectacle.

One morning, in May 1915, I met Zohrap in front of Osman Bey Park in Pangalti.[10]

"Where are you going?" I asked.

"I'm taking my usual walk before lunch."

"Would you like me to walk with you?"

"Why not?"

The sad expression on his face both surprised and disturbed me. My friend did not have his usual vigor, proud manners, and commanding voice. To avoid the subject, I reminded him of a few of his short stories, and told him that I had reread *Khghmchantki dzayner* (Voices of conscience), *Lur dzaver* (Silent pains), and *Kyanke inchpes vor é* (The way life is), and that they had given me a lot of pleasure.

"When will you publish the stories that weren't included in those volumes?"

"I don't know," he said. "First I'd like to bring out a special volume of the stories that appeared under the title "*Ejer ughevori me oragren*" (Pages from a travel journal) in *Azatamart*. They contain my whole philosophy of life."

Then we reminisced about the publication of *Masis* in May 1892, when we used to go to the Fogel tavern in Ghalatia (Galata) for lunch and discuss the subjects we wanted to include in *Masis*—sometimes we argued and tried to convince each other, often without success, but always without getting angry at each other.

---

8. One of the four islands in the Sea of Marmara, near Istanbul.

9. Another island in the Sea of Marmara, very close to Kinali, which is mostly inhabited by Armenians.

10. Residential neighborhood in Istanbul, inhabited mainly by Armenians at that time.

And so we examined the past and talked about what we remembered as we walked along Nishantash Road to Pangalti, until we were in front of the military school, by the tram line. I would continue in the direction of Osman Bey, and he would go the other way, down to Ayaz Pasha, where he lived.

It was already lunch time. We were still talking and did not want to part.

But Zohrap stopped.

"I still have a long way to go," he said. "I'll walk home. These walks are a lifesaver for me. They relieve my blood pressure. The doctor is afraid that I may suffer from angina. I often have pains around my heart; they press on my chest and make it hard for me to breathe."

He shook my hand and took his leave. I watched him as long as my eyes could follow him. He was walking nervously and quickly.

That was the last time I ever saw him.[11]

TO ZAPEL KHANCHIAN-TONELIAN FROM HRAND ASATUR[12]

Péra.[13] 7 April 1895

Zapel, why do hearts that love sometimes sadden suddenly for no reason? Why does a deep melancholy envelop me today, and the necessity of staying away from you weigh on me like a horrible yoke? The sky is blue and drenched in joyous sunlight; darkness enfolds me, a thick sorrowful darkness that engulfs all my feelings and all my thoughts. Black clouds obscure the brightness, but through a gap glimmers your undesigning love, like the North Star, forever constant. I don't know the reason for my soul's distress: I'm so tense, my nerves are so tightly wound, that I feel like crying all the time and sitting beside you, my hands in yours, pouring my tears

11. Grigor Zohrap was among the intellectuals who were taken away and killed by the Turkish government at the beginning of the Armenian genocide of 1915.

12. Grigor Hakobian, ed., *Zapel yev Hrand Asatur: sirayin namakner* (Zapel and Hrand Asatur: love letters) (Yerevan, 2001), 85–87. Translated by the editors of the present anthology.

13. A neighborhood in Istanbul.

into your bosom. In the cold gloom of my room, I feel that patience is abandoning me; I feel an irresistible yearning to be alone with you and pour my heart into yours.

Please, my Zapel, don't imagine that physical passion has upset my nerves. I swear that isn't the case. This is a purely spiritual feeling, in which passion plays no role. It is my yearning for you, my longing for your closeness. Ah, the longing! The longing is with me every hour, every minute . . . in my heart . . . this is what I suffer: an infinite suffering, like the tortures of the martyrs— exquisite and voluntary. This longing, saturated with single-minded enthusiasm, always raises my mind from the cares and anxieties of this world to you. I am always with you in my heart, my Zapel: in your room, in front of the table where we have spent so many unacknowledged hours abandoned to love's tender feelings. And I think about your daily chores, lessons, and domestic concerns, which you cope with so cheerfully despite your frail body, which can't endure too much. I am a quiet witness, with a bleeding heart, to your daily martyrdom. I suffer every minute of your pain and your tortured existence.

We are alone only a few minutes a week, my Zapel, and this diminishes me, kills me. I saw you on Tuesday and again last night. I was really happy to feel near you, listen to your bewitching voice, take you in with my eyes. The fear caused by the continuous deceit to prevent betrayal before strangers is ghastly. It's torture to raise a barrier to our feelings when they cry out to rush forth, to emerge, to proclaim the external objects of our affections for hours on end— when we have so much to tell each other about our lives and our hearts—and to avoid looking at each other when we so need to comfort each other with our loving gazes.

You cannot imagine, Zapel, how particularly difficult the deception I suffered last night was. I had such a deep desire to be near you and needed so much to forget myself in your lap—I felt for the first time as if I were a tedious annoyance, the trifle of a nightmare, to you. This is a fault that I confess to you, since I have decided to tell you everything I feel, sincerely, and not to conceal anything from you. And my nerves were so unstrung and I was so beside myself that when we were alone for a short while, I couldn't press you to my chest and quench my longing for you even once.

But when we parted, my Zapel, I took one consolation with me—your sweet letter, which in no time made me acquainted with your inner thoughts, with the stress in your caring voice, your love's desires and dreams and the blessing of your soul, the echoes of which still expand within my entire being.

Signed Hrand Asatur

Sibil (Zapel Asatur)

(1863–1934)

Zapel Asatur (née Khanchian) was born in Scutari (Üsküdar), a suburb of Constantinople. After completing parochial school she graduated in 1879 from the Armenian lyceum (*chemaran*) and supplemented her education, both in Armenian and French, with private tutoring. She dedicated her life to social activism and teaching literature. While still a young woman she was one of the founding members of the *Azganver hayuhyats enkerutiun* (Women's benevolent society, 1879–95, 1908–15), which undertook the task of opening schools for girls in the Armenian provinces. Her first teaching assignments were in the provinces, where she stayed for eight years before returning to her birthplace in 1889.

Although she began to write earlier, her first but least successful work, *Aghjkan me sirte* (The heart of a girl), a novel, appeared in serial form in the journal *Arevelk* (Orient) in 1891. Other short stories and articles followed. In 1892, as a contributor to *Masis,* she adopted the pen name Sibil (also Sibyle), by which she was known for the rest of her life. In 1901 she married Hrant Asatur (1861–1928), a writer and journalist of great merit, who, along with Grigor Zohrap (1862–1915), was coeditor of *Masis.* Their collaboration, particularly in the preparation of textbooks, contributed greatly to the development and refinement of modern Armenian.

In 1902 Sibil published her first collection of poems, *Tsolker* (Glimmers). This was followed, in 1905, by a collection of stories entitled *Knoch hoginer* (Souls of women), in which she depicts women in different family and social circumstances, delves into their souls, and lays bare the feminine heart, giving expression to its dreams, joys, and disappointments. She was a feminist, supporting Srbuhi Dussap's (1840–1901) strong stand for women's rights. In 1940 her students brought out her second volume of poetry, *Kertvatzner* (Poems). She also wrote a play, *Harse* (The bride), which was published posthumously.

Sibil lived at a time when three literary schools, romanticism, realism, and aestheticism, followed each other in quick succession in Armenian letters, and she was influenced by all without relying on any one of them. This is evident in her short stories, where the romantic mood of her early days appears to conflict with the realities that her heroes live. As for her poems, they are meticulously crafted and highly polished in their use of language, each word carefully selected to fit the artistic design. Indeed, according to some critics, the extreme care she exercised in composing poetry sometimes ices over the warmth and emotion the poem is supposed to convey.

She dedicated the greater part of her life to teaching Armenian language and literature. Her major contribution in this field was a series of textbooks, some prepared in collaboration with her husband: *Gortznakan kerakanutiun ardi ashkharhabari* (Practical grammar of modern Armenian), in three volumes (1877, 1899, 1902), and the highly acclaimed series *Tangaran Hayeren lezvi* (Treasure-house of the Armenian language), which had many subsequent editions. In 1902 she also published *Gortznakan dasentatsk franserene hay targmanutyan* (A practical course in French-Armenian translation, 1902).

Sibil, Srbuhi Dussap, and Zapel Yessayan (1878–1943) were the three most famous women writers and women's rights activists of the Revival Period.

FROM THE BRIDE[1]

On the stage of current "feminist" and "liberation" causes, in which claims are often voiced aggressively for effect and immediate action, The Bride *may appear bland and perhaps even old-fashioned.*

---

1. Zapel Asatur (Sibil), *The Bride* (New York, 1987), 60–63, 54–59. Translation and introduction by Nishan Parlakian and afterword by Anne Paolucci.

But for those who grasp the value of historical evolution in such matters, the play is not only an interesting point of departure, a beginning of awareness of women as individuals who are sharply sensitive to the need to mold relationships and values in their own terms but, for its time, a bold statement too.

. . . Arusyak, the young bride in this play, has come with an impressive wedding gift (her father is very wealthy). But this fact doesn't ingratiate her with her sister-in-law (Hanumik) and mother-in-law. On the contrary, they seem bent on finding fault with her, humiliating her, proving her flighty and immodest. Her dowry provokes the unmarried sister-in-law's envy and hatred since Hanumik has not yet been successful in attracting a suitor. Ideally, Arshak should have married his sister off before taking a wife himself. In this and other ways, Zabel Asatur— the woman playwright and journalist, author of The Bride—*puts the excesses of her society to a subtle test.*

. . . Asatur deftly portrays the young Arusyak trying to find her bearings in her husband's house. Trapped by the jealousy of her sister-in-law, the formal demands of her mother-in-law, the rigid way of life they insist upon, the young bride learns to be cheerful in the face of veiled accusations and insults and never complains to her husband. She is sustained by his complete devotion to her; and we are reminded in many ways that theirs is a marriage of love (something contrary to all propriety). The fact that her substantial dowry has enabled the family to move from the country to the city and assume all the elegant trappings of their well-off neighbors doesn't mitigate the circumstances: Arusyak is the intruder who is making waves, who seems to outshine everyone, including and especially the unmarried sister-in-law, Hanumik. . . . Arusyak will never talk back to her husband or speak against his family; Hanumik will never say openly what it is that gnaws at her or confess to her personal greed and envy. The crises bring out the best and worst in the two women. To preserve themselves within the social bonds they cannot escape, they must find their true stride and use all their energies in a way that does not jolt reality. Of course, in Hanumik's case reality is shattered with the knowledge of her thefts—the money she has diverted from her brother's account into a secret one of her own, and the silver pieces she has stowed away to hide and keep for herself before the house and all its belongings are sold to pay Arshak's debts.

Anne Paolucci, President, Council on National Literatures

SCENE 11

(*Arshak, Arusyak*)

ARSHAK: (*Speaking to himself.*) The commandment is clear. Honor thy mother. Blessed is the son who does so. "Open your eyes," she said. If I hadn't, how would I have found out that there's a thief in my home and that thief—I'm sorry to say—is my own sister. All very sad, very sad, but let her take what she wants and leave. She can have the silver, the gold, all the valuables I own. I don't care. But I don't know how I will bring myself to look her in the eye let alone talk to her. Oh, she's used to this. She's absolutely without shame. She'll probably accuse someone else. . . . I've got to put an end to this disgraceful episode. I've got to tell her I know everything. Yes, I'll take these things and hide them. She'll try to find them. Let's see what happens. . . . (*He picks up the silver and carries it out of the room.*)

SCENE 12

(*Hanumik, Arusyak*)

HANUMIK: (*She tiptoes in, looks around for the silver without success, grows confused, then frustrated and angry as she approaches Arusyak with a menacing look, muttering all the while to herself.*) You, you . . . you . . . thief. I've caught you! I've caught you red-handed! I've got you all right!

ARUSYAK: (*She doesn't see her.*) There, I've managed to finish this letter before Arshak returns. I was afraid he'd catch me at it. (*She takes out an envelope and addresses it, speaking out loud as she writes the words.*) Monsieur Zareh Tatosian, Smyrna. (*She places the letter in it and seals the envelope.*)

HANUMIK: (*Comes up close.*) I caught you!!!

ARUSYAK: (*Startled, standing.*) You frightened me, Hanumik. (*She takes the envelope from the table and puts it in her pocket.*)

HANUMIK: What are you afraid of? I don't eat up people! "Courage in a thief doesn't last long." Isn't that true?

ARUSYAK: (*Annoyed.*) I don't know what you're talking about—

HANUMIK: No, you don't know anything! Why should you know anything? You thought I was asleep! You never dreamed I'd be right here in this room! . . . If guilt were a sable coat, no one would want to wear it! All right! I'll spell it out for you: Where did you put the silver? What happened to the silver?

ARUSYAK: (*Calm now, cold.*) How would *I* know—?

HANUMIK: (*Shouts.*) You're going to return that silver right now, *now!* If you don't, I'll shout and scream and wake up everybody. I'll wake all the servants. I'll disgrace you in front of everyone!

ARUSYAK: You're raving, Hanumik! What have I got to do with your silver? Look for it where *you* put it.

HANUMIK: I put the pieces right there, here on the floor, next to the set. I was going . . . to polish them, but Mother called and I left them and ran upstairs. And now I come back to find them stolen.

ARUSYAK: Who would steal them? You've probably forgotten where you put them.

HANUMIK: I'm not like you, I don't forget where I put things! You're not going to fool me with that kind of talk! Bring out the silver or I'll bring out something else! (*Arshak appears on the threshold.*)

SCENE 13

(*Arusyak, Hanumik, Arshak.*)

ARUSYAK: (*Doesn't see Arshak.*) You're very confused tonight, dear sister. I don't want to hurt your feelings, but I certainly can't help you. I haven't laid eyes on the silver!

HANUMIK: (*Runs at her, yelling.*) Where is it? Where is the silver?

ARSHAK: (*He comes forward slowly, calmly, the silver in his hands.*) Here it is. And I've been here too, for an hour. I saw a thief come in, open the closet, take out the silver, start to carry it off, and then, hearing footsteps, drop everything to the floor and run off. I picked up the silver and hid it. (*Mrs. Tiruhi enters after a few seconds of silence.*)

SCENE 14

(*Mrs. Dirouhi, Arusyak, Arshak, Hanumik.*)

MRS. TIRUHI: What is all this! A thief! In my house? What else can possibly happen to us! Arusyak, you must have left the window in this room open again.

ARUSYAK: Did you see who it was, Arshak? Couldn't you catch the thief?

ARSHAK: I saw who it was with my own eyes, Arusyak, but I was so ashamed I could not stop it.

HANUMIK: You were imagining things. There's no thief here. I took the silver from the closet to clean and polish. I couldn't sleep so

I came down to take it up to my room. But if you want to catch someone at something, ask your wife what is in the envelope she hid in her pocket when she saw me.

ARUSYAK: I don't know what the thief and the robbery have to do with the envelope. You seem very confused tonight, Hanumik.

HANUMIK: Why not let us see the envelope so we can tell whether I'm confused or not! What's there to hide?

MRS. TIRUHI: I won't have secrets in my house! Secrets are evil.

ARUSYAK: And what if I've hidden something good?

MRS. TIRUHI: Good or bad, I must know what you're hiding.

ARSHAK: You have no right, Mother. My wife's secret is her own.

MRS. TIRUHI: Arshak, my son. What did I tell you a little while ago? Open your eyes. Look around you. Obviously I have some reason for suspicion or I wouldn't speak this way. How do I know what's going on in this house? You leave in the morning and are away all day. Your wife goes to her room and writes. What is she writing, writing all the time?

ARSHAK: Mother, she's writing a novel.

HANUMIK: So tell me, is that the novel in her pocket?

ARUSYAK: No, what's in my pocket is not a novel. It's a letter. But please don't ask me to show it to you.

HANUMIK: I knew all along you wouldn't dare show it!

ARSHAK: Please, Arusyak, let them have it and put an end to suspicion.

ARUSYAK: So, they really *do* suspect me of something!

HANUMIK: If you want to put it that way, yes! We have our suspicions about you!

ARUSYAK: Well then, take it. (*She pulls out the letter and throws it on the table.*)

HANUMIK: (*She seizes it, reads the name and address out loud.*) Monsieur Zareh Tatosian, Smyrna. (*Triumphant.*) Now! Do you understand, brother?

MRS. TIRUHI: (*Strikes her head with both hands.*) Oh, my poor poor boy—!

HANUMIK: A disgrace, that's what it is! (*She hides her face in her hands, while Arusyak smiles, her arms crossed at her breast.*)

ARSHAK: (*Extracts the letter from the envelope and reads out loud.*) "My dear cousin. I beg you, if you can, without any delay, to pass the enclosed letter to my mother and to please keep it from my father. I would consider this a great favor for which I shall be most grateful." (*To his mother and sister.*) Well, what have you got to say?

ARUSYAK: Don't bother reading the letter to my mother. Here, Arshak, let me have it—

HANUMIK: No! The first letter is obviously a cover. It has no purpose. The secret is the other letter. Go on, read it if you dare.

ARSHAK: (*Reads.*) "Dear Mother, you always said I should turn to you when I needed help. I am following your wish in writing to you now. But you need not worry. I have no problems and you mustn't be uneasy. Actually, I have a very good life here. You know how much I love my Arshak and he loves me. I couldn't ask for more in this world. The trouble has to do with material concerns. I need some money to help out someone, but I don't want either my husband or father to know about it. I'm sure you will approve of what I'm doing once you learn about it. I need a few hundred pieces of gold. Please, I beg you, send me what you can quickly and you'll make your only daughter very happy." (*He throws the letter on the table, extends his arms and embraces his wife while Mrs. Tiruhi and Hanumik hang their heads down in shame.*)

CURTAIN

A LETTER FROM SIBIL (ZAPEL ASATUR) TO HRAND ASATUR[2]

5 April 1895, Wednesday night
My Dear Hrand,

I've never been so happy as I was the last time we met; how I enjoyed how charming you are with others: our silent stares across the distance that separated us made me feel as if your heart beat within mine, and I was seduced as it were by the resonance of your voice, which came to me with all the sweetness of your lips and

---

2. Grigor Hakibian, ed., *Zapel yev Hrant Asatur: sirayin namakner* (Zapel and Hrand Asatur: love letters) (Yerevan, 2001), 80–82. Translated by the editors of the present anthology.

soul. And my secret concerning you reached a mysterious height in my mind. There it was: the sheer grandeur of the intense and irrational worship of an ideal being, on whom all the admiration of my eyes and all the desires of my soul were focused. Because of my undying love for you, I was proud: pleased that others too could see your matchless talents; I feel confident, however, that no one in the world will ever be able to appreciate them as much as I do. My darling Hrand, the only quality I possess in comparison to you, who have so many, is my ability to understand you much better than anyone else, and your expression of the tender feelings nurtured in your sweet heart for your family and your mother that day transported me much more than all your declarations of love for me.

You don't know, Hrand, how attractive you are when you express such feelings, and perhaps that's why I love you. I am so used to seeing heartless, selfish, ill-mannered people around me that I wonder if you're not a fantasy: one of those fantasies that one raises in the heart and can never give up until the grave. I admire you, I worry about you, and my love increases from day to day, from hour to hour, like a flame fanned by the wind: forever growing, widening, spreading. But it would smother, it would waste away if you were less gentle and less kind. If I love your face, Hrand, it's because it's an angel's face; if I love your eyes, it's because I can see through their unsoiled clarity fearlessly, without doubt. And I kiss your lips because I know that they pronounce no lies. My love is a reasonable love, because by loving you I love all superior things in the world—they infuse and intoxicate me more and more, and take over my mind in such a way that I am no longer responsible for my own thoughts; I am metamorphosed completely—my faith and my consciousness—which took years and years to develop— shatter within me, and all is overwhelmed but one thing: stamped on my soul is the wish, the desire to make you happy. And I want to do great things for you; I want my weakness to be as great as my love; would you like me to tell you more? I wish that you didn't love me, so that my suffering could make me worthy of you. Then come the foolish desires and dreams. My soul's imagination, for which nothing is ever enough, expands.

There are moments when it seems to me that the relationships of human love are very imperfect: you have to become the person you love, be capable of placing your soul inside his soul and never detaching your gaze from his gaze, so that nothing from outside might tarnish the sanctity of perfect devotion between the two of you. And then I think that if that were possible life would seem too short to express so much love. Oh, what more, what else! I am filled with so many wishes—perplexed, dim—which contain the dream of the infinite: what they have in common is my dream of devoting myself to never-ending worship of you.

This is what I live for, and I look back with wonder on the time of my life when your image was not present. How was I able to endure that void in my life? It is clear that in the few short years I've known you, I've lived a hundred times more than in all the rest of my life, because of the love in my heart, where tears are worth more than frivolous happiness.

I am indebted to you, my Hrand, not for your love (because I don't really expect that), but for your existence, just as the least creature hidden in the dewy grass is indebted to the sun, not because the latter loves it, but because it warms and illuminates it. My heart is filled with warmth and feels the need to bless you, and that, perhaps, is the best indication of its ability to fly and glorify.

Signed Zapel

Levon Manuelian (Manveliants)

(1864–1919)

Born in Nerkin Agulis in Nakhijevan, Manuelian was a poet, playwright, novelist, and educator. After completing his elementary education in that village, where Raffi (1837–88) was one of his teachers, he studied at the gymnasium in Tiflis and then at the University of Moscow (1886–90). After graduating he taught at the Gevorgian Seminary in Etchmiadzin and at the Nersesian school in Tiflis. Between 1897 and 1903 he worked as a librarian at the Armenian Philanthropical Association in Baku, where he developed enough courage and knowledge to venture on the first of three chapters of his *Rusahay grakanutyan patmutiun* (History of Russian literature), which was completed later (1909–12), after he had finished *Banasteghtzutiunner yev poemaner* (Poems and narrative verses, 1899–1909). His poems are often monotonous and almost always mournful and sad. His last teaching position was at the School of Commerce in Alexandropol (now Giumri), where he taught until his death in 1919.

Manuelian began his career as a lyrical poet but also developed as a prose writer and a playwright. His writings are filled with the anguish of his nation and a yearning for freedom. He was the first to introduce the genre of dramatic poetry to Armenian literature, in works such as *Galilé yev Milton* (Galilee and Milton), *Potorik* (Storm), *Dep i ver* (Upward, 1902), and *Sasuntsi Davit yev Msra Melik* (David of Sasun and

Msra Melik), which was published in 1940. The subject of *Dep i ver* is Khachatur Abovian's climb to the summit of Masis (Mount Ararat).

His plays—*Tigranuhi* (1892), *Doktor Yervand Boshayan* (1900), *Nkarich Tashchian* (Tashchian the painter, 1903), *Veratznvatze* (The reborn, 1906), and *Magda* (1913)—represent a major contribution to the development of psychologically realistic Armenian drama. The subjects of some of his plays are taken from the historical past, while others reflect contemporary life.

In 1897, five years after he published his mythical-historical tragedy *Tigranuhi*, he brought out his voluminous novel *Khortakvatz kyank* (Shattered life), which depicts the tragic existence of a talented individual who devotes his life to the arts. In fact the novel reflects the collision of the individual and capitalism, and the subsequent defeat of the individual.

By virtue of his expression of smoldering national anguish and his insistence on the importance of the concept of freedom, as well as for his important contribution to the genre of dramatic poetry, Manuelian deserves to be reckoned an interesting figure in the growth of Armenian literature.

FROM SHATTERED LIFE[1]

Part One: Hopes and Dreams

The hall of the theater was full of spectators. It is impossible to describe the tumultuous crowd. The Armenian intelligentsia of Tiflis occupied the orchestra seats: mostly intellectuals, men of letters, teachers, and so on. The notable figures of the community, the wealthy ones, were seated comfortably with their families in the boxes. The lights of the vast chandeliers reflected off earrings, bracelets, gold chains—all set with precious stones—and opera glasses. Sparkle filled the theater, flooding the hall like waterfalls. There were no empty seats, even in the "gods": the section where young theater addicts usually sat.

Everyone had come to see the greatest of Armenian actors; this evening he would perform a fabled play by the genius of the north. The crowd was quiet, waiting impatiently for the curtain to rise.

---

1. Levon Manuelian, *Khortakvatz kyank* (Shattered life) (Tiflis, 1897), 3–15. Translated by the editors of the present anthology.

Suddenly the door opened and in walked a twenty-one-year-old youth: tall and gallant, with a bold but worried appearance. His black curls formed cascades of swirls on his head and prominent forehead. From afar he looked handsome, as the furrows on his young face were not noticeable. He wore a dark blue suit, and the long ends of a sky-blue tie tumbled on his chest.

He raised his eyes to one of the boxes and spotted a young woman. He immediately lowered his head when he realized that the woman had turned her opera glasses on him. That means she's here too, the young man concluded, and walked toward the eighth row.

Artashes Voskerchian was his name. For reasons of economy he usually bought tickets in the gods. When the play or the actor was particularly interesting, however, he made an exception. For tonight's performance he had parted with his last kopeck for a seat in the orchestra. He would have done this even if it meant that he would have to go without eating the following day.

He took his seat and removed from his breast pocket a copy of the play: *Hamlet*. He opened it to the second scene of the first act. He read a little, then put the still open book on his knees. He raised his head and gazed at the chandelier, and in the flood of sparkling light who knows what he was thinking.

Twelve minutes had already gone by, and the curtain was still closed. As a result of this delay, spectators in the gods, always the most uncontrollable section of the theater, began impatiently shouting:

"Show time! Show time!"

At last the curtain went up. At midnight, on the moonlit terrace before Elsinore Castle, a couple of armed guards, Bernardo and Francisco, appeared. Bernardo paced continuously, as if walking on thorns. Francisco did not move; his posture, his voice, his manner of speaking—none of them was adapted to the mysterious silence of the night. The actors were young, inexperienced novices.

In the early eighties, to be sure, we had an excellent theater troupe, quite well funded and boasting several notable talents—a troupe whose first three seasons constituted a distinct era in the history of our theater. That period is over. The leading lights scattered and began to perform on their own rather than as a company. But the past successes of the troupe and their deserved reputation remained alive in the hearts of art-loving young people. This new generation of theater people, unprepared and inexperienced, tried to replace the old troupe. A few members of the old theater troupe tried to direct and otherwise help out the new generation from time to time. This was, however, an occasional occurrence and did not really serve to consolidate the new company. They had no stars and no directors, and the neophytes had to rely on individual taste, individual reflection. The public, though, having tasted the esthetics of true entertainment, demanded that the troupe improve, and the new company could not satisfy these demands.

When, in the following scene in the royal castle, the smiling king and queen appeared with the councilors in their colorful costumes, the court, and finally Hamlet—in mourning, dressed in black from head to toe, his curly hair falling on his shoulders, his head bowed, his melancholy eyes staring at the floor, and his hands crossed on his chest, expressing agony—the theater resounded with applause. This was repeated when the ghost of his murdered father appeared at the end of the act: as if his blood had frozen in his heart, his left hand resting on his chest, which rose and fell with his laborious breathing and quavering voice of deep agony.

As for Voskerchian. . . . A shudder beginning at the roots of his hair traveled along his spine and through his entire body; he felt a sting in his nostrils; his eyes watered and tears glided over the wrinkles of his face, one after the other. During the intermission the audience filled the lobby. Brimming with fresh impressions of the play, everyone was having a lively conversation. From all corners the name of the great actor echoed.

Artashes Voskerchian was, as usual, the last out of his row. He joined an enthusiastic group walking through the orchestra in the direction of the stage. The place was still thundering with continuous applause.

"Adamian! Adamian! Bravo! Bravo!"

When he entered the lobby he looked for someone to talk to. He spotted a group of acquaintances at the far end, near the wall. Pushing his way in their direction and making repeated excuses, he finally managed to free himself from the crowd.

"Good evening! I was looking for you," he said, wiping the sweat off his forehead with a handkerchief he held in his left hand as he shook his friends' hands with the other.

"Well, what do you think so far?" he asked, addressing Garegin Zarikian.

"It's fabulous, of course, replied his friend. "Why, is this the first time you've seen Adamian perform?"

"Yes, it's my first time. I am so delighted, so very delighted. . . ."

"Yes, I can see that: it's obvious," added Zarikian, looking at him pleasantly.

At that moment Ashkhen, Garegin Zarikian's sister, who had been strolling arm-in-arm with another young woman, back and forth in the lobby, walked up to them with her friend. She greeted Voskerchian with a couple of words and said:

"I'd like to introduce my friend, Miss Mariam Vartumian. This is my brother."

"I'm pleased to meet you, Garegin Zarikian."

Mariam's tender eyes met Zarikian's gentle ones for the first time; at once a vague but warm feeling filled the hearts of these two young people. Their gazes met and lingered for a long moment, full of tenderness and intimacy—and then they found themselves unable to look at each other deliberately, even as the young woman continued talking with Garegin. Smiling radiantly, she focused her eyes on his sister instead. And when Zarikian spoke he looked down, or anywhere but at her face.

Ashkhen also introduced her friend Mariam to Artashes Voskerchian, who had wanted to be introduced to her for a long time.

"We're neighbors," said Artashes, holding the young woman's delicate white hand in his own lean, bony one.

"Are you neighbors? I didn't know that," said Ashkhen, staring first at Voskerchian and then at her friend.

"Yes, of course. Mr. Voskerchian sometimes plays the violin, and I listen from our window."

"Artashes plays?" Ashkhen asked, surprised that her brother had never mentioned it to her.

When Mariam mentioned that she had listened to Voskerchian play, the latter began to wonder what she really meant—was she mocking him or flattering him? He made the following modest remark:

"Maybe Ashkhen thinks I'm a real musician. I don't, however, deserve the name. I don't play well. It's kind of her to think so. It's true that I have a violin I bought for five rubles. I've struggled with the instrument for months, but I've come to the conclusion that I lack musical talent. I'm surprised our young friend had the patience to listen to me rather than fleeing from the sound."

"All right, all right, enough of your modesty!" responded Ashkhen jokingly. "Tomorrow night, bring your violin to our house. I'll be your critic or judge or whatever you call it."

The music in the lobby stopped and the bell summoned the audience back to their seats. Already the lobby was almost empty. Voskerchian resumed his seat. Ashkhen and her brother were in their seats too; they were looking up at the box where Miss Vartumian would soon enter.

Ashkhen was talking to her brother, keeping her eyes on that particular box, which was still empty. Finally a tall woman entered first, Miss Vartumian's aunt, wearing a diamond tiara that glittered in the rays of the chandeliers. Then the young woman came in, followed by a neatly dressed young boy.

While the curtain was rising, Mariam took advantage of the opportunity to focus her opera glasses on Garegin Zarikian, who automatically raised his head and saw her.

There were two people on the stage: Hamlet and Polonius. The former pretended to be crazy in order to exasperate the old man. The latter pretended to be even crazier, and let the young prince mock him—just as a grandfather allows his naughty grandchild to pull his white beard. The dialogue was subdued: to grasp the fine details of the scene the audience had to be extremely attentive, and absolute silence was needed. In a theater, though, there are always unexpected distractions, with the result that the audience focuses its attention on the stage only during scenes of great emotion or boisterous scenes in which the actors brandish their swords. When, on the other hand, it is necessary to follow the actors' delivery in order to comprehend what is being said, some people begin to yawn, turn their heads to the right and left, talk with their neighbors, or blow their noses.

Artashes Voskerchian was upset more at the impolite behavior of his friends and acquaintances than he was at missing the subtleties of Adamian's performance.

The third act, however, made him forget everything. He was now aware only of the powerful effect of the artist's talent. The varying modulations of the actor's voice, the sweetness with which he delivered the mother tongue, his delicate psychological nuances, his intelligent gestures and thoughtful movements. When he recited the famous soliloquy "To be or not to be," it was as if his liberated soul ascended to the heavens and then descended back to earth—to the scene of endless torments. And when he confronted Ophelia, it was as if he dug out his love from the bottom of his heart with a red-hot iron, then dropped it at her feet and, lifting it up again, embraced it. At such moments the audience entered the illusion completely. It was as if a magic wand had been waved, and hundreds of hearts beat in unison, all of them, without exception, young and old, under the mighty spell of a great actor.

The curtain fell. The auditorium was agitated. Applause, bravos, the stamping of feet on the floor. . . . The curtain rose again, then fell, and rose again. The actor was tired, but they called him back on stage. From the boxes, from the orchestra, from everywhere flowers poured on the actor's head, at his feet, all around him. People in the front row of the orchestra showed their approval with bravos and applause, and the actor responded with his hands pressed against his chest to express his thanks.

In the lobby, the audience was in a very buoyant mood. Everyone was expressing excitement:

"Oh, it was fabulous!"

"It was marvelous!"

"Absolutely unequaled!"

In another spot, a couple of Adamian's colleagues were talking. One of them was saying: "Do you remember the days when Adamian didn't know how to control himself on stage? It was our doing: we were the ones who made him what he is. But the so-and-so acts amazingly well now."

"Yes, he is excellent, beautiful!" agreed the other, his eyes burning with jealousy. And in his voice the cardiologist would easily have been able to discern the tremolo of repressed fury. "He is very good, but I don't think there's any reason for the public to go crazy. It's really weird. There should be a limit, even to expressions of appreciation."

Near the door that served the first rows of the orchestra, a group of young men and women was listening to a couple of gentlemen discuss Adamian's performance. One of them was Sevumian, the other Azatian; they worked for the same newspaper. The subject of their conversation was the dagger that Adamian had held during the famous soliloquy "To be or not to be." Sevumian was insisting that the dagger was completely superfluous, belonging more to the Hamlet tradition than to Shakespeare's *Hamlet.* The other was trying to defend Adamian, pointing out several justifications. Not far from them stood Ashkhen and Mariam, listening to the discussion.

Zarikian stepped out to smoke. When he returned, he noticed that Sevumian and Azatian were being introduced to Miss Vartumian. They started to chat about Adamian's performance. Garegin was surprised to hear Mariam's sound appraisal of the play. Until then, he had been charmed by the young woman's beauty. Now, it seemed, she was also well read and intelligent.

A few minutes after the first bell, Artashes Voskerchian hurried over to them. He was happy: he was smiling and his eyes were glittering.

"Where have you been? We couldn't find you," Garegin said to his friend. "I thought you were at the bar, having a beer. But I didn't see you there either."

"What are you talking about: bar? beer? I was with Adamian. With Adamian!"

"You were with Adamian? You mean you went backstage?" asked Ashkhen, interrupting Azatian, who was in the midst of a veritable tirade against the newspaper *Zhamanak* (Time).

"Yes," replied Voskerchian. "I went and introduced myself to him. I shook his hand, offered my congratulations a thousand times, and left . . . but I wouldn't advise anybody else to go there, because that Ophelia, who was like an angel on stage, was nothing but a made-up doll backstage." Voskerchian was chuckling at his own acerbic observations, enjoying himself. As soon as they heard the last bell ring, he stopped talking and immediately stepped into the stream of people heading in the direction of his seat. When the curtain rose he was already seated.

For the rest of the play, Voskerchian followed Adamian's performance with the greatest attention, and applauded and shouted loud bravos with all the others. Even as the crowd was thinning out while the audience left the auditorium, a group of gymnasium students and other adolescents gathered in front of the stage, urging Adamian with thunderous shouts and applause to take a tenth curtain call. Voskerchian was not going to be outdone; he was soaked in sweat and his throat was raspy and sore.

He also participated in the ovation that took place in the street when hot-blooded young theater lovers pushed the horses aside so that they themselves could pull the carriage of their beloved actor.

Hovhannes Hovhannisian

(1864–1929)

Born in Vagharshapat (now Etchmiadzin), Hovhannes Hovhannisian studied in Yerevan, at the Lazarian Institute in Moscow, and at Moscow University (1884–88). He spent a year traveling in Europe (Constantinople, Paris, Vienna, and London), and for many years taught Russian language and literature, general literature, and Greek at the Gevorgian Seminary in Etchmiadzin. During the Soviet period he held various administrative positions in the fields of education and culture. His first collection of poems appeared in 1887, followed by two other volumes, in 1908 and 1912, which established him as the initiator of a new trend in poetry. In the words of Kevork Bardakjian: "His wistful, impersonal yearning that captured the mood of the age was a marked change from the patriotic poetry of Rafayel Patkanian and that of his teacher Smbat Shahaziz. Nature, love, patriotism, exhortation for his nation not to be given to despondency, some historical figures, and the Armenian massacres of mid-1890s inspired Hovhannisian's gentle, lyrical verse."[1]

---

1. Kevork B. Bardakjian, *A Reference Guide to Modern Armenian Literature, 1500–1920* (Detroit, 2000), 179–80.

Among the subsequent masters of this mode were Hovhannes Tumanian (1869–1923) and Avetik Isahakian (1875–1957).

Hovhannisian translated a number of works by Homer, Goethe, Schiller, Heine, Hugo, Pushkin, Lermontov, and others. Various collections of his works have been published, but the main compilation, *Yerkeri zhoghovatzu* (Collected works) was published in four volumes in Yerevan, from 1964 to 1968.

Araxes Came Devouringly[2]

Araxes came devouringly,
Swept o'er her boulders scouringly—
Where shall I lay my aching head
Bowed down with grief o'erpoweringly?

Oh my Araxes, flow serene;
Tell me, hast thou my sweet love seen?
My heart's desire is unfulfilled;
Arax, hast thou more happy been?

Mount Ararat with clouds is veiled,
My love is lost, my hope has failed.
For pity's sake an answer give
To my sad heart with grief assailed.

I sob and weep the livelong night;
Till dawn I watch—I watch and write;
Arax, ere sunrise gild thy waves
To thee I bring my spirit's blight.

Upon the rocks the sunbeams dart,
Red flames devour my mourning heart;
Those eyes and brows have left with me
A sorrow which shall ne'er depart.

---

2. Hovhannes Hovannesian, "Araxes Came Devouringly," in *Armenian Legends and Poems,* ed. and trans. Zabelle C. Boyajian (London, 1916; reissued New York, 1958), 77.

A GENTLE SLEEP[3]

Ah, give me a gentle sleep
So I may drift far away from life
To a world where laughter,
Where love are always bright.

Let delicate roses be my pillow,
The soft new grass my bed,
And their fresh young fragrance
Let me always breathe with joy.

And before me, brilliantly,
Let the clear stream flash,
And, like Eden, spread
Freshness all around me.

And may dawn find gladness for me
In the tender sun of spring,
And at night let the gleaming moon
Move slowly across my brow.

And may the silken-eyed maiden
Lilt her song at my ear,
And, disheveled, dally at my neck
Tenderly, lovingly, caressingly.

And may eternal happiness
Embrace my soul—unquenched I go.
Ah, grant me a gentle sleep
That I may drift away, far away.

---

3. Hovhannesian, "A Gentle Sleep," in *Armenian Poetry Old and New*, ed. and trans. Aram Tolegian (Detroit, 1978), 149.

Aleksandr Tzaturian

(1865–1917)

The poet and translator Aleksandr (Alexander) Tzaturian was born in Zakartala (Azerbaijan), to a poor family. He was three years old when his father died. This is how he describes the conditions in which he spent his early childhood: "My mother and I lived in a dilapidated house in a poor and obscure corner of town. The stove was lit and we had a hot meal only once a week, on Sundays. The only happiness I had in my childhood was my mother's exceptional love for me. She worked very hard as a washer woman to keep us alive. Though she was illiterate, she had an instinctive desire to see me educated."[1] He attended local schools and in 1881 graduated from the public middle school. Before that, however, his mother, exhausted and spent, had died, leaving him alone and helpless. With the assistance of Arshak Agapian, one of his teachers, he went to Tiflis to attend the Nersisian Academy, but his application was refused. He then entered the Mikayelian vocational school, but had to withdraw because of his fragile health. In 1885 he tried to attend the Gevorgian Academy in Etchmiadzin, but that attempt also failed. All during this time he worked at diverse jobs—as a letter carrier, an errand boy,

---

1. Quoted in Minas Teololian, *Dar me grakanutiun: 1850–1920* (A century of literature), vol. 1 (Boston, 1977), 408.

and even a construction worker—while educating himself in literature and languages. In 1887 he became private tutor to the children of an Armenian merchant in Nizhni-Novgorod and moved to Moscow with the family. This provided him opportunities to make the acquaintance of intellectuals and university students, and to address the public. He contributed to the periodicals *Handes grakan yev patmakan* (Literary and historical review) and *Murch* (Hammer), using various pen names.

Tzaturian's writings are deeply influenced by the vicissitudes of his life. Love, patriotism, exile, the plight of the working class and the downtrodden, and the vices of society are the recurrent themes of his writings, which are expressed in powerful imagery and with deep sincerity. In some of his works, such as "The Stepchildren of Life," "The Beggar," and "The Song of the Poor before Death," he exposes the selfishness and corruption of "elite" society, whereas other works such as "Where Art Thou, O Nightingale of Armenia?" and "It Is Enough, O My Nation!" sing about his dream of the emancipation of his homeland. In the mood of the 1905 Russian revolution, he envisioned "the big battle between labor and gold" and sang about the heroic fight of the "brigades of labor" and "the lullaby of the woman laborer." His love poems, though woven delicately, reflect the underlying conflict between the restraints of traditional "ethics" and the dream of individual freedom and happiness. Some of his nature poems, such as the series *Ghrimi albomits* (From the Crimean album, 1896–98), are allegories of social life; another series, *Grchi hanakner* (Literary jokes, 1901), consists of humorous poems.

His poems were very popular and a number of them have been set to music; songs such as *"Ay vard"* and *"Mi lar, blbul,"* addressed to the rose and the nightingale, are still sung. In general, his poems reveal the psychology of a man who was unfulfilled, not in terms of his own ambitions, but in terms of his dreams for his nation, his homeland, and humanity in general. His poems were collected in two volumes, published in Moscow in 1891 and 1898 respectively.

Tzaturian has to his credit a number of translations from Armenian to Russian and vice versa. He helped Yuri Veselovsky select and translate excerpts for his *Armenian Literature* (1893), produced a translation of Gabriel Sundukian's play *Pepo,* translated the works of a number of Russian poets in two volumes (1906), and contributed to the compilation of Valery Briusov's anthology *Armenian Poetry* (1916).

His health began to deteriorate rapidly, and he headed south to Tiflis for treatment. He died in 1917. His works were printed in three volumes in Yerevan: *Entir banasteghtzutiunner* (Selected poems, 1937), *Yerker* (Works, 1948), and *Namakner* (Letters, 1961).

DON'T CRY, BULBUL[2]

Don't you cry, bulbul,[3] don't you droop
    Because the cold storm
Tore off and carried away from the bush
    The beautiful rose, the red rose.

Days will pass—it will return again,
    A new spring, a rose-bearing spring,
And having forgotten the old pain,
    You'll sing of love to the rose again.

But O, for the singer of life,
    Orphaned in early years,
Who commits to the hard earth
    His lovely, beloved rose:

No spring is in store for the singer,
    For he cannot love a new rose—
He must weep, he must mourn
    Until he sings no more.

THE ARMENIAN POET'S PRAYER[4]

O God, 'tis not for laurel wreaths I pray,
For pompous funeral or jubilee;
Nor yet for fame beyond my life's decay—
All these my country will accord to me.

One favor, Lord of Heaven, I implore—
One that my land to me will never give:
Grant me a crust of bread, or else such store
Of grace that I on air may learn to live!

---

2. Aleksantr Tzaturian, "Don't Cry, Bulbul," in *Armenian Poetry Old and New,* ed. and trans. Aram Tolegian (Detroit, 1979), 145.

3. Nightingale.

4. Aleksantr Tzaturian, "The Armenian Poet's Prayer," in *Armenian Legends and Poems,* ed. and trans. Zabelle C. Boyajian (London, 1916; reissued New York, 1958), 43.

Gegham Ter-Karapetian (Msho Gegham)

(1865–1918)

Gegham Ter-Karapetian, better known as Msho Gegham and by the pen names Asoghik and Tatrak, was, like Tlkatintsi (1860–1915) and Ruben Zardarian (1874–1915), a major writer of Armenian provincial literature. He was born in the village of Heybian, in the province of Mush. He was educated in the venerated monastery of St. Karapet (Glakavank), under the care of Mkrtich Khrimian Hayrik (1820–1907, Patriarch of Constantinople 1869–73) and Srvandzdiants (Garegin Srvandztian (1840–92, primate of Mush and abbot of St. Karapet). These two writers were major influences on him.

In 1883 he went to Etchmiadzin to resume his studies at the Gevorgian seminary. After two years, however, he returned to Mush without graduating and entered public life. He was appointed secretary of the Armenian diocese in 1888 and enthusiastically devoted himself to the education of the Armenians of Mush.

His marriage in 1892 to a woman named Kiulizar (Gülizar), from the village of Kars, was rather eventful. Musa Beg had abducted Kiulizar, and the entire population of the province of Taron revolted against him, filing a suit of protest to the government in Constantinople. Msho Gegham was among those who liberated her. Musa Beg was sentenced to exile, but members of his family tried to persecute Msho Gegham, who fled to Diyarbekir and stayed there until 1896, working as the secretary of the local Armenian diocese.[1]

When he eventually returned to Mush, Msho Gegham resumed his post at the Armenian diocese. In 1908, directly after the proclamation of the Ottoman Constitution, he was elected deputy to the Ottoman National Assembly, representing the region of Taron. His frequent visits to the capital were a turning point in his writing career, and he became known in the literary circles of the capital. Between 1895 and 1914 he contributed to several Armenian dailies and periodicals of Constantinople, including *Masis, Hayrenik* (Fatherland), *Biuzandion* (Byzantium), *Arevelk* (Orient), *Manzumé* (Verse), *Biurakn* (Thousand-source), *Zhamanak* (Time), and *Surhandak* (Courier). As a result of their publication in diverse journals and newspapers, his writing has not been collected into one volume, except for a few saved from oblivion by being published in Paris as *Daroni ashkharh* (The world of Taron) by the Friends of Martyred Writers, in 1931. It is to be hoped that one day soon his complete works will be collected, in recognition of his unique talent as an Armenian provincial writer.

Msho Gegham wrote several short stories, chronicles, and novels. *Tiratsun yev zhamkoche* (The altar boy and the sexton) is his principal novel.[2] He also wrote reflections on the death of his daughter, Haykanush, and several short stories, including *"Sargis aghbaar"* (Brother Sargis), *"Hoviv Karo"* (Karo the shepherd), and others. The theme of his prose is his native province, the hardships of the Armenian peasants, their traditions, manners, and behavior, their wanderings and exile, and contemporary social conflicts; the latter theme is well developed in *Hoghayin hartse hayabnak nahangneru mej* (The land question in provinces with Armenian populations, 1911), in which he writes about the confiscation of Armenian-owned land during the reign of Sultan Abdul-Hamid II (reigned 1876–1918), and exposes the policy of persecuting Armenians.

Other important works from a national point of view are *Mshu gavarakan lezvi barer* (Words from the Mush dialect), *Msho muratatur surp Karapet vanke* (The wish-fulfilling monastery of St. Karapet in Mush), and *Aprilyan yegherne* (The April genocide), along with collections of popular songs, fables, and traditions. Although some of these

---

1. See H. Mesrop Chanashian, *Hay grakanutyan nor shrjani hamarot patmutiun, 701–1920* (Concise history of modern Armenian literature, 1701–1920) (Venice, 1973), 322–24. See also Armenuhi Ter-Karapetian, *Kiulizar, nshkharner Msho Geghamen* (Kiulizar: pieces by Msho Gegham) (Paris, 1946).

2. Published in *Arevelk*, 3700–52 (1896).

remain in manuscript form, they are a veritable treasure trove for provincial dialect studies and history.

Gegham is an authentic provincial voice, writing in his own unique style and in the local provincial dialect. He portrays village life with all its constricted daily experiences, emotions, ambitions, and insignificant antagonisms. He describes the virtues and imbalances of the village—on one hand, the hard rustic life, the industriousness, the plow and the hoe, the Bible and religious zeal, youthful love, the thirst for learning, and traditionalism; on the other hand, the exploits and injustice of the crook, the landlord, and the village chief, jealousy, futility, and, above all, the ruined homes of the exiles.

Armenian provincial writers are social historians, dialectal and literary ethnographers. Gegham's main contribution to Armenian letters was to introduce the purity of provincial expression at a time when the realists were open to its absorption. Chanashian calls him the photographer of Mush, who portrayed the lives and the true characters of villagers in all their beauty, emotion, passion, and glory—like Thomas Hardy, the English Victorian novelist. The reader at once becomes aware of the family life, traditions, and principles of the Armenian peasant. The Taron dialect and the mixed local idiom add to the richness of the Armenian language, although they are now difficult to understand.[3] Gegham could not have achieved the same effect had he shrunk from using this particular idiom and dialect. He was free of foreign influence, since he did not know even a bit of any European language. Whatever he produced came from himself and his homeland, pure and unadulterated.[4] For all these reasons, he has earned a place in Armenian literature, as have the few other literary provincialists whose works embellished the realist movement of the time.

FROM A MOONLIT JOURNEY TO MUSH[5]

In early August the sun intensifies its heat considerably over the plains of Mush. During that time, sun stroke, tremors, and

---

3. See Chanashian, *Hay grakanutyan*, 324.

4. See Hakob Martayan, "*Hamaynapatker Hay mshakuyti*, 1852–1920" (The panorama of Armenian culture, 1852–1920), *Marmara* (Istanbul), Monday, 11 June 1965, 2.

5. Gegham Ter-Karapetian (Msho-Gegham), "*Lusnak gisherov ughevorutiun me i Mush*" (A moonlit journey to Mush), in *Taroni ashkharh, patkerner u patmvatzkner* (The world of Taron: images and stories) (Paris, 1931), 23–25. First published in *Masis*, 3925 (1889). Translated by Arminé Keuchguerian and edited by the editors of the present anthology.

fever begin to visit every house and hut, not only in the villages but especially in the towns, for townsfolk are usually less resilient and tough. This year, however, there has been less illness and suffering than last year, since the summer illnesses came late, at the time of the "cool moon,"[6] which is the protector and guardian against them.

This year the farms are in better condition. They have flourished and are more prosperous; the fields and barns are filled with profitable produce. Hunger has disappeared. You do not see children eating grass. "God has taken pity on the people," they say. Yes, instead of the Persian wind, which devoured the mossy bushes last year, the south wind blew this year, cool and fresh, full of bliss and blessings, engendering crops in the fields and hope in the hearts of the people. The south wind, our south wind, is the friend of the tiller and the sower. The south wind is held sacred by the reaper, "It's not a wind," they say: "it's the breath of God's compassion, blowing over mountain peaks and hills, over stones and plowed land, over the rose, and over human beings." I do not mark the deadly silence of last year; instead, there is a smile on every face, joy in the housewife's heart, and the children play happily.

It was on one of these summer days that we embarked on a pilgrimage to the Red Church, north of Mount Serki. It was impossible to travel during the day, as the road is usually dusty: you are suffocated by storms and parched by the heat of the sun. And if, as frequently happens, there is no wind, nature seems to seethe. We decided to travel after dark, by the light of the moon. We were three friends, all riders. A young, armed Kurd accompanied us on horseback. The moon was not yet full; the stars were shining; the night was cool and still. In another fifteen minutes we would be out of Gheypyan, the village we were leaving. To the right was Antzar,[7] the Kurdish village. And sure enough, there were no trees or bushes. The village was behind us, and we passed through its pasture land. To our left we could see the farm of the Patriarchal Society of Akn, which I think must have been inactive by then.

We had already left the village limits behind and were on the promontory. The horses were exhausted: they needed rest; they

---

6. The Armenian expression is *hovun lusnake*.
7. *Antzar* means treeless in Armenian.

were sweating and irritated. There was no moon. Although it was hard to see, the road was smooth and even. We were quite fearless, having confided ourselves to God and being on a pilgrimage: "The shrine protects the pilgrim," as women on pilgrimage say. We rested for half an hour on the soft, silky grass of the mountaintop, and then continued our journey.

The Red Church was not far. We rode through another Kurdish village and entered the traditional church grove. Bears sometimes took refuge among those lofty poplars. This time, fortunately, there were no bears. We dismounted. There was a pile of stones and earth. That was the church. Although it was red, the color was quite faded and weathered. In fulfillment of our vows, we crossed ourselves, and while we knelt facing east, our Kurdish traveling companion made obeisance facing south. They consider it a shrine and respect it; they also make oaths about it: "Don't cut the trees in the grove," they say, "or the curse will befall you." I wonder who originated the curse and who imprinted this strong dread in their hearts, that they should keep it alive even among these ruins.

After we left the ruined church, our Kurdish companion took us to the healing spring. There we washed our faces and drank of the fortifying water, which was supposed to soothe pain and cure illness.

It was past midnight when our guide invited us to his people's tents to rest until morning. So we went to the Kurdish area, in the Zozas, half an hour away. We went through leafy poplar woods, sometimes walking on stones, sometimes trampling tender young plants, and arrived at the tent ground, beside the flow of a cool stream. There was life everywhere; wherever we looked we saw excitement and gaiety. Here there was a fire, over there a candle, in yet another place they were singing a Kurdish lullaby; some were eating, others sleeping; sheep and cattle were everywhere, and clamor and shrieking came from all corners. Soon several large dogs surrounded us, and groups of people emerged from the tents. According to their custom, when they had determined who we were, they welcomed us. Then we went to the tent of their chief, whom we knew, and spent the night there. After such a long and tiring night and in such exceptionally fine weather, we slept soundly until morning.

Vrtanes Papazian

(1866–1920)

Born in Van in 1866, Vrtanes Papazian was a prolific writer, critic, historian, and translator. Despite his Western Armenian origin, his works belong to Eastern Armenian literature. After his schooling in Van, he studied at the Gevorgian seminary in Etchmiadzin, from which he graduated in 1888. He then began his peripatetic life, first going to Shamakh and then to Baku, trying his hand at odd jobs. Around this time his literary career began, with publications in *Ardzagang* (Echo) and *Mshak* (Tiller). In 1891 he published *Patkerner Turkahayeri kyankits* (Scenes from the lives of Armenians in Turkey), in two volumes, in which he gives touching descriptions of the persecutions and lives of Western Armenians.

Between 1891 and 1895 Papazian studied literature and history at the University of Geneva, while continuing to write novels and short stories. Following his years in Geneva, he returned home, where he taught for a while. Papazian found it difficult to remain in one place; his adventurous nature and curiosity took him to many cities, towns, and villages in the Middle East, the Caucasus, and Iran, collecting popular tales and becoming intimately acquainted with Armenian life and customs in all these different places. He was later able to draw on these experiences for material for his stories and novels.

Papazian's preferred themes are the relationship between the rich and the poor, and social injustice. He is always on the side of the oppressed, defending the destitute regardless of nationality. He knows the people he talks about well—their pains, worries, concerns, and so on—and he draws on this knowledge chiefly in his descriptions, rather than using it to create individual idiosyncrasies.

Papazian's works consist mainly of novels, short stories, and plays, although he also wrote tales and vignettes. Among his stories are "*Khat-Sapa*" (1890) and "*Santo*" (1898), both based on the lives of Armenian gypsies; "*Turisti hishoghutiunner*" (Tourist memories, 1895); "*Khente*" (The fool, 1903); "*Gaghtakanner*" (Immigrants, 1894). About twenty of these stories were published in Shushi in 1911.

From a literary point of view, his novels and novellas are the most interesting of his works. *Tomas Botsaris* (1891), based on contemporary Greek life; *Azerfeza, Alemgir,* and *Asi* (1903), a reflection of Iranian life; and *Emma* (1901), inspired by the student environment and mirroring contemporary morals and mores. *Emma* is a good example of Papazian's treatment of characters. These are thinkers like himself rather than full-blooded examples of their ideals. That is why they often seem faded and superficial. *Haji Bek* (1891) is based on Armenian revolutionary life connected to the history of Western Armenians.

Zhayre (The rock) is one of his best loved plays. In this psychological drama about Armenian rustic life, the rock represents despotism and tyranny. At times Papazian shows an almost Rousseauian faith in the noble and natural strength of the peasant. He portrays the landlord as a tyrant and exploiter of men. His principal concern is humanitarian as well as nationalistic. *Arshaluys* (Dawn, 1905), a play inspired by the life of Armenians in Turkey, was published under the pen name Vardges.

Many consider *Lur-da-lur* to be Papazian's best work. It is a prose poem, a Kurdish ballad, a warm and lyrical story of the lovers Haso and Zakhlé, in which the author passionately protests inequality and human injustice. Its central idea is that human injustice must not be allowed to stifle the most noble feeling of humanity, love.

It is important to recognize and appreciate Papazian's optimism: he believed that others would turn his exposure of the conditions of tormented people into a source for publicizing and improving their situations.

He was a philosophical writer rather than a philosopher, and in this vein he also wrote scholarly works. *Hay Boshanere* (The Armenian gypsies, 1899) is a study of Armenian gypsies. *Vtak* (Brook) is a collection of writings on literary philology produced in collaboration with other Armenian writers. *Vardanants paterazm* (The battle of Vardanants, 1910), *Artashes II* (1910), *Gagik II* (1910), *Sahak yev Mesrop* (Sahak and Mesrop, 1910), and *Patmutiun Hayots grakanutyan* (History of Armenian literature, vol. 1, 1907; vol. 2, 1913) are other important, nonliterary creations.[1] In Teolelian's words, *Patmutiun Hayots grakanutyan* is "a handy book of quick sketches."[2] Papazian also translated several stories by Alphonse Daudet.[3]

Vrtanes Papazian represents a mixture of several literary qualities, and his works display both romantic and realistic traits with no individual, idiosyncratic quirks. There is, however, a kind of final message in his writings, especially in the stories and novels: perhaps their own idealism helps create a sense of hope in a better future.

Papazian died in difficult financial circumstances in 1920.

THE SOURCE[4]

There was a king in far-off India who delighted in putting up huge buildings, palaces, mosques, schools, towers, pyramids, and wonderful gardens. Not only did he enjoy building, but he really enjoyed watching the work of his craftsmen, inspiring them with encouraging words, distributing generous rewards, and standing beside them to examine their doings.

One day, as, with a group of his top ministers, he watched the workmen shouldering heavy stones with great effort, he noticed that one of them lifted huge stones with no help from anybody and went about his work singing happily all the time. The workman could not be described as huge and powerful. Yet, while the others moaned under their burdens, while the most sturdy and stalwart among them were rather sad and solemn and could move forward

1. See H. Mesrop Chanashian, *Hay grakanutian nor shrjani hamarot patmutiun, 1701–1920* (Concise history of Armenian literature: the modern period, 1701–1920) (Venice, 1973), 175–78.
2. Minas Teolelian, *Dar me grakanutiun, 1850–1920* (A century of literature, 1850–1920) (Boston, 1977), 1:445.
3. French novelist (1840–97).
4. Vrtanes Papazian, "The Source," in *The Great Armenian Short Stories*, trans. Sarkis Ashjian (Beirut, 1959), 62–66. Revised by the editors of the present anthology.

only with great difficulty, this remarkable workman shouldered the big stones with the utmost ease and moved them quickly, singing and smiling all the while. He mounted the steps with great agility and contentment. The king was amazed. And so were his ministers. Who was this man, who carried out the heaviest task smiling and singing and without even the thought of a sigh? Where did he get his strength? What was the secret of his happiness and endurance? Surely some mysterious power turned that rather weak body of his into a source of energy and vitality, by dint of which he had become more active, more dynamic, and more daring than the rest of the workers.

"Tell me, my friend," the king addressed his chief minister, "how do you explain this enigma? What is the secret of his cheerfulness and toughness? The other fellows whine and moan under lesser burdens, while that rather weak-bodied fellow goes about his work with such quickness and joy!"

The chief minister brooded deeply about the question put to him, but he could not find an answer.

"Speak up, my counselors," said the king, turning to the rest of his ministers: "whichever of you can find the answer to this question will become my favorite and my dearest friend!"

But who could tell what only God and the workman in question knew?

"My Lord," said one of the ministers, "order the fellow to take on heavier tasks. Let's see if he still sings under different conditions. Maybe he is even more powerful than he appears to be now."

And the king ordered the workman to position the pedestal of a huge pillar all by himself. The workman approached, looked at the enormous stone, and then, after calling on the great and powerful name of God, he bent down and, with one single movement, rolled it to the side of the pillar. And after wiping his sweating face, he placed the pedestal under the pillar.

Everyone was dumbfounded. There certainly was something mysterious, a secret power, that aided the workman. And, more certainly still, neither the king nor his ministers possessed even the tiniest amount of that power. The king called the extraordinary workman, gave him a great deal of money, and asked him: "What is the source of your power, my brave workman?"

"I really don't know, my Lord," smiled the hero, "all I know is, that I'm happy, I don't have any sorrow, I work cheerfully, and I live in joy. . . ."

The king could understand nothing from these words, so he ordered his counselors to a meeting where their major task would be the unraveling of this secret. And he set them a time limit of five days.

The greatest wizards of the state exerted their minds in search of a reasonable answer. At last the oldest among them asked to withdraw, and, after watching how Hasan (for that was the workman's name) worked until evening, he approached him and accompanied him to his house. Then he asked to be invited in.

"I am penniless, my Lord," said Hasan: "my dwelling is no more than a miserable hut; how could I dare to invite you to sit at my poor table?"

"Never mind about that, my son. I want to see your hut and your wife, your child, and your everyday life. I want to see whether you really don't have any troubles at all; I want to see if you're always happy, cheerful, and singing."

And Hasan took the old minister to his modest hut. As they walked in, a young and most glorious woman appeared at the door, an angelic baby in her arms. She came forward, embraced her husband, and kissed him with obviously exemplary love, then handed him the baby and admitted them, smiling and happy the whole time. She prepared supper and fed her husband with such care, and caressed him with such unaffected love, that tears came to the eyes of the minister, who could not remember ever having been so moved in his life.

After supper, which was eaten in an atmosphere of joy and cheerfulness, the father took his child in his arms and played with him, amusing the baby a great deal. The child filled the hut with his silvery laughter and charmed the minister. As for the exemplary wife, she entertained her weary husband with so much adoring love and tenderness that the minister, genuinely transported, exclaimed: "As God and the Prophet are my witnesses, I have never seen such a loving, wonderful wife in all my life!"

"And you have probably never seen such a loving husband either," added the woman, putting her head on the breast of her husband: "my husband loves me, and we are happy, content, and satisfied. The world's injustice can't cross our threshold because it's afraid of love and peace. Sorrow and pain remain foreign to us because Love is our physician and savior. . . ."

"As God and His Prophet are my witnesses, woman, you're right: there is no greater physician and encourager than unstained, everlasting Love, which creates heroes with its tender smile, breaks down rocks, and removes obstacles. The whole world is unable to withstand its power, and sorrow is but an insignificant dwarf compared to Love. You're right, woman: I see now where the source of your husband's power lies. Power is the offspring of Love and Love is the power that is able to move mountains, to change the world, to annihilate injustice, and to turn every thorn into a rose."

So spoke the minister, and he left Hasan's home in amazement. He went directly to see the king and told him all that he had seen. The king was much surprised and did not believe his minister's words, because he had never experienced pure Love. In fact, he had never loved. All he could do was inspire fear in people. So he could not realize the strength of Love, because all he had seen around him was flattery; nobody had ever really loved him.

"You're out of your mind, you addle-brained old goat!" he shouted, "do you think Hasan's strength comes from that? Who is more loved than I? Don't you see how everyone bows to me? Don't you know how many wives and children I have? How can you say that none of them loves me? . . ."

The old minister bowed and held his peace; he was afraid the king would order his death if he tried to say anything further.

"Get out of my sight! Get out of here!" shouted the king with great contempt: "you're a dreamer, you've already lost your mind. You'll shortly see how mistaken your conjectures have been. Behold, I order you, right here and now, first of all to bring the man's wife and child to my harem. If his wife be as beautiful as you say, I'll keep her for myself, and you'll see that it won't affect Hasan's power in the least!" And he gave an unconditional order to carry out this wish.

Five horsemen surrounded Hasan's hut immediately; they forced the door open and went in, in the dead of night. They turned everything upside down and dragged Hasan's wife and child to the king's harem.

On the following day the king stood near the building where Hasan started his daily work, sad, unsmiling, and tearful. Everyone gathered there waited for him. Hasan bent down and tried to move a large stone, but he could not. He tried a smaller one, and he failed again. His arms were paralyzed, his knees were trembling, and he could not move even a small stone.

He raised himself and, his hands empty, fell down in utter dejection and crawled along the ground, sighing mournfully: "There is no strength left in me!"

Hakob Hakobian

(1866–1937)

Hakob Hakobian, the founder of proletarian poetry in Armenian and a revolutionary activist, was born in Gandzak (presently Ganja in Azerbaijan) to a worker's family. He received his early education at the local Armenian parish school and Russian gymnasium but was forced to discontinue his studies in 1886 for financial reasons. He worked for a year as an apprentice in a pharmacy in Tiflis then moved to Baku, where he worked seven years in the oil industry, first as a laborer then as an accountant. His experiences in Baku forged his strong sense of identity with and devotion to the working class.

In 1893 he moved permanently to Tiflis and worked as an accountant in various institutions. In 1901 he became chief accountant of the Commercial Bank of Tiflis, a position in which he remained until 1921, the sovietization of Georgia, when he was appointed commissar of all the banks in the city. He joined the Communist Party in 1904 and participated in the 1905 Russian revolution. In 1911 he was sent to Geneva, Paris, and Berlin to establish contacts with exiled revolutionaries.

In 1914 he edited and published the first almanacs of Armenian proletarian literature, *Karmir mekhakner* (Red carnations) and *Banvori albom* (The worker's album), and edited the literary monthly review *Darbnots* (Forge). In 1922 he founded the Association of Armenian

Proletarian Writers, was later promoted to administrative positions in the writers' unions of Georgia and Armenia, and in 1934 was elected to the Administrative Council of the Writers' Union of the USSR.

Hakobian was one of the early revolutionary idealists, fighting vehemently for the rights of the working class, the exploited, and the abused. His literary output consists mainly of poetry that flows directly from his heart in sincerity and faith. Even though his skill as a poet is no match for his revolutionary enthusiasm and ardor, the genuineness and candor of his feelings have earned him great respect. His pre-Soviet poems have been published in various collections, such as *Ashkhatanki yerger* (Songs of labor, 1906), *Heghapokhakan yerger* (Revolutionary songs, 1907), *Nor aravot* (New morning, 1910), and *Banasteghtzsutiunner* (Poems, 1912).

During the period of Soviet rule, his works went through a number of editions. They were eventually compiled into a four-volume set titled *Yerkeri zhoghovatzu* (Collected works, 1955–58).

My Land[1]

However much I wish to climb to your heights,
    magnificent mountains,
And hold tightly to your fresh and snow-covered sides;
    However much I wish
    To fly up and higher,
Climb the air like an eagle,
O untried mountains, I can't
    Forsake my land,
That wallows in filth and despair,
    Suffering without end;
I must choose the earth of the needy,
    The oppressed and forlorn.
Where pain and deprivation, clinging together,
    Seek a way out.
And you, bright stars,
    However potent your magic,
Your rapturous gleaming,

---

1. Hakob Hakobian, "My Land," in *Armenian Poetry Old and New*, ed. and trans. Aram Tolegian (Detroit, 1979), 153–55.

However you capture my dreaming soul
And carry me far to your heaven-world,
 Yet I cannot, I cannot leave my land—
By my own will I'm bound to my homeland,
To the unending cry of my people,
 To their grief and sorrow.
They call out to me:
 "Come, poet,
 Sing our sorrow,
 Become our friend."
Oh, how good it is to fly up to the sky,
 Forget pain and hardship;
To float and soar beneath the brightness of the moon,
 And touch the stars—
But the gaunt wraith
Of our bleak life,
An evil spirit
Alive with warning and protest,
Issues commands:
"Come down from your dream of heaven,
 Become one with life,
 You have songs of pain to give it."
And I will come down—it is hard
To ignore my people, it is hard.
My soul is scattered among my people,
My nerves are woven with their nerves.
 No other path
Can lead to meaning for me ever,
And however much your charms allure,
 Oh heaven and stars,
There lives a browbeaten, needy world,
 Oppressed, forlorn
 It is that earth I choose—
There, clinging together, grief and want
 Seek a way out.

Tigran Kamsarakan

(1866–1941)

Tigran Kamsarakan was born in Constantinople and attended the Aramian school, where his teacher of Armenian was Khachatur Misakian, later one of his severest critics. He made his literary debut in 1884, publishing columns, short stories, and translations in the local press.

The work that brought him fame and notoriety was his first and only novel, *Varzhapetin aghjike* (The teacher's daughter), written in 1888 and serialized in Arpiar Arpiarian's *Arevelk* (Orient). This was the first realistic novel of the time, and aroused so much controversy that even the author was momentarily tempted to discontinue its publication. In fact, the novel provided a focus for the debate between romanticism and realism. While conservatives condemned it as "an attempt to vulgarize literature," many others, such as Arpiar Arpiarian (1852–1908), Hrant Asatur (1862–1928), and even writers from Eastern Armenia such as Perch Proshian (1837–1907) and Shirvanzadé (1858–1935), greeted it with enthusiasm.

Varzhapetin aghjike portrays an unhappy marriage in which virtue and vice, personified by Astghik and Aram respectively, are treated in their various manifestations. It also exposes, with exceptional courage, the immorality of some wealthy families. The novel's sharp realism, however offensive to certain readers, was the main cause of its success.

In the words of Hrant Asatur, "Kamsarakan was the first to write a realistic novel, at a young age when one looks at life through lights and flowers, and reality is mixed with dreams. He did not yet have the experience to penetrate the deep secrets of the human heart, but his first impressions had the charm of freshness. He was not wandering in the realms of imagination; he was just depicting what he saw and what he knew."[1] Or, in Kamsarakan's own words: "The French writer Alphonse Daudet (1840–97) became my inspiration, even my closest friend, but mainly an 'advisor,' to whom I never said anything: it was he who told me everything. . . . Only after reading his *Fromont jeune* (Young Fromont, 1874) and *Jack* (1876) was I tempted to write my own novel, which, though weak in art and naïve, nevertheless possesses a sincere and genuine realism."[2]

This novel was an unexpected revelation at the time, when such masters of realism as Arpiarian and Zohrap had published only a few short stories. Despite some weaknesses, it captured the public's imagination, and is still widely read.

Among his short stories are "*Nvard*" (a proper name, 1886), "*Gratune*" (The bookstore, 1889), "*Yaro*" 1892), "*Hovkul*" (a proper name, 1892), and "*Enkuyzin koghove*" (The basket of walnuts, 1892).

During the 1895 massacres of Armenians, he fled Constantinople and took refuge first in Egypt and then, in 1919, in Paris. In 1910, in collaboration with Mikayel Kiurchian (Gürdjian), he wrote *Prkank* (Ransom), a play dealing with a real-life event, which was staged in Egypt, Constantinople, Baku, and Paris. He continued to send occasional articles to various journals for several years, but eventually he abandoned literature for a career in business. He died in Vichy, France.

FROM THE TEACHER'S DAUGHTER[3]

Chapter 2

In the past, when teachers were not such a heavy burden on the modest revenues of our schools as they are in modern times,

---

1. Hrant Asatur, *Dimastverner* (Portraits) (Constantinople, 1921), 254.

2. Quoted by Minas Teoleolian in *Dar me grakanutiun* (A century of literature), vol. 1 (Boston, 1977), 374.

3. Tigran Kamsarakan, *Varzhapetin aghjike* (The teacher's daughter) (Yerevan, 1956), 29–44. Translated by the editors of the present anthology.

specialists in Armenian were very well paid. In our school curricula, subjects such as philosophy, rhetoric (which is now the study of literature), and logic (I do not understand why it has been separated from philosophy, when it is an integral part of it) adorned the advanced studies programs along with algebra, which was not yet called *hanrahashiv* or *grahashiv*.[4]

The Armenian specialists used to teach philosophy, rhetoric, and logic. Some of them used to teach rhetoric and logic quite successfully, but when it came to philosophy, they taught it rather . . . philosophically! In the best schools, the highest grade wrote letters in *grabar* (classical Armenian). Naturally the most talented students could find poetic inspiration in the letters of the Mkhitarists. The philologist might perhaps find a few rare copies of a richly-bound collection of these letters in bookstores, printed by Kiurkchian in 1858 and "dedicated to discerning minds."

Having to talk about prose and poetry drove our *patvelis* mad; they reduced the entire charm of literature to questions related to sex and nature; they were stale, old-fashioned academics who understood language but not literature: they lacked soul.

The students of the *Chemaran* (academy) were taught by such an honorable *patveli,* whom Paronian, the Armenian satirist, had honored by including his likeness in *Azgayin jojer* (National big wigs). His presumption had increased in proportion to his size. When he was not ridiculing modern creative works he was deploring them, and you may be sure he referred to them as *palekhchiakan*.[5] In his opinion, modern literature deserved to be consigned to Hell. It was quite doubtful he could see any farther than the end of his nose when it came to questions related to literature. And that is an understatement.

One day, a student who had been endlessly parsing long sentences had the audacity to ask the *patveli* to assign a subject for composition. The enraged *patveli* replied:

"You little so-and-so, have you ever been in a house on fire, that I can ask you to describe the experience? Have you ever been in a sea swell, that I can ask you to describe a storm? All you can tell me is how the world appears to a little newborn jackass!" His

---

4. Armenian names for algebra.
5. The jargon or cant of fish mongers (Armenian-Turkish).

reply was not terribly poetic, nor a literary jewel, but this famous observation of the *patveli*'s would forever be remembered by his students at the time. Meanwhile, many beautifully phrased pieces have evaporated from their minds.

K . . . (the *patveli*) was unshakeable. Consequently, he continued to make his students translate the proverbs of Aesop and Nasreddin Hoja[6] into modern Armenian. And so the students were educated, learning stories about foxes, cats, roosters, mice, and who knows what tales of the devil.

Fifteen years before my story opens, the old *patveli* resigned his post at the *Chemaran* in Scutari (Üsküdar),[7] following a grammatical dispute. He had invented a compound word out of three words (the names of two small beasts), and another word of nineteen letters, and had presented them as authentic Armenian words. The national press of the time, especially *Meghu*[8] had ridiculed him with biting sarcasm.

The post of Armenian specialist at the academy now had to be filled. There was in Scutari an Armenian youth association, the purpose of which was to sing the national songs, dance, and, finally, to have a good time, with the aim of breaking the silence and making their voices heard in community affairs. The association was led by R . . . Agha, who was the church choir master and had studied the songs of the nation: "Mother Araks," "Farewell," etc., were among the best songs in the repertoire of the association. "A new song! a new song!" was always being demanded of the choir master. He reminded them, however, that before there could be a melody one needed a verse.

One of the members of the association, Gabrielian, brought the long-sought lyrics to a meeting and asked for permission to recite them. Then, if they liked them, R . . . Agha would have them set to music.

Gabrielian was a sensitive young man and had a soft voice. When he finished reciting the first two stanzas, the heart of everyone there was pulsing, and he was enveloped in a cocoon of admiration. By the time he had finished reading, their souls were swept

---

6. A humorous character in Turkish folk literature.
7. A section of Istanbul on the Asiatic side of the Bosporus.
8. An Armenian periodical published in Constantinople (1856–62; 1870–74).

away on currents of adulation. It was a sad, gripping piece. The author had created a beautiful allegorical line that was regularly repeated at the end of each stanza. This allegorical invention was the essence of the poem—and that poem remains a rare gem in the Armenian songbook to this day.

When Gabrielian finished reading, he was quickly surrounded by other members.

"It's Peshiktashlian," said some.

"No, it's Durian," said others.

And from their seats at the back of the hall other members rushed to the stage where Gabrielian was still standing, jumping over tables and knocking over chairs. He had not revealed the name of the poet. He answered each suggestion made by the rising voices around him with a smile, as if he enjoyed hearing all the wrong answers to the riddle he had just presented.

"Tell us who wrote it! Tell us!" the crowd insisted.

In a clear, resounding voice, Gabrielian revealed the name: "Andranik Fenerchian."

They had never heard this name. The members of the association looked at each other. Each asked if any of the others knew or had ever heard the name. All in vain. Everybody murmured the name over and over: "Andranik Fenerchian, Andranik Fenerchian."

Although they did not recognize the name, they recognized the poetic power of that particular piece. No matter who the author was, they already acknowledged him as a poet. They wanted to reward Andranik Fenerchian, to get to know him.

It was a fairly easy task for Gabrielian to introduce him to his friends. Fenerchian gave a few excellent talks. Imagine: during the early years of the Armistice my father's Armenian soul had already become extremely sensitive! Fenerchian could compose verses in seconds; there could not have been more unmistakable proof of literary talent. "Find some way to reward him!" became the endless refrain of this youthful association. The daring opinion was that Andranik Fenerchian should be appointed the next Armenian specialist at the Academy. A few weeks after this bold project was launched, something unexpected happened: the Armenian youth association succeeded in persuading the board to accept

Fenerchian's appointment. It was said that a member of parliament from Scutari, S. Terterian, had appointed a candidate of his own to the Board of Directors of the Academy, promising a twenty per cent increase in salaries, and this man had proposed Andranik Fenerchian. As they had been in the past, the board was naturally influenced by intermediaries of such national stature.

Nothing changed. The poet Andranik Fenerchian would comfortably fill K . . . *Patveli*'s chair and read his own delicate verses in the same classroom where the echoes of Nasreddin Hoja's tale of the mouse were still reverberating. Soon Andranik Fenerchian entered the classroom. First he was curious to know what his predecessor had asked the class to prepare. So he asked:

"What have you prepared for today's lesson?"

"The *patveli* assigned us a subject to write a letter about," the class replied in unison.

"What kind of subject?"

"We had to write to a friend in Izmit and ask him to send us some cheese."

"Cheese?" exclaimed Fenerchian, completely taken aback.

"Yes, cheese," replied the students.

With a scornful expression on his face, the teacher said:

"Well, we'll salt that subject down. Can it."

Then he examined the students' notebooks. There he found that their last translation from classical Armenian had been the rooster's tale: while eating his food in the gutter, the rooster finds a pearl. Andranik Fenerchian read the whole thing with an enigmatic expression on his face and then, suddenly, he closed the notebook and began to talk.

First of all, he suggested in a couple of words that an instructor be called Teacher, not *Patveli*, which was Armenian for honorable. "This is because," he said, "as long as he is not known as a dishonorable person, we have no right to deny any man the title honorable or *patveli*. Naturally, teachers are not the only honorable people in the world, so why are they the only ones we call *patveli?*" Then the new teacher explained the new goal he would set for the class: "to develop poets for the nation."

After these preliminary remarks, like a true academic ready for his first class, Andranik Fenerchian assumed an earnest expression and completely forgot about telling the students to "can" the subject of the letter they had been asked to prepare. The students still had smiles on their faces.

The lecture he gave was very well prepared. His eloquent delivery conveyed his views on literature. A few members of the board and some of the other teachers were there to listen to the first lecture of the newly appointed Armenian specialist of the Academy. They were all in awe when Andranik Fenerchian delivered his lesson with admirable fluency and musicality of expression. But how astonished they all were and what a deep impression he made when he suddenly grabbed a student's notebook and pointed with excitement to the fable of the rooster and the pearl, at the same time loftily intoning, "And, gentlemen, poetry flies so very high that it will never descend to the gutter where the rooster thrusts his beak. It is as fragrant as that hideous sewer is foul. No! We should look for poetry in a red rose!"

The effect of that conclusion was immeasurable. Andranik Fenerchian still paid periodic visits to the standard literary theories, but he presented them in a new way. All the old, outmoded views were left behind. After no more than three lessons, the students christened their teacher *Votanavorchi,* the versifier.

It was not only in the field of literature that Fenerchian was a revolutionary. He was addressed not as *patveli,* but as Monsieur Fenerchian. And instead of the traditional *chiuppe,* or academic gown, he wore a classic redingote or frock coat, the collar of which was so very greasy that people thought it was made of velvet.

Whether he was called Versifier or something else really made no difference. Antranik Fenerchian's lucky star had begun to shine the day he was appointed Armenian specialist to the Academy. A French academician does not enjoy so much prestige as the Armenian specialist at an Armenian academy. The French academy has much more than one member, whereas the Armenian *chemaran* has only one Armenian specialist.

And so our Armenian specialist relinquished his responsibilities at the Narekian school in Péra and settled in Scutari, near its magnificent cathedral, where he had lived before. He might not have moved were it not for S. Terterian's advice, based on political considerations: it would be a good idea for Fenerchian to become part of the local community and try to win their hearts.

The teacher, the Armenian specialist of the Academy, began to enjoy financial and moral advantages. An endless flood of letters from various school directors invited him to lecture. The directors of foreign schools where Armenian was taught heard about his reputation and wanted him to teach in their educational centers. The Armenian students of the French school in Kadiköy[9] certainly remember Monsieur Fenerchian, as the French Brothers who ran the school used to call him, forgetting to pronounce the *e*, Fnerchian.

A teacher's income did not come from the school alone; teachers used to give private lessons to the families of the nobles known as *Amiras*.[10] This had a double advantage: first, they were well paid, and second, they got to know these prosperous aghas and could consequently rely on their influence to keep their teaching posts in the schools.

And Antranik Fenerchian, with all his charm, which was always part of him when he talked, could not afford to seem disagreeable to the "great aghas." He knew full well how to exploit their weaknesses. Physically speaking, there was nothing unsympathetic about him: he had a trim figure, a little on the short side, a black beard, and lively black eyes; actually, he was quite pleasant to look at. He had become his students' idol. This handsome teacher was dazzling, and the poetry he produced fascinated the students and captivated their hearts. The Armenian specialist was not without respect outside the Academy either; on the contrary, the citizens of Scutari, whether literate or not, sang his praises and seemed to forget his predecessor, perhaps in so doing remaining faithful to a national characteristic.

Such were the honors paid to Antranik Fenerchian—and the national poet proudly accepted them all as his due. He had, after all, reason to be proud. Every hour in his day was taken up. The Academy, the Agapian and Mezpurian schools, other schools within the neighborhood, and non-Armenian educational establishments all brought him a fine round sum of money, such as might make a retail merchant jealous. He taught in the evenings too; as if to justify his nickname, Versifier, he used to refer to his evening responsibilities by repeating, with a smile:

9. Small municipality near Scutari, on the Asiatic side of Constantinople.
10. Lord, man of high class—a title given by the sultan to notable Armenians.

> He who toils in the night so dark
> Later enjoys the golden spark!

By the end of the school year the teacher had bought the house he had rented, and Astghik, who was then ten years old, had enrolled in A . . . ian school, where her father also taught, as a boarder. Before long he had changed his greasy frock coat, and Srbuhi Hanim,[11] as he called his wife, was proud to have a young maid under her command. Lady luck, as they said, had smiled on her as well as on the teacher.

But no smile lasts forever, and neither does luck. Lady luck's smile is never permanent. The day came when people began to ask whether Fenerchian was an Armenian specialist or a poet. From then on his luck assumed a solemn expression, and the smile disappeared.

In the seventh year of his employment, when the poet's dazzle had already faded, one of the Academy students was angrily telling his friends:"For me Fenerchian is a bard. He is talented and has a powerful imagination, but he is no Armenian specialist, not at all." And his classmates remained silent.

On another day another student started complaining about the way the teacher corrected classical Armenian, pointing out that the man used the preposition *ent*[12] incorrectly. The complaints multiplied and went beyond the confines of the school. One day, when the teacher was now crying instead of smiling, the Academy's board of directors met to discuss a very important issue. The students of the higher grades had presented a written complaint against the teacher of Armenian philology, accusing him of incompetence in Armenian studies. They had attached a few of Andranik Fenerchian's personal writings to the written protest; they contained four mistakes, all of them double underlined, including the word *patker* (picture), which was misspelled.

"And how heavily he has pressed on the misspelled letter," said one of the board members, referring to the letter *e* in *patker*.

"Usually you get rid of someone by grabbing his arm and throwing him out, and it wouldn't be that difficult to grab the

---

11. Madam in Ottoman Turkish and Arabic.
12. To, on, over, by, about, etc.

teacher by his arm and kick him out," added another member derisively.

An equally discerning board member said, "No, leave his arm alone; he uses it to fly fast and high; it's better that he leave in good faith."

They continued joking around, but when Andranik Fenerchian received the letter from the board asking him to resign, the joking came to an end. He took it hard. Years later, pretending to confuse Armenian's two *e*-sounds, this is how he expressed his bad luck:

> Many good things from *e* result;
> Because of it my abode was spoilt.

But he wrote these lines very late—too late: when his pretensions had been shattered. Being deified for seven years had given him a blind self-confidence; he certainly regretted the loss of his honorable post, but he refused to use slavish means to get it back. S. Terterian promised to support him and get his job back, but the word *patker* remained a permanent obstacle to the teacher's return to teaching. "You pressed so hard on the *e* that my voice is very weak in its defense."

Fenerchian did not, in fact, much mind such sardonic remarks and did not pay much attention to the advice a few worthy citizens gave him. His deeply rooted pride would not permit him to beg. When he had been appointed to the post in Armenian philology at the Academy seven years ago, he had been uneasy about his inadequate qualifications, but as his reputation grew, he became convinced, in fact intoxicated with the idea, that he was a great talent! And if nobody appreciated him, it was not his fault.

As if the letter from the *Chemaran* were contagious, within a few months the teacher had received a pile of similar letters from all the institutions where he taught. It was as if they had agreed among themselves; every letter politely said the same thing: "the board requests that you cease your visits. . . ." Yes, the calamitous *patker*, which had delineated the entire question of the teacher's competence, became the subject of daily conversation within educational circles, and in August the teacher received a huge bundle of letters; he sweated as he read them, not because of the hellish August heat but because of the letters' weighty content.

Plans for the following school year are finalized in August.
Normally, August is the month for registering in our schools, and
the completion of the previous school year gives the boards a
chance to put in place any new projects they have planned. Consequently, in August the boards, each of which had been angered
by teacher Andranik's knowledge of Armenian philology, were all
communicating the black news—the news of his unemployment—
to him at the same time, on reams of white paper.

It was time for Andranik Fenerchian to think seriously about
his suitability for the job. The letters from the various boards were
piled on his desk; they outnumbered the student compositions he
used to bring home to correct. One day Andranik Fenerchian tried
to count on his fingers the schools where he was still teaching, out
of the thirteen that had employed him; he started at the little finger
and stopped at his ring finger. There must be a mistake! He counted
again and again, but whenever he got to that finger he stopped. In
his anger he yanked the finger so forcefully that it almost broke.
No, there was no mistake: only two, two schools, were left: the
school in Kum Kapu and the college of the French *frères*. It was
discouraging. Teacher Andranik, however, knew how to console
himself: "Well, times were hard, and it wasn't every board that
could afford to pay an Armenian specialist of his caliber." And
besides, within a month and a half his private lessons, which had
been interrupted by the summer break, would begin again.

Betrayal. It was October; only two of his six students were
continuing their lessons. His pride would not allow him to go to
the other parents and request them to continue their lessons in Armenian. He made a small concession to the trustees of the school,
proposing a slight cut in his salary. Each of the trustees made all
sorts of promises, but none of them materialized.

The teacher finally realized that the trustees had asked him
to resign for reasons other than economy. For the first time he
felt the blow that the board of the *Chemaran* had dealt him. He
decided to get revenge. He had already been elected representative
to a meeting of the National Assembly; there he criticized the management of the Academy, attempting to redeem what was left of his
good name. The attempt failed. Once again the story of *patker* was
brought up, negating what was left of his reputation.

To add to the growing heap of the teacher's misfortunes, the two remaining schools, the one in Kum Kapu and the French school, sent belated letters, also announcing that Armenian studies were no longer on their curricula.

The teacher had not saved up, and considering that he was the poet Andranik Fenerchian, his extravagance was relatively understandable. He earned much and he spent much, like those who suddenly find themselves transported from rags to riches: they spend as if they were taking revenge for their former deprivation.

And the devil of poverty—if there is a god of wealth—peeked into the house through the teacher's window. Andranik Fenerchian's wife, Surpik Hanim, saw that the devil was extremely ugly —so ugly that nothing ever portrayed in all the pictures of Hell equaled him in ugliness.

In order to reduce the anxiety, the diligent woman doubled her economy, which had been absent from their home for many years. She fired her maid, Iskuhi, and for the time being she became the Iskuhi in her kitchen. Surpik Hanim was a God-fearing woman. In her eyes, where one could discern nothing but kindness, there were traces of beauty. She was always pleased with her husband, and agreeable and engaging. Not a word of reproach against her husband for the poverty they were suffering! She pretended not to feel or notice anything, with fervent affection. The teacher treated her in the same way—well, he was not an evil man, Andranik Agha: he felt sorry for his wife.

The woman was enterprising: they could live like that for a century, if need be: poor but happy. But Astghik, a laurel wreath on her head and clutching a piece of yellow parchment, her diploma, would return home filled with hope and bubbling over with ideas. . . .

Avetis Aharonian

(1866–1948)

Born in a village near Igdir (now in Eastern Turkey), Avetis Aharonian spent his childhood there, on the shore of the Araxes River, facing Mount Ararat (Masis), the two topographical symbols of Armenian national consciousness that were to hold him under their spell throughout his literary life. In his memoirs, *Im girke* (My book), written in 1927, he said, "Masis was my first teacher. All those who are born in the Ararat valley live under the irresistible charm of that magic mountain from the day of their birth. When I first opened my eyes I beheld Masis at our gate and its shadow hanging over my head."

After attending the local elementary school, he studied at the Gevorgian seminary in Etchmiadzin, then found the means to continue his education at the University of Lausanne, where he studied history and philosophy (1898–1901). He spent the next two years in Paris, where he audited courses in literature at the Sorbonne. On his return from Europe in 1902, he was already known as a writer because of articles he had published in various periodicals. From 1907 to 1909 he was superintendent of the Gevorgian seminary. He was arrested by the czarist government in 1909 and confined in the infamous Metekh prison, where he fell ill. After his release in 1911, he moved to Europe.

In his student days in Switzerland he had been enlisted into the Armenian Revolutionary Federation by Kristapor Mikayelian (1859–1905), one of the founders of the organization. By 1917 he had emerged as a political figure. He returned to the Caucasus and was elected chairman of the Executive Council of the Armenian National Council in Tiflis. In 1918, soon after the declaration of independence which created the First Armenian Republic, he led a delegation to Istanbul for talks on the Treaty of Batum, and the following year he headed the delegation of the Armenian Republic to the Paris Peace Conference. In the same year he became the president of the Armenian Parliament in Yerevan, and in 1920 he signed the Treaty of Sèvres, which was later superseded by the Treaty of Lausanne. After the establishment of the Soviet regime in Armenia, he moved to France permanently. In 1934, in the course of a lecture in Marseille, he suffered a stroke that left him paralyzed for the rest of his life.

The short stories and novellas that make up the better part of his literary output focus on the Armenian village, with its sufferings and heroism. His anguished characters are imbued with patriotism and a yearning for freedom. Though he depicts scenes of violence and misery, his plea is not for submission but for the courage to oppose and revolt, an element of character which he weaves skillfully into the nature of his heroes. His first collection of short stories, published in Moscow in 1899 under the title *Patkerner* (Images), was based on the fate of the Armenian peasants who were exiled and massacred during the 1877–78 Russo-Turkish war. Many of his subsequent stories and short novels were published in various periodicals: to mention a few, *Ariunot ttkhmore* (The blood-stained leaven, 1902), *Kheghchere* (The wretched, 1902), *Mrrki surbe* (The saint of storm, 1903), *Khavari mej* (In darkness, 1910), *Mokhirneri takits* (From beneath the ashes, 1910), *Partvatzner* (The defeated, 1912), and *Hayrenikis hamar* (For my fatherland, 1920). After settling in Marseilles, he wrote a series of reminiscences of village life, such as *Yerb dziunn é ijnum* (When the snow is falling, 1925), *Katushke* (1926), and *Aragilnere* (The storks, 1927).

His work in other genres comprises a novel, *Lrutiun* (Silence, 1904); a play, *Artsunki hovite* (The valley of tears, 1907), based on the theme of the struggle for emancipation; *Azatutyan chanaparhin* (On the road to freedom, 1908), a notable patriotic and ideological treatise; two travelogues, *Italiayum* (In Italy, 1903) and *Shveytsarakan giughe* (The Swiss village, 1913); *Im girke* (My book), an autobiographical work in two volumes (1927, 1931); and critical studies on two important revolutionaries, *Kristapor Mikayelian* (1926) and *Andranik* (1927).

He is best, however, in his short stories and novellas, in which, as Kevork Bardakjian says, "his main preoccupation is not so much examination of the reasons for his heroes' misery as psychological analysis, probing the tortured depth of the human soul. . . . His solicitude for his fellow countrymen and for human suffering are revealed in his haunting descriptions, which are further dramatized by his notable skill in depicting nature."[1]

His prose is poetic, his style and language representing the best of Eastern Armenian. The two literary figures who influenced him were Khachatur Abovian and Raffi. His collected works were published posthumously in ten volumes (1947–51) in Boston, on the initiative of his son, Vardges Aharonian.

JUDGMENT[2]

Many years have passed, but the memory of that extraordinary judgment remains seared into my mind.

That evening my father returned from the vineyard, leading a little calf by its tether. He had a bundle of fresh grass under his arm. I noticed that his sheepskin hat was pushed back on his head, exposing his dark, wrinkled forehead. He had tucked up his sleeves more than usual. He had forgotten to button his cuffs: he usually buttoned them after he finished working in the vineyard. Furthermore and most significantly, his right hand held his crooked stick in a visibly threatening way as he led the calf by its tether.

All these signs were ominous. There was not the least doubt that my father was angry, and when he returned from the vineyard in an angry mood it was a sure sign that someone in our household had done something wrong. Who was the guilty one? I started to turn this question over in my mind.

"Tie up the calf," he ordered me sternly, not addressing me by name.

That was another bad omen.

I went over to him and took the calf's tether from his hand. While tying it up, I reviewed the events of my day. I remembered everything item by item. Early in the morning I had taken our

---

1. Kevork B. Bardakjian, *A Reference Guide to Modern Armenian Literature, 1500–1920* (Detroit, 2000), 186–87.

2. Avetis Aharonian, "Judgment," in *Great Armenian Short Stories*, trans. Sarkis Ashjian (Beirut, 1959), 162–69. Revised by the editors of the present anthology.

harvest workers their breakfast, and I had returned home about
noon. I had not done anything all that bad, so far as I knew. True,
I had destroyed a sparrow's nest in the crevice of a wall and driven
her little ones away, but neither my father nor anybody else could
have known that, since it had happened in a far-off field, and not a
single soul had seen me do it. I had deliberately stepped on the dung
cakes baked by our neighbor Nupar, an old woman, just for fun.
The old woman had been angry and shouted at me. That, however,
had also remained a secret: otherwise Nupar would have come
to our house to complain with her endless curses. I had gone to
the cotton fields after lunch; young girls and women were picking
cotton there with my mother and two sisters. I had remained there
until dusk, busily chasing butterflies and birds. So I had spent the
second half of the day much more innocently, doing small services
for people who needed my help. I had brought fresh water to the
pickers, and I had chased the crows that tried to eat their food.
After reviewing this rather happy day, I tied up the calf and entered
the hall with an easy conscience. There my sisters were preparing
the beds. Meanwhile my father had put down the bundle of grass
and sat down, after putting his stick and his hat aside. My mother
was washing the milk pail, getting ready to milk the cows. I kept
my eyes on my father. He seemed uneasy. He rubbed his forehead
and, turning to my sister, he asked: "Look here, what way did that
damned fellow take the cows this morning: towards the vineyard,
or towards the pasture?"

"That damned fellow" was my brother, my senior by eight
years.

"I can't say, Father: he was so far ahead of us this morning,
we couldn't catch up with him," answered my sister.

"No doubt he took them by the lane to the vineyard—he always
does," I exclaimed light-heartedly, without expecting my statement
to be of any special use. "I have no doubt it was him! Who else could
it have been! Damned fellow—evil incarnate; who else would dare
to do what he has done?" muttered my father.

That brother of mine was the youngest of the children born to
my father by his first marriage. He was a stubborn, silent, dark,
and brooding fellow. He disliked us and we disliked him. He was
already about eighteen, but he was still the same melancholy, re-
served fellow. Maybe the reason for our dislike of him was this
very reserve. But my father had other reasons to dislike him: "He

always hangs his head, and I don't like that. He's done that ever since he was a small child. People who go around with their heads down all the time are usually dangerous to fall out with," observed my father. That was not all, though. Something else absolutely infuriated my father: whenever my father called him, he never answered by saying, "Yes, Father?" Instead, he would utter a dull "Huh?" which sent my father into a fury: "Can't you call me Father? A thousand curses on your stinking head! Let your tongue be tied forever!"

No, sir, he would never call his own father Father.

And that was not all. That most unusual boy never spoke a word to our father. And when forced to summon Father, he said, "Hey!" instead, and that only when it was absolutely necessary. So whenever a stranger asked him to call our father, this extraordinary brother of ours came in and loitered by the door for a few moments, flushed and perplexed. We all understood the reason for his presence and held our breaths as we uneasily awaited the blessed moment when he would utter the charming word *Father*. Our expectations in that direction were always frustrated. His lips remained shut, and his malevolent exclamation "Hey!" came as a disappointment to us all. My father gave him a silent glance, filled with sorrow and indignation, and then, shaking his head, he turned to my mother: "Did you hear the confounded boy, woman? He refuses to call his *own* father Father. May your tongue be tied forever, damned scoundrel!"

That astonishing lad knew full well what troubles, privations, and pains his hardy stubbornness had earned him, but he remained the same: bearing insults, curses, hatred, and spite in perfect calmness and utter silence. So we had gradually turned him into our scapegoat. Every disorderly act or sin committed, both inside our home and outside, was deliberately heaped on him. I and my sisters were especially cruel to him. He never complained, never tried to justify himself. He remained stone silent.

Fortunately, my father, although very strict, was very, very kind-hearted, good, and charitable. All his discontent and anger ended with his baring his complaints to my mother, and thus relieving his sad heart.

My brother watched over our cattle in the fields all day. When he came back in the evening and my father scolded him for some offense (the author of which was usually me or one of my sisters), he would approach the breadbasket without paying any attention to him, take a loaf, place it under his arm, and walk out, leaving my father to continue cursing and complaining as long as he wished.

I was the most unjust of all towards this lonely, silent, and rebellious boy. He was often scolded and punished because of my secret perversity. I was the spoiled child of the family. I was naughty, and full of life, energy, and trickery too. People said I was intelligent and talkative, in marked contrast to my brother. My father had great hopes for my future. I knew all that and I was proud of it; and I was always unjust to my poor brother. . . .

So, after very carefully sifting through the day's events, I came to the firm conclusion that my father's wrath could not be directed at me.

The cows returned from the field. My brother walked back in their train, with bent head and dark, suntanned face as usual. He drove the cows into the shed, except for the ones that were about to be milked. Then he placed his stick in a corner, sat in his usual place—the single step leading up to the hall—turned his back on us, and started to shake sand out of his sandals and pick burrs off his socks. My mother was milking the cows, helped by my sisters. My father turned to him and asked: "What direction did you walk in when you took the cattle to the field this morning?"

My father's voice was shaking. He nearly choked on his excitement. I had never seen him so angry. I drew back in fear. My brother was silent.

"Have you been stricken dumb or what? Answer me! Did you go into the vineyard? Yes or no?"

My brother went on shaking his sandals.

"Look here, son," said my father, turning to me, "go and fetch the bundle of grass I brought back with me: there's something important in it."

I went and got the bundle of grass, undid it, and took out a rather large, fresh vine branch with green bunches of grapes on it. I was almost petrified. I had broken that branch myself, not that day but the previous evening. I had broken it and had not said a word about it. I had pulled on the branch and it had broken. My father had found it and thought it had been broken early that morning.

My guilt was two-fold. To begin with, I had broken a precious vine that my father took extreme care of. The vine had been brought from far away. It was the kind that yielded large bunches of yellow grapes. They matured more quickly than other grapes, and the wine made from them was eventually used for the Mass of thanksgiving when the grapes were blessed on the Feast of the Blessed Virgin. And furthermore—which was most important and most unforgivable—whoever had broken the vine had certainly eaten some of the grapes that were on it, and they had most definitely not yet been officially blessed by the priest, according to the enduring tradition of the age-old Armenian Church. We were still fasting. My brother looked at the branch in my hand out of the corner of his eye, glowered at me, bowed his head, and kept silent. I was frozen to the spot and I could not raise my head either. It was I who was being judged, not my brother.

"Tell me," my father continued, becoming more and more furious, "you damned scoundrel, since when does an Armenian Christian eat grapes two weeks before the Feast of the Blessed Virgin? Don't you know that it's strictly forbidden by the Church? Look what you've done! It would have been better if you'd broken your hand instead of this branch!"

My whole body was trembling and the bunch of grapes was shaking in my hand. Every word my father said pierced my heart like an arrow and made a painful, bleeding wound. I was so confused I felt I could not move a step, and the branch seemed to have stuck to my hand, where it would remain glued wherever I fled in the world. I did not have the courage to confess that I had broken the branch and not my brother. I so wanted someone to tell everybody the truth. At the same time, I was angry at my brother: why did the blockhead not defend himself? Why did he not say that he was innocent and had never gone into the vineyard? The confounded fellow kept stone-silent, while I shivered all over with unspeakable torture. My mother intervened: "No need to get so excited about a branch, dear: such things happen all the time. How do you know it isn't the work of thieves?"

"Once a woman, always a woman: do you know what you are prattling away about?" my father retorted: "how could a thief know the exact place where that particular vine matures earliest? I tell you, the thief is from this house, the thief is no other than this damned, hateful fellow, who's so dumbstruck with guilt that he can't say a word!"

"And you, boy," said my mother, turning to my brother, "why do you keep silent so pigheadedly? Can't you see that your father's angry? Well, just say a few words and explain that it wasn't you. Do you think your mouth will be scorched with fire if you open it to say a few words?"

My brother remained silent.

He finished cleaning his sandals and gave me a spiteful and sorrowful glance. I felt like melting away on the spot. It would be better for me if the ground had opened and swallowed me up. He knew perfectly well that I was the guilty one, and he seemed pleased to see that by an amazing coincidence my father had put the symbol of guilt into my hands: that infernal branch, which burned my fingers. He felt how tormented I was and savored my agony in silence. No punishment had ever been so severe as mine was, so he kept silent, even if that awful silence of his earned him a cruel beating.

I looked at him, at that cocky, stubborn chap, at his dark, sorrowful eyes whose expression forever remained a mystery to me. I looked at his tight lips, which expressed such a strong will. I examined his intelligent, weather-beaten face, I stared at his coarse, chapped hands and his rather stooped back, and I saw the whole picture in a fundamentally new light. The poor boy had run left and right, among stones and thorns, in the scorching sun for days, weeks, months, nay years. And he had been rewarded by so many similar odious trials, because of my sisters and me. An enormous affliction weighed on my heart like a heavy black stone. My lips trembled more and more, and I felt like crying, shouting, and beating my head with my fists. But I bit my lips and controlled myself when I saw him preparing to leave. The tempest would end with his exit. It was always like that. He stood up and made for the door to the yard, without so much as taking his usual loaf of bread from the breadbasket. He walked past my father, who was following his movements closely. Lightning flashed in my father's eyes. He was pale. He was breathing heavily, like a busy bellows. His stick twitched in his hand. He had never looked so ruthless and dreadful before.

"Is he going to hit my brother?" I wondered. "No, that's impossible: father is too good and generous." And it seemed that if he struck him I would go mad with pain and cry out at the top of my voice. "Will he hit him or not?" I repeated in my mind, unable to take my eyes off my father's stick. "Will he raise his stick or not? will he hit him or not. . . ." I saw nothing else, thought of nothing but that yellowish stick. And I saw the terrifying stick rise above my father's head, waving threateningly in the air. . . .

"No, no, Father, Father, don't, please don't. . . ." The words stuck in my throat. I threw myself between my father and my brother, but it was no use. I was too small and frail to stop my father. The rod bludgeoned my brother's back; it rose again and fell once more on his back, with the same violent rush. My brother remained motionless, as if glued to the ground. He did not utter a word of complaint. He was as silent as before. He looked at my father with infinite woe. He felt the sore spot on his back with his right hand, and two teardrops hung from his gloomy dark eyes, then these two drops flowed down and remained glistening on his cheeks.

Something like a dark, oppressive horror descended upon the house, made even more suffocating by the silent tears of my brother.

I was virtually destroyed.

My father stood shaking, staring in front of his feet, as if he did not grasp what had happened. And the burden, the awful burden of that scene weighed and weighed on my bosom to the point of bursting it. I could no longer resist, and shouted: "It's me, it's me! It's me who's guilty of the whole business. I broke the branch. I stole the grapes; he did nothing wrong. . . ."

Everybody was dumbfounded. The sky seemed to crash down on their heads. My mother dropped the milk pail, which tumbled down and spilled milk all over the ground. My sister was so stupefied that she let the calf loose, and the calf rushed to its mother's teats. My father raised his head, stared at me with wide-open eyes, and retreated a few steps, as if he had seen a poisonous snake; then he took his forehead in both hands and, shaking from head to foot, remained absolutely silent. He walked over to my brother a little while later, put his hand on his back, and hugged him, saying: "I wish I'd broken my hand, Son; I wish my hand had withered. . . ." And turning to me, he said: "As for you, may God. . . . What shall I do with you? You've sent my soul to perdition! may God. . . .

Oh! . . ." He could say no more. He had no desire to curse me, and he began to weep like a child.

"I won't do it again, Father! I won't do it again, Father! Never, never, never again!" I said.

My brother wiped his eyes with his forearm. He sat down on the ground, took his head in his hands, and again remained silent. That night my father could not get to sleep for a long time. He sighed and tossed in his bed. I was sleepless too. My body and soul were both on fire. I pulled the quilt over my head and wept and wept, for a long time.

Nar-Dos (Mikayel Hovhannisian)

(1867–1933)

Mikayel Hovhannisian, better known as Nar-Dos, was born to a poor family in Tiflis. He received his elementary education in the parish school of the Armenian quarter of Havlabar. He manifested a strong desire and aptitude for education, but schooling was something his parents could not afford. His application to the Nersissian school was refused, probably for financial reasons. He attended a few other schools, but could not complete any of them because he lacked means. He went to a vocational school to learn a trade but abandoned it after a year; his vocation was elsewhere: in literature. It is amazing that this youth, despite his lack of formal schooling, became one of the best writers from Eastern Armenia: the secret obviously lay in his constant and resolute efforts at self-education.

He began working for various newspapers as a proofreader, copy editor, and translator. In 1890 he became a regular contributor to *Nor-Dar* (New age), a respected Tiflis daily with national, literary, and political content, founded in 1883 by Spandar Spandarian. He soon became the editor of the paper's literary section. *Nor-Dar*'s conservative stand made it the frequent target of its liberal rival, *Mshak* (Tiller), which seldom missed an opportunity to attack *Nor-Dar* with ideological assaults. Nar-Dos managed to keep clear of this strife, however, and remained with *Nor-Dar* until 1906. It is assumed that his pen name, Nar-Dos, is derived from *Nor-Dar.* After *Nor-Dar* ceased to publish in 1816, he worked for various other papers, where his meticulous editing was greatly appreciated.

He began to write creatively in the early 1880s. After trying his hand at poetry, he wrote a few plays, which show the influence of Gabriel Sundukian. Then he shifted to stories and novels, such as *"Chshmarit barekame"* (The true friend, 1886), *"Nuné"* (1886), *"Bararern u vordegire"* (The benefactor and the adoptee, 1887), and others, which concentrate on moralistic themes, with heroes who are prepared to sacrifice their lives for the good of society. He concentrated on the sector of city life in which children have no childhoods and women slave to support their families. His short novel *Anna Saroyan* (1888), one of his better works, dramatizes the collapse of a family distinguished by an obsession for material gain and self-complacency.

In 1891 a new era in his literary output began, characterized in particular by deep psychological analyses of his heroes. The focus of his works turned to the individual, the human element, seen from moral and social points of view. Plot and action no longer interested him, but rather the psychological profiles of his characters, because therein lies the source of discord and conflict. His short novel *Spanvatz aghavnin* (The slain dove, 1901), which basically represents the tragic life of the Armenian woman, was the first work he wrote with this new approach.

Among his best works are *Paykar* (Struggle) and *Mahe* (The death), published almost simultaneously in 1912. This is what the author says about *Paykar:* "I have tried to depict various characters from among the social activists of the time (the 1890s), all drawn from real life. My aim was to picture the conflict between the conservatives and liberals, the so-called *Nor-Dar*-ites and the *Mshak*-ites."[1] The fact is that the book goes much deeper than this simple explanation suggests: it touches important social issues, portrays the major and minor dramas of life, and reveals the depths of the human soul and its life-and-death struggle.

Again, in the novel *Mahe,* says the author, "I wanted to portray the problem of life and death from the opposed viewpoints of an optimist, who is filled with active enthusiasm, and a pessimist, who is fraught with apathy."[2] Nar-Dos contrasts the idealistic aspirations cherished by some youth with the attitude of those who readily succumb to Schopenhauer's philosophy of pessimism. He also deals with other situations of social

---

1. *Yerkeri liakatar zhoghovatzu* (Complete Works) (Yerevan, 1950), 8:296.
2. Ibid.

and psychological conflict. The novel is an important work of Armenian critical realism.

Among his later works is the story "*Anhet koratze*" (Lost without a trace, 1920) which depicts the aftermath of the First World War, *Verjin Mohikannere* (The Last of the Mohicans, 1930), and translations of Tolstoy's drama *The Living Corpse* and Dostoevsky's *Poor Folk*.

After the Sovietization of Georgia and Armenia in 1920, Nar-Dos remained in Tiflis and continued his literary pursuits undisturbed. He became a member of the Writers' Union in Tiflis, then vice president, then honorary president; he was also an associate member of the Writers' Union of Armenia. In 1931 the forty-fifth anniversary of his literary life was celebrated with great pomp. He was planning an extensive novel, *Nor marde* (The new man), which was to deal with the 1914–18 war and its consequences, but illness overtook him and it remained unfinished. He died in Tiflis.

HOOPOE[3]

Asatur, the gunsmith, was a man of about forty. He wore an old jacket, with a leather belt around his waist. His face was rather swollen, owing to his inveterate drinking. He was known to the whole quarter by the nickname of Hoopoe.[4]

One evening he was on his way home after closing his shop, which was no larger than a chicken coop. In one hand he held a jug that could hold half a demijohn of wine. The inside of the jug was almost black from long use. In the other hand he carried a small package wrapped in a red handkerchief. The package contained some fried fish, a few green onions, a bunch of red radishes, and two loaves of bread, which thrust their tapered ends from the package like two long ears.

It was about sunset. The unbearable summer heat had some-what abated, yet the atmosphere was heavy with the smell of dust baked by the sun. The women of the quarter sat barefoot in groups

3. Nar-Dos (Mikayel Hovannesian), "Hoopoe," in *Great Armenian Short Stories,* trans. Sarkis Ashjian (Beirut, 1959), 142–50. Revised by the editors of the present anthology.

4. A salmon-pink bird with black and white wings and tail, a large erectile crest, and a long, slender, downward-bending bill.

before their houses after the heavy work of the long summer day. They had let their head kerchiefs fall loosely on their half-exposed bosoms. They were busy with talk, which was, of course, no more than idle gossip. Dirty children, bareheaded and barefoot, ran helter-skelter in the streets, shouting loudly enough to deafen any-one who heard them. They reminded one of so many flies, buzzing about in all directions. "Hoopoe!" one of them suddenly shouted.

Hoopoe paid no attention to the call, and that, it seemed, was very natural for him. He went on his way undisturbed. Sweat trickled from under his hat, running along his ears and dropping onto his weary shoulders.

"Hoopoe! Hoopoe!" shouted a second, third, fourth, and even-tually all the street urchins, resulting in an uproar capable of un-nerving even the most cold-blooded man. Hoopoe could stand it no longer. Without deigning to turn his head, he started to rain terrible curses on the shouting children behind him. The children seemed to have anticipated precisely that, and their shouts in turn rose in pitch and amplitude. They interspersed their shouts with shameless laughter and reciprocal curses that they had learned from their elders. Some of them went so far as to throw stones at him. But Hoopoe proceeded on his way without so much as thinking of defending himself, although he saw the stones whizzing past him right and left and landing on the ground, raising the dust. His only reaction was to maintain his choice, coarse insults. To judge from appearances, he would have continued indifferently on his way until he got home, if one of the stones had not hit one of his feet. His foot must have been badly hurt, for suddenly he stopped, put down his package and wine jug, picked up a big stone, rolled his bloodshot eyes, and made ready to hurl it with all his strength. Just then, however, the children ran off and disappeared into the side streets.

Hoopoe swore a blue streak. "Why do you run away like cow-ards? So you want to fight with stones, eh? Why don't you come back then? Eh? A body can't even go about his business in peace without these nasty little sons of bitches showing up and daring to get in the way! Why do you get in my way? What have I done to bother you? Eh? Why don't you let me go home in peace? Damn you all!"

He dropped the stone, wiped his forehead with his index fin-ger, then waved the finger threateningly. He bent down and, still cursing, rubbed the spot where the stone had touched his foot. "Hey! Mr. Asatur, what's the matter? What's eating you?" asked one of his acquaintances, who passed without stopping.

Hoopoe looked at him, picked up his jug and package from the ground, and as he followed him began to complain:

"Tell me this: is it right, what they do? Those pups never leave me in peace to go about my business. They shout and cry, 'Hoopoe! Hoopoe!' Tell me, am I their age? What gives them the right to make fun of a man my age?"

"Why take it so seriously? They're only children, after all. You mustn't pay any attention to what they say," retorted his acquaintance, walking on with hasty steps and leaving Hoopoe behind.

"Of course I never pay attention to them, but what about the stones they throw at me?" complained Hoopoe. But his acquaintance no longer heard him, since he had turned into one of the side streets and vanished out of sight.

⚓

The whole quarter had given Asatur the gunsmith the nickname Hoopoe. In their choice of this name for him they had been inspired by the popular proverb that went: "The hoopoe bird stank, but he thought that it was his nest that stank." And Asatur the gunsmith did, in fact, stink: that is to say, he was a very nasty, quarrelsome fellow. The people in his quarter had a hand in his making, though: they insisted on provoking him with that undesirable appellation, sending the poor man into frequent rages.

Hoopoe would not be reconciled to anyone. There was not a single neighbor, either at the market or in his quarter, with whom he had not quarreled and by whom he had not been roundly licked. Every day was a continuous battle with his wife. He beat his wife and his wife beat him. They hit each other until either they exhausted themselves doing so or the neighbors came and separated them. He feared no one but the police, having experienced, through the intervention of the latter, the rat-infested prison cells. The local police chief had personally beaten him more than once, making blood pour from his nose and mouth. Hoopoe was a drunkard. But we must say that he drank only wine, and first-rate red wine at that. He did not care for arak, and if ever he had occasion to drink that oriental brandy he writhed his face into such a disgusted expression that one felt sure he was going to throw up. He was very particular in his choice of food. He disliked foods with sauces. He particularly disliked peas. His usual food consisted of greasy boiled meat, roast beef, fresh onions, red radishes, and white bread. And he always managed to scrape together enough money to buy those rather costly foodstuffs, because he was skilled in his trade and so clever that he could easily sell a rusty, good-for-nothing dagger or gun to a European tourist at a good price, persuading them that they were buying an exquisite, very valuable antique.

He had been using his wine jug for the last fifteen years. He carried this beloved jug empty to work in the morning, and brought it back filled with excellent wine in the evening. He was so fond of this jug that on Saturday nights, after swallowing its contents, he set a lit candle on it. "My blessing resides in this jug," he said: "as long as I drink wine from this wonderful jug of mine, my work can only bloom and prosper!" Once his elder son, a lad of six, accidentally touched his jug with his foot. The jug toppled over and had Hoopoe not managed to grab hold of it, it surely would have broken to pieces. Hoopoe lost his temper over this, and he beat the boy so cruelly that he surely would have died if Hoopoe's wife had not succeeded in snatching him from his father's clutches. Fortunately, the jug was already empty; otherwise, he would surely have given a share of the beating to his wife too.

When he reached home, his wife was not there. Outside, at the bottom of the wall, his son was making a house out of pieces of wood. The boy was wearing nothing but a long, dirty shirt with tails.

"Where's your mother?" he asked.

The child stood up, stared at the package his father had brought home, and answered: "She went to the Pakratians' house."

Hoopoe's eyes glared angrily. "So she's there again, is she?" and, cursing, he went in, placed his jug and package on the table, and turned back to his son: "Go tell her to come home at once!"

His son, who had followed him in, still staring at the package in his father's hand, turned and ran out.

"Pakratian's house! Now! Well; very well," he said to himself aloud, "I'll soon show you what you get for visiting Pakratian! I'll teach you a much needed lesson! You think Asatur is already dead, do you? You think he is no longer on the face of the earth, eh? You think he can put up with other people fooling around with his wife, eh? You think that because everyone calls me Hoopoe I've lost all sense of honor, do you?" And in his anger he took off his hat, threw it to the ground, and stamped on it violently. And then, continuing to address icy threats to his wife's absent person, he removed his belt, took off his jacket, trousers, shoes, and stinking socks. He positioned himself near the door and began wiping off his sweat. He waited impatiently for his wife. After a while he went over to his jug and drank copiously. When he had quenched his thirst, he set the jug back on the table. Then, without opening the small package wrapped up in his handkerchief, he cut off the dry end of one of the loaves and started to munch on it.

The boy, who had gone to fetch his mother, bounced back in like a ball, and, panting all the while, said: "Mother said she'll come soon." Now the poor child was staring at his father's mouth, which went on chewing the heel of bread.

"Huh!" roared Hoopoe and, still chewing on the piece of bread, he once more stretched out his hand to the jug. After that he sat down on the couch and raised the jug to his burning lips several more times before his wife returned. At last his wife appeared in the doorway. She was plump and good-looking enough. She had yellow, frayed shoes on her feet. She wore no socks. She had a baby in her arms.

"Here I am, so tell me what you want," she said boldly. To judge from her appearance, she seemed perfectly aware of what lay in store for her: in all probability, one of their habitual brawls.

"So you wonder what I want, do you?" said Hoopoe, who had taken a fresh draft from his jug and now wiped his mouth on the sleeve of his shirt. He walked over to his wife, grabbed hold of her hand, glared at her menacingly, and asked: "Now, tell me where you've been!"

"I've been to the Pakratians'," she answered in the same undaunted manner.

"What were you doing there?"

"What do you think I was doing there? They had laundry to do and they told me about it so I could go over and finish the job by tomorrow morning."

"Laundry! Don't tell me! Laundry, eh? Laundry. You have no one to care for you, you have no husband to care for your needs, you go hungry and thirsty, so you need to do other people's laundry, is that it? You think I no longer inhabit this nasty world: dogs and jackals have torn me to pieces, is that it? Will you kindly tell me why my wife has to do other people's laundry? I can buy and sell hundreds of Pakratians, and yet my wife has to do his laundry, is that how it is? He's a respectable government official, is that it? To hell with his position!" (Here Hoopoe poured out inspired insults on the Pakratians). "What laundry are you talking about, my good woman? Do you think you can fool me with your lies so easily? Why don't you come right out and say that you . . . you! Come over here and look at me, will you?" (Hoopoe dragged his wife into the house, lowered his voice, bent his head, and muttered through clenched teeth:) "Why not just tell me you went there to commit adultery, eh? Is what I say slander and lies? Tell me, tell me again that it's a lie, why don't you?"

His wife took courage and freed herself from his grasp.

"You're a madman, that's what you are," she said disdainfully, and turned her back to go out.

But her husband grabbed her strongly by the arm, so she could not move from her place. "Stay where you are!" he yelled, "Where are you off to like that? Do you think you can escape punishment at my hands by simply going out? Now I'll show you what kind of madman I am! Do you think you can save your skin so easily? So you believe I'm dead and gone the way of all flesh, and that makes it all right for you to talk back and commit adultery with that bastard, is that it? Yes, yes, yes. Tell me I'm dead, will you? For Heaven's sake! Tell me I'm dead and done for, will you?" And each time he repeated "I'm dead, am I?" he gave his wife a terrible blow, letting his fists fall where they might: on her head, her shoulders, her waist. . . . His wife had bowed her head to avoid blows to her face, while with one hand she tried to hold her baby to her bosom, and with her free hand she tried to grab her husband's arm.

Hoopoe grew even more enraged, and the blows became still more violent.

"You fool of a Hoopoe, what do you want from me?" screamed his wife, wailing.

The baby at her breast started to cry. The other child had withdrawn to a corner and watched the familiar scene in silence.

"I have to beat you with a big stick, woman!" Hoopoe shouted at last and, leaving his wife, he started to search the room for a stick. He failed to find what he was looking for, and his eyes fell on his heavy boots. He picked up one of the boots, which was heavily hobnailed. Meanwhile his wife placed the baby on the bed and grabbed the wine jug to arm herself for the fight.

"Hit me if you can, and I'll break this jug over your head!" she shouted boldly.

"Damn it!" muttered Hoopoe and, letting go of his heavy foot gear, he rushed to snatch the jug from her hands. But she was too quick for him: she kicked aside the boots and ran from the house, jug in hand. Her husband followed in a fury.

They raised such a racket that the neighborhood women and children gathered to enjoy the familiar sight. Hoopoe ran after his wife, who held the jug tightly in her hands. Hoopoe was bare-headed, barefoot, and in his underwear.

The din that filled the air was beyond description, as the women burst out laughing, the children shouted, whistled, and screamed "Hoopoe!" and the young men of the quarter roared in concert, "Atta boy, Hoopoe! Go get her, Hoopoe! Atta boy!"

Hoopoe ran through the uproar, his eyes fixed on the jug in his wife's hands. His shirt flapped in the air. Wine sloshed about in the jug and spilled to the ground in small quantities. The distance between husband and wife gradually narrowed, because the jug slowed her down. When only a few steps separated them, she raised her hands and, without stopping, smashed the jug to the ground with all her might. It shattered into pieces, and the wine it contained erupted like a deep dark-red rose. The thick, heavy bottom of the jug remained where it had fallen, but the thin walls broke into a thousand pieces, scattering left and right. The red wine stained the ground, resembling coagulated blood. The thirsty, sunburnt ground sucked it up almost immediately.

Hoopoe was shaken to the very bottom of his soul. He stopped at once. He felt as if he had been knocked down. His eyes grew dim. Losing control of himself completely, he bent down, picked a big stone from the ground, and hurled it with an awful fury at his fleeing wife. It struck her at the waist. She screamed desperately, mechanically ran a few more steps, and then fell in a heap to the ground.

There was a sudden lull in the tumult. Everyone seemed petrified.

Levon Bashalian (Pashalian)

(1868–1943)

Born in Constantinople, Levon Bashalian received his education at the Perperien (Berberian) school. He began his literary career in journalism, in such progressive periodicals as *Masis, Arevelk* (Orient), and *Hayrenik* (Fatherland). He collaborated with Arpiar Arpiarian (1852–1908) and Grigor Zohrap (1861–1915), and his short stories and novellas soon established his position in the realist movement. He was a member of the Hnchakian Party when the government began persecuting political parties in 1890, and he fled to Paris for safety. During the 1896 massacres he was forced once again to seek refuge abroad, this time in London, where he joined Arpiarian in founding and editing *Nor kyank* (New life, 1898–1901), a literary and political bimonthly that was the mouthpiece of the Reformed Hnchakian Party. This paper was later merged with *Hnchak*, the Party's official organ. In a letter from London to Arshak Chopanian (Arshag Tchobanian, 1872–1954) dated 4 July 1898, he describes their (his and Arpiarian's) gloomy financial situation, which was so bad that they did not know where their next meal would come from. "This is the third time," he says, "that my watch has been at the pawnbroker's."[1]

---

1. *Arevmtahay groghneri namakani* (Letters of Western Armenian writers) (Yerevan, 1972), n.p.n.

The year 1902 was a turning point in Bashalian's life. He all but abandoned literature and went to Baku as an employee of a French oil company, where he remained until the Bolshevik Revolution of 1920. He then returned to Paris and settled there. In 1922–23 he was a member of the Armenian National Delegation to talks connected with the Lausanne Peace Treaty. He visited Soviet Armenia in 1924 as a member of the Central Committee for Armenian Refugees and the Armenian General Benevolent Union, to organize the construction of settlements, schools, and hospitals. In 1928 he founded a bilingual monthly review for the French Armenian community, *Le Foyer* (The hearth, 1928–32), which lasted until 1932. He died in Vichy, France.

Although his literary output was small, Bashalian is one of the most noted realists of the epoch. All his subjects are taken from real-life events and situations, fraught with sadness, disappointments, and broken hearts and lives. His sharp observation, restrained expression, and his gift for straightforward narration, without literary flourishes, makes his stories simple, captivating, and impressive. His stories and short novels include *Hmayatape* (The disillusioned); *Dratsuhin* (The neighbor woman, 1888); *Verjin hambuyre* (The last kiss); *Nor zgeste* (The new outfit, 1890); *Terterin ukhte* (The vow of the priest), which was made into a short film in Armenia; *Aghavniner* (Pigeons, 1894), and *Tseghin dzayne* (The voice of the people, 1898). His other works consist of news reports, newspaper columns, and memoirs. His works were scattered in various periodicals until 1939, when his stories were collected into a volume titled *Noraveper yev patmvatzkner* (Short novels and stories), published in Paris, with an introduction by Arshak Chopanian.

ANGEL[2]

Many a time I saw her in our house. She would come over to sew one of my sister's dresses. From the first time I saw her, she left a deep impression on me, a mixed feeling of admiration and compassion that came from her charming beauty and the persistent sadness of her melancholy eyes. Her eyes were very dark, but it was the white surrounding that darkness that made her eyes so inviting. She had dark chestnut-colored hair, so abundant that you

2. Levon Bashalian, "Angel," trans. Chris Keseci, *Ararat* (Autumn 2001), 35–36.

would not know what to do with it. She had a delicate and graceful nature. But what would touch my heart the most was her lusterless eyes, which made me think they were always tearful.

Her name was Angel and she had to be twenty-five years old. She was a serious girl, so concerned with her work that you would think she was mute. When she spoke, you got the feeling that this girl was destined for a socially better position, where she could let her talents shine. I have no doubt that she went to school, because she spoke clean and pure Armenian, she knew a little French, and she was capable of playing the piano.

After the first days of cautious acquaintance, we quickly became friends—or should I say more honestly, I became her friend. To my gallant compliments, she would respond with a sad smile, which would encourage me more than discourage me because it would give me the opportunity to see her beautiful tiny white rows of teeth. I thought I would eventually be able to subdue her. I did not know anything about her. I heard that she was once engaged and that the engagement was broken for reasons I didn't know, reasons which I never sought to know, because it had only been seven or eight months since they arrived in our village, and they led a very solitary life, she, her father, and her mother, in one corner of the village. It is not to justify myself, but not to forget to say either, that my feelings were not a mere cold whim or naughtiness but rather feelings of love, where I would think of a little or a great deal of poetry. I thought it was going to be easy to console the heart of that wonderful, sad girl.

And from the first day, I did not make any progress. I doubled my compliments and she equally doubled the sadness of her smile. I do not know why I still had yet to dare to move from expressions to actions.

When I found myself away from her, I would have these foolish desires, and I would suddenly make a definite decision to carry out these desires. But when the opportunity to see her presented itself, I would stand a few steps away from her with my secret enthusiasm. The wish of having that beautiful statue in my arms was burning within me. And the unfulfillment of that wish was frustrating me.

One day I could not endure it any longer; without noticing the suppliant expression in her look and instead of my usual words of affection, I moved closer to her, and my hand became buried in her hair. She jumped up to free her hair from my touch, and in a soft voice said, "What you did was not a good thing, Mardik Effendi."

What's more, she had a humble attitude. She had nimble movements when she bent down and lifted her head to free her hair from me. My being was moved, but since my attempt was unsuccessful, my anger motivated me to exclaim: "Don't you have a heart? Are you a heartless person?"

I said it and regretted it. Her big dark eyes became filled with tears and with a reproachful expression became fixed on me.

"Excuse me," I sincerely said, "if I hurt you, but if you are rattled, say so, don't shy away."

"No, no, I don't have anything to say," she replied. "You said it well: I don't have a heart, or I don't have one particularly now, for me there is nothing left in this life—no pain, no happiness."

"Have you had much grief?" I asked, suddenly remembering the vague knowledge I had of her past life.

She didn't reply.

My curiosity was awakened. I desired to know that sad girl's secret.

"I think you were engaged some time ago," I said. "Were you severely hurt?"

She appeared to be making a great effort to control herself, and she finally said, "Yes, I have grieved. Why do you ask? My life is a sad story."

And at my expectant look, she continued, "Two years after I finished school, I was engaged. I was nineteen years old then. I had learned a lot; like many people I didn't have great expectations for myself. Our family was not very well-to-do. My father was an employee in a warehouse, and he didn't make much. Therefore, he wanted very much to have me engaged. I became engaged to a young man from the village. Arsen Tigranian was his name. Maybe you have read about his sad end in the newspapers. I knew him before we were engaged. I would always see him on the street. I encountered him everywhere I went—and I could feel that he loved me. When he began to visit our house regularly and our engagement was decided within our family circle, it was then when I completely understood how much he loved me. He was twenty-six years old and he worked in a warehouse as a clerk. I don't think he earned much, but it didn't matter to me. He wasn't very handsome, but he had an ordinary complexion. He was a serious and sad young man. He would stare at my face for long periods of time without saying anything. In that stare he would put all of his love and tenderness. I didn't love him with all of my heart, but I would respect him.

"It was under these circumstances that he suddenly stopped coming to our home. I heard that my father had someone tell him not to visit our house again. The Sunday he was told this, he came to our house, but my mother saw him coming from a distance when she went upstairs, and kept the door closed. I was told that I would be engaged to someone else, a bright, well-to-do young man who saw me outside and liked me.

"They besieged me from all sides. You would think they were competing with each other to see who could say worse things about Arsen. They said he had a quick temper; he could not even support himself, how could he support a wife? Moreover, he is a very quiet man; anybody living with him would get sick of him. To make a long story short, one or two months later I was engaged again. I returned the gold ring Arsen gave me. He did not accept it and sent it back, saying I should keep it as a souvenir of him.

"You see it's the ring on this hand.

"As I was saying, I was engaged for a second time. You'll say, of course, that I fell in love very quickly. Maybe you have good reason to say so. But have you ever thought about the ailments of the human heart? My separation from Arsen hurt me very much, especially the sad premonition I had of how hard a blow this would be for him. But I was weak. The first few days I completely resisted my parents, but I became discouraged and my strength to resist ran out. They said so much, they did so much, that I couldn't think any longer.

"My second fiancé was a thirty- to thirty-five-year-old man, a very merry, happy-go-lucky man. The fact that he had a pharmacy, they would say, meant he was well-to-do. There is no need to give you his name; he is now married and has children. He had a hand-some face; he was youthful and healthy. Whenever he entered our house, he would bring joy in with him. My father and mother espe-cially liked the idea of his being my fiancé. As for the feelings I had for him, I was not very sure. But I would get great pleasure from him, so much so that gradually I would forget about the remorse that came with the sad memory of my separation from Arsen. For the first four to five months, my conscience would torment me, especially since I heard the poor young man was very discouraged because of what happened and was very sad. But later I calmed down, because his mother noticed her son's condition and engaged him to another girl.

"From then on, I gave myself to my new fiancé. Frequently we would go for a walk, all of us together, but more often just the two of us alone, and he had so many jokes and so many funny things to say that I would hold myself from dying with laughter. Soon our engagement was over and we were busy preparing for the wedding.

"One Sunday evening, an evening that I will never forget. . . ."

She uttered a deep sigh and there was a cold silence, then she continued.

"One Sunday evening, I went out for a walk with my fiancé, as was our custom. He was telling a funny story again and I held his arm with my head close to his. I listened to him with a smile, then suddenly I saw Arsen. I had not seen him since our separation. I had a pale appearance and had grown thin. He looked directly into my eyes, and in his stare I saw everything: sadness, bitterness, supplication. I was left with half a smile on my lips. He must have seen my careless gaiety, because his arms were folded in hopelessness and his face contracted so much that I thought he was going to cry. He stopped and we continued to walk, but from the corner of my eye I saw his trembling hand reach to the back pocket of his coat. I don't know how it happened, but I had the feeling something terrible was about to happen; so I closed my eyes and embraced my fiancé like crazy. I put my head on his shoulder, leaning on him, when suddenly we heard the explosion of a firearm, only five or six steps away."

Her eyes grew even larger, and in them you could read the horror of the shocking scene so vividly that you felt it was all happening at that moment. Her discolored face became animate and a light red spread over her pale face.

"From every direction people came running. I didn't have the courage to turn and look behind me. I had a need to flee that place before another second passed. My fiancé was curious and wanted to stay but I pulled him away by the arm. When we arrived home I left my fiancé in the hall with my parents while he told them about the events that had taken place. I had a headache and a nervous shock. I retreated to my room, where on my bed I began to cry like mad.

"That night I could not sleep, nor the many nights after. As soon as I would go to bed, I would suddenly see Arsen's sad and serious face that gave me a pleading look, and I would see his hand reach into his pocket and pull out the revolver, put it into his mouth, and fire. The sound of the revolver would always ring in my ears, always deep in my head, always resounding in the bottom of my heart. I forgot to tell you, when they lifted him off the street, he was already dead: he had indeed emptied the revolver into his mouth. It was I who prompted his death.

"How did I not know that he was not an ordinary man? I didn't care that he could not cope with the pain in his heart. He was one of those rare men who either love or die. His love for me was not a whim, but an irresistible need of his heart. I didn't give any importance to all of this; I brushed him off. How did I not understand his heart? Subsequently, I comprehended the magnitude of his love, and in my repentance, I now love him, after he died for me. Only now do I understand his boundless love. Poor boy, he thought he could forget about me or that is what he believed he could do, for I heard later that he had gone to his fiancée's house only once, but could not bring himself to step inside. At last, when he saw me on the road, he perceived complete nothingness in his ruined life and he executed his awful intention. Surely he was tormented by these thoughts for a long time; if not, why did he carry the revolver in his pocket? He wanted me to see his death, so that his bloody condemnation would punish me.

"After all of this, it is not likely for me to live with someone else, to be happy and joyful. The next Sunday my fiancé came, but I could not see him. My father and mother had heard what had happened and knew the reason for Arsen's suicide. When I told them I wanted to break off the engagement and to tell my fiancé not to come to our house, they could not argue with me. I simply detested my second fiancé, especially when envisioning the images of the two men. The next month, I heard, my fiancé proposed to someone else.

"Since then many years have passed. Many men have wanted me, but I refused them all. Whenever my mother and father pressure me to marry someone, I mention Arsen's name and they don't make a sound. I have dedicated myself to his memory, and I live with his memory. All I have from him is this ring, and I will wear it to my grave. Now do you understand why I am so sad? You flirt with me fervently and with the enthusiasm of a young man, but now will you understand how distant your words are for me? I didn't want my father and mother to support themselves alone— therefore, excluding honor and other feelings, I became a seamstress to have a livelihood and help my family. What did I care about anything else? I don't have any wishes or ambitions. My heart is dead."

She stood up, gathered her materials, and mechanically put them into the bundle. Then she extended her hand.

She said, "Good-bye."

I could not find the words to respond.

Hovhannes Tumanian

(1869–1923)

The dean of Eastern Armenian poets, Hovhannes Tumanian, was born in the village of Dsegh in the district of Lori, northern Armenia, the eldest of eight children. His father, Ter-Tadevos, was a priest and of noble descent, and Hovhannes saw him as a model. "The best and greatest thing I ever had in my life was my father," he states in a biographical note. He spent his childhood in the breathtaking magnificence of Lori. His impressions of the people of this region, their legends and customs, and the beauties of nature that surrounded him later became a powerful source of inspiration and were vividly recreated in his works.

He received his early education in the local parish school. In 1883 he moved to Tiflis, where he attended the Nersisian school, the best educational institution of the time, but his studies were cut short in 1887. The following year he married, and eventually he had ten children to raise and educate. He worked for a while in the Armenian diocesan office and then in a publishing house, but he was obviously not cut out to be a functionary. In 1893 he abandoned his job and dedicated his life entirely to literature. In his autobiography he has this to say of that period: "With deep sadness I look back on those five hellish years of my past."

By this time Tumanian had begun to contribute to various journals, and his first collection of poems was published in 1890. The famous Russian poet Valery Bryusov (1873–1924) described him as "largely self-educated, and an extremely well-read man, if not systematically so, . . . a southern type in whom two principles, fun and genius, are astonishingly synthesized."[1] Tumanian's favorite authors were Shakespeare, Byron, Pushkin, and Lermontov.

His earliest poems, written in the 1880s, deal with popular and patriotic themes and bear the influence of Ghevond Alishan (1820–1901) and Rafayel Patkanian (1830–92). His first book of poetry, *Banasteghtzutiunner* (Poems), which appeared in 1890 and was followed by a second volume in 1892, marked a turning point in Armenian poetry, but it took about a decade for this to be recognized and his work to be emulated by his contemporaries.

His principle was "Look to nature and the people." By the turn of the century, in a large number of new works and in revisions of some of his older ones, he had begun to focus poetry on real life and real people. His works in various genres—narrative poems, legends, short stories, epic poems, and tales—depict the social and psychological conflicts of village life and Armenian reality in general, drawing themes from national traditions, long-standing customs, and even superstitions. The Armenian soil and the psyche of the Armenian people—their pains, joys, virtues, and moral values—found expression in his works. These essential elements are expressed with utter sincerity and transparency, qualities that characterized the man himself. Each of his lyric poems forms part of what he called "the biography of a soul" and enshrines a thought that makes the reader ponder the meaning of life. His characters are simple villagers, bent to their difficult daily tasks, in whom he discerns a strong individuality, a wealth of emotions, and a popular wisdom that often help them withstand the cruel realities of life—though sometimes they succumb to them. The passions, pains, and joys of his heroes continue to stir his readers.

Tumanian was prolific. His earliest narrative poems are *Maron* (1887) and *Loretsi Sakon* (1889). In the former, Maro, caught in a forced marriage, frees herself, but, hounded by society, eventually kills herself. In the latter, Sako, a strong but naïve youth who is driven by superstition and ignorance, imagines that he is pursued by evil beings and ends up

---

1. Quoted in Arra M. Garab, ed., *Hovhannes Tumanian: A Selection of Stories, Lyrics, and Epic Poems* (New York, 1971), 11.

losing his mind. *Anush* (1890, revised 1901–2), which is considered Tumanian's masterpiece and was made into an opera by Armen Tigranian in 1912, has a simple plot. Saro and Mosi are friends, and Saro and Mosi's sister Anush are in love. One feast day Saro and Mosi engage in a traditional wrestling match; Saro gets carried away and topples Mosi to the ground. To avenge his public humiliation, Mosi hunts Saro down and shoots him dead. Anush goes insane and throws herself into the turbulent waters of the River Debed.

"Surprisingly, some have construed the poem (and a number of other works dealing with similar themes) as a nostalgic elegy for yesteryear. If there is any nostalgia here on the part of Tumanian, it is for noble love and the moral purity that characterized the peasantry. In all other respects, it is a total negation of outdated and disastrous notions of honor and tradition. In *Anush,* as in other works revolving around similar subjects, Tumanian's characters are entrapped by conventions; they have no life of their own beyond the long-standing code of behavior, and are thus victims of ineluctable fate. . . . This has been seen as a manifestation of Tumanian's realism, which assumes even greater sophistication when it documents the ravages of money and industrialization on this essentially backward and conservative society."[2]

In 1902 Tumanian compiled the third cycle of the popular epic *Sasuntsi Davit* (David of Sasun), which depicts David's adventures following his return from Egypt.[3] Tumanian's version is based on three ancient variants, and it is considered the best. *Tmkaberdi arume* (The capture of Fort Tmuk, 1902), based on an incident that occurred during Nadir Shah's invasion of Armenia in the eighteenth century, is full of valor, fraud, patriotism, and treachery, and served as the basis of Alexander Spendiarian's opera *Almast.*

Among Tumanian's most notable works are *Akhtamar* (1954); *Shunn u katun* (The dog and the cat, 1908); *Parvana* (Mayfly, 1903); *Gikor* (1907), the moving story, often adapted to film, of a boy (the title character) who is uprooted from his native village, only to wither away in the big city; *Vosku karase* (The pot of gold), *Tern u tzaran* (The master and the servant, 1910), and *Hskan* (The giant), all written in 1908; *Katil me meghr* (A drop of honey, 1909); *Kaj Nazar* (Nazar the brave, 1912);

2. Kevork B. Bardakjian, *A Reference Guide to Modern Armenian Literature, 1500–1920* (Detroit, 2000), 181.

3. For text see vol. 2 of the present anthology, 990–1019.

Aghavnu vank (The dove monastery, 1913); and *Tagavore yev charchin* (The king and the peddler, 1917).

In the long poem *Depi anhune* (Journey to infinity, 1894) and in the numerous quatrains he wrote in his later years, Tumanian contemplates the eternal issues of life and death and explores the multiple facets of reality and human destiny. His long unfinished poem *Hazaran Blbul*[4] deals with the philosophical and aesthetic role that art plays in the perfection of men and society. His essays on and studies of the lyric poets Nahapet Kuchak, Naghash Hovnatan, and Sayat-Nova are important contributions to literary criticism. He translated a number of works by Pushkin, Byron, Lermontov, and Longfellow. Many of his works have been translated into Russian, all the languages spoken in the former Soviet Union, French, English, German, Spanish, Italian, and a number of eastern languages.

Early in the 1900s Tumanian became seriously involved in social and humanitarian activities aimed at establishing harmony and friendship among various ethnic groups in the Caucasus. In the period 1905–7, when the Armenians and the Tatars were at war with each other, he worked tirelessly to end hostilities. These activities brought him into conflict with the government, and he was twice imprisoned (1908–9 and 1911–12). The 1915 genocide in Western Armenia was a terrible blow to him, but he dedicated himself to organizing relief for refugees and orphans. He visited Alashkert and Van, which were devastated by the Turks, became president of the Armenian Aid Committee (1921–22), and in this capacity visited Constantinople in 1921.

In 1899 Tumanian organized a literary club in Tiflis, with some fifteen prominent literary figures. The club was called *Vernatun* (the upper room), as they held their meetings on the fifth floor of Tumanian's house. In 1908 the club was closed by the government. In 1912 Tumanian founded the Caucasian Society of Armenian Writers, which lasted until 1921. In 1918 he lost both his brother and his beloved son, the latter was a volunteer soldier in the war. In late 1922 his health deteriorated and he was moved to Moscow for cancer treatments. He died on 23 March 1923; his body was brought to Tiflis and buried in the Armenian cemetery there.

Tumanian is cherished as a poet by all Armenians. He received many honors from the Armenian state, and his collected works have gone through many printings, both in Armenia and in the diaspora.

---

4. A mythical bird of Armenian legend that represents the reawakening of nature and is also a symbol of beauty and harmony.

MY FRIEND NESO[5]

1

We village children were always happy together.

There was neither a school for us, nor lessons to learn. We were as free as birds and played all day long. Ah, how we played! What good friends we were, and how we all loved each other! When we'd feel hungry we'd run home for a chunk of bread and a piece of cheese from the crock, and then we'd be off again. Sometimes we would gather in the evenings to talk and tell stories.

One of the boys was named Neso. He knew so many stories and fairy tales that there just was no end to them.

On summer moonlit nights we'd sit around in a circle on the logs piled in our yard and gaze enchantedly at Neso's face. He would become handsome with inspiration. He told us stories about Gun-Pen, about the bird of paradise and the kingdoms of Light and Dark.

"Come on, Neso, tell us another story. The one about the blind king, and the one about the parrot, and about the bald man and the beardless man."

2

One day they opened a school in our village. My parents sent me to school, as did about twenty or thirty others. Tuition was three rubles a year, and that is why many village children whose parents could not pay the fee were excluded. Most of my friends, including Neso, were not going to go to school.

We were being separated for the first time in our lives, and the school and the teacher were the ones who were separating us. Now, for the first time, we were given to understand that some of us were better off, while others were poor. I can still hear Neso's wail as he rolled in the dust and cried: "I want to go to school, too!"

And I can still hear his father's voice, shouting: "For God's sake, can't you understand! I don't have the money! If I had three

---

5. Hovannes Tumanian, "My Friend Neso," in *We of the Mountains: Armenian Short Stories* (Moscow, 1972), 59–62. Translated by Fainna Glagoleva.

rubles I'd buy grain with it, so's you wouldn't all be hungry. I don't have the money!"

Neso and my other friends who were not at school would come around and cluster at the threshold, peeping in to have a look at us. But the teacher would not let them in. He chased them away. He wouldn't even let us play together during recess. He said that outsiders had no business playing with schoolchildren. My friends would walk off, sit down outside school and wait till we were let out. Then we would all walk home together.

Gradually during that first year I made new friends at school. By the end of the year Neso and my other friends who were not at school no longer waited outside for me.

3

I attended our village school for two years. Then my father took me to the neighboring town and enrolled me in the secondary school there. This was a new world to me. All the houses had red roofs, and the townspeople were all dressed in fine, clean clothes. The school, too, was large and beautiful, and instead of one teacher, as we had back home, there were several, one of whom was a woman. This was a pleasant surprise to me.

In conformity with my new surroundings and school, my clothing, too, underwent a change. Now I wore a beautiful, clean, town school uniform. Thus transformed I returned to my village for my holidays. When Neso and my other old friends heard I was home they came by first thing in the morning, hanging about, trying to peep in. I went out to greet them. I don't know what we said to each other, but I do remember that our old camaraderie was gone. The first thing they noticed was my uniform. Neso cocked an eye at my short regulation shirt and said: "It looks like they pulled the feathers out of your tail!"

Everyone laughed. I was offended, but said nothing. Then Neso felt the cloth of my jacket, and all the others followed suit. They all exclaimed at the softness of the material. It was then that I first really took notice of their clothes, of how filthy and torn they were. Indeed, the entire village appeared poverty-stricken and filthy to my eyes.

4

Two years later my father took me to a big city and enrolled me in a still larger school. When I returned from there my former playmates, now grown-up, came over, greeted me as did the other peasants and stood to one side respectfully, as they did. Just once during our conversation, when someone asked me whether I recalled our days together at the village school, Neso spoke up.

"Do you remember the way we used to sit around on the logs in your yard at night and tell stories?" he asked.

"How could I ever forget that! That's one of the nicest things I remember."

I thought Neso seemed pleased, yet he remained at a distance, a stranger.

However, when the time came for me to return to the city my father hired a horse for me from Neso's father. Neso was supposed to accompany the horse that I would ride. When we set out, I on horseback and Neso in his rags and decrepit sandals on foot, I felt miserable. After we had gone but a short way I said I preferred to walk and dismounted. We proceeded, either walking together or taking turns riding. Neso was pleased, but I realized that he did not understand my feelings of fairness and comradeship, but, rather, considered me foolish for walking. I felt hurt, but worse was yet to come.

We stopped on the way to have a bite. When we came to cutting the watermelon, I handed Neso my pocket knife. Then, when we were ready to start out again, I noticed that it had disappeared. Neso swore he had returned it and that I had put it in my pocket. Though I knew for a fact that he had not, I went through my pockets. Finally, we set off. It was obvious that he had taken the knife, and later people saw it on him. As we continued on our way my heart ached, not for my lost knife certainly, but for that far greater loss I had sustained and of which my companion was ignorant.

When we reached our destination and Neso was to return, I bought him a length of cotton for a jacket beside the fee for hiring the horse. He greeted this with, "But won't you give me a tip?"

I was terribly embarrassed. I tipped him. However, from then on, every time I recalled the days of my childhood and the moonlit nights as we sat on the logs with Neso telling us stories, my heart would fill with pain and pity.

5

"Neso is poor. . . . Neso is ignorant. . . . Neso is crushed by the hopeless poverty of village life. . . . If he had had an education, if he had been properly brought up and provided for, he might have turned out to be a much better person than I."

This is what I say to myself now when I think of Neso and try to absolve him, to raise him in my eyes and love him as I once did in my childhood. I want Neso always to appear to me as he was in those quiet, starry, moonlit nights, but I find this impossible, I cannot. Immediately another picture, one that is shameful and oppressing, comes to mind.

Having completed my education and made a place for myself in the world, I again returned to my native village. The village square was crowded and noisy that day. Neso stood bound to a post in the center of the square, his head hanging in shame.

I was told that he was being punished for stealing. I intervened on his behalf and he was released. But in my mind's eye I still see him standing there in the scorching sun, bound to a post, his head hanging as the crowd rumbled. Such things as stealing and flogging were commonplace in our village, but I cannot forget this event: Neso sitting on the logs on moonlit nights, telling us stories. Neso so pure and sweet, my childhood friend.

AKHTAMAR[6]

Every night, in secret
a boy walks from his village
on the shore of Lake Van
into its sea.

Without a boat or a sail
with virile arms parting

---

6. *"Akhtamar,"* in *Anthology of Armenian Poetry,* ed. and trans. Diana Der Hovanessian and Marzbed Margossian (New York, 1978), 160–62.

the water, he swims toward
the island floating in front,

where a single, bright light
like a beacon from a lighthouse
on the dark island
guides him on his way.

Beautiful Tamar builds the fire
on the beach nightly,
and waits impatiently
in the shrubbery nearby.

· ·

The heavy sea curls and roars,
but the boy's heart is buoyant.
He fights the pounding water
that shouts in his ears.

Tamar's heart heaves with the water
as she hears the waves breaking,
as she burns with the taper
burning in the dark.

Silence now. On the dark shore
one black shadow
finds the other and there
is one shadow again.

Only the waves of Lake Van
touch the shore and move now.
They go back to sea grumbling
with muffled news.

As if they were whispering
to the stars arched above them
about the virginal Tamar,
calling her shameless names.

While the waters murmur and gossip
time runs out for the two.
One enters the rough sea,
the other prays, left behind.

· ·

"Who is he anyway
so brave and so brash,
so drunk with his love
that he dares the sea by night?

He crosses from foreign shores
to kiss our Tamar?
What does he think we are
to give her up?"

The sullen boys of the island
defy the stranger and one night
stamp down the fire
that Tamar has lit.

And Tamar's lover,
swimming, is lost in the dark.
The wind lifts his sighs.
Akh! Tamar, he calls.

Under the steep rocks
in the frightening darkness
where the wild sea shouts
Akh! Tamar, he cries.

In the morning the waters,
rippled only now, and calm,
wash him ashore.
On his cold lips two words
are frozen forever,
"Akh! Tamar,"
the island's new name.

MY SONG[7]

I have treasures without measure.
I have wealth that has no bound.

---

7. Ibid., 159.

Many graces are showered on me,
opulence you cannot count.

Beautiful is my trove of treasures,
filling my heart, free and wide.
Whatever I give
(love is endless) comes back multiplied.

I am dauntless. I am fearless
of temptation and of thieves.
I shower back on the envious
only what I have received.

I've been wealthy. I was lucky
since the bright day of my birth,
knowing the path I travel
is a one-way road on earth.

I have treasures without measure,
I have wealth and luck that's rare
There's no limit. There's no boundary
to heaven's riches made to share.

Yervand Otian

(1869–1926)

Yervand Otian (Odian) was born in Constantinople to an aristocratic family. His uncle, Grigor Otian (1834–87), a prominent figure in the Reform Movement, and his aunt, Yevpimé Avetisian (Anaïs, 1871–1950), the poet-writer, greatly influenced his literary development. At the age of ten he went to France and Italy with his uncle, and the following year he went to Romania, where his father served as consul of the Ottoman Government. On his return to Constantinople, he studied at the Perperian (Berberian) school for about two years (1883–84), but most of his education was acquired from private tutors and the family's rich library. The 1896 massacres obliged him to flee his birthplace. He went to Egypt by way of Athens, settled in Paris for three years, then moved on to London, Alexandria, Bombay, and back to Alexandria.

In 1908, when the Young Turks came to power and the second Ottoman Constitution was affirmed, with its apparent promises of liberty and justice, Otian returned to Turkey, in the hope of putting an end to his wanderings. But in less than seven years, in 1915, he was forced on a death march to the Syrian deserts, along with hundreds of thousands of his countrymen. He was one of the few who survived. He returned to Constantinople and eventually settled in Cairo, where he died in 1926.

Yervand Otian was a prolific and restless writer. With rare exceptions, he resided in any one place scarcely long enough to become acquainted with it. From 1888 to 1896 he wrote for the papers *Arevelk* (The Orient), *Masis,* and *Hayrenik* (Fatherland). In almost every city he stayed in, he founded, either alone or in partnership, a newspaper, including *Azat khosk* (Free speech), *Azat bem* (Free tribune), *Tertik* (Pamphlet), *Manana* (Manna), *Shavigh* (Pathway), *Ignat Agha* (a satirical weekly), *Arev* (Sun), and others. The brief life of these papers kept him from establishing a clear literary and artistic direction. His livelihood depended on his writing; thus he wrote incessantly and in haste, and seldom or never took time to revise or reedit his work.

The literary climate of the time and his varied talents led him to the genres of the novel, the short story, the chronicle, drama, satire, and memoirs. Contemporary characters and everyday life formed the background and often the very substance of his novels and stories, which are full of mystery and political intrigue. For him the plot was of primary importance; psychological considerations played a secondary role. He was a keen observer and a skillful storyteller, and he earned a place in Armenian literature primarily as a satirist. Some consider him equal to Hakob Paronian (Baronian, 1841–93). Paronian's satire, however, is forceful and piercing, aimed particularly at merchants, council members, political activists, and pseudo-intellectuals, and exposing hypocrisy and self-glorification. The working class is entirely absent from his works. Otian's is more sophisticated, closer to humor. Nonetheless, his *Azgayin yerespokhannere* (National deputies) and *Heghapokhakan makabuytzner* (Parasites of the revolution) are reminiscent of Baronian's *Azgayin jojer* (National bigwigs) and *Metzapativ muratskanner* (Honorable beggars) respectively. In a sense, Otian was Paronian's pupil.

Otian's more popular works include *Entanik, pativ, baroyakan* (Family, honor, morality); *Taghakanin kine* (The parish councilor's wife); *Mijnord ter-papan* (The matchmaker-priest); and *Yes drsetsi chem arner* (I won't marry an outsider). All these novels expose the ills of society and the vice in human nature; the last focuses on the contempt of the self-styled "pure bred" Constantinople Armenians for Armenians in the provinces. Other works, such as *"Abdul Hamit yev Sherlok Holms"* (Abdul Hamid and Sherlock Holmes), a detective story; *Saliha Hanem kam banake brnavorin dem* (Saliha Hanem, or the army against the tyrant), a novel of "Ottoman revolutionary life"; *Matniche* (The traitor); and *Tiv 17 khafiyen* (Spy number 17), reflect on the regime of the Young Turks, World War I, and the 1915 massacre of Armenians. *Paterazm yev khaghaghutiun kam entanekan namakani* (War and peace, or family letters) consists of the letters exchanged between two brothers, one in the army, who lives in peace, and the other married, who lives in a constant state of strife. *Tasnerku tari Polsen durs, 1896–1908* (Twelve years away from Constantinople, 1896–1908), is a book of reminiscences. *Zavallen* (The poor soul) is a vaudeville-type play, and *Charshili Artin Agha*, written in collaboration with Mikayel Kiurchian (Gürdjian, 1879–1965) is a satirical play on the conflict of wills between an old-fashioned, uneducated, wealthy merchant and his equally uneducated wife, who assumes the manners of high society.

Otian's masterpiece is the trilogy *Enker Panjuni* (Comrade Panjuni), which consists of three sequential novels: *Arakelutiun i Tzaplvar* (A mission to Tzaplvar, 1910), *Panjuni Vaspurakani mej* (Panjuni in Vasburakan, 1914), and *Panjuni daragrutyan mej* (Panjuni in exile, 1924), relating the adventures of a Marxist propagandist who audits social sciences in Geneva, returns to Constantinople, and, finding the field crowded, sets himself the task of mobilizing the Armenian proletariat against the bourgeoisie and the capitalists, none of which truly existed in the Armenian provinces, especially in the rural areas. There is neither passion nor bitterness nor alarm in Otian's narrative, which exposes the absurd activities of this bizarre character through caricature.[1]

The first collection of Otian's works appeared in Yerevan in 1934, followed by four other editions in 1956, 1960–63, 1978, and 1988.

FROM COMRADE PANJUNI[2]

In Lieu of a Preface

If I were a plagiarist, I would not feel it necessary to write these few explanatory lines and, without making a sound, I would represent as my own that packet of letters which by some happy chance fell into my hands and which I want to make available to the public.

There are twelve of these letters, written in the course of one year. In the manuscript the language more nearly approaches the

---

1. Kevork B. Bardakjian, *A Reference Guide to Modern Armenian Literature, 1500–1920* (Detroit, 2000), 168.
2. Yervand Otian, *Comrade Panjuni*, trans. Jack Antreassian (New York, 1977), 19–36.

Caucasian Armenian idiom. However, I felt it fitting for the convenience of the reader to convert it, as much as possible, into the modern vernacular. Besides, the writer himself is a pseudo-Russian Armenian, having been born in Turkey.

If these letters are read as satiric essays, that fault is surely not the writer's. For the real author is an Armenian socialist revolutionary of resounding faith, fortified by firm principles, who has explored the most remote boundaries of sobriety and there entrenched himself.

The letters appear to be directed to a central body, on whose behalf the correspondent has apparently been assigned to do his missionary work.

Signed Yervand Otian

Tzaplvar, September 15, 1908
Dear Comrades:

As soon as I received your instructions, I hastened to depart from Arabkir. After traveling for four days and staying overnight in the villages of Shepik, Vaghshen, Krani and Mashkert, I reached the village of Tzaplvar, which in my opinion offers the most receptive environment for our propaganda.

Tzaplvar is a thoroughly Armenian village, with twenty families, set in a beautiful and fertile valley through which the Jrberik stream runs. The villagers for the most part are prosperous, diligent and hard-working. Unfortunately, they did not endure much suffering under the old regime, and for this reason have not been greatly impressed by the new one. They were persecuted on occasion, but mainly by the Kurds of the neighboring Komrash village.

It should not be necessary for me to say that Tzaplvar is buried in profound ignorance, particularly on socialist matters. I have been here for fifteen days, having embarked on my propaganda work immediately upon my arrival, and I haven't yet been able to insinuate into the minds of these villagers the massive crimes of capitalism, the imperative need for workers' syndicates and the just demands of the proletariat. But I have not despaired. On the contrary, their lack of understanding inspires me to greater efforts in advancing our propaganda.

What makes my mission especially difficult is that clear-cut class distinctions do not exist in Tzaplvar. Or it is more exact to say that the villagers have no consciousness of such distinctions. It will be my first job to emphasize class divisions, and show them what their own specific needs are, and the means by which they may be secured.

I must prepare these ignorant villagers for class struggle, and that's not a simple job.

For the past two weeks I have been in continuous contact with all the inhabitants of the village, and I have been trying, in my own mind, to arrange them according to the classes to which they would naturally belong.

The village has an elderly priest, Rev. Sahak, who represents the clericalism of the Middle Ages, with all its dark ignorance and obscurantism. It is essential to mount a continuing offensive against him.

The bourgeoisie of Tzaplvar is represented by Res[3] Sergo and his satellites. That contemptible bourgeois has three fields, two cows, one donkey and two goats, a wealth amassed through centuries of oppression imposed on impoverished villagers. Yet, amazingly, this man enjoys a good reputation in the village, and is respected by all, even by those who should be his natural enemies. Imagine how dulled by ignorance these poor wretches must be. Need I add that Rev. Sahak dines at Res Sergo's home a few times a week? The eternal alliance between capitalism and clericalism against the proletarian class! But patience, everything will fall into its proper place.

The entire working class of Tzaplvar consists of the blacksmith Mko, who is also the iron monger.

Two days ago Res Sergo's donkey lost a shoe, and that contemptible bourgeois was forced to call Mko. I tried very hard to persuade Mko to call a general strike, and leave Res Sergo's donkey shoeless. That would certainly have stunned the privileged classes. But unfortunately, Mko wouldn't go along. Apparently our propaganda has not yet had its expected effect. No matter. If it did not succeed this time, it will another. A general strike is indispensable in Tzaplvar to demonstrate and dramatize the practical effects of our propaganda.

---

3. Reference to *reis,* meaning chief (Arabic).

Tomorrow I leave for the Kurd village of Komrash where I will stay a few days to preach cooperation between the Armenians and Kurds. The Kurds are our natural allies. We must effect a reconciliation with them and use them whenever possible for the victory of the principles we stand for. But these are matters for the future.

Send me a little money.

Tzaplvar, October 2, 1908
Dear Comrades:

I write this letter in a happy frame of mind, with the joyous anticipation that I will be able to present you with actual successes in my next communication. The preliminary steps were truly difficult, but I have great hope for the future.

The Kurds of Komrash gave me a good reception. I remained with them four days and found that they are very well disposed towards us. They grasped my observations on expropriation far more readily than those blockheads in Tzaplvar. They expressed willingness to consider for immediate implementation the issue of forceful seizure of the properties of the rich bourgeois exploiting class. I cautioned them not to move too fast, that it would be best to wait a bit. In any event the village of Komrash is a fertile field for our work.

One amazing incident will illustrate the magnificent character of these Kurds. After I left their village on horseback and was riding alone through the Kanli Ova Valley on my way back to Tzaplvar, the same Kurds in whose homes I was a guest, who had accorded me every hospitality and honor, suddenly appeared, fully armed, and fell upon me and robbed me, leaving me almost as naked as the day I was born.

"But why didn't you do this while I was still among you?" I asked, amazed.

"You were our guest then," Kelesh Mko explained, "but once you left the village, it became another matter entirely."

This answer contains a fundamental principle of honor which is worthy of serious thought.

Returning to Tzaplvar, I continued my mission with energy and enthusiasm. At present I have enlisted a devoted follower who in the near future can be a source of great strength to us. He is known in the village by the name of Khev[4] Avo. He is a brave young man of 18 years, who has been cast out of his father's house for a number of reasons that should not concern us. The villagers generally do not seem to like the young man very much, persisting in regarding him as doltish and immoral—the effect no doubt of the still surviving spirit of the clericalism of the Middle Ages, narrowed further by selfish bourgeois attitudes. Because, in their absence, he has picked up a few things from the homes of some villagers; because, in coming across Krpo[5] Sekho's daughter alone in the fields, and urged by the most natural of feelings, he cultivated relations with her; because, when Rev. Sahak refused outright to give him a loan he had asked for, Khev Avo undertook to punish his indifference by stoning him; so that the poor boy is looked upon as a kind of idiotic evil-doer, persecuted and hounded as a result. It is always the same story. Either you have to humble yourself like a slave before the dirty bourgeoisie and hang your head before their self-serving prejudices, or you will suffer persecution by their whole corrupt gang. But he who laughs last, the French adage tells us, laughs best.

From the very first I could see that Khev Avo was a good prospect who could be helpful to us. I undertook to advise him, to instruct him, preach to him, with the result that he has become a reliable and committed revolutionary socialist. Khev Avo is prepared to play an important part in our revolutionary ranks in Tzaplvar.

The other day two Kurds from Komrash paid me an unexpected exchange visit. There was not enough food in the house to prepare an adequate dinner for them. I explained this to Khev Avo.

"Don't worry," he reassured me and left. A little later he returned with two plump chickens, both of which we cooked and ate. I don't remember ever having eaten tastier chicken. My guests and I insisted that Avo tell us where he managed to secure such fine birds on such short notice.

"I stole them from Res Sergo's garden," Avo said, "and his wife and daughters-in-law were even there at the time."

---

4. Crazy (Armenian).
5. Boorish fellow (Armenian and Turkish).

We all howled with laughter. The Kurds marveled at Avo's cleverness, while I was thinking that at last the centuries-old oppressed were rising and in a practical way attempting to become masters of what was rightfully theirs.

We have also attracted Sments Vardan to our party in Tzaplvar. He is one of Res Sergo's farm-hands, and only the other day was fired by that filthy creature, who accused him of being lazy and of stealing. I invited Vardan to visit me; I insisted that he not acknowledge that dismissal and demand, by force if necessary, that he be rehired. It was impossible to persuade him.

"No," he said. "It is better if I beg for his forgiveness, if I ask Rev. Sahak to intercede on my behalf. Res Sergo is not a bad man, and he will forgive me."

See how deep in slavery we are buried.

For hours I pleaded with him to reject such a servile act, and we finally agreed that I would apply directly to Res Sergo and demand that a tribunal of honor be created to consider the matter. Vardan agreed, but Res Sergo obstinately and categorically rejected our just demands. Yesterday I prepared a threatening ultimatum to that awful creature and had Khev Avo deliver it. It developed that Rev. Sahak was to visit me and discuss the matter further.

If satisfaction is not given to our demands, then our tactics will take a different turn.

It would be a very easy matter for Khev Avo to set fire to Sergo's sheepfold and barn, in the event that his provocation is carried to the extreme.

Send me a little money.

Tzaplvar, October 20, 1908
Dear Comrades:

As I suspected, and as I suggested in my previous letter, the trouble between Res Sergo and Sments Vardan became extremely serious.

You know that Vardan was working for Res Sergo as a cultivator, and the latter had him thrown out on the grounds that he was lazy and immoral, and that I had immediately leaped into the breach in order to protect the rights of the helpless proletariat.

Rev. Sahak, as intermediary, approached me on behalf of Res Sergo, and informed me that while Res Sergo was dissatisfied with the worker, he was sorry for the poor man's wretched circumstances and was ready to forgive him and permit his return, on condition that I guarantee his integrity and diligence.

I could immediately see that the clericalism of the Middle Ages, agrarian capitalism, and the village bourgeoisie had already begun to retreat before the thundering forces of the revolution. That was our first victory in Tzaplvar, and it was necessary to exploit it to the full.

Sments Vardan, who was present at our negotiations, was affected by the priest's words, began to thank him profusely, and with his arms extended prayed for the health of Res Sergo, and wanted to kiss Rev. Sahak's hand to express his deep gratitude.

I severely reprimanded the servile creature and ordered him out of the room. When we were alone, I said to the priest, "In no way do Res Sergo's concessions satisfy our demands."

"What else do you want," Rev. Sahak answered, "as long as Res Sergo agreed to take Vardan back?"

"That is a matter of secondary importance," I explained."The really vital issue is one of principle."

And I began to expatiate on the position of socialism concerning agriculture. I told him that the villager can save his home and land only by turning them into collective property and collective productivity; while with individual property, the villager is destined for bankruptcy. And to support my arguments I cited the theories of Engels, Kautski, Marx, Shishko, Prampolin, Chernov, Vikhlianev and others.[6]

Poor Rev. Sahak, his eyes opened wide, trying to penetrate the blindness of centuries, stared at me in a dazed stupor, now and then muttering incoherently.

"But what has all this to do with Sments Vardan's dismissal?"

And finally he asked for a definite answer which he could communicate to Res Sergo. In order to avoid possible denials and distortions, I presented in written form the following minimum demands, as the basis for future negotiations:

---

6. The author is making fun of the pedantry of Panjuni by inventing some of these names.

(1) Res Sergo must pay Sments Vardan his rightful wages for the time he was prevented from working; (2) Increased wages and shorter working hours; (3) A pension for the cultivators; (4) Accident insurance; (5) Res Sergo must guarantee to keep Vardan employed for at least twenty years; (6) Res Sergo must make a substantial gift to the treasury of our revolutionary party in recognition of its services in settling this dispute.

As you can readily see, I shifted the entire matter to the level of high principle.

Rev. Sahak left, rocking his head sadly. A few days passed and I received no answer at all. Vardan began to show signs of impatience.

"Since Res Sergo has forgiven me, let me go back to work," that idiot kept repeating, wanting in this selfish manner to trample the rights of millions of proletarians, for his own personal profit.

Finally, seeing that the answer was being deliberately delayed, I sent Khev Avo as our representative to obtain a definite word from Res Sergo. It appears that our comrade Avo, who has the fine mettle of a revolutionary, used somewhat strong language and was beaten and thrown out of Res Sergo's house. A little later Rev. Sahak also came to me and told me that Res Sergo doesn't want even to hear Vardan's name again.

That was plainly a declaration of war. The combined forces of capitalism and obscurantism were pressing heavily on the weary shoulders of the proletariat. It was impossible to remain silent in the face of this deliberate provocation. The very same night I prepared the following proclamation, which at dawn today Khev Avo posted on the church wall:

"Working class of Tzaplvar, the alarm has sounded, the dispute between Sments Vardan and Res Sergo is known to you all. In spite of our party's peace-making efforts, agrarian capitalism has declared implacable war against the proletarian cultivators. It would be shameful for us to remain silent; it would be shameful to remain indifferent. The dark forces of Tzaplvar are organized and aimed at shattering the rights of the working class and undermining the new freedom which we have secured with so much sacrifice.

"Workers of all the world, Are you going to permit one contemptible bourgeois in Tzaplvar to trample the rights of sixty million workers? Impossible! All for one. One for all. This must be our motto. The workers of all the world are invited to a great protest meeting on Sunday in Mgrents' barn. Speakers will be Comrade Panchuni, Comrade Avo, and the martyr of agrarian capitalism, Sments Vardan. Down with capitalism, down with obscurantism, long live socialism, long live the proletariat, long live May first."

Unfortunately, today is a weekday and all the villagers left for the fields early in the morning. Another drawback is that I'm the only one in Tzaplvar who can read or write. Even the priest doesn't know how to read. In spite of this I had hoped that the announcement would excite a shocking awakening in the villagers when they returned from the fields in the evening. But only a little while ago Khev Avo came running in and blurted out between gasps:

"They've torn down the paper from the church wall. . . ."

I couldn't believe my ears. With Avo I went to ascertain the truth of this grave development. Yes, it was so! The proclamation was torn to pieces, with barely a few fragments left which evil hands had failed to rip from the wall because they had been firmly glued. Avo had spared neither flour nor water when he posted the announcement.

Who could have committed this sacrilege? The villagers were all in the fields; there was no one near the church. The treachery had to have been worked in a very sly manner. In any event it became obvious that Reaction was not giving up. On the contrary, with this new attack, it was violently increasing its provocation. We could not retreat. I decided to organize a counter demonstration immediately. I returned home. I gave Avo a long stalk, with a red cloth tied to one end. Sments Vardan threw his tools on his shoulder, and I stepped out in front of them, and in this manner we stormed down Tzaplvar's main streets.

When we reached Rev. Sahak's house, I suddenly began to sing:

> *Debout, les damnés de la terre*
> *Debout, les forçats de la faim!*

I think it was the first time that the song of revolutionary socialism was heard in Tzaplvar. The children who had been left at home, hearing the workers' battle cry, came running to join us, and our parade took on majestic proportions.

When the demonstrators arrived at Res Sergo's house, feelings had reached a high pitch.

"Boys," I exhorted, "smash the windows of that traitor's house." But, regretfully, Res Sergo's windows had no glass; otherwise, the shattered panes would surely have given them something to talk about.

Khev Avo, who had become more and more excited, appeased his resentment by throwing rocks at Res Sergo's donkey which was grazing in the field. In his fervor, he even drew his knife and wanted to attack the beast, but I forbade it, not wishing to allow useless blood-letting.

Finally, the crowd dispersed, content with what had been done.

As you can see, the situation is very tense in Tzaplvar. Let us see what the consequences will be. We have sworn to press the battle by every means.

Send me some money soon.

P.S.: At the last moment, even as I was sealing my letter, I was informed that our proclamation had been torn down, not by the dark forces of reaction, but by that old witch Maro's goat, which ate it, apparently savoring the watered flour that was rubbed on the back.

The general situation is unchanged. The meeting will definitely be held on Sunday.

Levon Shant

(1869–1951)

Levon Shant's life spans a period of considerable change in the history of Armenian literature. His career spans the literary revival, the Romantic period, the realist and aesthetic movements, the 1915 genocide, the post-genocide diaspora, and three decades of Soviet Armenian literature.

Born Levon Nahashpetian in Constantinople, he later changed his surname to Seghbosian, after his father, and adopted Shant as his pen name. He was orphaned at the age of six, and his paternal aunt became his legal guardian. He was educated in Scutari (Üsküdar) and at the Gevorgian seminary in Etchmiadzin (1884–91). There he was exposed to Eastern Armenian, hence the unusual depth and range of his literary expression and grammatical construction. Later (1893–99) he continued his education in the German universities of Leipzig, Munich, and Jena. He then taught in Armenian schools in the Caucasus (1906–11) and in Constantinople (1911–13). While in the Caucasus (in Tiflis) he attended the literary salons of Hovhannes Tumanian (1869–1923) and befriended several contemporary writers.[1] He was fortunate enough to be in Europe in 1915, when the Ottoman government rounded up

---

1. See G. Aznavurian, "*Levon Shanti namaknere Hovhannes Tumanianin*" (Levon Shant's letters to Hovhannes Tumanian), in *Patmabanasirakan handes* (Journal of philological history), 1 (1982): 201–17.

Armenian writers and intellectuals, sent them to the interior, and brutally slaughtered them. Shant lived, but with a burning memory of the
tragedy that affected his nation so cruelly. He became preoccupied with
Armenian history and the disunity that characterized it, a subject he
treated in his plays of this period. *Inkats berdi ishkhanuhin* (The princess
of the fallen castle, 1923), written in Tehran, was the product of this
particular period. A historical play set in the twelfth century, it shows a
keen awareness of the political intrigues, internal discord, and savagery
of the era.

From 1918 to 1920 Shant continued to shuttle between Europe and
the Caucasus, engaged in politics on behalf of the Armenian Republic.
His ties with the republic did not last: he was disillusioned with the
decline of Armenia following the establishment of the Soviet regime.
After five years in Marseille and a brief stay in Egypt (1929), he settled
in Beirut, where, in 1950, he helped found the Armenian *Chemaran,* a
well-known Armenian secondary school, which he directed for the next
twenty years.

Levon Shant's first prose piece was *"Mnak barovi irikune"* (Farewell
evening, 1891). During his student years he wrote the novels *Leran
Aghjike* (The mountain girl, 1893) *Yeraz orer* (Dream days, 1896), *Dur-
setsinere* (The outsiders, 1896), *Verzhin* (1898), *Derasanuhin* (The actress, 1898), and *Dardze* (The conversion, 1899), as well as a collection
of poems, *Yerger* (Songs, 1894). All these works express Shant's social
and national reflections. Despite his prolific output and the popularity
of his poetry and novels, they are now among his less frequently read
works.[2] His novel *Hokinere Tzaravi* (Thirsty souls, 1945), although a
work of a more mature period and correspondingly more serious and
reflective, belongs to the same category.

Shant believed that the writer, the public activist, and the intellectual should struggle against prejudices and all that thwarts progress and
reform. His beliefs are expressed through his characters, who are mostly
people who refuse to give up: if they fail they try once more to prevail;
they tear down in order to build again; they are destined to struggle without end; in Teoleolian's words, they are "disciples of unceasing labor."[3]

Drama was Shant's favorite genre. The subjects of his first realistic
plays, *Yesi marde* (The egotist, 1903), *Urishi hamar* (For others, 1903),

2. See Kevork B. Bardakjian, *A Reference Guide to Modern Armenian Literature,
1500–1920* (Detroit, 2000), 195.
3. Minas Teoleolian, *Dar me grakanutiun: 1850–1920* (A century of literature:
1850–1920) (Boston, 1977), 1:513.

and *Chambun vra* (On the way, 1904), are mainly drawn from life. *Yesi marde* contrasts patriotism and egotism through two characters, one of whom, Setrak, a young man educated in Europe, is ready to sacrifice himself to change his friend. *Urishi hamar* focuses on love and family relationships. Siran, a sensitive and sincere young woman, sacrifices her own happiness for her father, brother, and sister. In *Chambun vra*, Vahram, a young man devoted to his country and under obligations, is prepared to separate from the girl he loves to serve the nation. The ending is characteristically tragic: the girl, unable to endure their separation, commits suicide.

Shant wrote more serious plays on subjects partially drawn from history. In *Hin Astvatznere* (The old gods, 1912), his best play, he sets the real world aside and enters the realm of thoughts and ideas. This play treats the clash between body and soul. The theme of love, temporal and spiritual, dominates the drama. *Kaysre* (The emperor, 1916) is based on the story of Byzantine emperor Nicophorus II Phocas (d. 969) and his successor, John I Tzimisces (d. 976), who was Armenian in origin, and their struggle for power. Shant used historical facts as a backdrop, but the play is mostly the product of his imagination, complete with complex amorous and revenge plots. *Shkhtayvatze* (The chained one, 1921) is derived from medieval history: the revolutionary events and militant efforts to defend the city of Ani. It centers around King Artashes's son, Artavazd I. The theme is once again a struggle for power and the uprising of the working class against the princedom. *Inkatz berdi ishkhhanuhin* (The princess of the fallen fortress) is set in Cilicia and focuses on the vengeful acts of Princess Anna, a beautiful, brave Armenian. Her husband and two sons are killed by Kogh Vasil and she is taken by force to his palace, where she commits suicide in order to rejoin her husband and sons. *Oshin Payl* is also based on historical events: the tragic story of Prince Oshin of the fortress of Korikos, who has fallen in love with Rita, the daughter of Prince Smbat. The play is filled with intriguing events of betrayal and sacrifice surrounding a tangled love-revenge story.

As a novelist and poet Shant produced mainly rudimentary literary experiments to express his national and social ideas—the writer as leader—and so the majority of these works inevitably have a didactic tone. But in his plays one can see the author being transformed and developing his own means of expression, while at the same time introducing a mature depth of meaning, all under the influence of European literature.

Shant died in 1951 and was buried in Beirut.

FROM ANCIENT GODS[4]

ACT 1

SCENE I

(The summit of Sevan. A ruin amid the rocks. Twilight.

(FATHER SUPERIOR is seated on a rock, his chin resting on his hand, as he pensively looks down. From under a partially destroyed arch, the MAN IN WHITE emerges. FATHER SUPERIOR is tall, has thick, graying hair, and is bareheaded. The MAN IN WHITE is likewise bareheaded and has long black hair and a splendid black beard, braided in the Assyrian manner. For a moment they stare at each other in silence.)

MAN IN WHITE: *(Jeeringly.)* Oh, how you survey your kingdom!

FATHER SUPERIOR: Who are you?

MAN IN WHITE: Behold that sight! See those few, small flimsy cells. Didn't you build them? And that chapel which you've built in haste! And lastly, look at your new church, whose dome soars upward day by day, and on top of which, with your own hands, you shall soon affix the cross.

FATHER SUPERIOR: Yes, if the Lord so wills it.

MAN IN WHITE: Look and take pride! Isn't that all born of your selfish will?

FATHER SUPERIOR: Who are you?

MAN IN WHITE: You, garbed in black! Why have you gathered those black-robed and black-souled people about you? Why have you come to this ancient isle?

FATHER SUPERIOR: Who are you?

MAN IN WHITE: Arise, arise! Drive that miserable, morose throng back to life again. Get out, *you* who want to dry up the senses and suppress all passions. Out of this isle, you who are enemies of all beauty, all life and movement, all strength and creation. Out! Do not defile this holy paradise of my gods!

FATHER SUPERIOR: There is no paradise here! I founded my monastery on this piece of rock. Hereafter, this isle shall be called a desert.

---

4. Levon Shant, "Ancient Gods," in *Modern Armenian Drama*, ed. Nishan Parlakian and S. Peter Cowe (New York, 2001), 189–215. Translated by Anne T. Vardanian.

MAN IN WHITE: A desert? On the bay of this smiling sea, facing this brilliant sun? Go away! The spot you tread upon is an ancient altar of the gods! Away! I speak to you from the threshold of the ancient gods.

FATHER SUPERIOR: From the ruins of the ancient gods!

MAN IN WHITE: Men like you piled up these stones. They have been destroyed, but the temple of life is indestructible, as is life itself. Stones will crumble, names will change, hut the gods endure forever!

FATHER SUPERIOR: Here died your gods!

MAN IN WHITE: Here and wherever man treads, they shall he immortal and eternal.

FATHER SUPERIOR: Here died your gods, and, upon their ruins, I built my God's temple. Look, see the apex of the dome, almost completed, still visible in the dusk. There reigns only the spirit; there reigns the breath of God alone.

MAN IN WHITE: There reigns the instrument of suffering and death!

FATHER SUPERIOR: It is suffering that elevates the soul and torment that cleanses it. And the most unfathomable mystery of life is death.

MAN IN WHITE: Suffering is the submission to a life of pain, and the willful waste of life is death.

FATHER SUPERIOR: Through you speaks primitive mankind.

MAN IN WHITE: It's ailing mankind that speaks through you!

FATHER SUPERIOR: Enough! Who are you that speak so profanely? Be gone! There is no place on this island for you and your gods.

MAN IN WHITE: This island is also part of the world. Oh, you bewildered fool, pay homage to the eternal gods!

FATHER SUPERIOR: Go away!

MAN IN WHITE: Accept them and pay homage!

FATHER SUPERIOR: Go away!

MAN IN WHITE: The day will come when you will accept their power. (*He disappears.*)

FATHER SUPERIOR: (*Looks about uncomfortably.*) Who was that? He vanished! An apparition, a doubt? No, never! The world cannot enter this island. The world shall never enter this island. Never.

SCENE 2

(*A courtyard in front of the church under construction. On one side of the stage there is an open door frame, through which several wooden*

ladders are seen. Here and there are planks, partially carved stones,
a sieve, and tools. Upstage center there are trees through which one
catches a glimpse of the sea. Throughout this scene the wind is blowing.
Occasionally there is a vigorous gust of wind. The rustle of leaves and
the distant, muffled sound of the sea are heard.)

Part 1

(*One or two* STONE CUTTERS *run through the trees toward the sea. The*
SEXTON *passes swiftly through the upstage area, carrying a long pole on*
his shoulder. Out of the church emerges MONK ADAM, *who struggles to*
pull a rope out of the church.)

MONK ADAM: (*Fervently.*) God help us! May God help us!

STONE CUTTER: (*He enters from the direction of the sea, drying his*
   hands. His legs and arms are bare.) Drop it, Father, drop it! There's
   no need for it. They got out. They all made it to the shore.

MONK ADAM: All? All of them, you say? Even those who fell overboard?

STONE CUTTER: All of them, though we'd completely given up hope.
   We stood there dumbfounded and helpless. It's such a furious sea!
   We said, "Now it'll smash the boat against the rocks on shore and
   shatter it to pieces with all on board." My God, they got away
   lightly!

MONK ADAM: Glory to you, holy Mother of God! And who fell overboard? Were there many?

STONE CUTTER: Only two, our young monk and a young lady.

MONK ADAM: Young lady? What young lady?

STONE CUTTER: The prince's daughter.

MONK ADAM: Oh, was she with the prince, too? Well, is she alive? Is
   she conscious?

STONE CUTTER: Yes, it seems so. Her father and his men took her to
   Father Abbot's cell. You should have seen how pale the prince
   was!

MONK ADAM: Poor man! Why did they embark in weather like this?

Part 2

(*Enter* MONK ANTON, MONK MOVSES, *and the* OLD MONK.)

MONK ANTON: Wait, wait, let me catch my breath! Don't keep asking
   me what happened next. What followed was awful! Ooh, my
   arms feel like they're going to fall off!

(*He sits on a high rock. During the course of the dialogue that follows,*
those present gather about MONK ANTON *as he relates the events. A few*

LABORERS *and* MONKS GHAZAR, DAVIT, *and* ZAKARIA *also enter and join those listening.*)

MONK MOVSES: Get on with your story.

OLD MONK: Wait, son, until he catches his breath.

MONK ANTON: (*Briefly covers his face with his hands, then suddenly looks up, taking his hands away.*) We were already halfway across. Again and again we climbed to the top of the waves and were hurled down below. All on the boat clung to their places, pale and stiff. The young monk and I were pulling at the oars with all our might. When I turned my head and glanced around, I saw that we were approaching the shore! The oncoming waves, smashing against the rocks, were like mountains of foam rising before us. Why hide my fear? My heart sank. I said, "It's all over." Yet, hope against hope, I forcefully bent to my oars, repeating again and again, "Oh, Lord Jesus." I told everyone, "Sit tight, don't be frightened!" Suddenly, just as I said this, I saw one enormous wave approaching from the distance. It looked as though it was torn from the shore and was heading straight for us. (*Standing up.*) And the rest. . . . Oh, how can I describe it? I only know that all of a sudden the boat listed sharply at the crest of the wave overhanging the gaping abyss. Then we heard a sharp cry. It seemed as if something fell out of our boat and slipped into the sea. The prince cried, "My daughter, my daughter!" There was chaos and confusion. I hardly knew what had happened when the young monk jumped up from my side, flung off his waistband, and leaped into the water. The boat swayed violently, and I was left with one oar. It's a good thing a wave was driving us to the island shore, but I knew that the rip tide would push us out again. If you hadn't thrown us the ropes in time, we'd all have been lost. A half-minute longer . . . just a half-minute, and it would all have been over!

OLD MONK: A miracle from God!

MONK ADAM: And the young lady?

MONK ANTON: (*Proudly.*) Our young monk rescued her!

MONK ADAM: He swam back with her?

MONK DAVIT:: Yes, he did! He brought her ashore!

MONK MOVSES: You mean the young monk can swim so well?

MONK DAVIT: But when did he learn? Who would have thought it!

MONK MOVSES: It's a miracle!

OLD MONK: I tell you the hand of God is in this!

MONK ADAM: But really, why did you set out in this weather, Father Anton?

MONK ANTON: I warned them at Tsamakaberd not to. Our saintly princess herself pleaded along with us, but no one took any heed. Her brother, the prince, ordered his men to board the boat. "If you're afraid, don't come," he said. How could I refuse? I said, "It's God's will."

MONK MOVSES: Well, what about his daughter?

MONK ANTON: She's another one, just like her father!

OLD MONK: No! This was the will of the Mother of God. (*Straightening himself up on his cane, excitedly.*) Who can we thank for building this shrine dedicated to the Mother of God? Our saintly princess, of course. Who keeps this monastery in good repair? Who has built our cells? Who in time of need has consistently helped the prayerful servants of the Mother of God?

VOICES: It's true, it's true!

MONK ZAKARIA: May God bestow long life on our patron, the saintly princess!

OLD MONK: She, who has left all courtly life and pleasures, her children, her palace, and has come to the feet of the Mother of God in the solitude of her castle by the shore, to dedicate her remaining days to self-denial and prayer.

MONK DAVIT: Long live our pious saint!

OLD MONK: Yes, because of the princess's dedication, the Mother of God performed this miracle for us, by rescuing the princess's brother and his daughter from the waves. Let all those wanting in faith observe and be convinced that our Mother of God does not turn away from her servants and her worshipers. May we be generous with our prayers, and may she be generous with her blessings upon us and our saintly princess. Glory to the name of the Mother of God! Glory to the name of her only begotten Son, forever and ever!

THE GROUP: Amen!

VOICES: The prince! The prince!

Part 3

(*Immediately the group divides itself into two parts. They line up and stand by humbly. The PRINCE and FATHER SUPERIOR enter with a few followers and MONKS.*)

PRINCE: (*Heading directly toward the building.*) So this is the church so loved and cherished by my sister. It's a cozy little church, and rather pretty. (*To his followers.*) I said that I would see this church today, and, despite the adverse elements, I am here now, safe and sound.

FATHER SUPERIOR: That was a bold step you took, Your Grace!

PRINCE: Your desert is one thing, Father Superior, but outside this cloister it's quite different. Out there, the world belongs to men of daring! And, after all, who knows when I'll pass through these parts once more? I have so many things to attend to. I felt I ought to see my sister's church at least once. Shouldn't I kiss its holy altar before going back?

FATHER SUPERIOR: You might have come tomorrow, Your Grace.

PRINCE: Tomorrow? I'm taking leave of my sister tonight!

FATHER SUPERIOR: Are you crossing over again today?

OLD MONK: Do not tempt God, Your Grace!

PRINCE: God forbid! We have a few hours on the island. I hope the sea will calm down by then.

FATHER SUPERIOR: If you are not concerned about yourself, you ought to be thinking of your child, at least.

PRINCE: My daughter is up to the task! She was frightened a bit and took in some of your Sevan water. That's all. She's young, she'll get over the shock. But her experience will always stay with her. After all, I gave her an exciting storm to treasure in her youthful storehouse of memories.

OLD MONK: You shouldn't toy with life, Your Grace!

PRINCE: What do you really know about life, old man? You've lived so long, you've forgotten life is just a game.

OLD MONK: Life, my son, is a cross we must bear on our shoulders till the Lord calls us. The Mother of God spared you this time. Don't transgress in that way again!

PRINCE: And I'm thankful to her, Father. I'm on a pilgrimage to her shrine and haven't come empty-handed. I am donating an embossed oak door and a velvet curtain embroidered in gold thread to this shrine of the Holy Mother, for the main altar.

OLD MONK: Bless you! The name of your house shall never be erased from these walls!

PRINCE: Moreover, I have ordered my steward to send ten measures of wheat from my barns to your desert every year, as long as my house stands. May you enjoy it, and may you include my parents and children in your prayers!

VOICES: God bless the memory of your parents! May your fields and orchards be bountiful! God keep your children! May God increase your estate and your fortune!

PRINCE: And now (*to* FATHER SUPERIOR), where is the young monk?

FATHER SUPERIOR: Coming, your Grace. I've sent for him. Ah! Here he is now.

Part 4

(*The* YOUNG MONK *enters, accompanied by* MONK SIMON *and a* SCRIBE. *He is dejected, his face immobile, his eyes downcast and rather listless.*)

PRINCE: (*After briefly studying the* YOUNG MONK.) What a handsome lad you are, and how young!

FATHER SUPERIOR: He is the youngest in our order, Prince.

PRINCE: Oh, if only you were not garbed in that black cassock, then I'd know what to do. I'd give you my favorite stallion. I'd give you my very own sword, which for thirty years has served me faithfully. And I'd take you into my palace as my very own son. My black stallion would have been a fitting gift for you. And your hand, I see, would have quickly gotten accustomed to my sword. Had my horse and sword not sufficed, I'd have given you my daughter . . .

FATHER SUPERIOR: Your Grace!

PRINCE: . . . whose life you saved today. She'd already be yours by right. In the outside world whatever you lay hands on is yours.

FATHER SUPERIOR: Your Grace!

PRINCE: I know, I know. This holy monastery is not the place for this kind of talk. But what can I do? I want to give him something. I want to do something to show my gratitude somehow to this selfless, valiant hero! What a pity! That black cassock binds my hands! (*Moving closer to the* YOUNG MONK.) My son, your prince stands before you impoverished and utterly powerless to repay you. What I'd like to say would seem inappropriate here, what I'd like to give would be useless to you here.

FATHER SUPERIOR: All we need is the sun to shine on you and your daughter.

PRINCE: (*To the* YOUNG MONK.) Well, then, I remain indebted to you. It's not a good feeling. I'm not accustomed to being indebted. At any rate, give me your hand. Here's mine. It has never been weak before our enemies and has never committed an unjust act. It is only proper that you take it in your own, which today rescued

my daughter from the waves. (*The* PRINCE *firmly clasps the* YOUNG
MONK'*s hand.*) Father Superior, let's go into the church.
(*The* PRINCE, FATHER SUPERIOR, *several followers and* MONKS *enter the
church.*)

MONK SIMON: (*Gently taking the* YOUNG MONK'*s arm.*) Let's go. We
should go now so you can rest a little. Your color is completely
gone, and I sense your body is still trembling. (*Half supporting the*
YOUNG MONK, *he leads him offstage.*)

Part 5

MONK GHAZAR: (*Approaching* MONK ADAM, *in a thoughtful manner.*)
Now, how long does the young monk have to do penance before
the doors of the church are open to him again?

MONK ADAM: Do penance? Why?

MONK GHAZAR: Well, hasn't he touched a woman?

MONK ADAM: But . . . but in a situation like this—

MONK GHAZAR: It's all the same, a sin is always a sin. (*More thoughtfully.*) I saw them, clinging to each other as they emerged from
the waves. The prince's men practically forced the girl out of his
arms!

MONK ADAM: (*Angrily.*) You're speaking nonsense!

SCENE 3

Evening. The YOUNG MONK'*s cell. A low, small room with plastered stone
walls. Upstage center there is a simple wooden bed; on it is spread a piece
of rawhide and a hard rough pillow. A coarse coverlet has partially
fallen to the floor. In the middle of the room stands a low, wide bookstand, upon a piece of old carpet. On the bookstand, there is a large open
manuscript. On one side of the room there is a rough wooden table; on it
are a black wooden cross, a clay water jug, and an oil lamp that flickers.
Opposite the table is the entrance to the room. The* YOUNG MONK'*s cassock
hangs from the wall at the head of the bed.*)

PART I

(*The* YOUNG MONK *is sitting on the edge of his bed; his hands are folded
across his chest, and he stares at the floor. Next to him, on a low wooden
stool, sits the* BLIND MONK, *erect and immobile, both hands on his cane,
his head held high.*)

BLIND MONK: Where are your thoughts, young monk? (*Startled, the*
YOUNG MONK *raises his head.*) Wandering again?

YOUNG MONK: Yes, I know it's a sin, a great sin. No, I'm not going to think about it anymore! There's no need to! I must erase this day from my mind, everything, everything, the sea, the wind, the boat, the waves, oh, those waves! (*Suddenly he jumps up.*) But what a wonderful thing it was to fight them. They push their wet breasts against you, splashing their foam against your face, blinding you. One of them leaps on your shoulder, another rolls across your chest. One pushes, the other pulls, crushing you. And all of them, all of them, want to drag you under. And you, always on the surface, rocking with their undulations, overcome all their attempts to draw you into the deep with controlled arm strokes. Ah, for that fight!

BLIND MONK: Fighting is about life, Brother. This is a desert.

YOUNG MONK: Yes, a desert! (*Contrite.*) I have sinned against you, my God; I have sinned.

BLIND MONK: Careful! Examine yourself well, Brother, pray!

YOUNG MONK: (*Kneeling in front of the cross.*) I'm a lost sinner, save me, Lord. I'm an abject transgressor, help me, Lord. I'm drowning, take my hand, Lord. I'm adrift in the sea of sin, in the sea . . . the sea. (*He rises, covering his face with both hands.*)

BLIND MONK: Say it, say it! (*The YOUNG MONK suddenly uncovers his face and looks directly at the BLIND MONK's statue-like face.*) Say it. Out with it!

YOUNG MONK: Say what?

BLIND MONK: What's out there in the deep!

YOUNG MONK: The deep, the deep.

BLIND MONK: Say it, say it!

YOUNG MONK: Who can see that far into the deep? Who can speak about the deep?

BLIND MONK: I . . . I can see. I can speak!

YOUNG MONK: You, a blind man can see? (*Sarcastically.*) Then speak! Tell me what you see.

BLIND MONK: (*Staccato.*) In the boat, when the oar in your hand was cutting through the water, who was there in your soul?

YOUNG MONK: (*Frightened.*) Quiet!

BLIND MONK: For whom was your heart throbbing? What was the word clinging to your lips, when everyone around you was calling out to God in the midst of the storm?

YOUNG MONK: (*Horrified.*) I wish your eyes were open so you could not see!

BLIND MONK: When all glances were turned toward heaven, when all were awaiting help from above, where were your eyes fixed? And before whom did your soul genuflect?

YOUNG MONK: Be quiet, be quiet! You have no right to see everything! You can't see into everything.

BLIND MONK: (*Pitilessly.*) Speak! What was your desire? What were you seeking?

YOUNG MONK: (*Pleading.*) I don't know, I don't know anything . . . that's enough!

BLIND MONK: And in the sea, when she, like a serpent, was wrapped around your neck, her body against your body, her breath against your breath, as you cut through the waves, tell me you still don't know what it was you desired!

YOUNG MONK: (*Dreamily.*) I remember, I remember! With all my being I wished that there would be no end to that watery road, that there would be no end to that moment!

BLIND MONK: Impious!

YOUNG MONK: (*Shattered.*) But it did come to an end!

BLIND MONK: And you reached the shore. Then, when they took your burden out of your arms, you, exhausted, fell to the sand, you a lifeless corpse!

YOUNG MONK: That's true! That's just how I felt.

BLIND MONK: Even now, you are a corpse. A body from which the breath of God is gone!

YOUNG MONK: Oh, my God, I've lost my soul!

BLIND MONK: (*Standing up.*) Fall to the ground and lament. Wear the sackcloth and repent. But first, go at once to Father Superior and confess.

YOUNG MONK: Confess? To Father Superior? What? Why? Oh, anything, but that one thing. Never. Never! And you, too, Father, you won't, you—

BLIND MONK: No. I'm blind, deaf and dumb; but go yourself to Father Superior, and willingly confess.

YOUNG MONK: (*Sharply.*) To Father Superior? Never!

BLIND MONK: Are you afraid?

YOUNG MONK: No, but . . . but. . . .

BLIND MONK: Of course! You want to secretly venerate your little new goddess in a distant corner of your heart.

YOUNG MONK: Have pity, have pity on me . . . you merciless—

BLIND MONK: And you, do you pity yourself? You heathen, remember the commandment, "Thou shalt have no other gods before me.[5]

YOUNG MONK: Shalt not have . . . shalt not have.

BLIND MONK: "Thou shalt not make unto thee any graven image, or any likeness of anything that is in heaven and above, or that is in the earth beneath, or that is in the water under the earth."

YOUNG MONK: (*Trembling.*) "Or that is in the water under the earth."

BLIND MONK: (*Slowly walking toward the door.*) "For I, the Lord thy God, am a jealous God, visiting the iniquity of the fathers upon the children. . . ." (*He goes out.*)

PART 2

YOUNG MONK: (*Goes to the crucifix and kneels in front of it and, with arms out-stretched, fervently prays.*) Save me, Oh God, for the waters are coming into my soul. I sink in the deep mire, where there is no respite; I am come into deep . . . into deep waters, where the floods have overwhelmed me.[6]

(*He becomes weaker and weaker, and bows his head on his chest.*)

PART 3

(*Slowly the table and the cross become enveloped in mist; everything becomes hazy and blurred. Against the background of this mist, a girl's form gradually becomes visible. She appears to have just emerged from the water, dressed in a simple, delicate and close-fitting white tunic. Her hair is loose and damp, with a few strands of seaweed entwined in it. The YOUNG MONK raises his head slightly. Suddenly he sees her and leaps to his feet in terror.*)

YOUNG MONK: (*Backing away.*) You. . . . You?

SEDA: Yes, me. . . . Weren't you expecting me?

YOUNG MONK: My God!

SEDA: You're alone?

YOUNG MONK: I . . . I am always alone.

SEDA: And now I've come as your companion. And I've come like this, at midnight, so we could be alone, you and I. You, my hero . . . my sun . . . my savior!

YOUNG MONK: That's enough!

---

5. Exod. 20:3–5.
6. Ps. 69 [68 LXX]: 1–2.

SEDA: Why? Isn't it because of you I am alive now, since you saved me from the deep and gave me back life? And how sweet is that life you gave me! All these years I've lived . . . seventeen in all, I had no idea how precious life is. lucre we were, there iii the waves. My hair is still damp . . . Take it in your hand take it . . . here, stroke it. (*The* YOUNG MONK *backs up, bewitched by the sight of the girl.*) You have such strong, agile arms. How aroused I still am, despite my fatigue.

YOUNG MONK: (*Attempting to prevent her.*) Young lady! pite my fatigue! (*She attempts to sit on the* YOUNG MONK'*s bed.*)

SEDA: (*Sitting on the edge of the bed.*) I am "young lady" to my servants. I am "young lady" to our subjects. My lord must address me in some other manner.

YOUNG MONK: Seda!

SEDA: Oh, my! You know my name!

YOUNG MONK: That's the name your father used.

SEDA: Yes, Seda is my name. And what is your name?

YOUNG MONK: They call me Brother.

SEDA: But before . . . before . . . when you were in the world and of the world?

YOUNG MONK: My world has always been the monastery ever since I came of age.

SEDA: Oh, how chilly it is here. How cold I am!

YOUNG MONK: You're cold?

SEDA: Put something 'round me to warm my soul.

YOUNG MONK: I don't have anything.

SEDA: (*Without turning her head, she points to his cassock, hanging on the rear wall.*) That would do.

YOUNG MONK: My cassock?

SEDA: I'm cold!

YOUNG MONK: My cassock?

SEDA: You hesitate! But you did not hesitate to risk your life for me. You did not hesitate when you plunged after me into the raging waves.

YOUNG MONK: No, I did not hesitate. That was different.

SEDA: Yes, that was different! There it was a battle in the stormy sea! Here, it is quiet and peaceful . . . like a grave. Oh, how chilly it is here. I'm so cold! (*She stands up. The* YOUNG MONK *runs toward the cassock. His hand reaches for it, but again he hesitates and stops.*)

SEDA: (*Pleading.*) Bring it, here . . . here . . .

(*The* YOUNG MONK *suddenly grabs the cassock and turns toward the girl, who has already disappeared. He remains immobile, holding the cassock in his outstretched hand.*)

PART 4

(*Offstage, the* SEXTON's *voice is heard, in a monotone, as he calls worshipers to the service in a melancholy chant. The sound grows gradually closer. The cassock falls from the* YOUNG MONK's *hands.*)

YOUNG MONK: (*Mumbling.*) Jesus, . . . (*He tries to kneel before the cross, but jumps back like a madman.*) No! No! What if she suddenly appears again? (*He turns his face toward the bed.*) Oh, my God has turned away from me! (*Sobbing, he falls to the foot of the bed and buries his face in the bedding. Outside, the* SEXTON's *chant continues, gradually becoming more and more distant, eventually fading away.*)

Curtain

Yerukhan (Yervand Srmakeshkhanlian)

(1870–1915)

Born Yervand Srmakeshkhanlian in Khasgiugh (Hasköy), an Armenian suburb of Constantinople, the writer known as Yerukhan received his elementary education at the local Nersesian school, where he distinguished himself as an uninterested and slothful student. In 1886 he was moved to the newly opened Kedronakan lycée in the city, where Minas Cheraz (1852–1929) was the principal and Arshak Chopanian (Arshag Tchobanian, 1872–1954) was a classmate. This is what he says in his autobiography: "Throughout my school life I was not a lazy, but a slack and uninvolved pupil. I particularly hated arithmetic and those who taught it. . . . In composition, I was incapable of developing a topic; my sentences were lame and lifeless. I had no desire to write. My compositions were so short that my teacher used to call them telegrams." Eventually he was dismissed from school as an unpromising student. Poor and needy, he found a job as an errand boy; but that too was short-lived. Then came his father's stern order, "Go and earn your living, or else. . . ." For the next two and a half years he applied extraordinary efforts to educate himself by reading everything, both old and new, that he could get hold of and also learning French. His efforts were rewarded. In 1890 he was appointed to *Arevelk* (The Orient) as translator and was later assigned to editorial work. The first short stories he wrote captured the attention of the public and he began to collaborate with other papers as well.

When the Armenian massacres broke out in Constantinople in 1896, he fled, along with other writers, to Varna, Bulgaria, where he founded the periodical *Shavigh* (Pathway). In 1904 he moved to Egypt, where he worked as journalist, editor, and teacher both in Alexandria and Cairo, and contributed articles and stories to various Armenian periodicals. He married, and in 1908, upon the declaration of the new Constitution of the Ottoman Empire, returned to Constantinople. His literary and community activities reached a new height as he became editor-in-chief of *Arevelk,* school teacher, and delegate to the Armenian National Assembly. In 1913 he was appointed principal of the Kedronakan school in Mezire, in the province of Kharberd (Harput). In 1915, when the genocide began, he was arrested, imprisoned, tortured, and put to death, with many other intellectuals. His entire family perished in the death march to the Syrian desert.

Yerukhan belongs to the group of realists who immediately followed Arpiar Arpiarian (1852–1908) and Grigor Zohrap (1861–1915). Hakob Oshakan (1883–1948), the famed literary critic, considered him the one who "succeeded the best" among them. His characters are common people—fishermen, laborers, porters, the poor, those of humble origin— and he depicts them in everyday life, with their struggles, loves and hatreds, joys and sorrows, in their own world and in their own speech. He does not make comments, does not moralize, does not draw conclusions. He condenses a situation, a behavioral or psychological temperament, through terse, concentrated, but eloquent expression.

The work for which he is most noted is the novel *Amirayin aghjike* (The amira's daughter),[1] first serialized in a periodical and published posthumously in book form in Constantinople in 1929. The differences in nature and morals among the three main characters in the novel— Arshak, Sofi, and Hambik—create an enormous contrast of attitudes and notions. Arshak personifies the wealthy, and is in the depths of moral depravity; Sofi exemplifies pure love that somehow becomes tainted with passion; and Hambik, though poor, is a model of moral integrity, for which he suffers until his death. The entire novel develops around these

---

1. *Amira,* derived from the Arabic *amir* (prince, commander, noble, or chief), was the title given to a class of wealthy Armenian dignitaries in the service of the sultans and in the higher echelons of Ottoman bureaucracy who acted as bankers for viziers, pashas, and tax collectors. The *amira* wielded considerable power within the Armenian community.

and a few other characters interconnected by love, denial, jealousy, and virtue. *Amirayin aghjike* is a realistic representation of the family life of some wealthy households in Constantinople at the time.

Only two of Yerukhan's books were published in his lifetime: *Kyankin mej* (In life, 1911), a collection of short stories, and *Harazat vordi* (Legitimate son, 1913), a short psychological novel. The first collection of his works was published in Paris by the Friends of the Martyred Armenian Writers in 1942.

CRAYFISH[2]

He was seen about ten at night. His raucous, appalling voice imposed itself on the wild current of the hurly-burly seething in the streets of Galata.[3] He had large, corn-covered feet in big boots, flattened at the ends until they scarcely accommodated his bare feet; that was why the skin on his soles had turned to leather: it was continuously chafed by the dust and mud of the streets. His strong legs moved in his narrow wool pants. He had a wide wool belt, which nearly covered his abdomen. He wore the same jacket both summer and winter, and the same vest. The latter could be buttoned to cover his chest, but the fisherman, desiring to show off his well built body, left it unbuttoned, exposing his manly, hairy chest. He wore his black whiskers in shapely curls that nearly reached his ears. His cheeks were ruddy, weather-beaten, and tanned. He had fiery eyes which, gimlet-like, seemed to bore into those on whom they chanced to fix. His gait was proud. To look at his posture one would think he was deliberately challenging people to a fight. He suddenly stepped in from the street and announced the contents of his basket: "Crayfish, crayfish, fresh crayfish!"

Oh! With what admiration and devotion he fondled the red crayfish arranged in apple-pie order in his basket! He declared he cherished every one of his crayfish as the apple of his eye.

One of the customers who enjoyed Mirik's talk very much noticed one day that he was wearing new shoes instead of the ones he had worn for such a long time. He mockingly asked him

---

2. Yerukhan (Yervand Srmakeshkhanlian), "Crayfish," in *Great Armenian Short Stories,* trans. Sarkish Ashjian (Beirut, 1959), 71–74. Revised by the editors of the present anthology.

3. A business district in Istanbul.

the reason for this unexpected change. Mirik was confused by the question, and his look reminded one of the guilty perplexity of a schoolchild caught committing an offense. He looked around him before giving an answer, and his gaze fell on a young lady who sat with a young man two tables away. She had heard the question, and she too waited for his answer.

"The other ones were worn out," said Mirik with a slow, deep sigh, and he grabbed his basket and left the beer parlor immediately. He was not seen there for about two weeks. Whenever he passed there, he cast a furtive glance through the opening of the door and then hastened away. But one night, as he was looking in again, he put his hand to his forehead, thought for a moment, mustered his courage, ventured in, and started to make his usual round, murmuring in a low voice to the customers at the tables: "Crayfish, red crayfish."

The young couple was there again. The girl wore a dark dress. She was a charming brunette with jet-black hair. They came there about three times a week. When Mirik approached them, the young woman turned to her friend and said, "Buy me some crayfish."

A smile glided over Mirik's thick lips. He lifted up his basket, mixed the crayfish dexterously, and said, with hardly noticeable excitement in his voice: "You've never tasted such crayfish in your life, sister. I'll give you the best ones." And he filled her plate with the largest crayfish, in such abundance that there was not an inch left empty on the plate.

"How much?" asked the young man.

"Money?" said Mirik, rather surprised. "No, I don't want money right now. If you like them, you can pay me some other day."

And taking his basket, he ran out.

The young woman wolfed down Mirik's red crayfish. She crushed and chewed the delicate shells of the crayfish with her small teeth. The young man sitting with her observed her in surprise: "Goharik, I never knew you loved crayfish so much."

"Oh! yes, I sure do like them," answered the young woman. "My father used to bring us crayfish quite often when we were children."

Two nights later Mirik entered the beer parlor with a brand new tarboosh on his head. He had apparently got rid of his old hat, which was greasy as well as worn. He had arranged his belt in a neat and attractive fashion around his strong waist. And his basket, instead of hanging carelessly from his right side, was gracefully borne in his sinewy hands. The customers noticed the changes that Mirik had undergone in the space of a few weeks, and were amazed. His manners and words were no longer awkward and uncivil. He no longer gave his crayfish the loving look of times gone by. Whenever anyone asked for some, he doled them out in generous handfuls, accepting the money in a casual way. And he left the beer parlor in a rather broken and dejected spirit.

When he came in that night he walked right up to the young woman's table, smiled, and asked her if she had liked the crayfish.

"They were delicious. I want seconds, please: give me some more."

Mirik dished out crayfish as abundantly as before.

And then a curious idea took hold of him. He reckoned himself out of place, with his coarse, vulgar clothing. Clothes meant a lot to women. He went straight to a store that sold ready-made clothes. He bought the kind of narrow suit that his gigantic, proud frame had always despised. His new clothes seemed rotten, insignificant, and miserable to him. He made a comparison, and realized the excellence of his broad, tough old clothes. He had parted with them in spite of himself. He had denied his past, and by putting on new clothes he had undergone a repulsive metamorphosis. He stood before the mirror and could not recognize himself in the reflection: who was that foreign-looking young man looking out of the mirror at him?

He paid for the suit and walked out of the shop. He was hopeless and glad at the same time. He cleaned his basket diligently; then he placed in it the largest and reddest crayfish and entered the beer parlor with a throbbing heart in his bosom and a broad smile on his lips. He did not shout "Crayfish, crayfish" in his stentorian voice as before.

Goharik sat intimately with her boy-friend. She looked sad; she had the appearance of someone suffering from a secret pain. Dispensing with his usual coarse manners, Mirik approached their table, trying to imitate the refined manners of a dandy. He made a deep bow to them, and said with a smile: "You've never eaten such crayfish in your life before, I assure you, miss." And he started to pour the red crayfish onto her plate.

At Mirik's polished appearance, however, the young woman's face suddenly darkened and took on a forbidding expression. That face expressed the bitter sorrow of someone undergoing an unpleasant disappointment. And while the fisherman filled her plate, the young woman asked: "Why have you changed your clothes?" And after a moment's hesitation she added, "I don't want any more crayfish!"

Khnko Aper

(1870–1935)

Atabek Khnkoyan, who wrote under the pen name Khnko Aper, was born in the village of Gharaboya.[1] He received his primary education in his birthplace and then in Alexandropol (later called Leninakan, now Giumri). Between 1890 and 1910 he taught in various Armenian schools in Transcaucasia. He contributed to the periodicals *Ashkhatavor* (The laborer), *Nor askhatavor* (The new laborer), *Aghbiur* (The fountain), *Machkal* (The plowman), *Hayastani ashkhatvaruhi* (The Armenian worker-woman), and *Hasker* (Spikes), a monthly magazine for children.

Following the establishment of the Soviet regime, he settled in Armenia, where he resumed his career as a writer and educator. He wrote several textbooks to teach Armenian children their mother tongue, including *Mer Dbrotse* (Our school) and *Karmir arev* (Crimson sun).

Khnko Aper wrote mainly children's literature: fables, legends, and lyric and narrative poems. His original writings and translations make a total of 120 books. *Giughatsin yev arje* (The peasant and the bear, 1909), *Gogh makin* (The lamb thief, 1911, 1941, 1970), *Pesatsu muke* (Mouse,

---

1. The village has been renamed Khnkoyan, after him; it is in the region of Spitak.

the intended bridegroom to be, 1912), *Arakner* (Parables, 1917, 1930, 1937), *Tranvaye Yerevanum* (The Yerevan streetcar, 1934, 1936), *Mknern inchpes grvetsin katvi tem* (How the mice fought the cat, 1936), *Khozn u agrave* (The pig and the crow, 1940), *Gayln u katun* (The wolf and the cat, 1957), and *Mkneri zhoghove* (The council of the mice, 1957, 1964, 1972, 1979) are among his best known works. Khnko Aper's use of dialect and popular language are part of the literary charm of his prose and poetry.

He was buried in the Komitas Pantheon in Yerevan.

THE GOLDEN SPINDLE[2]

Once upon a time there lived a woman who had two daughters. One was beautiful but lazy, the other ugly but industrious.

The mother loved the beautiful daughter very much; she made the ugly daughter always spin wool.

One day when the latter was standing near a well, the yarn broke and the spindle fell into the well. Crying her heart out, she ran to her mother and told her she had let the spindle fall into the well.

"I don't want to hear any more about it," the mother said. Go, bring back the spindle—or else!"

The girl did not know what to do. Heartbroken, she ran to the well, bent down, and peered over the edge, when suddenly she fell headfirst into it. When she regained consciousness and opened her eyes, she saw a beautiful meadow. A brightly shining sun lit up the green trees and the flowers: roses and carnations and hyacinths, and the flower known as crowned nightingale. These few words are all the description I will give you; you can imagine the rest.

The girl felt happy, and started to walk beside the meadow. She walked and walked, and came to a *tonir*[3] full of freshly baked bread. From inside the oven the loaves were screaming: "We're burning,

2. Khnko Aper (Atabek Khnkoyan), *"Voski ilike"* (The golden spindle), in *Arevelahay grakanutiun* (Eastern Armenian literature), ed. Simon Simonian (Beirut, 1965), 598–99. Translated by Nairi Bahlavuni and edited by the editors of the present anthology.

3. Oven, earthen stove, tandour.

we're burning! Hey, you, girl! come and save us! Take us out of the oven!"

The girl bent down and picked up the loaves closest to the walls of the oven, removed them, and spread them out to cool a bit, then lay the others on top of them, and went on her way.

She walked and walked, until she came to an apple tree. The tree was moaning like a sick person and crying out: "I'm . . . I'm dying. My burden is heavy, my apples too many, my branches to be pitied. Shake me, shake me, rock me, rock me tight."

The girl heard and took pity on the apple tree, shook it well, piled up all the apples, and went on her way.

She walked and walked, and this time she came to a house. She went in and saw a sick old woman lying in bed.

"My dear girl, you came just in time. You are so welcome to my house. I'm a childless woman, with no one to take care of me, no one to look after me. I feel sick; please take care of me until I get well."

The girl stayed with the sick woman, gave her good care, looked after her, washed her, and made her sweat until she got well.

When the old woman recovered and was on her feet again, she said to the woman, "Granny, let me go and look for my spindle. I have to find it. I left a lot of work behind. I feel homesick."

"Very well, my girl. It's a good thing to love one's home. Let's go and find your spindle."

They started to walk, hand in hand. They walked and walked, and came to a closed gate. The old woman said, "Gate of Destiny, we salute you! Open! Shower down golden raindrops. Make this girl beautiful; turn her hair to gold. This little girl of ours is so industrious, never afraid of work; make her spindle golden too."

When she had said this, the gate opened and they both went in.

Suddenly golden drops of rain started to shower down, forming golden pools on the girl's head. She grew golden-haired and beautiful, was clad in a lovely silk dress, and metamorphosed she turned into a partridge.

The old woman took the golden spindle, gave it to the girl, kissed her, and said, "You earned this by taking good care of me: it is your reward for your work."

No sooner had she spoken than the gate closed and the old woman disappeared. The girl closed her eyes and opened them again to find herself in front of her house. The dog and the cat ran out to her and the rooster began to sing:

> *Tsughrughu,*[4] my hens and chicks,
> Look at the partridge who has come to give us grain!
> It's the golden-haired girl: her hair is covered with gold.
> Her spindle too has turned to gold.
> You know who has made her so:
> The sick old woman has adorned her so!
> *Tsughrughu,* my hens and chicks,
> She has come to give us water and grain.

The golden-haired girl went in to her mother and sister, who welcomed her with open hearts, for she had brought them a lot of gold.

The golden-haired girl told them what she had seen and heard during her ordeal. The mother sent her favorite daughter to the well to spin the wool. The lazy girl started to spin and spin. Then she deliberately threw the spindle into the well and threw herself headfirst after it.

When she regained consciousness she saw the same meadow. She walked and walked beside the meadow, and came to the same *tonir.* Loaves were screaming from inside, "Take us out of the fire! We're burning, we're burning!"

The lazy girl said, "What do I care if you're burning? Who wants to get dirty by covering her hands with ashes?"

She walked and walked, and came to the apple tree. "I'm dying. My burden is heavy; shake me, rock me, make my apples drop. They are ripe for picking."

"Ah, that's not my problem. You say you're dying? Well, go ahead! Why should I care? I'm going to get golden hair and bring home gold."

She walked and walked, until she came to the old woman's house, and she began to work for her.

The first day she woke up early, cleaned the room, and tidied the place up, doing whatever the sick woman asked. The second day she did not feel much like working. The third day even less. The fourth day she did not even bother to move. The old woman got tired of her. Still feeling sick and moaning with pain, she took

---

4. Cock-a-doodle-doo.

the girl to the Gate of Destiny and said: "Gate of Destiny, open! Cough up a gift for this girl. She is so lazy, a smoke-blackened pot would be most fitting. May she be blackened with smoke and return home covered with soot!"

When the lazy girl got home, the rooster began to crow:

> *Tsughrughu,* my hens and chicks,
> I wonder where this one has been and where she came from.
> This black creature has come in vain:
> She went away white and came back black,
> Went away beautiful and came back bedeviled.
> Come out! Look who's back!
> She won't give us water or grain.
> *Tsughrughu,* my hens and chicks.

And this is how the hardworking daughter became a beautiful golden-haired girl, while the lazy one grew pitch black and ugly. I do not know how many times they tried to wash her white, but she never got any whiter. Pitch black is what she was, and pitch black is what she remained.

Vahan Malezian

(1871–1966)

The writer, poet, and social activist Vahan Malezian was born in Sulina, Romania, but that same year the family moved to Constantinople. He received his education at Hakob Gurgen's private school, then attended law school, from which he graduated in 1895. In 1896 he moved to Mersin, Cilicia, where he was imprisoned for a year on charges of revolutionary activity. He spent his life in different parts of the world: Cairo (1898–1923), Brussels (1923–27), Paris/Marseilles (1927–45), and New York (1945–47); he eventually settled in Nice in 1948. In Cairo he was one of the founders of the *Sahmanadrakan Ramkavar* (Constitutional Democratic) Party, which later merged with other organizations to form *Ramkavar Azatakan Kusaktsutiun* (the Armenian Democratic League). He held administrative positions in the Armenian General Benevolent Union, which was founded in Cairo in 1906.

His literary activities began in the late 1880s with a set of poems that appeared in *Masis* and *Arevelk* (The Orient). His first collection of poems was published in 1890 under the title *Mrmunjk* (Murmurs), followed in 1892 by *Anitzyale* (The cursed), a verse narrative. His most productive years were the ones in Cairo, where he wrote both prose and poetry that was later collected in various volumes, such as *Keronner* (Candles, 1912), *Taragri me hushatetre* (Notebook of an exile, 1915),

Antsatz orer (Days gone by, 1927), and *Karapi yerge* (The swan song, 1949). His numerous articles, memoirs, letters, and other material have been compiled in two volumes: *Chambus vra* (On my way) and *Chambus tzayre* (At the end of my way), published in 1950 and 1955. He also translated works by Victor Hugo (1802–85), Henri Barbusse (1873–1935), Maurice Maeterlinck (1862–1949), and others. In 1956, on the occasion of his eighty-fifth birthday, a commemorative volume dedicated to his life and accomplishments was published in Paris.

FROM IN THE FIELDS[1]

I love to wander in the fields alone, all alone; I often go there to be self-contained.

How sweet it is to live within yourself once in a while; how sweet to forget everything and everyone around you sometimes— to live only within yourself—with your self. You can see so much within yourself: the deep earth within you, an entire world, even the universe!

Away from the city, where an infernal din combines with the human swarm, beautiful fields spread out at the foot of the mountains or beside the sea.

Birds warble much better in the fields; the enchanting chirping of the dales sounds so much more pleasing. There the flowers open all by themselves in the spring. All by itself the immense and dappled carpet is woven, the green elegance of which enchants the soul.

I love to wander in the fields alone, all alone.

Sometimes for hours I stroll down the summits and pause before magnificent dwellings, just to admire them.

I pick flowers by the roadside; I make a bouquet of wild flowers, and the birds and the butterflies, jealous of my bouquet, swarm round my head.

And when I feel that I am tired, I stretch myself out on the green, cool grass like a carefree soul who is happy to be alive.

---

1. Vahan Malezian, "*Dashterun mej*" (In the fields), in *Hogii Dzayner* (Voices of the soul) (Paris, 1949), 14–16. Translated by the editors of the present anthology.

✦

The air, transformed by the heat of the glittering sun, steams from the earth like vapor, and an invisible fire spreads over the glowing, fragrant grass and flowers, which are sprinkled with sweet dew, and over the earth.

The warm air has the taste and scent of kisses; I savor it, gradually forgetting the world and enjoying only the wavering sensitivity that calls forth the absent soul of my beloved.

And exalted, feeling happy from the bottom of my heart, I drink in the air, more intoxicating and sweeter than all the beverages that have ever wet my lips.

And so I remain there, basking in the fields where the flowers blossom by themselves and the birds sing much better, for quite a while; I remain motionless, distracted, refusing to open my eyes to the light, refusing also to close them in sleep, while they tremble and smolder, stirred by the delight of a reverie.

THE BLOUSE[2]

The blouse of a beloved woman is a flower, like the flowers of the equator, magical and heady. A flower that takes its scent from that voluptuous paradise, the bosom of a beautiful woman.

There is something indiscreet about that flower when it gets into someone else's hands. It is as though, unprotected, it reveals everything; every crease reveals all that it has seen. In the hands of a lover it is like a confession: a betrayal, the enjoyment of which intoxicates the enamored soul with a secret happiness.

The delightful fragrance given off by the blouse of a beloved woman comes from her warm, white body and permeates its silky folds. And in a lover's hands, trembling with pleasure, that blouse turns into a ballad, a flower so attractive and so sensual that no garden, not even Eden, has ever been so adorned.

Its entire life, the luckiest of all lives, has been but a touch, a caress; the echoes of a feverishly beating heart forever throb there; how many pleasing tremors have palpitated its folds! From her

---

2. "*Pluze*" (The blouse), in *Hogii Dzayner*, 11–12. Translated by the editors of the present anthology.

snowy neck, embraced by its collar, the coolness of wet kisses has flowed with the softness of warm ether; and how much desire have its meticulous pleats and unseen slits provoked, the accomplice of over-excited fingers and unwise lingering?

It is as if the blouse has become a body that you can feel beneath your ardent fingers, and, troubled and delirious, you hear everything that the rumpled ribbons and the rounded hollows and the perspiration stains enticingly whisper.

And from the blouse, which spills out under a flood of foolish kisses, arises the sweetest and headiest of all fragrances—the private scent of a beautiful woman—and that moist scent, permeating every fiber and fold, recalls dreamt-of pleasures and provokes dreams of unforgettable bliss.

My soul too is pale like your blouse, my sweet one, but it is full to the brim with your love, to the depths of its yellowish folds and its hidden recesses: love that you inspired permeates all my shivers and tears. My soul can tell of nothing that has taken place without folding in memories of your love, like the secretive pleats of your blouse.

I possess so much! A voice within me sings to you, my inner eye always beholds you; and my love-burnt kiss swoons between your breasts.

Anaïs (Yevpimé Avetisian)

(1872–1950)

The poet Yevpimé Avetisian, who wrote under the pen name Anaïs, was born in Constantinople to an aristocratic family known as Hovivian (Chopanian), who originated in the Armenian province of Akn. She received her education at the Makruhiyats school, then attended a French private school. She perfected her Armenian under special tutors, Tovmas Terzian (1840–1909) and Khoren Narpey (Narbey, 1832–92), two well known writers of the day. Her first poems appeared in the periodical *Masis* in 1893, followed by other works, both prose and poetry. During Abdul Hamid's years of terror she moved to Switzerland and remained there until the declaration of the new Ottoman constitution of 1908. Returning to her homeland, she took up her literary activities and continued to contribute to the periodicals *Masis, Arevelyan mamul* (Oriental press), *Biuzandion* (Byzantium), and others. After World War I she joined the staff of the women's magazine *Hay kin* (Armenian woman) and became a strong voice in support of women's issues, particularly in the field of education. In 1922 she moved to Paris, where she remained and continued writing for the rest of her life.

A collection of her poems, *Ayg u verjaluys* (Dawn and dusk), was published in Paris in 1942. Her autobiography, which contains a great deal of information about important events and figures of her time, was published, also in Paris, under the title *Hushers* (My recollections) in 1949.

FROM MY RECOLLECTIONS[1]

You have asked me, my dear, to tell you the story of my life. What is one leaf among all the leaves of a forest? "Pass through this life like a gust of wind, leaving nothing behind you."

Who has ever had the guts to tell the story of his life sincerely?

Who among us has not stumbled in this world of hardship, had moments of dejection or even of wickedness? Since you are so eager to know, I shall offer you this confession, which I have written for you only (although nobody can guess where any piece of writing will end up), and perhaps when you read it I may no longer be around, but will have departed this earth. Remember, then, that memory can leave no legacy but its truth, its timeless truth.

You know, I have never been inclined to judge myself with leniency; therefore, I shall speak without any effort to glamorize, without reticence, but audaciously.

Some pages of a book are filled with light; others are shaded with the murkiness of dusk. Shadow and light embrace each other on the road of humanity. So do not blame me when bitter melancholy is glimpsed within the folds of my soul.

The upper section of Beshiktash (a suburb of Constantinople) is situated on the side of a mountain that is adorned with lime blossoms and beautiful jack pines. I was born there on a stormy night in February 1872, in a splendid white house surrounded with gardens.

My father, Hakob Chopanian, owned the house. The Chopanian family had come to the city from Akn, and from its earliest days had produced intellectuals, scientists, and poets as well as businessmen; it was divided into two branches: major and minor.

---

1. Anaïs (Yevpimé Avetisian), *Husheres* (My recollections) (Paris, 1949), 7–13. Translated by the editors of the present anthology.

There is a legend about the Chopanian-Hovian families:

Hundreds of years ago, there lived in Akn a man and a woman, well-to-do and famous. Beginning soon after their marriage, they had twelve sons. Each of them died after only a year. After the death of their last child, discouraged and full of anguish, they moved to a remote village and endured their sorrow there.

One summer evening, a priest from the south turned up on their doorstep. He was a tall, gentle cleric. He was not like other clergymen: it was as if the hem of his coat dripped saintliness. He spoke in a soothing voice:

"Don't be so sad," he said: "you have cried enough. Soon you'll have another son, and this one won't die. But don't baptize him before he's forty days old; then I'll come and baptize him myself." And with that he disappeared.

The couple knelt and, with tears in their eyes, began to pray.

Within a year they had a beautiful boy. They waited forty days. On precisely the fortieth day the mysterious priest arrived and christened the child. He named him Hoviv. When he had baptized the child he handed him to his mother and said: "Take your child. He will have a happy life and become the founder of a great dynasty, and his name will be remembered for a long time."

Many members of the Chopanian family are named Hoviv. One of my cousins is named Harutiun-Hoviv, although he does not use his second name. Hovhannes Chopanian has a certificate signed by Father Karapet, primate of Akn in the eighteenth century, that he found in the prayer book of his father, Hovhannes Agha Chopanian. The certificate proves that the father of the child christened Hoviv, mentioned above, was a Rubenian prince. When the Rubenians were defeated, enemies kidnaped him and left him in an unplowed field. A shepherd named Puzam found him, adopted him, brought him to Akn, and there took care of him. The prince, unaware of his origins, tried to make his way in life, and he did. He married the daughter of a respectable family and became the father of Hoviv after losing twelve children, as I have told you. And that same Hoviv, who is thus descended from the Rubenians, is Patriarch Hovian, a member of the Chopanian family.

At least that is what Father Karapet's certificate says. . . .

♦

Arshak Chopanian (Arshag Tchobanian)! With the writing of this name my thoughts take wing, flying back over the intervening years to those fabled times when we used to have our morning tea under the arbor in our garden beside the musk-smelling Ohlamur forest. The adolescent Arshak, who lived in a beautiful suburb called Yeni Mahallé, used to pass by on his way to Makruhiyan school, his schoolbag under his arm. The face of the young man, already a poet, used to light up at the sight of our white roses.

My father was a council member at the Armenian church in Beshiktash. As he was interested in children's education, he often visited the school in the neighborhood. The teachers there talked about a talented student who had the same name as he— Chopanian. Srapion Tghlian, the teacher of Armenian literature, in particular expressed admiration for the alert boy who showed early signs of immense literary talent.

Memory takes me from Beshiktash to the Kedronakan school, where Arshak delivered the first fine writings from his desk to the Armenian press. They were like the dazzling rays of a sunlit day.

Now his fabulous literary creations, his gem-like studies of the Armenian minstrels, his poetry, his rose-scented *Roseraie,* the dancing lines of his verse, bring back my dear, sweet impressions of his earliest inventions.

Chopanian's involvement in public life was a major hindrance to his literary production. Despite his commitments, however, he has produced works of enormous literary merit: they adorn his white locks like the priceless gems of an everlasting crown.

In Paris, Chopanian has superbly enhanced the prestige of Armenians in the eyes of the French. The rest I leave to his biographers. One would need volumes to write about his life and literary achievements. The fantastic, almost crazy enthusiasm that the liberation and the armistice created was almost boundless.[2]

Lectures were given everywhere, and there were performances of new plays, such as *Azatutian Ayke* (The dawn of liberation); all the *zurnadjis*[3] of the royal court, the great spies, etc., with all their wicked manipulations, were portrayed on the stage . . .

---

2. Ibid., 140–43. The liberation and armistice refer to the Ottoman Constitution of 1908 that promised liberty and justice.

3. Oriental clarinet players (Turkish).

even our cowled Ormanian patriarch. The people adored these performances, and the playwrights were rewarded generously.

The sultan gave fabulous, very European banquets for ambassadors and ministers. It was said that the sultan's gallant treatment of women was exceptional.

Apparently the fan of the British ambassador's wife broke during one of the banquets and the sultan had caused the accident. The chivalrous monarch immediately took the damaged fan from her and, with a cordial smile, put it in his pocket. A few days later the fan was returned to her, exquisitely repaired: the damaged part was covered with diamonds arranged to form the sultan's initials! Of course, the gracious lady admired the taste of the Turkish sovereign.

The days went by as rapidly as the waters of a clear river rush through the confines of a flower-bedecked valley. All the intellectuals and revolutionaries who had been sent into exile were gradually returning. They received special treatment and recognition from Armenians, as if their names were surmounted with halos, followed by crowns of thorns. They gave lectures and speeches in Armenian, and the public lapped up their words.

There were many likable figures among these revolutionaries in addition to the ones we had known previously. It was a real treat to associate with them, listen to the details of what they had done, get excited by their expectations, and be reinvigorated by their mission. Those who were leading intellectuals greeted the Armenian intellectuals of Istanbul like real brothers, appreciating everyone according to his true merit. A few of them were elected as members of parliament. It was both amusing and strange, though, to think that the sultan, who hated Armenians, would see them comfortably seated in the chairs of the National Assembly and the Senate.

It was the opening of parliament. There had been a great deal of preparation. From the palace all the way to the assembly building the roads were decorated with flags. Along the route of the procession, windows and balconies that offered a good view were worth a fortune.

Most of the inhabitants had come out in the street hours before the procession, even the previous night, in order to secure a good spot to watch from—people of all nationalities, all races, all religions, old and young, women, children . . . perhaps even the handicapped . . . all of them had come out of their homes. They all patiently waited for hours to see the sovereign pass—a sovereign who had made every effort not to show himself to his people!

Péra. The guardhouse on Taksim square was decorated very ostentatiously. The crowd there was extremely dense. Noratunkian's home was right across Taksim Square from the garrison. Their windows were the best place to watch the procession from. Members of the elite families of Péra had accepted my sister's kind invitation to come and sit at these windows. I was on the top floor, seated beside a pleasant Turkish woman at a wide window. Her husband, an intellectual and an honest government official, had died in exile, another of Sultan Hamid's victims. She made very prudent, wise comments on the events of the day; I wondered how she could view these things objectively and make such wise observations.

Abdul Hamid was seated in a carriage drawn by two horses. He was wearing a coat over his gold-encrusted uniform. Through the open front one could see the wide red ribbons of his decorations. Facing him respectfully was Kâmil Pasha, the vizier. He also was wearing a coat over his uniform. The sultan looked distracted but healthy. In contrast to his usual fatigued appearance, he seemed rejuvenated. It was even said that Mavroyani Pasha had given him a treatment to reinforce his strength. The carriage advanced slowly, in contrast to the usual haste after Friday prayers, when the carriage of the royal *selamlik*[4] raced from the mosque as if fleeing. The cavalry escort, in their dazzling uniforms, followed the sovereign. Then an endless row of carriages with assorted occupants, an impossible mixture of people: the imam, the Greek priest, the rabbi, and the Armenian sexton, as if at the moment of departure they had been shoved haphazardly into the carriages: one could not imagine a more heterogeneous procession!

I asked the Turkish lady beside me what she thought the sultan was thinking at that very moment.

"It's very easy to guess," she replied. "He is probably wondering how and by what means he'll be able to topple all these people,

---

4. The part of a Turkish house or palace set apart for men.

lock up the representatives of the Assembly, exile or bribe them, send back those who have returned or throw them from Saray Burnu[5] to the bottom of the sea, and thus reestablish absolute rule.

Her conjectures were realized on March 31, 1909.

---

5. Literally the tip of the palace (Turkish). The sea in front of the Palace of Topkapi is very turbulent.

Arshak Chopanian (Arshag Tchobanian)

(1872–1954)

Arshak Chopanian (commonly spelled Archag Tchobanian, as in French), poet, translator, literary critic, philologist, journalist-publicist, and playwright, was born in Beshiktash, a suburb of Constantinople, to a family whose origins go back to the historic city of Akn (Kemaliye) on the banks of the Euphrates River. When he was about a month old, his mother died, and thus his childhood lacked a mother's tender care. He later expressed this privation in one of his early poems, "*Adami vishte*" (Adam's grief), in which Adam, who has been watching Eve cradle her child in her arms, raises a complaint to God saying, "O Lord, why did you not give me a mother?"

He received his education at the local Makruhiyan school and at the newly founded (1886) Kedronakan lycée (1887–91), where his teachers included Minas Cheraz (1852–1929), Tovmas Terzian (1840–1909), and Yeghia Temirchipashian (Demirdjibashian, 1851–1908), who soon noticed literary abilities in this bright student and encouraged him to develop his talents. In 1889, while still a student, he began to write poetry and to translate French authors such as Daudet, Zola, Flaubert, Maupassant, and Théophile Gautier. He was published in the *Arev-elk* (The Orient) daily. He owed his mastery of French to two French women who tutored him in his childhood. After graduating summa cum laude from the lycée, he took up a teaching position and became a regular contributor to the *Hayrenik* (Fatherland) daily, where such writers as Arpiar Arpiarian (1852–1908), Levon Bashalian (Pashalian, 1868–1943), Grigor Otian (1834–87), and Hovhannes Shahnazar, all members of the editorial board and proponents of realism, guided him to a literary career. His first essays in prose and poetry were published in 1891, in a booklet titled *Arshaluysi dzayner* (Sounds of dawn), followed in 1892 by a collection of poems called *Trtrumner* (Shudderings). These were followed by *Tughti parke* (The glory of paper, 1892)—a psychological novella—and his first play, *Mut khaver* (Dark strata, 1893), which was successfully staged. The honorarium he received from this play enabled him to visit Paris in 1893, and there he made the acquaintance of such famed literary figures as Émile Zola, Alphonse Daudet, François Coppée, Jean Lorrain, Henri Baüer, and Madame Caroline Séverine, with whom he had maintained a correspondence. When he returned home in late 1894 he assumed the editorship of *Tzaghik* (Flower), but in 1895, when the Armenian massacres broke out, he and other intellectuals moved to Paris. He remained there for the rest of his life.

His early works reveal a tendency to romanticism, but in the late 1880s, when he joined the Arpiar Arpiarian group, he gradually shifted to realism, after toying for a while with the Parnassians'[1] maxim, "art for art's sake"; he never entirely abandoned romanticism, however. His realism was more accentuated in his later poetry, such as *Kertvatzner* (Poems, 1908), *Hayreni knar* (The ancestral lyre, 1925), *Banasteghtzutiunner* (Poems, 1949), as well as in prose such as *Tghu hoginer* (The souls of children, 1923), *Patkerner* (Images, 1940), *Kyank yev yeraz* (Reality and dream, 1945), and in his two plays, *Bambasank* (Gossip, 1950) and *Hrashke* (The miracle, 1952).

He was a prolific and multifaceted author, and wrote in many genres: poetry, essays, short stories, plays, philological studies, and literary criticism. In 1894 he published the collected works of the poet Petros Durian (1851–72), meticulously based on the original manuscripts, with an in-depth analysis of the work. This was instrumental in reviving Durian's poetry, the popularity of which was diminishing twenty years after his premature death. In 1907 Chopanian published an extensive critical study of Mkrtich Peshiktashlian (Beshiktashlian, 1828–68), which included a collection of his poems. His *Demker* (Portraits) in two volumes

---

1. A group of young French poets (1866–76) who challenged the old romantics (Hugo, Lamartine, and so on) and promoted an impersonal lyricism, expressed by the formula "art for art's sake."

(1924, 1929) contains critical essays on a number of contemporary writers. In his important scholarly study of Grigor Narekatsi (Gregory of Narek), the tenth-century mystic, he considers *Matyan voghbergutyan* (Book of lamentations) as an aesthetic and humanistic creation hidden under the guise of religious mysticism, and places it among the great works of world literature.[2]

Chopanian was also an indefatigable researcher of medieval Armenian poetry. By digging through numerous old manuscripts he compiled a treasury of *hayrens*—short poems or songs of secular reflection that constitute a daring and brilliant poetic genre[3]—and published them in two volumes, *Nahapet Kuchaki divane* (The collected poems of Nahapet Kuchak, 1902), and *Hayrenneri burastan* (Garden of *hayrens*, 1940). This work of discovery and compilation and his study of the bardic poetry of Naghash Hovnatan (1661–1722) were major contributions to modern knowledge of Armenian literature.

In 1898 he founded *Anahit*, a review of literature and research that opened a new era in Armenian journalism and played a prominent role in Armenian letters, art, and philology; it is also known for its longevity (1898–1911, 1929–49), an amazing achievement for a one-man initiative. It constituted a chronicle of Armenian life and gathered around itself the foremost intellectuals of the day.

He rendered another great service by introducing Armenian history, art, and literature to French intellectual circles through lectures and articles in periodicals such as *Revue Blanche, Revue des Revues, Revue Encyclopédique,* and others. Outstanding among these was his series of lectures titled "History, Art, Literature, and the Armenian Question," organized under the aegis of Anatole France (1844–1924), whom he had won over to the Armenian cause. Chopanian's translations of Armenian poetry into French, published under titles such as *Poèmes arméniens, anciens et modernes* (Armenian poems, ancient and modern, 1902), *Chants populaires arméniens* (Popular Armenian songs, 1903), *Les trouvères arméniens* (The Armenian minstrels, 1906), and *Poèmes* (Poems, 1909), eventually culminated in *Roseraie d'Arménie* (Rose garden of Armenia, 1918–29), a three-volume work that is truly a masterpiece.

His connections to prominent literary figures enabled him to launch an aggressive campaign to heighten the awareness of the French government and public vis-à-vis the atrocities committed against Armenians in the Ottoman Empire. The first article, published in *Mercure de France* in

---

2. For Gregory of Narek, see volume 2 of the present anthology, 274–307.
3. For a discussion of *hayrens,* see volume 2 of the present anthology, 1028–32.

1896, is titled "*Les Massacres d'Arménie, Témoignages des Victimes*" (The Armenian massacres: victims' accounts). It is an eyewitness account of the massacres ordered by the Red Sultan, Abdul Hamid, and has a preface written by Georges Clémanceau, a prominent politician and later (1906–9, 1917–20) prime minister of France. His other works on the Armenian cause are: *L'Arménie; son passé, son histoire, sa littérature, son rôle en Orient* (Armenia: its past, its history, its literature, its role in the east, 1897); *Zeïtun, depuis les origines jusqu'à l'insurrection de 1895* (Zeytun, from its origins to the rebellion of 1895, translated from Aghassi, 1897); *Le peuple arménien, son passé, sa culture, son avenir* (The Armenian people: its past, its culture, its future, 1913), with a preface by Denys Cochin of the French Academy; *L'Arménie sous le joug turc* (Armenia under the Turkish yoke, 1916); *La France et le peuple arménien* (France and the Armenian people, 1917); *La femme arménienne* (The Armenian woman, 1918); *La nation arménienne et son oeuvre culturelle* (The Armenian nation and its cultural achievement, 1945); and articles in various periodicals. In recognition of his work he was awarded a medal of honor by the French Academy.

His hectic career did not allow him time for family life; he lived alone, in a modest room in Paris, and dedicated his existence to his ambitious projects. He remained active until 1954, when he died in a car accident in Paris.

FROM GREGORY OF NAREK[4]

I

The contemporary part of Armenian literature is almost wholly unknown in France—that literature in modern Armenia which developed under the influence of European literature, and which includes some great novelists, poets and humorists of real originality. Of the ancient part, the more considerable, little is known, except the historical works. The French Armenists, Saint Martin, Dulaurier, Brosset and Langlois, have translated the greater part of the Armenian chroniclers and historians. The French critic has appreciated the documentary importance of these works, where are to be found in abundance details concerning

---

4. Arshak Chopanian, "Gregory of Narek," *Armenia* 3, no. 4 (February 1907), 8–10. Translated by Y. R.

the numerous peoples of the Orient who have traversed Armenia, and, above all, information concerning the Sassanides, the Byzantine empire, and the crusades. But until now the restoration of the purely literary side of this literature has been neglected. The translations of the historians, some of whom, like Yeghishé and Moses of Khoren, are almost epic poets, have not been made with the aesthetic care which they deserve. They are published in inaccessible forms, as scientific documents; and there has never been any attempt to make the French public acquainted with the poetic part of this literature. And yet notwithstanding the lack of breadth and of variety, resulting from the continually agitated existence of the people, Armenian literature, in which many Oriental influences have blended together with a curious complexity, with the Greco-Roman thought as the predominant influence, is far from being devoid of interest from the aesthetic point of view.

Since there remain but a few fragments of the ancient rhapsodic poetry of pagan Armenia, Armenian literature from one end to the other is imbued with the Christian spirit. It was founded after the adoption of Christianity in Armenia (fourth century), by the Armenian clergy educated in Greece and in Syria, who began to introduce Occidental civilization into their country by translating the Bible and the books of the Fathers: then by writing theological and historical books. They had their successors, who continued the intellectual work in the same direction, through the political confusion, until the ultimate loss of independence. It is therefore, taken together, a church literature, like the Byzantine and Syrian literatures. It is composed of chronicles penetrated by a spirit of Christian fatalism; of religious commentaries, of meditations, of mystical, didactical, allegorical and descriptive poems, and of translations of Greek and Syrian works, of books of sorcery, of mathematics, of astrology, of medicine and of morality. And if the long series of Armenian chroniclers are of an incontestable documentary value, this vast accumulation of poems, religious or descriptive, is interesting from the richness and brilliance of its form, from the depth and nobleness of its inspiration.

All this lyric part remains unknown in France. Nothing has been translated of the hymns or of these poems, except some fragments, in a mediocre version, which has been translated in "Christian Armenia and her Literature," by Felix Nevé, the Belgian Armenist.

While waiting for this gap in the French library of foreign literatures to be filled, we wish to present to the French public one of the most original of the mystic poets of Armenia, the monk Gregory of Narek, or, according to the Armenian form, Grigor Narekatsi (950–1003). "He is indeed one of the purest glories of this ancient church," writes Eugène Boré[5] in speaking of Narekatsi. But so far nothing has been done to popularize him in our Occident. It would be rendering a high service to sacred literature to translate the works of this great theologian and mystic. Dulaurier desired it with all his heart, because he could understand their worth from his extensive knowledge of Oriental authors.

In its execution, the work of Narekatsi, of an extreme boldness of expression and a depth of sentiment that no other of our poets has attained, gives a most typical note of Armenian poetic enthusiasm, and merits in other ways to be known as one of the most original pages of the mystic poetry of humanity.

THE BOND[6]

All things are bound together by a tie
    Finer and subtler than a ray of light;
Color and sound and fleeting fragrances,
    The maiden's smile, the star-beam sparkling bright,
Are knit together by a secret bond
    Finer and subtler than a ray of light.

Sometimes an urn of memories is unsealed
    Just by a simple tune, or sad or gay;
Part of the past with every quivering note
    From its dark sleep awakens to the day,
And we live o'er again a long-past life,
    Just through a simple tune, or sad or gay.

Some flowers bring men and women back to mind;
    A well-known face smiles on us in their hue;

5. *Correspondence et mémoires d'un voyageur en Orient* (Correspondence and memoirs of a voyage in the Orient) (Paris, 1840).

6. Arshak Chopanian, "The Bond," in *Armenian Poems*, ed. and trans. Alice Stone Blackwell (Boston, 1917), 175–76.

Their bright cups, moved by the capricious wind,
  Will make us dream of eyes, black eyes or blue;
We in their fragrance feel a breath beloved;
  Flowers bring back men and women whom we knew.

The summer sea recalls fond, happy hours;
  We in the sunset see our dead once more;
In starlight, holy loves upon us smile;
  With our own griefs the stormy thunders roar;
The zephyr breathes to us a name adored;
  We in the sunset see the dead once more.

All things are bound in closest unison,
  Throughout the world, by many a mystic thread.
The flower and love, the breeze and reverie,
  Nature and man, and things alive and dead,
Are all akin, and bound in harmony
  Throughout the world, by many a mystic thread.

To the Moon[7]

Why am I not the thin white cloud
  That, floating soft and slow,
Veils the pure splendor of your face
  'Neath its transparent snow?

Or one of those unnumbered stars—
  Bees that in heaven's height
Flit 'round you, seeking honey there,
  O shining Rose of light?

Why am I not the dark-browed mount
  Where you a moment stay,
Ere spreading your broad, viewless wings
  To soar through heaven away?

Why am I not the forest deep,
  Where, dropping through the air,

---

7. Ibid., 177–78.

'Mid foliage dark slip in and hang
    Threads of your golden hair?

Why am I not the tranquil sea
    On which your beams descend,
Where molten diamonds and fire
    And milk and honey blend?

Alas, why am I not at least
    That cold tomb of the dead,
On which your rays so tenderly
    Their tears' bright sadness shed?

ODE TO MY NATIVE TONGUE[8]

You flow like a boundless river, sprung from the lofty summits of everlasting mountains and rushing forth into the sunshine with life-giving freshness from time immemorial, singing through the ages, O beautiful, sweet tongue of my native Armenia. Your origin is shrouded in mystery, in the mists of ageless mountains. Through the majestic shades of the legends you bring, we still perceive the bright form of Hayk, the godlike hero, as he stands over your rushing fountain like a stately oak tree, casting his manly and paternal gaze upon you as he raised his mighty arm against tyranny for the first time. Like children looking in wide-eyed wonder at a garden of lilies, we marvel to behold the luminous beauty of Ara the Fair, which spreads along your shores like the daybreak and slowly fades away with unsullied purity.

A hundred races, from the mightiest to the weakest, the most civilized to the most savage, have traversed your shores. Many of them tried to restrain your flow and reduce you to a trickle, but they were buried in the dust of their brutish footprints, and perished forever. But you took from each of them a shade, a hue, a tint, and a scintilla, enfolding them to your bosom, adding them to the splendor of your attire, and continuing your course through the ages with vigor and resolve.

---

8. Arshak Chopanian, "*Geghon i pativ Hay lezvin*" (Ode to my native tongue), in *Kyank yev yeraz zhoghovatzu ardzakneru* (Life and dream: a collection of prose pieces) (Paris, 1945). Translated by the editors of the present anthology.

Who will make us hearken again to the solemn music, the lyric poems, and the valiant victory songs of your golden days, with which your waves resounded when the steed of triumph trotted proudly on your soil, the mighty hands of Tigran and Trdat holding the reins? All these lie sleeping in the darkness of time. They were echoed, however, in the majestic symphony you fashioned from Mesrop's divine breath, when, refreshed by your abounding streams, fortified by your bold, meandering lunges, armed with the power of the sun within you and with the thrill of the visions rebounding in your soul and the courage of the races watching over you, you brilliantly emerged to shine in the fullness of your splendor, as your frolicking waves reflected the shimmering rainbow of my native land.

One day you were shaken by a storm. Your seething waters, black, roaring, and gashed by lightning, unleashed an unaccustomed song: a song that was deep and strong, raging and harmonious, loftily harsh and tenderly apprehensive, a song that proceeded from the trumpets of archangels and resounded over the gaping horrors of hell. This was the spirit of Narek the Ascetic passing. . . .

Much, much later, one moonlit night your waters blossomed with light-flowers of matchless delicacy. Your pallid ripples, gently caressed in an ecstasy of rapture, in a shower of glittering silver, sang a song of love and blessing. Shenohali's heart was beaming down on you.

Then came days of great distress. Glory and power departed from your shores. Heavy anguish settled in your soul and deadly winds rent your bosom. Torrents of bloody rain poured down on you, turning your waters crimson. Woeful heaps of bodies floated on your waves. Your shimmers were defiled and shrouded in the putrid colors of decay. For a while you felt the dark wings of death hovering over you. But your inner force vanquished death and quickened you with new life, making you younger than ever. A renewed spring, a brighter sun shone upon you, and turned your waters crystal clear, as lustrous as mother-of-pearl. A gentle breeze refreshed your bosom, and the light of morning showered you with roses and lilies. Gardens blossomed on your banks, and nightingales came to perch in your cool and perfumed shady places, there to warble their amorous songs. These were our bards, with their sad, sweet melodies. . . .

And today, after flowing through a thousand places and a host of diverse circumstances through countless ages, after experiencing the greatest glories and the deepest sorrows, you flow on, ever stronger and clearer, O sweet, magnificent tongue of my native Armenia! Your infinite course has not tired you and you have not aged, because you possess the secret of eternal youth. To the gilded splendor of the garment you wore in the ancient days of your glory, you have now added the delicate grace of your bards, our mothers' undescribable tender glances and the shining brazen armor of your resolute heroes. Sometimes your garb reflects the dreadful red of our harrowing tragedies, sometimes the bright radiance of our noble aspirations. Wherever you rushed forth, as with a multitude of mouths you sang of freedom, and you sang it in a deep, strong, rich voice which quavered the entire East. And now, your song dawns like a diamond through shrouding darkness.

O native tongue! Mirror of benevolence, valor, compassion, and sweetness! You are our heart, our soul, and our blood. You are our being, our glory, and our honor. You are one of the most glorious manifestations of the universal force. As long as there is life on earth, you will triumphantly pursue your noble course through the endless meadows of time.

Artashes Harutiunian

(1873–1915)

The poet and literary critic Artashes Harutiunian was born and educated in Malgara, Turkey. He settled in Constantinople in 1912 and was rounded up by the Ottoman leadership in 1915 and slain shortly thereafter. *Lkvatz knar* (Abandoned lyre, 1902) was his first collection of poems. *Yerkunk* (Childbirth, 1906) followed it four years later. *Nor knar* (New lyre, 1912), his third collection, was written under the influence of the French *symboliste* movement—his verse here expresses images and colors, always in concise and concrete terms. His enthusiasm for the *symboliste* poets and his efforts to imitate them were beneficial, allowing him to introduce a new psychological depth to Armenian poetry during the first decade of the twentieth century.

Harutiunian's main importance centers around his profound comprehension and appreciation of, and his efforts to promulgate, Armenian provincial literature. He made a further contribution as a literary critic. *Dimastvernere* (Portraits) is a collection of critical pieces published in various periodicals on such figures as Yeghia Temirchipashian (Demirdjibashian, 1851–1908), Matteos Mamurian (1830–1901), Shirvanzadé (1858–1935), and others. These writings include such literary studies as "*Indra yev ir nerashkharhe*" (Indra and his inner world), "*Daniel Varuzhan yev ir nor girke*" (Daniel Varuzhan and his new book), "*Gavari kyanken*" (On life in the provinces), and so on, which, containing neither emotional outbursts nor philosophical dissection, provided education in literary criticism, which Harutiunian regarded as a creative endeavor, for Western Armenian scholars.

FROM ART AND LITERATURE[1]

The poetry of love has a right to exist in every literature. The subject can never be exhausted. We wait only for the poet to find a new string on which to sound the tumults of his heart. We then listen to him with the utmost pleasure and sometimes even with gratitude. This despite the fact that many consider the genre childish. Is it not the case that to people with such temperaments all poetry may seem childish? It is a matter of personal opinion.

I think that poets are no less responsible for the common opinion that poetry is a vacuum that resounds with trivial echoes. There are many bad poets; despite these, however, there is still poetry. The thing is that in order to understand poetry one has to be a bit of a poet oneself. And to understand love one must possess a heart that is capable of loving. I know many pedants who are immature and are condemned to stay that way; they insist that their limited intellectual sensitivity is an unerring touchstone for all values—for example, deriding poetry—and thus they imagine that in so doing they have gained in importance. In their devastating ignorance, they have pronounced the dreaming poet immature, whereas they are minuscule in comparison. And love has nothing to do with learned, aged, or serious and practical people; love belongs to hearts capable of loving; love is the grace of youth; it is life's very purpose; therefore, "Sing of love" as Solomon says.

There was a time when criticism was likened to what a schoolteacher does when he corrects his students' compositions: pointing out mistakes, correcting errors, citing rules, and imposing conventions were what the literary critic excelled at. His particular role in

---

1. Artashes Harutiunian, "*Grakanutiun yev gegharvest*" (Art and literature), in *Ardzak ejer yev kertvatzner* (Prose pages and poems) (Paris, 1937), 159–70. Translated by the editors of the present anthology.

this area was a proud, overturning role. As if the works were things that needed correction! This unattractive business of finding spots and stains, of pointing them out, and of making an issue of them continues to be a task that rejoices the sad, dry hearts of school masters.

A literary work, as a work of art, is a complete, created entity, expressed according to the independent and individual rules of a particular sensitivity. The role of criticism is to understand and explain, and, if necessary, to love and to make others love. The critic is an appreciator, and his task is limited to the intrinsic merits of the object he is criticizing. The best ability he could possess would be the ability to understand completely what the ordinary appreciator can understand only incompletely. His soul, his mind open wide their doors to all expressions presented to him— even though they differ from his own—in all their individualistic independence and free sensibility. Within these limits, there is no place for absolute judgments, and consequently there are no means of judgment either. There are only individualities, each composed differently and hence each reflecting the realities of the world differently. The critic's job is to understand and affirm the degree to which the aspects he looks into are effective. When the critic encounters felicitous expressions, his duty is to enthuse and to be enthused. His is the happiness of the explorer who finds hidden treasure. It may happen that what he finds is nothing but worthless charms and tawdry beads. Alas, precious stones are rare. He should not, however, get upset at that, nor should he be irritable and ask why things are that way. In fact, he must not permit himself to say that things could have been any other way. Rather, he will try to say that he knows that things are precisely like that because they could not have been any other way, despite our wishes or even our exasperation. The critic raises altars, weaves laurels, erects temples for worthy deities, the number and diversity of whom serve only to make the pantheon more attractive. Aware of his high calling as a devoted priest, it is his mission to instruct the faithful and win believers to his divinities.

Ruben Vorberian

(1873–1931)

The poetry of Ruben Vorberian reflects the sensitivity of the Armenian soul that longs for the homeland, its houses, its sky—a condition afflicting both poet and reader. In this respect he recalls the "graveyard school" of pre-Romantic English poetry.[1] His expressions of sincere, deep feeling and melancholic nostalgia for what is old, the past, and childhood strike chords beyond the range of other Armenian romantics.

Vorberian was born in Malatya, Turkey, and educated at Euphrates College in Kharberd (Harput), at the time one of the foremost educational establishments in Asia Minor. He received his Armenian education under Tlkatintsi (1860–1915) and Ruben Zardarian (1874–1915), and joined them as an exponent of provincial Armenian literature.

Vorberian moved to Constantinople in the early 1890s. Following a decade of teaching in Constantinople and Smyrna (Izmir), he went into business in Djibouti (1903–20). During the long years he spent away from home he maintained contact with the Armenian periodical press. He wrote mainly about his passionate yearning for his homeland. He

---

1. The graveyard school consisted largely of imitations of Robert Blair's long poem *The Grave* (1743) and of Edward Young's *Night Thoughts* (1742–45); it reached its culmination in Thomas Gray's "Elegy Written in a Country Church-Yard" (1751).

spent his final eleven years in Paris, but after 1923 he was bedridden as the result of a stroke, unable even to use a pen.

His first work, *Hishatakats tzaghikner* (Flowers of memory, 1893), brings out the romantic poet immersed in years gone by. It contains both verse and prose poetry, full of romantic motifs and sentimentality, but without significant imagination. His thin volume *Tzpankner* (Ripples) was published in 1906 under the pen name of Ruben Alikian. The first poem, "*Depi andund*" (Toward the abyss), is reminiscent of Byron's *Childe Harold's Pilgrimage,* "an idea conceived in complete isolation, cajoled, aggrandized, loved, and worshiped—a meditative peregrination through lands not yet visited by Harold," the later poet says, "weaker than Harold, but more afflicted than he."[2] The pilgrimage goes to the far corners of Asia, to the Far East, to the cradles of great religions. It is an ambitious work, engendered by patriotic aspirations. The hero, like Harold, is restless and worn, self-exiled, and gloomy.

In *Ovasis* (Oasis, 1920), Vorberian reveals the troubled but imaginative mind of the poet, who mourns his ruined homeland with deep anguish and pessimism. His lyricism is more pronounced here than in the early poems. There is more artistry, and an agitated emotionalism pervades such poems as "*Giughis chamban*" (The road through my village), "*Nor tnaks*" (My new hut), "*Gna*" (Go), and "*Vardenin*" (The rosebush). The influence of the English Romantic poets Byron and Shelley is readily discernible. Vorberian's study of Byron was published in *Bazmavep* (*Polyhistor*) in 1932.

FROM ALL THE WAY TO ARGAEUS[3]

Fulfillment of one's destiny.[4]

These words are repeated, repeated again and again, ten thousand times recorded in the inmost recesses of my soul; in a way

---

2. H. Mesrop Chanashian, *Hay grakanutyan nor shrjani hamarot patmutiun, 1701–1920* (A short history of modern Armenian literature) (Venice, 1973), 214. Vorberian translated sections of Byron's Childe Harold.

3. Ruben Vorberian, "*Minchev Erchias*" (All the way to Argaeus), in *Ovasis* (Oasis) (Paris, 1938), 7–14. Translated by the editors of the present anthology. Argaeus (presently known as Erciyas) is the highest mountain (12,848 feet) in Asia Minor.

4. "All the Way to Argaeus" and "Beyond Argaeus" are products of the last days of my time in Izmir. They form the first rings of the chain that links me to the desert and an authentic depiction of my wandering existence at the time. I wrote their closing lines in Djibouti and I reproduce them here for my own benefit, in order that I might not forget the climb to the heights that preceded my plunge into this terrible dark solitude." (Ruben Vorberian)

they anesthetize my heart, lessening the pain of separation and the weeping and sorrow that go with it.

Fulfillment of one's destiny.

You have a meager few hours to spend with your loved ones; all too soon the rising sun will light up the skies; a few friendly rays will soon creep over you, and yet you have no sense that tomorrow or in the days that follow tomorrow, whether cloudy or bright, these glimmers will forget you and leave you to turn to dew, alone under different stars, which will shine on you from behind foreign mountains and from unknown skies.

All other thoughts have disappeared, undiscerned in the mist, and before you leave your cottage, you have the impression that you have already departed: the train speeds whistling away and you, lying in the coach, speed with it, and you climb the mountains or complete the steep descent alone.

All alone!

And no one who leaves home for the first time, whether in pursuit of petty or extravagant dreams or to temper the boredom of an ambitious life, can ever feel the bitterness of this word. It is the only word that these two classes cannot understand. It is understood only by the wayward nightingale, which flies over and across the mountains and comes to a place where it builds a nest in a hollow for itself, its mate, and its young ones, and then an innate weakness turns the bird aside from its usual path and it fixes its tiny eyes on something vague and amorphous and flies off, leaving its loved ones behind.

Fulfillment of one's destiny.

These words course through the veins like cocaine—you shudder and press your loved ones to your bosom; the deadening of feeling continues. And you feel that the separation is more depressing than your strength or ability can cope with. A vague feeling that has no name. The train whistles, departs; your eyes well up with tears and you do not know why, because you still do not think of yourself as isolated and alone, and you come to the bay, and this, your beloved Cordelia, brings to mind the glowing, sweet smelling, unforgettable Cordelia of your halcyon days, which faintly sparkles and then disappears. But you remain, and life goes on.

And yet you continue to dream for hours. Through tear-filled eyes you discern the sky-high peaks of Sibyl, from the precipice of which a little valley descends to Manisa. Not far from that is the weeping Niobe, who looks out at you from her rocky abode. Beyond that, and beyond even that . . . there is only icy loneliness . . . you shut your eyes and return home.

Ah, I assure you, that is when the real torment begins. Now that you have left it behind, everything seems dear to you: your cottage, your small room, the huge, unfeeling mirrors, the little cat, and even the tree or two that grow by the door—even though, perhaps, you never noticed the rustling of their leaves in your whole life.

The train speeds on. The icy winds cool your fevered brow. With somber heaviness evening shadows stretch out along the valleys. But you feel their pressure for only a minute, and are already speeding away from them: beautiful houses, which cast shadows on your life no more than momentarily.

Villages scattered here and there. Precipice, ascent, descent, and another steep ascent on the way to Uşak. About twenty tunnels, iron bridges that seem suspended in midair. And to think that it is now a splendid Sunday evening—that the bay sleeps calmly in the arms of the goddesses of the harbor of Izmir, and the atmosphere is lazy with a sweet intoxication.

The night, they say, is the consoler of despondent souls. Those who are far from home will understand me very well when I say that instead of consoling me night sows fires in the depths of my existence. Unconsciously I begin to hate the daylight. Daylight, which revealed to me the distant mountain chains that lay between my home and my self, irritated and stung my body painfully. And so I feel a certain sadness descend upon me when night falls; I stand beneath it, tense, with lips tight and contracted. I stretch my head out of the coach window. It is a curious night: cold, bitterly cold.

I try to focus my gaze in the familiar darkness that confronts me, and search. I try to sort out my memories of the day—the first day of my journey—and do not succeed. No, I see nothing. I have traveled all day, and have not distanced myself even a smidgen: I am back there; I cannot leave my home behind. Up above, a few stars shine out of the darkness, winking at me mockingly. I do not look at them, although I wince at their derision. My hands begin to tremble. Everything disappears. For hours, the train speeds on, whistling savagely. It is almost eight o'clock. Now and then the half-shut leaves in the forests seem to glitter with faltering hope—

which escapes, like the last gasp of a dying person. A cottage, more cottages, hamlets, villages, sometimes all of them together. I feel that I am getting depressed; I am depressed. I bow my head and begin to weep. Otherwise, I would go out of my mind; the sigh I have been suppressing all day dissolves in those teardrops. I sink deep into self-oblivion, but I am startled back to reality. A friendly hand squeezes my own. I am comforted. Oh! Never before in all my days has friendship been so welcome. Never have I been so much in need of it. And that friendly squeeze gives me the chance to collect myself and think a little about the rising of the sun when I left home; that was now hours ago.

"May God be with you, *Hayrik* (Father)."

In the darkness I feel the presence of the great "I am." I feel that God, whom you have loved and known more simply than I have, to whom you have unconsciously prayed for me, is following me, your dear son. And I too whisper a prayer, hesitantly. I am not sure exactly what I told the great Eternal; I know only that He heard my voice, weak like the voice of all mortals, and I felt sure that I would travel over this same line once again in the near future, on the day of my return, and would joyfully greet the flaming dawn which would light up for me the road to my modest, happy cottage.

♣

Perhaps my friends find it rather unusual that I am submitting for publication these purely personal impressions of the first day of my journey. I thought it right, however, to proclaim that such sentiments, intangible but nevertheless eternal, exist, and that human beings, regardless of how completely they have to surrender to the tumult of the harsh world, still have moments when their hearts reexperience an ardent longing for the past, their brows cloud with reverie. . . . The past is made up of two types of days: the happy and the sad. I know of no intermediate state. We recall both types with sadness, because they are gone and will not come back again. . . . And I have no doubt that is why no artist has ever painted or sculpted the goddess of memory without obscuring her brow with a melancholy cloud.

Once Uşak has been left behind, one is overcome by something like drowsiness: the route is more monotonous, the country almost flat. At the end of the trip you remember, as if from a dream, Afyon Karahisar; Eskişehir, its black rocky hills jutting up out of the flat terrain, where the railway joins the network; and, finally, historic Enkiuri (Ankara), with its famous Red Monastery. Despite its tasteless square houses and narrow winding streets, one feels a certain empathy with this town; I do not know why. Perhaps because Mother Nature has endowed it with a milder, smoother, clearer atmosphere, a sort of diffused radiance that touches the heart.

The mountains are crowned with small patches of snow. I look at them like a stranger, our old friendship forgotten. As I sit in the hotel garden, I cannot take my eyes off the splendid sunset—one that can light up the skies of Eastern countries only. Clouds piled one on top of another and edged with ribbons of silver glide in splendid panoply beyond the mountain peaks. A double railway track abruptly slithers like a snake from the foot of the hill toward the unknown. Beyond this point the ascent begins for me: an ascent, with a few tiny descents, to the timeless mountain plains. Beyond this point the distant: Oh! the ever-increasing distance from my loved ones.

Another day—a keen interest awakens in the traveler's heart. Gradually the trees come to an end and a volcanic barrenness begins: red, yellow, rows of brown hills, vast fields devoid of vegetation and the color green. The day continues to pass by, and what a day! The hours pass, we climb, we ascend higher and higher, and the air gets more and more biting. I reflect that in Smyrna everything was green, and continue my journey.

Hardly two days have passed, and there it is: the Halys River can be seen in the distance, with its muddy, turbid waves; it gushes forth from the foot of the hills and plunges into the depths of formidable stony chasms. I look down from the bridge with apprehension, as if at the unsettled, turbulent days of early spring. Compared to the latter the Halys is only a brook, a worthless, babbling brook, but all the same it is still intimidating. At one end of the bridge a sculptor unfamiliar with antiquity has erected a crouching marble lion with the face of a sphinx, gazing at the mountains across from it. Past centuries draw nearer, making a hushed and reverent journey to the river to which the ancients attached the word *deity*.

Beyond the river is Idé-Belin with its familiar plateau, and then once more the monotony of gray fields; they are scattered with flattened ruins, their tops lying ignominiously on the ground. During long journeys such flatness depresses the traveler. It can never satisfy the spirit, especially when unrelieved by abysses through which the savage clamor of a river floods and surges.

Beyond Kirshehir the scenery changes significantly. The wind blows harder and the earth is dotted with gloomy, dark, lead-colored patches. Everywhere there are traces of an extinct volcano, and when one sees them one feels the scorching fires. And the earth seems to tremble. One hour, two, three. A road leaps over a mountain, as though the road also were curious—a large, stony, very rough road. The coach has now reached the top of the hill; I examine my surroundings: the horizon has now expanded on three sides. One sees farther into infinity. Across from me, behind the incessant hillocks, I can see a round patch of white cloud. In the limpid blue of the sky the presence of that monolithic, motionless, fixed piece of cloud seems strange. I am engrossed, like one who dreams. A little more time goes by: half an hour, an hour. And suddenly in the fog, in the vastness, its contours disappearing, on this side of infinity stands a mountain—a mountain soaring into the sky.

It is Argaeus.

With profound emotion—awe mixed with a kind of adoration— I take it in. It seems to be approaching me, coming right at me; I dare not lose courage, for it seems to crush my very existence, and I think it will end up falling on me.

I needed that. This shock—which only majestic mountains can create in children who have run away from the foot of mountains and are beside themselves with fear—has sent an electric charge through my soul. What I experienced was like a great shudder from one who has been asleep and unfeeling for many long years, has wandered the shores of a sluggish and peaceful bay, and has begun no longer to feel the urgent stirring of life in his soul. A new life was beginning to course through my veins. The mountain understood me. I no longer think that those enormous rocky masses that sprout from the bowels of the earth and are eternally immovable have no soul. Their brows require snow and arctic winds to assuage the fieriness of their volcanic past. They are closer to infinity than we, who are only traveling through life as we pass near their bases; they have more opportunity and enough time to learn the mysteries of the precipice.

Argaeus does not rise alone, like other mountains. A chain of hills surrounds it: a procession of pagan priests, and Argaeus himself is the high priest, wearing an ivory crown around which drift and sigh the age-old mists. We have begun our long descent, and race like horses on their homeward journey. Closer to Argaeus, closer to the lofty mountain, which, like all dreams, is slowly evanescing. The little hills that obscured it from our view disappear one by one, and now the mountain rises in its entirety before my eyes—glorious, towering sublimely.

The silent, superb, and noble colossus has enlarged me, like Mont Blanc, "which has the charm to arrest the dawn," as the poet says.

For a moment let me move in spirit from afar to its twin peaks. From that height I look around at the surrounding world.

The muddy Halys, whose frenzied and impatient waves rush past below. Caesarea (Kayseri), with newly sprouted greenery, Talas, Everek, and several villages relieve the gray monotony of the volcanic land that spreads out before me.

The red river continues on its course: a twisting, doubling, and meandering course; it flows through barren or overpopulated shores right up to the sea that most merits the name of Black.

The sea. From this rocky height I can see all the way to the sea, which reaches out for my soul, and I feel my heart pounding within my bosom.

"May God be with you, *Hayrik*."

The echo of your stammering, boyish voice has come and found me here, my son. In this barren wilderness, man, like a lofty mountain, is also nearer to God. I also feel the centuries passing here, somber and mournful.

The thought of the universal "I am" is enough to strip Argaeus of its majesty. For the spiritual outsoars the greatest heights in the world. Argaeus and its white-haired peaks are not enough for the spirit. All the same, I am thankful to you, O mountain! that you have brought back the memory of my youth. With my soul raised to your summit, I once more see myself, a pale-faced lad who, decades ago, traveled from a great distance, unselfconsciously, and roamed a hostile, soulless, alien land, seeking my fortune.

Ruben Zardarian

(1874–1915)

A master of Western Armenian prose, Ruben Zardarian was born in Siverek (Diyarbekir) in 1874 and moved with his family to Kharberd (Harput) when he was two years old. After completing his primary education he studied under the renowned educator and writer Tlkat-intsi (1860–1915). Under his influence Zardarian became an enthusiastic devotee of Armenian provincial literature.

His writing career began in 1892 while he was a teacher at Tlkat-intsi's private school and continued when he moved on to teach in other schools. He was arrested as a suspected revolutionary in 1903, but he was soon freed, and a year later he was appointed principal of a school in Manisa. This position did not last long, however: Zardarian was jailed again, and he and his family fled to Plovdiv (Bulgaria). In 1906 he founded the *Razmik* (Plebeian) newspaper. Encouraged by the optimism generated by the proclamation of the Ottoman Constitution of 1908, he returned to Constantinople and began to publish the *Azatamart* (Freedom battle) daily in 1909, together with friends in the Dashnak (Armenian Revolutionary Federation) party. The tragic events of 1915 put an end to the paper, and Zardarian was arrested by the Young Turk regime on the night of April 24, 1915. He was put to death shortly thereafter.

His works consist of editorials, literary articles, short stories, and prose poems, which comprise provincial scenes and descriptions of local life, scattered through various newspapers and periodicals. As early as 1890, while he was still in Kharbert, he contributed to a number of periodicals, such as *Shirak, Tzaghik* (The flower), *Arevelyan mamul* (The eastern press), *Masis,* and others.

His publications include *Tsaygaluys: ardzak ejer* (Daybreak: prose pages, 1910), one of his most important works. This is a collection of his writings from the period before the proclamation of the Ottoman Constitution. According to the author, the title refers to the period when deep darkness enveloped the Armenian mind and literature. Except for a few revolutionary pieces, such as "*Ter lsé mezi*" (Hear us, O Lord) and "*Pahaknere artun yen*" (The guards are awake), most of the twenty-nine pieces in the volume are about nature, often treated in a symbolic and semi-philosophical way, and always reflecting village experiences that occur in a peaceful, free, and happy atmosphere. *Meghraget* (Honey river, 1914) is a series of readers. "*Yekeghetsiin ariutze*" (The lion of the church), written under the pen name Ezhtahar, is a long short story that was probably not included in *Tsaygaluys* because of its length. "*Put me jur*" (A bit of water) is another short but noteworthy story, about an Armenian grandmother who embodies the psychology of the superstitious, fanatic, and ignorant women of the provinces.

Zardarian's literary skill in dealing with subject, style, and poetic language is evident in *Tsaygaluys.* His poetic sensitivity enhances the beauty of his prose. His style is carefully wrought: his works are never hasty pronouncements. He is often a psychologist, trying to probe the inner secrets of man. He is a realistic narrator, capable of sustaining interest to the end. His descriptions are often poetic, colored with romantic sentiment and symbolism.

"A Sultan in His Heart," "The Bride of the Lake," "How Death Came to Earth," "The Truthful Boy," and "When Men Did Not Die" are among his works that have been translated into English. His writings have also been translated into French, Italian, and Russian. Several critical studies of Zardarian's works have also been published.

THE SEVEN SINGERS[1]

The hand of an unknown artist wrote on a piece of scroll:
Seven singers they were, seven unknown, homeless minstrels.

---

1. Ruben Zardarian, "The Seven Singers," in *Great Armenian Short Stories*, trans. Sarkis Ashjian (Beirut, 1959), 55–61. Revised by the editors of the present anthology.

They were seven singers and they carried seven musical instruments, and every instrument had seven times seven melodies.

They were drunk with all the wines of the vineyards of life. That was the reason their lips were so sensitive and imbued with so much sweetness. That was likewise the reason their songs were scented with the balm of all those mysteries whose everlasting jets water the gardens of the human soul, filling them with unearthly tremors.

Six of them were disciples and the seventh was their master; he had curly white hair that flowed abundantly onto his shoulders. And the seven singers were blind, every one of them, because blindness was sacred in those remote times and it imparted to poets (so writes the hand of the unknown artist) the light of the suns of wisdom instead of the rays of our sun: the light of the suns of wisdom, which is far brighter than that of our sun, radiates from the unreachable skies of the soul in its eternal and divine splendor.

They were gathered on that day to sing the words of their lyric perfection. Each one of them would play on his own instrument and the master would reveal to them the last mystery of art and wisdom, and then he would let them go to the seven corners of the earth. They were to go forth and greet all sorrows and joys, wherever they found them, with the strength of all the languages of the heart. They would talk to all the feelings and consciences of mankind, wherever they met them.

The famous wine of Armenia was laid in green clay pitchers and seven white porphyry cups were filled to the brim, one for each of the minstrels.

♣

The first ode was played on the flute, by the minstrel whose black hair was crowned with a fresh rustic wreath, woven of ivy leaves and multicolored field flowers.

". . . . Sweetness my song, and my song for the world. I am the breeze that comes down from the hilltops. I am a nightingale who has no homeland. Woe unto the heart that has no laughter! Woe unto the land that has no nightingales! A heart without a minstrel is like a dried-up fountain or an endless night. My voice and song are for you, O happy among men, who carry the golden jars of the dawns of Eden on your shoulders. Yes, my friend, my song is for the likes of you. Stop at every step and drink to excess of the sensuousness generated by the contents of your jars, like the blessed cranes that fly in mirth and while a-wing, in midair, sip the dewy syllables of heavenly harmony. I have dipped my lips in the honey of the pomegranates of Akn, and I have washed my soul in the attar of the red roses of Shiraz. My song has the power to reach even the grave and catch the ears of the dead, so that they tap their bones in time. And when my breath passes over deserts, it causes the flowers of creative life to bloom, even in the burning sands. I know of one force in the universe, which is the fountainhead of all sources, the beginning and the very end of all existence. . . ."

And the cups were raised and the singing voices repeated in harmony: "It is Love, it is Love, it is Love!"

The second minstrel, who wore a coronet of woven laurel leaves on his head, touched the strings of his harp and sang:

"The morning passes as a dream lifts from the eyes of a babe, and the evening dies in the arms of darkness like the wink of an eye. But the sun of noontide makes the soil fertile, allowing it to deliver its gifts to the world in a perfect, accomplished, and total way. I sing of the secret of the skies and of the earth. I sing of the secret that preserves the eternity of the gloriously green forests and points the mountain peaks at the stars. I sing of that which the wise men sang in marble stones in the temples of Athens: precisely of that which is the very glory of men and forces women to prostrate themselves before it, moves them to yield themselves, casting away all their divine weapons! My song is the glorification of life and of that single law that existed yesterday and in the yesterday of yesterdays and will certainly exist tomorrow and eternally. I know of one strength only, which is the strength of all strengths, the perfection of all the arts, and the key to all the mysterious vaults of the universe. . . ."

And the hands raised the wine cups and the seven minstrels sang full-throated and harmoniously: "It is Power, it is Power, it is Power!"

The third minstrel raised his lute. He had a coronet of daisies, pinks, and violets around his head. He sang in a ringing and vibrating voice: "I come to thee, I kneel before thee, and I raise my soul to thee, O divine goddess, who created the songs of all the centuries gone by, thus becoming the smiling rainbow which unites all past and all future times, all times, indeed, that moan with sorrow and affliction. I come to thee as, descending from their thrones, kings came imploringly, and as shepherds came, forgetting their flocks in the valleys. I come to thee as the armies of dreamers and the immortal dreams of great poets came to thee, and as surely as caravans of ever-youthful generations will come. O, hear me! I tell you all: there is but one single temple raised above all the victories in the entire universe! It is the supreme temple, whose god is immortal and whose adoration is the religion of all religions, and it shall reign forever! The day my god dies, the sun will lose its light, life will lose its attraction, and the world will become an accursed palace, whose pillars will shake and totter, and whose foundations will quake and tremble, and from that accursed palace men will flee terror-stricken, as flocks of wild beasts flee the boundaries of a prairie that is on fire. I come to thee, O goddess; touch thy fingers to my instrument and let its song be the clear understanding of all intricate mysteries. . . ."

And seven wine cups clashed and the group sang melodiously: "It is Beauty, it is Beauty, it is Beauty!"

The fourth minstrel, who had a single vine leaf thrust in his curls, placed his bagpipe under his arm and sang as follows:

"I was exceeding sorrowful and behold I found my cheek resting on the pillow of mirth. I was weary and exhausted as the wheel spinning under the feet of the potter, and behold my blood boiled in my arms and made them as strong as steel. Everything is torture and vanity, Love, Power, and Beauty included. The river passes away and its pebbles remain behind. I know how to hold eternity on my lips and to rise above the tempests of life with wings the likes of which were sought in vain by all the saints, prophets, oracles, and wizards! My feet trod all the ways of the world and I found people everywhere busy burying their dead. Some were following a coffin and mourned already; others were preparing for a funeral and knew it not. I stood at the crossroads and invited the sorrowful to consolation and to the talisman of happiness. I told them Love was more fleeting than the wind. I warned them Beauty died sooner than dew vanishes from the chalice of a lily. I underlined for them the hard fact that the day comes when all feelings and regrets fill the heart with bitterness and gall, more mortal than poison and more corrosive than copper rust. There is no wisdom at all in tears and sorrow. There is one wisdom only—oblivion: forgetting sorrow, affliction, tears, heaven, and hell. Join me, and drink wisdom from my goblet. . . ."

And the seven minstrels echoed in full voices, as if repeating the last line of a sacred hymn: "It is Wine, it is Wine, it is Wine!"

A red rose thrust into his hair, the fifth minstrel sang to the accompaniment of his guitar:

"My strings have a thousand tongues, those thousand tongues have a thousand hearts, and each of those hearts is as large as an ocean! O sun, sacred sun! O Earth, wonderful Earth! I am ready to lay down my life both for thy thorn and for thy rose, for thy mist, and for thy clear sky! Woe unto the mountain where no tempests break; woe unto the heart where no sufferings seethe. No mountain can be clad in green without tempests! And a heart without sorrow is nothing but a rock, containing not a single drop of water. Happy is the Earth when it rejoices and sad is the Earth when it mourns. Fill up the goblet then, wine steward, and let us give the great masters the share of glory that is due to them. Ladder and staircase shall be destroyed and the ground shall rise to the heavens, and the skies shall tumble down and turn to dust and smoke. Let us give the great masters that share of glory that is their due, because they taught us the tale of happiness, along with all the other tales. . . ."

And seven pairs of ardent lips vibrated in a long chorus: "It is Song, it is Song, it is Song!"

A coronet made of rather faded pale leaves around his head, the sixth minstrel sang thus, ringing his petaur:

"Glory to all that the gods scattered upon the earth and upon the waters and in the heavenly spaces, with their generous and radiant hands. Blessed are those who have seen the light of the stars. Blessed are those who have breathed the morning air. Blessed are those who have had tears and laughter. Blessed are those who have slept and awakened. Behold, there is blessedness in this law alone: whatever has crossed this Earth or its waters or has crossed the heavens but once, passing through the paths of the sun but once, has become a god already. But only once, because one's turn comes but once, and whoever has come will return no more, and whoever has wept or laughed shall no more know sorrow or laughter, and whoever has felt thirst and hunger has already tasted of supreme and immutable felicity. Blessed is the arm that acted once on this earth. Blessed is that voice that once echoed in this world. Enjoy whatever there is, enjoy whatever you find, because you find the only truth in doing so. That is the way the waters flow: from innumerable sources, whether turbid or clear, flooded or frosted, under rain or rainbow. . . ."

And the red wine wafted its sweet scent and the song of the seven minstrels rang warm and throbbing: "It is Life, it is Life, it is Life!"

All six of them were disciples and the seventh was their master, who had curly white hair that flowed abundantly onto his shoulders. And the master raised his castanet, kissed it three times, touched it to his forehead, and then sang this song:

"You are entering the gates of those halls from which I have already passed, and behold, I have returned—I have returned after drinking from the six goblets in turn. I come from the feasting table of the world, where I have embraced Love in my arms and felt the magic of Beauty with all its charms. I have beheld Power, which swept past me like a neighing Arabian steed. I drank Wine from all the tables and I gave ear to all the Songs sung by the singers of all singing times. I have sailed on the seas of Life, O minstrels, and I have saluted all the harbors, one by one. And I have counted all the dawning stars and the clusters of them on all the horizons. I am convinced that Love is immortal, yet I know that the human heart is doomed to turn to dust. I am aware that Beauty is eternal, yet I know full well that night strikes its dark seal on the eyes that behold it. I have not the shadow of a doubt that Power, Wine, Song, and Life are balanced on an abyss. . . . And when I drank wine, terror did not loose its grip on me, and when I wished to sing songs of mirth, awe petrified my soul, and I concluded forcefully that no true song of real happiness was ever sung on this earth. Behold my fingers, which tremble, behold the tables, which are empty, and behold your boon companions, who leave! Others come to take their places, and the new arrivals take up what the old ones have already finished. This is Life and this is my song! You all sang of what you had to sing of. And I did not tell you how things really are because Love, Power, Beauty, Wine, Song, and Life are real. And certainly Death is real, together with those things and above them. Let all these realities shine together everywhere, like the seven colors of the rainbow. Let them send their rays into your souls, and let them shed their light from the strings of your individual musical instruments. And hear me, O minstrels: I have not told you the whole truth. All I have told you has been nothing but the mystery of the perfection of art. . . ."

The wine bubbled in the porphyry goblets, and the seven minstrels sipped their last drafts from the green jugs, the handiwork of a skillful potter. They kissed the master's instrument and took leave of each other.

They made their way to the seven corners of the world to greet, with the power of all languages (so writes the hand of the unknown artist), all kinds of sorrow and mirth, wherever they happened to find them. Their mission was to talk to the human soul in cities and villages, palaces and huts alike. There is no need to mention their names, since the world will be repeating their song forever!

Onnik Chifté-Saraf

(1874–1932)

The journalist and writer of short stories known as Onnik Chifté-Saraf was born Hovhannes Abisoghomian Aspet in the Constantinople suburb of Scutari (Üsküdar). He received his education at the Aramian school in Kadikiugh (Kadiköy), then continued at the Kedronakan lycée, but financial constraints forced him to quit school and work as a clerk to a merchant. His first articles appeared in the daily *Surhandak* (Dispatcher) in 1900. The following year he was invited by Arpiar Arpiarian (1852–1907) and Grigor Zohrap (1861–1915) to contribute to *Masis,* where his first short stories were published. In 1902–3 he traveled through Italy, Switzerland, France, and England, acquainting himself with literary trends, and returned home with rich impressions. There followed a fertile creative period. He became a regular contributor to a number of periodicals in addition to *Masis,* such as *Tzaghik* (Flower), *Arevelyan mamul* (Eastern press), *Shirak, Hay grakanutiun* (Armenian literature), *Biuzandion* (Byzantium), Teodik's *Almanachs,* and others. He also served as an elected member of the Armenian National Assembly. At the start of the First World War he was drafted into the Turkish army and was thus spared the horrible fate met by most of his writer colleagues in April 1915.

In 1919 he founded a weekly paper *Hay mitk* (Armenian mind), which, though it had only a brief life, reflected at length and in depth upon the aftermath of the genocide. In one article he says: "As the tattered remnants of six hundred years of slavery and suffering, what we lived through these four horrendous years was the sum total of the misery of that entire period. Now our generation, beheaded of its intellectuals, dismembered, stricken at the heart, humpbacked and aged, is left like a paralyzed and stunned invalid." In the same year he was teaching in an Armenian orphanage that sheltered hundreds of children retrieved from deportation camps. He was so closely associated with these children that in 1920, when the orphanage moved to the Greek island of Corfu, he moved with them. The literature he produced during the following years was strongly influenced by the psychological devastation caused by the genocide. At this time he signed his works Hovhannes Aspet.

In 1923 he was in Marseille, as principal of the Armenian National School, and in 1928 in Geneva, as a teacher, where he remained for the rest of his life.

Realism was the dominant trend when he started his literary career, and Grigor Zohrap was the undisputed master. "His name has a gravitational attraction," he wrote in 1901. "There is a charm in the way he writes, the way he thinks, and the way he lives."[1] Zohrap's influence on Chifté-Saraf's earlier stories is particularly strong. His own aesthetic principle, however, is that nature and life conceal such a wealth of unequaled beauties in their depths that even the strongest poetic imagination cannot rival them. There are few characters and little action in his short stories, but plenty of love, emotion, and passion. His heroes are compassionate lovers of good, beauty, and harmony, and always of a lyrical disposition. Because he was an admirer of Émile Zola, some critics claimed to detect a trace of naturalism in his realism.

Although Chifté-Saraf wrote a great number of articles, reports, travel notes, meditations, and sketches, he made his fame with short stories, of which some of the best known are "*Chermaknerov*" (Clothed in white), "*Metz 'Ayo'n*" (The big yes), "*Hogineru prkutiun*" (Salvation of souls), "*Bazhanumi gishere*" (The night of separation), "*Speghani*" (Healing ointment), "*Zeytuntsi patanin*" (The youth of Zeytun), and "*Khachelutiun*" (Crucifixion). His best known work is *Miamiti me arkatznere* (The adventures of a naïve young man, 1908), his only novel, which depicts the prodigal life of a youth who inherits considerable wealth from his Scrooge-like uncle. Eventually he comes to his senses and

---

1. *Masis* 20 (1901): 309.

returns to his ancestral values. The novel consists of twelve chapters, each giving a description and psychological analysis of a stage in the gradual transformation of his heart and mind.

Chifté-Saraf's works remain scattered in various periodicals. In 1981 a partial collection of his works, including *Miamiti me artatznerw*, was published in Yerevan.

CRUCIFIXION[2]

I have a friend: young, beautiful, and educated. I have been teaching her English for some time now. One day when I went to give my lesson as usual, I saw that she was all dressed up, her hat on her head, waiting to go out. Naturally, I was surprised, and asked:

"Where are you off to?"

"I was waiting for you," she replied coquettishly.

"I hope not for a lesson," I said with a smile, to accentuate my remark.

"No," she retorted with another smile beaming on her youthful lips, "not for a lesson, just for some personal business. I hope you'll be kind enough to come with me, because I'll need your advice in this business. I'm sure you'll make certain things go more smoothly for me."

"I'll be pleased and honored."

"That means we can go."

"But where?"

"To the refugee camp in Haydarpasha."[3] And so we set out from Moda to go there.

On our way, my student explained that she was thinking of choosing a little orphan to adopt.

"We're very lonely at home," she said: "My brother goes to work every day and is terribly busy. My brother's a nervous person and solitary in his habits. I'm left alone, and of course my lessons and handicrafts are not enough to occupy me fully. I hope that

---

2. Onnik Chifté-Saraf, "Khachelutiun" (Crucifixion), in *Yerker* (Works) (Yerevan, 1981), 95–105. Translated by the editors of the present anthology.

3. A suburb on the Asiatic shore of Istanbul.

having a child in our home might bring joy and gaiety, and at the same time, I'll be doing a good deed that will not really add much to our regular budget. I think that if adoption were to catch on, it would lessen the nation's burden and the orphans would grow up in better surroundings and be educated."

We had a very interesting conversation on the subject all the way to the camp. She also expressed earnest and well thought out ideas about how to handle the tattered beings who had succeeded in being saved from the great calamity.

The camp was situated in the middle of an open field and consisted of hundreds of tents. There was a huge crowd of tormented men, women, and children; there was constant movement—coming and going, people busily going about their affairs—giving the impression of a bustling village.

We applied to the supervisor of the camp. After giving him her name, address, and status, my friend said: "I'd like an eight or ten-year-old girl who has no father or mother, not even any relatives."

"We have many!" the supervisor answered; her request had probably surprised him.

Realizing his surprise, I intervened: "The young lady's question was quite understandable, because we see that in or outside every tent there are families with children. She thought that perhaps real orphans would be hard to find or that you'd have to look for them."

"No," replied the supervisor. "Naturally some families have their children with them. Many, however, have lost their children, under so many unfortunate circumstances. The real abandoned orphans have been divided up among the families while they wait to be sent to orphanages or to be adopted. Unfortunately, the latter category is rather small. Of course, some people, especially the middle-class crowd, come here with splendid promises to adopt, but what they really have in mind is to use the children to perform household chores: these are difficult times; it costs a lot to hire servants. And it's not surprising that some of the children escaped and returned to the horrible camp conditions, considering life here a thousand times better than what they had with those families!"

As he explained the situation, he led us to the center of the camp. There he told a few of his subordinates to fetch a group of orphans. A little later they lined up: a pitiful, barefoot, disheveled group of eight- to ten-year-old girls; there were about twenty of them.

"All of them were brought here from Deir Zor,"[4] he said.

They all seemed unhappy. If they had not been afraid of the supervisor, you would have expected them to run away.

"Some of these children," explained the supervisor, "were adopted, but they escaped and came back to us. They couldn't put up with the treatment they received. And when the other girls hear about this they'd rather all go to an orphanage together as a group. In their unhappiness they feel instinctively that if they ever separate they'll be much more miserable, even under similar conditions. That's why they seem frightened and depressed. This one in particular has run away and come back here three times; now she never wants to leave her friends again."

The one he was talking about was half-hidden behind her friends. We asked her to come closer, but she refused, and had to be brought almost by force. She was wrapped in dirty, black, lice-ridden rags: barefoot, with greasy hair, frowning eyes, and rebellious behavior.

"I'm sure you'd like a pretty little orphan," added the supervisor with a worried look. "Usually well-to-do adopters ask that. But the others, the middle-class adopters, don't make that much of a fuss, because what they have in mind is different. That's why this little one was adopted three times without much hesitation, but she couldn't stay, and she doesn't want to leave again."

My friend thought for a brief moment and said: "It shouldn't matter at all whether they're pretty or not. The child has experienced the misfortune of losing her parents and relatives. You'd have to be rather hard-hearted and inconsiderate to cause the child unhappiness by passing her by in favor of a better-looking orphan." And she asked the supervisor to send the others away and complete the paper formalities for the adoption of the girl.

When the formalities were finished we put her in a little carriage and went home. On the way, the tears that had been welling up in her brown eyes slid down her cheeks, which were caked with

---

4. Syrian desert where Western Armenian families were transported during the 1915 persecutions.

thick black dirt. But she did not say a word. And we asked her nothing. I think that if she had not been conscious of my presence, my beautiful friend would also have cried. Both of us gazed out the side windows, trying to occupy our minds with what was happening on the streets.

It was a nice day, and a lot of people were out for a stroll. Every face reflected the unbounded happiness brought on by the end of the war.

. . . .

For the first few days the poor girl remained silent. She even maintained the sad expression on her face. They asked her many questions, but received no reply; the only thing they heard her say was that in Deir Zor the Arabs had called her Miriam. My friend was getting desperate. On the third day I asked to talk to the little girl. Her mood had already started to change a bit, because she had realized that the home she was living in was not like the three she had run away from.

I began by asking if she wanted to return to camp and telling her that if she did want to she would not have to run away.

"No," she said, and began to cry again.

I thought that was enough for our first conversation; I put a bag of chocolates in her lap.

The wild child was becoming tame.

Through subsequent questioning I discovered that she did not remember her parents' and brothers' names. She did not recall the name of her village either. She looked to be about eight years old at most. So she must have been four when they were transported. She was all mixed up: she vaguely remembered that she had six or seven brothers and sisters, and that one of them was younger than she was. She also remembered that all the girls in her village had gone to work in a big house every day—probably a silk mill. She remembered that at home she had been called Azniv. For a child who had been only four at the time, to remember even this much was a lot.

Besides this she remembered nothing about her family, her village, how they got to Deir Zor . . . how she had traveled there through immense provinces and the desert—completely abandoned, alone—and how an Arab *pahlavaji*[5] had adopted her. She

---

5. A baker of baklava—a sweet oriental pastry.

remembered her suffering very well though: the difficult times she spent with the Arabs. And so, at her tender age, she had justifiably become an obstinate, inflexible misanthropist.

They beat her constantly. It was such a simple and customary thing. They expected her to work beyond her capacity and strength. They used to give her a bucket made from a gasoline can to fetch water with. She had to walk to a deserted place about half an hour from the village, where there was ample but shallow water. She had to walk through the water to a place where it was deep enough to half fill the bucket, and then she had to fill it up bit by bit using a smaller container: if it was not full to the brim she would be punished with a sound beating.

Woe to innocent Armenian childhood during those tragic times! Your unimaginable privations and untold suffering were all that was needed to fill your nation's cup of bitterness!

Azniv—that is what they call her now—said that when the English came for her, she refused to go with them, because she was afraid that the *giaours*[6] would kill her. She kept saying that she was an Arab, not an Armenian, but another Armenian girl who was a little older insisted that her friend was an Armenian, and in the end the British left with both of them.

In Deir Zor she learned Arabic and forgot the little Armenian she had known. The British took her to Aleppo and placed her in an orphanage. There the children were taught Armenian by "Misses," as Azniv called them. In fact, she speaks broken and childish Armenian. Her vocabulary is rather limited and mixed with Arabic words.

From the very first day, a pair of glass earrings glittering on the dirty ears under her lice-ridden hair had caught my attention. I asked who had given them to her, the Arabs?

"No," Azniv replied. "In Aleppo, when the 'Misses' took us out for a walk, they gave us each five *kurush* to buy whatever we wanted, and I bought these earrings."

The savage was becoming tame, but at a cost: during the first month or two, she had several nervous spells, during which she would grow silent and assume a pensive, severe expression. Terrifying memories came back to her, and absolutely nothing interested her: neither fruits, nor sweets, nor toys. The only thing that affected

---

6. Term applied by Muslims to unbelievers, especially Christians.

her was the threat of returning her to the camp; we resorted to it when the spell had gone on for just too long. These fits gradually abated. And today Azniv has become a sweet, gentle little girl who is only mixed up when she recalls bad things, and who always has a beautiful Armenian song on her lips.

Once, during my English lesson with my friend, Azniv was sitting beside the stove as usual, pretending to recite the alphabet to herself, but she was listening to us instead.

My student read something about "the baby and the nurse." I asked her if she knew the meaning of *baby*. She replied that she did not.

And suddenly, Azniv, unable to contain herself, shouted over from her little corner: "I know!"

"What does it mean, girl? Out with it!"

"It's an orphan."

My heart ached, and I asked: "How do you know?"

"When we were in Aleppo, the 'Misses' called us babies, and when we came here, people called us orphans."

We continued the lesson and finished it feeling very sad.

One day I said to her: "Azniv, if you're good, on New Year's Day we'll give you presents."

"New Year's? What's New Year's?"

"Don't you know what New Year's is, girl?"

"No."

Again my heart ached.

"My dear girl, New Year's is a day of joy. It comes once a year, and good little girls get presents then."

She looked at me with a thoughtful and serious expression and asked with a sudden glitter in her eyes: "*Bayram?*[7] Is it the Armenian *Bayram*?" She started to jump up and down.

And tears flooded into everyone's eyes.

Another day, Azniv looked quite out of sorts. My student friend gave her a little doll. Azniv's eyes and face lit up. The joy she felt at that moment was unimaginable. What kind of instinctive mood, what kind of inherited memory was suddenly awakened within her,

---

7. The two major Islamic festivals: the first *bayram* is the three days following the fast of Ramadan; the second is the four days that begin seventy days later. Also national holiday, festival, or festivity.

prompting her to embrace the doll with love and care and cover it with a shower of kisses!

From that day on, Azniv never suffered another severe spell.

One day I read in the paper that the world would come to an end in a week. We laughed at the news. I remarked that there was nothing disagreeable about the news, since we would all die together and there would be no need to leave each other or mourn each other's death. And then a sob burst out from the corner of the room near the stove.

"I don't want to die," Azniv was sobbing.

What had life given her, this poor little girl? But still, the instinct for life reverberated within her. And I noticed that as she cried she pressed the doll to her chest.

Our appetite for joking melted away, and our eyes filled with tears once more.

On New Year's Day, in addition to her other presents, Azniv received a second, bigger doll. Her joy had no limits. The big doll had wedding dresses with silver threads, and even a bed. It opened and shut its eyes. It moved its arms and legs. Azniv was beside herself.

Now Azniv played with her dolls every day, almost always; she played in the small side room that had been given to her. And I gave her a series of large, colored religious pictures. She chose two of these pictures, and the rest she wrapped up and put aside.

In one corner of her little room she made a place for her dolls, and above the dolls' bed she placed the picture of the baby Jesus in the manger. Near them she had made a place for herself, with pillows, colorful boxes, the presents she had received, candles, toys, and many other things. And over them all she placed the large colored picture of the Crucifixion of Christ.

One day, when I visited her room unexpectedly, I noticed what she had done and, filled with amazement, I asked her: "Azniv, what is this picture? Do you know?"

"No."

"Then why have you put it here?"

She did not reply, but bowed her head.

"You have so many other pretty pictures," I said. "Take this one down, put up another one."

"No," she said again, without raising her head.

I felt that if I insisted she would start crying. Without another word, I left the room.

After that day I visited her room many times. The picture of the Crucifixion was always there. Azniv would be sitting next to her dolls, busy at the new skill of embroidery she had just learned. How was it that this poor little soul, who had experienced the worst kind of crucifixion and had lost everything in this world, nevertheless, through some inner instinct, had selected this from among many other pictures and given it an honored spot on her own altar, always working or rocking her dolls in her arms before it, her eyes forever fixed on the suffering One nailed to the cross?

One day, when Azniv was in an extremely good mood, I suddenly asked her: "My child, when are you going to replace this picture with another one?"

"When I get married," she replied quietly, blushing unconsciously. And I am sure that when that time comes she will replace it, led by a similar instinct, with the picture of the blessed Resurrection. Because when "this only remnant of her age-old ancestry" becomes a bride, that immortal age-old ancestry will rise from its grave!

Yevterpé (Zaruhi Kalemkiarian)

(1874–1971)

Born in Constantinople, Zaruhi Kalemkiarian received her education at a local Aramian school and started writing poetry at the age of seventeen. Her early poems were published in the periodical *Tzaghik* (The flower) under the pen name Yevterpé. Her first collections of poetry, *Nvakk yevterpia* (Yevterpean tunes), *Zartonk* (Revival), and *Mrmunj* (Murmur) appeared between 1892 and 1894. She continued to write after her marriage, but under a new pen name, K. Zaruhi. Under this name she published a series of short stories and prose poems in various periodicals, such as *Biuzandion* (Byzantium), *Arevelyan mamul* (The eastern press), *Shant* (Lightning), *Vostan* (The city), and others. After the First World War she moved to New York, where she settled permanently. There she contributed to the periodicals *Lraber* (News bearer), *Paykar* (Struggle), and *Hayastani kochnak* (Bell call to Armenia).

During her lifetime she published the following collections of prose: *Tornikis girke* (My grandchild's book, 1936), an account and impressions of her travels from New York to Constantinople; *Kyankis champen* (The course of my life, 1952); and *Orer yev demker* (Days and portraits, 1965). Some of her works were collected into a volume titled *Haskakagh* (Gleaning) and published in Yerevan in 1965.

AGONY OF A HORSE[1]

Early in the morning they had beaten the old sick horse. The heavy odor of the last breath of its agony, and of its wounded, scar-crossed body filled the barn with a terrible heaviness. All the other horses, a tender and sorrowful look in their big shining eyes, seemed to understand the torment of their unfortunate friend.

Early in the morning, its pitiless and violent master, having lost his last hope for the horse's recovery, drove it out of the barn, and prodded and pushed it stumbling down the hill. For years it had spent all its strength, the last spark of its energies, bearing heavy burdens over the high and rocky hills of Prinkipo,[2] every day from dawn to the last moment before dark, depleted, heaving and groaning.

Early in the morning with the first rays of the sun, I was awakened by the sounds of its tumbling, almost in front of my window. And straining through the resounding thuds was the hoarse and helpless rattling in its throat. I leaped to the window from my bed; beyond the slope I could see only the shadow of the man, creeping away like a criminal, and below, the pitiful agony of the horse.

All day I stayed close to the window, The wounds, where the horse's body had been ripped by stones, left traces of blood on the ground. The wretched creature shifted restlessly, its whole body soaked and gleaming with sweat. The dampness around its eyes gave the dying animal's face the mournful aspect of crying.

A few workingmen passed, recognized the horse, and gently prodded it with sticks, trying to bring it to its feet—now moving its head, now trying to roll it over on its legs—but the horse could not gather enough strength for the effort. Its hind legs stood stiff as sticks, with life already drained out of them. The men gave up and went on their way, and left before my eyes this picture of torment. . . .

The struggle of life and death stormed for the last time in the wretched animal. With a supernatural effort, it hobbled to its feet, swaying like a drunken man, unable to control the huge mass of

---

1. Zarouhi Kalemkiarian, "Agony of a Horse," *Ararat* 11, no. 3 (Summer 1960): 11. The name of the anonymous translator is unknown.
2. Present-day Büyük Ada. An island in the sea of Marmara near Istanbul, Turkey.

its body on its numbed and feeble legs. It stumbled toward the wall of our house, the great body, shivering, rammed against the wall, three times, four times, the painful rattle in the throat, the teeth jammed together, the glitter gone from half-closed eyes. The will to live, the frenzied dread of death stirred in it for the last time as it drove against the wall again, its head down, tumbling on its back, its legs stuck straight in the air, and a last breath hissing through clamped teeth.

The stiffened body was no longer sensitive to pain or annoyance. Hundreds of insects crawled over the lifeless hulk, dogs gathered around it, barking, howling, sniffing, sensing that it was dead but not daring to tear it apart.

A vision of people succumbing to physical and spiritual torment came to me suddenly, and I thought that, in this condition, without breath and without motion, the horse had found its place. . . .

All day long, I was drawn to the window again and again to look on this picture of death.

In the deepening darkness soon after the sun went down, they buried the horse. They tied a rope around its legs and dragged the heavy and stiffened body down the slope. A couple of curious boys followed and, as funeral attendants, dogs surrounded the wretched animal's carcass.

Indra (Tiran Chrakian)

(1875–1921)

In 1895, when the Realist Movement had waned, the inactive literary scene of Constantinople was given a shot in the arm by an exceptional writer known as Indra. Born Tiran Chrakian in Constantinople, he studied at the celebrated Perperian (Berberian) school in the same city. After teaching in Constantinople and Trebizond (Trabzon) for a short time, he went to Paris to develop his interest in painting and his skills both as an artist and as a writer. After travels to Geneva and Egypt, he returned to his native city and resumed his teaching and literary activities.

In 1906 he published *Nerashkharh* (Inner world), which he wrote between 1898 and 1900. The book was disparaged by critics, who failed to appreciate the originality and brilliance of Indra's literary perception. In two series of articles, "*Nerashkharn ir heghinaken ditvatz*" (*Nerashkharhe* as seen by its author, 1906) and "*Kartzikner yev kartzoghner*" (Opinions and believers, 1908), that he wrote for *Biuzandion* (Byzantium), the author went to considerable length to interpret his work for the literary public and defend himself. In effect, these pieces constitute a literary apology.

Indra wrote essays, travel impressions, and articles for various Armenian periodicals. *Nochastan* (The cypress grove), a slim volume of sonnets, appeared in 1908. Shortly thereafter Indra set aside his literary career, gradually withdrew from society, and became a zealous preacher. During World War I he served with the Turkish army as a translator and clerk. In 1915, when Armenian intellectuals were rounded up by the Ottoman government for exile and eventual execution, Indra was arrested but succeeded in escaping slaughter. These events affected his mental state. "In 1921, the Kemalists arrested him and sent him into exile. According to one of his companions, Indra went insane during the march from Konya to the interior and died shortly after crossing the Tigris to Diyarbekir."[1]

Indra's major work, *The Inner World,* although a brilliant literary accomplishment, is little known. It seems a collection of scattered impressions, but is in fact a unified whole; indeed, it can be viewed as a work of philosophical analysis, full of spiritual reflection and spiritual wisdom. The reader discovers not only Indra's mind but the whole man, with all his desires, deliberations, loves, and anxieties, on a universal level.

The Cypress Grove, on the other hand, is not a very successful literary attempt. The restrictions of the sonnet form imposed restraints on both his feelings and his thoughts. In fact, *The Inner World,* although written in prose, contains more poetic flights than these poems. Indra, it seems, could not give adequate expression to his inspirations without freedom from the conventions of literary genres.

A considerable amount of critical attention has been devoted to Indra and his works. These help reveal the unique light that is there to discover in his special universe.

FROM THE INNER WORLD[2]

It is the sound of the wind, the sound of the wind coming from the cypresses in the dense night. Behind the closed window, in the midnight light of my lamp, which keeps burning unaffected by the strong hum of the wind, I am dreaming, drawn by its flame, all alone and motionless, surrounded by the floating lace of tobacco puffs that rise around its clear glass, cloud-like, to disappear within

---

1. Kevork B. Bardakjian, *A Reference Guide to Modern Armenian Literature, 1500–1920* (Detroit, 2000), 377.
2. Indra (Tiran Chrakian), *Nerashkhhar* (Inner world) (Beirut, 1955), 53–57. Translated by Abraham Terian.

the low-spirited lamp of my loneliness. There is not a sound within the sleeping house. The folds of the curtain wave unsteadily. Some blissful integration emerges between the tranquility of a normal anguish, the ordinary and quiet heaviness displayed by the furniture and the objects, and the room's resident concealed behind and blended with their respective outlines, in his other-worldliness, in deep thought, in unbounded detachment. A few high branches of the cypresses, knotted, disorderly, stick out with a fearless shiver, as from a dry, waterless pot, and their scattered, senseless shadow on the wall plays an illogical, hushed piece of harp music driven by the wind. My uncovered inkwell lies shy beside the lamp that tempers its darkness with a purplish glow. Closed books. A studded ball, curled like a porcupine in front of me, holds the time-honored spike-pens near the edge of my desk. Pictures, few and far between, adorn the walls. The portrait of a distant teacher hangs from a dry branch of a reddish tree. Over there, that of the late Adamian, in the role of Hamlet; and another, of my late father. The one beneath, is the Tower of Kephren; and there, the Sphinx. Other objects over there. . . . What a sound! The deep hum is coming from distant places; it keeps coming, bellowing, huffing and puffing, agonizing, mighty, sudden and strange. I feel happy, thrilled by its enormity. What a windy night!

The skin of a jackal is spread on my couch; its snout stretching, the ears raised, blind, flat, lost! Outside, from among the cypresses, a howl is heard. The ears of the dead jackal could hear the barking of its friends through the unruly moaning of the branches about to snap. Poor beast, sleep uninterrupted in your eternal death. Let the realism of my room be a mausoleum for your wild and free spirit, a surrealistic substitute for your lost, subterranean den in this very windy night.

There are other things here that belong to me. They are mine, though they subject me to a sweet enslavement. My travel bag, empty, dusty, hanging from the wall. Outside, the delightful ferocity of the wind at night. Where are the unknown, uninhabited, rocky wilds of the outdoors? Where are the unknown waves? Instead of the salty foam of splashing waves, the ceiling dust covers the travel bag. I remember. . . . indeed, I feel the smell of the leather, the lost joy of a past experience, all alone, something inexplicably and blissfully animistic, in the smell of the leather, an earthly joy, yet full of the ecstasy of visions that freely embrace the cosmos in its entirety.

O, how come I didn't notice it? On the glass of the dark window, between the drapes that open into the night, there is a glaring shadow; it is my silhouette. That's me! It is my self. What an excitement—if not sadness! It is my self silhouetted against the darkness of the cypresses. It is the self. I look at it, my incorporeality, as if it were my body. It seems to be my ideal being, an outward reflection of my real being. The calm interplay between its pliable yet controlled lines, combined with the precarious grief of the dark contours, blend well with the essence of the tumultuous darkness of the space behind, from where my tilted head, as in a portrait by Rembrandt, gets traced on papyrus, the night of the cypresses permeating through its transparency.

For a moment, I grieve over my body, its thorough and dear affinity to me; I feel sorry for the explicit relationship it has with me. As always, to the end, I will pity my virgin earthiness, my maidservant body. Perhaps this compassion is also because I foolishly desire the detachment of that image from my real existence, my captive condition, which keeps reflecting itself in everything I desire or plan. That image seems ideal, for it is my identity, recovered at night in the loneliness of my room, floating among the cypresses, with ethereal density and substantiality in the tumultuous night, like an embossed, magnificent icon of a saint, taking shape under a heavenly light from beyond this world.

None of the objects in my room could divert my attention to the present, the real; they all are sad, poor antitypes of unboundedness. I fancy incomparable trajectories. They traject like paths emanating from darkness, shadowy paths, and which end up being inundated with light. The starting point of these paths is my miserable self, and their end is God. . . .

⚓

. . . . I had wanted, I would have wanted—what a silly wish—I would have wanted from there, from the southern heights, a rupture in the clouds and for the sun to appear; the skies blue, the blue sky to appear a little from there. Then I would not have been so sad, so listless, had the sky appeared now from an opening in the clouds. I must lower my head and work now, to start on the enormous work of drawing a small picture assigned to me. Now, adding to my misery is the lack of optimistically perceived abilities. What am I capable of doing? The awareness of this adds to my misery now, an unmanageable complication. Everything, everything magnifies my frailty: be it the cypresses that sway, the grass that bends with the wind, the enormous joy of noisy birds, the still objects sunk in the shadow of my room, everything—the sound of the wind sighing, even all my mental images, my memories on which I have pity and which I despise, the groaning sounds heard from afar, the colorless silence where my hearing submerges itself in bewilderment, and where, once more, gently, the top of the cypress sways; even the things I do not like, especially those things I like, they all whisper, they become silent, they scream at my frailty. And motionless, listless, I think they are telling me my faults.

My soul is full of friendly feelings. I feel with a pathetic poverty that a certain view of life, of the struggle for life, has been submitted to my awareness instead of another view of life, of the impossible life. I see myself in social terms, in the way men and women perceive one another. What am I? A laughable hobo who thinks he can withdraw from society and from its most foolish institutions, one who is still inclined to think that he can be aloof, that is to be over and above others in the world of the living who are blissfully deemed "successful"? That he can be great without stealing and without becoming fat, that he can remain unaffected by the misery of the rules dictated by society? Ah, thoughts on life do not materialize, they do not converge like breathless dogs packed beside the garbage piles!

There is nothing that can save me from little things; they persist with great stubbornness, reminding one of the proverbial saying about the ferocious lion stung by a fly. Hence I realize that nothing is small—as in nature so also in society, and that all the big things are under the dominion of the little things. The little matters are the agony of the great—if not their constant joy. Every living person should make an irrevocable resolution to respect all beings ignoble to one's heart; one should always acknowledge the greatness of their uncrushable and surprising drive for life. There is nothing more pathetic than to feel oneself to be great. Ah, would that humility were as rampant as ignorance!

And there is nothing comforting but an emptiness that is sad, puzzling and gloomy. The birds have fled from this sky, they have disappeared; who knows where the singing birds are gone. But the dogs are in the street, sniffling, filthy, stubborn, roaming around. With a domesticated wildness they are in the streets, wandering. From the rainy distance their barking is sometimes heard, strident and piercing. Whereas the birds, I do not know where they are. Not one desire, not a song. And I feel myself wearily miserable, filthy with the rest of the world, full of unqualified, seemingly unobjective hatred that puzzles me. As though a mole is ceaselessly crawling through my soul, and I no longer love anyone.

♣

What I see everywhere is greed, poverty, the pointed chins of hatred; the real, genuine, skyless, incapable of smiling, smile-denying, sunken and flat cheeks of hatred. After all, when the sky is blanketed, a cock's cry is heard. And even the cock's cry is a sad outcry which tries to prolong itself but ends embarrassingly. Ah, how painfully annoying is this distant call of a vendor! The commotion of the city reaches me like a damp and ominous roar, it penetrates me, and I cannot do anything. Could it be that a grievous, terrifying mortality is staring at me from outer space? The man is screaming again, his sorrowful voice stretching with a terrible vexation. This utterly miserable man is about to die now.

The wind blows, the cypresses bend, they sway with an inexplicable grief. The cypresses call on the blue sky, but the sky is dim. My window has a grayish light which makes me think of sad and disorderly things. Today the powerlessness of all objects is obvious, their frailty, and all of my overwhelming poverty. There is nothing else; only the falsehood of all things, their shakiness and filth. I feel a general sorrow, the sorrow of everything.

And the pains sneak in, they multiply. In my heart, my head, I feel their parasitic crawl—the short, soft yet cruel crawl of mud-dwelling creatures cutting furrows through me. And fixing my eyes on the gray shadow of the pouring rain, pouring into the dark folds of the cypresses, I mumble to myself that I no longer love anyone. And to be saved from these meaningless sorrows, even from this picture, the total ugliness of myself—the totality of abominable deception, the dismal mendacity that cannot be erased—to remove the whole commotion of myself with a calm effort, I gently mumble to myself that today too is time to die.

Mari Svachian (Svadjian)

(Nineteenth–twentieth centuries)

Despite lengthy critical commentary on the work of Mari Svachian, almost no information is available on her life. It seems she was born in Constantinople in the second half of the nineteenth century and fled to Europe after the 1896 atrocities against the Armenians of that city. Beyond that, there is mention of her having joined her son in Alexandria and Cairo in 1983, when he was giving concerts there.

She began her literary career as a novelist and short story writer with the *Hayrenik* (Fatherland) daily, and beginning in 1897, while she was in Europe, she contributed to *Nor Kyank* (New life). It is not difficult to discern the traces and influence of her peripatetic life in her works.

She was undoubtedly influenced by the flourishing contemporary enthusiasm for mostly adventurous short stories and novels. Mari Svachian's first novel, *Hayhuyi me i Paris* (An Armenian woman in Paris), a sad story mixed with realistic and romantic passages, was published in *Hayrenik*. Her second novel, *Brni amusnutiun* (Forced marriage), the story of Matilt, who marries at the relentless insistence of her wealthy but bankrupt father, was also published in *Hayrenik*.

Svachian's other novel is *Amira* (A title given by the Ottoman sultans to prominent Armenians). It is the narrative of Herodik Amira, who leaves his son, Mkrtich Bey, a huge legacy. The son spends it unwisely, but Amira's grandson, Armenak, saves the family. He introduces French customs into the family by marrying Lucia, who is Belgian. *Amira* was translated into French by Frédéric Maclaire and published, together with other Armenian pieces, under the title *Petite biblothèque arménienne* (Little Armenian library), in Paris in 1927.

"*Khamsin*," which is reproduced in the present anthology, is an example of her brief short stories. Among her other well-known short stories are "*Grav me*" (A wager, 1893), "*Bakhtin kamkove*" (Fortune willing, 1893), "*Aparanchane*" (The bracelet, 1893), "*Hin havatke*" (Faith of our fathers, 1893), "*Manushaki taghare*" (Manushak's flower pot, 1894), "*Tznndyan tzare*" (The Christmas tree, 1894), "*Yerazi me khorhurte*" (Mystery of a dream, 1895), "*Harse*" (The bride, 1895), "*Yerek patker*" (Three pictures, 1897), "*Ariune*" (Blood, 1898)—which describes incidents occasioned by the massacre of Armenians—and "*Zavake*" (The child, 1898).

Mari Svachian succeeds in reflecting woman's psychology and deep emotions, with spirited descriptions and light poetic passages. Her writings are aimed at the liberation of the Armenian woman, above all at obtaining for her the freedom and the right to choose her own husband. She also advances the belief that evil is not innate; sins, whether of intention or of deed, are the result of social conditions. Her narrative style is simple and natural, which at times creates a certain monotony.

KHAMSIN[1]

The blue sky over Cairo darkened as the dazzling rays of the sun put on mourning. Yellow grains of sand began to rise, and the *khamsin*,[2] the terrible *khamsin* blew fast and strong.

The hot air swirled the dust and scattered it in the air, blinding the eyes of passersby. It gradually grew fiercer. It was blowing in from the desert—howling, yelling, rolling, right up to the city. The shutters of houses banged against each other; windowpanes rumbled; sand piled up in front of houses with phenomenal speed.

People took shelter in their homes. They shut everything. They sat cross-legged on their cushions and waited for the storm to cease.

---

1. Mari Svachian, "Khamsin," *Anahit* 3 (1899): 104–6. Translated by the editors of the present anthology.
2. A strong wind that characterizes the fifty-day period that follows the forty days of most severe winter, ending at the vernal equinox.

How many days would it last? The *khamsin* was the plague of the exuberant people of Cairo. It prevented them from going out, from going to musical cafés. With what pain and boredom they stared at each other! Perhaps this damned wind would last three whole days!

The wind continued to blow, with wavering and monotonous whistles. It looked as if smoke were rising from the ground. The dust climbed up, up, and seemed like metal filings flung in the face of the sun. The air was dense. An unbearable nervousness took hold everywhere. Far away, the boundless, unknown desert was gradually disappearing in smoke.

In the British barracks there was great concern. General James Mott, a newcomer, had ridden off on his horse in the morning and, although it was almost dark, had not yet returned.

James Mott was the young, second son of a lord. He had a restless vitality that made him determined to create a certain position and standard of living for himself. From his very first day in Egypt he roamed everywhere, with insatiable curiosity. He found everything in the city of the Pharaohs appealing. The weather, the night, the women's stares, the young brunettes like young partridges, troubled his northern temperament.

Caught in the storm, James whipped the horse. Enraged by the blows of the whip, the fine animal seemed to float through the air in a fast-paced, regular gallop, its tail straight out behind it. The Englishman continued on his way, as if borne along on the air. His imagination was excited by the wind's long assault—everything he had seen since the very day of his arrival in Cairo flickered before his eyes. The palm trees rustled. The region watered by the muddy Nile seemed to be in flux under the onslaught of the weather. He remembered a musical café where he had spent a night.

There was a young woman there. A young woman of the desert. She had large black eyes, as though charred by the sparks of her gaze. She had gazed at him. He could see the stage and the hall filled with people, glittering under the lights. The air was thick; the dancer moved her little feet, swayed her colored hands in the air, and began her dance. Her body was slender and petite, moving to the rhythm of the music; her supple waist folded into segments; her eyes, half closed now, stared deeply at him, as in that café a few days earlier.

James continued speeding homeward. The illusion was becoming more concrete; he could even hear the voice he had heard there. The young woman was getting more and more excited and sweat poured down her forehead. The applause of the spectators inflamed her more and more. It seemed to him that he heard the applause of the crowd, disagreeable noises that deafened his ears.

He had arrived home.

He had a little white summer house beside the dead waters of the Nile. The garden, filled with flowers and other plants, went all the way down to the river. As he unlocked the door, a light smile covered his face.

"What a fool," he muttered, "daydreaming about a poor fellah [peasant] girl!"

He pushed the door open nervously. But a black mass moved toward him through the darkness so boldly that even the horse shied. Her voice full of tears, a girl whispered something in Arabic. James recognized her and pushed her back, almost in anger. It was Fatimé, the dancer, the partridge, who had been on her way to her father's home, had been caught in the storm, and had taken shelter there.

The girl stretched an arm covered with gold bracelets up in the air. The silk cloak covering her from head to foot slipped aside, and her foot became visible. There was a small wound on it. Her body exuded a fine fragrance. She focused her dark, black eyes on the young man, gazing at him with unremitting innuendo. She moved her little fingers again, and again she showed her foot.

In an attempt to end the scene, James grabbed her by the shoulders and pushed her inside.

Fatimé was looked after there for three days. On the fourth day, early in the morning, without informing the servants, the young Englishman sent her away. He felt calmer; his agitation had disappeared, or at least that is what he thought.

After days, weeks, months of summer, with Cairo burning under blazing skies, the officers of the garrison got together one night. They reminisced about their native land, all of them sad and nostalgic as they talked about their memories. Were they all going to die under these everlasting star-studded skies? They emptied bottles of champagne and chatted disconcertedly.

No, it was not possible to live like this anymore. The burning hot air had had an evil effect on them. Even the flowers in the garden were slack, drooping their heads in the dusky moonlight.

The Nile unrolled like an endless, silvery ribbon. In the distance, on the opposite bank, a flat plain stretched to infinity. James Mott did not speak; he ceaselessly twirled his shaggy blond moustache.

Suddenly he rose to his feet. His tall frame cast a giant black shadow on the ground. He looked up at the moon, glowing with absolute tranquility in the middle of the sky. With exasperated steps he walked to the garden gate. The sand slithered under his feet. He opened the door and stretched out his arms into the loneliness.

A woman, supple as a tiger, threw herself at him, kissing him, crying, whining. "I love you," she repeated softly. She had been coming for months and knocking with perfect regularity at his door.

The servants took her for a beggar and frequently chased her away. But she always came back and put her ear against the keyhole, in the hope of at least hearing his voice.

"Darling," she murmured, "darling!" She put her arms around his neck. "Please don't send me away anymore, please don't. . . ."

James was drunk and not himself. He stood there in the glimmering moonlight, motionless. He listened.

"Quiet," he said suddenly. "Don't speak, and don't be afraid."

The young man had tried so long to resist his unhealthy passion. Every night in his bed he was tormented with thoughts of her. Was it really love? He laughed. A flame consumed his body; it was a strange feeling, difficult to diagnose. All his senses seemed to come alive, and he tumbled into the fire.

No, it was not love.

He must assiduously resist such feelings. A fellah girl. A girl of the desert. What could she be to him, after all?

But before long a shade would pass over his face. Once again he would work himself into an unbearable state. He would run to the window and try to breathe some clean, fresh air. And at once he would catch sight of a shadow, almost impossible to perceive, motionless, but always looking at him.

It was Fatimé. Leaning against a tree. Her long black eyes forever looking upwards. He would hear her tearful voice. He would shut the window and walk away. He would go and cower in a corner. It was as if the slender arms of the fellah woman were pursuing him. A thin film of sweat covered his forehead.

In the morning, however, he would smile again; he would admonish himself; he would treat himself with contempt. But alas! at night his burning dreams would revisit him.

And now, tired of struggling against himself, he let the girl envelop him like a snake. Now he was hers. He was tied to her, to the land, to the air and the water too. Sometimes, like a refreshing token of the past, he recalled life in England. But it was no longer possible to divorce himself from that heated atmosphere, from those sparkling eyes.

"I also drank of the waters of the Nile," he used to tell himself, "and they inflamed my blood."

Avetik Isahakian

(1875–1957)

The third of the four most renowned poets of the time—with Hovhannes Hovhannisian (1864–1929) and Hovhannes Tumanian (1869–
1923) before him and Vahan Terian (1885–1920) after him—Avetik
Isahakian was born in Alexandrapol (present-day Giumri, Armenia), received his early education in local schools, and then attended the Gevorgian seminary in Etchmiadzin (1889–92), where student unrest put an
end to his studies. During the period 1893–95 he audited courses at
the University of Leipzig, before returning home for family reasons. In
1896 he was accused of revolutionary activities, imprisoned, and exiled
to Odessa. He was released the following year and found his way to the
University of Zurich, where he studied literature and philosophy. He
returned home in 1902. In 1908 he was arrested again under the same
accusations, but was released shortly thereafter. By 1911 he had become
fed up with the harassment of the czarist police and fled to Europe,
where he spent the next twenty-five years, moving around from place
to place, including Vienna, Zurich, Geneva, Berlin, and Venice, and
eventually settling in Paris. In 1926 he paid a visit to Soviet Armenia,
and ten years later he moved there and stayed for the rest of his life.

His first book of poetry, *Yerger u verker* (Songs and wounds) appeared in 1897, followed by *Hin-nor yerg u verkerits* (From old and new
songs and wounds, 1902) and an enlarged edition of *Yerger u verker*
(1908). His poetry is profoundly lyrical, characterized by a mixture of

fervent emotion and philosophical thought. His main themes are love, nature, motherly devotion, the homeland, social injustice, and human destiny. The love that he celebrates in its various manifestations is rather disquieting: a fleeting, elusive love that captivates him, speaks to him through the most tender emotions and the beauties of nature, then vanishes, leaving the poet in a sad and pessimistic mood. The pain within him gradually grows into a universal cry against the vanity of life.

Isahakian's inspirations came from the life of the Armenian people, and he wrote for them, at times in their own dialects, and in a style reminiscent of medieval *ashughs* (minstrels). His poetry was obviously affected by his native province of Shirak, which was famed for its *ashughs*. A large number of his poems have been set to music and maintain their popularity.

His philosophical concerns about the destiny of man are reflected in his long poem, *Abu Ala al-Mahari*,[1] published in 1911. The great poet Abu Ala al-Mahari has seen the world, with its good and evil, and has sat at the tables of the rich and the poor. One night, disgusted with human society and the injustice of the world, he leaves Baghdad, never to return, and heads for the sun, the symbol of light and righteousness. As his caravan progresses through the desert, he delves deeper and deeper into the bitterness of his soul, pouring out his utter disillusionment with friends, women, love, wealth, the city, man-made laws, and power. He disdains human society, and his perturbed soul is in search of a haven. His goal is to reach the sun and be transported by it into an ideal and eternal existence. Certain critics see in this poem the influence of Nietzsche and Schopenhauer, while others detect a reaction to the abortive Russian Revolution of 1905.[2] The work has been translated into numerous languages.

Isahakian was a prolific writer. In addition to his lyric poems, he also wrote narrative poems, such as *Alagiazi maniner* (Tunes of Alagiaz, 1917), an exquisite poem, full of love, joy, and sadness, set against a backdrop of popular traditions. The epic poem *Sasma Mher* (1922) is an abridgement of the fourth cycle of *David of Sasun*. His parables, of which he wrote a large number—including *Mayre* (The mother, 1946), *Mor sirte* (The mother's heart), *Hayreni hogh* (The native soil), and *Attilan*

---

1. Named after Abu-al-'Ala' al-Ma'arri (973–1057), the Syrian poet. He lost his sight in early infancy as a result of smallpox. In 1007 he visited Baghdad, where he made the acquaintance of literary circles. In 1009 he returned to Ma'arri, where he spent the rest of his life. Isahakian's *Abu Lala Mahari* is based on this prototype.

2. See Kevork B. Bardakjian, *A Reference Guide to Modern Armenian Literature, 1500–1920* (Detroit, 2000), 184.

yev ir sure (Attila and his sword)—are mostly based on oriental tales and traditions. His short stories, such as *Hamberanki chibukhe* (The pipe of patience, 1928), are mostly derived from local incidents. He also wrote numerous tales, for example, *Agha Nazar* (1912), and many fables. His only novel, *Usta Karo* (Master Karo), was unfinished; it begins with a depiction of life in Shirak and reflects the author's concerns about the destiny of the people. Another important work is *Im husherits* (Reminiscences, 1946), wherein Isahakian describes a number of his contemporary writers.

His works have been published in Yerevan, in numerous editions and various collections: *Yerger* (Works, in two volumes, 1939–40; and in one large-format volume, 1955); *Hatentir* (Selected works, 1943, 1958, 1975); *Yergeri zhoghovatzu* (Collected works, in four volumes, 1950–51; and in six volumes, 1973–79); and many individual titles. His works were extremely popular because people saw themselves in them, with their joys, sorrows, and traditions masterfully woven into poetry. This is why he was popularly known as *Varpet* (Master).

His return to Soviet Armenia in 1936 was the beginning of a new epoch for him. In Europe he had been a supporter of the new state, an active participant in the Committee of Aid to Armenia, and a correspondent to various papers. During World War II his pen was active in sustaining the morale of the people and contributing to the war effort. In 1943 he was elected a member of the newly founded Academy of Sciences of the Armenian SSR; in 1944 he was elected president of the Union of Soviet Writers of Armenia, a position he held until his death. In 1945, at the celebration of his seventieth birthday, he was awarded the Lenin Medal and the title Writer Emeritus. In 1946 he won the USSR State Prize for literature. In recognition of his contributions to Armenian verse, the Avetik Isahakian Literary Prize for Poetry was established in Yerevan in 1980.

SAADI'S LAST SPRING[3]

Spring had come.

It was one of those springs that transform the earth. Saadi,[4] poet of joy and sadness, had seen one hundred such springs.

---

3. Avetik Isahakian, "Saadi's Last Spring," in *We of the Mountains: Armenian Short Stories* (Moscow, 1972), 44–47. Translated by Fainna Glagoleva.
4. Saadi (c. 1184–c. 1291), Persian poet and prose writer, author of *Bustan* (Orchard) and *Gulistan* (Rose garden), which came to be regarded as classics of Persian literature.

Saadi awoke early that morning. He went out into the flower-ing orchard on the bank of the Ronnabad River to hear the nightin-gale sing once again and to witness again the miracle of spring.

He gazed at the field of Shiraz, adorned by nature's gift of roses and deep in its morning slumber. It was veiled by a fragrant white fog.

Saadi sat down on a beautiful rug beneath a flowering jas-mine. He held a green-red rosebud in his trembling hands a while and whispered softly: "As a young maiden smiles upon the lover who embraces her, so does the rose part its lips for the morning breeze."

Though Saadi was now very old, his soul still saw and heard, through half-closed lids and ears, the wondrous events and images of this world, the songs and silences of the unknown distances: for the magic spirit of poetry, the Zmrukht[5] bird that made its nest on top of Mount Kaf in the Kingdom of Stars, still spoke to him.

Light-eyed, grey-feathered nightingales trilled, singing their en-chanting rubaiyat, burning with the fire of love, and their songs echoed in Saadi's heart.

The virgin breath of a caressing breeze brought the roses greet-ings from far-off enamored roses, and Saadi's soul understood these declarations of love.

"A loving heart will always understand the words of Nature. The world is full of harmony. Its enamored intoxication is immor-tal," he recalled the words he had uttered long ago.

Carried away by the nightingale's song and the beauty of the red roses, Saadi breathed in their entrancing fragrance and, intox-icated by it, he closed his eyes; as in a dream he saw the world reflected in his own heart.

He saw the still rivers of India, adorned by sacred lotuses.

He saw the wise elephants, pensive in the jungle thickets. And in the golden palaces of Delhi he saw the lovely maidens with crimson flowers in their blue-black hair.

He saw the stormy plains of Turan and the terrible villains with flaming swords, carried aloft on the wings of the storm.

He saw the desert as well, scorched by the sun, with mounted Bedums chasing fleet-footed gazelles under the keen eyes of soaring eagles.

---

5. Emerald (Armenian).

He also saw the endless caravans of pilgrims; he saw them kneeling, praying and singing before the gates of Mecca.

He saw the famous wonders of ancient Egypt, the blue crystals of vast seas and the velvet-skinned maidens of Damascus with their shimmering bodies; their supple, caressing arms had embraced young Saadi like a necklace.

Saadi sighed and opened his eyes.

"Alas, my hundred years have flown by like a sweet dream, like one night's vision; the years have flown by like a moment, for you have always been my companions, you fairy-tales, nightingales and roses, and you sisters of the roses, maidens full of bliss!"

The sun broke forth from the heavenly gardens that sparkled with flowers, and the grasses, leaves, stones and cliffs glittered, for the night had strewn diamond dust over them all.

Saadi's gaze was deep as he looked at the blue heavens and the birds soaring in the gold of sunrise.

He looked upon them with wonder and awe.

"Truly, the world is a miracle, a fairy-tale; it is eternally wondrous and beautiful.

"Each day I look out upon the world and each day I am amazed anew, as if I were seeing it for the first time; the world is familiar, yet wonderful, old, yet ever new, new with an eternal and inexpressible beauty equal only to itself."

Saadi again looked out upon the world, at the multiform and magical play of nature and noticed two doves, stepping with coral-red feet upon the green meadow as they billed and cooed; and again Saadi spoke aloud:

"The world is enchanted, everything in it is under the spell of a magic wand in the hand of an invisible sorceress, and all has turned into a fairy-tale.

"The world rushes on headlong, falling apart and ever changing; but what recreates and rebuilds this magnificent world again, spreading this wonderful fairy-tale before us?

"What makes the gazelle, its heart weary with love's passion, clamber up the sharp cliffs, breaking its horns on the rocks?

"What makes the rose burst its emerald sheath and emit such sweet fragrance?

"What makes a human being break forth from the unknown and acquire flesh and blood in order to think and suffer, to feel the flames of our scorching desires and never want to die?

"Ah, love, you unconquerable force, you sweet tyrant, long have I known you! And yet, never was I able to fully comprehend your depth and your essence."

Saadi's intuition told him that this was to be his last spring.

His last spring!

The garden gate opened.

Yielding her snow-white body to the caresses of the breeze, Naziat of Shiraz, Saadi's beloved, who often came to him, entered. Her lips, as heady as wine, the whiteness and heat of her naked arms had often delighted the sleepless nights of the centenarian poet.

Saadi loved her with all his youthful, unfading heart, having drawn her in letters of gold in his immortal *Gulistan*.

Naziat approached, her arms filled with roses, and greeted him, herself as fragrant as a rose.

The poet was sad. Sadness lay on his pale lips.

"What grieves you, oh most happy of mortals?"

Saadi was silent.

"I love your wistfulness, O Saadi; your sadness is wise; for have your heavenly lips not said that pearls are born of wounds and the fragrance of incense is sweet as it burns."

Saadi gazed upon her with a faded smile.

"Look, I have brought you roses, velvet roses from my garden."

She showered Saadi with roses, and touched the poet's sad face with the tips of her bright fingers.

"The roses which you gave me, O heavenly maiden, were always the best roses in the world and never faded."

"Yes, Saadi. 'Why, as one breathes in the fragrance of a rose, must one think of its short life? Remember its fragrance and then you will soon forget that it has long since faded.' " Naziat repeated the poet's once-spoken words in her silvery voice.

And her hair that called up dreams fell on Saadi's face as she sank down beside him; then a fragrant breeze blew through the orchard, its rainbow wings fluttering: it was the wondrous wings of the Zmrukht bird fluttering in the air as Saadi stroked Naziat's dreamy hair with a faltering hand.

Then Saadi cast a glance from the bottom of his soul upon the fairy-tale world ablaze around him; he glanced at the bright smile of the lovely maiden, and a hot tear burned his old heart; then, taking the girl's small hand in his, he kissed it and pressed it against his fluttering heart.

"Write my last words on the last page of my *Gulistan* with your own small hand:

"'We are not born of our own will, we live in wonder and die in anguish!'"

ABU ALA AL-MAHARI[6]

Seventh Canto

And Abu-Lala's caravan came to rest at the edge of the Arabian desert,
And the camels knelt, tired and exhausted.

The free and untenanted shores of the horizon were ablaze,
Darkness gathered up its velvet skirt, and the sky shimmered with crimson flames.

Abu-Lala sat in solitude, resting his head against a rock of sapphire,
And fixed his gaze on the shimmering distance, his soul stilled and quieted.

"Oh, how free I am now, how boundlessly free! Is it possible for this desert
To contain within its vast embrace my endless, everlasting freedom?

"No human eye could see me, no human arm could reach me here.
O Freedom, heady perfume of the enchanting roses of Paradise!

"Crown me with your enchanting roses, enkindle my soul with your flaming torches,
O Freedom: immortal Koran sung by the dazzling nightingales of Paradise!

---

6. Avetik Isahakian, *Abu-Lala Mahari* (Yerevan, 1975), 41–46. Translated by the editors of the present anthology.

"Inviting rock, golden orb of wisdom, a thousand greetings to
you!
O unspoiled wasteland, where man has never desecrated man,
may you be for ever blessed!

"Extend for ever, spread your yellow seas of sand upon the
nations,
Bury all mankind: all palaces and hovels, towns and villages,
markets and fortresses.

"With your raging winds, spread the reign of freedom over all
the world,
Let the majestic golden rays of the rising sun spread freedom
over all the globe."

With thousands upon thousands of wonders and fiery allure-
ments,
The sun rose, glorious and glowing with a thousand swirls of
rose-infused satin.

And beneath the torches of the sun, the shores of the desert
spread out, ablaze with flames,
Like enormous lion skins, glittering gold.

"O cup of golden, universal intoxication and blessedness,
O abundant fountain of delight, charms, and fiery wine!

"O manifold and universal feast, source of jubilation, O benevolent sun,
Here is my soul, a thirsty bud: sprinkle it with your unwatered
wine.

"Make me drunk with your happiness, wisdom, and eternity;
allow me to forget the past,
Letting me slumber, and replace it with the splendor of your
perfumed dreams.

"Make me drunk, make me drunk with your immortal wine,
That I may forget man, falsehood, and gloom, forget for ever
evil and sorrow.

"Make me drunk with your grandeur, make me drunk with
your radiant ecstasies,

O invincible champion against darkness, mother of springs, sea of happiness.

"O unique goodness, my only love, my only saint, O maternal bosom,
You are forever loving, the vanquisher of death, the only wholly magnificent beauty.

"You are my love, you are my love. Burn me with ardent love, wound me,
Spread your hair of sparkling gold over me, and caress me.

"Make my lips bleed with the searing sting of your kiss,
Reveal your dazzling bosom, which radiates happiness, and I shall fly to you, ablaze with love.

"Let my ears grow deaf, that I may hear no longer the tumult of the world,
Let my eyes grow blind to this world, that I may never look back and see mankind again.

"Soar to the sun, my noble caravan, through endless ages:
Carry me to its glowing, fiery bosom, that I too may become a sun for all eternity!

"O mother-sun, place upon my shoulders the golden sheen of your splendorous mantle,
That, drunk with love of your shining glories, I may soar victoriously to you.

"O mightier than God, my only love, my only mother, my maternal bosom,
O unique goodness, sole blessedness, the only wholly majestic beauty!"

The Final Canto

And the camels, cleaving the fiery waves of the desert sea like golden boats,
Sailed swiftly toward the flaming, radiant distance.

No simoom with fiery wings could have matched their galloping pace,

No speeding arrow shot by an uncouth Bedouin could have hit
the fleeting caravan.

Fresh breezes from the oasis engendered a keen desire for
lively songs,
And fountains of milk plashed in the dreams of their virgin
hearts:

The shimmering fairies of legend and the soft rustle of palm
trees
Greeted him with kisses and beckoned him with secret
promises.

But Abu-Lala did not wish to hear their calls of love, nor the
sweet rustling:
He was flying insatiably toward the sun, himself as bright as it.

Meanwhile, the seraphim, with new visions of a thousand illusions and charms,
Ran off with his bewitched soul on the golden wings of radiant
dreams.

The camels, strong and free of harness, with fiery impulse
Surged recklessly forward, as if in the furor of frenzy.

Under the searing rays of the sun the camels were joyfully
ablaze,
The camel bells tinkled merrily and free, and sparkled in the
glittering light.

Abu-Mahari stared at the sun with the unblinking eyes of an
eagle
And sped on without sleep, his soul imbued with light, ablaze
with the flames of bliss.

Behind him the naked desert spread out in the bosom of light,
While above his head the sun was beckoning, its sapphire hair
spread out in the infinity of space.

And Abu-Mahari, the great poet, the golden sheen of the mantle upon his shoulders,
Sped relentlessly, victorious and majestic, toward the sun, the
immortal sun . . .

Suren Partevian

(1876–1921)

Originally named Sisak Partizpanian, the writer known as Suren Partevian was born in Kadiköy in Constantinople. After attending the Perperian (Berberian) and Kedronakan schools, he fled to Europe to escape
the Armenian massacres of the mid-1890s. For a short while he audited
literature courses at the Sorbonne and the Collège de France in Paris,
returning to Constantinople in 1908. He contributed to a number of
periodicals: *Shirak, Azg* (The nation), *Vaghvan dzayne* (The voice of tomorrow), *Dashink* (Alliance), *Dzayn hayrenyats* (The voice of the homeland), and others, always writing in a contentious voice, as in "*Kharazan*"
(The whip, 1901).

Following the proclamation of the Ottoman Constitution he settled
in Izmir, editing and directing the journal *Dashink*. There he published
Killikian arhavirke (The Cilician terror, 1909), in which he realistically depicted and protested the horrible ordeals of the Armenians of
Adana and Mersin. His next realistic work was *Kaykayum* (Destruction,
1910), a description of deported Armenians and the gradual decline
of their psyches in exile. Within a year Partevian brought out another
book: *Hayuhin* (The Armenian woman, 1911), which used a variety of
scenes and stories to depict the sufferings, animosities, and heroisms of

Armenian women. He also wrote a few plays and *Yekiptahayu taretsuytse* (Egyptian-Armenian almanac, 1914).

Partevian was a disciple of Grigor Zohrap's realistic school. His main literary contribution is his fiction. His books and articles may fail, perhaps, to withstand intense literary scrutiny, but he remains a master of language, pleasant style, and rhetorical prose.[1] He spent his final years in Egypt and died in Alexandria.

The Vow[2]

Winter is approaching. . . .

The last winds of autumn begin to moan lamentably at being stirred up yet again: our banished souls, betrayed by fatherless, alien nights.

This is the confused symphony of sounds unknown to nature that, with extreme force, awakens within us the fresh anxiety of pain-wracked sacred distances; it brings us the sad tiding that incurable and irrevocable losses are perilously close and suddenly fills our tempestuous thoughts with furious suspicions and terrifying impressions.

Winter is approaching. . . .

O, the heart-rending significance, the death-like weight and enormous fatalism of these three common words! They seem a distant, inaudible barking that echoes in our throbbing brains, as if inviting us to prepare for the funeral of mighty, revered Anguish. . . . But our trembling awareness revolts violently against that evil idea, and refuses to mourn that inconceivable eventuality.

Winter is approaching. . . .

And once more our Fatherland, naked and wounded, will be wrapped in a shroud. The accursed Road of Infamy will be closed, and the unburied corpses that line it will be entombed beneath countless gravestones of ice. The bloodstains will disappear from

---

1. See Minas Teoleolian, *Dar me grakanutiun: 1850–1920* (A century of literature) (Boston, 1977), 1:598–60.
2. Suren Partevian, "Ukhte" (The vow), in *Navasart*, ed. Daniel Varuzhan and Hakob Siruni (Constantinople, 1914), 171–72. Translated by the editors of the present anthology.

the earth of the homeland. Under the roofs buried in snow, hearths that suffocate forgotten elegies and frozen lives will once more smolder in the dark. And within the all-enveloping rattling of the storms the exhausted and pitiful cries of far-off Armenian agony will be rent asunder, will be drowned out.

Winter is approaching. . . .

And so the time passes, without mercy and with no return; years fly by despite our pains and expectations: monotonously, heedlessly, and with unrelenting deception, which makes us dizzy when we realize it and think about it in moments of exalted meditation. And then our hearts are strained by unusual burdens, burdens of lead: we feel them beating heavily in our breasts and they give rise to the anxious doubts that crowd our minds.

"Where are you going? . . . When will you get there? . . . Will you ever arrive?"

Terrible questions!

We try to remember once more, to look steadily at the past. We try to measure the road we have trod, the long years of suffering and of struggle that reach back into the dark abysses of the past like a long chain. Then we turn our faces in the direction of what lies far ahead of us, we focus the frenzied gaze of our Ambition; we try to pierce the barred and impenetrable horizon of the future—to note, to calculate the length of the road, to see how much more we have to bear. And our inadequate eyes cloud with tears. And our souls, swollen with grief, are overcome for a while and succumb.

Behold! . . . So much blood, so much destruction, so much sac-rifice, so much effort, and so much deceit lie behind us. . . . And ahead of us the uncertain and the unknown. . . . And we bleed, to be demolished once more, to be sacrificed once more, to be obsti-nate and aspire once more. . . .

It is the tragic and painful moment of self-abandonment and discouragement. . . . The slave, protesting savagery, has faltered on the road to freedom. But he never quits. Once his steps have been set in motion, he feels that there is no return, and to deviate from his path is tantamount to suicide. He bends his legs, clenches his teeth, and keeps walking, walking, forever impractical and defiant—without unmanly giddiness and unsuitable sentiment—

always forward, his earnest brow to the horizon, self-confident and stern.

And this mighty walker once again, like a refrain, repeats his noble, unyielding steps.

Yes, it is necessary to bleed once more, necessary to be demolished once more, necessary to be sacrificed once more, necessary to be obstinate once more, necessary to aspire once more. . . .

Shushanik Kurghinian

(1876–1927)

Shushanik Kurghinian was the first revolutionary female poet in Armenian literature. Born in Alexandropole (present-day Giumri, Armenia) to a poor family, she received her early education at the local Arghutian girls' school, then at the Russian pro-gymnasium. Despite her desire for higher education, her parents could not afford to give it to her, and she struggled to compensate for this by educating herself. Her talent for writing manifested itself early in life: her first poems were published in 1899 in the literary weekly *Taraz,* and in 1900 her first short story appeared in the children's magazine *Aghbiur* (Fountain), both published in Tiflis. In 1903 she moved to Nor Nakhijevan (now Rostov-na-Donu), an area in southern Russia that was seething with revolutionary turmoil. Profoundly influenced by the 1905 revolution, she adopted the cause of the working class and enchanted them with the magic of her poetry. In 1907 she published her first collection of selected works, *Arshaluysi ghoghanjner* (Tinkles of dawn). As one of the poems in the collection says, "I sing the anguish of men, and the pain of the wretched who has no one and not a morsel of bread; I sing the agony of enslaved hearts and the tears of black nights." Her two best known poems, "*Hangtsrek jahere*" (Extinguish the chandeliers) and "*Banvornere*" (The workers), which exhibit rebellion against social injustice, are included in this collection.

Other poems, such as *"Geghjkuhu mormoke"* (The anguish of a peasant woman), *"Artzvi sere"* (Eagle's love), and *"Vorpes knkush mayisyan vard"* (Like a delicate May rose) are dedicated to the women's cause.

Some of her other works were suppressed by tsarist censorship. From the late 1910s to the October Revolution, she continued to write and participate in social projects, but her activities were curtailed by fragile health. In 1921, the year after the sovietization of Armenia, she moved back to Giumri, her native city. In 1925 she traveled to Kharkov and Moscow for medical treatment and returned home disappointed. In 1926, after the Giumri earthquake, she settled in Yerevan, where she was welcomed with great enthusiasm by literary circles. She died the following year, at the age of fifty-one.

Kurghinian's poetry has two distinguishing characteristics. One is the revolutionary ardor for which she is famed. In this respect she stands with Hakob Hakobian, her contemporary. The other is her delicate lyricism, which reminds one of Hovhannes Tumanian and Avetik Isahakian, also her contemporaries. The melding of these elements is, however, so successful that her poems are infused with exquisite charm.

Her works were published posthumously in Yerevan, in a number of volumes: *Hatentir* (Selected works, 1939, 1978), *Yerkeri zdoghovatzu* (Collected works, 1947), *Banasteghtzutiunner* (Poems, 1971), and *Banasteghtzutiunner, artdzak ejer, piesner, namakner* (Poems, prose, plays, letters, 1981).

THE WORKERS[1]

Here we are, on the march—
Tattered jackets, smudged and soiled,
Crumpled caps and filthy hair,
Mostly jaundiced, base, and barefoot,
Sometimes washed-out, sometimes unperturbed,
Sometimes starved, sometimes trodden down,
With mute, unending torment, deeply lined,
The poisonous revenge of crabbed contempt—

---

1. Shushanik Kurghinian, "Banvorner" (The workers), in *Hayreni ghoghanchner-tzaghkakagh Sovyetahay grakanutyan* (Voices of the homeland: an anthology of Soviet Armenian literature), ed. R. H. Aristakesian and H. Kh. Poghosian (Yerevan, 1985), 91–92. Translated by the editors of the present anthology.

Uncontrollable fury.
Still, with the soul-wrenching pain of growing old too soon,
Faces covered, seeking to breathe fresh air,
And hoping for a life that is worthy of mankind,
Still, with the sorrow of deep wounds in our hearts—
    We are on the march. . . .
We, the workers of potbellies,
Layers of fat, and heaps of gold,
    We, the exploited tillers. . . .
We, the workers of torment, tears,
Half-starved tenacity, prison, exile—
    Inseparably united. . . .
We, the workers, frightened of life,
Shabby goods in life's marketplace—
    Sold for a pittance. . . .
Oh, monstrous leeches on human livelihood,
Vile stranglers of creation;
You senseless, slumbering moles
Of the corrupt desire for riches;
You shameful, grave digging,
Ill-famed hangmen of sacred liberty:
You are all bloodsuckers,
Soul-snatching demons of embryonic hopes;
You feed your pampered self-esteem
With our afflicted faces, starved with distress;
    Your bloated bodies. . . .
Is it not the truth that,
With every drop of our blood,
Our salty, bitter sweat,
Our endless flood of mournful tears,
Our strong, enduring arms,
Our backs, bent with constant care,
You watch us every minute?
With dreadful fear of untimely death
    You feed yourselves,
    You flourish and grow fat. . . .
And for our labors only a few scant crumbs
And offensive haste for the starving masses.
You tell humanity that we are the bastards

And you the select champions
> Of elegance and corrupt existence. . . .
Yes, here we are, and on the march—
From age-old grief, the crucible of woe,
From persecution, the chains of slavery,
> And forgotten classes. . . .
To quash the glories of the master,
The throne of tyranny—the chains of bondage—
To level the path for the likes of us,
Who are worthy of the call and of equality—
> And so we are on the march. . . .

Arandzar (Misak Kuyumchian)

(1877–1913)

Born Misak Kuyumchian (Kuyumdjian) in Talas, Caesarea (Kayseri), Arandzar received his education at the Sanasarian school in Karin (Erzurum), then went to Europe, where he graduated from the University of Zurich. In 1907 he attained a position as principal of the Armenian National School in Alexandria. After the proclamation of the 1908 Ottoman Constitution, which seemed to promise freedom and justice, he moved to Constantinople and was soon appointed principal of the Armenian school in Adana, Cilicia, at which post he remained until his premature death in 1913.

His first short stories appeared in 1903–4 in the periodical *Murch* (Hammer), published in Tiflis, then he began to contribute to both East and West Armenian newspapers as he gained more and more recognition. He mainly wrote short stories and novellas with a vein of humor. His first collection of such works was published in 1905 under the title *Vshti tzitzagh* (Smile of anguish). This was followed in 1907 by a drama, *Prkichner* (Saviors).

In a number of his stories he depicts the condition of the Armenian people in Turkey under the rule of the sultans and defends their struggle for freedom, at the same time rejecting the reckless schemes of the political parties. This stance is reflected in such stories as *"Kakhaghanen . . . amusnutiun"* (From the gallows to the marriage-altar), *"Burdi vacharakanutiuns*" (My wool business), "*Moruki santre*" (The beard comb), "*Yerku patker*" (Two pictures), and so forth. He was an absolute realist, who believed that the aim of literature was to serve life and to express the feelings and ambitions of the people as they really are: hence his criticism of writers who tried to mix realism with aestheticism.

THE STORY WITHIN THE STORY[1]

Atom Vorbuni woke up very late that Sunday. While he was still in bed, lying on his back, having a restless dream with his eyes open, the street had already begun to get noisy from the crowd of those returning from church. "Well, this won't do," he cried suddenly, leaping out of bed. "I won't be able to resolve anything until I take pen in hand."

He put on his socks and pants and approached the wash basin, rolled up his shirt sleeves but suddenly turned back, chuckling: "No, my muses are deserting me, it's better if I finish my work and then wash up."

He put on his jacket too and, after straightening his long hair and attractive fresh beard with a careful stroke of the hand in front of the mirror hanging from the opposite wall, he sat at his desk.

A volume of Maupassant's novels and sheets of paper, fresh and used alike, were scattered about his desk, around a lamp whose dried-up wick attested to his having stayed awake the previous night, until the wee hours. And, indeed, after finishing reading one of Maupassant's stirring novels the night before, with a deep sigh, and inspired by its influence, Vorbuni, already one of the brilliant representatives of the new literary school of Constantinople despite having newly entered the literary arena, had begun to write a short story, which he hadn't finished, despite a long vigilant effort that lasted until two o'clock in the morning. He had a very disturbed sleep that night: as for the heroes of his as yet half-finished short story, he wasn't satisfied with the description of one of their faces; he was annoyed by the insufficiently powerful depiction of

---

1. Arandzar (Misak Kerovbé Kuyumchian), "*Noravepin noravepe*" (The story within the story), in *Zhoghovatzu yerkeri* (Collection of works) (Tiflis, 1905), 8–12. Translated by Aris Sevag.

another's feelings. They had goaded and woken the poor writer up a few times; each time, he had removed the pencil and paper from beneath his pillow and, under the light of the candle that was waiting on his bedstand, he had jotted down the corrections that suggested themselves. However, what tormented him the most was the short story's ending. A few different conclusions had come at the same time and besieged his much tortured imagination, one "better" than the other, one more exciting than the other, and now he didn't know which one to choose. However, he had eventually to finish the piece, as a month had passed since his byline had appeared in the papers.

Sitting down at his desk, Atom gathered the sheets that had countless cross-outs and corrections in hand; even he would have difficulty reading them, if he hadn't memorized them by now through frequent reading. He read over the entirety once and edited the text according to the notes taken during the night; then he read it again and jumped out of his chair, unable to hold himself back from admiration.

"There's no question, it's good; now, if I could only figure out how to make this goddamned conclusion work. . . ."

Right away he imagined those sloppily scribbled pages of his printed cleanly and with special care on the front page of a newspaper, with his name printed in large letters A. VORBUNI. . . . Then the considerable impression that would be spread around him. Many an acquaintance would be shaking his hand in the street, exclaiming "What a wonderful piece you wrote, Monsieur Vorbuni!" Many a girl would shed tears in secret, and many sweet smiles would be flashed at him by the lasses he knew. . . . And, having become giddy from this blissful prospect of tomorrow, Atom began to go around the room, skipping more than running, when suddenly the door opened.

"My gosh!" cried out an elderly woman upon entering. "I've been knocking on the door for half an hour. Didn't you hear? What were you doing?"

"I'm busy, mom, don't disturb me," replied the poet in an irritated voice.

"What work have you got again on a Sunday, my son? You didn't come to church either. Aren't you at all God-fearing? How can you sleep so late?"

"I'm telling you, leave me alone, mom, don't you understand?"

Suddenly noticing the table lamp, his mother cried out, "Don't tell me you stayed up all night again, now did you? You're going to die, my son; either you're going to die or you're going to drive yourself crazy on account of all this reading. How many times have I told you to go to bed before midnight?"

"Enough is enough, mom, for Christ's sake just go, you don't understand anything," Atom replied, raising his voice even higher.

The poor woman took the lamp and left the room, muttering under her breath, "You think that you're the only one who's got intelligence. You don't listen to anybody else."

"For crying out loud, how can I create literature with people like this around me?" an exasperated Atom shouted, closing the door, and returned to his desk.

Holding his head in his hands, he calmed himself down for a while, gathered his thoughts and picked up the pen. He wrote a few lines, crossed them out, wrote again, but the accursed ending wouldn't take shape. Gradually increasing his concentration, the poet began to engage in a monologue out loud.

"Shall I have them get married or not? Shall I have them get married or not? . . . I'll have them get married. . . . No, I won't have them get married. . . ."

Suddenly, however, a voice interrupted his concentration. . . . Again someone was knocking on the door, rapidly and firmly.

"For Christ's sake," shouted Atom, angrily pulling the chair away from the desk, "what is it now, mom? Can't you just leave me in peace?"

"Hey, aren't you going to open the door?" said a voice from the other side.

Immediately recognizing the voice of his friend Tigran Asapian, Atom hastily gathered up the sheets of paper, stuck them in the drawer, went and opened the door.

"What were you doing in there?" asked the visitor, running the head of his finely crafted walking stick through Atom's beard. "I kept knocking on the door but you didn't hear me and, besides, it was shut tight."

"Do you think he's got his wits together so as to hear the sound of knocking at the door?" Atom's mother chimed in as she stood in the hallway. "Again he's writing something for the newspaper."

"Drop the subject, brother, don't ask," answered Atom, shaking his head after closing the door. "I've begun writing something, but I can't finish it because of all the interruptions. If it's not someone leaving the room, it's someone else entering it. . . ."

"Could it be that I too am interfering with you?"

"No, no, not at all; please, sit down, I'm glad you came; I'm on the verge of finishing my story; the only thing is that I'm not sure how to end it; now give me some advice."

"Very well, read me what you've written so far."

Atom removed the sheets of paper from the drawer; holding them in one hand, he turned them to one side and the other, hesitating from time to time, and replied:

"No, my friend, last night I wrote it in a hurry, over a span of some thirty minutes. I haven't edited it yet so it's better if I don't read it."

"Never mind, my friend, read it anyway; I've written something which I brought to read to you."

"If that's the case, you read yours first."

"Now don't be so coy; since you were going to read yours, go ahead and do so."

"No, no, you're better off reading it after it's published; the printed version makes a more powerful impression on the reader than the manuscript version. I'll just read the beginning now, then I'll tell you the rest, and you can state your opinion."

Atom situated himself more comfortably in his chair, coughed a few times to clear his throat, and began reading:

" 'The sweet morning coolness had begun to caress the beautiful nature of summer with the light wings of the balmy zephyr, and the sun, bloodying its mother's womb, was crawling out and, appearing through the thick leafy branches of the trees in the grove as if through a prism, it was scattering its flaming needles on the light-blue mirror of the sea. An intoxicating fragrance of jasmine and carnation permeated the air, and nice bird aubades were making a mad current run through the air, with circuitous turns. At that moment, a creature of striking color and enticing scent was strolling along a path that ran like a ribbon the length of the sea, stirring the fine dust. You'd think it was Astghik who was taking a walk in the morning mist, after having taken her bath. A soft ray of the dawn's light was kissing the feminine milky white nape of her neck, where the lovely curls of her long hair were caressing her soft flesh with delicious drunken strokes.' "

"How is it?" asked Atom, sticking the sheets of paper into his pocket.

"Aren't you going to continue?"

"This is the beginning. I'll tell you the rest but, before doing so, I want to hear your opinion regarding this introduction."

"I can sincerely say that it is quite good. The description of the sunrise, in particular, is marvelous, but the phrase 'who was taking a walk' doesn't quite make it; it ruins the effect of the narration. You've got to avoid using such trite, banal explanations. You've got to create totally new, picturesque phrases. For example, how would it be if you change that sentence as follows: 'her beauty was making a procession through nature.' "

"Oh, that's a marvelous image!" exclaimed Atom, jumping up from his chair. "Her beauty was strutting; that is to say, she was taking her beauty for a walk through nature with the solemnity and divinity of a procession . . . but is there a word 'strutting'?"

"What difference does it make?" replied Tigran, a little offended. "If it doesn't exist, we'll make it up; after all, the other wordsmiths aren't any more literate than us, are they?"

"That's not even in doubt," said Atom and, taking the sheet of paper out of his pocket immediately made the correction as decided. Excited by the praises he heard, he got up and, putting his hand on Tigran's shoulder, said:

"Now listen as I tell you the plot of my story. As you found quite beautifully, that girl who is strutting her beauty, whom I've named Nvard, is the daughter of a wealthy family which has gone to their summer home in a seaside village. Nvard, who is an educated girl with a sensitive and poetic heart (you're picturing an angelic creature like our . . . Vardanush, aren't you?), is in the habit of taking a walk every morning along the seashore. During one of those walks, she meets Mushegh, a young fisherman, who captures Nvard's heart with his handsome, masculine and typically Oriental looks and physique. This fellow, in turn, is enraptured by the girl's beauty and, finally, one day they bare their hearts to each other in a moment of seclusion in the grove. However, when the girl tells her parents about her love, they become very angry and absolutely refuse to give their approval. Now, I've gotten this far, for what it's worth, but I don't know if I should have them get married or not. Sometimes I think like this: One day, the girl goes out on a boat, there's an accident which the fisherman fellow sees, he rushes into the sea and saves her, whereupon the distraught parents give their daughter to him in marriage. Other times, I think about ending the story in a tragic manner like this: Nvard returns to town with her parents, who keep such a tight leash on her that Mushegh can't see her; the pain in her heart leads to tuberculosis, and she dies from that. Mushegh, in turn, receiving the news of his sweetheart's death, drowns in the sea or goes insane. . . ."

"Never mind about his going insane," suddenly exclaimed Tigran who had grown quite weary listening to the entire story.

"Why, what's wrong with that?" asked a surprised Atom.

"There's nothing wrong with that, except my story also ends with insanity, so why don't you select another ending? As it is, yours is so much like my short story here and there that it's as if you've taken it from mine."

"How could I have taken it from you, my wily friend, when I haven't yet seen what you've written?"

"I'm not saying that you've taken from me. That similarity results from our belonging to the same literary school; as it is, there are many differences as well. For example, the name of the heroine in my story is Satenik; the hero's name is Mihran; in my story, the boy and the girl fall in love at dusk, whereas in yours that happens at dawn; you have them falling in love in the forest whereas, in mine, that happens in a boat, etc. However, it won't be good if the endings are similar."

"Well, what do you say now, how shall we proceed?"

"How are you going to proceed? In my opinion, having them get married makes it kind of blah; that kind of ending is characteristic of the old Romantic school, whereas novels written in the new Realistic vein always have a tragic ending."

"So you're saying that I shouldn't have them get married; having him go insane is already in your story. Well then, how do I end this story? Shall I have him drown in the sea?"

"That's the best solution, since the fellow is a fisherman to begin with."

"Well, what about the girl? Should she die from tuberculosis or commit suicide with a pistol?"

"With a pistol? That's not a bad idea; that way, a heroic element will enter into the picture. . . . But, no, let her die of tuberculosis; that's a softer and more heart-rending ending. In particular, you can put a nice descriptive passage in it, about how the girl melted down like a candle owing to her illness."

"True enough, that would make a spectacular ending. So that takes care of that. Now let's read yours," exclaimed Atom, clapping for joy.

And so the two friends began to read the other story, which, in fact, differed from the first only in terms of the details cited shortly before by the author. And it is superfluous to mention that, during the reading, Atom repaid his friend's compliments with interest.

⁌

Two days later, Atom Verbena left an editorial office, with newspaper in hand and a blissful smile on his face. He was walking along the streets with a triumphant gait, and it seemed to him that the attention of all the pedestrians was focused on him; for that reason, he was looking down at the ground so as not to appear immodest. His short story had been published that day, with the following editorial note:

"In the current issue we are publishing a marvelous and touching story by our talented contributor A. Verbena, which, we're certain, will elicit tears of emotion from the eyes of our sensitive readers."

And, in the same issue of the same paper, there was the following note as well:

"In tomorrow's issue, we shall publish a sublime short story by our well-known contributor Tirana Asapian."

Mikayel Manuelian (Manvelian)

(1877–1944)

The actor, playwright, and story writer Mikayel Manvelian was born in Agulis, Nakhijevan, and began his career as an actor with Armenian theater groups in Tiflis in 1895. He acted in more than a hundred plays and became an important figure on the Armenian stage. He usually played the principal characters in famous plays by internationally known dramatists, and was celebrated for his interpretations of such roles as Shylock in Shakespeare's *Merchant of Venice*, Karl von Moor in Schiller's *Die Räuber* (*The Robbers*), and the Blind Monk in *Hin astvatzner* (Ancient gods) by Levon Shant (1896–1951). His 1909 season in Constantinople was crowned with great success and earned him much admiration.

Melancholy, questioning, anguish, worry, and disappointed idealism were constants in Manvelian's interpretations both as an actor and as a writer. These characteristics, with a few clever twists, are well represented in his short story "Baghd" (Luck, 1904).

His collection of stories, *Eskizner* (Sketches), was published in Tiflis in 1904. His other works consist of several short plays that were popular with Armenian theater groups, including *Sheghvatzner* (The misled) and *Ush é* (It's late) in 1907, *Depi paylogh luyse* (Toward the shining light) in 1909, *Vosdayn* (Canvas) in 1912, *Hekyat* (Fable) in 1914, *Hrabukh* (Volcano) in 1915, and *Getstsé kyanke* (Hurrah for life) in 1919.

From the advent of the Soviet regime in Transcaucasia until the end of his life, Manvelian worked with the Shahumian Theater in Tiflis. As well as being a very well-known actor and intellectual, he also made a contribution to Armenian letters, especially in the field of drama. He was awarded the Medal of the Red Flag in recognition of his spectacular career.

Luck[1]

He had been unable to attend even his university lectures that day.

He had roamed here and there all day long, unable to concentrate on anything at all. He had had nothing substantial between his teeth for the last three days. Tea, bread, and cheese had been his only nourishment. And today he did not even have that. The only thing left were a few lumps of sugar. What upset him most was that he had no tobacco. He got up from his bed, where he had stretched out for a little rest. He inspected every corner of the room, to see if he could find at least a butt to quench his craving for a smoke. In the past his searches had rewarded him with a stub, which he had then smoked. Today he could find nothing that would procure him the pleasure of at least a few puffs. He threw himself once more on the bed. Why are they so late in sending me money? What are they thinking of? He fumed as he thought of his family back home.

It was almost four in the afternoon. He was terribly hungry. What could he do? He had already borrowed too much from his friends. He was ashamed to ask them again. He was afraid of losing face. He got up. He tried to read, but was unable to do so: his head felt as heavy as lead. He decided to go out. He quickly put on his coat and took his hat. At least I can fool the landlady this way, he thought. When he had no money for lunch he always tried that trick: he went out at lunchtime, lingered in the streets for half an hour or so, and came back with a toothpick between his lips, as if he had eaten lunch somewhere else. He reached the street.

---

1. Mikayel Manvelian, "Luck," in *Great Armenian Short Stories*, trans. Sarkis Ashjian (Beirut, 1959), 75–78. Revised by the editors of the present anthology.

He did not know where to go. The weather was wonderful. The sun shone brightly. Powerless to melt the thick snow, the rays of the sun made no more than a token effort. He crossed Tverskoy Alley and, turning to face the way he had come, sat on one of the public benches. What was he going to do now? Where could he borrow some money? The demands of the stomach are uncompromising. He turned this way and that, as if sitting on thorns. Oh, for a cigarette! He was on the point of begging a cigarette from the pedestrians passing nearby. That, however, would be too much! To stand up, to go home and try to sleep would be the best thing. But he knew very well that he would be unable to sleep on an empty stomach. How wonderful it would be to be back in Armenia, he thought. If my mother saw me starving like this. . . . He had been far from home for the past two years. He was a student. But he had never been caught in such dire straits before. I hate living like this! To hell with this life; to hell with being a student! He mechanically traced a figure-eight on the ground. . . .

It seemed like a dream. What a coincidence, what a stroke of luck! You could say it dropped right from heaven: not far from where he sat, half-buried in the snow, lay a silver ruble. He looked 'round. He bent down, picked it up, slid it into his pocket without looking at it, and hurried home, as if pursued. He went to his room. His heart was beating violently. He took the coin out of his pocket, as if distrusting its tangible reality. Yes, it was a silver ruble. He seemed to forget his hunger for the moment. What did I come home for? he thought, and he hurried out again. He approached the entrance of a restaurant, and stopped. It would be better to buy a few things and eat my fill at home. Maybe I'll ask the landlady to prepare them for me. And without further ado he went to the nearby store.

"What would you like?" asked the shopkeeper.

"Half a pound of sugar and ten kopecks' worth of tea."

The man handed him his order. "Anything else I can do for you?"

"Two packs of cigarettes. A box of matches and half a pound of cheese, please. And another half-pound of cookies."

"Anything else?"

"That'll be all, thanks."

The first thing he did was open one of the packs of cigarettes and greedily start to smoke. Meanwhile the shopkeeper wrapped the package and handed it to him, saying:

"Here you are, sir."

"How much do I owe you?"

"Sixty-four kopecks."

He handed the man the silver ruble and waited for his change, all the while smoking his cigarette in utter bliss. He stood there holding his package. For a moment he was so pleased and elated at the thought of the feast he was going to make of what he had just bought, when he got home, that he was ready to kiss both the shopkeeper and his assistant, as well as the plump, pie-eyed woman who was standing near him. But suddenly it seemed to him that the shopkeeper got it into his head that the money he had handed him was not really his, that it was a silver coin some-one had dropped on Tverskoy Alley, and that he had found it by chance. . . .

The shopkeeper looked at the coin for a few moments, struck it against the marble table top a few times, and then fixed his eyes on the young man.

"I think this coin is false," he said, and handed it back to him.

Mouth wide open in surprise, the student stared at him, bewildered and unable to understand what he was saying.

"This is a counterfeit coin," repeated the shopkeeper.

"A counterfeit coin," the student repeated, as if he failed to grasp the meaning of the man's words.

"Yes, it's counterfeit, that's what it is: counterfeit."

"But, how can that be, my friend?"

His eyes darkened and he felt his legs give way beneath him. "Counterfeit: a counterfeit coin!"

"Do you remember who gave it to you?"

"Yes, certainly, most certainly I do."

Happy to find a way out of the awkward situation, he blurted out, "I'll take it back immediately and get a good one. I'll be back in a minute." He picked up the coin, placed his parcel on the counter, and was on his way out.

"You still have the two packs of cigarettes," the shopkeeper reminded him.

"Oh! Yes, yes, take this one; as for the other, I'm very sorry, I've already opened it. I'm sorry. I have no more money on me. I'll bring you the money in a moment."

"That's all right. I believe you."

"You know I was given this ruble just a little while ago. I'll go right away and change it for a real one. What impudence! What robbery!"

"That's all right," replied the shopkeeper, "take it easy, sir."

Derenik Temirchian (Demirdjian)

(1877–1956)[1]

The novelist, poet, and playwright Derenik Temirchian was born in Akhalkalak (now in Georgia) and received his early education at the local parish school and at a private school in Ardahan. In 1892 he enrolled at the Gevorgian school in Etchmiadzin, where his literary inclinations were encouraged and guided by his teacher, the poet Hovhannes Hovhannisian (1864–1929). He continued his studies at the Nersisian school in Tiflis and graduated in 1898. He settled in Tiflis in 1900, joined the *Vernatun* (Upper room) literary club (founded by Hovhannes Tumanian, 1869–1923), and got to know the intellectual elite. He went to Moscow (1903) to study music, and then (1905–10) to the University of Geneva, where he majored in pedagogy. Upon graduation he returned to Tiflis and dedicated himself to teaching. He moved permanently to Yerevan in 1925, and was appointed secretary of the arts department of the Institute of Arts and Sciences.

Like many writers, Temirchian began his literary career by writing poetry. His early poems were scattered in the periodical press and were gathered into book form in 1899, followed by a second volume in 1913. The mood of his earlier poems is pessimistic: not yet sure of himself and searching for the causes of injustice in society, he employs vague and abstract symbolism. By contrast, later works such as "*Garun*"

(Spring, 1920) reveal a more penetrating analytic capability, a deeper understanding of the psyche of his people, and a greater affinity with his readers.

The years of transition to the Soviet era, 1918–20, were crucial for Armenian writers and intellectuals in general. Derenik Temirchian was one of those who made the transition very cautiously and with tact: he tried to avoid politically motivated literature and to probe deeper into human behavior. By then he had almost abandoned poetry for prose. The stories he wrote in the 1920s, such as "*Hangsti tane*" (At the rest home), "*Kayarani Akobe*" (Akob of the station), and the novellas *Rashid* and *Nigyar,* contain characters that exemplify the new social order.

One of his best known plays, *Kaj Nazar* (Nazar the brave, 1923), ridicules those who acquire power by accident, turn into cruel despots, and eventually fall into disgrace. Although others (for example, Tumanian and Isahakian) also wrote adaptations of this folk tale, Temirchian's version gained wide popularity, not only for its entertainment value, but also for the political message it conveys in more ways than one. While some saw *Kaj Nazar* as a tyrant, others viewed him as a victorious ruler. The play was staged in Armenian theaters in Yerevan, Tiflis, and Baku the same year it was written, and it was made into a film in 1940.

Another of his plays, the comedy *Napoleon Korkotian* (1934), drew particular attention and displeasure from the authorities. Kevork Bardakjian finds its story reminiscent of Nikolai Gogol's *Revizor* (1836), a brilliant satire on bureaucracy. Temirchian's comedy mercilessly exposes corruption in a *sovkhoz,* an economic institution created by the new system. Official critics panned the play as a distortion of the "bright realities" of Soviet life.

Temirchain was very concerned with the historical and cultural past of his people and with their destiny. These concerns became more pronounced in time, and they were dominant themes in his works of the thirties, when interest in patriotism and the nation's past were still regarded by the state as expressions of "bourgeois nationalism." The Soviet Union exhibited a tendency to cut people off from their past and traditional culture in an effort to promote and advance the formation of the "Soviet man." The drama *Hovnan metzatun* (Hovnan the landlord, 1919) touched on the events of 1915 and their impact, and the short prose piece "*Girk tzaghkants*" (Book of flowers), which was inspired by the medieval poet Kostandin Yerznkatsi (c. 1250–1315) and published posthumously, in 1985, stresses the continuity of Armenian culture through the story of an illuminated manuscript.

In 1938 Temirchian wrote a patriotic drama, *Hayreni yerkir* (Fatherland), which was brilliantly staged the following year. It depicts the political life of Armenia in the eleventh century, when the Bagratuni king, Gagik II, fought against Byzantine forces that had laid siege to the capital, Ani, and defeated them with the assistance of an army commanded by Vahram Pahlavuni.

Temirchian's masterpiece is his sweeping historical novel *Vardanank*, which he completed in 1943. That such a strongly patriotic novel was allowed to be published was a result of the Second World War: the Soviet Union, at war with Germany, needed this kind of literature to lift the spirits of the people. The book was based on the battle of Avarayr in 451 AD. For centuries Armenians have believed that this battle, in which the martyr-hero Vardan Mamikonian was pitted against Vasak the traitor, ensured the preservation of Christianity. Temirchian looks at the event from a political angle: Vasak remains a traitor, but one with a political agenda. The novel recreates the social and cultural atmosphere of the era and is written in excellent Eastern Armenian.

After the war Temirchian wrote stories on the theme of reconstruction, such as *Hanun kyanki* (For the sake of life, 1949), *Tun* (Household, 1949), and *Hush-aghbiur* (Source of memories, 1950). In his later years he began to write a novel about Mesrop Mashtots, but it remained unfinished. He also wrote stories for children, including *Puy-puy mkike* (Puy-puy the mouse, 1934), *Arjuk-lrjuk* (The little bear, 1944), and *Tz-tapar* (Sparrow dance, 1947). Moreover, he translated the first volume of Nikolai Gogol's *Dead Souls*.

Temirchian's works have been published both as individual volumes and in various collections, and they have been translated into Russian, French, English, and German. His complete works, in fourteen volumes, were published in Yerevan from 1976 to 1978. He received a number of medals for his literary achievements, and, in honor of his contributions to Armenian literature, the Derenik Temirchian State Literary Prize in Prose was established in Soviet Armenia in 1980.

KING ARAM[2]

We lived in a small town in Armenia. I was five years old at the time. My world consisted of our yard, our neighbors, and their children. But what a glorious world, full of thousands of wonders!

---

2. Derenik Temirchian, "King Aram," in *Great Armenian Short Stories*, trans. Sarkis Ashjian (Beirut, 1959), 96–15. Revised by the editors of the present anthology.

I was friends with two girls: two sisters who were both a bit older than I was. Their names were Sandukht and Khosrovidukht. I was with them all day long. We played, talked, and ran all over the place together. I had never met their father; that amazed me very much. Did they perhaps have no father? Once, when I asked them this, they answered that they had one and that his name was King Aram.

"King Aram?"

This curious answer made me wonder even more.

"All right, but where is he?"

"He's not home."

"Why doesn't he come home?"

"He'll be back one of these days."

King Aram! That was very interesting indeed!

King Aram lived almost next door, right under our noses, and I had never known who he was! For one thing, I had never seen a king in my life, let alone lay eyes on an Armenian king! But why was he away? Why did he not return to our town? Where was he wandering? What was he doing elsewhere, for heaven's sake? What kind of king was he? What type of men were kings? Interesting, engrossing: he must be a very curious creature indeed! When my excitement over these questions calmed down a little, I asked a few people how it was that the father of Sandukht and Khosrovidukht happened to be a king. One evening I asked my mother why their father was a king while my own was a simple carpenter.

"Well, he does something different: after all, he's King Aram," my mother said, thinking she had explained all there was to explain. But there were still doubts in mind, and they bothered me constantly—rather major doubts. I could not stifle my curiosity. I wanted to see King Aram as soon as possible. I kept turning the question over in my mind, trying to picture him in my mind's eye. It is almost impossible to relate everything I imagined him to be. He was sure to have a gold crown on his head, wear purple garments, and have a belt studded with pearls, from which would hang a magnificent sword in a diamond-encrusted sheath; he would have a scepter in his hand, or an orb. That was what kings looked like, as far as I could tell from the pictures I had seen. No, really: it would be wonderful to get a glimpse of King Aram.

I started to look on Sandukht and Khosrovidukht in quite a different light. Their names acquired fresh meaning for me. They became mystical creatures, legendary heroines. Their features, clothes, and manners were rather royal and stately. They no longer belonged to this temporal world. And then I thought: how interesting it would be to hear Sandukht and Khosrovidukht talking with their father. There was no doubt that King Aram would answer them. What kind of vocabulary would he use? Just imagine: King Aram was their father! Oh how happy, happy, happy they were! How was it that I had failed to recognize my friends' royal lineage until that day? Oh, it was quite simple: they had kept it a secret from me. What nobility! Their simplicity had already begun to work its wonders on me!

They were rather poor. We often heard about their family quarrels and hardships. Their mother, a sturdy, melancholy creature, would sometimes refuse to give them something, God knows what, and they would insist on having it. And sometimes it happened that she beat them. But in spite of their misery and indigence, I looked upon their life as one that was lavish, opulent, and extremely happy. After all, it was the house of King Aram. And all of the fantastic events and persons in Armenian history that I had ever heard of became crystallized in that family.

One day, while I was playing with King Aram's daughters, so absorbed in our play that I had completely forgotten their exceedingly noble birth, Khosrovidukht shouted: "Here comes Father, Sandukht—look!"

The two sisters ran to the corner of the street, where their father's silhouette was outlined. In other words, King Aram was arriving in all his glory. The girls grabbed hold of his hands, and all three started to make for home. Quickly, with a pounding heart, I ran up to them and scrutinized the new arrival with wide eyes. He was a thoroughly common man, with a yellowish beard and curly dark hair. He wore a dirty, greasy sheepskin hat: the kind of hat worn by the poorest villager. His jacket had been patched. He had sandals on his feet and carried a bulging bundle on his shoulder. My surprise knew no limits. I lost all measure and proportion. I approached King Aram all the same and accompanied him to his house, staring at him all the while. On arriving at the threshold of his abode, King Aram lowered the bundle from his shoulder, stooped, and walked through the low doorway of his hut. I did not dare go in. And my friends did not come out, busy as they were with their father the king. I went home and broke the great news to my mother: "Mother, King Aram has come to town!"

"Is that so?" My mother smiled kindly, and said no more.

I remained in the yard. I could tell that a conversation was underway in the king's house by straining my ears, but I could hear no more than confused and indistinct gibberish. Did the mysterious King Aram never talk, or talk very quietly? At any rate, I did not hear him speak a single word. I went home, sat on the windowsill, and peered at King Aram's windows. Inside there was a dim, mysterious light. Shadows played on the walls, with unaccountable symmetry. Was that King Aram's shadow, perhaps? Look! Now the shadow of a waving hand moved across the wall! Whose hand was that? They were probably talking over there, even though I could not make out a single word. There was no doubt about that. Absolutely! And of course, they were talking in the presence of King Aram. And maybe they were addressing him in person. Oh, how enchanting it would be to hear their talk! What questions did they put to him, and what did he answer? To hear and see all that would be like witnessing the most glorious wonder of wonders on earth! What an unforgettable, historic event that would be!

My brain was teeming with these ideas when I heard my mother calling me. She told me to go to bed. I got into bed and dreamed of King Aram and his daughters for a long time, until sleep wiped the magnificent vision from my eyes.

The next morning I woke up quite late. A few rays of sun had fallen on my face. I jumped up, ran to the window, and looked in the direction of King Aram's house, where a solemn silence reigned. I got dressed and went out into the yard. King Aram was now more magical for me than he had been yesterday, despite his curious clothes and poor hat, which were rather unsuitable for a king. I burned with a tremendous desire to hear King Aram's voice and words. Just at that moment the door opened and King Aram made his appearance, large as life. Yes, it was King Aram himself, talking with a certain peasant who had approached him, God knows by what miracle. I asked myself whether the fortunate peasant had approached the king at night or very early in the morning. King Aram looked into the house and gave an order (I could not make out whom he addressed this order to, his wife or his daughters): "Do exactly what I told you." And then he turned back to the peasant and said, "Let's go!"

They walked past me. I ran up to them and looked at King Aram very closely. His glance seemed very sad and mysterious to me. The two sisters did not come out of the house.

King Aram walked the length of the street, turned the corner, and disappeared from my sight like a legendary being. Where was he going, and on what mission? This too was an inscrutable, baffling riddle to me, which my childish fantasy nevertheless wrestled with.

I had already started to avoid the two sisters. They had become unapproachable, alien beings to me. I tried to linger on street corners, harboring in my heart the wish to meet King Aram and hear him talk. Oh! If I could only hear him once, and see what a great speaker he was!

That wish was at last satisfied. He entered his yard with a few villagers the following evening. They walked past me in silence and entered the king's house. The two sisters went in too, and did not reappear. I slowly crept up to their window on tiptoe and began to listen. They had started an exuberant conversation. I could not make out the words, though. I was startled by the voice of one of the peasants, who roared like thunder. I saw King Aram's queen near the window, where the kettle glistened. She filled the cups with tea and carried them away. One peasant roared all of a sudden: "To the health of everyone here. May God grant you all a long life!"

"May God hear your wish," answered a voice, whose identity remained unknown to me.

They laughed, and the talking grew louder. I stepped closer to the window. The roaring peasant began to sing. His voice was wavering now. Suddenly he stopped short and said: "Tell the story again, for God's sake!"

"He's told it once already. How many times do you want him to repeat it?" was the response.

"For God's sake, King Aram, tell it again," insisted the roaring peasant.

The voices died out. And then King Aram's voice was heard:

"The letter arrived a month ago. The King of China wrote to the Armenian people, saying: 'It is a historical fact that the famous Armenian Mamikonian warrior princes, so well known throughout Armenia for their valor and wisdom, originated in our country, China. Send us, therefore, one of their descendants, so that he may lay claim to the treasures left them by their ancestors. Needless to say, all those treasures will be the rightful property of the glorious country of Armenia."

"Where are the descendants of the Mamikonian princes now?"

"That's what we're trying to find out."

"Oh! Splendid!" everybody said. "God bless you, King Aram," roared the peasant, "Fill the glasses again, please!" And he sang again in his tremulous voice.

When the song ended, King Aram spoke again:

"The letter was brought to us by the Chinese Prince Khin-kho. It was written in Chinese ink (which never smudges) on priceless parchment and enclosed in a scroll case."

"What about the ocean? How did he cross the sea?" asked the stalwart peasant.

"He sailed past the shores, so that England might not get wind of the secret," explained King Aram.

I felt a flush of pleasure.

"May God hear your words, King Aram!" shouted the same peasant. "Come on, boys, fill your glasses again!"

I felt I was in fairyland. And when I went to bed, I felt I was in an enchanted world! Where was the Chinese prince now? Would they ever find the descendants of the Mamikonian princes? How could one be an eyewitness to all these things?

Years passed. I became a discreet adolescent, and the riddle of King Aram was unraveled to me. The secrets of the King of China and the Mamikonian princes were also revealed to me. It was very simple: King Aram was a common teacher, who gave private lessons to children in churchyards or clubhouses in several neighboring villages. He taught the basic "three Rs" and supported his family on what he was paid. He was a kind, friendly man, devoted to his family. But, as I came to understand, he really enjoyed gathering the villagers together and telling them stories. He told them of imaginary events, massacres, victories, and miracles. God knows what glowing descriptions of the bloody slaughters carried out by heroic Armenian kings he had made up for them. No doubt he always exaggerated the number of slain enemies enormously. His unbridled imagination ascribed unlimited heroism and valor to the Armenian kings. And the villagers, more out of sympathy for him than out of belief that his stories were true, had nicknamed him King Aram, which was not out of place or devoid of respect for a popular teacher. Curiously, he never felt his pride wounded when they called him King Aram. And that name had come in from the villages and been echoed all over town, reaching the very ears of his two innocent daughters. For me King Aram was stripped of his charm and became simply Aram the teacher. He talked to me about events that happened in the villages, he talked about current affairs and about many other happenings that for the most part had taken place nowhere but in his chimerical imagination.

He was simply a dreamer.

He could create three or four events every day and describe them in the most gruesome detail, without so much as winking an eye. Where did all this fantasy come from? What drove him to conjure up such impossible, even coarse and whimsical apparitions? Maybe he had material expectations. But what material reward was to be had? There was neither material reward nor spiritual satisfaction, since the villagers did not believe him. They simply laughed up their sleeves and went their way.

Siamanto (Atom Yarchanian)

(1878–1915)

Atom Yarchanian, a poet of protest and rebellion, was born in Akn, a town not far from Kharberd (Harput), on the Euphrates River in historic Western Armenia. (The name Siamanto was given to him by Garegin Srvandztiants [1840–92], after the name of the hero of one of his stories.) At the age of thirteen, after he completed the local elementary school, he and his father moved to Constantinople, where he attended the Mirijanian school in Kumkapu then the Perperian (Berberian) school in Scutari (Üsküdar). Horrified by the 1894–96 massacres, he left for Egypt, and went from there to Geneva and then Paris, where he audited literature courses at the Sorbonne (1897–1900). Back in Geneva, he established ties with the Armenian Students' Association, intellectuals, and revolutionaries. It was an atmosphere that formed his worldview and encouraged his literary abilities.

His first poem, "*Mahvan tesil*" (Vision of death), known also as "*Kotoratz*" (Carnage), and a few others were published in various periodicals in 1898. These poems were deeply influenced by reports of massacre, and they were an early indication of the direction his poetry would take. His first collection, a slim volume titled *Diutsaznoren* (With heroism, 1902), introduced him to a wider public. It was addressed mainly to youth, evoking scenes of destruction and carnage from the massacres of the mid-1890s and launching a defiant call to join the struggle for freedom.

Siamanto's second volume of collected poems, *Hayordiner* (Armenian youth), published in three cycles (1905, 1906, 1908), presents a transition from mystical symbolism to a realistic depiction of the gruesome events to which Armenians had been subjected for centuries. His heroes are from the new generation, called upon to struggle for liberation and to fight with steadfast determination until victory is attained.

In contrast to the first two, his third collection, *Hogevarki yev huysi jaher* (Gleams of agony and hope, 1907), is subdued; it even manifests some lyricism. It seems now he was exhausted with scenes of massacre, hatred, and vengeance. He became more introspective, lamenting his loved ones, his destroyed home—as in the poems *"Artsunkneres"* (My tears), *"Hayreni aghbiur"* (The ancestral fountain), and *"Ap me mokhir, hayreni tun . . ."* (A handful of ashes, my native home . . .)—and all the loves and hopes he cherished in his childhood, now vanished in the wake of destruction. In the poems *"Dzerkert indz yerkare"* (Stretch out your hands to me), *"Aspetin yerge"* (The knight's song), *"Huysin hamar"* (For hope), and others, the poet reaches out to his loved ones to gain power for the final struggle.

Siamanto remained in Europe till 1908, when the Young Turks seized power in the Ottoman Empire and adopted a new constitution that promised equality and freedom to all. Siamanto was among the Armenian intellectuals who returned to Constantinople with high hopes for a better future. The following year, however, the Young Turks carried out a terrible massacre in Adana (Cilicia), killing more than 30,000 Armenians. Deceived and disillusioned, Siamanto wrote *Karmir lurer barekames* (*Bloody News from My Friend*), published in Constantinople in late 1909. It consists of twelve incidents reported to him by a medical doctor, which he recast into narrative poems depicting scenes of horrendous barbarism, such as *"Pare"* (The dance), *"Khache"* (The cross), and *"Kuyre"* (The blind man). In the words of Peter Balakian: "It is extraordinary to see how, in writing about the genocide with such blunt realism, Siamanto wrote poems that are remarkably modern in their concreteness, their unromanticized view of the world, their daring risks with vernacular, their ways of using the epistolary episode, and eyewitness-like reportage."[1]

Since the Armenian homeland was being depopulated by persecutions and frequent massacres, Siamanto decided, in 1909, to go to the United States, where some fifty thousand Armenians had already taken

---

1. Siamanto, *Bloody News from My Friend,* ed. and trans. Peter Balakian and Nevart Yaghlian (Detroit, 1996), 20–21.

refuge, and launch a campaign to persuade them to return. For this purpose he wrote a book, *Hayreni hraver* (Invitation to the homeland), consisting of twelve appeals that reflected the pain and anguish of the homeland. His mission failed, and he returned to Constantinople. In 1911 he joined the new literary movement initiated by Daniel Varuzhan (1884–1915), whose *Hetanos yerger* (Pagan songs) became a source of inspiration for many. In contrast to traditional Christianity's counsel of submission and pacifism, the new movement advocated power, force, and self-assertion, taking as models the kings and warriors of pagan Armenia. In 1912, on the occasion of the celebration of the 1500th anniversary of the invention of the Armenian alphabet, Siamano wrote an eloquent poem in praise of its originator, "*Mesrop Mashtots*," which is one of his best works.

Realism and symbolism are interwoven in his poetry, the main characteristics of which are the use of free verse and the power of expression that emanates from his creative inspiration, inner stress, visionary imagination, and rich vocabulary.

In 1915 he was rounded up with other intellectuals by the Turkish authorities, sent to the interior, and brutally killed.

His complete works have been published in various editions in Paris, Beirut, Boston, and Yerevan. Some of his poems have been translated into several European languages.

PRAYER TO ANAHIT[2] ON THE FEAST OF NAVASARD[3]

Goddess, I purge my conscience of all slothful religions.
And I walk proudly in sacred slippers toward you.
Open the marble gates of your temple. Let me bruise my fore-
    head on the door.
Open the altar and give back to me the hot strength
of my Artaxian forefathers.

Hear me, golden mother, fertile sister, sister of virtue,
donor of abundance, patroness of Armenians.

---

2. The most important deity after Aramazd. Anahit was an appropriation of the Persian goddess Anahita.

3. "Prayer to Anahit on the Feast of Navasard," *Ararat* 17, no. 4 (Autumn 1976): 9. Translated by Diana Der Hovanessian.

Hear me on this morning of the feast of Navasard[4]
when your people rejoice.
Allow me to kneel and pray before your idol.

Listen, miraculous rose, goddess of golden feet,
white bride of nocturnal light, lover of the sun,
nakedness with a body of light, sail of Aramazd,[5]
let the sun burn on your altar again.

I believe in you, as I stand on the hills of Bakrevand.
I, the centuries old worshiper of God, come armed with a spear.
I am your son, here as a supplicant apostle,
begging you to hear my lyre of Hayk, a lyre born
from the soil of Koght.

I come in the robes of a pilgrim, bearing green
balsam branches and gold rosewater
in a silver pitcher to anoint your breasts.
And here with the rosewater are tears
mourning your destruction.
Deers follow my shadow as I come to you.

Let the pagan life flow again from the hills.
Let tall sons of the sun wear brocade
and arch their bows, planting their spears,
fastening their swords into necks of the bulls
on the threshold of your altars.
Let a white flock of doves fly from the shoulders
of fertile young Armenian brides toward your statue once
    more.
Let the fountains of Vardavar[6] come to life and flow,
and let sixteen-year-old girls rise to dance,
offering their magical bodies to you, goddess of chastity.

Take your revenge now, after twenty centuries,
oh my goddess, Anahit, now as I throw
into the fires of your altar the two poisonous arms

---

4. In the Armenian calendar the year begins on the first day of the month
Navasard (meaning New Year's Day), which corresponds to August 11. See Hacik-
yan, *The Heritage of Armenian Literature*, vol. 1, chapter on Armenian mythology.
    5. The supreme and omnipotent deity, the creator of heaven and earth in
Armenian mythology.
    6. Transfiguration of our Lord (Armenian).

of my cross. And I celebrate you, oh golden mother,
by burning the polluted bone from the rib
of the Illuminator.

I beg of you, oh powerful, unequaled beauty,
give your body to the sun and be fertilized,
give birth to a formidable god for the Armenians.
For us, from your diamond-hard uterus bear an invincible god!

1914

THE GLORY OF INVENTION[7]

Mesrop![8] You stand an unshatterable
diamond rock against time,
against the Armenian centuries.
You, an undiscovered lighthouse
illuminating the unformed brains
of children, and igniting the genius.
You, the clatter of the chisel,
whose hours, whose minutes carve statues
for the museum of the intellect.
You, the sleepless watchman,
you, the visionary titan of
each word of ours, each utterance
from the cradle to the grave.
You, the creator of dialect and dialogue,
prince of words,
You, the permanent watermark,
the generating father of substance,
you, wheel of light, invitation to faith,
boundless forest, a forest rising on our native soil,
sudden as a storm rising, a forest of solid trees,
each of whose branches is a harp for our breath.
Each one a trumpet for our battles, each

---

7. "The Glory of Invention" (excerpts), *Ararat* 17, no. 4 (Autumn 1976): 10–11. Translated by Diana Der Hovanessian.
8. Mesrop Mashtots (c. 362–440), the inventor of the Armenian Alphabet.

a barricade against scourges.
You, inexhaustible field of wheat, you, free bread.

· ·

You, the titled prophet
forecast by the Greeks,
you, the solitary magistrate
to whom Armenians roar Hosannah!
Hosannah! they cry also
to Sahak[9] of Parth, your contemporary
pontiff of Vagharshapat.
Hosannah to King Vramshapuh[10]
for supporting, like two buttresses,
your discovery,
one with his cross, one with his sword.
Pace by pace, they walked with you,
to open the door of literature
to let in the dawn of Ararat.

· ·

And from which germinating seed,
which unsprouted flower,
from what air, what voiceless accent,
what colorless word, which rootless
stripling did you create
the harmonious alphabet?
Thus, from the golden threshold
of the fourth century until now,
the Armenian spirit fuses
with Armenian blood.

· · · · · · · · · · · · · · · · · · ·

You, a passionate monk, man of God,
brother of the mind, sister of the harp,
allow me to drink from your cup.

Today, nourished by your holiness

---

9. Sahak Partev (348–439), the son of Catholicos Nerses and descendant of St. Gregory the Illuminator.

10. With the support of King Vramshapuh and the active assistance of Catholicos Sahak, Mesrop Mashtots set himself to accomplish the great task of inventing the Armenian alphabet.

I, a tardy harpist, undeserving but
grateful bring you the soul
of your people as a mirror.
The fire in my eye is from the fiery eye
of your people. My words are harvested
from their hearts.
Whatever you read on my forehead
and in my smile,
I have written with their hope.
Therefore, allow me to climb your gold ladder
step by step, crown by crown, as your son,
the son of your thought,
to sing this song.

1913

THE DANCE[11]

Her blue eyes drowned in tears,
the German witness to the horrors tried
to describe the ash fields where Armenian life had died:

"This untellable thing I'm trying to say
I saw with my pitiless human eyes
from the hellish window of my safe house.
While I gnashed my teeth in terror and frustration
my eyes stayed open and pitiless.
I saw a garden city change into ash heaps.
Corpses piled to the tops of trees.
And from the waters, from the springs,
from the brooks and from the roads,
the roar of your blood.

It is the voice of that blood that still speaks
in my heart. Don't be disgusted,
but I have to tell this story

---

11. "The Dance," *Ararat* 17, no. 4 (Autumn 1976): 8. Translated by Diana
Der Hovanessian.

so that people understand the crimes
man to man. Let all the hearts of the world hear.
That morning with death shadows was a Sunday,
the first useless Sunday to rise over those bodies.

I had been in my room all night, tending,
from evening until morning, a girl I knew
stabbed my knives. I bent over her agony,
wetting her death with my tears.
Suddenly I heard from a distance
a black mob of men, whipping, leading twenty girls.
Twenty young women, pushed into my vineyard
while the men sang lewd songs:
'When we beat the drum, you dance!'

And their whips began to crack ferociously
against the flesh of the Armenian women
who longed for death. Twenty
of them, hand in hand, began their dance.
Tears flowed from their eyes, as if from wounds.
And I envied the dying girl
who could not see, but who cursed
with her harsh breathing the universe,
poor beautiful Armenian girl
giving wings to her dove-white soul,
while I shook my fists in vain against
the mob below, 'You must dance, faithless heathen
beauties. Dance, with open breasts, to death,
smiling at us without complaints!

Fatigue is not for you. Nor modesty.
All the way to death, dance with lust, with lewdness.
Our eyes are thirsty for your forms and for your deaths.'

Twenty handsome girls fell to the ground exhausted.
'Stand up' the roar thundered behind the snake-like
whirling swords. Someone brought a bucket
of kerosene. Oh human justice
I spit at your forehead. Then they doused those twenty brides,
shouting
'You must dance. And here's a fragrance

Arabia does not have.' And with a torch,
they set on fire the naked flesh.

The charred corpses rolled toward death
through the dancing. From my fright
I shuttered the window as if against
a hurricane. And I asked the dead girl in the room,
'How shall I dig out these eyes of mine? How?' "

1909

Vahan Tekeyan

(1878–1945)

The poet Vahan Tekeyan was born in Ortagiugh (Ortaköy), a suburb of Constantinople. He attended the Nersesian and Perperian (Berberian) schools and then transferred to the Kedronakan (1891–94). He was obliged to cut short his education when he was sixteen and started working as a clerk. In 1896 he became a sales representative and embarked on an itinerant life, which, over the course of the next few years, took him to England, France, Germany, and eventually Egypt (1903). In Egypt he joined the Hnchakian political party, but after dissension broke out in the ranks, he joined the Ramkavar (Democratic) Party, with which he remained for the rest of his life. While living in Egypt he contributed poems and literary essays to various papers. In 1905 he founded his own literary monthly, *Shirak* (1905–07), in Alexandria, with Mikayel Kiurchian (Gürdjian, 1879–1965) and Arpiar Arpiarian (1852–1908) as coeditors. This paper later (1909) reemerged in Constantinople.

In 1908, attracted, like many other intellectuals, by the freedoms promised in the new Ottoman Constitution, he returned to Constantinople. In 1911 he was a delegate to the election and enthronement of Catholicos Gevorg V in Etchmiadzin. He was elected a member of the Armenian National Assembly and was sent to Caesarea (Kayseri) for a short while as principal of an Armenian school. In 1914 he became the permanent representative of the National Assembly to the Patriarchate of Jerusalem and so was spared the horrors of the genocide. Back in

Cairo in 1915, he collaborated in the founding of *Arev* (The sun), a political, social, and literary daily that he edited intermittently over the course of its long life. In 1919 he went to Paris as a member of the Armenian National Delegation, headed by Nupar Pasha, that presented the Armenian case to the Congress of Paris.

Busy as he was with political and public activities, Tekeyan did not neglect his literary pursuits. Between 1920 and 1923 he was again in Constantinople, where he edited a daily, *Zhoghovurdi dzayn* (The people's voice), and established, with the collaboration of Hakob Oshakan (1883–1948) and Kostan Zarian (1885–1969), the literary monthly *Bardzravank* (1922), with the aim of gathering around it the intellectuals who survived the genocide. The same year he was called to fill the principal's position at the Kedronakan lycée. In 1923 he traveled back and forth between Greece and the Middle East to oversee orphanages and ensure the proper education of Armenian children. The decade 1924–34 was filled with new assignments, numerous trips between Cairo and Paris, and an abundant output of literary works, in addition to serving in his position as supervisor of the teacher training school of the Melkonian Institution in Cyprus. In 1936 he again assumed the editorship of *Arev* in Cairo, and a year later he helped launch a daily, *Zartonk* (Revival), as the organ of the Liberal Democratic Party in Beirut. His hectic life, with more literary output, more editorial work, and more civic duties, continued unabated until 1945, when he died in Cairo.

Tekeyan's literary career began in 1892, when some of his essays were published in the periodicals *Hayrenik* (Fatherland) and *Tzaghik* (The flower). His first collection of poems, *Hoger* (Anxieties, 1901), contains the love songs of his early youth: lyrics written in a melancholic mood that would stay with him for a long time. In this first book he is still in search of himself and reveals his anxieties.

His second volume of poetry, *Hrashali harutiun* (Splendid resurrection, 1914), considered one of his better works, embodies the maturity he attained through the "resurrection" of his inner self, a miracle achieved through poetry. It revives the past, with its pains, longings, and hopeless dreams. The most vibrant chord in these songs is that of love; it is, however, a privately cherished love, restrained, and with an object not revealed. Nostalgic memories of past loves, sadness, and solitude, and meditations on life and death, courage, and injustice are among the themes of the collection.

Tekeyan's third volume, *Kes gisheren minchev arshaluys* (From midnight to dawn, 1919), includes poems written between 1914 and 1918, the most tragic period endured by the Armenian nation. Despite the pain and sorrow that weighed so heavily upon his heart as a result of the barbaric destruction of his people, he maintained restraint and dignity in his poems, even though the messages of revolt and anguish they contain are very powerful.

The volume *Ser* (Love, 1933), which marked the fortieth anniversary of his literary debut, is, despite the title, has less to do with love than with patriotic sentiments, issues of life and death, compassion, human relations, and philosophical meditations and abstractions. *Hayergutiun* (Songs of Armenia and Armenians, 1943), brings together a number of older poems previously scattered in the periodical press, along with a few new ones. His last work, *Tagharan* (Song book, 1944), is a song of love that alternately celebrates its joy and its bitterness.

Tekeyan's poetry is distinguished by restraint of feeling and depth of thought. A melancholic mood permeates his verse, reflecting his inner soul, which was burdened with sadness. This is attributable in part to the circumstances of his life and in part to the influence of the French symbolists Baudelaire and Verlaine, who were his favorite poets. He is known as the master of the Armenian sonnet, his favorite form of poetry: a condensation of thought and feeling into fourteen lines. His language is simple but perfect, each word and rhyme chosen with the utmost care. "In his poetry, each word is subjected to intense scrutiny, in order to squeeze the maximum meaning and emotion out of it."[1]

In addition to poetry, short stories, essays, columns, travel notes, and numerous editorials, Tekeyan also left a volume of translations, which includes works by several French poets, particularly Baudelaire, and a number of Shakespeare's sonnets. The publication of his complete works began in Cairo in 1949, but only volumes 3, 4, 5, 7, 8, and 9 have appeared. Individual volumes have been published in Beirut (1954, 1958, 1978) and Yerevan (1958, 1978).

IT IS RAINING, MY CHILD[2]

It is raining, my child. All the autumn is wet
like the eyes of those love has betrayed.
Close the window, shut the door and return
to sit here beside me in this room.

---

1. Edmond Y. Azadian, *Portraits and Profiles*, ed., trans., and intro. Agop J. Hacikyan and Edward S. Franchuk (Lewiston, N.Y., 1995), 104.

2. Vahan Tekeyan, "*Kandzrevé tghas*" (It's raining, my child," in *Sacred Wrath: The Selected Poems of Vahan Tekeyan*, ed. and trans. Diana Der Hovanessian and Marzbed Margossian (New York, 1982), 28.

Does it rain in your heart? Does a storm churn
in your soul? No, you're too young to mourn
the pains of circumstance,
or sunlight that has turned to gloom.

But you are crying, dear child,
suddenly in this dark,
heavy tears for no reason I know,
except being the victim of life—
your innocent tears have to flow.
Cry then; let them be used up. And grow.

1901

To the Armenian Nation[3]

I know it. Only too well. You do not need this.
But here, again, I give myself to you,
page by page. Forgive this useless gift.
What can you do with poems? They are not food.

Let the adolescent write himself out. That is allowed.
But what about the grown man who insists
on stringing lines and meters, to hang
on them the dim lanterns of his heart?

I know you do not expect anything; you never have.
Except the inexpressible tribulation
of your children staying yours.

But take these anyway. To discard. To forget—
these pieces of a heart, worn out
with the burden of burdening you.

1925

Ode to Verlaine[4]

In this world of words, no one besides
you kept the sacred and profane

---

3. Ibid., 11.
4. Ibid., 27.

side by side, and innocent
of wrong or right, Verlaine.

You were like the vast forest, ready
to disclose secrets to those who camped.
You were for the dark shadows of
the soul's miner a golden lamp.

What mysteries your murmurs tell.
What ideas you raise. What hidden doors
where we kneel, while you praise,

like a cursed priest, the flowers of sin—
all from the safe chapel
that you stay within.

1904

Dark Hours[5]

I

Was it all wasted? Starting from the first
sun of childhood, when we pressed you into our heart,
nurtured you with the sweet overflow of milky dreams,
and for your sake hammered a bargain with hell?

We traded with the devil for lives so that you
could be heaven, fatherland, you, dangling between
abyss and sky, dizzy cradle, glorified plague, fire
warming the soul and house eternally in flames.

How many times has your rainbow arched from sky to pit,
and how often from the abyss has a huge column risen to tease
us into useless climbing again and again?

How often, with only defeat, and sliding back
for those of us who wrapped ourselves around its shaft
only to fall back in agony, again, again?

1922

---

5. Ibid., 48–49.

PRAYER ON THE THRESHOLD OF TOMORROW[6]

Look, New sprouts push through the fields.
But which are thorns and which are wheat
I do not know. Perhaps to the appetite
that is sated all is chaff
while to the hungry all is wheat.

Undistinguishable sounds, blows, footfalls
thud in the distance, an agonizing attack
where the oppressed plant red
flames with their blood.
And the rains sweat and expand
into floods that shake the walls
of the oldest dams.

Lord, now is the time to send
your wisdom and kindness
to the tortured who, although
they have forgotten, need you as they hurl
themselves closer to the precipice.

Oh, God, who trimmed the wick of the mind
and poured the oil of life, do not let
your lamps be overturned.
Let them illuminate paths to your truth.

Plant love in the eyes of today's
and tomorrow's mighty. Do not let
their hearts close.

And do not let the hearts of the child
and the aged be strangers
to tenderness and hope.

Let the struggle of our time be short.
Let it be settled with justice.

Let the fortress of egos,
that huge barricade,

---

6. Vahan Tekeyan, "Prayer on the Threshold of Tomorrow," trans. Diana Der Hovanessian, *Ararat* 17, no. 2 (Spring 1976): 23.

crumble. And let every treasure
go to every man. Let every garden
gate be open. But let no flower be crushed.
No single branch fall.

DEAR BROTHER IN THE BOND: A LETTER OF TEKEYAN TO VARUZHAN[7]

1906, February 13, Alexandria
Dear brother in the bond,
Some time ago I received your letter and along with it the poem
you sent for publication. There are few letters that I would have
replied to with such pleasure, there have been few times that I have
had such a great desire to commence a new correspondence—and
yet it has been more than three months that I have not written to
you. Explain it as you like; I don't wish to offer the usual excuse of
being busy and having various problems; it seems to me more that
a natural kind of destiny has held back my pen till now, and today it
is only this that impels my pen—with an instinctive and irresistible
force—to cut at once across the span of distance and the dark road
of unacquaintance, to greet you fraternally, personally (as though
we were face to face).

Today I read your poems in *Geghuni*. I liked them so much and
was filled with so much admiration that I hesitate to express my
thoughts in words for fear of appearing feeble. Besides, I think that
it might perhaps be a sign of immodesty on my part to praise you
to yourself; for—contrary to the well-known jealousies between
fellow-craftsmen, am I not just a bit, a very little bit(!), a sharer
in your glory, considering that it was I who for the first time—I
think—announced your newborn, authentic talent?

This pleasureful, yet pride-inspiring, consideration does not
prevent me from expressing that great joy which I experienced
with your sheaf of poems. Apart from the art, which is nearly
perfect, it is the freshness of spirit shaping the art, the sincerity

---

7. Vahan Tekeyan, "Dear Brother in the Bond . . . ," in "Veronico Varoujan
Remembers" by Shoghere Markarian, *Ararat* 19, no. 1 (Winter 1978): 20–21. See
the poems of Daniel Varuzhan in the present anthology.

and the boldness, which captivate me. Fortunate for you that upon your mouth of inspiration you have no halters, that you enjoy the supreme fortune, being yet so young, of marking the path of the happiest age with the traces of imperishable flowers

Believe me! Write, write now! Sing now! Full and strong, without reservation, any hopes and any feelings that pass through your being. Songs now still can nourish, and they are natural and beneficial; the songs of adolescence are the froth which appears on the surface of life just coming to a boil, the froth which is skimmed off and kept, like the first film of foam upon the *miuron*[8] cauldron. I know how those first pure and strong songs—since they remained repressed in the heart of a hypersensitive boy, then poisoned it, then were transformed into perpetual mist, cutting off his eyes from the spectacle of life—turned into weakness and enfeebled his legs forever upon the path of life Perhaps this was not the only reason, but what sadness to constantly recall unsatisfied desires, attempting to conceal beneath one's breast the cold corpse of adolescence, which ought to have been interred, and upon which a robust youth ought to have flowered.

I am sure that you will be spared this bitterness. In your verses I already sense the vigorous natural development of a life to which, with all my fraternal soul, I wish love, strength, and success.

After expressing all my sincere and ardent admiration to you, I wouldn't want to introduce any criticism in this letter of mine. You will be surprised that in the current issue of *Shirak,* which will reach your hands at the same time, your poem which you sent me doesn't appear. Regarding this, let me say immediately that, being perhaps more demanding of you in consideration of your renown, after reading it over several times, I decided not to publish it, for in spite of some strong and fine lines, I found the thing as a whole weak, and in some places particularly incomprehensible. Clarity in poetry is not my favorite quality, but I desire—and it is requisite— that *I* at least understand what might be considered obscure by others. Beginning with our very first issue I have wanted to have your contributions, but taking into consideration your relationship with the people in Venice, in order not to be untactful, I have

---

8. Chrism, holy oil (Armenian).

refrained from proposing this. After this issue we hope to continue *Shirak* in Cairo in a new arrangement. If you should wish to write to me, send along some poems to the following address: V. Tekeyan, c/o K. G. Melkonian, Cairo. We will recompense you as much as we can.

Yours affectionately and devotedly,

Signed Vahan Tekeyan

Zapel (Zabel) Yesayan

(1878–1943)

Zapel Yesayan, née Hovhannesian, was born in Scutari (Üsküdar), a suburb of Constantinople, to a large family of modest means. Her father, an educated man, had a great influence on her. As she states in her autobiography: "My adolescent idealism was nourished by his reasoning, which gradually succeeded in ordering the confused and chaotic state of my mind. Violent confrontations took place within me, followed by victories as well as defeats, plunging me into extreme and contradictory states. But under the influence of my father's words some degree of harmony would be introduced within me and gradually I would reach a state of internal balance and synthesis."[1]

She graduated from the local Surb Khach (Holy Cross) Armenian school in 1892, and showed strong inclinations to literature. Her first prose poem, "*Yerg ar gisher*" (Night song), appeared in the periodical *Tzaghik* (The flower), published by Arshak Chopanian (Arshag Tchobanian, 1872–1954). In 1895 she went to Paris, studied literature and philosophy at the Sorbonne and the Collège de France, and began to contribute short stories, literary essays, articles, and translations in

---

1. In Zapel Yesayan, *The Gardens of Silahdar and Other Writings,* ed. and trans. Ara Baliozian (New York, 1982), 85–86.

both Armenian and French to various periodicals, such as *Mercure de France, Anahit, Masis,* and *Arevelyan mamul* (The eastern press). In the meantime she married the painter Tigran Yesayan. She returned to Constantinople in 1908 and took an active role in the community, joining various literary, political, benevolent organizations, and women's groups as a staunch advocate of feminism.

During the first decade of the twentieth century she published a number of short pieces in various periodicals. These demonstrated her literary talent and helped to spread her fame. The most important are *"Spasman srahin mej"* (In the waiting room), which depicts the plight of a young mother; *"Skiutari verjaluysner"* (Twilights of Skutari, 1905), in praise of nature; *"Keghtz hancharner"* (Phony geniuses, 1909), a sarcastic and contemptuous portrayal of a few famous contemporary writers— Suren Partevian (1876–1921), Siamanto (1878–1915), and Tiran Cherakian (Indra, 1875–1921); *"Hlunere yev embostnere"* (Conformists and dissidents), which deals with sociopolitical issues; and *"Shnorhkov mardik"* (Decent people, 1907), an exposé of the degenerate bourgeoisie.

In 1909, after the massacres in Adana, the Patriarchate sent her to Cilicia on a fact-finding and mercy mission as the representative of the Aid Committee. Her report, *Averakneru mej* (Among the ruins, 1911), is an account of the atrocities. Her novella *Anetzke* (The curse) and the two short stories *Safieh* and *Nor harse* (The new bride), both written in 1911, also draw on those tragic events.

In 1915, during the mass arrests and displacement of intellectuals, she fled first to Bulgaria then to Tiflis, where she involved herself with efforts to shelter the refugees and orphans who were pouring into the Caucasus from Western Armenia. During this time she wrote *Zhoghovurdi me hogevarke* (The death pangs of a nation, 1917), the testimony of a genocide survivor, and the novel *Murati chambordutiune Svazen Batum* (Murat's journey from Sivas to Batum, 1917).

Her novellas, *Verjin bazhake* (The last cup), *Andzkutyan zhamer* (Hours of anxiety), and *Hogis aksoryal* (My exiled soul), written between 1916 and 1919 and considered among her best pieces, deal with the inner life of heroic women, including herself, who are caught in unhappy marriages, in the clash between individual liberties and social conventions, or in the inconsistencies of human relationships within the context of culture, literature, and art. The strong personality she reveals in her writings is that of a free thinker; emancipated from prejudice, she comes across as a rebel, sometimes unhappy even with herself. *Verjin bazhake* is a psychological study of a woman in love; *Andzkutyan zhamer* is the story of a disharmonious marriage, with all the suffering that entails; and

Hogis aksoryal depicts a painter who believes she will be delivered from all her anxieties when she attains perfection in art.

Yesayan was a wholehearted supporter of Soviet Armenia, and in the novel *Nahanjogh uzher* (Retreating forces, 1923) she describes the social and political conditions of the time. She visited Soviet Armenia in 1926 and shortly thereafter published her impressions in *Prometheus azatagrvatz* (Prometheus unbound, 1928). In 1933 she settled in Yerevan. She taught French literature at Yerevan State University and in 1934 took part in the first All-Union Congress of Soviet Writers in Moscow. To this period belong her two exquisite works, *Kraké shapike* (The shirt of fire, 1934) and *Silahdari parteznere* (The gardens of Silahdar, 1935), a captivating autobiography. Her last work was a novel, *Barba Khachik* (Uncle Khachik), published posthumously in 1966. Her other works include essays on literature and art and translations of, among others, Maurice Maeterlinck's *La sagesse et la destinée* (Wisdom and destiny) and *La mort* (Death).

Yesayan's final years are shrouded in mystery. Soviet sources give 1943 as the year of her death. It is assumed she was a victim of Stalin's purges. Collections of her works have been published in Yerevan (1937, 1959, and 1977), Beirut (1972), and Antilias (2 vols., 1987).

FROM SHIRT OF FIRE[2]

At the time I was barely ten. We lived in a one-story, ramshackle, wooden structure in Scutari, not far from Bülbül Deresi (Nightingale Gulch).

In summer and winter, the dark, muddy waters of the river tumbled sluggishly into the gulch. I will never know why it had such a poetic name. Probably because on the opposite bank there was a Turkish cemetery in whose evergreen and melancholy cypress trees nightingales had built their nests.

---

2. Yesayan, "Shirt of Fire," in *The Gardens of Silihdar and Other Writings*, 33–38. All footnotes by Baliozian, unless otherwise indicated.

"Shirt of Fire" was first published in Yerevan in 1934; shortly thereafter (1936) it was translated into a number of Soviet languages, including Russian. It is a short (about eighty pages) autobiographical novella and generally regarded as one of Zapel Yesayan's best works. The introductory pages have been translated here. It will be noted that the locale is the same as that in *The Gardens of Silihdar*, but viewed, as it were, through a glass darkly.

My childhood was spent on the banks of that gulch, with whose stench every youngster in the neighborhood was well acquainted, having inhaled it even in his cradle.

In the summer, when the south wind blew, the adults frowned with distaste and the word spread that it was the *lodos*.[3] That word filled me with horror. In those days my mother was more irascible than usual and my father's spent eyes reflected unfathomable despair. Any insignificant occurrence became a pretext for Mother to mount a savage attack on Father's improvidence. In the oppressive atmosphere of our home, complaints and shouts of despair rang out incessantly, interrupted only by hissing slaps that stung my brothers' and my cheeks. The stench of Bülbül Deresi became even more unbearable, and when, once in a while, a gust of wind brought a different kind of whiff from the cemetery on the other bank of the gulch, Mother would hasten to lock us in, saying with a look of mystery and alarm on her face: "Don't go out today—looks like the Turks buried another one of their carrion."

At night, when Father and Mother spoke about their endless problems, Mother's words were more bitter than usual, and Father's replies more disheartening. "For heaven's sake," Mother would cry out, pounding her knees to emphasize her hopelessness, Why don't you do something and get my poor, innocent children out of this hell?"

But it was no use. There was no way out for us. Like an incurable disease, destitution had found a permanent place in our home.

My father was a yarn-dyer in a textile factory. Every morning he rose before sunrise, walked to the factory, prepared the dyestuff, and in the summer heat and winter cold and wind, carried skeins of yarn down to the beach, washed them, and then carried them all the way up to the factory again, still dripping wet on his shoulders, his face moist with sweat and blood.

Even with the six children she had to look after and no one to help her with the other household chores, Mother worked too, weaving cloth on a hand loom.

When, during the long winter months, our bedding was spread on the floor, and we all went to sleep one by one, my mother, with

---

3. Southwest wind, southwesterly gale (Greek).

the aid of a small lamp, kept on working late into the night. My father lay down on the covers and dozed off, but once in a while he opened his eyes and exchanged a few words with my mother. My brothers and sisters would be asleep by then. But being a light sleeper myself, I tried to follow their conversation.

Though exhausted, my mother continued working with teeth clenched, speaking all the while of the many problems that beset us—money lenders who were threatening to knock on our door the following day, the coal-dealer who had refused to sell her any more coal on credit, the baker who early that day had refused to stop by our house and make his customary delivery. My father sighed and cursed poverty. Roused to a fury, my mother interrupted her work, stood up and cried out: "A shirt of fire! That's what poverty is, a shirt of fire!"

In the semidarkness of the room, it seemed to me as though my mother, with her slender frame, fiery eyes, and chin thrust out defiantly, was struggling against invisible forces. Like someone possessed, she looked wildly around her, and my father followed every one of her movements with sleepy eyes, and slowly reached for his aching feet that trembled in their damp tattered socks.

My mother's anger, though I could not understand its meaning, always caused a sense of deep anxiety in me. My heart tightened and I wanted to shout. I knew, yes, I knew very well, that a heavy sorrow lay on us all, even if it was the grown-ups who carried its burden, sometimes with patience, sometimes with rebellion. That sorrow was like a twin brother who had come into the world with us and was growing with us. It was only much later that I understood it was destitution in its many horrible, multi-faceted disguises, and ever since then I have taken it upon myself to defeat that monster.

At the time, however, I was young and immature. When I heard my parents use such expressions as "just to eke out a living," or hope against all hope that "things may get better soon," I couldn't understand that they were already working as hard as they could, and that even if things did get better, our lives and the lives of people like us would never improve.

At school, the words of our teachers, legends inscribed in fine calligraphy on the walls, the stories we were told or read in our textbooks, aimed at persuading us that "with study and application one can achieve anything in this world." Impervious to such admonitions, my brothers spent most of their time and energy playing games and brawling in the streets. Attending classes was for them an unpleasant duty, and the instant school ended they shot out like bullets, became absorbed in their games, and woe to him who stood in their way.

Though sometimes I followed their games from a distance with jealous admiration, I didn't take part in them because I preferred to go home and study. Mother was indifferent to my diligence and to my brothers' mischievous behavior—so long as she was left alone. I don't recall a single tender, motherly kiss or affectionate smile. Ah! let them say what they will; let them deliver speeches and write about the sweet memories of childhood. . . . These are people who know nothing about the struggle for life. My mother had no time for such nonsense. When my baby sister began to wail and screech in her cradle my mother's face registered annoyance, not concern. When the noise became unbearably loud, she would pick up the child and nurse her with a hollow stare until the baby had its fill.

I understand now that life was not easy for my mother and that she worked so hard to keep us alive that she was drained of all affection. But at the time, my childish soul longed for a little tenderness and my mother's grim face filled me with resentment. I had acquired a purpose in life, however, and I consoled myself with it, feeling strong and confident of my future.

One particularly cold winter, my little sister Arusyak fell ill. She was eight years old. Though none of us saw anything out of the ordinary in her, everyone else said she would grow up to be a very attractive girl.

"I'll tell you a secret if you promise not to tell Mother," she said to me one day shortly after she fell ill.

I nodded in agreement.

"You mustn't tell anyone else either," she added.

"All right, I promise."

"I'm going to die soon," she said, smiling a happy smile.

"You must be mad!" I said horrified. "What kind of talk is that?"

"I just know it," she replied, "and I'm very happy about it. They will put me in a white box with blue ribbons, and I'll go straight to heaven. I was told this by an angel. I was also told I'll turn into an angel myself."

"Enough of that nonsense!" I shouted. "It's all lies, I tell you, *lies!*"

"Actually it wasn't an angel who told me; it was Zaruhi," she said with a gasp. "Whenever little ones die, she said, they go straight to heaven."

"That lying hussy! If that's the way it is, then why doesn't she drop dead herself? I tell you she lies. . . ."

It seemed to me that if my sister stopped believing that story, she wouldn't die.

"Nothing but lies," I said again. "Ask anyone you want. One mustn't die. Listen to me, Arusyak: you know what happens to you after you die? You turn into a corpse, they dig a hole in the ground, they bury you, and you turn into dust, that's all! Zaruhi told you a fib."

"But why, why?" my sister said, now in tears, putting her head against my shoulder.

"You'll get well, you'll see," I said caressing her hair. "When we grow up, we'll go to work together, we'll have a nice garden, and in the garden we'll plant lots of rosebushes. . . ."

Arusyak didn't agree with that at all, and looking straight at me said between sobs:

"I want jasmines. Also an almond tree. We *must* plant an almond tree—they have such nice flowers! There is nothing in this world I love more than an almond tree in bloom."

"All right, all right. We'll plant rosebushes, jasmines, and an almond tree—if that's what you want. But first tell me you don't believe that dumb story Zaruhi told you."

Arusyak rested her head against her pillow, reflected a moment, heaved a sigh, and said:

"It was a nice story all the same."

"*Lies, lies!*"

"So what? When I grow up, I'll write about it."

Arazi (Movses Harutiunian)

(1878–1964)

Movses Harutiunian, who wrote under the pen name Arazi, was one of the pioneers of proletarian literature. He was born in Shulaver (present-day Shahumian, in Georgia), received his early education at the local school, and completed middle school in Tiflis, where one of his class-mates was the noted revolutionary Stepan Shahumian (1878–1918), whose ideas had a strong influence on him. In 1899 he moved to St. Petersburg and enrolled in the Institute of Technology. There he was imprisoned for five years (1901–5) for participating in student protests. In 1906 he returned to Tiflis and began to publish his first articles in the monthly *Murch* (Hammer), which was the forum of most of the demo-cratic thinkers of the time. While the socialist revolution was fermenting he published a number of short stories, such as *"Menavor laptere"* (The solitary lantern, 1912), *"Verjin yeraze"* (The last dream, 1912), *"Kisat tune"* (The unfinished house, 1913), *"Viravor trchune"* (The wounded bird, 1913), and *"Ariunot dzaghikner"* (Blood-stained flowers, 1916). During World War I he collaborated with Hakob Hakobian (1866–1937) to edit and publish two collections of proletarian literature, *Karmir mekhakner* (Red carnations) and *Banvori albom* (The laborer's album).

His works written after the revolution, in the 1920s and '30s, dwell mainly on the themes of rebuilding the country and the effect of the new ideology on the psychology of the people. Short stories such as *"Enker Mukuch"* (Comrade Mukuch, 1924), *"Lusni shogherov"* (By the light of the moon, 1932), and *"Jrvezhi tsolkum"* (In the reflection of the waterfall, 1933) are but a few examples from this period. His novel *Ayrevogh horizon* (The blazing horizon, 1940) depicts the student disturbances, labor movements, and general unrest that characterized the beginning of the century. During World War II Arazi published two collections of short stories, *Hayreniki kanche* (The call of the Fatherland, 1942) and *Anhaghtnere* (The invincibles, 1944). His historical novel, *Israel Ori* (1959), is about the seventeenth-century Armenian emancipation movement.

Arazi was awarded a number of medals by the Armenian SSR and was twice elected deputy of the Supreme Soviet. A collection of his works, in three volumes, was published in Yerevan in 1955–57.

IN THE CAGES[1]

He went to the same telegraph office every day.

Over the course of the years, those streets had become habitual to him, like his home. Even the thoughts he had on his way to the office had become habitual.

When he reached the crossing, he wondered, "Does it really matter which road I take? Life has harnessed me to its heavy burden, so no matter where I turn there's no way out.

"No! This important question must be resolved!" he would repeat to himself as he walked through the public park. "Whose life is it, that I have to drag it around as my own? But there you have it! I am dying from day to day instead of living for my wife and child who, like me, also have pale faces and broken hearts.

"Who is all this for?" he would ask over and over again, slowing his pace. "Here! I know. . . . It's for the rich and carefree lucky couple who gaily walk into the telegraph office, snatch the pen from each other's hand, write and erase and write again. . . . They send funny telegrams and nonsense: 'Congratulations on your name

---

1. Arazi (Movses Harutiunian), "In the Cages," in *Hatentir Yerker* (Selected works) (Yerevan, 1948), 9–13. Translated by Ardashes H. Shelemian and edited by the editors of the present anthology.

day; we are all well, so is our little imp of a puppy.' They congratulate, give thanks for the life they enjoy . . . but I curse . . . as I stay
up all night wiring their entertaining burden to its destination.

"Money! Money!" he repeated as he entered the telegraph office: "Money would change everything, money would solve everything. . . . Money would free me from these unbearable surroundings, it would free me from unsuitable, backbreaking labor."

"There you are, you damned cages!" he said, as he entered his
disgusting office, where the old man who was always the first one
there sat reading his small penny newspaper.

"Good day! Anything new in the paper today?" he asked the
old man.

"Nothing of interest . . . but it's work and more work for us."

"But, imagine," Melanian said, "winning two hundred thousand dollars in the lottery, taking wing and flying from this stinking
cage once and for all, taking a tour around the world. . . ."

"O! You're so lucky you can dream: you're still young. For me,
that's all behind me. There was a time I used to dream too, but I've
never seen such a determined dreamer as you. You have such a
strong desire to be rich, that sometimes it makes me wonder. And
mind you, if it comes true some day, the very next day you will
start putting us, your fellow workers, down. . . . That's how life is:
one day, well dressed and with an arrogant air, you will turn up
at our small counter and bawl out rudely: 'What a disgrace! Why
wasn't my telegram delivered on time?' Not content to show your
ignorance of the unspeakable weight of work on our shoulders,
you will have the audacity to send for the manager. Yes, all of that
might happen one rainy fall day. . . . But let's say no more about
your scheming fantasies. . . ."

A customer's hand clasping a blue telegram form appeared in
the small opening on the countertop. That interrupted their conversation, and the usual clamor in the office resumed.

The poor old fellow was sad; his face looked like that of a troubled child. They had had a strange argument about those imaginary
riches. He felt bitter whenever he thought of what Melanian had
said about the lottery. He wrote the receipt mechanically, while he
continued the argument in his mind: "He wants to make himself
rich at the expense of thousands of people. No: forget your determined dream and evil treachery!"

✦

Melanian was on his way home today, walking along his habitual route, lost in thought. He seemed to be hurrying to his room to solve whatever was torturing his mind.

The house, which had no opening to admit the sun, was dark. He had kept one of the two rooms for himself. It looked like a space governed by sad spirits. His wife and daughter had already conformed to his moods, for want of a better model. For hours he paced up and down in the room, thinking, thinking . . . wearing out the small rug beside the table.

That evening, having surrendered to his thoughts, he paced his room with special dedication. He was irritated by the noises in the street occasioned by the upcoming holiday. He could not get his conversation with the old man out of his head.

"Old man," he said, "whenever I mention becoming rich you argue with me and discourage me."

And he imagined the old man sitting in his cold little room, chain-smoking . . . with a sadly dribbling dirty teapot on the table beside his . . . reminding him of the old days. . . .

He went up to the old man and whispered in his ear: "Old man, do you know that you're preventing me from getting rich?"

Instantly the old man sprang up and retorted angrily: "And you! you're going to ruin our lives: you want to get rich and ride on our shoulders. . . ."

And much to his surprise, all of a sudden he saw the boiling pot blow off steam . . . hundreds of people with raised hands lined up behind the old man, threatening and shouting, "Who do you think you are! You're ruining our lives! . . ."

Suddenly Melanian was melted by the heat of the enormous crowd, and he joined them. "I'm with you!" he shouted, "I support you!"

✦

He walked into the other room, where his wife and children stood in amazement, and exclaimed in a loud voice, "I'm yours! We'll all stick together."

The little girl—who had been busy making colored paper ornaments for the Christmas tree—and his wife were stunned.

He hugged his daughter, who, filled with joy and surprise, ran over to him, thinking that the upcoming holiday was the cause of her father's elation, and put the red chain she was holding around his neck.

He sat in the chair, his face glowing as though he had just completed a difficult task. The boiling pot was still blowing out steam, as if it had heated up under the pressure of the argument, and exclaiming, "We're all together; all of us together!"

—New Year's was near.

Buried in his work, Melanian incessantly tapped on the machine, wiring congratulatory messages. He seemed to be in charge of controlling the bustle outside. His powerful imagination transformed the uproar into the cries of millions of people. The machine tapped out congratulations, one after the other. It seemed to be something else—a bigger holiday on the earth—with huge bells clanging from ocean to ocean around the world. . . . And he was standing high up in a tower, calling out to the crowd of millions: "Straighten your bent backs, make the withered grass green again. . . . There are no more cages. . . . You are free!"

Aram Antonian

(1879–1951)

Novelist, historian, and journalist Aram Antonian was born in Constantinople and received his education in Armenian and French schools. He contributed to the periodical press, edited the literary magazines *Tzaghik* (The flower) and *Luys* (Light), and the satirical reviews *Karapnat* (The gallows) and *Kharazan* (The whip). He also edited the Armenian daily *Surhandak* (The dispatcher). His best known works include *Drami koghin tak* (Under the cover of money, 1904), a novel that was serialized in *Surhandak; Chshmartutyune* (The truth, 1909), a novella; *Kavé ardzanner* (Clay statues, 1910), a satirical novella; and a biography of Alexander Shirvanzadé, published in 1911 on the occasion of the fortieth anniversary of the beginning of the latter's literary career. Antonian also published a textbook of Armenian language and literature, *Gandzaran* (The treasure house, 1912), that was widely used in Armenian schools. His most outstanding work is *Patkerazard endardzak patmutiun Palkanian paterazmin* (A comprehensive illustrated history of the Balkan War, 5 vols., 1912–13). He witnessed the 1915 genocide and wrote about his experiences in a collection titled *Ayn sev orerun* . . . (In those dark days . . .), published in 1919. He also published texts of secret telegrams from the Ittihadist (Young Turks) leaders transmitting ciphered orders for the Armenian relocations and massacres in 1915.

These were published in Boston in 1921 in a volume called *Metz vochire: haykakan verjin kotoratznere yev Talat pasha; pashtonakan heragirner* (The great crime: the recent Armenian massacres and Talaat Pasha: the official telegrams).

In 1928 Antonian moved to Paris. He was appointed director of the Nuparian Library, which operated under the aegis of the Armenian General Benevolent Union, and collected an extensive amount of material related to Armenian history, art, and literature. He remained in this position until the end of his life.

IN THOSE BLACK DAYS . . . [1]

There's nothing . . .

A

It was the third morning that we were waking up on that Karluk elevation, under a large black goat-hair cloth which, attached to the ends of two unhewn stumps, was stretched out above us, like a tent. There were more than fifty of us under that tent: men, women, and children, jumbled together, pressed up against each other, in a veritable ocean of fleas and a thousand kinds of maggots.

All the refugees being driven toward Meskené over the last seven months had camped at the summit of that bald, rocky mountain, and every single caravan had brought the fleas accumulated along the roads and left them there before descending into the desert. The ground was a mosaic of dirty and unrecognizable shades, consisting of pieces of rags, bits and pieces of woolen clothing, and ribbons of faded silk fabrics, stuck in the hardened earth; as flooring, that mosaic had covered the entire space. And, on those ruins of last year's clothing, those horrible parasites were crawling and jumping, like the bubbles forming the foam of a boiling liquid.

The people had already become used to them, and sometimes they would pull and remove one of those rags and, laughing, show it to those next to them. The fleas on them were boiling, seemingly buzzing like an army of bees milling the length of the honeycomb.

---

1. Aram Antonian, "*Ban chka* . . . (There's nothing . . .), in *Ayn sev orerun: patkerner* (In those black days: images) (Boston, 1919), 3–6. Translated by Aris G. Sevag.

Aleppo was facing us, barely half an hour's distance away but, for us, it was the forbidden city, as we were under special surveillance and could not go away from Karluk. Nearby, almost ten minutes' distance away, at the end of an avenue lined with dwarf pistachio trees, was a huge reservoir, but we were obliged to submit to a thousand kinds of formalities in order to go there and wash up, and again we could not head towards the reservoir without being accompanied by a gendarme. And, as such, early in the morning, the still sleepy gendarmes were not all that disposed to "taking the animals to water," as they used to say, laughing.

But we had other work to do, anyway. Before cleaning our bodies, we had to clean our clothes because myriads of fleas must have laid their nests in them during the night.

Besides our tent, there were three other goat-hair tents on the summit. These were government tents, all of them open on all four sides during the summer and winter alike. And, in that accursed place, the heat was as murderous as the cold. They formed a crescent, practically one next to the other, and in the semicircle formed by them rose the private tents of the well-to-do refugees—some were square, others were pointed, a few were round and dome-shaped, in the Armenian Catholic style, made of white or green cloth, but faded, sometimes completely earth-colored, on account of having remained under the sun, rain and snow for a long time.

People were slowly emerging from the tents, going as far as the opposite side of the mountain, and, gradually divesting themselves of their clothes in the hot sun, they began to clean them, which they were obliged to do, sometimes three or four times daily, like a regular job. The reason was that otherwise they would not be able to endure. A few persons had brought little brooms with them; others, hair or clothes brushes; they would simply brush the fleas off their clothes and undergarments. It was already difficult to chase away those armies any other way. It was also difficult to kill them because there were so many of them. They would remain piled up on the ground, one upon the other, like a countless multitude of white ants. You'd think it was a large moving rug the way it floated.

Very seldom did one try to squash them with the heels of his shoes but soon he would be forced to stop because, if he succeeded in killing a portion of them, this time, other more numerous groups, spreading out on his shoes, would begin climbing up the length of his pants.

It was only the little boys who would most effectively massacre them when they happened to get hold of a newspaper or other piece of paper of any kind. They would immediately set it on fire and throw it on the countless multitudes. And, those hapless boys being of an age of adorable unconsciousness, their little hearts, orphaned from the merriment of all the previous year's recreational activities, would become filled with boundless joy when those myriads of fleas, being successively roasted, would crackle under the influence of the flames and jump like sparks escaping from rockets.

A true fireworks display, which would make their deprived souls rejoice, and transform those ordinarily sad and tragic groups of children into a hodgepodge of crazy leaps and bounds, dances and especially shouts of joy.

B

... A rifle shot suddenly brought us out of the mind-torturing reverie to which we were still subjected in the form of that disagreeable and murderous activity, which was a torture in itself.

It had been quite some time since we were surprised by the sounds of firearms, as we had become totally accustomed along the way to the ill-boding whistle of bullets that passed by our heads, sometimes even singeing our hair. We were not frightened by the sound of that firearm. However, the commotion that arose in the camp and our curiosity forced us to turn around and look back.

Immediately there were three or four more shots, then a collective simultaneous fusillade by ten gendarmes, who had taken up positions along the right side of Karluk and were aiming at something, but we couldn't see what it was.

The elevation there was totally steep, thus concealing the descent that ended at the highway which went down to Meskené. Apparently the object of the fusillade, which we couldn't see, was located on that downward incline.

We got up and hastened to advance. But a gendarme, a torrent of curses streaming from his mouth, ordered us not to go forward.

Then they again fired a collective fusillade but apparently that too was futile because they were upset and were cursing. They ceased firing their weapons from that point on. Two of them ran all the way to the nearby guard house and, jumping onto their respective horses, galloped down the side of the mountain.

A woman was screaming near a tent, surrounded by five or six other women, who were struggling mightily to restrain her.

"They shot and killed him!" she was screaming, short of breath.

"No, don't worry, nothing happened," said the others in an attempt to reassure her. But it was obvious that they too weren't sure of what they were saying because each time they managed to calm her down a bit and take a deep breath, right away a curse rolled off the tips of their tongues:

"May they break into pieces! . . . may they not see another day, another sun! . . ."

Those curses were undoubtedly for the gendarmes shooting that fusillade.

However, that woman wasn't the type to stay calm for long. They were barely able to restrain her before she would again put up a struggle, trying to break the chain of arms that were holding her back. If she were to break free, there's no doubt that she would rush upon the group of gendarmes who, by now, had ceased firing and were looking intently down the mountain.

Her gaze never got separated from them, and the flames of a horrific hatred were shooting from her eyes.

The others wouldn't release her; they would even torment her while attempting to restrain her thus, because they knew that if they did let her loose, she would run right up to the gendarmes, insult and hit them.

And they would kill her too.

The drama, of which we were spectators, was simple, not requiring any explanation. But again we asked what was happening.

"It's nothing," one person said.

Entering Aleppo was strictly forbidden to those who were in that hell called Karluk. The son of that screaming woman, a lad who was barely fourteen years old, had fled a short while ago. They had a relative in town, and he was going to see that person, for sure. A gendarme had seen him and informed his comrades who, in turn, had fired their rifles at the boy.

"Who knows, maybe they killed him. . . ."

And the man who gave us this information saw fit to add:

"It's nothing . . . it's nothing. . . ."

They were killing a boy . . . he was the woman's . . . only son . . . she was giving voice to the frightful pain in her heart . . . she was becoming consumed with anxiety which, by now, had turned to despair . . . a life was being extinguished . . . there was no justification for the crime but it was being committed in the most unmerciful manner and there would be no regret . . . the gendarmes were committing it as a recreational sport . . . they were laughing while killing! . . . they were capable of killing them all, always as recreation, laughing! . . .

"It's nothing . . . it's nothing," said the man once again.

And, indeed, what were these little dramas compared to the horror that the people had gone through?

C

A little ways off, however, it seems that the scene was becoming totally engrossing since the groups of refugees were no longer paying much attention to the prohibition of the gendarmes; gradually they approached the sides of the mountain and, milling around each other, they were stretching their necks to fix their restless and terrified gaze downwards.

We approached and began to look, in turn.

The real drama was unfolding at precisely that moment.

The boy had not been hit. All those bullets had been fired in vain down that rough slope, on which each mound of earth afforded the protection of a rampart. But those two gendarmes had galloped and cut off the path, by which the lad would continue his descent in order to reach the highway. And now they were ordering him to descend and surrender.

But the lad wasn't moving from where he was. The dread caused by the firing of the fusillade had nailed him to the spot. His trunk and head, seemingly resting on motionless legs stuck in the ground, constantly kept turning, first one way, then the other, with feverish speed. With each movement of the head, his eyes were examining his surroundings with restless glances, as if seeking an escape route. Sometimes, a sudden shudder would shake his entire body, perhaps at those moments when the glance of his eyes, not seeing an escape route during his quick scrutiny, became hopelessly focused upon himself, and his lids slowly closed, just as a newly perched bird closes its wide-opened wings.

The poor little fellow! He closed his eyes in order not to see the gendarmes who had come and cut off his path to freedom. But, after closing his eyes, it seems a momentary dream was starting for him, and that somewhat of an introspection, of course, was a more horrible thing; it was showing him the frightening passages of the entire martyrdom to which he would be subjected, once he was caught in their clutches, such that he immediately opened his eyes, opened them very wide, to return to the light a minute earlier, in a haste to avoid that already imminent prospect.

And he was panting, yes, he was panting . . . from the exhaustion brought on by his mad-dash descent perhaps, or from fear? . . .

The gendarmes continued to order him to descend, assuring him that they weren't going to do anything to him, but the little fellow didn't trust them. Who knows what he had seen since being snatched from his nest, along those endless roads of slaughter, in which the most frightful share of torture had fallen to the children.

People were encouraging him from above:

"Go," they were shouting, "go down, they won't fire at you!"

Did they really trust the words of the gendarmes, or were they trying to save their own skins by attempting to "bring in line" one who was caught in a "crime" like that? It was more a case of them making an attempt to win the gendarmes' favor. And perhaps, at the time they were giving that advice, all of them were certain that the punishment for the young lad would be a terrible one. That was how bad the concern to save their own skins had made these people!

However, the lad persisted in not descending. The poor kid, of course, sensed what awaited him and was trying as much as possible to prolong those minutes of uncertainty and risk, as well as freedom.

At that point, one of the gendarmes rode forward toward the mountain. But the mountain was steep. The animal was barely able to advance a few steps and stood on its hind legs, its hoofs stuck in the ground, causing a twin current of soil and stones to move down the mountain. The horse's standing that way had occurred so unexpectedly that the gendarme almost fell off it. He barely managed to maintain his balance by clinging to the animal's mane.

Although the horse inclined, it could no longer remain on that steep site and retreated, again creating a considerable torrent of soil and stones.

We had lost sight of the young lad while observing that scene. When we turned our attention toward him, we saw that he was sitting on the ground behind one of the crests, hunched over, his right arm curved around his eyes like a belt, so he wouldn't see the frightful image of the impending calamity.

As the horse retreated, he lifted his head and looked down; then, turning toward us, he gazed at length at the crowd milling around on the sides of the mountain. There was something so expressive in that glance! . . . Were those eyes really looking, or were they shouting, pleading? . . .

The helpless lad was asking for help!

Help! . . . but all of us wanted . . . the desperate situation of that little fellow, his soul crushed, facing that terrible danger was such a heartrending thing!

And yet . . . I don't remember a more exhaustive torture than being seized with the irresistible desire to help someone subjected to such a danger as that and not being able to do anything at all. . . .

There was so much hatred in us at that moment toward those gendarmes, when that poor kid was conveying that silent plea from the frightful depths of his fear, with that mad and maddening look in his eyes.

Powerless hatred—the most supreme of tortures! . . .

Mikayel Kiurchian (Gürdjian)

(1879–1965)

The writer, translator, and journalist Mikayel Kiurchian[1] was born in Constantinople and received his education at the Nersesian and Perperian (Berberian) schools. He witnessed the 1894–96 massacres, and in 1896 he moved to Egypt and settled in Alexandria, where he worked as a court clerk until 1905, when he became an employee of the Ottoman Bank, in which position he remained until 1935. In 1905 he also collaborated with Vahan Tekeyan to found the literary magazine *Shirak;* he was also a cofounder of the daily *Arev* (The sun), which he edited from 1920 to 1923.

Kiurchian wrote essays, columns, short stories, satires, and editorials on social and political issues, mostly for the periodical press. Apart from contributing to the publications he founded or edited, he also contributed to Armenian papers published abroad—in Paris, London, Smyrna, and even St. Petersburg—under a variety of pen names. Unfortunately, a large part of this work remains uncollected.

---

1. For most of the information in this biographical sketch, the editors are indebted to Edmond Y. Azadian's *"Mikayel S. Kiurchiani grakan dimagitse"* (The literary portrait of Mikayel S. Kiurchian), in Mikayel Kiurchian, *Martik Agha,* ed. Henrik Bakhchinian (Yerevan, 1999), 282–309. See also Edmond Y. Azadian, *Portraits and Profiles,* ed., trans., and intro. Agop J. Hacikyan and Edward S. Franchuk (Lewiston, N.Y., 1995).

One of his most popular satirical works, coauthored by Yervand Otian, is the comedy *Franko-turkakan paterazme* (The Franco-Turkish War), also known as *Charshele Artin Agha* which was first staged in Alexandria in 1903. It ridicules the life led by a wealthy family of the provincial class by having the husband, Artin Agha, adhere to his provincial manners and customs while his wife, Yevpimé, puts on aristocratic airs. The play's hilarious scenes and clashes strengthen its social message. It has been staged hundreds of times, in both Armenia and the diaspora, and is still a favorite. "Kiurchian's humor is rarely so explosive as that of a Paronian (Baronian); he prefers the ridicule that runs deep to the raging flood. In his humorous works the comical passages are peppered with subtle observations, often underlined by the use of succinct, witty puns."[2]

After Otian's death Kiurchian wrote a sequel to this play, *Ksan tari verj* (Twenty years later, 1961), in which the family moves to France and the comedy continues in a European context. He also collaborated with Otian on the comedy *Herosakhaghe* (The contest of heroes, 1928); his drama *Prkank* (Ransom), coauthored by Tigran Kamsarakan, depicts a father who sacrifices himself for the future happiness of his daughter.

Kiurchian enjoyed literary friendships with Tiran Chrakian and others; rather parsimoniously, he guarded in his mind and heart the psychological satisfaction he derived from these associations, seeming to forget that there were always readers and literary historians who were thirsty for information, who were eager to know about these men.

"Kiurchian's pen is versatile, and he has a multifaceted mind. He has written in nearly all literary genres and has succeeded in leaving his distinctive mark of unsurpassed craftsmanship on each of them."[3] Besides what he wrote for the stage, he also produced a number of short stories and novellas, such as *"Hrashki me patmutyune"* (The story of a miracle), *"Anunin gishere"* (Name-day night, 1963), *"Nor lat"* (The new outfit), *"Anjnjeli matyane"* (The indestructible book), and *"Entanik me"* (A family), which mostly revolve around social issues. Among his allegorical legends *Kiatibin yeraze* (The clerk's dream) is the best known. His prose poetry, composed in his mature years and collected as *I khorots srti khosk end pashtelvuyn* (Words to my beloved, from the bottom of my heart, 1960) is imbued with naïve romanticism. Although for many years most of his time was taken up with writing editorials, reviews, studies, and commentary on local and immediate issues, he also found time for translations. His favorite French writer was Alphonse Daudet, whose *Tartarin de Tarascon* he translated in his younger days; this was later

---

2. Azadian, *Portraits*, 101.
3. Ibid., 94.

serialized in the daily *Arev*. In many of his writings he dealt with issues of human behavior, the inner self, and human destiny.

Kiurchian started writing his masterpiece, the novel *Martik Agha*, in his youth, but he never finished it. The earlier chapters were published (1898–99) in Arpiar Arpiarian's *Nor Kyank* (New life) in London, and they testified from the very start to the author's intellectual scope, literary taste, and grip on the art of narration. But publication was discontinued because of the uproar it created. The author reverted to the novel only as he approached the end of his life, in response to the urgings and encouragement of his literary friends. It was only through the efforts of the philologist Harutiun Mekerian that a completed version of this novel saw the light in 1999, a century after Kiurchian wrote its first pages. The novel draws inspiration from the revolutionary movement, which provided ample material, heroic and sublime as well as sarcastic, for a number of contemporary writers. Its hero, Artin Agha, is a wealthy merchant, boastful and very conservative, who is duped by a fanatical and corrupt revolutionary, Levon Surian, into joining his party. Artin Agha joins the party first out of fear, and then false promises. This was a time when the revolutionary parties were fighting each other. Events, plots, and personalities, in all their good and evil aspects, are depicted vividly in the novel.

Kiurchian was a realist rather than an idealist. For a writer of his character, idealism would probably have been a restraint on his freedom of expression. He had tasted the bitterness of Turkish despotism, and his only idealism consisted of fighting against that despotism.

Many of his works, written over a span of seventy years—works which would fill several volumes—remain scattered in literary journals and newspapers: destined, perhaps, to be forgotten. In his later years Kiurchian could not find time to revise or reedit his writings for publication, despite his friends' promptings. His collected papers are kept at the Museum of Literature and Arts in Yerevan. He died in Cairo at the age of eighty-six.

THE NEW OUTFIT[4]

Born poor, raised poor, and possessing a voracious addiction to food and drink that ate away indeed most of his earnings—or,

---

4. Mikayel S. Kiurchian, "*Nor Lat*" (The new outfit), in *Anunin gishere yev ayl patmvatzkner polsahay barkeré* (The name day and other stories of Istanbul-Armenian manners) (Cairo, n.d.), 38–51. Translated by the editors of the present anthology.

if you like, it devoured the flesh, leaving only his bones to care for his other needs—Merker the blacksmith had not seen a new set of clothes since he was a kid, except on others. And because even the humblest person needs something to look forward to, besides earning his daily bread, if he is going to go on living, from time immemorial Merker had looked forward to getting himself a new suit. But he did not know for sure when he would be able to get his hands on one; otherwise, he would have gone around daydreaming: his gaze eternally fixed on the object of all his desires. Like all people whose ideals are difficult to attain, he was in no hurry: these people live under the sway of a sweet hope that at last, one day, they will achieve their goal—it is just a matter of time and money—and so it was for our man. Money! That was a bit of a problem. How was he supposed to put together a fair sum of money to buy new togs? And suppose he had the money: how would he ever be able to keep it? As they say, in his hands it would turn not into salt, but into *oghi*,[5] and would drain away. It is true that on at least a few occasions the blacksmith's rough hands had had the pleasure of holding gold. Then, for a moment, he had considered realizing his dream through the miraculous power of Mammon, but it had proved too much for him—in fact, it would have meant not eating and especially not drinking, not being able to buy drinks for friends, but instead going and spending the money on a new suit—in other words, he might as well die!

After a few temptations such as this, he made up his mind: he would never accomplish the heroic feat of buying a new suit of clothes with his own money and with his own hands. Once this conviction was firmly developed, he was left to rely completely on outside intervention—for which he was now waiting.

It so happened that an exciting and agitated period of parish electioneering sprang up in the village where Merker lived. I do not know exactly how many different political factions began crusades under the banner of various liberal ideas and principles or under this or that effendi's or bey's noble aegis . . . this is not what our story is about. During the election campaign, of course, the tavern was a strategic center of propaganda and activity, where alcohol served as fuel and occupied a central position on the scene of parish

---

5. The Armenian name for the alcoholic drink variously known as raki, arak, ouzo, etc.

life. There men launched their campaigns; there they also mixed the heady wine of nationalism with *oghi,* which was quite different from mixing it with water. Merker—who was as popular as his wide, thick pants and picturesque swear words and within the measure of his drunkenness, which was enormous—was approached by all the rival parties as a much-needed candidate, whose collaboration had to be obtained at any cost. He was thrilled and delighted, feeling that the long-sought providential chance to attain his old object of desire was approaching—he would be part and parcel of a new parish council. This election, he thought, would get him not a *khalpakh* (calpac), but a damn good set of togs. Everyone said that the struggle would be violent and the victory difficult, and he worked like a dog.

One night, in the intimacy of a bottle of *oghi,* Merker reflected on this matter for a long time. After comparing the chances of the parties that were trying to win him over and calculating what each was likely to do for him, he decided in favor of the political faction that could offer him most in these two areas. He went and presented himself in person to the leader of the party: a true bigwig, who, having regained his memory on that particular day, recognized Merker, remembered his first name, family name, and profession, gently asked how he was, politely offered him a cup of coffee and a cigarette rolled by his own hands, then, after delivering a vague speech on the sacred rights of the people, added a few indulgent words in praise of Merker, like digestion pills after a heavy meal. Emotionally Merker, as a true man of the people, stood up, placed his hairy hand on his broad chest, and solemnly promised his unreserved collaboration and that of his friends. The effendi stroked his beard and expressed his thanks; not content to leave it at that, he promised Merker that if he won, his gratitude would be translated into the ringing language of gold.

Merker then declared, with the haughty pride of a person who could never be bribed, that he would not accept money for doing his duty—he would do all for the sake of the Effendi—it was because of his love for the effendi that he wanted to get into this business. . . . But. . . . If the effendi nevertheless wanted to do something to express his satisfaction, perhaps he could give him a suit.

"Very well," said the other, surprised, and he smiled. "If that's what you want. I'll dress you up from head to toe: a new outfit, from shoes to fez!"

And the agreement was signed! For the entire campaign Merker worked with extraordinary enthusiasm, to the point that his surprised friends sat up and took notice. Never during any previous contest had he worked so willingly, outspokenly, confidently, and selflessly. Never had he drunk and talked so much, shaming all his friends; they did not know that he brought to this task the effort and fury inspired by the approaching realization of a long-sought ideal—the hope and passion of at last attaining it. . . . As fresh as the next parish council, the daily expectation of a new suit worked miracles on his rhetoric and *oghi*-soaked activities. He made a tremendous contribution to the victory of his party, which got its complete slate of candidates elected.

That night Merker drank until dawn, buying drinks in honor of the newly elected parish council and at its expense. . . . Like a soldier under arms, he slept in his old suit; needless to say, his dreams were of an entirely different cut and color.

The following day a man sent by the effendi took Merker to a shoemaker's and a shirt maker's shop, then led him to a clothing store. For a moment the blacksmith was tempted to leave his old clothes there, the worn-out, soiled mementos of a past life. A devout and pious thought stopped him, though: he would give them to a poor man. He put his old clothes back on, had the new ones nicely wrapped up, and returned home; in fact, it is important to say, he returned triumphantly. That evening he decided to dress up and go out.

You can imagine the difficulties he had: putting on the tight shoes, the trousers, the starched shirt, and especially the high, starched collar. A few buttons popped and a few noises that suggested torn fabric were heard in response to his clumsy and impatient efforts. Finally, his patience, which had had a few moments to catch its breath in the wake of a few effective curse words, was on the verge of disappearing altogether, when he more or less managed to bring the painful operation to an end.

His eyes fell on his old clothes, which were scattered all over the place. He remembered his intention to give them to a poor person, but now this did not seem like such a good idea. Why? Even he did not know. Was he reluctant to part with clothes that had been broken in by years of wear and tear? It is important to mention that despite the elegance of his new clothes, he did not feel any contempt for the old ones; rather, he felt like a kind and considerate soul who has suddenly become rich but would never snub the humble friends of bygone days.

He picked up his old clothes and, with caring hands, hung them one by one on the wall. Creased with thousands of wrinkles and tattered with age—it was a pitiful sight, and he wept with bent head—there was so much familiarity and use in what he saw, in the creases and stains, that he felt a sort of tenderness for them and was almost embarrassed that his new clothes seemed to mock their sorry state. His feeling of affection gradually grew into a moral and philosophical meditation, and like all simple people he began to talk to himself out loud:

"Merker Agha, keep them, keep these clothes. . . . Keep them always before your eyes, to remind you of your previous state. . . . Don't get uppity just because you have new clothes. . . . But always be careful that you never need to wear the old ones again. . . ."

But as he was walking out the door, he had a comical thought: leaping and grimacing like a clown, that thought, ungodly and sarcastic, ridiculed his moment of serious reflection and stuck out its tongue in disrespect: "Keep them, my son, keep them: tomorrow's another day. Who knows what will happen? One day you'll decide to sell your new clothes and wear the old ones again. . . ."

When he emerged from the door, he was a totally different man, both inside and out: a new man. If we agree with Sterne[6] that a man may see the world differently after shaving than he did before, why should a new outfit not change a man's outlook on life too, especially when it is the first one he has ever had? Someone from the same neighborhood who was passing by saw Merker from a distance and took a hesitant step in his direction, but did not dare to suppose that this man dressed in his Sunday best, as if for a party, was the Merker he knew: Merker, the constantly drunken, brawling, cursing, faithful frequenter of taverns. He doubted his judgment for a moment, but put it down to mistaken identity.

But where are you going, Merker? It did not cross his mind to go to his usual hangouts. Was he shy of his old friends or was it the pride of a new identity? Or was it an attempt to preserve the splendor of his new outfit and protect it from stains? All of these

---

6. Laurence Sterne (1713–68), English novelist and clergyman.

were possibilities. . . . The truth is that the idea did not appeal to him, nor he to it. He decided to go to the village casino, a place not frequented by ordinary people—they were always well-dressed there. Now, since clothes make the man, his outfit would give him the right to enter and would secure him an honorable place among that stylish crowd. So on he went!

Anyone who happened to pass by and see Merker dressed like that, full of unbounded pride and wearing a triumphant expression on a face swollen with self-satisfaction, and who happened to notice, on the other hand, the tortured nature of his movements and gait would have to be rather naive not to guess that he was face-to-face with a man who was wearing a completely new outfit for the first time in his life. Poor Merker, who used to move freely in worn, loose clothing, was now obliged to subject his body to the strict discipline of a new, narrow outfit's constrictions. He had to change the style of his usual free verse, unmeasured, capricious steps; otherwise, they could create absolute havoc with the limits imposed by his narrow trousers. He took tentative, imprecise steps, as short as possible. He, who had often thrown his large overcoat over his shoulder with the bold self-assurance of an old Spanish nobleman, was now constricted in a tight jacket. He felt the heavy fabric against his back, his shoulders, under his arms, and this severe *manière d'attaque* irritated him, making him itch all over. Then he could not stop squirming, could not stop rolling his shoulders from side to side as if scratching his back. He constantly reached for his armpits, to loosen the fabric pressing against or around them. He was also tormented by his shoes. His feet looked odd to him—so shapely, long, and narrow—he did not feel certain that he was firmly planted on the ground. But it was his neck that caused the greatest discomfort: the collar that encircled his neck like a snake. Ah, there he was literally collared and imprisoned: he made quite a sight, violently moving a finger from right to left and left to right as he tried to enlarge and loosen the collar to let in a bit of air, to make a little more room for the strangulated neck it contained. And what about his hands? His poor hands; he did not know what to do with them, or where to put them: his trouser pockets were too tight to admit more than his fingers! Maybe he could put them in his jacket pockets—but they were too high. He could let them dangle at his sides, but his hands were so broad and rough that the sight of them against the fashionable light color of his suit would shame him.

Then there were his meticulous and never-ending efforts to avoid getting the clothes dirty: the morbid desire for cleanliness that had suddenly infected him! To preserve the suit from dust and mud, he had rolled up his pant legs—much higher than needed. No matter what he did, or how attentive he was, or how sure his steps were, a clumsy step, the carelessness of a carriage driver or a passerby would quash all his efforts. . . .

After walking awhile, he would realize that things were not as they should be, and would take from his pocket a large red and white handkerchief—the most unspeakably common and most colorful betrayal of the respectable decency of his outfit. . . . And he would inevitably find a speck of dust here, a bit of mud there. . . . Where did it come from? How did it get there? And with all his strength he would begin to shake, rub, and clean. . . . This became an obsession. He held his handkerchief by one corner. Every five or ten steps he flicked it against his cuffs, his shoes, sometimes his jacket, whipping them violently, from right and left, with haphazard blows. These exertions and the tightness of his outfit made him sweat, and he raised the soiled handkerchief from his feet to his brow. He removed his fez so he could clean and wipe his face and forehead, then stuck the handkerchief into his collar to dry his neck—then, with a sigh of satisfaction, he continued on his way.

But all the same, he was happy: happy with the feeling that he had become a new person, a physical sensation that his outfit's cleanliness and stylishness had given him.

"After all, I'm somebody too!"

He would experience an immediate sense of pride on seeing himself as comparable and equal to the "proper gents" in the street, whom he had longed to be like for years.

On the way he narrowly escaped a couple of fights: one with a passerby who had stepped on one of his shoes and soiled or scuffed it, another with a mule driver who had splashed a fair amount of mud on his pants. The latter would have been in deep trouble, had he not galloped away on the animal, pursued by a barrage of colorful language and threats from Merker. He went to a nearby fountain, dipped his handkerchief in the water, wiped and cleaned his pants, and let the spot dry in the sun—an operation that took half an hour.

⁜

That evening Merker did not turn up at a café or tavern. His friends wondered: was he sick, perhaps exhausted by the frenzy of the election?

The next day a strange rumor circulated in the neighborhood: the incredible news of Merker's metamorphosis. There was more than one eyewitness: trustworthy people. Then it was discovered that he had disappeared the night before, and the secret motive for his actions during the parish election contests thus came to light.

"To get a new suit of clothes!"

That night all of Merker's friends and acquaintances gathered at the café he usually frequented, waiting patiently with their bottles of *oghi*. They bubbled over with expressions of interest, wild conjectures, wisecracks. . . . Was he coming? . . . Was he not coming? . . . Why had he not showed up the previous night?

"Out of shame?"

"No, out of pride. . . ."

"Ah, Merker, ah. . . ."

They tried to imagine Merker as he now appeared. The lucky few who insisted that they had seen him, albeit from afar, immediately became centers of attention. They had to tell every group, every new arrival, what they had seen, and this encouraged them to exaggerate, invent, fill in details, out of a desire to please. It became a wondrous tale in their mouths, and earned them glass after glass of *oghi* from their audience.

"Oh, how we wish he'd come. . . ."

"You think he'll come? . . ."

But time passed and Merker was late. Disappointment. The *oghi* flowed more slowly—it was also waiting. They had to think up a speech. A few volunteers went in search of Merker, the deserter, promising to bring him back by force if need be—a suggestion that was loudly applauded by everyone there.

Barely half an hour later there was a sound of rejoicing outside and a unanimous shout arose inside.

"He's coming. . . . It's Merker. . . ."

And sure enough, a moment later Merker made his entrance into the café—one friend holding him by his left arm, another by his right, and led by a third—but it could hardly be considered a triumphal entry. Everyone there rose to his feet, however, gathered round him, and greeted him with laughter and polite phrases.

The confusion caused by Merker's entrance was beyond description. Everybody was laughing loudly as they came, one by one, to shake Merker's hand, pat him on the shoulder, and inundate him with wishes of "wear it in good health." The poor man blurted out a few confused, unintelligible syllables in a strangled voice.

Ah, Merker! He looked irresistibly ridiculous in his new clothes. It was impossible to take him seriously, to feel respect for his expensive clothing. And his bearing; his pitiful, tortured appearance in his new outfit, like the startled shame of a person caught doing wrong.

"Ah, Merker, ah. . . ."

When the uproar had simmered down a bit, Merker was offered a chair with exaggerated politeness.

"Pray be seated, Merker Agha. . . . Why are you standing? . . . Come and sit by me. . . . We haven't had a good chat for a long time."

Merker, nervous and sweaty, took out his handkerchief and wiped off the chair that was offered him—oh no, he was not going to get his new clothes dirty!—then sat uneasily, making sure not to lean against the back of the chair.

"Why don't you sit more comfortably, brother?" someone suggested mischievously.

"Good evening, boys," Merker finally managed to choke out. "Good evening. . . ."

"Good evening, Merker Agha! Welcome—a thousand times welcome! What a surprise to find you here. . . . It's an ill wind that blows no good! Dammit all, you seem to have forgotten us. . . . Where've you been the last couple of days? . . . We have to send an escort to get you to come. . . . Just because you have new togs, you shouldn't forget your old friends!"

"I was a bit under the weather," Merker stammered in a barely audible voice.

"Eh, I hope you feel better. . . . May you wear it in good health! . . . What a smart suit. . . . May you wear it long enough to wear it out, may you reduce it to tatters. . . . May your endeavors bring you many others. We pray the Lord bless us with many more parish councils, and you with as many new clothes. . . ."

A unanimous burst of laughter followed the last remark.

"Well, but this isn't nearly good enough!" said someone on the edge of the crowd: "We have to drink to these clothes. . . . They have to be toasted . . . don't you think, brothers?" he asked the gathering.

"You're right! We have to toast them, we have to. . . ."

For the first time Merker felt like himself, and in his usual voice he added, "What do you mean? Of course, we'll have a drink! Hey, Kirakos! give them whatever they want: *oghi,* wine, cognac. . . ."

General enthusiasm, the placing of orders, bravos, applause, full bottles!

But Merker was not comfortable sitting there; he who used to sit comfortably in a chair, used to slouch, shift about, put his elbows on the table and stretch his arms, enjoy freedom of leg and hand movements and exercise them over a large area, was now sitting on the edge of his chair, motionless, almost compacted: his legs touching each other, his torso trim and straight, his hands on his knees, embarrassed and still.

"Relax, Merker!" said one of his friends.

"I *am* relaxed," the poor man replied, and moved a little as if to settle himself more comfortably.

The assembled well-wishers emptied their glasses: "To Merker and . . . long live his new clothes!"

Merker half-emptied his glass and carefully set it down beside him. Not only his clothing, but also his manners and habits had changed: as if along with his new outfit he had acquired a secret instinct that forbade him to drink and move as before . . . to say nothing of his constant worrying about getting his clothes dirty. He was afraid that if he drank too much he would lose control . . . and then what would happen to his clothes?

Merker's cronies noticed his uncharacteristic abstemiousness and poise, if that is the right word, and they protested.

"What's this? . . . Something new? . . . No, that's too much. . . . Drink up, man. . . ."

He had to drink the other half of the glass. He dared not touch the *mezé* (sweetmeats). What if a drop of oil or something greasy fell on his outfit and left a stain? He made do with a piece of cheese.

"What's this—don't you like *mezé* any more?"

Someone offered him a forkful of *plaki*.[7] Merker pushed his chair back in terror, spread his legs, stretched his trunk forward, opened his lips wide, and carefully accepted it into his mouth. None of this, of course, went unnoticed: nudging each other with their elbows, winking and smirking, his companions forced him to drink, and whenever he drank everyone offered him *mezé*, despite his refusals and protests of "I've had enough."

Merker was well aware of the mischievous game they were playing, and his discomfort increased. He was no longer the old Merker in the eyes of his friends, but had become a new butt of humor. He rose to his feet and said: "I have a headache. Goodbye. Drink as much as you want; I'll pay for it later," and hurtled himself out of the café before the others had time to grab him, like someone breaking out of prison.

After he had gone, those who had dragged him there entertained the others further by telling them how they had succeeded in getting hold of him. They had spotted him in a seashore café, in a crowd of distinguished aghas and madams. Ah, this was the *coup de grâce!*

"Ah, Merker, ah!"

When he got home, as if rescued from an awkward meeting, Merker savagely tore the new suit off. "O God, what a disaster!"

What was the point of the past two days of suffering, putting aside cherished habits, dressed from head to toe in new clothes, forgetting how to walk, to move, to drink . . . and, as if all this were not enough, his friends' mocking sniggers, the echoes of which were still ringing in his ears.

Suddenly his eyes caught sight of his old clothes, still hanging where he had put them. . . . Ah, there they were! His old clothes: familiar, broken in! They looked so friendly, and in their sinuous creases there was so much sadness, reproach . . . the expression of an outcast. The moment he saw them he was overwhelmed with understanding and once more he felt profoundly the roomy comfort and unbounded freedom his body had once known A great turmoil occurred within him, as if a mysterious surge of spiritual forces was beginning, like a tidal wave, to return to shore.

---

7. A stew of beans with oil and onions (Greek).

Suddenly he had a thought. He put a hand into the pocket of the new trousers. . . . "Let's see how much money I have left. . . ." And he spread on the table a few poor *metaliks* and *kurushes* in all. "Well, what did you expect? You haven't worked for three days . . . playing the great agha. . . ."

♠

The next evening, everybody waited with great interest to see whether Merker would come. Exactly at his usual time, the blacksmith walked in, with his original, natural appearance, dressed in his old clothes.

After a moment of surprise, questions and snickers began to fly everywhere.

"Eh, what about your new clothes? What happened to your new clothes?"

"Oh, I've got them right here," said Merker, jingling something in his pocket, and he took out a handful of money and laid it on a table. The bright glitter and silvery noise wrested an exclamation of admiration from everyone there.

"Here they are: my new clothes. . . . I sold them, my friends! . . . I'm rich tonight . . . drink as much as you want! Eat! Hey, Kirakos! bring . . . bring whatever they want. Long live our council members!" From then on Merker lived comfortably in his old clothes, without ambition or desire. . . . He had eaten his fill from the dish called realized ambition, which is often charred—the fire of reality burns that intensely. . . .

Gegham Barseghian

(1883–1915)

Gegham Barseghian, writer and journalist, was born in Gedik Pasha, a suburb of Constantinople, attended the local Mesropian school, and continued his studies at the Kedronakan lycée until 1896. He spent a year in Paris, where he followed courses in the social and political sciences. His first literary essays, written 1900–3, were scattered in the periodical press of the time. He became first a columnist and then editor of two daily papers, *Surhandak* (The dispatcher) and *Azatamart* (The fight for liberty), where most of his writings were initially published. For about a year (forty-one issues during 1909–10) he was also responsible for publishing the literary review *Azdak* (The monitor). In 1914 he joined Kostan Zarian (1885–1969) and Hakob Oshakan (1883–1948) to form the editorial board of a new monthly literary magazine, *Mehyan* (The temple), of which only seven issues saw the light. Barseghian maintained the editorship of *Azatamart* until 1915, when he was arrested along with other intellectuals, deported, and killed in the Armenian genocide.

Barseghian wrote short stories, prose pieces, and lyrical impressions. His works reflect pure idealism of thought, sentiment, integrity of expression. He believed that Armenian literature should spring straight from the Armenian soul and the Armenian soil. The writer must be able to sense the heartbeat of the land and the people if he wants his work to be a genuine representation of his environment. Barseghian's perfectionism is reflected in his language, choice of words, style, and expression, revealing tendencies of aestheticism. In some of his allegorical writings, such as *Aparni kaghakin khuzarkiche* (The prober of the future city[1]), *Spasumes kakhaghani vra* (As I wait on the gallows), and *Mesian kuga* (The Messiah is coming), he praises human willpower. His complete works were published in Paris in 1931 by the Society of Friends of Martyred Writers.

JOURNAL[2]

15 June, 191

Art is freedom, says one of the dictums of *Mehyan*.[3] Literature is independence, I add, and the greatest independence, the most valuable, is man's inner independence, whereby we can exist within ourselves without any interference; there we are our own sovereign: the sovereign of our thoughts, of our imagination, and of the confined or unconfined world of our feelings.

As this is true of our creative works, it is also true of our pronouncements on the works of others. Whether we are right or wrong in these pronouncements is not a problem. All is acceptable as long as we are absolutely sincere. If writers or critics feel themselves pressured by relationships, dependencies, intrigues, fears, or considerations of the outside world, they have not succeeded in finding independence in the literary world either. They are slaves, blasphemers.

Is the concept of literary independence infectious, and do the borders of literary independence extend among and around us, and when? There is no clear answer to that, so long as people are people, even if they are artistic and literary luminaries.

While waiting for it to arrive, let us smooth the way.

---

1. This and the following two titles are collected in Gegham Barseghian's *Amboghjakan gortze* (Complete works) (Paris, 1931).

2. Gegham Barseghian, *"Oragir"* (Journal), in *Amboghjakan gortze* (Complete works) (Paris, 1931), 77–78. Translated by the editors of the present anthology.

3. Mehyan meaning "pagan temple," a monthly literary review published in Constantinople in 1914.

6 June, 1914[4]

Six years ago, in 1908, it must have been one of those days—
I can't remember what day it was now—a crowd of mourners
drifting through the morning mist walked from Samatya to Balikli[5]
along the silent, narrow, uneven streets, accompanying Metzarents's[6] mortal remains, which we then confided to the earth. The
blood of our past, present, and future fraternity, of our irrevocable
loss, dripped in our footprints. . . .

And now an irresistible longing has come over me and made
me seek his two volumes. Here they are before me, *Tziatzan* (Rainbow) and *Nor Tagher* (New odes), which he autographed and gave
to me. But his dedication and signature are not there anymore.
I remember—Oh, what a hard duty!—I tore them out . . . as a
precaution. In those days, when he was alive, we were always
threatened with political persecution. If they came to arrest me or
searched my home, perhaps they would think that Matzarents was
a close friend of mine, so it was prudent to get rid of his handwriting.
Oh, a very harsh necessity. . . .

Whenever I read him, I am with him at that very moment—
with his dreams and desires, with his profuse and earnest images,
which he composed with such undiluted enthusiasm and exalted,
exuberant speech at the altar of nature—until death in its grim
progress carried him off and silenced him: death pursued him,
a soul vibrant with the desire to live, unlike Léon de Belle, the
French poet, who pursued death. He committed suicide in Paris.

One day, if we devote a whole issue of *Mehyan* to Metzarents—
which we are planning to do—I know that once again, and much
more brilliantly this time, the poetic talent of this young man will
be established—his pure, clear talent, which sounded new notes in
our poetry and showed such promise, such promise. . . .

And today is the anniversary of his death. That means it is All
Souls' Day. I read one of his poems: *Merelots* (All Saints' Day):

> One wintry day, alone, all through the snow,
> The snow a tomb, in the tomb of my soul was borne

---

4. Ibid., 81–84.
5. Suburbs of Istanbul.
6. Misak Metzarents, Armenian poet (1886–1908).

An unsoiled early love, which of a smile was born:
A milky rose, that froze beneath the snow.

In springtime, blossoming in kisses,
A damask rose, drunk with the fevered sunshine's heat,
Languished—another love: that love, O Deity,
I buried, without hope, as it begged for life.

At summer's end, I dropped beneath autumnal leaves
My yellow rose, which sprouted from a glance.
I picked it up; it had become mere memory.
I tossed it aside, as something that was worthless.

I go now, every All Souls' Day,
To their icy marble tombs,
And pray, bewildered and in fog astray,
Crazed by their memory, still and mute.

And my mind, itinerant mendicant priest,
Says heavenly words and crosses itself,
But when I raise my eyes again from earth,
My soul remembers them not in the least.

But my soul, our soul, can never forget him, and once again today—as we anticipate the communal visits that it is our duty to pay certain very dear graves, to express our admiration with a few testimonials—I go to seek him in those corners where he took the burden of his dreams when he went for a walk and where our little group used to meet to read and chat. Late this afternoon I shall go to Samatya, to that very neighborhood he used to pass through, we used to pass through, along garden paths bordered with plants. And the shadows of grief and mourning descended, shivering and gradually becoming days of dismay. While fireflies, golden sparks from an invisible bonfire, glittered in the dark.

In the silence and the darkness, the bonfire of our souls burned brightly.

Hakob Oshakan

(1883–1948)

The writer, critic, and teacher Hakob Oshakan was unique in Western Armenian literature for the impressive quantity of his literary output and for his sharp criticism of scores of other writers. He was born Kiufechian (Küfedjian) in Sölöz, near Brusa (Bursa), to a poor family. At five years of age he lost his father, and the task of supporting five children fell entirely to his mother, a worker in a silk-spinning mill. He completed his elementary education in the local Gevorgian school and attended the seminary in Armash for a year (1899–1900), studying under Yeghishé Durian (1860–1930). Although a gifted boy with a quick mind, he had to discontinue his education and return to Brusa, where he taught at the local school. In 1902 he published a short story, *"Arajin artsunke"* (First tears) in *Arevelk* (The Orient) of Constantinople. It contains subtle criticism of school board members, and he was immediately dismissed from his teaching position. He found another, however, in the nearby village of Marmanchek, where he spent six years, fully participating in and studying village life. One of his collections of short stories, *Khonarhnere* (The humble), published in 1920, depicts genuine village characters, probing their psychological depths and unfulfilled yearnings.

In 1908 Oshakan was in Constantinople and actively engaged in journalism, contributing bold ideas and often controversial criticism to

numerous papers and periodicals. Lacking a formal university education, he was self-taught: he mastered French and Turkish and learned
a bit of German, which later helped to save his life. He was very well
versed in Armenian literature and closely acquainted with the works of
western masters such as Balzac, Proust, Zola, de Maupassant, Stend-
hal, Dostoyevsky, and Joyce. His passionate writings, which reflect his
strong personality, and his criticism, often trenchant and excessive, and
directed against scores of writers, made him lifelong enemies as well as
admirers.

In 1914 Daniel Varuzhan (1884–1915), Kostan Zarian (1885–1969),
Gegham Barseghian (1883–1915), and Oshakan got together to publish
a literary magazine, *Mehyan* (Temple), which aimed at injecting a new
breath of freedom and self-reliance into Armenian literature. It glorified
acts of valor and strength after the example of the pagan Armenian
kings, as opposed to the subservience taught by the Church. The 1915
massacres shortened the magazine's life: Varuzhan and Barseghian were
killed, the others survived. Oshakan managed to escape to Bulgaria
disguised as a German military officer. In 1919, when Constantinople
was under the occupation of the Entente powers, he returned, and was
appointed teacher at the Kedronakan lycée. In 1922, along with Vahan Tekeyan (1878–1943), Kostan Zarian, Shahan Perperian (Berberian, 1891–1956), and Gegham Gavafian (Kavafian, 1888–1959)—all
survivors of the 1915 massacre—he founded a new literary monthly,
Bardzravank, which attracted the best writers. But this too was short-
lived. In 1924 he was in Egypt, then in Cyprus, where he taught Armenian literature and creative writing at the Melkonian Institute. In
1934 he was in Jerusalem, teaching the same subjects at the St. James
seminary. He remained there until 1948, when he died during a visit to
Aleppo.

Oshakan was a prolific writer. His works constitute an imposing
monument, though a good part of what he wrote still languishes in newspaper archives. He tried his hand at almost every literary genre, from
short stories to scholarly works, essays, novels, plays, literary criticism,
textbooks, poetic drama, and autobiography; it cannot be said, however,
that he succeeded in all of them. His short stories, tales, and novellas
have been collected into various volumes. In *Khonarhnere* (The humble,
1920), the stories "*Doksan*," "*Topich*," "*Baghdon*," and "*The Turkoman
girl*" present passionate visions of the human soul in a decaying village.
"A thematic kinship marks his novels, wherein there emerges in varying
shades one other cardinal element to Oshakan's creed: 'blood,' by which
he meant heredity, atavistic patterns, customs, myths and traditions,

and overall racial characteristics."[1] *Khorhurdneru mehyane* (The temple of mysteries, 1922) is a collection of legends and tales; and *Yerb patani yen* (Adolescence, 1926) includes three love stories: *"Maro," "Albom"* (The album), and *"Bulbul"* (The nightingale). The novel *Tzak Ptuke* (Pot with a hole)[2] stands out among his works. It is built around the myths of love, beauty, and death that steer the human will and reason through passion and betrayal to a tragic destiny. Some of his other novels, such as *Süleyman Effendi* (1985), *Haji Abdullah, Shahbaz,* and *Haji Murat,* are shorter and faster-moving, contrasting the Turkish philosophy of life with Armenian national traits.

Oshakan also wrote a number of plays, including *Yerb mernil gitenk* (When we know to die), *Orn orerun* (Day of days), and *Minchev ur* (How far?), few of which have been staged. There is little action in his plays, and the dialogues are not very effective. Three of them were published posthumously: *Nor psake* (Modern marriage), *Knkahayre* (The godfather), and *Akloramarte* (The cock fight); they deal with married love, dishonor, and patriotism and corruption, respectively. To these he added a number of verse plays, called *Knarakhagher* (Lyrical plays, 1983), one of which is based on the life of Stepannos Siunetsi (d. 735), the metropolitan of Siunik who was killed by a harlot.

He left two important testimonies to his lifelong profession as a teacher of Armenian literature: *Hay grakanutyun* (Armenian literature, 1942), which has gone through three editions, and the monumental work *Hamapatker arevmtahay grakanutyan* (Panorama of Western Armenian literature, 10 vols., 1945–82).

Oshakan's literary career spanned two crucial turning points in the literary history of modern Western Armenia. The first was the period 1900–15, when Armenian literary sensibility had attained a certain maturity and had enough self-confidence to launch into pure literary theory. . . . The second was the period 1930–45, when a new crop of diaspora writers filled the void left by the 1915 massacres, asserting their own identities and rejecting many traditional values and their representatives. Oshakan lived through both historic epochs and was intimately involved in the war of ideas.[3]

---

1. Kevork B. Bardakjian, *A Reference Guide to Modern Armenian Literature, 1500–1920* (Detroit, 2000), 173.

2. A colloquial expression best translated into English by Bardakjian as "the incontinent woman."

3. Vahé Oshakan, "The Genius of Hakob Oshakan," *Ararat* 24, no. 1 (Winter 1983), 16.

Oshakan's masterpiece is the novel *Mnatsortats* (Remnants), planned as three volumes, but only two were completed (Cairo, 1932–34). The plan was to cover the years 1890–1915, the most crucial period of recent Armenian history, culminating in the third volume with the great massacre. The novel focuses on the human soul, intergenerational conflicts, the transformation of character by extreme conditions, and philosophical and psychological analysis. To research the third volume, Oshakan went to Aleppo in 1948, with the intention of visiting Deir el Zor in Syria, in order to see the site of the carnage for himself. The morning he was to have gone to the village, he suffered a fatal heart attack. This was around the time when the fiftieth anniversary of the start of his literary career was to be celebrated. He was buried in Aleppo with great pomp.

TOPICH[4]

"Tonight there's going to be a storm, fellas; pull the boat ashore," he said, throwing his head back.

A little later, a few fellows wearing white *shalvars*[5] and shirts came out from the rear of the cottage. And walking with a roll, they went down and pulled the boat ashore.

Topich got up from where he was sitting and, leaving the shade of the plantain, he stood with his hands on his hips. His eyes were scanning the sun and Gurlei-Kar. For a moment, there was a look of uncertainty about him; then he headed for the cottage.

When he came out, he was holding a long black bottle in one hand and a bundle of bread in the other.

A short distance from the cottage, Topich sat down on the nice hot ground, leaning up against the trunk of a thick oak tree. It seemed like the sun was on fire amidst the trees at the top of the mountain, and pale yellow colors appeared and disappeared over the waters.

Topich thrust the bottle into the sand. His bare feet in the sand gave him mild pleasure; with care, he opened the bundle and spread his cape out alongside it. He put the bread and the wooden cup

---

4. Hakob Oshakan, "Topich," *Ararat* 25, no. 1 (Winter 1983), 42–47. Translated by Aris Sevag.

5. Baggy trousers tied at the ankles.

filled with olives on the cape, and removed a large coffee cup from his sash—the kind of cup from which the Turks drink it straight! He began to look off into the distance. Meanwhile, his hands had independently removed the cork from the bottle, filled the large cup with the "blessed fluid" and drawn it up to his lips. With his gaze constantly directed at the blood-red sun, he picked up a piece of bread and some olives and brought them to his mouth.

This was Topich's moment of enjoyment in the evening.

What a man that fisherman had been!

And with those cupfuls bringing relief, warmth, and pleasure to his innards, somehow, for some reason, he began to reminisce about days gone by.

He didn't remember his boyhood very well. He recalled only their crazy mule, which had been so close to him and which he had loved so dearly. He was irked by the recollection of Duman-Daghi gorge where he had given the mule to Circassian brigands.

Then his adolescence—without color, marked by uncertainty—barely brightened, sweetened by the glances of a few girls.

Then his young manhood—the period of adventures, scuffles, naive exploits, during which the scimitar had never left his sash and the double—barreled shotgun had always hung from his shoulders. . . .

Topich picked up the cup, tossed the *raki*[6] down the hatch with such a motion that could be considered unusual for that tired man who had gotten worn out over his hair turning white. That delusion of reliving his youth also lit a flame in the depths of his eyes.

And he relived his fights with the Turks, the Albanian robbers, and the Georgian brigands. And the magnificent dark areas of the grand mountains, the periods of silence of the desolate defiles became quite vivid in his mind. There too he had shed his blood. The reflections of the mountain fires and the echoes of the screams of fighting revived his faded imagination.

Oh, what good old times those were!

The smoke was thinning out over the cottage; the sun had taken on more of a yellowish tinge. The fishermen, lying on the bent grasses, were resting.

---

6. Arak, ouzo—an alcoholic drink having an anise or licorice flavor.

The waters were burning bright red in the twilight. The breeze coming from the olive groves brought sweet, relaxing smells. From time to time, little fishes would jump up out of the water amidst a golden lustre on the water's surface and, after getting refreshed, they'd fall back into the lake again.

Topich loaded his pipe and, with his hand resting on the crook of his elbow, he lay all stretched out on the still hot sand. . . .

He was at home now—in his room, with his bride who was removing his *shalvar.* Then the soft delights of the bed, then the infinitely tasty pleasures of their kisses.

As long as his mother was alive, the tranquility and happiness of their home knew no bounds. He used to keep his wife in "milk and honey." He used to bring the first mountain fruits and the first harvest of the fields home to his mother and wife.

One day his mother died. Topich followed behind her coffin with a pain not understood by him. Like the rest and along with the rest, he cried over that old woman.

For a few days, her shadow wandered through the rooms; her shadow seemed almost alive but, little by little, the life went out of that shadow and his wife filled the whole house.

And, oh, how he loved that wife of his!

♦

Topich plummeted to the recesses of his heart.

They were alone in the large house.

His wife's cheeks had gotten nice and plump. And the moments of intense passion in their love life; the hugging on the stairs and under the windows; their kissing each other behind the protective cover of the curtains; and countless kinds of love play they found; the innocent taps that left round marks on the cheeks; the little pinches that caused roses to bud on her breasts; their passionate embraces. . . .

Every evening, his wife would prepare his *raki* on a little table.

"My son, you shall drink your *raki* at home," his mother had said to him, kissing him on the forehead before she died, and the words of that luminous deceased one still had an effect on him.

And when his wife would come over and sit beside him, after lighting the lamp, Topich would say to her with great fondness and with laughter in his soft boyish eyes:

"Wife, fill my glass with *raki!*"

And his wife, with a joyful smile on her face, would fill his small glass and lift it to his mouth.

Then, in a flash, he saw himself in the cafés and bars, with groups of drunks. The bottles were coming and going; the time passed. In the deserted and rundown shop, their games and songs were still degenerating into commotion. Shivering and staggering along from wall to wall, he'd reach home; ashamed of himself, he'd go upstairs, at the top of which he wouldn't find his wife. Once he was in the bedroom, his misty eyes would cast a sweet smile upon the sleeping countenance of his wife. Softly he'd kiss her on the cheeks and wake her up.

"Wife, fill my glass with *raki!*"

And his wife, with a heavy heart, would fill his glass.

And then came worse days.

Drunken brawls, the defamation of his reputation, the effrontery of the tough guys he had once made tremble in fear, the humiliation of getting beaten up in cafés, his name hardly worth a nickle. . . .

Topich refilled his pipe and, in the dark, thought he definitely saw the gleam of eyes that were full of hatred. His entire body shook as those eyes became part of a face, a forehead, and with the hair falling into place, persons emerged. And those human heads were laughing through the smoke in disdain.

Topich rubbed his eyes with the back of his hand. A thin stream of salty tears flowed from beneath the tiny wrinkles, wetting his face. Violently he grabbed the glass of *raki* and gulped it down.

The fluid warmed his innards a bit. However, as if by some compelling force, his mind wished to go back in time, despite his obvious attempts to the contrary, despite his scratching his head for a long long time, and despite his wanting to make the old lips playfully move. After each movement, he found himself in his past, in the period of his life, to which he would never have wished to return; he was even afraid of the loneliness of that memory.

Days . . . weeks went by without work. Unaccustomed to working, he was forced to earn his daily bread stealthily by going on nocturnal raids. There was no longer any peace at home. Sometimes, in the middle of the night, strangers wearing odd clothes would remain in his room for hours.

♦

Bits of history, fragments of life came to his mind. In all of them too, the ignominy of the women having gone to Constantinople was execrable to the same degree; the fallen ones of Yüksek-Kaldirim were among them also.

After his wife had fled, things got worse for Topich. He fell, generally speaking, into the humiliating category of beggar-drunkards. For a glass of *raki,* he had to endure hours of ridicule. This fall would have continued for sure if a comrade-in-arms hadn't pulled him away from the edge of the precipice.

"Come on, Topich, let's leave the village. I'm going to Pazar Creek; there we can get hold of a good skiff. We'll catch some fish, we'll dive into the water and have a good time."

With passive modesty, the drunk went down to the shore of the lake.

There life was lonesome. The song of the vast expanse of water, the skittering of the big birds on the waves, the soft sighs of the rushes undulating in the lake, the absence of people and, in particular, a sudden feeling of misanthropy that was growing inside changed him.

With pleasure, he circled around on the water in his broken-down boat. On the shores, he stretched out his nets under the white sun. He felt the turning of something in his stomach on the first few nights, the spasm of an incomprehensible need, but the fatigue brought on by the motion of the waves soon made him sleepy. Without realizing it, he forgot about the *raki.*

And, little by little, the boy of the old days, the days of youth, came alive in him.

The dignity of his name, which had fallen into the mud and died, came and found him again at the shore of the lake. In his bold actions, he knew enough to set a real standard, by which the fighting men can be separated from the flock of cowards, rash and crazy ones. He again shook down the Turkish tough guys who were becoming unbearable on his turf. He spread terror at night in the fields; in broad daylight, he even killed a dervish with a hatchet whom he had caught casting a spell on an Armenian boy.

And, again, his name became decent, cleansed of its dirt. He didn't go to the village at all. He felt disgusted when darkness came upon the village lying in repose on the side of the mountain, and the blinking lights would flutter in the night like a distant heart.

The inappropriateness of being near his village and encountering so many of the villagers became clear to him and he crossed over to the other side of the lake.

He worked for many years among groups of fishermen and became quite experienced in that trade. He got to know the air and the sea like the palm of his hand. With the money he saved, he managed to eventually have his own hut, along with his own boat and nets.

For all practical purposes, he was happy.

Over fifty, he was past his prime. The cloak he had bartered in exchange for fish made his bones look larger than they actually were. His thick white *vardiks,* made of canvas and "roasted" on the sand, expressed fatigue. He didn't yearn for the glamor and crazy flings of youth. . . .

For years he lived in this monotonous way.

All summer long, he used to rise at the break of day, wearing his white *shalvars.* For a while, he would observe the position of the stars appearing from Chengiler way and, for a long time, his gaze would remain fixed upon the "Three Brothers." His soul would sweeten from the dull brightness of the stars; generally speaking, the moonlight made him sad. As he looked at its large disc, especially during the later phases, the memory of a distant scene came alive in him. Then, when the first red lights would start to spill from the crest of Bash-Kiraz, Topich would call the fellows, one by one, by their nicknames, which bore strong resemblances to the character and past of the men who worked with him.

And the fellows would all get up. One would be half asleep; another, in the midst of a coughing spell; a third in a squat position, moaning.

The boat moved slowly, gliding out toward the open sea and Topich, standing in the bow and holding the wheel, would furtively make the sign of the cross and then command in a pleasant voice:

"Come on, boys, lower the ropes."

The threads of the net would hang quietly for a bit on the silent surface of the water as if softly caressing it; after rocking to and fro for a while, they'd melt in the sea and Topich, his eyes turned toward the rising sun, would remain kind of dreamy and content. . . .

Thirty years passed like this. Not once did he go to Nor-Giugh. Once a year he'd climb up to Soloz or Gurle during Easter: he'd go to church and take a bunch of candles up to the altar in front of the Virgin Mary. He didn't pray—he didn't know any prayers—but he felt lighter in spirit as the sweetness of the songs and lights, the incense and fluttering candlelight expanded and swelled under the wide arches.

He wouldn't look at the face of a woman; he felt ashamed. After spending a day there, he'd return in haste to his hut.

There he lived. Close to sixty, he felt a dissolution in his flesh which made him uncomfortable. It seemed to him that his arms were getting longer and heavier with the passage of time. And his rock-like breastplate seemed mushy and rotten to him.

Prior to the beginning of that decline, he very seldom had the heart to think about his wife. The mere visualization of her affected him so much that he would break out in a cold sweat. Forgotten pleasures would come and gnaw at his heart, shake his soul, and he would always picture the little table at home, the flask of *raki,* the cute little glass, his wife while filling. . . .

"Wife, pour me a glass of *raki!*"

However, sound wouldn't come out of his throat and, in his soul, he'd hear his wife saying as she offered her lips:

"Hey, let my mouth be your appetizer!"

He would experience the monotonous torment of this scene and become bathed in sweat.

After the age of sixty, there was no longer any pleasure in this life of the outdoors and solitude. He felt cold in his bones. The fear and anxiety of approaching old age upset the tranquillity he felt having fled from society.

Gradually he got used to the *raki.* During the first few days, it produced a dreamy taste in his mouth. And memories stirred in his head. However, it was pleasurable for the old man to confine his boat in the midst of the reeds, put the bottle in the broken-down boat and drink, drink drop by drop, sucking the essence of the *raki.* There were many little islands of reeds in the lake and he liked to listen to the sounds of their watery songs, see his boat rocking in the little foamy bubbles that floated on the water surrounding their thin stalks.

And the *raki* softened his spirit and tempered the cold that stalked through his bones. He could drink for days without getting drunk.

"Fellows, this is medicine for the soul," he used to say to them when he was in good spirits.

However the joy or, more accurately, the carefree brightness would desert his face. The coldness of his white hair, the sorrow of his sagging face, and the thickness of his enervating tongue began to weigh on him.

In this manner, several more years passed.

From one year to the next, his hut got emptier. Many of the group had died and newcomers would barely tolerate that old man who used to have jugs of *raki* lined up under his pillow. Instead of catching fish, he used to drink, with the jug of *raki* thrust into the sand and with his back smack up against a thick bare tree trunk, and look out beyond Chengiler, below which the Sea of Marmora turned bluer.

He didn't know what had happened to his wife there. He wasn't thinking about what could happen. The shame engendered by this thought pierced his soul. For a long time, he would remain engulfed in the smoke of his pipe, not to see a form that wished to take the shape of his wife in front of his eyes.

After she had gone to Constantinople, he had received word about her. She had been seen in the homes of the rich; she had turned into a full, roly-poly woman. Then worse things had been whispered to him about her. Actually he didn't know anything about her.

Now he was suffering over not having a wife. The hut that had sheltered him for years now seemed cold to him. What was going to happen to him in the end? For sure, a snowstorm or wind would choke him in the throat or crafty water would drown him at the hands of one of its daughters, as she had done to the fisherman in the fairy tale. This nevertheless would still be a happy ending. What if death were late in coming, if his hands and feet were to fail him, if his eyes closed the world to his soul, if. . . .

There was no end to these suppositions. And he was dreaming of himself in his home—with a full beard, surrounded by his children and grandchildren, sitting on a large cushion in one corner of the hearth. And his wife by his side, holding the bottle of *raki*. And his favorite expression took shape on his lips:

"Wife, fill my glass with *raki!*"

The sun had disappeared even from the high mountains.

Reflections of red clouds on the lake cut up the darkness. A hot silence was expanding on the waters under the wind which had gotten milder. From amidst the plantain, the May bird was filling the mystery of that time of evening with a more delicate sweetness.

Along the length of the shore, the outline of the green reeds became blurred, forming a dense stretch of blackness the size of men and spreading out like endless armies, one behind the other. Thin fires glowed red in the dark on the plains of Chengiler and Nor-Giugh. From afar, the mournful song of the little bells—monotonous yet crying—of the herds returning to the village revived the shudder in Topich. The animals were going home.

And he didn't know how his eyes became filled with a dampness of salt and fire all of a sudden. He wanted something, something, and he again picked up the glass and swallowed its contents to calm the tempest raging in this soul of his.

A little while later, a tongue of flame leaped out of the open door of his hut and, in the dark, a touch of apricot flickered on the pointed ends of the reeds, producing a sad fleeting undulation on the sand. The fellows were boiling their evening fish.

It had gotten darker. And Topich was still looking at the ash-bound lake and the mountains with red backs which were about to disappear.

Without warning, he felt a strange and unexpected sensation. Something incomprehensible touched his flesh and was gone. He turned around to see if there was anybody. There was no one, but he put his ear to the ground.

The sound of tired footsteps dragging along struck his ear. He waited. The steps became more firm, more decisive, and drew nearer to him. Topich again turned around.

A woman was standing, wearing city dress. The evening darkness had made her face unrecognizable.

However, that total appearance wasn't altogether unfamiliar to Topich. All of a sudden, he saw beyond the exterior of those clothes and in a manner so close to his heart, which is the same for all men, with his soul irradiating, he seemed to recognize that body which old age and darkness had considerably reduced.

It was his wife. Having given her youth to Stambul, having emptied her breasts in unspeakable places, she was bringing her wrinkles and her shriveled nose back to the village, to her husband.

Topich recognized his wife. He couldn't understand the meaning of her return. The longing in him was so great and his heart so noble that he forgot about Stambul and its filth; he forgot her entire past and, extending the bottle and glass to her, slowly murmured in a soft and touching voice as if crying:

"Wife, fill my glass with *raki!*"

Daniel Varuzhan

(1884–1915)

The celebrated poet Daniel Varuzhan was born Varuzhan Chpugkyarian in Brgnik, a village near Sebastia (Sivas). He described his early life as follows:

> I spent my childhood in our native village, dreaming in the dark shadows of willow trees or mischievously throwing stones at ducks from the river bank. When I was barely old enough to chase butterflies, I watched my father leave the village as a *pandukht* (emigrant) to Constantinople, and my mother would sit with me in the long, harsh winter evenings, inflaming my imagination with stories of Janissaries and wolves as the wind howled in the chimney like a demon. In 1896, the time of the massacres, when I had just learned to read the Missal in the village school, they took me to Constantinople, where after a desperate search for my father amidst the bloody horrors, I found him shut up in a prison, falsely accused.[1]

From 1896 to 1902 Varuzhan attended the school of the Mkhitarist fathers in Constantinople. As he was as a brilliant and promising student, he was sent from there to the Murat-Raphaelian school in Venice

---

1. Teodik, *Amenun taretsuytse* (Everyone's almanac) (Constantinople, 1909).

(1902–5). He pursued his higher education at the University of Ghent, in Belgium (1905–9), where he studied economics and the social sciences and became acquainted with Italian and French literature. He also developed an appreciation of Flemish art. Ghent was an industrial city, and there he witnessed firsthand the inequalities of the social system and the lot of the working class. His favorite author was the Belgian poet Émile Verhaeren (1855–1916), who advocated the brotherhood of man and the emancipation of the working class, themes that Varuzhan later dealt with in some of his own poems, such as "*Banvoruhin*" (The workwoman), "*Mernogh banvore*" (The dying worker), "*Mekenanere*" (The machines), and "*Mayis mek*" (The first of May).

He returned home to his native village, and for three years he taught Armenian in the Aramian school in Sebastia (Sivas, 1909–11) and the parish school in Tokat (1911–12). In 1912 he was back in Constantinople with his family, and was put in charge of the Lusavorchian school of Pangalti, where he dedicated himself to literary pursuits and lecturing. In 1914 he collaborated with Hakob Siruni (1890–1967) to found *Navasard*, which was intended as an annual review of arts and literature. Only one issue was published. Varuzhan was among the intellectuals arrested by the Turkish police on the night of April 24, 1915. He was deported to Çankiri and murdered.

Varuzhan's poetry is national and universal at the same time. He formulated his approach to poetry at a young age:

> In our literature the mode of artistic expression should be Armenian, but its foundation, its basic idea, should be universal; in other words, the poet, the heart: Armenian; the philosopher, the mind: universal. In this way our evolution will proceed in progressive steps, without losing its unique national character. . . . The line of our glorious ancestral civilization has been broken for centuries; now it is time to pick it up and continue.[2]

This was his poetic creed, and he tried to observe it faithfully in all his works. His first collection of poetry, *Sarsurner* (Shivers, 1906), reveals his sensitivity to pain and suffering—not just his own, but that of humanity—and his intense desire to relieve it. Probing the real causes of human suffering, the poet depicts the inherent conflict in his own heart between the harsh reality of the present and a lovely dream of the future.

The second collection, *Tseghin sirte* (The heart of the nation, 1909), deals with different concerns and aspirations. The Armenians who lived

---

2. Daniel Varuzhan, *Namakani* (Letters) (Yerevan, 1965), 151.

under the Ottoman yoke and had been subjected to countless persecutions, atrocities, and massacres were now dreaming of freedom. Reaction to centuries of subservience to despotic rule was bursting forth like a song of protest. As Varuzhan himself put it, "When the entire Armenian nation was being drowned in a nightmare of fire and famine, I chose to sing out the heart of the nation, whose throbbing I felt in my own heart and blood."[3]

The prologue is a lengthy poem, "Nemesis," dynamic and filled with artistic imagery, which describes the carving of a statue of the goddess of retribution, an idol that the author calls on his people to worship until the tyranny is over, and then to destroy it. The three sections of the book, "*Baginin vra*" (On the altar), "*Krkesin mej*" (In the arena), and "*Diutsaznaveper*" (Epic poems), represent, in dramatic poetry, the holocaust of the people, their struggle for survival and revival, and their acts of heroism.

Although the liberties promised by the 1908 Ottoman Constitution were never realized, they created a relaxed atmosphere in Constantinople for a short while. During those years a new movement started in Western Armenian literature, which was known as *hetanosakan sharzhum* (the pagan movement) and was headed mainly by Varuzhan. In 1912 he published a new collection of poems called *Hetanos yerger* (Pagan songs, 1912), together in the same volume with a group of poems called "*Goghgotayi tzaghikner*" (Flowers of Golgotha). The aim of the "pagan movement" was to revive the spirit of the pre-Christian era, when strength, bravery, and beauty were idolized. Varuzhan did not portray paganism in its essential aspect, but only in certain selective characteristics, such as glory, power, and the enjoyment of life and physical beauty, characteristics that he saw as parts of the romantic ideal he was building. As Edmond Y. Azadian has observed, "his glorification of the past . . . was a philosophical and artistic introspection which made the actual hardships of the time seem more bearable: ironically, he worshipped and glorified the past in order to conquer the future."[4] In *Hetanos yerger*, woman is portrayed as a source of beauty and joy in glittering imagery (sometimes controversial) through poems like "*Harche*" (The concubine), "*Ov Lalagé*" (O Lalagé), and a few others. The second part of the book, in which Émile Verhaeren's influence is felt more strongly, deals with the human suffering caused by injustice, exploitation, and moral corruption. By dividing the book into two sections, the first on pleasure and the

---

3. Ibid., 207.

4. Edmond Y. Azadian, *Portraits and Profiles*, ed., trans., and intro. Agop J. Hacikyan and Edward S. Franchuk (Lewiston, N.Y., 1994), 42.

second on suffering, the author was probably establishing a psychological link between the two: the ideal and cruel reality.

His last work, *Hatsin yerge* (The song of bread, 1921) is a lyric poem about tilling the earth to produce bread, the staff of life; it depicts every stage in the process, from plowing the furrows and sowing the grain to putting the loaf on the table. In those years the Armenian peasant's life was miserable. Living in half-ruined huts and deprived of sustenance, the men were forced to move to the large cities, where they languished in rotten hostels. *Hatsin yerge* is an idealized portrayal of village life, hence an appeal to the *pandukht* (émigré) to return to his native soil to make it flourish. Similar appeals were launched by other writers, such as Ruben Vorberian (1874–1931) Ruben Sevak (1885–1915), and Siamanto (1878–1915). The manuscript of *Hatsin yerge* was confiscated by the Turkish police when they arrested the author, but it was recovered through bribery after his murder and published in 1921. Varuzhan had planned to write a sequel, *Giniin yerge* (The song of wine), but he did not live long enough to fulfill this plan.

His works have been published as individual volumes, selections, or complete collections in numerous editions. Many of his poems have been translated into French, Russian, English, German, and Italian. On the occasion of the centenary of Varuzhan's birth, Edmond Y. Azadian summed up Varuzhan's importance to Armenian literature by saying that he "placed his people's ordeals and their anguish within a universal context. And thus . . . , elevated by the greatness of the Armenian nation, [he] raised it even higher: there was, in his words, 'Deep in his soul, vast as a pond, / The earth-scented, life-giving sap of the universe.'"[5]

THE RED SOIL[6]

Here in a plate on my desk is a gift,
a handful of soil, a clump from the fields
from my fatherland. The giver thought
he gave his heart and did not know
he gave with it the hearts of

---

5. Ibid., 49. The quoted lines of poetry are from Varuzhan's poem "Nemesis," from *Tseghin sirte* (The heart of the nation).

6. Daniel Varuzhan, in *Ararat* 19, no. 1 (Winter 1978): 20. Translated by Diana Der Hovanessian.

his forefathers. I look at the soil,
sometimes for hours. My pupils
dilated, silent, sad, focus as if my stare
could pull and release roots from the fertile
earth. I think that perhaps this rust-red
color does not come from chemical laws
of nature. But being a sponge of wounds
this soil has drunk too from life, from
sun, and as a defenseless element
has turned red, being Armenian soil.
Perhaps palpitating in it still are centuries
of ancient glory. Perhaps there are throbbing
sparks from the iron hooves of victorious
Armenian troops. In it still
living that original strength that formed
breath by breath, my life and yours
giving us, as if with a confident hand,
the same dark eyes and similar souls.
In it also is the glitter of an ancient spirit,
an old epic hero, or the sweet tears of a virgin.
Or perhaps molecules of Hayk[7] can be found,
dust from Aram,[8] and bright rays from the stars
buried with the eyes of Ananias.[9]
On my writing table there is a nation,
an ancient nation speaking to me
from this soil where dawn was born.
It animates my soul like a sudden
planting of torrid stars in the blue
infinity, it irrigates my soul with lightning.
The chords of my nerves shiver
with a trembling that furrows the mind
with more creative furrows than
the sun-drenched spring winds ever bring.
And I feel in my brain the passage of remembrances
from souls still red with wounds

---

7. Ancestral epic hero.
8. Ancestral epic hero.
9. Reference is to Anania Shirakatsi, seventh-century Armenian scientist. See
The Heritage of Armenian Literature, vol. 2.

and with lips still calling vengeance.
And I keep this soil, this dust with more love
than my soul would someday greet
the ashes of my body in the winds.
This emigrant piece of Armenia,
this relic of victorious ancestors,
this talisman and gift grasps, claws
my heart.
Facing the sky from its place on a book
it seems to touch me at the very hour
of smiles, love, or at the majestic moment
of a poem's birth. It precipitates a cry,
sometimes, a roar, and sometimes
it arms my fist with my soul.

THE ORIENTAL BATH[10]

The inner door moves languorously, lazily
swings open slowly into the green domed bath
whenever the thick ebony is struck
with a mallet like a gong. It sweats,
creaking wearily behind the parade of houris
who enter slowly, regally. They are naked,
exotic, all beautiful with arms folded
under the brown buds of their breasts.

Their wooden sandals, inlaid with mother-of-pearl,
slap and echo over the tile. And the heave
of their breath and the ring of their voices
change into drowned chimes.

Their glimmering dark eyes are stars swimming
in the dark fog. The steam wraps
their bodies with damp veils, and
the bodies seem to swell with the sweat.

---

10. *Anthology of Armenian Poetry,* ed. and trans. Diana Der Hovanessian and
Marzbed Margossian (New York, 1978), 153–57.

They are houris, houris, bathing, dangling,
dipping legs into water from the marble slabs.
Some lie dreaming, half asleep in the water.

The white sun rays from the light-diffusing dome
sift down like a pearly rain. And vapors float.
Oriental swans are swimming in a silver sea.

Towels cling like seaweed to thighs and are finally
discarded and the bodies look like statues.
Hair comes down, unties, braid by braid,
like the sea, and sometimes, pin by pin it
sheds grains of jewels.
. . . .
A hundred faucets open, one after another
in a hundred marble pools bubbling,
gurgling. And dark vapors rise
like a fine ash, wave by wave. The empty tubs
come to life and waters sing with a sweet
ringing voice. The women bathe,
gathered around the bathtubs as if they
were Gaia's favorites, as if embracing
each other, mixing breasts, flushed arms,
sparkling legs and navels, navels
that are urns for essence where the scent
of dissolved musk can be diffused.
. . . .
And the bubbling water flows and the beauties swim.
Their skin catches fire like the petals
of the burning rose as they pour water
over the fire, their eyes languid
as one arm pours the water and one arm
supports their breasts.

Now, they hurry out, one by one, flame
by flame breathlessly, ripened into blooming
by the steam, like red tulips.

Oh, those damp curls that reach bare chests.
Oh, those soaked curls that shed pearly dews.
How can I describe the sweet smell,

the aura, the radiance, when toweled dry,
you dress like goddesses?

I want to kiss your fingers which you dip
deep into the wooden henna bowl now
as if into a red bloody heart.
I want to kiss your hair that is anointed
with incense and will spread scent
tonight on your pillows.

I want to kiss those cloud-like eyelashes,
those painted brows. And to kiss throat,
clavicle, chest, with the golden necklaces which
become a bright chandelier of light
when the chains reach the breast,
a chandelier over a marriage bed.

Let me kiss too the navel where you keep
the hashish of Arabia and the musk of Africa.

Laden with jewels you walk home
and the pavement becomes freshened where you step.

Let the cool air nip your chin, pinch your cheeks.
From the damp towel, from your floating skirt
let the fragrance of thyme arise, perfuming
the street and the square.

And the left-over food you carry home
in a cup, covered with a towel,
let it too release exotic spice
so the street of the oriental city will know
that May, that Spring, with sweet damp
blossoms is walking by.

THE LAMP[11]

Fill oil into the lamp, dear daughter.
Trim its wick, *Hars*,[12] so we can go.

---

11. Ibid., 157.
12. Bride or daughter-in-law (Armenian).

I hear the wagon turn into the yard.
I hear the wheels stop beside the well.

Hurry, *Hars.* Our soldier is home now.
My boy is back with us. He's home.
Light the lamp so we can see the hero's
laurel on his brow.

Light it, *Hars.* Hold it high.
Wait. What is that blood in the wagon?
Who is that lying pale and still?
Put out the lamp, *Hars.* Put out the light.

Tigran Cheokiurian (Chögürian)

(1884–1915)

Born in Gümüshhané, Turkey, Tigran Cheokiurian spent some of his childhood years in Trebizond (Trabzon), but he was orphaned at an early age. He found shelter in the orphanage of Karmir Vank in Angora, and in 1898 he was transferred to an Armenian orphanage in Constantinople. He attended the Perperian (Berberian) school, graduated in 1907, and began to teach in the same institution, as well as at the Chemaran school in Skutari (Üsküdar). In 1911, in collaboration with Mikayel Shamtanchian (Shamdandjian, 1874–1926), he founded an arts and literature review called *Vostan* (The city), in which he published most of his works. These include travel notes under the title of *Chambus vra* (On my way); an essay on Shirvanzadé (1858–1935); and a number of translations from Guy de Maupassant's *Boule de Suif* (Ball of fat), Leonid Andreyev's *Krasnyi smekh* (The red laugh), and a few plays by Henrik Ibsen and George Bernard Shaw. A collection of his short stories was published in 1910 under the title *Hayreni dzayner* (Voices from the homeland). *Herose* (The hero, 1911), a novella, depicts a bogus revolutionary who exploits patriotic feelings. Cheokiurian's most important work is the novel *Vanke* (The monastery, 1914), which features a celibate priest caught in a conflict between religious commitment and the attraction of love. The novel is written in diary form.

In 1915, at the age of thirty-one, Tigran Cheukiurian was deported with a number of other Armenian intellectuals and killed.

THE MONASTERY[1]: THE DIARY
OF AN ARCHIMANDRITE

A

November. . . .

I've been here for two weeks now. The onerous impressions of the first few days began to lighten, and my solitary life as an archimandrite, which was almost too monotonous, assumed its customary course.

But why should relocation affect me like this? The fact that I suffered quite a bit from the boredom and incertitude of the first few days cannot be hidden from the confidential pages of my diary.

I had lived the monastic life as a pupil in Armash; then I had relished that completely during the days of my trial as deacon. I had come to know the noble yet sad feeling of voluntary deprivation. I had become very familiar with my shadow in the barrenness of desolate cells, when the excessive thirst of penitence was filling my heart with dreams of victory, because I thought that hierarchical elevation would follow me, making me the possessor of floral garb woven with gold, rings and a pectoral cross, with which our ignorant and decrepit bishops are laden. Why shouldn't I hold out hope now too, since I am twenty six years old, still a young man?

When I ended up in Constantinople, I thought that I was taking leave of my days as a monk; the hustle and bustle, the hectic pace of urban life, which I had dreamed about for many years and from which I now have pleasant memories, was beginning; I would become a preacher in a secondary neighborhood while I was very young, practically timid. Now, barely having established loose relationships and enjoyed a warm family atmosphere, I've ended up in this monastery, in the recesses of a province, far from the city, in the bosom of solitary nature.

---

1. Tigran Cheokiurian, *"Vardapeti me orgire"* (The diary of an archimandrite), in *Vanke, herose* (The monastery, the hero) (Paris, 1933), 15–21. Translated by Aris Sevag.

Gloomy impressions filled my first days, especially the nights; it seemed to me that I would not be able to tolerate this new monastic atmosphere. Constantinople, its rich scenery, its streets, where I used to promenade my black shadow in an invariable manner but full of the emotion attached to secular desires, my cell, my friends were calling me. I made a vain appeal to the feeling of my obligation because a sacred task is weighing upon me; I have been sent here as director of this newly opened orphanage, as father to one or two dozen of the myriad orphans who will come to seek shelter under this protective roof, as victims of the brutal massacres.

That thought at least had the capacity of quieting me but I don't know why I was remaining unfeeling; I think I cried a few nights too. As it is, moving from place to place has always weighed on me; I had this susceptibility even during the days of my childhood.

But, after the first week, I gradually found my equanimity and now I am convinced of the idea of getting used to the monastery. Perhaps one day I will like it, as it is not as solitary as I thought; from one day to the next, I meet new people.

I've already become friendly with the abbot, a man who has most likely reached the age of sixty, if he hasn't passed it already. He has a red face like the cloth used to hold a cross; his honey-colored and oily eyes barely sparkle; and his black beard has begun to turn gray—in a word, the invariable appearance of a buffalo. His extremities and the upper part of his body are plump; one day, will I become like him, a corpulent beast, and will my life end ingloriously like this, within the bare walls of a monastery? Never, since the title of His Eminence, of which this man boasts, doesn't satisfy me.

Perhaps I am very ambitious, but one of my obliging and knowledgeable teachers, Orumian, always used to repeat, "ambition is the most forgivable of sins."

However, the abbot does not appear to be an odious man; I'm content with the reception he's accorded me; he's amusing. It is surprising that he hasn't been affected by the national catastrophe and doesn't nurture hope for the success of the orphanage; in fact, he shows somewhat of a reluctance toward it. Never mind, it is unsuitable to ask for more from him; apparently life has taught him more than school, yet he hasn't graduated from the former with all that high honors. He's quite ignorant too; he isn't knowledgeable about the new discoveries in Armenian studies; the best source he could rely on, in response to one or two of my incidental questions of a historical-critical nature, was Movses Khorenatsi. This Khorenatsi is a ridiculous primary source; I think it was in *Handes Amsorya* (Monthly review) that I read a critical article about him, entitled "*Patmutiun stuyn Movsesi Khorenatsvo*" (The false history of Movses Khorenatsi), to the effect that what he wrote was more of a tale than a book of history.

At any rate, I hope that I will be able to get along with Abbott Vardan, whose name, like him, is short too.

B

November. . . .

Two days ago, I made a more successful discovery: I met a stout elderly person in the monastery courtyard, and was barely able to curb my laughter; teetering like the mast of a ship caught in a storm, he was walking with the aid of a cane; he couldn't have been a pastor because he was wearing an old worn-out western outfit; I thought perhaps he was a superintendent but he didn't have a cruel face. He left me in a state of doubt so I approached him with hesitation.

"Greetings, brother. . . ."

"Greetings, holy father. . . ."

That's all it took. We sat on one of the steps of the belfry tower that stood in the courtyard. After a few questions designed to make our acquaintance, our conversation began to drift to various matters.

First, we discussed the monastery, and while my conversational companion was filling me in with information, I was observing his face. It was august without the severity that age, suffering and the pessimism of old age can put on a face. Between his long hair and the yellowed whiteness of his flame-shaped beard, his face, with its prominent lines, was weakly wrinkled and dark; an aquiline nose, curving noticeably, was inclined toward the black line of his mouth. That hardy face became oddly softer with his eyes, whose blue sweetness had still not extinguished the spark, which, as I understood later, flows from an intelligent and inquisitive rationality. . . .

I discussed the orphanage that was to be newly established. . . .

"It's difficult to maintain an orphanage here," chimed in my conversation partner, "but those poor kids can be sheltered for a while; the abbot is lazy and inimical to such undertakings; the only thing is not to become despondent, my son. . . ."

The words "my son" could insult the dignity of my friar's status but, as spoken by this man, they fill me with filial love; indeed, I bear the heart of a child, a timid, sensitive yet ambitious lad. These traits are not a credit to me; one day, I shall change completely.

I severed the thread of the conversation, to distance the old man's grievous relation with the bloody days of the past few years; suddenly I asked:

"Are there many manuscripts in the monastery?"

I was barely able to finish my sentence; I saw that this hunched-over old man sat up straight, smiled and, noticing my confusion, assured me cheerfully:

"The manuscripts are my friends, my family and my children. A family that has a few hundred members. . . ."

"I lost my wife and children sixteen years ago; then, as a result of an accident, one of my legs became crippled; I came here as a disabled teacher to help the abbot. For months, I was tormented by the tears of loneliness and longing; a monastery is no place for a teacher accustomed to commotion.

"One day—that day would turn out to be the day of the resurrection of my lost heart—I found a few trunks in one of the church closets. I opened them to find a random assortment of dusty and torn apart books; I dusted them off while examining them more closely; their contents also tempted me; my affinity for them soon followed and, finally, I became filled with a deep love for them.

"They were illustrated manuscripts, parchment books of psalms, books of fables, medical books, and love ballads penned by minstrels. Pursuing my researches, I also found pictures of rare beauty, and until now the monastery has not been ungrateful as regards my investigations. I cannot explain my ardent feeling towards them; what I have is a true love affair with those sheets of paper and parchment. . . ."

"But that is not in vain; I remember that, during my childhood, I used to look with profound admiration and veneration at the floral letters drawn by our Reverend Andreas; for hours I would gaze at them, trying to copy them; my failure would barely be contented with tears of anger and shame.

"In this wretched monastic life, I shall perform the vain role of faithful protector of those treasures until my death, with a contented heart, always reading the wisdom and jewels of love of the ancients and gazing insatiably at the illustrated manuscript page and the simple yet sensitive hues of a picture. I don't expect the day to come when I will become sated from that."

The flapping of the turtledoves' wings in flight arrested his enthusiasm, and he rose to go down to the river's edge.

"We'll get together many more times," he said. "We can become good friends. I too was longing to meet someone with a noble soul."

Comforted, I took leave of him; these pages of my diary should be the echo of my sincerity. I think that this person is precious for me; he's a friend, even a father; I would have loved art although I don't understand much about it.

Oh . . . his name? . . . Yes, it was Yeghiazar, whereas I told him mine was Artak.

Ruben Sevak

(1885–1915)

Ruben Sevak, poet, prose writer, and physician, was born in Silivri, a town not far from Constantinople. His family name was Chilinkirian. He received his education at the local Askanazian elementary school, the American middle school in Partizak (Bahçecik), the Perperian (Berberian) College in Constantinople (1901–5), then at the University of Lausanne, where he studied medicine and from which he graduated in 1911. He married a German woman and had two children. He practiced medicine in Lausanne until 1914, when, before the start of the First World War, he and his family moved to Constantinople. On the fateful night of April 24, 1915, he was arrested along with many other Armenian intellectuals. They were sent to concentration camps in Chankiri and Ayash, led from there in small groups to desolate places, and brutally killed. Ruben Sevak, Daniel Varuzhan (1884–1915), Siamanto (1878–1915), and two other companions comprised one such group. "According to the testimony of the carriage driver, they were taken to a remote valley and were ordered to take off their clothes so they would not be damaged; the assassins then tied each victim to a tree and murdered them in cold blood with their daggers."[1]

---

1. G. Palakian, *Hay Goghgotan* (The Armenian Golgotha) (Vienna, 1922), 1:149–51.

Ruben Sevak started writing poetry while he was still a student at the Perperian College. He collected his early poems and two prose pieces— one a study titled "*Hisusi kyanke*" (The life of Christ) and the other a graduation essay on "*Marde*" (The man)—into a notebook and titled it *Dzayner* (Sounds). It was never published during his lifetime. It surfaced in print, as a booklet edited by Alexander Topchian, in Yerevan in 1992. The contents of this booklet reveal the beginnings of a depth of thought and an aesthetic that matured and flourished in Sevak's later works.

The only book Sevak published during his lifetime was *Karmir girke* (The red book, 1910), comprising three lengthy dramatic poems inspired by the massacres of Adana. He planned to publish three further volumes in sequence: *Siro girke* (The book of love) was to include his personal emotions, his joys as well as the sadness of love; *Kaose* (Chaos) was to depict the destiny of contemporary society; and *Verjin haye* (The last Armenian) would probably have contained his patriotic poems. His life was cut short before he could complete this plan; *Siro girke* and his other poems, however, were published in a collection of his works in Jerusalem, in 1944. Another important work of his, standing completely apart from his poetry, is *Bzhishkin girken prtsvatz ejer* (Pages torn from the diary of a physician), comprising short stories based on real-life situations that depict various aspects of human suffering and at times philosophize on religion, science, and human destiny.

Ruben Sevak's literary output, both poetry and prose, was widely scattered in the periodical press, as was the case with many other writers of the time. While in Lausanne, where he spent most of his adult life, he contributed to a number of journals. He wrote about love and nature, and on social, national, and patriotic themes; he revolted against social injustice and corruption, and he championed universal harmony. Though some critics discerned neoromantic tendencies in his works, he did not, in fact, belong to any literary school. In poetic aestheticism and imagery he may not have reached the level of some of his contemporaries, such as Misak Metzarents (1886–1908), Siamanto, and Varuzhan; however, he had a unique appeal to his readers. He brought a fresh breath and a new viewpoint to Armenian literature at the turn of the century.

His works were published posthumously, as individual volumes or as collections: *Bzhishkin girken prtsvatz ejer* (Pages torn from the diary of a physician) in Salonica (1925), in Jerusalem (1943), in Paris (1946), and in Beirut by the *Zartonk* daily (1951); *Kertvatzneru havakatzo* (Collected poems) in Jerusalem (1944); *Yerker* (Works) in Yerevan (1955, 1985, and 1995); *Ruben Sevak yev Prtsvelik ugheghner* (literally, Ruben Sevak and brains to be ripped out) in Paris (1985); *Yerker* (Works) in Antilias (1986); *Ruben Sevak, antip ejer ashakertakan tetrerits* (Ruben Sevak:

unpublished student writings) in Yerevan (1992); *Ruben Sevak antip ejer* (Ruben Sevak: unpublished writings) in Yerevan (1995); and *Namakani* (Letters) in Yerevan (1996). It should be noted that the various collections published under the title *Yerker* have different contents and are not reeditions.

THE CRANE[2]

It was a cold winter day. Outside, the freezing wind whipped the faces of the passersby. And the thick snow blinded their eyes.

We were sitting in a friend's room, just a few friends, all of us expatriates. The door creaked and the cold wind swept into the room. It was Karo; he was coming from the cemetery.

"Brrrr," he said, "it isn't fit for a dog out there. How could a man pick such a day to die on?"

A bit later the door opened once more. A few other late arrivals came in, all of them friends. They had waited in the snow until the corpse was completely buried; they had even said a few words of farewell to the unknown dead man.

Who knew, who would ever know the thousand and one pages torn from the drama of life and death that today we buried under the snow in a foreign hole? Without a name, like the body of a dead bird. . . .

"I didn't know him either," one of us said, "but the people at the hotel knew that he was an Armenian and tried to find an Armenian doctor to have a look at him. After looking for only a week, they found me. When I entered the room, the shutters were closed. But bit by bit I made out a face in the darkness: long, angular, a greenish-yellow pattern of darkness and light, a Rembrandtian head.

"The second thing I noticed in the blackness was bone-colored fingers, which stretched out to me and grasped my hand with clammy tenacity, as if there were not a drop of blood in his body. The eyes had already lost their glitter—black within blackness, they could not be discerned.

"When I got more accustomed to the semi-darkness, I saw spots of blood on his beard: splotches of congealed red blood. The

---

2. Ruben Sevak, *Yerker* (works) (Antilias, 1986), 379–81. Translated by the editors of the present anthology.

warm exhalation of a slaughtered animal poured from his mouth. He breathed slowly and deeply, as if an invisible knife had slashed his lungs from the inside, from top to bottom.

"What kind of treatment could I give to this body that was almost dead? But he made an effort to speak; a cough choked his words, but I plucked a word from his hoarse, rasping cacophony: " 'The *Krunk*' (crane). . . ."[3]

"And I sang for him. Who doesn't know '*Krunk*': the '*Krunk*' of all travelers whose eyes look back . . . and beyond . . . the '*Krunk*' of all whose necks are bent and of all who follow endless roads. . . . And it seemed to me that he flew back to his homeland and was refreshed, and he cried. . . . He had entrusted the *Krunk* with all the yearnings of his heart. . . ."

When the story ended we were all silent. There was something terrible in this student's destiny; he had set out to return to his homeland, and on his way he had died, and was now buried in a country he had never seen before. . . .

The tuberculosis had been there, inside of him, for centuries, waiting for years, until all of his hopes were realized, all of his studies completed, and all of his efforts and work were terminated, before it began its awful labor, delivering its crucial blow at a crucial moment. . . . Ah, what a nasty, disagreeable illness!

"Doctor," somebody said, "when we uncovered his face at the cemetery, it was as black as ink. . . . Why is that?"

But the doctor did not speak; no one spoke.

Silence once again fell on us like a stone, this time heavier than before. To break the ice, someone else said: "Hey boys, it's Armenian New Year tomorrow. . . ."

But who was in the mood to think of New Year? We could hear snow smacking on the windowpane, as if the dead youth's fingers were tapping on the window. . . . In this cold he had escaped from his grave and wanted to join us. And you never know what that nameless and unknown dead young man had for all of us—a symbol or a warning. . . .

And as a matter of fact, at that very moment we all felt the presence of death: death, the unknown and horrifying, came to the student, the laborer, the believer, and the agnostic, to both the healer and the healed. . . .

---

3. A well-known Armenian folk song.

We were going to be somebodies, to be educated, to carry light to our dark world: lies, lies, lies! Which of us was not filled with the age-old breath of death? Was not thinking about himself and suspecting himself of. . . .

What noble sentiments could be found among those young souls, who did not even believe in the bonds of prayer that unite the dead and the living? Thus, each of us remained isolated within himself. . . .

But suddenly, from an unlit corner, arose a low tremulous song: first as a solo, then rising from multiple lips—a tender and overpowering song, like a funeral song, pleading like a prayer, a lofty and graceful song, which broke the ice, melted the tears, warmed the hearts, and united all the souls, all the cares, all the sorrows, all the sadness.

The homeless lad's heart is wounded, and his lungs afflicted with consumption.

The bread he eats is bitter and the water is cursed. . . .

Krunk, Krunk, from every corner of the world, from every chamber of every heart, how many heavy tidings are tied to your legs? And yet you can still fly! How many deaths have been tied to your wings, *Krunk?* And yet on those wings you still fly forward!

And when the doctor made a sign and we all stood up as a sign of respect for the dead, I had goose flesh all over my body at the thought that at that moment, far, far away, in a place far over the seas and mountains, an old mother and a white-haired father, their faces wreathed in smiles and hope, were watching the road for the young man we knew would never return, never ever return. . . .

And, trembling now, I joined my voice to the others, as if I were singing the death-scented song into his mother's ear. . . . On the roads of exile an entire people was dying anonymously—that song contained enough grief to poison the entire world, and enough sweetness to make the stones weep.

Lausanne, 1913.

LETTERS FROM A STUDENT[4]

We are living through black days again. Days of horror. Telegrams announce new calamities every hour. Massacres; and if not

---

4. Sevak, *Yerker,* 552–54. Translated by the editors of the present anthology.

massacres, fires; and if not fires, famine; and, what is most terrifying, epidemic! The press increases the toll of mourning every day. Just this evening I read in the paper a letter from a well-known Swiss woman, Lucie Borel, who for many years has devoted herself to the education of Armenian children in Cilicia. This selfless woman describes how a deadly peace had settled at last over this *dead city* and the Red Cross was getting organized to take care of the wounded, when suddenly a new and unprecedented outburst broke out among the mob; they torched the fabled Armenian school, which had opened its doors to thousands of wounded people. Borel adds, "Suffice it to say that the new council has given orders not to kill anymore, but to burn everything. . . ."

Everything! What is there left to burn, anyway?

Yesterday I noticed a crowd gathered in front of a newspaper office and walked over to see what they were looking at. New photographs had arrived and had just been printed: thousands of miserable people strung out along the seashore; beds in churches; pieces of human bodies, feet; the corpse of a mother, and an infant taken from her slit-open belly; the Mediterranean, choked with corpses; old people lying on the ground; orphaned little girls; misery, suffering everywhere. . . . Armenians, Armenians, Armenians. . . . They tore my heart to pieces. In that curious crowd, I was the sole representative of this miserable people. I was walking away from that blood-drenched scene when a short conversation stopped me in my tracks. It was between two little girls, seven or eight years old.

"What are these pictures?" asked the younger.

"They're slaughtering the Armenians. . . ."

"Why?"

The older one stopped, totally confused. Did she know *why?* She had only heard, from the cradle on, what her parents said about the Armenians as they talked with each other in the evenings. *Why?* What a bewildered, petrified, stunned thought: that colossal *Why?* That crimson *Why?* which burst from the soul of a seven-year-old girl. That insurgent, monumental *Why?* that flowed from her mouth as naturally as crystal clear water from a spring. The wisdom of the very young. . . . So many of us, the "adults," "respected" people, and "thinkers" of the nation, have not yet thought about the basic question that troubled the brain of that child. Ah, but they might discover unpleasant things beneath that little word, things that could harm their interests, like the worms beneath a stone. . . .

This Saturday a Swiss magazine contained a very bitter satire on this subject: "God created the donkey to be vilified and the Armenians to be slaughtered. . . . The regime in Turkey changes, so massacre the Armenians; the Sultan is deposed, so massacre the Armenians; *sheriyat*[5] is to be imposed: a good excuse for massacring the Armenians. None of these things, however, appears so strange to us as the mournful 'docility' with which the Armenians greet these massacres. When is this nation going to learn *to resist, like a human being?*"

And it's true: this essential virtue—*to resist, like a human being*—seems foreign to the Armenian heart. Not only among God-fearing churchgoers—the incense addicts, the ignorant artisans—but even and especially among our intellectuals. Take the press: believe it or not, during the last few months the European press has covered the wounds of the Armenians more closely than the Armenian press of Istanbul! The international political press has unanimously agreed on the number of people massacred, which is over thirty thousand. "The Cihan River alone dumped three thousand Armenian corpses into the Mediterranean," report the officers of French battleships. European witnesses report the most horrifying realities on the very day they take place.

Stupefied and petrified, we await the Istanbul Armenian papers, in the expectation of finding more detailed news or at least of taking comfort in reading a powerful protest. . . . The papers arrive, and turn upon us once again the blank arrogance which forever characterizes the Istanbul intelligentsia. . . . Our papers continue their paralyzed existence. We even read newspapers and magazines in which, right before the massacres in Cilicia, there are endless lewd love poems, stories about betrothals, and much more. . . . The entire Armenian press should have been swathed in the black of mourning or splashed with the red of blood, or, if it could not reveal or say everything, it should have shut up. . . . At the least, they should not have written those extremely pessimistic, destructive, depressing eulogies. Those who died consciously and heroically do not need tears; they do not need hired professional

---

5. Canonical obligations (Arabic).

mourners or advice. The eulogies should be read over the eulogizing editors. Nations have an inborn instinct to struggle for self-defense and the perpetuation of the race. The press should not pervert that instinct into pessimism, mourning, and unassuageable anguish and pain at such horrifying times. It is not fatalism that will save oppressed nations, and this is what our press is forgetting!

Every day the foreign press, especially the Swiss dailies, publishes a complete list of donations received for the massacred Armenians. Where are our people? The Armenian papers publish endless lists of donations made (in lieu of flowers) in memory of our *worthies*. Should we not expect the same papers to present this seven-times martyred nation with countless lists of donations, in lieu of flowers, in memory of the thousands of massacred Armenians? The provinces—the much-reviled provinces—the provinces have given their mite. When will feelings of national awareness be aroused within the souls of the people of the capital? When will they feel compassion?

And when, especially, will they begin *to resist, like a human being?*

Vahan Terian

(1885–1920)

Vahan Terian, one of the most important and best educated poets in Armenian literature, was born in the village of Gandza in the Armenian province of Akhalkalak. After finishing the primary school of his native village he went to Akhalkalak to study for another two years before moving to Tiflis and eventually to Moscow to complete his education.

In art and language Terian excelled the majority of his predecessors. The music of Terian's poetry is pure and simple, like an Armenian melody, and its structure, like traditional Armenian architecture, is simple, unified, and compact. His masterful and varied metrication produces symphonic harmony.

His deep interest in languages, including Latin and Greek, and literature led him to the works of the European masters. Paul Verlaine (1844–96) was one of his favorite foreign poets, and he was deeply influenced by the principles of French symbolism. Terian started writing while he was still a student at the Lazarian College in Moscow, where he also began his involvement in social and political movements. The Armenian liberation movement, the confiscation of Armenian religious properties in Russia (1903), the uprising in Sasun (1903–4), and the Russo-Japanese war (1904) influenced the thinking of the future poet.

The first Russian Revolution (1905–6) generated a great deal of turbulence among the students, to the point that the college was temporarily obliged to suspend classes. Vahan Terian's experience of these events added revolutionary zeal to his literary talent, and he eventually became an ardent promoter of national and international emancipation projects.

The year 1905 was crucial in Terian's life. He and a few close friends left Moscow for the Caucasus, passed through Tiflis, and arrived in Shirak, with the intention of engaging in revolutionary work. In one of the villages of that region Terian met the poet and writer Avetik Isahakian (1875–1957) and spent several unforgettable days with him in the latter's home. In 1906 Terian returned to Moscow a new person, regenerated both psychologically and ideologically. Upon his return he entered the University of Moscow to study philology. Because of his close relationship with Russian Social Democrats he was arrested and put in jail for a brief period, but the incident did not change his conduct and thinking. He devoted all his efforts to literary, social, and political activities.

His first book of poetry, *Mtnshaghi anurjner* (Twilight dreams: book 1), appeared in Tiflis in 1908. The date of this publication is rather significant, as the first book of poems by Misak Metzarents (1886–1908), *Tziatzan yev nor tagher* (Rainbow and new verses), was also published in Constantinople that year, heralding the birth of two outstanding poetic talents whose names would soon be included among the great masters of Armenian literature.

Terian's book introduced unprecedented artistic beauty into Eastern Armenian poetry. After reading Terian's manuscripts, Hovhannes Tumanian (1869–1923) wrote to him: "You are a poet. I rejoice at your entrance to a literary career. You are most welcome."[1] Around the same time, Tumanian also remarked to Avetik Isahakian (according to the latter's memoirs): "[Terian's lyricism] is exceptional, almost a novelty in our poetry. Although the images are scarce and spare, the language is clean and pure, like the chime of a silver bell. . . . At any rate, he has a definite place in our pantheon." Isahakian replied: "They are marvelous pieces, expressing crystalized feelings in flawless forms. This is true, unadulterated lyricism." In the opinion of many critics, Terian's language will remain one of the most perfect and beautiful in all of Armenian literature

---

1. This and the following two quotations are cited in Simon Simonian, *Arevelahay grakanutiun* (Eastern Armenian literature) (Beirut, 1965), 626.

and the most flawless and exquisite realization of Eastern Armenian letters: "a polished, measured, vivid, and literary Armenian, which, like holy basil, has gathered within it all the fragrances of the long history of our language."[2]

Terian's greatest inspirations were the Armenian people, his birthplace, and his parental home. Despite his later life in big cities and his studies in Russia, he always remained faithful to his Armenian roots.

In 1910, in collaboration with Poghos Makintsian (1884–1938) and Tsolak Khanzadian (1886–1935), he began editing the *Garun* (Spring, 1910–12) annual. Around it he gathered many Eastern Armenian collaborators and contributors, including Avetik Isahakian, Hovhannes Tumanian, and Shirvanzadé (1858–1935). Upon the closure of this publication, Terian founded the Pantheon Press, but unfortunately it did not last long.

Terian truly believed that the hope of the Armenian nation was a pan-Russian revolution. He was extremely saddened by the Armenian massacres and the ensuing 1915 genocide, and wrote several poems on those tragic events. During this period he made friends with Maxim Gorky (1868–1936) and collaborated with him on an anthology of Armenian literature, helping him to select and translate the works. The anthology was published in 1916. At the same time, as a result of heavy intellectual commitments, work, and financial difficulties, his health began to fail. Despite his illness, soon after the 1917 revolution his support of the Bolshevik uprising earned him an important post with the Commissariat for Armenian Affairs, based in Moscow. He assumed his responsibilities enthusiastically, organizing assistance for Armenian refugees and planning a huge publishing project, which had always been his dream. The *Communist* newspaper of Moscow was founded through his efforts. His fragile health continued to deteriorate, however, and he died in Orenburg, on his way to Central Asia, on January 7, 1920.

His first book of poetry, *Mtnshaghi anurjner* (Twilight dreams), was followed by *Gisher yev husher* (Night and memories), *Voski hekiat* (The golden fable), *Veradardz* (The return), *Voské shghta* (The golden chain), *Yergir Nayiri* (Nayiri homeland), and *Katvi drakht* (Cat heaven), as well as a number of scattered poems in the periodical press. He also made several translations and wrote essays, articles, and reports. His more than five hundred letters, half of which have been published, are also noteworthy. Terian's works had numerous printings and have been rearranged under different titles throughout the twentieth century.

---

2. Ibid., 623.

I LOVE YOUR DARK AND WICKED EYES[3]

I love your dark and wicked eyes, as deep
as the mysterious evening is deep, and dark
as the spell that dusk casts. I love the vast
seascape of your eyes where sin
hesitates like twilight before flickering past
where luck and chance have been.
I love your eyes, their drunken golden haze,
eyes that magnetize the lost like wordless beams
and torture the soul with their pitiless
caress. I love their dark and mysterious depths.

COMING TO TERMS (OR RECONCILIATION)[4]

Let us live in the present today
and not be afraid to admit
our wretchedness. Let us not blame fate,
nor dwell on what we regret.

Without pretense, let us acquiesce
to what our dying hearts understand.
We are bereft and orphaned apart;
let us not be ashamed.

Let us forgive each other with love,
not blame. Let us not calculate.
Say we won't covet, say we won't judge
but accept without rancor or pain.

Let us pity and not torment,
reciprocate kindness with kind.
Let us make up for our past mistakes
and respect the brevity of time.

---

3. Vahan Terian, "I Love Your Dark and Wicked Eyes," in *Coming to Terms*,
ed. and trans. Diana Der Hovanessian (New York, 1991), 9.

4. "Coming to Terms," in *Ararat* 32, no. 1 (Winter 1992): 9. This poem and
the next one are included in Terian, *Coming to Terms*.

IN THE STYLE OF SAYAT-NOVA[5]

Don't label yourself sinful or unwise—
love's wounds cleanse the soul and open the eyes.

Don't bemoan the blows that fate often deals—
Pain heightens the power to feel and to heal.

And if love leaves, don't curse its birth—
Keep it a clean memory, without its hurt.

Exult in both joy and grief. Death comes
when the heart cools and becomes numb.

For what is done—waste no regret.
Remorse is for what's not done or said.

Vahan Terian asks: Why shut the door
while a fire still burns, even a small flame?

How many fires have been tamped in error?
A thousand pities. And what a shame.

CAROUSEL[6]

Turn and turn again, carousel.
Your tunes are old familiar tunes.

It is an old familiar story
about the spell a smile can cast
across a lifetime, across pink mists,
a warm smile that can heat the soul.

The words that pledge love end in kisses
with words that praise the sweet, sad world.
Do we use them, knowing we are lying?
Do they use us to be heard?

Spin and spin again, carousel.
I am long familiar with your song.

---

5. Ibid. Sayat-Nova (1720–95) is an Armenian troubadour.
6. "Carousel," in Der Hovanessian, *Coming to Terms*, 20–21.

Once there was a land, distant and golden.
Once a world blessed by the sun.
Once there were illusions, now faded.
Once they shone in glory. Now they're gone.

Is it you or the world that changed
with suffering and sorrow's tears?
Let the dream go. It deceives you gilding
the past and the by-gone years.

Turn and turn again, carousel.
Your path is an old familiar route.

In that far-off world the song
I sang was one we all knew:
"I love you but you don't love me."
How banal and predictable. Now.

"Time beyond reaching," say the verses;
"Waltz me again," says the tune.
Such an old tired story full of
night, a kiss and the moon.

Spin again slowly, carousel.
I know your tune.

Do you know the secret they are singing
at the frenzied banquet as they dance?
Do you know the song without end or beginning?
"Yesterday I was, today your turn, tomorrow
someone else will be."

Turn and return, carousel.

THIS TIME LIKE A SISTER[7]

Listen, at least like a sister this time.
Look, all my fantasies are erased.
One last time, come with calm and your grace
to understand my torment and pain.

---

7. "This Time Like a Sister," in ibid., 31.

I am so tired of evasion and games,
and need the touch of a sisterly hand.
I crave your outspoken and candid words.
Come. Even if it's just pity I gain.
I plead for friendship, and want to remain
in your heart where good memory stays.
How can it be that this blaze which stirs
my soul kindles no warmth in yours?

FAREWELL SONG[8]

Every moment with sorrowing love I say farewell,
I say farewell to the sun, blazing in my heart.

I say goodbye to men everywhere, evil and kind,
I say goodbye to Adam's afflicted and orphaned sons.
Farewell to my close and distant friends,
Farewell to the enemies who watch me.

To the sky's blue, the sea's living green, the forest darkness,
To the light inside a spring cloud, I bid farewell.

To the shining chain of my memory, my nights and my pain,
To the larks in golden fields, I say farewell.

And goodbye to the unopened flowers, to the souls yet un-
kindled,
To the lively, playing children, farewell.

I am going to a darker earth, a remote land, I will not come
back,
Remember me well in your hearts. I say goodbye, farewell.

THE GALLOWS[9]

At daybreak he walked up the gallows
—Sunrise, O bloodied dawn—

---

8. Vahan Terian, "Farewell Song," in *Armenian Poetry Old and New*, ed. and trans. Aram Tolegian (Detroit, 1979), 255. The original title of this poem is "*Hra-zheshti gazel*" (Farewell ghazel).
9. "The Gallows," in ibid., 253.

The priest and soldiers waited there,
They stood pale and silent beside him

The old priest did not remember a single prayer,
His heart was dark with curses.
In the grey fog of dawn
The sunrays scattered aimlessly.

The officer shifted left foot to right—
Did he remember his distant mother?
The black night began to pale, then take color,
The sun began to gild the hills and valleys.

At dawn he walked up the gallows
—Sunrise, O bloodied dawn—
The priest and soldiers waited there,
They stood pale and silent beside him.

Kostan Zarian

(1885–1969)

Kostan Zarian, poet, novelist, critic, teacher, scholar, editor, polyglot, and world traveler, was born Kostan Yeghiazarian in Shamakhi (now in Azerbaijan). His father was a respected general in the Russian army, after his death (when Kostan was four) the family moved to Baku, and Kostan began to study at the local Russian gymnasium (1890–95). He and his elder brother were sent to Paris, where he studied (1895–1901) at the Collège de Saint-Germain. He continued his education at the University of Brussels, from which he graduated with a doctorate in literature and philosophy. By this time he was already publishing French poems in Belgian periodicals and earning a living by giving lessons in Russian.

In 1911 Zarian had a memorable talk with Émile Verhaeren (1855–1916), the Belgian poet, which was to change his life. Zarian recounts the meeting as follows:

> At that time the French press was accusing Verhaeren of excessive use of "Belgianism." I thought there was a germ of truth in this criticism, and I once said as much to Verhaeren. He smiled and said: "Recite the Lord's prayer." And all of a sudden my distant childhood woke up in my memory. I recalled the words of my native, and almost unknown, language and began to recite the prayer in Armenian. "There you

are," Verhaeren said, evidently pleased. "Well, poetry is one endless prayer."[1]

This episode resolved him to learn his native tongue. He went to Venice, where from 1911 to 1913 he studied classical and modern Armenian, along with Armenian culture and history, with the Mkhitarists. He writes: "I realized that language is simply part of the blood that circulates through one's body; one doesn't learn it, but simply discovers it."[2]

In 1913 Zarian was in Constantinople, where he collaborated with Daniel Varuzhan (1884–1915), Hakob Oshakan (1883–1948), Gegham Barseghian (1883–1915), Siamanto (1878–1915), and a few others to found a literary magazine, *Mehyan* (The Temple), which would serve as a rallying point for young writers. Its initial success was short-lived. The beginning of World War I in 1915 gave the Young Turk's government the opportunity to launch their scheme of exterminating the Armenian population of Turkey. Most of the intellectuals were killed, but Zarian fortuitously escaped the fate of his colleagues and took refuge in Bulgaria, Greece, and eventually Rome, where he stayed for a while. In 1916 he published a long poem in Italian, *Three songs*,[3] a section of which, "*La Primavera*" (Spring) was set to music by Ottorino Respighi (the piece was first performed in 1923). While in Italy Zarian was a member of the Society for the Freedom of Oppressed People, published poems, delivered lectures, and, in 1919, made a tour of Turkey, Georgia, and Armenia as a correspondent for an Italian newspaper. In 1920, during the Allied occupation, he established himself in Constantinople and in 1922, together with Vahan Tekeyan (1878–1943), Gegham Gavafian (1888–1959), and Shahan Perperian (Berberian, 1891–1956), he published another short-lived magazine, *Bardzravank* (Hilltop monastery), which he called "an observation post in a burning forest." At this time he published his first book of poems in Armenian, *Oreri psake* (The crown of days, 1922), which has been described as "expressing varying and contrasting moods, captured with vivid imagination through sensations and impressions of light, color, and sound."[4]

---

1. Quoted in Kostan Zarian, *Bancoop and the Bones of the Mammoth*, ed. and trans. Ara Baliozian (New York, 1982), x–xi.

2. Ibid., xi.

3. The poem was originally written in French. The Armenian version was published in Vienna in 1931, under the title *Yerek yerger aselu hamar vishte yerkri yev vishte yerknki* (Three songs that sing of the sorrows of the earth and the sorrows of the heavens).

4. Kevork B. Bardakjian, *A Reference Guide to Modern Armenian Literature, 1500–1920* (Detroit, 2000), 198.

In 1922 Zarian moved to Soviet Armenia, where he stayed for three years, teaching comparative European literature at the newly organized University of Yerevan. In 1925, as a result of certain disappointments, he asked permission to leave the country. From then until 1961 he lived the life of an émigré, wandering through Italy, France, the United States, and the Middle East, editing the French-language *La Tour de Babel* (The tower of Babel) in Paris and (in 1946) the English-language *Armenian Quarterly* in New York, and teaching at Columbia University, and the American University in Beirut. In 1935 he met and married a young American artist, Frances Brooks. From 1935 until the outbreak of World War II he lived on the island of Corfu, where he met the English novelist and poet Lawrence Durrell (1912–90), who later published an account of his conversations with Zarian in *Prospero's Cell* (1945).

During this period Zarian produced some of his best works. *Antsorde yev ir chamban* (*The Traveler and his Road*, serialized 1926–28) is based on his travels, impressions, and reflections from the last months of his stay in Constantinople (1922) to the end of his sojourn in Soviet Armenia (1925). His patriotism was genuine, and he had faith in Armenia despite the misery of the time. He scorned Armenians who denied Armenia's spiritual heritage and mission in world history and turned to the West for help and guidance. Zarian believed that Armenia, though poor and abandoned, still had the potential to regenerate.

Tatragomi harse (The bride of Tatragom, 1930) recounts, in verse, an episode that occurred during the atrocities in Sasun at the turn of the century. Hovan, a patriot and newlywed, joins the resistance fighters to defend Sasun against the marauding Kurds. He leaves behind his wife, Sana, who, after waiting for years, eventually gives in to the blandishments of a Kurd. Hovan's comrades in arms decide that Sana must die and that he should carry out the verdict. This book, published in Yerevan in 1956, raised sensitive social, cultural, and traditional issues.

Bankoope[5] *yev mamuti voskornere* (*Bancoop and the Bones of the Mammoth*, 1931–34), an extensive work, consists of impressions of Soviet Armenia interspersed with vivid images, encounters, conversations, philosophical reflections, and a search for the Armenian soul. Zarian attaches great importance to the distinctive characteristics of his country and its people, particularly to its language as a mode of thought.

---

5. Conflated form of *Banvorakan cooperative* (Workers' cooperative).

Long before Jean-Paul Sartre's[6] famous statement in October 1945 regarding *littérature engagée*,[7] Zarian spoke of the connection between a writer and the society in which he lives. Some of the most powerful pages of *Bancoop* deal with the role of the artist. Zarian views the artist as an "integrated man" for whom supra-personal problems are a personal concern: he doesn't draw a line between his individual existence and his community, since . . . he has completely and passionately identified himself with his people."[8]

Zarian's best known novel is *Nave leran vra* (The ship on the mountain, 1943). The author uses an interesting allegory to represent the enormous challenge of reviving Armenia in the years of the First Republic (1918–21). He likens the task to moving a ship overland, from the shores of the Black Sea to Lake Sevan, a scheme conceived by the hero of the novel, Ara Herian, an enterprising sailor. The ship gets stuck in the mountains of Kanaker. Another character, Mikayel Tumanian, builds a boat on the shores of Lake Sevan. The allusions are to the pre-Soviet and Soviet eras. Zarian's main concern for the revival of Armenia is to foster self-reliance and rally national elements, regardless of political persuasion. The book covers important Armenian realities of the day, and the author is not sparing of incisive cultural, social, political, and philosophical observations. It was published, with some revisions, in Yerevan in 1963 (followed by a Russian translation).

Kghzin yev mi mard (The island and a man, 1955), which Zarian called a novella, may also be described as poetic fiction or a series of impressions, ideas, emotions, and reminiscences based on a diary kept in the spring and summer of 1950, when Zarian and his wife were on vacation on the island of Ischia in the gulf of Naples. There they again met Lawrence Durrell, who wrote an ode and an essay, "Constant Zarian—Triple Exile,"[9] on Zarian.

In 1961 Zarian moved to Armenia for the second and final time. He was awarded a post at the Charents Museum of Art and Literature in Yerevan, giving lectures, writing, and preparing a projected edition of his collected works, which did not materialize. He died in Yerevan in 1969, about a month short of his eighty-fifth birthday.

---

6. Jean-Paul Sartre, French philosopher and writer (1905–80).

7. Literally, literature that is engaged or involved: literature that emerges from, reflects, and influences the issues of its time.

8. Kostan Zarian, *Bancoop and the Bones of the Mammoth*, ed. and trans. Ara Baliozian (New York, 1982), xviii.

9. Published in *Poetry Review* 43, no. 1 (January/February 1952).

Most of his works are still unpublished in book form, with the exception of *Bancoop*, which was published posthumously in 1987 in Antilias, Lebanon. There is a French translation of *Nave leran vra*, translated by P. Ter-Sarkissian in 1986. Selections from three of his books, *The Traveler and His Road, Bankoope and the Bones of the Mammoth,* and *The Island and a Man,* have been translated into English by Ara Baliozian and published in 1981, 1982, and 1983, respectively.

ISTANBUL[10]

The passage through the Bosphorus is as pleasant as browsing through a favorite book.

The crowded descent of wooden huts on the slopes of the hills. Green gardens and the melancholy monologues of solitary cypresses. The feminine sounds and rapid movements of countless boats and ferries. The proud stance of palaces and the epic row of mosques.

It is beautiful and grand.

Constantinople: a golden cloak fallen from the tormented body of history—multicolored stones, splendid ornaments, all mixed with bloodied rags, rubbish dumps, open wounds.

The marbles of Byzantium, the towers of Genoa, the brooding palazzos of Venice, Moslem crescents, grisly tragedies, starry nights, mournful dawns. Blood, diamonds, and the sparkle of blunted swords.

The Ottoman state is no longer. Yildiz Kiosk[11] is no longer hosting an international set of gamblers, swindlers, confidence men, and similar riffraff. In dance halls, the wives of the sultans are on sale; and the Turks are renouncing their religion and race.

The stench of stagnant pools of water, the noise of street vendors, the howl of journalists.

Byzantium has been transferred to Moscow.

Intimidated by the wrath of the world, Turkey is now cowering in some dark corner of Asia. Armenia has taken a backward step. And everybody is busy sharpening his knives.

---

10. Zarian, *Bancoop,* 18–22. Footnotes are by Baliozian unless otherwise indicated.

11. The Star Pavilion: Abdul Hamid II's villa situated on a hill in Beshiktash, a suburb of Istanbul.

The bells of the Kremlin can be heard around the world.

Where is the Mamikonian dynasty?[12]

Where is Emperor Basil, and Theodora, and Theophano?

In those days too slaughter and famine had scattered the Armenians all over the world. But lo, one day, a stout-hearted, virile man rose from under the rubble, took hold of his staff and, turning his face to the wind, strode toward the land of emperors. A knapsack on his back, his clothes in tatters, a heart full of daring, he crossed Constantinople's Golden Gate and, covered with dust, entered the city exhausted, went into the vestibule of St. Diomedes, lay on the floor, and promptly fell into a deep sleep.

Around midnight, the abbot of the monastery was shaken from his sleep by a voice calling to him: "Rise and open the gate of the church before the emperor!"

Immediately the monk rushed out and, seeing no one but that wretched Armenian on the floor, realized he had been dreaming and went back to bed. But soon that same voice rang out again and issued the same command. Again the monk dashed out and in despair returned to bed. In the deep silence, the voice rang out for the third time, louder than ever, and a mighty fist struck the monk.

"Rise," the voice commanded, "and go to the man lying in the vestibule, and invite him in. *He* is the emperor."

Startled and shivering, the monk went out and welcomed the stranger in, washed his body, gave him new clothes, and told him of his destiny.

"Behold Thy servant, O Lord," said the Armenian pilgrim. "Command and I shall obey."

"Thou art he who shall be emperor," said the monk bowing low before him.

The thought occurs to me now that there can be no nobler mission in life then to carry this message to the barefooted Armenians in the streets of Istanbul.

A nation that has severed its ties with its destiny and can no longer hear its command might as well be dead. When souls are deaf and minds extinguished, when life becomes a heavy burden

---

12. A noble Armenian family that produced several rulers, generals, and saints, the most famous of whom is the fifth-century AD *sparapet* (commander-in-chief) Vardan Mamikonian.

on one's shoulder, a mantle of mist descends on the horizon and men turn into orphans and mendicants, the heart darkens its sun, and the mind its daring.

"Thou art he who shall be emperor. . . ."

The ship reminds me a little of Abovian Street. Heavy, yawning, slothful, gloomy.

All of Europe now appears to me as an impoverished merchant. Its arrogance extinguished, its daring folded up like a handkerchief. Cowardly, without a dream, devoid of hope, its protruding, grocer's paunch stuck out, its breathing labored, its masts creaking like a village cart, it creeps along with eyes fixed on the next harbor, after calculating ten times the amount of expense required to cover each nautical mile.

Sacks of nuts, cackling hens crammed into cages, and a couple of cows with bewildered eyes.

Contraband. Silk stockings, little glass and metal trinkets, and rows of multicolored packages of cigarettes lined up on shelves.

The wrinkles on the seamen's faces are deep, their shoulders sagging, and when at dusk they try to sing, the melody emerges from their torn throats with a tired groan, like the unsuccessful flight of a bird with a broken wing.

Wads of Turkish liras and Greek drachmas held between prying, black fingernails and square, thick thumbs. Furtive, sly glances, hoarse voices, and loud, forced laughter.

This Europe has been waiting before Istanbul now for many days. On its gangway stand Turkish policemen spying on the void and the silence.

Below, lazily swaying row-boats that sell such things as cherries, *kasseri* cheese, *pasterma*,[13] *chiroz*,[14] glass ornaments, cigarettes, and postcards.

In order to bring in this wretched merchandise, the Russian passengers lower a bucket tied to the end of a rope and, dangling it before the nose of the hawker, they haggle for a long time over the price. Finally, Galata,[15] with its reek of cadaver burning on a pyre and the taste of sugar-coated ordure, is hauled up, and the boat continues to sway for hours on end.

---

13. Spicy and garlicky oriental variant of pastrami.
14. Small, dried mackerel.
15. A business district in Istanbul (the editors).

I reflect that, in the course of years, that reek, that insidious taste, and that lazy swaying of the boat, like a complex chemical solution, seeped into the very flesh of the people of the Orient and dissolved their souls, spun webs in their brains, and sealed their souls tight. The pincers of tyranny, opium, servility, the fatiguing breath of the *lodos*[16] wind, the ubiquitous presence of blood and death, the habit of covering up crime with a false adjective and smile—all these things combined to cast the human soul down the ladder of all moral values and into the infernal realm of the stomach and superficial sensations, where there is nothing but muck and mildew, and where life is constantly engaged in deceiving itself.

Today even the Turk is running away from Istanbul. He is moving his capital city deeper into the mainland, instinctively freeing himself not only from the meretricious stimulations of the Bosphorus, the shabby simulacrum of Parisian life, and the residues of European civilization, but also from its religious and linguistic mannerisms. He wants to return to his mountains and speak once more the rude and uncouth, but also simple and manly, language of his ancestors. He is hurling aside the gawdy overcoat spun with the artificial gold of Arabic, Persian, Italian, and French expressions, styles, and epithets, replacing it with the rough garments spun with the cotton gathered with his own hands, from his own fields.

And what about us?

There are those who grieve over Istanbul. They speak with the cadence of a decrepit island in the putrid Venetian lagoon,[17] where Péra,[18] Latinism, the graveyard of a defunct grammar and vocabulary sparkle with the glare of cheap ornaments, and under a fraudulently seductive facade, conceal an awesome intellectual and spiritual squalor. Beneath that impenetrable darkness we call "the light of Europe," death advances—as it did for the Armenian communities of Transylvania, Poland, and Italy itself.

How fortunate that our people back home, even our university students, cannot understand that language. There, our words are

---

16. The name of a humid, southerly wind which blows across the Mediterranean Sea.

17. San Lazzaro; a small island in Venice, home of the Mkhitarists, an independent religious order founded by Mekhitar Petrosian (1676–1749). See the overview at the beginning of volume 3 of the present anthology (the editors).

18. Business and residential district in Istanbul, present-day Beyoğ lu (the editors).

bound to mountains, fields, and rivers hurtling down ravines. Clear, bright, direct. As for Istanbul and its mentality: let it decay and slowly breathe its last. Istanbul fell because it could not create its own culture. History placed its merciless foot on that smeared mirror which reflected only the squalor of the West and the East, and with one kick smashed it to bits.

Constantinople became Istanbul. And when our Levantines[19] say "nation," "homeland," "language," what they actually mean is the filth and din of Galata, a piece of *pasterma,* and a slab of *kasseri* cheese.

THE MAN[20]

I am the man—with a valise, some books, an umbrella, and a trench-coat. Here I am.

Here I am at last.

It is Saturday.

The spring—as always in these parts—seems to be out of breath from haste. With vibrating wings open wide, it shudders, scorches, and scurries about noisily.

Here I am too, like the spring, as if on urgent business. But why? Who knows. That's the way it is with men. Even when they stand still, they pulsate with movement, rushing headlong on the whirling wheels of their minds and raging inner fires.

And behold the island.[21]

Pine trees, rocks, gardens. Like all islands around the world, this one too is a big boat of stone traveling through storms and centuries. And the boat's cargo is a dream from the depths of time, its nose against the unknown, its sails open wide, its heart restless.

Perhaps that is why, throughout my life, I have always sought out islands. Islands are uncontrollable desires and irresistible longings—secluded, solitary, detached from the rest of the world.

It is Saturday.

---

19. From Levant, a name applied to the countries along the eastern shore of the Mediterranean, including Greece, Turkey, Syria, Lebanon, Palestine, and Egypt.

20. Kostan Zarian, "The Man," in Ara Baliozian, ed. and trans., *The Island and a Man* (Toronto, 1983), 19–22. Footnotes by Baliozian, unless otherwise indicated.

21. The island is Ischia, at the northwest entrance to the Bay of Naples.

At last I am here.

The men of this island are mostly fishermen, sailors, and vintners with bushy eyebrows and an intent, far-off look in their eyes. They speak with sudden bursts of emotion. Even the swallows are impetuous here. They invade the skies in enormous flocks. They soar noisily and with the speed of arrows.

I greet this world. The yellowish church on the edge of the short peninsula, and all the other churches whose towers jut out from the huddled mass of houses, and the sea that prances off on blue steps, the hills, the big mountain.

The cone of the volcanic mountain dominates the island.[22] Its heavyset body, which is the island itself, is anchored in a centuries-old and adventure-filled history. Its present life, however, is mired in obsolescent customs and senile traditions. Faithful to these traditions, and to its filth and squalor, its epidemics and secret vices, it lies idly under the blistering sun, avoiding all unnecessary exertions. It lives a slow, passive, lethargic existence. But dig into the earth and you will uncover layers upon layers of history: tombs filled with pottery, weapons, and an endless succession of peoples and races driven here from the four corners of the sea.

I stand on the beach and gaze into the distance.

Where am I going to stay? I don't know yet, and I don't much care.

On the beach some women are washing their clothes. Once in a while they stop and with arms akimbo exchange a few words; they laugh, after which they return to their work. Around them a few children are throwing pebbles into the sea. The women scold them with hoarse, stentorian voices.

Seated in a fishing boat, an old man is smoking contemplatively.

We chugged along for quite some time to reach this island. At the harbor on the mainland,[23] we were told it wasn't far—"Over there, see?" they said, pointing a finger. And yet, we had to travel for hours and hours.

The small propeller of the white steamer churned the indigo sea furiously. Covered with countless buildings, the hills on the coast piled skywards. In the distance, a tall mountain kept us in its sights.

22. Monte Epomeo, rising to 2,581 feet (788 meters). An extinct volcano.
23. Naples.

The air was clear and bright. Like big sea-birds, boats with white and tan sails floated on the waters.

When we reached the end of the bay, the sea became agitated as if it had suddenly remembered a disturbing thought. It fretted and fussed, got upset, ran excitedly to and fro, grabbed the vessel with powerful hands, rocked it, after which it calmed down, lay on its back, and with hands folded behind its neck, stared at the sun.

Island mountains are invariably crowned by the ruins of old castles. Silent, brooding, grim, they tower like petrified ghosts, waiting for the dialogue of the winds. Colossal sagas from the past perch on their massive ramparts and groan.

When we approached the first island (Procida), our steamer awakened and tooted with a ridiculously incongruous thin whistle. A pompous song with an affected delivery blared forth from its loudspeaker. The cluster of men and women waiting on the pier below stirred and began to walk up the gangplank.

Like rickety props on a stage, the brightly colored houses all along the waterfront seemed to be made of papier maché.

The faces of the people were interesting to look at too. A confusing and complex mishmash of races. Big, swollen eyes, as shiny as olives, with slightly upturned ends, gazing with the regal dignity of Egypt's Nefertiti. Heads like those unearthed from the sands of Ur in Mesopotamia. Bodies with rounded, sloping shoulders.

It was eerie, viewing that superimposition of ghosts. A familiar experience. A quick glance at a man's face suddenly reminds me of a distant world where I have been at one time and I am glad I am there no longer. In such moments, I seem to catch a glimpse of beckoning seawaves from the other side of my subconscious.

We left, veered a little, and were confronted with this island.

Misak Metzarents

(1886–1908)

The poet Misak Metzarents was born Misak Metzaturian in the village of Binkian, near the city of Akn (Egin, presently Kemaliye, Turkey). It is said that he was a shy, sensitive, and quiet child, who was enchanted with the beauties of nature. He attended the local elementary school for two years and, beginning in 1894, when the family moved to Sebastia (Sivas), he spent another two years at the Aramian school there. In 1896 he was enrolled as a boarding student in the Anatolia College of Marzovan; during this time (1896–1901) he began to bloom as a student, and his poetic abilities became manifest. In 1902 the family moved to Constantinople, and Misak continued his education at the Kedronakan lycée. In 1905 he was forced to discontinue his studies because of his rapidly worsening tuberculosis. He died on July 4, 1908, at the age of twenty-two.

He began writing in 1903, and his early essays were published in various journals, including *Masis, Hanragitak* (The encyclopedist), and *Arevelyan mamul* (The eastern press). He collected his early student poems in a handwritten notebook titled *Babakhumner* (Heartbeats). He is best known, however, for two collections of poems, *Tziatzan* (The rainbow) and *Nor tagher* (New songs), both published in 1907 with an interval of only a few months. His entire literary output consists of over 130 lyric poems, about ten prose poems, a few short stories, and a couple of articles defending himself against his critics. He may also have attempted a few translations in verse of works by foreign authors.

Metzarents redefined Western Armenian poetry around the turn of the century. The kind of poetry promoted by Mkrtich Peshiktashlian (Beshiktashlian, 1828–68) and Petros Durian (1851–72) a generation earlier had already faded in popularity, and a group of traditionalists were trying to impose themselves upon the public. But this young poet from the provinces sang a new song that enthralled audiences with its delicate human emotions, love for mankind, admiration of the splendors of nature, and dreams of a harmonious world.

Some critics have tried to draw a parallel between Petros Durian and Misak Metzarents, who were both aware of their impending fate and died at the same age and of the same disease, albeit a generation apart. There was, however, an enormous contrast between them. Whereas Durian rebelled against his fate and used his poetry to express his bitterness in the most forceful manner, Metzarents had a gentle and resigned nature and did not allow the thought of premature death to color his poetry. On the contrary, until the end of his days he sang about the ultimate harmony between the human soul and nature.

Although Metzarents's poetry bears some traces of classical romanticism, it also shows signs of symbolism; a number of his poems evoke subtle relations and affinities between sound, sense, and color. His poetic imagery is exquisite and his language refined modern Western Armenian, enriched with new compound words of his own making.

Metzarents's poems went through numerous editions after his death. A few individual poems have been translated into English, French, German, Russian, Italian, and Spanish. His published prose writings and manuscripts were collected by Toros Azatian (1898–1955) and published in 1934 under the general title *Voski arishin tak* (Under the golden vine arbor).

A Winter's Serene Night[1]

To your kiss my window is open, oh Night.
Allow me to absorb all your glittering hues,
The soggy magic of your chilly dews
And the soft-flowing milk of your voluptuous light.

---

1. Misak Metzarents, "A Winter's Serene Night," in *Selected Armenian Poets*, ed. and trans. Samuel Mkrtchian (Yerevan, 1993), 114–15.

Oh Night. So serene, so wonderful, and whole.
Flow into my heart like an enchanting tide,
Pour out drop by drop the honeyed sprays you hide
And spill them softly into my warming soul.

Deceitful voices ceased. I would never falter
To drain your precious nectar greedily;
I wish the hours of the day would never bother me,
That I could ever kneel beside your altar.

Oh I would kneel there and never would complain.
Saying a thousand prayer to your power;
As long as your sparkles come down like a shower
My eyes forget the nadir once again.

Oh fascinating Night! Receive me to your bliss.
Receive me, oh most mystical calm.
Receive my breath and my imploring psalm
And my soul's burning, everlasting kiss.

My chamber is filled with memories so bitter.
The unrestrained lechery of yesterday's breeze:
Still the wrinkles are mourning with the trees
The fury of its kindness and infamous glitter.

Rush in furiously. Flow, spread, roll and creep
into my chamber as to console a mourner.
Let your saintliness spill into each corner
That I might awake from an ancient sleep.

To your kiss my window is open, oh Night.
Allow me to absorb all your glittering hues.
The soggy magic of your chilly dews
And the soft-flowing milk of your voluptuous light.

NAMELESS[2]

Oh wild flower, what's your name?
Oh you, standing in the shade

---

2. Ibid., 116.

Of a deep green briar fence
That will never, never fade.

Oh white flower, what's your name?
Tell me, who is missing you?
Tell me, don't you tremble gently
When the breeze is kissing you?

Oh proud flower, what's the name
Of the fairy gone away?
She just passed you by and vanished,
Leaving here a gentle spray.

Do you know, oh flower, the name
Of the tremble that just came?
Of the voice that calls my name?

THE HUT[3]

I wish I were a hut
On a road in some field,
Or a hut below some hill—
A wayside place for travelers
Alone on their way.
I wish I could call my concern
To the harried travelers,
And on the winding golden road
Make them welcome,
Smoke billowing from my chimney.

I wish I could give comfort
To weary travelers,
And in exchange for their greeting
Do them a thousand kind turns.
Yes, do a thousand good turns,
The fire logs crackling,
The crop of the fertile fields,
All the fruits of autumn
And milk and honey and wine.

---

3. Misak Metzarents, "The Hut," in *Armenian Poetry Old and New*, ed. and trans. Aram Tolegian (Detroit, 1979), 244–45.

I wish I might listen till daybreak
To their praise of the fire,
The song of the traveler at evening,
And, asleep, wrapped in dreams,
I wish I could send off at daybreak
The nightfall comer.

And I wish I might hear at daybreak,
Cordial and happy,
The praise of one who comes at nightfall,
And, at daybreak, see
And wonder all through the night
About the departure of the one who comes at evening.

And patiently all through winter, too,
I wish I might stand along the roadside
With my arms outstretched wide
And in the stance of a beaming beckoner,
Offer with warmth and ready cheer
My fatherly invitation to a frostbitten traveler—
I wish I could always be taken for
The one who beckons travelers to his door.

Oh, if only I could be, could ever be
On a road in some place,
At the foot of some hill,
So that for those who travel
I could be the waiting hut.

PRAYER FOR THE NEW YEAR[4]

Give me, my God, that kind of happiness
that has no self. Let me gather it like flowers
in other people's eyes.

Give me, oh Lord, an impersonal joy
which like a child's sparkler tints
the onlooker's face.

4. Misak Metzarents, "Prayer for the New Year," in *Anthology of Armenian Poetry*, ed. and trans. Diana Der Hovanessian and Marzbed Margossian (New York, 1978), 130–31.

Give me, oh Lord, an impersonal joy
to hang like ribbons braided with bells
on each door I pass.

Let me build altars out of words
of those I love and echo them
like cymbals of brass.

Give me an impersonal joy
to share like the stars dispersed
across the skies.

Let it be happiness
that does not drown laments
of those in pain

and not the kind of joy confined
within *my* self alone.
Let every loaf upon my plate be blessed

with a crossed pair of joys.
And like the sun going west
let me spread sunlight, Lord.

Let me lower it on waters
as one lowers nets and plant it
in earth's furrows like a plow

and like the rain
shower it
over the thirsty crowd.

And having found it, let me stay
the hunter of the ideal. Give me the grace
to know its true worth

like the sailor on the life raft.
Let me gather it from the souls
of common and uncommon man

and give it back.

1907

Aharon Taturian

(1886–1965)

Aharon Taturian (who wrote under the single name Aharon) was born in Ovacik, a village in Nicodemia (Izmit), in Turkey. After attending the village school, he continued his education at the Mkhitarist school in Constantinople and the Murat-Raphaelian school in Venice. Upon graduation he chose to become a schoolteacher, a profession he practiced for most of his life.

His literary contributions to *Bazmavep* (*Polyhistor*), *Azdak* (The monitor), *Azatamart* (Freedom fight), and other periodicals started as early as 1909. A few years later, in 1914, he became a member of the literary movement centered around *Mehian* (Temple), a magazine founded by Daniel Varuzhan (1884–1915), Hakob Oshakan (1883–1948), and Kostan Zarian (1885–1969). Their purpose was to start an Armenian renaissance, waking the nation from centuries of slavery and darkness to reconnect to the great pre-Christian past, and encouraging it to stand on its own feet and not tolerate tyranny, whether from its own corrupt leadership or the Turkish government.[1]

As an officer in the Ottoman army, Taturian was preserved from the purge of April 24, 1915. In 1822 he went to Bulgaria to resume his

---

1. Shant Norashkharian, "Taniel Varoujan," http://www.umd.umich.edu/dept/armenian/literatu/varoujan/html

education. After a couple of peripatetic moves in 1928, he ended up in Paris, where he lived alone until his death. He gave up his former ties with the Armenian press in the Middle East in order to retain his links to the greater Armenian collectivity.

Taturian published three volumes of collected poems during his lifetime: *Magaghatner* (Scrolls, 1938), *Pohemakank* (Bohemian songs, 1939), and *Sosyats antar* (Forest of plane trees, 1948). Two other volumes appeared posthumously: *Yerkner Yerkir* (The earth was in labor, 1957) and *Karmir avetaran* (The red gospel, 1959). His poems echo the anguish of human souls and lay bare the state of the poor in a world of contradictions. As a result of his personal life and the tragic destiny of his people, He expressed a dark pessimism.

Taturian was a careful poet—extremely particular about language—sometimes to the point of exaggeration. He was a staunch aestheticist and handled his language artistically, choosing vocabulary to reflect his feelings and ideas accurately. Occasionally he even invented his own words. He was almost the last representative of the aestheticist generation.

ANCIENT LONGING[2]

I trod all foreign thoroughfares
Without asking where they came from, where they led;
Sometimes I picked thorns, and sometimes roses,
But I could not find the road that led to you, Armenia.

I drank from all foreign fountainheads,
Without asking whence the waters hastened;
I quenched my heartache with their dew,
But I could not find your fount, Armenia.

I endlessly perused all foreign books
Without asking what they had to offer me;
Closing them, I sometimes wept and sometimes laughed,
But I could not find a way to read Armenia.

I took to heart all foreign sorrows
Without asking why they throbbed from time to time;

---

2. See Aharon Taturian, "*Hin Karot*" (Ancient longings), *Sosiats antar* (Paris, 1949), 33. Translated by the editors of the present anthology.

I ignored them, or mourned them one whole day,
But I could not forget your woes, my dear Armenia.

MY SHOES[3]

On the streets of my city and the trails of my village
We walked tirelessly, with no complaints, needless to say.
With dust on your brow and sparks in your eyes,
We obeyed each summons to misery together.

Endlessly, from morn to night you wrote upon the ground
The fiery story of my life and chanted all its verses.
Perhaps now no one else can recognize your soundless words,
which twist about my trembling legs like ivy.

Over your dark abyss is stretched the dream—a delicate
    thread—
And I a skilled tightrope walker, practiced and proficient.
Unhappy shoes! You must know that roads still lie ahead.
And one day, when we separate, I'll weep with all my heart.

---

3. Taturian, "*Koshikners*" (My shoes), in *Pohemakank* (Paris, 153), 149. Translated by the editors of the present anthology.

Hakob Mndzuri

(1886–1978)

Mndzuri was born Hakob Temirchian (Demirdjian) in the lesser village of Armtan, west of Yerznka (Erzincan). After a short period of schooling in his native village, he finished his elementary education in Constantinople and then attended Robert College. In 1907 he returned to his birthplace, but seven years later, on the eve of World War I, he moved back to the capital and remained there.

His first story was published in *Masis* in 1906. He contributed short stories, fables, pastoral scenes, and memoirs to local newspapers and periodicals, as well as to Armenian journals published abroad. The outstanding characteristic of his writing is its pastoral nature, and he has a very special place in Armenian provincial literature.

Mndzuri's stories were collected under the following titles: *Kapuyt Luys* (Blue light, 1958 and 1968); *Armtan* (Armudan, 1966); and *Krunk, usti kugas* (Crane, where do you come from? 1974).

We conclude this biographical introduction in Mndzuri's own words, from an interesting autobiographical sketch and self-assessment he wrote in 1957.[1]

---

1. See *Hamaynapatker hanrapetakan shrjani Istanpulahay grakanutyan* (Panorama of Istanbul Armenian literature during the republican period) (Istanbul, 1957), 43–44. Translated by the editors of the present anthology.

✦

"I was born on a Thursday: October 16 in the year 1886, in Armtan, in the province of Yerznka (Erzincan); the village had seventy houses. There were two Armtans: the big one was ten minutes away, and had three-hundred homes. I come from the little one. It was on the left bank of the Euphrates, in other words, opposite the Mndzuri Mountains. Akn was the nearest town. Akn was the end of the world for us village folk, with all its inviting, colorful riches. This province is still vivid in my mind, down to the last detail of its villages, appearance, population, mentality, psychology. . . .

"I completed my primary education in the village school. When I came here to Constantinople from the village, I knew more French than anyone who finishes the fifth grade nowadays. Here, after finishing elementary school in Galata, I attended Robert College until the end of my second year. The schools I attended had no reason to be proud of me, and I have no fond memories of them either.

"Schooling did not form me; I formed myself. I did not get very much out of school: in fact, nothing. I took care of my own *montage*. My passion for reading, for reading everything, did that. My tools were adequate. My French was very good, and my English was not bad either. Fortunately, I went to Robert College when I was a young boy. In the college library and in the library of the Armenian students' association I found what I wanted. There I became acquainted with writers from Eastern Armenia and abroad. There I read the Russian masters, in English translations.

"I like writers who caress my soul. Writers whose words I have long been waiting for. Regardless of genre: poems, stories, novels, reviews, true stories, or intellectual, philosophical pieces. Any work can intoxicate me, provided it contains the alcohol I crave. My first literary work was a story—or a sketch, as we called it at the time—from village life, entitled "*Hars u kesur*" (Bride and mother-in-law. It appeared in *Masis* in 1906. Up to the armistice that ended the First World War, everything I wrote was *l'oeuvre de jeunesse* (the work of youth). It was only after that that I really began to write.

"I have written about three things: the village, my times, my reflections. I have written most about the village. I have presented it through fables, pastoral pieces, and short stories. In my pastoral works I take an overview of the patrimony—a field, a valley, a vineyard, a mountain chain, a river—and I try to picture it as clearly as possible, as if I have seen it only yesterday. Or a summer rain, an autumn or summer evening, something that I know well as it existed there: how they used to speak, act, do things, a donkey, a piece of stone, a road, a man. I talk about them, I describe them, I elaborate on them. All I want is to render the exact moment accurately and bring it to life. It is not photography. I live through them.

"Besides the village there is our times: my times as a writer. I write about everything that has happened around me. Then come my reflections, in which I talk about my opinions of my times, about this or that event, about what I have seen. In all I have written 125 stories, 24 pastoral pieces, 15 fables, and 37 reflective pieces. My writing is my autobiography. I am in my every story and in everything I say. I have lived through it, and with it.

"I thought of collecting my writings together into books, but the books did not materialize. I leave them where they are: in the dailies, in the magazines."

THE FIRST BORN[2]

My mother used to tell me over and over again, "Oh, you . . . couldn't you have waited a little longer. . . . Couldn't have come in the evening and be born? You came to this world on the ground, in the field. Woe to me, what am I supposed to do now?

"Now what should I do, this is my firstborn, I don't know how to handle it. I have brought no swaddle with me, not even a piece of cloth, I said to myself. While you were still wet I placed you on the grass and ran for the bread bag. I took the bread out and wrapped the bag around you. It didn't work. I took my jacket off and covered you with. It didn't work either."

"Where, where was I born?" I asked.

"In the mountain," she said, "in the valley of the blue gorges below our fields."

"How could you manage carrying me all that distance?"

"Don't ask me," she used to say and go on, "I thought you might not survive, you may die. Should I have abandoned you at the mountain? I decided to take you home no matter what. You were born during the grass harvesting time, during the week of Lent of *Vardavar* (feast of Transfiguration), the month for plowing,

---

2. Hakob Mndzuri, *"Arjinek"* (The firstborn), in *Krunk usti kugas* (Crane, where do you come from?) (Istanbul, 1974), 103–9. Translated by Ardashes Shlemian and edited by the editors of the present anthology.

the hay and the vineyards. Those three things had to be done during that month. We had to plow the field. There ought to be someone beside the plowman to help clean the reeds from the bundles and throw them away, otherwise the reeds would grow again. If plowing were not done how could we sow in autumn?

"As always early in the morning, on the day you were born, everybody was out, gone to the fields. My brother-in-law and your father left for the fields. 'Bride' said the granny, 'our folk are going to gather grass, you too go with them, to the mountain and pick the grass. Pick the grass at the valley near our field and on the mountain by the blue gorge. Let's be the first to be there. Take bread and your sickle, and set out. I bring the donkey over in the afternoon, we load and we come home.' 'Done! I'll go,' I said.

"I was pregnant with you; it was the final weeks. 'Anyway, these are not your final days,' said your granny, 'It will not happen today or tomorrow, you have one week and even more.'

"I walked up to the mountain. My eyes tickled under the sun. It was all white bryony all the way up to the top. As if they were sown. Those were not only the kind of bryony at the Our Brook and Our Akn valley. Of divers colors. White, green, yellow, crimson. Most of them were crimson as if an embroidery covered the mountain's surface. There were also some foxtails. The tufts' touch on your fingers was so delicate, like the down of a partridge, like silk.

"I pulled a pile. As I was pulling a second pile my back started aching. I thought it would pass. Yesterday also I had pains but they went away . . . they come and go, I said. They didn't go away. I stopped picking. I put the sickle aside. I sat down. I looked around for our people. They weren't around. I went down. Across, over the hilltop I noticed people. . . . I thought to cry out for the Kurdish women. I decided to wait a little more. I felt giddy. The valley darkened. What's this, what's happening to me, I said. You came into the world. Your umbilical cord broke off. You became detached from me.

"What should I do now? Where do I go? I exclaimed. Now, what can I do alone? I asked myself. You were on the ground. There was no wrapper, not even a piece of cloth to cover you with. It is not going to survive, it will die, I said again in my mind. I got up, I left you. I reached for the bread bag, poured the bread onto the ground, also the salted berry of terebinth and walnuts I had taken as it was the Lent of *Vardavar*. I took the bag and wrapped you with it. You made a sound . . . you cried. It is not dead. . . . It is alive, I said to myself.

"That didn't help. I took off my jacket and packed you in it. I had no strength left. I lifted you up and took you in my arms. I started. I had no hope for you. But still I kept walking. Were you a girl, or a boy? I was too afraid to check. A horseman passed by me He had a white silken turban on his head. Was he from Hasunavan? I changed my course in order to avoid him.

"I took the direction of Yerku Karuk up the hill. I did not want anybody seeing me. No strength was left in my arms. I sat down. Oh, my God, oh Mary, give me strength, I said. You were silent in the packing. What happened, is it dead? I wondered. I was afraid to open my bundle and see. I stood up again. I said, even if I die, no matter what, I'll walk. I started toward Yerku Karuk, from there to the Dervish slopes, to the stables and then to the valley, passed by Teghutsi's tall walnut tree, to the threshing-floor of the barn, to the doorway, and the door. It was shut. Teghutsi, the neighbor next door, saw me.

"Bride, weren't you gone with our folks to pick the grass?" she asked.

"I did," I said. "After leaving our field behind, I separated from them. I left the reaping half done. My cockerel was born. I took him and brought him home. I am afraid to look to see if he is dead or alive.

"She became perplexed. She ran to me. 'Woman! What are you saying?' she yelled. She took the bundle in her arms and took me to their home. 'Come on, come on! Let's hurry up!' she said. She spread a haircloth on the floor. She covered it with a sheet. She warmed up sand and spread it upon the sheet. She undressed me. She laid me down. I do not know what happened thereafter.

"In the afternoon, your granny takes the donkey out to the doorway. 'Certainly she has done with picking by now,' she says to herself and tries to mount it. She is too old. She starts following the donkey. Whenever you mount the donkey and do not jostle with your heels and let it go by its whim, do you think the donkey will move? It is an ass; does it walk? It takes two steps and stops.

"Slowly, at the donkey's own pace finally they make to the field. She starts wondering. She walks down to the valley. The harvest is bundled but there is no one around. She sees the sickle left on the ground. The breads, the berries, and walnuts are all scattered on the grass. The bag is missing. She is puzzled. 'I wonder if something happened to her?' she asks herself. She goes to our folks and asks, 'What happened to our bride, do you know?' 'She was picking grass. For a while we left for the other side of the mountain and when we came back there was no sight of her.'

"She approaches the Kurdish women up on the summit and asks them but they are not much help either. With the donkey in front of her, your granny decides to return home. She reaches Khachi Tar and notices Arkhan of Khnkents in their broad-bean field.

"'Arkhan, have you seen our bride passing by?' she asks him. 'No!' he says, 'I saw her this morning together with your people on their way to pick grass. Why? What happened?'

"'Women! I sent her down to Kapuyt Kapan to pick grass. Then at noon I would take the donkey over, to load it together and come home. So I was there now; the bride was not there in the valley, down under the field, neither up at the mountain. She has picked the grass, has some six or seven bundles made. The sickle is left there on the ground, the walnuts and the breads spread over the field. I have a thousand and one things passing through my mind!'

"Your granny returns to the village and comes home. She is informed of the birth and the whole story."

My poor *mayrik* (mother) had not been able to open her eyes for two days. She was not even able to give birth in her own home. She had slept in the home of our folks. As she took a deep breath and exhaled they all said: "Oh! Let the mother get well and get on her feet. If the baby boy dies, so what! It's the first, let the mother bring another."

For two days Tprents's bride, and the bride of our folk had come to breast-feed me. Guess what! I was a guzzler from the first moment on. Whoever crammed my mouth with her breast, I clung to it and sucked with great appetite.

The third day my mother learns that I was not dead, I was alive. That I was not a girl either, but a boy!

Hakob Antonian

(1887–1967)

The poet and translator Hakob Antonian was born in Constantinople. After graduating from Robert College he became secretary and translator for Henry Morgenthau, the US ambassador to Turkey. He later moved to the United States to continue his studies. In 1921 he graduated from New York University with a degree in law.

Antonian contributed to various Armenian periodicals: *Shant* (Lightning), *Biuzantion* (Byzantium), and *Paykar* (Struggle) among others. His first book of poems, *Biureghner* (Crystals), was published in Constantinople in 1921. His second book (1960) has the same title; it contains both poems in rhymed metrical verse and prose pieces. Antonian also translated works by Shakespeare, Hugo, Lamartine, Verlaine, Baudelaire, and Shelley.

Not much has been written about him, despite his many poems, prose pieces, and translations. He died in New York City.

MOMENTS[1]

I live moments, moments furious and feverish,
When, like a horse, free of reins and foaming,

---

1. Hakob Antonian, *"Paher"* (Moments), in *Biureghner: kertvatzner, tarkmanutiunner, ardzak ejer* (Crystals: poems, translations, prose pages) (Beirut, n.d.), 22. Translated by Arminé Keuchguerian and edited by the editors of the present anthology.

I want to run with unrestrained desire
Through the path of my existence, undaunted and without fear.

I respect these moments of great exertion
—Moments of sound, electrifying activity—
Which gently rock the basic blunted reflex
Of my wicked struggle in the times gone by.

I live moments, moments of mute meditation,
When, like a river, majestic and frothy,
I want to flow undaunted from the depths,
Through countless complex courses of my covert thoughts.

I love these moments of sublime reflection
—Moments of priceless, luminous contemplation—
That make us human beings all unlike
The irrational creatures in the universe.

I also live moments, moments of satisfying sensations,
When, like a flower, fragile and delicate,
I inwardly shudder—sometimes without stirring—
Aflutter at even the slightest hint of a breeze.

Oh, I adore these moments of deep emotion
—Sweet moments, teeming with tenderness.
It is through them that life, so full of lament,
Acquires its sober shades, great value, and its grace.

1912

The Waves[2]

Standing on the shore, I dreamily watched
The waves, which with harmonious pace
Roll in and then succumb to the pebbles of the beach,
Dissipating there in endless heaps of foam.

I wondered why they rush to reach
The brink that is their final end.

---

2. "*Aliknere*" (The waves), in ibid., 35–36. Translated by Arminé Keuchguerian and edited by the editors of the present anthology.

Why do they quit the so-dynamic sea
And rush to land to be so quickly dashed?

I pondered why they wish so avidly
To put an end to their swelling, uncurbed passage.
Do they not hear the anguish of their dying friends
Moving the heart with such deep sympathy?

Abandoning myself to these most mournful thoughts,
I gloomily reflected on the foaming waves,
When suddenly, out of their surging spew,
There seemed to come a voice, which thus addressed me:

"Wayfarer, is it fair to censure us
When, driven on by a relentless power
That wishes us to meet a mandatory death,
We hasten to the shore, to meet our fatal end?

"Don't you humans also, just like us,
Walk steadily and with the self-same haste
Toward death and the brink, the bosom of infinity,
There to meet the certain, constant end of life?

"Why don't you stop, and why do you produce
New offspring who repeat your actions,
Set off once more on the same dread course
Toward death and the brink, the bosom of infinity?"

The voice from the foam by then had ceased to speak,
When I, in a daze and groping clumsily,
Wandered about, along the shore of the sea,
Repeating to myself: "Why don't we stop?"

1913

Stepan Zorian

(1889–1967)

Stepan Zorian, writer and novelist, was born Stepan Arakelian in Gharakilisa (now Vanadzor, in Armenia) and received his education in the local Russian school. In 1906 he moved to Tiflis, where he worked as a journalist for *Surhandak* (The dispatcher, 1909–11) and *Mshak* (The tiller, 1912–19). In 1919 he settled in Yerevan, where he occupied a number of posts, such as editor-in-chief of the State Publishing House (1922–25), literary adviser to the Institute of Cinematography (1930–34), secretary of the Writers' Union of Armenia (1950–54), and other cultural, administrative, and political positions—both locally and in some all-union organizations. In 1965 he was elected to the Academy of Sciences of the Armenian SSR and became a member of the editorial board of the Soviet Armenian Encyclopedia.

His first collection of short stories appeared in Tiflis in 1918 under the title *Tkhur mardik* (Sad people). This collection brought a new quality to the genre by examining of the inner life of ordinary people who are depressed by the harshness of their daily lives. He characterizes his heroes not through their physical actions, but through their psychological and moral lives, which the author depicts with acute details. His subsequent volumes of short stories, such as *Tsankapat* (The fence, 1923), *Paterazm* (War, 1925), *Krak* (Fire, 1927), and *Arajin orer* (First days,

1930), deal with a wider variety of issues and characters: good and bad, honest and dishonest. Clashes occur because of avarice and dishonest deals, and sometimes very insignificant issues have serious consequences. Regardless of the subject matter, the prose is charmingly lyrical.

Zorian is considered one of the pioneers of Soviet Armenian literature. His earliest works from the Soviet era are the two novellas *Heghkomi nakhagahe* (The chairman of the revolutionary committee, 1923) and *Gradarani aghjike* (The girl at the library, 1925), and the novel *Amirianneri entanike* (The Amirian family, written 1921, published 1963), in which fathers are pitted against sons and the traditional against the progressive, in a revolutionary setting. These three works are based on the dramatic events of the years 1918–21. The female characters in particular are adorned with the virtues of morality and nobleness.

In the postrevolutionary period (the 1930s) Zorian concentrated on the theme of constructing the country. His main heroes are builders and laborers, who parade through books such as *Vardadzori komune* (The Vardadzor commune, 1930) and *Spitak kaghake* (The white city, 1932), in the latter of which he creates ideal "socialist" characters and emphasizes the ideological and psychological changes that affect their attitudes and views about life. One of his better works is *Mi kyanki patmutiun* (The story of a life, 2 volumes, 1935–39), which paints a picture of a particular era of Armenian life in all its moods, colors, and contradictions.

During World War II Moscow tacitly encouraged patriotic literature, and Zorian, like Derenik Demirchian (1877–1957), seized the opportunity. He began his famed trilogy of historical novels, *Pap tagavor* (King Pap, 1944), *Hayots berde* (The fortress of Armenia, 1959), and *Varazdat* (1967). These novels are based on the agitated political conditions of fourth-century Armenia, reevaluated from a socialist point of view. *Hayots berde,* which comes first in historical subject matter, encompasses the time of Arshak II, King of Armenia (350–368), who, in collaboration with Catholicos Nerses the Great, initiated numerous social and cultural reforms. He was, however, firmly determined to rally the feudal lords, some of whom were rebellious, others self-serving, around the central power, and he was very harsh with those who did not comply. *Pap tagavor* covers the time of King Pap (369–374), Arshak's son, who carried out his father's policies and fought vigorously to curtail the immense power and possessions of the Church, which, by that time, was itself acting like a feudal institution. The third book, named after King Varazdat (374–378), advocated self-reliance. In their historical content, analysis, and reinterpretation of events, their lively characters, flowing prose, and literary artistry, these volumes—particularly the first two—are among the best of their genre.

Stepan Zorian was a prolific writer. He also has to his credit a number of translations, the most notable being Tolstoy's *War and Peace* and works by Turgenev (1818–83), Garshin (1855–88), Stefan Zweig (1881–1942), and others. Most of his works were published several times and also translated into foreign languages during his lifetime. He died in Yerevan. An annual state prize for translations to or from Armenian, established in 1980, was named after him. His *Yerkeri zhoghovatzu* (Collected works), in twelve volumes, was published in Yerevan from 1977 to 1990.

GRANDFATHER AND GRANDDAUGHTER[1]

Grandfather Yeprem was very, very old.

For a long time now his eyes no longer saw, he was hard of hearing, and his head bobbed continuously, like a ripe sunflower. Also his cold, parched hands trembled, so that whenever he ate his soup or drank his milk, the food always dropped onto his white and somewhat greenish beard. Besides this, Grandfather Yeprem could not walk for long. When he felt like amusing himself in the front garden, he called his granddaughter, Astghik, and with her help, stick in hand, he took a slow walk under the trees.

Grandfather Yeprem was very, very old.

At home they did not like him very much and did not give him everything he wanted to eat. Yet he loved all of them, and above all he loved the youngest, Astghik. He told her tales, fables about other boys and girls, and explained why the stars fell from heaven. Astghik worshiped him. She grasped him by the hand and led him among the trees, and she told him how every tree was growing and how the strawberry bushes were thriving. But Astghik was very sorry that Grandfather could not see all this; she pitied him and loved him all the more. One thing, however, did not please her at all: Grandfather used to get sick very often. And now for three weeks Grandfather had been ill.

For the past few days he had wanted to go out to amuse himself in the sun, but Grandmother would not let him go: she objected that

---

1. Stepan Zorian, "Grandfather and Granddaughter," in *Great Armenian Short Stories,* trans. Sarkis Ashjian (Beirut, 1959), 86–91. Revised by the editors of the present anthology.

he would catch a cold. Astghik was astonished that Grandmother so cruelly refused Grandfather. And one day Grandfather went out unexpectedly. Astghik remembers that day very well. It was a Sunday. Her mother and grandmother had gone to church, and Father was downtown. When Astghik came in from the street, she saw him sitting on his bed, groping for something with trembling hands.

"What are you looking for, Grandfather?"

"My clothes," he answered, trembling.

She gave him his pants, jacket, cap, and shoes. He dressed with shaky hands, grabbed his walking stick, went out to the verandah, and sat there on the bench, in the sun. His face seemed very strange to her that day. She looked at him and wondered why he was so distracted and what he was listening to in that unusual way. And Grandfather really was listening to something. A few years of blindness had made his hearing keener, so he distinctly heard the hum of the bees in the air, the merry rustle of the poplar leaves, and the solemn chime of the church bells, which reverberated in the air and then stopped and fell to the ground. The sound of the bells revived dead memories in Grandfather Yeprem's soul, and he pictured himself as a child, on his way to church with his father on Easter Sunday. Then he saw himself, as if in a vision, as young and healthy, walking to his wedding with a young, beautiful girl on his arm. And finally he saw himself as a grown-up man, mowing grass in the field with a sickle. Remembering all this, Grandfather smelled the new-mown grass, opened his mouth, and breathed deeply. Astghik, who had been watching her sick grandfather all this while, was rapt in sudden wonder at the sight of her grandfather's face drawn in exaltation.

"Astghik?"

"Yes, Grandpa?"

"Take me to the orchard, will you?"

"What about catching cold?" she asked, looking into her grandfather's blind eyes and wavering.

"I won't catch cold, my dear child; let's go."

Grandfather and granddaughter entered the orchard. His hand in his granddaughter's, he followed her and asked about the trees: whether they had all bloomed.

"They have, Grandpa, they have."

"Can you see fruit on the trees?"

"Yes, Grandpa, a whole lot."

"That's good, my darling daughter, that's very good."

They continued talking, and arrived at the end of the small orchard, from which a gate opened onto the street. Grandfather stopped there and breathed again.

"Let's go home, Grandpa: you may catch cold and Grandma will be angry then."

"No, darling, I won't catch cold," he reassured her, and took another deep breath. After standing like that for a while, Grandfather asked: "The field is not far from here, is it, Astghik?"

"No, Grandpa, it isn't."

"Since it's near, my child, kindly take me to the field; you can pick yourself some flowers."

Astghik was delighted. "Yes, Grandpa, there are so many lovely flowers in the field."

A few minutes later the villagers looked on in great wonder from their yards as the sick Grandfather Yeprem, holding his granddaughter's hand, walked to the field. For a long time they walked through the fresh grass. Grandfather staggered at every step but never tired, and Astghik, holding his hand firmly, led him and directed him all the while: "This way, Grandpa. There's a stone right in front of you, Grandpa. Try to step over here, Grandpa."

And the decrepit man, obedient to his granddaughter's voice, carried out all her directions and followed where the girl led. After walking a long way, he stopped and asked how far they had come.

"We're at a wonderful spot, Grandpa: so many beautiful flowers out here," Astghik answered.

Grandfather breathed deeply and asked again: "The forest is nearby, my dear, isn't it?"

"Yes, Grandpa, it's very close; do you see it, Grandpa?"

Grandfather raised his eyes and listened without replying. He wanted to hear the forest's murmur. And the whisper of the forest clearly reached his ears. It reminded him of the steady rumble of the rivers. How amazing the murmur of the forest is, thought Grandfather. It rustled the same way when he was a young man, it whispered that way when he was a full-grown man. It will be the same forever! Now he sat on the green grass with a sad sigh, and Astghik began to pick flowers and chase butterflies.

Sitting in the same position, he continued to listen. Now, along with the rustle of the forest, his ears clearly made out the gurgle of the brook. How many well remembered times he had sat having lunch on its banks during harvest season! The twitter of birds caught his ears: larks were singing in the meadow. He heard the sweet rustle of the grass and the fresh breath of the bushes swaying in the wind, and from far away came the tinkle of the church bells again . . . it mingled with the harmonious rustle of the forest. How magically the forest rustles! He wanted to pray, but no words of prayer came to his mind. After listening to those friendly, familiar voices, he bent over and bowed his head to the ground. For a long time he kissed the ground covered with fresh grass, and tears he could not control flowed abundantly down his cheeks. Yet a little, yet a little more, and he fell down on the grass, all his forces spent. After a little while, when Astghik returned to her grandfather with a huge bunch of flowers, she was very puzzled why her grandfather had lain down that way. Why on earth was he sleeping like that, she thought, and she called his name out loud. But Grandpa did not respond. Then Astghik went closer to him and moved his hand: "Grandpa, hey, Grandpa!" she repeated, stroking his cheeks and head, "get up, let's go, Grandpa. Grandma will be angry. . . ."

But Grandpa did not wake up. And Astghik went on shaking his hand and his head, begging him to get up. But Grandpa did not make any movement. Realizing he had no intention of walking home, she decided to run home all by herself and tell them that Grandpa was asleep and would not wake up!

But Grandpa was not sleeping. They went and found him dead in the field.

When Astghik heard this, she could not believe he was dead. She could not believe that they would take him away and he would never come back.

Who then would sleep in his bed, she thought. Who would put on his clothes?

And when the priests took him to church for the funeral service the following day, Astghik hoped he would return. But now darkness had fallen and still there was no Grandpa to be seen. And when they closed the house doors at bedtime, Astghik grew extremely sad and wept bitterly under the quilt. She wept and pondered hard on why they had closed the house doors. Don't they know that Grandpa could return? Perhaps even now he's back and is waiting anxiously at the door! She wept and all the while wondered who would lead Grandpa to the fields again. Don't they know that he can't see and his feet may stumble against a stone or he may walk into the pools of water?

Ah! Would that a good boy or girl, thought Astghik, would lead her dear Grandpa there. . . .

Hakob Siruni

(1890–1973)

Hakob Siruni (Jololian, also spelled Chololian) was born in Adapazar, a town near Constantinople. After completing the local school, he successively attended the Esayan and Kedronakan schools in Constantinople and studied law at the State University (1909–13). He was imprisoned for a brief period as an "undesirable," but he managed to escape the arrest and massacre of Armenian intellectuals on April 24, 1915, by concealing himself. In 1922 he moved to Bucharest, Romania, and settled there.

His early writings consist of poetry and prose, some dramatic pieces, essays, and translations of foreign literature, and appeared in various periodicals.

In 1914 Siruni and Daniel Varuzhan (1884–1915) founded a yearbook of literature and art called *Navasard*,[1] which gathered around it some of the best intellectuals from both Western and Eastern Armenia. The first number, comprising 340 pages, was the only one to see the light. Type was set for the second number, but before press time it was destroyed in the horror of 1915. In 1923 in Bucharest, Siruni attempted to revive this review under the same name and to maintain the same high

---

1. The first month of the Armenian calendar.

standard with the collaboration of writers who survived the genocide. Unfortunately, it ceased publication in 1926.

After the First World War Siruni became actively involved in the diminished community of intellectuals in Constantinople, carrying out organizational work and editing papers. After moving to Romania, he became very active in the Armenian community and expanded his journalistic activities by founding, editing, or contributing to a score of papers in Armenian, Romanian, and French. He established close ties with Nicolaï Iorga (1871–1940), historian, scholar, and political figure, who was also well versed in Armenian studies and translated a number of works from Armenian to Romanian. For many years Siruni taught Armenian language (classical and modern) and history in Romanian and other East European institutes of research, and brought archival material to light.

He published an impressive number of books, all in Romanian: *A Chronology of Armenian Cultural History* (1935–41), *The Unknown Raid of a Group of Turkish Bandits in Romania in 1769* (1940), *Romanian Princes at the Sublime Port* (1941), *A Chronological History of Armenians from Ancient Times to 859* (1942–43), *Armenia As Seen by Turkish Geographers* (1965), and *The Tanzimat and the Armenians* (1966). He founded and edited a quarterly journal of Armenian studies (1935–38), also in the Romanian language, which later (1941–43) became a yearly publication. He translated works by Daniel Varuzhan, Misak Metzarents (1886–1908), and Hovhannes Tumanian (1869–1923), among others, into Romanian, and, reciprocally, translated into Armenian the works of Romanian authors such as Mihail Eminescu (1850–89). His *Ruminahay kronikon* (Romanian-Armenian chronicle) (1933–34) and *Kaghvatzkner Kamenitsi hayeri zhamanakagrutiunits, 1430–1611* (Excerpts from the chronology of Armenians of Kamenets, 1430–1611) (1936) are valuable historical works. Siruni's major historical work is *Polis yev ir dere* (Constantinople and its role), in four volumes (1965, 1970, 1987, 1988), which is still unrivaled both in terms of coverage and scholarship.

Along with the Romanian scholar Vlad Banateanu, Siruni was cofounder of the Society of Orientalists, where he headed the department of Armenian studies and of which he became the honorary president in 1971. He was one of the editors of the society's journal, *Studia et Acta Orientalia.* He was also very active within the Armenian community of Bucharest, as president of the *Komitas* musical society, founder of the Armenian House of Culture, and in other capacities. He maintained very close ties with the Soviet Republic of Armenia, particularly between 1965 and 1971. He died in Bucharest at the age of eighty-three.

THE CARAVAN[2]

We once asked the dervish why he never went into the mosque. In fact we had never seen him go into the building. He used to stand in the courtyard of the mosque and sell water. On days when the *Mevlûd*[3] was read in the mosque, he did not often look into the mosque, which was completely filled with worshipers. He made fun of those who came rushing up late to the mosque, afraid that Allah would distribute His bounty only on those who were already inside and that they themselves would remain empty-handed.

On that morning the *Mevlûd* was to be read in the mosque. All the good Muslims from the surrounding villages thronged into our mosque in order to be present at the reading, which was to commemorate the souls of those who had fallen on the battlefield. The war on the *giaours*[4] had ended recently and there had been many victims from our village, the son of Murtaza Agha among them. It was Murtaza Agha himself who had asked the muezzin to read the *Mevlûd*. He had also invited the good Muslims of the surrounding villages to the ceremony. Who could refuse Murtaza Agha's invitation? He was the richest man in all the villages. He used to send special telegrams to the mighty Sultan of Turkey. Furthermore, he was also a hero, who had fought for the glory of Allah in four major wars.

The dervish was in the courtyard of the mosque when people arrived for the ceremony. When Murtaza Agha solemnly walked in, the dervish was busy feeding bread to the dogs and he did not bother to move. Only the beggars who were lined up before the gates of the mosque opened their palms. Murtaza Agha distributed silver coins from his purse to the prostrate wretches at his feet.

The *Mevlûd* began. The dervish was playing with his dogs and talking to them when we approached him, and one of us asked him

---

2. Siruni (Hakob Chololian), "The Caravan," in *Great Armenian Short Stories,* trans. Sarkis Ashjian (Beirut, 1959), 43–54. Revised and abridged by the editors of the present anthology.

3. A poem written by Suleiman Chelebi that depicts the birth of the prophet Muhammad. Also a religious meeting held in memory of a deceased person, during which the *Mevlûd* is chanted.

4. Term applied by Muslims to nonbelievers, especially to Christians.

why he did not go into the mosque. The dervish knitted his brows, as he usually did when people disturbed his peace.

"My children, Allah is not in the mosque. He has never been inside it. The mosque was built by men, who thought that Allah would come there if they only called for Him. My children, I don't enter the mosque because Allah never goes there. And nobody knows where Allah is."

He cut short his talk. The muezzin was up in the minaret and called loudly, "*Allahu akbar:* God is great. . . ."

The dervish laughed. "They have not seen God, but they measure His greatness all the same."

And when the muezzin had ended his call, the dervish told us the story of the caravan.

♠

"Once the wise men of Baghdad summoned a great meeting to define the nature and properties of Allah. The question had been heatedly discussed that year in the *medresseh:* the Muslim theological school. They wanted precise knowledge of God's exterior appearance and nature. The discussions often ended in violent quarrels, because they couldn't convince each other. The matter was brought to the Caliph of Baghdad. He ordered the wise men of the city to convoke a great meeting to solve the problem. The quarrel in the *medresseh* had upset the entire country.

"When the gates and the windows were closed, an awful silence reigned in the hall. A wild crowd waited outside in the streets, to hear the verdict of the wise men.

"They too had violent discussions. The first speech was made by Hoja Nejibellatif. His fame in the metropolis of the Caliphs was great. Everybody bowed in reverence when he broke the silence:

" 'The face of Allah is like the sun, and He lets His light shine on great and small, poor and rich, good and evil alike. He belongs to all. There is no need to torment the soul with fatigue and suffering, since the sun sheds its bounty upon all alike.'

"Then another hoja got to his feet and said: 'Allah is like a lion. He is good to those who recognize Him and bow before His might. But He is unforgiving when people are proud in His presence. It is foolish to mock the power of the lion and disregard his will and desires.'

"Another one rose and prepared to speak, when all of a sudden a pitiful, wretched old man, who had squeezed himself into a corner of the hall, gave out a loud laugh. 'You stupid men, what makes you think that Allah even exists?'

"Everybody was horror-stricken, but they could not silence this hunchbacked old man whom no one knew.

"The wretched old man shouted again: 'There is no Allah! Men have invented Him to frighten and confuse each other. Men have created that fairy tale to frighten the devil that is within them, because they are unable to vanquish it through their own power.'

"A new horror crept into the hearts of the wise men. Why was this horrible old wretch cursing God? A whisper ran through the hall. No one could muster enough courage to expel him from their midst.

"The wretched old man went on, in a voice that trembled with emotion: 'You have come here to define the features of Allah— before you have found Him. In vain have you gathered here. You, the silliest men in Baghdad, you, you, you cannot create an Allah!'

"The wise men heard him in silence, waiting for him to finish. Yet he did not stop speaking. He told them the parable of the caravan, and they all listened to him, holding their breath.

♦

"'Centuries ago, people were afraid of being alone in this immense world. They had no force with which to contend against the powerful elements of nature. The thunder that rent the clouds, the tempest that played havoc with what they had made and planted, and the flood that swept away their villages filled their hearts with terror. Men suffered and were unhappy because they were not the masters of their days, and they were horrified at uncertainty of the morrow.

"'Once plague visited the villages. People fled to the plains in terror. They gathered together and tried to find a means of salvation. Who sent them those miseries? Who poured the flood on their villages or carried off their dear ones? They resolved to find that stranger, and they gave the unknown the name Allah. So the caravan marched on, in search of Allah.

♦

"'They walked for many days. Their souls were laden with sorrow, but nature continued to mock at their sorrow. They had fled the plague, yet other diseases harvested their ever-increasing number. From every village they passed a new caravan joined theirs. One night they had not enough energy left to go on. All through the day they had struggled against a tempest that had chased and buffeted them. Fatigue soon closed their eyes. Their slumber was plagued by nightmares, and when everyone was thus suffering even in their dreams, they heard an awful cry. A child woke up the caravan with his shouts. He had not been able to sleep, and he had given himself over to contemplation of the stars, trying to count them. Then all of a sudden he had seen something in the shadows, something unexplainable, gigantic, and horrible. It must have been Allah Himself. And he shouted to everybody. They all got up, with eyes still heavy from their troubled sleep, and knelt facing the direction that the child indicated. A sort of pleasurable terror seized them all. What sacrifices did they not promise in return! And what happiness: they would have no more sorrows in the morning! This important vigil lasted until morning. And when the sun rose, they raised their eyes to look on Allah. But Allah was not there. Their disappointment made them seethe with rage, and they beat the child to death: the poor thing had taken a good-for-nothing mountain for Allah.

⚴

" 'They walked on and on for years, and every day fresh caravans of disappointed people joined them. The worldly order had brought nothing but misery to men. Everyone grumbled at the unending calamities, and they wanted to show the Unknown their wounds and ask for pity.

" 'They continued walking, weary and brokenhearted. The more years passed, the more anguish and misery thrived on earth and the more the number of the caravans increased. They were all looking for Allah, Who would heal their wounds. One day the earth shook violently. The mountains belched forth fire and the earth split open in many places. Everyone thought it was the end of the world, and they all called out Allah's name for help.

" 'They walked day after day and night after night, but they could not find Allah. They often had the illusion that at last they had found Him. They thought they heard Allah's voice when they heard thunder. Who would bring peace to their parched souls? Who would take pity on this caravan, which moved on year after year in the hope of finding happiness?

" 'Once the wise and the old of the caravan held a meeting to reach a conclusion. All the discussions proved abortive and vain. They failed to find the means to ease the wounds of the caravan, and they hadn't the faintest idea where help would come from. So they concluded that their pains had been sent to them by a distant Allah, of whom they neither knew the name nor the dwelling place. They all knelt down to pray to that Allah, that He would be so kind as to judge that they had gone through enough sorrow and suffering.

" 'And that caravan still marches on. It has walked for centuries and still it has not found Allah. The unknown Allah always hides His face, and people utter His name in vain, walking on, day and night. Only once did they believe that they had found where He was. An infant had seen the throne upon which Allah sat in a dream. When they reached the place indicated by the infant, they saw that the throne was vacant. You simpletons! You sit here and argue about Allah's attributes and nature. There is no Allah. Men have not found Him yet!'

♦

"When the old man finished his story, the wise men of Baghdad bowed their heads. They were silent and bewildered. No one dared break the silence or meet his neighbor's eyes. They were ashamed. Allah had been destroyed in their souls, and they were afraid. The unknown force which reigned in their earthbound souls was no longer there.

"The crowd down in the streets began to grow restless. It was already night, and the wise men had failed to announce their decision. The Caliph grew angry waiting for their answer.

"The old man noticed the poor wise men, who had no strength to move from their places. Allah had left their hearts vacant. He had blown away all their knowledge. And now they looked at the old man, hoping that he would show them a way out, a new light. How could he bear to leave them in such blindness?

"The old man was moved; he pitied them. He regretted his lack of consideration. He had thought that he was bringing them the light, but all he had done was to extinguish the dim glimmer that glowed in their souls. He stood up. At the sight of his wrinkled face, the hundred wise men of Baghdad felt an awful shudder. He walked peacefully to the door and then he said to them, calmly and kind-heartedly:

" 'Get up and set forth in search of Allah at once. Let what the caravan suffered be a guiding example to you. Unless your passions take you where Allah has hidden Himself, you cannot find Him. Cleanse your souls. Renounce the world and set forth after you have done so. Only on these conditions will Allah agree to remain on His throne when you reach Him!'

"The old man closed the door behind him and departed. It was only then that the wise men of Baghdad thought to ask his name. But the old man did not return, and they could not learn his name. But tradition says that he may have been Allah Himself, because the crowd that waited outside did not see him leave the hall. The only thing they saw was that the door opened and a luminous shadow glided out and disappeared.

"The meeting of the wise men soon ended and they broke up. The crowd outside was howling and waiting for their decision. And when the wise men began to depart with heads bowed in shame and silence, the crowd became enraged with fury and lynched several of the wise men. As for the Caliph, when he heard the news, he was infuriated. Tradition says that he hanged the wise men who had managed to escape the wrath of the crowd. He had them executed outside the walls of the city, in the early hours of the morning."

⚓

The dervish breathed deeply. He had ended his story. And he added:

"Now do you still insist on asking why I never enter the mosque? I don't enter it because Allah is not to be found there. And He will never enter it unless someone carries Him in, by bearing Him in his soul. Nations and peoples have come and gone, and they have all had their Allahs. All of them have passed away—both the peoples and the Allahs they created. They died because men had made their gods out of their own flesh and had put their own hearts into the breasts of their own Allahs. And nobody carried Allah in his soul."

⚓

The dervish was silent. The *Mevlûd* was over and people started coming out of the mosque. We took to our heels, because we were afraid of being seen with the dervish. We never returned to the courtyard of the mosque again.

Hrach Zardarian

(1892–1986)

One of the significant figures of post-genocide Armenian literature, Hrach Zardarian was born in Kharberd (Harput). His father was Ruben Zardarian (1874–1915), another noted writer, who was massacred on the eve of the Armenian genocide. As a result of his father's wandering life, Hrach Zardarian lived in many different cities and was educated in several distinguished Armenian schools, including the Yesayan and Kedronakan schools in Constantinople, the Sanasarian in Erzurum, and the Gevorgian in Etchmiadzin. After graduating, he moved to Paris, where he audited courses in literature at the Sorbonne; he graduated with a degree in dentistry from the University of Paris.

Zardarian is remembered for his two novels, *Mer kyanke* (Our life, 1934) and *Vorbatsogh mardik* (Orphaned men, 1954). His numerous short stories are scattered through the Armenian periodic press and occupy an important place in modern Armenian literature. In his novels and short stories he depicts the life of the Armenian people, with their tragedies, anxieties, passions, old and new morals, and the like. In *Mer kyanke* he describes the decaying social, moral, and family values of the new generation through the stories of two families and two protagonists. *Vorbatsogh mardik* is about the psychological struggle of Armenians in the diaspora, unequivocal failures, decadence, national degeneration, and so on. Zardarian's message is that Armenian life is on the road to deterioration. The scenes he paints are among the most moving in post-genocide Armenian literature, expressed in masterly literary language. His short stories also reflect the moral and social perceptions of the generation of Armenians who ended up in Paris: some were shocked by what they find there, others were startled, many indifferent, but all of them struggled. . . .

Zardarian's other major work, *Zhamanak yev khorhurtk iur* (Time and its mysteries, 1955), deals with philosophical, ethical, social, and cultural questions. His stories and philosophical writings make him an important figure in twentieth-century Armenian diaspora literature.

Grandmother and Grandson[1]

"Get up and get dressed; we're going to town," commanded his grandmother, prodding Avetis's shoulder with the tip of her foot.

Her grandson, who was not yet completely awake, was so angry he wanted to shout.

His grandmother had been treating him like that for quite some time now; it was getting worse with every passing day. A sudden fright seized Avetis. He jumped to his feet and buttoned his short trousers. His grandmother rushed in again, pulled the jacket he was about to put on out of his hand, and threw it aside.

"Didn't I tell you we were going to town? Wear your new clothes."

Avetis put on his sailor suit. He waited, with his hands in his pockets, in the courtyard. He raised his head every now and then to see if his grandmother was coming. The tip of his nose and his chubby cheeks shone, and a lock of wet hair drooped over his forehead. His face wrapped in concentration, he stood like a miniature philosopher. "It's always like this. . . . They make me wait in the courtyard for hours. 'Hurry up! hurry up!' but they're never ready."

He suddenly caught sight of his mother at a second-floor window, looking at him with pale eyes. "It's been a week," he said to himself, "why won't they let me into my mother's room?"

---

1. Hrach Zardarian, "*Mamn u tore*" (Grandmother and Grandson), in *Ardi Hay grakanutiun* (Modern Armenian literature) (Paris, 1939), 101–13. Translated by the editors of the present anthology.

For a week the house had been full of whispers, the atmosphere rather uneasy; and no one paid any attention to him. As for his grandmother . . . the only thing she had not done yet was beat him, but her pushing and shoving were gradually getting worse. There it was; it was coming. She grabbed his hand and walked with long strides. Avetis doubled his pace until they got to the train station. His grandmother had not said a word the whole way.

He thought it over, again and again. His stomach hurt, but he did not want to moan. Just before they got off in Paris, his grandmother handed him a parcel and said, "Take this. No, in your other hand. When I make a sign, give it to the man."

"What man?"

"You'll see."

"What kind of sign, Grandma?"

"I'll give your hand a little squeeze. Don't start up with more questions, Avetis."

He was really tired when they got there. There was a sweet smell in the room. There were big paintings on the walls and a huge chandelier hung from the ceiling. It had large glass crystals, like the one in the church. He had never seen such a beautiful living room—except in *Madame*'s house: her living room was even bigger and more beautiful than this. He had thought they were going to *Madame*'s place. But here, who knew what would happen? *Madame* always kissed him and gave him chocolate, and last time she even put a banknote in his pocket—money, a large sum. Later his grandmother took the bill away from him, but that did not matter: he still liked that place very much.

What was that little boy over there in the corner doing? He was trying to put his index finger on top of his middle finger. In a second Avetis put his four fingers on top of one another, thrust his thumb under them, and held out his hand so the little boy could see it. His mother gently turned the boy's face away. Avetis's grandmother pinched his bottom and immediately made him sit next to her on the chair.

They waited a long, long time, leaning their backs against the wall. When drowsiness overcame Avetis—he was so bored—he slid slowly down the wall, rested his head on Grandma's foot, and went to sleep. But suddenly, as if pulling a tooth, Grandma yanked on his arm, jerking him to his feet in a single movement. The maid opened the door and a man came in, like a berserk goat rushing out of the barn, his hands in the air and holding a pen and a letter. His eyes seemed at odds with each other: one looked right and one looked left.

"What do you want? Who are you? Who's this?" he fired off the questions at the boy's grandmother.

"Doctor, please, I beg you; you can save us—help my daughter. She's melting away like a candle before our eyes."

"What daughter? What candle? Who are you? What do you want?"

"My daughter, my daughter. I think Mr. K. has written to you about her; my daughter: send her somewhere . . . before it's too late—a sanatorium."

"Somewhere, somewhere. . . . Mr. K. has written. . . . He writes. Poets write; they don't know what else to do. A poet . . . of no consequence. . . . It's easy to say 'Send here somewhere.' Have you got money, cash? We need money. There isn't a *centime* in the association's coffers."

"Doctor, please, please! I throw myself at your feet: save my daughter; you're our only hope! As long as we live we'll pray that the sun will shine on you." Grandma was nervously squeezing Avetis's hand, so the boy thought it was time, and decided to present the parcel ceremoniously to the doctor. His grandmother realized his mistake, and pushed the parcel and her grandson away.

"I've never received anything but ingratitude for everything I've done for Armenians. They're bunch of dirty, ignorant liars; crooks: the whole lot of them! They shame me in front of strangers. They don't have the least bit of *éducation* at all. You'd think all of them had come down out of the mountains or escaped from asylums! I'm ashamed to admit I'm Armenian, to tell you the truth."

"My dear doctor, in the past we were also. . . ."

"I know, I know, I know. . . . In short, there's no money, no money. Ah!"

This time Avetis thought it was definitely the right moment: Grandma had squeezed his hand again. He took the parcel from under his arm and held it up to the doctor, who was crumpling the poet's letter of recommendation in his hand. Again Grandma swept both the little parcel and the little boy away with a single movement.

"Doctor, I kiss your feet! you are the glory of our nation. . . . Let me come and be your servant for the rest of my life. . . . Rather than watch my daughter. . . ."

"There's no money, woman! do you un - der - stand? There's no cash, no money!"

"Look here, doctor. . . ."

Avetis was shaken. His eyes were glued to his grandmother. It seemed to him that Grandma changed suddenly. She held her head erect, her body swelled up, her voice grew terribly hard.

"Look here doctor, do you want me to raise my skirt and start begging. . . ."

His grandmother could not continue. It was impossible for Avetis to tell what she was thinking. He did not know why she had bowed her head and was staring at the floor. Meanwhile the doctor . . . in silence . . . pretended to read the wrinkled letter. . . .

Then Grandma began to wipe her eyes. In a completely different voice, her first voice, she said:

"We have sold everything we had that was worth even a *centime,* doctor, even my engagement ring, which I didn't touch even when we were starving. My son has been unemployed for the last eight months. They kicked him out of *Régie* Renault. It's the same with my two nephews. They live with us; they're orphans. There was only my daughter to support us: she sewed all day and all night to bring home enough money for a dry crust of bread, and now she also. . . ."

"What do you want me to do, woman? Do you think I have time for such stories? Everyone who comes here begging tells similar stories. . . . *Voyons, voyons* a bit of *éducation.* . . . Leave your *adresse* here; I may send you Dr. Gavazian, but I don't promise anything. You mustn't count on it."

These last words sounded as if they came from the other end of the corridor, because the doctor, after tossing the wrinkled letter in the direction of the kitchen, left the room as he spoke.

It was dark. At the station Avetis bumped into and was bumped by the rushing crowd, but he managed to keep up with his Grandma. She was silent, weeping ceaselessly, wiping her eyes, and blowing her nose. Mrs. Hakobian, their neighbor, saw them come into the compartment and sat beside Grandma. She received no reply to all the questions she asked. Only once Grandma exclaimed:

"Our great men! May God save us, even Abdul Hamid's officers were more. . . . It took an entire day to see one great man. . . . Now, my daughter—who knows?—may. . . ."

♠

Avetis lifted his head and saw a huge car coming his way, filling almost the entire street. All at once he recognized it, and ran inside. They did not have enough time even to plump up a cushion before the *Madame* came in, accompanied by a doctor. How he had changed. . . . It was *the* doctor! You would never know it was the same man. His eyes were even busier: one darting to the left and the other to the right. . . . Smiles and sweetness dripped from his face.

"Come here, let me have a look at you," he said to Avetis, and began to twist his ears lightly, "What's your name?"

"Avetis Kuyumchian. My mother and grandmother call me Avetik, and my uncles Avto."

Well, let me see, what nationality are you? *Attention!* If you answer correctly I'll give you this package. This package here."

The *Madame* smiled quietly, her lips glowing like honey.

"I'm Armenian."

"Eh, bravo! bravo! the package is yours. You see, you should always remain Armenian and be proud that you're Armenian. You belong to a great nation. Never forget it, whatever you do.

The doctor looked from Avetis to *Madame* as he talked. Noticing she was looking at a large photograph, he added in a low voice, "I think he was a revolutionary. He was killed, wasn't he?"

"He was an honorable man," *Madame* replied gently.

After a short pause Avetis spoke up, his eye shining, glazed with emotion. "This was for you," he said to the doctor, and gave him the parcel he had carried through the city for an entire day.

"What's this? Let's see!" said the doctor with exaggerated surprise as he opened the package. "Oh, how nice! But you should give it to *Madame;* she was the one who brought you the toys."

Avetis blushed, took back the delicately embroidered tablecloth, and presented it to the *Madame*. She sat Avetis on her lap, kissed him on both cheeks, and whispered sweet words in his ears, even sweeter than the stories his Grandma used to tell him when she was in a better mood and used to kiss him more than his mother.

"Who made this? There is so much work in this. . . ."

His mother had embroidered it; who else? This was nothing: she had embroidered much bigger, more beautiful ones than this, his mother.

Ha! Wouldn't he like to go and spend a few weeks at *Madame*'s house and become her little boy? There he'd have a room full of toys. The ones she had brought with her were nothing—a train on long tracks, a bicycle, blocks for building castles, a big horse, a sleigh. . . . Sweets and chocolates too. Did he want to become her son? If he wanted to, in a while he could hop into her car with her and go back to Paris. . . . No! No, Avetis did not want to.

He had not been allowed to see his mother's face for several weeks. His uncles no longer lifted him onto their shoulders; no one spoke a word to him; it was as if he no longer lived in the house. Grandma did not talk to him: no more stories, figs, or almond sweets. Still Avetis did not want to leave the house, to go away; he did not want to be *Madame*'s boy, no matter how frightened he was as he now pressed and glued himself against Madame's bosom.

The doctor came down and took out his watch; there was a little commotion. Then, a bit later, the doctor and *Madame* got into the car. The engine coughed, groaned, growled, and they left.

⚓

The next day, almost at the same hour, another big automobile stopped in front of Avetis's door. This one had big red crosses on its sides. Avetis was walking around the car and examining it when a nurse came out of their house and signaled to the driver. Despite his limited French, Avetis understood very well what the nurse said to the driver: "She won't make it to the hospital," she said, shaking her head ominously. Avetis did not know exactly what was up, but the car, the nurse, and her words really frightened him, and his heart started beating faster and faster.

He heard somebody in the house call his name. He ran in. His grandmother was pacing the floor like an enraged bull in a circus, then she turned around and ran to him. Trouble, big trouble. Then—oh, what a novelty!—he was allowed to see his mother! One of his uncles took his mother by the shoulders and sat her up in the doorway. His mother fixed her eyes on him and looked long. Her face was as white as the newly painted house across the street. And she had become smaller, a lot smaller. Her black eyes had become feverish, restless, like a pair of black mice. Unable to stand it any longer, his mother beckoned their neighbor, Mrs. Hakobian, to come closer and said something to her. The neighbor asked the nurse something and she agreed. Suddenly, three people rushed over to Avetis and in a second removed his shoes and socks; then, lifting him like a feather, they carried him over to his mother. His mother summoned all her strength, took one of his feet in her hands, and planted her jaundiced lips on the sole. And what a kiss it was. . . .

Avetis felt as if he would never be able to free his foot from his mother's grasp and lips. It lasted a long, long time. . . . Finally the nurse interrupted and separated them. But his mother succeeded in making her agree to let the boy stay in the doorway a little longer. From around her neck she removed the chain with its little heart-shaped pendant set with little stones. She gave it to their neighbor, Mrs. Hakobian, who turned to the nurse and whispered a question. The nurse replied: "You'll have to boil it for ten minutes," then she repeated, not in her usual voice, "ten minutes."

Then they led the boy away from her. Nobody paid any further attention to him. And when his grandmother saw them carrying the stretcher out the door, she suddenly ran up, gesticulating and making strange noises like a madwoman, and threw herself over the stretcher. Four or five people could barely control her and take her back into the house; she was like a frenzied cow that refuses to step across the threshold of the slaughterhouse.

The doors of the car with the red crosses on its sides slammed shut, roared, growled, and left.

That evening Avetis sat on the carpet for a long time. Later that night he was frightened awake by a dream. He had felt a strange pain in his chest, as if a nail had been driven into it. He rubbed his eyes for a moment and went into the other room, to be close to his grandmother. Grandma had fallen asleep sitting down. She was snoring horribly, at the same time making strange movements in her sleep. From time to time a sudden sharp movement caused her to bang her head on the wall. Her hair had fallen over her face, making her look like a madwoman. Avetis felt so bad, so very bad. He looked around him and asked: "Where have they taken my mother?"

His grandmother did not answer. She did not know whether these sounds were those of a buzzing fly or her grandson.

"Where have they taken my mother?" he asked again, more alarmed.

Grandma did not even bother to open her eyes.

"I want to know: where have they taken my mother?" he asked again, shouting and tugging on Grandma's skirt.

His grandmother woke from a shadowy nightmare; her eyes wide like those of a cow, she slapped Avetis across the face.

Such a terror fell on her grandson's heart that all others, all the previous terrors of his life put together, came nowhere close to what he felt now. He covered his face with both hands and ran from the room. He went into the next room and quickly went to bed, with his clothes and shoes on. In order to muffle the sound of his voice, he hid his head under the covers. He cried and cried, but his tears did not soften his resentment, which had no limits. That is when he began, over and over, as solemnly as if pronouncing a verdict, to repeat: "Tomorrow I'll go to *Madame* and become her son."

Matteos Zarifian

(1894–1924)

Lyric poet Matteos Zarifian was born in Constantinople, in the suburb of Gedik Pasha. He first attended the local Armenian school, then the Perperian (Berberian) school, followed by the American school in Partizak (Bahçecik), Robert College in Constantinople, and back to the Perperian, which he completed in 1913. His wanderings from school to school were the result of his rebellious nature and his critical attitude toward favoritism. After graduation he taught for one year in Adana (Cilicia), where early signs of tuberculosis were discovered. He spent some time in Lebanon, hoping that the moderate climate would benefit him. At the outbreak of the First World War in 1914 he was conscripted into the Ottoman army, and shortly thereafter was confined to a military hospital. In 1919 he worked as an interpreter for the British Army, stationed in Constantinople, and taught for a while at the Perperian school, his alma mater.

Up until 1919 he was known for his athletic abilities; no one suspected that he had the makings of a poet. However, the publication of his first collection of poems, *Trtmutian yev khaghaghutian yerger* (Songs of sadness and peace) in 1921, followed by a second volume, *Kyanki u mahvan yerger* (Songs of life and death), a year later, earned him fame. His romantic verses struck a responsive chord, particularly in the hearts of the younger generation, and they maintain their appeal even today. Zarifian's literary career was the shortest among Armenian poets: from 1919 to 1923. He died of tuberculosis in 1924.

Zarifian's poetry displays a distinctly different attitude and philosophy from that of Petros Durian (1851–72) and Misak Metzarents (1886–1908), who both died of the same disease and at a similarly young age. Durian's attitude was that of a rebellious spirit fighting against death; Metzarents, in contrast, charmingly evoked nature, sound, and color, and displayed boundless sympathy for mankind. Zarifian's approach was entirely different: he is reconciled with the idea of death; he is sad and quiet, but not hopeless; he lives with the memories of past loves, and dreams of loves that he knows will never be realized. He has no bitterness, only the melancholy of sadness: as he says in one of his poems, "I have no shore to land on; the game of life is lost." Kevork Bardakjian expands on this: "Death overtook Zarifian before he could refine his poetic gift into a distinct style. His romantic poetry is intensely subjective and revolves around unrequited sentiments in matters of the heart, mental anguish, unfulfilled dreams, and a yearning for tranquility. He faced death with courage, although in many poems sentimentality and self-pity are a touch too obvious."[1]

In addition to his two collections of poetry, which comprise some 140 poems, Zarifian left unpublished poems, a diary, and letters that were collected and edited jointly by his sister (Siran Seza) and Vahé Vahian and published in his collected works in Beirut in 1956. His poems have been published in various editions in Constantinople (1921, 1922), Aleppo (1946), Jerusalem (1951), Beirut (1956), Yerevan (1965), and Antilias (1990).

THE CRAZY BOY[2]

1

When we sat down quietly, face to face,
That crazy boy—whose countenance in the evening
Seems to be a melancholic poem that pours into your heart—

---

1. Kevork B. Bardakjian, *A Reference Guide to Modern Armenian Literature, 1500–1920* (Detroit, 2000), 162.
2. Matteos Zarifian, "*Khente*" (The crazy boy), in *Trtmutyan yev khaghaghutyan yerger* (Songs of sadness and peace) (Constantinople, 1921). Translated by Abraham Terian.

That crazy boy, looking into my eyes,
Told me:

2

—Ah, the story of my soul, see, how simple it is!
That morning I had returned to the woods
To pick wild flowers.
For when at night beneath the moon I sit to dream,
I always hold a flower in my hand
To pluck the petals one by one.
So, that morning, I had returned
To the deep and dark woods
To pick wild flowers;
That's when I found her. . . .
Ah, you'll ask, "Who was she?"
Wait a minute, I'll tell it all.

3

That girl, bending over the pond,
A sweet song on her lips,
With a twig in her hand was drowning a butterfly.
I had not seen her face.
How I pitied the feeble insect!
Its wings were so white,
As though it had a virgin's soul. . . .
So, I went quickly to the pitiless stranger,
And when I reached her
—"Please," I said—
My whole face, I'm sure, had turned white by my grief—
"Please," I said, "stop that game quickly.
"Do you not see that it is but a feeble butterfly?
"It is a sin, it is a sin to drown it in the dark water;
"Its wings are so white,
"As though it has a virgin's spirit. . . ."

4

She pulled back the twig, ended her song.
Quietly she looked into my eyes. . . .
Ah, I died from my grief!
Such lovely eyes she had:

As though she had a rose's spirit. . . .
Quietly she was looking—
Very quietly was she looking;
Her eyes gently blinking, she was thinking.
Then suddenly she laughed out loud,
And with a voice which was music, so deep,
In the woods so deep,
She said to me
—"Take it, take it to you.
"I bestow it.
"Take it, take it to you;
"The butterfly to you. . . .
"And you to me
"In lieu of my gift.
"Pale boy, from the depth of your heart
"What will you give . . . ?"

5

I had wild flowers,
Colorful, pretty, very pretty.
So I gave her one—she laughed. . . .
Then two—she laughed. . . .
Then all, I gave them all.
She refused, she laughed. . . .
—"Ah, it's so little, pale boy!
"Only wild flowers to me?
"Look, your butterfly on a twig
"Shall come to life again.
"Its wings are so white,
"As though she has a virgin's soul.
"Only wild flowers he gives.
"It's little, it's too little, pale boy. . . ."
Thus she sighed—
Her voice itself a heavy sigh.
What a twinkle in her eyes when she said
"Pale boy, pale boy . . . !"

6

I clasped my hands.
—"But I have nothing else.

"I'm a poor poet in the village," I said.
"In the daytime I weave sad songs in the woods,
"And at night, when I sit beneath the stars to dream,
"I pick wild flowers.
"I'm a poor, ignored poet in the village. . . ."
—"Are you a poet? Poor? Ignored?
"Do you in the daytime, lying quietly in the woods,
"Weave songs, many songs. . . .
"And at night,
"With those boyish eyes, of a sick boy, a sweet boy,
"Do you dream beneath the stars . . . ?
"Ah, how nice is he!
"A poet is he!
"Poor, ignored, dark-eyed poet is he . . . !"
Thus she spoke, and with sea calmness in her eyes
She opened her arms very wide. . . .

7

Those arms. . . .
Of what, of what were they made . . . ?
Of violets, of jasmine white as snow?
And her lips of red roses? Of flame? Of Love . . . ?
Such gloomy eyes she had,
As though she had the soul of a star. . . .
Ah, I now wonder why I didn't die there,
When with those flower-scented and snow-white arms
She hugged my bent neck
And with her rosy, aflame lips
She kissed my hair first, then my eyes, then my lips . . . !
—"Pale boy," she sighed in my ears,
"Wouldn't you for my white-winged butterfly
"Give me your poor boy's, poet boy's
"Heart; wouldn't you give me your heart . . . ?"

8

Tell me, should I have given it or should I have not?
How, how shouldn't I have given it . . . ?
Do not forget that we were alone in the woods.
It was so quiet, it was so dark. . . .

Also do not forget, I beg,
The stupor of her bewitching
With which she was rocking my soul.
She had such deep eyes,
As though she had the soul of a sea. . . .
So I gave her;
She laughed and laughed as I gave. . . .

9

She had such glaring eyes,
As though she had a tiger's soul. . . .
Ah, her look, that stare—Like an enchanting, moony twilight,
Like a pitiless, teasing death . . . !
She laughed and laughed as she said:
—"Pale boy, you redeemed your butterfly,
"How well you did;
"And gave your heart in lieu of it,
"How well you did.
"Didn't I know, didn't I,
"That for me
"Your heart is yet another butterfly . . . ?
"Ah, let's see who'll redeem it . . . !
"When to that great sea—that dark sea"
I take it to drown.
"You surely know the name
"Of that great sea—the Love Sea—you, poet in the dark,
"Of that dark sea, the deep sea. . . ."

10

Thus she spoke as she took my heart and went away;
As though a laughter broke in the woods.
When I found myself alone with the pines,
I seemed to be foolish:
I laughed and wept, laughed and wept.
Then, feeling sick, looking at the ground,
I went and sat on my doorstep.
And although no stars could be seen,
My ruined soul

Began its play with the flowers in the dark. . . .
Instead of a dream, only a grumble it had now.
And while on my knees petal by petal
The feeble flowers were dropping,
I was thinking of the dark woods
And of the girl. . . .
Ah, how I wept
That day,
Deeply, so deeply . . . !

11

And thus,
From that strange morning to this day,
Not a day
Was I able to weave sad songs in the woods;
Not a night even for dreams beneath the stars—
However brief;
Yet so much pain. . . .
Every moment I feel I am drowning,
Fallen in that great sea;
You surely know the name—Love—
Of that dark sea, the deep sea.
And that girl on the water's edge,
A sweet song on her lips,
Laughs. . . .
I sigh, I plead, I plead so hard.
Still,
A sweet song on her lips,
She laughs.

12

But she's not alone
Who torments
My poor soul
So very much. . . .
See, even the trees laugh, the waves too;
The sky especially,
When the color of the clouds fades in the evening.

See, see, how every color
Laughs boisterously
When at the verge of death. . . .
From every thing—listen carefully—
It's the same word that proceeds:
—"Feeble boy, he suffers in vain;
"No cheers for him again;
"Lost is his life's game. . . ."

13

This is how that crazy boy
Recounted the story of his soul.
When he finished telling it,
He stood over the rock where for hours we sat
Against the sea
And with eyes fogged by a heart-tearing bewilderment,
Laughing and weeping,
He kissed my entire face.
I bent down my equally colorless forehead
And with fear—
As though I were suddenly found before a ruined sanctuary—I
    kissed his pale hand. . . .

Vahan Totovents

(1894–1938)

Vahan Totovents was born in Mezre, a town near the city of Kharberd (presently Harput, in Turkey) in Western Armenia. He finished the local Kedronakan school (1907), one of the most prestigious schools in the province, having studied under Harutiun Tlkatintsi (1860–1915), the founder of the school, and Ruben Zardarian (1874–1915). In 1908 he went to Constantinople, where he published his first booklets, *Averak* (Ruins) and *Sring* (Flute). In 1909 he went to Paris, then to New York. He studied at the University of Wisconsin (1912–15), taking courses in literature, history, and philosophy. Equipped with French, English, and a considerable knowledge of the world's classical literature, he went back to serve his people.

Totovents joined the Volunteer Corps and helped defend Van and Erzurum against the Turks. He also assisted Hovhannes Tumanian (1869–1923) in his efforts to settle the refugees. In 1917–18 he edited the Tiflis daily *Hayastan* (Armenia), which had been founded by General Andranik (1865–1927), commander of the first Caucasian Volunteer Corps. *Hayastan* promoted the rights of West Armenian refugees and unified action against the common enemy, but it lasted only one year. During the general's stay in Transcaucasia, Totovents acted as his secretary and actively participated in the cultural life of Tiflis, Constantinople, and other Armenian centers. In 1920 he visited Constantinople, southern Europe, and the United States for a second time. He returned to Armenia permanently in 1922.

Totovents's literary life was hectic. He occupied various editorial positions and for a time (1924–26) taught at the University of Yerevan, but he dedicated most of his time to writing. Like many writers, his early efforts were poetry, and he published two slim volumes, *Voghb anmahutian* (Lament on immortality, 1917) and *Arevelk* (Sunrise, 1918), but he soon turned to prose, in which he excelled. Among his most important works are: *Doktor Burbanian* (1923), a short satirical novel about a political propagandist and braggart; and a number of dramatic plays, such as *Mahvan batalion* (Battalion of death, 1923), *Poghpati chash* (Meal of steel, 1924), *Nor Biuzandion* (New Byzantium, 1925), *Hrdeh* (Fire, 1927), *Yerku sur* (Two swords, 1930), and *Mokhrakuyt* (Pile of ashes, 1936). His most celebrated play is *Nor Biuzandion,* the plot of which unfolds in Constantinople after Duzian Amira and some of the male members of his family were beheaded in 1819 by Sultan Mahmut II (1785–1839). The ensuing tragic events illustrate the evils of a society ruled arbitrarily by a despot. The play won an all-Union prize, was translated into several languages, and was staged in many cities in Armenia and abroad, including Paris.

Totovents's short stories earned him great popularity. In the collection *Amerika* (1929) he wrote about his experiences in and impressions of the United States, including, of course, the dehumanizing effects of capitalism and the plight of the blacks, which struck a chord of sympathy in his heart. *Baku* (3 volumes, 1930–34) was a less successful novel, though in the same vein as *Amerika;* it reflects the revolutionary upheavals and proletarian struggle in Transcaucasia early in the century and how they affected peoples' lives. The shorter novel *Hovnatan vordi Yeremiayi* (Jonathan, son of Jeremiah, 1934) depicts the life of a potter-sculptor and praises human creativity, art, and liberty. The book deplores fossilized views and values and religious intolerance.

One of Totovents's best works is *Bats kabuyt tzaghikner* (Pale blue flowers, 1935), a touching story of an unconventional marriage between a prostitute and an orphaned youth in a remote region steeped in conservative traditions. In 1980, under the directorship of Henrik Malian (b. 1925), Armenfilm of Yerevan made a movie of the story under the title *Ktor me yerkink* (A piece of sky).

A work that surpasses all of his others is *Kyanke hin hrovmeakan chanaparhi vra* (Life on an old Roman highway, 1933): "Consisting of fragmented memories of [Totovents's] birthplace, it is written with broad strokes in robust colors and sharp contrasts. In a trenchant, warm style, sparingly laden with lyrical metaphors and imagery, with thinly veiled nostalgia, poignant emotions, humor, and sarcasm, he evokes a quotidian routine, mores, intriguing characters and events, and glimpses into the mentalities of ruler and ruled."[1] This has been translated into Russian, English, and French.

In addition to the works mentioned above, Totovents wrote other stories, plays, and prose, an autobiographical novel titled *Hrkizvatz tghter* (Burned papers, 1934), and essays on Alexander Shirvanzadé (1930) and Hovhannes Tumanian (1931); he also translated Shakespeare's *Richard II* and *Antony and Cleopatra*.

Totovents died in 1938, a victim of the Stalinist purges. His works were published in Yerevan in 1957, and a 2–volume set appeared in 1988–89.

THE DIVINE COMEDY[2]

After replacing the receiver in its cradle, our boss approached me and suggested:

"Go over immediately to Mr. Finkelstein's right away, and take a look at the oriental rugs he has to be cleaned and mended."

"All right," I said, and hurried off to Mr. Finkelstein's mansion at once.

Mr. Finkelstein was one of the greatest millionaires in the United States. My expertise in oriental rugs had taken me to many glorious palaces in America, but I had never visited Mr. Finkelstein's mansion until that day.

Mr. Finkelstein's mansion was in the aristocratic quarter, on the highest point of the hill; it was surrounded by many kinds of trees; the trimmers of skilled gardeners had touched practically every branch of those trees, shaping them into artificial forms.

I had scarcely passed through the gate when two black men, who kept watch over Mr. Finkelstein's gardens, made their stately appearance. I immediately handed them our firm's business card, and they let me in. At the entrance of the mansion I was welcomed

1. Kevork B. Bardakjian, *A Reference Guide to Modern Armenian Literature, 1500–1920* (Detroit, 2000), 216.

2. Sarkis Ashjian, ed. and trans., *Great Armenian Short Stories* (Beirut, 1959), 92–95. Revised by the editors of the present anthology.

by a beautiful young serving maid, whose white cap was the only indication of her social position. I greeted her and showed her our card. The maid ushered me in, asked me to wait in the hall, and, card in hand, left.

Everything in the hall was very simple but expensive. In the front part of the hall a marble bust of Mr. Finkelstein rested on a high pedestal. There was not a single wrinkle on his face. It must have been a bust of Mr. Finkelstein when he was young. Or perhaps he had told the commissioned artist to give him a youthful face, I mused.

The fireplace contained a few symmetrically shaped pieces of wood. A red electric bulb shone on them from behind to make it look as if they were on fire. A stormy sea could be glimpsed through the branches of the treetops that thrust up in front of the windows on the right. And directly beyond the sea could be seen the roof of the neighboring mansion. There is no sea in this city, so what sea am I looking at? I wondered as I focused my attention on the scene, and then I noticed that the waves were not moving—it was merely a decoration, a seascape painted on the windowpane.

The crimson velvet curtains in the far corner of the hall parted and in came an old woman, who was dressed very plainly. She had a sickly, waxen face. The illusion I had experienced by looking at the painting of the lake made me think, through the association of ideas, that the woman who had stepped onto the scene was an artificial decoration too, so portrait-like was her face. But no, she was a real woman, as was clear when she started to talk:

"So, you've come to see our oriental rugs, right?"

"Yes, ma'am," I answered, standing up.

"Well, let's go in then."

I followed her. She led me to the library and asked me to mend, wash, and iron the oriental rugs there.

"All right," I answered mechanically, for I was distracted for a moment by the books in the library.

All the literature of the world was there: the classics of all the civilized nations, in gilt volumes that were all the same size and identically bound. In addition, the books were arranged chronologically, with every century well represented. Greek literature, for example, stood in impeccable rows at the top of the western wall, in covers as blue as the sky of Hellas. Not a single Greek author was omitted. I envied wealthy people for the first time in my life. Books, and books, and more books; that has always been the ever-hopeful dream of my life. I must ask the old lady to let me cast an eye over all the books, I thought, when I noticed that the old woman had already gone. I followed her out to the hall and went to our firm to get a car to carry the rugs to be mended and washed.

By the time I returned I had decided to ask her to let me see at least the large volume of Dante's *Divine Comedy* upon which was conspicuously stamped: "Royal Edition." I had long heard that such a luxurious edition existed, with magnificent drawings. This is doubtless that famous edition, I mused.

When I returned to Mr. Finkelstein's mansion, I was welcomed by the same charming maid.

"What a quiet house," I said to her as we walked along the corridors, by way of breaking the ice and eventually steering the conversation in the direction of the books.

"Yes, very quiet, and very sad too," she answered.

"Sad? Why, no, on the contrary: this is a nice, quiet, peaceful place," I remarked.

"There's no one in this big house but Mr. Finkelstein and his old wife. I don't have much to do here, so I get bored and find it a sad, a very sad, place. My job is to usher in visitors and then accompany them to the main gate. That's all I'm here for. Their meals are delivered by restaurants, so I have nothing particular to do out here. Sometimes I get so bored I think of quitting and not having any job, provided I'm surrounded by noise and people, you know?"

"Why don't you try reading?" I asked, with barely suppressed impatience: "Read, read, my friend! Oh! If I only had the time, and books to read!"

"I read, and I read a lot," answered the maid, "I've already finished the last number of *The Blue Book*, and I could certainly give it to you to read, if you'd like."

"I don't need *The Blue Book*," I said and I took her by the hand before we entered the library. She did not resist. "Don't be afraid," she whispered. "I have to ask you something," I said.

"Go ahead," she answered, with a broad, satisfied smile.

"First let me collect the rugs, and then I'll tell you about it," I said. I rolled up the rugs and handed them to the black man to put in the car. Then I walked over to her and said: "Young lady, please allow me to look at that large volume, Dante's *Divine Comedy*."

The maid stared at me in amazement, grinned, and then broke into loud laughter. After she had calmed down a bit she said:

"Please, please: go ahead and have a look."

I ignored her inappropriate laughter and picked up the Royal Edition. It was surprisingly light. I tried to open it but had no success. I turned it left and right in my endeavors to unfasten it. My efforts were in vain. The maid went on with her ruthless laughter. Incensed with rage, I threw Dante to the ground.

"All the books you see are made of cardboard: there are no pages in them; the whole thing is nothing but sheer make-believe; you'd better take my *Blue Book* if you want something to read," said the maid.

"Thank you very much indeed," I answered, and walked out of the hall.

I could still hear her cruel laughter ringing from the corridor.

Azat Vshtuni

(1894–1958)

Vshtuni (né Karapet Mamikonian), one of the pioneer poets of the new era, was born in Van in Western Armenia. He received his primary education at the local Yeramian Aramian school. He continued his secondary studies at the Kedronakan lycée of Constantinople (1908–11) and then went to Paris, where he audited courses in literature and philosophy at the Sorbonne. In 1914 he returned to Tiflis and participated in the "Armenian volunteers' movement." Between 1919–20 the Armenian Soviet republic sent him to Iran and Iraq to organize the emigration of Armenians to their homeland. In the following years Vshtuni edited several periodicals: the *Murch* (Hammer, Yerevan 1922), *Dirkerum* (At the ramparts, Tiflis 1924), and *Murch-Mangagh* (Hammer-scythe, Northern Caucasus and Rostov, 1926–27). For a while he was the president of the first Writers Union of Armenia and occupied other official positions.

Vshtuni wrote poetry as well as ballads and songs: *Srtis lareren* (From the strings of my heart, 1915) and *Banasteghtzutiunner* (Poems, 1918); the basic motifs of these are love, homeland, compassion, the rage of the oppressed, and protest against the perpetrators of the genocide. His "*Banvorakan gaylerg*" (Laborers hymn), "*Enchazurkner bolor yerkirneri, miatsek*" (Proletarians of all countries, unite), "*Pokrik lragravachare*" (The little newsboy), "*Berkrank*" (Joy), "*Garnanakanch*" (Call of spring), and other works all published in 1917 signal the beginning of his poetic maturity with a fresh voice.

Vshtuni echoed the rebirth of Armenians and their advancement through socialist reform, together with other themes and political principles. His writings demonstrate unique poetic forms and freshness of expression. *Neo Orientalia* (1923), *Salamnamé* (1924), *Arevelke hur é hima* (The east is burning now, 1927), *Banasteghtzutiunner* (Poems, 1929), *Yerker* (Works, 1935), *Ram Roy* (1936), *Lusademin* (At the sunrise, 1939), *Entir yerker* (Chosen works, 1941), *Yerb kaytzake paylatakum é* (When the thunderbolt is flashing, 1942), *Hatentir* (Selected works, 1944), and other books of poetry and versified narratives are among his works that have been translated into Russian and other languages of the Soviet republics.

THE CAMEL[1]

Dedicated to the workers of Iraq

Yesterday,
in our boundless desert,
you,
my dearest camel,
you raised your neck high,
and tried to kiss the *shems*—the sun.

Yesterday,
in the oasis of El Sam,
my confidant,
my dearest,
when night came—deep and boundless—
you and I
read the turquoise verses of the sky.

Do you remember
that I kissed you
on the eyes,

---

1. Azat Vshtuni, "*Ughte*" (The camel), in *Hayreni Ghoghanjner* (Chimes of the homeland) (Yerevan, 1985), 180–84. Translated by the editors of the present anthology.

my friend,
my confidant,
my dearest?

My friend in labor,
wet with sweat and lonesome roads,
you remember, don't you:
you and I were drenched in sweat,
for me, for you, for everyone
the days were arduous,
windy and scorched by the sun;
we were naked and famished.
But our eyes were smiling
and looked to a distant tomorrow:
toward the sunrise, born of the womb,
of a dark night
We walked the desert
steadfast
sturdy
solid
and satisfied.

Today
you no longer lift high your neck.
Why?
Today
your walk is unsteady,
your steps are slow.
Why?
Today
you no longer miss,
my dearest,
the *shems*—the sun.
Why?

Today
the azure letters of the sky
are faded.
Why?
Who took hold of you

today, and parted you from me?
Why?

With bent neck
and questing eyes
scouring the dark sand,
whose footprints
do you seek?

Why is there
grief in your gaze,
my dearest,
a starless night in your aspect,
and rage?
There are strange footprints
in the sand;
there are drops of the blood
of your loved ones in the sand;
there are tear drops
of your loved ones in the sand.

Who was the stranger with a deceitful smile?
Who was the stranger in burnished arms
who stepped on the burning sand?
My dearest,
there are drops of the blood
of your dear ones in the sand.
Our sun-burnt deserts today
know the wetness of distant seas
and of unhappy far-off lands.
Our endless deserts today
know the hubbub of unfamiliar circuses
and the frowns of gawking strangers.

To the deserts of our fathers
foreigners have come
by sea and ocean roads.

They have crossed from land to land,
from sea to sea,
and have arrived from the oceans,

where there are no camels,
and only beavers swim.
Strangers have joined the hyenas of our deserts,
eager to chop your body to pieces,
my dearest.

Who was that
who placed the heavy load
upon your back?
What?
Now
strangers whip you,
as if to replace my kisses,
my dearest.

Who humbled the proud bearing of your neck?
What!
Do these outsiders think
you are a beast of burden?

Tell me, dearest,
my friend of sweat, labor, joy
and roads:
When,
when at last will you flash your dusky glare?
When,
when at last will creep before your eyes
these hyenas of the desert of your homeland?

When,
when at last will I see
your neck stretched forth to the sun
in your rippling, and steam-blown
new desert?
When,
when,
when?

Beniamin Nurikian

(1894–1988)

Born in the village of Hiuseynik, near Kharberd (now Harput, in Turkey), Beniamin Nurikian attended the local elementary school, then moved to the Kedronakan school in Kharberd, where he studied under Tlkatintsi (1860–1915), the foremost representative of provincial literature and founder of the school. Tlkatintsi awakened in him a love for Armenian literature. In 1913 Nurikian left his native village for the United States, in quest of a college education. He delayed this pursuit for more than two years, however, until he earned some money as a factory worker. He entered Columbia University in 1916 and graduated in 1922 with an M.A. in literature and history. He settled permanently in the United States.

His first literary work was a translation (1930) of Mark Twain's *The Prince and the Pauper,* but Nurikian's principal literary career began when he started contributing articles and essays to the various newspapers of the diaspora. In 1936 he and Andranik Andreasian (1909–96) founded a monthly review of literature and art, *Nor gir* (New writing), in New York, to promote Armenian literature in the United States. In 1939 it became a quarterly under the editorship of Nurikian, and its publication continued until 1954. This journal played an important role in rallying a number of contemporary writers, such as Vahé Hayk, Aram Haykaz, Zaven

Siurmelian, and Karapet Sital. It published special issues on Hakob Oshakan (1946, Nos. 3, 4) and Komitas (1950, No. 1), included a critical analysis section, and frequently published excerpts from world literature in translation.

Nurikian's first volume of short stories, *Aygekutk* (Vintage), was published in New York in 1937. This was followed by *Pandukht hoginer* (Souls in exile) and *Karot hayreni* (Yearning for the homeland), published in Yerevan in 1958 and 1978, respectively. Two main themes dominate his short stories. One is the attraction of his native village, its scenes and events, its enchanting landscape, its customs and mores—which he knew so well and recalls so vividly. These idealized portrayals of the rustic past, however, are in sharp contrast with the reality of a depression-ridden society. The second major theme is the emotional and economic hardships and the cultural distress of his uprooted countrymen, the survivors of 1915, who now live in the United States and feel the serious threat of assimilation and consequent loss of their Armenian identity. Nurikian believed that Soviet Armenia was a symbol of survival and a source of hope for some of those survivors.

Love for the simple people and sympathy for the weak, expressed in clear and fluent language, are outstanding characteristics of Nurikian's writings. A large amount of his prose and translations still remains scattered in the periodic press. A fourth volume of stories, *"Ariunogh srter"* (Bleeding hearts), remains unpublished.

THE SUN FOR YOU[1]

Ellis Island. A small slice of land that projects into the mouth of upper New York Bay. Exactly where the Hudson River falls exhausted into the bosom of the Atlantic and joins it. This little infant of an island, covered with gray, cold buildings, is a mass of black rock—a kind of threshold planted in the waters of New York, where many are obliged to stop for a while, or a week if need be: voiceless immigrants—all of them woven of the same cloth—who arrive third-class at the gates to America.

These gates open a few inches at a time to admit newcomers to a process of enumeration—counting and long examinations—that

---

1. Benyamin Nurikian, "Areve kezi" (The sun for you), in *Nor gir* (New writing) (New York, 1984), 33–36. Translated by the editors of the present anthology.

is sometimes as painstaking as searching for a hair in an egg yoke, and about as amusing.

"Where were you born? How old are you? Is your skin black, white, or yellow? Do you believe in God and monogamy? How much money do you have in your pocket? Let's have a look at your eyes. Bare your chest. Stick out your tongue."

Stick out my tongue? Are they going to measure it? I ask myself with a feeling of utter surprise and doubt intermingled, the like of which I have never experienced before.

"Your tongue!" the interpreter repeats.

The doctor diligently examines the tongue that dangles like a wick before his eyes and shakes his bald head.

"He has a cold, a bad one. He might be consumptive."

And, a yellow ticket now stuck on my chest, I am admitted to the island hospital.

I want to say "Hello, America!" or at least stammer out something, but my mouth is paralyzed, and my desire remains unexpressed. I have traveled for forty days and forty nights, on five different seas and a huge ocean . . . and at last I have arrived at the entrance to a new, a very new country, where the only thing I have been offered is a hospital bed, cold and white.

"Hello, New World," I murmur at last. And I pull the covers up to my chin. And worry.

If they send me back. . . . Let them! I'll go home and there, in the warm presence of my mother and father, I'll pick up the silver string of my adolescence, which I left behind forty days ago. Let them send me back! At least I'll get rid of this lump of yearning that fills my throat and is gradually choking me. No, America: I'll take my greeting back, sling my bundle over my shoulder, and go home, right now, if. . . .

But America is the place I dreamed about only yesterday—beautiful dreams. Here she is, under this white hospital ceiling, which crushes me like a fallen meteorite. Beside this radiator, which sometimes lets off steam and hisses. The nurse places the little thermometer under my tongue to find the cause of all my bodily pains.

America is here. Around the electric light fixtures that make halos on the white ceiling. Outside, the ships whistle and shriek "America! New York!"

For a moment I forget New York, and America too. A question pops into my head. Who are my neighbors, my fellow patients?

My history and geography lessons, long dormant, impatiently come pushing and shoving into my mind.

Spain. If Ferdinand and Isabella had not married, the Genoese Columbus would not have been able to discover America.

Who are my friends?

Germany. Gutenberg invented printing.

But who are my friends?

Portugal. Magellan circumnavigated the globe and, at the cost of his own head, proved that the world is round, swollen like a pumpkin at the waist.

But who are my friends?

A voice, a dusty voice—Adam's perhaps or Noah's—whispers in my ear.

"People, ordinary people."

And my foreign friends are silent; they suffer from a common pain and are in bed like me. All of them voiceless creatures. They do not even acknowledge each other's presence, let alone take stock of the kind and measure of each other's pain in order to pass a word of consolation from one bed to the next.

A repeated drumming, a half-stifled cry, a deep cough that cannot be restrained and echoes with a coppery noise; from time to time words rise from the pillows, from every corner of the ward. And a newly born intimacy spreads the warmth of its breath everywhere. People, ordinary people. . . . I turn my face on my pillow and look over at my neighbor. He is a young man, with no mustache. He looks back at me with a painful smile that is worth a thousand words of greeting. I feel my eyes crinkle into a slight smile at this sudden discovery of a lost brother—a sharer of my pain. "How are you?" I want to ask. My friend answers only with his sad, sweet gaze, which dwindles and goes out like the light of a wick when there is no more oil in the lamp. Outside the ships whistle, raging against the fog.

The lights in the ward all go out at once. The halos of light vanish from the white ceiling. Pulling the blanket all the way up to my face, I try to make New York vanish as well. America too. I try to fall asleep. But my neighbor is restless. The dry cough that echoes like metal rends his chest from time to time. And a painful

"Ah!" escapes from the depths of his soul. He says something in his native language, perhaps worn-out bits of words; only two syllables strike my mind and sear into it: "Ma . . . ma. . . ."

I have slept scarcely at all; my eyes gape helplessly. Let them gape; I can sleep during the day; what else have I got to do?

The nurse comes, does something near my neighbor's bed, mumbles something, and goes away.

It is morning. The ceiling of the ward turns white. My neighbor is still moaning and gasping.

A light cough and a hoarse rale can be heard in the distance, as the woes of the hospital awaken and salute each other, as though inquiring after each other. And they grow lighter, of course, lighter. An "Ah!" released from the heart, a cough released from the lungs, a couple of teardrops fallen from the eyes: these are the inheritance of Adam, and are precious: even death retreats from them, even death.

A patient props himself up on his elbows and tries to sit up. His dry, emaciated fingers grip the iron railing of the bed and he looks out the window. What could he be looking at? The frolicking sea, the ships that shuttle back and forth. The Statue of Liberty, which, with a raised torch in one hand and a book in the crook of the other arm, rises up over the black waters; and the sun, which shows its fresh face behind the forest of tall buildings that is the city of New York. A familiar, very good-natured face, that of the sun, which comprehends every language and understands all pains.

The patient tightens his fingers and utters a sigh through dry lips—this time directed at the sun. His hands loosen, his arms slide down, and he strikes his head against the headboard. He is terrified. His half-swallowed call of longing . . . freezes on the tip of his tongue: "Ma. . . ."

I bury my head beneath my pillow and cry. Muffled sobs reach my ear, from every corner of the ward, from every pillow.

The sun stands for you, far-off, unnamed mother. Many have cried for their *gharip*[2] sons before you, far-off, unnamed mother . . . the sun is you.

February, 1939.

---

2. Person away from home, immigrant, exile.

Hamastegh (Hambardzum Gelenian)

(1895–1966)

Hamastegh (Hambardzum Gelenian) was born in Perchench, a village in Kharberd (Harput). He spent his childhood in this pastoral atmosphere, which was later to appear in his works as a symbol of security. After completing the local village school, he continued his education at the Kedronakan school in Meziré, where he was exposed to the powerful influence of the writers Tlkatintsi (1860–1915) and Ruben Zardarian (1874–1915), who inspired him to become an aestheticist, always in love with the natural surroundings of his birthplace. Following graduation he taught at his village school for a year, then followed his father to the United States. He never became comfortable with life in North America, however.

Despite his innate propensity, talent, and passion for literature, he had to confine his reading and writing to his spare time while working in factories and shops to earn a living. The impressions of his village childhood remained vividly alive and inspiring in the imagination of the future writer. In 1917 the *Hayrenik* (Fatherland) daily of Boston published his first poem. At around that time he began to contribute to *Piunik* (The phoenix), a monthly journal published in Addis Ababa.

In 1920 a meeting with Shirvanzadé in New York opened a new creative phase. The great dramatist convinced Hamastegh to portray realistic scenes based on life in his birthplace. *Tapan Margar* was the product of this opportune encounter. Hamastegh thus found his real creative vocation. Years later, in Paris, Shirvanzadé told Avetik Isahakian: "I saved Hamastegh."[1]

Other sketches and short stories followed until 1931, when Hamastegh began to write his two-volume novel, *Spitak Dziavore* (The white horseman), which was finished and published in 1952. His specific intention in writing this novel was to emphasize the tragic Armenian destiny in the midst of Turkish and Kurdish incursions during the First World War, and to underline the strength of Armenian resistance and the centuries-old dream of life lived in peace.[2] The novel is overly long, but despite its shortcomings, it is full of interesting episodes and successful descriptive passages.

Hamastegh also wrote long poems, such as *Simon yev Kiro* (Simon and Kiro), which was probably intended as a heroic poem in the tradition of *David of Sasun*, and *Chamchov karkandak* (Raisin cake). His stories, published in *Hayrenik* beginning in 1921, were collected in two volumes, *Kiughe* (The village: Boston, 1924) and *Andzreve* (The rain: Paris, 1929), which established his reputation as an Armenian writer. In them he breathes life into the memories of his native soil and reflects the simplicity of its people, who constitute his very special dramatis personae. At times they find themselves under American skies, but the great national tragedy and the author's memories of his homeland are never far from the foreground.

Hamastegh's publications include *Kaj Nazar yev tasnerek patmvatzkner* (Nazar the brave and thirteen other stories, 1955); *Aghotarane* (The prayer book, 1957), a poetic work based on personal spiritual experiences; and *Srbazan katakergutiun* (The divine comedy), also called *Tomar makiakan* (1938), which had previously appeared in *Hayrenik* but was republished in 1960 as a separate volume under the title *Aytzetomar*.

In his later years he wanted to visit Armenia, but his doctors would not permit him to undertake the long trip because of his heart condition. He died in the United States during festivities organized for the fiftieth anniversary of the beginning of his literary career.

---

1. Reported in Mesrop Chanashian's *Hay grakanutyan nor shrjani hamarot patnutiun, 1701–1920* (Concise history of Armenian literature: the modern period: 1701–1920) (Venice, 1973), 348.

2. Ibid., 349.

THE BLUE BEAD[3]

Two bleary eyes, a gaunt figure, always holding a broom: that was Karuk's aunt.

"Karuk!" she always shouted. Her eyes could not see well. She often mistook him for the piece of cloth spread on the opposite wall or the ewer left out in the sun.

Karuk was on the roof near the garret. He was busy making a kite. He had already tied the two sticks together and now he was gluing on the paper and preparing the tail. He needed a large roll of string to fly his kite far up into the sky, to the poplars, to the distant hills. He knew quite well where his aunt kept her string. While making his kite he had a few flights of fancy: What if it were possible for him to ride on the kite, so the wind would carry him over the poplars? He wished this would happen on a summer afternoon. Women gathering firewood, men binding sheaves, oxen at work, dogs in the village streets, hens on the fences, washerwomen spreading laundry on the rooftops, all, all would look up in rapt fear and wonder; they would surely recognize him, and they would say, "It's Karuk, Sako's son! Just look at him! It's a miracle, a downright miracle! . . ." What did he care if his aunt, broom in hand, threatened him? Among all these people, there would also be Maran, who would see him from her roof. . . .

"Karuk!"

It was his aunt's voice again.

Oh, how he wished loudly beating drummers would come out of the haylofts, that St. Sarkis would pass by and walk straight into the village with his boisterous chorale of animal musicians all bleating away! That would help drown out the voice of his wretched aunt, and he would be left in peace. Failing this, he would at least like to have a cat at his disposal, whose tail he could so strongly slam in the roof door that the cat would howl so loudly it would drown out his aunt's voice so completely that it would not reach him. Afraid of his aunt's threats, he jumped down off the fence, crept up to her, and was standing right beside her when she

---

3. Hamastegh (Hambardzum Gelenian), "The Blue Bead," in *Great Armenian Short Stories,* trans. Sarkis Ashjian (Beirut, 1959), 151–56. Revised by the editors of the present anthology.

prepared to call him once more. She ordered: "Karuk, fly like a bird: fetch me some yeast from your grandmother's. And hurry back!"

Karuk neighed and turned his face up into the air like a horse, and began to run. His grandmother's house was not very far. From their roof they often saw his grandmother spreading laundry on the roof of her house. Karuk took the longer path by the meandering brook, and, sure of his speed, he ran in a manner reminiscent of a noble horse. There were some children playing with a toy water mill on the bank of the brook. From poplar twigs they had made a wheel, and as the water ran over it the mill turned. Karuk asked them to grind his wheat first.

"No, we can't," objected little David, pretending to be a miller.

"You *can*," insisted Karuk.

"We *can't*," answered the other.

Karuk pushed the wheel over, and the twigs it was made of broke into pieces. The water carried away the water mill, as a flood destroys and carries off a golden temple in a story. Karuk was older than his friends. Who could stand up to him? Again he began to run like a noble steed. He was already in the vicinity of Maran's vineyard. He wanted to see Maran and show her how he could run like a noble steed. It was wonderful.

Often Maran would be there, near the wall, with her small calf. It was good that he remembered. He knew of a lapwing's nest in Maran's pear tree. Karuk had not touched its eggs. He did not want to destroy them when he could watch their mother hatching them. He climbed up the tree, rolled up his sleeves and thrust his hand into the nest. The lapwing flew out all of a sudden. The eggs were warm, colorful, and spotted. He did not touch them. It was the lapwing in Maran's pear tree. He went on his way to fetch the yeast.

He was near Arakel's yard. Near the kennel, the bitch waited with hanging udders. Karuk entered the kennel to see how big the litter was. Then he went on his way to fetch the yeast. He stopped in front of the butcher's for a moment. He wondered why the butcher did not cry out the price of the meat. If only *he* were a butcher, he would think up many wonderful ways to attract customers! He went on his way to fetch the yeast. When he entered the shop, he heard his aunt talking to his grandmother: "What can I do, for heaven's sake? God doesn't take my soul to save me from this vagabond!" she complained.

She had waited for Karuk for a long time, and in the end she had gone to fetch the yeast herself. She took the yeast, grabbed him by the hand, and marched him home, extremely angry. Now they were walking past Maran's open door. Oh, how he hoped Maran would not be there, so he would be saved the humiliation of being seen in that miserable state! Maran's mother was sweeping the front yard when his aunt came by, stopped, and began to complain about Karuk's mischievous deeds.

"They are still quite young, my dear," said Maran's mother. "They change when they grow older. For the last couple of days, Maran has had a blister right on her breast. My poor only child is sick."

The aunt let go of Karuk's hand. Her anger seemed to vanish, and in the authoritative tone of an old woman, she prescribed the treatment needed for the abscess: "Cover it with a piece of onion. Make sure you fry the onion well. Then take some soap, mix it with olive oil, and crush it with a mortar and pestle. Daub the mixture on the fried onion, then bind it over the abscess. When you do this, it will penetrate the abscess and suck out the pus."

"Where will I get olive oil, my dear friend?"

"I have some at home. I'll send Karuk with it."

"For God's sake, send Karuk with it and I'll do what you say. Last night the poor child couldn't sleep a wink."

A little later, a small dusty bottle in his hand, Karuk entered Maran's house. Her mother was preparing the onion. Maran lay on the bed, dozing. Karuk spoke in a low voice so he would not wake her up. Oh, what a burning desire he had to see the abscess on Maran's breast! Karuk heard his aunt's voice: "Karuk!"

"Your aunt is calling you, Karuk," Maran's mother reminded him.

Karuk lingered a little. He wanted to see the abscess when Maran's mother applied the onion to it.

"Karuk!" It was his aunt's shrill voice again.

Karuk remembered that his aunt was already cross with him because of the yeast. He prepared to go, in order to avoid making her angrier. Maran moved in her bed.

"Karuk!"

"Your aunt's throat will burst with shouting, lad," remarked Maran's mother.

Karuk left. Oh, how ardently he wished to see Maran's abscess!

The villagers did not need a calendar: when they saw Karuk going barefoot, it meant spring was near and warm weather had blessed the earth with its presence. When Karuk's pants were torn to his knees, it meant summer was at hand. When he fished for crabs under the bridge, it meant it was autumn. That summer Karuk had had no record of outstanding mischief. The only mischief he did was to eat all the cherries on Makar's cherry tree. When he and Maran were playing once, he had asked for a kiss and been refused. Maran had even told her mother about this; her mother had reported the news to his aunt, and his aunt had given him a sound thrashing.

One autumn day when Karuk was fishing for crabs under the bridge, he found a blue bead. He threaded a string through it and hung it around his neck to protect himself from the evil eye and from stinging nettles. His aunt said that a blue bead was the safest way to ward off the evil and jealous eye. Karuk told his playmates a lot about the miracle-working bead. Maran was one of his playmates too. She even asked him if she could hold the bead just once.

As usual, that day Maran took the calf to the vineyard and was making a daisy chain when all of a sudden Karuk jumped over the fence.

"You know, if you wear this bead, even the cold can't bite you," said Karuk, opening his eyes wide. "If you play knuckle-bones, all the luck will be on your side. If you fall from a tree, you'll never get hurt. And the flood can't carry you off, and fire can't burn you if only you wear this bead!"

What yarns he told! Maran was fascinated with the bead.

"Karuk, will you lend me the bead?"

"Never. I'd never give it to you, even if you gave me a hundred gold pieces."

"Just for one single day," Maran continued to plead, with a shy feminine smile. The bead's blue color seemed a much deeper blue to her. There was a certain warmth in that bead. How marvelous it would be if she could have it for only one day!

There was nobody in the vineyard. They could occasionally hear the birds flap their wings. Karuk and Maran were altogether alone. Karuk felt a warm desire in that solitude. Maran seemed more beautiful to him when she asked for the bead with a shy smile.

"Maran," Karuk said, and then he was silent. It seemed as if his voice came from far away.

"What is it, Karuk?"

Karuk could not say it. He was enveloped in warmth, like the blue bead in Maran's hand. Ah, he could not say it! What if she refused. . . . He bent down and murmured in her ear: "If you give me a kiss, I'll give you the blue bead."

Maran blushed. She cast her eyes down. How could she ever agree? What if her mother heard of it? No! She did not want it. But once she had the bead in her hand, she no longer wanted to give it back to him. The bead grew warmer in her hand, and its color seemed more enchanting. But what if her mother found out?

"Then give me back my bead," demanded Karuk.

Maran did not want to part with the bead. How nice and wonderful it was! Tomorrow she would hang it around her neck!

Karuk swore a thousand oaths.

Maran remained silent. She seemed not to agree.

"Give me back my bead," Karuk insisted again.

"Here," replied Maran, blushing, and with a pleasant pout she offered her cheek to Karuk's lips. . . .

Oh, how warm Karuk's lips were, warmer than the blue bead which burned in her hand. . . .

Yeghishé Charents

(1897–1937)

Yeghishé Charents was born Yeghishé Soghomonian in the Western Armenian city of Kars (now in Turkey) to a carpet dealer's family. He received his early education in the local Armenian elementary school, then attended the Russian high school (1908–12). He was a lonely child and spent much of his time reading. He greatly admired the work of Vahan Terian (1885–1920), and the first book he acquired was Terian's *Poems*, which he purchased with a ruble taken from his father without permission. Another time his father bought him a new outfit, which he sold, and with the money he bought a dictionary and a copy of Movses Khorenatsi's *History of the Armenians*.

When World War I broke out in 1915, Charents joined the Armenian Volunteer Corps in support of the Russian war effort on the Russian-Ottoman front. He was sent to Van, where he witnessed the genocide of the Armenian people. In September 1916 he went to Moscow to study literature at the popular Shaniavski University, where the intellectual milieu played an important part in fostering his revolutionary ideas. In 1918–19 he took arms for the second time, in support of the Red Army in the civil war. He served in Tsaritsin, in the northern Caucasus, and in 1920 settled in Yerevan. Charents's university education was incomplete, but he compensated for it with incessant reading and independent study.

Charents wrote his first poem, *"Tzaghiknere hez tekvum en kamu orori takin"* (The flowers gently bend under the lullaby of the wind), in 1912, when he was fifteen, and it was published in the Tiflis journal *Patani* (Adolescent). This was followed by *"Yerek yerg tkhradaluk aghjkan"* (Three songs for a pale, sad girl, 1914) and two poetry collections, *Hro yerkir* (Land of fire, 1913–16), and *Tziatzan* (Rainbow, 1917), in which he tried to analyze human suffering as he searched for an idealistic world. At this time a number of Russian writers, including Aleksandr Blok (1880–1921) and Valery Bryusov (1873–1924), formed the Russian symbolist movement under the influence of the French symbolists, and this affected Charents's earlier works.

In the second decade of the century writers and poets were still evoking heroes, images, and visions from past glories, hoping to inspire the people to rise up and fulfill the ancient dream. Charents's lyric poem *"Kaputachya hayrenik"* (Blue-eyed fatherland, 1915) is a reflection of this attitude, which prompts him to sing about an illusive Armenia: "O, my faraway, blue-eyed sweetheart."

Soon after the publication of this work he fought with the volunteer army in Van and saw firsthand the death and destruction wrought on the Armenian people. Under the impressions of these dreadful events he wrote his famed poem *"Danteakan araspel"* (Dantean legend, 1916), which he dedicated to three comrades-in-arms who fell in the battle. He was now firmly convinced that what would save Armenia was the October Revolution, which he wholeheartedly supported. In 1918–19, while fighting in the Red Army, he wrote two long poems, *"Soma"*[1] and *"Ambokhnere khelagarvatz"* (The frenzied masses), each full of revolutionary ardor. The former is emotional and romantic praise of the revolution that was supposed to put an end to the old world order, and the latter the battle cry of the masses on the march to liberation. The Turkish onslaught on Armenia in the autumn of 1920 moved him to begin the series *Mahvan tesil* (Vision of death), with the title borrowed from Siamanto (1878–1915).

Some months after Soviet rule was established in Armenia in 1920, Charents began to work at the Ministry of Education as director of

---

1. In Indian mythology a sacred and intoxicating drink prepared from the juices of a certain plant and drunk by gods and mortals alike to confer inward fire and immortality. It is said to have been brought to earth by the daughters of the sun and is itself worshiped as a deity, represented by the moon.

the Arts Department. In 1921–22 he wrote *"Amenapoem"* (Everyone's poem), which became a classic of revolutionary poetry, and *"Charents-namé,"* an autobiographical poem. In the meantime he married Arpik Ter-Astvatzatrian and took her to Moscow for a short visit.

A new world order required a new guideline for literature. On his return from Moscow, Charents, along with Gevorg Abov and Azat Vshtuni, published a declaration in *Soviet Armenia* (14 June 1922), known as "The Manifesto of the Three," in which they expressed their opposition to "bourgeois nationalism" in favor of "proletarian internationalism," and advocated a literature full of "action, the class struggle, machines, the sexual instinct, and the color red." This trend was obviously influenced by the Russian futurists[2] Viktor Khlebnikov (1885–1922) and Vladimir Mayakovski (1893–1930), both of whom Charents knew well, and also by the activities of the Russian LEF (Left Front of the Arts) organization. This implied rejecting previously written Armenian literature. The movement did not last very long, however.

In 1922 Charents again went to Moscow, to study at the Institute of Literature and Arts founded by Valeri Bryusov (1873–1924). In 1924–25 he went on a seven-month trip abroad, visiting Turkey, Italy, France, and Germany and becoming acquainted with European values, literary and social trends, and noted intellectuals. His trip was arranged by Alexander Myasnikian, who occupied a prestigious position in the government of Soviet Armenia; himself an accomplished poet, he was a great admirer of Charents's poetry.

When Charents returned from his European trip, he discovered that many things had changed. He founded a union of writers, named November, but the central government soon decided to incorporate all writers, including those who had reached prominence before the revolution, into one organization, which became the Armenian Writers Union in 1926.

In the same year Charents published *Yerkir Nayiri* (The land of Nayiri), a politically charged satirical novel based on characters and events that occurred in Kars, his native city, from just before the outbreak of World War I until its occupation by Turkish invaders. Indeed, the three stages of the evolution of the land of Nayiri describe Armenia: first as a romanticized vision, then as a land groaning under incompetent

---

2. Futurism was a radical, early twentieth-century movement in Italian and Russian art and literature. It maintained that the sources of inspiration for the artist or the writer should be cities, technology, and machines, and that the laboring classes are the creators of the future.

leaders, and eventually as a shattered dream, symbolized by the fall of Kars. What remained of Nayiri, however, was now a Soviet Socialist Republic, and was being built anew. The characters in the novel are drawn with so much affection that it could be called a patriotic, even nationalistic work, and some party officials began to look upon it with disfavor.

Charents attracted more frowns with *Tagharan* (Songbook), a collection of lyric poems in imitation of the style of Sayat-Nova (c. 1720–95). This was an abrupt return to the tone of the earlier literature, at a time when Soviet writers had to follow the party line. The last poem in this collection is the most popular, and it has been set to music: "*Yes im anush Hayastani arevaham barn em sirum*" (I love the sun-tasting fruits [or name] of my sweet Armenia), The ambiguity arises from how the *r* in *barn* is written. According to the official edition of his works (Yerevan, 1962, 1:246), Charents must have used the word to mean "fruit."

In September 1926, having shot and slightly wounded a sixteen-year-old girl (for motives that have never been clear), Charents found himself condemned to eight years of imprisonment in the Yerevan House of Correction; however, because of his wife's death during childbirth in January 1927, and his ensuing distress, he was released a week after she died. The same year he published his prison journal under the title *Hishoghutiunner Yerevani ughghich tnits* (Memories of the Yerevan House of Correction) and a collection of forty-four quatrains that he titled *Rubaiyat*. The following year he had kidney surgery and became addicted to morphine, which was prescribed to ease his suffering.

From 1928 to 1935 Charents was artistic director of the State Publishing House. He encouraged new talent and commissioned a group of scholars headed by literary historian Manuk Abeghian (1865–1944) to edit a comprehensive version of the national epic, *David of Sasun*. In 1930 he published *Epikakan lusabats* (Epic dawn), which consisted of the poems he wrote from 1927 to 1930. This, too, represented a return to the old, a tribute to the art of Hovhannes Tumanian and Vahan Terian. A gap was opening up between Charents, who now advocated literary freedom, and other writers, who followed the party line in literature.

In 1931 Charents married Isabella Niazian; the first of their two daughters was born in 1932 and named Arpenik after his first wife, the second, Anahit, was born in 1935.

His last collection of poems, *Girk chanaparhi* (The book of the road), was dedicated to his daughter Arpenik. It was printed in 1933, but its distribution was delayed by the government until 1934, when it was reissued with certain revisions. In this work Charents lays out the panorama of Armenian history and reviews it cycle by cycle. The first cycle, "*Sasuntsi Davite*" (David of Sasun), is a retelling of the Armenian national epic, which the author uses as an allegory of the revolution. Armenians were once more in the situation described in the epic: the people were expecting Mher to lead them to freedom but were deceived; instead a group of Dzenov Ohans took charge.[3] The second cycle, "*Patmutyan karughinerov*" (At the crossroads of history), expresses Charents's bitterness and disappointment over Armenia's leadership, particularly during the eighteenth and nineteenth centuries, and ends with the sarcastic observation that in order to be saved Armenia should perhaps attempt, like the camel in the parable, to pass through the eye of a needle (Matt. 19:24). The next poem, dedicated to his friend Aksel Bakunts, is an imaginative recreation of the last night of Khachatur Abovian's life (1809–1948) before his mysterious disappearance. The long poem "*Mahvan tesil*" (Vision of death), inspired by Dante's *The Divine Comedy*, is a trip to hell to identify thinly disguised national heroes, writers, and founders of the liberation movement of the nineteenth century and the first two decades of the twentieth. For some he has affection, for others sarcasm and irony, but the overall message is that the way to liberation is through revolution. The last poem of the cycle is Charents' famed "*Patkam*" (Message), which contains a cryptic message: the second letters of each line spell out "Oh Armenian people, your only salvation is in your collective power."

From his early days Charents was an ardent revolutionary, and he remained so to the end of his life. But he became disillusioned when the Soviet Union betrayed Armenia by signing the treaties of Moscow (16 March 1921) and Kars (13 October 1921) with Kemalist Turkey. In 1929, when the borders were already permanently set, the Soviet Armenian historian Bagrat Borian (1882–1939) wrote: "The greatest land sacrifices were made in favor of Turkey at the expense of Armenia. With the treaty of Kars Armenia was auctioned off, in the Soviet-Oriental policy, for the sake of world revolution."[4] Charents was gradually returning to nationalist feelings.

---

3. In the fourth cycle of the epic, the legendary hero Pokr Mher (Mher the Younger), is expected to bring deliverance to the people, but is treacherously imprisoned in a cave, with the expectation that one day he will emerge and fulfill his mission. In Charents's version Mher comes out of the cave and leads the people to freedom. In the epic Dzenov Ohan (loud-voiced Ohan) represents those who talk a good game but in practice render servile obedience to despots. See the section on the medieval Armenian epic in the overview to volume 2 of *The Heritage of Armenian Literature*.

4. Diana Der Hovanessian and Marzbed Margossian, "Yeghishe Charents: His Life, His Poetry and His Times," *Ararat* 20, no. 1 (Winter 1979), 59.

By this time he had gained considerable fame and prestige in literary circles. As always, this raised a wave of jealousy and antagonism among lesser writers and inept commissars, who did not hesitate to condemn him with nationalism, disobedience of the party line, unconventional behavior, and a host of other real or imagined sins. This was the era of Stalin and Beria, when dissidents were silenced. In 1935 Charents was dismissed from the executive committee of the Writers' Union in Yerevan, and friends such as Aghasi Khanjian (1901–36), the first secretary of the Armenian Communist Party, and Aksel Bakunts (1899–1937) were exiled and executed. He wrote a moving poem on Bakunts, which was published in 1967, thirty years after Charents's death. One evening in early 1937 he was arrested and imprisoned on charges of insulting a high government official. On November 29th of the same year he died or was killed under mysterious circumstances.

Soon after Stalin's death, Anastas Mikoyan (1895–1978), a high-ranking government official, rehabilitated Yeghishé Charents, along with other writers, in a speech delivered on 11 March 1954. At this time also a considerable amount of Charents's writings that had been kept in a tin container and buried underground were revealed and carefully studied. Charents's daughter Anahit played an important part in this process.

Charents was and still is unsurpassed as an Armenian poet. His turbulent life and restless genius seem to have been the motivating factors of his rich and abundant literary production. Collections of his works and individual titles have been published in numerous volumes in Yerevan. Many of his works have been translated into Russian, French, English, Spanish, and almost all the languages spoken in the Soviet Union. The scholarly edition of his collected works, in six volumes, was published in Yerevan from 1962 to 1968. However, his complete works have still not been published because more material continues to surface.

FROM LAND OF NAYIRI[5]

(*This excerpt describes the day of the declaration of war in the dull provincial town of Nayiri, and the noisy demonstration of the Nayiri philistines, organized by the local tsarist powers and the bourgeoisie—the beginning of a great historic tragedy.*)

---

5. Yeghishé Charents, *Yerkir Nayiri* (Land of Nayiri) in *Ararat* 20, no. 1 (Winter 1979), 67–70. Translator anonymous.

The city of Nayiri was basking, that morning, in its lazy, peaceful Sunday rest. The bell of the Church of Apostles rang peacefully and serenely. Those who loved prayer went to church; but most of the citizens went out into the park, or sat in front of the locked stores, engaged in inane conversations. Some went to the coffeehouse owned by Telfon Seto, or to that of Yegor Arzumanov; others to the club. There was quite an assemblage in the club, that day: Sergei Kasparich, the city doctor; Osep Narimanov, the justice of the peace; Aram Antonych, the school inspector; Maruke, Kinturi Simon, who loved to move among the "worthies"; Khadji Onnik Manukoff Effendi, the anglomaniac merchant; and a few other citizens. They were playing preference, macao, and baccarat. They liked to play, and the games usually went on in a solemn silence, broken from time to time by ejaculations such as "pass," "twenty-eight," or "deal." But despite their utter absorption in the game, many of the players—and especially Sergei Kasparich and Osep Narimanov—felt somehow out of sorts. They often looked towards the door or the window, as though they felt a draft—despite the pleasant July weather. The trouble was that a certain "thing," to which they were all accustomed, was missing—if one may call a live and respected person a "thing." General Alesh was not at the club. There was no life in the club without him, especially as the second spirit of the club—Mazut Amo[6]—was also missing. . . . Before he started playing Osep Narimanov had asked—no; that's not how it happened: as he entered the club, Osep Narimanov had shouted joyously, as he always did:

"My sincere compliments, Alesh Nikitich!" . . . But there had been no answer, for the simple reason that Alesh Nikitich was not there. Osep Narimanov was stunned. A whole series of suspicions rose up before him on the instant; in the first place, General Alesh had promised, on leaving the club at 4 a.m., to come back at 10 in the morning and continue an interrupted game of macao, and in the second place, General Alesh had been looking in a peculiar way, lately, at Olga Vasilyevna Zheltokudraya Tykva, who belonged to him, Osep Narimanov, and to none other—and General Alesh had better look out!

These thoughts had barely taken shape in Osep Narimanov's mind when his friend, the school director Aram Antonych—about

---

6. Mazut is diesel oil. Charents uses it satirically.

whose wife the justice of the peace was so worried—came in hurriedly. Seeing that everyone had already started playing, Aram Antonych came up to Osep Narimanov, took him by the arm, and asked him to make a pool.

"My sincere compliments!" cried Osep Narimanov, sincerely gratified. "And how is Olga Vasilyevna, Aram Antonych?"

Osep Narimanov seemed only now to remember that it was already three days since he had seen Olga Vasilyevna; and that yesterday at six in the evening, when he came, as usual, to "call on" her (Aram Antonych was usually in his school at that hour), the maid had declared that Olga Vasilyevna was not receiving. As soon as he remembered this fact, his eyes blurred, and he was about to remove his clouded gaze from the shining eyes of Aram Antonych when. . . .

"Olga Vasilyevna sends you her greetings," said Aram Antonych with a mysterious smile; and then, bending down, he whispered: "The city midwife, Aksiona Manukovna, swore to us yesterday that this time it will be a boy."

A heavy stone rolled from the heart of Osep Narimanov. "So my long years of intimacy with Olga Vasilyevna have not been wasted," he thought happily; and he pressed Aram Antonych's hand with a friendly grip, saying:

"I shall have the honor to stand godfather to little Kolya—do you understand, Aram Antonych—it simply must be Kolya!" And both sat down to play.

"But where on earth is Alesh Nikitich?" asked Aram Antonych a moment later, as he dealt the cards. But everyone was busy playing, and nobody answered—although they all felt his absence. Doctor Sergei Kasparich glanced at the window, as though there were a draft; but he realized that this was not the cause of his discomfort, and silently went on playing.

And then, at about twelve o'clock or so, General Mesh and Amo Ambartsumovich rushed hastily into the club. They flew in like bombs, hurried to the tables, messed up the cards, and threw them to the floor. . . . Everyone jumped up, surprised and confused. But Kinturi Simon—although he had lost more than anyone, and therefore had the greatest cause for indignation—decided that the "fellows" had got drunk; so he threw down his cards, got up, and yelled foolishly:

"Hurrah! Hurrah! Hurrah!"

"Have you gone mad?" cried the doctor, angrily banging with his fist on the table. "What's the matter?"

Before the others had even come to themselves, Amo Ambartsumovich raised his arm and signed for attention. And. . . .

"War!" declared Amo Ambartsumovich, in a barely audible voice. Silence, awe and wonder settled over the room.

General Alesh also wanted to say something—he had already raised his arm; but under the influence of the silence which had come over them all, he stopped still and could not speak. The eyes of Aram Antonych also remained still, fixed on the raised arm of General Alesh. A comical, frightened smile was frozen on the face of the club monkey—Kinturi Simon. Sergei Kasparich raised his hand to his lips and coughed mechanically—a dry official cough, such as usually attacked him during consultations. Then General Alesh and Mazut Amo told everything they knew of what had occurred.

It seemed that about seven or eight o'clock that morning, when Amo Ambartsumovich was still asleep, suspecting nothing, a messenger had come to call him to the district commander, on extremely important business. He was requested to bring Alesh Nikitich with him. The latter when notified had dressed immediately and rushed to Mazut Amo's house; and together they had gone to the home of the district commander. At this unaccustomed hour of the morning, the district commander had received his guests extremely amicably, and had informed them that "*by the will of God and of our most august monarch,*" Russia *had declared war*—a war which had been forced on her. . . . As a matter of fact, *the infamous German Kaiser Wilhelm II had declared war on Russia.*

The district commander had explained to Alesh Nikitich and Mazut Amo that it was necessary to organize a demonstration, and to explain to the people the great, incalculable importance of this event.

Amo Ambartsumovich's report had the effect of thunder on his listeners. They threw down their cards and left the club, headed by General Alesh.

"Friends, it is time to begin," said Amo Ambartsumovich, stopping at the entrance to the club.

"What?" asked Kinturi Simon. He thought it was time to begin . . . the war.

"You shall see in a moment," answered Amo Ambartsumovich significantly, going back into the club. Kinturi Simon followed him. They came out of the club holding a large portrait of the tsar; they were followed by a club waiter, who set down a green card table in front of the club. A crowd gathered around the table.

"Friends!" shouted Mazut Amo, raising his arm.

Everyone was turned to stone, with gaping mouths. A real marvel—a wonderful person—this Amo Ambartsumovich—Mazut Amo!

From the dizzy height of his pedestal—the green card table—Amo Ambartsumovich announced to the great crowd of citizens assembled about him the news of war. With flashing eyes, from the height of his table, Mazut Amo cursed and berated the base German Kaiser, Wilhelm II. It seemed to the store-keeper Kolopotyan, who was standing in the crowd, that the German Kaiser must be a mortal enemy, a personal creditor of Mazut Amo's; to the barber Vasil, who was standing a little distance apart, Wilhelm appeared as a blood-thirsty monster. Nor did Mazut Amo forget to bring to the attention of the gathering the important circumstance, told him by the district commander, that our all-powerful prince and emperor had many times telegraphed to Wilhelm, proposing a *peaceful* settlement of their *misunderstandings;* but that, unfortunately, his efforts had been in vain. In conclusion, Mazut Amo called upon those present to come to the aid of their common fatherland in this critical hour, and to make willing sacrifices, not hesitating at small privations to help the fatherland.

"And so, long live our prince and emperor, and his valorous army! Down with the German Kaiser, Wilhelm the Second! Hurrah!"—thus did Mazut Amo conclude his historic speech, which to his great surprise, was received in utter silence. But you must not think that the people kept silence on purpose; no, of course not. They simply *did not know* that one must respond in such cases. But now General Alesh came into the breach. With an agility that could never have been expected from such a corpulent old man, he climbed up onto the green card table, stood next to Mazut Amo, waved his hat, and shouted "Hurra-a-a-ah!" He was echoed by a fearful roar from Sergei Kasparich, Osep Narimanov, and Kinturi Simon; and then the crowded park resounded so loudly that even Maruke, who had already left his partners and gone into the crowd, was confused for a moment, and almost took off his hat and roared. But of course Maruke did not actually do this. From the very first day he took a peculiar stand towards what was happening around him—but of that later.

The park was still thundering with joyous shouts when a military orchestra sent by the district commander began to play *God Save the Tsar.* All heads were bared. After the hymn, Osep Narimanov shouted to the crowd "Long live our beloved Prince Nicholas the Second! Hurrah!"—and again General Alesh and Mazut Amo began to shout and wave their arms on the green table. Then, after long applause and shouting, they got off the table; and a procession, led by these two respected townsmen, left the park and went along Main Street towards the home of the district commander. When the procession, accompanied by the military band, passed the coffee-houses owned by Telefon Seto and Yegor Arzumanov, the citizens inside left their games of cards and dominoes, poured out into the street, and stood in front of the coffee-houses until the procession had passed.

"What sort of a row is this?" asked the undertaker Knok, who held the queen of diamonds in his hand.

"Bread's gone up again," answered Telefon Seto, confidently; and he went back into the coffee house, shaking his head. "I can't see what all the noise is about," he said inside, addressing the empty space; but there was no answer, for everyone was out on the street watching the demonstration. "Bread's gone up again, so they're raising a row," he repeated, when his customers had come back inside to resume their interrupted games. "What else could it be?" answered Krivoi Artur; and the Nayirians thoughtfully nodded their heads.

However, some of the customers of the coffee-houses—such as Abomarsh, the storekeeper "Liar," Katolik Daniel, and others— noticed that the procession was led by such respected Nayirians as General Alesh and Mazut Amo; and they joined the crowd themselves, and went along with the procession. It soon became clear that the crowd was going to the district commander, to express its readiness and its loyal feelings; and Abomarsh felt that this was an extremely desirable and necessary act . . .

"Up to what age will the draft go?" asked Katolik Daniel.

"God alone knows, that depends on how many they need," answered Abomarsh, gloomily; and both speakers seemed to grow sad: they walked silently, with their eyes fixed on their shoes.

It was a hot Sunday. The sun shone brightly. The clear, cloudless sky hung over the town like a sky-blue plate. The playing band was followed by townspeople dressed in many-colored holiday clothes. To the children, most of whom went in front of the band, this spectacle, which of course they did not understand, seemed a merry holiday. The ten- or twelve-year-old son of Khadzhi Onnik Manikoff Effendi, who was known throughout the town for his pranks, marched alongside of the drummer, like a conqueror, and made believe he was a soldier, beating time:

"One-two-one-two-one-two!"

The procession finally reached the home of the district commander. The orchestra played *God Save the Tsar* and the district commander came out onto the porch. "Hurrah!" shouted the crowd led by General Alesh; and then a deathlike silence came over all. Everyone looked at the district commander. He was lean and long, and resembled a cane with an onion head. After looking out from the porch in silence at the gathered crowd for about two minutes, this tall district commander raised his hand to his lips and pretended to cough, and then spoke, in a dry, jerky, typically military voice:

"War! Prince Wilhelm Second! Our duty to serve our country and the throne! Long live! Down with! Hurra-a-ah!"

Again the crowd caught up the cry; again the orchestra played *God Save the Tsar*. And again . . . Mazut Amo spoke. Their faces shone with pride, like blooming roses. What would happen to Nayiri, pray tell us, if it were not for Amo Ambartsumovich—this leading light, Mazut Amo. It would be crushed and effaced; it would vegetate in the darkness of ignorance. He alone had "moved the cart from its place," despite all difficulties. He rescued them now again. In the name of the townspeople, Mazut Amo expressed full readiness to fight to the last drop of blood in defence of the throne and country. He knew quite well what language to use. A snaky tongue he had, Amo Ambartsumovich—Mazut Amo! . . .

After Mazut Amo, the district commander expressed his thanks to the grateful citizens, and suggested that they break up and go home. General Alesh, Amo Ambartsumovich, Osep Narimanov and the doctor were invited upstairs to dine. The crowd broke up. Some went home to eat; some to the coffee-houses—either that of Telefon Seto or that of Yegor Arzumanov; and many went to the city park, to kill time for the rest of the day.

It was thus, noisily and pompously, that this bloodthirsty guest, later to be called the World War, was met by the city of Nayiri; met with deep serious ceremony as becomes every real city. And for this the city was indebted above all to its worthy son Amo Ambartsumovich Asaturov—Mazut Amo.

The next day was Monday; everyone woke at dawn and went about his business, just as usual. Nothing had changed and nothing had occurred—unless we consider as an "occurrence" the insignificant circumstance that General Alesh, Mazut Amo, and their friends felt rather tired and worn out that morning—as they usually felt after drinking a lot. But to most of the townspeople—and especially to the merchants—it seemed that the talk of war which had taken place the day before was nothing but a harmless Sunday joke; Sunday was gone and Monday was at hand—and that was that. Time to get back to business. Of course, they spoke of the war at times—but only in passing, as of something that did not concern them. Thus passed one day—two days—three days. Thus passed the entire week. But very gradually the distant war made itself felt in full even in this far-off city of Nayiri. Yes, in full.

I LOVE THE SUN-BAKED TASTE OF ARMENIAN WORDS[7]

I love the sun-baked taste of Armenian words,
their lament like ancient lutes, the bend
of blood-red flowering roses in the accents,
the lilt of Nayirian steps still danced by girls.

I love the arch of skies, the faceted waters
running through its syllables; the mountain

---

7. Yeghishé Charents, *"Yes im anush Hayastani arevaham barm em sirum"* (I love the sun-baked taste of Armenian words), in *Anthology of Armenian Poetry*, ed. and trans. Diana Der Hovanessian and Marzbed Margossian (New York, 1978), 198–99.

weather, the meanest hut that bred this tongue.
I love the thousand-year-old city stones.

Wherever I go, I take its mournful music,
its steel forged letters turned to prayers.
However sharp its wounds, and drained of blood,
or orphaned, for my homesick heart there is no other balm.

No blow, no mind like Narek's, Kuchak's.
No greater utterence. No mountain reach
like the peak of Ararat.
Search the world there is no crest so white.
So like an unreached road to glory. Masis.
(No other language tells my want.)

1920–21

OCEAN SONG[8]

Refrain:
> Sing, poet, sing, sing the wind's song.
> Sing love and struggle's song.
> Sing like a storm, like a simoom,[9] sing.
> In your heart don't let it die, the song!

I remember the ocean in the tempest's hour
Rocking at its breast the endless waters,
And there was thunder in the abyss—a fearful wind howling
Sang a savage song.
Its song rang with boundless grief
And the shoreless longing of a titan soul
Which, crazed with the ocean's imperious dark,
Called out with unending love.
A heart illimitable, maddened, called;
Howling, it called its love
Who fled singing from the center of the storm

---

8. "Ovkiani Yerge" (Ocean song), *Ararat*, 73. Translated by Diana Der Hovanessian.

9. A hot, dry, dust-laden wind blowing at intervals in the African and Asian deserts.

And flew pealing to the ends of beyond.
An escaper roaring from the midst of the winds,
His lofty lover never finding,
Desolate wind, amazing in his grieving,
Sang victory's song far away.
It was wind and water's battle bleak,
The love of two enemies, one another enrapturing,
Giant simoom of a love without rest
That gave battle's song to the wind.

It was the triumphal hymn of shoreless passion,
Heroic song of love without end,
And in surrender to that love's victory hymn
The fierce wind sang to the assault.

Refrain:
 A boundless grief, an endless love
 Burned you in life with its final infinity
 Like that wind howling, calling,
 The fierce blast from the dark.

That love shook you like the crashing wind
Crushing the breakers in its cruel career
And passed from your heart in this hour of battle
Like an anger-roused procession marching,
And like lightning it exploded on your thoughts
Like a flash, cachinnating, wind-rattling,
And your thoughts reared mountainous, oceanic,
And your wind-pursued love roared thunder.

ODE FOR THE DEAD[10]

With anguish I watch you leave,
you who will not be returning,
you who will stay forever
in silence and out of touch
with the pulse of the universe,

---

10. "Ovkiani Yerge," 77. Translated by Diana Der Hovanessian.

you who will not taste again its fragrance
nor feel the heave of its voice.

You will become instead
part of its earth and water
as all of us will. Our luck
and lot are the same.
Only the souvenir differs,
that unbuyable legend that stays behind
to fill all beating hearts with yearning.

Days turn to ashes, stars turn to ashes.
The suns die and turn to ashes.
Spring blackens to ashes. Its greenness
all ashes, bud and enflamed rose
and all the flowers with the sad names.
But the souvenir? Does it generate light
from light? Flame from flame?
The souvenir that rose from action
settles like a haze over simmering water.
It stays and is never consumed.

The souvenir echoes the days you used.
It reflects and is reflected. It shoots
up along the banks of roads you passed, sprouts
in the hot noon, falls with dew on new flowers
as the ultimate gift.

It lifts up from your heart, from your thoughts,
even from your blood and your last breath.
But it does not belong to you.
Just as my audacious lines no longer
belong to me the minute
they arrive on paper.

The souvenir, like the ray of the sun
or the light of the dead star,
reaches out from the day past.

Let the dead sleep the sleep of oblivion.
Something will glow forever,
burn in eternal light.

It is what is left behind in life,
in the fire of the souvenir.

Hairdresser's Charms[11]

The woman sits brooding, waiting
for the hairdresser to conjure up
a new vision in the silver mirror,
acknowledges herself with dead eyes
from under her blond hair, wondering what can be made
lovable in the strange face staring back.

The mirror mocks her too but sadly
like death making an inspection, taking inventory.
But the hairdresser hovers like love,
like a strange friend, working miracles.

The smile is a smirk. Powders, sprays in hand
for the sorcery, the charms, the spells that are for sale.

The twinkling scissors, intimate, working against
the clacking clock, wicked
with its staccato beat, striking
with sharp strokes like a shower of sizzling hail.
The invoker of spells, the maker of magic,
performs the old art.

And in a little while the woman
will rise with an unwilling smile,
a stranger even to herself
to approve such transformation,
that she will use to enslave, torture and torment.
Believe, oh woman, in the magic you see here.
I am a poet and know that in this somber world
this analgesic, this balm, is the only true charm left.
It is the gloss, the glow, rising from sham.

---

11. "Varsaviri hmaykner" (Hairdresser's charms), in ibid. Translated by Diana
Der Hovanessian.

Toros Azatian

(1898–1955)

Toros Azatian (who wrote under the pen name Azatuni), writer, poet, and journalist, was born in Apuchegh, a village in Akn, Western Armenia. He was educated first in the local Narekian school and then in Chmshkatzag (Chemishkezek in Turkey). He embraced writing as a career at a very young age. His poems were published in three volumes under the series title *Aghpiur anmahutyan* (Fountain of youth, 1926, 1927, 1933). His prose works consist of memories and images from the villages, and they were collected in *Krasnak* (Forty days, 1930). His travel impressions, prose poems, and a series of village scenes appeared in Istanbul in 1936.

Azatian also published a periodical called *Astghaberd,* (1951–53) to promote Armenian studies. His biographical studies were published as separate volumes: *Misak Metzarents, ir kyanke* (Misak Metzarents, his life, 1922); *Voski arishin tak* (Under the golden vine-arbor, 1934), a collection of Metzarents's prose work; *Komitas vardapeti kyankn u gortze* (Father Komitas's life and work, 1931); *Komitas Vardapeti knarergutiun-nere* (Father Komitas's poetry, 1939); and *Zhamanakakits demker: Zabel and Hrand Asatur* (Contemporary figures: Zabel and Hrand Asatur, 1937). In addition, he coauthored, with H. Acharian, A. Khachaturian,

K. Pasmachian (Basmadjian), G. Manukian, and S. Shamlian, an important study of Armenian family names, published in Istanbul in 1937. Between 1925 and 1932 he and M. Chukhachian (Chukhadjian) edited the yearbook of Holy Savior Armenian National Hospital. He also founded the *Mshakuyt* (Culture) publishing house.

Azatian assumed editorial responsibility for several dailies and periodicals, and took charge of many different literary sections and supplements, including *Zartonk* (Enlightenment, 1932–33) and *Arevelk havelvatz* (Supplement to The Orient, 1932). He also contributed to the Armenian press outside Istanbul.

He taught at the Pezazian (Bezazian) school and was secretary of the Armenian Patriarchate of Istanbul for many years.

SOLITUDE[1]

I am sitting in a public park.
Beneath an arch of woven green branches.
Silence surrounds me, and tranquility fills my soul.
The early morning hour refreshes me.

The sun smiles constantly upon the prospering land. Far away, the waters of the Bosporus flow on with countless waves, wearing diamond-studded robes. On the mountain tops, the mist has just begun to dissipate. Green piles, washed and transformed into objects of beauty, cast off the veil that covered them.

A tower rises up from the sea to remind me of the death of a princess.[2] I want to forget that bitter episode, thereby preserving the peace that fills my soul.

Suddenly Constantinople begins to breathe and come to life before my eyes, and memories of its past invite me to a conversation. I decline, for suddenly I feel quite indisposed. I close my eyes to listen to the bird songs, which at that moment bring me relief, like prayer. I quickly pull myself together and look around. A few passengers are standing beneath the awnings, others in the shade of trees, as if to emphasize my solitude.

---

1. Toros Azatian, "Arandznutiun" (Solitude), in *Zmrukhte patmuchan* (Emerald tunic) (Istanbul, 1936), 160–61. Translated by Ardashes Shlemian. Edited and footnoted by the editors of the present anthology.
2. Reference is to Leander's Tower in the Sea of Marmara.

I turn my attention back to nature. I wind my soul like an incessant hurdy-gurdy, played against the backdrop of distant scenes and unarticulated feelings.

But my exaltation does not last for long. Why? I sense, experience a change within me. The tranquility that filled my soul has left me. I ponder how to calm the storm of my unsettled soul.

The shadow of a sailboat on the water catches my attention. An inexplicable sorrow gradually suffuses my existence. What connection can there be between the shadow of a sail and my soul?

Happy sailboat! No matter how strong your arms, no matter how brisk and steady the wind that fills your sail, you will not be able to stick this course: you would sink, you would disappear, if, at this moment, you found yourself in the turbulent waters of my soul.

Suddenly there is music. The sounds of jazz jostle my existence, tearing my mental obsessions to pieces. A joyful atmosphere has sprung to life, and I am not a part of it. I have no desire to share the mood of the crowd. Couples glide across the dance floor, watched attentively by the crowd.

The proximity of this gaiety does not appeal to me, but becomes more and more inimical to my sorrow. I leave, like a startled bird. I go away, seeking tranquility for my soul.

Shavarsh Narduni

(1898–1968)

Journalist, philologist, and prolific writer Shavarsh Narduni was born in Armash, an Armenian village in Izmit, Turkey. He was educated in the local school before moving to Adapazar to study at the Kedronakan. After the end of the First World War, he entered the Medical Faculty of the University of Istanbul, but he was soon expelled for political reasons. He later resumed his medical studies in Paris; after graduating in 1927 he worked for a while at a mental hospital in Amiens.

Narduni began writing pastoral songs and verses at an early age, but he later destroyed these juvenile writings, along with other early literary experiments. His literary interest eventually focused on prose, where it remained for the rest of his life. At the initiative of various associations and publishers, his *Alpom hekyatneru* (Album of fables: Athens, 1927), *Meghediner, meghediner . . . hekyat yev banasdeghtzutiun* (Melodies, melodies: fables and poems, Paris, 1933), *Yerusaghem, Yerusaghem* (Jerusalem, Jerusalem, Paris, 1938), *Baner, baner, inch baner* (This and that, Paris, 1951), and similar works appeared from time to time. In general, these are all based on experiences, images, and sweet and painful recollections from his native village. There is a kind of idealized nostalgia and melancholy in his recollections of his birthplace; his folktales, stories, and vignettes of human love are retold in an elegant manner.

His collection *Nartyan patarag* (A Narduni offering) was published by his friends in Beirut in 1968, on his seventieth birthday, a day before his death. Another collection of his writings, *Grakan tsolker* (Literary reflections), was published posthumously in 1975. Other works, indeed the bulk of his literary, philological, historical, and linguistic writings, remain scattered in the Armenian dailies and periodicals of the time.

Narduni wrote short prose pieces, tales, stories, recollections, observations, and reflections. Not all of them, however, are of the same high quality.

For more than a quarter of a century Narduni published *Hay buyzh* (The Armenian remedy), a monthly magazine, as a testimony to his devotion to his vocation as a medical man.

THE TOWER OF BABYLON[1]

And this was how it was in the land of Shinar.

From the entrance of the valleys of Babylon to the valley of Sokot, and from the west to the Sea of Isles, an immense circular area, the radius of which was the length of the three-times-seven "Sabbath-day roads," was filled with white tents, like a fleet of Phoenician sailing ships. Glittering Babylon was deserted: Babylon, which seemed to float like a magnificent raft on two silver arms of water, was now adorned with snow-white canopy. No one could be seen in the windows where once harlots sat, calling Assyrian merchants to pleasure from behind orange curtains that drooped as gently as eyelashes. All, all had left for Shinar, where seventy-seven kings had gathered their peoples to build a tower to a height that no waters could reach: the Amorites, the Edomites, the Babylonians, the Caridarbians, the Arvadites, the Samaritans, the Zuzims, the Casluhims, the Hamathites, the Goreans, the Ludians, the Somians, the Elamites, the Scythians, the Phrygians, the Sabeans, the Cappadocians, the Gomorrhans, the Sodomites, the Jebusites, the Salemites, the Gheledians, the Parthians, and the Armenians.

King Godolagomorrh, who reigned over the people of Elam, sat in Beglam, on the banks of the river Gozan. The river meandered

---

1. Shavarsh Narduni, "The Tower of Babylon," in *Great Armenian Short Stories* (Beirut, 1959), 37–42. Translated by Sarkis Ashjian and revised by the editors of the present anthology.

through a grove of almond trees, the flaming flowers of which dappled the surface of the water like small lamps at the beginning of spring. In the garden where the king had struck his tent was a vast pool, shaped like a harp. The water of the river trickled into this pool through delicate pipes and created wonderful music. The king sat in the shadow of the almond trees all day long and listened to the chatter of his concubines; and he listened to the music of the harp, while his people carried turpentine trees from the valley of Elboran and cedars from the mountains of Lebanon for the construction of the tower.

King Ashtaroth, who reigned over the Chariadarbians, sat in Siddim. He mounted his horse and went to hunt quail and partridge in the summer mornings. The partridges fled until they grew weary of flight, then fluttered into a bush and wept. The mighty king drew near, stretched out his hand in childish delight, and closed it over an exhausted, living partridge. Then he sat under the high arches of the trees, roasted quail and partridge, and garnished them with honey-sweet grapes, while his people, who were all villagers, bore huge stones from the quarries of Mount Seir on their shoulders.

King Slalmaneser, who reigned over the Assyrians, sat in Dibon, the legendary city on the road leading to the Mount of Jeul, which looked like a crouching tiger, his awful eyes fixedly watching Salem. The king drank all day long to the sound of enchanting music, and then he entered his opulent seraglio to satisfy his lust for pleasure, while his people brought great quantities of oil from the valley of Siddim in jars.

Artavazd, king of the Armenians, lived on a hill, in a tent made of blue woolen cloth, the magnificent curtains of which were adorned with seven sardonyx clasps that glowed like the eyes of a wakeful watchman. While the king slept inside on sweet-scented, warm furs, his people made bricks for the tower. And the tower rose: an enormous, seven-sided building. It had already risen to three thousand measures above the ground, and its perimeter was seventy fathoms. Every five hundred measures, the tower terminated in a round terrace, from the center of which rose a new tower, a bit narrower than the one preceding it.

Gamaliel, a Babylonian scientist, declared in those days that at the end of three lunar months the tower would reach the bounds of heaven. Then the bowmen of Ochozias, the Armenian archers, and the brave Ghorreans would come forward to rend the blue curtain of heaven and drive Yahweh into slavery. For men had revolted against Jehovah, who had threatened them with death. They wanted to live long, to enjoy all the pleasures of life and the sweet flowers of sin. They wanted their names and their fame to last for generation after generation.

And the people worked and toiled, without ever grumbling. When night fell, they hung brilliant vessels filled with oil from the terraces of the tower, and the light illuminated the entire field of Shinar. And instead of taking their rest, the weary multitude came out of their tents to dance and amuse themselves. The smoke of baked fish and the smell of Egyptian garlic tantalized their nostrils. Then the Jewish girls danced, nearly naked, while the old people, tucking up their broad white cassocks, grabbed cymbals and trumpets, fifes and zithers, horns and bells and multi-stringed harps, and played on them, skipping after the girls. The Assyrians had long, wailing melodies, and the dances of their girls resembled twirling more than skipping. Very sad and sorrowful was their "Dance of Moods." The skin of the Edomites was the color of burnt brick. So one could not tell what they were wearing when they came out to dance at dusk. They were very lively, and their muscles quivered in their bodies. They always danced in pairs, and passionately. Oh, how wonderful was their dance called "The Night Storm." The man crouched down like a partridge unable to flap its wings, and movingly turned round and round, while the woman looked down from above, her arms outstretched, hanging like a vine-tree, and constantly changed the veils covering her bosom and face, and when she changed the veils the color of her bosom and face changed too. The partridge wailed under the stormy sky, the clouds glided speedily by, now covering the moon, now revealing it.

And so the people amused themselves in the peace of the night, until horns sounded from the top of the tower. Then they put out all the lights and went to sleep. Only one light remained, at the top of the tower, like a flower hanging in the sky. Sometimes that solitary lamp blazed up, stretching its fiery tongue into the sky, biting the wind-driven clouds, but it never went out. The master, Parula, often watched there, and had beatific visions.

He had wide, deep-blue eyes, full of feeling and mystery. He had lips that expressed human joy and divine wisdom. The kings had entrusted him with the construction of the tower, which would endure for centuries and into history, to immortalize their royal names. The higher the tower rose, the more Parula rejoiced, and he seemed to look across time, to the distant horizons of history. "No waters will be able to destroy its foundations; no tempest will be able to shake its gigantic structure, nor shall Yahweh ever be able to burn it to ashes. Humanity shall reign over time, like a god!"

Parula loved the tower, and he seemed to live only for the tower. But Parula's heart filled with a new love during the seventh year of construction. When the Scythians brought construction material from the northern countries, they also brought a wonderful, unearthly girl, as a present for the architect. Parula loved her beyond words and named her Sivan, after the month in which she had been brought to him.

Sivan was beautiful, like a cloud wrapped in sunlight. Her tresses spread over her bluish mantle like yellow broom flowers. Parula felt weak at the sight of the beautiful girl, and the vision of the heaven-soaring tower was soon wiped from his soul.

One night he had a disturbing dream. He was sleeping in a tent. Now and then he opened his eyes and looked about him. The curtain of the tent had been removed and he could see the white tower in the distance, as beautiful as a snow-covered mountain. Sivan stood in front of the tent and looked with great jealousy at the tower. And suddenly he heard Sivan address the tower: "I am beautiful—just look at me and see. I am beautiful and desirable; no sooner do a man's lips touch me, than they burn with sweet passion. My skin inflames the souls of men. And if I gaze at a man, not one of them is capable of choosing eternity over the present moment. Who is happier: the prince who gets drunk and rejoices in my warm arms, or your kings, whose names you try to engrave on history, you senseless heap?"

"Beauty belongs to the one who endures!"

"Happiness belongs to the one who lives!"

"My life will span centuries."

"A life like that of a wearied beggar, like that of a bored animal . . . whereas I, the beautiful Sivan, give delight to young men and dreams to everybody. . . ."

Sivan spoke with passion and excitement, while the tower answered with serene calm. At last Sivan grew mad with rage and

began to hurl stones at the tower. And suddenly—terror of terrors!
—the highest terrace was shorn off and fell down in pieces.

Parula awoke in anguish, and saw that Sivan slept by his side.
The moon up above looked like a water lily. He freed himself from
Sivan's naked arms, went out onto the balcony, and ascertained
that the tower remained standing in the field of Shinar, in all its
glory. He returned to his bed and stared at Sivan.

But the Council of the Elders had already noticed that the construction of the tower was not progressing at its previous pace. Various rumors troubled the people's minds. Jehovah gathered dark
clouds on top of Mount Seir. Torrential rains impeded the workers.

And the Council of Elders sent the sage Melchiras to Parula,
to suggest that the rate of construction of the tower should be
increased. Parula looked into the eyes of Sivan, in which he seemed
to read: "I am the tower. You will love nobody but me!"

But why, why could Parula no longer make the tower so strong
and beautiful, as he had when construction began? Parula was
exceedingly troubled when he saw that the new construction was
clumsy and unsatisfactory. But how beautiful Sivan was!

The people showed signs of uneasiness and the kings grew
disappointed. They could no longer harbor the cherished idea of
raising their names above the clouds. They could no longer think
of writing their names on the curtain of the sky, and they could
no longer disregard the laws of Jehovah, attain immortality, and
endure through centuries of history. Was it impossible to build a
tower to the stars?

"I am the tower," said Sivan, and by and by Parula forgot
the other tower, the one that stood on the field of Shinar and rose
three thousand measures above the ground. He had lost his skill,
and whatever he added to the tower was destroyed the following
day, unable to withstand the spring rain and the wind. And down
in the fields the people fought constantly with each other, out of
disappointment and boredom. Many wished to return to their own
countries, objecting: "It is useless. Everything is utterly useless, the
tower will never be completed."

Parula believed that the best, the only tower was his Sivan!

And one tempestuous morning, blasted by thunder and shaken
by winds, the gigantic tower shuddered and collapsed. And the
seventy-seven kings and their peoples ran off, as if pursued by
devils, and dispersed to the four corners of the world. . . .

Nshan Peshiktashlian (Beshiktashlian)

(1898–1972)

Nshan Peshiktashlian was born in Istanbul. His education did not go beyond elementary school. As a result of his lifelong reading, his observant and curious mind, and his creative imagination, which helped him develop his originality, he provided himself with the background and experiences necessary to become a prolific author of plays, verse, and prose pieces—but chiefly of satire, on which his fame rests.

He began to write at the age of twelve. Even in his earliest work he manifested a genuine inclination to and talent for satire. " 'He has turned tears into laughter,' confronting human weaknesses, defects, mistakes, and pretensions with the smile of a wise man."[1] He had an impressive talent for satire. Some critics have judged him rather harshly as a writer; others have ranked him with Hakob Paronian (Baronian, 1843–91) and Yervand Otian (1869–1926). Peshiktashlian's language is flexible, adapting to as many stylistic modes as his subjects require.

His literary output is both varied and prolific: *Enker Shahnazar* (Comrade Shahnazar, 1927); *Sidonna* (1928); *Rappi* (1932); *Yergitzakan* (Satire, 1933); *Hivandates* (Nurse, 1936); *Tzaghrankarner* (Satirical

---

1. Minas Teoleolian, *Dar me grakanutiun: 1920–1980* (A century of literature: 1920–1980) (Boston, 1977), 2:190.

sketches, 1942); *Mer partezen* (From our garden, 1947); *Hakob Oshakan* (1947); *Grikor Narekatsi yev Smbat II* (Grikor Narekatsi and Smbat II, 1950); *Nor tzaghrankarner* (New satirical sketches, 1954); *Huzume* (The emotion, 1953); *Momianere* (The mummies, 1954); *Taterakan demker* (Theater people, 1969); a voluminous work, *Hrashalur patmutiun Hayots* (The miraculous history of the Armenians), published posthumously in 1972; and other writings scattered in the pages of the Armenian periodical press. There is also a collection of unpublished works, which may one day be assembled and published.

In Lieu of a Preface[2]

THE SMILE

The smile is the most precious of the gifts that God gave only to mankind. But human beings must use and polish that gift. People with long faces are an affront to the Creator as well as to the people and other creatures around them.

Do you know why the Almighty Father blessed only humans with that gift? It carried a message from Him: "You alone, human creature, of all breathing beings in the world, have in your possession all the means necessary to make you feel happy. You alone can laugh and enjoy the abundance that nature provides for you."

Has the human being been happy? Has he laughed? No, he has neither laughed nor provided a good laugh to others. Through the centuries he has done his best to strangle his happiness with his own hands.

Now it is time for mankind to learn to smile, in order to rediscover the lost paradise.

It is time for the satirist to play the devil's advocate and help to raise a tribute to the God-given gift of the smile.

The smile is a bouquet of unfading golden lilies, handed to humans by a host of joyful spirits.

The smile is the star of the human soul, the ray of the body; the star is beneficial to the soul; the ray generates life. Blessed is he

---

2. Nshan Peshiktashlian, *"Zhpite"* (The smile), in *Mer Partezen* (From our garden) (Paris, 1947), 5–9. Translated by Nairi Bahlavuni and edited by the editors of the present anthology.

who is born under that star! Esteemed is he who is invigorated by that ray.

The smile gives us a sense of self-appreciation. It generates dynamic energy and blood circulation, the euphoria induced by red cells, and renders our dispositions robust.

Humans feel younger when they smile.

Thought becomes gilded, dreams are transformed into a sweet perfume, and hope radiates light.

The smile is the light of contentment, which is pleasing to God. The smile, then, is Christian. As much as if it wore a halo on its head.

The lotus grows in a swamp. The smile is a kind lotus, able to flower amidst misery and misfortune. The smile is the gold of the poor. It is gold engendered in the depths of our spiritual reservoirs. It must be refined and purified—in other words, not base, and devoid of the impurities of bitterness, envy, and meanness: just unadulterated gold. A coin minted of such gold cannot bear the image of an earthly ruler, but only the stamp of the One and Only, the Almighty.

"Render unto . . . God the things that are God's." Your smile is only on loan from Heaven.

The smile is a sweet perfume. It exhales the breath of the soul. Incense, myrrh, and holy oils burn in it, lighting up one's face and lending their sweetness to the glance.

We need to make others smile. We smile to make a woman return our smile. Good fortune is like a woman. You must smile at it before it smiles back at you.

The smile is a song of joy: a silent song, but an eloquent one.

It is a drop of honey that pours from the heart and spreads over the face. It is seen in the eyes, around the lips, and even on the skin. The eyes contain the twinkling of a star that bodes good news, the corners of the lips hint at exuberance, the skin gleams as if drenched in sun and oil.

Smiling is nourishing. It has been tasted. Two souls have often nourished each other with smiles. It has been examined and proven that one smile is as beneficial as a good orange or a bunch of incense-tasting grapes. Sometimes, even, the smile is life itself.

Know how to live, suffer, and, if necessary, die—but with a smile on your face. Those who smile will not easily give in to misfortune. The smile is invulnerable.

Become pedagogues of the merits of the smile. If you cannot be a pedagogue, be good students, and teach others to smile.

Keep your sorrow locked up in your eyes, in your soul, inside yourself. But perhaps it is best to let the prisoner free. Get rid of it. Drown it from time to time in good wine.

Smile, smile. . . .

And the world will be filled with swallows, nightingales, and doves.

It will be spring again, a new dawn, a new, sweet, soul-stirring song. Is a new twilight yet to come? The twilight too will be woven with smiles.

Misers smile . . . smile . . . smiles are free.

If all people on the globe were to cooperate, all together, in unison, and smile for a moment, everything would be saved. Believe me, believe me: disarmament, reconciliation, and peace would break out all over. The winds of joy would blow. The doves would go crazy. . . . They would perch on the nerves of politicians, form an arch over thousands of cities, and drop lotuses, lotuses. . . .

The Holy Spirit would appear, and even inanimate things would begin to smile and sing.

Aksel Bakunts (Aleksandr Tevosian)

(1899–1937)

Alexander Tevosian, known by the pen name Aksel Bakunts, was born in Goris, Armenia. He received his early education at the local parochial school and in 1910 was admitted as a boarding student to the Gevorgian seminary in Etchmiadzin, free of tuition, upon pleas to the catholicos by more than a hundred villagers. He graduated in 1917, well versed in ancient and modern Armenian literature, Russian, and history, particularly that of his own nation. He joined the Armenian volunteers and fought against the Turkish invaders in Erzurum, Kars, Surmalu, and finally in Sardarapat. From 1918 to 1920 he worked as a reporter and proofreader for various newspapers in Yerevan, then left for Kharkov, Ukraine, to study agriculture (1920–23). Upon his return he occupied various positions as an agronomist in Goris, and he settled in Yerevan in 1926.

His main interest, however, was always literature. He began writing very early. In 1915, while still a student, he published an article in the Shushi paper *Paylak* (Flash), satirizing the mayor of Goris; the young author was jailed for a month for his audacity. In 1918 he began to publish a series of booklets, consisting of a series of lectures on agriculture, under the general title *Giughatsu matenadarane* (The peasant's library). Between 1923 and 1925 he serialized such works as *Mer giugherum*

(In our villages) and *Gavarakan namakani* (Letters from the provinces), which dealt with village life and psychology, in the periodical press.

Bakunts produced his best works after 1925. The setting for most of them is the majestic mountain scenery of the region of Zangezur. His love of nature, the land, and the laborer were his main sources of inspiration. He was a skilled craftsman, working meticulously on his stories, experimenting and perfecting his style and penetrating deeper into the psychology of his heroes until he was satisfied. The first collection of short stories to win him renown was *Mtnadzor* (The dark valley, 1927). It included some of his best stories, such as "*Alpiakan manushak*" (The Alpine violet), "*Lar Margar*," and "*Mirhav*" (Pheasant). These tales portray, with an artist's skill and sensitivity, the drama of life, the clash of old and new, and the discrepancies between tradition, religion, and politics in remote rural areas. "*Alpiakan manushak*," the skillful story of a beautiful woman driven by jealousy, contrasts the beauties of nature and the harshness of human behavior. "*Lar Margar*" is the story of a survivor of the Turkish massacres who realizes his dream of settling in the Armenian homeland.

Hovnatan March (a proper name, 1927), is a semi-satirical work with political overtones. Though a number of years had passed since the Soviet revolution, the new ideology had not yet fully penetrated the entire country. Writers of the old school still called for literary moderation and attachment to tradition, and Bakunts belonged to this group.[1] His association with that movement later led to his demise.

A second collection, *Patmvatzkner* (Short stories), was published in 1928, followed by *Spitak dzin* (The white stallion, 1929). In 1929 Bakunts tried his hand at writing a novel, *Karmrakar* (The red rock), which revolves around conditions prevailing in the rural areas of Armenia at the turn of the century and how social change affected the pattern of life there; unfortunately, this novel remains unfinished. Another attempt at a novel was a fictional biography of Khachatur Abovian, *Khachatur Aboviani anhayt batsakayume* (Khachatur Abovian's mysterious disappearance), for which Bakunts carried out long and meticulous research. This too remains incomplete, although a few fragments from it were published in 1932.

The years 1932–36 were Bakunts's most productive. He worked hard to achieve artistic perfection of language and style and sharpen his

---

1. Other members of the group included the poets Yeghishé Charents (1897–1937) and Gegham Sarian (1902–76), and the prose writers Gurgen Mahari (1903–69) and Vagharshak Norents (1906–73).

sensitivities to the sights, sounds, smells, tastes, and textures of his people and their life. Stories like *"Sev tsleri sermnatsane"* (The sower of black furrows, 1933), *"Andzreve"* (Rain, 1935), *"Yeghbayrutyan enkuzeninere"* (The walnut trees of brotherhood, 1936), *"Keri Davon"* (Uncle Davo, 1936); and pieces such as *"Namak rusats takavorin"* (Letter to the king of Russia) and *"Bruti tghan"* (The son of the potter) deal mostly with themes related to the people, authority, and social and psychological clashes. In his last work, *Kyores* (an allusion to his birthplace, Goris, 1935), he paints a satirical portrait of the entire social structure, dealing with the clash of the old and the new in the pre-Soviet era; this work is similar in tone and intent to Charents's *Yerkir Nayiri* (The land of Nayiri). Bakunts attacks government officials and usurers, and he looks at the backwardness and poverty of the peasants under them with compassion and anger.

He worked for a while as a screenwriter at the Hayfilm movie studios in Yerevan, where he wrote the screenplays for three movies: *Sev tevi tak* (Under a black wing, 1930), *Tragedia Aragatzi vra* (Tragedy on Mount Aragatz, 1931), and *Zangezur* (1936). He also translated Nicolai Gogol's *Taras Bulba* from Russian (1934) and *Aghvesagirk* (The book of the fox), a collection of medieval fables from classical to modern Armenian (1935).

Bakunts was and still is considered one of the best Armenian short story writers. He was a good friend of Charents and shared some of his opinions, both political and literary; the difference was that while Charents was vocal and fiery, Bakunts was calm and composed. This did not save him from sharing Charents's fate, however. One night in 1937 Bakunts was arrested, taken from his home, and eliminated: where and how no one knows. All his manuscripts were destroyed at the same time.

After Stalin's death, Bakunts and a host of other victims were rehabilitated, and his works began to be published in Yerevan, in collections or as individual titles. Some of his works have been translated into Russian, English, French, and German.

THE ALPINE VIOLET[2]

The top of Mt. Kagavaberd is draped in clouds the year round. White drifts hide the jagged walls of the castle, with tall black

---

2. Aksel Bagunts, "The Alpine Violet," in *We of the Mountains: Armenian Short Stories* (Moscow, 1972), 12–21. Translated by Fainna Glagoleva.

towers emerging here and there. From afar it seems that sentries are patrolling the ramparts, that the great iron doors of the castle are locked and that at any moment a guard might challenge a stranger scaling the mountain.

But when the wind scatters the clouds and the white shreds dissolve, first the leaning top of a tower appears and then the overgrown walls, half-buried in the earth. There are no iron gates, there are no sentries.

Silence reigns over the ruins of Kagavaberd. The only sound is that of the turbulent Basut in the canyon below as it rushes along, polishing the blue quartz of the narrow bedrock. It seems that a thousand wolf-hounds are howling beneath the churning waters, gnawing away at their iron chains.

A hawk and a vulture have made their nests in the walls. At the first rustling footstep they fly up with wild cries and begin circling over the ruins. A mountain eagle joins them. Its beak is a curved saber, its claws are pointed spears, its feathers are a coat of mail.

The only flower that grows so high on Kagavaberd is the violet. It is blood-red, with a stem as red as the feet of a ptarmigan. The flower blooms among the ruins. When the clouds lie low upon the gloomy castle walls, the stem bends low to let the flower lay its head upon a sun-drenched rock. A bright beetle, bathing in the pollen, sees the flower as a swing and the world as a crimson blossom.

Far below, in the canyon on the opposite bank of the Basut, are several huts. In the morning columns of smoke rise from the circular openings in the roofs. Dissolving into blue ribbons, they disappear among the clouds. In the heat of noon a cock might crow in the village; an old peasant, yawning in the shade of his house and lost in his memories, draws figures in the sand with a stick

Time drags on both in the village and in the castle above. The years are like the changing leaves of a tree. Memories become confused. Now, as always, the river rushes by; above are the same rocks and the same mountain eagle.

How many generations have lived out their lives on the bank of the Basut? How many people have spread their tattered felt rugs here and covered their roofs with reeds? In spring, when the violet blooms on the slopes of Kagavaberd, how many have taken their goats and sheep up to the mountain pastures, then filled their saddle-bags with cheese, and, in winter, eaten it with bread made of millet?

One hot noon three men on horseback rode up the rocky slope of Kagavaberd. From their clothing and the way two of them sat in the saddle you could tell they were city men who had never seen the castle or the cliffs before.

The third man was their guide. While the first two clutched at their horses' manes and were bent over double to keep their seats, the third rider hummed a song as he swayed in the saddle, a song as melancholy and hopeless as the deserted canyon, as the gloomy cliff and the distant village.

The clouds that masked the castle would sometimes part like a curtain, now revealing walls, now covering the tops. The first rider could not tear his eyes from the walls. In his mind's eye he reviewed the legends about the castle, tales preserved in the parchment chronicles of the times when princes had ruled here, when horses in armor had trodden the path outside the iron gate and warriors brandishing their spears had returned from raiding parties. The eyes that peered through his glasses were those of a scholar. He could actually see the warriors and the chroniclers who had sung their praises, their sharpened reeds scratching words on the parchment, he could hear the hoof beats of those ancient steeds. How difficult it was for him to ride up the cliff which the former inhabitants of the castle had scaled as easily as mountain goats.

Finally, they reached the village. The first rider continued on his way. He was looking for the old road and noticed neither the children playing in the ashes of the campfires nor the goats that followed him with surprised eyes.

The second rider, a man in a felt hat, was not searching for the past on top of Kagavaberd. His possessions were a sharpened pencil and a thick drawing pad. As soon as a face or a charming corner with a moss-covered rock struck him he would begin to draw.

One rider was an archaeologist, the other was an artist. When they reached the first dwelling several dogs rushed out at them. Hearing the barking, some people appeared to stare at them from the doorways.

The children who were playing among the ashes watched the barking dogs chase after the horses. In vain did the guide try to shoo them off with his whip. The dogs accompanied them as far as the castle walls, and only then did they turn back and race down again.

The stones of the castle seemed to come alive: they were talking to the archaeologist. He approached each stone, crouched down to search for something, then measured it, jotting in his notebook, digging in the dirt with the toe of his shoe to reveal yet another shaped stone. Finally, he climbed the wall and stuck his head through a loop-hole in the tower. At the sight of the writing hewn in the wall he exclaimed loudly.

The guide, who had dropped his reins and was sitting by the wall smoking, jumped to his feet at the sound of the shout. He thought the man in the glasses had been bitten by a snake.

The artist was sketching the ruins of the wall and the pointed tower. When he had drawn the entrance to the castle his pencil stopped in mid-air, for the vulture, alarmed at the sound of his steps, had flown out of its nest. Now it circled over the tower. The other birds followed with a great flapping of wings.

The frightened horses pressed close together. When the archaeologist shouted down that he had discovered the burial vault of Prince Bakur, the artist did not know what he was talking about. He was following the flight of the vultures, the powerful flapping of their wings, and was fascinated by their curved, blood-red beaks. There was something majestic in their circling.

He did not notice when his hat slipped off his head and fell on top of a rock.

A peasant with a sickle stuck in his belt, a dirty kerchief tied round his head, and leaning on a staff, climbed the rocky slope and approached the guide.

He had seen the man in the glasses move a rock. When he asked the guide who these strangers were and what they were looking for among the ruins, the man was at a loss for any explanation. Then he said that it was written in a book that a large pitcher of gold coins was buried somewhere on top of Kagavaberd.

The peasant was lost in thought. Then he shrugged and climbed back down to the canyon to reap his field of millet. He spoke to himself as he walked along. What a stroke of luck it would be if he were to find the hidden treasure. How often had he sat on the very rock where the man in the glasses had moved. If he had only known about the treasure before his pockets would have jingled with gold.

Ah, how many cows he could have bought. . . . Thus occupied with his thoughts he reached his field. He took off his long jacket, cast aside the useless thoughts together with it, grasped a handful of millet and began to reap.

A violet was blooming among the ruins, but the archaeologist noticed neither the crimson flower nor the grass. All lay crushed beneath his boots.

The world to him was one great museum in which there was not a single living thing. He tore away the ivy that covered the rocks; with the tip of his stick he pulled out the violet that bloomed in the crevice and ran his hand lovingly over the stones, scraping away the dust that had eaten into the inscription. The artist, having sketched all the archaeologist was interested in, began to draw the ruins, the eagle's nest between the jagged rocks and the blooming violet at the foot of the wall.

They left the castle in the afternoon. Before starting down the ar-chaeologist walked around the ruins once again, making notations on his pad. Then he walked quickly to catch up with the others.

This time the guide led the way. If the archaeologist was think-ing about Prince Bakur and the parchment scrolls, if the artist was recalling the violet as he listened to the churning waters of the Basut, the guide dreamed only of a fresh flat-cake, of goat cheese and yoghurt.

He unsaddled the horses at the first dwelling, hobbled them, and entered through the narrow door. The hungry horses thrust their mouths greedily into the fresh grass.

Inside, sitting by the hearth near the entrance, was a small boy. He was roasting mushrooms in the hot ashes and was startled by the stranger. He did not know whether to run away, leaving his mushrooms to burn, or to pull them out of the ashes. At the approaching sound of his mother's bare feet he became bolder. Raking out a roasted mushroom, he set it to cool in one of the hearthstones.

His mother entered, pulled her kerchief down low over her eyes and went over to the corner. She extracted two pillows from a heap of bedding and proffered them to the visitors.

The guide took a tin of food from the archaeologist's knapsack.

"We are hungry, my sister," he said. "Would you give us some yoghurt, if you have any, and boil us some tea? We have our own sugar."

The woman went to the hearth, pushed the mushrooms out of the way and, bending low over the ashes, began to blow on them. The kerchief slipped from her head, revealing to the artist her white forehead, raven hair and dark eyes. He could not take his eyes from the smoking hearth and the woman bent over the ashes. Where had he seen this face before? It was the same marble brow, the same dark-violet eyes. When the woman rose to set a tripod over the fire her eyes and the white dust of ashes on her brows and hair were but inches away from him.

So many years had gone by! Could any two faces be so alike? Even the shape of their mouths was the same. This woman's face was tanned by the sun, but her eyes were the same as those of the other woman; they both had the same slim waist and lithe body. Moving swiftly and silently, the woman brewed their tea. Each time she bent, rose, or walked across the straw mats the silvery bangles on her sleeves tinkled like tiny bells and her long dress rustled softly.

The other woman had also worn dresses that rustled, but she had worn a grey coat and a black velvet hat with an orange hatpin as well. That woman was very far away now. Perhaps the Basut, flowing into another river, did eventually reach the sea where he had once sat on the sandy beach beside the other woman.

The guide opened the second tin of food. The archaeologist kept looking at the cloth and at the copper utensils that were set on it. The boy ate his mushrooms and then looked in wonder at the shiny can, waiting for the strangers to empty it. The guide noticed his glance and handed it to him. The boy began to shake it. A dog that had been lying outside swallowed the remaining morsel of meat and licked its chops. Then the boy rushed off to show his friends the shiny white can, a sight unseen in these parts.

The woman sat by the hearth, picking up the lid of the kettle every so often to see whether the water had boiled. She fussed with the fire, moving the sticks closer together, protecting her eyes from the smoke that rose like a cloud and escaped through the cracks in the reed walls.

The woman by the hearth whose knees were clearly outlined beneath her long dress seemed to the artist to be a sorceress who could see the future in the billowing smoke.

The other woman had never walked barefoot and had never sat by a smoking hearth.

The sea had heaved like bronze lava in the mornings, licking the rocks along the shore. And the woman in the black velvet hat had sat on the beach, drawing lines in the sand with the tip of her parasol and then erasing them. He had been breaking bits off the dry twig in his hands. The waves, tossing foam at their feet, had washed the bits of twig back into the sea. As they had sat there on the beach the woman had promised to marry him, and the world had suddenly become a boundless sea, with his heart a part of it.

Then other days had come. Life had torn them apart so suddenly. All that remained to him was the memory of her violet eyes, her grey coat, and the tip of her parasol with which she had written and then erased her promise in the sand.

The lid rattled. The woman took some saucers from a basket and set some painted glasses on the cloth. When she bent over it her long braid slipped over her shoulder. The woman at the seashore had had short hair, a white neck and translucent skin.

The boy came running in, carrying the empty can.

A group of children now stood in the doorway, staring openly at the strangers. There was no end to the child's joy when he was given the second can. This time he did not run off, but sat down on a mat. His mother poured him some tea, and the artist dropped a large lump of sugar into his glass. The boy was fascinated by the bubbles rising from the sugar. He stuck his finger into the glass to fish it out. Though the hot tea burned his skin he did not utter a sound. The archaeologist smiled, having apparently recalled a scene from mankind's past. The woman filled the kettle again and smiled happily at her mischievous son.

Her smile did not escape the artist. It was so familiar. When people resemble each other, their smiles are similar, too. First, the woman's upper lip trembled, then her lips parted and the smile lit up her eyes. The artist whipped his drawing pad from his pocket, leafed through the drawings of rocks and bas-reliefs, then deftly sketched the woman sitting by the fire.

The outline of her figure was familiar; in his mind's eye he had sketched it for many years.

No one but the boy saw the drawing in his pad. It seemed to the child that the white sheets of paper that belonged to the man in the felt hat mirrored every object, as did the clear waters of a spring.

A short while later the guide brought the horses by. He put on the bridles, tightened the bellybands, buckled on the saddlebag and went back in to say goodbye to the woman. She rose and quickly pulled her kerchief down over her forehead. Her fingertips brushed against his outstretched hand. The other two also offered her their hands but she bade them farewell by pressing her hand to her heart.

The artist gave the boy a few silver coins and patted his head.

Three horses made their way down the rocky slope of Kagavaberd to the valley below. Each of the three men riding down the mountain was lost in his own thoughts.

The violets were in bloom along the roadside. The artist leaned over in his saddle, picked a flower, and pressed it in his pad, on the page which had a drawing of a slim woman by a hearth.

Stones clattered under the horses' hooves and rattled down into the gorge.

A sea churned in the artist's mind. It would toss up on its shores first a pretty head in a black velvet hat, then a woman in a long dress with heavy braids hanging down her back, then the ruins of a castle and crimson flowers blossoming at the foot of its walls.

Twilight had fallen.

A man was climbing the same road up the mountain. A sickle was stuck into his belt. The man was tired. All day long he had been reaping the short stalks of millet and his back ached. And so his steps were slow, he leaned heavily upon his staff and stopped frequently to catch his breath. His knees trembled whenever he stopped. It was the same man whom the guide had told about the buried treasure of the castle. He had looked up from his field to see the riders coming down. It had seemed to him that the gold was in their saddlebags, gold which had lain buried for centuries under the very same stone on which he had sat while his goats and sheep had grazed among the ruins. Either because this thought gave him no peace or because he was so tired, he was as irritable as a hungry bear out on its evening hunt.

When he reached the first dwelling he kicked aside the dog that ran out to greet him, pulled the sickle from his belt and flung it into a corner. Then, leaning his staff by the hearth, he sat down on the mat.

The fire was smoking. The kettle was boiling. Two lumps of sugar lay on a pillow.

Before the reaper had time to take off his bast slippers and shake the chaff out of them, his wife entered. The bangles on her sleeves tinkled, and the folds of her long dress rustled. Her son hung on to her skirt, clutching the empty cans.

He ran up to his father to show him his treasures. Suddenly the man realized that the riders had been sitting on his mat. Then the boy showed him the silver coins the kind stranger had given him.

The man brushed the child away and threw down the cans. They rolled off, as did the boy. But the child jumped to his feet and picked them up again. Then he buried his face in his mother's skirt and wept. The father felt sorry for him. He called to him and asked to see the coins. The child came over, smiling through his tears, the coins clenched in his fist. Then he told his father that the stranger had had something shiny with white pages in his pocket. The man who had given him the coins had carried off a picture of his mother on one of the pages.

Jealousy, like a bolt of lightning, rent the peasant's seething soul. He opened his eyes wide. He turned pale. The woman looked at her son and flushed; her husband noticed the color rising to her cheeks. The next moment he was on his feet. His hairy hands grabbed the heavy staff and brought it down across the woman's back.

Her buttons tinkled, her long braids were cast aside. The kettle tipped over. The broken end of the staff flew off into a corner. The woman did not cry out, she merely writhed in pain. Holding her hand to her back she went out of the house, there to weep. The child followed her, still clutching the cans, and hid among her skirts.

The husband, grumbling all the while, had some millet cakes, then put his sheepskin hat under his head and stretched out on the mat.

Once again silence fell on Mt. Kagavaberd. The fires in the hearths died down as the blackness of night descended. The village dogs, shivering in fear of wild beasts, curled up outside the dwellings. The sheep lay down in the grass. The woman lay down on a mat, covering the child with a length of felt.

A cloud, like some giant snail, crawled down the mountain towards the huts.

Darkness covered the moss and the rocks as the dampness of night settled on the fleece of the sleeping sheep.

Dew fell upon the petals of the violet. A tiny beetle, heady from its fragrance, slept in the flower cup. And it seemed to the beetle that the world was a fragrant violet.

Aram Haykaz

(1900–1986)

Aram Chekemian was born in Shabin Karahisar. He appended the name of his brother to his own first name and wrote as Aram Haykaz thereafter. He was personally involved in the 1915 resistance struggles and eventually wrote their story. He experienced four adventurous years during the period of the deportations. After the end of World War I he worked as a shoemaker for a while, until one of his aunts made it possible for him to attend the Kedronakan school. There he was taught by Hakob Oshakan (1833–1948), the renowned writer and critic, who encouraged the young Aram to pursue a literary career.

Aram Haykaz wrote six important books: *Tseghin dzayne* (The voice of the nation, 1949); *Tseghin dzayne* (The voice of the nation, vol. 2, 1954); *Chors ashkharh* (Four worlds, 1962); *Pandok* (Hotel, 1967); *Karot* (Longing, 1971), *Chors tari Kiurtistani lernerun mej* (Four years in the Kurdish mountains, 1973); and *Yerjankutiun* (Happiness, 1978). He also published *Shapin Karahisari inknapashpanutyan patmutiune* (The story of the self-defense of Shabin Karahisar, 1957). In 1973 a collection of his selected works appeared in Beirut.

Aram Haykaz's works are unique in form and in depth, both results of his very sincere pen. He was interested in all things Armenian, but his works express deep-seated feelings and values. For example in

Pandok, Haykaz implies that longing is a universal sentiment experienced not only by exiled Armenians but also by exiles of all nationalities. He describes the lives of Armenian heroes, people, and events straightforwardly, with the utmost realism, reflecting life pure and complete. The lives of children and women constitute one of his major themes. Describing them with extreme simplicity, he reveals their inner thoughts and memories, and transforms them into immortal literary characters. He does not preach, but the reader is aware that this is an author who thinks.

Haykaz's work is suffused with a gentle, pervasive humor that often underlines human vanity while emphasizing the truly essential elements and the everlasting greatness of life. His humor also allows him to escape from the melancholy sadness of some of the situations he describes and create, in clear and transparent prose, characters who are self-sufficient and well-balanced.

HAPPINESS[1]

I am a happy man. Do not suppose, however, that I have more reason to be happy than others. . . . Lots of people are probably more fortunate than I am, but lots of people also have less reason to be happy than I have. . . . There is no such thing as fair distribution, ensuring everybody an equal portion of happiness. . . . The sun, the snow that falls from the sky, and the rain, even the crazy winds: all are dispensed unequally. I am also aware that just as there is no such thing as a cloudless sky, neither is there any such thing as a man without grief. The wine of our happiness is mixed with water.

Nevertheless, like a drunkard looking for excuses to drink, I seek excuses to be happy.

Years ago I had a neighbor whose name was Nshan: a drunk, but an infinitely kind person. He was a *kusaktsakan.*[2] He was very interested in national affairs. He thought that the way to pilot the ship of state to calmer waters was by placing the party he belonged to at the helm. And that if ever the national leadership fell into other hands, the nation would undoubtedly break up into pieces.

1. Aram Haykaz, *Yerjankutiun* (Happiness) (Beirut, 1978), 7–13. Translated by the editors of the present anthology.
2. A member of a political party.

After each election, whether the party he worshiped had won or lost, he always got drunk. If they won, he would drink to celebrate their victory, and if, God forbid, they lost—which was equivalent to a national disaster—he would drink to quench his deep, unending anguish.

And because he was happy in his drunkenness, on the average he had more happy moments than we did.

There is a fable from the western Orient. In it a traveler, in order to kill some time while he waits for a train in an unfamiliar village, takes a stroll through a cemetery near the station. As he reads the epitaphs on the tombstones, he is astonished to discover that the people of the village do not live very long. . . . Two years, four years, eight weeks, four days, etc. Anxious to find at least one exception, he asks the cemetery guard for an explanation. The latter replies that the number of days or years engraved on the tombstones has nothing to do with the age of those who enjoy perpetual rest beneath the stones.

"What, then?"

"It's the total of all their happy days," the man replies.

⚓

Now I also think that one day when I die, if someone should undertake to erect a stone over my grave according to the above principle, the total of all my happy days would be quite high—high enough to make others jealous.

In order to facilitate the task of those who might undertake such a job, I have begun to use a diary, marking with an x the happy days of my life.

Which days do I think deserve a cross? you may ask. Ever since the day our first mother, Eve, was expelled from Paradise—such a zealous God! . . . for a single apple?—is there any such thing as long-lasting happiness in this world?

I am convinced that there is. Happiness is a state of mind. There is no animal by that name. It cannot be seen; it cannot be touched; but it definitely exists. For instance, your happiness is absolute when your long-winded mother-in-law, who has been staying with you, begins to dust off her suitcase. . . . You experience happiness when your wife loses her voice one morning and the doctor says that she will probably not find it again for a month or forty days. . . . Then with a light heart you can open your diary and mark each of the next forty days with an x.

I said above that happiness is a state of mind. When I wake up early in the morning, still snug in the comfort of my bed, and before I open my eyes I hear the song of a wren or the whistle of a starling perched on my roof, I realize that it is a sunny day with blue skies. Someone else, perhaps, might remain indifferent to the song and the blue of the sky, and even feel grumpy at having been awakened by the birds.

On a wet, foggy March morning, when I wake up and peer at the yellow fog outside my window, I tell myself that spring is not far away and that soon the violets in my garden will bloom. I even seem to smell their fragrance, and my nostrils quiver. . . . Someone else in the same situation and conditions might say: "Oh, God! What a lousy day. . . ."

♦

Many years ago, after I got married and while my two children were still very young, I fell seriously ill. Naturally, as I lay in my hospital bed and thought about my situation, I was quite sad and miserable. My nurse was a plump, blue-eyed Irish girl, who did whatever she could to make my days more bearable.

It was near spring, I well remember, when she entered my room one morning and opened the shutters of my window, letting the sun stream in. She tossed a jovial "Good morning!" in my direction, crinkled her freckled little nose, smiled broadly, and announced that it was spring outside, the doves were cooing on the rooftops, the benches in the park were already occupied by sun-worshipers, and the buds on the trees were swollen, ready to burst in a few days.

She arranged my comforter and pillow and hurried out to fetch my breakfast. When she went out, it seemed to me that the sun's rays that had flooded my hospital room went with her. I scarcely had time to feel sad when she showed up with my breakfast tray and placed it in front of me, covered my shoulders with the comforter, looked me in the eye, and said:

"You'll soon be well."

"How do you know?"

"He told me so."

"Who's 'he'?"

"The sainted one. This morning, on my way to work, I stopped at the church and prayed."

"And 'he' told you I'd get better?"

"Yes."

It was some time ago, but I know that I smiled at that kind, sweet girl's naive faith. Who knows? perhaps, deep down inside I believed her good tidings.

How nice it is to have faith, I thought. I took her nice little comforting hand and gave it a tender kiss.

I expressed no doubts about the saint's assurance that I would get better. I turned things over in my mind for a moment and then, I do not know why, I felt obliged to give her an explanation.

"Look, my dear Emma, you're such a kind woman; I'm not sad because I'm afraid of dying, believe me. If Gabriel comes for me today, to take me to my predetermined place, whether 'up above' or 'down below,' I won't ask him to come back again tomorrow. But I *would* like to live a few more years, so my children, who are still very young, will not be left prematurely without a father. I'm all too familiar with the hardships and compassion of being fatherless. . . . I know how it feels. . . . I want to look after them. . . . That's all I want."

"Don't worry: when I prayed to the sainted one, he told me that you'll soon be completely better and able to go home."

"When the day comes for me to go home, I'll miss you. And I'll come to see you sometimes."

"Oh, never mind. . . . They all say the same thing, and then. . . ."

"And then what?"

"And then they forget."

"Emma. . . ."

"Yes?"

"Emma, sweet Emma, my dear girl, let me ask you something. Don't answer if you don't want to, but I'd like to hear what you have to say."

"Shoot!" she said abruptly.

"I know that every morning on your way to work you go into the church to pray," I said, taking her hand in mine. "Now all I want to know is whether you pray for all of the patients. . . ."

I was going to add, "... or just for special ones?" but she did not let me finish. She grabbed the tray and, blushing slightly, ran out.

⚜

Several years later, on a holiday, I went with my wife and children to a seaside restaurant, beyond the city limits. We sat at a table near a window overlooking the sea and tried to decide what to order. Each of us chose a different dish. The air flowing in through the window brought with it the scent of the sea and seaweed. I filled everybody's glass, turned to my children, and said: "You've grown up now, my children. . . . Today you can have a bit of wine instead of milk." I raised my glass to my nose to smell the pungent perfume of the juice of the grape. "You know, kids, when I was barely your age, there was a fire in our city. My brothers, who were not yet scattered to the four corners of the world, and I ran with my father to put out the fire or to keep an eye on the stores so the Turks would not take advantage of the situation and loot them. A few hours later, we returned home. My father sent one of my brothers down to the cellar to fetch a jug of wine from the big barrel.

"'Aram, you go with him to hold the lamp,' he told me.

"The wine was dark red, almost black. We filled the jug and our bellies too, somewhat.

"When we get upstairs make sure you don't tell them we've already had some,' suggested my brother Levon, who eventually went to Russia and died there.

"'No, I won't say a thing,' I said, shaking my head.

"Upstairs we all chatted joyfully as we drank the wine, and we went to bed with calmed nerves. Ever since that day, whenever I drink red wine, I either begin to smell its bouquet or remember that night. . . . It's strange, how a fragrance or perfume, such an invisible and intangible thing, can remain so firmly fixed in my memory; it's almost incomprehensible. . . . It has now been half a century or so ago, but that aroma lingers in my memory."

I had barely finished my story when my daughter suggested a toast to the older and the younger members of our family. We clinked our glasses. Memories kept flooding back. To hide my emotions, I stood up and turned my back to them, pretending to look at the scenery. There was not a speck of cloud in the remarkably blue sky. The sea was calm. The waves barely lapped the shore. Blue jays fished for oysters, and a fast motorboat churned up a wake of foam as it sped out to open water.

"The world is full of beauty," I said to myself. "God seems to have known what He was doing when He set it in order."

"What are you daydreaming about? Come back to the table," said my wife.

"Forgive me."

The wine heated my brain and whetted my appetite.

When the waiter brought the bill at the end of a pleasant dinner, my son reached out, grabbed it, and put it in his pocket.

"Don't put it in your pocket, son; give it to me, so I can pay it before we leave."

"Papa, you're all my guests today."

"But. . . ."

"No buts! You're all my guests today."

"Why didn't you say so earlier? I would've ordered something expensive!"

We all laughed. I was happy. My son had grown up. He was making his own living now.

I opened up my diary; next to that day's date I firmly pencilled an x to indicate a happy day.

I do not know why, but I also thought of my blue-eyed Irish nurse, and my heartbeat quickened slightly. . . .

February 12, 1973.

Zareh Vorbuni

(1902–80)

Zareh Vorbuni was born Zareh Eoksiuzian (Öksüzian) in Ordu, a city in Turkey on the southeastern shore of the Black Sea. He received his early education at the local Movsisian school. His father was killed in the 1915 genocide, but his mother managed to flee to Sebastopol, Crimea, with their four children. After a year the family moved to Constantinople, where Zareh attended (1919–22) the Perperian (Berberian) school, and in 1922 they moved to France. They lived in Marseilles for two years, then in Paris (1924–30) and Strasbourg (1930–37). From his early days in France Zareh was an avid reader, acquainting himself with European intellectual trends and prominent works of French literature, particularly those of Marcel Proust (1871–1922).

Vorbuni belonged to the group of promising young Armenian intellectuals—among them Nikoghos Sarafian, Vazgen Shushanian, Shahan Shahnur, and Hrach Zardarian: mostly orphans of the genocide—who emigrated to France in the early 1920s and produced literature that derived its themes from the social, cultural, moral, and psychological distresses of the émigrés and their deep concerns about the eventual loss of their ethnic identity. In Paris he and Petros Zaroyan jointly edited two short-lived periodicals, *Nor havatk* (New faith, 1924) and *Lusabats* (Daybreak, 1938–39). In 1939, at the beginning of World War II, he was called up for service in the French army. He was captured and held prisoner of war in Germany until the end of the war in 1945.

Recollections of his prison days appear in a cycle of ten short stories called *I khorots srti* (From the bottom of the heart).

His first novel, *Pordze* (The attempt, 1929) depicts the hard life of an Armenian immigrant family of four plucked out of their native land and transplanted to Marseilles, where they suffer the impact of a totally strange environment. *Pordze* is the first volume of a quartet, intended by the author to be published under the collective title *Halatzvatznere* (The persecuted). However, the succeeding three volumes—*Teknatzun* (The candidate, 1967), *Asfalte* (Asphalt, 1972), and *Sovorakan or me* (An ordinary day, 1974)—were not published until much later. In *Teknatzun* the main character, Vahagn, embodies the tormented young generation that bore the psychological trauma of the genocide and remained its victims, leaving a moral legacy to the entire nation. In the other two volumes the author delves more deeply into the psychology of his characters, probing the sources of their anguish. However, almost all his characters, no matter how battered, are firmly determined to survive.

Of primary significance among Vorbuni's writings are his three volumes of short stories, *Vardzu seniak* (Room for rent, 1946), *Andzrevot orer* (Rainy days, 1958), and *Patmvatzkner* (Stories, 1966). In these poignant tales he bares the hidden emotions and mental anguish of his characters and deplores the disintegration of the Armenian identity as it gradually becomes a burden for the new generation. The subtle presence of the genocide is felt throughout these narratives.

In 1946 Vorbuni visited Soviet Armenia and recorded his impressions in *Depi yerkir, Husher hayrenike n hayreniken* (Memories from the homeland, 1947). Another important work is the novel *Yev yeghev mard* (And there was man, 1965). This title was later reused for a collection of his works published in Yerevan in 1967 that includes *Pordze, Yev yeghev mard,* and eight short stories.

During the fifty years between 1920 and 1970, Armenian literature revived in the diaspora, where new trends, new approaches, and a new philosophy were brought to bear on it. Zareh Vorbuni was one of the pioneers of that revival.

FROM THE PERSECUTED (THE CANDIDATE)[1]

Dear Miss Arshaluys,
Vahagn has passed away.

---

1. Zareh M. Vorbuni, *Halatzvatznere—Tegnatzun* (The persecuted: the candidate) (Beirut, 1967), 9–14. Translated by the editors of the present anthology.

Yes, Vahagn has passed away. Today a police car took the body to the morgue. If no one claims it in two days, the morgue may give his body to the medical faculty. The church refused to have anything to do with him, since he died by suicide. I forgot to mention that Vahagn committed suicide. Yesterday when I came back to the room after work, I found Vahagn lying on the floor. At first I thought he had stretched out on the floor to read the paper, as papers were strewn all around him, until I noticed the pool of cold blood. He had placed his left wrist on a pile of newspapers after slashing it with a razor blade. Then he had waited calmly for death, according to the expression on his face, which was, after all, the expression of a soul at peace. That is how it was, dear Miss.

I have now done my duty; at least what I considered my duty, for of late Vahagn was always talking to me about you, and now I realize that he was indirectly asking me to contact you. Please accept, dear Miss, my heartfelt condolences.
Masis Yerazian,
Paris, 24 April 1927.
P.S.: My address is on the envelope.

"Oof!" he sighed as he slid the envelope into the mailbox. He felt somewhat relieved. He had rid himself of a heavy burden. He had been up all night, searching for an appropriate style for the letter, and now he was pleased with its telegraphic tone. It gave it an official flavor, like news from the ministry of war: "Private So-and-So has fallen in the line of duty," or "Private So-and-So is missing in action." He felt, though, that he had placed a bit too much emphasis on his feelings: despite the letter's air of detachment, he had succeeded only in muffling the intensity of his emotions, not in concealing them completely. True, compared to his first attempts this version of the letter was considerably tighter. Significantly shorter. But still, it seemed to him that the way he had ended the letter invited a reply from the recipient, and that was precisely what he had been trying to avoid as he worked so hard through the night in his room, where the memory of the deceased was still fresh—even warm—as if he were still there, alive, lying on the wood floor, giving instructions after his death: as if he were guiding the pen, directing it to write what he wanted, with an insistence such as only the dead could manifest. He began the letter over and over again, trying out new ways of saying things as crumpled paper piled up on the floor. Then he had left the room and come here, to one of the cafés in Les Halles, where the hubbub drowned out, as it were, the interruptions of the deceased.

The daily commerce was already under way. The tumult created by the merchants and shoppers held the departed one at bay, and in this flood of light it was not possible to perceive his presence: he was reduced to a distant and now engaging murmur. And thus it was that he had been able to finish the letter, and he immediately walked out and dropped it into the mailbox.

That is when Minas exclaimed "Oof!" in relief, released from the reproaches of memory. He had walked only a few steps when he came to a sudden stop. He wanted to go back and retrieve the letter, but it was already too late. But if it was too late to get the letter back, it was also too early to go to work. The clock had just struck five. The protracted peals of the clock on the front of l'Église Saint-Eustache reminded him of signals from a ship, lost in the fog of this cold autumn morning—out there, far away, on the high seas. There was lots of time before six. It would not take him more than fifteen minutes to walk to where he worked on the Grand Boulevard.

He made a little detour from his usual route. He walked through the streets and the market crowded with huge piles of goods, inhaling the mingled smells of fruits and vegetables that filled the air. Near the Louvre he made another little detour to the tree-lined quay that bordered the river, where freight carts as big as ships created a veritable chaos as they rolled along, bringing dust-laden late fruits from the south to the capital. From there he would walk to the Jardins des Tuileries and past the Comédie Française, and the Boulevard de l'Opéra would take him all the way to the Opéra. There he would find the morning papers. He would buy one and read it by the light of the lamps along the boulevard as he walked to work, and would arrive at work at exactly six o'clock. His steps were slowed by thoughts that invaded the corridors of his mind like uninvited guests. Ever since Vahagn's unexpected act it had been impossible to check their invasion. He was used to working his mind all the time, and now that he had dropped the letter into the mailbox and calmed down, his brain opened its doors to an odd mixture of thoughts. He halted and leaned against the wall that ran beside the swollen waters of the Seine. There was a slight breeze. The cold off the water hit his face and he felt as if he had been awakened from sleep, for he had not slept all night. Lack of sleep had numbed his brain. The sound of a motor from the lead-colored waters caught his attention. A cargo vessel approached the bridge, lowered its funnel, and passed under it, like a man bending his head to walk under a low-hanging branch of a tree. His breast filled with childlike joy as he watched the vessel head toward the island; it would follow the right bank of the river to Notre Dame, Asnières, and beyond to Melun, or perhaps traverse rivers and seas to foreign countries. The river grew silent. The water, which had been divided by a wide furrow for a brief moment, closed up again, leaving only a gurgling scar that would soon enough disappear in the tumult of the day. Minas stirred. He would have to shorten his route if he surrendered to the morning spell of the waters.

He began to walk fast in order to make up for the time he had lost, or perhaps in order to avoid feeling the passage of time, and in his mind he started to go over the letter he had dropped into the box a short while ago. His brain had considered and gone over it so much all night that the entire letter was engraved on his mind. But he was still at the first line. How? How could he commit such a stupidity? I'm losing my mind, he thought, smacking his hand to his forehead. Minas, you don't know what you've done! How will you manage to dig your way out of this? He knew that it was possible to get back a letter, but by the time he finished work the letter would be almost halfway to its destination. He was worried, upset, his heart crushed; he felt that he had made a big mistake that was no longer possible to correct. Then he began to run for the train. There was no other way. The train was whistling and speeding—filling the air with smoke and fumes—free and unhindered, closing the distance, which it devoured piece by piece like thousands and thousands of neighing, whinnying horses.

The distance was trembling, horrified at this attack. Minas stopped for a moment. He rested. The train, like a captive army strung along the Dijon-bound platform, was panting softly, as though panting were forbidden. Suddenly the train started to move again, just as Minas reached the end of it. And now it was speeding away as if it were a holiday, a red-letter day on its way to some pleasure spot—laughing with amusement at the crazy fellow who had dared try to catch it.

He felt as if he were awakening from a dream when he noticed that he was in the Jardins des Tuileries; he looked like a dejected little boy. Anyway, he already felt that he had placed himself in a trap. Even with the first word he had given this woman a chance to close the trap around him. Why should she not do so? What would she have to fear now that she had lost her lover? There he was, the friend of the man she loved, standing before her with arms wide open and saying, "Dear Miss Arshaluys." Like a sign of welcome. An invitation. Vahagn is gone, but do not worry: I am here. "Dear Miss," as he had written initially, was really just right! Yes, *Miss* was quite innocuous all by itself, so why had he felt compelled to add her name: "Dear Miss Arshaluys"? His original salutation expressed a contained, neutral attitude: cold, distant, and it had been his instinct to stop there, at "Dear Miss"; it was the name that changed everything; it was the name that gave the conventional *dear* a possessive connotation. That *dear* seems to convey an effort to possess the owner of the name, in this case Miss Arshaluys. Why had he not realized that adding the name gave the word *dear* a touch of intimacy, despite his painstaking care to avoid precisely that?

As if that were not enough, the name on the envelope was Miss Arshaluys Aghvorikian, Paper Factory, Lansey. In an official letter one does not use the name. It gives an impression of intimacy, which can even seem unpleasant. Isn't that why, in the right corner of the page, under the date, one writes the first and family names of the addressee? As for the letter itself, it should begin with a simple "Mr." or "Miss." At the most modified by "Dear" or "Respected" or something of that sort. Suddenly he burst out laughing. He did not know why he was laughing. He realized, though, that laughing put him in a good mood. His heart grew lighter. He was amused at himself for going over the stupidities he had included in the letter— just going over them in his mind—no, after all, he was not going to shout them out loud, even if the street was deserted at such an early hour. . . .

Gurgen Mahari

(1903–69)

The novelist and poet Gurgen Mahari was born Gurgen Achemian in Van, Western Armenia, and attended the local elementary school. His education was cut short by the massacres of 1915, when, with thousands of other refugees, he fled to Eastern Armenia. He found refuge in orphanages in Igdir, Etchmiadzin, Dilijan, and Yerevan. Eventually he made it to the University of Yerevan, where he studied history and literature.

The poets who influenced him most in his youth were Vahan Terian (1885–1920) from the east and Daniel Varuzhan (1884–1915), Misak Metzarents (1886–1908), and Siamanto (1878–1915) from the west. Mahari's early poems began to appear in various papers in 1918, and his first book of verse, *Titanik* (Titanic), was published in 1924, followed by *Yerku poem* (Two poems, 1926), *Kesgisherits minjev aravot* (From midnight to morning, 1927), and a few other products of his formative years, when he was in search of a literary direction and artistic identity. By this time, however, he had already acquired recognition in literary circles. His fame grew wider with his book of poems *Mrgahas* (Fruition, 1933), which included some ballads and narrative poems; the verses all deal with such themes as love, nature, the homeland, national values, and the people. Yeghishé Charents (1897–1937) regarded this volume as a cornerstone of Soviet Armenian lyric poetry.

Like many of his contemporaries, Mahari was full of confidence in the new system, and he wrote *agitkas* (propaganda in various literary forms) in collaboration with proletarian writers. But this lasted only briefly. He became an associate of Charents, turned to lyric poetry, and began to assert his own literary creed, arousing the displeasure of his "comrades."

In the late twenties Mahari began to publish in prose, where it seems he was more at home. The first volume of his autobiographical trilogy, *Mankutiun* (Childhood, 1930), paints vivid pictures of his native Van and the most fateful years of the pre–World War I period. The second volume, *Patanekutiun* (Adolescence), also published in 1930, describes the destruction of Van, the deportations, and the mass exodus of Armenians to Eastern Armenia. The third volume, *Yeritasardutyan semin* (On the threshold of youth), not published until 1956, narrates the author's life in the early days of the revolution. All three volumes depict the story of a growing adolescent whose life is intricately interwoven with the tragic destiny of his homeland.

In August 1936, Mahari was arrested and exiled to Siberia for ten years. He was released in 1947, rearrested in 1948, and sent back to Siberia to live in virtual exile, performing menial labor in the pottery shed of a camp in Vologda, north of Moscow. In 1954, after Stalin's death, Mahari was rehabilitated and allowed to return to Yerevan with his Lithuanian wife, Antonia. No one offered convincing explanations for his seventeen years of exile. Later, he wrote the following lines of biting sarcasm in his famed novel *Tzaghkatz pshalarer* (Barbed wire in flower):

> During this time I matured; now I know many things I did not know before. Now I even know that I am a member of an underground nationalist—Trotskyite terrorist organization! Yes, I was someone, and I knew nothing about it. But now I know that I and a few other writers had secret meetings day and night, aiming somehow to sever Armenia from Russia. . . . Ah, if only my poor, widowed mother could have seen me here, she would have realized that all these years her faithful son had been a terrible monster.[1]

After his rehabilitation Mahari dedicated himself entirely to writing, presenting in simple and fluent prose the deeper emotions and delicate sensitivities of his characters, without abandoning his subtle humor.

---

1. Gurgen Mahari, "Tzaghkatz pshalarer" (Blossoming barbed wire), in *Sovetakan grakanutyun* (Soviet literature) (January, 1988), 57. Translated by the editors of the present anthology.

Lrutyan dzayne (The sound of silence, 1962) is a collection of short stories about life in the early decades of Soviet rule and some of the episodes
he witnessed in Siberia. Perhaps his best novel about his Siberian experience is *Tzaghkatz pshalarer* (Barbed wire in flower, published posthumously in 1988). According to one commentator:

> [This work] is a riveting memoire-novel of [Mahari's] time in Siberian
> labour camps in the Soviet Union during the 1930s and 1940s. Mahari
> reconstructs the monstrous apparatus of repression with characteristic
> wit and humour and unfolds the routine of everyday life through the
> tragic tale of love between an unskilled Azerbaijani worker, Mamo,
> and Lyudmila, a talented German artist. Every page of this book is
> permeated with Mahari's profound compassion and solidarity for the
> plight of fellow human beings.[2]

Mahari's last work was *Ayrvogh aygestanner* (Burning orchards,
1966), a novel based on historical documents that delves into the tragic
events of 1915, and the defense and eventual fall of Van. It is a strong
indictment of the Turkish plan to exterminate the Armenians but also
highly critical of the Armenian political leadership. Although it caused
polemical arguments between "academics" and "nationalists," it is one of
the finest novels in Armenian literature.

Gurgen Mahari was an original poet and a master prose writer. As
one critic puts it, "his prose was spontaneous, innocent, and colorful; he
knew the secret of telling the tragic with a smile, but the most characteristic element of his style was his sardonic humor."[3] Mahari died on
16 July 1969, in Lithuania; he was buried in Yerevan. A collection of his
works in five volumes was published in Yerevan from 1966 to 1990. Some
of his pieces have been translated into Russian, French, and English.

FROM BARBED WIRE IN FLOWER[4]

The brief days of Spring are felt even inside the potter's workshop, where the sun does not penetrate, yet through its dirty windows we can see the valley flooded with sunlight where a calm river

2. Eddie Arnavoudian, "Life in Stalinist Labour Camps: An Armenian
Writer-Prisoner's View," Armenian News Network/Groong (19 August 2002), 1–2.
14 August 2003, http://groong.usc.edu/Tcc-20020819.html
3. Garig Basmadjian, "Gurgen Mahari" *Ararat* 20, no. 1 (Winter 1979), 99.
4. Gurgen Mahari, "Barbed Wire in Flower," ibid., 102–4. Translated by Garig
Basmadjian.

bends its way. Mamo and I go there to fetch water for the needs of the workshop.

At this time of the year, after having prepared the clay, the greatest delight for me is to take off my shoes and socks, run down the valley barefooted, sit on the grass next to the water and wash my feet.

This dreamy period however did not last more than a month, because during the second half of June the workshop was closed down, and everyone—without discrimination—was taken to work in the fields until late autumn.

For the first few days the armed guards in the watchtower did not like my sitting barefoot at the riverbank. I even heard them whistle twice. But they soon realized I had no intention of escaping and left me alone with my pacific occupation.

I sat at the riverbank for about fifteen minutes blessing the creation of the world, blessing my birth, forgetting all bitterness and my miserable self. I gave freedom to my spirit, which flew far away from the workshop. Even the armed guards could not guess that I, with all my essence, was away, infinitely away from their borders. I was transported back to my childhood and the Hayots Valley, the Khoshap River. Then, already an adolescent, I am in Yerevan on the banks of Hraztan. I was quenching the yearning for the rivers of my birthplace with Hraztan and my yearning for Van with Yerevan. Even this was too much for them. . . .

They even deprived me of that, when one night they decided that I was a criminal and jailed me in one of the narrow cells in the basement of a five-story tufa[5] building.

I hear buckets clanking and without turning my head I know that Mamo is going down the valley with four empty buckets in his hands. This dry and discordant clanking brings me back to reality. The dream is over. There remains the watchtower with its armed guards, Mamo with his four buckets, and I holding my worn-out shoes.

Potter's workshop. My workshop! I have not forgotten you and shall never forget. For if my early childhood was buried under the fortress of Van, my youth was shattered in your debris.

---

5. A stone of volcanic origin that comes in various shades, used for buildings and monuments in Armenia.

I remember when Autumn spread its gray wings on your court-yard and the rain beat at your dirty windows, you smelled of earth and clay, and the earth was innocent as the man working with it.

The clay was tortured under our bare feet so that Ashot Dayi could make plates out of it and give them to thousands of prison-ers saying: "Take this . . . it is my body. Eat whatever they put in them and remember that it's man who creates earthenware and not God."

I now believe that God has created man who, even when forced to abandon everything, continues to cry liberty. That same God has sent another earthly god, almighty as well, on a special mission to earth so that he may crush millions of people under his iron boots, pulverize them, turn them into clay, and mold them in such a way that they even forget the word liberty.

The new god would create this new man in his own image, breath-ing life into him and promising him a new Eden. The new man would be full of fear, weak-kneed, pompous and brutal. He would be punished for loving and glorified for being ruthless. The statue of his creator would be erected in all stations, at every square, in every city and village. Towns and factories would bear his name. All the writers would write about him, the poets sing his praise, the artists paint his portraits, the scientists work in his name, the soldiers fight according to his commands. So that all the country would sing Hosanna and he, never quenched, would continue to drink the brine of glory. . . .

An impenetrable darkness covers the barracks. If an invisible hand switched on the non-existent electricity and the barracks was flooded with light, you would be witness to an unbelievable phe-nomenon if you looked closely at the faces of the sleeping prisoners.

The prisoners smile in their sleep. Yes, they smile with a real and human smile. There is the bitter smile, the sweet, the childish, the cynical, the doubting, and some smile to the point of erupting into laughter.

The prisoners smile. Repressed and suffering all day long, in their sleep they give freedom to their pent-up feelings and dream with carefree abandon. They go back to their homes, they embrace their families, their friends. They eat the food which they were dreaming about during the day. They go to a beer parlor with their friends and it so happens that they meet there the barracks' inspector or the chief of the camp serving them beer dressed in a white apron. . . . And the dream ends.

That night I must not have smiled.

"I declare it clean-up day" said Ashot Dayi. "Let's put the work-house in order. Prepare the clay so that tomorrow we can start to work with new vigor. It would be great if we could have a bottle of vodka after work. . . ."

The devil stirred in me.

"Ashot Dayi" I said, "you are omnipotent. You can take an apple of immortality out of your pocket at this very moment, if you wanted. But to find a bottle of vodka . . . that is beyond your powers."

"Don't make me mad, you crook! If I decide to find it, I'll find it. I'll dig it out of the earth."

As we sit down to eat, the miracle takes place. The bottle of vodka sits on the table. It would be useless to say that I didn't believe my eyes and that my mouth fell open with amazement. For years it has been said that alcohol does not penetrate the prisons and the barbed wires. For years on end this irrefutable reality has been discussed and proven. For years on end we have celebrated New Year's Eve with boiled water. Now all of a sudden this terrible, terrific Ashot Dayi. . . .

"Let's drink this glass to the health of the prisoners. They say there is a country in the world that has only one little prison. Its sole aged guard is fed up because he has no work to do. And when someone is jailed in that country, a black flag is hoisted on the prison. Let it be like that here too.

"Let's drink to the health of our fellow prisoners. They are innumerable. Ah, they are too many. What has happened? Why? What an astonishing tale. How could there be so many prisoners in this country of justice and order? This is but a rumor. A big lie. They have filled the prisons with innocent, useful people. Why this enormous injustice? There must be someone who simply doesn't like people who are correct, straight, kind, outspoken. And they are destroyed with his orders."

Ashot Dayi stops. A cricket chirps in one of the corners of the workshop. I have known Ashot Dayi within these barbed wires for many years. That night he was different. This terribly superb Ashot Dayi.

"To the health of all our prisoners" he repeated. "Whether they are dead or alive, it is the same, because the dead are always with us and the living are dying. . . ."

The first glass left a great impression on me. After eight years of privation, it was a reawakening of all the vodka glasses I had emptied in my life. I found myself in blazing, burning flames lifted off the ground and into the air. The faces of Ashot Dayi and Jonas became misty, and the workshop and the whole world with it changed place and swam into the unknown. Ashot Dayi's voice slowly brought me back to myself.

"I drink for the sick justice. Its condition is serious but it won't die. When justice is sick, man becomes poor, miserable, petty. He wears two faces. He becomes evil, obnoxious and egotistical. He licks the boots that crush him, says things contrary to his true nature, carries out works and missions with which he disagrees. But he nevertheless carries them out because justice is sick."

"Let's drink to that great day when the last prisoner will leave the last prison. Let man turn the prisons into schools and let all the space taken by the prison camps turn into wheatfields."

"Let the day come when all statues of the *Father of the People* disappear from all cities and villages. But let one statue stand forever. The one with icy feet still standing on my heart. It happened in the north, not far from the camp on a small hill of ice that could be seen from the barracks. They placed a young prisoner there and showered him with water brought in buckets. The water froze in seconds and there arose before my very eyes a human statue. That was the only monument that I know of erected to the millions of prisoners dead or dying. Let that monument remain standing forever. It is the frozen shriek of all innocent prisoners. Let human generations hear his voice and never forget it. And may they never allow history to repeat itself."

The feast is over. Our heads are filled with iron and other heavy minerals. From between burning lashes we look at each other, trying to remember when and where we have met. But I hear the broken voice of Ashot Dayi: "Behave yourselves. Stand up and let's go back to work. . . ."

You're on your own, take care of yourselves. I'm dying. Two people are carrying me by my feet and head. The one holding my head is okay. I have no complaint. I can't say the same for the one holding my feet. He must be an interesting fellow. He is performing a physiological experiment on me. This individual must surely have the intention of writing a medical thesis. . . . He simply is tickling the bottom of my right foot as if to verify whether someone dying of thirst can laugh. . . . Please don't try to convince me that it was only an illusion. He was with all seriousness t-i-c-k-l-i-n-g me.

The wind blows above the high fence and through the barbed wires. The snow freezes on the wires and on their thorns. It seems they are in flower as the apple tree is in Spring.

The wind blows above the high fence and through the thick barbed wire. The barbed wire sings. Its song is rusty and full of blood. And the blood is black.

ON GUARD, PEOPLE[6]

I carried my life like a flag
up from the dark pits
where Tartarus forged my soul and guts.
If I were helpless as an orphan
I was as proud as only an orphan can be.

I lost everything without crying.
That became life's meaning. And magic.
I left my books to the small teeth of mice,
and hibernated for seventeen years.

When I woke to grope my way back to life,
the single-headed devil,
who cannibalized a million heads,
had entered his mausoleum.

But our Anti-Christ stood
sullen and cruel, ruling Yerevan,

---

6. Mahari, "Barbed Wire in Flower," 104–5. Translated by Diana Der Hovanessian.

ignoring the moan of Kanaker mountain
where foreign steel boots cut into its heart.

For the first time in Armenia
the fraudulent poet praised the work of Satan,
trading pens for intrigue's dagger,
trading ink for muck,

flattering even the executioner
who had plucked the children of light,
Charents, Khanchian, Bakunts,
out of the light.

While his victims sat helpless in jails
he struck them in the back; then
crawled up their pedestals
like a puny Nero, a clown.

I lived and lived long enough to see
Nebuchadnezzar fall from his peak.
I saw the steel corpse sawed apart
and dismembered arm, neck and knee.

I carried my burden like a flag
up from the dark pits
where I had forged my guts in the furnace.
If I were helpless as an orphan
I was as proud as only an orphan can be.

My life and my pen were returned to me.
And now with the strength
of my robbed springtime I shout:
Hey, people, be careful. Look around.

It can happen. Be mindful
of those who never left the pits
but stayed sacrificed to the furies,
helpless as orphans, majestic as saints.

Shahan Shahnur

(1903–74)

Shahan Shahnur[1] was born Shahnur Kerestechian (Keresdedjian) in Istanbul. His mother was the sister of Teodik (1873–1928), the well-known author of *Amenun taretsuytse* (Everbody's almanac), to which Shahnur began to contribute at a very young age.

In 1921 he graduated from the local Perperian (Berberian) College with a diploma in literature. Two years later he emigrated to Paris, where financial difficulties obliged him to work as a retoucher of photographs. At the same time he audited literature courses at the Sorbonne.

As a young boy he was weak and complained of chronic migraines. In 1936, as a result of his worsening health, he was hospitalized for four and a half months in Salpêtrière, where he was treated for bone disease. Three years later, in 1939, his illness became so intense that he was subjected to surgical intervention. Unfortunately, the operation

---

1. The following biographical sketch and commentary was written (in Armenian) by Krikor Keusseyan especially for the present anthology and was translated by the editors. Keusseyan is a writer and the author of several books, including a collection of correspondence between Shahan Shahnur and Krikor Keusseyan, *Namakani* (Letters), vol. 1 (Boston, 2001).

left permanent scars. Shahnur wrote: "Another reason for me to prefer literature to my life: in my works suffering always has an end!"[2]

That same year, France declared war against Germany. The threat of German invasion led some hospitals to shut their doors, and Shahnur, still in bandages, was forced to move to the Pyrenees, in the south of France. There—in Pau, Pessac, and other places—under the unbearable conditions in certain hospitals and clinics, his Golgotha began. At times he was at death's door. Before leaving Paris in 1936, he decided to destroy all his writings. Shahnur, who was a perfectionist, feared that he might never return to Paris and that his writings, including two advertised volumes, might be published without his final approval. His deep disillusionment with French Armenian circles may have been another reason for this "house-cleaning."

Not until 1959 did he find real and permanent refuge, at the newly opened *Home arménien* for senior citizens in Saint-Raphaël, on the Côte d'Azur, where he lived for the rest of his life. There his health became relatively stabilized.

⚜

Shahan Shahnur began his writing career with the publication of the novel *Nahanje arants yergi* (Retreat without song) in 1929, it had first appeared in the Paris daily *Haraj* (Onward). It was an instant success, demonstrating a new voice, a new style, a contemporary subject, and a new approach that imbued Armenian literature with passion by presenting both sides of the issues it dealt with. This novel was part of a projected series called *Patkerazard patmutiun Hayots* (Illustrated history of Armenians), and the titles of the remaining three volumes are listed in the book.

In 1932 Shahnur created a scandal by publishing an excerpt, "*Puynuzlunere*" (The horned ones), from his unpublished novel *Vordik vorotman* (Sons of thunder), in *Menk* (Us). That novel was among the works he eventually destroyed. In 1933 he published a volume of short stories, *Haralezneru davachanutiune* (The plot of the *haralez*),[3] which revitalized the Armenian short story. Over the next six years he contributed various writings—literary, critical, theoretical, national, and so on—to the Armenian press, especially to *Abaka* (The future). Pieces like *Azatn Komitas* (Komitas the liberated), *Vaveratughte* (The document), *Vepin shurj* (On

---

2. *Tertis kiraknorya tive* (The Sunday edition) (Beirut, 1958), 20.
3. In Armenian mythology the *haralez* were dogs that revived fallen heroes by licking their faces.

the novel), *Liuksempurki pahapannere* (The guardians of Luxemburg), *Verjin khosks chapazantsutiun é* (My last words are exaggerations), *Lragir* (Newspaper), *Ardar gndakaharutiun me Yerevani mej* (A just execution by shooting in Yerevan), *Avag urbat* (Good Friday), *Avur hatsi karot* (In need of daily bread), and others embodied the evolution of his thinking. His sharp analyses and bold, unsparing criticisms helped shape the literary atmosphere of the nation.

After emigrating to France, Shahnur also wrote in French under the pen name Armen Lubin. Beginning in 1932 he contributed to the French periodical press. In 1942, his first opus, *Fouiller avec rien* (Digging with nothing), consisting of twelve poems, appeared in Paris. This was followed by the poetry collections *Le passager clandestin* (The clandestine passenger, 1946), which received the Prix Rivarol; *Sainte patience* (Holy patience, 1951); and *Les Hautes terraces* (The high terraces, 1957); the *Transfert nocturne* (Transfer by night, 1955), the only collection of his prose works in French; and *Feux contre feux* (Fighting fire with fire, 1964), a book of poems that includes a short prose piece. The last was awarded the Cardin-Geoffroy Renault prize for poetry. In 1968 Shahnur published another volume under the same title (*Feux contre feux*); this is a selection of works from his books in French to that date. Shahnur also received the Prix Max Jacob. In addition, on the initiative and with the support of his French colleagues, a collection of his French works, *Armen Lubin, Les logis provisoires* (Armen Lubin: Temporary accommodations), was published posthumously. It includes two poems that were left out of his previous publications.

Shahnur's French works have been praised by French writers, one of whom, Henri Thomas (1912–93), has said: "Anyone searching for the true character of mid-century French poetry will certainly one day come across this 'foreigner' at the very heart of this poetry, which he enkindles and which illuminates his smile."[4]

Shortly before settling into *Home arménien*, Shahan Shahnur revised a number of his writings from the '30s and published them as *Tertis kiraknorya tive* (The Sunday edition, Beirut, 1958). The book was heralded as Shahnur's return to Armenian literature. It was followed by *Zuyg me karmir tetrakner* (A pair of red notebooks, Beirut, 1967). *Bats tomar* (Open register, Paris, 1971) and *Krake koghkis* (My burning side, Paris, 1973) contain some new and a number of revised older writings.

---

4. *Feux contre feux* (Fighting fire with fire) (Paris, 1964), back cover.

Following Shahnur's death, the *Harach* (Onward) daily of Paris published *Sirt srti* (Heart to heart, 1995), a collection of the author's works gleaned from the Armenian press.

Shahan Shahnur is a brilliant figure in post-genocide Armenian literature. He stimulated interest in Armenian life with his very first novel and continued to charm and provoke with his subsequent works. He became an important writer early in his life, and his impressive influential literary output is unequaled in Armenian prose of the diaspora.

His fierce and deeply defiant resistance to established conceptions, of which his inflexible atheism is an example, is part of his greatness. In *Nahanje arants yergi* (Retreat without song), as well as in his short stories and literary criticism, he scrutinizes the scattered fragments of the Armenian people after the genocide: the young and the old, their psychoses and their bitterness.

The novel is structured as a love story; it depicts the life and torment of the Armenian youth who were cast away from Istanbul into the streets of Paris following the Armenian genocide: their confusion amidst the splendor of a foreign language, their psychological and linguistic retreat and alienation. What makes the work especially shocking is the author's departure from the supposed lessons of a number of historical phenomena, particularly those related to the immediate Armenian past. Like his contemporary surrealists, Shahnur seriously questions national and traditional concepts and values, even certain sacred cows. From the perspective of a people deprived of their homeland, evicted from their lands, and massacred, he points to insiders who are partly responsible for the tragedies; he is unsparing in his criticism of them as incompetent and short-sighted leaders. His unhappiness corresponds to his limitless anguish, his wounded spirit, which opened new public wounds. Some critics consider him a talented but "cursed" writer.

Shahan Shahnur is a unique and original master of literary expression. His engaging artistry confers and secures the success of his subject matter and enhances the value of his controversial judgments. His language is clear and radiant but at the same time vigorous and colorful; his style is light and sparkling, lively and compact, emitting rays of genius. He is able to create fully developed situations and turn others upside down. Shahnur is a stylist. He plowed new furrows in Armenian literature with his masterful works of re-creative prose and his ever-curious mind.

His work is also invaluable as genuine testimony for the new reality of Armenian life.

FROM RETREAT WITHOUT SONG[5]

4

The young refugees, most of them mere boys who ended up on the sidewalks of Paris, had formed a close-knit bunch during the months immediately following the Armenocide. However, their boundless love and fondness for each other diminished and they drifted apart over time. These Armenian lads had been uprooted from their birthplaces, families and futures; in those days, having lost their way, they clung to one another until a certain amount of time had passed, when they found direction and approached manhood. However, the fast-moving years gradually brought about their separation. Being in the formative stage of their lives, they took different paths, as if driven by a fan; the difficulty in earning their daily bread, the demands of life and, especially, the hustle and bustle of their new environment all blew upon this weak group and scattered them, like feathers in the wind. With her irresistible charm, Marian approached each of them and dragged them off hither and thither. Regardless of place, the victor was always the same; it was always Nanette, the granddaughter of the likes of Manon, Ninon and Nana. Some of the lads got married; many of them lived with their girlfriends. They stopped going to the Armenian church; the number of letters written by them decreased and, of course, their distant mothers cried.

There are only small groups left now, consisting of true, sincere friends. The Armenian spirit still shines in the junction of their souls, although this whirlpool has caused it to pale as it declines toward extinction. Nevertheless, that spirit will shine until it becomes extinguished.

It was just such a group that these five youths formed, and today's get-together is surely their final one. It is the final one because Misak is set to depart. While earning his daily bread, he

---

5. Shahan Shahnur, *Nahanje arants yergi* (Retreat without song), trans. Aris Sevag (Paris, 1920), 134–42. Kevork Bardakjian has the following to say about the novel: "[The novel] still stands out as perhaps the most powerful landmark of Armenian Dispersion literature, epitomizing its turbulent emergence." Kevork B. Bardakjian, *A Reference Guide to Modern Armenian Literature, 1500–1920* (Detroit, 2000), 240.

went to dental school at great sacrifice and finally succeeded in earning his diploma. Now he is going to Marseilles where he will work with his uncle who's a shoemaker there. Petros shall depart too. No explanation is being given as to when, where and why. Of course, Petros would not condescend to confess, not even to his buddies, that he planned to run after Nanette. Yes, starting from the day after the get-together, Petros would wait, with ever-increasing impatience, for Nanette's approaching steps, Nanette's approaching fragrance. He waited and waited, out of breath, in torment, in love, but she didn't come, she never returned. And the longing for that absent golden head, gradually taking on more form, color and fragrance, easily dispelled defenseless thoughts. Thus, with the magnified and exaggerated deliberations receding in order to serve a second purpose, the other fellows left him by himself, with his love, with his sweetheart Nanette. Now too his energies are depleted, so is his pride, and he shall run to the others' increasing warmth. What will the others do? Hrach knows how to prepare Oriental dishes very well, with plenty of cooking fat, the expenditure of a few francs, and buffoonery. Indeed, everything in this two-room apartment screams of the absence of a woman, but he had arranged the dinner table with a neatness that is extremely praiseworthy for a male, but which now has the appearance of a pile of ruins. Plates, remnants of food, appetizers mixed together, half-empty glasses, breadcrumbs, and, on the floor, wine bottles rolling underfoot.

They ate and drank their fill. Their bodies now stood erect around the table, the chairs creaked, and cigarette smoke wafted. Every time they get together like that in Hrach's room, they first speak about letters having arrived from "home" and business; they tell each other their experiences and romances with girls; then they argue at length over the latest crimes and trials having taken place in Paris, only to end them with song. The song following the first glasses of wine is "*Yes siretsi mi zuyk acher*" (I loved a pair of eyes), and that strident chorus ends with "*Her yer karanlik*" (Everywhere is dark). Now they're all silent. Suren breaks the silence. His contracted eyes have an extraordinary shine to them, and the manner of burying his fingers in his hair betrays his state of mind. Of the five youths, he is the one with the highest intelligence. His buddies have a certain reverence and admiration for his extensive knowledge, which, incognito, seemingly dominates the glances of those simple fellows. He is someone who is destined to become a full-fledged writer, yet he doesn't write because he reads and smiles. He very rarely expresses himself in this social circle, to which he comes only to give satisfaction to a camaraderie different from intellectual intercourse. It seems, however, that the wine weakened him and imparted an amazing sincerity to his words. He let his thoughts loose in an unrestrained manner, propelled them, speeded them up, and let them become accented and more intense under warmth.

Suren looked askance at Petros and said:

"Just look at you, you sure didn't make much of yourself. . . . Photographer . . . ain't worth a dime. We have had and we now have good photographers, masters of form, in every country, but what about the essential, the sublime, and the beautiful? You too are a perfect embodiment of the Armenian people. The Armenians have good painters but not a style or school of painting. The Armenians have good actors but not dramaturgy; they have indefatigable travelers but never a navigator. The Armenians have delightful poets but not a school of literature. They have gods but not mythology, praiseworthy revolutionaries but not a revolutionary movement. The Armenians have had freedoms but never independence."

Then, emptying his wine glass with one gulp, he continued rapidly without drying his lips.

"The Armenians are sterile, barren, infertile. The Armenians are empty, fruitless, vain, futile.

"They don't have the right to live since they haven't been born.

"One day perhaps they'll be born, and with a different color than we hoped for—red, yellow or black. However, we, this segment of the Armenian people, are condemned to perish.

"We haven't been born. 'Boy, cocktail!' "

No sooner than his glass was filled, it was emptied.

"I'm telling you, certain that I will become understandable since all of you, in turn, have had a tragic love at one time or another.

"A lover, especially a tragic and sensitive lover, shall inevitably think about death at least once. He will want to fall down at the feet of his sweetheart, to fall into her arms, struck by death, and breathe his last. He will want to see and enjoy the excitement and anxiety of that indifferent girl. Oh, what satisfaction he will derive from seeing her cry, supplicate and try to save him! . . . However, it is useless, in vain; it's too late and the lad shall die; his eyes shall gradually close, he shall go, depart from this earth. And, of course, after his death, he shall enjoy the pain of his sweetheart. Of course.

"And we, and I, behold, have that same merciless joy, a boundless glee, like an infectious drunkenness prepared with poisons. The most barbaric grimace to gain revenge, to steal pleasure from another's pain and suffering. Let him cry now, grind his teeth, wring his hands—he, our nation, the Armenians. Let our leaders write, talk, shout in meetings, scream, in vain, to no avail. All of us shall become degenerates; all of us shall become assimilated.

"Like others, we too buried our religion and faith during the course of the war. The hope of an independent country melted away and became lost in the fortress city given up. And now the greatest and most fundamental pillar keeping us afloat, the family, is being assailed. The Armenian girls remained cut off, abandoned; it was they who were necessary for our blood, despite their ugliness, dry pride and tendency to immediately become mothers and grow old. These are advantages for someone else other than a youth. . . .

"That youth saw French girls, German, Italian, Greek and Russian girls too. One day he imbibed the fragrance of one of them, and the next day another's; one night he stayed in this hotel; another morning he descended the stairs of another hotel; he was loved a few times until he too loved one day, closing a door behind him.

"Now Armenian girls appear in his memory with two heavy legs and a slight mustache.

"Who cares?

"It's better to become assimilated than to live without the stamp of heels.

"All our grandfathers are eunuchs; they haven't been able to sculpt anything on flesh; they haven't been able to sculpt anything with flesh. There is a major deficiency among us, which they should have known to compensate for. We haven't lived in Armenia; its soil and air are unfamiliar to us; its mores and customs haven't shaped us and, naturally, we love only our birthplace; i.e., foreign skies. The endless successive generations of our forefathers haven't been able to save us; they haven't been able to give us that great love. All boasts evaporate; true patriotism needs—especially in our case—a past, greatness, examples.

"I said, the idea of a fatherland is quite often a heel.

"The idea of a fatherland is quite often a hero.

"The idea of a fatherland is quite often folklore.

"We have substituted duplicity for that great lie—Our entire history is proof thereof.

"We have substituted tillers for heroes—Our empty fingernails are proof.

"We have substituted combatants for collective effort—Proof is all our monasteries.

"We have substituted tears for the screams of guts—Proof is all our poets.

"We have substituted brides for divine passion—Proof is all our *raki* drinkers.

"We have substituted molds for ideology—Proof is all of our books.

"We have substituted pugnacity for struggle—Proof is all our political parties.

"We have substituted this for that!—Proof is our soul.

"Assimilate, assimilate, assimilate! 'Boy, cocktail!' "

They filled his glass and he drank. Misak said:

"It's a good thing that you don't say these things to others; they'll immediately call you a traitor, a renegade, a degenerate. It's not your fault, however; it's the wine speaking. I think it flowed a little too much. . . ."

"Don't worry, he's not drunk," responded Petros with his best attempt at solemnity. "These are not the statements of a drunk or a traitor. On the contrary, I would like our *aghas* to hear these statements and, instead of barking or cursing, to finally grasp the seriousness of the prevailing atmosphere and think in terms of remedy, if the possibility exists . . . if the possibility exists. . . ."

Nikoghos Sarafian

(1905–73)

Nikoghos Sarafian was born aboard a ship on its way from Constantinople to Varna. He received his early education in Armenian and French
schools in Bulgaria and Rumania. During World War I he and his family
fled back to Varna, and following the Armistice in 1919 they moved to
Constantinople. There Sarafian attended the Kedronakan school until
the Kemalist takeover; soon after that he left for France in 1923 and
settled permanently in Paris. After working at a number of different jobs,
he chose to make his living as a typesetter.

Despite having a limited and critical readership, especially in the
beginning, Sarafian produced an impressive amount of work. His poetry
has been collected into five volumes: *Anjrpeti me gravume* (The conquest
of a space, Paris, 1928); *14 kertvatz* (Fourteen poems, Paris, 1933);
Teghatvutiun yev makentatsutiun (Ebb and flow, Paris, 1939); *Mijnaberd*
(Citadel, Paris, 1946); and *Mijerkrakan* (Mediterranean, Beirut, 1971).
He also wrote a novel, *Ishkhanuhin* (The princess, Paris, 1934), the story
of a Turkified girl married to a pasha, which is quite different from the
rest of his work in terms of tone and emotions. His other prose works
are a collection of reflections, *Venseni antarnere* (The Vincennes woods,
Paris, 1988), an account of an inner journey in which he treats issues
such as war, politics, and the destiny of his nation, Soviet Armenia; and

several short stories. His travels and his experiences in Russia as an adolescent influenced his outlook and consequently his writing, particularly in *Anjrpeti me gravume, Teghatvutiun yev makentatsutiun, Mijerkrakan,* and *Venseni antarnere.*

Sarafian was influenced by such diverse sources as the Danish philosopher and writer Søren Kierkegaard (1813–55), French literature of the late nineteenth and early twentieth centuries, symbolism, existentialism, and surrealism. Many of his poems are recollections of his childhood, reconstructed through the use of symbols and metaphors which are at times difficult to follow. His poetry is very personal and individual, but its symbolism raises it beyond the world of occurrences: a collective voice is heard—a chorus of pain, agony, and sadness. Many pieces reflect on, among other things, the Armenian destiny, Armenian diasporan psychology, mechanized progress, and the tragedies and afflictions of Armenian life.

It took Sarafian a long time to secure himself a place among the important writers of Armenian literature. In the beginning he was unfairly criticized, and Soviet Armenians were unfamiliar with his work. He was blamed for theatrical innovation and artificial expression. It is evident that for many his writing was difficult to understand: his obscure images and ideas alienated readers unfamiliar with his method of juxtaposing seemingly unconnected images to form a dense mosaic. Now, however, he is credited with having created a new mode of poetic composition; he offered a new means of writing Armenian poetry, as if older poetic traditions had been exhausted.[1] To underscore the importance of his contribution to Armenian poetry, he is one of the few writers born after 1900 to be included in this anthology.

ON THE ROAD TO INSOMNIA[2]

Sometimes a dream comes to disturb sleep,
which stops, then, like a watermill struggling
with a corpse that floats downstream to stick
on the axle of the turning wheel.

---

1. For more information see Kevork B. Bardakjian, *A Reference Guide to Modern Armenian Literature* (Detroit, 2000); Krikor Beledian, *Cinquante ans de littérature Arménienne: 1922–1972* (Fifty years of Armenian literature: 1922–72) (Paris, 2001); and Marc Nichanian, *Writers of Disaster*, vol. 1 (Princeton and London, 2002).

2. *Anthology of Armenian Poetry*, ed. and trans. Diana Der Hovanessian and Marzbed Margossian (New York, 1978), 236–37.

And other times, the dream drops like loose stool
on its pajama-wrapped creator, decays his sleep.
Or like a mysterious rope around his neck
yanks, and makes him fall awake.

Or like a secret agent, the dream stops him short,
pulling him off a happy road
to shiver back to life, innocent but
perspiring a guilty sweat.

And like a monkey, eating only the fruit's skin,
the dreamer takes the vision instead of deep sleep
and swallows down its poison like a sedative,
only to be turned over to insomnia.

(1927)

AT FAREWELL[3]

This morning, in the algae of my arteries
your gaze swims like a fish, Marie.
And I feel the sad bubbles
and the deafening gulp of its jaws.

My train is snapped from the city like smoke.
I see the city lights, like a burning plane,
jumping now like a slaughtered chicken
running in the distance.

Your gaze waits in silence while the roar
of transatlantic ships pass. Be compassionate,
Marie, when you judge this heart.
It is not really made of tile.

Your handkerchief is a dove fluttering sacred
blessings. I drown putting out my regrets
for our old days. Marie, forgive me
for my wandering, my inherited disease.

(1927)

---

3. Ibid., 240.

BIBLIOGRAPHY

Works in Armenian

Abeghian, Artashes. "*Raffii azdetsutiune hetaga serundneri vra*" (Raffi's influence on the following generations). In *Raffi, keanke, grakanutiune, hishogiutiunner* (Raffi, his life, literature, memories). Paris, 1937. 88–93.

Abeghian, Manuk. *Yerker* (Works). Yerevan, 1970.

Abovian, Khachatur. *Verk Hayastani. Voghb hayrenasiri* (Wounds of Armenia: lamentation of the patriot). Yerevan, 1955.

———. *Yerker* (Works). Moscow, 1897.

Acharian, Hrachya. *Patmutiun Hayots nor grakanutyan, B shrjan* (History of Armenian literature, 2nd period). Yerevan, 1957.

Achemian, Mkrtich. "*Moloryale*" (The sinner). In *Trtrun hanger* (Fluttering rhymes). Constantinople, 1908.

———. *Trtrun hanker, khunki burumner, anzat hatvatzner, luys yev estverk, garnan hover* (Fluttering rhymes, scents of incense, connected segments, light and shadows, winds of spring). Constantinople, 1908.

———. *Zhpitk yev artasuk* (Smiles and tears). Constantinople, 1909.

Achemian, Shahé. *Tetrak aghotits* (Prayer book). *Etchmiadzin* LVI, no. 1 (January 2000): 97–101.

Adonts, Nicolas. " '*Davit Bek' vepi patmakan hime yev gaghaparakan arzheke*" (The historical basis of the novel "*Davit Bek*" and its ideological value). In Abeghian, *Raffi, keanke, grakanutiune, hishogiutiunner*. 122–48.

Aghababian, Suren. "*Grakanutiune hayrenakan metz paterazmi tarinerin*" (Literature in the years of the Great Patriotic War). In *Sovetahay grakanutyan patmutiun* (History of Soviet Armenian literature). Yerevan, 1965. 2:9–63.

Aghayan, Ghazaros. *Yerker* (Works). Yerevan, 1979.

Anaïs. *Hushers* (My recollections). Paris, 1949.

Antonian, Aram. *Ayn sev orerun: patkerner* (In those black days: images). Boston, 1919.

———. *Gandzaran* (Treasure-trove). Constantinople, 1912.

———. *Gandzaran* (Treasure-trove). Constantinople, 1919.

———. *Harutiun Shahrikian.* Constantinople, 1910.

Antonian, Hakob. *Biureghner* (Crystals). Beirut, n.d.

Arakelian,G. *Hay zhogovurdi mtavor mshakuyti zargatsman patmutiun* (History of the Armenian people's cultural and intellectual development). Yerevan, 1975.

Arandzar. *Zhoghovatzu yerkeri* (Collection of works). Tiflis, 1905.

Arazi (Movses Harutiunian). *Entir yerker* (Selected works). Yerevan, 1948.

Arevmtahay groghneri namakani (Letters of Western Armenian writers). Yerevan, 1972.

Aristakesian, R., and H. Kh. Pogharian, eds. *Hayreni ghoghanjner: tzaghkakagh, Sovyetahay grakanutyan* (Native chimings: anthology of Soviet Armenian literature). Yerevan, 1985.

Artzruni, Grigor. *Grigor Artzrunu ashkhatutiunnere* (Works of Grigor Artzruni). Tiflis, 1904.

Asatur, Hrant. *Sahmanadrutiun yev Hay zhoghovurdn* (Constitution and the Armenian people). Constantinople, 1879.

———. *Dimastverner* (Portraits). Constantinople, 1921.

Assadurian, Hagop. *Serundnere mkhatsogh* (The smoldering generations). Tenafly, N.J., 2000.

Avetisian, Zaven. *"Vepi karutsvatzkayin sherteri verlutzutiune. Muratsani Gevorg Marzpetuni vepe"* (Analysis of the structural layers of Muratsan's *Gevorg Marzpetuni*). In Edward Jrbashian et al., *Grakan steghtzagortzutiun: verlutzutyan ughinere yev skzbunknere* (Literary creation: paths and principles for analysis). Yerevan, 1983.

———. *Hayots patmavepi poetikan* (Poetics of the Armenian historical novel). Yerevan, 1986.

Azadian, Y. Edmond. *Portraits and Profiles.* Ed. and trans. Agop J. Hacikyan and Edward S. Franchuk. Lewiston, N.Y, 1955.

Azatian, Toros. *Zmrukhté patmuchan* (Emerald gown). Istanbul, 1936.

Aznavurian, G. *"Levon Shanti namaknere Hovhannes Tumanianin"* (Levon Shant's letters to Hovhannes Tumanian). *Patma-banasirakan handes* (Journal of philological history) I (1982): 201–17.

Barseghian, Gegham. *Amboghjakan gortze* (Complete works). Paris, 1931.

Bashalian, Levon. *Noravepner yev patmvatzkner* (Novellas and short stories). Intro. Arshak Chopanian. Paris, 1939.

Basmajian, Gabriel. *"'Agapi' arevmtahayots arajin vepe yev ir antzanot heghinake"* (*Agapi,* the first Western Armenian novel and its unknown author). *Abaka* 6:9 and 7:11 (7 and 28 July 1997). Reprinted in *Marmara* (22 August 1997).

———. *"Hayatar Turkeren mamul"* (Armeno-Turkish literature). *Abaka* 12 (31 March 1997): 7.

Bournoutian, A. George, trans. and intro. *The Chronicle of Abraham Kretatsi.* Costa Mesa, Calif., 1999.

Chamchian, Mikayel (Father Michael Chamich). *History of Armenia: From BC 2247 to the Year of Christ 1780, or 1229 of the Armenian Era.* Trans. Johannes Avdall. Calcutta, 1827.

Chanashian, V. Mesrop. *Hay grakanutyan nor shrjani hamarot patmutiun: 1701–1920* (Concise history of Armenian literature: 1701–1920). Venice, 1973.

———. *Patmutiun ardi Hay grakanutyan* (History of modern Armenian literature). Venice, 1953.

Charents, Yeghishé. *Yerker* (Works). Yerevan, 1932.

———. *Poemner* (Narrative poems). Yerevan, 1955.

Cheokiurian, Tigran. *Vanke, herose* (The monastery, the hero). Paris, 1933.

Cheraz, Minas. *Grakan pordzer* (Literary experiments). Constantinople, 1874.

———. "Loksandra Pandelis." *Armenia* 3, no. 4 (February 1907), 18–24. Trans. A——S.

Chifté-Saraf, Onnik. *Yerker* (Works). Yerevan, 1981.

Chilinkirian, Grigor. *"Kinn tasnyevinnerord darun mej"* (The nineteenth-century woman). In *Chashak ardi matenagrutyan* (Selections in modern Armenian literature). Constantinople, 1888.

Chopanian, Arshak. *Kyank yev yeraz: zhoghovatzu ardzakneru* (Life and dream: collection of prose pieces). Paris, 1945.

Danielian, Karlen. *"Ayl ardzakagirner."* In *Hay nor grakanutyan patmutiun* (History of modern Armenian literature). Yerevan, 1964. 3:589–654.

Durian, Petros. *Tagher, namakner* (Poems, letters). Venice, 1959.

Durian, Yeghishé. *Srbazan knar* (Sacred lyre). Jerusalem, 1936.

———. "The Travelers of Emmaus." *Sion* 34, no. 9 (September–October 1971): 330–32.

Dussap, Srbuhi. *Mayta.* Constantinople, 1924.

———. *Siranush.* Constantinople, 1925.

Galemkerian, Zaruhi. *Haskakagh* (Gleaning). Yerevan, 1965.

———. *Kyankis chamben* (From the course of my life). Antilias, 1952.

Ghapantsi, Petros. *Hayreniki yev bnutyan yerker* (Songs of the homeland and nature). In Shushanik Nazarian, ed., *Petros Ghapantsi.* Yerevan, 1969.

Ghukasian, Zaven. *Zhamanakakits sovetahay vepe (1953–1963)* (The contemporary Soviet Armenian novel: 1953–1963). Yerevan, 1964.

Grigorian, Hrachya, et al., eds. *Entir ejer Hay grakanutyan hnaguyn zhamanaknerits minjev mer orere* (Selected pages from Armenian literature from ancient times to our days). Yerevan, 1946.

Hakhumian, Tigran. "Derenik Demirchian." In *Sovetahay grakanutyan patmutiun* (History of Soviet Armenian literature). Yerevan, 1965. 2:105–67.

Hakobian, Grigor, ed. *Zapel yev Hrant Asaturner: sirayin namakner* (Zapel and Hrant Asatur: love letters). Yerevan, 2001.

Hakobian, Hakob, Shushanik Kurghinian, Movses Arazi. *Yerker* (Works). Yerevan, 1982.

———. *Yerkeru zhoghovatzu* (Collected works). Yerevan, 1958.

Harutiunian, Artashes. *Ardzak ejer yev kertvatzner* (Prose pages and poems). Paris, 1937.

Hayrapetian, Srbuhi P. *Hrant Asatur kyanke yev gortze* (Hrand Asatur: his life and works). Los Angeles, 1979.

Hisarian, Hovhannes. *Nern kam kataratz ashkhharhi* (Antichrist, or the end of the world). Constantinople, 1867.

Indra. "The Inner World." *Ararat* 19, no. 1 (Winter 1978): 16–17. Trans. Garig Basmadjian.

———. *Nerashkhharh* (Inner world). Beirut, 1955.

Ishkhan, Mushegh. *Ardi Hay grakanutiun* (Modern Armenian literature). Beirut, 1982.

Kamenatsi, Hovhannes. *Patmutiun paterazmi Khotinu* (A narrative of the war of Khotin). Yerevan, 1964.

Kamsarakan, Tigran. *Varzhapetin aghjike* (The teacher's daughter). Yerevan. 1956.

Karnetsi, Hovhannes. *Tagharan* (Songbook), ed. Shushanik Nazarian. Yerevan, 1962.

Keusseyan, Krikor. *Gir yev gitz.* (Writings and drawings). Boston, 1998.

———. *Namakani: namakner Grigor Keosseyani* (Letters from Shahan Shanur to Krikor Keusseyan). Boston, 2001.

Khachikian, S. Levon. *Hay zhoghovrdi patmutiun* (History of the Armenian people). Yerevan, 1972.

Khrimian, Mkrtich. *Amboghjakan yerker* (Complete works). New York, 1929.

Kiurchian, Hrand Melkon. *Amboghjakan yerker. I. pandukhti kyanken* (Complete works, I: from the life of an expatriate). Paris, 1931.

Kiurchian, S. Mikayel. *Anunin gishere yev ayl patmvatzkner Polsahay barkeré* (Name-day night and other stories from the life of Istanbul Armenians). Cairo, 1903.
———. *Martik agha.* Yerevan, 1999.
Kurghinian, Shushanik. *Hayreni ghoghanjner—tzaghkakagh Sovetahay grakanutyan* (Chimes of the homeland: an anthology of Soviet Armenian literature), ed. R. H. Aristakesian and H. Kh. Poghosian. Yerevan, 1985.
Leo. *Grigor Artzruni.* Tiflis, 1903.
———. *Meliki aghjike* (Melik's daughter). Boston, 1933.
———. *Rusahayots grakanutiune skzbits minjev mer orere* (Eastern Armenian literature from the beginning to our times). Venice, 1904.
———. *Yerkeri zhoghovatzu* (Collected works), 8 vols. Yerevan, 1966–85.
Mahari, Gurgen. *Sovetahay grakanutyan entir ejer* (Selected pages from Soviet Armenian literature). Yerevan, 1960.
Malezian, Vahan. *Hogii dzayner* (Voices of the soul). Paris, 1949.
Mamurian, Matteos. *Anklyakan namakani kam Hayu me chakatagire* (English letters or the destiny of an Armenian). Smyrna, 1881.
———. *Sev lerin marde* (The man from Black Mountain). Izmir, 1909.
Manukian, Saribek. "Yervand Otian." In *Hay nor grakanutyan patmutiun* (History of modern Armenian literature). 5 vols. Yerevan, 1979. 5:660–99.
Manveliants, Levon. *Khortakvatz kyank* (Shattered life). Tiflis, 1897.
Margarian, Hakob. *Tigran Kamsarakan.* Yerevan, 1956.
Margossian, Marzbed, ed. *Nor gir yev ir ashkhatakitsnere* (New writing and its collaborators). New York, 1984.
Martayan, Hakob. *Hamaynapatker Hay mshakuyti—ardi shrjan 1852–1920* (Panorama of Armenian culture—modern period), *Marmara* (October 5, 1964–September 4, 1965).
Metzarents, Misak. *Banasteghtsutiunner, tziatzan, nor tagher* (Poems: rainbow, new verses). Venice, 1959.
Mirzabekian, J. *Mesrop, Taghiadian, kyanke yev steghtzagortzutiune* (Mesrop Taghiadian: his life and work). Yerevan, 1971.
Mkhitarian, M. H., ed. *Hay parberakan mamuli matenagitakan hamahavak 1794–1980* (Select bibliography of the Armenian periodical press 1794–1980). Yerevan, 1986.
Mkrtchian, Vahagn. *Dasakanner yev zhamanakakitsner* (Classical and contemporary figures). Los Angeles, 2001.
Mndzuri, Hakob. *Krunk usti kugas* (Crane, where do you come from?). Istanbul, 1974.
Movses Khorenatsi. *Hayots patmutiun* (History of the Armenians), trans. into Modern Armenian by S. Malkhasiants. Yerevan, 1940.
Mrmrian, Harutiun. *Tasnyevinnerord dar yev Hovhannes Prusatsi Teroyents* (The nineteenth century and Hovhannes Teroyents of Brusa). Constantinople, 1908.
Muradian, H. B. "Khachatur Abovian." In *Hay nor grakanutyan patmutiun* (History of modern Armenian literature). 5 vols. Yerevan, 1962. 1:363–478.
Muratsan. "*Gevorg Marzpetuni,*" *Armenian Review* 5:1 (Spring 1952): 143–48.
———. *Noyi agrave, arakyale* (Noah's crow, the disciple). Yerevan, 1954.
———. *Yerkeri zhoghovatzu* (Collected works). Yerevan, 1965.
Nanumian, Ruzan. "Mesrop Taghiadian," in *Hay nor grakanutyan patmutiun* (History of modern Armenian literature). 5 vols. Yerevan, 1962. 1:318–63.
———. *Mesrop Taghiadian, kyanke yev gortze* (Mesrop Taghiadian: his life and work). Yerevan, 1947.

———. "Tzerents," in *Hay nor grakanutyan patmutiun* (History of modern Armenian literature). 5 vols. Yerevan, 1962. 3:500–33.

———. *Tzerents*. Yerevan, 1961.

———. "Vrtanes Papazian." *Sovetakan grakanutiun* (Soviet literature) 5 (1955), 121–28.

———. *Vrtanes Papazian, kyanke yev steghtzagortzutiune* (Vrtanes Papazian: his life and work). Yerevan, 1956.

Norents, Vagharshak, and Soghomon Taronetsi, eds. *Matteos Zarifian, yerker* (Works of Matteos Zarifian). Yerevan, 1965.

Nurikian, Beniamin. "*Areve kezi*" (The sun for you), in *Nor gir* (New writings). New York, 1984.

———. *Pandukht hoginer* (Expatriate souls). Yerevan, 1958.

Ohanian, Ashot. "Leo." In *Hay nor grakanutyan patmutiun* (History of modern Armenian literature). 5 vols. Yerevan, 1964. 4:345–73.

———. *Leoi gegharvestakan steghtzagortzutiune* (Leo's literary creation). Yerevan, 1969.

———. *Vrtanes Papazian*. Yerevan, 1976.

Ordayan, V. Y., and Shavoyan, A. H. *Hayots Lezu* (The Armenian language). Yerevan, 1973.

Oshakan, Hakob. *Hamapatker arevmtahay grakanutyan* (Panorama of Western Armenian literature), vols. 1–5 (Jerusalem, 1945), 53, 54, 56, 62; vol. 6 (Beirut, 1968); vols. 7–10 (Antilias, 1979), 80, 82.

———. *Hayots grakanutiun* (Armenian literature). Jerusalem, 1957.

———. "*Mardots kovn i ver.*" In *Raffi, keanke, grakanutiune, hishoghutiunner* (Raffi, his life, his literature, memories). Paris, 1937.

———. *Vahan Tekeyan*. Beirut, 1985.

Otian, Grigor. "*London yev Paris*" (London and Paris), *Hatntirk ardi tohmayin grakanutyené* (Selections from modern national literature). Constantinople, 1908, 164–68.

———. *Sahmanadrakan khosker u charer, dambanakanner, maheru artiv grvatzner* (Constitutional pieces and speeches, funeral orations, eulogies). Constantinople, 1910.

Otian, Yervand. *Yerkeru zhoghovatzu* (Collection of works). 5 vols. Yerevan, 1960–62.

Paghtasar Dpir. *Taghikner siro yev karoti* (Songs of love and longing). Yerevan, 1958.

Palakian, G. *Hay Goghgotan* (The Armenian Golgotha). Vienna, 1922.

Papazian, Vrtanes. *Patmutiun hayots grakanutyan* (History of Armenian Literature). Tiflis, 1910.

———. *Yerkeri zhoghvatzu* (Collected works). Yerevan, 1958.

Parsamian, Mkrtich. "*Raffi: kensagrakan teghekutiunner*" (Raffi: biographical information). In *Raffi, keanke, grakanutiune, hishogiutiunner* (Raffi, his life, literature and memories). Paris, 1937. 7–24.

Partevian, Suren. *Kaykayum* (Destruction). Izmir, 1910.

Pashalian, Levon. "Angel," trans. Chris Kesici. *Ararat* 34, no. 3 (Autumn 2001): 34–36.

Perperian, R. H. "The Blind Youth's Grief," trans. J. J. Barsamian. *Armenia* 3, no. 8 (July 1907): 3–5.

———. *Khohk yev Hushk* (Reflections and memories). Vienna, 1904.

Peshiktashlian, Mkrtich. *Banasteghtzutiunner: charer* (Poems: speeches). Venice, 1956.

Peshiktashlian, Nshan. *Enker Shahazar* (Comrade Shahazar). Paris, 1927.

Peshtimalchian, Grigor. *Lusashavigh . . .* (Path of enlightenment). Constantinople, 1848.

Petrosian, Yeghishé. *Raffi, keanke yev steghtzagortzutiune* (Raffi: his life and work). Yerevan, 1959.

Proshian, Perch. "*Mikitan Sakon*" (Sako the publican), in *Hatsi khndir* (A matter of bread). In *Hay grakanutiun* (Armenian literature). Yerevan, 1984. 46–54.

———. *Shahen vipasanutiun* (Shahen, a novel). Tiflis, 1883.

Raffi (Hakob Melik Hakobian) (Signed as Pavstos). "*P. Haykunu kritikan yev 'Kaytzer'e.*" In *Raffi: yerkeri zhoghovatzu* (Raffi: collected works). 10 vols. Yerevan, 1964. 10:67–147.

———. "*Vipagrutiune rusahayeri mej*" (Eastern Armenian Fiction). In *Vepikner yev patkerner* (Novellas and images). Tiflis, 1891. I:vi–xiv.

Raffi: kyanke, grakanutiune, hishoghutiunner, luys entzayvatz tznuntyan hariuramyakin artiv, 1835–1937. (Raffi: his life, literature, memories; a commemoration of the occasion of the one-hundredth anniversary of his birth). Paris, 1937.

Roshka, Stepanos. *Zhamanakagrutiun kam tarekank yekeghetsakank* (Chronicle, or church annuals). Vienna, 1964.

Samuelian, Khachik. *Raffi: hamarot aknark* (Raffi: brief consideration). Yerevan, 1957.

Sarinian, Sergei. "*Haykakan romantizmi hartsi shurje*" (About the Armenian romanticism). In *Grakan ditoghoutiunner* (Literary observations). Yerevan, 1964. 153–94.

———. "Muratsan." In *Hay nor grakanutyan patmutiun* (History of modern Armenian literature). 5 vols. Yerevan, 1964. 4:124–82.

———. *Muratsan.* Yerevan, 2004.

———. *Raffi. Gaghaparneri yev kerparneri hamakarge* (Raffi, his ideas and characters). Yerevan, 1985.

———. *Raffi.* Yerevan, 1957.

———. "*Raffu steghtzagortzutiune*" (Raffi's work). In *Raffi. Yerkeri zhogovatzu* (Raffi, collected works). Yerevan, 1983. 1:9–38.

Setian, Hovhannes. "Lament." In *Hay grakanutiun* (Armenian literature), ed. Hakob Oshakan. Jerusalem, n.d.

Sevak, Ruben. *Ruben Sevak yev prtsvelik ugheghner* (Ruben Sevak and brains to be ripped out). Paris, 1985.

———. *Yerker* (Works). Antilias, Beirut, 1986.

Sev-vost. *Leran vogin* (The spirit of the mountain). Constantinople, 1920.

Shahaziz, Smbat. *Hraparakakhos dzayn* (The reporter's voice). Moscow, 1881.

———. "My Beloved Children." *Armenia* 3, no. 4 (February 1907): 12–13. Trans. Z. C. Boyajian.

Shahnur, Shahan. *Nahanje arants yergi* (Retreat without song). Paris, 1920.

Shant, Levon. *Hin astvatzner* (Ancient gods). Boston, 1917.

Shirvanzadé, Aleksandr. "Raffi: Hakob Melik Hakobian." In *Raffi, keanke, grakanutiune, hishogiutiunner* (Raffi, his life, literature, memories). Paris, 1937. 36–47.

———. *Yerkeri Zhoghovatzu* (Collected works). Yerevan, 1961.

Shmavonian, Harutiun. "*Madrasi Hayots*" (To the Armenians of Madras), *Azdarar* (Monitor) I (Madras, July 1794). Reprint, Lisbon, 1970.

Shtikian, Suren. *Hay nor grakanutyan zhamanakagrutiun, 1865–1875* (Chronology of modern Armenian literature: 1865–1875). Yerevan, 1991.

———. "*Zhamanakagrutiun*" (Chronology). In *Hay nor grakanutyan patmutiun* (History of modern Armenian literature). 5 vols. Yerevan, 1979. 5:973–99.

Simonian, Simon. *Arevelahay grakanutiun* (Eastern Armenian literature). Beirut, 1965.

Siruni, H. J. *Polis yev ir dere* (Constantinople and its role). Vols. 1, 2, 3, 4. Beirut, 1965, 1969, 1987, 1988.

Stepanian, Hasmik. *Hayatar turkeren grakanutiun, aghbiuragitakan usumnasirutiun* (Armeno-Turkish literature, source study). Yerevan, 2001.

———. *Hayatar turkeren grkeri matenagitutiun, 1727–1968* (Bibliography of Turkish language books in Armenian characters, 1727–1968). Yerevan, 1985.

Surkhatian, ed. *Hay grakanutiun, Arevelahay XIX i yev XX i arajin karort, artsak yev chapatzo nmushner* (Armenian literature in the nineteenth and the first quarter of the twentieth century: prose and metrical samples). Yerevan, 1926.

Svachian, Harutiun. "August Guiné." *Meghu* (The bee) 1, no. 1 (15 September, 1856), 19–24.

Svachian, Mari. "Khamsin," *Anahit* 3 (1899): 104–6.

Taghiadian, Mesrop *Gegharvestakan yerker* (Artistic works). Yerevan, 1965.

Tamrazian, Hrand. *Hay knnadatutiun* (Armenian criticism). Yerevan, 1992.

Temirchipashian, Yeghia. *Yerker* (Works). Yerevan, 1986.

Teoleolian, Minas. *Dar me grakanutiun* (A century of literature). 2 vols. Boston, 1977.

Terian, Vahan. *Grakan tsolker* (Literary reflections). Venice, 1956.

———. *Yerker* (Works). Yerevan, 1989.

———. *Yerkeri zhoghovatzu* (Collected works). Yerevan, 1960, 1961, and 1963.

Ter-Karapetian, Gegham. *Taroni ashkharh patkerner u patmvatzkner* (The land of Taron, images and short stories). Paris, 1931.

Teroyents, Hovhannes. *Banadat* (Critic). Constantinople, 1860.

Terzian, Tovmas. *Banasteghtzutyants amboghjakan havakatzo* (Complete collected poems). Venice, 1929.

Tlkatintsi. *Giughin kyantke* (Village life). Yerevan, 1966.

Tumanian, Hovhannes. *Yerkeri Zhoghovatzu 1881–1922* (Collected works, 1881–1922). Yerevan, 1950.

Tzerents (Hovsep Shishmanian). *Yerkeri havakatzo* (Collected works). Yerevan, 1957.

Tzovak, V. S., et al. *Hamaynapatker hanrapetakan shrjani Istanpulahay grakanutyan* (A panorama of Istanbul Armenian literature during the republican period). Istanbul, 1957.

Vanandetsi, Hovhannes. *Arpiakan Hayastani* (The light of Armenia). Constantinople, 1836.

Vanandetsi, Sargis. *Metzn Nerses kam Hayastani barerare* (Nerses the Great, the patron of Armenia). Jerusalem, 1887.

Varuzhan, Daniel. *Namakani* (Letters). Yerevan, 1965.

Vorberian, Ruben. *Ovasis* (Oasis). Paris, 1937.

Vorbuni, M. Zareh. *Halatzvatznere-Teknatzun* (The persecuted—the candidate). Beirut, 1967.

———. "*Mahazd*" (Obituary), *Kam* 1 (Paris, September 1980): 15–74.

Voskanian, N. A., et al. *Hay girke 1512–1800 tvakannerin* (Armenian literature between 1512 and 1800). Yerevan, 1988.

Vshtuni, Azat. "*Ughte*" (The camel), in *Hayreni Ghoghanjner* (Chimes of the homeland). Yerevan, 1985.

Yerukhan. *Novelner* (Novellas). Yerevan. 1965.

Zardarian, Hrach. "*Mamn u tore*" (Grandmother and grandson). In *Ardi Hay grakanutiun, zhoghovatzu* (Modern Armenian literature, collected works). I:101–13. Paris, 1939.

Zardarian, Ruben. *Tzaygaluys hatvatzner* (Dawning fragments). Venice, 1983.

Zorian, Stepan. *Patmvatzkner* (Stories). Yerevan, 1980.

Works in English and Other Languages

Abovian, Khachatur. "*Verk Hayastani*" (Wounds of Armenia). *Ararat* 23, no. 4 (Autumn 1982): 8–10. Trans. Sonia Harlan and Hovrig Jacob.

Alexanian, Elena. "19th Century Armenian Realism and Its International Relations," *Armenia* 13 (1984): 45–64.

Alonso, Amado. *Ensayo sobre la novela histórica.* Madrid, 1984.

Altoonian, Janine. *La Survivance.* Paris, 2000.

Antreassian, Jack, ed. and trans. *Voice of Conscience: The Stories of Krikor Zohrab.* New York, 1983.

———, and Marzbed Margossian, eds. and trans. *Across Two Worlds: Selected Prose of Yeghishé Charents.* New York, 1985.

Arnavoudian, Eddie. "Life in Stalinist Labour Camps: An Armenian Writer-Prisoner's View." Armenian News Network/Groong (14 August 2003) (19 August 2002), 1–2. http://groong.usc.edu/tcc/tcc-20020819.html

Arnot, R., and F. B. Collins, eds. and trans. *Armenian Literature, Comprising Poetry, Drama, Folklore and Classical Traditions.* London, 1908.

Asatur, Zapel. *The Bride.* Trans. Nishan Parlakian. New York, 1984.

Ashjian, Sarkis, ed. and trans. *Great Armenian Short Stories.* Beirut, 1959.

Attwater, Donald. *The Penguin Dictionary of Saints.* 2nd ed. London, 1983.

Balakian, Nona. *A New Accent in Armenian Fiction. The Armenian-American Writer.* New York, 1958.

Baliozian, Ara, ed. and trans. *The Armenians, Their History and Culture.* New York, 1980.

———. *Zohrab: an Introduction.* Kitchener, Ontario, 1985.

Bardakjian, Kevork B. *A Reference Guide to Modern Armenian Literature, 1500–1920.* Detroit, 2000.

Bashalian, Levon, "Angel." *Ararat* 42, no. 4 (Autumn 2001): 35–36. Trans. Chris Keseci.

Basmadjian, Grig "Gurgen Mahari." *Ararat* 20, no. 1 (Winter 1979): 99.

Beledian, Krikor. *Cinquante ans de littérature arménienne en France: 1922–1972.* (Fifty years of Armenian literature in France: 1922–1972). Paris, 2001.

Blackwell, Alice Stone, ed. and trans. *Armenian Poems Rendered into English Verse.* Boston, 1917.

———, ed. and trans. *Armenian Poems Rendered into English Verse.* A facsimile reproduction of the 1917 edition. Delmar, N.Y., 1978.

Bournoutian, George. *Armenians and Russia, 1626–1796.* A Documentary Record. Armenian Studies Series No. 2. Costa Mesa, Calif., 2001.

———, ed. and trans. *The Chronicle of Abraham of Crete (Patmutiun of Katoghikos Abraham Kretatsi).* Costa Mesa, Calif., 1999.

———. *Eastern Armenia in the Last Decades of Persian Rule, 1807–1828.* Costa Mesa, Calif., 1982.

———. *A History of the Armenian People: Prehistory to 1500 AD.* Costa Mesa, Calif., 1993. Vol. 1.

———. *A History of the Armenian People: 1500 AD to the Present.* Costa Mesa, Calif., 1994. Vol. 2.

————. *A History of Qarabagh: An Annotated Translation of Mirza Jamal Javanshir Qarabagh's Tarikh-e Qarabagh.* Costa Mesa, Calif., 1994.

————. *History of the Wars: 1721–1738 (Abraham Yerevantsi's patmutiun pateraz-matsn).* Costa Mesa, Calif., 1999.

————. *The Khenate of Erevan under Qajar Rule 1795–1828.* Costa Mesa, Calif., 1993.

Boyajian, Zabelle C., ed. and trans. *Armenian Legends and Poems.* London and New York, 1916.

Burt, Daniel S. *What Historical Novel Do I Read Next?* Detroit, 1977.

Butterfield, Herbert. *Historical Novel.* Cambridge, 1924.

Carmont, Pascal. *Les amiras, seigneurs de l'Arménie ottomane.* Paris, 1999.

Chopanian, Arshak. *Chants populaires arméniens* (Armenian popular songs). Paris, 1903.

————. "Gregory of Narek," *Armenia* 3 (February 1907): 8–13. Trans. from French by Y–R.

————. *La nation arménienne et son oeuvre culturelle.* Paris, 1945.

————. *Profiles.* 2 vols. Paris, 1921 and 1929.

Cross, F. A., and E. A. Livingston, eds. *The Oxford Dictionary of the Christian Church.* Oxford, 1982.

Dadrian, N. Vahakn. *The History of the Armenian Genocide.* Providence, R.I., 1995.

Der Hovanessian, Diana, and Marzbed Margossian, eds. and trans. *Anthology of Armenian Poetry.* New York, 1978.

————, eds. and trans. *Eghishe Charents: Land of Fire: Selected Poems.* Ann Arbor, Mich., 1986.

————. *Sacred Wrath: The Selected Poems of Vahan Tekeyan.* New York, 1982.

Donoyan, Armen, ed. and biographer. *Classical Armenian Short Stories.* Translated by Sarkis Ashjian. Glendale, Calif., 1992.

Doody, Margaret Anne. *True Story of the Novel.* New Brunswick, N.J., 1996

Emin, Joseph. *Life and Adventures of Emin Joseph Emin.* Calcutta, 1918.

Etmekjian, James, ed. *An Anthology of Western Armenian Literature.* New York, 1980.

————. *The French Influence on the Western Armenian Renaissance.* 1964. Reprint, New York, 1978.

————. "The Historical Novel." *Ararat* 36, no. 4 (Autumn 1978): 39.

————, trans. "Mayta." *Ararat* 19, no. 2 (Spring 1978): 39.

————. "Toros Levoni." *Ararat* 19, no. 4 (Autumn 1978): 40–43.

————. "Western European and Modern Armenian Literary Relations up to 1915," *Armenia* 13 (1984): 64–92.

Fernández Prieto, Celia. *Historia y novela: poética de la novela histórica.* Pamplona, 1998.

Feuchtwanger, Lion. *House of Desdemona, or Laurels and Limitations of Historical Fiction.* Trans. Harold A. Bisilius. Detroit, 1963.

Garab, M. Arra, ed. *Hovhannes Tumanian: A Selection of Stories, Lyrics, and Epic Poems.* New York, 1971.

Hacikyan, J. Agop, et al., eds. and trans. *The Heritage of Armenian Literature: From the Oral Tradition to the Golden Age.* Detroit, 2000.

————. *The Heritage of Armenian Literature: From the Sixth to the Eighteenth Century.* Detroit, 2002.

Hairapetian, Srbouhi. *A History of Armenian Literature from Ancient Times to the Nineteenth Century.* Delmar, N.Y., 1995.

————. *Hrant Asatur.* Los Angeles, 1979.

Hewsen, Robert. "Khachatur Abovian: Father of Modern Armenian Literature." *Ararat* 13, no. 4 (Autumn 1982): 5–6.

Hovannisian, G. Richard, ed. *The Armenian People: From Ancient to Modern Times.* 2 vols. New York, 1997.

Injejikian, Hasmig. "Sayat Nova and Armenian Musical Tradition." M.A. thesis, McGill University, 1990.

Isahakian, Avetik. *Abou-Lala-Mahari.* Trans. Zabel C. Boyajian. New York, 1948.

———. *Selected Works.* Trans. Mischa Kudian. Moscow, 1976.

Ishkhanian, R., ed. *The Armenian Literature in Foreign Languages.* Yerevan, 1971.

Jitrik, Noé. *Historia e imaginación literaria; las posibilidades de un género.* Buenos Aires, 1995.

Kudian, Mischa, ed. and trans. ———. *Retreat without Song.* London, 1982.

———. *Soviet Armenian Poetry.* London, 1984.

———. *The Tailor's Visitors.* London, 1984.

Leo. *History of Armenian Printing.* Vol. 1, revised. Tiflis, 1945.

Lukács, György. *The Historical Novel.* Trans. Hannah and Stanley Mitchell. London, 1965.

Manzoni, Alessandro. *On the Historical Novel.* Trans. Sandra Bermann. Lincoln, Neb., 1984.

Mata Induráin, Carlos. *"Retrospectiva sobre la evolución de la novela histórica."* In *Novela histórica. Teoría y comentarios.* Pamplona, 1995.

Matthews, Brander. *The Historical Novel and Other Essays.* New York, 1901. Reprint, Detroit, 1969.

Mkrtchian, Samuel, ed. and trans. *Selected Armenian Poets.* Yerevan, 1993.

Muratsan. "Gevorg Marzpetuni," *Armenian Review* 5 (Spring 1952): 143–48. Trans. anonymous.

Nichanian, Marc. *Writers of Disaster: The National Revolution.* Vol. 1. Princeton, N.J., and London, 2002

Norashkharian, Shant. "Taniel Varoujan." http://www.umd.umich.edu/dept/armenian/literatu/varoujan/html (accessed 16 July 2003).

Orel, Harold. *The Historical Novel from Scott to Sabatini: Changing Attitudes toward a Literary Genre, 1814–1920.* New York, 1995.

Oshakan, Hakob. "Dobij." *Ararat* 35, no. 1 (Winter 1983): 42–47. Trans. Aris Sevag.

Oshakan, Vahé. "A Brief Survey of Armenian Literature," *Armenia* 13 (1984): 28–44.

———. "Cosmopolitanism in West Armenian Literature," *Armenia* 13 (1984): 194–213.

———. *The English Influence on West Armenian Literature in the Nineteenth Century.* Cleveland, Ohio, 1982.

———. "The Genius of Hakob Oshakan." *Ararat* 24, no. 1 (Winter 1983): 16.

———. Otian, Yervand. *Enker B. Panjuni* (Comrade Panjuni). Trans. Jack Antreassian. New York, 1977.

———. *Manana* (Manna). Constantinople, 1914.

Parlakian, Nishan, and Peter Cowe, eds. *Modern Armenian Drama.* New York, 2001.

Paronian, Hakob. *Balthasar.* Trans. E. D. Megerditchian. Boston, 1930.

———. "The Honorable Beggars." *Ararat* 20, no. 2 (Spring 1979): 43–48. Trans. Aris Sevag.

———. *The Honorable Beggars.* Ed. and trans. Jack Antreassian. New York, 1980.

———. *The Perils of Politeness.* Ed. and trans. Jack Antreassian. New York, 1983.

Perperian, Reteos. "The Blind Youth's Grief." *Armenia* 3, no. 8 (1907): 3–5. Trans. J. J. Barsamian.

Raffi. *The Fool.* Trans. Donald Abcarian. New Jersey, 2000.

———. *The Fool.* Trans. J. S. Wingate. Boston, 1950.

Refik, Ahmed. *Anadoluda Türk Aşiretler* (Turkish tribes in Anatolia). Istanbul, 1932.

Rowe, Victoria. *A History of Armenian Women's Writing.* Amersham, Buckinghamshire, 2003.

Shant, Levon. *The Princess of the Fallen Castle.* Trans. H. Baytarian. Boston, 1939.

Sharasan. *The Armenian Theater and Its Actors in Turkey, 1850–1908.* Constantinople, 1915.

Shirvanzadé, Alexandre. *Evil Spirit.* Trans. Nshan Parlakian. New York, 1980.

Shishmanian, H. *Toros Levoni: Armenian Stories.* Boston, 1917.

Siamanto. *Bloody News from My Friend.* Ed. and trans. Peter Balakian and Nevart Yaghlian. Detroit, 1996.

———. "Mother Tongue." *Ararat* 17, no. 4 (Autumn 1976): 6. Trans. Mischa Kudian.

———. "The Prayer of an Armenian Poet." *Ararat* 17, no. 4 (Autumn 1976): 7. Trans. Martin Robbins.

Sndukian, Gabriel. *Bebo.* Trans. E. D. Megerditchian. Boston, 1931.

———. "The Ruined Family," *Armenian Literature.* Trans. F. B. Collins. New York, 1901.

Spang, Kurt. *"Apuntes para una definición de la novela histórica."* In *Novela histórica. Teoría y comentarios.* Pamplona, 1995.

Tashjian, H. James. *My Name Is Saroyan.* New York, 1983.

Tebbel, John. *Fact and Fiction: Problems of the Historical Novelist.* Lansing, Michigan, 1962.

Tekeyan, Vahan. "Dear Brother in the Bond . . . ." *Ararat* 19, no. 1 (Winter 1978): 20–21.

Terian, Vahan. *Coming to Terms: Selected Poems.* Trans. Diana Der Hovanessian. New York, 1991.

Tolegian, Aram, ed. and trans. *Armenian Poetry Old and New: a Bilingual Anthology.* Detroit, 1979.

Totovents, Vahan. *Scenes from an Armenian Childhood.* Trans. Mischa Kudian. London, 1962.

———. *Tell Me, Bella.* Ed. and trans. Mischa Kudian. London, 1972.

Tumanian, Hovhannes, "My Friend Neso," in *We of the Mountains: Armenian Short Stories.* Trans. Fainna Glagoleva. Moscow, 1972.

Werfel, Franz. *The Forty Days of Musa Dagh.* New York, 1935.

Wesseling, Elizabeth. *Writing History as a Prophet: Postmodernist Innovations of the Historical Novel.* Amsterdam and Philadelphia, 1991.

Yevterpé (Zaruhi Kalemkiarian). "Agony of a Horse." *Ararat* 11, no. 3 (1960): 11. Trans. anonymous.

Zarian, Kostan. *Bancoop and the Bones of the Mammoth.* Selected and trans. Ara Baliozian. New York, 1982.

INDEX

Aballino (J. H. Zschokke), 89
Abdul Aziz, 21, 25, 226
Abdul Hamid yev Sherlock Holmes
  (Abdul Hamid and Sherlock
  Holmes / Y. Otian), 104
Abdul-Hamid II, 14, 21, 25, 26, 58,
  342, 566, 683
Abdul-Mejid I, 13, 21
Abeghian, Manuk, 68, 72, 106
Abov, Gevorg, 960
Abovian, Khachatur, 68, 75, 85, 89–90,
  211–14, 293, 317, 354, 355, 377,
  551, 594, 962; education of, 211–12
Acharian, Hrachya, 106
Achemian (Adjemian), Mkrtich, 78,
  362; *The Misguided*, 363–65 (text)
Adana, 60
Adonts, Nikoghayos, 106
aestheticism, 81–82
Afghanistan, 37
Agapi (H. Vardanian), 59, 59n. 53
Agapian, Arshak, 562
Aghabekian, Marcos, 305
Aghaton, Mkrtich, 56, 199
Aghayan, Ghazaros, 68, 69, 81, 292,
  317, 383–85, 420, 481; *Tork Angegh
  and Haykanush the Fair*, 385–98
  (text)
Aghbelian, Nikol, 106
Aghbiur (Source), 383
Aguletsi, Andreas, 471
Aharonian, Avetis, 79, 592–94;
  Judgment, 594–611 (text); short
  stories of, 593
Aharonian, Vardges, 594

Ahmed III, 5, 22
Aïvazovski, Gabriel, 336, 337
Akbar, 36
Akhtark (Astrological treatise), 43
Aksorakane (The exile / A. Shitanian),
  103
Alafranca (K. Narpey), 338
Alamdarian, Harutiun, 68, 195–96,
  196n. 1, 211; *Dream*, 197–98 (text);
  Spring, 196–97 (text)
al-Armani, Ali ibn Yahya Abul-Hasan,
  34
al-Armani, Bahram, 34
al-Armani, Hassan, 34
Alashkert, 25, 26
Alemgir (V. Papazian), 104
Aleppo, 30, 35
Alexander I (Tsar of Russia), 9, 337
Alexandria, 34, 35
Alishan, Ghevond, 53, 54, 62, 74, 91,
  229–31; *The Lily of Shavarshan*, 231–
  33 (text), 231n. 2; *The Nightingale*,
  234–35 (text); translations by of
  Western classics, 230
al-Jamali, Avdal, 34
al-Jamali, Badr, 34
Almast, 621
Almast (S. Mupahiachian), 432
al-Rumi, Vardan, 34
Amerika (V. Totovents), 936
Amira (M. Svachian), 728–29
amiras, the, 19, 659n. 1
Amirayin aghjike (The amira's daughter
  / Y. Srmakeshkhanlian), 659–60

Amusinner (Spouses / G. Sundukian), 270

Anahit, 82

Anaïs. *See* Avetisian, Yevpimé

Anatolia, 14n. 18, 18, 26

Andreas Yerets (Andreas the priest / G. Ter-Hovhannesian), 99

Andreasian, Andranik, 946

Andrianatsi, Karapet, 46

Andrikian, Nerses, 102

Andunde (The precipice / A. Shitanian), 103

Andzevatsi, Khosrov, 230

Angliakan namakani (English letters / M. Mamurian), 306, 306n. 3, 307–15 (text)

Anhetatatz serund me (A vanished generation / G. Zohrap), 79

Anii kortzanume (The destruction of Ani / B. Ayvazian), 101

Anin tzakhvetsav (Ani is sold / B. Ayvazian), 101

Anitzyale (The cursed / A. Shitanian), 103

Ankiuratsi, Hovhannes, 45

Anna Saroyan (H. Hovhannisian), 603

Antonian, Aram, 804–5; as editor of literary periodicals, 804; *In Those Black Days*, 805–11 (text)

Antonian, Hakob, 900; *Moments*, 900–901 (text); *The Waves*, 901–2 (text)

Anush (H. Tumanian), 621

Apaga (Future), 431

Aper, Khnko, 664–65; *The Golden Spindle*, 665–68 (text)

Aptakk (Slaps / H. Svachian), 330

Ara Keghetsik (Ara the fair / A. Haykuni), 92

Arabo yev Andranik (Arabo and Andranik / A. Shitanian), 104

Arajin Hogeghen kerakur hayazgi yerakhaneri hamar (First spiritual food for Armenian children / S. Nazarian), 220

Arajin terevk (The first leaves / R. Perperian), 429

Aramian, Janik, 48

Arandzar. *See* Kuyumchian, Misak

Arandzar Amatuni (H. Svachian), 331

Ararat, 69, 238, 316, 383

Araskhanian, Avetik, 81

Araxia kam varzhuhin (Araxia, or the school teacher / S. Dussap), 400

Arazi. *See* Harutiunian, Movses

Archbishop Abraham, 32, 33

Ardzagang (The echo), 76, 93, 346, 481

Ardzern banasteghtzutiun hamarotyal (Short manual of poetry / Y. Hurmuzian), 72

Arev (The sun), 104, 784, 812

Arevelian mamul (Eastern press), 58, 306, 306n. 2, 307, 372

Arevelk (The east [Orient]), 78, 261, 264–65, 453, 658, 659

Arevmutk (Sunset [Occident]), 265, 292

Argatzk Tigrana (The adventures of Tigran), 72–73

Arghutian, Hovsep, 8, 160

Arik Haykazunk (Brave Armenians / H. Svachian), 331

Ariuni chambun vra (On the bloody road / S. Biurat), 102

Ariuni dzore (Blood canyon / S. Biurat), 102

Armenia, 1, 8n. 8, 643, 962; as battleground between Persian and Ottoman empires, 1–6, 2n. 1, 29, 109n. 1; Catholicism in, 20; conservative and liberal intellectuals in, 471; Eastern, 5, 6, 9–12, 22, 67–70; education in, 63–64, 67–69; emancipation movements, 6–9; famine in, 2; genocide in, 14, 27–29, 87, 104, 482, 622; massacre at Adana, 27; National Constitution of, 20–22, 226, 341–42; in the nineteenth century, 84–85; partition of, 5; peasantry of,

15–16; revolutionary parties in, 76, 86; social, economic, and political conditions in, 14–16; Western, 12–14, 25–26. *See also* Armenian diaspora; Armenian Question, the

Armenian Benevolent Society, 286, 480

Armenian cultural revival (the *Zartonk*), 42–43, 48, 56, 495–96; in Eastern Armenia, 67–70; and journalism, 56–58; and the origins of printing, 43–50. *See also* Armeno-Turkish literature; Armenian literature; Mkhitarist Order (Mkhitarist Fathers)

Armenian diaspora, 29–30, 42, 108; to the Crimea, 38–40; to Egypt, 34–35; to India, 35–38; to Jerusalem, 32–34; to the Middle East, 30–31; to Transylvania, 42; to the Ukraine and Poland, 40–42. *See also* Armenian cultural revival

Armenian historical fiction (nineteenth-century), 84–85; antecedents and development of, 85–86; historical drama, 84n. 80; historical novelists, 88–106 passim; historical novels, 86–88; typology of, 88

Armenian language: classical (*grabar*), 61, 71; contributing factors to the spread of, 63–67; middle, 61; modern, 61–62

Armenian literature, 70–73, 70n. 61; and aestheticism, 81–82; and the *hetanosakan sharzhum* (pagan movement), 845–46; literary criticism, 106; and neoclassicism, 70–71; poetry, 106–7, 108; provincial, 82–84; and realism, 77–81; and romanticism, 74–76; and symbolism, 82; twentieth-century, 106–8. *See also* Armenian historical fiction (nineteenth-century)

Armenian Orthodox Church, the, 6, 11, 20, 31

Armenian Patriarchs of Jerusalem, 32n. 40

Armenian Question, the, 22–27, 77

Armenians, in Constantinople, 16–18, 17n. 23, 28–29; massacre of, 27; social conditions of, 18–19, 490. See also *amiras*, the

Armeno-Turkish literature, 58–59, 58n. 51; newspapers and periodicals, 59–60; translations, 64–67

Arpiakan Hayastan (Sunlit Armenia / H. Vanandetsi), 73, 185, 185–88 (text)

Arpiarian, Arpiar, 57–58, 78, 79, 452–54, 519, 580, 611, 659, 783, 814; *I Have Seen So Many*, 454–58 (text); short stories of, 454

Arshak (M. Peshiktashlian), 287, 297

Arshak II (K. Narpey), 338

Arshak II (T. Terzian), 381

Arshak yerkrord (Arshak the second / P. Minasian), 73

Arshaluys (Dawn / V. Papazian), 521

Arshaluys Araratian (Dawn on Ararat), 56

Arshaluys kristoneutyan hayots (The dawn of Christianity in Armenia / G. Alishan), 230

Artzruni, Grigor, 69, 75, 79, 346, 420–22, 452; *A Couple of Words on the Education of Girls*, 422–27 (text)

Artzvi Vaspurakan (The eagle of Vaspurakan), 57, 237, 372

Artzvik Tarono (The eaglet of Taron), 57, 237, 372

Arutiun yev Manuel (Arutiun and Manuel / G. Aghayan), 384

Asatur, Hrand (Hrant), 57, 78, 518, 531–32, 541, 580, 581; *Grigor Zohrap*, 532–38 (text)

Asatur, Zapel (Sibil), 74n. 68, 78, 80, 81, 518, 532, 541–42; as a feminist, 542; *Letter to Hrand Asatur*, 547–49 (text); publications by, with her husband, 542

ashkharhabar, 85, 89

Ashot Yerkat (B. Ayvazian), 101
Ashtaraketsi, Nerses, 68, 195, 354
Asi (V. Papazian), 104
Aské anké (About here and there /
    H. Svachian), 331
Aspet, Hovhannes Abisoghomian. *See*
    Chifté-Saraf, Onnik
Assises d'Antioch (Assises of Antioch),
    230, 230n. 1
Association of Armenian Proletarian
    Writers, 577–78
Astghaberd, 975
Atamnabuzhn arevelyan (The oriental
    dentist / H. Paronian), 405
Atrpet. *See* Mupahiachian, Sargis
Austria, 25
Avarayri artzive kam Vardanank (The
    eagle of Avarayr, or Vardanank /
    S. Biurat), 102
Avazakapete (The bandit chief /
    A. Shitanian), 103
Avedikian, Gabriel, 54
Avetaber (Messenger), 57
Avetisian, Yevpimé, 673–74;
    contributions to periodicals, 673;
    My Recollections, 674–79 (text)
Avgerian, Harutiun, 52
Avgerian, Mkrtich, 54
Aydnian, Arsen, 62
Ayrvogh horizon (Burning horizon /
    M. Harutiunian), 105
Ayvazian, Bagrat, 101
Ayvazian, G., 60
Azadian, Edmond Y., 845
Azatamart (Freedom battle), 701, 826
Azatian, Toros, 886, 975–76; *Solitude*,
    976–77 (text)
Azatutyan hamar: Zeytuni vrezhe (For
    liberty: the revenge of Zeytun /
    S. Biurat), 102
Azatutyan zhamer (Hours of freedom /
    S. Shahaziz), 377–78
Azdak (The monitor), 826
Azdarar, 37, 49
Azerfeza (V. Papazian), 104

Azganver hayuhyats enkerutiun
    (Women's Benevolent Society), 541
Azgaser (The patriot), 89, 203
Azgaser Araratyan (Ararat patriot), 203
"*Azgayin harajdimutiun*" (National
    progress / K. Misakian), 224–25
    (text)
Azgayin jojer (The big wigs of the
    nation / H. Paronian), 405
Azgayin natenadaran (The national
    library), 54
Azgayin sahmanadrutiun (The National
    Constitution), 43
Azgayin tshvarutiun (National misery /
    M. Nalbandian), 293

Babakhanian, Arakel, 100–101, 506–8;
    historical writings, 507; short novels
    of, 506–7
Baghdasar, Dpir, 156
Baghnesi bokhcha (Bath bag /
    G. Sundukian), 270
Baghramian, Movses, 37, 147–48, 160,
    161
Bagratuni, Arsen, 52, 53, 72, 286, 400
Bagratunis, the, 30
Bakunin, Mikhail, 292, 292n. 2
Bakunts, Aksel, 963, 988–90; *The
    Alpine Violet*, 990–99 (text)
Baldazarian, Ghukas, 64
Balkan War (1912), 27
Balkans, the, 2, 6, 24, 26, 405
Baltazarian, Ghukas, 56
Banasteghtzakan yerker (Poetic works /
    S. Biurat), 102
Banasteghtzutiunner (Poems /
    G. Aghayan), 384
Banasteghtzutiunner (Poems /
    H. Tumanian), 620
Banateanu, Vlad, 911
Bante bant (From prison to prison /
    S. Biurat), 102
Banti hishatakaran (Prison memories /
    Movsisian), 481
Barboni, Michelangelo, 45

Bardakjian, Kevork B., 292, 559, 594, 928, 1026n. 5

Bardanes, Philippicus, 39

Bardzravank (Hilltop monastery), 784, 831, 875

Bargirk haykazian lezvi (Dictionary of the Armenian language / M. Sebastatsi), 51, 62

Barkhudarian, Mkrtich, 76

Barseghian, Gegham, 83, 826–27, 831, 875; *Journal,* 827–29 (text)

Bartoli, Antonio, 45

Basa, Dominicus, 44

Bashalian (Pashalian), Levon, 57, 78, 79, 107, 454, 611–12; *Angel,* 612–18 (text); stories and novels of, 612

Bats kabuyt tzaghikner (Pale blue flowers / V. Totovents), 936

Bayazit, 4, 25, 26

Bazmavep (Polyhistor), 51, 57, 229

Beg, David (Davit), 5, 7, 175n. 2, 347

Beg, Musa, 565

Begun, Maryam, 36

Bghde (P. Proshian), 355

Bishop Hovakim (Primate of Brusa), 17

Bishop Nerses of Ashtarak, 9

Biurat, Smbat, 102–3

Biuzandian (Byzantine), 56

Blok, Aleksandr, 959

Borian, Bagrat, 962

Bournoutian, A. George, 26

Bovis, Juan Batista, 45

Bravo of Venice, The (J. H. Zschokke, trans. M. G. Lewis), 89

Brooks, Frances, 876

Brosset, Marie, 110

Bryusov, Valery, 563, 620, 959

Bulgaria, 24, 42

Burgeren (From the pyramids / S. Biurat), 102

Burma, 37, 38

Burton, Richard, 66

Buzand, Pavstos, 52, 71

Byron (Lord Byron), 55

Byzantium, 34, 39

Cairo, 35

Calcutta, 37–38; printing in, 49

Cana, Tomas, 37

Casmir the Great, 40

Cathedral of St. James, 33

Catherine the Great, 6, 12, 42; and the annexation of the Crimea, 39

Catholicos Abraham Kretatsi. *See* Kretatsi, Abraham (Abraham of Crete)

Catholicos Abraham II Khoshabetsi, 109

Catholicos Gevorg IV, 68, 237

Catholicos Gevorg V, 783

Catholicos Hakob IV Jughayetsi, 6–7, 45

Catholicos Matteos II Izmirlian, 460

Catholicos Mikayel I Sebastatsi, 6, 44

Catholicos Mkrtich Khrimian. *See* Khrimian, Mkrtich

Catholicos Movses III Tatevatsi, 45

Catholicos Simeon I Yerevantsi. *See* Yerevantsi, Simeon

Catholicos Stepanos V Salmastatsi, 6

Catholicos Yeprem I Dzorageghtsi, 50

Caucasian Society of Armenian Writers, 622

Chamchian, Mikayel, 53, 174–75

Chamurchian, Teroyents Hovhannes Patveli, 59

Char nerboghakan i surb khachn Kristosi (Eulogy on the Holy Cross of Christ / H. Vanandetsi), 184–85

Charek, Aram, 81

Charents, Yeghishé, 107, 958–63, 990, 1013; *Hairdresser's Charms,* 974 (text); *I Love the Sun-Baked Taste of Armenian Words,* 970–71 (text); *Land of Nayiri,* 963–70 (text); *Ocean Song,* 971–72 (text); *Ode for the Dead,* 972–74 (text). *See also* "Manifesto of the Three"

Cheokiurian, Tigran, 852–53

Cheraz, Minas, 62, 380, 459–60, 518, 531, 658, 680; *Loxandra Pandelis,* 460–66 (text)

Chifté-Saraf, Onnik, 709–11; contributions to periodicals, 709; *Crucifixion,* 711–18 (text); influence of the Armenian genocide upon his life and work, 710; short stories of, 710

Chilinkirian, Grigor, 62, 65, 66, 306, 366–67; translations by of European authors, 367

Chivelekian, T., 60

Chopanian, Arshak, 57, 78, 80, 83, 106, 107, 497, 612, 658, 680–83; *The Bond,* 685–86 (text); early works of, 681; *Gregory of Narek,* 683–85 (text); historical contributions of, 682; *Ode to My Native Tongue,* 687–89 (text); *To the Moon,* 686–87 (text); translations by of French authors, 680

Chrakagh (The gleaner), 69, 220

Chrakian, Artin, 35

Chrakian, Tiran (Indra), 80, 81, 381, 722–23

Christianity/Christians, 32, 33, 34

Church of the Holy Sepulcher, 33

Church of St. Mary, 33

Cilicia, 24, 28, 34, 41

Cicilian Kingdom, 30, 31, 35, 61

Clémanceau, Georges, 683

Cleopatra, 34

Complete Works (M. Nalbandian), 294

Congress of Berlin, 26, 92–93, 93n. 88; Article 61 of, 77, 77n. 72

Congress of Vienna (1814–15), 23

Constantinople, 25, 35, 62, 65, 74, 79, 82, 85; fall of, 17n. 22, 43, 48; missionaries in, 20; printing in, 56–57, 59–60, 129. *See also* Armenians, in Constantinople

Crete, 24

Crimea, the, 38–40

Crimean War (1853–56), 10, 13–14n. 15

Critica (Criticism / M. Nalbandian), 293

Dadrian, Vahakn, 23

Darbnots (Forge), 577

Dashink (Alliance), 744

Datastanagirk (Book of judgments / Gosh), 41

Da'ud, Karapet Artin Pasha, 31

Daudet, Alphonse, 581, 813

Davanutiun chsmarit yev ughghapar havoto srpo yekeghetsvo Hayastanyats yev im sharadroghis isk (Confession of the true and orthodox faith of the Armenian Holy Church and myself / S. Yerevantsi), 152n. 1, 152–55 (text)

Davit Bek (H. Hakobian), 94, 95, 347

De Propaganda Fide, 44, 120

Demirdjian, Derenik. *See* Temirchian, Derenik

Depi Yltez (Toward Yiltiz / S. Biurat), 102

Diakaputnere (Body snatchers / S. Biurat), 102

Dimastverner (Portraits / H. Asatur), 532

Ditak Biuzandian (The Byzantine observer), 56

Ditsabanutiun (Mythology / M. Taghiadian), 204

Divan (H. Hisarian), 281

Djerideyi Sharkiye (Eastern journal), 60

Djivelekian, T., 60

Dodokhian, Gevorg, 327–28; *Swallow,* 328–29 (text)

Dpir, Astvatzatur, 47–48

Dpir, Paghtasar, 63, 128–29; *Money,* 129–30 (text); *Song,* 130 (text)

Drakhti entanik (The family of paradise / M. Khrimian), 238

Durian, Petros, 62, 74, 75, 440–42, 442n. 2, 681, 886, 928; *Complaint,* 442–44 (text); historical tragedies of, 441; *The Lake*, 444–45 (text); *My Death*, 445–46 (text)

Durian, Yeghishé, 81, 500–502, 830; as a poet, 501–2; as a scholar, 502; as a teacher, 502; *The Travelers of Emmaus*, 502–5 (text)

Durrell, Lawrence, 876, 877

Dussap, Srbuhi, 74–75, 74n. 68, 287, 399–401, 518, 542

East India Company, 36, 38

Eastern Question, the, 22–23

Egypt, 34–35

Ejer ughevori oragren (Pages from a travel journal / G. Zohrap), 519

Eli mek zoh (Yet another victim / G. Sundukian), 269

Eliza, kam Verjin arevelyan paterazmi zhamanak teghi unetsatz depk me (Eliza, or an incident that occurred during the recent eastern war / A. Haykuni), 92

Émile (Tlkatintsi), 83

Emin, Hovsep (Joseph), 7–9, 37, 43, 160, 168; *Life and Adventures of Emin Joseph Emin—1726–1809*, 168–73 (text)

Emin, Mkrtich, 68

Emma (V. Papazian), 571

Endhanur yekeghetsakan patmutiun (General church history / H. Teroyents), 200

Entertsasirutiun (Love of reading / N. Zorayan), 247

Erzrumtsi, Khachatur, 72

Etchmiadzin, 9, 11, 42, 110. *See also* Holy See of Etchmiadzin

Etmekjian, James, 519

Evelina (G. Artzruni), 422

Fatma (A. Shitanian), 103

Fitzgerald, Edward, 66

France, 9, 12

futurism, 960n. 2

Gabamachian, Simon, 67

Gaghtnik siraharats kam Ararata aytselum (Lover's secret, or visitor to Ararat / H. Karian), 91

Galanus, Clemens, 20

Galfayan, Ambrosius, 336–37

Galfayan, Khoren. *See* Narpey, Khoren

Gandz lezvin hayots kam bararan Stepanian (A treasury of the Armenian language, or Stepanos's dictionary / S. Roshka), 120

Gandzaketsi, Kirakos, 230

Ganja, 6, 9

Garnan hover (Winds of spring / M. Achemian), 362

Garun (Spring), 868

Gavafian, Gegham, 831, 875

Gelenian, Hambardzum, 951–52; *The Blue Bead*, 953–57

Georges Dandin (Molière), 270

Georgia, 2, 3, 5, 9

Georgian Church, 11

Gevorg Marzpetuni (G. Ter-Hovhannesian), 99–100, 101, 472, 472–79 (text)

Ghapantsi, Petros (Peter of Ghapan), 128, 156–57; *To My Honorable Nation, Under the Metaphor of the Rose*, 157n. 1, 157–59 (text)

Gharadaghtsi, Poghos, 203

Gharip akhpere (The expatriate / A. Shitanian), 103

Ghlijents, Avetis, 46

Girk aghotits vor kochi zbosaran hogevor (A book called spiritual recreation / S. Yerevantsi), 152

Girk kerakanutian (A grammar book / P. Dpir), 129

Girk vor kochi partavchar (A book called acquittal / S. Yerevantsi), 152

Gishervan sabre kher é (A sneeze at night is good luck / G. Sundukian), 269

Gladstone, William, 459

Gnuni (A. Shitanian), 103

Gochunian, Misak, 60, 60n. 55

Gogol, Nikolai, 268

Gorky, Maxim, 868

Gosh, Mkhitar, 41, 61

Grakan pordzer (Literary essays / M. Cheraz), 460

Grakan yev imastasirakan sharzhum (Literary and philosophical movement), 448

Granjon, Robert, 41

"graveyard school" of English poetry, 693, 693n. 1

Great Bandit, The (J. H. Zschokke), 204

Great Britain, 9, 12, 25, 26; influence of in India, 37–38

Greece/Greeks, 16, 32, 33; Greek uprising, the, 13

Greek Orthodox Church, 39

Gregorian Calendar, 44

Grkuyk vor kachi yergaran (A booklet called the song book / P. Ghapantsi), 156–57

Grots-brots (Bookworm / G. Srvandztiants), 373

Grotto of the Nativity, 33

Gurgen, Hakob, 62, 669

Haghags pordzakan hogebanutyan char (Lecture on experimental psychology / S/ Nazarian), 220

Haghags umemn Merser kochetysal Sahak mankan (On the youth Sahak, called Merser / H. Karnetsi), 180

Haghags Varvar anun ariasirt aghjkan (On a courageous girl called Varvar / H. Karnetsi), 180

Hai, Abdul, 36

Hakobian, Hakob, 577–78; as editor of Armenian almanacs, 577; *My Land,* 578–79 (text)

Hakobian, Hakob Melik (Raffi), 76, 79, 81, 86, 93–98, 345–48; criticism of, 97; literary influences, 93–94; self-awareness of, 97

Hakobjan, Melik, 110

Hamarot meknabanutiun tramabanutian

(Concise commentary on logic / P. Dpir), 129

Hamarot patmutiun (Abridged history / K. Gandzaketsi), 230

Hamarotutiun patmutyan Movses Khorenatzvo (Summary of Movses Khorenatsi's history / P. Dpir), 129

Hamastegh. *See* Gelenian, Hambardzum

Hamataratz ashkharhatsuyts, 47

Hamidiye, the, 26

Hamov, hotov (With taste, aroma / G. Srvandztiants) 374

Handes Amsorya (*Handes amsoria*), 51, 57

Handes grakankan yev patmakan (Literary and historical review), 76

Handes nor hayakhosutyan (Review of Modern Arenian S. Nazarian), 220

Hangatz Yekeghetsin (The muffled church / N. Andrikian), 102

Harem (M. Hakobian), 346

Harse (The bride/ Z. Asatur), 542, 542–47 (text)

Harutiunian, Hovhannes (Tlkatintsi), 495–97, 565, 693, 935, 946; plays of, 497; short novels of, 496; *The Village and the Winter,* 497–99 (text)

Harutiunian, Movses (Arazi), 105, 799–800; *In the Cages,* 800–803

Harutiuninan, Artashes, 83, 690–91; *Art and Literature,* 691–92 (text)

Hasan-Jalalian dynasty, 470n. 1

Hatsi khndir (A matter of bread / P. Proshian), 355, 356–61 (text)

Hatsin yerge (The song of bread / D. Varuzhan), 846

Hatt-i Sherif-i Gülhane (Edict of the Rose Chamber), 13–14

Hay busak (Armenian flora / G. Alishan), 54, 230

Hay buyzh (The Armenian remedy), 979

Hay kin (Armenian woman), 673

Hay mitk (Armenian mind), 710

Hay vankere (Armenian monasteries / H. Asatur), 532

Hayastan (Armenia), 56–57, 199; editorship of, 261, 935; name change of, 261

Hayastan Mayr (Mother Armenia / H. Svachian), 331

Hayguyzh (Bad tidings from Armenia / M. Khrimian), 237

Hayi vrezh (Revenge of the Armenian / A. Babakhanian), 100

Hayk, Vahé, 107, 946

Hayk diutsazn (The epic hero Hayk / A. Bargratuni), 53, 72

Haykakan endhanur patmutiun (General Armenian history / S. Biurat), 102

Haykakan namakani (Armenian letters / M. Mamurian), 306

Haykaz, Aram, 107, 946, 1000–1001; *Happiness*, 1001–6 (text)

Haykuni, Armenak, 92

Hayots berde (The fortress of Armenians / S. Zorian), 106, 904

Hayots patmutiun (History of the Armenians / A. Babakhanian), 507

Hayrenik (Fatherland), 57–58, 78, 453, 728

Hayrik. *See* Khrimian, Mkrtich

Hazarpeshen (The wine jug / K. Abovian), 212–13

Hegel yev ir zhamanake (Hegel and his time / M. Nalbandian), 293

Heracle II, 8

Herzen, Aleksandr, 292, 292n. 1

Hetanos yerger (Pagan songs / D. Varuzhan), 845–46

Hin havatk kam hetanosakan kronk hayots (The ancient beliefs or pagan religion of Armenians / G. Alishan), 54, 230

Hisarian, Hovhannes, 59n. 53, 280–81

Hishatakaran (Records / S. Yerevantsi), 152

Hishogutiunner Vardanants toni artiv

(Recollections from the Feast of Vardanank / S. Shahaziz), 378

History of the Armenians (Khorenatsi), 47, 62

History of the Jewish War (Josephus, trans. Stepanos Lehatsi), 50

History of Napoleon Bonaparte (H. Vardanian), 91

History of Stambol (Keomiurchian), 18

"Hisus vordi" (Jesus the Son / Shnorhali), 46

Hiurmiuz, Yedvard, 52, 53, 72

Hiusis (The north), 317

Hiusisi artzive (The northern eagle / B. Ayvazian), 101

Hiusisapayl (Northern lights), 69, 75, 219–20, 291, 377

Hnakhosutiun ashkharhagraken Hayastani (Archeology of geographic Armenia / G. Inchichian), 53–54

Hnchak, 611

Hnots-norots (Of old and new / G. Srvandztiants), 374

Holy See of Etchmiadzin, 36, 41–42; printing in, 49–50

Holy Translators' School, 34

Hovhannisian, Hovhannes, 76, 81, 559–60, 734, 765; *Araxes Came Devouringly*, 560 (text); *A Gentle Sleep*, 561 (text)

Hovhannisian, Mikayel (Nar-Dos), 602–4; *Hoopoe*, 604–10 (text); stories and novels of, 603–4

Hovnatan, Naghash, 128

Hovsep geghetsik (Joseph the fair / T. Terzian), 380–81

Hovvakan sring (Pan pipes / Y. Durian), 501

Hovvakan sring (Shepherd's pipe / G. Aghayan), 384

Hravirak Araatian (Convoker to Ararat / M. Khrimian), 236

Hravirak yerkrin avetiatz (Convoker to the Promised Land / M. Khrimian), 237, 242–45 (text)

Hripsimé (T. Terzian), 381
Hromeakan pargev (A gift from Rome / S. Voskanian), 264
Hunanian, Vardan, 42
Hungary, 42
Hunon (P. Proshian), 355
Hushikk hayrenyats hayots (Memories of the Armenian homeland / G. Alishan), 91, 229–30

I petes zargatselots (For the use of the educated / A. Bagratuni), 54
Im dzeratetre (My notebook / H. Paronian), 406
Im kyanki glkhavor depkere (The major events of my life / G. Aghayan), 385
Inchichian, Ghukas, 53–54
Inchichian, Karapet, 367
India, Armenian community in, 7, 11, 72
Indra. *See* Chrakian, Tiran
Innesunvets: ariuni mejen (The bloodbath of ninety-six / S. Biurat), 102
Iorga, Nicolai, 911
Iran, 9, 10
Iravakhoh (The arbitor / H. Teroyents), 200
Iravunk (Rights), 103, 297
Isahakian, Avetik, 76, 106, 560, 734–36, 867, 952; *Abu Ala al-Mahari*, 735, 740–43 (text); *Saadi's Last Spring*, 736–40 (text)
Isfahan, 5, 22
Islam, 24; Islamic nationalism, 14
Israel Ori (M. Harutiunian), 88, 105
Iutiuchian, Karapet, 57, 65, 66, 74, 77, 261–62; translations by of French literature, 262; *The Task of National Advancement*, 262–63 (text)
Ivanhoe (W. Scott), 86

Jakhjakhian, Manuel (Manvel), 52, 53, 73
Jalaleddin (H. Hakobian), 87, 94, 347
Jambr (S. Yerevantsi), 151–52

Janissaries, the, 2–3, 2n. 3, 12, 13, 16
Javahir (S. Mupahiachian), 432
Javanshirs, 6
Jews, 16
Journal asiatique de Constantinople (Asiatic journal of Constantinople), 280
Jughayetsi, Hakob (Hakob of Julfa). *See* Catholicos Hakob IV Jughayetsi
Jughayetsi, Hovannes, 45
Justinian, 32
Justinian II, 39

Kaghakavarutyan vnasnere (The dangers of politeness / H. Paronian), 406
Kakhaghanen yetk (After the gallows / A. Shitanian), 103
Kalemkiarian, Zaruhi (Yevterpé), 719; *Agony of a Horse*, 720–21 (text)
Kamalian, Sargis, 102
Kamenatsi, Hovhannes (John of Kamen), 141–42
Kamenets-Podol'skiy, 40–41
Kamsarakan, Tigran, 78, 79, 104, 107, 453, 580–81; short stories of, 581
Kananian, Gevorg, 317
Kandvvats ojakh (Ruined family / G. Sundukian), 270, 270n. 1, 270–79 (text)
Kaos (Chaos / A. Movsisian), 80, 481
Karabagh, 3, 5, 6, 9
Karakashian, Matatia, 62
Karapetian, Onnik, 429
Karapetian, Petros, 429
Karapetian, Shahan, 429
Karian, Hambardzum, 91
Karim Khan Zand, 6
Karmatanents, Hovhannes, 45
Karnetsi, Hovhannes, 180–81; *Hymn to Love (Ten)*, 181–82 (text); *Hymn to Love (Fifteen)*, 183 (text); *Song One*, 181 (text)
Katina (H. Svachian), 331
Kaytzer (Sparks / H. Hakobian), 87, 94–95, 98, 345, 347

Kechian, Biuzand, 78, 531

Kensagrutiun hayots yepiskoposats i lehs (Biographies of Armenian bishops in Poland/ S. Roshka), 120

Keomiurchian, Yeremia Chelepi, 17–18, 47

Keoroghli (G. Aghayan), 384

Kerakanutiun (Gramar / S. Roshka), 120

Kerakanutiun haykazian lezvi (Grammar of the Armenian language / G. Peshtimalchian), 189

Kerakanutiun haykazian lezvi (Grammar of the [classical] Armenian language / M. Chamchian), 174–75

Kertvatzner (Poems / Z. Asatur), 542

Kesaratsi, Khachatur, 45

Keusseyan, Krikor, 1022n. 1

Kghzin yev mi mard (The island and a man / K. Zarian), 877

Khachagoghi hishatakarane (Racketeer's memoir / H. Hakobian), 94, 347

Khamsay melikutiunnere (The five melikdoms of Khamsay / H. Hakobian), 95, 347

Khanjian, Aghasi, 963

Khansanamian, Levon, 101–2

Khanzadian, Tsolak, 868

Kharnapntiur tomari (Confusion of the calendar), 44

Khatabala (Quandary / G. Sundukian), 269

Khente (The fool / H. Hakobian), 86, 87, 94, 347, 348–53 (text)

Khev Karapet (Crazy Karapet / S. Mupahiachian), 432

Khikar, 57, 406, 406n. 3

Khlebnikov, Viktor, 960

khodjas, 22

Khorenatsi, Movses, 47, 52, 53, 71, 89, 175, 348, 385

Khorhrdatetr (Missal), 50

Khortakvatz kyank (Shattered life / L. Manuelian), 551, 551–58 (text)

Khosrov metz (Khosrov the great / P. Minasian), 73

Khosrov yev Makruhi (Khosrov and Makruhi / H. Hisarian), 280

Khrimian, Mkrtich (Hayrik), 12, 21, 25–26, 57, 62, 77, 236–38, 372, 405, 459, 496, 565; *Crowned by Grandpa in the Field,* 238–42 (text); exile to Jerusalem, 238; *Invitation to the Promised Land,* 242–45 (text)

"*Kilikia*" ("Cilicia"), 227–28 (text)

King Arshak II, 904

King Arshak III, 298n. 2

King Artavazd II, 34

King Herakl, 50

King Hetum II, 46

King Pap, 298n. 2

King Sigismund I, 41

King Tigran the Great, 32

King Tigran II, 34

King Vachagan, 89

King Vladislav III, 40

King Vladislav IV, 40

Kipchaks, the, 59n. 54

Kish, Nicholas, 47

Kiurchian, Melkon, 489–90; *The Emigrant's Life,* 490–94 (text)

Kiurchian, Mikayel, 78, 783, 812–14; *The New Outfit,* 814–25 (text)

Knar pandukhtin (The expatriate's lyre / K. Narpey), 337

Knnakan kerakanutiun ashkharabar (A critical grammar of modern Armenia / A. Aydenian), 55

Koghbatsi, Yeznik, 71

Kolot, Hovhannes, 63

Kornack (M. Peshiktashlian), 286–87

Kostandnupolso hayere yev irents patriarknere (The Armenians of Constantinople and their patriarchs / H. Asatur), 531–32

Kouymjian, Dickran, 3

Kretatsi, Abraham (Abraham of Crete), 49, 109–10

Krtutiun kaghakavarutyan (Education in civility / G. Peshtimalchian), 190

Krunk (Crane), 372

Krvatzaghik (Battle-flower /
P. Proshian), 98
Krvatzaghik (A bone of contention /
P. Proshian), 355
Kurats dastiarakutiun (The education
of the blind / K. Misakian), 224
Kurghinian, Shushanik, 81, 748–49;
The Workers, 749–51 (text)
Kuyumchian, Hovannes, 31
Kuyumchian, Misak, 752–53; *The
Story Within the Story,* 753–59 (text)
Kyanke hin hrovmeakan chanaparhi vra
(Life on an old Roman highway /
V. Totovents), 936–37

La Réforme (Reform), 265
Lambronatsi, Nerses, 52, 61
L'Arménie-Armenia, 459
Lazarian, Hovhannes, 160
Le Foyer (The Hearth), 612
Lebanon, 13, 31
Lehatsi, Simeon, 41
Lehatsi, Stepanos, 41
Leo. *See* Babakhanian, Arakel
Leopold I, 7, 41
*Leran vogin: Hay yeritasardi me
arkatznere metz paterazmi entatskin*
(The spirit of the mountain: the
journey of a young Armenian during
the Great War / Sev-Vost), 104
Lerntsinere (Mountaineers /
A. Babakhanian), 100
Levon Metzagortze (T. Kamsarakan),
104
Levoni vishte (Levon's grief /
S. Shahaziz), 378
Lewis, Matthew Gregory, 89
*Life and Adventures of Joseph Emin, an
Armenian, The* (Emin), 8–9
L'Orient inédit (The unpublished east /
M. Cheraz), 460
Lusabats (Daybreak), 1007
Lusaber (Lucifer), 453
Lusashavigh (The path of
enlightenment / G. Peshtimalchian),
190, 190–94 (text)

Lusignan, Gwiton, 66
Luys yev stverk (Light and shadow /
M. Achemian), 362
Lur-da-lur (V. Papazian), 571
Lvov, 40, 42; printing in, 45

Maclaire, Frédéric, 729
Madjmuayi Havadis (New magazine),
59
Madras, 37; printing in, 48–49
Madras Group, 8, 8n. 8, 43, 148, 151,
161; members of, 160
Mahari, Gurgen, 1013–15; *Barbed
Wire in Flower,* 1014, 1015, 1015–20
(text); *On Guard, People,* 1020–21
(text)
Mahmud II, 2n. 3, 13
Mahmut II, 48, 936
Mahtesi, Marcos, 48
Makintsian, Poghos, 868
Malezian, Vahan, 669–70; *The Blouse,*
671–72 (text); *In the Fields,* 670–71
(text); translations by of European
authors, 670
Malkhasiants, Stepan, 67, 68
Mamluks, the, 30, 33, 34–35
Mamul (The press), 60
Mamurian, Matteos, 56, 65, 78,
86, 91–92, 292, 305–7, 366,
367; English publications, 306;
translations of European authors,
307; translations of Voltaire, 306
Manana (Manna / G. Srvandztiants),
374
"Manifesto of the Three" (Abov,
Charents, and Vshtuni), 960
Manuelian, Levon, 81, 550–51;
dramatic poetry of, 550–51; plays of,
551
Manuelian, Mikayel, 760–61; as an
actor, 760; *Luck,* 761–64 (text)
Manzumei Efkâr (Course of opinion),
60
Marash, 27
Marcus Antonius (Mark Anthony), 34

Mardik yev irk (Men and Objects / R. Perperian), 429

Maronite Church, 31

Mart (Battle), 453

Martik Agha (M. Kiurchian), 814

Marzvanetsi, Grigor, 47

Mashtots, Mesrop, 30

Masis, 57, 74, 78, 82, 261, 372, 452, 518, 532, 541

Masyats aghavni (Dove of Masis), 337

Matniche (The informer / A. Shitanian), 103

Matnutiun (Betrayal / H. Svachian), 331

Mayakovski, Vladimir, 960

Mayta (S. Dussap), 400, 401–3 (text), 518

Meghapart, Hakob, 43, 44

Meghu (The bee), 57, 74, 292, 330, 372, 405, 471

Meghu Hayastani (The bee of Armenia), 69, 101, 220

Mehyan (The temple), 83, 83n. 77, 107, 826, 827n. 3, 831, 875

Mekerian, Harutiun, 814

Meknutiun aghotits pataragin (Interpretation of the prayers of the Mass / K. Andzevatsi), 230

Meliki aghchike (Melik's daughter / A. Babakhanian), 100–101, 508–16 (text)

meliks, 5, 6–7, 507; melikdoms, 5–6n. 6

Merelahartsuk (The necromancer / M. Nalbandian), 293

Mesrop Mashtots (D. Temirchian), 105, 776

Metzapativ muratskanner (Honorable beggars / H. Paronian), 406, 407–19 (text)

Metzarents, Misak, 80, 81, 106, 867, 885–86, 928; *The Hut,* 888–89 (text); *Nameless,* 887–88 (text), *Prayer for the New Year,* 889–90 (text); *A Winter's Serene Night,* 886–87 (text)

Metzn Nerses kam Hayastani barerare (Nerses the Great, patron of Armenia / S. Vanandetsi), 297, 298–304 (text)

Metzn Sahak Partev yev ankumn Artashri Arshakunvo (Sahak Partev the Great and the fall of Artashir Arshakuni / G. Srvandztiants), 373

Mi kani khosk im entertsoghnerin (A few words to my readers / S. Shahaziz), 378

Michael VIII Palaeologus, 17

Mihrdat (S. Vanandetsi), 297

Mikayelian, Kristapor, 593

Mikayelian-Chakikian, Grigor, 49

Mikoyan, Anastas, 68, 963

Minasian, Petros, 73

Minin khosk, miusin harse (A bride promised to one but given to another / M. Nalbandian), 293

Miutiun (Unity), 297

Mirichanian, Mkrtich, 184

Mirror of Calcutta (*Hayeli Kalkatian*), 37, 49

Mirzayan, Sargis. *See* Vanandetsi, Sargis

Misakian, Khachatur, 223–24, 580

missionaries, 20, 57, 64

Mkhitarist Order (Mkhitarist Fathers), 45, 47, 50–52, 67, 72; and the development of the Armenian language, 54–55; and education, 55; publishing of Armenian classics, 52, 61–62; publishing of history and philology, 53–54, 57; publishing of poetry, 52–53, 72; publishing of Western classics, 52, 64–65; two branches of, 51–52

Mnatsortats (Remnants / H. Oshakan), 833

Mndzuri, Hakob, 894–96; *The First Born,* 896–99 (text)

Mohammed II, 17

Moldavia, 24

Monastery of the Holy Cross, 39

Monastery of St. James, 33; seminary within, 33–34
Monastery of St. Sarkis, 46
monophysite communities, 32
Montenegro, 25
Morea, 50, 51
Moscow, 85
Movsisian, Aleksandr (Shirvanzadé), 421, 480–83, 952; *For the Sake of Honor,* 483–88 (text); novels of, 481–82; plays of, 482–83; plays made into films, 483
Mrmrian, Harutiun, 200
Mserian, Grigor, 66
Mshak (The tiller), 69, 75, 79, 93, 95, 100, 270, 346, 420, 422, 471, 506, 602
Muhentisian, Hovannes, 48
Mupahiachian, Sargis (Atrpet), 431–32; contributions to periodicals, 431; *Tzhvzhik,* 432–39 (text)
Murad IV, 24n. 31
Murat, Mkrtich, 39
Muratsan. *See* Ter-Hovhannesian, Grigor
Murch (The hammer), 69, 81
Musa Dagh, 28, 28n. 38, 30
Musayk Araratian (The muses of Ararat), 72
Musayk masyasts (Muses of Masis), 92
Muslims, 2, 110n. 1
Mustafa III, 18
Myasnikian, Alexander, 960

Naghash, Mkrtich, 44
Nahanje arants yergi (Retreat without song / S. Shahnur), 1023, 1025, 1026–30 (text)
Nakhashavigh krtutian (Introduction to education / K. Abovian), 212
Nakhijevan, 3, 4, 5, 6, 9, 10
Nakhijevan, Nor, 40
Nalbandian (Nalpantian), Mikayel, 68, 69, 75, 291–94; *Days of Childhood,* 295–96 (text); *Freedom,* 294–95 (text); revolutionary activities of,

292; translations by of European authors, 293
Nalbandian, Vahan, 106
Nalian, Hakob, 128
Nar-Dos. *See* Hovhannisian, Mikeyel
Narduni, Shavarsh, 978–79; *The Tower of Babylon,* 979–83 (text)
Narek (Narekatsi), 43
Narekatsi, Grigor (Gregory of Narek), 52, 682
Narpey (Narbey), Khoren (Khoren Galfayan), 78, 336–38, 673; *Armenia,* 33–39 (text); at the Congress of Berlin, 337; *The Exile to the Swallow,* 339–40 (text); translations of Lamartine, 336
Navasard, 107, 844, 910
Nave leran vra (The ship on the mountaintop / K. Zarian), 877
Nazarbekian, Avetis (Lerents), 81
Nazarian, Shushanik, 180
Nazarian, Stepanos, 68, 75, 219–20, 291, 377; beliefs concerning Christianity, 220; *On Childhood,* 220–22 (text)
Nedelka (A. Shitanian), 104
neoclassicism, 70–71
Nerashkharh (Inner world / T. Chrakian), 722, 723, 723–27 (text)
Nerkin hamozum (Inner conviction / S. Voskanian), 264
Nern kam kataratz ashkharhi (Antichrist, or the end of the world / H. Hisarian), 280, 281–85 (text)
Nerses of Ashtarak, 10
New Julfa, 30, 36, 43, 44; printing in, 45
Newspaper, 56
Niazian, Isabella, 961
Nicholas I (Tsar of Russia), 10, 11
Nicholas II (Tsar of Russia), 11–12
Nkaragir azgayin dastiarakutyan (The nature of national education / N. Zorayan), 247

Nochastan (The cypress grove / T. Chrakian), 722–23

Nor bargirk haykazian lezvi (New dictionary [lexicon] of the Armenian language), 54, 67

Nor dar (New age), 69, 471, 602–3

Nor gir (New writing), 946–47

Nor havatk (New faith), 1007

Nor Kyank (New life), 453, 611, 814

Nor tetrak vor kochi hordorak (A new booklet, called Exhortations / M. Baghramian), 8, 48, 147–48, 148–50 (text), 161–62

Nouvelles Orientales (Eastern short stories / M. Cheraz), 460

Novel of Alexander (pseudo-Callisthenes), 86

Nupar, Poghos, 35

Nuparian, Mesrop, 65, 66, 77, 306–7, 367

Nurikian, Beniamin, 107, 495, 946–47; short stories of, 947; *The Sun for You,* 947–50 (text)

Olimbiada (Olympiado / A. Haykuni), 92

Orhnyal gerdastane (The blessed dynasty), 79

Ori, Israel, 7, 7n. 7

Orlando, Stephan, 45

Ormanian, Malachia, 500

Oshagan, Vahé, 80

Oshakan, Hakob, 79, 83, 106, 107, 659, 784, 826, 830–33, 875, 1000; *Topich,* 833–42 (text)

Oskan Petrovichn en kyankume (Oskan Petrovich in the afterlife / G. Sundukian), 269

Osman II, 141

Ostrovski, Aleksandr, 268

Otian, Grigor, 21, 62, 65, 77, 226, 292, 341–42, 630; *London and Paris,* 342–44 (text)

Otian, Yervand, 79, 87, 104–5, 107, 630–32, 813; *Comrade Panjuni,* 632–41 (text); contributions to

periodicals, 631; popular works of, 631–32

Ottoman Constitution (1908), 489, 845

Ottoman Empire, 17, 23–24, 40–41, 43, 775; Armenian suffering under, 23–24; brutality of, 23, 23n. 30; conquest of Syria, 30; decline of, 12, 26; revolts against, 13, 24; rule of Western Armenia, 12–14; as the "sick man of Europe, 25, 25n. 33; and the *Tanzimat* period, 13–14, 21, 23, 24; treaty with France, 30. *See also* Ottoman/Persian empire, rivalry of

Ottoman/Persian empire, rivalry of, 1–6, 2n. 1, 109n. 1; and the Black Sheep/White Sheep, 2; campaigns of 1553–55, 3–4; forced displacement of Armenian population during, 4–5

Paghtasar aghbar (Brother Balthazar / H. Paronian), 406

Palian (Balian), Nikoghayos, 342

Pantukhti namakner (Letters of a pilgrim / M. Kiurchian), 490

Pap Tagavor (King Pap / S. Zorian), 88, 106, 904

Papazian, Andreas, 64

Papazian, Vrtanes, 69, 79, 87, 104, 421, 570–72; scholarly works of, 571–72; *The Source,* 572–76 (text)

Papik yev tornik (Grandfather and grandson / M. Khrimian), 238

Papikian, Astvatzatur, 51

Parap vakhti khaghalik (Leisure entertainment / K. Abovian), 212

Paraser (Fond of glory / R. Patkanian), 318

Paris Peace Conference (1856), 13–14, 21, 33, 593

Parnassians, the, 681, 681n. 1

Paronian (Baronian), Hakob, 57, 78, 79, 80, 404–7, 440, 631; contributions to periodicals, 405

Parrot, Friedrich, 211

Partevian, Suren, 744–45; *The Vow*, 745–47 (text)

Paruyr Haykazn (Paruyr the Armenian / H. Hakobian), 94, 96, 96n. 91, 347–48, 347n. 3

Parzabanutiun kerakanutian karcharot yev diurimats (A simplified grammar, concise and easy to understand / P. Dpir), 129

Parzatumar (The calendar), 43

Pasha, Ibrahim, 30, 35

Pasha, Ismail, 35

Pasha, Mohammed Ali, 30, 35

Pashalian. *See* Bashalian, Levon

Paskevich, Ivan, 10

Pasmachian, Grigor, 18

Pataragatetr (The Missal), 43

Patkanian, Gabriel, 91, 316

Patkanian, Rafayel, 68, 91, 316–18, 377; *The Vacant Yard*, 320–26 (text); *The Woe of Araxes*, 317, 318–20 (text)

Patkanian, Serovbé, 67, 316

"*Patkerapashtutiun*" ("The worship of images" / H. Teroyents), 200–202 (text)

Patkerner Tiurkahayeri kyankits (Scenes from the lives of Armenians in Turkey / V. Papazian), 570

Patmutiun Hayots (History of the Armenians / M. Chamchian), 53, 175, 175n. 1, 175–79 (text)

Patmutiun hin Hndkastani hanhishatak daruts anti i hardzakumn mahmetakanats (History of Ancient India from immemorial ages to the invasion of Mohammedans / M. Taghiadian), 204

Patmutiun: Kataghikos Abraham Kretatsi (The chronicle of Catholicos Abraham of Crete / A. Kretatsi), 110, 111–19 (text)

Patmutiun Parsits (History of the Persians / M. Taghiadian), 204

Patmutiun paterazmatsn vor yeghev hosmantsvots i vera kaghakatsn hayastanyayts yev parsits (History of

the wars fought by the Ottomans over Armenian and Persian cities / A. Yerevantsi), 131, 132–40 (text)

Patmutiun paterazmin Khotinu, i zhamanaks sultan Osmanian tachkats, yev i katoghikosutyan Hayots Melkisedi srpo Etcmiadzni (History of the war of Khotin in the time of the Turkish sultan Osman, during the Patriarchate of Melkised, the Armenian Catholicos of holy Etchmiadzin / H. Kamenatsi), 141, 142–46 (text)

Patmvatzkner (Short stories / M. Kiurchian), 490

Pechevi, Ibrahim, 3–4

Pepo (G. Sundukian), 268, 269–70

Perperian, Reteos, 62, 78, 380, 400, 428–29, 448, 518, 519; as founder of the Perperian school, 428; *The Blind Youth's Grief*, 429–30 (text)

Perperian, Shahan, 831, 875

Persia, 282n. 5, 507n. 1; and the Ottoman empire, 1–6, 2n. 1, 29, 109n. 1

Peshiktashlian, Mkrtich, 24, 62, 65, 74, 250, 286–88, 292, 297, 380, 399, 681, 886; *A Plaint*, 288 (text); *Spring*, 290 (text); translations by of European authors, 287; *We Are Brothers*, 289–90 (text), 289n. 2

Peshiktashlian, Nshan, 984–85; *The Smile*, 985–87 (text)

Peshtimalchian, Grigor, 189–90, 223

Peter the Great, 5, 7

Peterazme (The war / A. Shitanian), 103

Petrus, Jacob, 38

Pillars of Hercules, 282, 282n. 4

Pitt, William, 8

Piunk (The phoenix), 951

Pluz, Hovhannes, 61

Polozhenie, the, 11

Pope Clement XI, 51

Pope Gregory XIII, 44

Pope Pius IV, 44

Pope Urban VIII, 120
Pordz (Essay), 470
Proaeresius, 347n. 3
Proshian, Perch (Hovhannes Ter-
  Arakelian), 68, 69, 76, 98, 293,
  354–56, 420
Ptuyt me Polso tagherun mej (A
  stroll through the quarters of
  Constantinople / H. Paronian), 406

Qajars, 6

Raffi. *See* Hakobian, Hakob Melik
Raphael, Edward, 37
Razmik (Plebeian), 701
realism, 76–77; Armenian, 77–81
Respighi, Ottorino, 875
Roman Catholicism, 6, 41–42, 44–45;
  in Armenia, 20, 31
Romania, 24, 25
romanticism, 73–74; Armenian, 74–76
Roshka, Stepanos, 41, 120–21
Roslin, Tovos, 40
Rumeli, 18
Rusinian, Nahapet, 21, 62, 65, 226–27,
  330, 342; as an educator, 227; as
  translator of French literature, 227
Russia, 25–26, 99; and unification with
  Eastern Armenia, 9–12
Russian Orthodox Church, 11
Russo-Iranian War (1804–13), 9
Russo-Swedish War (1700–21), 7
Russo-Turkish War (1877–78), 10, 25,
  593
Russo-Turkish wars (1768–74,
  1787–91), 6
Ruzan kam hayrenaser oriord (Ruzan,
  or the patriotic damsel / G. Ter-
  Hovhannesian), 99, 470

Safavid dynasty (1502–1736), 2;
  decline of, 5, 22
Saghmosaran (Psalter), 44, 45, 50
St. Gregory the Illuminator (church),
  17, 50, 298n. 2
St. Nerses, 298n. 2

St. Sarkis (church), 17
Sakayan, S., 60
Saladin, 33
Salbi (H. Hakobian), 97, 97n. 93
*Saliha hanem kam Banake brnavorin
  dem* (Saliha Hanem, or the army
  versus the tyrant / Y. Otian), 104
Samuel (H. Hakobian), 94, 96, 348
Samuelian, Khachik, 97n. 93
Sanasarian, Mkrtich, 63, 337
Sandukht (T. Terzian), 380
Sarafian, Nikoghos, 1007, 1031–32; *At
  Farewell*, 1033 (text); *On the Road to
  Insomnia*, 1032–33 (text)
Sargsents, Sedrak (Tevkants), 98–99
Sarhad, Khoja Israel, 37
Sarsurner (Shivers / D. Varuzhan), 844
Sasune ayrvum e (Sasun is burning /
  B. Ayvazian), 101
Sasunen yetke (After Sasun / S. Biurat),
  102
Scott, Sir Walter, 86
Sebastatsi, Mkhitar, 46, 50, 54
Sefilents tune (The house of Seflis /
  M. Mamurian), 306
Selim I, 2–3, 2n. 2, 33; conquest of
  Egypt, 35
Selim III, 13, 21
Seljuks, the, 30; invasion of Armenia,
  39, 40
Sepoy Mutiny, 38
Ser yev azatutiun (Love and liberty /
  G. Sundukian), 270
Serbia, 25
Setian, Hovhannes, 78, 467; *Lament*,
  468–69 (text)
Sev haghtanak (Black victory /
  B. Ayvazian), 101
Sev hogher (Black soil / P. Durian), 441
Sev lerin marde (The man from Black
  Mountain / M. Mamurian), 91–92,
  306
Sevak, Ruben, 846, 858–60; *The Crane*,
  860–62 (text); *Letters from a Student*,
  862–65 (text)
Sev-Vost, 104

Shah Abbas the Great, 4–5, 22

Shah Ismail I, 2, 3

Shah Nadir, 5–6, 110, 110n. 2

Shah Tahmasp, 3, 4

Shahamirian, Hakob, 48, 78, 160, 161

Shahamirian, Shahamir, 37, 48,
160–61

Shahaziz, Smbat, 68, 377–78; *Dream,*
379 (text)

Shahen (P. Proshian), 98, 355

Shahenn i Sipr kam Gaghtakan haye
(Shahen in Siberia, or the Armenian
expatriate / S. Sargsents), 98–99,
98n. 100

Shahnur, Shahan, 108, 1007, 1022–25;
writings in French of, 1024

Shant, Levon, 79, 80, 81, 107, 642–44;
Ancient Gods, 645–57 (text); plays of,
643–44; student writings of, 643

Sharaknots (Hymnal), 50

Shavigh (Pathway), 659

Shekerchian, Grigor, 223

Sheref, Abdurrahman, 14

Shi'ite Moslems, 2, 4

Shinakani namakner (Letters of a
peasant / M. Kiurchian), 490

Shirak, 453, 783, 812

Shiraz, Hovhannes, 374

Shirvan, 4

Shirvanzadé. *See* Movsisian, Alexsandr

Shishmanian, Hovsep (Tzerents), 62,
68, 74, 88, 91, 92–93, 250–51

Shitanian, Armen, 103–4

Shmavonian, Harutium, 37, 48

Shnorhali, Nerses, 34, 44, 52, 61, 180

Shoghokorte (The flatterer /
H. Paronian), 405

Shtemaran pitani giteliats (Warehouse
of useful knowledge), 56

Shushan Shavarshana (Shushan of
Shavarshan / G. Srvandztiants), 373

Shushanian, Vazgen, 1007

Sibil. *See* Asatur, Zapel

Sion (Zion), 34, 501

Sirak yev Samuel (Sirak and Samuel /
M. Khrimian), 238

Siranush (S. Dussap), 400

Siruni, Hakob, 844, 910–11; *The
Caravan,* 912–17 (text); Romanian
publications of, 911

Sis, 31

Sital, Karapet, 947

Siurmelian, Zaven, 946–47

Siyar, Farrukh, emperor in Delhi, 37

Skizbn yerkants (The onset of labor /
P. Proshian), 98

Smbat arajan (Smbat the first /
P. Minasian), 73

Smyrna, 28–29, 29n. 39, 48, 62, 64,
65; printing in, 56

Sobieski, John, 41, 41n. 45

Soperk haykakank (Armenian stories /
G. Alishan), 54, 230

Sophia (K. Misakian), 224

Sos yev Varditer (Sos and Verditer /
P. Proshhian), 293, 355

Spannvatz hayre (The assassinated
father / A. Babakhanian), 100

Sparapet, Mkhitar, 5, 7

Sparapet, Smbat, 61

Spendiarian, Alexander, 621

Srbazan knar (Sacred lyre / Y. Durian),
502

Srmakeshkhanlian, Yervand
(Yerukhan), 79, 380, 454, 658–60;
Crayfish, 660–63 (text)

Srvandztiants, Garegin, 57, 83,
372–74, 496; *Lament Over the
Heroes Fallen in the Battle of Avarayr,*
374–76 (text); literary career,
373–74; religious career, 373

Storagrutiun hin hayastaniayts
(Description of Armenia /
G. Inchichian), 53

Stverk haykakank (Shadows of the
homeland / K. Narpey), 337

Suleiman (the "Magnificent"), 3

Sultan Hamit (A. Shitanian), 103,
103n. 106

Sundukian, Gabriel, 68, 76, 80,
268–70, 420, 603

Sunni Moslems, 2

Surhandak (The dispatcher), 826
Surhandak Costandnupolso
    (Constantinople courier), 56–
    57
Surmelian, Khachatur, 54
Svachian, Harutiun, 57, 75, 292,
    330–31; *August Guiné*, 331–35 (text)
Svachian, Mari, 728–29; *Khamsin*,
    729–33 (text)
swallows, 384n. 1
Symbolist Movement, 82
Synod of Etchmiadzin, 11
Syria, 30

Tabriz, 3, 4, 10
Tahmaz Ghuli Khan, 109
Tagavorats zhoghov (The meeting of
    kings / M. Khrimian), 238
Tagharan (Song book), 43–44, 47
Tagharan (Song book / V. Tekeyan),
    785
Tagharan pokrik (A small book of odes
    / P. Dpir), 128
Taghiadian, Mesrop, 85, 89, 203–4;
    Diary, 207–10 (text); *Lazy Pupil*,
    206–7 (text); *Parables*, 204–6 (text);
    translations by of Western classics,
    203
Taghk (Poems / A. Bagratuni), 53
Taghk mkhitarian vardapetats (Poems
    by Mkhitarist Fathers), 53, 72
Tamara (A. Shitanian), 104
Tangaran (Treasure house / H. Asatur
    and Z. Asatur), 532
Taparakan haye (The wandering
    Armenian / A. Shitanian), 103
Taparakan hayu vordin (The wandering
    Armenian's son / A. Shitanian),
    103
Tarerk hayeren kerakanutyan
    (Elements of Armenian grammar /
    A. Bagratuni), 54
Taretsuyts (Yearbook / N. Rusinian),
    227
*Tasnevinnerord dar yev Hovhannes
    Prusatzi Teroyetz* (The nineteenth

century and Hovhannes Teroyents
    of Brusa / H. Mrmrian), 200
Tatakhman gishere (The night of
    breaking Lent / A. Babakhanian),
    100
Tatragomi harse (The bride of Tatragom
    / K. Zarian), 876
Tatron (Theater), 60, 297, 405
Tatron barekam mankants (Theater, the
    children's friend), 405
Taturian, Aharon, 891–92; *Ancient
    Longing*, 892–93 (text); *My Shoes*,
    893 (text)
Tchernishevski, Nicolai, 292
Teghagir hayots metzats (Topography of
    Greater Armenia / G. Alishan), 230
"Teghekutiunk tntesagitutyan vra"
    (Information about political
    economics / N. Zorayan), 246
Tekeyan, Vahan, 80, 81, 106, 107,
    783–85, 812, 831; contributions to
    periodicals, 784; *Dark Hours*, 787
    (text); *Dear Brother in the Bond*,
    789–91 (text); *It is Raining, My
    Child*, 785–86 (text); *Ode to Verlaine*,
    786–87 (text); *Prayer on the Threshold
    of Tomorrow*, 788–89 (text); *To the
    Armenian Nation*, 786 (text)
Temirchian, Derenik (Demirdjian),
    68, 69, 88, 105, 765–67, 904; *King
    Aram*, 767–73 (text)
Temirchipashian, Yeghia
    (Demirdjibashian), 66, 78, 80,
    380, 447–49, 519, 680; *The Song of
    the Vultures*, 449–51 (text)
Teodoros Rshtuni (H. Shishmanian),
    93, 251
Ter-Arakelian, Hovhannes. *See*
    Proshian, Perch
Terdjümane Efkâr (Translation of
    opinions), 60
Ter-Hovhannesian, Grigor
    (Muratsan), 99–100, 470–72;
    short novels of, 471–72
Terian, Vahan, 76, 106, 734, 866–68;
    critical opinion of, 867–68; *Carousel,*

Terian, Vahan (*continued*)
870–71 (text); *Coming to Terms,* 869
(text); *Farewell Song,* 872 (text); *The
Gallows,* 872–73 (text); *I Love Your
Dark and Wicked Eyes,* 869 (text); *In
the Style of Sayat-Nova,* 870 (text);
This Time Like a Sister, 871–72 (text)
Ter-Karapetian, Gegham (Msho
Gegham), 83, 565–67; contributions
to periodicals, 566; *A Moonlit
Journey to Mush,* 567–69 (text);
novels and short stories of, 566
Teroyents, Hovannes, 56, 65, 199–200,
261; translations by of Western
classics, 200
Terzian, Tovmas, 62, 65, 74, 77,
78, 380–81, 467, 673, 680; *The
Chraghan Palace,* 381–82 (text)
Terzntsi, Hovhannes, 44, 64
*Tesaran handisitsn Hayka, Arama,
yev Arayi* (Scenes of splendor
depicting Hayk, Aram, and Ara /
H. Vanandetsi), 73, 185
Teteyan, Harutiun, 66
Tetrak vor kochi Nshavak (A
booklet [tract] called Target /
S. Shahamirian), 8, 161
Tevkants. *See* Sargsents, Sedrak
Tevosian, Alexsandr. *See* Bakunts,
Askel
Thomas, Henri, 1024
Three Songs (K. Zarian), 875, 875n. 3
Tiapart kam vanakan (Convict or
monk / A. Shitanian), 103
Tiaparte (The convict / A. Shitanian),
103
Tiflis, 68, 69, 75, 85
Tigranian, Armen, 621
Tikin yev nazhisht (The lady and the
maid / R. Patakanian), 318
Timurian, Minas, 317
Tknutiunk hayrinasiri (Wakefulness of
a patriot / K. Misakian), 224
Tlkatintsi. *See* Harutiunian,
Hovhannes
Tlkurantsi, Hovhannes, 44

Tokhatetsi, Abgar Dpir, 44, 47
Tokhatetsi, Minas, 41
Tokhatetsi, Sultanshah, 44
Tonatsuyts (Calendar of feasts /
S. Yerevantsi), 50, 152
Topchian, Alexander, 859
Tork Argegh, 385
Toros Aghbar (Brother Toros /
G. Srvandztiants), 374
Toros Levoni (H. Shishmanian), 88,
92, 251, 252–60 (text)
Torosowicz, Nicholas, 42
Totovents, Vahan, 935–37; *The Divine
Comedy,* 937–40 (text)
Tovmajan, Yeghia, 52, 73
Tramabanutiun (Logic / S. Roshka),
120
Tramabanutiun kam arvest banakan
(Logic, or the art of reason /
G. Peshtimalchian), 189
Transcaucasia, 4
Treaty of Amasya (1555), 4
Treaty of Gulistan (1813), 9
Treaty of San Stefano (1878), 25, 77,
77nn. 71–72
Treaty of Turkmanchai (1828), 9
Treaty of Zuhab (1639), 5
Tsaygaluys: ardzak ejer (Daybreak:
prose pages / R. Zardanian), 702
Tseghin sirte (The heart of the nation /
D. Varuzhan), 844–45
Tsetser (The moths / P. Proshian), 355
Tsolker (Glimmers / Z. Asatur), 542
Tumanian, Hovhannes, 68, 69, 76, 81,
106, 355, 560, 619–22, 642, 734,
935; *Akhtamar,* 626–28 (text); *My
Friend Neso,* 623–26 (text); *My Song,*
628–29 (text); narrative poems of,
620–21; notable works of, 621–22
Turgenev, Ivan, 292
Turkey, 9, 13–14, 27, 962
Turki aghjike (The Turkish girl /
K. Abovian), 213
Tutak taghiadiants (The Taghiadian
parrot / M. Taghiadian), 204
Tzaghik (The flower), 82, 366

Tzaturian, Aleksandr, 81, 562–63; *The Armenian Poet's Prayer*, 564 (text); *Don't Cry, Bulbul*, 564 (text); periodical contributions of, 563; translations by of Russian authors, 563

Tzerents. *See* Shishmanian, Hovsep

Tzeretsi, Matteos, 45–46

Tzitzagh (Sneer / H. Paronian), 406

Ughevorutiun i Kavkasia (Travels in the Caucasus / A. Arpiarian), 453

Ughevorutiun i Kostandnupolis (Travels to Constantinople / G. Chilinkirian), 367, 367–71 (text)

Ughghakhosutiun (*Orthologia:* correct speech / N. Rusinian), 227, 330

Unitors, 20, 20n. 26

Urbatagirk (Friday book), 43

Urhayetsi, Matteos, 34

Vahan (M. Peshiktashlian), 287

Vahan Goghtnatsi (G. Alishan), 91

Vahan Mamikonian (A. Babakhanian), 100

Vahanants paterazme (The war of Vahanants / D. Temirchian), 105

Vahanian, Srbuhi, 287

Vahé (M. Peshiktashlian), 287

Van, 3, 4, 24, 27, 57; resistance of to the Turks, 28; schools in, 64

Van Sichem, Christoffel, 46

Vanandetsi, Hovhannes (John of Vanand), 73, 184–85

Vanandetsi, Matteos, 47

Vanandetsi, Sargis, 297

Vanandetsi, Tovmas, 47

Vanguyzh (Bad tidings from Van / M. Khrimian), 237

Vani haydukner (The fighters of Van / A. Shitanian), 104

Vanke (The monastery / T. Cheokiurian), 852, 853–57 (text)

Varazdat (S. Zorian), 106, 904

Vard yev Shushan (Rose and Lily / P. Durian), 400, 441

Vardanank (A. Babakhanian), 100, 507, 507n. 1

Vardanank (D. Temirchian), 88, 105, 767

Vardanian, Hovsep, 59, 59n. 53, 59, 91

Vardapetaran kroni (Source book of religion), 220

Vardenik (Rose garden / K. Narpey), 337

Vardovian, Hakob, 441

Varuzhan, Daniel, 80, 81, 106, 831, 843–46, 858, 875, 910; *The Lamp*, 850–51 (text); *The Oriental Bath*, 848–50 (text); and the pagan movement (*hetanosakan sharzhum*), 845–46; poetic creed of, 844; *The Red Soil*, 846–48

Varzhapetian, H., 60

Varzhapetian, Nerses, 25, 77, 77n. 73, 459, 518

Varzhapetin aghjike (The teacher's daughter / T. Kamsarakan), 79, 580–81, 581–91 (text)

Varzhutiun entertsanutyan (Exercise in reading / N. Zorayan), 247

Vasak (D. Temirchian), 105

Vashkharun (The usurer / A. Shitanian), 103

Vegharavor herose (Hooded hero / S. Biurat), 102

Vehapetian, Matteos, 291

Vep Vardgesi (The story of Vardges / M. Taghiadian), 89, 204

Vep Varsenka (The story of Varsenik / M. Taghiadian), 89, 204

Verhaeren, Émile, 844, 874–875

Verjaluysi dzayner (Sounds of twilight / M. Khrimian), 238

Verjin berde: kottatsogh verker hayutyan srtin mej (The last fortress: wounds stabbing at the Armenian heart / S. Biurat), 102

Verjin verker (The last wounds / A. Babakhanian), 100

Verk Hayastani kam Voghb hayrenasiri (Wounds of Armenia, or lamentation of the patriot / K. Abovian), 75, 89–90, 97, 98, 213–14, 214–18 (text), 293

Vernatun, 622, 765

Veselovsky, Yuri, 563

Vichenian, Serobé, 21

Virgenia (S. Vanandetsi), 297

Vkayabanutiun srbuyn Sandkhto (The martyrdom of St. Sandukht / M. Taghiadian), 204

Voch vok chi karogh nakhasahmanutyan pokhel (No one can alter the order established by Providence), 90–91, 90n. 86

von Bismarck, Otto, 25

Von Dyck, Christopher, 46

Vorberian, Ruben, 265, 693–94, 846; *All the Way to Argaeus*, 699–700 (text), 694n. 1

Vorbuni, Zareh, 108, 1007–8; *The Persecuted*, 1008–12 (text)

Vorogayt parats (Snare of glory / H. Shahamirian), 8, 37, 48, 161, 161–67 (text)

Voskanian, Stepan, 21, 65, 77, 264–66, 292; character of, 265; education at the Sorbonne, 264; translations by of European authors, 266; *Our Shortcomings*, 266–67 (text)

Voski Akaghagh (The golden rooster / H. Hakobian), 95, 347

Voski dar Hayastani (The golden age of Armenia / H. Vanandetsi), 73, 185

Vostan (The city), 852

Vshtuni, Azat, 941–42, 960; *The Camel*, 942–45 (text)

Wallachia, 24

Wilhelm, Johann (Prince of Düsseldorf), 7

World War I, 28, 34, 87

Woskar, Khoja Petrus, 37

Yarchanian, Atom (Siamanto), 774–76, 846, 858, 875; *The Dance*, 780–82 (text); *The Glory of Invention*, 778–80 (text); *Prayer to Arahit on the Feast of Navasard*, 776–78

Yepimendes i Vospor (Epimendes in the Bosphorus / K. Misakian), 224

Yerevak (Saturn), 60

Yerevan, 3, 4, 5, 6, 9, 10

Yerevantsi, Abraham (Abraham of Yerevan), 131

Yerevantsi, Simeon (Simeon of Yerevan), 8, 49, 151–52

Yerevantsi, Voskan, 46

Yerkeri zhoghovatzu (Collected works / H. Hovhannisian), 560

Yerkragortzutiune vorpes ughigh chanaparh (Agriculture is the right path / M. Nalbandian), 293

Yerkragunt (The globe), 448

Yerku kuyr (Two sisters / G. Aghayan), 384

Yerku terov tzara me (A servant of two masters / H. Paronian), 405

Yerkunk innerord daru (Ninth-century labor pains / H. Shishmanian), 93, 102, 251

Yernjak (Common / A. Haykuni), 92

Yerukhan. *See* Smakshkhanlian, Yervand

Yervand (P. Minasian), 73

Yes nshanatz ei (I was engaged / R. Patkanian), 318

Yesayan, Tigran, 793

Yesayan, Zabel, 74n. 68, 79, 542, 792–94; contributions to periodicals, 792–93; novellas of, 793–94; *Shirt of Fire*, 794–98 (text)

Yev alyn kam nor Diogines (Etcetera, or the new Diogenes / G. Sundukian), 269

Yevropa (Europe), 57

Yevterpé. *See* Kalemkiarian, Zaruhi

Yltezen Sasun (From Yildiz to Sasun / S. Biurat), 102

Yltezi pompan (The Yildiz bombing / S. Biurat), 102

Young Turks, the, 27, 775

Yusufian, Poghos, 35

Yüzbashi, Avan ("Captain Avan"), 5

Zakaria Dzagetsu Orere (The days of Zakaria Dzagetsi / L. Khansanamian), 102

Zanazan targmanutiunk (Diverse translations / M. Achemian), 362

Zardarian, Hrach, 108, 918–19, 1007; *Grandmother and Grandson*, 919–26 (text)

Zardarian, Ruben, 64, 78, 83, 495, 497, 565, 693, 701–2, 918, 935; *The Seven Singers*, 702–8 (text)

Zarian, Kostan, 83, 107, 784, 826, 831, 874–78; *Istanbul*, 878–82 (text); *The Man*, 882–84 (text)

Zarifian, Matteos, 80, 81, 107, 927–28; *The Crazy Boy*, 928–34 (text)

Zaroyan, Petros, 1007

Zartonk (Revival), 784

Zbosaran hogevor (Spiritual recreation / S. Yerevantsi), 49–50

Zeytun, 24, 24n. 31, 27

Zeytuntsi vardapet (The priest from Zaytun / S. Biurat), 102

Zhamanak (Time), 60

Zhamanak yev khorhurd yur (Time and its mystery / M. Khrimian), 238

Zhamanakagrutiun (Chronology / P. Dpir), 129

Zhamanakagrutiun kam tarekank yekeghetsakank (Chronicle, or ecclesiastical annals / S. Roshka), 120–21, 121–27 (text)

Zhayre (The rock / V. Papazian), 571

Zhbitk yev artasuk (Smiles and tears / M. Achemian), 362

Zohal (Saturn), 59, 199

Zohrap, Grigor, 57, 78, 79, 380, 400, 448, 452, 517–20, 532, 538n. 11, 541, 611, 659, 710; *Armensia*, 520–30 (text); contributions to periodicals, 518; short stories of, 518–19

Zohrapian, Hovhannes Vardapet, 46

Zola, Émile, 103, 103n. 105

Zorayan, Nikoghayos, 21, 62, 65, 246–47; *Association*, 247–49 (text)

Zorian, Stepan, 106, 903–5; *Grandfather and Granddaughter*, 905–9 (text); short stories of, 903–4; translations by of Russian authors, 905

Zschokke, Johann Heinrich, 89, 204

Zul-Qarnain, Mirza, 36

Zvarchakhos arakk parsits (Humorous Persian fables / M. Taghiadian), 204

PERMISSIONS ACKNOWLEDGMENTS

Portions of the following works have been reprinted by permission

Kevork B. Bardjakian, compiled with intro., *A Reference Guide to Modern Armenian Literature, 1500–1920* (Detroit: Wayne State University Press, 2000). Selection of quotes and bios.

Aram Tolegian, compiled and trans. with intro., *Armenian Poetry Old and New* (Detroit: Wayne State University Press, 1979). Selections of poems.

Diana Der Hovanessian and Marzbed Margossian, trans. and eds. with intro., *Anthology of Armenian Poetry* (New York: Columbia University Press, 1978). Selections of poems.

Diana Der Hovanessian and Marzbed Margossian, trans. and eds. with intro., *Sacred Wrath: The Selected Poems of Vahan Tekeyan* (New York: Ashod, 1982), 28.

Diana Der Hovanessian, trans. and ed. with intro., *Coming To Terms,* poems by Vahan Terian (New York: Ashod, 1991). Selections of poems.

George A. Bournoutian, trans. and ed. with intro., *The Chronical of Abraham of Crete* (Costa Mesa, Calif., 1999), 11–23.

George A. Bournoutian, trans. and ed. with intro., *History of the Wars (1721–1738),* by Abraham of Erevan (Costa Mesa, Calif., 1999), 11–27.

Hakob Shahamirian, *Snare of Glory* in *Armenian Reporter International,* March 16, 23, 30, 2002. Aris Sevag, trans.

Donald Abcarian, trans. *The Fool* by Raffi (Reading and New Jersey: Gomidas Institute, 2000), 206–17.

Nishan Parlakian and S. Peter Cowe, eds. with intro., a portion of "Ancient Gods," trans. Anne D. Vardanian in *Modern Armenian Drama* (New York: Columbia University Press, 2001), 189–215.

Ara Baliozian, trans. and preface, intro. by S. Yapoudjian, *The Gardens of Silihdar and Other Writings* by Zabel Yesayan (New York: Ashod, 1982), 33–38.

Ara Baliozian, trans. with intro., *Bancoop and the Bones of the Mammoth* by Kostan Zarian (New York: Ashod, 1982), 18–22.

Ara Baliozian, trans. with intro., *The Island and the Man* by Kostan Zarian (Toronto: Kar, 1983), 19–22.

Nishan Parlakian, trans. with intro., *The Bride* by Zabel Asatur (New York: Griffon House, 1987), 54–59.

Jack Antreassian, trans. with intro by Michael Kermian, *Comrade Panchooni* by Yervand Otian (New York: St. Vartan, 1977), 19–36.

Jack Antreassian, trans. with intro. by Michael Kermian "Armenissa," in *Voice of Conscience: the Stories of Krikor Zohrab* (New York: St. Vartan, 1983), 44–57.

From *Ararat* Quarterly

Diana Der Hovanessian, trans. selection of poems in *Ararat* 12, no. 2 (Spring 1976); 17, no. 4 (Autumn 1976); 20, no. 4 (Winter 1979); 25, no. 1 (Winter 1983); 32, no. 1 (Winter 1992).

Sonia Harlan and Hourig Jacob, trans. a section, *Wounds of Armenia* by Khachatur Abovian in *Ararat* 23, no. 4 (Autumn 1982): 8–10.

James Etmekjian, trans., a section, Toros Levoni by Tzerents, *Ararat* 19, no. 4 (Autumn 1978): 39.

James Etmekjian, trans., a section, *Mayta* by Srbuhi Dussap, *Ararat* 19, no. 2 (Spring 1978): 39.

Aris Sevag, trans., "Honorable Baggers" by Hakpb Paronian, *Ararat* 20, no. 2 (Spring 1979): 43–48.

Aris Sevag, trans., "Topich," by Hakob Oshakan, *Ararat* 24, no. 1 (Winter 1983): 42–47.

Nishan Parlakian, trans., a section, *Patvi Hamar* by Aleksandr Shirvanzadé, *Ararat* 15, no. 1 (Winter 1974): 19–22.

Kris Keseci, trans., "Angel," by Levon Bashalian, *Ararat* 42, no. 168 (Autumn 2001): 35–36.

Garig Basmadjian, "Barbed Wire in Flower," by Gurgen Mahari, *Ararat* 20, no. 1 (Winter 1979): 102–4.

Yeghishé Charents, a section, "Land of Nairi," *Ararat* 20, no. 1 (Winter 1979): 67–70. Trans. anonymous.

Vahan Tekeyan, "Dear Brother in the Bond . . . ," *Ararat* 19, no. 1 (Winter 1978): 20–21. Trans. anonymous.

Zarouhi Kalemkarian, "Agony of a Horse," *Ararat* 11, no. 3 (Summer 1960): 11. Trans. anonymous.

Samuel Mkrtichian, ed., *Selected Armenian Poets* (Yerevan, Samson, 1993). Selections of poems.